International Business

Environments and Operations

Fifteenth Edition

Global Edition

John D. Daniels

University of Miami

Lee H. Radebaugh

Brigham Young University

Daniel P. Sullivan

University of Delaware

PEARSON

Boston Columbus Indianapolis New York San Francisco Upper Saddle River
Amsterdam Cape Town Dubai London Madrid Milan Munich Paris Montréal Toronto
Delhi Mexico City São Paulo Sydney Hong Kong Seoul Singapore Taipei Tokyo

Editor in Chief: Stephanie Wall
Senior Editor: Kris Ellis-Levy
Senior Acquisitions Editor, Global Editions: Steven Jackson
Head of Learning Asset Acquisition, Global Editions: Laura Dent
Associate Editor, Global Editions: Toril Cooper
Project Editor, Global Editions: Arundati Dandapani
Program Manager Lead: Ashley Santora
Program Manager: Sarah Holle
Editorial Assistant: Bernard Ollila
Director of Marketing: Maggie Moylan
Director of International Marketing: Ann Oravetz
Senior Marketing Manager: Erin Gardner
Marketing Assistant: Gianna Sandri
Marketing Manager, Global Editions: Kristin Borgert
Project Manager Lead: Judy Leale
Art Director: Steve Frim
Text Designer: Black Horse Designs
Cover Designer: Jodi Notowitz
Cover Photo: © Ohmega1982/Shutterstock
VP, Director of Digital Strategy & Assessment: Paul Gentile
Digital Editor: Brian Surette
Digital Development Manager: Robin Lazrus
Digital Project Manager: Alana Coles
MyLab Product Manager: Joan Waxman
Digital Production Project Manager: Lisa Rinaldi
Senior Manufacturing Controller, Production, Global Editions: Trudy Kimber

Credits and acknowledgments borrowed from other sources and reproduced, with permission, in this textbook appear on the appropriate page within text.

Pearson Education Limited
Edinburgh Gate
Harlow
Essex CM20 2JE
England

and Associated Companies throughout the world

Visit us on the World Wide Web at: www.pearsonglobaleditions.com

Authorised adaptation from the United States edition, entitled International Business, 15th edition, ISBN 978-0-13-345723-0 by John Daniels, Lee Radebaugh, and Daniel Sullivan, published by Pearson Education © 2015.

ISBN 10: 1-292-01679-5
ISBN 13: 978-1-292-01679-5

British Library Cataloguing-in-Publication Data
A catalogue record for this book is available from the British Library

10 9 8 7 6 5 4 3 2
15

Typeset in 10/12 Palatino by Integra Software Services Private Limited
Printed and bound by Courier Kendallville in United States of America

Brief Contents

Preface 24
About the Authors 40

PART ONE: Introduction 43

1 Overview of International Business and Globalization 43
An Atlas 74

PART TWO: National Environmental Differences 87

2 Culture 87
3 Governmental and Legal Systems 129
4 Economic Systems and Market Methods 179

PART THREE: Connecting Countries through Trade and Factor Movements 229

5 Trade and Factor Mobility Theory 229
6 Trade Protectionism 271
7 Economic Integration and Cooperation 301

PART FOUR: The Global Monetary Environment 339

8 Markets for Foreign Exchange 339
9 Factors that Influence Exchange Rates 371
10 Global Debt and Equity Markets 407

PART FIVE: Corporate Policy and Strategy 441

11 Ethics and Social Responsibility 441
12 Strategies for International Business 475
13 Evaluation of Countries for Operations 525
14 Modes of Trading Internationally 561
15 Forms and Ownership of Foreign Production 611
16 The Organization and Governance of Foreign Operations 653

PART SIX: Functional Management and Operations 697

17 Global Marketing 697
18 Global Production and Supply Chains 737
19 Global Accounting and Financial Management 771
20 Global Management of Human Resources 807

Contents

Cases with [globe icon] denotes a case that emphasizes a country, cases with [building icon] denotes a case that emphasizes an industry or company.

Preface 24

About the Authors 40

• PART ONE: INTRODUCTION 43

1 Overview of International Business and Globalization 43

CASE: The Globalized Business of Sports 44

Introduction 47

How Does *International Business* Fit In? 47

The Forces Driving Globalization 48

Factors in Increased Globalization 49

The Costs of Globalization 54

Threats to National Sovereignty 55

Environmental Stress 55

Growing Income Inequality and Personal Stress 56

Point-Counterpoint
Is Offshoring Good Strategy? 56

Why Companies Engage in International Business 58

Expanding Sales 59

Acquiring Resources 59

Reducing Risk 59

Modes of Operations in International Business 60

Merchandise Exports and Imports 60

Service Exports and Imports 60

Investments 61

Types of International Organizations 61

Why International Business Differs from Domestic Business 62

Physical and Social Factors 62

The Competitive Environment 64

Looking to the Future
Three Ways of Looking at Globalization 65

CASE: Transportation and Logistics: The Case for Dubai Ports World 66

Summary 71

Key Terms 71

Endnotes 72

An Atlas 74
Map Index 82

• PART TWO: NATIONAL ENVIRONMENTAL DIFFERENCES 87

2 Culture 87

CASE: Saudi Arabia's Dynamic Culture 88

Introduction 92
The People Factor 92
Cultural Awareness 93
A Little Learning Goes a Long Way 94
The Idea of a "Nation": Delineating Cultures 95
The Nation as a Point of Reference 95
How Cultures Form and Change 95
Sources of Change 95
Language as Both a Diffuser and Stabilizer of Culture 96
Why English Travels So Well 98
Religion as a Cultural Stabilizer 99
Behavioral Practices Affecting Business 100
Issues in Social Stratification 100

Does Geography Matter?
Birds of a Feather Flock Together 101

Work Motivation 103
Relationship Preferences 106
Risk-Taking Behavior 107
Information and Task Processing 108
Communications 109
Spoken and Written Language 109
Silent Language 111
Dealing with Cultural Differences 112
Host Society Acceptance 112
Degree of Cultural Differences 113
Ability to Adjust: Culture Shock 113
Company and Management Orientations 114
Strategies for Instituting Change 115

Point-Counterpoint
Does International Business Lead to Cultural Imperialism? 115

Looking to the Future
What Will Happen to National Cultures? 118

CASE: Tesco PLC: Leveraging Global Knowledge 120

Summary 125
Key Terms 125
Endnotes 126

3 Governmental and Legal Systems 129

CASE: China—Complicated Risks, Big Opportunities 130

Introduction 133
The Political Environment 134
Individualism Versus Collectivism 135
- Individualism 135
- Collectivism 136

Political Ideology 136
- Spectrum Analysis 137
- Democracy 138
- Totalitarianism 139

The Standard of Freedom 140
Trends in Political Ideologies 141
- Engines of Democracy 142
- Democracy: Recession and Retreat 143
- Authoritarianism's Surge 145

Looking to the Future
Political Ideology and MNEs' Actions 146

Political Risk 148
- Classifying Political Risk 149
- Classes and Characteristics of Political Risks 149

Point-Counterpoint
Proactive Political Risk Management: The Best Approach 151

The Legal Environment 153
- Types of Legal Systems 154
- Trends in Legal Systems 155
- Implications for Managers 157
- The Confound of Democracy's Retreat 157
- Which Rule When? 158

Legal Issues in International Business 160
- Operational Concerns 160
- A Key Relationship: Wealth and Regulation 162

Strategic Concerns 163
- Country Characteristics 163
- Product Safety and Liability 164

Legal Jurisdiction 164
Intellectual Property 164
The Basis of Political and Legal Differences 165
Historical Legacies 165
Economic Circumstances 166
Cultural Orientation 166
The Potential for Cross-National Convergence 167
CASE: It's a Knockoff World 168
Summary 171
Key Terms 172
Endnotes 172

4 Economic Systems and Market Methods 179
CASE: The Comeback Accelerates 180
Introduction 184
New Markets, New Perspectives 184
International Economic Analysis 187
Does Geography Matter?
Consequence of Change in Arctic Sea Ice 188
Economic Freedom 189
Economic Freedom Today 190
The Value of Economic Freedom 191
Trends in Economic Freedom 191
Types of Economic Systems 194
Market Economy 194
Command Economy 195
Mixed Economy 196
Looking to the Future
State Capitalism: Detour or Destination? 197
Assessing Economic Development, Performance, and Potential 199
Measures of Economic Performance 200
Adjusting Analytics 201
Performance and Potential: Alternative Interpretations 204
Point-Counterpoint
Growth: Positive and Productive? 207
Economic Analysis 209
Inflation 209
Unemployment 210
Debt 211

Income Distribution 211
Poverty 212
The Balance of Payments 215
Elaborating Economic Analysis with Global Indices 215
CASE: The BRICs: Vanguard of the Revolution 217

Summary 222
Key Terms 222
Endnotes 223

• PART THREE: CONNECTING COUNTRIES THROUGH TRADE AND FACTOR MOVEMENTS 229

5 Trade and Factor Mobility Theory 229

CASE: Costa Rica's Trade Evolution 230

Introduction 233
Laissez-Faire Versus Interventionist Approaches to Exports and Imports 233
Theories of Trade Patterns 234
Trade Theories and Business 234
Factor-Mobility Theory 234
Interventionist Theories 235
Mercantilism 235
Neomercantilism 236
Free-Trade Theories 236
Theory of Absolute Advantage 236
Theory of Comparative Advantage 239
Theories of Specialization: Some Assumptions and Limitations 240
Trade Pattern Theories 242
How Much Does a Country Trade? 242
What Types of Products Does a Country Trade? 243
With Whom Do Countries Trade? 246

Does Geography Matter?
Variety Is the Spice of Life 247

The Statics and Dynamics of Trade 248
Product Life Cycle (PLC) Theory 248
The Diamond of National Competitive Advantage 250
Factor-Mobility Theory 252

Point-Counterpoint
Should Nations Use Strategic Trade Policies? 253

Why Production Factors Move 255
Effects of Factor Movements 256
The Relationship Between Trade and Factor Mobility 258

Looking to the Future
In What Direction Will Trade Winds Blow? 260

CASE: LUKOIL: Foreign Trade and Investment 262

Summary 267
Key Terms 268
Endnotes 268

6 Trade Protectionism 271

CASE: The U.S.-Vietnamese Catfish Dispute 272

Introduction 275
Conflicting Results of Trade Policies 275
The Role of Stakeholders 275
Economic Rationales for Governmental Intervention 276
Fighting Unemployment 276
Protecting "Infant Industries" 277
Developing an Industrial Base 278
Economic Relationships with Other Countries 279
Noneconomic Rationales for Government Intervention 282
Maintaining Essential Industries 282
Promoting Acceptable Practices Abroad 282

Point-Counterpoint
Should Governments Impose Trade Sanctions? 284

Maintaining or Extending Spheres of Influence 285
Preserving National Culture 286
Instruments of Trade Control 286
Tariffs 286
Nontariff Barriers: Direct Price Influences 287
Nontariff Barriers: Quantity Controls 289
Dealing with Governmental Trade Influences 292
Tactics for Dealing with Import Competition 292
Convincing Decision Makers 292
Involving the Industry and Stakeholders 293
Preparing for Changes in the Competitive Environment 293

Looking to the Future
Dynamics and Complexity 293

CASE: Doing Business in Singapore 294

Summary 298
Key Terms 298
Endnotes 298

7 Economic Integration and Cooperation 301

CASE: Toyota's European Drive 302

Introduction 304
The World Trade Organization—Global Integration 305
GATT: Predecessor to the WTO 305
What Does the WTO Do? 306
The Rise of Bilateral Agreements 307
Regional Economic Integration 308
Geography Matters 308
The Effects of Integration 309
Major Regional Trading Groups 311
The European Union 311
The North American Free Trade Agreement (NAFTA) 317
Regional Economic Integration in the Americas 320

Point-Counterpoint
Is CAFTA-DR a Good Idea? 322

Regional Economic Integration in Asia 324
Regional Economic Integration in Africa 326
Other Forms of International Cooperation 327
Commodity Agreements 328
Commodities and the World Economy 328
Consumers and Producers 328
The Organization of the Petroleum Exporting Countries (OPEC) 329

Looking to the Future
Will the WTO Overcome Bilateral and Regional Integration Efforts? 331

CASE: Unilever Goes East 332

Summary 336
Key Terms 337
Endnotes 337

• PART FOUR: THE GLOBAL MONETARY ENVIRONMENT 339

8 Markets for Foreign Exchange 339

CASE: Going Down to the Wire in the Money-Transfer Market 340

Introduction 342
What Is Foreign Exchange? 343
Players on the Foreign-Exchange Market 343

How to Trade Foreign Exchange 345
Some Aspects of the Foreign-Exchange Market 345
Global OTC Foreign Exchange Instruments 345
Size, Composition, and Location of the Foreign-Exchange Market 346
Does Geography Matter? Foreign-Exchange Trades and Time Zones 349
Major Foreign-Exchange Markets 351
The Spot Market 351
The Forward Market 352
Options 353
Futures 353
The Foreign-Exchange Trading Process 353
Banks and Exchanges 354
Top Exchanges for Trading Foreign Exchange 356
How Companies Use Foreign Exchange 356
Business Purposes (I): Cash Flow Aspects of Imports and Exports 357
Business Purposes (II): Other Financial Flows 358
Point-Counterpoint Is it OK to Speculate on Currency? 359
Looking to the Future Where Are Foreign-Exchange Markets Headed? 361
CASE: Do Yuan to Buy Some Renminbi? 362
Summary 367
Key Terms 368
Endnotes 368

9 Factors that Influence Exchange Rates 371
CASE: El Salvador Adopts the U.S. Dollar 372
Introduction 374
The International Monetary Fund 374
Origin and Objectives 374
The IMF Today 375
The Global Financial Crisis and the IMF 376
Evolution to Floating Exchange Rates 376
Exchange-Rate Arrangements 377
Three Choices: Hard Peg, Soft Peg, or Floating Arrangement 379
Hard Peg 380
Soft Peg 380
Floating Arrangement 380
The Euro 381
Pluses and Minuses of the Conversion to the Euro 382

Point-Counterpoint
Should Africa Develop a Common Currency? 384

Determining Exchange Rates 385
Nonintervention: Currency in a Floating-Rate World 385
Intervention: Currency in a Fixed-Rate or Managed Floating-Rate World 386
CASE: The U.S. Dollar and the Japanese Yen 387
Black Markets 389
Foreign-Exchange Convertibility and Controls 389
Exchange Rates and Purchasing Power Parity 391
Exchange Rates and Interest Rates 394
Other Factors in Exchange-Rate Determination 395

Forecasting Exchange-Rate Movements 395
Fundamental and Technical Forecasting 396
Fundamental Factors to Monitor 396

Business Implications of Exchange-Rate Changes 397
Marketing Decisions 397
Production Decisions 397
Financial Decisions 398

Looking to the Future
Determination of Exchange Rates—Exploring the Case of Singapore's Monetary Policy as a Model for Sustainable Economic Growth 398

CASE: Welcome to the World of Sony—Unless the Falling Yen Rises Again 399

Summary 404
Key Terms 405
Endnotes 405

10 Global Debt and Equity Markets 407

CASE: GPS: In the Market for an Effective Hedging Strategy? 408

Introduction 411

The Finance Function 412
The Role of the CFO 413

Capital Structure 413
Leveraging Debt Financing 413
Factors Affecting the Choice of Capital Structure 414
Debt Markets as a Means of Expansion 416

Global Capital Markets 416
Eurocurrencies and the Eurocurrency Market 416
International Bonds 418
Equity Securities 420
The Size of Global Stock Markets 421

Taxation of Foreign-Source Income 425
International Tax Practices 425
Taxing Branches and Subsidiaries 426
Transfer Prices 428
Double Taxation and Tax Credit 429
Dodging Taxes 430
Offshore Financing and Offshore Financial Centers 430
What Is an OFC? 430
Point-Counterpoint
Should Offshore Financial Centers and Aggressive Tax Practices Be Eliminated? 432
Looking to the Future
The Growth of Capital Markets and the Drive by Governments to Capture More Tax Revenues by MNEs 433
CASE: Does the Devil Really Wear Prada? 434
Summary 437
Key Terms 438
Endnotes 438

• PART FIVE: CORPORATE POLICY AND STRATEGY 441

11 Ethics and Social Responsibility 441
CASE: Ecomagination and the Global Greening of GE 442
Introduction 445
Stakeholder Trade-Offs 445
The Foundations of Ethical Behavior 446
Why Do Companies Care About Ethical Behavior? 447
The Cultural Foundations of Ethical Behavior 447
Relativism Versus Normativism 448
The Legal Foundations of Ethical Behavior 449
Legal Justification: Pro and Con 450
Extraterritoriality 450
Ethics and Corporate Bribery 451
Corruption and Bribery 451
The Consequences of Corruption 452
What's Being Done About Corruption? 452
Point-Counterpoint
Are Top Managers Responsible When Corruption Is Afoot? 455
Ethics and the Environment 456
What Is "Sustainability"? 456
Global Warming and the Kyoto Protocol 457
Does Geography Matter?
Where Small Carbon Footprints Mean Big Business 459

Ethical Dilemmas and the Pharmaceutical Industry 460
Tiered Pricing and Other Price-Related Issues 460
Taking TRIPS for What It's Worth 461
R&D and the Bottom Line 461
Ethical Dilemmas of Labor Conditions 462
The Problem of Child Labor 463
What MNEs Can and Can't Do 464
Corporate Codes of Ethics: How Should a Company Behave? 464
Motivations for Corporate Responsibility 465
Developing a Code of Conduct 465
Looking to the Future
Dealing with Ethical Dilemmas in the Global Economy 466
CASE: Anglo-American PLC in South Africa: What Do You Do When Costs Reach Epidemic Proportions? 467
Summary 471
Key Terms 471
Endnotes 471

12 Strategies for International Business 475
CASE: Zara's Strategy for Value Creation in the Global Apparel Industry 476
Introduction 481
Industry Structure 482
Industry Change 483
Perspectives on Strategy 484
Approaches to Value Creation 485
Cost Leadership 486
Differentiation 486
The Firm as Value Chain 487
Managing the Value Chain 489
Configuration 489
Does Geography Matter?
Clusters and Configuring Value Chains 491
Logistics 496
Coordination 497
Looking to the Future
The Rise of Robots 498
Change and the Value Chain 500
A Case in Point 500

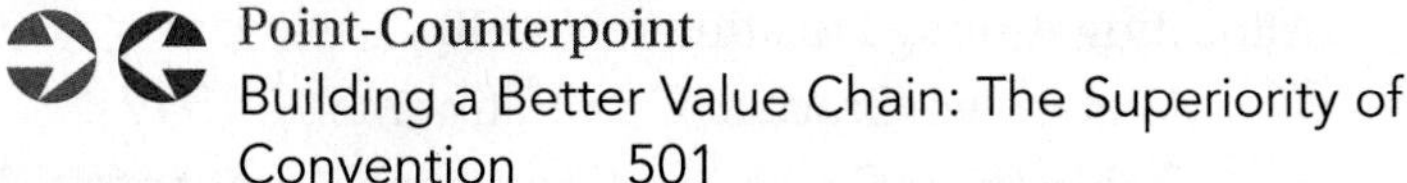
Point-Counterpoint
Building a Better Value Chain: The Superiority of Convention 501

Global Integration Versus Local Responsiveness 503
Pressures for Global Integration 503
Pressures for Local Responsiveness 505
When Pressures Interact 507

Types of Strategy 508
International Strategy 509
Multidomestic Strategy 511
Global Strategy 512
Transnational Strategy 513

CASE: The Mobile Money Revolution: A Look at Safaricom's M-Pesa 515

Summary 518
Key Terms 519
Endnotes 519

13 Evaluation of Countries for Operations 525

CASE: Burger King 526

Introduction 530

How Does Scanning Work? 532
Scanning Versus Detailed Analysis 532

What Information Is Important in Scanning? 532
Opportunities: Sales Expansion 532
Opportunities: Resource Acquisition 534
Risks 537

Does Geography Matter?
Don't Fool with Mother Nature 540

Collecting and Analyzing Data 543
Some Problems with Research Results and Data 543
External Sources of Information 544
Internally Generated Data 545

Country Comparison Tools 545

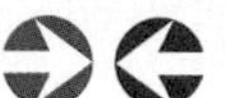
Point-Counterpoint
Should Companies Operate in and Send Employees to Violent Areas? 545

Grids 547
Matrices 548

Allocating Among Locations 548
Alternative Gradual Commitments 549
Geographic Diversification Versus Concentration 550
Reinvestment and Harvesting 551
Noncomparative Decision Making 552
Looking to the Future
Will Prime Locations Change? 553
CASE: The LEGO® Group 554
Summary 557
Key Terms 558
Endnotes 558

14 Modes of Trading Internationally 561
CASE: SpinCent: The Decision to Export 562
Introduction 564
Exporting 566
Who Are Exporters? 567
The Matter of Advantages 567
Characteristics of Exporters 568
Why Export? 569
Profitability 569
Productivity 570
Diversification 570
Export: Initiation and Development 571
Sequences and Increments 571
Born Globals 572
Interaction: Time and Place 573
The Wildcard Role of Serendipity 575
Approaches to Exporting 575
Which Approach When? 577
Importing 578
Who Are Importers? 578
Input Optimizers 578
Opportunistic 578
Arbitrageurs 579
Characteristics of Importers 579
Why Import? 579
Specialization of Labor 580
Global Rivalry 580
Local Unavailability 580
Diversification 580

Point-Counterpoint
Exporting E-waste: A Useful Solution? 581

Importing and Exporting: Problems and Pitfalls 584
Financial Risks 584
Customer Management 585
International Business Expertise 586
Marketing Challenges 586
Top Management Commitment 586
Government Regulation 586
Trade Documentation 587

Importing and Exporting: Resources and Assistance 588
Government Agencies 590
Export Intermediaries 591
Customs Brokers 593
Freight Forwarders 595
Third-Party Logistics 596

Reconciling Opportunity and Challenge: An Export Plan 596

Looking to the Future
Technology and International Trade 599

Countertrade 601
Costs 601
Benefits 602
CASE: A Little Electronic Magic at Alibaba.com 602

Summary 605
Key Terms 605
Endnotes 605

15 Forms and Ownership of Foreign Production 611

CASE: Meliá Hotels International 612

Introduction 618

Why Exporting May Not Be Feasible 619
When It's Cheaper to Produce Abroad 619
When Transportation Costs Too Much 619
When Domestic Capacity Isn't Enough 619
When Products and Services Need Altering 620
When Trade Restrictions Hinder Imports 620
When Country of Origin Becomes an Issue 620

Noncollaboration: FDI 621
Reasons for Foreign Direct Investment 621
Acquisition Versus Greenfield 622

Why Companies Collaborate 623
Alliance Types 623
General Motives for Collaborative Arrangements 624
International Motives for Collaborative Arrangements 625

Types of Collaborative Arrangements 627
Some Considerations in Collaborative Arrangements 627

Point-Counterpoint
Should Countries Limit Foreign Control of Key Industries? 628

Licensing 629
Franchising 630
Management Contracts 631
Turnkey Operations 632
Joint Ventures 634
Equity Alliances 634

Problems with Collaborative Arrangements 635
Relative Importance 635
Divergent Objectives 636
Questions of Control 637
Comparative Contributions and Appropriations 637
Culture Clashes 638

Managing International Collaborations 638
Country Attractiveness and Operational Options 638
Problems of Switching Modes 639
Learning from Experience 639
Dealing with Partners 640

Looking to the Future
Why Innovation Breeds Collaboration 641

CASE: The oneworld Airline Alliance 642

Summary 648
Key Terms 648
Endnotes 648

16 The Organization and Governance of Foreign Operations 653

CASE: Building a Global Organization at Johnson & Johnson 654

Introduction 657

Changing Situations, Changing Organizations 658
Building a "Magical" Organization 659

Organization Structure 659
Vertical Differentiation 660
A Dynamic Balance 660

Horizontal Differentiation 662
Functional Structure 662
Divisional Structures 662
Matrix Structure 665
Mixed Structure 666
Neoclassical Structures 666
Changing Times, Changing Strategies, Changing Structures 667
The Ideal of Boundarylessness 668
Network Structure 669
Virtual Organization 671
Pitfalls of Neoclassical Structures 671
Coordination Systems 672
Coordination by Standardization 672
Point-Counterpoint
Hierarchy: The Superior Structure? 673
Coordination by Plan 675
Coordination by Mutual Adjustment 677
Control Systems 679
Bureaucratic Control 679
Market Control 679
Clan Control 679
Control Mechanisms 680
Which Control System When? 681
Organization Culture 681
A Key Piece of the Performance Puzzle 681
Culture's Increasing Importance 682
Building an Organization Culture 683
Organization Culture and Strategy 684
Looking to the Future
The Rise of Corporate Universities 685
CASE: Hyundai Motor Company: Expanding Organizational Excellence 687

Summary 691
Key Terms 692
Endnotes 692

• PART SIX: FUNCTIONAL MANAGEMENT AND OPERATIONS 697

17 Global Marketing 697
CASE: Tommy Hilfiger 698

Introduction 700
Marketing Strategies 700

Marketing Orientations 701
Segmenting and Targeting Markets 703

Product Policies 704
Why Firms Alter Products 704

Point-Counterpoint
Should Home Governments Regulate Their Companies' Marketing in Developing Countries? 705

Alteration Costs 707
The Product Line: Extent and Mix 708

Pricing Strategies 709
Potential Obstacles in International Pricing 709

Promotion Strategies 713
The Push-Pull Mix 713
Some Problems in International Promotion 714

Branding Strategies 715
Worldwide Brand Versus Local Brands 716

Distribution Strategies 717
Deciding Whether to Standardize 718

Does Geography Matter?
Is Necessity the Mother of Invention? 718

Self-Handling or Not? 719
Distribution Partnership 720
Distribution Challenges and Opportunities 720
E-Commerce and the Internet 721

Managing the Marketing Mix 723
Gap Analysis 723

Looking to the Future
Evolving Challenges to Segment Markets 725

CASE: Grameen Danone Foods in Bangladesh 726

Summary 732
Key Terms 733
Endnotes 733

18 Global Production and Supply Chains 737

CASE: Apple's Global Supply Chain 738

Introduction 740
What Is Supply Chain Management? 740

Global Supply Chain Strategies 741
Factors in Supply Chain Strategy 742

Supplier Networks 746
Global Sourcing 747
Major Sourcing Configurations 749
The Make-or-Buy Decision 750
Point-Counterpoint
Should Firms Outsource Innovation? 750
Supplier Relations 752
The Purchasing Function 752
Information Technology and Global Supply-Chain Management 753
Electronic Data Interchange (EDI) 753
Enterprise Resource Planning/Material Requirements Planning 753
Radio Frequency ID (RFID) 754
E-Commerce 754
Quality 755
Zero Defects 756
Lean Manufacturing and Total Quality Management (TQM) 756
Six Sigma 757
Quality Standards 758
Foreign Trade Zones 759
General-Purpose Zones and Subzones 759
Transportation Networks 760
Looking to the Future
Uncertainty and the Global Supply Chain 761
CASE: Samsonite's Global Supply Chain 762
Summary 768
Key Terms 768
Endnotes 768

19 Global Accounting and Financial Management 771
CASE: Parmalat: Europe's Enron 772
Introduction 776
The Crossroads of Accounting and Finance 776
Differences in Financial Statements Internationally 778
Differences in the Presentation of Financial Information 779
Accounting Objectives 780
Factors Affecting Accounting Standards and Practices 781
Cultural Differences in Accounting 782
International Standards and Global Convergence 784
Mutual Recognition Versus Reconciliation 784
The First Steps in Convergence 785
The International Accounting Standards Board 785

Point-Counterpoint
Should U.S. Companies Be Allowed to Close the GAAP? 787

Transactions in Foreign Currencies 788
Recording Transactions 788
Correct Procedures for U.S. Companies 789

Translating Foreign-Currency Financial Statements 790
Translation Methods 790

International Financial Issues 793
Capital Budgeting in a Global Context 793
Internal Sources of Funds 794
Global Cash Management 795

Foreign-Exchange Risk Management 797
Types of Exposure 797
Exposure-Management Strategy 798

Looking to the Future
Will IFRS Become the Global Accounting Standard? 800

CASE: Dell Mercosur: Getting Real in Brazil 801

Summary 805
Key Terms 805
Endnotes 806

20 Global Management of Human Resources 807

CASE: Globalizing Your Career 808

Introduction 811

Human Resource Management 811
HRM and the Global Company 812

Strategizing HRM 813
A Case in Point: GE's Evolution 813

The Perspective of the Expatriate 814
Who's Who 814
Trends in Expatriate Assignments 814
Cost Considerations 817
The Enduring Constant 817

Staffing Frameworks in the MNE 818
The Ethnocentric Framework 818
The Polycentric Framework 819
The Geocentric Framework 821
Which Framework When? 822

Managing Expatriates 823
Expatriate Selection 824
Expatriate Assessment and Preparation 827
Point-Counterpoint
English: Destined to Be the World's Language? 829
Compensating Expatriates 833
Repatriating Expatriates 837
Managing Repatriation 839
Expatriate Failure 840
Looking to the Future
I'm Going Where? The Changing Locations of International Assignments 841
CASE: Banglalink: Staffing the Bangladeshi Operation 842
Summary 846
Key Terms 846
Endnotes 846
Glossary 853
Company Index 863
Name Index 867
Subject Index 877

Preface

This textbook is one of the best-selling international business textbooks in both the United States and the rest of the world. Widely used in both undergraduate and MBA level courses, this text has had authorized translations into Spanish, Chinese, Thai, and Russian, and it will soon be in Albanian, Korean, and Macedonian as well. This textbook set the global standard for studying the environments and operations of international business. The elements of success that have driven this performance anchor our efforts to make this edition the best version yet. We believe these efforts result in a textbook that provides you and your students the best possible understanding of what is happening and is likely to happen in the world of business.

AUTHORITATIVE, RELEVANT, CURRENT

Students, faculty, and managers praise this book for its compelling balance between rigorous, authoritative theory and meaningful practice within the context of a fresh, current analysis of the international business environment. Indeed, this book not only describes the ideas of international business but also uses contemporary examples, scenarios, and cases to make sense of what managers do and should do. We include multiple insights and real-world examples, which we base on our research, discussions with managers and other stakeholders, opinions of students and professors, and observations from traveling the world. Since 2010, the authors have traveled individually to more than 45 countries, only a few of which overlapped. We traveled to every region and nearly every continent, which provided significant insights we were able to use in this edition. We believe no other textbook comes close to successfully blending a comprehensive review of international business theory with exhaustive attention to what happens in the many parts of the global market. We are confident that this new edition, by making international business ideas and practices more meaningful than ever before, will give students a comprehensive, current view of international business in the twenty-first century.

RELEVANT MATERIALS THAT ENGAGE STUDENTS

AUTHOR-WRITTEN CASES

An enduring strength of this text is its in-depth case profiles of cutting-edge issues in international business. This edition introduces new cases and updates and revises the remaining. All 40 cases are unique and, with few exceptions, are personally researched and written by the text's authors. As such, we believe they set the standard for integration of theory and practice in an international business textbook on the following three levels:

1. *Level of Analysis*: Cases engage an extensive range of topics from environmental, institutional, country, industry, company, and individual perspectives. No one perspective dominates; all are represented and, hence, create a meaningful representation of the world of international business.
2. *Scope of Geographic Coverage*: Cases cover topics in settings that span the globe; no region is unaddressed, no major market is neglected.

3. *Scope of Company Coverage*: Cases look at various issues from a range of company perspectives, notably companies headquartered in all regions of the world, from large MNEs to small exporters, from old-line manufacturers to emergent cyber businesses, from companies that make products to those that deliver services.

Opening Case Each chapter starts with a provocative case written to set the stage for the major issues covered in the chapter. Designed to grab the student's attention, these cases look at fascinating issues in a way that makes students want to understand the ideas and concepts of international business. These cases, by variously taking the point of view of individuals, companies, governments, and institutions, give a great sense of the richness of the ensuing chapter. Material from the opening cases is then integrated with chapter discussions that we highlight in the text.

Closing Case Each chapter closes with a rich, elaborate case that integrates the ideas and tools presented in the chapter. The closing cases aim to put the student into a situation that asks, given certain circumstances, what should be done. Called on to analyze issues and decisions for which the chapter prepares them, students can then grapple with many of the opportunities and challenges of international business.

NEW CASES IN THIS EDITION

We have extensively updated *all* the cases from the previous edition so that students will find them relevant and rigorous. In addition, we have included several entirely new cases:

- Chapter 1: Logistics and Transportation: The Case of Dubai Ports World
- Chapter 6: Doing Business in Singapore
- Chapter 7: Unilever Goes East
- Chapter 12: The Mobile Money Revolution: A Look at Safaricom's M-Pesa
- Chapter 18: Samsonite's Global Supply Chain
- Chapter 19: Dell Mercosur: Getting Real in Brazil

LOOKING TO THE FUTURE 

Each chapter offers future scenarios that are important to managers, companies, or the world. The topic of each *Looking to the Future* feature alludes to ideas discussed in the chapter in a way that prompts students to engage their imagination about the future of the world.

POINT-COUNTERPOINT 

To reinforce our strong applications orientation, we have included a separate feature in every chapter that brings to life a major debate in contemporary international business and globalization. We use a point-counterpoint style to highlight the diversity of perspectives that managers and policymakers use to make sense of vital issues.

The give-and-take between two sides reinforces this textbook's effort to link theory and practice in ways that will undoubtedly energize class discussion.

GEOGRAPHY AND INTERNATIONAL BUSINESS 

In appropriate chapters, we have included "Does Geography Matter?" sections. Some of the geographic variables we include to help explain the chapters' content are country location, location of population and population segments within countries, natural resources and barriers, climate, natural disasters, and country size.

NEW TOPICS AND CHAPTER CHANGES

Although it is a tired cliché, every instructor of international business knows the world is changing in many and often unpredictable ways. We wake up to the same challenges you do, trying to make sense of what we read, hear, and see in the global press. Our effort to make sense of this leads to an unconditional effort to improve and update the text to reflect the latest knowledge and practice of international business. Most notably, among the many changes in this edition are the following:

PART ONE: INTRODUCTION

- Updated opening case, such as including the cost and company sponsorship of the London Summer Olympics (Chapter 1)
- Brought in new examples of determining product origins because of their mixed composition, such as the example of Swiss chocolate (Chapter 1)
- Extended discussion of economic uncertainties (oil prices and economic recession), especially as they affect the value of international trade and investment (Chapter 1)
- Explained how countries' sizes influence their degree of globalization (Chapter 1)
- Introduced the concept of inshoring (Chapter 1)
- Presented example of how border cooperation enhances efficiency, e.g. dam between Brazil and Paraguay, and how lack of standards create inefficiencies, e.g. trans-European rail service (Chapter 1)
- Illustrated global economic cooperation with example of G-20 countries (Chapter 1)
- Introduced additional downsides of offshoring, such as the loss of higher skilled jobs and the possible inattention to process techniques when relying on cheap labor (Chapter 1)
- Illustrated job shifts because of technology with example of airline cockpit crews (Chapter 1)
- Revised the closing case to include an in-depth study of a Dubai based logistics and transportation company (Chapter 1)

PART TWO: NATIONAL ENVIRONMENTAL DIFFERENCES

- Updated the opening case on Saudi Arabia, such as with illustrations of women's changing roles in the work force, Olympics participation, and possible changes in driving prohibitions (Chapter 2)

- Emphasized the advantages and problems of using multi-cultural teams (Chapter 2)
- Introduced the concept of deal-focused versus relationship-focused societies (Chapter 2)
- Discussed the growth of bicultural and multicultural individuals (Chapter 2)
- Expanded the coverage of laws to include underutilized societal groups, such as women on European boards, ethnic work quotas in Malaysia, and university racial quotas in Brazil (Chapter 2)
- Used Korea to show strain of using needed foreign workers while maintaining traditional cultural values (Chapter 2)
- Illustrated how poor translations affect business with example of Chinese contracts with foreign companies (Chapter 2)
- Showed how ethnic conflict may lead to the dissolution of the United Kingdom and Spain as we know them today (Chapter 2)
- Included a new closing case on Tesco that discusses how the company used multicultural teams to transfer knowledge among countries (Chapter 2)
- Expanded profile of the importance of the political system; particular attention paid to implication of political affairs in Russia (Chapter 3)
- Streamlined discussion of collectivism and individualism; greater emphasis given to their implication to the business environment (Chapter 3)
- Revised profile of political freedom and its implication to rights of individuals and organizations (Chapter 3)
- Detailed update of trends in political ideologies, the play of long-run trends in recent developments and circumstances (Chapter 3)
- Expanded coverage of democracy and totalitarianism within the context of changing degrees of political freedom (Chapter 3)
- Updated profile of the drivers of the recession retreat of democracy; profile of current assessments as provided by Freedom House as *Economist Intelligence Unit* (Chapter 3)
- Updated profile of the drivers of the surge in totalitarianism (Chapter 3)
- Revised interpretation of the implication of political ideological change and MNEs' actions (Chapter 3)
- Streamlined discussion of political risk; reset table to better represent classes and characteristics of political risk (Chapter 3)
- Updated developments in the legal environment; greater emphasis given to business implications of legal change (Chapter 3)
- Profiled ongoing trends in the basis of rule, highlighting the scale and scope of the rule of law versus the rule of man (Chapter 3)
- Streamlined discussion of the interaction of the basis of rule and the practice of democracy worldwide (Chapter 3)
- Reported latest World Bank data on the ease of doing business worldwide; particular attention paid to critical startup, operational, and shutdown activities (Chapter 3)
- Streamlined discussion of the strategic implications of legal environments to the activities of MNEs; particular attention directed toward the ongoing play of intellectual property specification and protection in established versus emerging economies (Chapter 3)

- New section developed to better present the basis for political and legal differences among countries. Provides students a systematic profile of the basis for cross-national differentiation. New section highlights the potential for cross-national convergence in political and legal outlooks and orientations (Chapter 3)
- Updated case profile of intellectual property violation and counterfeiting in the world today; reset case to highlight economic, political, and social dynamics of counterfeiting and intellectual property piracy; emphasized angles of political and legal ambiguity that reflect location effects. Data points updated to report most recent statistics (Chapter 3)
- Updated and expanded opening case, emphasizing the ongoing and accelerating comeback of emerging economies and its growing scope of implication to Western economies (Chapter 4)
- Contextualized discussion of economic trends and anomalies that shape the perspectives brought to bear to assess the performance and potential of international markets; designed to illustrate that systematic principles guide assessment of differentiated markets (Chapter 4)
- Streamlined specification of key assumptions anchoring international market analysis (Chapter 4)
- Updated assessment of ice melt rates in the Arctic ice cap and their implication to economic development (Chapter 4)
- Revised discussion of the centrality of economic freedom in international market analysis; precise specification of components of economic freedom (Chapter 4)
- Revised discussion of the current state of economic freedom and predominant trends (Chapter 4)
- Assessment of the concerns and constraints that motivate national governments to reduce individuals' economic freedom (Chapter 4)
- Revised presentation of materials profiling types of economic systems (Chapter 4)
- Updated assessment of the scale and scope of state capitalism; direct evaluation of the ongoing debate regarding whether state capitalism is a detour or destination for established and emerging markets (Chapter 4)
- Summary discussion in chart profiling various specifications of emerging economy clusters (Chapter 4)
- Expanded discussion of broader conceptions of economic performance and potential, with additional emphasis given toward measures of sustainability—most notably Net National Product, Genuine Progress Indicator, and Human Development Index—and stability, most notably Your Better Life Index, Gross National Happiness, and Happy Planet (Chapter 4)
- Stronger connections drawn between economic performance and national potential (Chapter 4)
- Streamlining of the Point-Counterpoint, "Growth: Positive and Productive?" to more directly stress test the comparative benefits and costs of growth (Chapter 4)
- Revised coverage of key components of economic analysis, with particular attention given to include inflation, unemployment, debt, income distribution, poverty, and the balance of payments (Chapter 4)
- Expanded coverage of the base-of-the-pyramid concept as well as discussion of the multidimensionality of poverty (Chapter 4)

- Addition of section to discuss the explanatory usefulness of global indices to evaluate the economic potential of international markets; particular attention given to the Global Competitiveness, World Competitiveness, Global Innovation, and the Where to Be Born Indices (Chapter 4)
- Reference throughout chapter evolving implication of global credit crisis, particularly in Western economies (Chapter 4)
- Addition of new case that evaluates trends, opportunities and constraints in the BRIC markets with an overt sensitivity of the relevance of those markets to fellow emerging economies (Chapter 4)
- Updated statistics throughout chapter (Chapter 4)

PART THREE: CONNECTING COUNTRIES THROUGH TRADE AND FACTOR MOVEMENTS

- Updated trade and demographic figures for the opening case on Costa Rican trade and the closing case on LUKOIL's foreign trade and investment (Chapter 5)
- Brought in the recent upsurge in trade among developing countries, mainly due to Chinese and Indian demand for raw materials (Chapter 5)
- Added a map comparing U.S. states' GDPs with those of countries to demonstrate why the U.S. is a major trader with a low dependence on foreign trade (Chapter 5)
- Compared homogeneous and differentiated products in terms of the importance of distance in explanation of countries' trading partners (Chapter 5)
- Included new map showing recent major destinations of immigration (Chapter 5)
- Brought in new examples of technology that is causing shifts in global trade patterns, such as robots with cameras that displace agricultural pickers and fracking for natural gas that displaces petroleum trade (Chapter 5)
- Discussed the effect of ethnic networks on trade patterns (Chapter 5)
- Updated the opening case on U.S.–Vietnamese disputes on catfish trade, such as with later figures and the 2012 U.S. repeal on inspections of Vietnamese catfish (Chapter 6)
- Replaced old with recent export restrictions to maintain domestic supplies (Chapter 6)
- Brought in the effect on workers in exporting countries when importing countries impose an optimum tariff (Chapter 6)
- Introduced the Committee on Foreign Investment in the United States (CFIUS) (Chapter 6)
- Augmented discussion of trade sanctions with examples of recent trade bans with Iran (Chapter 6)
- Discussed the problem and documentation needed to explain a product's origin, such as with imports when animals were born in one country, raised in a second one, and slaughtered in a third (Chapter 6)
- Showed how the image of a country's products changes when some of its exported products are rejected for health or safety reasons (Chapter 6)
- Dropped the U.S. Cuban trade case, and introduced the case of Doing Business in Singapore that examines the pro-business climate in the country (Chapter 6)

- Updated the Toyota case to reflect its expansion into Europe, and replaced the case of Walmart with one on Unilever's ASEAN connection and the company's subsequent growth in the region (Chapter 7)
- Focus on the importance of bilateral and regional trade agreements at the expense of program on WTO talks, especially on the Doha Round (Chapter 7)
- Updated the progress in different regional trade agreements and introduced new talks between the U.S. and the EU (Chapter 7)
- Included the addition of Croatia to the EU in 2013, an updated status of other expansion moves in the EU, and the importance of the Schengen Area and monetary union (the Euro) as two important areas of focus in Europe (Chapter 7)
- Update of the differences between the EU and NAFTA regarding rules of origin (Chapter 7)
- Added a discussion of new regional agreements being discussed in Latin America (UNASUR) and Asia (the Trans-Pacific Partnership) (Chapter 7)

PART FOUR: THE GLOBAL MONETARY ENVIRONMENT

- Revised opening case to include information on sources and destinations of migration as well as the role of remittances of foreign workers in Dubai (Chapter 8)
- Update of players on the foreign-exchange market to demonstrate the changes that have occurred (Chapter 8)
- Updated size, composition, and location of the foreign-exchange market according to the latest BIS survey (Chapter 8)
- Updated the end-of-chapter case on China's revaluation of the yuan and how China is gradually opening up the market for trading yuan and using Hong Kong as a place to test changes in the role of the yuan in the global financial system (Chapter 8)
- New information on the global financial crisis as it expanded in 2012–2013 and especially the challenges in Europe (Chapter 9)
- Update of exchange rate agreements to fit with the new definitions (Chapter 9)
- Discussion of the Greek financial crisis and its spread to other southern European countries and the efforts of the European Union to find a resolution (Chapter 9)
- Updated the closing case to reflect the falling value of the yen in the fall of 2012 after several quarters of sustained rise in the value of the yen against the dollar and its impact on Sony's competitive position (Chapter 9)
- Added a new Chapter 10 on global capital markets to strengthen PART FOUR: The World Financial Environment (Chapter 10)
- Updated the opening case to discuss the expansion of GPS into Europe and the challenges they face with new financial market regulations (Chapter 10)
- Updated data in Chapter 10 to reflect changes in the size of capital markets resulting from the drop in global equity values in the 2010–2012 period (Chapter 10)
- Included additional information on international tax issues and tax haven countries as a result of the global efforts to go after MNEs that are perceived as avoiding paying a fair share of taxes (Chapter 10)
- Updated the closing case on Prada's IPO in Hong Kong and why Asia is so important for the luxury goods market (Chapter 10)

PART FIVE: CORPORATE POLICY AND STRATEGY

- Updated initiatives by the UN and EU to combat bribery as well as expanded coverage on U.S. anticorruption efforts (Chapter 11)
- Discussed the impact of the slowing global economy on the ability of countries to comply with the Kyoto Protocol and the slowdown in the progress of the Protocol to expand its coverage globally (Chapter 11)
- Added new examples of global sustainability initiatives by SMEs as well as larger MNEs (Chapter 11)
- Updated opening case profile of Zara for latest performance data and strategic moves; streamlined presentation of materials (Chapter 12)
- Revised discussion of drivers of industry change to better reflect contemporary examples in established and emerging markets (Chapter 12)
- Revised introduction given reviewers' comments to better anchor the concept of strategy in the international market (Chapter 12)
- Profile of key examples that link generic concepts of strategy and industry structure to the activities of MNEs (Chapter 12)
- Refined discussion of the cost leadership and differentiation strategy in international markets (Chapter 12)
- Streamlined specification of the value chain and anchored more directly within the context of global operations (Chapter 12)
- Reset discussion of the Industrial Organization perspective relative to ideas developed within the context of Great by Choice viewpoint (Chapter 12)
- Updated profile of key factors that shaped the configuration of value chains (Chapter 12)
- Reset graphics to better communicate the concept and components of the value chain (Chapter 12)
- Expanded discussion of force that shaped the configuration of value chains to reflect ongoing technological innovations (Chapter 12)
- Expanded discussion of configuration moderators to better capture the implication of labor demographics, dynamics, and costs (Chapter 12)
- Emphasized geographic aspects of strategy and international market by profiling the moderating effects of business clusters (Chapter 12)
- Added discussion of the lexicon of location perspectives to better interpret the configuration of value chains (Chapter 12)
- Added new Looking To The Future profile of the rise of robots and their potentially dramatic implications to the conception of value chain configuration and coordination (Chapter 12)
- Updated the profiles of Samsung and Sony, as an interactive scenario that illustrates the dynamic give-and-take of strategy and global markets (Chapter 12)
- Expanded profile of the dynamic of change in competitive competencies resulting implications to configuring and coordinating the value chain in international markets (Chapter 12)

- Updated and streamlined presentation of the pressures posed by global integration and local responsiveness in the conception of strategy and the configuration and coordination of value chains for international markets (Chapter 12)
- Broadened discussion of integration and responsiveness pressures to reflect predominant trends among emerging markets (Chapter 12)
- Reset discussion of the international, multi-domestic, global, and transnational strategies to reflect new ideas and revised principles introduced in preceding sections (Chapter 12)
- Revised summary chart to integrate and organize the key characteristics of the international, multi-domestic, global, and transnational strategies (Chapter 12)
- Introduced Safaricom's M-Pesa as an example of a mobile technology firm setting its sights on emerging markets as good value-chain strategy (Chapter 12)
- Juxtaposed the opening and closing cases (Burger King and LEGO) and updated figures and locations for both (Chapter 13)
- Bolstered discussion of company and country bargaining positions because of access to unique resources (Chapter 13)
- Enhanced discussion on lack of accuracy on countries' data, including how different methodologies lead to different results (e.g., Chinese 2012 GDP data) (Chapter 13)
- Examined the need to consider risks throughout the supply chain, including location of secondary suppliers (Chapter 13)
- Gave opposing thoughts of preferring versus avoiding countries with weak protections of intellectual property rights (Chapter 13)
- Added evidence that access to knowledge is enhanced by locating in knowledge-producing countries (Chapter 13)
- Included the factor of stress for people working in countries with violence (Chapter 13)
- Updated opening case on Burger King's international expansion to include its new entries into Morocco, Russia, and Slovenia (Chapter 13)
- Enriched discussion in opening case to better profile the opportunities and constraints posed by export options to small and medium-size enterprises (Chapter 14)
- Highlighted connection between international business activity and the steadily expanding scale and scope of export and import (Chapter 14)
- Revised sections regarding the characteristics and classes of exporters and differential export motivations (Chapter 14)
- Reset coverage of export development perspectives, emphasizing the sequential nature of the incremental internationalization viewpoint as well as the dynamism of the born global perspectives (Chapter 14)
- Applied data-driven analysis to evaluate the interaction between export development perspectives; evaluated the leading import and export part of the United States to stress test discussion (Chapter 14)
- Expanded discussion of the primary approaches to exporting (Chapter 14)
- Streamlined and updated discussion of the export of electronic waste (Chapter 14)
- Expanded sections on who importers are and why they import (Chapter 14)
- Expanded coverage of the pitfalls and problems that challenge importers and exporters; fortified discussion by tapping data analytics provided by various United States agencies (Chapter 14)

- Identification of key points of difficulty that complicate international trade; directly adopted the perspective of small and medium-sized enterprises (Chapter 14)
- Better organized discussion of the resources available to international traders; emphasized the growing scale and scope of technologies and their moderating influence on the decision to import and export (Chapter 14)
- Sharper specification of the theoretical components that anchor an export plan (Chapter 14)
- Updated profile of the technology of trade and its application to the potential and practice of export and import (Chapter 14)
- Further streamlined coverage of countertrade and it role as a facilitator of international trade (Chapter 14)
- Updated closing case to reflect contemporary developments (Chapter 14)
- Updated statistics throughout the chapter (Chapter 14)
- New opening case, map, and figures on Meliá Hotels International, a company using multiple operating modes for its international operations (Chapter 15)
- Enhanced coverage of market failure as a reason for using FDI as an operating mode (Chapter 15)
- Added Lenova's acquisition of IBM's PC division as example of cultural collision when combining managers from the two companies (Chapter 15)
- Brought in leasing as an alternative to FDI in foreign expansion (Chapter 15)
- Introduced the concept of coopetition (Chapter 15)
- Revamped discussion on how to divide compensation in collaborative arrangements (Chapter 15)
- Showed change in turnkey leadership because of growth in Chinese companies' operations (Chapter 15)
- Presented new example of equity alliance, e.g. management contract of Port of Antwerp with a port facility in India (Chapter 15)
- Illustrate how shift in a partner's product line emphasis puts strain on partnership arrangements, e.g. IBM with Toshiba (Chapter 15)
- Indicated how home market trust influences trust in foreign collaborations (Chapter 15)
- Indicated the resurgence in importance of conglomerates (Chapter 15)
- Updated the ending case on the oneworld Alliance, such as by discussing the complexity of the proposed merger between American Airlines and US Airways because of their membership in different airline alliances (Chapter 15)
- Streamlined opening case profile of Johnson & Johnson to directly reference elements of organization structure, systems, and culture that are discussed in the chapter (Chapter 16)
- Reset and updated discussion of macro environmental trends that influence contemporary interpretations of organizing the MNE (Chapter 16)
- Clarified discussion of classical and neoclassical structures to emphasize key points of form, functionality, overlap, and differentiation (Chapter 16)
- Updated company examples regarding adoption or abandonment of classical organization structures (Chapter 16)
- Structured discussion of neoclassical structures to reflect ongoing developments driven by technological innovation, behavioral economics, and virtuality (Chapter 16)

- Reset graphic representation of network structure to better communicate dimensions and dynamics (Chapter 16)
- Streamlined interpretation of coordination and control systems; developed richer explanations within the context of practices (Chapter 16)
- Broadened discussion of coordination systems to reflect changes precipitated by technological innovations and expanding interpersonal connectivity (Chapter 16)
- Fortified discussion of organization culture by strengthening connection between its outlook, forms, and functionality and the MNE's strategy (Chapter 16)
- Updated profile of the rise of corporate universities and their role in developing and sustaining organization in the MNE (Chapter 16)
- Streamlined profile of The Hyundai Motor Company in the closing case to better highlight the role of its founding mission and enduring principles as it expands through organizational excellence (Chapter 16)

PART SIX: FUNCTIONAL MANAGEMENT AND OPERATIONS

- Updated the opening case on Hilfiger, such as with newer operating figures and the company's use of Disney characters to promote its children's line (Chapter 17)
- Illustrated the use of global team members to develop more globally standardized products (Chapter 17)
- Enhanced discussion of companies' approaches to sell simultaneously to different income levels, such as Diageo's and SABMiller's sale of a cheaper beer in some African countries (Chapter 17)
- Gave new examples of standardized products aimed at a global niche, e.g. Red Bull and Ferrari (Chapter 17)
- Showed how companies can adapt their competencies to foreign markets, such as Hermés' use of its luxury silk competence to sell saris in India (Chapter 17)
- Added the importance of social media using Web 2.0 in word-of-mouth product acceptance (Chapter 17)
- Inserted new examples of brand name changes to better fit sounds, meaning, and visual acceptance in other languages (Chapter 17)
- Enhanced reasons for national differences in negotiating prices (Chapter 17)
- Mentioned new U.S. Supreme Court rulings permitting U.S. sales in the gray market (Chapter 17)
- Updated ending case on Grameeen Danone Foods in Bangladesh, such as by showing newer demographics and recent sales growth (Chapter 17)
- Introduced a new case discussing Apple's Global Supply Chain (Chapter 18)
- Restructured the chapter on global supply chain to introduce the concepts of global sourcing at the beginning of the chapter (Chapter 18)
- New discussion on contract manufacturing as a way to source parts and final products (Chapter 18)
- Discussed the problems of a company like Apple using a supplier like Foxconn to manufacture high-end products in China and possibly losing control of intellectual property and creating a competitor (Chapter 18)
- Discussion of principles from *The World Is Flat* to illustrate offshoring, outsourcing, and supply-chaining and other ways information technology is changing global supply chains (Chapter 18)

- Updated the opening case to reflect how Parmalat has recovered from its corporate corruption scandal (Chapter 19)
- Updated trends in the convergence of accounting standards through IFRS and negotiations with the U.S. FASB and explained why it will be difficult, if not impossible, for the U.S. to adopt IFRS in place of U.S. GAAP (Chapter 19)
- Updated the differences in American and European responses to the adoption of IFRS (Chapter 19)
- Moved the discussion of global debt and equity markets to Chapter 10
- Focused on operational issues in international finance, such as capital budgeting, the internal flow of funds, and foreign exchange risk management (Chapter 19)
- Dropped a case on H&M's global strategy and added a new case about Dell's success in Brazil (Chapter 19)
- Refined the idea of globalizing your career as reported in opening case; expanded the diversity of viewpoints on the usefulness, responsibilities, opportunities and costs of the expatriate experience (Chapter 20)
- Emphasized the growing connection between the MNE's success in planning its strategy and the quality of its HRM programs in general, its expatriate management in specific (Chapter 20)
- Profiled trends in expatriate processes given consequences of global financial crisis and the call to contain the escalating expenses (Chapter 20)
- Highlighted implications of the changing workplace and workforce of globalization to the use of third-country nationals, reverse expatriates, and different genders and demographics (Chapter 20)
- Revised discussion of the ethnocentric, polycentric, and geocentric approaches to expatriate staffing; adjusted discussion for changing interpersonal connectivity through unfolding technological innovations (Chapter 20)
- Streamlined discussion of the linkage of expatriate selection to the matters of professional and personal characteristics (Chapter 20)
- Expanded data that substantiate key competencies and key concerns of expatriates (Chapter 20)
- Profile of changing compensation patterns given globalization of compensation standards as well as growing pressures to economize (Chapter 20)
- Expanded and elaborated discussion of the role of English in the world of business, specifically testing the proposition that English is destined as the default language of the world (Chapter 20)
- Added section and table data profiling the scale and scope of various forms of language in the world (Chapter 20)
- Fuller explanation of the causes and consequences of expatriate failure; repositioned section to reflect reviewers' suggestions on chapter flow (Chapter 20)
- Expanded section on the evolving location mix of expatriate assignments, emphasizing the shift from established to emerging locations (Chapter 20)
- Updated coverage of the general characteristics and peculiar attributes of the Bangladeshi market (Chapter 20)
- An indepth look at staffing Bangladesh's most successful mobile telephony operator, Banglalink (Chapter 20)

ENGAGING IN-TEXT LEARNING AIDS

We believe a powerful textbook must teach as well as present ideas. To that end, we use several in-text aids to make this book an effective learning tool. Most notably, each chapter uses all of the following features:

CHAPTER OBJECTIVES AND SUMMARY

Each chapter begins with learning objectives and ends with a summary; both tie directly to the chapter material. This linkage helps students prepare for the major issues within each chapter and appreciate their general relationships, and reinforces the important lessons of the chapter material.

CONCEPT LINKS

Throughout each chapter, as warranted by discussion in the corresponding text, we highlight in the margin how ideas from previous chapters link to the ideas being discussed. This cumulative series of concept links helps the student build an understanding of the connections among concepts across chapters. This feature also facilitates student understanding when instructors do not assign all chapters.

CASE ICONS  

Although all of our cases are primarily issue-oriented, new icons now enable easy identification of the focus of the chapter opening and closing cases. Know at a glance if a case is more focused on a specific country or on company or industry issues, or, when both icons are present, if it will provide both a country and company/industry focus. The identifying icons appear in both the extended table of contents and in the opening and closing cases within the chapters themselves.

CASE LINKS

Another effort to help students better interpret the connections among ideas and practices is encompassed in our latest innovation. Specifically, as warranted by discussion in the corresponding text, we highlight with text shading and icons how those ideas being discussed elaborate ideas that were presented in the opening and closing cases of that chapter.

KEY TERMS AND POINTS: BOLDING, MARGINAL NOTES, AND GLOSSARY

Every chapter highlights key terms; each key term is put in bold print when it first appears. Key learning points are also highlighted in the adjoining margin. These terms and others are then assembled in an end-of-chapter list and into a comprehensive glossary at the end of the book.

CASE QUESTIONS

The opening and closing case of each chapter stipulates several questions to guide students in applying what they have learned in the chapter to the reality of international business. We have found in our classes that the questions at the end of the case go a long way toward putting the case into perspective for students. In addition, they make for great assignment activities, directing students to respond to questions with information presented in the specific case as well as the chapter. Select questions are also available as assisted graded writing prompts in MyManagementLab.

POINT-COUNTERPOINT  

This feature, as we have already discussed, is compelling not only for class discussion, but also for specific assignments. These assignments may include requiring students to take sides in debates or to apply arguments to specific countries.

MAPS

Geographic literacy is essential in international business. Thus, we have not only included a map section between Chapters 1 and 2, but we incorporate maps throughout that show both locations and other information.

INTERNATIONAL BUSINESS MINI-SIMULATIONS

Students can apply the concepts they've learned and exercise their decision-making skills in real-world scenarios via the online mini-simulations found in MyManagementLab. Created in collaboration with experts in the field, eight mini-simulations covering the following topics will be available for fall 2014 courses: Global Culture and Diversity, Management in a Global Environment, Organizational Structure, Globalization, International Ethics, Legal Differences, Outsourcing, and Tariffs, Subsidies, and Quotas. Sign into MyManagementLab.com or ask your Pearson representative for more information.

CURRENCY AND READABILITY

We have always prided ourselves on being current in the research and examples we cite in the chapters. The 15th edition is no exception; in fact, we believe our coverage goes beyond that of any other IB text. If you examine the endnotes for any chapter, you will see that we include both classic and the most up-to-date materials from both scholarly treatises and the popular press. If you examine the list of companies in the "Company Index and Trademarks," you will see that our citations are numerous and include large and small firms from a variety of industries based in countries throughout the world. These citations illustrate to students the practical reality of the theories and alternative operations we describe.

We have made a special effort in this edition to improve the readability of the extensive materials we present. First, we make a point of putting authors' names (except for classics such as Adam Smith) only in the reference section rather than in the chapters' prose. We have simply seen too many students try to remember names rather than concepts. Second, we have engaged a copy editor to improve the language and flow of materials.

INSTRUCTOR SUPPLEMENTS

Instructors can access downloadable supplemental resources by signing into the Instructor Resource Center at http://www.pearsonglobaleditions.com/Daniels.

- **Instructor's Manual**
- **Test Item File**—over 100 questions per chapter, including multiple choice, true/false, short answer, and essays. The Test Item File includes questions that are tagged Learning Objectives, Learning Outcomes, and AACSB Learning Standards to help measure whether students are grasping the course content that aligns with AACSB guidelines.
- **TestGen Software**
- **PowerPoint Slides**
- **Image Library**

Need help? Our dedicated Technical Support team is ready to assist instructors with questions about the media supplements that accompany this text. Visit **http://247pearsoned.custhelp.com** for answers to frequently asked questions and toll-free user-support phone numbers.

LEARNING MANAGEMENT SYSTEMS

2014 QUALITATIVE BUSINESS VIDEO LIBRARY

This selection of videos showcases International Business concepts, as well as those from other business disciplines. These videos and many more are found in MyManagementLab.

ACKNOWLEDGMENTS

Every author relies on the comments, critiques, and insights of reviewers. It is a tough task that few choose to support. Therefore, we want to thank the following people for their insightful and helpful comments on the fourteenth edition of *International Business: Environments and Operations*, which helped guide us in preparing the fifteenth edition.

MARK BAYLOR, University of Delaware
ALI KARA, Pennsylvania State University
LOUIS MELBOURNE, Florida International University
SHAD MORRIS, Ohio State University
JOHN O'BRIEN, University of Denver
AJAYI RICHARD, University of Central Florida
SHIRI TERJESEN, Indiana University
ANTHONY PAPUZZA, University of Colorado, Boulder

In addition, we have been fortunate since the first edition to have colleagues who have been willing to make the effort to critique draft materials, react to coverage already in print, advise on suggested changes, and send items to be corrected. Because this is the culmination of several previous editions, we would like to acknowledge everyone's efforts. However, many more individuals than we can possibly list have helped us. To those who must remain anonymous, we offer our sincere thanks.

We would also like to acknowledge people whom we interviewed in writing cases. These are Brenda Yester (Carnival Cruise Lines); Omar Aljindi, Nora al Jundi, and Talah Tamimi (Saudi Arabia's Dynamic Culture); Mauricio Calero (Ecuador: A Rosy Export Future?); Raul Arguelles Diaz Gonzales and Francisco Suarez Mogollon (Walmart Goes South); Jonathan Fitzpatrick, Julio A. Ramirez, Arianne Cento, and Ana Miranda (Burger King); several executives at American Airlines and oneworld who wish to remain anonymous (The oneworld Airline Alliance); and Ali R. Manbien (GPS: In the Market for an Effective Hedging Strategy). In addition, we would like to thank several people who authored or co-authored cases for us and Mary Yoko Brannen and Terence Mughan at the University of Victoria for Tesco PLC: Leveraging Global Knowledge (Chapter 2), Fidel León-Darder and Cristina Villar at Universitat de València for Meliá Hotels International (Chapter 15), Jon Jungbien Moon at Korea University for Grameen Danone Foods in Bangladesh (Chapter 17), and Manuel Serapio at the University of Colorado at Denver and Steve Katsaros, founder and CEO of Nokero for Nokero: Lighting the World (Chapter 18); others who helped with administrative and research matters include Melanie Hunter, Maddison Daines, Lisa Curlee, Allison Johnson, and Katie Cooper Redding.

It takes a dedicated group of individuals to take a textbook from first draft to final manuscript. We would like to thank our partners at Pearson Prentice Hall for their tireless efforts in bringing the fifteenth edition of this book to fruition. Our thanks go to Editor in Chief, Stephanie Wall; Senior Acquisitions Editor, Kris Ellis-Levy; Program Manager Team Lead, Ashley Santora; Senior Marketing Manager, Erin Gardner; Project Manager Team Lead, Judy Leale; Program Manager, Sarah Holle; and Project Manager, Ann Pulido.

Pearson gratefully acknowledges and thanks the following people for their work on the Global Edition:

Contributors:

VALERIE GOBY, Zayed University in Dubai
BERSANT HOBDARI, Copenhagen Business School
DENNIS LEE, Shantou University Business School
STEFANIA PALADINI, Coventry University
HAMED SHAMMA, The American University in Cairo

Reviewers:

AZIZ BAKAY, Gediz University
TUNG LAI CHENG, Wawasan Open University
STEPHEN J JONES, Bangor University, Wales
LYDIA KERNEVEZ, ESSCA School of Management, France
ANDREW TAN, Singapore Polytechnic
HELENE TENZER, Tübingen University

About the Authors

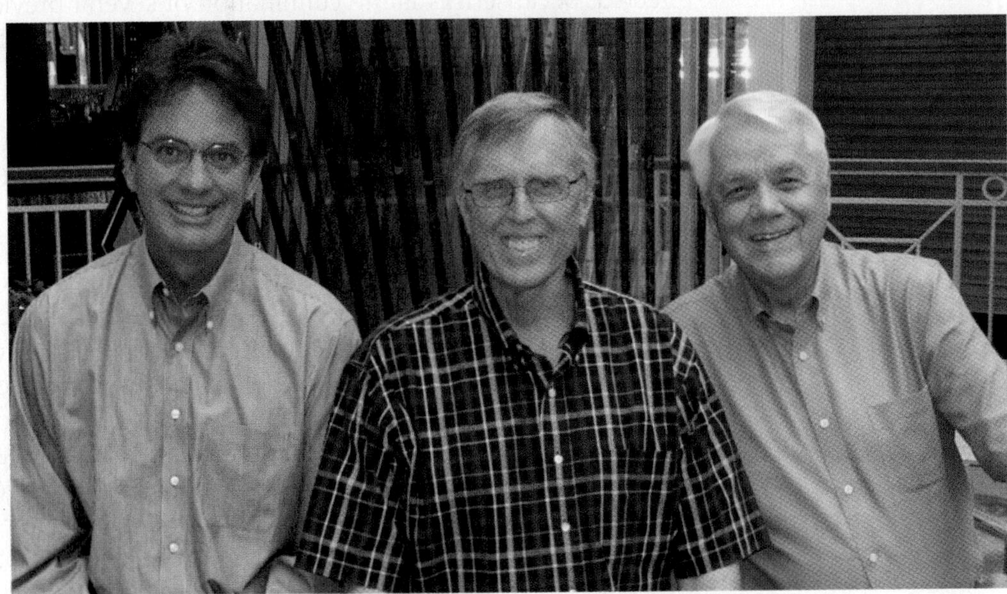

From left to right: **Daniel Sullivan, Lee Radebaugh, John Daniels**

Three respected and renowned scholars show your students how dynamic, how real, how interesting, and how important the study of international business can be.

John D. Daniels, the Samuel N. Friedland Chair of Executive Management emeritus at the University of Miami, received his Ph.D. at the University of Michigan. His dissertation won first place in the award competition of the Academy of International Business. Since then, he has been an active researcher and won a decade award from the *Journal of International Business Studies*. His articles have appeared in such leading journals as *Academy of Management Journal, Advances in International Marketing, California Management Review, Columbia Journal of World Business, International Marketing Review, International Trade Journal, Journal of Business Research, Journal of High Technology Management Research, Journal of International Business Studies, Management International Review, Multinational Business Review, Strategic Management Journal, Transnational Corporations*, and *Weltwirtschaftliches Archiv*. Professor Daniels has published 15 books, most recently *Multinational Enterprises and the Changing World Economy* (coedited with Ray Loveridge, Tsai-Mei Lin, and Alan M. Rugman), three volumes on *Multinational Enterprise Theory*, and three volumes on *International Business and Globalization* (all co-edited with Jeffrey Krug). On its 30th anniversary, *Management International Review* referred to him as "one of the most prolific American IB scholars." He served as president of the Academy of International Business and dean of its Fellows. He also served as chairperson of the international division of the Academy of Management, which named him Outstanding Educator of the Year in 2010. Professor Daniels has worked and lived a year or longer in seven different countries, worked shorter stints in approximately 30 other countries on six continents, and traveled in many more. His foreign work has been a combination of private sector, governmental, teaching, and research assignments. He was formerly a faculty member at Georgia State University and The Pennsylvania State University, director of the Center for International Business Education and Research (CIBER) at Indiana University, and holder of the E. Claiborne Robins Distinguished Chair at the University of Richmond.

Lee H. Radebaugh is the emeritus Kay and Yvonne Whitmore Professor of International Business and former Director of the Whitmore Global Management Center/CIBER at Brigham Young University. He received his M.B.A. and doctorate from Indiana University. He was a faculty member at The Pennsylvania State University from 1972 to 1980. He also has been a visiting professor at Escuela de Administracion de Negocios para Graduados (ESAN) in Lima, Peru. In 1985, Professor Radebaugh was the James Cusator Wards visiting professor at Glasgow University, Scotland. His other books include *International Accounting and Multinational Enterprises* (John Wiley and Sons, 6th edition) with S. J. Gray and Erv Black; *Introduction to Business: International Dimensions* (South-Western Publishing Company) with John D. Daniels; and seven books on Canada-U.S. trade and investment relations, with Earl Fry as co-editor. He has also published several other monographs and articles on international business and international accounting in journals such as the *Journal of Accounting Research, Journal of International Financial Management and Accounting, Journal of International Business Studies,* and the *International Journal of Accounting*. He is the former editor of the *Journal of International Accounting Research* and area editor of the *Journal of International Business Studies*. His primary teaching interests are international business and international accounting. Professor Radebaugh is an active member of the American Accounting Association, the European Accounting Association, the International Association of Accounting Education and Research, and the Academy of International Business, having served on several committees as the president of the International Section of the AAA and as the secretary treasurer of the AIB. He is a member of the Fellows of the Academy of International Business. He is also active with the local business community as past president of the World Trade Association of Utah and member of the District Export Council. In 2007, Professor Radebaugh received the Outstanding International Accounting Service Award of the International Accounting Section of the American Accounting Association, and in 1998, he was named International Person of the Year in the state of Utah and Outstanding International Educator of the International Section of the American Accounting Association. In 2012, Lee was honored when the award for the top article published in the *Journal of International Accounting Research* in the past decade was named the Lee H. Radebaugh Notable Contribution to International Accounting Research.

Daniel P. Sullivan, Professor of International Business at the Alfred Lerner College of Business of the University of Delaware, received his Ph.D. from the University of South Carolina. He researches a range of topics, including globalization and business, international management, global strategy, competitive analysis, and corporate governance. His work on these topics has been published in leading scholarly journals, including the *Journal of International Business Studies, Management International Review, Law and Society Review*, and *Academy of Management Journal*. In addition, he has served on the editorial boards of the *Journal of International Business Studies* and *Management International Review*. Professor Sullivan has been honored for both his research and teaching, receiving grants and winning awards for both activities while at the University of Delaware and, his former affiliation, the Freeman School of Tulane University. He has been awarded numerous teaching honors at the undergraduate,

M.B.A., and E.M.B.A. levels—most notably, he has been voted Outstanding Teacher by the students of 17 different Executive M.B.A. classes at the University of Delaware and Tulane University. Professor Sullivan has taught, designed, and administered a range of graduate, undergraduate, and nondegree courses on topics spanning globalization and business, international business operations, international management, strategic perspectives, executive leadership, and corporate strategy. In the United States, he has delivered lectures and courses at several university sites and company facilities. In addition, he has led courses in several foreign countries, including China, Hong Kong, Bulgaria, the Czech Republic, France, South Korea, Switzerland, Taiwan, and the United Kingdom. Finally, he has worked with many managers and consulted with several multinational enterprises on issues of international business.

CHAPTER 1

Overview of International Business and Globalization

OBJECTIVES

After studying this chapter, you should be able to

1. Define *globalization* and *international business* and explain how they affect each other
2. Grasp why companies engage in international business and why its growth has accelerated
3. Discuss globalization's future and the major criticisms of it
4. Illustrate the different ways a company can accomplish its global objectives
5. Recognize the need to apply social science disciplines to understand how international and domestic business differ

MyManagementLab®
Improve Your Grade!
When you see this icon, visit **www.mymanagementlab.com** for activities that are applied, personalized, and offer immediate feedback.

© corocota - Fotolia.com

The world's a stage; each plays his part, and takes his share.

—Dutch proverb

CASE The Globalized Business of Sports

Sports may be the most globalized legitimate business in the world.[1] Historically, most players and teams in most sports have competed only on their own home turf; today, however, fans demand to see the best, and "best" has become a global standard. Satellite TV brings live events from just about anywhere in the world to fans just about anywhere else. This gives the key players in the sports-promotion business—team owners, league representatives, and sports associations—broadened audience exposure, expanded fan bases, and augmented revenues, especially through advertising that cuts across national borders.

Nevertheless, competition among teams sponsored by national sports federations goes back more than a century, most notably the World Cup in football (soccer) and the Olympics. More national organizations participate in these events than there are countries in the United Nations. And probably more people follow these competitions than follow most of the goings-on at the UN. In fact, you were likely part of the record global television audience for at least some of the 2010 World Cup in South Africa and the 2012 Summer Olympics games in London. (The chapter's opening photo shows Wenlock, the London games' mascot, dressed as a Queen's Guard. Hundreds of thousands of stuffed mascot toys were made in China and shipped to the games.)

How do these international competitions relate to business? Cities and countries compete to host the events in order to attract tourists and publicize to the world (especially potential investors) the opportunities that might exist for business. In turn, global companies pay for marketing rights as sponsors, such as the $957 million paid by eleven companies for the London Olympics. For instance, Coca-Cola's Facebook page enabled millions of Facebook visitors from dozens of countries to upload videos dealing with the games. Finally, individual athletes compete not only for medals, but also for lucrative contracts to endorse products. Michael Phelps' swimming successes have led to contracts with Visa, Omega, Hilton, Procter & Gamble, Under Armour, Subway, and HP.

While the participation in the Olympics and the World Cup has long been global, the location of competition has been less so, largely because of the cost of staging the events. This is now changing. The 2010 World Cup was the first in Africa. The first South American Olympics is scheduled for Brazil in 2016, and the first Middle East World Cup is slated for Qatar in 2022.

THE INTERNATIONAL JOB MARKET

Because more fans expect to see the world's best teams and players, the search for talent has become worldwide. You can now find U.S. and European professional basketball scouts in remote areas of Nigeria looking for tall high-potential youngsters. Baseball agents have opened live-in training camps for teenagers in the Dominican Republic in exchange for a percentage of any of their future professional signing bonuses. Keep in mind, though, that assembling talent is necessary but insufficient for making a sports business successful. Shrewd marketing and financial management are crucial too. For instance, the Barcelona football club, arguably the best professional soccer team in recent years, has turned to young business graduates to help turn around its financial problems.

Most of today's top-notch athletes are willing to follow the money wherever it may take them. For example, many of the best Brazilian soccer players are with European teams that offer much higher payrolls than their Brazilian counterparts. England's professional soccer league (Premiership) includes players from about 70 countries, which helps improve the caliber of play and increase the TV fan base outside England.

How the ATP Courts Worldwide Support

If you're a fan of individual sports, you've probably noticed that players are globe hoppers. Take tennis. No single country boasts enough interested fans to keep players at home for year-round competition, yet today's top-flight tennis pros come from every continent except Antarctica. For 2013, the Association of Tennis Professionals (ATP) sanctioned 64 tournaments in 31 countries. It also requires member pros to play in a certain number of events—and thus stop over in a number of countries—to maintain international rankings.

Because no tennis pro can possibly play in every tournament, organizers must attract enough top draws to fill stadium seats and land lucrative TV contracts. So tournaments compete for top-billed stars, not only with other tournaments but also with such regular international showcases as the Olympics and the Davis Cup. Prizes for two weeks' worth of expert serving and volleying can be extremely generous (about US $2.55 million for the 2013 singles champions of the Australian Open).

Remember, too, that tournaments earn money through ticket sales, corporate sponsorship agreements, television contracts, and leasing of advertising space. The more people in the stadium and TV audience, the more sponsors and

MAP 1.1 Examples of National Sports

Some 33 countries have either defined a national sport by law or de facto have a national sport. Some national sports are shared by more than one country, such as cricket by six former British colonies in the Caribbean. Some others have been established to protect an historical heritage, such as tejo in Colombia. Note also that Canada has two designations, one for winter and one for summer.

Source: The information on sports was taken from Wikipedia, http://en.wikipedia.org/wiki/National_sport (accessed January 30, 2013)

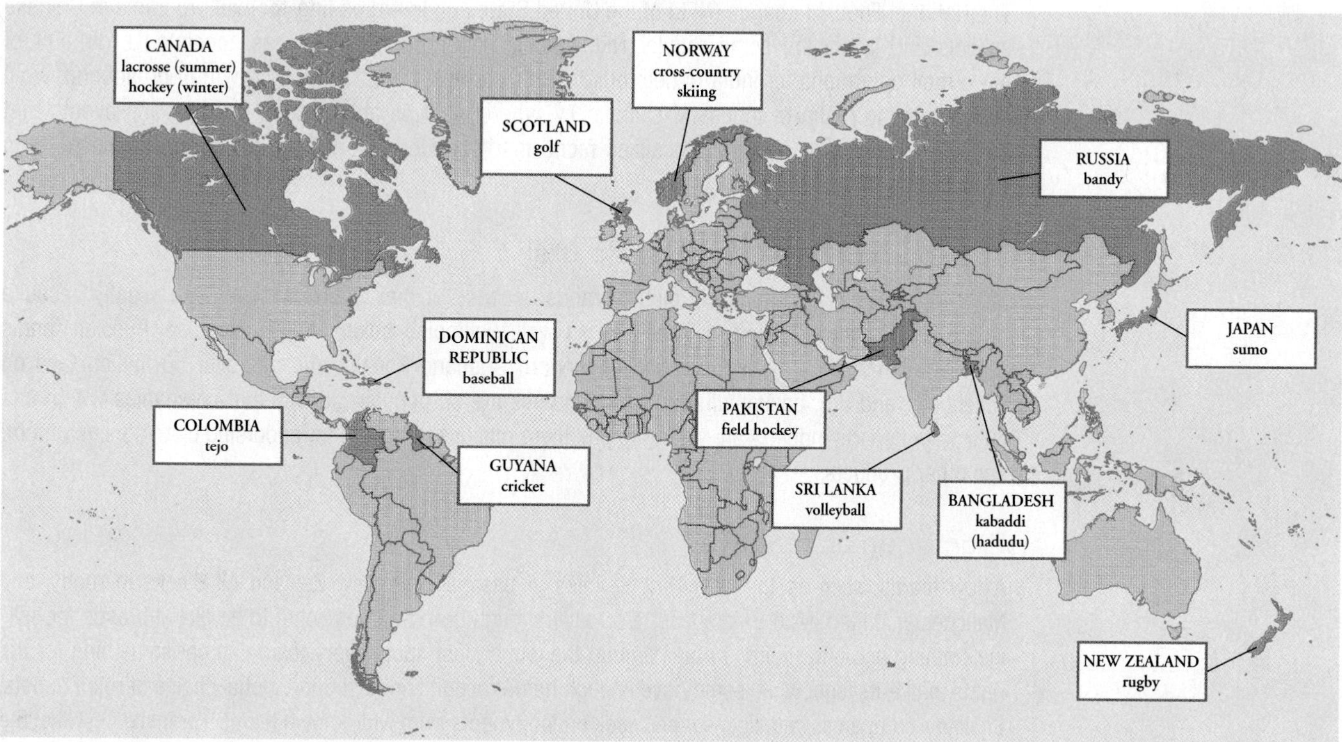

advertisers will pay to get their attention. Moreover, international broadcasts attract sponsorship from international companies. The partner and sponsor list for the 2013 Australian Open tennis tournament included a South Korean automaker (Kia), a Dutch brewer (Heineken), a Swiss watchmaker (Rolex), a French clothing company (Lacoste), and a U.S. sporting goods firm (Wilson). Such sponsorship of world-watched sporting events generally pays off in a higher market growth rate.

From National to International Sports Pastimes

Some countries have legally designated a national sport as a means of preserving traditions; others effectively have one. Map 1.1 shows a sample of these. However, other sports have sometimes replaced national sports in popularity, such as cricket replacing field hockey as India's most popular sport.

The International Baseball Federation now has over 100 member countries, even though baseball was popular only in its North American birthplace for most of its history. As TV revenues flattened in North America, Major League Baseball (MLB) began broadcasting games to international audiences. Increased exposure not only broadened the global fan base, it also showed youngsters all over the world how the game was played. As late as 1986, only 14 percent of MLB players were born outside the United States; by 2013, that number had climbed to over 28 percent. The average MLB clubhouse is now a bastion of multilingual camaraderie, with players and coaches talking baseball in Spanish, Japanese, Mandarin, and Korean as well as English.

THE WIDE WORLD OF TELEVISED SPORTS

Not surprisingly, other professional sports groups have expanded their global TV coverage (and marketing programs). Most viewers of Stanley Cup hockey watch from outside North America. Fans watch NASCAR races (National Association for Stock Car Auto Racing) in more than 120 countries and NBA games in about 200. If you lived in Tunisia and enjoyed simultaneous access to multiple TV channels, you could watch more hours of NBA action than there are hours in the year.

TV isn't the only means by which sports organizations are seeking foreign fan bases and players. The National Football League (NFL) of the United States underwrites flag-football programs in Chinese schools and is playing some regular NFL games in Europe. The NBA has appointed a director of basketball operations for India to help build youth leagues there. With the growth of broadband, we'll soon enter the realm of thousand-channel TV, where we'll be able to tune into sporting events that currently appeal only to highly localized niche markets. How about Thai boxing or Japanese sumo wrestling?

The Top-Notch Pro as Upscale Brand

Many top players are effectively global brands because of their sports success and usually because of good looks and pleasing personalities as well. Philippine boxer Manny Pacquiao, Russian tennis pro Maria Sharapova, Portuguese soccer forward Cristiano Ronaldo (he has over 50 million fans on Facebook), and U.S. basketball star LeBron James are so popular globally that companies within and outside the sports industry are willing to pay them millions of dollars for endorsing clothing, equipment, and other products.

Promotion as Teamwork

A few teams, such as the New York Yankees in baseball, the New Zealand All Blacks in rugby, and Manchester United (Man U) in soccer also have enough brand-name cachet to be global brands for selling clothing and other items to fans around the world. Just about every team can get something for the rights to use its logo, while some have enough name recognition to support global chains of retail outlets. Similarly, companies both sponsor and seek endorsements from well-known teams. For instance, Nike, the U.S. sports shoes and apparel giant, has fought hard to become the top sportswear and equipment supplier to European soccer teams. The success of this campaign has stimulated Nike's international sales to become greater than those in the United States.

Many nonsports companies, such as Canon (cameras, office equipment), Sharp (consumer electronics), and Carlsberg (beer), sponsor teams mainly to get corporate logos emblazoned on uniforms. Still others, such as United Airlines in Chicago, pay for the naming rights to arenas and other venues. Of course, teams themselves can be attractive international investments. For instance, the owners of the Boston Red Sox baseball team (U.S.A.) bought the Liverpool Football Club of the United Kingdom.

Sports and You

What does all this mean to you as a sports fan? Chances are you fantasized at one time about going pro in some sport, but you've probably given up that fantasy and settled into the role of spectator. Now that pro sports has become a global phenomenon (thanks to better communications), you can enjoy a greater variety—and a higher level of competition—than any generation before you.

That's the upside, but we must point out that people don't always take easily to another country's sport. Despite many efforts, cricket, although popular in countries that were British colonies for centuries, has never become popular elsewhere. (In post-colonial United States, it was popular, but it gradually gave way to baseball.) Nor has American football gained much popularity outside the United States. A former NFL lineman expressed a reason: that rules for cricket and American football are so complicated that one must learn them as children. However, basketball and soccer have traveled to new markets more readily because they are easier to understand and require no specialized equipment.

Further, there is disagreement about the economic effect of successfully winning a bid to host big international competitions such as the World Cup and Olympics. On the one hand, they help spur tourism, foreign investment, and infrastructure construction, and improvement of blighted areas that will speed future economic growth. (The cost of building facilities for the 2012 London Olympics was about $15 billion.) On the other hand, in light of threats from global terrorism the cost of security has skyrocketed, while hosts may have to spend on stadiums and facilities that have no use afterward. Many competitions have ended with substantially increased local and national debt.

Nor is everyone happy with the unbridled globalization of sports—or at least with some of the effects. Brazilian soccer fans lament the loss of their best players, and French fans protested the purchase of the Paris Saint-Germain (PSG) football club by the Qatar Investment Authority. ■

CRN
Case Review Note

QUESTIONS

1-1. Professional athlete A is a star, and professional athlete B is an average player. How has the globalization of professional sports affected each of these both positively and negatively?

1-2. As you read the chapter, identify and show an example of each international mode of operations that is illustrated in the globalization of professional sports.

INTRODUCTION

International business consists of all commercial transactions between two or more countries.

- The goal of private business is to make profits.
- Government business may or may not be motivated by profit.

Globalization refers to the widening set of interdependent relationships among people from different parts of a world that happens to be divided into nations. The term sometimes refers to the elimination of barriers to international movements of goods, services, capital, technology, and people that influence the integration of world economies.[2] Throughout history, wider human connections have expanded people's access to more varied resources, products, services, and markets. We've altered the way we want and expect to live, and we've become more deeply affected (positively and negatively) by conditions outside our immediate domains.

The opening case shows how far-flung global contact allows the world's best sports talent to compete, and their fans to watch them, just about anywhere. Likewise, managers in almost every industry consider ever more distant places as sources of supplies and markets. As consumers we know from "Made in" labels that we commonly buy products from all over the world, but these labels do not tell us everything. So many different components, ingredients, and specialized business activities from different countries go into products that it's often a challenge to say exactly where they were made. Belgium is renowned for its chocolate, but a Belgian Neuhaus bonbon includes ingredients from the Ivory Coast, Philippines, Ecuador, São Tomé, and Venezuela.[3] Because Apple ships its iPhones from China, they appear to be Chinese products, but less than 4 percent of their value is created in China.[4]

HOW DOES *INTERNATIONAL BUSINESS* FIT IN?

Studying international business is important because

- Most companies either are international or compete with international companies.
- Modes of operations may differ from those used domestically.
- The best way of conducting business may differ by country.
- An understanding helps you make better career decisions.
- An understanding helps you decide what governmental policies to support.

Globalization enables us to get more variety, better quality, or lower prices. Our daily meals contain spices that aren't grown domestically and fresh produce that's out of season in one local climate or another. Our cars cost less than they would if all the parts were made and the labor performed in one place. All of these connections between supplies and markets result from the activities of **international business,** defined as all commercial transactions, including sales, investments, and transportation, that take place between two or more countries. Private companies undertake such transactions for profit; governments may undertake them either for profit or for other reasons.

The Study of International Business Why should you study international business? Simply, it makes up a large and growing portion of the world's business. Global events and competition affect almost all companies, large and small, regardless of industry. They sell output and secure supplies and resources abroad, and they compete against products, services, and companies from foreign countries. Thus, most managers need to take into account

FIGURE 1.1 Factors in International Business Operations

The conduct of a company's international operations depends on two factors: its objectives and the means by which it intends to achieve them. Likewise, its operations affect, and are affected by, two sets of factors: physical/social and competitive.

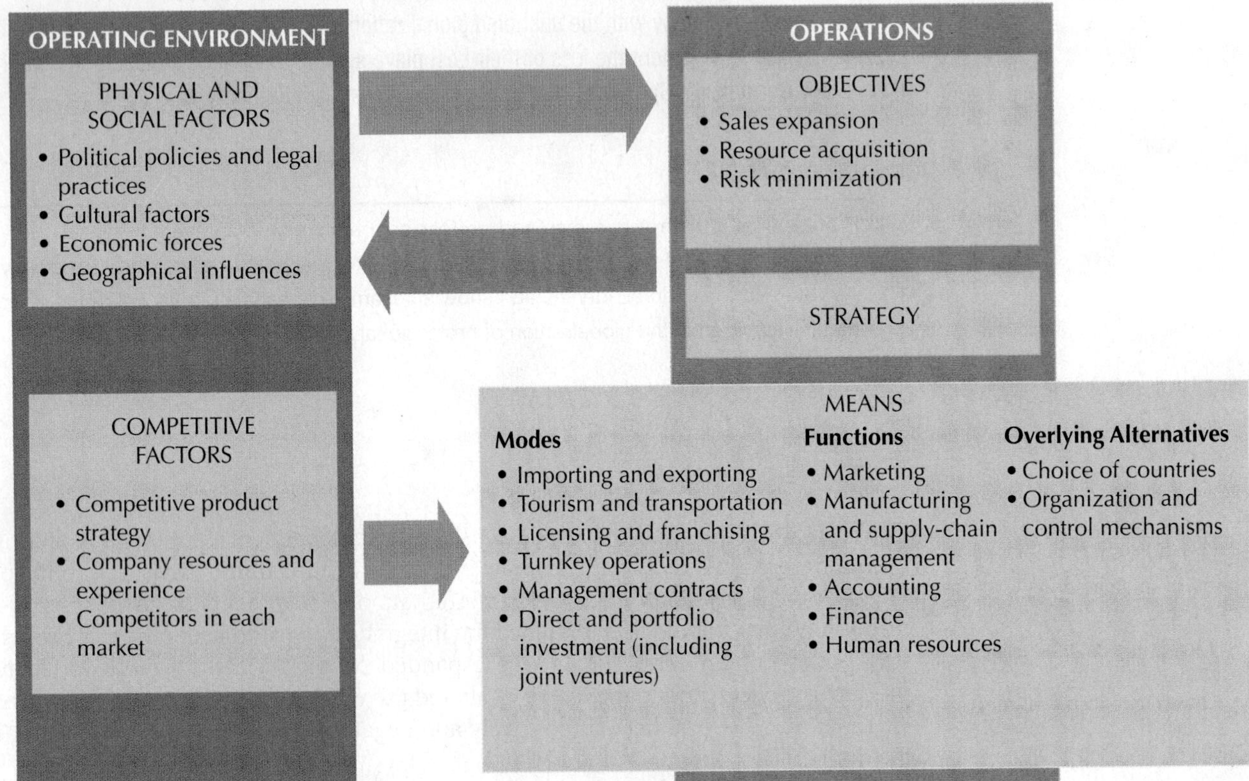

international business when setting their operating strategies and practices. Like the NBA teams in the opening case, which search globally for talent and additional markets, as a manager in almost any industry you'll need to consider (1) where you can obtain the best required inputs at the best possible price and (2) where you can best sell the product or service you've put together from those inputs.

Understanding the Environment/Operations Relationship The best way to do business abroad may not be the same as the best way at home. Why? First, when your company operates internationally, it will engage in *modes* of business, such as exporting and importing, which differ from those it uses domestically. Second, physical, social, and competitive conditions differ among countries and affect the optimum ways to conduct business. Thus, international companies have more diverse and complex operating environments than purely domestic ones. Figure 1.1 outlines the set of relationships between international environments and operations.

Even if you never have direct international business responsibilities, understanding some of the complexities may be useful to you. Companies' international operations and their governmental regulations affect overall national conditions—economic growth, employment, consumer prices, national security—as well as the success of individual industries and firms. A better understanding of international business will help you make more informed decisions, such as where you want to work and what governmental policies you want to support.

Globalization
- Has been growing.
- Is less pervasive than generally thought.
- Has economic and non-economic dimensions.
- Is stimulated by several factors.

THE FORCES DRIVING GLOBALIZATION

Measuring globalization is problematic, especially for historical comparisons. First, a country's interdependence must be measured indirectly.[5] Second, when national boundaries shift, such as in the breakup of the former Soviet Union or the reunification of East and West

Germany, domestic business transactions can become international ones and vice versa. Nevertheless, various reliable indicators assure us that economic interdependence has been increasing, at least since the mid-twentieth century. Currently, about 25 percent of world production is sold outside its country of origin, compared to about 7 percent in 1950. Restrictions on imports have generally been decreasing, and output from foreign-owned investments as a percentage of world production has increased. In periods of rapid economic growth, such as most years since World War II, world trade grows more rapidly than world production. However, in recessionary periods, such as that which began in 2008, global trade and investment shrink even more than the global economy. In fact, the world was less connected economically in 2012 than in 2007.[6]

At the same time, however, globalization is less pervasive than you might suppose. In fact, many Americans find it hard to believe that only about 15 percent of the value of goods and services bought in the United States comes from other countries. In much of the world (especially in poor rural areas), people lack the resources to connect much beyond their isolated domains. Such isolation is changing quickly, though; witness Africa, where telephone connectivity has increased markedly since the advent of mobile phones.[7] Only a few countries—mainly very small ones—either sell over half their production abroad or depend on foreign output for more than half their consumption. This means that most of the world's goods and services are still sold in the countries in which they're produced. Moreover, the principal source of capital in most countries is domestic rather than international.

Granted, these measurements address only *economic* aspects of global interdependence. Various studies have made more comprehensive comparisons by including, say, people-to-people contacts through travel and communications, technological interchanges, government-to-government relationships, and acceptance and adaptation of attributes from foreign cultures such as words from other languages.[8] Despite these ranking differences, the studies' results have several commonalities:

- *Size of countries*—Smaller countries tend to be more globalized than larger ones, mainly because their smaller land masses and populations permit a lower variety of production.
- *Income of the countries' populations*—Countries with higher-income populations tend to be more globalized than those with lower-income populations because their citizens can better afford foreign products, travel, and communications with people they have met abroad.
- *Variance among globalization aspects*—Although a country may rank as highly globalized on one dimension, it may be low on another, such as the United States being high on technological scales but low on economic ones.

FACTORS IN INCREASED GLOBALIZATION

What factors have contributed to the growth of globalization in recent decades? Most analysts cite the following seven factors:

1. Increase in and application of technology
2. Liberalization of cross-border trade and resource movements
3. Development of services that support international business
4. Growth of consumer pressures
5. Increase in global competition
6. Changes in political situations and government policies
7. Expansion of cross-national cooperation

Of course, these factors are interrelated, and each deserves a closer look.

Increase in and Application of Technology Many of the proverbial "modern marvels" and efficient means of production have come about from fairly recent technical advances. These include new products, such as hand-held mobile technology devices, as well as new applications of old products, such as guar beans from India now being used in oil and natural gas mining.[9] Thus, much of what we trade today either did not exist or was unimportant in trade a decade or two ago. Why have technical developments increased so much? More than half the scientists who have ever lived are alive today. One reason, of course, is population growth. But another is rising productivity—taking fewer hours to produce the same thing—which frees up more people to *develop* new products because fewer people can *produce* them. This rising productivity also means that on average people can buy more, including the new products, by working the same number of hours. The entry of new products into the market creates a need for other complementary products (such as cases and apps for smart phones), thus accelerating the need for scientists and engineers.

Many new products, as well as new ways to produce old ones, cannot easily take place in a single country. Much new technical innovation takes so many financial and intellectual resources that companies must cooperate to take on portions of development. These efforts may necessitate collaboration among and dependence on firms in different countries that have financial resources and specialized capabilities. A noteworthy example of interdependent technology, and one you may have watched on worldwide TV transmission, was the 2010 rescue of Chilean miners. Success would have been unlikely without the innovations and products from a variety of countries: the Center Rock drill bit from the United States, a high-strength cable from Germany, a super-flexible fiber optics communications cable from Japan, and a special cell phone from South Korea.[10]

Once new products are developed, the optimum scale size of production seldom corresponds with the market demand in a single country. Consequently, companies may need to sell both domestically and internationally in order to spread the fixed developmental and production costs over more units of production.

Advances in Communications and Transportation Strides in communications and transportation now allow us to discover and desire products and services developed in far parts of the world. Meanwhile, the costs of these improvements have risen more slowly in most years than costs in general. A three-minute phone call from New York to London that cost $10.80 in 1970 costs less than $0.20 today, while a call using Voice over Internet Protocol (VoIP) is virtually free.

Innovations in transportation mean that more countries can compete for sales to a given market. The sale of foreign-grown flowers in the United States used to be impractical; today, however, flowers from as far away as Ecuador, Israel, the Netherlands, and New Zealand compete with each other for the U.S. market because growers can ship them quickly and economically.

Or recall the opening case. Innovations allow individual athletes and teams to go head to head at venues around the world and sports media to broadcast competitions to fans everywhere. If it weren't for modern means of transportation and communications, a tennis pro couldn't play in Morocco right after finishing a tournament in Miami, and advertising wouldn't generate enough prize money to induce the pro to do all that traveling.

Improved communications and transportation also enhance a manager's ability to oversee foreign operations, such as more easily visiting foreign facilities and communicating with managers therein. Thanks to the Internet, companies can immediately exchange pictures of samples. Even small companies can reach global customers and suppliers. However, you may ponder the following question: Has the Internet been a bigger force in globalization than the laying of the first trans-oceanic cable across the Atlantic in 1858 that reduced communication time from 10 days to a matter of a few minutes?

Liberalization of Cross-Border Trade and Resource Movements To protect its own industries, every country restricts the movement across its borders of not only goods and services but also the resources—workers, capital, tools, and so on—needed to produce them. Such restrictions, of course, set limits on international business activities and, because regulations can change at any time, contribute to a climate of uncertainty. Over time, however, most governments have reduced such restrictions, primarily for three reasons:

1. Their citizens want a greater variety of goods and services at lower prices.
2. Competition spurs domestic producers to become more efficient.
3. They hope to induce other countries to lower their barriers in turn.

Services that Support International Business Companies and governments have developed a variety of services that facilitate global commerce. Take sales in a foreign country and currency. Today, because of bank credit agreements—clearing arrangements that convert one currency into another and insurance that covers such risks as nonpayment and damage en route—most producers can be paid relatively easily for goods and services sold abroad. When Nike sells sportswear to a French soccer team, a bank in France collects payment in euros from the soccer team when the shipment arrives at French customs (probably from somewhere in Asia) and pays Nike in U.S. dollars through a U.S. bank.

Growth in Consumer Pressures More consumers know more today about products and services available in other countries, can afford to buy them, and want the greater variety in quality, price, and characteristics that access to them offers. However, because greater affluence is spread unevenly, both among and within countries as well as from year to year, consumers' ability to avail themselves of this variety differs substantially. As a result, more companies are now responding to those markets where incomes and consumption are growing most rapidly, such as China.

Greater affluence has also spurred companies to spend more on research and development (R&D) and to search worldwide—via the Internet, industry journals, trade fairs, and trips abroad—for innovations and products they can sell to ever-more-demanding consumers. By the same token, consumers are more proficient today at scouring the globe for better deals, such as searching the Internet for lower-priced prescription drugs abroad.

Increase in Global Competition The present and potential pressures of increased foreign competition can persuade companies to buy or sell abroad. For example, a firm might introduce products into markets where competitors are already gaining sales, or seek supplies where competitors are getting cheaper or more attractive products or the means to produce them.

In recent years, many companies have merged or acquired operations to gain the efficiencies to better compete, such as the publishing merger between the Random House division of the German firm Bertelsman with the Penguin division of the U.K. firm Pearson, or to become large enough to compete with or become global leaders, such as the merger between the Brazilian chilled and frozen food firms Perdigão and Sadia.[11]

So-called **born-global companies** start out with a global focus because of their founders' international experience[12] and because advances in communications give them a good idea of where global markets and supplies are. Take SoundCloud, a Swedish audio-sharing Web service. Of its two co-founders, one was born in England and the other in Sweden. The two moved to Germany within months after the firm's start-up and soon broke into the U.S. market, where they also secured $50 million in financing.[13] Many new companies locate in areas with numerous competitors and suppliers, a situation known as **clustering** or **agglomeration.** They quickly observe how their competitors benefit from foreign opportunities. And because suppliers and human talent gravitate to these areas, they gain easier access to the resources needed for international moves.[14]

Regardless of industry, most firms and individuals have to become more global; in today's competitive business environment, failure to do so can be disastrous. Once a few companies have responded to foreign opportunities, others inevitably follow suit. And they learn from each other's foreign experiences. As the opening case suggests, for example, the early success of foreign-born baseball players in U.S. leagues undoubtedly spurred U.S. basketball and football organizations to look for and develop talent abroad.[15]

Changes in Political Situations and Government Policies For nearly half a century after World War II, business between Communist countries and the rest of the world was minimal. Today, only a few countries do business almost entirely within a political bloc. In fact, political changes sometimes open new frontiers for international business, such as Myanmar's cessation of military rule that has influenced international companies to seek footholds there. Nevertheless, governments still prefer international business with certain countries and even deny such business with others for political reasons, such as many countries' sanctions against doing business with Iran because of its efforts to develop nuclear capabilities.

Governments seem more willing to support programs, such as improving airport and seaport facilities to foster speed and cost efficiencies for delivering goods internationally. They also now provide an array of services to help domestic companies sell more abroad, such as collecting information about foreign markets, furnishing contacts with potential buyers, and offering insurance against nonpayment in the home-country currency.

Expansion of Cross-National Cooperation Governments have come to realize that their own interests can be addressed through international cooperation by means of treaties, agreements, and consultation. The willingness to pursue such policies is due largely to these three needs:

1. To gain reciprocal advantages
2. To attack problems jointly that one country acting alone cannot solve
3. To deal with areas of concern that lie outside the territory of any nation

Gain Reciprocal Advantages Essentially, companies don't want to be at a disadvantage when operating internationally, so they petition their governments to act on their behalf. Thus, governments join international organizations and sign treaties and agreements for a variety of commercial activities.

Some treaties and agreements allow countries' commercial ships and planes to use certain of each others' seaports and airports. Some cover commercial-aircraft safety standards and flyover rights; some protect property, such as foreign-owned investments, patents, trademarks, and copyrights. Countries also enact treaties for reciprocal reductions of import restrictions (remaining prepared, of course, to retaliate when another party interferes with trade flows by raising trade barriers or cutting diplomatic ties).

Multinational Problem Solving Governments often act to coordinate activities along their mutual borders by building highways, railroads, and hydroelectric dams that serve the interests of all parties. The adjacent photo shows a dam between Brazil and Paraguay. (However, there are still border inefficiencies. For instance, trains between Italy and Sweden must change locomotives three or four times because of different national systems.)[16] They also cooperate to solve problems that they either cannot or will not solve by themselves. First, the resources needed to solve a problem may be too great for one country to manage; sometimes no single country is willing to pay for a project that will also benefit another country, as witnessed by Japan and the United States sharing the costs of ballistic-missile defense technology. In any case, many problems are inherently global—think of global climate change or nuclear proliferation—and can't be easily addressed by a single country. That's why cooperative efforts have developed to fight the spread of diseases such as malaria, to set warning systems against such natural disasters as tsunamis, and to take action on environmental problems such as global warming.

Second, one country's policies may affect those of others. Higher real-interest rates in one country, for example, can attract funds very quickly from individuals and firms in countries with lower rates, thus creating a shortage of investment funds in the latter. Similarly, a country may manipulate the value of its currency so that companies abandon suppliers in one country for those in another, with an undervalued currency thus contributing to unemployment in the abandoned country. To coordinate economic policies in these and other areas, the

The Itaipu Dam is a joint project between the governments of Brazil and Paraguay and is on the Parana River separating the two countries. It is the largest hydroelectric generating facility in the world, and its height is equivalent to a 65-story building.
Source: Shutterstock

most economically important countries meet regularly to share information and pool ideas. The most notable coordination, known as the Group of Twenty or G20 countries, consists of 19 of the world's most important countries plus representation from the European Union of its members not included in the 19. These countries account for over 80 percent of the world's production and trade as well as about two-thirds of the world's population. The adjacent photo shows representatives at a 2012 meeting in Mexico.

Areas Outside National Territories Three global areas belong to no single country: the noncoastal areas of the oceans, outer space, and Antarctica. Until their commercial viability was demonstrated, they excited little interest for either exploitation or multinational

The G20 (Group of 20) countries meet to discuss global conditions. Shown here at a 2012 meeting in Los Cabos, Mexico are the heads of state from the 19 member countries plus the European Union.
Source: epa european pressphoto agency b.v./Alamy

cooperation. The oceans, however, contain food and mineral resources and constitute the surface over which much international commerce passes. Today, we need agreements to specify the amounts and methods of fishing to be allowed, to address questions of oceanic mineral rights (such as on oil resources below the Arctic Ocean), and to deal with piracy of ships.

Likewise, there is disagreement on the commercial benefits to be reaped from outer space. Commercial satellites, for example, pass over countries that receive no direct benefit from them but argue that they should. If that sounds a little far-fetched, remember that countries do charge foreign airlines for flying over their territories.[17]

Antarctica, with minerals and abundant sea life along its coast, attracts thousands of tourists each year, has a highway leading to the South Pole, and has thus been the subject of agreements to limit commercial exploitation. However, there is still disagreement about the continent's development—how much there should be and who does it.

Much of the cooperation we've described has been undertaken by international organizations, which we discuss in more detail in later chapters, especially in Chapter 7.

THE COSTS OF GLOBALIZATION

Although we've discussed interrelated reasons for the rise in international business and globalization, remember that the consequences of the rise remain controversial. To thwart the globalization process, *antiglobalization* forces regularly protest international conferences and governmental policies—sometimes violently and sometimes by using instruments of globalization to make the protest. Figure 1.2 shows such a use of globalization humorously. We focus here on three issues: *threats to national sovereignty, environmental stress,* and *growing income inequality and personal stress.* We revisit these and others in more depth later; watch for them also in several of our Point-Counterpoint features.

ANARCHY
Len
"The internet means we can organise anti-globalisation demos across the planet."

FIGURE 1.2 Social networks are global by nature and are used to reach an ever expanding audience. The cartoon implies using globalization to stem globalization.
Source: Len Hawkins/CartoonStock

THREATS TO NATIONAL SOVEREIGNTY

Critics of globalization claim

- Countries' sovereignty is diminished.
- The resultant growth hurts the environment.
- Some people lose both relatively and absolutely.
- Greater insecurity increases personal stress.

You've probably heard the slogan "Think globally, act locally." In essence, it means that local interests should be accommodated before global ones. Some observers worry that the proliferation of international agreements, particularly those that undermine local restrictions on how goods are produced and sold, will diminish a nation's **sovereignty**—its freedom to "act locally" and without externally imposed restrictions.

The Question of Local Objectives and Policies Countries seek to fulfill their citizens' economic, political, and social objectives by setting rules reflecting national priorities, such as those governing worker protection and environmental practices. However, some critics argue that individual countries' priorities are undermined by opening borders to trade. For example, if a country has stringent regulations on labor conditions and requires clean production methods, cheaper production may occur in countries with less rigorous rules. The result, by opening borders to trade, may be that the strict country must either forgo its labor and environmental priorities to be competitive or face the downside of fewer jobs and economic output.

The Question of Small Economies' Overdependence In addition, critics say that small economies depend so much on larger ones for supplies and sales that they are vulnerable to foreign mandates, including everything from defending certain positions at the United Nations to supporting a large economy's foreign military or economic actions. Nobel economist George Akerlof has noted that consequences of this dependence are intensified by poor countries' inadequate administrative capacity to deal with globalization.[18] These countries are also concerned that large international corporations are powerful enough to dictate their operating terms (say, by threatening to relocate), exploit legal loopholes to avoid political oversight and taxes, and counter the small economies' best interests by favoring their home countries' political and economic interests.

The Question of Cultural Homogeneity Finally, critics charge that globalization homogenizes products, companies' work methods, social structures, and even language, thus undermining the cultural foundation of sovereignty. In essence, they argue that countries have difficulty maintaining the traditional ways of life that unify and differentiate their cultures. Recall in our opening case that despite countries' designation of national sports to maintain tradition, some are losing out to imported sports anyway. Fundamentally, many critics feel helpless when it comes to stopping the incursion of foreign influences by such means as satellite television, print media, and Internet sites.[19]

ENVIRONMENTAL STRESS

Much criticism of globalization revolves around the economic growth it brings. According to one argument, growth consumes more nonrenewable natural resources and increases environmental damage—despoliation through toxic runoffs into rivers and oceans, air pollution from factory and vehicle emissions, and deforestation that can affect weather and climate. In addition, globalization opponents contend that by buying from more distant locations, the added transportation increases the *carbon footprint*, which refers to the total set of greenhouse gases emitted. They point further to the more than 1000 container ships plying the seas, each of which pollutes as much as 50 million cars do because of reliance on heavy oil as a fuel.[20]

The Argument for Global Growth and Global Cooperation Not everyone agrees with such a conclusion. Others argue that globalization has positive results for both sustaining natural resources and maintaining an environmentally sound planet. Global cooperation, they say, fosters superior and uniform standards for combating environmental problems, while global competition encourages companies to seek resource-saving and eco-friendly technologies, such as automobiles that use less gas and emit fewer pollutants.

The positive effects of pursuing global interests, however, may conflict with what a country's citizens think is best for themselves. Consider the effect of global pressure on Brazil to help protect the world's climate by curtailing logging activity in the Amazon region. Unemployed Brazilian workers have felt that job creation in the logging industry is more important than climate protection outside Brazil.

GROWING INCOME INEQUALITY AND PERSONAL STRESS

In measuring economic well-being, we not only look at our absolute situations but also compare ourselves to others. We generally don't find our economic status satisfactory unless we're doing better *and* keeping up with others.

Income Inequality By various measurements, income inequality, with some notable exceptions, has been growing both among and within a number of countries. Critics claim that globalization has affected this disparity by helping to develop a global superstar system, creating access to a greater supply of low-cost labor, and developing competition that leads to winners and losers.

The superstar system is especially apparent in sports, where global stars earn far more than the average professional player or professionals in sports with a more limited worldwide following. It also carries over to other professions, such as business, where charismatic top people can command many times what others can.

Although globalization has brought unprecedented opportunities for firms to profit by gaining more sales and cheaper or better supplies, critics argue that profits have gone disproportionately to the top executives rather than to the rank and file. Nobel economist Robert Solow supports this criticism by arguing that greater access to low-cost labor in poor countries has reduced the real wage growth of labor in rich countries.[21] And even if overall worldwide gains from globalization are positive, there are bound to be some losers in either an absolute or relative sense (who will probably become critics of globalization). The speed with which technology and competition expand globally affects the number of winners and losers along with the relative positions of individuals, companies, and countries. As an example, relocation of U.S. manufacturing jobs to China and India has helped the latter grow more rapidly than the United States, thus lessening the U.S.'s *relative* economic leadership over those countries.[22] Likewise, some displaced workers have lost economic and social standing relative to workers whose jobs were not moved. The challenge, therefore, is to maximize the gains from globalization while simultaneously minimizing the costs borne by the losers.

Personal Stress Certain repercussions of globalization can't be measured in strictly economic terms. What about the stress imposed on the people whose relative economic and social status suffers, or those who fear the loss of their jobs?[23] There is some evidence that the growth in globalization goes hand in hand not only with increased insecurity about job and social status but also with costly social unrest.[24] Further, although few of the world's problems are brand new, we may worry about them more now because globalized communications bring exotic sagas of misery into living rooms everywhere.[25]

Point — Is Offshoring Good Strategy?

Point **Yes Offshoring** is the dependence on production in a foreign country, usually by shifting from a domestic source. *If offshoring succeeds in reducing costs, it's good.* This is happening with many companies. Most branded clothing companies locate offshore to have work done by cheaper sewing machine operators. Many investment companies, such as Fidelity in India, are hiring back-office workers in poor countries to cut the cost of industry research. What good are cost savings? It's basic. If you can cut your costs, you can cut your prices or improve your product. Thus, by offshoring work to India, Claimpower, a small U.S. medical-insurance billing company, cut costs, lowered the prices it charges doctors, quadrupled its business in two years, and hired more U.S. employees because of the growth.[26]

What's the main complaint about offshoring? Too many domestic jobs end up abroad. As we discuss this, keep in mind that employment results from offshoring are difficult to isolate from other employment changes. Sure, unemployment in most high-income countries has increased substantially since 2008, but this was probably due mainly to improvements in production technology and the global recession. Let's try to pinpoint direct results of offshoring.

IBM is a good example. More than 70 percent of its nearly 400,000 employees are based outside the United States. By shipping some of its programming work abroad, IBM saves a tidy $40 an hour per worker—which comes out to $168 million a year.[27] If IBM failed to enact such cost savings, analysts agree that its competitors in low-wage countries, such as Infosys from India, could underprice IBM with competitive products and services.[28] Moreover, when you become price-competitive, you sell more both at home and abroad. You may also increase sales abroad if you locate near foreign customers. As you *create* jobs in this process, you improve your chances of survival.[29] IBM, for instance, is actually saving jobs by offshoring. Again, it's basic business: Cost savings generate growth, and growth creates more jobs.[30]

Not just any jobs, either: This process lets companies create more *high-value* jobs at home—the ones performed by people like managers and researchers, who draw high salaries. When that happens, demand for qualified people goes up. In the United States, that process has already resulted in a higher percentage of white-collar and professional employees in the workforce. These are *high-income* people, and more of them are employed as a result of sending *low-income* jobs to countries with lower labor costs.[31]

Further, offshoring is a natural extension of *outsourcing,* the process of companies' contracting work to other companies so that they can concentrate on what they do best.[32] This contributes to making a company more efficient. What is the difference, then, of outsourcing to a domestic versus a foreign location?

Admittedly, workers do get displaced from offshoring, but *aggregate* employment figures show that these workers find other jobs, just like workers who get displaced for other reasons. In a dynamic economy, people are constantly shifting jobs, partly due to technology. The prevailing employment for U.S. women was once as telephone operators; direct dialing technology changed that. Passenger aircraft used to carry five cockpit crew members; technology eliminated the need for the navigator, flight engineer, and radio operator. On the near-future horizon, pilotless passenger aircraft and package-carrying drone helicopters will reduce the cockpit crew to one or even zero,[33] while driverless cars will reduce demand for traffic policemen, auto insurers, emergency room personnel, and makers of such products as road signals and guard rails.[34]

What all this means is that the shifting of jobs is commonplace, and shifting because of outsourcing is no different from doing so for any other reason. In any case, because there are bound to be upper limits on the amount of outsourcing work a country can do, the direst predictions about job loss are exaggerated: There simply aren't enough unemployed people abroad who have the needed skills *and* who will work at a sufficiently low cost. Further, as production increases in outsourced facilities abroad, wage rates go up there.

Offshoring isn't for all companies or all types of operations. Some firms are bringing many operations *back* from abroad, a situation known as **reshoring**, because of such factors as poor quality, consumer pressure, concerns about competitive security, and advantages of locating production near technical development. In fact, about a fifth of the companies that have gone to offshoring now say that the savings are less than they expected.[35] That brings us back to what we said explicitly at the outset: Offshoring works when you cut operating costs *effectively.*

Is Offshoring Good Strategy?

Counterpoint

No Some things are good for some of the people some of the time, and that's *almost* the case with offshoring. Unfortunately, it is good for only a *few* people but not for *most.* I keep hearing about the cost savings, but when I buy goods or services I rarely find anything that's cheaper than it used to be. Whether buying a Ralph Lauren shirt, getting medical services from a doctor who is saving money through Claimpower, or having Fidelity manage my assets, I have seen no lower prices for me. Instead, the lower production costs have resulted in higher compensation for already high-paid employees and for shareholders. Further, Claimpower's growth had to be at the expense of other companies in the business, not because of growth in the number of people getting medical services but because of its price decreases.

One study took a close look at 16 high-income countries and found that, in aggregate, the percentage of national income going to labor has gone down while the percentage of national income going to profits is up.[36]

Here's a key problem: When you replace jobs by offshoring, you're exchanging *good* jobs for *bad* ones. Most of the workers who wind up with the short end of the offshoring stick struggled for decades to get reasonable work hours and a few basic benefits, such as healthcare and retirement plans. More important, their incomes allowed them to send their kids to college, and the result was an upwardly mobile—and productive—generation.

Now many of these employees have worked long and loyally for their employers and have little to show for it in the offshoring era. Yes, I know governments give them unemployment benefits but these never equal what the employees had before, and they run out.[37] On top of everything else, they may have no other usable skills, and at their ages, who's going to foot the bill for retraining them? The increase in what you call "high-value jobs" doesn't do *them* any good. Further, when *reshoring* occurs (usually because managers didn't think through the offshoring decision adequately in the first place), you can bet they re-hire domestic workers at less cost than before they offshored those jobs.

Offshoring may lead to short-term cost savings, but many studies indicate that it merely diverts companies' attention from taking steps to find innovative means of more efficient production, such as better operating techniques and machinery.[38] Concentrating on these latter alternatives may cut costs, increase production, and maintain the jobs that are going abroad.

While we're on the subject of job "value," what kinds of jobs *are* we creating in poor countries? Because countries are competing with lower wages, it encourages them to keep wages from rising, a sort of race to the bottom. However, multinational enterprises (MNEs) no doubt pay workers in low-wage countries more than they could get otherwise, and I'll grant that some of these jobs—the white-collar and technical jobs—are pretty good. But for most people, the hours are long, the working conditions are barbaric, and the pay is barely enough to survive. When you use such suppliers, your reputation can suffer. Recently in Bangladesh, workers were killed when locked doors prevented their escape from a fire, and others were killed when their ramshackle workplace building collapsed. There is also little job security. As salaries creep up where companies are offshoring, the companies merely move to even cheaper places to get the job done. For instance, this is what happened to workers in the island country of Mauritius. As soon as Mauritians began to think they might expect a better way of life, MNEs found workers elsewhere to do their sewing.[39]

Admittedly, in a dynamic economy, people have to change jobs more often than they would in a stagnant economy—*but not to the extent caused by offshoring.* There's still some disagreement about the effects of offshoring on a country's employment rate. Researchers are looking into the issue, but what they're finding is that more of the so-called better jobs are also being outsourced. A study of 4,700 major U.S. and European organizations showed that 750,000 finance, IT, and other high-level jobs will be offshored between 2012 and 2016.[40] So are we really creating higher-level jobs at home? Here's the bottom line: In countries like the United States, workers simply aren't equipped to handle the pace of change when it means that jobs can be exported faster than the average worker can retrain for different skills.

WHY COMPANIES ENGAGE IN INTERNATIONAL BUSINESS

Let's now focus on some of the specific ways firms can create value by going global. Take another look at Figure 1.1, where you'll see three major operating objectives that underlie the reasons for engaging in international business:

- Expanding sales
- Acquiring resources
- Reducing risk

Normally, these three objectives guide all decisions about whether, where, and how to engage in international business. Let's examine each in more detail.

EXPANDING SALES

Pursuing international sales usually increases the potential market and potential profits.

A company's sales depend on the desire and ability of consumers to buy its goods or services. Obviously, there are more potential consumers in the world than found in any single country. Now, higher sales ordinarily create value, but only if the costs of making the additional sales don't increase disproportionately. Recall, for instance, the opening case. Televising sports competitions to multiple countries generates advertising revenue in excess of the increased transmission costs. In fact, additional sales from abroad may enable a company to reduce its per-unit costs by covering its fixed costs—say, up-front research costs—over a larger number of sales. Because of lower unit costs, it can boost sales even more.

So increased sales are a major motive for expanding into international markets, and many of the world's largest companies—such as Volkswagen (Germany), Ericsson (Sweden), IBM (United States), Michelin (France), Nestlé (Switzerland), and Sony (Japan)—derive more than half their sales outside their home countries. Bear in mind, though, that international business is not the purview only of large companies. In the United States, 97 percent of exporters are small and mid-sized firms (SMMs), which account for about a third of U.S. direct export value. Further, many sell products to large companies, which install them in finished products slated for sale abroad.[41]

ACQUIRING RESOURCES

Foreign sources may give companies
- Lower costs.
- New or better products.
- Additional operating knowledge.

Producers and distributors seek out products, services, resources, and components from foreign countries—sometimes because domestic supplies are inadequate (as with crude oil shipped to the United States). They're also looking for anything that will create a competitive advantage. This may mean acquiring a resource that cuts costs, such as Rawlings's reliance on labor in Costa Rica—a country that hardly plays baseball—to produce baseballs.

Sometimes firms gain competitive advantage by improving product quality or differentiating their products from those of competitors; in both cases, they're potentially increasing market share and profits. Most automobile manufacturers, for example, hire design companies in northern Italy to help with styling. Many companies establish foreign R&D facilities to tap additional scientific resources.[42] They also learn while operating abroad, and they acquire product knowledge for entering new markets at home, such as what PepsiCo is doing in order to enter the fast-growth U.S. yogurt market.[43] Further, the diversity of employees and operations bring companies new perspectives.

REDUCING RISK

International operations may reduce operating risk by
- Smoothing sales and profits.
- Preventing competitors from gaining advantages.

Operating in countries with different business cycles can minimize swings in sales and profits. The key is the fact that sales decrease or grow more slowly in a country that's in a recession and increase or grow more rapidly in one that's expanding economically. During 2011, for example, Gap's North American sales fell 5 percent, but this was mainly offset by its sales growth of 11 percent elsewhere.[44] Moreover, by obtaining supplies of products or components both domestically and internationally, companies may be able to soften the impact of price swings or shortages in any one country.

Finally, companies often go international for defensive reasons. Perhaps they want to counter competitors' advantages in foreign markets that might hurt them elsewhere. By operating in Japan, for instance, Procter & Gamble (P&G) delayed foreign expansion on the part of potential Japanese rivals by slowing their amassment of resources needed to enter into other international markets where P&G was active.

Similarly, British-based Natures Way Foods followed a customer, the grocery chain Tesco, into the U.S. market. This move expanded its sales and its relationship with Tesco. Moreover, it reduced the risk that Tesco would find an alternative supplier who might then threaten Natures Way's relationship with Tesco in the U.K. market.

MODES OF OPERATIONS IN INTERNATIONAL BUSINESS

When pursuing international business, an organization must decide on one of the suitable *modes of operations* included in Figure 1.1. In the following sections, we discuss each of these modes.

MERCHANDISE EXPORTS AND IMPORTS

Merchandise exports and imports are usually a country's most common international economic transactions.

Exporting and importing are the most popular modes of international business, especially among smaller companies. **Merchandise exports** are tangible products—goods—that are sent *out* of a country; **merchandise imports** are goods brought *into* a country. Because we can actually *see* these goods as they leave and enter the country, we sometimes call them *visible exports* and *imports.* The athletic shoes that an Indonesian plant sends to the United States are exports for Indonesia and imports for the United States. For most countries, the export and import of goods are the major sources of international revenues and expenditures.

SERVICE EXPORTS AND IMPORTS

Service exports and imports are international nonproduct sales and purchases.

- They include travel, transportation, banking, insurance, and the use of assets such as trademarks, patents, and copyrights.
- They are very important for some countries.
- They include many specialized international business operating modes.

The terms *export* and *import* often apply only to *merchandise.* For non-merchandise *international earnings,* we use the terms **service exports** and **service imports** and are referred to as *invisibles***.** The provider and receiver of payment makes a *service export;* the recipient and payer makes a *service import.* Services constitute the fastest growth sector in international trade and take many forms. In this section we discuss the most important:

- Tourism and transportation
- Service performance
- Asset use

Tourism and Transportation Let's say that the Williams sisters, Venus and Serena, and some U.S. tennis fans take Air France from the United States to Paris for the French Open tennis tournament. Their tickets on Air France and travel expenses in France are service exports for France and service imports for the United States. Obviously, then, tourism and transportation are important sources of revenue for airlines, shipping companies, travel agencies, and hotels.

The economies of some countries depend heavily on revenue from these sectors. In Greece and Norway, for example, a significant amount of employment and foreign-exchange earnings comes from foreign cargo carried on their shipping lines. Tourism earnings are more important to the Bahamian economy than earnings from export of merchandise. (As we'll see in our closing case, regional legislation and diplomatic relations affect the work of Dubai Ports World.)

Service Performance Some services, including banking, insurance, rental, engineering, and management services, net companies earnings in the form of *fees:* payments for the performance of those services. On an international level, for example, companies may pay fees for engineering services rendered as so-called **turnkey operations,** which are construction projects performed under contract and transferred to owners when they're operational. The U.S. company Bechtel currently has turnkey contracts in many countries, such as expanding a copper facility in Chile, building a commuter railway in England, and constructing public housing in Gabon. Companies also pay fees for **management contracts**—arrangements in which one company provides personnel to perform general or specialized management functions for another, such as Disney's management of theme parks in France and Japan.

Asset Use When one company allows another to use its assets—such as trademarks, patents, copyrights, or expertise—under contracts known as **licensing agreements,** they receive earnings called **royalties**. For example, Adidas pays a royalty for the use of the Real Madrid football team's logo on jackets it sells. Royalties also come from franchise contracts. **Franchising** is a mode of business in which one party (the *franchisor*) allows another (the *franchisee*) to use a trademark as an essential asset of the franchisee's business. As a rule, the franchisor (say, McDonald's) also assists continuously in the operation of the franchisee's business, perhaps by providing supplies, management services, or technology.

INVESTMENTS

Dividends and interest paid on foreign investments are also considered service exports and imports because they represent the use of assets (capital). The investments themselves, however, are treated in national statistics as separate forms of service exports and imports. Note that *foreign investment* means ownership of foreign property in exchange for a financial return, such as interest and dividends, and it may take two forms: *direct* and *portfolio.*

Direct Investment In **foreign direct investment (FDI),** sometimes referred to simply as *direct investment,* the investor takes a controlling interest in a foreign company. When, for example, U.S. investors bought the Liverpool Football Club, it became a U.S. FDI in the United Kingdom. Control need not be a 100 percent or even a 50 percent interest; if a foreign investor holds a minority stake and the remaining ownership is widely dispersed, no other owner may effectively counter the investor's decisions. When two or more companies share ownership of an FDI, the operation is a **joint venture**. (There are also non-equity joint ventures.)

Key components of portfolio investment are

- Noncontrolling interest of a foreign operation.
- Extension of loans.

Portfolio Investment A **portfolio investment** is a *noncontrolling* financial interest in another entity. It usually takes one of two forms: stock in a company or loans to a company (or country) in the form of bonds, bills, or notes purchased by the investor. They're important for most companies with extensive international operations, which routinely move funds from country to country for short-term financial gain.

TYPES OF INTERNATIONAL ORGANIZATIONS

Basically, an "international company" is any company that operates in more than one country, but we have a variety of terms to designate different types of operations. Highly committed international companies usually draw on multiple operating types. Companies work together—in *joint ventures, licensing agreements, management contracts, minority ownership,* and *long-term contractual arrangements*—all of which are known as **collaborative arrangements**. The term **strategic alliance** is sometimes used to mean the same, but it usually refers either to an agreement that is of critical importance to one or more partners or to an agreement that does not involve joint ownership.

An MNE (sometimes called MNC or TNC) is a company with foreign direct investments.

Multinational Enterprise A **multinational enterprise (MNE)** usually refers to any company with foreign direct investments. This is the definition we use in this text. However, some writers reason that a company must have direct investments in some minimum number of countries to be an MNE. The term **multinational corporation** or **multinational company (MNC)** is often used as a synonym for MNE, while the United Nations uses the term **transnational company (TNC)**.

Does Size Matter? Some definitions require a certain size—usually giant. However, a small company, usually described within the United States as having fewer than 500 employees, can have foreign direct investments and adopt any of the operating modes we've discussed.

Although most small companies remain small, some, if successful, become medium or large companies.[45] Vistaprint is a good example. Founded in 1995, its sales grew to $6.1 million in 2000 and to over $1 billion in 2012 with operations mainly in North America and Europe.

WHY INTERNATIONAL BUSINESS DIFFERS FROM DOMESTIC BUSINESS

Although foreign external environmental differences are problematic

- Some anecdotes of failures are merely myths.
- They must be weighed against domestic opportunities and risks.
- Understanding social science disciplines and how they affect all business functions helps assure success abroad.

Let's now turn to the conditions in a company's *external environment* that may affect its international operations. Earlier we indicated that the best way of doing business abroad may differ from that in a company's domestic environment. Although there are many anecdotes illustrating operational problems when companies have failed to consider foreign environmental differences, these differences are not so daunting that they prevent success. First, some of the anecdotes are merely myths that have been repeated so often their truths are seldom challenged. Second, gaining start-up success domestically is also problematic almost anywhere in the world; thus when companies look objectively at their domestic opportunities and risks, foreign entries may seem less formidable. Third, a good understanding of what one will encounter helps reduce operating risks, and smart companies don't form or develop the means to implement international strategies without examining the conditions abroad that are indicated in the left-hand side of Figure 1.1 and organized into the following categories:

- *Physical factors* (such as a country's geography or demography)
- *Social factors* (such as its politics, law, culture, and economy)
- *Competitive factors* (such as the number and strength of a company's suppliers, customers, and rival firms)

In examining these categories, we delve into the realm of the *social sciences,* which helps in explaining how external conditions affect patterns of behavior in different parts of the world.

PHYSICAL AND SOCIAL FACTORS

The physical and social factors we show above can affect how companies produce and market products, employ personnel, and even maintain accounts. Remember that any of these factors may require a company to alter its operation abroad (compared to domestically) for the sake of efficiency.

Natural conditions affect

- Where different goods and services can be best produced.
- Operating risks

Geographic Influences Managers who are knowledgeable about geography are in a position to determine the location, quantity, quality, and availability of the world's resources, as well as ways to exploit them. The uneven distribution of resources throughout the world helps explain why different products and services are produced in different places. Further, countries differ in size of landmass and population.

Again, take sports. Norway fares better in the Winter Olympics than in the Summer Olympics because of its climate, and except for the well-publicized Jamaican bobsled team (whose members actually lived in Canada), you seldom hear of tropical countries competing in the Winter Olympics. East Africans' domination in distance races is due in part to their ability to train at higher altitudes than most other runners.

Geographic barriers—mountains, deserts, jungles, and so forth—often affect communications and distribution channels. And the chance of natural disasters and adverse climatic conditions (hurricanes, floods, droughts, earthquakes, volcanic eruptions, tsunamis) can make business riskier in some areas than in others while affecting supplies, prices, and operating conditions in far-off countries. Keep in mind also that climatic conditions may have short- or long-term cycles. For instance, recent melting of Arctic ice floes along with new ship technologies have allowed more ships to use a Northwest Passage to cut transport costs by saving as much as 15 days at sea.[46]

Finally, population distribution and the impact of human activity on the environment may exert strong future influences on international business, particularly if ecological changes or regulations cause companies to move or alter operations.

Politics often determines where and how international business can take place.

Political Policies Not surprisingly, a nation's political policies influence how international business takes place within its borders (indeed, *whether* it will take place). For instance, Cuba once had a minor-league baseball franchise, which went the way of diplomatic relations between Cuba and the United States back in the 1960s. Several Cuban baseball players are now members of professional U.S. teams, although most of them had to defect from Cuba to play abroad. (Even more Cuban boxers than baseball players have defected.)

Obviously, political disputes—particularly military confrontations—can disrupt trade and investment. Even conflicts that directly affect only small areas can have far-reaching effects. The 2002 and 2009 terrorist hotel bombings in Indonesia resulted in a decrease in the country's international tourism revenue and investment capital because individuals and businesses abroad perceived it as too risky.

Each country has its own laws regulating business. Agreements among countries set international law.

Legal Policies Domestic and international laws play a big role in determining how a company can operate abroad. *Domestic law* includes both home- and host-country regulations on such matters as taxation, employment, and foreign-exchange transactions. British law, for example, determines how the U.S.-investor-owned Liverpool Football Club is taxed and which nationalities of people it employs in the U.K. Meanwhile, U.S. law determines how and when the earnings from the operation are taxed in the United States.

International law—in the form of legal agreements between countries—determines how earnings are taxed by *all* jurisdictions. International law may also determine how (and whether) companies can operate in certain places. As we point out in our closing case, strong bilateral agreements and good legalese is an important part of the trade flow that allows unhindered movement of Dubai Ports World's ships across the seas. When transactions between countries involve disputes, such as whether a French football team must pay Nike for imported uniforms when it questions the quality, the contract usually specifies the country's law that will make the determination.

Finally, the ways in which laws are *enforced* also affect a firm's foreign operations. In the realm of trademarks, patented knowledge, and copyrights, most countries have joined in international treaties and enacted domestic laws dealing with violations. Many, however, do very little to enforce either the agreements or their own laws. This is why companies not only must understand agreements and laws but also must determine how fastidiously they're enforced in different countries.

Countries' behavioral norms influence how companies should operate there.

Behavioral Factors The related disciplines of anthropology, psychology, and sociology can help managers better understand different values, attitudes, and beliefs. In turn, such understanding can help managers make operational decisions abroad. Let's return once again to the opening case. Although professional sports are spreading internationally, the popularity of specific sports differs among countries, while rules and the customary way of play for the same sport sometimes differ as well. Because of tradition, tennis's grand slam tournaments are played on hard courts in Australia and the United States, on clay in France, and on grass in England. A baseball game in the United States continues until there is a winner, while Japanese games end with a tie if neither team is ahead after 12 innings. Presumably the reason for the baseball difference is that the culture of Japan values harmony more than U.S. culture does, whereas U.S. culture values competitiveness more than the Japanese do.

Economics explains country differences in costs, currency values, and market size.

Economic Forces Economics explains why countries exchange goods and services, why capital and people travel among countries in the course of business, and why one country's currency has a certain value compared to another's. Recall from our opening case that the percentage of non-U.S.-born players on major-league rosters has been on the rise. Although players from the Dominican Republic form the largest share of non-U.S.-born players, the

idea of putting a major-league baseball team there isn't feasible because too few Dominicans can afford the ticket prices necessary to support a team. Obviously, higher incomes in the United States and Canada enable major league teams to offer higher salaries that attract Dominican players.

Economics also helps explain why some countries can produce goods or services for less. And it provides the analytical tools to determine the impact of an international company's operations on the economies of both host and home countries, as well as the impact of the host country's economic environment on a foreign firm.

THE COMPETITIVE ENVIRONMENT

Companies' competitive situations may differ by

- Their rankings among countries.
- The competitors they face by country.
- The resources they can commit internationally.

In addition to its physical and social environments, every globally active company operates within a competitive environment. Figure 1.1 highlights the key competitive factors in the external environment of an international business: product strategy, resource base and experience, and competitor capability.

Competitive Strategy for Products Products compete by means of *cost* or *differentiation strategies*, the latter usually by:

- developing a favorable *brand image,* usually through advertising or from long-term consumer experience with the brand; or
- developing *unique characteristics,* such as through R&D efforts or different means of distribution.

Using either approach, a firm may mass-market a product or sell to a niche market (the latter approach is called a *focus strategy*). Different strategies can be used for different products or for different countries, but a firm's choice of strategy plays a big part in determining how and where it will operate. Take Fiat, an Italian automobile company that competes with its best-selling models by using a cost strategy aimed at mass-market sales. This strategy has influenced Fiat to shift some fabrication of engine plants to China, where production costs are low, and to sell in India and Argentina, which are cost-sensitive markets. At the same time, Fiat has centered its production of its Alfa Romeo, Ferrari, and Maserati vehicles in Italy because these compete with a high-priced focus strategy that requires access to both the expertise and image of high technical competence. Whereas the competitive U.S. market has not been conducive to a mass-market Fiat brand strategy, Fiat sells over a quarter of all its Ferraris in the United States and is selling its Fiat 500 (a sort of boutique car) in the United States with a focus strategy. Its U.S. strategy will widen if it merges with Chrysler.

Company Resources and Experience Other competitive factors are a company's size and resources compared to those of its competitors. A market leader, for example—say, Coca-Cola—has resources for much more ambitious international operations than a smaller competitor like Royal Crown. Royal Crown sells in about 60 countries, Coca-Cola in more than 200.

In large markets (such as the United States), companies have to invest much more to secure national distribution than in small markets (such as Ireland). Further, they'll probably face more competitors in large markets than in small ones. Conversely, national market share and brand recognition have a bearing on operating in a given country. A company with a long-standing dominant national market position uses operating tactics that are quite different from those employed by a newcomer. Such a company, for example, has much more clout with suppliers and distributors. Remember, too, that being a leader in one country doesn't guarantee being a leader anywhere else. For example, in terms of global market share, Toyota and General Motors see-saw in the number one and two positions, but in many countries they hold neither of these top two positions.

Competitors Faced in Each Market Finally, success in a market (whether domestic or foreign) often depends on whether the competition is also international or local. Large commercial aircraft makers Boeing and Airbus, for example, compete almost only with each other in every market they serve. What they learn about each other in one country is useful in predicting the other's strategies elsewhere. In contrast, the British grocery chain Tesco faces different competition in almost every foreign market it enters.

Looking to the Future

Three Ways of Looking at Globalization

At this juncture, there's a big difference of opinion on the future of international business and globalization. Basically, there are three major viewpoints:

- Further globalization is inevitable.
- International business will grow primarily along regional rather than global lines.
- Forces working against further globalization and international business will slow down the growth of both.

Globalization Is Inevitable

The view that globalization is inevitable reflects the premise that advances in human connectivity are so pervasive that consumers everywhere will know about and demand the best products for the best prices regardless of their origins. Those who hold this view also argue that because MNEs have built so many international production and distribution networks, they'll pressure their governments to place fewer restrictions on international movements of goods and means to produce them.

Even if we accept this view, we must still meet at least one challenge to riding the wave of the future: Because the future is what we make of it, we must figure out how to spread the benefits of globalization equitably while minimizing the hardships placed on those parties—both people and companies—who suffer from increased international competition.

The *Wall Street Journal* posed a question to all living Nobel Prize winners in economics: "What is the greatest economic challenge for the future?" Several responses addressed globalization and international business. Robert Fogel said it's the problem of getting available technology and food to people who are needlessly dying. Both Vernon Smith and Harry Markowitz specified the need to bring down global trade barriers. Lawrence Klein called for "the reduction of poverty and disease in a peaceful political environment." John Nash felt we must address the problem of increasing the worldwide standard of living while the amount of the earth's surface per person is shrinking.[47] Clearly, each of these responses projects both managerial challenges and opportunities.

More Regional Than Global Growth

The second view—that growth will be largely regional rather than global—is based on studies showing that almost all of the companies we think of as "global" conduct most of their business in home and neighboring countries.[48] Most world trade is regional, and many treaties to remove trade barriers are regional. Transport costs favor regional over global business. For example, largely because of rising and uncertain oil prices that raise transport costs, Mexico is on track to displace China as the largest exporter to the United States.[49] And regional sales may be sufficient for companies to gain scale economies to cover their fixed costs adequately. Nevertheless, regionalization of business may be merely a transition stage. In other words, companies may first promote international business in nearby countries and then expand their activities once they've reached certain regional goals.

Globalization and International Business Will Slow

The third view argues that the pace of globalization will slow, or may already have begun collapsing.[50] In light of the antiglobalization sentiments mentioned earlier, it's easy to see that some people are adamant and earnest in voicing their reservations. The crux of the antiglobalization movement is the perceived growing schism between parties (including MNEs) who are thriving in a globalized environment and those who aren't. For example, in the 2010-2012 period, about 870 million people, or about 12 percent of the world's population, were chronically undernourished.[51]

Antiglobalists pressure governments to promote nationalism by raising trade barriers and rejecting international organizations and treaties. Historically, they have often succeeded (at least temporarily) in obstructing either technological or commercial advances that threatened their well-being. Recently, antiglobalization sentiments have grown in many countries, such as law changes in some U.S. states that hinder activities of undocumented aliens, the deportation by France of ethnic Roma (gypsies), the evacuation in Italy of immigrants to protect them against local residents, and gains by Sweden's anti-immigration Democrat's Party.[52] In Brazil and South Africa, the governments have authorized domestic companies to copy pharmaceuticals under global patent protection. Bolivia and Venezuela have nationalized some foreign investments, and Canada prevented the Malaysian state energy firm, Petronas, from buying Progress Energy, a natural gas producer. The sparring between pro- and anti-globalists is one reason why the globalization process has progressed in fits and starts.

Other uncertainties may hamper globalization. First is the question of oil prices, which affect international transportation because they can constitute more than 75 percent of operating costs on large ships.[53] In early 2008 global oil prices rose 44 percent, fell 74 percent by the end of the year, more than doubled by the end of 2010, and rose another 7.9 percent in 2011. Many U.S. companies, such as furniture manufacturers, have responded by reshoring rather than facing transport cost uncertainty.[54] Second, the economic recession and lingering unemployment since 2008 have led countries to enact measures to protect their work forces.[55] Third, safety concerns—property confiscation, terrorism, piracy of ships, and outright lawlessness—may inhibit companies from venturing abroad as much.

Finally, one view holds that for globalization to succeed, efficient institutions with clear-cut mandates are necessary; however, there is concern that neither the institutions nor the people working in them can adequately handle the complexities of an interconnected world.[56]

Going Forward

Only time will tell, but one thing seems certain: If a company wants to capitalize on international opportunities, it can't wait too long to see what happens on political and economic fronts. Investments in research, equipment, plants, and personnel training can take years to pan out. Forecasting foreign opportunities and risks is always challenging. Yet, by examining different ways in which the future may evolve, a company's management has a better chance of avoiding unpleasant surprises. That's why each chapter of this book includes a feature that shows how certain chapter topics can become subjects for looking into the future of international business. ■

CASE Transportation and Logistics: The Case for Dubai Ports World[57]

The world economy and global trade has been gradually growing since the recession of 2008–2009. Growth is coming from Europe and Japan where trade is stronger than expected, from China and India where high growth rates continue to be recorded, and from less developed countries where trade is primarily based on petroleum and basic commodities. The global transportation and logistics industry is one of the most important factors that contributes to the expansion of trade and logistics. Thus, it is important to understand how business is done in this industry and know more about the trends in the transportation and logistics industry.

Several factors have led to the growth in the transportation and logistics industry: the separation of raw materials, labor and production, decline in tariffs, import restrictions, and exchange rate controls are some of the main factors that led to this growth. These factors have resulted in an increased demand for transporting raw materials, unfinished goods, and finished goods in the global economy. These trends have increased the demand for global transportation and logistics services. For the year 2010, it was estimated that there was a total of 545 million TEU (twenty-foot equivalent unit) that was handled globally, an increase of 113 percent over the year 2000.

The Transportation and Logistics Industry

Ports play an important role in the transportation and logistics industry. They provide quality services, advanced technologies, and skilled labor that lead to increased productivity. The World Bank has developed a logistics performance indicator (LPI) for around 150 countries. The LPI measures the different dimensions of supply-chain performance in the different countries such as customs clearance procedures, quality of trade-related infrastructure, quality of transport services, timeliness of delivery, and ability to track and trace consignments. The World Bank has also highlighted the influence that government policies have on logistics performance. Countries that attempt to develop policies to improve supply-chain activities find themselves scoring higher on the LPI than countries that do not pay attention to such policies.

Logistics has in the past focused on reducing barriers to trade, and on governmental procedures implemented regarding getting clearance for goods at customs. While the laws and regulations are important, they are not enough to advance the industry that includes various stakeholders working and interacting together. It is also necessary to develop policies that integrate all elements of the supply chain so that various players can easily manage different steps of their business. This aspect has been lacking lately and arguably should be given more attention. An approach that centers on all the policies will have a major impact on the productivity and efficiency of the logistics business. This requires bringing all the integrators together in the

MAP 1.2 Where Dubai Ports World Operates

Dubai Ports World operates in more than 65 terminals across 6 continents. On the map below, some of these major locations have been indicated.

Source: Data from "Dubai Ports World" at http://web.dpworld.com/images/DP_World_Brochure_2013_Eng.pdf (accessed January 2013).

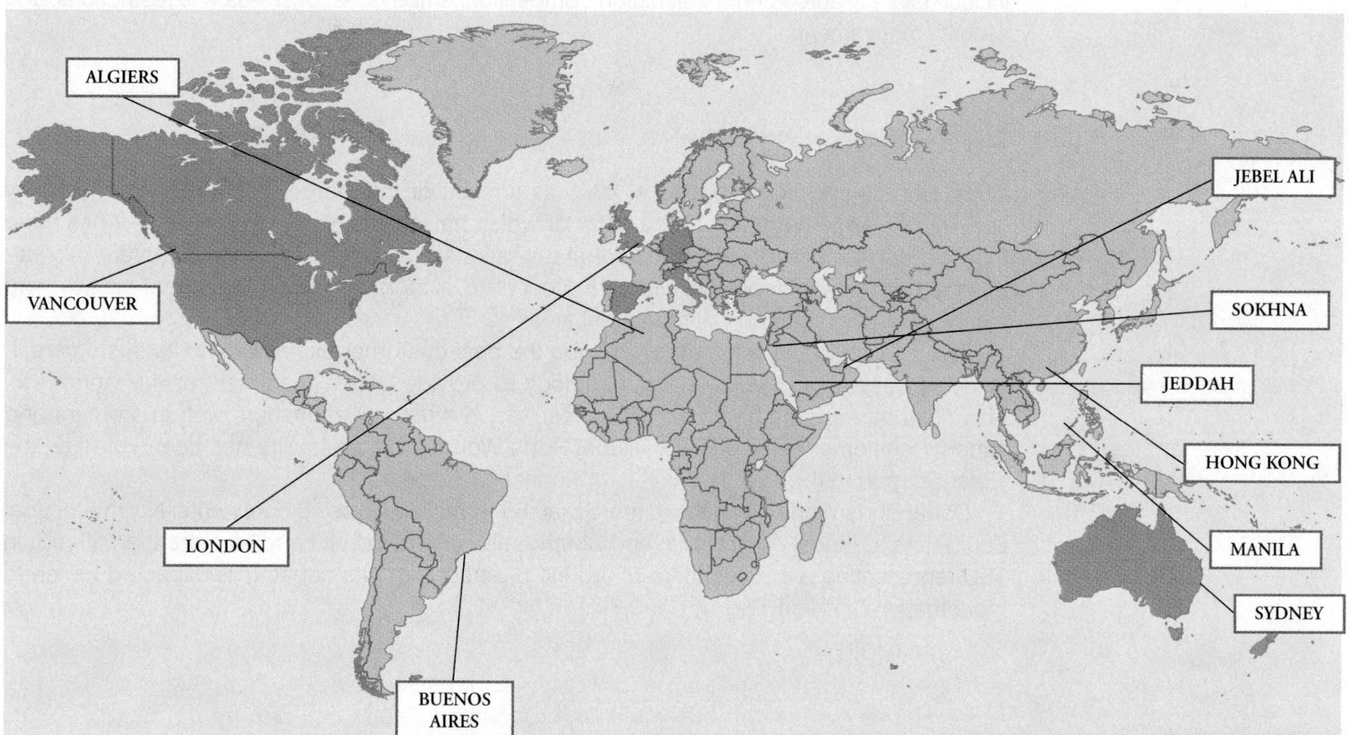

logistics chain: cargo handling, storage, warehousing, freight services, air road, and courier. This should result in an improvement in the global supply chain business.

Developing Logistics Clusters

Logistics clusters are geographically concentrated sets of logistics-related activities. They are known to have high transportation services, low transportation costs, and an efficient flow of goods. According to the *World Financial Review,* governments around the world are investing significant resources in developing logistics clusters.

The advantages of such clusters are economies of scope, economies of scale, economies of density, better service, and price stability. They also bring value by generating other business activities and bring in new jobs. These benefits create a positive feedback loop attracting more companies to them, resulting in further cost reduction and better efficiency.

Developing logistics clusters requires investment in seaports, airports, railways, and highways. This helps in improving the overall infrastructure of a nation. Examples of leading logistics clusters include Singapore, the Netherlands, Los Angeles, Dubai, Sao Paulo, and Aragon. These clusters are also referred to as logistics parks, transport centers, logistics platform, and logistics centers.

Doing Business in Different Countries

Local or domestic policies may affect the logistics operations in various markets. Some of these policies may raise costs, reduce efficiency, give preferential treatment for local or public owned corporations, and put limitations on investment in certain activities. These policies can significantly impact the supply chain, which may add costs to a firm and also affect the business activity.

Foreign countries may introduce restrictive policies such as importing raw material as opposed to processed products where the processing might be more efficient. Other restrictions include bilateral agreements that distort competition, embargoes, business visa restrictions, and security requirements.

About Dubai Ports World

Dubai Ports World was founded in 2005 as a result of the merger of Dubai Ports Authority and Dubai Ports International, the latter of which having been founded in 1999. It has more than 28,000 employees across its global operations. Excellence and innovation are two values the company embodies in its commitment to customers, profitable global growth, and responsible corporate and personal behavior.

Dubai Ports World attempts to provide the best customer experience to its customers. It heavily invests in its people and technology to provide better customer service worldwide. This customer-oriented approach has resulted in strong relationships with customers and superior customer service levels. Dubai Ports World Jebel Ali facility has been voted as the "Best Seaport in the Middle East" for 19 consecutive years.

Dubai Ports World operates in more than 65 terminals across 6 continents: North America, Europe, Asia, Africa, Australasia, and South America. In 2012, it handled more than 56 million TEU representing a market share of around 8 percent and its capacity is expected to rise to more than 100 million TEU by 2020.

Dubai Ports World is among the top three global terminal operators. It is one of the new players in the global market, with an aggressive growth and acquisition strategy. The majority of its business comes from emerging markets in South America and Africa. Their global expansion initially started in the Middle East, then extended into major ports in India. One of the major expansions for Dubai Ports World took place in 2006 when it acquired Peninsular and Oriental Steam Navigation Company (P&O) of the United Kingdom in 2006, for US$ 7 billion.

This was considered highly controversial by many in the United States, because it included a number of ports in the U.S. as well. These ports were sold shortly after they were purchased.

The Overseas Environment

Operating in various markets offers opportunities as well as challenges. The opportunities include access to new markets, access to natural resources, and innovative technology. The industry remains dynamic and profitable where emerging markets experience a significant growth in business. Governments are constantly aspiring to open their ports to logistics companies to facilitate economic growth and jobs. Logistics companies offer blue-collar, white-collar, and no-collar jobs while also providing opportunities to open new businesses.

Dubai Ports World faces challenges with regard to the complexity of operating in certain countries such as Africa, where the supply chain is an expensive and time-consuming activity. Transportation costs comprise up to 75 percent of the retail price in markets such as Malawi, Rwanda, and Uganda. For example, transporting a car from China to Tanzania could cost around $5,000 while transporting the same car from China to Uganda would cost $9,000.

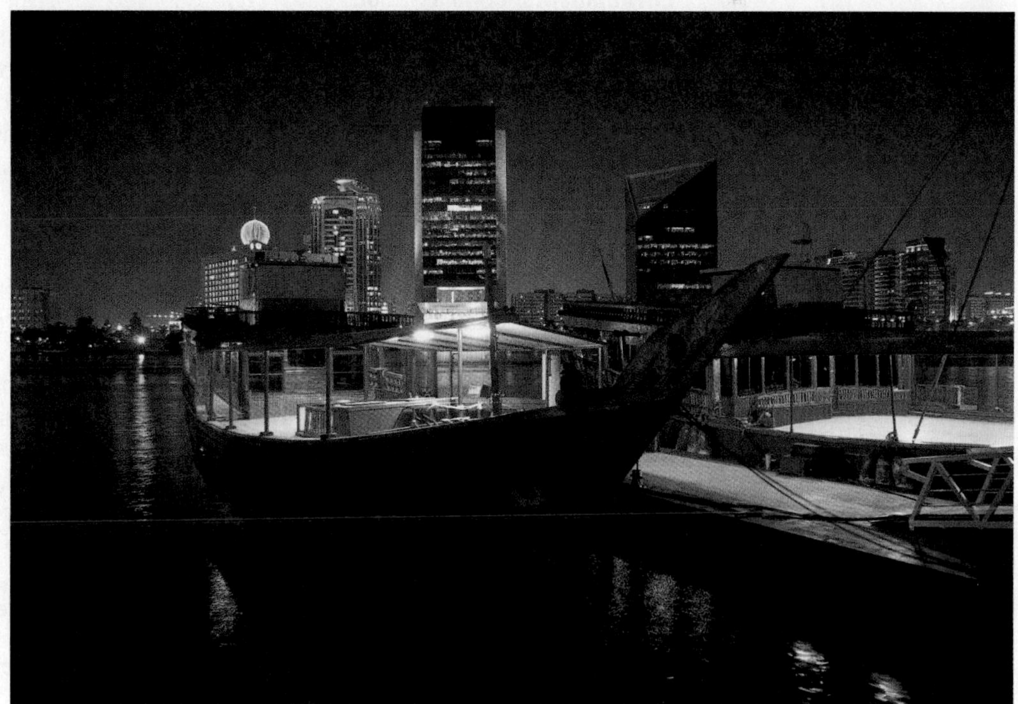

Dubai Ports World's mission is to use a global approach in local business environments, and of course to offer good value and service to their customers.
Source: © ewlyn - Fotolia.com

Finding the Right Skills

The logistics industry is primarily a people's business. Around 25 percent of the costs of logistics are labor costs. Thus, it becomes essential to attract, train, and motivate qualified people at all levels. One of the first issues that Dubai Ports World faces when it operates in a foreign country is finding qualified and skilled labor. There is usually a low supply of qualified candidates, low wages, low industry profile, and poor working conditions.

Risk Issues

Addressing risk in the supply chain is becoming a priority for businesses. Supply-chain risk can be caused by various disruptions: environmental risk such as natural disasters; geopolitical risk such as threat of attacks and terrorism; economic risk such as currency fluctuations, demand shocks and supplier failings; technological risk such as outage in IT and telecommunication systems, etc. Risk can be controlled by conducting scenario analyses, collaborating with the different players by sharing information, identifying vulnerabilities and synchronizing back-up plans.

Technology in Business

Dubai Ports World has been keen to use advanced information technology tools to facilitate its business. It has been using mobile technology to make life easier for customers by saving time and money. They also use mobile technology for their employees. Issues such as labor deployment, vessel arrival and gate appointments are communicated via mobile devices. This is linked to the human resource department which assigns labor to points of work, which results in more efficient work. Recently, this technology enabled container shipping lines to access bay and stowage, which helped reduce port call time.

Environmental Considerations

The presence of logistics companies may result in air pollution. This increases the health hazards around those clusters. Thus, there is always a tradeoff between the economic benefits of logistics operations and the hazards of their effects on the environment and health of the surrounding community. There are "green innovations" in logistics operations and processes that are ultimately minimizing the negative effects of logistics operations on the environment.

The Future

The logistics industry has high prospects for growth as the global economy grows. There are several matters that need attention to support this growth. There is a need for more comprehensive logistics policies that bring the various components of logistics together: land transportation, railway, shipping, commerce, and finance. More coordination is needed between these institutions. Additionally, more investment in logistics infrastructure such as roads, rail, and shipping is needed to ease traffic congestion, reduce costs and air pollution. Thirdly, people issues are becoming increasingly prominent and need to be addressed by those with the right skills in order to ensure high quality services throughout the industry.

The future of Dubai Ports World looks promising. It continues to sustain its growth by penetrating new markets while offering a unique customer experience. Its people remain the key stakeholder responsible for delivering the best service. Dubai Ports World is a global leader in logistics and transportation.

QUESTIONS

✪1-3. What global factors have contributed to the growth of the transportation and logistics industry? How have they contributed to this growth?

1-4. What steps has Dubai Ports World taken to benefit from global economic changes?

✪1-5. What economic factors influence the success of the international transportation and logistics industry?

1-6. How can logistics companies increase business with countries in Europe, Asia, or Africa?

1-7. What threats exist for Dubai Ports World? How would you overcome these threats?

1-8. Discuss some of the legal issues that have faced Dubai Ports World? How has this affected their operations in the United States and other places?

SUMMARY

- Globalization is the ongoing process that deepens and broadens interdependence among countries. International business is a mechanism to bring about globalization.
- International business has grown rapidly in recent decades because of technological expansion, liberalized government policies on cross-border movements (goods, services, and the resources to produce them), the development of services to facilitate international transactions, consumer desires to buy foreign products and services, increased global competition, changing political situations, and cooperation in dealing with transnational problems and issues. Because of these factors, companies use foreign countries increasingly as a source of both production and sales.
- Many critics feel that globalization weakens national sovereignty, promotes growth that is detrimental to the earth's environment, and skews income distributions.
- Offshoring—transferring production abroad—is controversial in terms of who benefits when costs are reduced and whether the process exchanges good jobs for bad ones.
- Companies engage in international business to expand sales, acquire resources, and diversify or reduce their risks.
- A company can engage in international business through various operating modes, including exporting and importing merchandise and services, making direct and portfolio investments, and entering into collaborative arrangements with other companies.
- Multinational enterprises (MNEs) are companies with foreign direct investments. Sometimes they are referred to as multinational corporations or companies (MNCs) or transnational companies (TNCs).
- When operating abroad, companies may have to adjust their usual methods of carrying out business. This is because (a) foreign conditions often dictate a more suitable method and (b) some international operating modes differ from those used domestically.
- Because country environments differ from each other, international managers must have a working knowledge of the basic physical and social sciences that impact operations: geography, political science, law, anthropology, sociology, psychology, and economics.
- A company's competitive strategy and resources influence how and where it can best operate. Likewise, from one country to another, its competitive situation may differ in terms of its relative strength and which competitors it faces.
- There is disagreement about the future of international business—that globalization is inevitable, that it will be primarily regional, and that its growth will slow.

KEY TERMS

agglomeration (p. 51)
born-global company (p. 51)
clustering (p. 51)
collaborative arrangement (p. 61)
foreign direct investment (FDI) (p. 61)
franchising (p. 61)
globalization (p. 47)
international business (p. 47)
joint venture (p. 61)
licensing agreement (p. 61)
management contract (p. 60)
merchandise export (p. 60)
merchandise import (p. 60)
multinational corporation or company (MNC) (p. 61)

multinational enterprise (MNE) (p. 61)
offshoring (p. 56)
portfolio investment (p. 61)
reshoring (p. 57)
royalty (p. 61)
service export (p. 60)
service import (p. 60)
sovereignty (p. 55)
strategic alliance (p. 61)
transnational company (TNC) (p. 61)
turnkey operation (p. 60)

ENDNOTES

1 ***Sources include the following:***"The Swedish Model," *The Economist* (October 27, 2012): 56; Kim Daekwan,"The Global Impacts of World Event Sponsorships on Firm Market Performance: A Hierarchical Linear Modeling Approach,"*Proceedings of the 54th Annual Meeting of the Academy of International Business* (Washington: June 30 – July 3, 2012);"Percentage of Foreign Players Rises,"(April 5, 2012) http://espen.go.com/mlb/story (accessed December 7, 2012); Mike Esterl, "Olympics Sponsors Go for the Young," *Wall street Journal* (July 3, 2012): B8; Andrew Zimbalist,"Is It Worth It?"*Finance & Development* 47:1 (March 2010): 6–11; Harald Dolles and Sten Söderman (eds.), *Sport as a Business: International Professional and Commercial Aspects* (Houndsmills, UK: Palgrave Macmillan, 2011); Mark Mulligan,"Football, Funding and MBAs,"*Financial Times* (December 13, 2010): 11; Roger Blitz,"Sports Organisers Play High Stakes Games,"*Financial Times* (September 29, 2010): 7; Jeremy Kahn,"N.B.A. in India, In Search of Fans and Players," *New York Times* (December 28, 2010): B13; George Vecsey,"When the Game Absorbs the Globe,"*New York Times* (April 1, 2007): A+; Simon Kuper,"Lost in Translation,"*Financial Times* (February 2–3, 2008): p. life & arts 2; Matthew Graham,"Nike Overtakes Adidas in Football Field," *Financial Times* (August 19, 2004): 19; L. Jon Wertheim,"The Whole World Is Watching,"*Sports Illustrated* (June 14, 2004): 73–86; Wertheim Jon,"Hot Prospects in Cold Places,"*Sports Illustrated* (June 21, 2004): 63–66; Grant Wahl,"Football vs. Fútbol,"*Sports Illustrated* (July 5, 2004): 72; Wahl,"On Safari for 7-Footers,"*Sports Illustrated* (June 28, 2004): 70–73; André Richelieu,"Building the Brand Equity of Professional Sports Teams,"Paper presented at the annual meeting of the Academy of International Business, Stockholm, Sweden (July 10–13, 2004).

2 For a good discussion of the versatility of the term *globalization,* see Joyce S. Osland,"Broadening the Debate: The Pros and Cons of Globalization,"*Journal of Management Inquiry* 10:2 (June 2003): 137–54.

3 Amy M. Thomas,"Brussels: The Chocolate Trail,"*New York Times* (December 25, 2011): tr7.

4 Andrew Batson,"Not Really'Made in China,'"*Wall Street Journal* (December 16, 2010): B1–B2.

5 Günther G. Schulze and Heinrich W. Ursprung,"Globalisation of the Economy and the Nation State,"*The World Economy* 22:3 (May 1999): 295–352.

6 "Globalisation Going Backwards,"The *Economist* (December 22, 2012): 105 referring to conclusions by the DHL Global Connectiveness Index.

7 "Africa's Economy: Bulging in the Middle,"*The Economist* (October 20, 2012): 43.

8 For example, see OECD, *Measuring Globalisation: OECD Economic Globalisation Indicators* (Paris: OECD, 2005); Pim Martens and Daniel Zywietz,"Rethinking Globalization: A Modified Globalization Index,"*Journal of International Development* 18:3 (2006): 331–50;"The Globalization Index,"*Foreign Policy* (November–December 2007): 68–76; Raab, M., Ruland, M., Schonberger, B., Blossfeld, H.-P., Hofacker, D., Buchholz, S., et al. (2008)."GlobalIndex: A Sociological Approach to Globalization Measurement,"International Sociology 23(4): pp. 596-631;"KOF Globalization Index, 2011,"http://globalization.kof.ethz.ch/ (accessed November 5, 2012).

9 Gardiner Harris,"Tiny Bean, Crucial to Halliburton, Lifts India Farmers from Mud,"*New York Times* (July 17, 2012): A1+.

10 Daniel Henninger,"Capitalism saved the Miners,"*Wall Street Journal* (October 14, 2010): A19.

11 Jeffrey A. Trachtenberg,"Book Deal a Tale of Reunions,"*Wall Street Journal* (November 5, 2012): B4; and Antonio Regalado and Lauren Etter,"Brazil Food Merger Creates Export Giant,"*Wall Street Journal* (May 20, 2009): B2.

12 See Rodney C. Shrader, Benjamin M. Oviatt, and Patricia Phillips McDougall,"How New Ventures Exploit Trade-Offs among International Risk Factors: Lessons for the Accelerated Internationalization of the 21st Century,"*Academy of Management Journal* 43:6 (2000): 1227–47.

13 Mark Scott,"Companies Born in Europe, but Based on the Planet,"*New York Times* (June 12, 2012): B7.

14 Stephanie A. Fernhaber, Brett Anitra Gilbert, and Patricia P. McDougall, "International Entrepreneurship and Geographic Location: An Empirical Examination of New Venture Internationalization,"*Journal of International Business Studies* 39:2 (2008): 267–90.

15 Dan McGraw,"The Foreign Invasion of the American Game,"*The Village Voice* (May 28–June 3, 2003) (accessed June 4, 2007).

16 "Charlemagne: Coming off the Rails,"*The Economist* (October 20, 2012): 51.

17 Susan Carey,"Calculating Costs in the Clouds,"*Wall Street Journal* (March 6, 2007): B1+.

18 His views are discussed in Joellen Perry,"Nobel Laureates Say Globalization's Winners Should Aid Poor,"*Wall Street Journal* (August 25, 2008): 2.

19 Lorraine Eden and Stefanie Lenway,"Introduction to the Symposium Multinationals: The Janus Face of Globalization,"*Journal of International Business Studies* 32:3 (2001): 383–400.

20 Christopher DeMorro,"One Container Ship Pollutes As Much As 50 Million Cars,"(June 3, 2009), accessed September 14, 2012.

21 His views are discussed in Joellen Perry,"Nobel Laureates Say Globalization's Winners Should Aid Poor,"*Wall Street Journal* (August 25, 2008): 2.

22 Steve Lohr,"An Elder Challenges Outsourcing's Orthodoxy,"*New York Times* (September 9, 2004): C1+; Paul A. Samuelson,"Where Ricardo and Mill Rebut and Confirm Arguments of Mainstream Economists Supporting Globalization,"*Journal of Economic Perspectives* 18:3 (Summer 2004): 135–47.

23 An examination of this subject may be found in Arne Kalleberg, "Precarious Work, Insecure Workers: Employment Relations in Transition,"*American Sociological Review* 74:1 (2009): 1–22.

24 Bernhard G. Gunter and Rolph van der Hoeven,"The Social Dimension of Globalization: A Review of the Literature,"*International Labour Review* 143:1/2 (2004): 7–43.

25 Jagdish Bhagwati,"Anti-Globalization: Why?"*Journal of Policy Modeling* 26:4 (2004): 439–64.

26 Craig Karmin,"Offshoring Can Generate Jobs in the U.S.,"*Wall Street Journal* (March 16, 2004): B1.

27 William M. Bulkeley,"IBM Documents Give Rare Look at'Offshoring,'" *Wall Street Journal* (January 19, 2004): A1+; William M. Bulkeley,"IBM to Cut U.S. Jobs, Expand in India,"*Wall Street Journal* (March 26, 2009): B1.

28 Richard Waters,"Big Blueprint for IBM,"*Financial Times* (March 3, 2009): 14.

29 N. Gregory Mankiw and Phillip Swagel,"The Politics and Economics of Offshore Outsourcing,"NBR Working Paper No. 12398 (July 2006); Kristien Coucke and Leo Sleuwaegen,"Offshoring as a Survival

Strategy: Evidence from Manufacturing Firms in Belgium," *Journal of International Business Studies* 39:8 (2008): 1261–77.

30 Matthew J. Slaughter, "Globalization and Employment by U.S. Multinationals: A Framework and Facts," *Daily Tax Report* (March 26, 2004): 1–12; Olivier Bertrand, "What Goes Around, Comes Around: Effects of Offshore Outsourcing on the Export Performance of Firms," *Journal of International Business Studies* 42:2 (February/ March 2008): 334–44.

31 Robert C. Feenstra and Gordon H. Hanson, "The Impact of Outsourcing and High-Technology Capital on Wages: Estimates for the United States, 1979–1990," *Quarterly Journal of Economics* 114:3 (1999): 907–40.

32 Alan S. Brown, "A Shift in Engineering Offshore," *Mechanical Engineering* 131:3 (2009): 24–29.

33 "An Internet of Airborne Things," *The Economist* (December 1, 2012): Monitor 3.

34 Paul Markille, "Cars on Autopilot," *The Economist* (The World in 2013 special issue): 152.

35 Timothy Aeppel, "Coming Home: Appliance Maker Drops China to Produce in Texas," *Wall Street Journal* (August 24, 2009): B1+; Linda Tucci, "Offshoring Has Long Way to Go," *CIO News Headlines* (June 2, 2005): n.p.; Paulo Prada and Niraj Sheth, "Delta Air Ends Use of India Call Centers," *Wall Street Journal* (April 18–19, 2009): B1+; Adrianna Gardella, "A Company Grows, and Builds a Plant Back in the U.S.A." *New York Times* (October 12, 2011): B9.

36 Tali Kristal, "Good Times, Bad Times: Postwar Labor's Share of National Income in Capitalist Democracies," *American Sociological Review* 75.5 (Oct 2010): 729–63.

37 Deborah Solomon, "Federal Aid Does Little for Free Trade's Losers," *Wall Street Journal* (March 1, 2007): A1+.

38 Paul Windrum, Andreas Reinstaller, and Christopher Bull, "The Outsourcing Productivity Paradox: Total Outsourcing, Organisational Innovation, and Long Run Productivity Growth," *Journal of Evolutionary Economics* 19:2 (2009): 197–232.

39 Carlos Tejada, "Paradise Lost," *Wall Street Journal* (August 14, 2003): A1+.

40 "The Hackett Group; New Hackett Research Forecasts Offshoring of 750,000 More Jobs In Finance, IT, Other Key Business Services Areas by 2016," Investment Weekly News (April 14, 2012): 612.

41 Small Business Export Association, 'New Report: SME Exports Support 4 Million Jobs," (December 6, 2010) www.nsba.biz/content/3647.shtml (accessed December 21, 2011); and "Rep. Sam Graves Holds a Hearing on U.S. Trade strategy and Small Business Exporters," Political Transcript Wire *[Lanham]* 17 (May 2012): n.p.

42 Heather Berry, "Leaders, Laggards, and the Pursuit of Foreign Knowledge," *Strategic Management Journal* 27 (2006): 151–68; and Jaeyong Song and Jongtae Shin, "The Paradox of Technological Capabilities: A Knowledge Sourcing from Host Countries of Overseas R&D Operations," *Journal of International Business Studies* 39:2 (2008): 291–303.

43 Diana Cimilluca and Mike Esterl, "PepsiCo Nears U.S. Yogurt Deal," *Wall Street Journal* (October 14, 2011): B3.

44 Devon Maylie, "Gap Sells Style in South Africa," *Wall Street Journal* (March 20, 2012):B1+.

45 Aaron Chatterji, ""Why Washington Has It Wrong," *Wall Street Journal* (November 12, 2012): R1+.

46 "Ships Take to Arctic Ocean as Sea Ice Melts," www.msnbc.com/id/39394645/ns/world_news-worldenvironment (accessed September 28, 2010).

47 David Wessel and Marcus Walker, "Good News for the Globe," *Wall Street Journal* (September 3, 2004): A7+.

48 Alan M. Rugman and Cecelia Brain, "Multinational Enterprises Are Regional, Not Global," *Multinational Business Review* 11:1 (2004): 3; and Alain Verbeke and Liena Kano, "An Internalization Theory Rationale for MNE Regional Strategy," *Multinational Business Review* 20. 2 (2012): 135–52.

49 "The Rise of Mexico," *The Economist* (November 24, 2012): 14.

50 John Ralston Saul, "The Collapse of Globalism," *Harpers* (March 2004): 33–43; James Harding, "Globalisation's Children Strike Back," *Financial Times* (September 11, 2001): 4; Bob Davis, "Wealth of Nations," *Wall Street Journal* (March 29, 2004): A1; Harold James, *The End of Globalisation: Lessons from the Great Depression* (Cambridge, MA: Harvard University Press, 2001).

51 Food and Agricultural Organization of the United Nations (FAO), *The State of Food Insecurity in the World, 2012* (Rome: FAO, 2012).

52 Peter Mayer, "Yearender: Europe Toughens Attitudes on Immigrants," *McClatchy – Tribune Business News* (December 15, 2010): n.p.

53 D. Ronen, "The Effect of Oil Price on Containership Speed and Fleet Size," *The Journal of the Operational Research Society* 62:1 (January 2011): 211–16.

54 Larry Rohter, "Shipping Costs Start to Crimp Globalization," *New York Times* (August 3, 2009): 1+.

55 Annie Lowrey, "An Increase in Barriers to Trade Is Reported," *New York Times* (June 23, 2012): B1+.

56 On the schism between those who thrive in a globalized environment and those who don't, see Jagdish Bhagwati, "Anti-Globalization: Why?" *Journal of Policy Modeling* 26:4 (2004): 439–64; Roger Sugden and James R. Wilson, "Economic Globalisation: Dialectics, Conceptualisation and Choice," *Contributions to Political Economy* 24:1 (2005): 13–32; J. Ørstrøm Møller, "Wanted: A New Strategy for Globalization," *The Futurist* (January–February 2004): 20–22.

57 ***Sources include the following:*** The public-private infrastructure advisory facility (PPIAF), Port Reform Tool Kit, http://www.ppiaf.org; Le Rossignol, Marie-Helene, 2007, Global Terminal Operators: an overview, Washington DC. http://www.dpworld.com; Outlook on the Logistics and Supply Chain Industry 2012, World Economic Forum, Containerization International Yearbook 2010; "Logistics Clusters: The Feedback Loop Leading to Economic Growth and Jobs," "Logistics Clusters: Delivering Value and Driving Growth," *The World Financial Review*, http://www.worldfinancialreview.com/?p=2265 (October 15, 2013).

An Atlas

Satellite television transmission now makes it commonplace for us to watch events as they unfold in other countries. Transportation and communication advances and government-to-government accords have contributed to our increasing dependence on foreign goods and markets. As this dependence grows, updated maps are a valuable tool. They can show the locations of population, economic wealth, production, and markets; portray certain commonalities and differences among areas; and illustrate barriers that might inhibit trade. In spite of the usefulness of maps, a substantial number of people worldwide have a poor knowledge of how to interpret information on maps and even of how to find the location of events that affect their lives.

We urge you to use the following maps to build your awareness of geography.

Map 1 World View page 75
Map 2 Africa, page 76
Map 3 Europe, page 77
Map 4 Asia, page 78
Map 5 North America, page 79
Map 6 South America, page 80
Map 7 Oceania, page 81
Map Index, pages 82–85

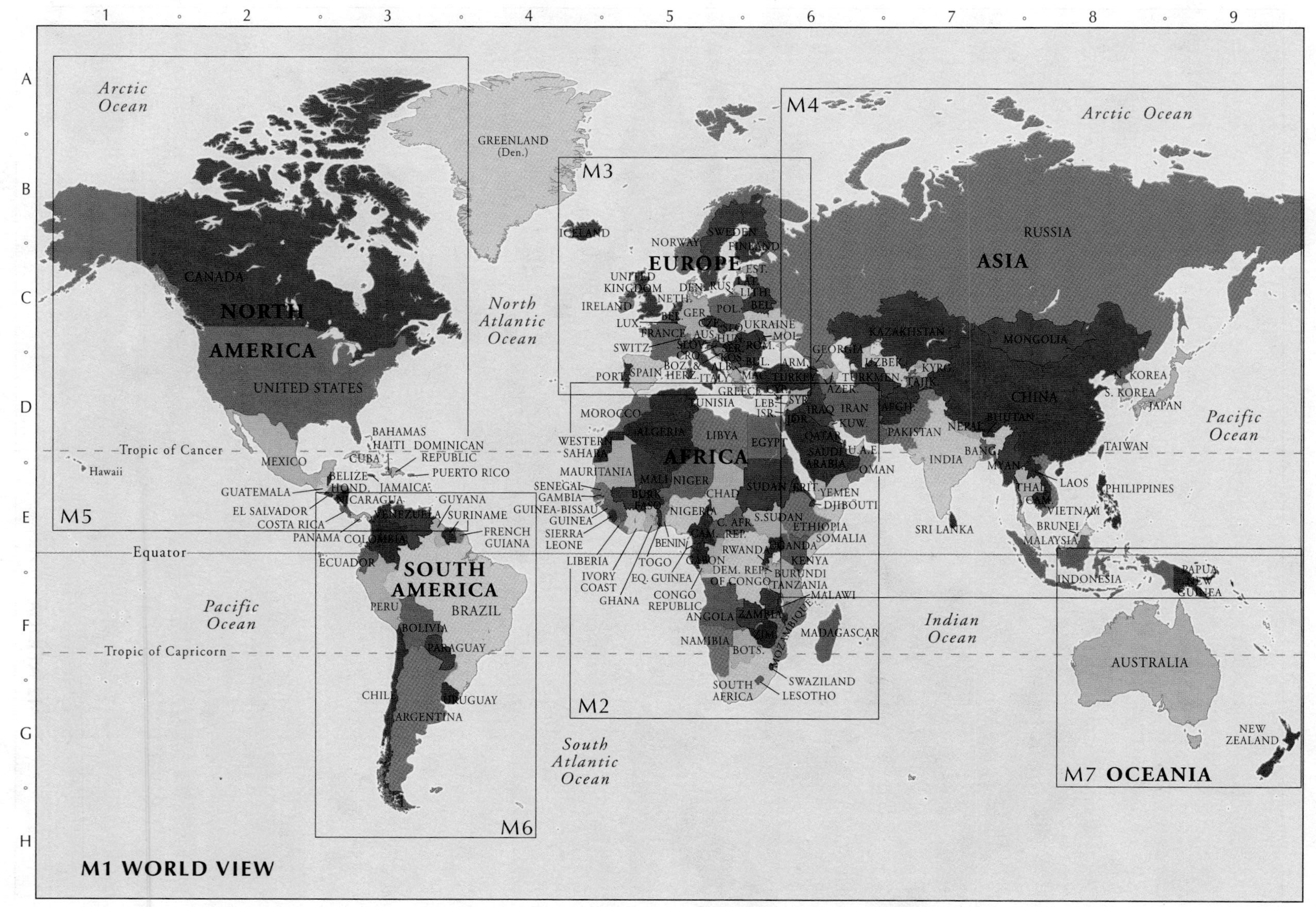
M1 WORLD VIEW
NORTH AMERICA
SOUTH AMERICA
EUROPE
AFRICA
ASIA
M7 OCEANIA
M2
M3
M4
M5
M6
Arctic Ocean
North Atlantic Ocean
South Atlantic Ocean
Pacific Ocean
Indian Ocean
Tropic of Cancer
Equator
Tropic of Capricorn
CANADA
UNITED STATES
MEXICO
GREENLAND (Den.)
Hawaii
BAHAMAS
CUBA
HAITI
DOMINICAN REPUBLIC
PUERTO RICO
JAMAICA
BELIZE
HOND.
GUATEMALA
EL SALVADOR
COSTA RICA
PANAMA
GUYANA
SURINAME
FRENCH GUIANA
ECUADOR
PERU
BRAZIL
BOLIVIA
PARAGUAY
CHILE
ARGENTINA
ICELAND
IRELAND
UNITED KINGDOM
NORWAY
SWEDEN
FINLAND
EST.
LITH.
POL.
GER.
UKRAINE
MOL.
ROM.
FRANCE
SWITZ.
LUX.
SPAIN
PORT.
ITALY
GREECE
TURKEY
GEORGIA
ARM.
AZER.
MOROCCO
WESTERN SAHARA
MAURITANIA
SENEGAL
GAMBIA
GUINEA-BISSAU
GUINEA
SIERRA LEONE
LIBERIA
IVORY COAST
GHANA
TOGO
BENIN
NIGERIA
NIGER
MALI
ALGERIA
TUNISIA
LIBYA
EGYPT
CHAD
SUDAN
S.SUDAN
C. AFR. REP.
EQ. GUINEA
CONGO REPUBLIC
DEM. REP. OF CONGO
ANGOLA
NAMIBIA
BOTS.
SOUTH AFRICA
SWAZILAND
LESOTHO
ZAMBIA
MALAWI
MOZAMBIQUE
MADAGASCAR
TANZANIA
BURUNDI
RWANDA
KENYA
ETHIOPIA
SOMALIA
DJIBOUTI
YEMEN
OMAN
U.A.E.
QATAR
SAUDI ARABIA
IRAQ
IRAN
KUW.
LEB.
ISR.
KAZAKHSTAN
PAKISTAN
INDIA
NEPAL
BHUTAN
BANG.
SRI LANKA
RUSSIA
MONGOLIA
CHINA
N. KOREA
S. KOREA
JAPAN
TAIWAN
PHILIPPINES
LAOS
VIETNAM
BRUNEI
MALAYSIA
INDONESIA
PAPUA NEW GUINEA
AUSTRALIA
NEW ZEALAND

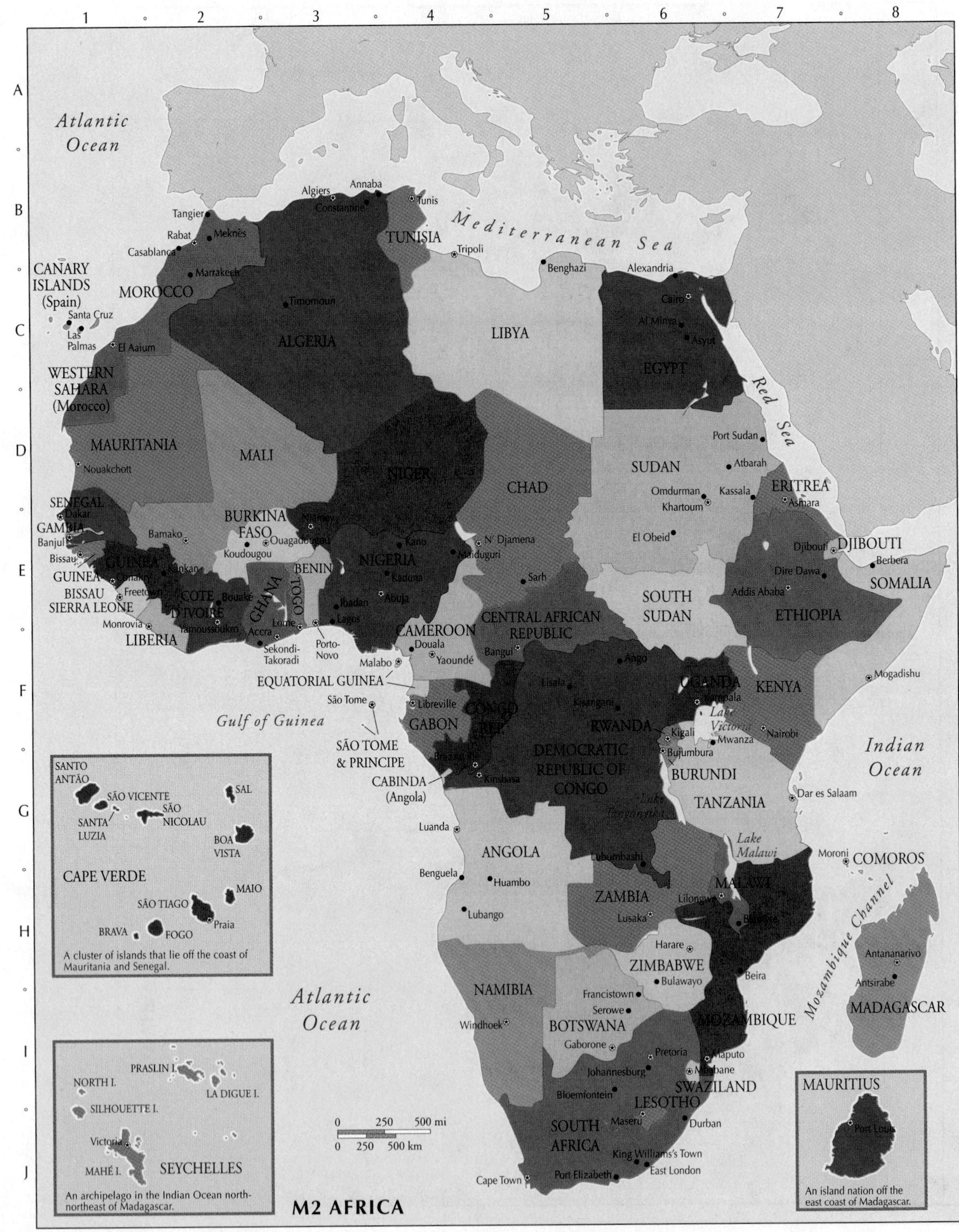
Atlantic Ocean
Mediterranean Sea
Red Sea
Gulf of Guinea
Indian Ocean
Mozambique Channel
CANARY ISLANDS (Spain)
MOROCCO
WESTERN SAHARA (Morocco)
MAURITANIA
MALI
ALGERIA
TUNISIA
LIBYA
EGYPT
SUDAN
SOUTH SUDAN
CHAD
NIGER
NIGERIA
SENEGAL
GAMBIA
GUINEA-BISSAU
GUINEA
SIERRA LEONE
LIBERIA
COTE D'IVOIRE
GHANA
TOGO
BENIN
BURKINA FASO
CAMEROON
CENTRAL AFRICAN REPUBLIC
EQUATORIAL GUINEA
SÃO TOME & PRINCIPE
GABON
CONGO REP.
DEMOCRATIC REPUBLIC OF CONGO
CABINDA (Angola)
ANGOLA
ZAMBIA
MALAWI
MOZAMBIQUE
ZIMBABWE
NAMIBIA
BOTSWANA
SOUTH AFRICA
LESOTHO
SWAZILAND
MADAGASCAR
COMOROS
TANZANIA
BURUNDI
RWANDA
UGANDA
KENYA
ETHIOPIA
ERITREA
DJIBOUTI
SOMALIA
Lake Victoria
Lake Malawi
SANTO ANTÃO
SÃO VICENTE
SANTA LUZIA
SÃO NICOLAU
SAL
BOA VISTA
MAIO
SÃO TIAGO
Praia
BRAVA
FOGO
CAPE VERDE
A cluster of islands that lie off the coast of Mauritania and Senegal.
PRASLIN I.
NORTH I.
LA DIGUE I.
SILHOUETTE I.
Victoria
MAHÉ I.
SEYCHELLES
An archipelago in the Indian Ocean north-northeast of Madagascar.
MAURITIUS
Port Louis
An island nation off the east coast of Madagascar.
0 250 500 mi
0 250 500 km
M2 AFRICA

M3 EUROPE
Arctic Ocean
Norwegian Sea
North Sea
Baltic Sea
Barents Sea
Atlantic Ocean
Denmark Strait
Bay of Biscay
English Channel
Irish Sea
Black Sea
Adriatic Sea
Tyrrhenian Sea
Ionian Sea
Aegean Sea
Mediterranean Sea
Strait of Gibraltar
Lake Ladoga
JAN MAYEN IS. (Denmark)
FAEROE IS. (Den.)
SHETLAND IS. (U.K.)
ORKNEY IS.
BALEARIC IS.
CORSICA
SARDINIA
SICILY
CRETE
ICELAND
Reykjavik
NORWAY
SWEDEN
FINLAND
RUSSIA
DENMARK
UNITED KINGDOM
IRELAND
NETHERLANDS
BELGIUM
LUXEMBOURG
GERMANY
FRANCE
SWITZERLAND
LIECHTENSTEIN
AUSTRIA
CZECH REP.
POLAND
SLOVAKIA
HUNGARY
SLOVENIA
CROATIA
BOSNIA & HERZEGOVINA
SERBIA & MONTENEGRO
KOSOVO
MACEDONIA
ALBANIA
GREECE
BULGARIA
ROMANIA
MOLDOVA
UKRAINE
BELARUS
LITHUANIA
LATVIA
ESTONIA
RUS.
PORTUGAL
SPAIN
ANDORRA
MONACO
ITALY
SAN MARINO
VATICAN CITY
MALTA
TURKEY
CYPRUS
Murmansk
St. Petersburg
Kostroma
Moscow
Tula
Smolensk
Orel
Kursk
Helsinki
Tallinn
Riga
Vilnius
Kaliningrad
Minsk
Homyel'
Kiev
Dnipropetrovsk
Lvov
Chernivtsi
Chisinau
Mykolayiv
Odesa
Bergen
Oslo
Stockholm
Göteborg
Malmo
Copenhagen
Glasgow
Edinburgh
Belfast
Dublin
Manchester
Liverpool
Birmingham
London
Amsterdam
The Hague
Brussels
Liege
Luxembourg
Hamburg
Berlin
Essen
Düsseldorf
Bonn
Frankfurt
Stuttgart
Munich
Leipzig
Dresden
Gdansk
Bydgoszcz
Warsaw
Lódz
Wroclaw
Krakow
Prague
Brno
Vienna
Linz
Bratislava
Budapest
Debrecen
Arad
Timisoara
Bucharest
Le Havre
Paris
Le Mans
Limoges
Bordeaux
Lyon
St. Etienne
Toulouse
Nîmes
Marseille
Geneva
Bern
Zurich
Milan
Turin
Padova
Venice
Genoa
Florence
Livorno
Rome
Naples
Bari
Taranto
Palermo
Messina
Valetta
Ljubljana
Zagreb
Sarajevo
Belgrade
Pristina
Skopje
Tirana
Sofia
Thessaloniki
Piraiévs
Athens
Istanbul
A Coruña
Porto
Lisbon
Madrid
Barcelona
Valencia
Sevilla
Granada
Málaga
Cartagena
0 300 mi
0 300 km

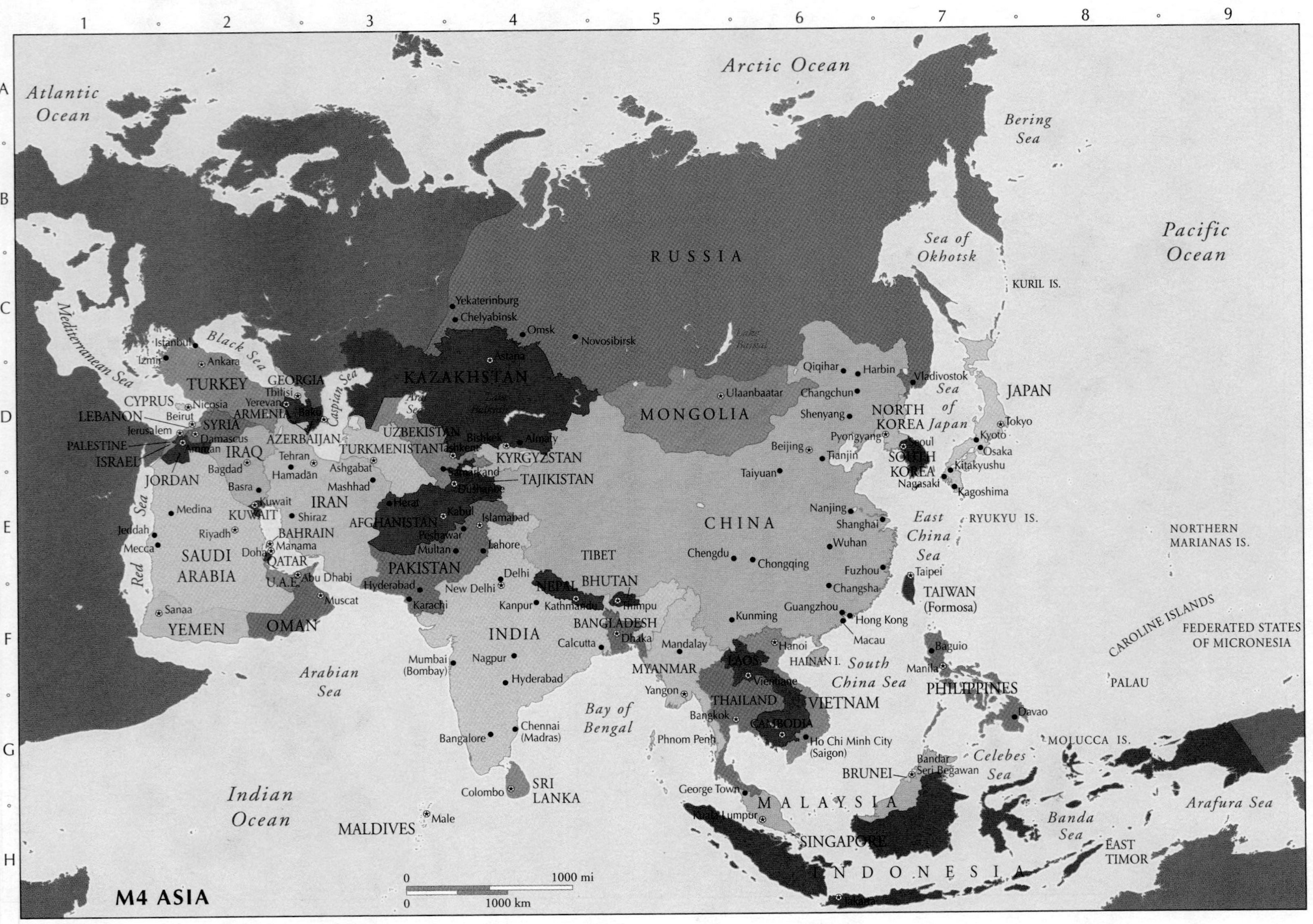
1 2 3 4 5 6 7 8 9
A B C D E F G H
Atlantic Ocean
Arctic Ocean
Bering Sea
Pacific Ocean
Sea of Okhotsk
KURIL IS.
RUSSIA
Mediterranean Sea
Black Sea
Caspian Sea
Red Sea
Yekaterinburg
Chelyabinsk
Omsk
Novosibirsk
Astana
KAZAKHSTAN
Istanbul
Izmir
Ankara
TURKEY
GEORGIA
Tbilisi
Yerevan
ARMENIA
Baku
CYPRUS
Nicosia
LEBANON
Beirut
SYRIA
Jerusalem
Damascus
PALESTINE
ISRAEL
Amman
AZERBAIJAN
UZBEKISTAN
TURKMENISTAN
Tashkent
Bishkek
Almaty
KYRGYZSTAN
TAJIKISTAN
Dushanbe
IRAQ
Bagdad
Tehran
Hamadan
Ashgabat
Mashhad
JORDAN
Basra
Kuwait
KUWAIT
IRAN
Shiraz
Herat
Kabul
Islamabad
AFGHANISTAN
Peshawar
Multan
Lahore
BAHRAIN
Manama
Doha
QATAR
U.A.E.
Abu Dhabi
Muscat
Medina
Jeddah
Mecca
Riyadh
SAUDI ARABIA
Sanaa
YEMEN
OMAN
PAKISTAN
Hyderabad
Karachi
Delhi
New Delhi
Kanpur
Kathmandu
NEPAL
BHUTAN
Thimphu
TIBET
BANGLADESH
Dhaka
Calcutta
INDIA
Mumbai (Bombay)
Nagpur
Hyderabad
Bangalore
Chennai (Madras)
Arabian Sea
Bay of Bengal
Colombo
SRI LANKA
Indian Ocean
MALDIVES
Male
MONGOLIA
Ulaanbaatar
Qiqihar
Harbin
Changchun
Shenyang
Vladivostok
Sea of Japan
JAPAN
NORTH KOREA
Pyongyang
Seoul
SOUTH KOREA
Beijing
Tianjin
Taiyuan
Tokyo
Kyoto
Osaka
Kitakyushu
Nagasaki
Kagoshima
RYUKYU IS.
CHINA
Nanjing
Shanghai
Wuhan
Chengdu
Chongqing
Fuzhou
Changsha
East China Sea
Taipei
TAIWAN (Formosa)
Kunming
Guangzhou
Hong Kong
Macau
Hanoi
HAINAN I.
South China Sea
Mandalay
MYANMAR
Yangon
LAOS
Vientiane
THAILAND
VIETNAM
Bangkok
CAMBODIA
Phnom Penh
Ho Chi Minh City (Saigon)
Baguio
Manila
PHILIPPINES
Davao
NORTHERN MARIANAS IS.
CAROLINE ISLANDS
FEDERATED STATES OF MICRONESIA
PALAU
MOLUCCA IS.
BRUNEI
Bandar Seri Begawan
Celebes Sea
George Town
Kuala Lumpur
MALAYSIA
SINGAPORE
INDONESIA
Jakarta
Banda Sea
Arafura Sea
EAST TIMOR
0
1000 mi
1000 km

M4 ASIA

Arctic Sea
GREENLAND
ELLESMERE I.
PARRY IS.
BANKS I.
VICTORIA I.
BAFFIN I.
Beaufort Sea
Baffin Bay
Davis Strait
Labrador Sea
Bering Sea
Gulf of Alaska
Hudson Bay
CANADA
UNITED STATES
MEXICO
Pacific Ocean
Atlantic Ocean
Gulf of Mexico
Caribbean Sea
NEWFOUNDLAND
Gulf of St. Lawrence
BERMUDA
BAHAMAS
WEST INDIES
CUBA
JAMAICA
HAITI
DOMINICAN REPUBLIC
BELIZE
GUATEMALA
HONDURAS
EL SALVADOR
NICARAGUA
COSTA RICA
PANAMA
HAWAIIAN ISLANDS (U.S.)
EASTERN CARIBBEAN
VIRIN ISLANDS (U.S. & Br.)
PUERTO RICO
ANGUILLA
ANTIGUA & BARBUDA
ST. KITTS & NEVIS
MONTSERRAT (Br.)
GUADELOUPE (Fr.)
DOMINICA
MARTINIQUE (Fr.)
ST LUCIA
ST VINCENT & THE GRENADINES
BARBADOS
GRENADA
TRINIDAD & TOBAGO
CURAÇAO (Neth.)
BONAIRE (Neth.)
ARUBA (Neth.)
Port of Spain
San Juan
Santo Domingo
M5 NORTH AMERICA
0 2000 mi
0 2000 km

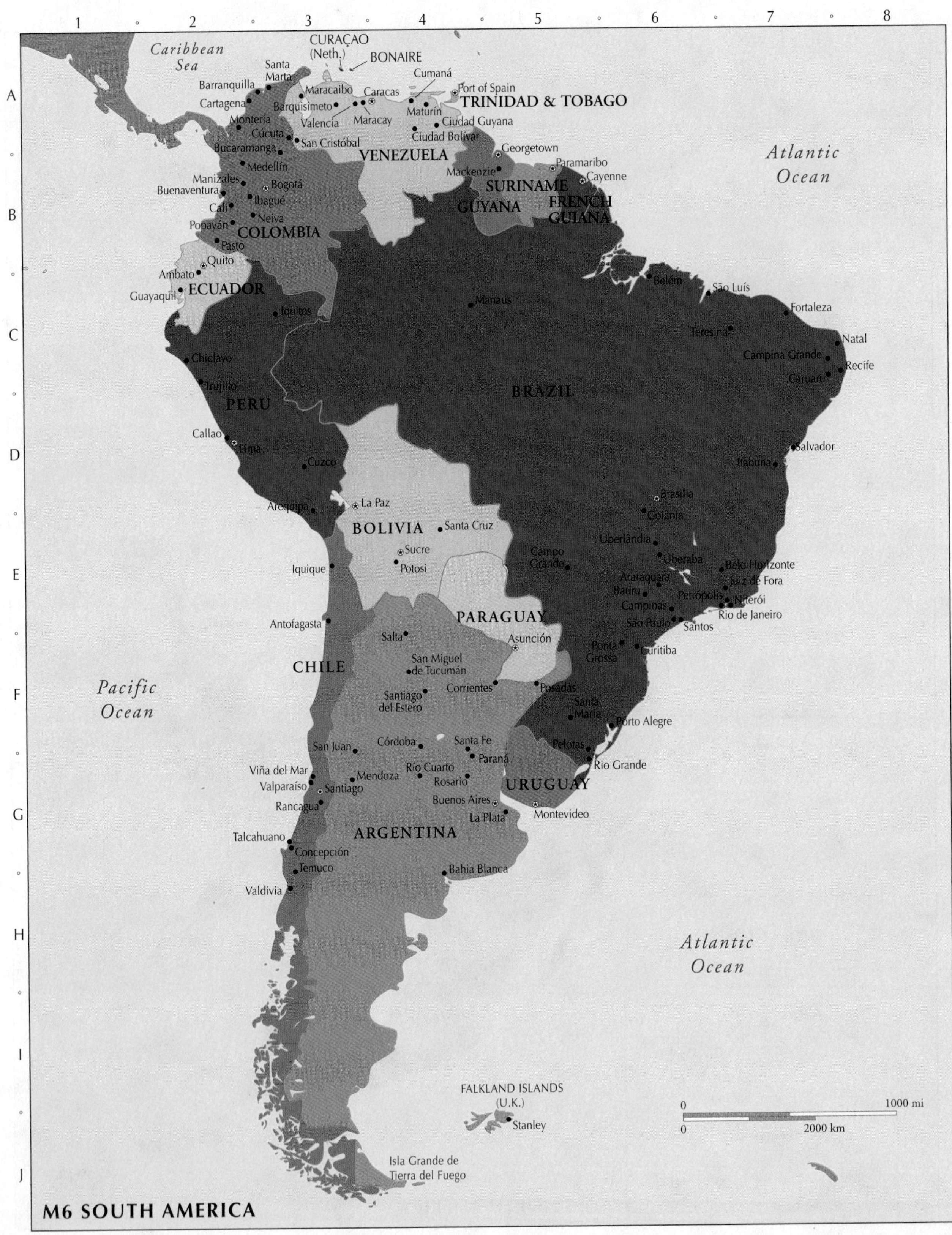
Caribbean Sea
CURAÇAO (Neth.)
BONAIRE
Santa Marta
Barranquilla
Cartagena
Maracaibo
Caracas
Cumaná
Port of Spain
TRINIDAD & TOBAGO
Barquisimeto
Valencia
Maracay
Maturín
Montería
Ciudad Guyana
Cúcuta
San Cristóbal
Ciudad Bolívar
Bucaramanga
VENEZUELA
Georgetown
Medellín
Paramaribo
Mackenzie
Cayenne
Manizales
Bogotá
Buenaventura
Ibagué
SURINAME
Cali
GUYANA
FRENCH GUIANA
Neiva
Popayán
COLOMBIA
Pasto
Quito
Ambato
Guayaquil
ECUADOR
Iquitos
Belém
São Luís
Manaus
Fortaleza
Teresina
Natal
Chiclayo
Campina Grande
Recife
Caruaru
Trujillo
BRAZIL
PERU
Callao
Lima
Salvador
Cuzco
Itabuna
La Paz
Brasília
Arequipa
Goiânia
BOLIVIA
Santa Cruz
Uberlândia
Sucre
Uberaba
Campo Grande
Potosí
Iquique
Belo Horizonte
Araraquara
Juiz de Fora
Bauru
Petrópolis
Niterói
Campinas
Rio de Janeiro
PARAGUAY
Antofagasta
São Paulo
Santos
Salta
Asunción
Ponta Grossa
Curitiba
San Miguel de Tucumán
CHILE
Corrientes
Posadas
Santiago del Estero
Santa Maria
Pacific Ocean
Porto Alegre
San Juan
Córdoba
Santa Fe
Pelotas
Paraná
Rio Grande
Viña del Mar
Río Cuarto
Mendoza
Rosario
URUGUAY
Valparaíso
Santiago
Buenos Aires
Rancagua
La Plata
Montevideo
ARGENTINA
Talcahuano
Concepción
Temuco
Bahia Blanca
Valdivia
Atlantic Ocean
Atlantic Ocean
FALKLAND ISLANDS (U.K.)
Stanley
0 1000 mi
0 2000 km
Isla Grande de Tierra del Fuego
M6 SOUTH AMERICA

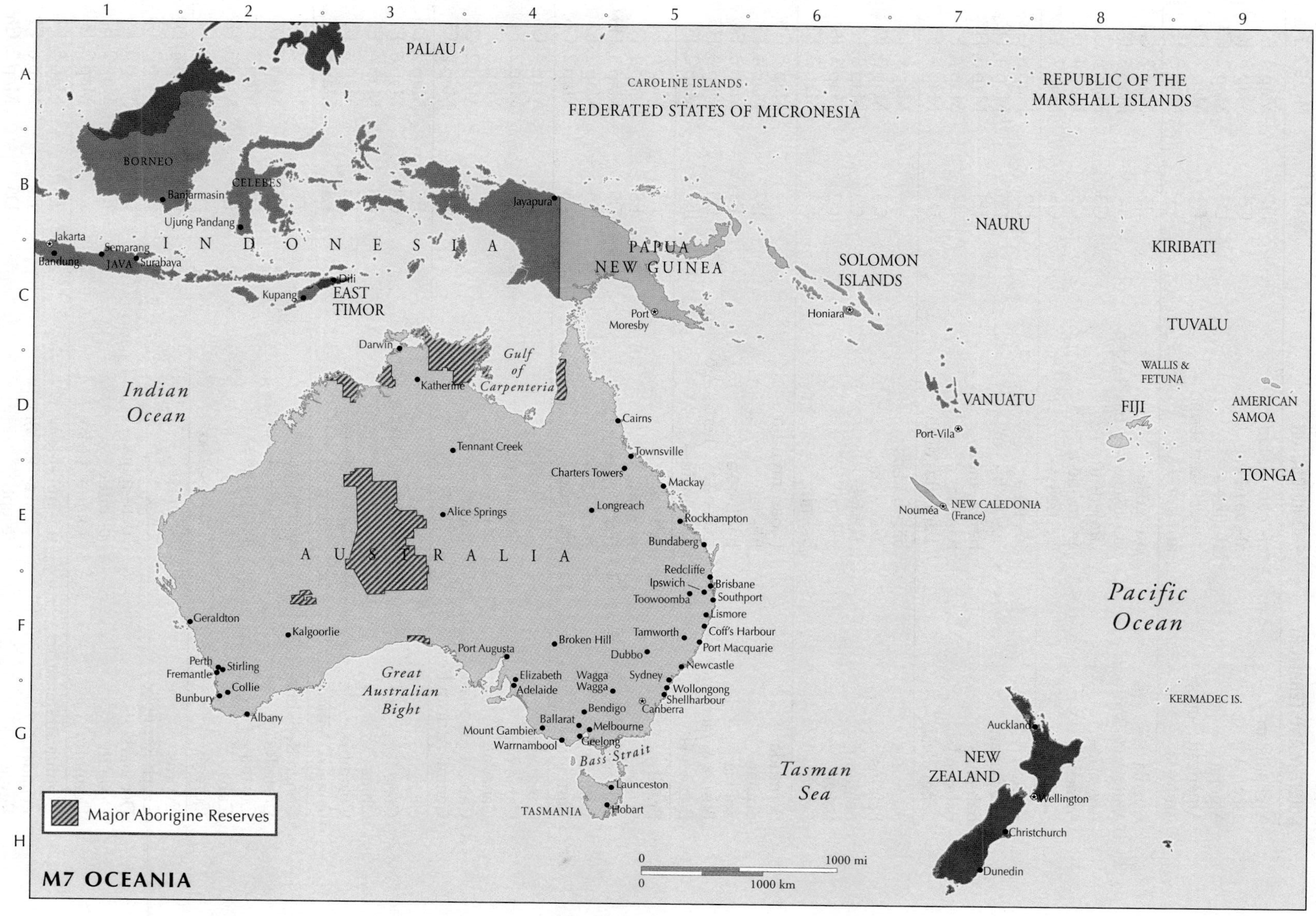
1 2 3 4 5 6 7 8 9
A B C D E F G H
PALAU
CAROLINE ISLANDS
FEDERATED STATES OF MICRONESIA
REPUBLIC OF THE MARSHALL ISLANDS
BORNEO
CELEBES
Banjarmasin
Ujung Pandang
Jayapura
Jakarta
Bandung
Semarang
JAVA
Surabaya
I N D O N E S I A
Dili
Kupang
EAST TIMOR
PAPUA NEW GUINEA
Port Moresby
NAURU
KIRIBATI
SOLOMON ISLANDS
Honiara
TUVALU
WALLIS & FETUNA
VANUATU
Port-Vila
FIJI
AMERICAN SAMOA
TONGA
Nouméa
NEW CALEDONIA (France)
Darwin
Katherine
Gulf of Carpenteria
Indian Ocean
Cairns
Tennant Creek
Townsville
Charters Towers
Mackay
Alice Springs
Longreach
Rockhampton
Bundaberg
A U S T R A L I A
Redcliffe
Ipswich
Brisbane
Toowoomba
Southport
Lismore
Geraldton
Kalgoorlie
Tamworth
Coff's Harbour
Broken Hill
Port Augusta
Dubbo
Port Macquarie
Perth
Stirling
Fremantle
Collie
Bunbury
Albany
Great Australian Bight
Elizabeth
Adelaide
Wagga Wagga
Sydney
Newcastle
Wollongong
Shellharbour
Canberra
Bendigo
Ballarat
Melbourne
Mount Gambier
Geelong
Warrnambool
Bass Strait
Launceston
TASMANIA
Hobart
Tasman Sea
Pacific Ocean
KERMADEC IS.
NEW ZEALAND
Auckland
Wellington
Christchurch
Dunedin
Major Aborigine Reserves
0 1000 mi
0 1000 km
M7 OCEANIA

COUNTRY AND TERRITORY	PRONUNCIATION	MAP 1	MAPS 2–7
Afghanistan	af-´gan-ə-,stan	D7	Map 4, E3
Albania	al-´bā-nē-ə	C5	Map 3, I6
Algeria	al-´jir-ē-ə	D5	Map 2, C3
American Samoa	ə-mer´i-kən sə-mō´ə	F9	Map 7, D9
Andorra	an-´dȯr-ə	—	Map 3, H2
Angola	an-´gō-lə	E5	Map 2, G4
Antigua & Barbuda	an-´tē-g(w)ə / bär-´büd-ə	—	Map 5, I3
Argentina	,,är-jen-´tē-nə	G3	Map 6, G3
Armenia	är-´mē-ne-ə	C6	Map 4, D2
Australia	ȯ-´strāl-yə	G8	Map 7, E4
Austria	´ȯs-trē-ə	C5	Map 3, G5
Azerbaijan	´az-ər-´bī-´jän	D6	Map 4, D2
Bahamas	bə-hä´-məz	D3	Map 5, H7
Bahrain	bä-´rān	—	Map 4, E2
Bangladesh	´bänJ-glə-´desh	D7	Map 4, F5
Barbados	bär-´bād-əs	—	Map 5, J3
Belarus	´bē-lə-´rüs	C5	Map 3, F6
Belgium	´bel-jəm	C5	Map 3, F3
Belize	bə-´lēz	D2	Map 5, I6
Benin	bə-´nin	E5	Map 2, E3
Bermuda	(´)bər-´myüd-ə	—	Map 5, G8
Bhutan	bü-´tan	D7	Map 4, F5
Bolivia	bə-´liv-ē-ə	F3	Map 6, E4
Bosnia & Herzegovina	´bäz-nē-ə / ´hert-sə-gō-´vē-nə	D5	Map 3, H5
Botswana	bät-´swän-ə	F5	Map 2, I5
Brazil	brə-´zil	F3	Map 6, D6
Brunei	brōo-nī´	E8	Map 4, G7
Bulgaria	´bəl-´gar-ē-ə	D5	Map 3, H6
Burkina Faso	bu˙r-´kē-nə-´fa˙-sō	E5	Map 2, E2
Burundi	bu˙-´rün-dē	E6	Map 2, G6
Cambodia	kam-´bd-ē-ə	E7	Map 4, G6
Cameroon	´kam-ə-´rün	E5	Map 2, F4
Canada	´kan-əd-ə	C2	Map 5, E5
Cape Verde Islands	´vard	—	Map 2, G1
Central African Rep.		E5	Map 2, E5
Chad	´chad	E5	Map 2, D5
Chile	´chil-ē	G3	Map 6, F3
China	´chī-nə	D8	Map 4, E5
Colombia	kə-´ləm-bē-ə	E3	Map 6, B3
Congo (Democratic Republic)	´känJ(´)gō	E5	Map 2, G5
Congo Republic	´känJ(´)gō	E5	Map 2, F4
Costa Rica	´käs-tə-´rē-kə	E2	Map 5, J7
Croatia	krō-´ā-sh(ē)ə	D5	Map 3, H5
Cuba	´kyü-bə	E3	Map 5, H7
Curaçao	´k(y)ür-ə-´sō	—	Map 5, J1
Cyprus	´sī-prəs	D6	Map 4, D2
Czech Republic	´chek	C5	Map 3, G5
Denmark	´den-´märk	C5	Map 3, E4
Djibouti	jə-´büt-ē	E6	Map 2, E7
Dominica	´däm-ə-´nē-kə	—	Map 5, I3
Dominican Republic	də-´min-i-kən	E3	Map 5, H8
Ecuador	´ek-wə-´dȯ(ə)r	E3	Map 6, C2
Egypt	´ē-jəpt	D5	Map 2, C6
El Salvador	el-´sal-və-´dȯ(ə)r	E2	Map 5, I6
Equatorial Guinea	ē-kwa´-tōr-ēal `gi-nē	E5	Map 2, F4
Eritrea	´er-ə-´trē-ə	E6	Map 2, D7
Estonia	e-´stō-nē-ə	C5	Map 3, D6

COUNTRY AND TERRITORY	PRONUNCIATION	MAP 1	MAPS 2–7
Ethiopia	´ē-thē-´ō-pē-ə	E6	Map 2, E7
Falkland Islands	´fȯ(l)-klənd	—	Map 6, J4
Fiji	´fē-jē	—	Map 7, D8
Finland	´fin-lənd	B5	Map 3, C6
France	´fran(t)s	C5	Map 3, G3
French Guiana	gē-´an-ə	E3	Map 6, B5
Gabon	ga-´bōn	E5	Map 2, F4
Gambia	´gam-bē-ə	E4	Map 2, E1
Georgia	´jȯr-jə	C6	Map 4, D2
Germany	´jerm-(ə-)nē	C5	Map 3, F4
Ghana	´gän-ə	E5	Map 2, E2
Greece	´grēs	D5	Map 3, I6
Greenland	´grēn-lənd	A4	Map 5, B7
Grenada	grə-nā´də	—	Map 5, J3
Guatemala	´gwät-ə-´mäl-ə	E2	Map 5, I6
Guinea	´gin-ē	E4	Map 2, E1
Guinea-Bissau	´gin-ē-bis-´au˙	E4	Map 2, E1
Guyana	gī-´an-ə	E3	Map 6, B4
Haiti	´hāt-ē	E3	Map 5, H8
Honduras	hän-´d(y)u˙r-əs	E2	Map 5, I7
Hong Kong	´hänJ-´känJ	—	Map 4, F6
Hungary	´hənJ-g(ə)rē	C5	Map 3, G5
Iceland	´ī-slənd	B4	Map 3, B1
India	´in-dê-ə	D7	Map 4, F4
Indonesia	´in-də-´nē-zhə	E8	Map 4, H7; Map 7, B3
Iran	i-´rän	D6	Map 4, E3
Iraq	i-´räk	D6	Map 4, D2
Ireland	´ī(ə)r-lənd	C5	Map 3, F1
Israel	´iz-rē-əl	D6	Map 4, D2
Italy	´it-əl-ē	D6	Map 3, H4
Ivory Coast (Cote D'Ivoire)	ī´və-rē	E5	Map 2, E2
Jamaica	jə-´mā-kə	E3	Map 5, I7
Japan	jə-´pan	D8	Map 4, D7
Jordan	´jȯrd-ən	D6	Map 4, D2
Kazakhstan	kə-´zak-´stan	D7	Map 4, D4
Kenya	´ken-yə	E6	Map 2, F7
Kiribati	kîr-ì-bàs´	—	Map 7, B8
Korea, North	kə-´rē-ə	D8	Map 4, D7
Korea, South	kə-´rē-ə	D8	Map 4, D7
Kosovo	´Ko-sō-vō	C5	Map 3, H6
Kuwait	kə-´wāt	D6	Map 4, E2
Kyrgyzstan	kîr-gē-stän´	D7	Map 4, D4
Laos	´lau˙s	D7	Map 4, F5
Latvia	´lat-vē-ə	C5	Map 3, E6
Lebanon	´leb-ə-nən	D6	Map 4, D2
Lesotho	lə-´sō-(´)tō	F6	Map 2, J6
Liberia	lī-´bir-ē-ə	E5	Map 2, F2
Libya	´lib-ē-ə	D5	Map 2, C4
Liechtenstein	lìk´tən-stīn´	—	Map 3, G4
Lithuania	´lith-(y)ə-´wā-nē-ə	C5	Map 3, E6
Luxembourg	´lək-səm-´bərg	C5	Map 3, G3
Macedonia	´mas-ə-´dō-nyə	D6	Map 3, H6
Madagascar	´mad-ə-´gas-kər	F6	Map 2, I8
Malawi	mə-´lä-wē	F6	Map 2, H6

COUNTRY AND TERRITORY	PRONUNCIATION	MAP 1	MAPS 2–7
Malaysia	mə-ˈlā-zh(ē-)ə	E8	Map 4, G6
Maldives	môlˈdīvz	—	Map 4, H3
Mali	ˈmäl-ē	D5	Map 2, D2
Malta	ˈmȯl-tə	—	Map 3, J5
Marshall Islands	märˈshəl	—	Map 7, A8
Mauritania	ˈmȯr-ə-ˈtā-nē-ə	D5	Map 2, D1
Mauritius	mȯ-ˈríshˈəs	—	Map 2, J8
Mexico	ˈmek-si-ˈkō	D2	Map 5, I5
Micronesia	mīˈkrō-nēˈzhə	—	Map 7, A5
Moldova	mäl-ˈdō-və	D6	Map 3, G7
Mongolia	män-ˈgōl-yə	D8	Map 4, D5
Morocco	mə-ˈräk-(ˈ)ō	D5	Map 2, B2
Mozambique	ˈmō-zəm-ˈbēk	F6	Map 2, H6
Myanmar	ˈmyän-ˈmär	E7	Map 4, F5
Namibia	nə-ˈmib-ē-ə	F5	Map 2, I4
Naura	näˈ-ü-rü	—	Map 7, B7
Nepal	nə-ˈpȯl	D7	Map 4, F4
Netherlands	ˈneth-ər-lən(d)z	C5	Map 3, F3
New Caledonia	ˈkal-ə-ˈdō-nyə	—	Map 7, E7
New Zealand	ˈzē-lənd	G9	Map 7, H7
Nicaragua	ˈnik-ə-ˈräg-wə	E3	Map 5, I7
Niger	ˈnī-jər	E5	Map 2, D4
Nigeria	nī-ˈjir-ē-ə	E5	Map 2, E4
Norway	ˈnȯ(ə)r-ˈwā	C5	Map 3, D4
Oman	ō-ˈmän	E6	Map 4, F2
Pakistan	ˈpak-i-ˈstan	D7	Map 4, E3
Palau	pä-louˈ	—	Map 7, A3
Palestine	pa-lə-ˈstīn	—	Map 4, D1
Panama	ˈpan-ə-ˈmä	E3	Map 5, J8
Papua New Guinea	ˈpap-yə-wə	F9	Map 7, C5
Paraguay	ˈpar-ə-ˈgwī	F3	Map 6, E4
Peru	pə-ˈrü	F3	Map 6, D2
Philippines	ˈfil-ə-ˈpēnz	E8	Map 4, F7
Poland	ˈpō-lənd	D5	Map 3, F5
Portugal	ˈpōr-chi-gəl	D5	Map 3, I1
Puerto Rico	ˈpōrt-ə-ˈrē(ˈ)kō	E3	Map 5, I2
Qatar	ˈkät-ər	D6	Map 4, E2
Romania	rō-ˈā-nē-ə	D5	Map 3, H6
Russia	ˈrəsh-ə	C7	Map 3, D7; Map 4, C5
Rwanda	ru̇-ˈän-də	E6	Map 2, F6
St. Kitts & Nevis	ˈkits / ˈnē-vəs	—	Map 5, I3
St. Lucia	sānt-ˈlü-shə	—	Map 5, I3
St. Vincent and the Grenadines	grènˈə-dēnzˈ	—	Map 5, J3
San Marino	sàn mə-rēˈnō	—	Map 3, H4
São Tomé and Príncipe	soun tōə-mèˈprēnˈ-sēpə	—	Map 2, F3
Saudi Arabia	ˈsau̇d-ē	E6	Map 4, E2
Senegal	ˈsen-i-ˈgˈl	E4	Map 2, D1
Serbia & Montenegro	ˈsər-bē-ə / ˈmän-tə-ˈnē-grō	D5	Map 3, H6
Seychelles	sā-shèlzˈ	—	Map 2, J1
Sierra Leone	sē-ˈer-ə-lē-ˈōn	E4	Map 2, E1
Singapore	ˈsinJ-(g)ə-ˈpō(ə)r	—	Map 4, H6
Slovakia	slō-ˈväk-ē-ə	C5	Map 3, G5
Slovenia	slō-ˈvēn-ē-ə	C5	Map 3, H5
Solomon Islands	ˈsäl-ə-mən	—	Map 7, C6
Somalia	sō-ˈmäl-ē-ə	E6	Map 2, F8

COUNTRY AND TERRITORY	PRONUNCIATION	MAP 1	MAPS 2–7
South Africa	´a-fri-kə	F6	Map 2, J5
South Sudan	sü-´dan	E6	Map 2, E6
Spain	´spāpn	C5	Map 3, I1
Sri Lanka	(´)srē-´länJ-kə	E7	Map 4, G4
Sudan	sü-´dan	E6	Map 2, E6
Suriname	su˙r-ə-´näm-ə	E3	Map 6, B5
Swaziland	´swäz-ē-´land	F6	Map 2, I6
Sweden	´swēd-ən	B5	Map 3, C5
Switzerland	´swit-sər-lənd	C5	Map 3, G4
Syria	´sir-ē-ə	D6	Map 4, D2
Taiwan	´tī-´wän	D8	Map 4, E7
Tajikistan	tä-´ji-ki-´stan	D7	Map 4, E4
Tanzania	´tan-zə-´nē-ə	F6	Map 2, G6
Thailand	´tī-land	E8	Map 4, F5
Togo	´tō(´)gō	E5	Map 2, E3
Tonga	´tän-gə	—	Map 7, D9
Trinidad & Tobago	´trin-ə-´dad / tə-´bā-(´)gō	—	Map 5, J3
Tunisia	t(y)ü-´nē-zh(ē-)ə	D5	Map 2, B4
Turkey	´tər-kē	D6	Map 4, D2
Turkmenistan	tûrk´-men-i-stàn´	D6	Map 4, D3
Tuvalu	tü´-vä-lü	—	Map 7, C9
Uganda	(y)ü-´gan-də	E6	Map 2, F6
Ukraine	yü-´krān	C6	Map 3, F7
United Arab Emirates	yoo-nī´tid à r´əb i-mîr´its	D6	Map 4, E2
United Kingdom	king´dəm	C5	Map 3, F2
United States	yu˙-´nīt-əd-´stāts	D2	Map 5, F5
Uruguay	´(y)u˙r-ə-gwī	G3	Map 6, G5
Uzbekistan	(´)u˙z-´bek-i-´stan	C6	Map 4, D3
Vanuatu	van-ə-´wät-(´)ü	—	Map 7, D7
Vatican City	vàt´ ì-kən	—	Map 3, H4
Venezuela	´ven-əz(-ə)-´wā-lə	E3	Map 6, A4
Vietnam	vē-´et-´näm	E8	Map 4, G6
Western Sahara	sə-hâr´ə	D4	Map 2, C1
Yemen	´yem-ən	E6	Map 4, F2
Zambia	´zam-bē-ə	F5	Map 2, H5
Zimbabwe	zim-´bäb-wē	F6	Map 2, H6

CHAPTER 2
Culture

OBJECTIVES

After studying this chapter, you should be able to

1. Understand methods for learning about cultural environments
2. Grasp the major causes of cultural difference and change
3. Discuss behavioral factors influencing countries' business practices
4. Recognize the complexities of cross-cultural information differences, especially communications
5. Analyze guidelines for cultural adjustment
6. Grasp the diverse ways that national cultures may evolve

© loiren - Fotolia.com

If you see men stroking their beards, stroke yours.

—Arab proverb

CASE Saudi Arabia's Dynamic Culture

Saudi Arabia (see Map 2.1), a land of contrasts and paradoxes, can be perplexing to foreign managers as they try to exercise acceptable personal and business behavior.[1] Its mixture of strict religious convictions, ancient social traditions, and governmental economic policies results in laws and customs that sometimes shift with little advance notice and vary by industry and region as dominant forces evolve. Many of these laws and customs contrast markedly with those in the home countries of the companies doing business there. Thus, foreign companies and the employees they send there must determine what these differences are and how to adjust to them. A brief discussion of the roots of Saudi traditions and a sample of both cultural norms and foreign operating adjustments should help you understand the importance of culture in international business.

A LITTLE HISTORY AND BACKGROUND

Although the land encompassing the Kingdom of Saudi Arabia has a long history, until recently most inhabitants' loyalty was primarily tribal rather than national. In most times past, invaders controlled a divided land. Nevertheless, the inhabitants have shared a common language (Arabic) and religion (Islam). In fact, Saudi Arabia is the birthplace of Islam and the location of its two holiest cities, Mecca and Medina. (The opening photo shows the Grand Mosque at Mecca.) Beginning in 1745, the Wahabi movement swept across and united most of the peninsula by calling for the purification of Islam through a literal view of the Koran. King Ibn Saud (1882–1953), a descendant of Wahabi leaders, took power in 1901, merged independent areas, created an entity that was both political and religious, and legitimized his monarchy and succession by being the defender of Islamic holy areas, beliefs, and values.

The growing importance of oil for Saudi Arabia, particularly since the 1970s, has led to rapid urbanization and given the government the means to offer social services such as free education. These changes have furthered its citizens' sense of a national identity, while diminishing their traditional ways of living. Since 1950, the rural population has decreased from more than 80 percent (about half nomadic) to less than 20 percent. Cities have also modernized physically. However, below the physical surface, Saudis hold attitudes and values that are neither like the norm elsewhere nor easily discerned.

Modernization has been controversial within Saudi Arabia. The liberal group, supported by an elite segment that has traveled abroad, wants such trappings from economic growth as greater choices in products and lifestyles. At the same time, the conservative group is supported by religious leaders and people who fear that modernization will upset traditional values and adherence to strict Koranic teachings. The government (the Royal Family) must balance these viewpoints while taking care not to overstep the acceptable boundaries of conservatism lest it become vulnerable to being replaced. For instance, it is well aware that Iran's Islamic Revolution was spearheaded in part by dissenters who viewed the Shah's modernization movements as corrupt and too secular. In 1979, a group largely marginalized by modernization seized the Grand Mosque of Mecca, which brought questions about the Royal Family's ability to protect Islam's holiest site. Meanwhile, liberals have been largely pacified by taking well-paid government jobs and slowly gaining the transformation they wish. The government has sometimes made tradeoffs to appease conflicting groups, such as requiring women to wear longer robes (women must wear *abayas* and men customarily wear *thobes*) in exchange for advancing women's education.

THE RELIGIOUS FACTOR

If your country maintains more or less strict separation between religion and the state, you will probably find the pervasiveness of religious culture in Saudi Arabia daunting. Religious proscriptions prohibit the sale or use of pork products and alcohol. During the holy period of Ramadan, when people fast during the day, restaurants serve customers only in the evening. Because Muslim men are called to prayer five times a day, restaurants such as McDonald's dim their lights and close their doors during those periods. Many companies convert revenue-generating space to prayer areas; Saudi Arabian Airlines does this in the rear of its planes, the British retailer Harvey Nichols in its department store.

However, there are regional differences. In the capital, Riyadh, women traditionally wear *niqabs* that cover their faces. But in the port city of Jeddah, which has more contact with foreigners and is less conservative, dress codes are more relaxed and fewer women wear them. Nevertheless, merchants routinely remove mannequins' heads and hands and keep them properly clad to prevent public objections. Starbucks franchises even altered the company logo and Coty Beauty its point-of-purchase exhibits in order not to display women's faces.

Rules of behavior may also be hard to comprehend because of the ways in which religious and legal rules have

MAP 2.1 Saudi Arabia and the Arabian Peninsula

The kingdom of Saudi Arabia comprises most of the Arabian Peninsula in Southwest Asia. The capital is Riyadh. Mecca and Medina are Islam's holiest cities. Jeddah is the most important port. All of the country's adjacent neighbors are also Arabic—that is, the people speak Arabic as a first language. All the nations on the peninsula are predominantly Islamic.

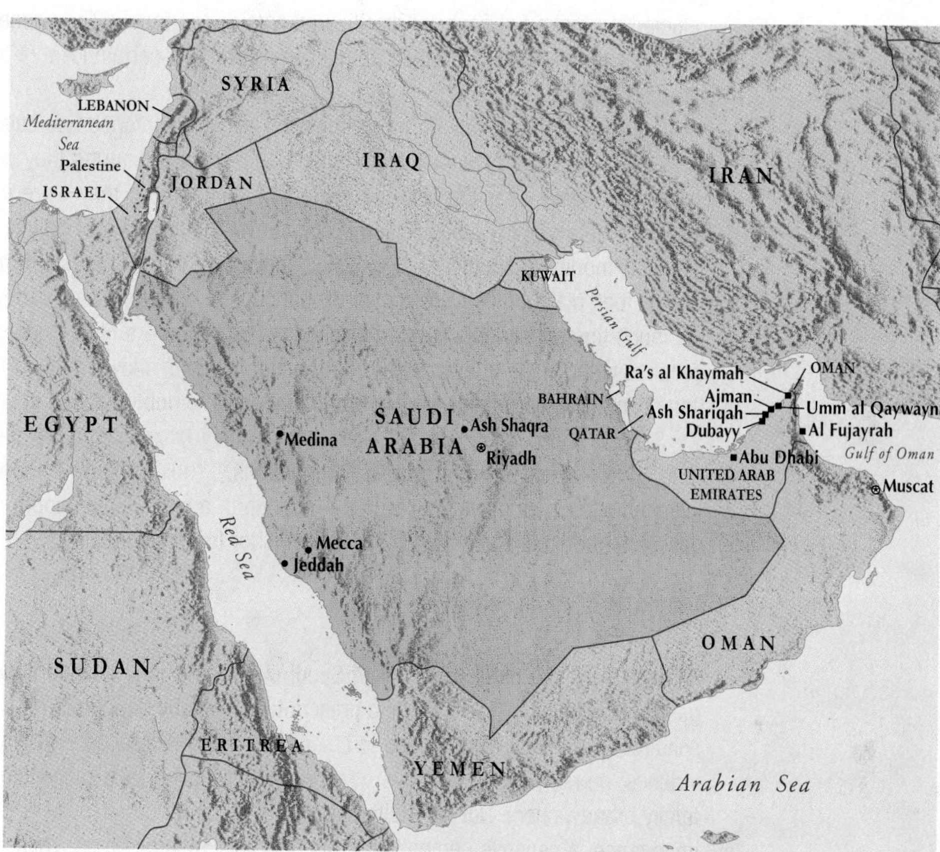

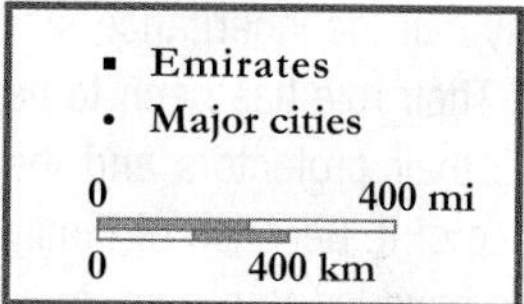

been adapted to contemporary situations. Islamic law, for instance, forbids charging interest and selling accident insurance (strict doctrine holds there are no accidents, only preordained acts of God). In the case of mortgages, the Saudi government gets around this proscription by offering interest-free loans. The government has simply eliminated the prohibition against accident insurance because Saudi businesses, like businesses elsewhere, need the coverage.

Nor are expected behaviors necessarily the same for locals and foreigners. Non-Muslim foreign women are not required to wear head scarves, although religious patrols may admonish them for not doing so. Saudi Arabian Airlines does not hire Saudi women as flight attendants (being in direct contact with men might tempt promiscuous behavior), but it hires women from other Arab nations. In addition, some compounds are inhabited largely by Americans and Europeans, who work in specialized positions and for foreign companies. To attract these needed specialists and investors, Saudi Arabia allows compound residents to dress and behave within the compounds much the way they do back home (alcohol, pornography, and drugs are still prohibited). However, in an example of a reverse dress code, some compounds prohibit residents and their visitors from wearing *abayas* and *thobes* in public areas.

TRADITIONAL FACTORS

Some Saudi Arabian traditions are probably the outgrowth of a tribal and nomadic past. For instance, the oft-quoted saying "Me against my brother, my brothers and me against my cousins, then my cousins and me against strangers" illustrates a family-centered society where trust of others is highly correlated with the degree of familiarity with them.

Given the trust factor, most Saudi businesses have historically been family owned and operated, preferring to hire family members or people they know well even though others might be better qualified. However, these companies have seen the need to partner with foreign firms to gain expertise. The process of partnering is usually lengthy because Saudis take time to know the foreigners well and are reluctant to make full financial disclosures outside the family. They generally prefer to get to know you well, perhaps invite you into their homes, and develop a certain level of friendship before ever turning to business details.

Not understanding this norm, a British publisher dispatched two salesmen to Saudi Arabia and paid them on commission. The salesmen moved aggressively, figuring they could make the same number of calls—and sales—per day as they made in Britain, where they were used to punctual schedules, the undivided attention of potential clients, and conversations devoted only to business transactions. To them, time was money. In Saudi Arabia, however, they soon found that appointments seldom began on time and usually took place at local cafés over casual cups of coffee. As far as they were concerned, Saudis spent too much time in idle chitchat and would even turn their attention to personal acquaintances rather than continue with business. Eventually, both salesmen began showing their irritation, and their Saudi counterparts came to regard them as rude and impatient. The publisher had to recall them.

Saudis' preference for dealing with people they know has led to a system known as *wasta*, which roughly translates into English as "connections." Thus, who you know helps a great deal in almost everything, such as moving a résumé to the top of a pile, gaining approval of a zoning request, getting a passport, and obtaining a visa to bring in a visitor from headquarters.

Gender Roles

Perhaps the most baffling aspect of Saudi culture to many outsiders is the expected role of people by gender. Based largely on a Koranic prescription whereby daughters receive only half the inheritance that sons receive, females are placed in a separate and often subservient position. Their role has been to be virtuous, marry young, and have offspring, while males take responsibility as their protectors and the family breadwinners. Not only is female virtue required, but also the appearance of it. Because of family importance, a negative perception of one member reflects on all. These beliefs have led to a number of proscriptions for women, such as no traveling abroad without permission of a male relative and no studying abroad without a male relative escort. Basically, non-kin males and females may interact personally only in "open areas," or in "closed areas" when the females are accompanied by a male relative. However, applying this restriction may seem a bit confusing to outsiders. For instance, restaurants are considered closed areas, and proprietors must maintain separate dining rooms and entrances for men without female companions. However, the food malls at most shopping centers are considered open areas where members of both sexes intermingle.

Nevertheless, several happenings since 2011 foretell possibly fewer future differences in gender requirements: women received future rights to vote and hold political offices, there was little intimidation when a group of women drove autos to protest their prohibition against driving, a Saudi prince spoke out in favor of women's driving as a means of limiting the number of foreign workers, a two-member women's team participated in the Olympics for the first time (but critics labeled them prostitutes for doing so), and prohibitions were lifted on female physical education classes in schools.

A 2008 royal decree lifted a ban on mixing men and women in the workplace, but the situation is complex. Male and female employees within the public sector work in separate buildings. When they must meet together, they do so within meeting rooms in the Governor's office, where they must use separate entrances. Men and women may work together within the private sector, but there are other limitations.

Although there are now more female than male university graduates in Saudi Arabia, only about 15 percent of the workforce is female. Why? The answer is partly cultural. Some women prefer traditional family roles. Some find driving restrictions to be too much of a hassle. And some families prohibit female members from working because of family honor ("What will people think?"). Economic factors blend with cultural ones as well, such as companies incurring the cost of providing separate entrances and toilet facilities. However, the genders do interact at work, especially in multinational companies. For example, Unilever's female brand managers, as long they adhere to dress codes, interact with male colleagues and meet with men from other companies. However, they are limited in traveling abroad on company business because they need permission from their male relatives. Some multinationals ease this problem by paying the travel costs for a male relative to accompany a woman abroad.

At one time, visas for single women to enter Saudi Arabia were nearly unobtainable. However, the Saudi Arabian General Investment Authority (SAGIA) has successfully attracted investments by MNEs that need visas to send female executives there for short- and long-term assignments. While these visas are not given automatically, they can be obtained—more easily for women over 40, but also possibly for younger women, especially with the use of *wasta.* The U.S. consulting company Monitor Group brought in American women in their twenties, and L'Oreal has sent its female human resources manager there.

Restrictions on gender interactions also lead to other adjustments. For instance, four young Saudis who had lived and studied abroad wanted to test the market potential for opening an upscale restaurant—the Java Lounge—in Jeddah. Ordinarily, it can be difficult to conduct such research in Saudi Arabia because limitations on male-female interactions restrain family-focused interviews. In this case, however, consultants interviewed apparently affluent families by approaching them in restaurants after noting how they comported themselves, whether they wore custom-made versus off-the-rack robes, what quality of wristwatches showed beneath long sleeves, and how well the men kept their beards—all indicators that researchers from outside the society would probably overlook.

At upscale U.S.- and U.K.-based department stores like Saks Fifth Avenue and Harvey Nichols, mixed shopping is allowed only on the lower floors. There, all salespeople are men (even those specializing in such products as cosmetics and lingerie), and there are no changing rooms or places to try cosmetics. Meanwhile, the upper floors are for women only, and female shoppers can check their *abayas* and shop in jeans or whatever they choose. (Meanwhile, the men who drove the women there can relax in a space the stores have set aside for them.) One problem: Because male managers can visit these upper floors only when a store is closed, they are limited in their ability to observe operations.

CULTURAL DYNAMICS

Almost all aspects of culture evolve, and Saudi Arabia is no exception. Take the case of women in the workplace. In terms of preparation, the first public school for girls did not open until 1960, and the government had to provide troops in one city because of protests that the schooling would negatively affect girls' religious and social values. Since then, the country has seen a gradual increase in years of study and curriculum offered for females. Economic need has spurred both changes in education and the use of education within the workforce. At the same time, critics have had to be persuaded that changes are compatible with women's roles. One of the first acceptances of working women (alongside men) was in the medical field because of the shortage of doctors, the high cost of separate male and female specialists, and the compatibility of healing with women's role as nurturers.

In addition, Saudi opinion and policy has been to reduce the heavy dependence on and cost of foreign workers. Thus, the government pays for foreign university education of its citizens while recognizing the disregard of much female talent.

The Saudi business world has seen much change. Consider that women own about 20 percent of all Saudi businesses, or that a woman is CEO of one of the country's largest concerns, the Olayan Financing Company. Three things will likely boost Saudi female workforce participation: (1) an increase in inward foreign investment, (2) more women studying abroad, and (3) women's psychological drive to prove themselves. Bear in mind, however, that changes tend to be uneven, particularly among geographic areas of the country and people of certain income and educational levels. ■

CRN
Case Review Note

QUESTIONS

2-1. Assume you are a manager in a multinational company that needs to send a team of three to five people to Saudi Arabia for about two weeks to investigate the feasibility of selling your products there. What advice should you give them to help assure that cultural problems do not impede their success in this task?

2-2. Assume your company is from North America or Europe and considering the establishment of an office in Saudi Arabia. What additional operating costs might it have to assume because of the Saudi culture?

INTRODUCTION

CONCEPT CHECK

In Chapter 1, we explained that behavioral factors, values, attitudes, and beliefs can be studied as keys both to cultural conditions and to ways of developing suitable business practices.

Our opening case illustrates companies' need to understand and be sensitive to ever-changing operating environments. Figure 2.1 shows how **culture**—learned norms based on the values, attitudes, and beliefs of a group of people—is an integral part of a nation's operating environment. Culture is sometimes an elusive topic to study. Why? Because people belong to different groups based on nationality, ethnicity, religion, gender, work organization, profession, age, political party membership, and income level, and each group comprises a culture. In this chapter, we emphasize *national cultures,* but also discuss how major cultural memberships differ among countries.

CONCEPT CHECK

Keep in mind our definition of *international business* in Chapter 1, where we stress that it involves "all commercial transactions"—sales, investments, transportation, and so forth—involving more than one country.

THE PEOPLE FACTOR

Business involves *people.* Every business employs, sells to, buys from, and is owned and regulated by people. International business, of course, involves people from different national cultures, which affects every business function—managing a workforce, marketing and transporting output, purchasing supplies, dealing with regulators, securing funds.

Cultural diversity can be a competitive advantage, but managing it can be difficult.

Cultural Diversity Chapter 1 explained how international business creates values and helps firms gain competitive advantages for themselves, such as acquiring knowledge-based resources abroad. But a company may also gain by nurturing the cultural diversity that international operations foster. As different nationalities come together through projects and teams, their diverse backgrounds, perspectives, and experiences often enable businesses to gain a deeper knowledge of products and services and how to create and deliver them. To keep team members from feeling threatened when expressing divergent viewpoints,

FIGURE 2.1 Cultural Factors Affecting International Business Operations

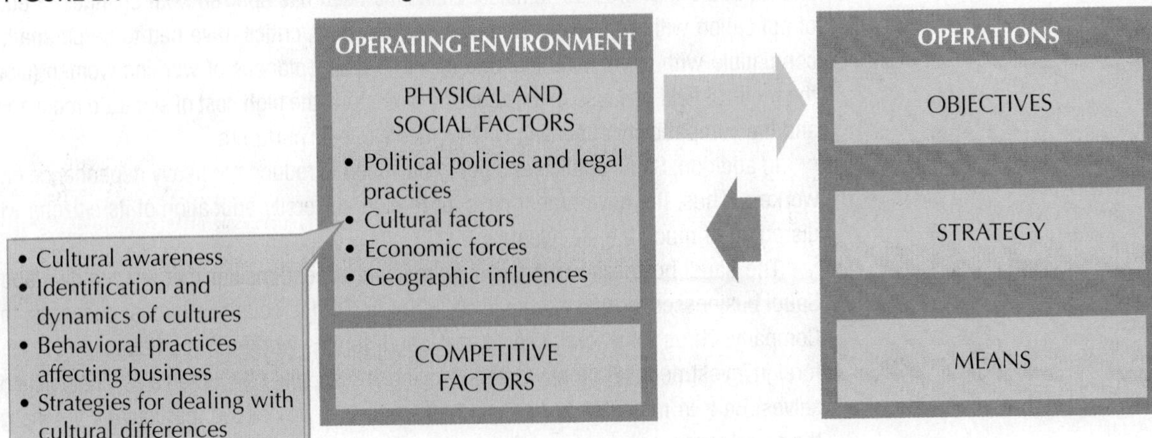

especially those from a minority nationality, leaders must strive to develop an open and non-threatening atmosphere.[2]

Successfully cultivating such diversity is difficult because individuals may interact with others as they do within their own cultures. A study of nationally diverse company teams found that some nationalities competed with other team members while others cooperated, some awaited precise directions while others took self-initiative, and some expected to divide tasks while others sought a team solution to each task. Another study found that language differences inhibited a common understanding of team roles, priorities, and sentiments.[3] The more successful teams worked to understand each other's cultures before dealing with the tasks at hand.[4] Yet a third study found that an expectation of high diversity among the teams led members to prepare more to deal with differences and keep open minds.[5]

Cultural Collision When divergent cultures come in contact, **cultural collision** occurs. In international business, the major problems of *cultural collision* arise under two conditions:

- When a company implements practices that are less effective than intended
- When a company's employees encounter distress because of difficulty in accepting or adjusting to foreign behaviors

Sensitivity and Adjustment A firm doing business in another country must determine which of that nation's business practices differ from its own and then decide what adjustments, if any, are needed to operate efficiently. This chapter first examines *cultural awareness*, especially the need for building it, and discusses the causes of cultural differences, rigidities, and changes. Next, it describes the major behavioral factors that affect the conduct of international business. Finally, it takes a look at the reasons why some businesses—and some individuals—do or don't adjust to other cultures.

CULTURAL AWARENESS

Almost everyone agrees that national cultures differ, but they disagree on what the differences are.

Most cultural variables—daily routines and rules, codes of social relations, language, emotive expression, concepts of luck—are universal. The forms of these variables, however, differ among cultures, and not everyone responds to them in the same way. Every national culture, for instance, features dancing, but types of and participation in dancing vary among and even within cultures.[6]

Problem areas that can hinder managers' cultural awareness are

- Subconscious reactions to circumstances.
- The assumption that all societal subgroups are similar.

No foolproof method exists for building cultural awareness.[7] Travelers remark on cultural differences, experts write about them, and international businesspeople note how they affect operations. Even so, people disagree on what they are, whether they're widespread or limited, and whether they're deep-seated or superficial. Nor is it easy to isolate culture from such factors as economic and political conditions. A survey measuring people's entrepreneurial attitudes, for example, could be influenced not only by respondents' risk-taking values but also by their economic conditions.[8] China's changing preference for male versus female offspring offers an example of cultural and economic interaction. Under the country's one-child policy, millions of families aborted female fetuses and put girls up for adoption. Why? Because males could carry on a family name (cultural), help work fields in rural areas (economic), and care for parents in old age (cultural and economic). Recently, however, China has seen a shift toward preference for female offspring. Why? Urbanization requires fewer male workers on farms (economic), while rising property values (economic) have taken a toll on families' tradition (cultural) of buying living quarters for sons before they can marry.[9]

Some cultural differences, such as acceptable attire, are fairly obvious; others aren't. And people in every culture often react to given situations by expecting the same responses they would likely get in their own. In our opening case, PRI's British sales reps expected their potential Saudi customers to be punctual and give them their undivided attention; in fact, the reps' compensation system discouraged them from spending much time on each business transaction. Their response was typical of countries with a **deal-focus (DF) culture**, where people are primarily task-oriented. The Saudis, meanwhile, had less compulsion to wrap things up; they regarded time spent in small talk at a café as a means to identify good business partners. They also put dealings with friends ahead of business dealings, a situation typical in a **relationship-focus (RF) culture**.[10] DF people may view RF people as time-wasters, whereas RF people may view DF people as offensively blunt.

A LITTLE LEARNING GOES A LONG WAY

CONCEPT CHECK

We stress in Chapter 1 that understanding cultural values, attitudes, and beliefs is often crucial in deciding when and how to alter operations in foreign countries.

Some people seem to have an innate ability to say and do the right thing at the right time, while others offend unintentionally or seem ignorant. Experts note, however, that business-people can improve their awareness and sensitivity and, by educating themselves, enhance the likelihood of succeeding abroad. Gathering research on another culture can be instructive. However, managers must assess information to determine if it perpetuates unwarranted stereotypes, covers only limited aspects of a country and its culture, or is obsolete. They should also observe the behavior of those people who have garnered the kind of respect and confidence they themselves will need.

Of course, cultural variations are too numerous to memorize completely. Just consider the many different ways to address people. Should you use a given name or a surname? Does a surname come before or after a given name? Do people take a parent's name as a surname? If so, is it taken from a parent's first or last name? If so, is it from one or both parents? Does a wife take her husband's name? What titles are appropriate for different professions? Note also that many languages have pronouns and verb forms (familiar and polite) that reflect status and familiarity. These can vary even among countries using the same language. Mistakes that may seem minor can nevertheless be perceived as ignorance or rudeness, thus jeopardizing a business deal. Fortunately, you can find country guidebooks based on people's experiences, including those by international managers. You can also consult with knowledgeable people at home and abroad.

Look at the other side of the cultural coin: Too often when we can't explain some difference—say, why the Irish consume more cold cereal than the Spanish do—we attribute it to culture without trying to understand it. (Perhaps the difference is simply that cereal companies have marketed more in Ireland.) Fortunately, we now have access to many recent studies on cross-cultural attitudes and practices that concern businesspeople.[11] Nevertheless, many attitudes, practices, and cultures remain unstudied.

Before reporting major research findings, we should emphasize a few common shortcomings:

1. Comparing countries by what people say can be risky. For one thing, responses may be colored by the very culture you're trying to understand. Some groups may be happiest when they're complaining; some respond with what they think you want to hear. In responding to degrees of agreement, say on a scale of one to five, some cultures are more apt to select the middle point, others the extremes.[12]
2. Researchers who focus on national differences in terms of *averages* may overlook specific variations within countries and believe in unrealistic stereotypes. For instance, the *average* Scandinavian may be uncomfortable with bargaining, but assuming that an IKEA buyer from Sweden doesn't expect to bargain on prices could be a grave mistake.[13] And of course, personality differences make some people outliers in their own cultures, with no certainty that they'll eventually integrate and conform to cultural norms.[14] Try scoring yourself on some common cultural comparison tests—ethnocentrism, individualism/collectivism, and power distance—to see how you compare with your national norm.[15]
3. Because cultures evolve, research may be outdated. Our opening case, for instance, details some changing Saudi attitudes toward women.

THE IDEA OF A "NATION": DELINEATING CULTURES

Let's examine why national culture is a useful but imperfect cultural reference for international business. Afterward, we'll take a look at why cultures evolve and discuss the influence of language and religion.

THE NATION AS A POINT OF REFERENCE

The nation is a useful definition of society because

- Similarity among people is a cause and an effect of national boundaries.
- Many laws affecting business are along national lines.

Nation provides a workable definition of *culture* because similarity among people is both a cause and effect of national boundaries. Laws governing business operations are largely along national lines. Within its borders, a nation's people chiefly share such essential attributes as values and language. The feeling of "we" casts foreigners as "they." National identity is perpetuated through rites and symbols—flags, parades, rallies—while the preservation of national sites, documents, monuments, and museums promotes a common perception of "we."

Managers find country-by-country analysis difficult because

- Subcultures exist within nations.
- Similarities link groups from different countries.

The Nation as Cultural Mediator Obviously, the existence of shared attributes doesn't mean everyone in a country shares all the same values and attitudes, or that each country is unique in all respects. Nations include various subcultures, ethnic groups, races, and classes, and a national culture must be flexible enough to accommodate such a mixture. In fact, a nation legitimizes itself by mediating its diversity;[16] those that fail to do so often dissolve, as happened with Yugoslavia. Yet a nation's shared and mediated characteristics constitute its national identity and affect the practices of any company that does business there. At the same time, some people (probably a growing number) are **bicultural** or **multicultural**, meaning that they have internalized more than one national culture. This occurs because they hold dual or multiple nationalities, have parents from another country, or have lived abroad at an impressionable age.

Cultural value systems are set early in life but may change through

- Choice or imposition
- Contact with other cultures

Certain cultural attributes can link groups from different nations more closely than groups in a given nation. People in urban areas differ in certain attitudes from people in rural areas; managers have different work attitudes than do production workers. Thus, Country A managers may hold work values closer to those of Country B managers than to those of Country A production workers. As a consequence, when international businesspeople compare nations, they must be careful to examine *relevant groups*—differentiating between, say, the typical attitudes of rural and urban dwellers, or between young and old people.

HOW CULTURES FORM AND CHANGE

Culture is transmitted in various ways—from parent to child, teacher to pupil, social leader to follower, peer to peer. Developmental psychologists believe that most people acquire their basic value systems as children, including such concepts as evil versus good, dirty versus clean, ugly versus beautiful, unnatural versus natural, abnormal versus normal, paradoxical versus logical, and irrational versus rational. These values are not easily changed later on.[17]

SOURCES OF CHANGE

Both individual and collective values and customs may evolve, however. Examining this evolution explains how a culture comes to accept (or reject) certain business practices—knowledge that is useful to companies attempting to introduce changes there. The important thing here is *change,* which may result from either *choice* or *imposition.*

" I say, if they want to live in this country, they should follow our culture . . .
By the way, what do you want for dinner - Mexican, Chinese or Italian ? "

FIGURE 2.2 Some aspects of a foreign culture are accepted easily; others not.

Source: Roy Delgado/CartoonStock

Change by Choice Change by choice may occur as a reaction to social and economic situations that present people with new alternatives. When rural people choose to accept factory jobs, for example, they change some basic customs—notably, working regular hours doesn't allow them the sort of work-time social interactions that farm work allowed.

Change by Imposition Change by imposition—sometimes called **cultural imperialism**—involves imposing certain elements from an alien culture, such as a forced change in laws by an occupying country that, over time, becomes part of the subject culture.

As a rule, contact among countries brings change; this is known as *cultural diffusion.* When the change results in mixing cultural elements, we have *creolization.* In many Asian countries, ethnic Chinese embody a mixture of Chinese and local cultures.[18] In the United States, the popularity of Mexican tortillas led to U.S. innovations in their use, such as tortilla chips and burritos. (Figure 2.2 offers a humorous example of creolization.)

Some groups and governments have tried to protect national cultures but have not succeeded entirely because people travel and access foreign information through a variety of sources. Further, protecting a culture may result in the disadvantage of limiting foreign contact, thus restraining the adoption of foreign technical advancements. Thus, most countries seek to preserve traditions that help maintain national cohesiveness while being open to changes that grow their economies. South Korea, for example, has recently become more multi-ethnic because it needs the influx of foreigners to work in globally competitive factories that bring domestic modernization and growth. To help maintain traditions, the government now sponsors programs and language centers to "Koreanize" the foreigners.[19] The photo on the next page illustrates another Korean means of bringing tradition to modern life.

LANGUAGE AS BOTH A DIFFUSER AND STABILIZER OF CULTURE

A common language within countries is a unifying force.

Like national boundaries and geographic obstacles, language limits people's contact with other cultures. Map 2.2 shows the distribution of the world's major language groups. Not surprisingly, when people from different areas speak the same language, culture spreads

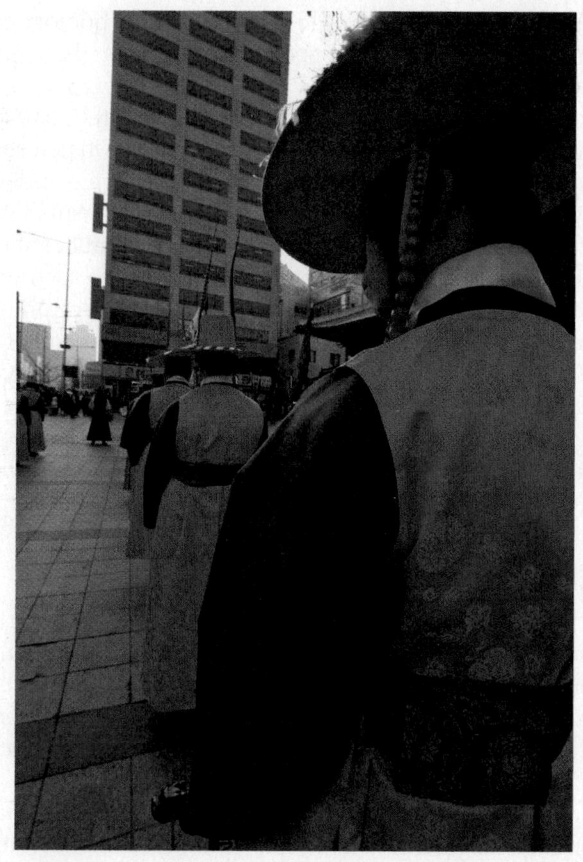

Although the buildings in the photo illustrate South Korean economic modernization, the members of the Royal Guard dress traditionally.

Source: © sandro lacarbona / Alamy

MAP 2.2 Distribution of the World's Major Languages

The people of the world speak thousands of different languages, but only a few of them remain important in the dissemination of culture. A significant portion of countries, for example, speaks English, French, or Spanish. But take a look at China: It's the only place where people speak Mandarin, but it's important in international business because the population of China comprises a lot of people. The classification "Regional" actually takes in two categories: (1) countries in which the dominant language is not dominant anywhere else (e.g., Japan) and (2) countries in which several different languages are spoken (e.g., India).

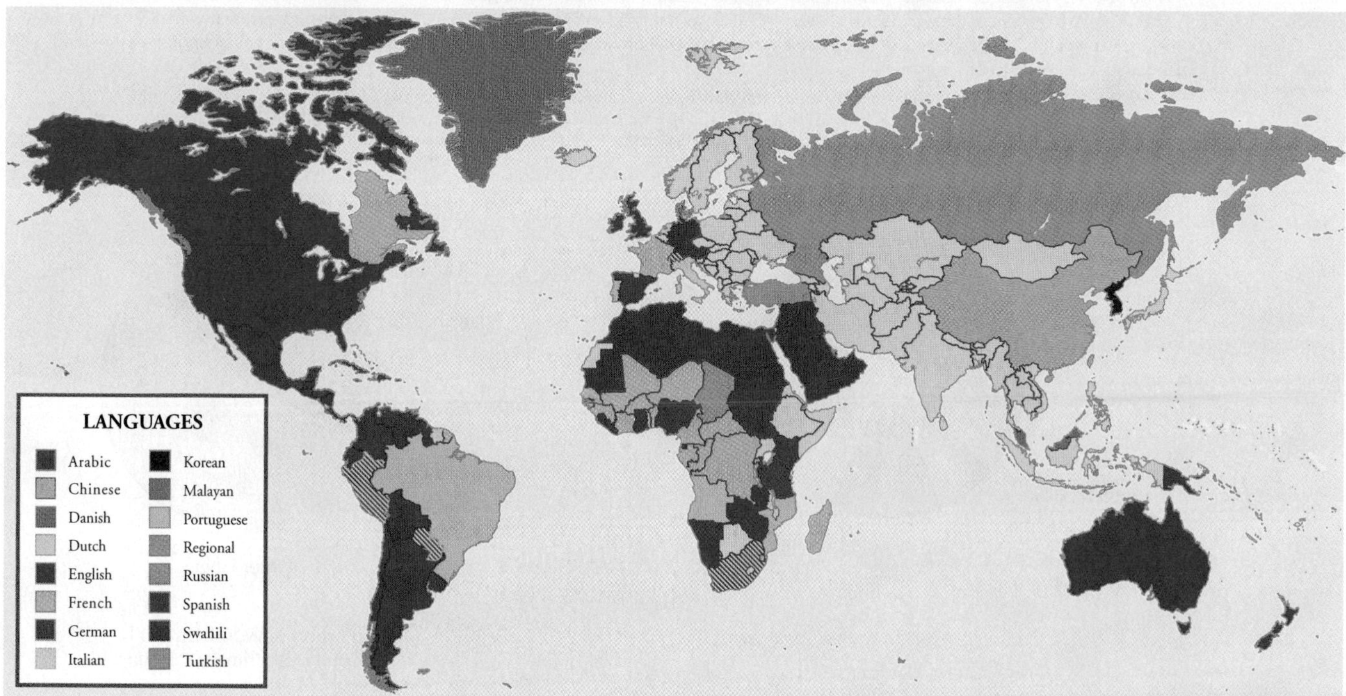

more easily. This helps explain the greater cultural homogeneity among English-speaking countries and among Spanish-speaking countries than *between* English-speaking and Spanish-speaking countries.

The map omits most of the world's approximately 6,000 languages because they are spoken by proportionately few people. Further, 50 to 90 percent of languages are expected to be extinct by the end of the 21st century.[20] When people understand only one language that has relatively few users—especially concentrated in a small geographic area—they tend to cling to their culture because they have little meaningful contact with others.

CONCEPT CHECK

As we observe in Chapter 1, improved communications and transportation are key factors in the increased international interactions that we know as **international business**.

Languages like English, French, and Spanish have such widespread acceptance (they're the most prevalent in 52, 21, and 21 countries and territories, respectively) that, as a rule, the native speakers don't feel the same need to learn other languages as do speakers of languages that, like Armenian or Bulgarian, are found only in limited geographic areas. Commerce is easier among nations that share the same language because there is no need to translate everything. Thus, when people study second languages, they usually choose those most useful in interacting with other countries, especially in the realm of commerce.

WHY ENGLISH TRAVELS SO WELL

In Figure 2.3, the pie chart on the right shows portions of worldwide output by language. As you can see, native English-speaking countries account for a third of the world's production, much more than any other language group—a fact that goes a long way toward explaining why English is the world's most important *second* language. Remember, too, that MNEs—which are largely headquartered in English-speaking countries—decide on the common language to use for communicating among their employees in different countries. Not surprisingly, it's usually English, because many of their managers either speak only English or have English as a second language. In addition, many MNEs from non-English-speaking countries have adopted English—the "international language of business"—as their operating language.

FIGURE 2.3 Major Language Groups: Population and Output

Native speakers for just a few languages—notably English—account for much more of the world's economic output than their population would indicate. Only 8 percent of the world's people speak English as their native (first) language, but the countries and territories where English is the most spoken native language account for 33 percent of global economic output, which helps to explain the prevalence of English as a second language when conducting international business.

Sources: The data for constructing the pie chart on the left came from by List of Languages by Number of Native Speakers," http://en.wikipedia.org/wiki/List_of_languages_by_number_of_native_speakers (accessed February 26, 2011); For constructing the pie chart on the right, the primary language by country came from "Languages Spoken in Each Country of the World," www.infoplease.com/ipa/A0855611.html (accessed February 26, 2011). The output per country and territory came from Central Intelligence Agency, The World Factbook, at www.cia.gov.

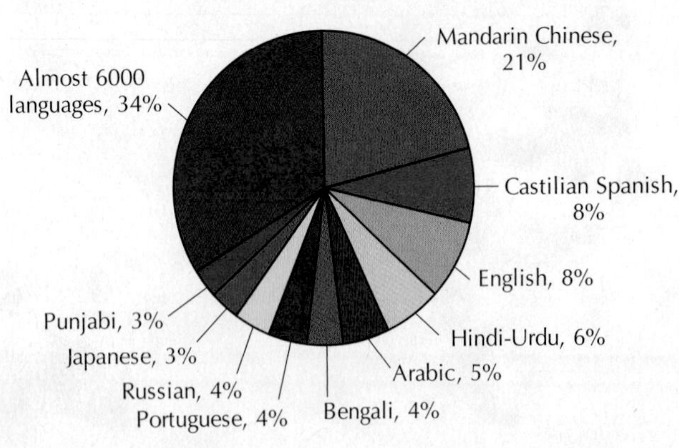

Portion of World's Native Speakers

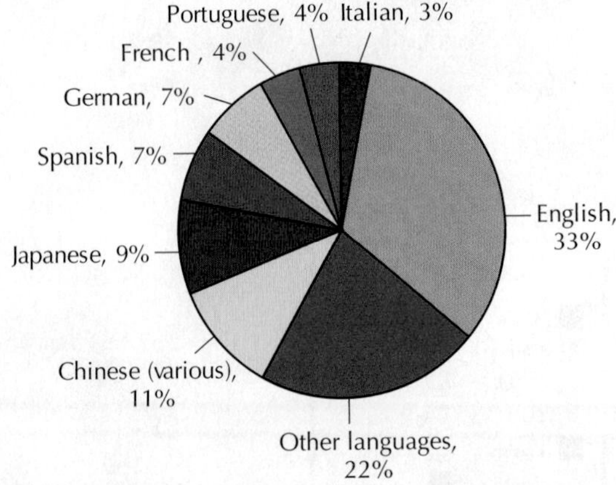

Portion of World Output by Countries' Primary Languages

However, downsides of this are that hiring decisions may overemphasize English language capability at the expense of task competence and that people with higher English language proficiency may dominate meetings even though their ideas are not as good.[21] Further, our ending case demonstrates that there are sometimes backlashes about accepting English as an operating language.

One prominent linguist has predicted that monolingual English speakers will eventually experience more difficulty in communicating worldwide. Why? Because the percentage of them will decrease, while the languages of such countries as China and India will grow rapidly along with their economies.[22] As is so often the case, history may teach us about this matter: Latin and French were once the languages of scholarship and diplomacy, respectively. Aramaic was once so dominant in the Middle East that conquering groups adopted the language rather than imposing their own.[23] But the use of these languages has long since been supplanted.

Nevertheless, for some time now, English words—especially American English—have been entering other languages. An estimated 20,000 can be found in Japanese. English travels so well partly because the U.S. media are so influential and because the United States originates a healthy percentage of new products and technology. When, say, a U.S. product enters a foreign market, its vocabulary often enters the language as well—sometimes in a strange form. In a Spanish-speaking country, for instance, you might see a sign announcing *Vendemos blue jeans de varios colores* ("We sell various colors of blue jeans"). At other times, the local language provides an Anglicized twist; thus, the French call a self-service restaurant *le self.* Finally, the intrusion of English into another language may result in the development of a hybrid tongue, such as "Spanglish" (Spanish and English) or "Chinglish" (Mandarin Chinese and English), which may ultimately become a distinct language.[24]

Note that some countries, such as Finland, prefer to coin their own new words rather than accept Anglicized items into their vocabularies. Because many countries see language as an integral part of culture, they regulate linguistic changes, such as requiring that all public signs be in the local language.

RELIGION AS A CULTURAL STABILIZER

Many strong values are the result of a dominant religion.

Map 2.3 shows the approximate distribution of the world's major religions. In many countries, the practice of religion has declined significantly; indeed, a few nations in northern Europe are sometimes called "post-Christian" societies. At the same time, religion has been a cultural stabilizer because centuries of religious influence continue to shape cultural values even in these societies.[25] Among people with strong religious convictions, the role of religion in shaping behavior is even stronger.

Many of these religions—Buddhism, Christianity, Hinduism, Islam, and Judaism—influence specific beliefs that may affect business, such as inhibiting the sale of certain products or the performance of work at certain times. McDonald's serves neither beef nor pork in India to keep from offending its Hindu or Muslim populations. El Al, the Israeli national airline, does not fly on Saturday, the Jewish Sabbath. In fact, religion has an impact on almost every business function. To be viewed legitimately, companies must take religious beliefs into account.[26]

Of course, not all nations with the same dominant religion impose the same constraints on business. In predominantly Muslim countries, for example, Friday is a day of worship, whereas in Turkey (a secular Muslim country that adheres to the Christian work calendar to keep in step with European business activity) it is a workday. In places where rival religions vie for political control, the resulting strife can cause so much upheaval that business activity suffers from property damage, broken supply chains, breaches in customer connections, and so on. Unfortunately, the problem is substantial. In recent years, religious violence has erupted in such countries as India, Iraq, Sudan, and Sri Lanka.

MAP 2.3 Distribution of the World's Major Religions

Most countries are home to people of various religious beliefs, but a nation's culture is typically influenced most heavily by a dominant religion. The practices of the dominant religion, for instance, often shape customary practices in legal and business affairs.

Source: The numbers for adherents are taken from "List of Religious Populations," http://en.wikipedia.org/wiki/list_of_religious_populations **

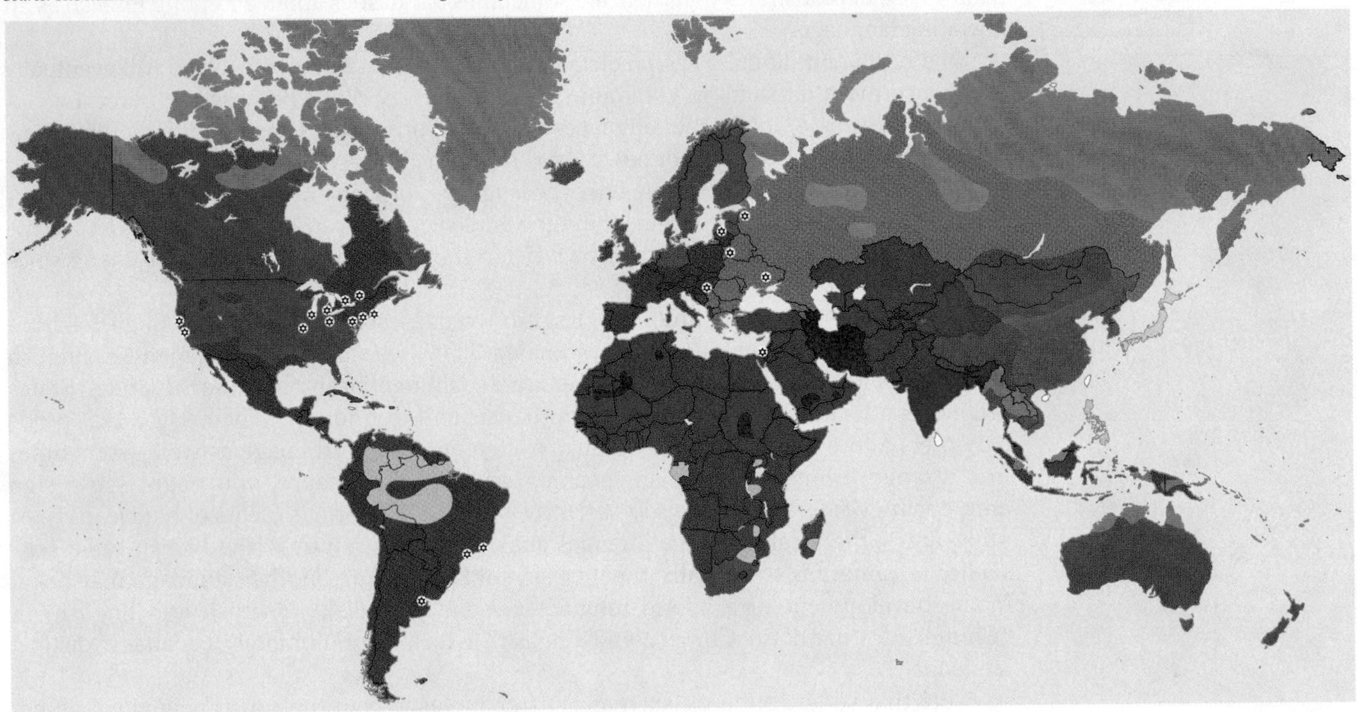

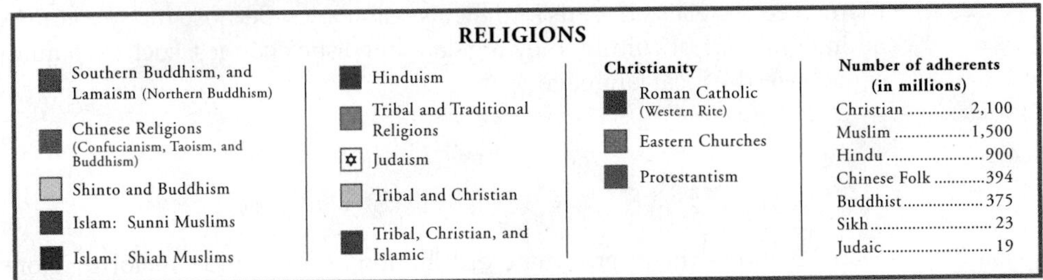

BEHAVIORAL PRACTICES AFFECTING BUSINESS

CONCEPT CHECK

In Chapter 1, we emphasize the importance of studying the behavioral factors that affect business conditions to help managers decide why and how they may need to alter operations in different countries.

Attitudes and values are composed of many *cultural variables,* which both researchers and businesspeople define differently, attaching various names to slightly different and sometimes overlapping concepts. Because of all these nuances in terms and concepts, there are thousands of possible ways to relate culture to business—far too many to cover in one chapter. We'll settle for hitting the highlights.

ISSUES IN SOCIAL STRATIFICATION

Every culture ranks some people higher than others. Such *social stratification* dictates a person's class, status, and financial rewards within that culture. In business, this practice may entail ranking members of managerial groups more highly than production group members. Social stratification is determined by (1) individuals' achievements and qualifications and (2) their affiliation with or membership in certain groups. These two factors interact, but the importance of one versus the other varies among cultures. Further, although this social stratification creates hierarchies, more formal cultures expect more status-oriented

Does Geography Matter?

Birds of a Feather Flock Together

Some groups of people are more isolated from the rest of the world, sometimes by natural barriers (rugged terrain, geographic remoteness), sometimes by others (unique languages, outmoded transportation and communications, xenophobia). Historically, natural conditions have been quite important in determining where people do and don't live. Take a quick look at any map and you'll see that a large portion of big cities are situated where waterways facilitate the interaction of people and interchange of goods.

Although many natural barriers are now less formidable because of airplanes and communication systems, they still play a role in determining which people are harder to get to know than others. In Papua New Guinea, the mutual isolation of tribal groups has resulted in about 800 different languages and has permitted little cultural diffusion. Similarly, natural conditions continue to affect physical cultures, such as clothing for native Inuits of the Arctic differing from the attire typically worn on Brazil's beaches. There is also evidence that these natural conditions, particularly temperature, have affected work values.[27] Then again, some places have traditionally enjoyed more-than-average outside contact. As we saw in our opening case, the Saudi port of Jeddah, having long experienced more external contact than the rest of Saudi Arabia, has a more liberal attitude toward dress than the interior.

Consider also the effect of proximity on cultural diffusion. Understandably, people generally have more contact with nearby groups than with remote ones. Take a look at Map 2.2. As you can see, most German-, Arabic-, and Spanish-speaking countries are more or less adjacent to each other. Likewise, Map 2.3 reveals that virtually all the world's major religions are geographically clustered. The notable exceptions to this have resulted from colonization and immigration. Both English and Spanish, for instance, spread to distant parts of the world during eras of European colonization.

Finally, cultural (and subcultural) clusters tend to confirm the old adage that "Birds of a feather flock together." Immigration patterns, for example, often reflect the tendency of people to go where they can find a subcultural support group. That's why there's a heavy concentration of Central American immigrants in the Los Angeles area; even if friends and family aren't already waiting there, they'll find affinities in language, diet, and general customs. Globally, we find many such patterns—Hong Kong Chinese in Vancouver, Canada, Algerians in Marseilles, France, and so on. ■

communications between the hierarchical levels. Higher-status individuals, for example, may be offended if people from a lower status address them by a first name or without using a title.

Businesses reward competence highly in some societies.

Individual Qualifications and Their Limitations In most societies, individual achievement is important, such as in choosing a successful athlete as a spokesperson to advertise sportswear. Similarly, in some nations, such as the United States, companies tend to base a person's eligibility for employment and promotion largely on individual achievements and qualifications. However, we shall see that this is not always the case even in the United States.

CONCEPT CHECK

In the opening case of Chapter 1, we discussed that many top sports players are effectively global brands as companies pay them to use and endorse their products.

Just as companies look for individual qualifications for choosing spokespersons for advertising, they also match spokespersons with the audience (group membership) they wish to reach, such as using older models for products aimed at older consumers. Societies look at these group affiliations differently, thus causing certain business functions to be carried out differently. Because Japan stresses cooperation over competition in the workplace more than the United States does, companies in Japan generally place more weight on seniority for employee promotion, thus favoring older employees.[28] Similarly, a study comparing banks' hiring, promotion, compensation, and staff-reduction practices showed that they differed by nationality on all four functions. When needing to reduce staff, for example, British banks were most prone to save costs by discharging on a performance-to-salary basis (targeting, say, a middle-aged manager with a high salary and average performance), whereas German banks were more concerned with minimizing personal hardship (targeting younger managers, regardless of performance, because they could find new jobs more easily).[29]

Group affiliations can be
- Ascribed or acquired
- A reflection of class and status

The above examples dealt with group memberships based largely on age, but there are many other ways to define memberships. Those determined by birth are **ascribed group memberships**, including gender, family, age, caste, and ethnic, racial, or national origin. **Acquired group memberships** include those based on religion, political affiliation, educational place and achievement, and profession.

Egalitarian societies place more importance on acquired group memberships.

The more egalitarian, or"open,"a society, the less group memberships determine rewards. However, laws may be designed to reinforce or undermine group differences, such as moves in Europe to require large companies to include women in at least 40 percent of their board membership.[30] In other cases, group memberships deny many people equal access to the preparation they need to qualify for jobs; an example is the lack of education for women that results in a lower literacy rate for them than for men in much of sub-Saharan Africa. The Nobel economist Amartya Sen referred to this exclusion of people from the workforce as *unfreedom* and pointed out its negative effect on economic advancement.[31]

Even when individuals qualify for given positions and no legal barriers exist to hold them back, opposition to certain groups—by other workers, customers, shareholders, or government officials—may limit their equal access to employment.

The following sections focus on some of the group memberships that influence how a person is viewed from country to country. An additional factor that is often important is a person's *social connections*,[32] which corresponds to the old adage, "It's *who* you know, not *what* you know."

Country-by-country attitudes vary toward
- Race and ethnicity
- Male and female roles
- Rules and expectations based on age
- Family ties

Ethnic and Racial Groups Laws may reinforce or undermine rigid stratification. Malaysia, for example, has political parties defined explicitly by three ethnic groups. It has also long maintained employment quotas for these ethnic groups—Malays, Chinese, and Indians—primarily to upgrade the economic position of Malays because, at the time of the country's independence, the Chinese and Indian minorities dominated business ownership and the professions, respectively.[33] The Malaysian system requires companies to maintain expensive record-keeping systems of their hiring practices; in fact, it has recently come under increasing criticism from within the country.[34] Likewise, Brazil, which has five official racial classifications in its census and many more terms to designate skin color, has racial quotas in universities and has been pressured to enact quotas for employment as well.[35] (But there has been no pressure for national football team racial quotas, where only competence counts.)

CRN
Case Review Note

Gender-Based Groups Country-specific differences in gender equality and attitudes toward gender are sometimes quite pronounced.[36] As you'll recall from our opening case, there are almost seven employed men for every employed woman in Saudi Arabia, and women are excluded from driving and from certain professions. Compare that employment figure with Norway, where only 1.1 men are employed for every woman. In Lithuania, more than 50 percent of both males and females agreed with the following statement:"When jobs are scarce, men have a better right to a job than women"; in Sweden and Iceland, the number was under 10 percent.[37]

In many parts of the world, however, barriers to gender-based employment practices are coming down, due to changes in both attitudes and work requirements. In the United States, one noticeable change is reflected in the number of people of one gender employed in occupations previously dominated by the other, such as more male nurses and more female physicians. But some of this change may be economic as males have gravitated to where there are jobs; few boys still say they want to grow up to be nurses.[38] Other economic factors matter as well. The decrease in production jobs requiring brawn and increase in jobs for people with specialized education, such as X-ray technicians and psychiatric caseworkers, has caused shifts in the relative demand for female employees and type of job for both genders.

Age-Based Groups Countries treat age groups differently, and each country expresses its attitudes toward age in different ways. All enforce age-related laws such as statutes applying to employment, driving privileges, rights to obtain products and services (alcohol, cigarettes, certain pharmaceuticals, bank accounts), and civic duty (voting, serving in the military or on juries). Sometimes the logic of these laws seems contradictory. In the United States, for example, people can vote, marry, drive, and die for their country before they can legally buy alcohol at age 21, whereas in parts of Switzerland one can legally buy alcohol at age 14.[39] U.S. firms bombard children with TV advertising, but Sweden prohibits ads targeted to children.

National differences toward employment age are substantial. Both Finland and the Netherlands enforce mandatory retirement ages, but with few exceptions (e.g., airline pilots) U.S. law specifically prohibits the practice. In Britain, age discrimination laws apply to everyone, regardless of age, whereas U.S. law is designed to protect only people over age 40.[40] When the proposition "When jobs are scarce, people should be forced to retire early" was put to people in different countries, almost three-quarters of Bulgarians agreed, but only 10 percent of Japanese.[41] Why this latter difference? For one thing, Japanese hold strongly to the assumption that there's a significant correlation between age and wisdom.

Family-Based Groups In some cultures, such as in much of Latin America, the most important group membership is the family. A person's position in society depends heavily on the family's social status or "respectability" rather than on individual achievement. Because family ties are so strong, there may also be a tendency to cooperate more closely within the family unit than in other relationships. In such cultures, not surprisingly, small family-run companies are quite successful; conversely, however, they often encounter difficulties in growing because owners are reluctant to share responsibility with professional managers hired from outside the family who may run the operation more efficiently. When its business culture is hampered by this state of affairs, a country (or region) may lack sufficient numbers of indigenously owned *large-scale* operations that are usually necessary for long-term economic development.[42]

WORK MOTIVATION

Not surprisingly, motivated employees are normally more productive than those who aren't. On an aggregate basis, of course, this influences companies' efficiency and countries' economic development. The following discussion summarizes studies showing major differences in how and why people in different nations are motivated to work.

The desire for material wealth is

- A prime motivation to work
- Positive for economic development

Materialism and Motivation When developing his *Protestant ethic* theory, Max Weber observed that predominantly Protestant countries were the most economically developed. He attributed this "ethic" to an outgrowth of the Protestant Reformation in sixteenth-century Europe, which reflects the belief that work is a pathway to salvation and that material success does not impede redemption. Although we no longer accept a strict distinction between Protestant and non-Protestant attitudes toward work and material gain, we do tend to adhere to the underlying values of Weber's concept: namely, that self-discipline, hard work, honesty, and a belief in a just world foster work motivation and, thus, economic growth.[43] As a matter of fact, on one hand there is evidence indicating a positive correlation between the intensity of religious beliefs per se (regardless of specific belief systems) and adherence to some attributes that lead to economic growth (say, confidence in the rule of law and belief in the virtue of thrift).[44] Moreover, strong evidence indicates that the desire for material wealth motivates individuals to perform the kind of work that leads to community-wide economic development.[45] On the other hand, values held by people with strong religious beliefs, such as maintenance of the status quo and predetermination, retard self-motivation to work for economic advancement.[46] Further, in societies such as Myanmar (shown in the adjacent photo) and Bhutan, a large portion of the population vanishes from the economic work force temporarily or permanently while living with few possessions in monasteries and nunneries and being supported by others.

Buddhist monks in Myanmar (Burma) line up to await lunches that are donated to them.
Source: Peter Zurek/Shutterstock

The Productivity/Leisure Trade-Off Some cultures place more value on leisure time than others. They push for working shorter hours, take more holidays and vacations, and generally spend more time and money on leisure activities. In a study of OECD (fairly high-income) countries, France and the United States offered an example of contrast. The French had 30 days mandated vacation; Americans had none. The French also spent more time per day eating and sleeping than Americans.[47] In the United States, there is still some disdain for people who work very little: people of privilege who appear to contribute too little to society and people who appear to be satisfied with a lifestyle maintained by social benefits. Americans who give up work (primarily retirees) often complain that they're no longer allowed to contribute anything useful to society—one reason for laws prohibiting mandatory retirement.

People are more eager to work if

- Rewards for success are high
- There is some uncertainty of success

Expectation of Success and Reward Motivation toward work is influenced by the perceived likelihood of success and its rewards versus failure. Generally, people have little enthusiasm for effort when the likelihood of success seems too easy or too difficult. Few would care to run a race against either a snail or a racehorse; in either case, the outcome is too predictable. Our enthusiasm peaks when uncertainty of success is high, such as the challenge of racing another human of roughly equal ability. Likewise, the reward for a successfully completed task—say, winning a fair footrace—may be high or low, and most of us usually work harder the more we expect success to lead to a higher reward.

Success and Reward Across Borders Performed in different countries, the same tasks come with different probabilities of success, different rewards for success, and different consequences for failure. In cultures in which the probability of economic failure is almost certain and the perceived rewards of success are low, people tend—not surprisingly—to view work as necessary but unsatisfying, mainly because they foresee little benefit to themselves. This attitude may prevail in harsh climates, in very poor areas, or in subcultures subject to discrimination. Likewise, if there is little difference in reward between working hard or not, there is less motivation to work hard. In Cuba, for instance, where public policy allocates output from productive to unproductive workers, there is not much enthusiasm for work. When high uncertainty of outcome is combined with the likelihood of a positive reward for success and little or no reward for failure, we find the greatest work enthusiasm.[48]

Performance and Achievement

The Masculinity–Femininity Index A study using the **masculinity–femininity index** found significant differences in attitudes toward achievement among employees in 50 countries. Those with a high-masculinity score admired successful work achievers, harbored little sympathy for the unfortunate, and preferred to be better than others rather than on a par with them. They shared a money-and-things orientation rather than a people orientation, a belief that it's better "to live to work" than "to work to live," and a preference for performance and growth over quality of life and the environment.[49]

Such attitudes help explain why an international company may encounter managers abroad who behave differently than expected or preferred. Let's say a firm in a high-masculinity country such as Austria sets up operations in a high-femininity country such as Sweden. Typical purchasing managers in Sweden probably prefer smooth social relationships and amiable, ongoing dealings with suppliers to, say, immediate lower costs or faster delivery. They may also place such organizational goals as employee and social welfare ahead of the Austrian firm's goals of minimizing workers' compensation.

The hierarchy of needs
- May differ among countries
- Is useful in deciding how to motivate differently among countries

Hierarchies of Needs According to the **hierarchy-of-needs theory** of motivation, people try to fulfill lower-level needs before moving on to higher-level ones.[50] As you can see from Figure 2.4, the most basic needs are *physiological*: food, water, and sex. We have to satisfy (or nearly satisfy) those before our *security* needs—safe physical and emotional environments—which must be satisfied before triggering social needs, or the motivational effect of *affiliation,* such as peer acceptance. Then we're motivated to satisfy our *esteem* needs—bolstering our self-image through recognition, attention, and appreciation. The highest-order need calls for *self-actualization*—self-fulfillment, or (to quote Robert Lewis Stevenson) "becom[ing] all that we are capable of becoming." Finally, the theory also implies that we'll typically work to satisfy a need, which, once satisfied, diminishes in value as a motivator.

What can the hierarchy-of-needs theory tell us about doing business in foreign countries? For one thing, research has shown that different cultures not only attach different degrees of importance to various needs, they also rank higher-order needs differently. Thus, the theory can help in distinguishing among the reward preferences of employees in different parts of the world. This is important because of differences in workforce composition.[51] In very poor countries, for example, a larger portion of workers are likely engaged in manual jobs; thus, a company can motivate a larger portion of them simply by providing enough compensation to satisfy their needs for food and shelter. Elsewhere, a larger portion of workers are motivated by other needs.

Compensation (even at low levels of income) cannot fully explain differences in work motivation. A long-term ethnographic study among a U.S. airline's back-office employees in

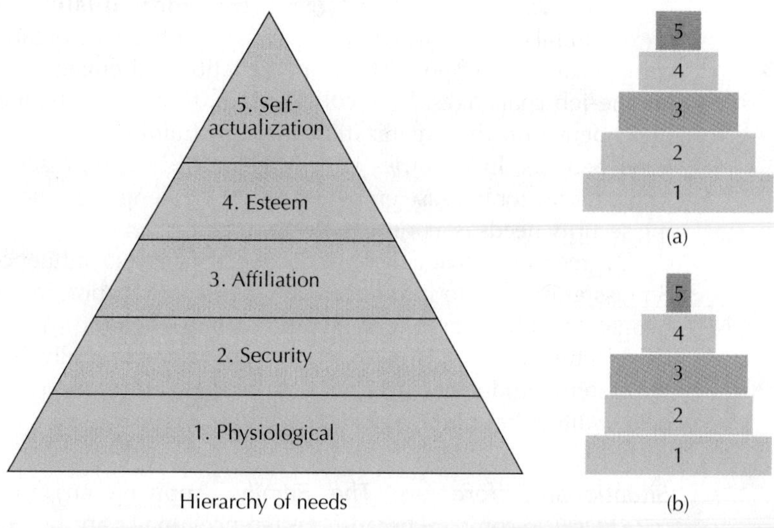

FIGURE 2.4 The Hierarchy of Needs and Need-Hierarchy Comparisons

The pyramid on the left represents the five-level hierarchy of needs formulated by Maslow. The two block pyramids on the right (a, b) represent two different groups of people—say, the populations of two different countries. Note that the block representing affiliation needs (level 3) is wider in (b) than in (a); conversely, the block representing self-actualization needs (level 5) is wider in (a) than in (b). In other words, even if we rank various needs in the same order (or hierarchy), the people in one country may regard a given higher-order need as more important (wider) than do people in another country.

three countries found that those in the United States and the Dominican Republic saw the job as a stepping-stone to higher-level positions. However, few in Barbados wanted a promotion because it would change their relationships with friends. U.S. workers usually dressed very casually because outsiders would not see them in the back office, but Barbadians dressed up to be seen going to what was considered a prestige job. In fact, the company offered Barbadian employees free company-owned bus transport, but the employees preferred to pay for slower public transportation where others could see them. The largely female staff in Barbados had low absenteeism and turnover rates because Barbados has a history of women working long-term. In the Dominican Republic, however, most female employees stayed on only until they married.[52]

RELATIONSHIP PREFERENCES

So far, we've discussed two categories of behavioral practices affecting business: social stratification systems and work motivation. Next, we examine some of the values underlying interpersonal differences in behavior.

There are national variations in the preference for autocratic or consultative management.

Power Distance From country to country, employee preferences tend to differ in terms of interacting with bosses, subordinates, and peers. Considerable evidence suggests that people perform better when the nature of their interactions fits their preferences. That's why companies are well advised to align management styles with superior-subordinate interaction preferences, which are known in general as **power distance**.

With *high* power distance, people prefer little consultation between the two tiers and one of two management styles: *autocratic* (ruling with unlimited authority) or *paternalistic* (regulating conduct by supplying needs). With *low* power distance, they prefer "consultative" styles.[53] What might happen, therefore, if a Dutch company assigned domestic managers, who typically prefer low power distance, to work in Morocco, where workers typically prefer high power distance? The Dutch managers might consult with Moroccan subordinates in an attempt to improve employee productivity. Unfortunately, subordinates may lose confidence in their superiors ("Why don't they know what to do?"), so that performance deteriorates rather than improves.

Interestingly, managers who prefer an autocratic style of superior–subordinate relationship are also quite willing to delegate and accept decision-making by a majority of subordinates. What they don't accept well is consultative interaction between the two tiers, which implies a more equal relationship between them. Clearly, worker-participation methods may need to be adjusted to fit different countries.

"Safe" work environments motivate collectivists. Challenges motivate individualists.

Individualism Versus Collectivism *High* **individualism** describes an employee's preference to fulfill leisure time and improve skills outside the organization, receive direct monetary compensation as opposed to fringe benefits, and engage in personal decision making and on-the-job challenges. *High* **collectivism**, in contrast, typifies an employee's penchant for dependence on the organization through training, satisfactory workplace conditions, and good benefits. In countries with high individualism, a self-actualization opportunity is a prime motivator because employees want challenges. In those with high collectivism, fulfilling security needs is a prime motivator.[54]

Degrees of individualism and collectivism also influence employee interactions. Levi Strauss attempted to introduce team-based production into several U.S. plants because its management had observed high productivity when the system was used in the highly collectivist culture of Japan. However, U.S. employees, especially the most skilled workers, detested the system; productivity went down, and Levi returned to a more individualistic system that better suited the culture of its U.S. workforce.

Situational Differences: The Family Applying any measure of *individualism versus collectivism* is complex because preferences may vary by situation.[55] Although Japan and

Mexico are both characterized as collectivist cultures, Mexico's collectivist preference is based more on kinship relations that do not carry over easily into the workplace.[56] Moreover, the Mexican concept of family sometimes includes not only the *nuclear family* (husband, wife, and minor children) but also the *vertically extended family* (members of several generations) and the *horizontally extended family* (aunts, uncles, and cousins).

Such differences can affect business in a variety of ways:

- Individualists in a family-oriented collectivists country may be less motivated to receive material rewards from their work because of dividing the rewards among more family members.
- Because relocation means that family members must also find new jobs, a worker's geographic mobility is limited. Even when extended families don't live together, mobility may be reduced because people prefer to remain near relatives.
- Interrelated familial roles may complicate purchasing decisions.
- Security and social needs may be met more effectively at home than in the workplace.

RISK-TAKING BEHAVIOR

Nationalities differ in
- Ease of handling uncertainties
- Degree of trust among people
- Future orientation
- Attitudes of self-determination and fatalism

Cultures differ in people's willingness to accept the status quo and control over destiny. The following discussion examines four types of *risk-taking behavior* that reflect these attitudes: *uncertainty avoidance, trust, future orientation,* and *fatalism.*

Uncertainty Avoidance In countries where **uncertainty avoidance** is high, most employees prefer to follow set rules even if they believe that breaking them may be in the company's best interests. They also tend to stay with current employers for a long time, preferring the certainty of present positions over the uncertainty of their future elsewhere.[57] When uncertainty avoidance is high, superiors may need to be more precise in their directions to subordinates, who typically don't want to be responsible for actions that counter what their superiors want.

Moreover, fewer consumers are prepared to risk being early product adopters. Gillette, for example, depends heavily on introducing new products, so it is likely better off to enter markets like Denmark and the United Kingdom, which rate low on uncertainty avoidance, before venturing into Belgium and Portugal, which rate high.

Trust Surveys measuring *trust* have found country differences in evaluations of such statements as "Most people can be trusted" and "You can't be too careful in dealing with people." Many more Norwegians than Brazilians, for example, regard most people as trustworthy.[58] Where trust is high, business costs tend to be lower because managers spend less time fussing over every possible contingency and monitoring every action for compliance and more time producing, selling, and innovating.[59] At the same time, the degree of trust may differ between what people consider their in-group and their out-group.[60] For instance, we discussed that in some family oriented societies, people have high trust of other family members, but low trust to people they do not know.

Future Orientation Cultures differ in their perceptions of the risks from delaying gratification. A **future orientation** (living for the future) is more pronounced in Switzerland, the Netherlands, and Canada than in Russia, Poland, and Italy.[61] In the former cultures, it may be easier for companies to motivate workers through such delayed-compensation programs as retirement plans.

Fatalism If people believe strongly in self-determination, they may be willing to work hard to achieve goals and take responsibility for performance. But if they're *fatalistic*—if they believe every event in life is inevitable—they're less likely to accept the basic cause-and-effect relationship between work and reward. In countries that rate high on fatalism, people plan less for contingencies, such as not buying insurance. Religious differences play a significant role in this regard. Conservative or fundamentalist groups, for instance, are more likely to view occurrences as "the will of God." Thus, managers are less apt to sway them with cause-and-effect logic than by making personal appeals or offering them rewards for complying with requests.[62]

INFORMATION AND TASK PROCESSING

"Beauty," we're often told, "is in the eye of the beholder." So, apparently, are perceptions and judgments, both of which are based on what people consider accurate *information.* Because different cultures handle information differently, the following discussion examines some of the ways in which people perceive, obtain, and process information.

Perception of Cues As a rule, we're selective in perceiving *cues*—features that inform us about the nature of something. We may identify things through any of our senses, and each sense can provide information in various ways, such as seeing color, depth, and shape through vision. People rely on cues that are partly physiological, and growing evidence suggests that evolution and genetics play a role in how different groups perceive.[63] Genetic differences in eye pigmentation, for instance, allow some people to differentiate colors more precisely than others.

Cultural differences, especially language, also reflect differences in perception of cues. The richness of a language's descriptive vocabulary allows its speakers to note and express very subtle nuances that speakers of a different language may not discern, or to perceive certain subjects more precisely than others. The Arabic language has many more words for camels, their body parts, and the equipment associated with them than other languages,[64] and Arabic speakers who work around camels can express nuances about them that most other people overlook.

It helps managers to know whether cultures favor

- Focused or broad information
- Sequential or simultaneous handling of situations
- Handling principles or small issues first

Obtaining Information: Low-Context Versus High-Context Cultures Researchers classify some countries (including the United States and most of northern Europe) as **low-context cultures**, in which people generally regard as relevant only firsthand information that bears directly on the subject at hand. Businesspeople will spend little time on small talk and tend to get to the point. In **high-context cultures**, people tend to regard seemingly peripheral information as pertinent and infer meanings from things said either indirectly or casually. They tend to follow these patterns in written communications as well, even in emails, and take them into account in international litigation.[65] Miscommunication can result as well. For example, because Japan is a high-context culture in which subordinates understand superiors' indirect instructions, Japanese managers have been challenged in conveying work expectations to their low-context United Kingdom subordinates, who expect more explicit explanations.[66] Even seemingly minor contextual differences may be misconstrued. For instance, on teams involving both Germans and Austrians, the low-context Germans were prone to say, "This is completely wrong" whereas the high-context Austrians would say, "This is a very interesting and important issue, but maybe we should also concentrate on this fact." The Austrians viewed the Germans as assertive and arrogant; the Germans viewed the Austrians as disorganized and less reliable.[67]

Information Processing Insofar as all cultures categorize, plan, and quantify, information processing is a universal activity. However, every culture has its own systems for ordering and classifying information. In U.S. directories, people's names appear in alphabetical order by last (family) name; in Iceland, they're organized by first (given) names (Icelandic last names are derived from the father's first name: Jon, son of Thor, is Jon *Thorsson,* and his sister's last name is *Thorsdottir,* "daughter of Thor"). To perform efficiently and work amicably in a foreign environment, you need to understand such differences in processing systems. Perhaps more important, different processing systems create challenges in sharing global data. Even the use of global personnel directories is problematic because of different alphabets and alphabetizing systems.

Monochronic Versus Polychronic Cultures Cultural differences also affect people's comfort with different degrees of multitasking. In **monochronic** cultures people may prefer to work sequentially, such as finishing transactions with one customer before dealing with another. Conversely, **polychronic** people are more comfortable when working simultaneously on a variety of tasks, such as dealing immediately with multiple customers who need service. Imagine the potential misconceptions when monochronic businesspeople see their polychronic counterparts as uninterested in doing business with them because they don't bother to give them their undivided attention. Further, when teams combine people from both types of cultures, the former sometimes feel that the latter delay results by wasting time.[68]

Idealism Versus Pragmatism Some cultures tend to focus first on the whole and then on the parts; others do the opposite. When asked to describe an underwater scene in which one large fish was swimming among some smaller fish and other aquatic life, most Japanese first described the overall picture, whereas most Americans first described the large fish.[69] Similarly, some cultures prefer to establish overall principles before they try to resolve small issues—an approach sometimes labeled **idealism**. Cultures in which people focus more on details than on abstract principles are said to be **pragmatic**.

These different approaches can affect business in a number of ways. In a culture of pragmatists (as in the United States), labor negotiations tend to focus on well-defined issues—say, hourly pay increases for a specific bargaining unit. In an idealist culture (as in Argentina), labor disputes tend to blur the focus on specific demands as workers tend to rely first on mass action, such as general strikes or political activities, to publicize basic principles.

COMMUNICATIONS

Cross-border communications do not always translate as intended.

We now look at problems in *communications*—especially translating spoken and written language. Problems occur not only when you shift from one language to another, but also when you communicate with someone from another country with the same official language. Finally, we discuss communication that occurs by means other than spoken and written language—a so-called "silent language."

SPOKEN AND WRITTEN LANGUAGE

Translating one language directly into another is not as straightforward as it may seem. Some words simply don't have direct translations. In English, for example, *children* may mean either "young people" or "offspring." In Spanish, *niños* and *hijos* distinguish between the two, and there is no word that encompasses both meanings that exist in English. Thus, despite recent great strides in the use of machines to translate, many errors still occur. Moreover, many translations—say, Galician into Welsh—go through an intermediate language, usually English.[70]

Language, including common word meanings, is constantly evolving. When Microsoft purchased a thesaurus code for its Spanish version of Word, the connotations of many synonyms had shifted by the time it implemented the software; some, in fact, were transformed into outright insults that alienated potential customers.[71] Of course, in any language words mean different things in different contexts. For example, the English word "old" can mean "former" or "long-standing."

Finally, remember that grammar is complex and the seemingly slight misuse (or even placement) of a word can substantially change the meaning. All of the following, each originally composed to assist English-speaking guests, have appeared on signs in hotels around the world:

FRANCE: "Please leave your values at the desk."

MEXICO (to assure guests about the safety of drinking water): "The manager has personally passed all the water served here."

JAPAN: "You are invited to take advantage of the chambermaid."

NORWAY: "Ladies are requested not to have children in the bar."

SWITZERLAND: "Because of the impropriety of entertaining guests of the opposite sex in the bedroom, it is suggested that the lobby be used for this purpose."

GREECE (at check-in line): "We will execute customers in strict rotation."

These examples offer a comical look at language barriers that usually result in only a little embarrassment. Poor translations, however, can cause commercial disputes; in 2011 the Shanghai Maritime Court dealt with almost 2000 such disputes between Chinese and foreign companies.[72] So choose your words carefully. Although there's no foolproof way of ensuring translations, experienced international businesspeople rely on such following suggestions:

- Get references for the people who will do your translating.
- Make sure your translator knows the technical vocabulary of your business.
- For written work, do *back translations:* Have one person go from, say, English to French and a second from French back to English. If your final message says what you said originally, it's probably satisfactory.
- Make sure that the tone, not just the words, fit both your own intentions and the expectations of recipients.
- Use simple words whenever possible (such as *ban* instead of *interdiction*).
- Avoid slang. American slang, especially words or phrases originating from sports—*off base, out in left field, threw me a curve, ballpark figure*—are probably meaningless to most businesspeople outside the United States.[73]
- When either you or your counterpart is dealing in a language other than your first language, clarify communications in several ways (repeat things in different words and ask questions) to ensure that all parties have the same interpretation.
- Recognize the need and budget from the start for the extra time needed for translation and clarification.

Be careful with humor because some lacks universal appeal. A Microsoft executive quipped to Indian executives that he really didn't have the qualifications to speak because he did not complete his MBA. The comment was badly received because Indians place high importance on education and on persevering rather than dropping out.[74]

Finally, even when all parties to a communication come from countries that share an official language, don't assume that understanding will go smoothly. Table 2.1, for instance, lists just some of the approximately 4,000 words that have different meanings in British and American English. What could go wrong? When Hershey's launched its Elegancita candy bar in Latin America, its expensive advertising campaign boasted about the *cajeta* in the product.

TABLE 2.1 Dangers of Misspeaking the Language(s) of Business

Below are a couple of short lists containing words used in business whose meanings are different in the United States and the United Kingdom—"two countries separated by a common language," as the British playwright G.B. Shaw once quipped. There are approximately 4,000 words with the potential to cause problems for people who—in theory—speak the same language.

United States	United Kingdom
turnover	redundancy
sales	turnover
inventory	stock
stock	shares
president	managing director

Unfortunately, although *cajeta* means "goat's-milk caramel" in Mexico, in much of South America it's vulgar slang for a part of the female anatomy.[75]

SILENT LANGUAGE

Of course, spoken and written language are not our only means of communicating. We constantly exchange messages through a host of nonverbal cues that form a **silent language**.[76] Recall from our opening case that in the process of conducting market research for the Java Lounge, researchers depended on several non-verbal cues to deduce who was affluent.

Silent language includes color associations, sense of appropriate distance, time and status cues, body language, and prestige.

Colors Colors are an interesting aspect of a culture's silent language. For a product to succeed, its colors obviously must be consistent with the consumer's frame of reference. Colors invoke distinct connotations in different countries, such as being lucky or unlucky or being associated with a specific business (e.g., yellow cabs in the United States and black ones in the United Kingdom). In most Western countries, black is a color for mourning death; in parts of Africa, it's white; in Thailand, it's purple. In the United States pink is used to denote femininity, while in Japan it denotes masculinity. United Airlines' promotion of a new passenger service in Hong Kong is an example of an effort that backfired because of color. Why? It handed out white carnations to its best customers, but Hong Kong residents give white carnations in sympathy for a death in the family.

Distance Another aspect of silent language is the accustomed distance people maintain during conversations or when conducting business. In the United States people customarily maintain a higher distance between each other than is typical in Mexico or elsewhere in Latin America. And except for handshakes, there is little or no touching in the United States, whereas touching one another in Mexico is quite common.[77] Thus, U.S. managers conducting business in Mexico may find themselves constantly moving backward to avoid the closeness their Mexican counterparts maintain. At the end of the discussion, both parties may well feel uneasy about each other without realizing why.

Time and Punctuality Different perceptions of time and punctuality also may create confusion. U.S. businesspeople usually arrive early for business appointments, a few minutes late for dinner at someone's home, and a bit later still for large social gatherings. In another country, the concept of punctuality in any or all of these situations may be different. A Latin American host may find it surprising and perhaps discourteous if a U.S. guest arrives only a few minutes later than the stated time for dinner.

Culturally, there are different ways of looking at time. People in English-speaking, Germanic, and Scandinavian countries tend to value time as a scarce commodity; if it's lost, it can't be recouped.[78] They tend to stick to schedules, even if taking longer would yield better results. In contrast, people who view time as an event prefer to take as long as necessary to complete a task to their satisfaction. In one case, the managers of a U.S. company competing for a contract were so confident of winning on the basis of better technology that they scheduled a tight, one-day meeting in Mexico City, thinking this was plenty of time for their presentation and questions. Unfortunately, the Mexican team arrived one hour after the scheduled start. Then, when one member of the Mexican team was called out of the room for an urgent phone call, the whole group got upset when the U.S. team tried to proceed without him. The competing French team, in contrast, allocated two weeks for discussions and won the contract with less sophisticated technology.[79]

Body Language Body language, or *kinesics*—the way people walk, touch, and move their bodies—also differs among cultures. Indeed, very few gestures have universal meanings. A Greek, Turk, or Bulgarian may indicate "yes" with a sideways movement of the head that could be construed as "no" in the United States and much of Europe. As Figure 2.5 shows, certain gestures may have several, even contradictory meanings.

FIGURE 2.5 Body Language Is Not a Universal Language

The fine line between approval and put-down: Very few gestures have universal meanings. In the United States, you'd probably be safe in approving of another person's statement by forming an O with your thumb and index finger (the so-called high sign). In Germany, Greece, and France, however, you'd be expressing a very different opinion.

Source: The meanings are based on descriptions in Roger E. Axtell, *Gestures* (New York: John Wiley, 1998). Reprinted by permission of John Wiley & Sons, Inc.

United States
It's fine

Germany
You lunatic

Greece
An obscene symbol for a body orifice

France
Zero or worthless

Japan
Money, especially change

Prestige Another factor in silent language relates to a person's status, particularly in an organizational setting. A U.S. manager who places great faith in physical things as cues to prestige may underestimate the status of foreign counterparts who don't have large, plush corner offices on high floors. Foreigners may underestimate U.S. counterparts who perform their own services, such as opening doors, fetching coffee, and answering unscreened phone calls.

DEALING WITH CULTURAL DIFFERENCES

After managers identify key cultural differences abroad, must they alter their customary practices to succeed there? Can people overcome culturally related adjustment problems when working abroad? There are no easy answers to these questions, but the following discussion highlights four issues that affect *degrees* of successful adjustment:

1. The extent to which a culture is willing to accept the introduction of anything foreign
2. Whether key cultural differences are small or great
3. The ability of individuals to adjust to what they find in foreign cultures
4. The general management orientation of the company involved

The following sections address each of these issues in some depth.

HOST SOCIETY ACCEPTANCE

Host cultures do not always expect foreigners to adjust to them.

Although our opening case illustrates the advantages of *adjusting* to a host country's culture, international companies sometimes succeed in introducing new products, technologies, and operating procedures with relatively little alteration. They pull it off either because what they're introducing does not run counter to deep-seated attitudes or because the host culture is willing to accept the foreign product or practice as an agreeable trade-off. Bahrain needs non-Muslim workers, so it permits the sale of pork products (ordinarily prohibited by religious law) as long as transactions are limited to special grocery store departments in which Muslims can neither work nor shop.

Sometimes the local society regards foreigners and domestic citizens differently. When staying overnight in Jeddah, Western female flight attendants can wear types of clothing publicly that local women cannot.[80] In other instances, local citizens may actually feel their cultures are being mocked when foreigners bend over backward to make adjustments, such as dressing in local traditional garb.[81]

DEGREE OF CULTURAL DIFFERENCES

When doing business in a similar culture, companies
- Usually have to make fewer adjustments
- May overlook subtle differences

Obviously, some countries are much like others, usually because they share many characteristics such as language, religion, geographic location, ethnicity, and level of economic development.

Cultural Distance A human values study comparing 43 societies on 405 cultural dimensions[82] could determine their *cultural proximity* by averaging the **cultural distance** separating them (number of countries apart) on each dimension. For instance, the United Kingdom is culturally close to the United States while China is culturally distant. When a company moves into a culturally similar foreign country, it should encounter fewer cultural adjustments than when entering a dissimilar country. An Ecuadorian company doing business in Colombia should expect to adjust more easily than if it were to do business in Thailand.

Even among similar countries, however, significant cultural differences could still affect business dealings. Moreover, managers may assume that such similar countries are more alike than they really are, and perhaps overlook important subtleties. Women's roles and behavior, for example, differ substantially from one Arab country to another even though the countries overall are culturally similar.

Hidden Cultural Attitudes Even if the home and host countries have seemingly similar cultures, people in the host country may reject the influx of foreign practices because they see them as additional steps that threaten their self-identities.[83] And with thousands of *minute* cultural dimensions, it may not be easy to discern operating impediments by comparing countries on the *broad* ones that are both obvious and studied. Disney had much more success in opening a theme park in Japan than in France, even though France is culturally closer to the United States. Why? First, France was very concerned about its separate identity, especially vis-à-vis the United States—encroachment of American English words into the French language, fast-food restaurants' threat to customary long lunches with traditional cuisine, U.S. companies' acquisition of French firms considered focal to French distinctiveness. Next, subtle differences separated the Japanese from the French. The Japanese were more receptive to Disney because (1) both Japanese children and adults perceived Mickey Mouse as a wholesome, nonthreatening figure, (2) the Japanese had a tradition of buying souvenirs on family excursions, and (3) Disney's reputation for super-cleanliness and smiling faces fit well with Japanese preferences for harmony and order. The French, in contrast, knew Mickey Mouse only as a comic-book conniver who'd been reformulated for the French market. They regarded Disney souvenirs as tacky and policies requiring personnel to dress uniformly and smile mindlessly as violations of personal dignity.[84]

ABILITY TO ADJUST: CULTURE SHOCK

International companies send personnel abroad for both short and long periods, subjecting them to potentially traumatic foreign practices. In fact, cultural practices all over the world are considered by many outsiders as downright wrong, such as polygamy, child marriage, the punishment of people (sometimes severe) for activities not considered crimes at home, and the public display of executed bodies. Both companies and individuals must decide if they're ready to work in places that countenance such practices.

Even in countries whose practices aren't necessarily traumatic to them, workers who go abroad often encounter **culture shock**—the frustration that results from having to absorb a vast array of new cultural cues and expectations. Even such seemingly simple tasks as using a different type of toilet or telephone, getting a driver's license, or finding where to buy specific merchandise can be taxing experiences at first. Our ending case shows that help from your fellow citizens who have already learned the different tasks can speed your understanding of them.

Some people get frustrated when entering a different culture.

Some people working in a culture significantly different from their own may pass through certain adjustment stages. At first, much like tourists, they're delighted with quaint differences. Later, however, they grow depressed and confused (the *culture shock* phase), so their effectiveness in the foreign environment suffers. Fortunately for most people, culture shock begins to ebb after a month or two as they grow more comfortable. In fact, some people experience **reverse culture shock** when they go back home, having become partial to aspects of life abroad that are not options back home.

COMPANY AND MANAGEMENT ORIENTATIONS

Whether and how a company and its managers adapt abroad depends not only on the host-country culture but also on their own attitudes. The following sections discuss three such attitudes or orientations: polycentrism, ethnocentrism, and geocentrism.

Polycentrist management may be so overwhelmed by national differences that it won't introduce workable changes.

Polycentrism A *polycentric* organization tends to believe that its business units abroad should act like local companies. Given the unique problems (and publicity about them) often inherent in foreign ventures, it's not surprising that many companies develop polycentric perspectives. However, polycentrism may be an overly cautious response to cultural variety, causing a firm to shy away from certain countries or avoid transferring home-country practices or resources that will actually work well abroad.

Look at it this way. To compete effectively, an international company—and its foreign units—must usually perform some functions differently from the competitors it encounters abroad in order to have an advantage over them. They may, for instance, need to sell and market new products or produce old ones differently. Thus, the overly polycentric firm may rely too heavily on imitating proven host-country practices and, in the process, lose the innovative edge it has honed at home.

Ethnocentrist management overlooks national differences and

- Ignores important factors
- Believes home-country objectives should prevail
- Thinks acceptance by other cultures is easy

Ethnocentrism *Ethnocentrism* reflects the conviction that one's own culture is superior to that of other countries. In international business, the term is usually applied to a company (or individual) so strongly committed to the principle of "What works at home will work abroad" that its foreign practices tend to ignore differences in cultures and markets. In turn, it underestimates the complexity of introducing new management methods, products, or marketing means, which likely leads to poor performance.

Before we go any further, we should point out that ethnocentrism isn't entirely an inappropriate way of looking at things. Obviously, much of what works at home will in fact work abroad. Further, concentrating on national differences in terms of *averages* overlooks specific variations within countries. A company may be able to deal with outliers even though the *average* person in the country has a strong cultural bias against what the company does in its home country. For example, although the average person in India has a strong cultural bias against eating meat, a company could sell meat products to the many Indians who do eat meat regularly or on occasion. Likewise, a company may identify partners, suppliers, and employees among a population minority whose attitudes don't fit the cultural average (there are always individualists in even the most collectivist societies).

Geocentric management often uses business practices that are hybrids of home and foreign norms.

Geocentrism Between the extremes of polycentrism and ethnocentrism, there is an approach to international business practices called *geocentrism,* which integrates company and host-country practices as well as some entirely new ones.[85] In our opening case, both Saks Fifth Avenue and Harvey Nichols have adjusted to Saudi customs (such as by setting aside women-only floors). At the same time, they've introduced home-country merchandising practices (what they sell) along with entirely new practices (providing lounges for the drivers of female customers).

Geocentrism requires companies to balance informed knowledge of their own organizational cultures with home- and host-country needs, capabilities, and constraints. Because it encourages innovation and improves the likelihood of success, geocentrism is the preferred approach for companies to succeed in foreign cultures and markets.

STRATEGIES FOR INSTITUTING CHANGE

Because people do not necessarily accept change readily, the management of change is important.

As we've seen, companies wanting to establish competitive advantages in foreign markets may need to operate in some ways differently from other companies in those markets, i.e., they introduce some degree of change into foreign markets. Thus, they need to bear in mind that people don't always accept change very readily, in either the home- or host-country market. The methods they choose for managing such changes are important for ensuring success.

Fortunately, we can gain a lot of insight by examining the international experiences of both for-profit and not-for-profit organizations. Moreover, a great deal of material is available on potential methods and so-called *change agents* (people or processes that intentionally cause or accelerate social, cultural, or behavioral change). The following sections discuss both experiences with and approaches to successful change, focusing on strategies in nine different areas:

- Value systems
- Cost-benefit analysis of change
- Resistance to too much change
- Participation
- Reward sharing
- Opinion leadership
- Cultural bridges
- Timing
- Learning abroad

We conclude with a discussion on the importance of learning as a two-way process—one in which companies transfer knowledge to and from both domestic and foreign markets.

Value Systems The more something contradicts our value system, the harder it is to accept. In Eritrea, for example, people eat less seafood than those in many other countries, despite having suffered several periods of agricultural famine while boasting a long coastline rich in seafood. One reason is economic. Because much of the population has traditionally not been able to afford the ice and refrigeration to prevent seafood spoilage, many adults have never developed a taste for seafood, worry about its safety, and believe it has a foul taste. Another reason is cultural: Eritrea's Cushitic speakers have religious taboos against eating fish without scales and insect-like sea creatures (including shrimp and crayfish). Thus, in trying to persuade these adults to eat more seafood, the Eritrean government and the United Nations World Food Program have faced formidable opposition. Among schoolchildren, however, whose value systems and habits are still flexible, officials have faced little opposition.[86]

Point

Does International Business Lead to Cultural Imperialism?

Point **Yes** The idea is pretty well accepted: International business influences globalization and globalization influences culture. Now, I have nothing against international business or globalization—at least part of it. What I don't like is *modern cultural imperialism,* which is what happens when the West, especially the United States, imposes its technical, political, military, and economic supremacy on developing countries.[87]

For years now, U.S. firms have been in the business of exporting U.S. culture—mostly through tactics that are rarely in the best interests of the national cultures it targets for economic domination. Because these firms nearly monopolize the international entertainment media, people all over the world are bombarded with U.S. movies, CNN, MTV, and the Disney Channel, not to mention the barrage of accompanying ads.

And what about the hordes of U.S. tourists who pay more for a night's lodging in a developing country than the hotel maid makes in a year? They'll tell you they're just taking a look at how the other half lives, but the fact is they're selling the U.S. lifestyle to a market that can't afford it and that's probably better off without it. Thanks to canned entertainment, nonstop advertising, and a sales force posing as tourists, culture shoppers in developing countries can sample U.S. possessions and practices to their hearts' content. Never mind that they come from a place (at least according to TV and the movies) populated mostly by the super-wealthy and by cops and psychotic malcontents whose daily lives are taken up with bullet-spattered body parts, round-the-clock sex, and inane family relationships. The lifestyle is seductive and promotes everything that's "Made in the U.S.A." That's why people everywhere are starting to behave and even talk like fictional Americans—after all, every speech from Manila to Managua is now peppered with U.S. slang. Along the way, people are letting their own cultural identities slip away.

Once they have a foot in the door, Western companies barge in to exploit the demand they've created, further destabilizing local cultures. In Mexico, Walmart thought nothing of putting up a superstore virtually next door to ancient ruins—eradicating the nearby street market—and bribing officials to alter zoning laws and sidestep required archaeological surveys, thereby destroying ancient artifacts with bulldozers and backhoes.[88] What's more, MNEs tend to cluster in urban markets, dragging workers away from rural areas to work under managers who speak only English and don't even allow time to go home for lunch.

I admit, if a country is rich enough, it can afford to resist cultural exploitation. Canada says no to foreign investment in culturally sensitive industries and makes sure there's Canadian content in local entertainment media. Finland discourages architecture that runs counter to tradition. France shuns outside languages and subsidizes a national motion picture industry. But even rich countries are affected. Some French TV programs and films are now being produced in English to cater to international audiences and more university courses are being taught in English, while some MNEs are contributing to the undermining of the French language in French-speaking Quebec.[89] In the developing world, where there's precious little cash for fighting off cultural extinction, people are at the mercy of foreign culture brokers.

Does International Business Lead to Cultural Imperialism?

Counterpoint

No You imply that people in poor countries passively accept everything they see in movie theaters and on TV. But they've turned their backs on a lot of products that international companies have promoted. Like most of us, they pick and choose.[90] You also imply that cultures in developing countries are the same. They aren't. They interpret what they see and hear—and what they buy—quite differently.

Like cultural purists everywhere, you've overlooked how cultural diffusion works. Through contact, culture heads in both directions and evolves. Way back between 100 BCE (BC) and 400 CE (AD), about 50 Mediterranean languages disappeared when people took up reading and writing in Latin and Greek.[91] Today, of course, very few of us converse in Latin, but that doesn't mean it's completely disappeared; it's evolved—namely, into the "Romance" languages.

I agree that many languages are in trouble today, and it's important to study them while they're still around. But the thing to remember is this: Most of them are giving way to dominant languages in the countries where they're spoken, such as Spanish, Mandarin, or Arabic. Of course, American English is seeping into other languages, but Americans have recently added a lot of foreign words as well. If you're a macho (Spanish) guy in charge of the

Counterpoint

whole enchilada (Spanish), for example, you're probably called the "head honcho" (Japanese).

Similarly, although U.S.-style fast food is almost everywhere, it has not entirely displaced local foods anywhere. When it comes to food, the result of international business is greater diversity for everybody. What we're witnessing is not "cultural imperialism" but cultural hybridization. In most countries, U.S. hamburgers, Japanese sushi, Italian pizza, Mexican tacos, and Middle Eastern pita bread coexist with the local cuisine. Mexico's Grupo Bimbo (owner of Sara Lee from the United States) sells tortillas in the United States and U.S.-style bagels in Mexico.[92]

Also, just because people in developing countries have taken a liking to soft drinks and fast food doesn't mean they've scrapped their traditional values. Moreover, some evidence suggests that, although young people are most likely to adopt elements from a foreign culture, they tend to revert to traditional values and habits as they get older. If that's the case, it's hard to argue that they're spearheading any permanent changes in their local cultures.[93]

As people seek to fulfill different wants, they must make trade-offs. But are people (and societies) worse off because they give up, say, lunch with the family to be able to afford certain consumer goods that will satisfy the whole family's needs? Globalization simply gives people more options. And tourism is also a two-edged sword. Rather than having a primarily negative effect, quite often it has helped maintain certain features of a traditional culture, such as the revival of traditional Balinese dancing because tourists want to see it.

A successful business, whether local or foreign-owned, must accommodate itself sufficiently to the culture in which it operates. This may mean revising plans to respond to local demands. Before Walmart finalized its construction plans in Mexico, executives consulted with anthropologists, reduced the store's height, and decided on a stone facade in a subdued color. Now it can be seen only from atop the pyramids. And while we're on the subject, you also failed to mention that the so-called traditional street market in question was peddling imported plastic goods rather than indigenous Mexican handicrafts. Many local residents had long complained about the lack of parking, stores that did not list prices, and rigged scales to inflate prices.

Cost-Benefit Analysis of Change Introducing products and practices abroad is sometimes costly, sometimes not. It can result in greatly improved performance, or only marginal change. Thus, a company must consider the expected *cost-benefit relationship* of what it does abroad. When U.S.-based Cummins Engine wanted to improve employee commitment in its Mexican plant, it succeeded by shutting down one day a year so workers could observe a religious holiday. On that day, Cummins hosts a celebration for employees and families at a cost that is much less than the benefits it has gained from improved performance.

Resistance to Too Much Change When the German magazine publisher Gruner + Jahr (G+J) bought U.S.-based *McCall's,* it immediately overhauled the magazine's format: changed editors, eliminated long stories and certain features, increased celebrity coverage, made layouts more robust, supplemented articles with sidebars, and refused discounts for big advertisers. Before long, morale declines led to greater employee turnover. More important, revenues fell because advertisers saw the change in format as too radical.[94] According to most observers, G+J might have obtained more employee and advertiser acceptance had it phased in its plans for change a little more gradually.

Participation One way to avoid problems like those encountered by G+J is to discuss proposed changes with stakeholders (employees, suppliers, customers, and the like) in advance. The discussion might help management assess the strength of the resistance, stimulate stakeholders to recognize the need for change, and ease fears about the consequences of changes. People might be satisfied that management has at least listened to them, regardless of the decisions it ultimately makes.[95]

Companies sometimes make the mistake of thinking that stakeholder participation in decision making is effective only with sufficiently educated people who are willing to speak up to make substantial contributions. Anyone who has had to deal with foreign aid programs can tell you that participation can be extremely important even in countries where education levels are low and power distance and uncertainty avoidance high.

Reward Sharing Sometimes a proposed change may have no foreseeable benefit for those whose support is needed. Production workers, for example, may have little incentive to try new work practices unless they see some imminent benefit for themselves. What can an employer do? It might develop the means of sharing gains with stakeholders both within and outside the company. For example, China National Petroleum has faced property damage from angry Iraqi farmers who have perceived problems without gains from living near drilling operations.[96] In contrast, a U.S.-Peruvian gold-mining venture won the support of skeptical Andean villagers simply by donating sheep to them.[97]

Opinion Leadership By making use of local channels of influence, or *opinion leaders,* a firm may be able to facilitate the acceptance of change. Opinion leaders may emerge in unexpected places. When Ford wanted to instill U.S. production methods in a Mexican plant, management relied on Mexican production workers rather than either Mexican or U.S. supervisors to observe operations at U.S. plants. What was the advantage of this approach? The production workers had more credibility with the Mexican workforce who would have to implement the new methods.[98]

Cultural Bridges Closely linked to opinion leadership are the attributes of people deciding about and then implementing changes abroad. People in the host country are persuaded not only by the details of a proposal, but also by their confidence in the presenters' technical qualifications, understanding of host-country constraints, and flexible attitudes toward reaching solutions. Bicultural and multicultural individuals may serve as bridges, especially if their cultures are from both the company's home and host countries. Even if the cultures are from other countries, these individuals may discern the new culture more quickly than unicultural individuals in much the same way that young bilingual children have an easier time than unilingual children in learning another language later on. Further, they have demonstrated empathy for divergent viewpoints and may be more positively perceived in the host country because of assumptions that they are not pushing an ethnocentric agenda.[99]

Timing Many well-conceived changes fail simply because they're ill-timed. A proposed labor-saving production method, say, might make employees nervous about losing their jobs no matter how much management tries to reassure them. If, however, the proposal is made during a period of labor shortage, the firm will likely encounter less fear and resistance.

In certain cases, of course, crisis precipitates the acceptance of change. In Turkey, for example, where family members have traditionally dominated business organizations, poor performance has stimulated a rapid change in this practice: rather than "running" the business, many families now serve in "advisory capacities" instead (often on the board of directors).

Learning Abroad Remember, as companies gain more experience in foreign operations, they may learn as well as impart valuable knowledge—knowledge that proves just as useful at home as in the host country. Such learning may concern any business function; however, access to R&D personnel is a particularly potent advantage in operating abroad. Nevertheless, if one goes abroad with the belief of already knowing everything, there is little chance to learn. But there are many examples of being open-minded with good results. For example, the merger between Renault and Nissan brought complementary strengths together. Renault brought its better financial management (typical of French firms) to Nissan. Meanwhile, Renault is learning more about Nissan's (and Japanese companies') ability to have functional groups work together to meet a common company objective.[100]

Finally, companies should examine economies and businesses abroad that are performing well in order to determine practices they can emulate. In India, for example, some large companies have performed extremely well recently, not in spite of but because of placing social missions and heavy investments in their employees.[101]

Looking to the Future

What Will Happen to National Cultures?

Scenario I: New Hybrid Cultures Will Develop and Personal Horizons Will Broaden

International contact is growing at a rate perhaps unimaginable a few decades ago—a process that should lead to a certain mixing and greater similarity among national cultures. At first glance, that's exactly what's happening. The mixing seems evident when one sees, say, a group of Japanese tourists listening to a Philippine band perform an American pop song in a British hotel in Indonesia. Likewise, combination languages such as "Spanglish" have emerged. The growing mix seems evident when people in every corner of the world wear similar clothing and listen to international recording stars alongside other people wearing local styles and listening to local recording artists. Competitors headquartered in far-flung areas of the globe are increasingly copying each other's operating practices, thus creating a competitive work environment that's more global than national. As companies and people get used to operating internationally, they should continue to gain confidence in applying the benefits of cultural diversity and globally inspired operating procedures to explore new areas in both workplace productivity and consumer behavior.

We'll also likely see people taking advantage of greater mobility and broadening their concepts of what it means to enjoy global or flexible citizenship.[102] Historically, most people who immigrated to foreign countries were able to return to their homelands perhaps once in their lives. They were thus compelled to accept the cultures of their adopted countries, sacrificing much of their native cultural identity in the process. Today, however, many who come to high-income countries to find work often obtain dual citizenship and maintain contact with their native cultures through travel, direct-dial phone calls, and Internet communications. On the one hand, these immigrants may tend to transfer culture in both directions, bringing greater diversity to both host and home countries. Further, as people travel more abroad, marriage among different nationalities increases; the number of Americans with foreign born spouses doubled between 1960 and 2010.[103] Evidence suggests that children in these circumstances are becoming bi- or multicultural, resulting in a class of international managers whose traditional ties to specific cultures are much looser than those of most people (witness CEO Carlos Ghosn of Japan's Nissan and France's Renault, a Brazilian of Lebanese extraction educated in France).[104] On the other hand, multiculturalism appears to be failing because immigrants no longer have to assimilate into the culture of their new residency, which could lead to more cultural strife within nations.[105]

Scenario 2: Although the Outward Expressions of National Culture Will Continue to Become More Homogeneous, Distinct Values Will Tend to Remain Stable

Beneath the surface of the visual aspects of culture (including most of the elements touched on in the previous section), people continue to hold fast to some of the basics that distinguish national cultures. In other words, although certain material and even behavioral facets of cultures will become more universal, certain fundamental values and attitudes will vary. Religious differences are as strong as ever; language differences still bolster ethnic identities. What's important is that such differences are still powerful enough to fragment the world culturally and stymie the global standardization of products and operating methods.

Scenario 3: Nationalism Will Continue to Reinforce Cultural Identity

If people didn't perceive the *cultural* differences among themselves and others, they'd be less likely to regard themselves as distinct *national* entities. That's why appeals to cultural identity are so effective in mobilizing people to defend national identity. Typically, such efforts promote the "national culture" by reinforcing language and religion, subsidizing nationalistic programs and activities, and propagandizing against foreign influences on the national culture. Further, even though people will be more internationally mobile, peer pressure will force them to adapt to their national cultures.

Scenario 4: Existing National Borders Will Shift to Accommodate Ethnic Differences

Several countries are showing more evidence of subcultural power and influence. Why? Basic factors include immigration and the rise of religious fundamentalism. Equally important seems to be the growing desire among ethnic groups for independence from dominant groups where they reside. Both Yugoslavia and Czechoslovakia have broken up for this reason, while ethnic groups in Britain and Spain (Scots, Catalons, and Basques) are currently pushing for independence. Meanwhile, some subcultures—such as the Inuits in the Arctic and the Kurds in the Middle East—transcend national boundaries and simply resist being "nationalized." Because they have less in common with their "countrymen" than with ethnic brethren in other countries, it's hard to assign them an identity on the basis of geographic circumstances.

Regardless of the scenario that unfolds in any given arena, international businesspeople must learn to examine specific cultural differences if they hope to operate effectively in a foreign environment. In the future, analysis based only on national characteristics won't be sufficient; business will have to pay attention to all the other myriad factors that contribute to distinctions in values, attitudes, and behavior. ■

Tesco PLC: Leveraging Global Knowledge

—*Mary Yoko Brannen and Terence Mughan*

David Potts stared out the window of the 747 as it taxied for take-off.[106] His first visit to China as CEO of Tesco Asia had been exciting but had posed a number of big questions. The United Kingdom-based retailing giant had been in Asia for a little over a decade and sales and profits were already comfortably outstripping the UK and other Tesco areas, including Central Europe and the United States. Yet it was also clear that every Asian market was unique. Thailand, Malaysia, and South Korea had been great successes (the adjacent photo shows a Tesco store in Malaysia), Japan and Taiwan less so. The sheer size of China and India put them in a category of their own. How, then, was this venture going to develop across such a huge continent? And how could he capture and direct the energy and growth of Tesco Asia so as to continue to strengthen its core operations in the UK? Maybe Tesco could find an innovative answer to this challenge. It had done so supremely in other circumstances since its great transformation in the mid-1980s.

Company Background

Jack Cohen, who died in 1979, founded Tesco in the aftermath of World War I by purchasing surplus military supplies and selling them to a working-class population. Headquartered since 1973 outside London, his company became a readily identifiable feature of the UK retail scene. Known as a "Pile it high, sell it cheap" retailer with outlets in almost every town and city, Tesco knew its place in the class-based pecking order of the UK market, in which chains such as Sainsburys and Marks & Spencer met the needs of consumers with more disposable income and more refined tastes.

In the midst of the recession of the mid-1980s, Managing Director Ian McLaurin became chairman and ushered in a new management team that changed Tesco and its market

The photo shows a Tesco hypermarket in Ampang, Malaysia.
Source: © Beaconstox / Alamy

position radically. Relying on a cohort of young, talented executives with a Tesco background and an innate understanding of the UK consumer market (Potts and the current and past CEOs Phillip Clarke and Terry Leahy), McLaurin made Tesco into a store to meet all shoppers' needs. In fact, Tesco crushed the competition, including the Walmart-backed Asda, in the UK market.

Tesco's approach to the challenge of becoming market leader was to improve in every aspect of its operations, including distribution, marketing, land acquisition, and product innovation. The key driver of this approach was a change in corporate culture to emphasize attention to people. The new management prized loyalty and commitment from staff and was determined to make Tesco the employer of choice in the retailing sector. Such an attitude manifested itself in a company language that was simple and clear: "Treat people how we like to be treated" for customers, "Listen, support and say thank you" among employees.

David Potts took this belief in language a step further by compiling a "Jargonbuster"—a corporate dictionary that banished obscure terms and acronyms and laid down exactly how simple words make for clear communication. Such simple, clear language was increasingly important in Tesco's UK home base as immigrants and people with multicultural backgrounds permeated both the workforce and customer demographics. In the course of the 1990s this desire for clear communication extended further to the customer interface as the company increased the size range of stores: the *Super* stores, the smaller *Express* stores in urban centers, and the large *Extra* stores carrying the widest range of merchandise. Tesco bolstered its own branded food product range by adding the "Value" line at the lower end and the "Finest" line at the top end. With the help of an aggressive marketing campaign dubbed "The Tesco Way," which was led by the "Every Little Helps" slogan and the Clubcard incentive scheme, Tesco gained invaluable customer data and overtook its local competition. During a six-year period with Terry Leahy at the helm, its sales and profits grew by over 300 percent, making it the largest internet retailer and private sector employer in the UK. Thus, it began actively looking to international markets for the next phase of expansion.

Internationalization

In 1995 Tesco entered the Hungarian market by acquiring the S-Market chain. In 1998 it ventured further to find a local partner in Thailand and established Tesco-Lotus. An innovative partnership in 1999 with Samsung in South Korea formed HomePlus, thereby creating the bedrock for a sustained Asian presence—despite a disastrous £11 billion failure in Taiwan when Tesco sought to sell all of its Taiwan sites but had to settle on swapping them for stores owned by Carrefour (a major competitor from France) in the Czech Republic and Slovakia.

Tesco initially entered most of its foreign markets with an ethnocentric approach that sought to replicate its home success and culture in foreign locations. In the smaller and less distant cultures of central Europe this had worked well: then came France. The fact that the first international setback happened across the Channel was no great surprise; UK competitors such as Marks & Spencer had also found the British-French cultural gap too wide to cross, even though France was Britain's nearest neighbor. In fact, making English Tesco's operating language was harder in France than in any other country in which it operated.

Another problem occurred when Tesco launched Taiwanese operations by parading its Britishness—complete with Union flags and Beefeaters—in front of the store, and hence learned a strong lesson about foreign market entry strategy. Determined to banish any signs of imperialism and restore the qualities of hard work, humility, and customer dedication in future ventures, the company resolved to move toward a more locally responsive stance in foreign markets.

This desire to grow internationally in a bottom-up, locally inclusive fashion characterizes Tesco PLC. Of the young executives who came through the ranks in the 1990s, almost all were "lifers": people who started on the bottom rung of the corporate ladder, stayed with the company, and worked their way up. None, however, was more of a lifer than David Potts, who left school at the age of sixteen to work in his local Tesco supermarket. Gaining experience by stacking shelves on the shop floor and gradually moving into management gave him a deep understanding of the store, its customers, and the challenges involved in meeting their daily needs. Tesco even institutionalized this philosophy in the practice of TWIST—Tesco Week In Stores—whereby all management level employees must work one week a year in a Tesco store so as to always stay close to the customer and the stores' basic operations. All other activities of the company, whether supplier management, executive meetings, or government relations, are built around this key process. Extending this philosophy to include a policy of growing local talent from the bottom up in its international subsidiaries was a natural next step. Now, as CEO Asia, Potts was facing the challenges of operating in 14 countries across Asia, Europe, and North America. (Map 2.4 shows the countries with Tesco operations as of 2013.)

The main challenge for Tesco lay both in identifying the global advantages of its foreign subsidiaries as part of the Tesco group and learning from them in ways that would reinvigorate its home country competitive advantage. As a member of the Board for several years, Potts had accumulated a vast working knowledge of international business as Tesco rapidly became the world's third largest food retailer. How could he go about managing flourishing growth in Asia while maintaining and even enhancing the competitive position of Tesco's UK home market? Was there a way to transfer Tesco's leading-edge data, purchasing, and distribution resources across its global operations while also learning from the best practices evolving from operations in its foreign subsidiaries? And would it be possible to do all this and still maintain a globally integrated corporate culture? Was this a job for a consulting company? Could outsiders help solve this puzzle?

As he pondered over his challenge, Potts's thoughts kept coming back to the fact that in 2010, for the first time in over two decades, Tesco was losing its competitiveness in its home market: UK sales figures were down .5% for the year. Still, worldwide profits had risen by 12.9%, a growth led by the performance in Tesco's Asian regional markets. Clearly there was a lot that Tesco might learn from its Asian subsidiaries. But how?

MAP 2.4 Tesco Locations and Its Cross-Cultural Project

The orange-colored countries on the map show Tesco's operations by country as of 2013. The arrows indicate the countries sending personnel to the United Kingdom to participate in the project. Note that Japan participated, but Tesco has since closed operations there.

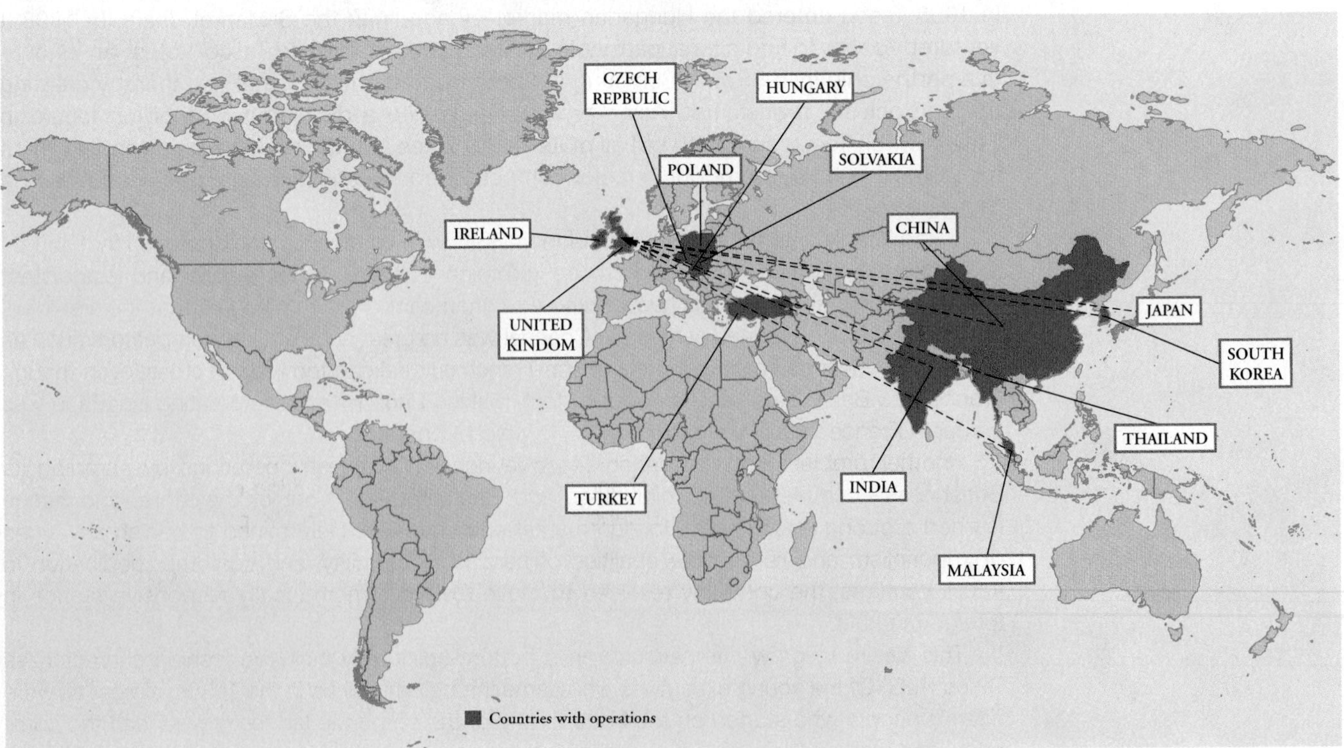

The Essence of the Tesco Project

Potts finally came up with a novel solution that was more consistent with Tesco's philosophy of building on its internal resources. Aware that declining growth at home is often a signal of complacency that can go unnoticed by people close to the situation, he decided to bring together a team of Asian managers who would visit Tesco in the UK to examine the home operations. As Tesco insiders they would be familiar with the company's mission, values, processes, and procedures and thus would be able to feel at home in the store context; as outsiders in the UK, they would be able to see things differently from the British managers, thereby bringing valuable insights from their home country perspective and sharing best practices that had evolved in their local markets. Potts called the project "The Essence of Tesco" and gave it a two-pronged strategic purpose: (1) to conduct a health-check of Tesco UK's current corporate state and determine what was and wasn't working; and (2) to compare and contrast that state with the processes and practices that had evolved in Tesco's Asian subsidiaries so as to learn from and leverage them globally for Tesco.

Nine managers were chosen from Tesco's six Asian subsidiaries: two each from Thailand, South Korea, and China—its largest Asian markets—and one each from Malaysia, Japan, and India. This Asian project team was then brought to the UK, trained in skills needed to observe and make sense of organizational behavior, values, and assumptions (a kind of corporate ethnography), and deployed for a three-month period to observe and work in 52 stores across the UK and Ireland. The task of helping Tesco reinvigorate home operations was not easy; nor had it been easy to find nine managers who could leave their job for an extended three-month period. In the end, the main criteria stipulated that team members had to have worked for Tesco for at least three years, had a working knowledge of English, and were store-level employees rather than country-level managers. The team was also assessed on various cultural adaptability skills needed to get by in a foreign environment, such as flexibility and openness, emotional resilience, and personal autonomy.

Three of the project team members were completely bilingual, having lived extensively in English-speaking environments; in fact, one had actually studied in England and thus had a deep cultural knowledge of the UK. These three proved very helpful to the team, especially with such practical things as opening bank accounts, navigating the public transportation system, setting up mobile phone contacts, shopping, and the like. The others had varying degrees of cross-cultural exposure and competencies in the English language. All were from group-oriented, high-context cultures, a fact that allowed teamwork to emerge quite naturally and ensured that the team would pay attention to unarticulated details—factors that proved invaluable for being able to see things in the stores that others from low-context countries might not notice. Team members' natural perceptual ability helped ensure that they would be able to act as organizational bridges between their home subsidiaries and Tesco UK.

This journey of nine Asian Tesco managers across the United Kingdom took place at a time when many British cities were shaken by riots and store looting. Still, the team compiled many pages of observances to use in creating their analysis of Tesco operations. Their exposure to British culture was intense on many levels. Two of them were actually locked in a Liverpool store during a riot and, though frightened, were impressed by the calm manner in which store managers handled the situation. The day-to-day experiences, though less exciting, were also very informative and gave rise to many comparisons and contrasts in implementing such core company values as customer focus in the UK and the home countries.

Brief anecdotes the team exchanged at the end of each working day can provide some insight into their findings. For instance, while watching a Tesco UK produce handler throw a bunch of bananas onto a display, Thai managers felt that UK standards were below what they were accustomed to. A Japanese project team member was shocked to learn that a UK fishmonger had only a couple of days' training before taking on the new role of learning to cut and prepare fresh fish, which was almost an art form in Japan and required several months of intensive training. Was Tesco still a place where everybody could develop a career? It certainly didn't seem so when the team exchanged stories of how one shop floor worker had never been enrolled in the career advancement program, or how another had been working at the same job-grade level for quite a few years. What were the reasons for this? By engaging with store staff, the project team found out that, although there was a clearly developed "Opportunity to Get On" program, an employee had to be willing to move geographically and/or take up a new job role in order to benefit from the program. The team uncovered many discrepancies between Tesco's espoused corporate culture and its everyday practices in the UK. Noting these discrepancies and asking follow-up questions, the project team members brought new perspectives to the company culture and were able to offer solutions from their own home practices.

In noting that Tesco UK does not take every opportunity to make the customer's experience as good as it can be, the Asian team offered suggestions about product promotions, family and community engagement, and customer service that would make UK stores more competitive. They provided great insights into taking advantage of the stock of market knowledge stemming from innovations that arose from the diverse partnerships forged in Asia. For example, by leveraging Samsung's technological strengths at Tesco Home-Plus Korea, Tesco-UK was able to come up with a smart phone app that could read bar codes off a panel shopping screen in the subway station and allow customers to easily shop online while waiting for their train. These and many other observations were absorbed by senior management in the form of a project report and in ongoing face-to-face meetings with the Asian team.

After almost two years, Tesco UK showed definite signs of reinvigoration at home. It employed 8000 new store personnel. It provided customer training to 250,000 staff members. Overall UK sales rose 1.8 percent. It has refreshed more than 300 of the UK stores, improved the bakeries in 850 stores, and increased online grocery sales by 12.8%. It has launched a club card and a T.V. channel, and the Tesco bank has 6.6 million account holders.

Tesco also continues to make great progress in Asia, which delivers twice the trading profits of continental Europe from only 33 percent more stores. The international strategy of the company has clearly moved beyond its ethnocentric past to become not only locally responsive but also capable of learning from its global operations. This is illustrated by the following statement on Tesco's web site:

> We will **win locally by applying our skills globally**. The key word here is "locally"—all retailing is local. But increasingly we are utilising the skill and scale of the Group to benefit the performance and competitiveness of each of our businesses around the world.

QUESTIONS

2-3. The United States and France are more culturally similar to the UK than are Thailand and South Korea, yet Tesco failed in the former two and has been highly successful in the latter two. How might you explain the difference?

2-4. In the context of global retailing, describe what you think is meant by "utilising the skill and scale of the Group."

2-5. What is the role of global teams in sharing best practices across a firm's global operations? What advice would you give to make the teams more effective?

2-6. What cultural skill sets are needed for individuals from multiple cultures to share best practices across the global group?

2-7. What are some things an MNE can do to facilitate knowledge sharing and global integration across its global businesses?

2-8. Look at the Tesco website. What exactly are its businesses and what do you think this tells us about its internationalization trajectory?

2-9. How would this business model translate into policies of recruitment, training and development, and career management across the Group?

SUMMARY

- *Culture* includes norms based on learned attitudes, values, and beliefs. Almost everyone agrees there are cross-country differences in culture, but most experts disagree as to exactly what they are.
- International companies and individuals must evaluate their business and personal practices to ensure that their behavior may fit with national norms.
- In addition to being part of a *national* culture, people are simultaneously part of other cultures, such as professional or organizational ones. Further, they may have more than one national culture.
- While studying other cultures is useful, there are problems in depending on self-reports to describe attitudes and values, assuming that everyone within a culture more or less fits the average, and depending on outdated information in dynamic situations.
- Distinct societies are often found within a given country. People also may have more in common with similar groups in foreign countries than with groups in their own countries.
- Cultural change may take place as a result of choice or imposition. Isolation from other groups, especially because of language, tends to stabilize cultures.
- People fall into social-stratification systems according to their *ascribed* and *acquired group memberships,* which influence their level of access to economic resources, prestige, social relations, and power. Individuals' affiliations may influence their qualifications and access to certain jobs.
- People work far more than they must to satisfy their basic needs for food, clothing, and shelter. They're motivated to work for various reasons, including the preference for material possessions over leisure time, the belief that work will bring success and reward, and the desire for achievement.
- There are national differences in norms that influence people's workforce preferences, such as whether they prefer autocratic or consultative working relationships, whether they prefer their activities to follow set rules, and how much they prefer to compete or cooperate with fellow workers.
- National differences in norms determine such behavioral factors as trust, belief in fate, and confidence in planning for the future.
- Failure to perceive subtle distinctions in culturally determined behavior can result in misunderstandings in international dealings.
- People communicate through spoken, written, and silent language—all governed by culturally determined cues. Cultural background also plays a major role in how people process information.
- Host cultures don't always expect foreign companies or individuals to conform to their norms. Sometimes they accommodate them because of trade-offs, sometimes they apply different standards to their behavior.
- A company usually needs to make fewer adjustments when entering a culture similar to its own, but it must be quite careful to heed subtleties both in host-country behaviors and in host-country perceptions of foreigners' behaviors.
- People living and working in foreign environments should be sensitive to the dangers of excessive *polycentrism* and excessive *ethnocentrism.* Usually, *geocentrism* is a safer approach.
- In deciding whether to make changes in either home- or host-country operations, a company should consider several factors: the importance of the proposed changes to every party involved, the cost and benefit to the company of each proposed change, the value of opinion leaders in implementing the changes, whether one can use people as cultural bridges, and timing.
- The future of national cultures may involve the emergence of new hybrid cultures, an adoption of similar visual aspects of culture while maintaining distinct values, the continuance of differences because of nationalism, and new nations based on prevailing cultural identities.

KEY TERMS

acquired group membership (p. 102)
ascribed group membership (p. 102)
bicultural (p. 95)
collectivism (p. 106)
cultural collision (p. 93)
cultural distance (p. 113)
cultural imperialism (p. 96)
culture (p. 92)
culture shock (p. 113)
deal-focus (DF) culture (p. 93)
future orientation (p. 107)
hierarchy-of-needs theory (p. 105)
high-context culture (p. 108)
idealism (p. 109)
individualism (p. 106)
low-context culture (p. 108)
masculinity–femininity index (p. 105)
monochronic (approach to multitasking) (p. 109)
multicultural (p. 95)
polychronic (approach to multitasking) (p. 109)
power distance (p. 106)
pragmatic (p. 109)
relationship-focus (RF) culture (p. 94)
reverse culture shock (p. 114)
silent language (p. 111)
uncertainty avoidance (p. 107)

ENDNOTES

1 We are particularly appreciative of personal insights given us by the following people in Saudi Arabia: Nora al Jundi, lecturer at Effat University; Omar Aljindi, consultant at Saudi Diyar Consultants; and Talah Tamimi, former executive at Saudi Investment General Authority. Additional Sources include the following: Sue Tibballa, *"Saudi Women Make History," New Statesman* 141:5118 (August 13, 2012): 17; "Saudi Prince Backs Letting Women Drive," *Miami Herald* (April 15, 2013): 11A;"Saudi Arabia: The Western Compound," americanbedu.com/2011/03/07/saudi-arabia-the-western-compound/ (Accessed March 15, 2011); Summer Said,"Saudi Activism Accelerates As Women Dare to Drive,"*Wall Street Journal* (June 18-19, 2011): A9; Abeer Allam,"Saudi Women Bridle at Business Rules,"*Financial Times* (May 22, 2009): 4; Karen Elliott House,"Pressure Points,"*Wall Street Journal* (April 10, 2007): A1+; Karen Elliot House,"For Saudi Women, a Whiff of Change,"*Wall Street Journal* (April 7, 2007): A1+; Roula Khalaf,"Saudi Women Carve a Place in the Future of Their Country,"*Financial Times* (January 25, 2002): 3; Steve Jarvis,"Western-Style Research in the Middle East,"*Marketing News* (April 29, 2002): International section, 37; Barbara Slavin,"U.S. Firms' Saudi Offices Face Manpower Issues,"*USA Today* (May 13, 2002): 5A; Colbert I. King,"When in Saudi Arabia...Do as Americans Do,"*Washington Post* (February 2, 2002): A25; Donna Abu-Nasr,"Saudis Begin to Show Wear and Tear of Life under Feared Religious Police,"*AP Worldstream* (April 28, 2002): n.p.; Cecile Rohwedder,"The Chic of Arabia,"*Wall Street Journal* (January 23, 2004): A11+.

2 Christian Tröster and Daan van Knippenberg,"Leader Openness, Nationality Dissimilarity, and Voice in Multinational Management Teams,"*Journal of International Business Studies* 43:6 (2012): 591–613.

3 Helene Tenzer and Markus Pudelko,"Language Differences as Impediments to Shared Mental Model Formation in Multinational Teams,"paper presented at the 54th Annual Meeting of the Academy of International Business (Washington: June 30-July 3, 2012).

4 Jeanne Brett, Kristin Behfar, and Mary C. Kern,"Managing Multicultural Teams,"*Harvard Business Review* 84 (November 2006): 84–91; Yaping Gong,"The Impact of Subsidiary Top Management Team National Diversity on Subsidiary Performance: Knowledge and Legitimacy Perspectives,"*Management International Review* 46:6 (2006): 771–98; and Aida Hajro, Markus Pudelko, and Christina Gibson,"Multinational Teams: Cultural Differences, Interactions, Organizational Context, and Performance,"paper presented at the 54th Annual Meeting of the Academy of International Business (Washington: June 30–July 3, 2012).

5 Vas Taras, Pawel Bryla, Dan V. Caprar, Alfredo Jimenez, Peter Magnusson, and Riikka Sarala,"A Comparative Analysis of the Effects of Different Forms of Team Diversity on Global Virtual Team Performance,"paper presented at the 54th Annual Meeting of the Academy of International Business (Washington: June 30–July 3, 2012).

6 David E. Brown,"Human Universals, Human Nature and Human Culture,"*Daedalus* 133:4 (Fall 2004): 47–54.

7 Tomasz Lenartowicz and Kendall Roth,"The Selection of Key Informants in IB Cross-Cultural Studies,"*Management International Review* 44:1 (2004): 23–51.

8 Ben Casselman,"Risk-Averse Culture Infects U.S. Workers, Entrpreneurs,"*Wall Street Journal* (June 3, 2013): A1+ shows how a variety of entrepreneurial indicators changed with the economy.

9 Patti Waldmeir,"Property Bubble Erodes China's Traditional Preference for Sons,"*Financial Times* (November 2, 2010): 1.

10 Richard Gesteland, *Cross-Cultural Business Behavior* (Copenhagen: Copenhagen Business School Press, 2012).

11 Four of the most significant are Geert Hofstede, *Cultures and Organizations: Software of the Mind* (New York: McGraw-Hill, 1997), which explores attitudes in 50 countries, primarily those concerning workplace relationships; Ronald Inglehart, Miguel Basañez, and Alejandro Moreno, *Human Values and Beliefs: A Cross-Cultural Sourcebook* (Ann Arbor: University of Michigan Press, 1998) analyzes political, religious, sexual, and economic norms in 43 countries; Robert J. House, Paul J. Hanges, Mansour Javidan, Peter W. Dorfman, and Vipin Gupta, eds., *Culture, Leadership, and Organizations* (Thousand Oaks, CA: Sage, 2004) examines leadership preferences in 59 countries. S, Schwartz," A Theory of Cultural Value Orientations: Explication and Applications," *Comparative Sociology* 5:2–3:(2006): 137–82.

12 Anne-Wil Harzing, Michelle Brown, Katherin Köster, and Shuming Zhao,"Response Style Differences in Cross-National Research," *Management International Review* 52:3 (2012): 341–63.

13 Mary Lou Egan and Marc Bendick, Jr.,"Combining Multicultural Management and Diversity into One Course on Cultural Competence,"*Academy of Management Learning & Education* 7:3 (2008): 387–93; and Paul Brewer and Sunil Venaik,"National Culture versus Individual Culture: The Importance of the Ecological Fallacy," paper presented at the 54th annual meeting of the Academy of International Business (Washington, DC, June 30–July 3, 2012).

14 Geert Hofstede and Robert R. McCrae,"Personality and Culture Revisited: Linking Traits and Dimensions of Culture,"*Cross-Cultural Research* 38:1 (February 2004): 52–88.

15 James W. Neuliep, *International Communication: A Contextual Approach*, 4th edition (Thousand Oaks, CA: Sage Publishing, 2009).

16 Robert J. Foster,"Making National Cultures in the National Acumen," *Annual Review of Anthropology* 20 (1991): 235–60, discusses the concept and ingredients of a national culture.

17 Harry C. Triandis,"Dimensions of Cultural Variation as Parameters of Organizational Theories,"*International Studies of Management and Organization* 12:4 (Winter 1982–1983): 143–44.

18 See Aihwa Ong, *Flexible Citizenship: The Cultural Logics of the Transnationality* (Durham, NC: Duke University Press, 1999); Leo Paul Dana, *Entrepreneurship in Pacific Asia* (Singapore: World Scientific, 1999).

19 Choe Sang-Hun,"In Changing South Korea, Who Counts as 'Korean'?"*New York Times* (December 7, 2012): A10.

20 Ariel Sabar,"Last Words,"*Smithsonian* (February 2013): 31–34.

21 Yadong Luo and Oded Shenkar,"The Multinational Corporation as a Multilingual Community: Language and Organization in a Global Context,"*Journal of International Business Studies* 37 (2006): 321–39; and Vesa Peltokorpi and Eero Vaara,"Language Policies and Practices in Wholly Owned Foreign Subsidiaries: A Recontextualization Perspective,"*Journal of International Business Studies* 43 (2012): 808–33.

22 David Crystal, *English as a Global Language* (Cambridge: Cambridge University Press, 1997): 1–23; Jon Boone,"Native English Speakers Face Being Crowded Out of Market,"*Financial Times* (February 15, 2006): 8.

23 Sabar, loc. cit.

24 Evelyn Nien-Ming Ch'ien, *Weird English* (Boston: Harvard University, 2004).

25 Inglehart et al., *Human Values and Beliefs*, 21.

26 Matthew Coy Mitchell,"Corporate Legitimacy across Cultural Contexts: Mapping the Cultural Schemata of Religio-Institutional Actors,"(Columbia, SC: unpublished PhD dissertation, Moore School of Business Administration, 2010).

27 Jong-Wook Kwon and Chuanxuan Shan,"Climate and Work Values: A Comparison of Cold, Warm, and Hot Regions in China," *Management International Review* 52 (2012): 541–64.

28 "When Culture Masks Communication: Japanese Corporate Practice," *Financial Times* (October 23, 2000): 10; Robert House et al., "Understanding Cultures and Implicit Leadership Theories across the Globe: An Introduction to Project GLOBE," *Journal of World Business* 37 (2002): 3–10.

29 Michael Segalla, "National Cultures, International Business," *Financial Times* (March 6, 1998): mastering global business section, 8–10.

30 James Kanter, "Renewed Push in Europe to Seat Women on Boards," *New York Times* (November 14, 2012): B3.

31 Amartya Sen, *Development As Freedom*, (Oxford: Oxford University Press, 1999): 192.

32 Fons Trompenaars, *Riding the Waves of Culture* (Burr Ridge, IL: Richard D. Irwin, 1994): 100–16.

33 "Putting the Malaise into Malaysia," *Asia Times Readers Forum*, at forum.atimes.com/topic.asp?topic_ID=9002& whichpage=10 (accessed May 27, 2007); Thomas Fuller, "Malaysia Vote May Rule on Racial Divide," *New York Times* (April 4, 2013): A10.

34 Clara Chooi, "Poor English Skills, Race Quotas in Way of Malaysian Prosperity, says ST," *The Malaysian Insider* (December 11, 2011): n.p.

35 "Black Women of Brazil," (November 20, 2011) www.blackwomen ofbrazil.com/2011/11 /(accessed November 23, 2012); "Affirming a Divide," *The Economist* (January 28, 2012).

36 Information on a number of gender-related indices can be found in UN Human Development Report (2011). *Gender Inequality Index*, pp. 139–42. Available at hdr.undp.org/en/statistics/gii/ (accessed 19 November 2012). For a discussion of the relationship between gender gaps and a number of cultural values, see Andy Bertsch and Gillian Warner-Soderholm, "Updating Cross Cultural Management: Exploring the Relationships between Cultural Values and Gender Inequality Practices," paper presented at the 54th annual meeting of the Academy of International Business (Washington, DC, June 30–July 3, 2012).

37 Inglehart et al., *Human Values and Beliefs*, question V128.

38 Shaila Dewan and Robert Gebeloff, "More Men Enter Fields Dominated by Women." *New York Times* (May 21, 2012): A1+; Josh Mitchell, "Women Notch Progress," *Wall Street Journal* (December 5, 2012): A3 citing Census Bureau data that showed women comprised about 10 percent of U.S. doctors in 1970, but 32 percent in 2010.

39 "Minimum Legal Ages for Alcohol Purchase or Consumption around the World," at www.geocities.jp/m_kato_clinic/mini-age-alcohol-eng-l.html (accessed May 28, 2007).

40 "The Employers Forum on Age," *Legal: Europe*, at www.efa.org.uk/legal/europe.asp (accessed May 27, 2007); Cindy Wu, John J. Lawler, and Xiang Xi, "Overt Employment Discrimination in MNC Affiliates: Home-Country Cultural and Institutional Effects," *Journal of International Business Studies* 39:5 (2008): 772–94.

41 Inglehart et al., *Human Values and Beliefs*, questions V129.

42 Francis Fukuyama, *Trust: The Social Virtues and the Creation of Prosperity* (New York: Free Press, 1995); Ana Paula Matias Gama, Jorge Manuel Mendes Galvão, "Performance, Valuation and Capital Structure: Survey of Family Firms, *Corporate Governance*12. 2 (2012): 199–214.

43 For a good overview of the literature on the Protestant ethic, see Harold B. Jones Jr., "The Protestant Ethic: Weber's Model and the Empirical Literature," *Human Relations* 50:7 (1997): 757–86. For evidence that other religions have equal or higher work ethics, see Yavuz Fahir Zulfikar, "Do Muslims Believe More in Protestant Work Ethic than Christians? Comparison of People with Different Religious Background Living in the US," *Journal of Business Ethics*105.4 (Feb 2012): 489–502.

44 Luigi Guiso, Paola Sapienza, and Luigi Zingales, "People's Opium? Religion and Economic Attitudes," *Journal of Monetary Economics* 50:1 (2003): 225–38.

45 See, for example, David S. Landes, *The Wealth and Poverty of Nations* (New York: Norton, 1998).

46 Hamid Yeganeh, "An Investigation into the Cultural and Religious Determination of National Competitiveness," paper presented at the 54th annual meeting of the Academy of International Business (Washington, DC, June 30–July 3, 2012).

47 David Gauthier-Villars, "France Wrests Title of Sleeping Giant," *Wall Street Journal* (May 5, 2009): A8.

48 Triandis, "Dimensions of Cultural Variation as Parameters of Organizational Theories," 159–60.

49 Hofstede, *Cultures and Organizations.*

50 Abraham Maslow, *Motivation and Personality* (New York: Harper & Row, 1954).

51 F. Pichler and C. Wallace, "What Are the Reasons for Differences in Job Satisfaction Across Europe?" *European Sociological Review* 25: (2009): 535–49.

52 Richard Metters, "A Case Study of National Culture and Offshoring Services," *International Journal of Operations & Production Management* 28:8 (2008): 727–47.

53 Hofstede, *Cultures and Organizations* 49–78; House et al., *Culture, Leadership, and Organizations.*

54 Hofstede, *Cultures and Organizations.*

55 Maxim Voronov and Jefferson A. Singer, "The Myth of Individualism-Collectivism: A Critical Review," *The Journal of Social Psychology* 142:4 (August 2002): 461–81.

56 See John J. Lawrence and Reh-song Yeh, "The Influence of Mexican Culture on the Use of Japanese Manufacturing Techniques in Mexico," *Management International Review* 34:1 (1994): 49–66; P. Christopher Earley, "East Meets West Meets Mideast: Further Explorations of Collectivistic and Individualistic Work Groups," *Academy of Management Journal* 36:2 (1993): 319–46.

57 Hofstede, *Cultures and Organizations.*

58 Inglehart et al., *Human Values and Beliefs*, question V94.

59 Srilata Zaheer and Akbar Zaheer, "Trust across Borders," *Journal of International Business Studies*, 37:1 (2006): 21–29.

60 Miriam Muethal and Michael Harris Bond, "National Contextt and Individual Employees' Trust of the Out-Group: The Role of Societal Trust," *Journal of International Business Studies* 44:4 (2013): 312–33.

61 Examples in this section come from the GLOBE (Global Leadership and Organizational Behavior Effectiveness) project. See Bakacsi et al., "The Germanic Europe Cluster: Where Employees Have a Voice," *Journal of World Business* 37 (2002): 55–68; Jorge Correia Jesino, "Latin Europe Cluster: From South to North," *Journal of World Business* 37 (2002): 81–89.

62 Ping Ping Fu, Jeff Kennedy, Jasmine Tata, Gary Yuki, Michael Harris Bond, Tai-Kuang Peng, Ekkirala S. Srinivas, Jon P. Howell, Leonel Prieto, Paul Koopman, Jaap J. Boonstra, Selda Pasa, Marie-François Lacassagne, Hiro Higashide, and Adith Cheosakul, "The Impact of Societal Cultural Values and Individual Social Beliefs on the Perceived Effectiveness of Managerial Influence Strategies: A Meso Approach," *Journal of International Business Studies* 35:4 (2004): 284–304.

63 Shirley Wang, "The Science Behind Why We Love Ice Cream," *Wall Street Journal* (November 9, 2010): D1+; and Nicholas Wade, "Human Culture, an Evolutionary Force," *New York Times* (March 2, 2010): D1+.

64 Benjamin Lee Whorf, *Language, Thought and Reality* (New York: Wiley, 1956): 13 claimed there are more than 6,000 words. "How Many Words Are There for 'Camel' in Arabic?" *Arabglot* (November 11, 2011) www.arabglot.com/2011/02/how-many-words-are-there-for-camel-in.html (accessed November 23, 2012) found many fewer, but nevertheless, many more than one would find in any other language.

65 "Legal Language," *The Economist* (November 10, 2012): 66.

66 Hyun-Jung Lee, Katsuhiko Yoshikawa, and Carol Reade, "Culture Under strain? Leadership Challenges of Japanese Managers in the UK and China," paper presented at the 54th annual meeting of the Academy of International Business (Washington, DC, June 30-July 3, 2012).

67 Hajro, Pudelko, and Gibson, loc cit.

68 Viviane A. Winkler and Ricarda B. Bouncken,"How Does Cultural Diversity in Global Innovation Teams Affect the Innovation Process?" *Engineering Management Journal* 23.4 (December 2011): 24–35.

69 Richard E. Nisbett et al.,"Culture and Systems of Thought: Holistic versus Analytic Cognition,"*Psychological Review* 108:2 (April 2001): 291–310.

70 "Babel or Babble?: Machine Translation,"*The Economist (Online)* (Jun 11, 2012).

71 Don Clark,"Hey, #@*% Amigo, Can You Translate the Word'Gaffe'?" *Wall Street Journal* (July 8, 1996): B6.

72 Wenting Zhou,"Translation Errors Cause Disputes over Contract Terms,"*McClatchy - Tribune Business News* [Washington] (March 23, 2012) accessed November 24, 2012.

73 Terry Mughan,"Culture and Management Crossing the Linguistic Rubicon,"*Language and Intercultural Training* 13:1 (Spring 1993).

74 Manjeet Kripalani and Jay Greene,"Culture Clash,"*Business Week* (February 14, 2005): 9.

75 Christina Hoag,"Slogan Could Offend Spanish Speakers,"*Miami Herald* (March 8, 2005): C1+.

76 Much of the discussion on silent language is based on Edward T. Hall, "The Silent Language in Overseas Business,"*Harvard Business Review* (May–June 1960). Hall identified five variables—time, space, things, friendships, and agreements—and was the first to use the term *silent language.*

77 Alberto Rubio Sanchez, Alejandro Pico, Lucette B. Comer, Purdue University,"Salespeople's Communication Competence: A Study of the Mexican Market,"*Journal of Business & Economic Studies*, Vol. 16, No. 1, (Spring 2010): 1–18.

78 For an excellent explanation of four ways to view time, see Carol Saunders, Craig Van Slyke, and Douglas Vogel,"My Time or Yours? Managing Time Visions in Global Virtual Teams,"*Academy of Management Executive* 18:1 (2004): 19–31. See also Lawrence A. Beer, "The Gas Pedal and the Brake: Toward a Global Balance of Diverging Cultural Determinants in Managerial Mindsets,"*Thunderbird International Business Review* 45:3 (May–June 2003): 255–70.

79 Trompenaars, *Riding the Waves of Culture,* 130–31.

80 Daniel Pearl,"Tour Saudi Arabia: Enjoy Sand, Surf, His-and-Her Pools,"*Wall Street Journal* (January 22, 1998): A1.

81 June N. P. Francis,"When in Rome? The Effects of Cultural Adaptation on Intercultural Business Negotiations,"*Journal of International Business Studies* 22:3 (1991): 321–22.

82 Inglehart, *Human Values and Beliefs*,16.

83 Amin Maalouf, *In the Name of Identity* (New York: Penguin Group, 2000): 26, asserts that people pinpoint the aspect of their identity that is most under threat.

84 Mary Yoko Brannen,"When Mickey Loses Face: Recontextualization, Semantic Fit, and the Semiotics of Foreignness,"*Academy of Management Review* 29:4 (2004): 593–616.

85 Mary Yoko Brannen and Yoko Salk,"Partnering across Borders: Negotiating Organizational Culture in a German-Japanese Joint Venture,"*Human Relations* 53:4 (June 2000): 451–87; Baruch Shimoni and Harriet Bergman,"Managing in a Changing World: From Multiculturalism to Hybridization—The Production of Hybrid Management Culture in Israel, Thailand, and Mexico,"*Academy of Management Perspectives* (August 2006): 76–89.

86 Geraldine Brooks,"Eritrea's Leaders Angle for Sea Change in Nation's Diet to Prove Fish Isn't Foul,"*Wall Street Journal* (June 2, 1994): A10; M.Y. Teweldemedhin,"The Fish Industry in Eritrea: from Comparative to Competitive Advantage,"*African Journal of Agricultural Research*, Vol. 3 (5),(May 2008): 327–33;"Taboo Food and Drink,"*Wikipedia*, en.wikipedia.org/wiki/Taboo_food_and_drink (accessed November 26, 2012).

87 John Tomlinson, *Globalization and Culture* (Chicago: University of Chicago Press, 1999).

88 David Barstow and Alejandra Xanic von Bertrab,"The Bribery Aisle," *New York Times* (December 18, 2012): A1+.

89 Sam Schechner,"C'est What? French TV in English,"*Wall Street Journal* (November 21, 2012): B8; Ian Austen,"Crackdown in Quebec: 'Le Gap'Won't Do,"*New York Times* (November 23, 2012): B1+; Maïa de la Baume,"Bid in France to Add Course in English Raises Fear for Language, *New York Times* (May 24, 2013): A10.

90 Nader Asgary and Alf H. Walle,"The Cultural Impact of Globalisation: Economic Activity and Social Change,"*Cross Cultural Management* 9:3 (2000): 58–76; Tyler Cowen, *Creative Destruction: How Globalization Is Changing the World's Cultures* (Princeton, NJ: Princeton University Press, 2002): 128–52.

91 Clive Cookson,"Linguists Speak Out for the Dying Languages," *Financial Times* (March 26, 2004): 9.

92 "Schumpeter: The Global Mexican,"*The Economist* (October 27, 2012): 70.

93 Adrian Furnham and Stephen Bochner, *Culture Shock* (London: Methuen, 1986): 234.

94 Patrick M. Reilly,"Pitfalls of Exporting Magazine Formulas,"*Wall Street Journal* (July 24, 1995): B1; James Bandler and Matthew Karnitschnig, "Lost in Translation,"*Wall Street Journal* (August 19, 2004): A1+.

95 Mzamo P. Mangaliso,"Building Competitive Advantage from Ubuntu: Management Lessons from South Africa,"*Academy of Management Executive* 15:3 (August 2001): 23–34.

96 Gina Chon,"China Faces Unexpected Problem Drilling for Oil in Iraq—Farmers,"*Wall Street Journal* (May 22, 2009): A6.

97 Sally Bowen,"People Power Keeps Peru's Investors in Check," *Financial Times* (February 6, 1998): 6.

98 Roberto P. Garcia,"Learning and Competitiveness in Mexico's Automotive Industry: The Relationship between Traditional and World-Class Plants in Multination Firm Subsidiaries,"unpublished Ph.D. dissertation (Ann Arbor, MI: University of Michigan, 1996).

99 Mary Yoko Brannen and David C. Thomas,"Bicultural Individuals in Organizations: Implications and Opportunity,"*International Journal of Cross Cultural Management* 10:1 (2010): 5-16; and David C. Thomas, Mary Yoko Brannen, and Dominie Garcia,"Bicultural Individuals and Intercultural Effectiveness,"*European Journal of Cross-Cultural Competence and Management* l:4 (2010): 315–33.

100 Mary Yoko Brannen,"Building Cross-Cultural Leadership Competence: An Interview With Carlos Ghosn,"*Academy of Management Learning & Education* (Special Issue on Cross-Cultural Management) (forthcoming 2013).

101 Peter Capelli, Harber Singh, Jitendra Singh, and Michael Useem, "The Indian Way, Lessons for the U.S.,"*The Academy of Management Perspectives* 24:2 (May 2010): 6–24.

102 Aihwa Ong, *Flexible Citizenship: The Cultural Logics of Transnationality* (Durham, NC: Duke University Press, 1999).

103 Neil Parmar,"A Global Love Affair,"*WSJ.Money* (Summer 2013): 12–13.

104 James Mackintosh,"A Superstar Leader in an Industry of Icons," *Financial Times* (December 16, 2004): 10.

105 James Wilson and Quentin Peel,"Multicultural attempts'Failed,' Claims Merkel,"*Financial Times* (October 18, 2010): 3.

106 Mary Yoko Brannen is Professor of International Business/Jarislowsky CAPI East Asia (Japan) Chair, and Terrence Mughan is Associate Professor of International Business. Both are at the Gustavson School of Business, University of Victoria, British Columbia, Canada.

CHAPTER 3
Governmental and Legal Systems

OBJECTIVES

After studying this chapter, you should be able to

1. Discuss the philosophies and practices of the political environment
2. Profile trends in contemporary political systems
3. Describe current trends in political ideologies and their implications to MNE's choices
4. Explain political risk management
5. Compare the relative benefits and drawbacks of proactive versus passive political risk management
6. Discuss the principles and practices of the legal environment
7. Profile trends in contemporary legal systems
8. Identify and describe key legal issues facing international companies

Every road has two directions.

—Russian proverb

CASE China—Complicated Risks, Big Opportunities[1]

From 1949 to the late 1970s, China was autarkic, championing a self-sufficient economy that relied entirely on its own resources. Leaders of the governing Communist Party believed that interaction with foreigners would corrupt China's politics and pollute its culture; hence, they prohibited FDI and restricted foreign trade. Near the end of the 1970s, however, China's leaders began rethinking this strategy. Realizing it was lagging the world, China enacted the Law on Joint Ventures Using Chinese and Foreign Investment in 1978 and effectively began building a socialist market economy that opened the country to the global market.

Since then, Chinese economic policy has been marked by steady market liberalization that has fueled its accelerating global trade and investment. Undeniably, the Chinese Communist Party (CCP) maintains its absolute monopoly on political power. As one Beijing scholar observed, "The Party (CCP) is like God. He is everywhere. You just can't see him."[2] Free market principles, however, increasingly shape the country's business environment.

Transformation has yielded astonishing results. Over the past three decades, China has prospered more from globalization than any other country, outsmarting and outperforming many on the world stage. Many of its citizens have moved from mud huts to high rises. Companies have turned from woeful enterprises into world-class multinationals. The country has accumulated the greatest financial reserves in the world. Consequently, many see its ascendency as a global event without parallel.

THE SIREN CALL OF CHINA

Compelling incentives attract foreign investors to China. Since the 1980s, MNEs have maintained a veritable gold rush there, ranging from manufacturing ventures and export processing to licensing agreements and service relationships. Total FDI in China—representing more than 600,000 ventures opened by companies from around the world—was nearly $1.7 trillion in 2012, while literally nonexistent in 1980. Why have so many rushed to China? Quite simply, they see stunning opportunities:

Market Potential With 1.34 billion citizens, China resets conventional analytics. Consider that the Walt Disney Corporation is building a $4.4 billion theme park and resort in Shanghai where 330 million people—more than the population of the United States—live within a three-hour drive or train ride. China's market scope steadily expands. Its economic growth has reduced the number of poor by more than a half-billion since 1981. Hundreds of millions more, though poor, see a brighter future. In 2010, 91 percent of Chinese citizens saw their economic situation as "good," compared to 52 percent in 2002.[3] Most domestic markets are in early high-growth stages. Many MNEs that came for low-cost workers stay for increasingly well-off shoppers.[4]

Market Performance Rapid economic development catapulted China from an also-ran in 1980 to the world's second largest economy in 2012; analysts see it becoming the world's largest sometime between 2016 and 2036.[5] Growing income spurs consumer spending. During the U.S. and British industrialization in the nineteenth century, real incomes per capita doubled in 50 years. China's did the same in nine years. Said a China expert, "Never before in history has so much wealth been created in such a short time."[6]

Infrastructure In a multiyear program, China is investing trillions of renminbi on housing, offices, highways, airports, seaports, waterways, dams, power grids, high-speed trains, and communication networks. Despite tremendous progress, it has far to go. For example, it lags in the number of airports with paved runways: 452, compared to 713 in Brazil and 5,194 in the United States. Moreover, 44 Chinese cities populated by more than a million people still have no mass-transit system other than buses.[7]

Resources China's well-educated population creates an immense pool of productive labor. Wage rates for unskilled labor are less those in many other countries—perhaps 5 percent of comparable costs in the United States, Japan, and Europe and a third of those in Mexico and Turkey.[8] Besides efficient factory workers, China boasts a large and growing number of productive, lower-cost brainworkers. In 2013, it added another $250 billion to its university infrastructure, and after doubling its number of universities over the previous decade, it plans to produce 195 million college graduates by 2020. China's current five-year economic plan directs millions to study alternative energy, energy efficiency, environmental protection, biotechnology, advanced information technologies, and high-end equipment manufacturing.[9]

Strategic Positioning China represents the biggest growth opportunity in the history of capitalism. The country is experiencing roughly ten times the economic acceleration, on more

MAP 3.1 China: The Inscrutable Market

With more than 1.3 billion consumers and a labor force of just over 800 million workers, China is attractive to foreign investors. One of every five people in the world lives in China, but the population is unevenly distributed. Approximately 50 percent of Chinese citizens live on just 8.2 percent of the country's total land. Even so, maintaining centralized control over the nation's political and legal affairs has traditionally been difficult. The vast distances between seats of authority helps local officials evade the watchful eye of faraway bosses.

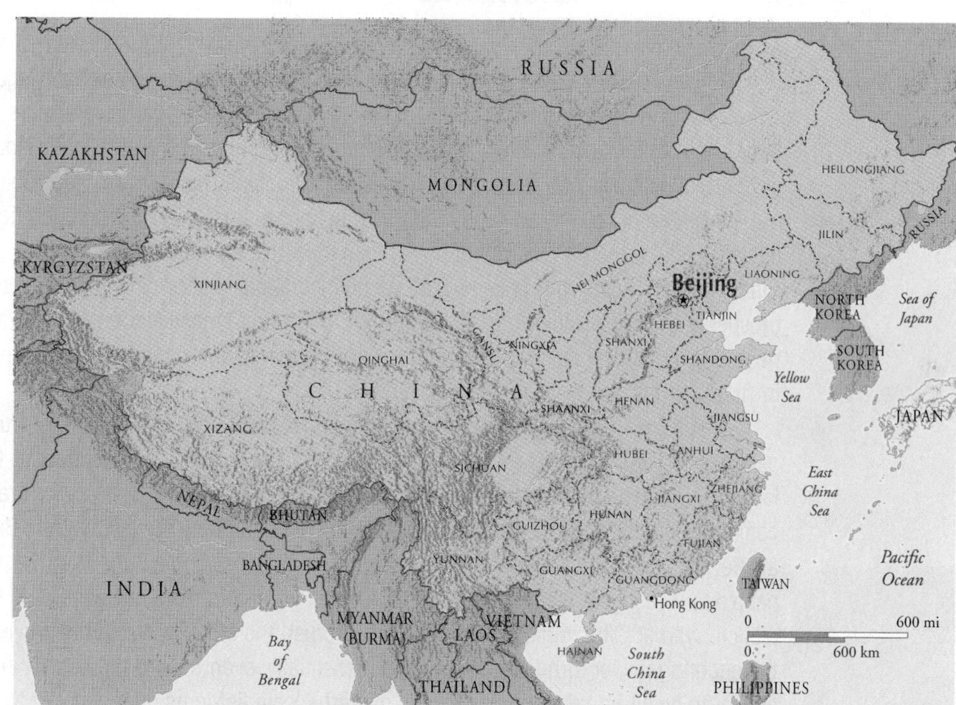

than 100 times the scale, resulting in an economic transformation that carries over 1,300 times the force of change than seen during the Industrial Revolution. MNEs are responding in kind: Ford plans to double its production capacity in China to 1.2 million vehicles by 2015, its most rapid expansion anywhere in 50 years; GE relocated its 115-year-old X-ray division from Wisconsin to Beijing; Yum! now looks to China for half its global sales and 40 percent of its operating profits. Bluntly put, "You are not a global player unless you are in China."[10]

THE COMPLICATION OF REALITY

Notwithstanding the hype and its hyperactive performance, complications tarnish China's appeal. Its political and legal systems make business operations a nebulous, frustrating process. In a nutshell, China practices "State Capitalism" whereby the government manipulates market activities to achieve political goals. Consequently, MNEs doing business in China often find themselves at a disadvantage. Ambitious Western firms such as Exxon Mobil, ABB, Caterpillar, and Vodafone purchased big stakes in Chinese companies. Political problems and legal difficulties short-circuited their plans. Eventually, like many others, they sold their stakes and reset their strategies.[11]

China's rapid emergence aggravates long-running idiosyncrasies. The resulting mix of ancient and contemporary outlooks creates many grey areas. Some observers argue that, when it comes to doing business in China, the number one rule is to throw away the rulebook. Sage foreign investors abandon the notion that Western ideas automatically work in China. The principle of forming a corporation "for any valid business purpose" does not exist there. Incorporating in China requires telling the government—in excruciating detail—who you are, what you want to do, how you plan to do it, how much you intend to invest, and how many jobs you will create. MNEs endure protracted negotiations in obtaining permission to open local operations. At each stop of the long march, national, provincial, and local officials ask how the investment encourages capital formation, promotes exports, creates jobs, and transfers technology. If you hit the right targets, only then does the government green-light your project.

DRAGONS AND SNAKES

As in China, centralized governments worldwide determine the path and pace of local economic development. China, however, poses a particularly tough case given that its political and legal systems impose many time-consuming tasks. Moreover, China tends to stack the odds against foreigners who are bold enough to forge ahead in the face of an elaborate government bureaucracy and a fledgling legal system.[12] "If the great invention of European civilization was a legal system," quipped an observer, "then China's was bureaucracy."[13]

Exasperated investors blame China's treacherous terrain on a bureaucratic system that regulates activity based more on arbitrary agendas than objective standards. Connections, not competencies, often matter more. Those who believe that economics should determine the efficient means of generating prosperity see this as illogical. Still, it is utterly logical to Chinese leaders who regard state control of business activity as the most reliable path toward harmonious prosperity—and, one mustn't forget, staying in charge of the show.

Foreign investors navigate often-mysterious political channels. The long-running conflict between central and local Chinese authorities further confuses issues. The vastness of the country means that local officials, whether headquartered in the smallest village or the largest city, are often left alone by their comrades in Beijing. Certainly, there are national laws, but how they move from Beijing to the provinces is a different story. "The center," notes one observer, often "has no control over the provinces. When it sends people to investigate illegal pirating of CDs, local governors block access to the factories."[14] As Chinese folklore warns, "The mightiest dragon cannot crush the local snake." This proverb captures the spirit of the enduring power struggle within China. Essentially, even though the central authorities in Beijing may appear to be all-powerful, the politics of powerful local fiefdoms often subvert their authority.

PRECISE LAWS OR AMBIGUOUS GUIDELINES?

China had no formal legal system in 1978 when it launched one of the greatest campaigns of legal reform in history. Ongoing developments have stabilized what had been an unpredictable, periodically chaotic legal environment. Still, China faces such ongoing challenges as legislative gaps, hazy interpretation, lax enforcement, and philosophical disagreements. Legislation is chock-full of ambiguities, says one Beijing-based lawyer, who thinks it will take 10 to 15 years to iron out many wrinkles.[15] Some are less optimistic, comparing the state of the Chinese legal system with that of the United States in the 1920s—then an antiquated composite of statutes and codes that took several decades to modernize.

Others note that, in the case of the Chinese system, even bigger problems reflect a difference in the concept of legality in that society. Western legal systems rest on the rule of law and its doctrine of legitimate regulations transparently administered by public officials who are held accountable for their just enforcement. In contrast, China practices the philosophy of the rule of man, seeing the right of the "man" (once in the person of the Emperor, today in the form of the CCP) to act free of checks and balances. Besides being the law, the CCP is seen as above the law and given the legitimacy bestowed upon it by its ostensible "mandate from heaven."[16] Rarely does the Chinese criminal court end with anything other than a guilty verdict. Rather, explained an FBI Special Agent and legal attaché at the U.S. Embassy in Beijing, "there is really no rule of law here...they (CCP) make a decision ahead of time to make a point."[17]

THE LEGALITY OF ILLEGALITY

China's legal practices combined with the growing pains of its novel legal institutions and evolving political norms challenges MNEs. A sensitive tripwire is the theft of intellectual property—patents, trademarks, copyrights, and so on. MNEs complain that relentless, widespread, and sophisticated robbery of their intellectual property fuels China's economic surge. Aggressive estimates link nearly a third of the Chinese economy to piracy.[18]

The FBI estimates that American companies lose hundreds of billions annually to counterfeiting. China continues to be the number one source country for counterfeit and pirated goods seized; in just the U.S., Chinese counterfeits accounted for 62 percent or $124.7 million of the total domestic value of seizure.[19] U.S. authorities, noting the rarity of legal punishment, charge Chinese officials with tolerating, if not encouraging, pirates.[20] Still, countries wage battle. The United States, for instance, has frequently appealed to various transnational institutions about China's "inadequate enforcement" of intellectual property regulations.[21]

What accounts for China's status as the world's premier counterfeiter? Analysts point to a mix of its quest to catch the West, collectivist orientation, rule-of-man legacy, and dubious enforcement of ambiguous laws—conditions that create a political and legal morass. Noted an observer, "We have never seen a problem of this size and magnitude in world history. . . . There's more counterfeiting going on in China now than we've ever seen anywhere."[22] Problems threaten to escalate. Government policies have "left a deep impression on companies that intellectual property is there for anyone to use it." Local and provincial authorities rely heavily on pirates to power local economic growth. Moreover, China excels in making high-quality knockoffs. As some say in Shanghai, "We can copy everything except your mother."[23]

WHERE TO NOW?

Inevitably, investors question how an opaque single-party political system bolstered by a murky legal environment can protect their rights. Some believe that external institutions will improve transparency. China's 2001 ascension to the WTO, for example, required it to accept rules on all sorts of business matters, including tariffs, subsidies, and intellectual property. And, granted, China has steadily amended its legal codes to comply with WTO standards. However, the struggle is not a shortage of regulations. Rather, China's sluggish enforcement, even in cases of outright violation, is the primary problem.

Despite intimidating political difficulties and confusing legal questions, legions of foreign investors fall sway to the siren call of China. Whether driven by bright forecasts, confidence in continued progress, or desperation to ride this megatrend, companies leave the sanctuary of predictable markets for the distinctive ways of the Middle Kingdom. Then, once they clear immigration and cross the modern-day Rubicon, they face the daunting task of interpreting China's political and legal systems. ■

CRN
Case Review Note

QUESTIONS

✪ **3-1.** Identify three compelling economic reasons to invest in China. Then identify three compelling political reasons to avoid doing so. Recommend a criterion one could use to trade off the opportunities of operating in China versus the risks of doing so.

✪ **3-2.** What sort of operational safeguards would you advise a company to adopt in order to better manage the risks of China's legal environment?

INTRODUCTION

Chapter 2 showed that the cultural issues facing international businesses differ from those facing domestic firms. This chapter carries the analysis forward, emphasizing that once a company leaves its home country it operates in markets with different political and legal systems. Some countries are similar; Australian companies would not find many surprises in New Zealand, for instance. In other cases, the differences are profound; an ill-prepared U.S. company would encounter shocks in Russia. Navigating among countries requires that MNEs study how political and legal circumstances overlap and differ. Determining where, when, and how to adjust business practices without undermining the basis for success is an enduring challenge.

FIGURE 3.1 Political and Legal Factors Influencing International Business Operations

The political and legal environments are broad-stroke concepts that defy straightforward classification. Nevertheless, managers emphasize key points, principally those identified here, to develop useful perspectives.

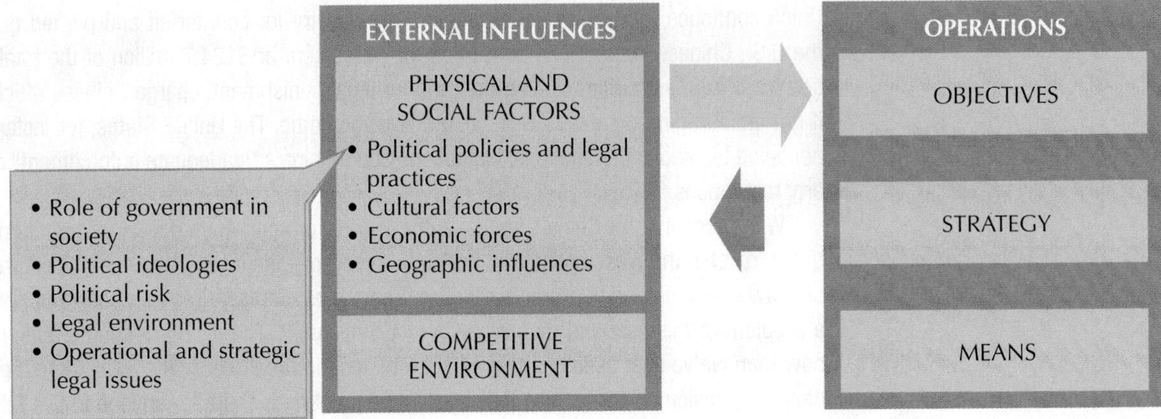

Managers study political and legal environments in order to adjust company activities to local circumstances.

Consider that a domestic company operates in a single national environment in which institutional policies are reasonably predictable. Operating internationally exposes its managers to diverse and conflicting pressures from wide-ranging groups in different nations. Variations increase the challenge of interpreting different philosophies, laws, and attitudes on political freedom, property rights, and legal responsibility. Consequently, effective managers begin with the realization that when it comes to politics and laws, countries' different ideas result in different political and legal environments. They position themselves to compete by understanding these differences, rather than ignoring or, worse, resisting them.

No matter where an MNE goes, the prevailing politics and laws affect its options and operations. China's political and legal environments, for example, require MNEs to rethink the best ways to acquire resources, make investments, adapt operating modes, and manage risk. Figure 3.1 identifies the political principles and legal outlooks that define a nation's business environment. This chapter will discuss how they influence the prevailing political ideology, shape the role of government, moderate the degree of political risk, and define the legal system.

THE POLITICAL ENVIRONMENT

Our opening profile of China shows that its evolving political and legal systems create a thriving business environment. Tens of thousands of foreign investors have entered its market, opened operations, managed activities, and earned profits. Still, the political system imposes hardships while the legal system complicates attempts to right wrongs. This situation is not unique to China. The interplay of political ideologies, conceptions of political freedom, legacies of legality, presumptions of fairness, and exercise of power makes for challenging political environments around the world.

Consider Russia, home to 142 million people. The world's largest country in terms of territory, it possesses vast natural resources and has a government that looks to foreign MNEs to help modernize its energy-dependent economy. Still, foreign investors face high hurdles. An executive at Swedish retailer IKEA explained that the Russian political environment is "a bit of a roller coaster.... [Y]ou don't know exactly what will happen tomorrow."[24] The roster of horror stories features well-known names. Authorities arbitrarily confiscated products of Motorola, charged PwC Russia with tax evasion on flimsy evidence, and arguably expropriated Yukos.[25] Doing business in Russia means you had better be "big enough to defend yourself against bureaucratic attacks [and]...ready to hold your nose when elections are rigged and political opposition is crushed."[26] Ironically, Prime Minister Vladimir Putin has promised a "dictatorship of the law," an approach that appeals to the majority of Russians who prefer strong leadership to vibrant democracy.[27] Others, however, see Russia trapped in lawlessness and legal nihilism. Accordingly, Transparency International rated Russia 133 out of 176 nations in its Corruption Perceptions Index.[28]

These sorts of situations require executives evaluate, monitor, and forecast the dimensions and dynamics of foreign political environments. They study how government officials exercise authority, legislate policies, regulate enterprise, and punish wrongdoers. They monitor how politicians are elected and whether and how they depart. They assess whether the rule of law or of man prevails. They gauge whether freedom is a practical ideal or a wishful abstraction. Then, based on their analyses, they forecast business scenarios, always mindful that political stability rewards investment while political uncertainty penalizes it.[29]

The goal of the political system is integrating the diverse elements of a society.

Whether targeting Afghanistan, Zimbabwe, or any of the more than 200 markets in-between, managers study a nation's **political system**—namely, the structural dimensions and power dynamics of the government that (1) specify institutions, organizations, and interest groups and (2) define the norms and rules that govern political activities. The mission of a political system is clear-cut: integrate different groups into a functioning, self-governing society. Likewise, its test is sustaining society in the face of divisive viewpoints. Success supports peace and prosperity, as we see in Sweden, Botswana, and Australia. Failure leads to instability, insurrection, and, ultimately, disintegration of the sort seen in Somalia, Afghanistan, and Libya.

The test of a political system is uniting society in the face of divisive viewpoints.

INDIVIDUALISM VERSUS COLLECTIVISM

CONCEPT CHECK

Chapter 2 showed that culture moderates the practices of international business. Many points of interpretation, both from an academic and managerial perspective, follow from the interplay of collectivism or individualism in a country.

Explaining the similarities and differences of political systems has intrigued a long line of thinkers, beginning with Plato and Confucius and moving on to Herodotus, Machiavelli, Smith, Rousseau, Marx, Gandhi, and Friedman.[30] Each wrestled with enduring philosophical issues: How should society balance individual rights versus the needs of the community to sustain a rational, righteous, and harmonious system? What is the basis of the state's authority over its citizens? Should society guarantee individual freedom in the pursuit of economic self-interest? Does society fare better when individual rights are subordinated to collective goals? Should society champion equality or institute hierarchy? Are individual rights inalienable or conferred by the collective? Engaging these and like-minded questions anchors interpretation of the political systems in terms of **individualism** versus **collectivism**.

INDIVIDUALISM

Individualism champions the primacy of the rights and role of the individual. Collectivism refers to the primacy of the rights and role of the group.

The doctrine of individualism emphasizes the primacy of individual freedom, self-expression, and personal independence (think of the declaration that we all have "certain inalienable Rights, that among these are Life, Liberty and the pursuit of Happiness").[31] It champions the exercise of one's ambitions while opposing regulations that overly constrain them. The government protects the liberty of individuals to act as they wish, as long their actions do not infringe upon the liberties of others.

The business implications of individualism are direct: every person has the right to make economic decisions largely free of rules and regulations. Countries with an individualistic orientation, such as Australia, Canada, Netherlands, New Zealand, the United States, and the United Kingdom, shape their marketplace with the idea of **laissez-faire**. Literally meaning, "leave it alone," a laissez-faire approach holds that the government should not interfere in business affairs; rather, the market should operate according to the neoliberal principles of free market fundamentalism. Left to their own devices, people regulate themselves in promoting economic prosperity and act fairly and justly to maximize personal performance without threatening the welfare of society.

Gaps between philosophical ideals and opportunistic behaviors often fan an adversarial relationship between governments and businesses in individualistic societies. Recent events dramatize this circumstance. The global financial crisis of the last decade revealed that some individuals and firms had maximized their interests at the expense of societal welfare. Long-running support of deregulation, privatization, and trade liberalization, advocated to maximize individual freedom of choice, ultimately proved destructive. Opportunistic behavior destabilized the marketplace and jeopardized system sustainability. In response, governments reset regulations to reduce market inefficiencies (such as deficient consumer knowledge or excessive producer power) that had given some individuals undue privilege. Ongoing market problems in such countries as Spain, Japan, Ireland, Greece, Portugal, and the United States push governments to restrain the individualism of free markets in order to protect the collective welfare.

COLLECTIVISM

Collectivism stresses that the needs of society take precedence over the needs of the individual.

The doctrine of collectivism emphasizes the primacy of the collective—e.g., a group, party, community, class, society, or nation—over the interests of the individual. No matter the importance of those who comprise it, the whole of the collective is ultimately greater than the sum of its individual parts. Today, we see collectivism in a range of countries, including Argentina, China, Vietnam, Japan, South Korea, Egypt, Brazil, Taiwan, and Mexico.

Collectivism in the business world holds that the ownership of assets, the allocation of resources, the structure of industries, the conduct of companies, and the actions of managers share a common goal: improve the welfare of all members of society. Business decisions are made by the group for the benefit of the group. Political systems that exhibit a collectivist orientation hold that government regulates the market to promote social equality, labor rights, income equality, and workplace democracy so that the "welfare of the nation takes precedence over the selfishness of the individuals."[32] In extreme cases, such as Venezuela or Saudi Arabia, political leaders severely limit property rights and regulate the mass media in order to control the business environment.

POLITICAL IDEOLOGY

A political ideology encapsulates the doctrine of political behavior and change. It outlines the procedures for converting ideas into actions.

The orientation toward individualism or collectivism fundamentally shapes a nation's political system and, hence, its **political ideology**. In theory, an ideology is an integrated vision that defines a holistic conception of an abstract ideal and its normative thought processes. For example, the ideal of freedom carries with it ideas about related principles, doctrines, goals, practices, and symbols. A political ideology stipulates how society ought to govern itself and outlines the methods by which it will do so.

In the United States, the liberal principles of the Democratic Party and the conservative doctrine of the Republican Party define their respective political ideologies—i.e., the former favors collectivist measures such as progressive taxation and strict environmental standards whereas the latter champions individualistic measures such as consumer choice and minimal regulation. Japan has a similar situation: its Democratic Party advocates social liberalism and its Liberal Democratic Party advocates conservatism. No matter the specific cause, an effective political ideology moves beyond describing a vision of a better, brighter future. Put simply, it specifies the means to achieve that ideal.

Pluralism holds that there are multiple opinions about an issue, each of which contains part of the truth, but none that contain the entire truth. Progress depends on negotiation and compromise.

Japan and the United States, like many other countries, have political parties that list smaller memberships than do the main parties. Consequently, most nations are pluralistic in which different political groups champion competing ideologies.[33] **Pluralism** also arises when two or more groups in a country differ in terms of language (Belgium), class structure (United Kingdom), ethnic background (South Africa), tribal legacy (Afghanistan), or religion (India).

A pluralistic system requires that officials negotiate policies. The bargaining process between competing groups dictates that politics follow multiple, shifting lines. Multi-criteria compromise, not single-minded consensus, is the order of the day. The resulting ambiguity complicates decision making for MNEs. Pluralism requires that managers assess the interplay among groups. Often, companies try to influence policy formulation. In the United States, for example, some companies fund political action committees that support preferred candidates or influence the legislative process.

SPECTRUM ANALYSIS

Figure 3.2 outlines a **political spectrum**. By specifying a basic conceptual structure, spectrum analysis guides the assessment of a complex issue—in this case, political ideology. Configuring ideologies along the central axis lets us model different ones relative to the others. The starting point is specifying credible ideas to anchor the endpoints. When those are reasonably set, we then position the others.

Determining the standard of "reasonably set" can prove difficult. The world exhibits a diversity of potential ideologies: anarchism, conservatism, secularism, environmentalism, liberalism, feminism, nationalism, socialism, theocracy, and so on. Cultural perspectives also moderate interpretation of such choices. From a Western perspective, for example, one commonly sees the endpoints defined as conservative versus liberal interpretations of democracy—i.e., Republican versus Democrat. Other endpoints command greater relevance in other contexts. A political spectrum in an Islamic country, such as Iran or Saudi Arabia, is likely bounded by theocracy versus secularism to reflect the role of the clergy in the government. In the case of Taiwan, parties that endorse Chinese reunification oppose those that champion Taiwanese independence. In Belgium, ends would reflect the ethnic and socioeconomic tensions between the Dutch-speaking Flanders region and the French-speaking Walloon region. In Canada, it would be inclusive nationalism versus Bloc Québécois's call for the sovereignty of predominantly French-speaking Québec.

Political freedom measures the degree to which fair and competitive elections occur, the extent to which individual and group freedoms are guaranteed, the legitimacy ascribed to the rule of law, and the existence of freedom of the press.

Although initially confusing, a common denominator integrates the diversity of political ideologies: namely, its vision of **political freedom**. This ideal originated in the practice of politics in ancient Greece and has since been inseparable from interpreting political action. Political freedom reflects the degree to which fair and competitive elections occur, the extent to which individual and group freedoms are guaranteed, the legitimacy ascribed to the rule of

FIGURE 3.2 The Political Spectrum

In practice, purely democratic and totalitarian systems are exceptions. Looking around the world, one sees many variations. For example, democratic systems range from radical on one side (advocates of extreme political reform) to reactionary (advocates of a return to past conditions). Likewise, totalitarian systems emphasize different degrees of state control. Fascism aims to control people's minds, souls, and daily existence, whereas authoritarianism confines itself to political control of the state.

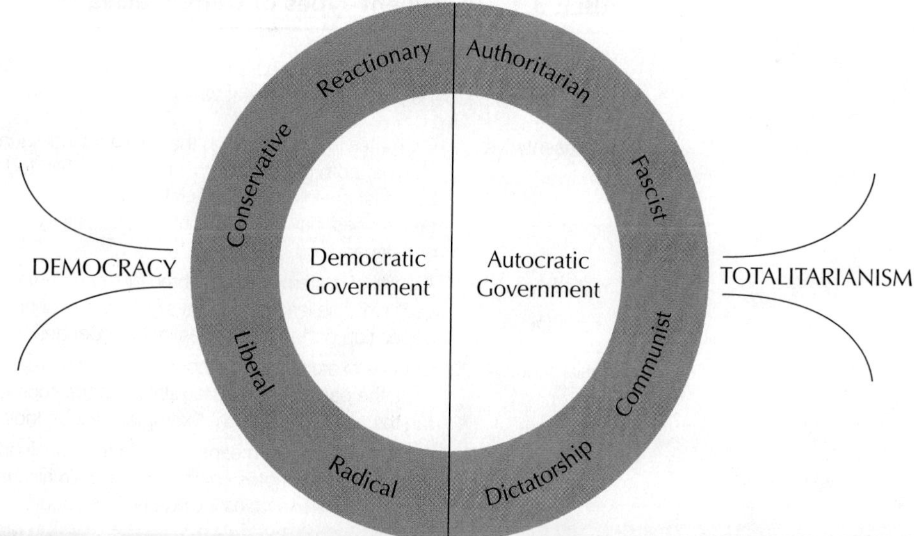

law, and the existence of freedom of expression. As ideologies differ, so too do interpretations of the ideal degree of freedom. Rather than an inalienable right, freedom is open to debate. As a result, the matters of where, how, and why a company invests and how it manages operations are alienable freedoms, subject to the ideology that anchors and influences the political system.

With these ideas in mind, Figure 3.2 sets the political spectrum, with democracy, with its call to preserve, protect, and defend political freedom, anchoring one endpoint and totalitarianism, with its call to control, constrain, and, suppress political freedom, the other.[34] The ideologies that fall between these endpoints interpret political freedom differently. Liberal ideologies, for instance, advocate the right of individuals; authoritarianism subordinates individual freedoms to the welfare of the collective. In the former, managers have many investment and operating options; in the latter, they have far fewer. Similar examples only reinforce our chief point: Freedom is the distinguishing characteristic of political ideologies. Some stress its primacy, others oppose it. Throughout all, MNEs study its implications to their decisions.

Each political ideology in Figure 3.2 is notable; we lack the space to stipulate each one here. However, understanding the ideals and means of the two endpoints, democracy and totalitarianism, helps one interpret the others.

DEMOCRACY

Democracy calls for participation by citizens in a fair and just decision-making process.

Abraham Lincoln held that **democracy** is a government"of the people, by the people, for the people." Modern-day democracies translate this ideology into the principles that all citizens are politically and legally equal, entitled to freedom of thought, opinion, belief, speech, and association, and command sovereign power over public officials.[35] A democratic government protects personal and political rights, civil liberties, fair and free elections, and independent courts of law.[36] These principles and practices institutionalize political freedoms and civil liberties that, by endorsing equality, liberty, and justice, support individualism.

Different legacies shape the performance of democracy in a nation. More practically, the scale and scope of modern society imposes logistical constraints, particularly when population size makes it impossible for all voters to participate directly. Table 3.1 shows that countries respond with different types of democracies. Notwithstanding variance, all advocate the authority of the many over the few. The future may see a resurgence of direct democracy. Evolving technologies increasingly support a virtual assembly of citizens who express their votes directly through electronic signature gathering or online polling processes.

TABLE 3.1 Prominent Types of Democracies

The elemental definition of democracy hails from the Greek *dēmokratía:* "rule by the people." As we see here, the rule of the people is practiced in different ways.

Representative	Originates in a constitution that protects individual freedoms and liberties. The law treats all citizens, both public and private, equally. Elected representatives hold ultimate sovereignty but must act in the people's interest. Officials represent voters and, while mindful of voters' preferences, have the authority to act as they see fit. Examples include the United States and Japan.
Multiparty	A political system whereby three or more parties govern, either separately or as part of a coalition. The leadership of a single party cannot legislate policy without negotiating with opposition parties. Examples include Canada, Germany, Italy, and Israel.
Parliamentary	Citizens exercise political power by electing representatives to a legislative branch referred to as the parliament. The legislature is the source of legitimacy for the various ministers that run the executive branch. Examples include India and Australia.
Social	Applies democratic means to guide the transition from capitalism to socialism. The government promotes egalitarianism while also regulating capitalism's tendency toward opportunism. Examples include Norway and Sweden.

Democracy and individualism are intrinsically related and mutually reinforcing; individualism legitimates principles of democracy and democracy supports standards of individualism.

Business Implications In a democracy, MNEs invest and operate based on economic, not political, standards. Business environments promote commerce, expand trade, and streamline exchange, both within and across countries. The signaling devices of market activities, not bureaucratic regulation, organize a productive business environment. Managers and consumers are free to do as they see fit. In political terms, freedom sanctions rights and liberties; in economic terms, it legitimizes profits and prosperity. Brazil, India, Indonesia, and Turkey provide cases in point. Their belief in central planning run by a strong state had led to stagnant if not failing economies 20 years ago. Now these countries are converting the energy of their emerging democracy into dynamic business environments.[37]

TOTALITARIANISM

A totalitarian system consolidates power in a single agent who then controls political, economic, and social activities.

A **totalitarian system** subordinates the individual to the interests of the collective. A single agent in whatever form, such as an individual, a committee, an assembly, a junta, or a party, monopolizes political power and uses it to regulate many, if not all, aspects of public and private life. The agent believes it has noble intentions, protecting people from the hazards of individual choice.[38] Fair game includes regulating residents' occupation, income level, interests, religion, and even family structure.[39]

A totalitarian government eliminates dissent through indoctrination, persecution, surveillance, propaganda, censorship, and violence. It tolerates few, if any, ideas, interests, or activities that run counter to state ideology.[40] There is no alternative for the simple reason that none is allowed to exist. In extreme situations, personal survival is linked to that of the ruling regime. Collectively, these conditions merge the interests of individuals with those of the state. Table 3.2 profiles types of totalitarian systems.

Totalitarianism and collectivism are intrinsically related and mutually reinforcing; collectivism legitimates principles of totalitarianism and totalitarianism supports standards of collectivism.

The dynamics of change in a totalitarian state highlight the means used to enforce its ideology. Rejecting preceding forms of society as corrupt, immoral, and beyond reform or redemption, a single leader advocates a new society that corrects wrongs, redresses injustice, and supports harmony. In place of private property, the state allocates power and status to reward supporters (who often monetize privileges through corruption). It uses propaganda, indoctrination, and incarceration to coerce citizens. State-controlled media filters

TABLE 3.2 Prominent Types of Totalitarianism

First recorded in reference to Italian fascism, "totalitario" stood for "complete, absolute, totalitarian" control by a dictatorial one-party state that regulates every realm of life. As we see here, the ruling agent can control society to different degrees.

Authoritarianism	Tolerates no deviation from state ideology. Day-to-day life reflects obedience to state authority; resistance incurs punishment. Officials regulate the political environment but pay less attention to the economic and social structure of society. Often lacks an ideology to politicize public and private life. Examples include Kazakhstan, North Korea, Chad, and Turkmenistan.
Fascism	Organizes a nation based on corporatist perspectives, values, and systems. Advocates a single-party state that controls, through force and indoctrination, people's minds, souls, and daily existence. Fascism calls for the merger of state and corporate power. There have been few fascist political systems; most prevailed during World War II.
Secular	A single-party government controls elections, tolerates dissent as long as it does not challenge the state, and suppresses other ideologies. The state does not prescribe an all-encompassing ideology. It grants limited individual freedoms provided one does not contest state authority or disrupt social harmony. Examples include China, Vietnam, and Venezuela.
Theocratic	Government is an expression of the preferred deity. Leaders claim to represent its interests on earth. Applies ancient dogma in place of modern principles. Strict social regulation and gender regimentation typically ensue. Examples include Iran, Afghanistan, and Saudi Arabia.

information, state-controlled education filters ideas, and state-controlled courts, police, and security suppress dissent. The cumulative result is a "virtual mind prison" in which the leader and the state fuse—one conforms or is cast out.[41]

CONCEPT CHECK

Recall our discussion in Chapter 2 of "Behavioral Factors Affecting Business." These variables change as people change—or as state authority influences them. Shaping people's behavior to support the state's interests leads an authoritarian government to manipulate norms, including work motivation, risk taking, communication practices, and consumption preferences.

Although remote to citizens in Western democracies, forms of totalitarianism prevail throughout the world. Some 2.5 billion people—roughly one-third of the world's population—live under such rule, with another 1.5 billion people residing in less draconian but still authoritarian political systems.[42] The citizens of such countries as Madagascar, Turkmenistan, Afghanistan, China, Iran, North Korea, and Saudi Arabia have few personal freedoms and civil liberties. The reemergence of powerful, single-party states worldwide reinforces totalitarianism: Russia suppresses individual freedoms through arbitrary governance; Venezuela restricts media that urge dissent; Iran corrupts its electoral process. Some see the political practices powering China's rise as endorsing authoritarianism.[43] Finally, leaders of such harshly governed countries increasingly display subtle finesse. Concludes Freedom House, "Our findings point to the growing sophistication of modern authoritarians. They are flexible; they distort and abuse the legal framework; they are adept at the techniques of modern propaganda."[44]

Authoritarian parties often rely on shadowy politics, skewed elections, and nefarious security agencies.

Business Implications Managers in totalitarian systems face markets that are radically different from those in democracies. Private enterprise, if permitted, supports state control of economic activities. For instance, the Chinese government, under the direction of the CCP, owns and manages large swathes of the economy. The state is the majority owner of 99 of the 100 largest publicly listed Chinese companies, 39 of which are among the 500 biggest in the world.[45] Similarly, 129 huge conglomerates in finance, media, mining, metals, transportation, communication, and so on answer directly to the CCP. Likewise, China's provincial and municipal officials control thousands of medium-sized and smaller ones.[46] Add it all up and you have an authoritarian system that rejects many of the practices found in a democracy.

Managers operating in such markets adjust decision making to the intricacies of political activities. Bluntly put, the government's imperative is sustaining state power, and economics and markets are handy tools with which to do so. The situation affects all companies, but typically hits foreign investors hardest. The state favors local companies at the expense of foreign competitors, providing them with favorable financial assistance, special tax programs, relaxed work regulations, and other benefits.[47] The state's intent to value and allocate resources in manipulating market outcomes for political purposes creates complicated risks and rewards. For example, China requires foreign enterprises to tolerate, if not facilitate, setting up Communist Party cells in their local operations—indeed, some local governments require that private companies contribute a share of their payrolls to finance Party activities.[48] The cells are there to educate and supervise the companies to behave lawfully, fulfill their social responsibilities, promote harmonious labor relations, and maintain social stability.

In recourse, MNEs strike deals that would be unthinkable elsewhere. Consider General Electric's 50–50 joint venture with Aviation Industry, a Chinese military-jet maker, to produce avionics, the electronic brains of aircraft. The deal required GE to take the risky but potentially lucrative step of folding pieces of its global operations into partnerships with a state-owned enterprise. Such deals had earlier proved troublesome, souring over concerns that Chinese partners, after gaining access to Western technology and expertise, became potent new rivals.[49] Even so, seeing China as its "second home market," GE reasoned the cost of missing the fast-growing Chinese aviation industry exceeded the potential risks. As GE's vice chairperson noted, "Staying out of China in hopes of keeping our intellectual property safe is obviously not an option."[50]

THE STANDARD OF FREEDOM

Freedom House identifies three types of political systems:

- Free.
- Partly free.
- Not free.

Freedom is a topic of enduring importance. Freedom House, an independent watchdog organization that promotes liberty worldwide, helps frame our interpretation. It stipulates, "Freedom is possible only in democratic political systems in which the governments are accountable to their own people; the rule of law prevails; and freedoms of expression,

MAP 3.2 Map of Freedom, 2013

Freedom House, classifying countries in terms of their degree of political freedom, identifies three types—Free, Partly Free, and Not Free. If you live in a country classified as "free," you enjoy a broad range of political rights and civil liberties. If you are a citizen of a "partly free" nation, your share of rights and liberties ranges anywhere from average to just below average. If your homeland is "not free," you enjoy few rights and liberties.

Source: Freedom House, "Map of Freedom 2013," at www.freedomhouse.org.

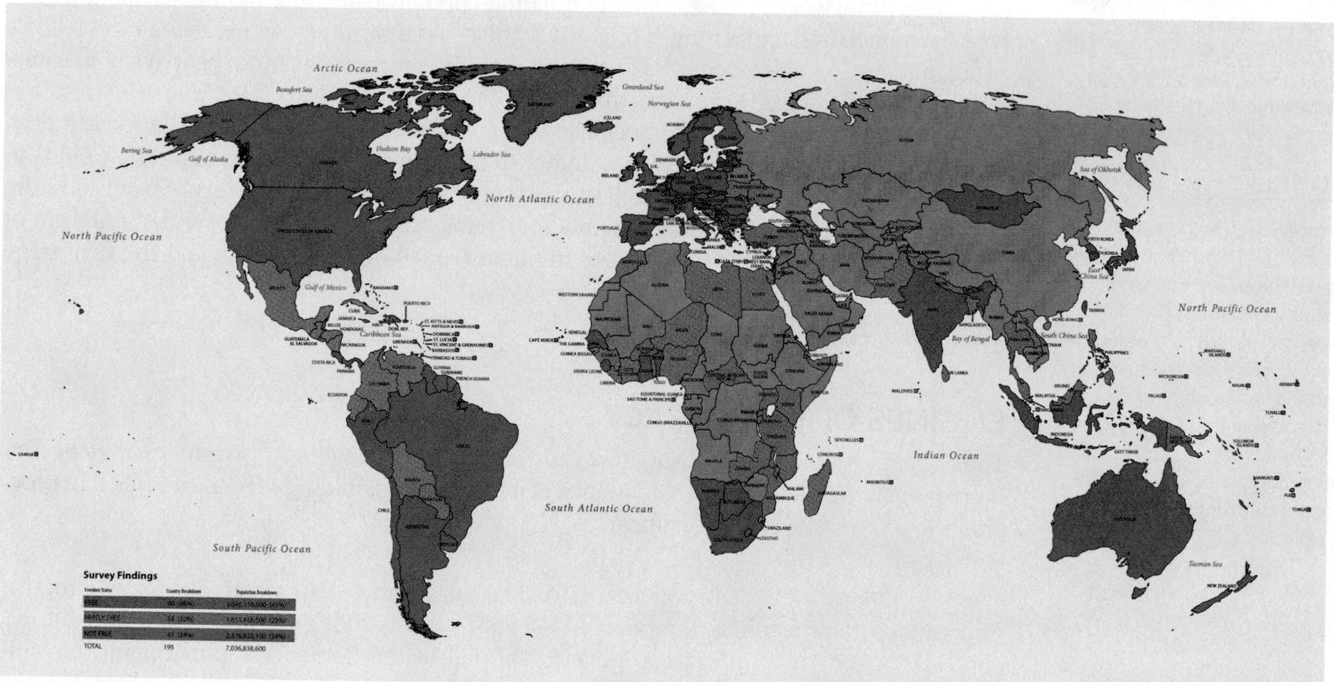

association, and belief, as well as respect for the rights of minorities and women, are guaranteed."[51] Since 1972, Freedom House has annually assessed the state of political freedom around the world,[52] applying measures derived from the Universal Declaration of Human Rights.[53] It identifies three types of systems:

- A *"free" country* exhibits open political competition, respect for civil liberties, independent civic life, and independent media. There are inalienable freedoms of expression, assembly, association, education, and religion. Examples include Australia, Brazil, India, and the United States.
- A *"partly free" country* exhibits limited political rights and civil liberties, corruption, weak rule of law, ethnic and religious strife, unfair elections, and censorship. Often, democracy is a convenient slogan for the single party that dominates within a façade of regulated pluralism. Examples include Guatemala, Pakistan, and Tanzania.
- A *"not free" country* has few to no political rights and civil liberties. The government allows minimal to no exercise of personal choice, relies on the rule of man as the basis of law, constrains religious and social freedoms, and controls a large share, if not all, of business activity. Examples include China, Russia, Saudi Arabia, Iran, and Vietnam.

Map 3.2 shows the distribution of freedom worldwide. In 2013, 90 countries were free (46 percent of all countries), 58 partly free (30 percent), and 47 not free (24 percent). Regarding population, approximately 3 billion people (43 percent of the global population) live in a free country, 1.6 billion (22 percent) partly free, and 2.5 billion (35 percent) not free.

TRENDS IN POLITICAL IDEOLOGIES

The second half of the twentieth century saw the steady diffusion of democracy. Between 1950 and 2009, the number of democratic political systems grew from 22 out of 154 countries (14 percent) to 90 out of 193 countries (47 percent). The number of nations that made

The Third Wave of Democratization refers to the third surge of democratically governed states in the 20th century. Ultimately, as this wave crested, the number of countries led by a democratic government significantly increased.

CONCEPT CHECK

In profiling "The Forces Driving Globalization" in Chapter 1, we noted the power of changing political situations. Until recently, we have witnessed the diffusion of democracy and the corresponding decline in totalitarianism. Growing acceptance of the legitimacy of democracy accelerated the expansion of international business.

the transition, particularly during the 1970s and 1980s, gave rise to the political phenomenon referred to as the **Third Wave of Democratization**.[54] During this period, more than 30 countries throughout Africa, Asia, Latin America, South America, and Eastern Europe abandoned totalitarianism for democracy. The quest for individual freedoms and civil liberties transformed the world. Societies began building fairer civic institutions, independent media, objective judiciaries, and stronger property rights.[55] As a result, today nearly half the world's population lives in a democracy of some sort. Put differently, today more people live in countries with democratic governments than at any time in history.

In doubling the number of democracies in two decades, the Third Wave of Democratization helped topple the Berlin Wall in 1989, demolish the Communist Bloc, and end the Cold War. Some saw the worldwide democracy surge symbolizing the "end of history." Specifically, the universalization of Western liberal democracy, reinforced by the market fundamentalism of capitalism, represented the endpoint of humanity's ideological evolution and the final stage of human government.[56]

ENGINES OF DEMOCRACY

The reluctance of totalitarian structures to fade gracefully requires powerful change agents. Beginning in the mid-1970s, a confluence of events began building several engines that powered the Third Wave of Democratization. Notably:

Regime Legitimacy The failure of totalitarian regimes to deliver economic progress undermined their legitimacy. Aggrieved citizens, weary of long-declining standards of life, contested the right of officials to govern. The fall of the Berlin Wall punctuated this epic change. Formerly communist countries shifted from collectivism to individualism, thereby spurring citizens to demand greater political freedom and civil liberty.

Various forces powered past the Third Wave of Democratization:

- Failure of totalitarian regimes to deliver prosperity
- Improving communication technology
- Economic dividends of political freedom

Communication Innovations Improved communications eroded totalitarian states' control of information. Technologies integrated disenfranchised people into the global village. Once it took weeks, if ever, for word-of-mouth of protests to spread; now, improving connections circulated news within hours.[57] Images of resistance and rebellion had snowball effects on pro-democracy campaigns worldwide. On a micro scale, we see similar effects linking protests in Chinese factories. Specifically, labor unrest has become more commonplace in China, as factories operating in highly competitive markets press their workers to improve productivity. Workers linked via mobile phones and the Internet, increasingly aware of their rights and common cause, increasingly challenge perceived injustices.[58]

Freedom's Consequences Freedom yielded economic dividends.[59] The median per capita gross domestic product, a measure of the standard of living, increased nearly sevenfold for free countries compared to not free countries. Growing wealth positively influences property rights, the rule of law, education opportunities, gender equality, media vigilance, and social tolerance.[60] Prosperity promoted the expansion of the middle class, whose burgeoning access to the uncensored news Thomas Jefferson's belief that "Information is the currency of democracy." Perhaps most critically, rising prosperity supported the political stability and faith in the future that anchors the democratic ideology.[61]

CONCEPT CHECK

Chapter 1 identifies the "Expansion of Technology" as a driving force of globalization. Advances in telecommunications liberated the flow of information, thereby challenging and changing political attitudes in many countries.

The multi-decade march toward greater political freedoms and expansive civil liberties fueled a belief in the inevitability of democracy—again, the so-called "end of history" scenario. For MNEs, this trend stabilized business environments, both at home and abroad. Growing stability encouraged them to expand their investment horizon to include markets that had previously been off-limits (notably, China, Russia, and Central and Eastern Europe). As a result, industries developed, middle classes emerged, globalization accelerated, and freedom flourished.

Thomas Jefferson reasoned, "Information is the currency of democracy." If so, then this satellite dish-covered exterior, atop a Kabul apartment's facade, plays a crucial role fortifying its performance.
Source: kzww/Shutterstock

DEMOCRACY: RECESSION AND RETREAT

Over the past seven years, long-running gains in political freedom have given way to wide-spread declines.

Democracy retains appeal worldwide—preferred by people in most countries, its allure energized by growing wealth and education, its legitimacy worldwide solidified by an expanding middle class.[62] Troubling data, however, question its momentum. Managers increasingly qualify their interpretation of political environments with the possibility that "history," rather than ending, is just beginning.

Several indicators show slowing adoption of democracy throughout the world.

A few years ago, longitudinal data on the slowing momentum of democracy indicated a "democracy recession." Now, data indicate that democracy is in retreat worldwide. In 1989, 41 percent of nations had an electoral democracy; in 1999, it was 63 percent; in 2012, down to 60 percent.[63] Figure 3.3 indicates an ominous shift over the past few years. Gains in freedom have given way to declines in freedom. Sham elections, police crackdowns, kangaroo courts, and persecution of dissidents gain traction. All speak to the stance taken by President Lukashenka of Belarus, who declared on the heels of a rigged election victory, "there will be no more mindless democracy in this country."[64] Worldwide, increasingly influential totalitarian regimes impose "forceful measures designed to suppress democratic reformers, international assistance to those reformers, and ultimately the very idea of democracy itself."[65] As a result, 2013 marked the seventh consecutive year in which political freedom declined worldwide—the longest consecutive period of setbacks in nearly 40 years.[66]

The State of Political Affairs The *Economist Intelligence Unit* (EIU) applies a broad measure to assess a nation's "texture of democracy." It notes that democracy, narrowly defined, is easily achieved—indeed, if merely holding elections were sufficient, virtually every country would qualify as a democracy. Rather, an effective democracy depends upon free and fair elections as well as supportive institutions and public attitudes that protect freedom. Assessing the "texture of democracy," therefore, involves 60 indicators of a country's electoral process and pluralism, civil liberties, government functioning, political participation, and political culture.[67] Countries are rated as either as a full democracy, flawed democracy, hybrid regime, or authoritarian regime.

The *Economist Intelligence Unit* identifies four types of political systems:

- Full democracy
- Flawed democracy
- Hybrid regime
- Authoritarian regime

The EIU evaluates democracy in 167 countries that, combined, are home to virtually the entire population of the world.[68] Analysis finds many are "democracies" in name only; just

FIGURE 3.3 Freedom in the World: Gains and Declines by Country, 2003–2013

The past decade shows a disturbing trend in the momentum of political freedom worldwide. Early on, gains in freedom exceeded declines. The past seven years have seen the opposite, with growing state authority reducing individuals' political freedom.

Source: Based on Freedom House,"Freedom in the World 2013: Democratic Breakthroughs in the Balance,"www.freedomhouse.org.

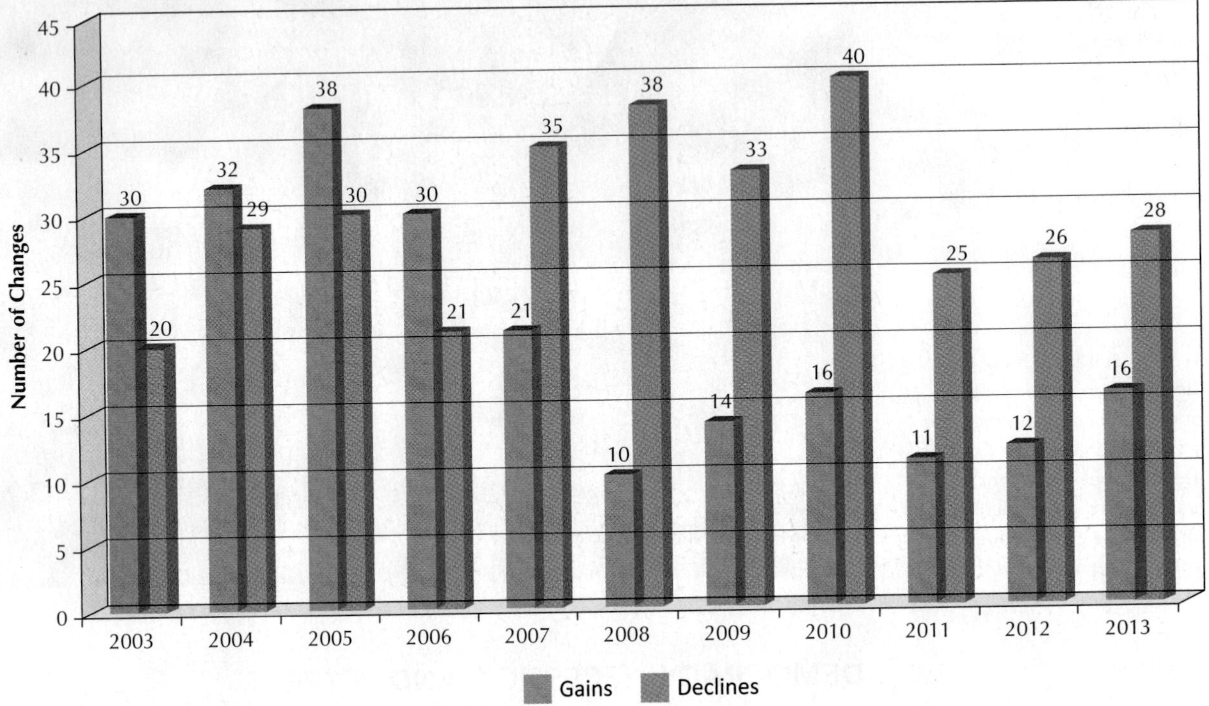

25 are full democracies, while 53 are "flawed democracies." Nineteen of the full democracies are found primarily in the West, with the remainder scattered in Latin America, Eastern Europe, and Africa. Flawed democracies predominate in Latin America and Eastern Europe. The fragility of institutional structures, political participation, and democratic cultures within many of these countries has led to significant backsliding. Likewise, corruption, violence, and drug trafficking encourage authoritarianism.

Of the remaining 89 countries, the EIU rates 36 as "hybrid regimes" that mix democratic and authoritarian practices. Procedural irregularities often corrupt free and fair processes. Hong Kong, for example, exemplifies a hybrid regime that manifests many trappings of a democracy, including an effective judiciary, civil liberties, independent media, and political parties. Still, authoritarian tendencies are evident. Consider its electoral process. Its Chief Executive (effectively its President) is chosen not by Hong Kong's 7 million residents but by a 1,200-person "Election Committee." The sense of a rigged system of political freedom without democratic accountability radicalizes its politics.[69]

Finally, 55 countries are judged authoritarian regimes. In many cases, they showcase institutions of democracy that are merely Potemkin designs. Day-to-day life displays the telltale marks of totalitarianism, including unfair elections, disregard of civil liberties, state-owned media, omnipresent state security, pervasive censorship, and a corrupt judiciary.

An Important Qualification Qualifying these results by demography adds some useful perspective. Like Freedom House, the EIU reports that about half of the world's population lives within some sort of democratic system. However, it notes that just 11 percent reside in countries with a functioning "full democracy." Furthermore, some 37 percent live in flawed democracies, 14 percent in hybrid regimes, and 38 percent in authoritarian regimes.[70] Westerners may presume that democracy prevails throughout the world, but presently only about one of every nine people lives in one.

AUTHORITARIANISM'S SURGE

In 1991, citizens in the former Soviet bloc countries celebrated the move from a single-party state to a multiparty political system. By 2009, support had fallen drastically, especially in poorer countries such as Ukraine, Hungary, and Lithuania.[71] By 2012, belief in democracy continued deteriorating in the wake of the global financial crisis as most countries in the region saw declining democracy scores.[72] Established democracies struggle as well. In the United States, the terrorist attacks of September 11, 2001, reset the standards of personal freedom, resulting in restrictions that raised questions about the moral authority of democratic ideals. Europe, meanwhile, struggles to preserve political freedom in the face of harsh austerity policies and the replacement of sovereign democratic processes with financial dictates from leaders of the EU and the European Central Bank.[73] Persistent economic struggles challenge the belief, strongly held since the fall of the Berlin Wall, that "freedom works."

Collectively, trends throughout the world show growing confidence in the authoritarian alternative, with countries growing skeptical of the virtues of a multiparty democracy and showing increasing interest in building single-party political systems. The EIU notes:

> Authoritarian trends have become even more entrenched in the Middle East and much of the former Soviet Union. Democratization in Sub-Saharan Africa is grinding to a halt, and in some cases is being reversed. A political malaise in east-central Europe has led to disappointment and questioning of the strength of the region's democratic transition. Media freedoms are being eroded across Latin America and populist forces with dubious democratic credentials have come to the fore in a few countries in the region. In the developed West, a precipitous decline in political participation, weaknesses in the functioning of government, and security-related curbs on civil liberties are having a corrosive effect on some long-established democracies.[74]

Powering the resurgence of totalitarianism are

- Strong states supporting strong performance
- Gaps in the principles and practices of democracy
- Economic insecurity following slowing growth
- Escalating debate of the meaning of democracy

Engines of Authoritarianism Several engines powered the Third Wave of Democratization. Likewise, the following forces promote totalitarianism today:

Political Economy of Growth Rising uncertainty questions the relationship between the level of economic development and democracy. The classic modernization hypothesis—that economic development is a pre-condition of democracy —is no longer universally accepted.[75] Consider China. Its economic performance since 1980 endorses its authoritarian, one-party system as an alternative to liberal, multiparty democracies. Concurrently, its model of a "people's democratic dictatorship" has steadily gained credibility worldwide.[76] For many poverty-stricken countries, patience with the not-yet-realized dividends of the "democracy advantage" thesis has worn thin. Some point to India, noting that its more than 60 years of nearly uninterrupted democratic governance rule has failed to improve health, education, or wealth for a majority of Indians.[77]

Rhetoric Versus Reality Democracy setbacks in Italy, France, UK, Spain, and the US give pause to some 70 strategically significant countries at the political crossroads. If democracy can't work there, how could it work here, they wonder.[78] Charges of hypocrisy against Western countries (owing to incursions in Iraq, Libya, and Afghanistan, along with the implications of antiterrorist activities for political freedoms and civil liberties) jumble democratic ideals. Double standards in foreign policy (i.e., some autocratic countries can be friends, such as Saudi Arabia, whereas others are foes, like Venezuela) corrode the credibility of democracy promoters.[79] Consequently, fewer than one in five West Europeans trust political parties, while only one in three regards governments and parliaments as trustworthy.[80]

Economic Problems The global financial crisis has complicated matters. High unemployment, slow growth, and rising debt, by threatening the middle class, has weakened belief in the effectiveness of democracy. Confidence in institutions has declined throughout the West. The International Labour Organization reports wavering belief that political policies in democratic states lead to a fairer and better future.[81] History shows that right-wing totalitarian movements generally draw popular support from the middle class seeking to preserve the status quo. Those who fall into poverty are politically hazardous. In the United States, for example, the worse the economy, the more people describe themselves as "right-wing."[82] On the other hand, left-wing totalitarianism often develops from working class movements seeking to overthrow wealthy oppressors—think of the tension between the proletariat and bourgeois in Marxism. Unless reversed, unemployment, debt, and anxiety erode confidence that democracy works.[83]

Who Defines Democracy? The legitimacy of Western notions of democracy travels poorly to societies with different ideals and institutions. Hu Jintao, former CCP chief and China's president, speaks of "democracy" with a different meaning from the one understood by Westerners. In his view, calls for multiparty democracy are taboo, opposition cannot officially organize, reform must obey the "correct political orientation," and "orderly" change must respect and preserve the authority of the CCP.[84] Similarly, Prime Minister Vladimir Putin, proclaiming himself "a true democrat," argues the West misinterprets the virtues of authoritarianism. He charges "some of the participants in the international dialogue believe that their ideas [of democracy] are the ultimate truth."[85] Western-style democracy, rather than promoting individual rights and civil liberties, is an ideological ruse that disguises vast inequalities. Likewise, Brazil's former President da Silva says that the primary advocates of Western-style democracy no longer speak for the world, having lost the moral authority to dictate solutions to developing countries.[86]

The engines of totalitarianism, considered in the context of democracy's retreat, raise the question: Has democracy run its course? If so, as we consider in our "Looking to the Future" box, what then might become of political ideologies and how might MNEs respond?

Looking to the Future

Political Ideology and MNEs' Actions

Like you, managers wonder what a political map of the world might look like in the next decade. Will democracy spread? Will totalitarianism gain more ground? Will new ideologies arise? It is tempting to regard these questions as academic straw men, best left to the folks in ivory towers. The latest data indicate they are anything but. As faltering political freedom and resurgent authoritarianism accelerate democracy's retreat, countries reset marketplaces and MNEs adjust strategies. Trends highlight the contemporary political ideologies competing for supremacy—namely, the Washington Consensus, the Beijing Consensus, and the Clash of Civilizations. What, pray tell, might these mean to managers?

The Washington Consensus

Named after the close of the Cold War for the free-market, pro-trade, and pro-globalization policies promoted by the United States, the Washington Consensus advocates democracy, political freedom, rule of law, and human rights.[87] As Washington became the global philosophical center in an America-dominated unipolar world, its idealized Consensus—promoted by executives, politicians, generals, journalists, and institutions—called upon countries to reform in ways that reflected the political economy of the United States. Powering this call was a set of interrelated beliefs: right-minded reform led to economic growth, which created a middle class that supported property rights, which in turn began institutionalizing the rule of law. Making those choices and implementing the necessary policies would institute, support, and sustain a legitimate democracy.

Successfully navigating this sequence, reasoned the United States, would build nations that steadfastly championed prosperity and peace. A world of nations practicing US-style pro-peace democracy arguably signified the endpoint of humanity's sociocultural evolution.[88] Ironically, promoting and protecting the Washington Consensus requires a powerful military; combined defense-related spending of more than $1.1 trillion in the U.S. exceeds that of all other countries combined.[89]

The Beijing Consensus

Alternatively, rather than the end of history, some say the growing appeal of the Beijing Consensus signals the next political era.[90] A euphemism for China's self-proclaimed "people's democratic dictatorship," this Consensus calls for a single-party system in which elected representatives, preapproved by the ruling party, oversee a nominal democratic system whose citizens, though granted the right to vote, cannot participate in decision making.[91] Elections, while free, are not fair. The CCP aspires to rule by consent, preferring benevolent persuasion to the iron fist. Still, it swiftly suppresses those who challenge its authority. Spontaneity in a single-party system, no matter how apolitical, symbolizes protest. As CCP officials explain, "Stability trumps everything."[92]

Unlike the ideologically interventionist Washington Consensus, the Beijing Consensus is ideologically agnostic. It prizes economic development and international trade as the means to generate growth, create wealth, and build a harmonious society. It uses fast-growing prosperity to subvert political choice, reasoning that people value higher wages, social stability, and economic security far more than political freedom. The Beijing Consensus does not pass judgment on another country's politics; in turn, it expects not to be judged. It advocates trade "with no strings attached" (which, in the case of the Washington Consensus, are democracy, freedom, human rights, and the rule of law). To this end, China invests throughout Asia, Africa, the Middle East, and South America free of demands for political reform.[93]

China's policy of harmonious stability within a single-party state has gained credibility worldwide, particularly given its strong performance in the wake of the global financial crisis. Said one analyst, "[T]he 'China model' of authoritarian capitalism is gaining currency. Governments from Syria to Vietnam have sung its praises."[94] Some argue that state control that weds liberal economics with single-party authoritarian politics, rather than the union of liberal economics and multiparty democracy, now represents the superior political path to prosperity and harmony.

The Clash of Civilizations

Spreading democracy in the Arab world, which is regularly rated the world's least free region, has been a long-running goal of the West. Indeed, an aim of the Iraq War was to build the luminous "city upon a hill" that would inspire peaceful democracy in the region. Efforts there, as well as pro-democracy movements in Tunisia, Egypt, Afghanistan, Libya, and elsewhere, have had limited success. Moreover, Western military involvement has raised questions about the legitimacy of democratic ideals throughout the region. Faltering institutions and changes in political sentiments hinder the transition to democracy in several Islamic nations, including Kuwait, Iran, Saudi Arabia, and the Palestinian areas.

Regional instability highlights the difficulty of promoting democratic political cultures, to say nothing of a functioning democracy. The discontent of the economically and politically disadvantaged, particularly among youth suffering extreme unemployment, mobilized the massive pro-democracy protests of the so-called Arab Spring. Although initially promising, study of the determinants and consequences of democratic transitions advise caution; violent uprisings struggle to institutionalize durable democratic change. Moreover, weak property rights and civil liberties continue constraining change, thereby thwarting democratic progress.[95]

Productive economies in the oil-rich Persian Gulf also stall the spread of democracy; it no longer appears that democracy is a necessary condition for prosperity. Furthermore, oil-based revenue entrenches an autocracy by removing the need to levy taxes and thereby reducing state accountability. Consequently, moderate Arab leaders contend that the transition from totalitarianism to democracy is, at best, "a slow process." Hardliners, meanwhile, vilify democracy.[96]

The reluctance of Islamic states to adopt democracy animates the "clash-of-civilizations" scenario. Irreconcilable cultural and religious differences between Islam and the West, goes this reasoning, will trigger a backlash against Western political ideals and their crystallization in the ideologically interventionist Washington Consensus.[97] Some speculate that an epic clash between oppositional civilizations will usher in a new political ideology based on cultural and religious ideals.

What's Next, Managers Ask?

Democracy's ongoing retreat questions long-cherished ideals. Managers study the direction that political ideologies might track. Will liberal democracy *à la* the Washington Consensus regain the commanding heights? Ongoing developments worldwide, led by an expanding middle class and supported by social networking channels, support that forecast.[98] Or will the one-party trademark of the Beijing Consensus set political standards? China's growing involvement in receptive countries worldwide supports that projection. To that end, when recently asked, "How satisfied are you with the country's direction?" 83 percent of Chinese reported satisfaction versus 31 percent in the United States, 19 percent in France, 15 percent in Britain, and 7 percent in Japan.[99] Finally, if countries bypass the American Way or the Chinese Path, might a clash of civilizations give rise to new ideas of political freedom?[100] Ongoing tensions in hotspots worldwide do not bode well.

Whatever the scenario, history reminds us that it matters. The first and second waves of democratization (1828–1926 and 1943–1962, respectively) were followed by periods of freedom backlash, democracy retreat, and backslides into authoritarianism. The end of the second wave saw more than 20 countries revert from totalitarianism, symbolized by the ensuing ideological war between Washington and Moscow. Hence, the question arises: Are we once again facing a cycle of transition and consolidation?[101]

Whatever the answer, only the ill-advised underestimate political change. If the Washington Consensus proves resilient, managers must adjust operations to the growing pains of countries that champion freedom, advocate human rights, and adopt the rule of law. Prosperity may come with difficulty, but there will be prosperity for many. If the Beijing Consensus predominates, managers must rethink business in a world that uses state controls to generate economic growth at the price of freedom. Prosperity may come easily, but its price will include individual freedoms. If ideologies transform as civilizations clash, the resulting social and religious orders will reset systems. Prosperity may prove a wild card as oppositional ideologies battle for the commanding heights. ■

POLITICAL RISK

Political risk refers to the threat that decisions or events in a country will negatively affect the profitability and sustainability of an investment.

Politics is always and everywhere dynamic. At different times, different parties champion different ideologies that endorse different political systems, with unpredictability ensuing. Consequently, investing and operating internationally exposes MNEs to risks that arise from a country's political system. This class of risk, referred to as **political risk**, is the potential loss arising from a change in government policy. More precisely, it is the risk that political decisions, events, or conditions will affect a country's business environment in ways that force investors to accept lower rates of return, cost them some or all of the value of their investment, or threaten the sustainability of their operation. Figure 3.5 identifies leading causes of political risk.

Two trends increase political risk worldwide. First, many fast-growing emerging markets are rife with flashpoints. Arbitrary legal systems, fragile institutions, volatile societies, and corrupt regimes fan instability. Many firms in these countries are state-run, pursuing political goals that complicate economic situations. Aggravating matters is the fact that political risks differ from market to market. In Venezuela, managers face economic nationalism; in Brazil, a manager needs to understand Congress's multi-party alliances; in China, the task is interpreting the power and play of the CCP; in Saudi Arabia, a manager must make sense of the internal relations of the ruling family. Hence, operating in these markets is quite different from the comparatively more predictable politics in Western democracies. Analytics that work in one country often travel poorly to others.

CONCEPT CHECK

Chapter 1 notes that some interest groups fear that globalization fatally weakens national sovereignty—that is, growing external control restricts a nation's right to act in its own interests. Here, we observe that this attitude often intensifies political risk. Foreign investors face higher risks when a host government becomes increasingly sensitive to threats to its sovereignty.

Second, the aftermath of the financial crisis aggravates political risk in both developed and developing markets. When the Berlin Wall collapsed, globalization steadily standardized the inconsistencies of politics across markets. Certainly, countries evolved at different rates. However, as many developed in the broad context of the Washington Consensus, managers could reasonably assume that the principles of Western-style political economy, not local quirks, would shape national affairs. The global credit crisis reset the equation. Now, local politics influence the performance of global markets and the actions of MNEs on a scale not seen in decades. If the crisis continues testing people's faith in democracy, companies face growing public challenge and political constraint.

FIGURE 3.5 Classes and Characteristics of Political Risk

The political risks of international business have telltale characteristics. Here, we see that they vary in terms of the intensity of their impact upon firm operations, belong to various classes , typically follow from the imposition of certain sorts of regulations, and have distinctive outcomes.

Scale	Class	Type	Outcome
Micro		Financial Anomalies	Regulatory policies that make it difficult for the company to get credit or arrange overseas loans.
	Systemic	Competing Perspectives	The host government's policies on, for instance, human rights, labor conditions, or environmental sustainability, create public relations problems for a foreign company at home.
		Unilateral Breach of Contract	The host government repudiates a contract negotiated with a foreign company or approves a local firm's doing the same.
	Procedural	Tax Discrimination	A foreign company is saddled with a higher tax burden than a local competitor.
		Restrictions on Profit Repatriation	The host government arbitrarily limits the amount of profit that a foreign company can remit from its local operations to the home office.
	Distributive	Destructive Government Actions	Unilateral trade barriers, often via local-content requirements, interfere with the distribution of products to local consumers.
		Harmful Action Against People	Local employees of a foreign company are threatened by kidnapping, extortion, or terrorist actions.
	Catastrophic	Expropriation/Nationalization	The host government or a political faction seizes a company's local assets. Compensation, if any, is usually trivial. Resurgent totalitarianism and resource nationalism increase this risk.
Macro		Civil Strife, Insurrection, War	Military action damages or destroys a company's local operations.

CLASSIFYING POLITICAL RISK

The evaluation of political risk often applies a macro-micro criterion. Macro risks affect all companies in a given country; micro risks are project-specific actions that affect individual, usually foreign-owned, companies. Figure 3.4 applies this approach but further qualifies the macro-micro division with the intensity level of the type of risk. We develop these characteristics in terms of the resulting classes of political risk: *systemic, procedural, distributive,* and *catastrophic*.

CLASSES AND CHARACTERISTICS OF POLITICAL RISKS

The political risks of international business have telltale characteristics. Here, we see that they vary in terms of the intensity of their impact on company operations, belong to various classes, typically follow from the imposition of certain sorts of regulations, and have distinctive outcomes.

The primary types of political risk, from least to most disruptive, are

- Systemic
- Procedural
- Distributive
- Catastrophic

Systemic Political Risk As a rule, a country's political processes aim not to punish specific companies arbitrarily. If they did, few would hazard the investment. More often, investors face political risk that follows from shifts in public policy. New political leaders, for instance, may adopt policies that differ from their predecessors'—say, reducing the individual benefit of business activity by increasing tax rates to improve collective welfare. In that case, new regulations will alter the macro environment for all. Similarly, a government may target an economic sector that it sees dominated by foreign interests, such as Venezuela's program to nationalize energy and media companies.[102] In both situations, politically motivated polices alter the macro environment, thereby creating systemic political risks that affect all firms. If democracy continues faltering, the likely rise in corruption, weakened property rights,

"Look, you've got to accept some curtailment of your freedom in exchange for increased security."

FIGURE 3.4 Today, a Question of Where Fiction Stops and Fact Starts

Source: Robert Mankoff/New Yorker Cartoon Bank/www.cartoonbank.com

unpredictably enforced laws, and freedom constraints will increase systemic political risk in many countries.

Systemic political risks, by influencing the macro business environment, affect the operation of all firms.

Systemic risks do not necessarily reduce potential profits. In fact, elections and policy shifts can create opportunities for foreign investors. In the past few years, for example, newly elected governments in Vietnam, Malawi, Estonia, and Guinea deregulated and privatized their previously state-controlled economies. Investors who accepted the risk of a public policy reversal and pursued the emerging opportunities prospered as freer markets developed in these countries. Our opening case traces a similar market pattern in China. Political trends encouraged pro-market reforms that reduced risks and created opportunities. Still, taking advantage of such opportunities, whether in China or elsewhere, calls for tough-minded analysis of the risk-return relationship.

Procedural political risk institutes impediments that constrain the flexibility of local operations.

Procedural Political Risk Around the clock, people, products, and funds move from point to point in the global market. Each move creates a procedural transaction between subsidiaries, companies, or countries. Political actions sometimes impose frictions that slow or stop these transactions. The repercussions of, say, public fraud or a partisan judicial system can raise business costs. Corrupt officials might pressure a foreign firm to pay additional monies to clear goods through customs or obtain a permit to open a factory. For example, Nigeria's notoriously challenging business environment is rife with procedural risks. "The entire state machinery exists to siphon off cash," said one observer. "Many functions of government have been adapted for personal gain. . . . A universe of red tape engulfs the economy. . . . In some Nigerian states, governors must personally sign off on every property sale; many demand a fee."[103] Politically motivated interference escalates expenses, thereby lowering returns. Procedural political risk is a micro risk—that is, it affects some but not all companies. Monitoring industry developments, minding the relative contribution of their firms to the local economy, and promoting solid citizenship help MNEs manage their exposure.

The dynamic of distributive political risk is the gradual elimination of the local property rights of foreign companies.

Distributive Political Risk Countries see successful foreign investors as agents of innovation and sources of prosperity. Often, as MNEs generate greater profits in the local economy, the host government may question whether it is getting its "fair" share of the rewards. In some situations, change is immediate. For example, rising silver prices led the Bolivian government to "dismantle the privatization model" governing its mining industry and expropriate all assets owned by private, largely foreign-owned mining companies.[104] Foreign MNEs, like Coeur d'Alene Mines and Pan American Silver, besides watching their share price plummet on the news, were given two weeks to prepare for state takeover of their Bolivian mines.

More often, officials launch programs of *creeping expropriation* whereby they slowly take a bigger share of the rewards. Methods vary, such as increasing barriers to transferring personnel into or profits out of the country. Gradually, through such techniques, the host government eliminates MNEs' local property rights. Generally, vigilance helps MNEs minimize exposure. Many also fight back, building global supply chains that diversify operations.

Chrysler, for example, deterred creeping expropriation in Peru because its local factory made about half the parts needed to assemble a car; importing the rest meant the local facility was useless if the government interfered with operations. Likewise, Japan's escalating tension with China (notably, consumer boycotts of Japanese products, anti-Japanese riots, and foreboding military confrontations) pushes Japanese MNEs to hedge their political risk. Some apply a "China-plus" approach whereby they backstop their supply chains, once anchored in China, with a shadow hub in another Asian market such as Thailand, Vietnam, or the Philippines. Although inefficient, alternative locations safeguard the Japanese firms' Asian operations in the event political hostilities flare.[105]

Sometimes the importance of the market leaves MNEs with few options. The United States, for instance, is not generally considered a hotbed of distributive political risk. If you're in the cigarette business, however, you're aware that the U.S. carries high degrees of political risk.[106] Its government battles cigarette makers (both domestic, like Philip Morris, and foreign, like British American Tobacco) on matters of taxation, regulation, business practice, and liability. Preserving market access requires that companies accept hard operational limits.

Catastrophic political risk devastates companies and countries.

Catastrophic Political Risk Catastrophic political risk includes political developments that adversely affect the operations of every firm in a country. It typically arises from macro flashpoints—ethnic discord, illegal regime change, civil disorder, insurrection—that disrupt society. Anti-state activities in Egypt in early 2011, for example, paralyzed its economy. Foreign commerce and domestic business all but halted, markets seized up, and supplies of all sorts vanished. Auspiciously, Egypt pulled back from the brink. In other situations, such as in failed states like Chad, Afghanistan, or Zimbabwe, spiraling disruptions triggered political conflicts that devastated the business environment for all firms.[107] By the fall of 2013, however, Egypt fell into a similar downward spiral. MNEs responded by suspending operations.

Point — **Proactive Political Risk Management: The Best Approach**

Point **Yes** Companies take politics seriously, fully aware that the actions of host governments affect the business environment. Consequently, MNEs face threats that demand political risk management strategies. All have a choice: They can apply a proactive or passive approach. Those who advocate active political risk management reason that the best defense is a good offense. In my opinion, they're right. Taking charge, predicting political problems, and controlling risks is the ticket to success.

WHAT TO DO Seasoned managers pull this off through two battle-tested tactics. First, they apply state-of-the-art statistical modeling to quantify political risks. Second, they stress-test their models, consulting experts on the political maneuverings in a particular country. This two-pronged approach, like good management in general, applies hard analysis and objective interpretation. It begins with the thesis that neither positive nor negative political events in any country are independent or chance events. Civil strife, creeping expropriation, regime change, ethnic tension, terrorism, and the like do not happen randomly. They unfold in observable patterns that bright folks applying sharp analytics can study to estimate the odds of future outcomes. An objective model that detects, measures, and frames scenarios moves a company ahead of the curve, preparing it to manage its political risk exposure.

WHAT TO WATCH Measuring the right set of discrete events is the key precondition of modeling political risk.

Specifically, this approach requires identifying valid indicators that one can measure reliably. Research identifies useful indicators: the number of military officers holding political office, pace of urbanization, frequency of government crises, degree of literacy, ethno-lingual fractionalization, and so on. Evolving methods fortify analyses. For example, sentiment analysis identifies emotionally charged words and phrases used in online communications. Comparing the relative frequency of positive and negative words used in millions of exchanges, feeds, and posts on the Internet produces a national as well as global map of how people "feel." Sentiment analysis, for example, indicated that people's resentment of autocratic rule was crossing critical thresholds in Egypt and Libya weeks before violence erupted.[108] Moreover, sentiment analysis confirms that the challenge is not identifying individual measures, but rather identifying the right mix. Once done, skillful statistical modeling can objectively estimate risk exposure.

WHAT TO ADD We concede a proactive approach has limits. Spreadsheet estimation, no matter how rigorous or extensive, carries analysis only so far. Reaching this limit need not halt analysis, however. One can complement quantitative measures with in-depth, country-specific qualitative indicators. Enriching interpretation requires perspectives and perceptions that intuitively understand a country's political drama in ways that numbers struggle to represent.

How do we apply this approach? A popular tactic is surveying country experts. Besides being mindful of quantitative factors, specialists add an understanding of the subtle intricacies of secondary data. They enhance analyses with their expertise on the subjective conditions in a country, adding a bit of wisdom to interpret what appears to others as idiosyncratic circumstances but, in their eyes, is a systematic pattern of political activities.

Integrating expert assessments into your political risk strategy is straightforward. Begin by running standardized interviews with experts to assess a country's political environment. If stuck, a useful starting point is the Internet; searching "political risk management" generates resources. Collectively, they support projecting realistic scenarios and logically assigning probabilities to reasonable outcomes—the hallmarks of proactive political risk management.

Proactive Political Risk Management: The Best Approach

Counterpoint

No Unquestionably, a proactive approach exhibits the hallmark of good management—enterprising, confident, and controlling. However, it fails to explain why many MNEs do the exact opposite, choosing to manage political risk passively by treating it as an unpredictable hazard of the business environment. They reason that no model, regardless of how brilliantly it has been conceptualized, how systematically it has been specified, and how precisely it has been administered, can consistently predict political risk. Granted, shrewd models extrapolate meaningful insights from economic, political, and social reports about who may take office, what polices may pass, and how these sorts of political events affect the business environment. Unquestionably, these insights make the political system and its risks understandable. They do not, however, make it predictable.

WHAT TO HEDGE Insights do not qualify as predictions precisely because of the intrinsic impossibility of reliably measuring messy, ill-structured situations. The political world is complex, its inalienable feature is ambiguity, and its tendency to change is absurdly high. Complicating matters are the innumerable variables and their interaction

Counterpoint

that shape a political system. This situation becomes more difficult as companies venture into emerging markets, each with its own political peculiarities. Going from the United States to Mexico may be a stretch, but that pales in comparison to expanding from the United States to, say, Saudi Arabia, Kazakhstan, Latvia, or Rwanda. No matter how powerful the spreadsheet or insightful the expert, the dimensions and dynamic of a political environment defy precise specification. Certainly, developing broad frameworks that anticipate unpredictable hazards makes good business sense. However, prudently managing political risk starts by rejecting the delusion that one can. The objective is protection, not prediction.

HOW TO HEDGE This, of course, raises the question: How do I hedge my company's exposure? Typically, MNEs applying a passive approach outsource the political risk-management process. They reason the best shield is buying political risk insurance—essentially, the best offense is a good defense. Consider the flexibility they get through this approach. They can purchase coverage that protects operations from an array of political risks, including government expropriation, involuntary abandonment, and damage from political violence. Furthermore, companies are not limited to a few carriers. A range of public agencies, international organizations, and private companies offer a variety of coverage options.

- Multilateral development banks (MDBs) are international financial institutions funded and owned by member governments that promote growth in member countries by providing financial incentives to potential investors. Reducing the capital at risk encourages firms to expand into otherwise unacceptably risky environments. Examples are the African Development Bank, the Asian Development Bank, and the World Bank Group.
- The Overseas Private Investment Corporation (OPIC) encourages U.S. investment projects overseas by protecting ventures against various forms of risk, including civil strife, expropriation, and currency inconvertibility. Increasingly, OPIC promotes investments in emerging markets that support U.S. foreign policy priorities.
- Private insurance companies underwrite political risk protection. Many cover "routine" distributive and procedural risks that involve property and income, such as contract repudiation and currency inconvertibility. Private insurers are reluctant to cover catastrophic risks that result from civil strife, insurrection, or war.

WHAT TO REALIZE Ultimately, we have no quarrel with the notion that prediction and control are touchstones of professional management. Still, politics are anything but predictable and controllable. Indeed, few, if any, predicted the political turmoil of the Arab Spring and the surprisingly swift collapse of the Mubarak regime in Egypt. And who would have called democracy's retreat a decade ago, especially when leading analysts were celebrating the "end of history?" Not to put too sharp an edge on it, but if one cannot predict these mega-events, then exactly what can one predict? Therefore, it just makes more sense—and, we might add, more cents—to resist the delusion of proactive management and opt for the practicality of passively managing political risk.

3-3. Given the choice between a proactive versus a passive risk management strategy, which approach would you recommend? Specify three reasons to justify your recommendation.

THE LEGAL ENVIRONMENT

As political ideologies differ among countries, so do legal systems. Thus, a key aspect of the international business environment is how a country develops, interprets, and enforces its laws. Businesspeople, understandably, champion consistency in laws from country to country. Uniform, transparent laws make it easier to plan where to invest and, once there, how to compete on competencies, not connections.

In theory, legitimate rules that apply without prejudice to individual or institutional behavior, regardless of political, cultural, or economic status, anchor an effective legal environment. Done justly, individuals and companies can make lawful decisions that support peace and prosperity; done arbitrarily, all suffer. "To distrust the judiciary," reasoned Honoré de Balzac, "marks the beginning of the end of society."

The legal system is the mechanism for conceiving, stipulating, interpreting, and enforcing the law in a formal jurisdiction.

The **legal system** specifies the rules that regulate behavior, the processes by which laws are enforced, and the procedures used to resolve grievances. Legal systems differ across countries due to variations in tradition, precedent, usage, custom, or religious precepts. Moreover, with the exception of the members of the European Union, countries rarely recognize the legitimacy of legal practices or court judgments from other nations. Concluded a legal scholar, "Products move very easily across borders. Legal judgments, not so much."[109]

Modern legal systems evidence three components:

- Constitutional Law
- Criminal Law
- Civil and Commercial Law

All things being equal, every legal system institutes rules that support business formation, regulate transactions, and stabilize relationships. Successfully doing so ensures that a society can pursue economic development and, when disagreements arise, resolve them without resorting to lawlessness. Modern legal systems share three components: (1) **constitutional law**, which translates the country's constitution into an open and just legal system, setting the framework for government and defining the authority and procedure of political bodies to establish laws; (2) **criminal law**, which safeguards society by specifying what conduct is criminal, and prescribing punishment to those who breach those standards; and (3) **civil and commercial laws**, which ensure fairness and efficiency in business transactions by stipulating private rights and specific remedies in order to regulate conduct between individuals and/or organizations. No single legal component in and of itself guarantees a functioning legal system. Success depends on the collective effectiveness of all in promoting philosophical integrity, procedural justice, and personal security.

CRN
Case Review Note

Aspects of each type of law bear upon MNEs' actions in a host country.[110] Our opening case, for example, shows how China's legal traditions and practices attract, retain, and deter foreign investment. Whereas Western investors are accustomed to transparent bankruptcy laws that protect creditors, Chinese law presently protects debtors. Likewise, one in six business practitioners in Russia has been prosecuted for alleged economic crime over the past decade; most cases have no plaintiff, acquittals are rare, and company assets are often expropriated by the state.[111] Russian law, contends critics,"is the property of those who enforce it, and written exclusively for them."[112]

TYPES OF LEGAL SYSTEMS

Managers face five types of legal systems in the world today:

- Common law
- Civil law
- Theocratic law
- Customary law
- Mixed

The type of legal system in a country determines the conduct of business transactions, the rights and obligations of those doing business, and the legal redress open to those who believe they have been wronged. Understanding the nuances of the system pushes executives to assess a variety of issues: Are laws based on abstractions or practicality? Do judges or juries pass judgment? Is justice based on objective principle or seen as the province of divinity? Do personal connections trump case facts? Peculiar as these questions sound, international business puts managers into different situations wherein different interpretations of these issues result in different standards that regulate the legality of their actions.

The globalization of business drives the standardization of laws across countries. Still, enduring philosophical outlooks and practical orientations result in different types of legal systems around the world. Map 3.3 identifies the primary types that prevail worldwide, namely: *common law, civil law, theocratic law, customary law,* and *mixed systems.*[113]

MAP 3.3 The Wide World of Legal Systems

Managers operating internationally face legal environments anchored in a variety of philosophies and principles. Here we see the world organized by predominant types of legal systems.

Source: University of Ottawa,"World Legal Systems," retrieved 4/15/2013 from www.juriglobe.ca/eng/index.php.

Note: Given that this is a Mercator projection, the scale approximates east-west distance at the equator; however, the farther you move from the equator, the more the east-west distance is distorted.

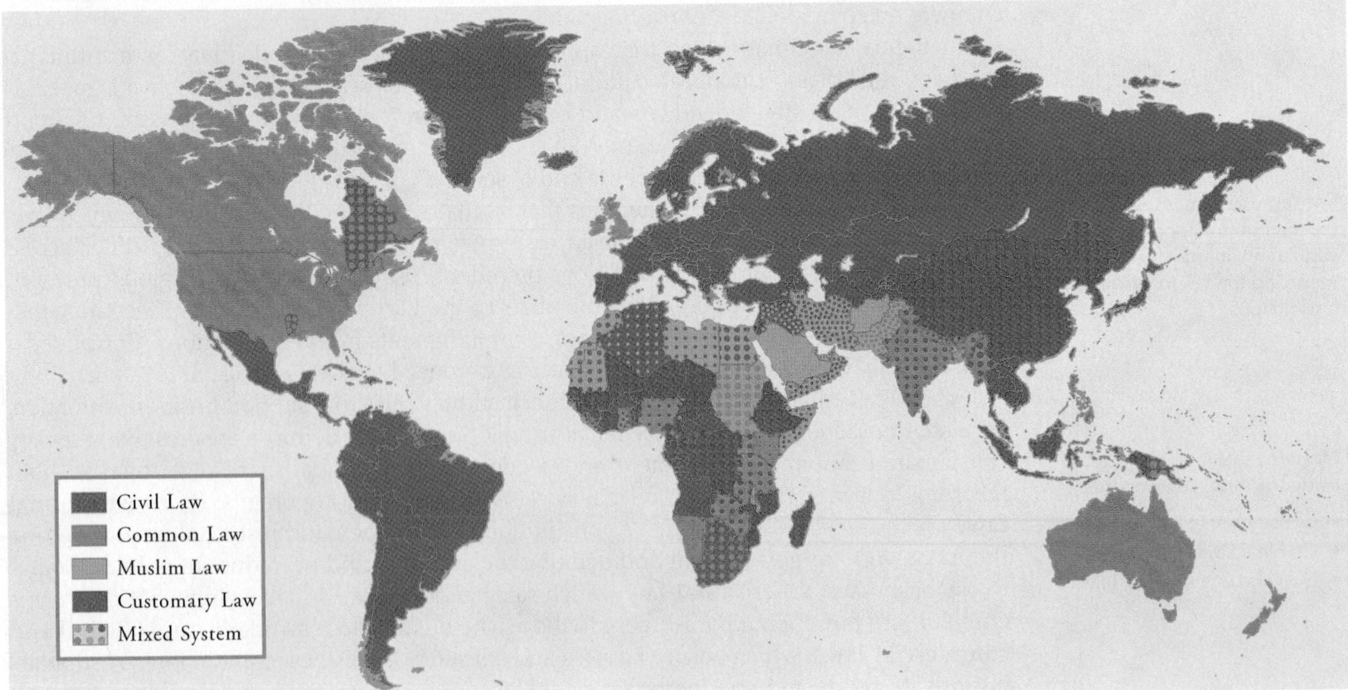

Common law is developed by judges through the decisions of courts.

Common Law A **common law** system relies on tradition, judge-made precedent, and usage. It respects established case law in resolving disputes. Judicial officials refer to statutory codes and legislation, but only after considering the rules of the court, custom, judicial reasoning, prior court decisions, and principles of equity. The doctrine of *stare decisis* is a distinguishing feature of the common law system—it obliges judges to respect the precedent established by prior court rulings.[114] The common law system has Anglo-American legacies; it prevails in, among others, Canada, the United States, India, Hong Kong, England, New Zealand, and Australia.

Civil law is based on strict application of statutory laws.

Civil Law A **civil law** system relies on the systematic codification of accessible, detailed laws. It assigns political officials, rather than government-employed judges, the responsibility to translate legal principles into a compendium of regulatory statues. Rather than create law, as they do in the common law system, judges apply the relevant statues to resolve disputes. In contrast to *stare decisis*, judicial officers in a civil law system are not bound by precedent. Precisely stipulated statutory codes, however, constrain their authority to interpret the law. Similarly, notaries public play minor roles in common law countries but are important gatekeepers as well as regulators of contracts and certificates in civil law systems. Civil law is the most widespread type of legal system in the world. It is used in various forms in approximately 150 countries, including Germany, France, Mexico, and Japan.

Theocratic law is based on the inspirations and instructions of religious teachings.

Theocratic Law A **theocratic law** system relies on religious doctrine, precepts, and beliefs. Ultimate legal authority is vested in religious leaders, who regulate business transactions and social relations based on their interpretation of a sacred text. For instance, Iran's president, Hassan Rouhani, defers to the final say of Iran's supreme leader, Ayatollah Ali Khamenei. Theocratic laws see no separation of church and state; government, law, and religion are one. The most prevalent theocratic system, Muslim or Islamic law (or *Shari'a*), is based on the Qur'an, the *Sunnah* (decisions and sayings of the Prophet Muhammad), the writings of Islamic scholars, and the consensus of legal communities in Muslim countries.[115] Muslim law prevails in the Middle East and northern Africa. However, modernists (e.g., Turkey, Indonesia), traditionalists (e.g., Kuwait, Malaysia), and fundamentalists (e.g., Iran, Saudi Arabia) advocate different interpretations of *Shari'a*.

Customary law is based on norms of behavior that gain legitimacy through long-term practice.

Customary Law A **customary law** system reflects the wisdom of daily experience or, more formally, enduring spiritual legacies and time-honored philosophical outlooks. It anchors legal systems in many indigenous communities, defining the rights and responsibilities of members. Legitimacy follows not from the stamp of a powerful person or sanctification by an institution, but from individuals recognizing the benefits of complying with community standards. Offenses are treated as torts—i.e., private wrongs or injuries rather than crimes against the state or society. Customary law prevails in many developing countries, particularly those in Africa.[116] Few nations operate under a wholly customary legal system. Instead, this type often plays a role in countries that have a mixed legal system.

Mixed System A **mixed legal system** emerges when a nation uses two or more of the preceding types. In a sense, legal pluralism results when two or more legal systems apply cumulatively or interactively. Map 3.3 shows that one finds most mixed legal systems in Africa and Asia. The Philippines, South Africa, and Guyana, for instance, follow a blend of civil and common law. Nigeria, Malaysia, and Kenya mix common, theocratic, and customary law. Bangladesh, Singapore, and Pakistan blend common and theocratic law. Indonesia, Djibouti, and Oman, conversely, blend theocratic law with civil codes.

CONCEPT CHECK

As we saw in Chapter 1, business environments vary. Granted, there are points of convergence, but conducting international business calls for recognizing the existence of fundamental differences across countries. Here, we stress that legal systems differ on a variety of principles and practices.

TRENDS IN LEGAL SYSTEMS

As the Third Wave of Democratization spread, the philosophy of individualism supplanted that of collectivism. Legally, this change promoted individual legal rights and instituted practices of due process. The law became more transparent, courts became more impartial, and officials became more accountable in many countries. Presently, democracy's retreat, by signaling the rise of strong states advocating collectivism, pushes managers to pinpoint likely changes in legal systems. Managers begin by accepting that authoritarian governments use the legal system to regulate business activity so that it unconditionally supports and sustains the state. There is no separation of law and state; the state uses the law to control public and private matters. Bluntly put, justice is not blind but arbitrary, oppressive, and state-serving.

Recall earlier observations on legal affairs in China. Doing business there, said an observer, means dealing with "a society that had...plenty of rules, but they were seldom enforced. China appeared to be run by masterful showmen: appearances mattered more than substance, rules were there to be distorted."[117] Moreover, the CCP's official status above the law further complicates determining what is right and what is wrong. China is not the exception. The Russian legal code is laced with ambiguities. Businesses, caution legal analysts, "cannot even keep track of the law, let alone decide whether to follow it."[118] Besides confusion, ambiguity renders the law as less about protecting the citizenry and more a tool of arbitrary and abusive state power.

CONCEPT CHECK

As developed in Chapter 2, a country's cultural orientation toward standards of accountability, equity, and fairness influences the prevailing principles in its legal environment.

The Basis of Rule Once relegated to the periphery of the global economy, emerging markets steadily command center stage. Their expanding markets increasingly frame managers' interpretation of legal trends. Most notably, the strong performance of emerging economies pushes managers to reassess the prevailing philosophical basis of law in order to understand how local officials will regulate the business environment. Specifically, the rise of emerging economies, along with their dissimilar conceptions of legality, requires that managers ask, "What is the *basis of rule* in a given country?" This question inevitably directs attention to the rule of man versus the rule of law.

The rule of man holds that the ruler, in whatever form, commands authority that is above the law.

The Rule of Man The **rule of man** holds that ultimate authority resides in a person whose word and whim, no matter how unfair or unjust, is law. For much of history, rulers and law were one and the same—the law was the will of the ruler, whether that ruler was called king, queen, lord, emperor, empress, shogun, czar, raj, chief, caliph, etc.[119] Today, these titles have largely given way to others, such as chairman, emir, comandante, generalissimo, dictator, supreme leader, or, in the case of North Korea, "Dear Leader." In whatever form and with whatever title, the rule of man defines a legal system in which the sovereign leader's actions are not restricted by a constitution, regulated by criminal codes, or open to opposition. For example, Saddam Hussein, former President of Iraq, imperiously declared that the "law is anything I write on a scrap of paper."[120] In China, furthermore, top-ranked party members accused of wrongdoing answer to the CCP first, not to the law of the land, precisely because "the Party sits outside, and above the law."[121]

The rule of man anchors the legal system in totalitarian states.

The rule of man is an instrumental device of totalitarianism. In effect, the sovereign leader creates the law, officials are the followers of the law, and the citizens its subjects. In such systems, the state uses the legal system to suppress threats to, and reward support for, its authority. Constitutional issues are discretionary, criminal law is arbitrary, and opportunism taints commercial and civil matters. The law is an apparatus of the state. Rather than deficient, justice is absent.

The rule of law holds that no individual is above laws that are clearly specified, commonly understood, and fairly enforced.

The Rule of Law The **rule of law** holds that no one, whether a public official or private citizen, is above the law. Thomas Jefferson, for instance, wrote in the Declaration of Independence that "all men are created equal" to hold forth that everyone, from kings to peasants, is subject to the same laws.[122] More symbolically, in front of courthouses worldwide stands a statue of a woman, carrying a sword and measuring balances, sometimes wearing a blindfold, sometimes with eyes closed. Her sword stands for the power of the court, her scales for the competing claims of the petitioners, and her blindfold signifies that justice is meted out objectively, without fear or favor, regardless of identity, power, or weakness. Justice is blind so that justice is impartial.

The rule of law holds that governmental authority is legitimately exercised in accordance with written, publicly disclosed laws. In such a system, citizens regard constitutional principles as legitimate, criminal codes as fair, and commercial/civil matters as just. Operationally, laws are clear, publicized, and protective of fundamental rights; they are developed, administered, and enforced transparently; all citizens have access to a competent, independent, and ethical judiciary; and all officials are accountable to the law of the land.[123] Rather than absent, justice is omnipresent.

Absent the rule of law, democracy struggles.[124] Operationally, it constrains state power and safeguards lives, liberty, and property. Instituting objective legal standards creates stability that encourages investment and growth. Finally, the rule of law defines the core of a just society and fortifies liberty. Protecting people from abusive and arbitrary government is vital, given that, as John Locke warned some three centuries ago, "Wherever law ends, tyranny begins."

IMPLICATIONS FOR MANAGERS

Originating in the Magna Carta of 1215, the concept of the rule of law anchored the legal evolution of many developed economies, most notably Great Britain, the United States, France, and Germany. Besides instituting a just political environment, the rule of law guarantees the enforceability of commercial contracts and business transactions while safeguarding property rights. Investors and companies rely on it to validate laws, codes, and statutes.

Uncertainty about the basis of law in a particular country complicates decision making in the MNE.

For example, in the West, property rights—namely, the exclusive authority to determine how one's property is used—are so taken for granted that they rarely cross our minds. We cannot say the same for many countries in Asia, Africa, the Middle East, and South America. There, the historic centrality of the rule of man makes the principles and practices of the rule of law odd abstractions. It has, at best, a negligible legacy in the legal traditions of many long-developing, now-emerging countries. As a result, property rights in countries like China, Venezuela, Saudi Arabia, Russia, and Vietnam are so arbitrarily protected that they are an enduring concern.[125] The rule of thumb for MNEs is straightforward: In countries where the rule of man is the basis of law, acceptable marketplace behavior is unpredictable. Managers stay alert to trumped-up charges, solicitation of bribes, and favoritism of local rivals.

Map 3.4 indicates that the rule of law prevails in wealthier, westernized countries—i.e., the United States, Canada, Japan, New Zealand, Australia, and most of Europe.[126] In contrast, the countries that fall in the long crescent that starts in northern Russia, cuts southward through China, circles down to South East Asia, moves on toward the Middle East, and extends through Africa over to South America show the far greater pervasiveness of the rule of man. Conclusion? The rule of man anchors the legal systems of many of today's emerging countries. Managers, eyeing these fast-growing markets, realize that where there is no formal law officially in place, society typically defaults to the rule of man.

THE CONFOUND OF DEMOCRACY'S RETREAT

The tendency toward totalitarianism in many developing countries complicates legal circumstances. Again, look at Map 3.4. Every country that Freedom House rates as "Partly Free" or "Not Free" lies along the "rule of man crescent." The same goes for countries rated as Hybrid or Authoritarian states by the EIU. Uncertainty about the basis of law and the goals of government in much of the world creates a disconcerting situation for managers. Operating in Western economies grants them the benefit of a consistent application of legitimate laws. Few developing countries offer such safeguards.

In Germany, for example, action taken by foreign firms against local companies that counterfeit their products consistently proves decisive. Violators are restrained and punished. In Belarus or Kazakhstan, however, the same sorts of legal actions typically prove pointless. There, as in other rule-of-man systems, writs, injunctions, and lawsuits are trapped in a slow-grinding legal machine that answers to the leader, not to legitimate legal standards.[127]

MAP 3.4 The Worldwide Practice of the Rule of Law

The *rule of law* holds that government authority is legitimate only when it is exercised according to written laws and established enforcement procedures. The coding of this map is based on the degree a country does so. Therefore, for example, the United States at the 90th percentile indicates the pervasiveness of the rule of law. Conversely, Venezuela's classification below the 10th percentile indicates the pervasiveness of the rule of man.

Source: Based on World Bank, *Governance Matters VI: Governance Indicators for 1996–2011*, retrieved April 15, 2013 from http://info.worldbank.org/governance/wgi/worldmap.asp See also Kaufmann D., A. Kraay, and M. Mastruzzi (2010), The Worldwide Governance Indicators: Methodology and Analytical Issues, retrieved April 15, 2013 from info.worldbank.org/governance/wgi/pdf/WGI.pdf. http://info.worldbank.org/governance/wgi/worldmap.asp

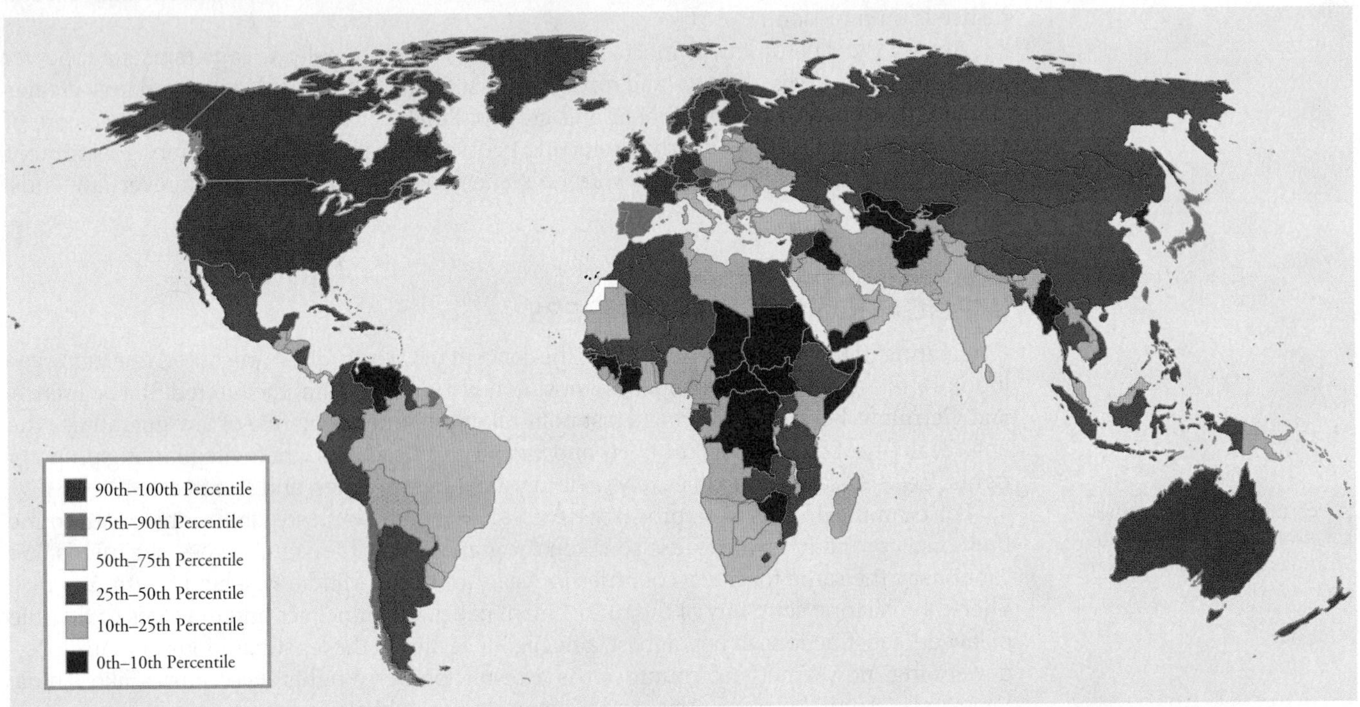

Violators in the good graces of the "man," whether Alexander Lukashenko of Belarus or Nursultan Nazarbayev of Kazakhastan, flourish.[128]

Certainly, a prudent MNE could opt to avoid such markets. In fact, this strategy had long been the case. Until 2000 or so, the question of the basis of law in developing countries was largely inconsequential. Markets in the West provided a wealth of opportunities for productive, profitable activity. Developing markets were on the periphery of the global economy, serving mainly as sources of raw materials. The occasional dispute between the adventurous Western company and the locals was typically resolved in the favor of the former. Now, slowing growth in the West, aggravated by the aftermath of the financial crisis, moves the fast-growing emerging economies to the center of the global market. Their supply of inexpensive, productive resources along with accelerating local demand is a siren call few MNEs can resist. As GE's CEO reasoned, "We've globalized around markets... Today we go to Brazil, we go to China, we go to India because that's where the customers are."[129] Going forward, the McKinsey Global Institute reports that 400 midsize emerging-market cities—many unfamiliar in the West—such as Sanaa, Ibadan, Ouagadougou, Chittagong, Kinshasa, and Bamako, will generate nearly 40 percent of global growth over the next 15 years. As a result, and as suggested in our opening profile of China, MNEs long accustomed to the rule of law increasingly operate in markets anchored in the rule of man.

WHICH RULE WHEN?

Some hypothesize that developing countries, especially fast-growing emerging economies like China, Argentina, Russia, Nigeria, Peru, Saudi Arabia, Thailand, and Malaysia, will follow the precedent of developed countries and eventually accept the legitimacy of the rule of law.

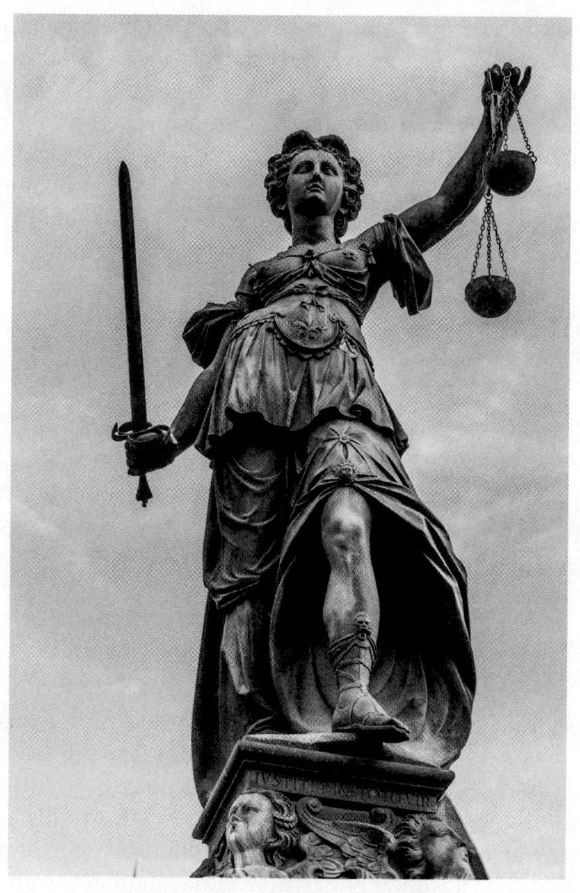

Lady Justice, here seen at Römer Square in Frankfurt, Germany, is an allegorical personification of the moral force of the rule of law.
Source: klickable/Fotolia

As Western countries moved from agrarian to industrial economies, their societies increasingly saw the need to sanction and protect property rights. Ongoing economic development, in turn, required a legal system that no longer appealed to the "man" in power but to the written law for guidance and resolution. Therefore, extrapolating from Western history, some presume that the shift from agrarianism to industrialism in developing countries will accelerate their adoption of the rule of law. The Third Wave of Democracy, with ideological change anchored in the Washington Consensus, bolstered this scenario.

CONCEPT CHECK

Chapter 1 suggests that democratic political systems grant MNEs the freedom to engage in their preferred modes of international business. Note, however, that democracy's retreat creates uncertainty about operating in particular countries. Nations use their legal systems to encourage, regulate, or prohibit certain modes.

Recent circumstances, however, complicate the projected progression. Democracy's retreat has slowed, if not reversed, progress precisely because the rule of law is antithetical to totalitarianism—one cannot be the "man" if one must answer to the law. More practically, China's economic performance tests the thesis that a positive relationship exists between the rule of law, economic growth, and prosperity.[130] China's status as the world's largest recipient of foreign investment over the past few decades, notwithstanding corruption within a system of crony capitalism administered by the absolute authority of the CCP, questions the necessity of the rule of law. Similar situations in Russia, Venezuela, Saudi Arabia, and Turkmenistan, among others, require foreign investors to qualify their forecasts. Now, the more plausible scenario is one in which emerging economies will arguably migrate from one basis of rule to another—that is, from rule of man to "rule *by* law" and its implicit notion that even the ruler is subject to the law. Growing cries from expanding middle class for stronger property rights, by improving the accountability of public officials, will then lay the foundation for society to accept the legitimacy of the rule *of* law.

Then again, in order to advise folks in emerging economies, one must qualify this interpretation in light of national legacies. The forecast of the rule of law as the inevitable end-state presumes that the particular legal philosophies of the West apply to countries throughout the world. Instead, some argue that the "West does not know best," reasoning that the

The growing confidence of emerging economies increasingly questions the long-running presumption that "the West knows best."

efficiency and stability of a progressive, autocratic ruler are often more important than the liberty and freedom of a messy democracy. Said one Western analyst, "One-party autocracy certainly has its drawbacks. But when it is led by a reasonably enlightened group of people, as China is today, it can also have great advantages."[131] Indeed, throughout its storied 5000-year history, Chinese civilization has never practiced democratic governance based on the rule of law. Instead, while dynasties periodically changed, each adopted authoritarian governance that imposed the rule of man. Consequently, managers watch and learn as changing economic environments, which we profile more precisely in Chapter 4, influence the basis of law.

LEGAL ISSUES IN INTERNATIONAL BUSINESS

Differences in political ideologies often pose operating problems. The fact that countries use diverse legal principles to regulate the business environment aggravates this situation. Moreover, new forms of business activity along with changing patterns of trade and investment put MNEs in uncertain legal situations. In the following, we profile legal aspects of day-to-day decision-making in the MNE.

OPERATIONAL CONCERNS

Operational concerns that managers face worldwide include

- Starting a business.
- Entering and enforcing contracts.
- Hiring and firing workers.
- Closing a business.

MNEs obey local laws on starting, running, and closing a business. Activities such as hiring workers, obtaining credit, protecting investors, paying taxes, trading across borders, and enforcing contracts must comply with applicable laws. In theory, business regulations are efficiently designed, easily accessible, and straightforwardly administered. Moreover, simple, well-designed work rules discourage corruption by removing the incentive to bribe regulators. The World Bank, along with the World Economic Forum, concludes that better business conditions consistently boost economic growth, job creation, and trade.

Despite these virtues, big companies and individuals often experience the opposite. Wal-Mart has run into a firestorm of controversy over its bribery practices in Mexico. In defense, Wal-Mart held that the convoluted, often contradictory Mexican legal code pushed it to protect its competitiveness with well-placed bribes.[132] Similarly, at the micro level, a Brazilian entrepreneur recalled his experience in starting up his first company in his home country, where obtaining authorizations, licenses, and permits to start a new business—from seven different ministries—took about 150 days. When he started a U.S.-based business, however,"within a week I had formed an LLC (limited liability corporation), incorporated in Delaware, and set up bank accounts."[133]

The globalization of markets progressively standardizes legal systems. Attracting foreign investors requires positive reputations and records. Memberships in international organizations accelerate this trend. The European Union requires all member countries to satisfy standards for the rule of law; the World Bank requires borrowers to agree to legal reforms; the WTO imposes a raft of legal obligations. Despite this convergence, enduring variability differentiates how countries regulate basic business operations. The World Bank evaluates several features of the business environment, studying how the role of regulation influences economic performance. Table 3.3 provides a cross-country snapshot of some of the variation involved in starting, running, and closing a business.

CONCEPT CHECK

A theme of the text is the linkages among individuals, companies, countries, and institutions. Here, we emphasize the importance of relationships between ideas and ideals, namely the interplay among a country's type of political system, its organizing legal philosophy, and its prevailing doctrine of law. Making these connections helps managers assess the systemic nature of the country's business environment.

Getting Started Starting a business involves activities such as registering a name, choosing the appropriate tax structure, obtaining licenses and permits, arranging credit, and securing insurance. Some countries expedite this process; others do not. For example, start-up is a straightforward process in Australia, requiring one registration procedure that encompasses tax, labor, and administrative declarations. Conversely, India imposes 13 procedural requirements, including regulations for bank deposits, court registration, health benefits, and so on. The upshot: it takes about two days to start a business in Australia but about 30 days in India.

TABLE 3.3 The Rules of the Game

The World Bank tracks micro-level characteristics of the regulatory frameworks in 185 economies. Comparative information on the rules of the game encourages officials to streamline their legal systems, thereby improving the efficiency of national business environments. Here we highlight data for a subsample of countries in terms of opening, running, and closing a business.

Economy	Starting a Business			Enforcing Contracts			Closing a Business		
	Number of Procedures[1]	Time (Days)	Cost (% of income per capita)	Number of Procedures[2]	Time[3] (Days)	Cost* (% of Claim)	Recovery rate (C on the $)	Time (Years)	Cost[5] (% of Estate)
Australia	2	2	0.7	28	395	21.8	80.8	1	8
Brail	13	119	5.4	45	731	16.5	17.1	4	12
Canada	1	5	0.4	36	570	22.3	90.7	.8	4
Chad	11	55	175.5	41	743	45.7	0	4	6
China	14	38	3.6	37	406	11.1	36.1	1.7	22
France	5	7	0.9	29	390	17.4	45.0	1.9	9
Germany	9	15	6	30	394	14.4	82.7	1.2	8
Guatemala	12	37	52.5	31	1459	26.5	27.5	3	15
India	12	29	46.8	46	1420	39.6	27.6	4.3	9
Japan	8	23	7.5	30	360	32.2	92.7	.6	4
Korea, Rep.	8	14	7.5	35	230	10.3	82.3	1.5	4
Russian	8	29	2.3	36	281	13.4	41.5	2	9
United States	6	6	1.4	32	300	14.4	81.5	1.5	7
United Kingdom	6	13	0.7	28	399	24.8	88.5	1	6

Source: Compiled from "Doing Business 2012," The World Bank.

Notes
[1] Number of procedures to complete before starting a business.
[2] Number of procedures that require interaction between the parties to the dispute or between them and the judge or court officer.
[3] Average number of days from when the plaintiff files the lawsuit in court until settlement.
[4] Average cost incurred during dispute resolution, including court fees and attorney fees.
[5] Average cost of bankruptcy process, including court costs, insolvency practitioners' costs, and associated expenses.

At least one can take comfort in avoiding the same in Suriname— starting up there involves 13 procedures spanning 694 days.

For the sake of clarity, we restrict our discussion primarily to first-order effects of day-to-day operations for a small to medium-size enterprise. Keep in mind that activities, such as a business start-up, can be quite complicated for large MNEs. For instance, when entering India, multi-brand foreign chains, such as Wal-Mart, Carrefour, IKEA, and Tesco, face a battery of regulations. Notably, they must operate as joint ventures, have no higher than a 51 percent ownership share, direct at least half of their capital investments into processing infrastructure, and open outlets only in cities that have at least 1 million residents.[134]

Making and Enforcing Contracts Once up and running, companies enter and enforce contracts with buyers and sellers.[135] The sanctity of a contract is vital to business transactions. The United Nations Convention on Contracts for the International Sale of Goods sets guidelines for negotiating and enforcing contracts. Still, standards vary across different legal systems. Countries using a common law system, for instance, encourage precise, detailed contracts, whereas those with a civil law system encourage less specific agreements.

Similar tendencies show up in contract-enforcement policies. Australia, Norway, and the United Kingdom impose the fewest number of enforcement procedures. Burundi, Angola, Bolivia, Cameroon, El Salvador, Mexico, and Panama require many procedures. Singapore needs 150 days to enforce a contract, the United States about 300 days, and Timor-Leste some 1,800 days. On average, across 185 countries, a firm is looking at 615 days to settle a contract dispute.

Hiring and Firing No matter where you are operating, you will have to hire and, when necessary, fire workers. One would think that common sense would guide legally appropriate decisions. Legal standards around the world, however, are rarely straightforward. Moreover, local laws cover virtually every aspect of employment—how workers are hired, what they are paid, how many hours they can work, and whether they can be fired.

Singapore, New Zealand, and the United States are among the countries with the most flexible labor-regulation statutes. China provides the most flexibility in hiring and firing and the greatest discretion in setting employment conditions (work hours, minimum wages, and benefits). In contrast, Angola, Belarus, and Paraguay restrict firing employees and impose generous severance payments.

Slow-moving bureaucracies often complicate business regulation. Mexico last overhauled its labor law in the 1970s; hence, sacking a worker after a year of employment costs three times as much as in Chile, and eight times more than in Brazil. Mexico's higher severance costs further constrain firms' flexibility.[136] Regarding bureaucracy, India's national government imposes 55 labor laws while its various states add another 150 or so. Its Industrial Disputes Act, for example, requires any company employing 100 or more workers to obtain state permission before firing anyone, even if it has hit hard times.[137]

Getting Out or Going Under Closing a business involves more than padlocking the doors. In the United States, for example, the Internal Revenue Service requires reporting the sale of assets, payments to subcontractors, and termination of retirement plans. In the West, the bankruptcy process is anchored in the English bankruptcy law of 1732, the first modern law to address this issue, and its progressive revision, beginning in 1800, by the United States.

Ireland, Japan, Canada, and Hong Kong make closing the doors both fast (between four to eight months) and cheap (between 1 and 10 percent of the estate). The situation differs in developing countries. India's lack of a comprehensive bankruptcy code complicates dealing with creditors, officials, and courts, which in turn discourages bankruptcy. Consequently, only four of every 10,000 firms go bankrupt in India, compared with 350 per 10,000 firms in the United States.[138] Bankruptcy in Indonesia, Vietnam, and Ecuador is slow (between five to eight years) and expensive (between 10 and 30 percent of the estate). Several countries, including Burundi, Sudan, Cambodia, Afghanistan, Guinea-Bissau, and Dominica, stipulate no standards to govern dissolution.

A KEY RELATIONSHIP: WEALTH AND REGULATION

CONCEPT CHECK

Chapters 1 and 2 note that income and wealth influence the actions that countries, both rich and poor, take to develop their business environments. Correspondingly, these factors also influence countries' approach to regulating MNEs local operations.

Data indicate an inverse relationship between a nation's general wealth and its regulation of business activity. In a nutshell, richer countries regulate less and poorer countries regulate more. In high-income countries (e.g., the United States, France, Japan), starting a business requires an average of 6.28 procedures, spans 18 days, and costs 7 percent of per capita income. Doing the same in middle-income countries (e.g., Mexico, Poland, Malaysia, China, India, South Africa), requires an average of 7.8 procedures, spans 36 days, and costs 28 percent of per capita income. Lastly, in low-income countries (e.g., Bangladesh, Ethiopia, Nepal), one is facing 7.5 procedures, a 90-day span, and 37 percent of per capita income. Furthermore, legal systems in wealthier nations tend to regulate operational activities more consistently than do those in poorer countries—as one would expect, given the prevalence of the rule of law in the former and the rule of man in the latter.[139]

Richer countries typically regulate business activities less. Poorer countries typically regulate more.

Table 3.4 identifies the top-ranked and bottom-ranked countries whose legal policies enact the most or least supportive business environments. In terms of the former, Singapore has developed a comprehensive legal code that fosters the most favorable business environment in the world. Conversely, the Central African Republic's legal shortcomings create the world's least favorable business environment. These rankings confirm an important relationship: most of the top-ranked countries in Table 3.4 have a democratic political system and a common or civil law legal system anchored in the rule of law. In contrast, most of the bottom-ranked countries exhibit authoritarian politics and a mixed legal system anchored in the rule of man.

TABLE 3.4 Easy Here, Hard There: Doing Business in Various Countries

The World Bank ranks 185 countries on their respective ease of doing business—the higher the score, the more favorable the business environment. Technically, the ease of business index averages the country's percentile rankings on ten dimensions: starting a business, dealing with construction permits, employing workers, registering property, getting credit, protecting investors, paying taxes, trading across borders, and enforcing contracts. Here we see the best and worst performers.

Country	Ranking	Country	Ranking
Singapore	1	Niger	176
Hong Kong SAR, China	2	Côte d'Ivoire	177
New Zealand	3	Guinea	178
United States	4	Guinea-Bissau	179
Denmark	5	Venezuela	180
Norway	6	Congo, Dem. Rep.	181
United Kingdom	7	Eritrea	182
South Korea	8	Congo, Republic	183
Georgia	9	Chad	184
Australia	10	Central African Republic	185

Source: Doing Business 2013, The World Bank, Retrieved August 15, 2013.

STRATEGIC CONCERNS

Strategic concerns that managers face worldwide include

- Product origin and local content.
- Marketplace behavior.
- Legal jurisdiction.
- Product safety and liability.
- Intellectual property protection.

Routine concerns focus managers' attention on the day-to-day operations of opening, running, and closing a business. Strategic concerns direct their attention to long-term issues that shape the competitiveness, profitability, and sustainability of the firm. A country's legal environment influences each aspect, shaping an MNE's strategic decisions on making a product, marketing it, and safeguarding its proprietary features. Let's inspect some key concerns.

COUNTRY CHARACTERISTICS

National laws affect the flow of products across borders. To determine charges for the right to import a product, host governments devise laws that consider the product's **country of origin**—the country where it was grown, produced, or manufactured. Some countries apply this policy to product labels, under the title COOL (country-of-origin labeling), to inform consumers and support local producers. National security concerns also shape country-of-origin regulations. Suspicion about the espionage capabilities of their communication products dog Huawei and ZTE. Both China-headquartered companies are marked by opaque governance and tight linkages with the Communist Party of China. National security concerns have led Australia, Canada, and US authorities to exclude their network equipment products from public contracts.[140]

CONCEPT CHECK

Recall from Chapter 2 that culture influences attitudes toward the development and ownership of ideas. Certain attitudes, particularly those toward workplace motivation and relationships, influence entrepreneurial behavior in a country. Likewise, attitudes toward collective and individual priorities shape a nation's competitive environment.

Politicians also enact regulations to protect jobs, appease voters, placate special interests, and preserve tax revenue. Not surprisingly, host governments prefer that MNEs make the greatest possible portion of their product(s) locally. Besides boosting local enterprise, technology transfers and knowledge spillovers support domestic innovation. To spur reluctant companies, governments enforce **local content** regulations. Brazil, for instance, levies a 30 percent tax increase on imported cars with less than 65 percent local content.[141] Likewise, Brazil requires foreign energy firms to spend 1 percent of gross revenue on local R&D.

PRODUCT SAFETY AND LIABILITY

Product safety regulations set by the European Union shape standards worldwide.

Countries regularly impose product-safety and liability laws that require an MNE to adapt a product or else forsake market access. As a rule, wealthier countries impose stringent standards, whereas poorer countries, reflecting developing legal codes and rule-of-man legacies, apply inconsistent ones. The European Union's product-liability directive shapes global standards.[142] It outlines the legal responsibility of manufacturers and stipulates the process of product-liability compensation claims. Then again, some MNEs proactively preempt the risk. The Danish toy maker Lego, for instance, noted consumers' fear of the possible toxicity of plastic toys made in China and did not open a factory there. Instead, Lego opted for factories in comparatively more expensive but less worrisome Mexico and Eastern Europe.[143]

LEGAL JURISDICTION

The addition of a choice-of-law clause to contracts between different parties in different countries is an effective legal safeguard.

Countries stipulate the criteria for litigation when agents—whether legal residents of the same or of different countries—are unable to resolve a dispute. Usually, in the face of a cross-national dispute, each company petitions its home-country court to claim jurisdiction in the belief that it will likely receive more favorable treatment. This situation is especially pressing when a MNE from a rule-of-law system has legal difficulties in a rule-of-man environment. Worry about legal proceedings in certain legal systems leads MNEs to specify a **choice-of-law clause** in contracts that stipulates whose laws, if necessary, govern dispute resolution. Importantly, it obliges both parties to negotiate a compromise in the event the law changes. Without binding arbitration agreements, companies and consumers travel in legal limbo. Unless the foreign company has local operations, determining legal jurisdiction does not hold it accountable to a nation's legal system.

INTELLECTUAL PROPERTY

Intellectual property is the general term for creative ideas, expertise, or intangible insights that grant its owner a competitive advantage.

In Adam Smith's time, countries drew strength from their agricultural prowess. Later, smokestack industries defined a nation's prosperity and power. Now countries look to their brainpower to create might, prestige, and wealth. We call the output of this brainpower **intellectual property (IP)**—the creative ideas, innovative expertise, or intangible insights that create a competitive advantage for an individual, company, or country. The growing power of ideas in the global economy has made the protection of intellectual property a flashpoint of controversy.

Intellectual property rights refer to the right to control and derive the benefits from writing (copyright), inventions (patents), processes (trade secrets), and identifiers (trademarks).

Mainstream thought holds that the right to claim ownership of intellectual property stimulates innovation. Transnational institutions—notably, the World Intellectual Property Organization (WIPO), along with governments and industry associations—push for stronger protection. The primary safeguard is an **intellectual property right (IPR)** that grants the registered owners of inventions, literary and artistic works, and symbols, names, images, or designs the right to determine the use of their property. In other words, an IPR grants the registered owner of a copyright the legal authority to decide who may use the property and under what circumstances. Essentially, an IPR constitutes a legally enforceable but limited monopoly granted by a country to the innovator. It specifies a period during which other parties may not copy an idea so that the innovator can commercialize it. MNEs invest great effort to safeguard intellectual property, relying on tools like patents, trademark registrations, and copyrights.

The predominant share of counterfeit products is made in countries in which the rule of man prevails.

The pervasiveness of piracy worldwide testifies to the difficulty of enforcing IPRs. Our closing case, "It's a Knockoff World," profiles these problems. Weak enforcement in some countries, particularly those marked by a rule of man bias and authoritarian politics, impose obstacles. Other problems arise because not all countries support the various agreements that protect IPRs—primarily, the Paris Convention for the Protection of Industrial Property and the Berne Convention for the Protection of Literary and Artistic Works, both created in the 1880s and updated periodically. The WTO's Trade-Related Aspects of Intellectual Property Rights (TRIPS) broadens protection while, more recently, the EU is moving toward a "unitary patent" recognized automatically in all member countries.

Matters of jurisdiction complicate protection. A U.S. patent, for example, establishes IPR only in the United States and its territories and possessions; it does not extend to foreign markets. Further, there's no shortcut to worldwide protection; companies cannot register a "global" patent, trademark, or copyright. Although an IPR sounds secure, enforcing it often proves difficult. For example, in the United States, companies can go after the makers and sellers, not users, of counterfeit goods.[144] Worldwide, governments claim to abide by these agreements and enforce IPRs. However, piracy increasingly threatens popular or pricey products.

THE BASIS OF POLITICAL AND LEGAL DIFFERENCES

A key theme of this chapter is that inalienable differences exist between countries regarding political practice and legal regulation. Students new to the study of international business often find it helpful to understand the historical, economic, and cognitive basis for these differences. As we just saw, IP is a critical component of the development of any economy, no matter how rich or poor. Whereas some countries steadfastly affirm strong protection, others are less inclined. Still others turn a blind eye, informally sanctioning piracy. Making sense of the differences in attitudes and outlooks, as would be the case for other political or legal issues, follows from making sense of the effects of *historical legacies, economic conditions*, and *cultural orientations*.

HISTORICAL LEGACIES

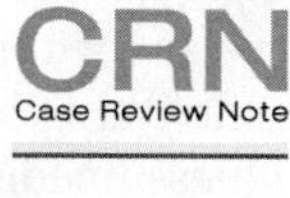

Most counterfeit goods are made in markets in which the rule of man is the *de facto* legal system. A return trip to China, given its legal tradition, its influence, and its sluggishness in protecting IP, highlights the scope of the problem. Officially, China has a battery of laws that comply with international standards for market access, nondiscrimination, and transparency. However, many Chinese citizens and officials question the legitimacy of laws passed by foreign governments. Hence, foreign-made laws are inconsistently enforced in the local marketplace. This gap between domestic traditions and foreign standards, explained a Chinese jurist, means that its IP laws "exist to protect Chinese IP from foreign IP."[145] This situation is not unique to China. The Asian Development Bank evaluated the performance of Indonesia, Malaysia, the Philippines, South Korea, and Thailand relative to the rest of the world on measures of good governance: accountability, political stability, government effectiveness, regulatory quality, control of corruption, and rule of law. Over the past decade, their performance has deteriorated on nearly every dimension.[146]

Countries that observe the rule of law, as opposed to the rule of man, more aggressively protect intellectual property rights.

Calls for China (as well as Vietnam, Russia, Chad, India, Malaysia, to name just a few of the many with similar records) to protect IP in the context of the rule of law may eventually prove successful. Still, few anticipate quick progress. Advised a partner of Jones Day Shanghai, the "trend in China is toward more transparency, but it's likely to be a 20-year process....even then, it will be far from the standards in the United States."[147] For China, the legal legacy of two millennia of the rule of man—or, in its current form, the rule of the CCP—suggests that such a change may be "one of the largest social infrastructure projects in the history of mankind."[148]

ECONOMIC CIRCUMSTANCES

The vigor of IP protection often reflects a country's stage of economic development. Just as poorer countries regulate less rigorously than richer countries, so too do they more weakly protect IP.[149] In the case of developed countries, folks reason that protecting IP is the best way to energize innovation. "If the stuff you create can be misappropriated," noted an analyst, "your incentive for continuing to create valuable IP diminishes significantly."[150] Strong protection has created extensive IP in the West. Individuals and companies from developed countries control virtually all IP rights: Presently, they hold nearly 95 percent of all patents worldwide. In addition, 80 percent of patents granted in developing countries belong to residents of wealthy countries.[151]

Generally, poorer countries protect intellectual property less vigilantly than do wealthier countries.

The evolving world economy, especially the market moves powered by emerging economies, alters transnational institutional structures and legal outlooks.[152] Popular perspectives in developing countries advocate less-stringent protection, arguing that IP rights are better interpreted as predatory, monopoly privileges that impose costs by:

- stifling the creativity, innovation, and emulation that support technological and cultural advance.
- inhibiting local development and lowering global welfare by constraining the use of existing knowledge.
- creating intellectual monopolies that protect business interests, bestow monopoly profits, and lessen the efficiency gains of free trade.
- inflating the prices that poor nations pay for products and processes that are available only from wealthy nations.
- stipulating licensing fees and regulatory burdens that increase the cost of idea creation and slow the diffusion of innovations.

In sum, goes this reasoning, property rights are a state-created privilege that impoverishes the majority in order to concentrate wealth and power among the privileged.[153] For example, in practical terms, critics in poor countries charge their rich counterparts with promoting strong IP protection to camouflage their intent to dismantle their generic drug industries.

Critics of intellectual property protection argue that granting monopoly rights imposes hardships, creates inefficiencies, and slows innovation.

This debate will twist and turn for many years. In the meantime, hard economics is likely the key determinant of a country's protection of IPRs. Poor people have little money to spend on necessities, let alone for expensive branded goods sold by foreign companies. In Kenya, where the average annual income is about $1,800, it should not come as a surprise that many Kenyans "think you have to cheat to survive."[154] One means of survival is buying pirated copies of products that improve productivity (i.e., software), fight illness (medicines), or provide relief (consumer products).

CULTURAL ORIENTATION

Different attitudes toward IP protection reflect cultural orientations. Individualist countries such as the United States and Australia regard personal property rights as intrinsically legitimate: if you create something, you should have the right to say who can use it or copy it for any given purpose. In contrast, collectivist countries such as South Korea, Thailand, and China extol the virtue of sharing over individual ownership: if you create something, it should improve the welfare of society. Asked about piracy in his country, for example, a South Korean diplomat explained, "Historically, Koreans have not viewed intellectual discoveries or scientific inventions as the private property of the discoverers or inventors. New ideas or technologies [are] 'public goods' for everybody to share freely. Cultural esteem rather than material gain [is] the incentive for creativity."[155]

Similarly, countries often interpret and enforce intellectual protection differently. For example, 2013 saw India's Supreme Court reaffirm Indian drug makers' right to apply a process that differed from that recorded by the registered owner to produce and sell drugs patented in other countries; in other words, Indian patent law protects only the "processes" by which drugs are made, not the drugs themselves.[156] Hence, Indian drug companies make copycat versions of many of the world's best medicines and sell them for far less. For example, leukemia treatment Gleevec, developed by Switzerland-based Novartis, costs patients up to $70,000 per year; the Indian generic versions run about $2,500 annually. Not surprisingly, India is the world's leading exporter of generic medicine. It, along with China, makes more than 80 percent of the active ingredients of all drugs used in the United States.[157]

Cultural attitudes influence the protection of intellectual property rights. Individualist societies are more vigilant than collectivist societies.

Today, technologies challenge the influence of individualism and collectivism in the use and abuse of IP. Among some demographics, whether in collectivist China or individualist United States, piracy is an increasingly mainstream behavior. On one hand, hard economics spurs theft; more poor people seek affordable options, egality notwithstanding. Alternatively, the prevalence of piracy among teenagers and young adults in rich and poor countries alike reflects evolving attitudes and technological opportunism. Said the general counsel for NBC Universal, speaking of illegal file downloading, "Young people, in particular, conclude that if it's so easy, it can't be wrong."[158] Improving technologies, by making piracy cheaper and easier, accelerate the violation of IP rights.

THE POTENTIAL FOR CROSS-NATIONAL CONVERGENCE

Convincing countries to protect IP confronts a potent mix of legal legacies, economic conditions, and cultural orientations. Institutional initiatives try to expedite stronger enforcement. The WTO, for example, gives wealthy countries a year to comply with its latest rules on IP but grants poorer countries five- to 10-year grace periods. Longer grace periods, the thinking goes, acknowledges economic realities while building awareness of the benefits of protecting IP. Rising piracy rates suggest these programs struggle to make a difference.

Ironically, calls for stronger protection hinge on the future success of companies in currently lax countries. History shows that countries that create IP—no matter their legal legacy, economic status, or cultural orientation—ultimately enforce property rights.[159] As countries evolve from idea consumers to idea creators, they invent products based on their own IP. At some point, countries cross the threshold where the benefits of protection exceed the gains from piracy. Observers note that the United States, today a staunch defender of IPRs, copied other countries' intellectual property when it was a developing country in the eighteenth century. Said one analyst, "American political independence was founded on the notion of economic self-sufficiency. And technology piracy became the premier tool to industrial development."[160] Inventing its own IP eventually led the United States to endorse the Paris and Berne Conventions, both of which originated in the 1880s. From then on, the U.S. has steadfastly advocated strong IP rights.

Countries that generate intellectual property are strong advocates of ownership rights.

Trends in China signal the start of this process. Long the factory floor of the world, China aims to be the new product lab. Presently, its patent office leads the world in patent applications; of the 2.14 million patent applications filed worldwide in 2011, 526,000 were filed in China, followed by the U.S. with 504,000, Japan with 343,000, and South Korea at 179,000. Although many Chinese patents file minor modifications, a growing share registers significant "invention" patents that grant the holder 20 years of protection (the same as in the West). Going forward, the Chinese government has a goal of 2 million domestic patent applications annually by 2015, with the aim of being one of the top two patent-owning countries by 2020.[161] Already, we see Chinese firms such as Huawei and ZTE battling each other over patent violations. Tension will likely escalate as Chinese firms, intent on protecting their expanding IP, demand the legal system police pirates. Right now, the signals from Chinese officials and companies are confusing—increasing piracy yet increasing patent activity.[162] The resolution of this conundrum—will China stay a pirate's paradise or become a property protector?—will shape IP practices throughout the world.[163]

CASE It's a Knockoff World

I stride toward ground zero of counterfeiting—the notorious Silk Market of Beijing. As do more than 10 million people a year, I enter a 35,000-square-meter, seven-level piracy temple, packed with nearly 2,000 small stalls staffed by thousands of hard-charging, take-no-prisoner vendors offering cheap knockoffs of the leading branded products in the world. Navigating a surreal bazaar gone wild, I scan stalls boldly displaying bogus Louis Vuitton luggage, Prada purses, Hugo Boss shirts, and Hermes scarves; depending on how well you negotiate, each can be had for an absurd fraction of the price of the genuine version. Moving on, stall after stall offers infamous "copywatches," Nike gear, Sony Jump Drives, Wii Remotes, Gillette razors, UGG footwear, Oakley sunglasses, Zeiss binoculars, Nikon lenses, North Face jackets—one after another, in a seemingly endless procession of premier brand names. Despite spot-on cosmetic resemblance, virtually all is counterfeit. Moving around, I come to digital zones, finding copies of software, music, games, and movies. Rack upon rack displays products from some of the best and the brightest minds of the world, now selling for ludicrously low prices—Microsoft Windows for about a buck, Microsoft Office for $0.75, Call of Duty or Wii Guitar Hero for a buck, Photoshop for two bucks, AutoCAD for five dollars. Each stall is packed with an ever-changing collage of customers—Germans, Indians, Canadians, Brazilians, British, Americans, and on and on—each getting past the initial shock, and many buying multiple titles.

—Daniel Sullivan's ramble through the Silk Market, Beijing, March 2012

Companies are dogged by piracy—the illegal imitating, copying, or counterfeiting of their registered products. It's a tense issue given that it cuts to issues of innovation, history, culture, politics, and prosperity. Making matters worse is that pirates, besides being everywhere, come in every form: individuals making unauthorized copies at work, imitators laboring in dingy sweatshops, and hardened criminals running global networks.

The problem, basically, is this: IP in the form of books, music, product designs, brand names, process innovations, software, film, and the like is tough to conceive but remarkably easy to copy. Moreover, notwithstanding moral shortcomings, pirates do not lack initiative or imagination. In our knockoff world, if it's being made, it's being faked. Counterfeiters leave no product category untouched. Fair game includes virtually everything—from the humble aspirin to the flashy Ferrari.[164] And, for the kicker, knockoffs sell for a fraction of the price of the real thing to eager buyers worldwide.

Big Money, Big Risks

IP theft is big business.[165] Globalization and the Internet fuel the perfect storm, the former moving much of the world's manufacturing to countries with poor IP protection, the latter providing cheap, easily accessible marketing platforms and distribution channels. The costs of counterfeit IP—e.g., lost sales, eroded consumer confidence, diminished brand reputation, dangerous products, enforcement expenses, and legal costs—is staggering. The International Anti-Counterfeiting Coalition (IACC) estimates that international trade in illegitimate goods runs more than US$600 billion a year—approximately 5 to 7 percent of world trade. ASIS International adds that the annual value of stolen corporate IP at $300 billion in the United States and over $1 trillion worldwide. Not surprisingly, piracy has grown more than 10,000 percent in the past three decades—it was $5.5 billion in 1982.[166]

Piracy grows because counterfeiting is astoundingly profitable; gross margins of 500 to 5,000 percent are common.[167] Counterfeit medicines are more profitable than heroin, copywatches may run a couple of bucks to make but sell for $20 in Beijing's Silk Market and $250 on Internet sites, and sales of high-end counterfeit software rival the return from cocaine trafficking.[168]

The lucrative rewards of piracy entice even notorious drug cartels to diversify. Mexico's La Familia and Los Zetas, for example, generate hundreds of millions of dollars selling counterfeit DVDs. Their expanding operations have made Mexico the pirate capital of Latin America. The cartels export so many bootleg movies to Central America, for example, that some studios have stopped shipping their products there. Also, whether buying it in Cancun, Cozumel, Monterrey, or Tijuana, the bootleg DVD more than likely bears a stamp indicating it was distributed by La Familia (a butterfly) or Zetas (a stallion).[169] Similarly, the cartels pirate software. La Familia sells counterfeit Microsoft software through kiosks, markets, and stores in the Michoacán region. Adding insult to injury, it stamps counterfeit Office discs with its "FMM" logo.[170]

Microsoft's predicament in China highlights common problems. Copies of the latest versions of Microsoft's Office and Windows programs are peddled in market stalls for a few dollars, a fraction of their retail price. Rampant software piracy means Microsoft's revenue in China in 2011 was just 5 percent of its U.S. sales—even though personal-computer sales in the two countries are almost equal. Explained its CEO, Microsoft's total revenue in China, with its population of 1.34 billion, is less than what it collects in the Netherlands, a country of fewer than 17 million.[171] This situation is not Microsoft's particular problem; thousands of companies in dozens of countries struggle with the same challenge.

Nothing Is Off Limits

Most think piracy is the problem of snobbish, expensive brands. Certainly, counterfeits target high-end brands—the top 10 brands counterfeited are Microsoft, Nike, Adidas, Burberry, Louis Vuitton, Sony, Lacoste, Reebok, Viagra, and Benson & Hedges. Luxury fakes, however, are just 4 percent of the counterfeit problem. The remaining 96 percent include every-day products. Nothing is off-limits; "If it's making money over here in the U.S., it's going to be reverse-engineered or made overseas."[172]

Increasingly, counterfeiting threatens global health and safety—counterfeit medicines annually kill tens of thousands and it's anyone's guess how much fake medicine is floating around the world today. Evidence indicates that the drug supply chain is a pirate's paradise. The Food and Drug Administration estimates that counterfeits account for 10 percent of all drugs sold in the United States. Studies of anti-infective treatments in Africa and Southeast Asia peg up to 70 percent as fake.[173] The United Nations estimates that half of the anti-malarial drugs sold in Africa are counterfeits. Imitations of Pfizer's best-selling drugs have been found in the legitimate supply chains of at least 44 countries.[174]

Waging a Multifront War

Companies, industry associations, and governments use a battery of weapons to wage war on counterfeiters. An enduring approach relies on dispatching squads of lawyers to search and destroy. Big companies lawyer-up to train customs officials on the nuances of their products, monitor the Web, prod Internet providers to take down copycat sites, and file injunctions against illegal sellers. UGG Australia began enforcing its IP upon realizing the prevalence of counterfeit boots. The company has shut down thousands of websites selling fake UGGs and blocked many thousands more online listings. Liz Claiborne Inc., owner of the Juicy Couture and Kate Spade brands, fight legions of websites selling counterfeits; it removed 27,000 auction listings of counterfeits in just a few months.

Some companies prefer high-tech assault. One approach embeds radio frequency identification (RFID) chips in the product packaging to allow precise tracking; IBM, 3M, and Abbot Laboratories are pacesetters. Others, like Oracle, provide software programs that track products from factories to consumers. In Ghana, mPedigree lets consumers use their mobile phones to check if the product is genuine or fake; buyers call in a special code embossed inside the package to the vendor, who then verifies its authenticity.[175] Moving forward, some anticipate weaving microscopic markers into the product's packaging.

Governments, fearful of losing tax revenues as well as pressures from legitimate businesses, aggressively enact tougher protection. The European Union ranks IP theft as a high priority.[176]

The United States has elevated software piracy from a misdemeanor to a felony (for 10 or more illegal copies made within a six-month period with a worth more than US$2,500) and boosted enforcement efforts by threatening to sanction notorious pirates with records of "onerous and egregious" IPR violations (including countries such as China, Russia, Argentina, India, Thailand, Turkey, and Ukraine). Likewise, its Federal Drug Administration has opened offices in China, India, South Africa, and Mexico, among others, in effect taking the fight to the frontier. On other fronts, rhetoric escalates. The U.S. Trade Representative, for instance, declared, "We must defend ideas, inventions, and creativity from rip-off artists and thieves."[177]

MNEs, officials, and trade associations lobby transnational institutions to devise stronger weapons. Industry associations, like the International Anti-Counterfeiting Coalition, spearhead efforts to toughen laws. Governments worldwide provide global services in public policy, business development, and consumer education. WIPO fortifies IP treaties and spurs members to bolster antipiracy efforts. Likewise, the WTO applies TRIPS to regulate enforcement, which requires all member nations of the WTO to protect and enforce IPRs according to global, not local, standards.

This fusillade of legal assaults, novel technologies, smarter investigations, diplomatic efforts, industry initiatives, consumer education, stronger IP policies, aggressive law enforcement, and concerted political, commercial, and institutional action, one would think, should prove more than sufficient. Then, to make things a bit more interesting, add in the firepower of the global reach of vigilant MNEs, high-profile legal proceedings, increased government cooperation, criminalization of piracy, and tougher trade agreements. Such a shock-and-awe campaign should devastate the pirates, right? Surprise, surprise: Piracy continues to grow at an increasing rate. For instance, in January 2009, Pfizer found counterfeit versions of 20 of its medicines in 81 countries. In July 2012, it found 60 such fakes in 106 countries.[178]

"The Bandits Are Everywhere"

The global cat-and-mouse game between MNEs and pirates, far from winding down, escalates. Booming piracy in big, fast-growing emerging markets like China and India spells big, fast-growing trouble. As more people enter the global market, many of them are eager to consume Western brands despite income constraints. Experts warn that the resulting quest for low prices turbocharges piracy.

In addition, crafty pirates quickly overcome IP defenses. They crack licensing codes, duplicate holograms, falsify email headers, set up anonymous post office boxes, and devise cryptocurrencies like bitcoins. Staying one step ahead of the IP police is a widespread competency. "Like drug trafficking, the counterfeiting problem is so massive [that] you don't know how to get a handle on it. The bandits are everywhere."[179] Worrisomely, successful pirates evolve into sophisticated entrepreneurs. "When you are dealing with high-end counterfeits, you are talking about organizations that have a full supply chain, a full distribution chain, a full set of manufacturing tools all in place and it is all based on profits."[180] Lamented one analyst, "Counterfeiting is like a balloon filled with water. You push it on one side but when you remove your hand, it bounces back even stronger."[181]

Piracy gets a huge boost from the increasing availability of counterfeit goods through Internet channels, such as P2P file-sharing sites, mail order sites, or auction sites. Outgunned and outfoxed, some companies surrender. Foley & Corinna, a high-end handbag maker, explained that as it noticed more and more Internet fakes, it stopped looking altogether. "It's just too frustrating. You can try to do something, but it's so big and so fast."[182] Then again, there are those who treat IPR as the price of doing business. Despite everyday piracy of his products in the Chinese market, an executive reasoned that the profitability of his legal sales more than offset the losses due to counterfeits.[183]

Is Piracy Inevitable?

The pervasiveness of piracy, in the face of aggressive lawyering, sophisticated tracking and tagging technologies, database software, and security controls, poses profound questions for protecting IPRs. Some worry that different legal legacies and political ideologies among countries complicate basic issues. TRIPS, by standardizing codes and norms, should have settled such troublesome issues. Legal and operational boundaries have limited its impact.

Others fear that the antipiracy war may already be lost. Evidently, a not-too-small number of consumers and businesses around the world have few ethical qualms about using counterfeits. Take software, for instance. Global software piracy is rampant. In 2011, the worldwide PC software piracy rate hit 42 percent. Put differently, of all the packaged software installed on PCs worldwide, 42 percent was obtained illegally, at a cost of US$63.4 billion in lost revenue (up from losses of $29 billion in 2003). For many nations, such as Armenia, Libya, Ukraine, Bolivia, China, and Zambia, software piracy rates top 80 percent. Even the best-behaved nations, like the United States and Japan, report software piracy rates north of 20 percent.[184] Consequently, Microsoft's biggest rival is not another software company—it is counterfeiters.

The global financial crisis has pushed more people to seek counterfeits. Similarly, some in collectivist cultures reason that IP holders should honor society by abandoning their profit-maximizing business models. Sharing knowledge, not protection, is the moral imperative. But, counter others, without protection, ultimately there will be no IP to share or, for that matter, steal.

QUESTIONS

3-3. Collectivism and individualism, democracy and totalitarianism, rule of law and rule of man: What do these concepts say about IPRs and the legitimacy of protection?

3-4. What is the relationship among governments, transnational institutions, and MNEs fighting piracy? Do they share similar or different motivations?

3-5. Can MNEs stop piracy without government help? Why would they prefer greater government assistance? Why would they oppose it?

3-6. Do you think consumers in wealthier countries versus those in poorer countries justify piracy with similar rationalizations? Why?

3-7. Can you envision a scenario where developers and consumers of IP develop a relationship that eliminates the profitability of piracy?

3-8. Put yourself in the place of a poor individual in a poor country struggling to improve the quality of your life. What thoughts might shape how you interpret the legality of IPRs?

SUMMARY

- Political and legal systems converge and vary across countries in terms of guiding principles and practical routines.
- Two standards anchor the assessment of a political system: the degree to which it emphasizes individualism vs. collectivism and the degree to which it is democratic vs. totalitarian.
- Individualism endorses the primacy of personal freedoms in the political, economic, and cultural realms. It champions the interests of the individual over those of society.
- Collectivism holds that the needs of society take precedence over the needs of the individual. It encourages state intervention to improve the welfare of the group at the expense of the individual.
- Political officials and agencies play an extensive to all-encompassing role in a collectivist society. They play a comparatively limited role in an individualistic society.
- Political freedom measures the degree to which fair and competitive elections occur, the extent to which individual and group freedoms are guaranteed, the legitimacy ascribed to the rule of law, and the existence of freedom of the press.
- Democracy champions the authority of the many over the few. A democratic government protects personal and political rights, civil liberties, fair and free elections, and independent courts of law.
- Totalitarianism champions the authority of the few over the many. The government exercises control over many to all aspects of life, the individual is subordinated to the state, and opposing political and cultural expression is suppressed.
- Recent data on the spread of democracy indicate it is in retreat. Democracy's retreat coupled with growing stagnation of freedom signals resurgent authoritarian governance.
- Political risk is the likelihood that political decisions, events, or conditions will affect a country's business environment in ways that (1) cost investors some or all of the value of their

investments, (2) force them to accept lower-than-projected rates of return, and (3) threaten the sustainability of local activities.

- The legal system specifies the rules that regulate behavior, the processes that enforce the laws of a country, and the procedure used to resolve grievances.
- Modern legal systems, in theory, endorse a system of constitutional law that institutes an open and just political order, a system of criminal law that safeguards the social order, and a system of civil and commercial laws that promote fairness.
- A common law system is based on tradition, precedent, custom, usage, and interpretation by the courts; a civil law system relies on a systematic collection of codes and statues that judges must follow; a theocratic legal system is based on religious precepts; a customary legal system follows the wisdom of daily experience; and a mixed legal system combines elements of the other systems.
- The rule of law endorses systematic and objective laws applied by public officials who are held accountable for their just administration. Operationally, no one is above the law.
- The rule of man holds that legal rights derive from the individual who commands the power to impose them. Operationally, the leader(s) is above the law.
- We see an inverse relationship between a nation's wealth and its tendency to regulate the various elements of the business environment.
- Primary legal issues in international business include product safety and liability, marketing practice, rule of origin, jurisdiction, and IP protection.
- Intellectual property is the creative ideas, innovative expertise, or intangible insights that give an individual, company, or country a competitive advantage. The strength of IPR protection within a country is moderated by its legal legacies, economic development, and cultural orientation.

KEY TERMS

choice-of-law clause (p. 164)
civil and commercial law (p. 153)
civil law (p. 155)
collectivism (p. 135)
constitutional law (p. 153)
common law (p. 155)
country of origin (p. 163)
criminal law (p. 153)
customary law (p. 155)
democracy (p. 138)
individualism (p. 135)
intellectual property (IP) (p. 164)
intellectual property rights (IPR) (p. 164)
laissez-faire (p. 135)
legal system (p. 153)
local content (p. 163)
mixed legal system (p. 155)
pluralism (p. 136)
political freedom (p. 137)
political ideology (p. 136)
political risk (p. 148)
political spectrum (p. 137)
political system (p. 135)
rule of law (p. 156)
rule of man (p. 156)
theocratic law (p. 155)
Third Wave of Democratization (p. 142)
totalitarian system (p. 139)

ENDNOTES

1 ***Sources include the following:*** Michael Sylvester,"Flaming Hoops," *Corporate Counsel: Market Report China* (2004): 171;"A Disorderly Heaven," *The Economist* (March 20, 2004): 12, U.S.;"Bulls in a China Shop," *The Economist* (March 20, 2004): 10;"China Slams US Piracy Complaint," *BBC News* (April 10, 2007); *The Economist,* Country Briefings: China, retrieved January 20, 2013 from www.economist.com/countries/China/ ; U.S. Department of State, Background Note: China, retrieved January 13, 2013 from www.state.gov/r/pa/ei/bgn/18902.htm Central Intelligence Agency, World Factbook, www.cia.gov/library/publications/ the-world-factbook/geos/ch.html (January 12, 2013). The pace of change in China's business environment makes any discussion of it hazardous. Regard this case as a set of educated generalizations about the kinds of problems encountered by would-be foreign investors in China from the 1990s to date.

2 Richard McGregor, *The Party: The Secret World of China's Communist Rulers* (Harper Collins, 2010): 1.

3 Pew Global Attitudes Project, Country's Economic Situation. Specific query:"Is the country's economic situation good or bad?" www.pewglobal.org/database/?indicator=5&survey=12&response=Good&mode=chart (Retrieved April 21, 2011).

4 Mark McDonald,"Disney to Asian Pirates: Knock It Off," *New York Times,* (July 11, 2012): C-1.

5 For example, the IMF and Nobel Prize winner Robert Fogel pegs 2016, Angus Madison of the OECD targets 2020, Price Waterhouse Cooper claims 2025, Goldman Sachs targets 2027, and the National intelligence Council of the United States targets 2036.

6 Erich Follath and Wieland Wagner,"Murder, Sex and Corruption: Beijing's Difficult Transition of Power," Spiegel Online, Retrieved January 17, 2013, from www.spiegel.de/international/world/murder-sex-and-corruption-beijing-s-difficult-transition-of-power-a-861837.html.

7 Gordon Orr,"What's in Store for China in 2013?" *McKinsey Quarterly,* January 2013.

8 "International Comparisons of Hourly Compensation Costs in Manufacturing, 2011" United States Bureau of Labor Statistics, Released December 19, 2012;"Manufacturing in India: The Masala Mittelstand," *The Economist,* (August 11, 2012):55. In addition, Monthly Labour Review of the US Bureau of Labour Statistics shows that in 2009, compensation of Chinese manufacturing workers was only $0.81 per hour in 2006—just 2.7 percent of comparable costs in the US, 3.4 percent of those in Japan, and 2.2 percent of compensation rates in Europe. While dated, they underscore the magnitude of the gap between China and the developed world. Moreover, as of May 2011, Apple has contracted with Foxconn to make their iPad 2s in China, where employees are reportedly paid 1,200 Yuan/month, or about $185 at current exchange rates (y/$ = 0.154), or, if we assume an average 8-hour/day, 250-day/year, (probably unrealistic assumptions), $1.11/hour. In contrast, the average U.S. manufacturing/mining/construction compensation is $32.53/hour as of December 2010, according to the Bureau of Labor Statistics.

9 Keith Bradsher,"China's Ambitious Goal for Boom in College Graduates," *New York Times,* (January 17, 2012): A-1. Martin

Dewhurst, Jonathan Harris, and Suzanne Heywood,"The Global Company's Challenge," *McKinsey Quarterly*, retrieved December 31, 2012 from www.mckinseyquarterly.com/The_global_companys_challenge_2979.

10 Personal Conversation, Daniel Sullivan and Peter Leung, Director, Nalco China, Beijing, March 1, 2011.

11 "Foreign Investment in China: Even Harder Than It Looks," *The Economist*, (March 23, 2011):64.

12 Chinese Negotiation: The Long Kiss Goodnight, retrieved May 14, 2009 from www.chinesenegotiation.com/page/2/.

13 "A Survey Of Business In China: A Disorderly Heaven," *The Economist*, retrieved March 24, 2011 from www.economist.com/node/2495184.

14 Ibid.

15 The goal is not judicial independence. Rather, the Chinese chief justice advocates out-of-court mediation as a favored means of settling civil disputes in ways that enhance social harmony. Criminal defendants, for example, have limited access to legal counsel, few rights to call their own witnesses, or even opportunities to contest testimony. Willy Lam,"Beijing Tightens Control over Courts," *Asia Times*, retrieved August 4, 2011 from atimes.com/atimes/China/MF25Ad02.html.

16 The notion of the "mandate of heaven" is a Chinese philosophical concept concerning the legitimacy of rulers. It is similar to the European concept of the divine right of kings. Both seek to legitimize rule from divine approval; however, unlike the divine right of kings, the Mandate of Heaven is predicated on the conduct of the ruler in question. It postulates that heaven blesses the authority of a just ruler, as defined by the Five Confucian Relationships, but disfavors a despotic ruler and would withdraw its mandate, leading to the overthrow of that ruler. The Mandate of Heaven would then transfer to those who would presumably rule best and the cycle would restart. Conveniently, the overthrow of the leader confirms that he had already lost his Mandate of Heaven (Source: en.wikipedia.org/wiki/Mandate_of_Heaven).

17 Personal Conversation, Daniel Sullivan and Kathy Stearman, Beijing (March 4, 2011).

18 "Oded Shenkar, *The Chinese Century*, (Upper Saddle River, NJ: Pearson Prentice Hall, 2006).

19 IPR Seizure Statistics, 2011, *U.S. Customs and Border Protection-Trade*, retrieved January 18, 2013 from www.cbp.gov/xp/cgov/trade/priority_trade/ipr/ipr_communications/seizure/.

20 Steven Weisman,"Before Visit to China, a Rebuke," *New York Times* (December 12, 2006): A-1.

21 Ibid.

22 "The World's Greatest Fakes," *60 Minutes*, quote by Dan Chow, www.cbsnews.com/stories/2004/01/26/ 60minutes/main595875.shtml, retrieved June 15, 2006.

23 "The Sincerest Form of Flattery," *The Economist* (April 4, 2007): 67.

24 "Business in Russia: Dancing with the Bear," *The Economist* (February 1, 2007): 23.

25 "BP in Russia: Dancing with Mr. Putin," *The Economist*, retrieved February 14, 2011 from www.economist.com/node/17967066?story_id=17967066.

26 "Business in Russia: Dancing with the Bear," *The Economist.*

27 "Russia's Weakened Democratic Embrace," *Pew Global Attitudes Project*, retrieved January 14, 2013 from (www.pewglobal.org/2006/01/05/russias-weakened-democratic-embrace/);"Russia's future: The cracks appear," *The Economist*." (December 10, 2011):13.

28 "Crocodile Tears," *The Economist*, (April 28, 2007): 44. Andrew Osborn, "Russia's Rule of Lawlessness," WSJ.com, retrieved January 20, 2011 from online.wsj.com/article/SB123758426519199313.html Corruption Perceptions Index 2012, retrieved from www.transparency.org/cpi2012/results, January 15, 2013.

29 Daniel Kaufmann, Art Kraay, and Massimo Mastruzzi,"Governance Matters IV: Governance Indicators for 1996–2004," *World Bank Policy Research Working Paper Series No. 3630* (May 2005).

30 Alan Ryan, *On Politics: A History of Political Philosophy from Herodotus to the Present*, London: *Allen Lane, 2012.*

31 Statement from the Declaration of Independence of the United States of America.

32 In Germany, before the adoption of liberal western economic ideas, its economic policy, so named "Gemeinnutz geht vor Eigennutz," held that that "the welfare of the nation takes precedence over the selfishness of the individuals" (www.stephenhicks.org/tag/gemeinnutz-geht-vor-eigennutz/).

33 Pluralism rests upon ideas drawn from the sociology of small groups. Translated to the level of a society, these ideas interpret the relationships and interactions between and within groups as they champion and contest political ideologies.

34 Hannah Arendt,"Totalitarianism," Part Three of *The Origins of Totalitarianism* (New York: Houghton Mifflin Harcourt, 1968), p. 164.

35 Practically, the ideology of democracy anchors a political system that grants voters the power to alter the laws and structures of government, to make decisions (either directly or through representatives), and to participate directly in elections.

36 More specifically, a democracy accepts the legitimacy of (1) freedom of opinion, expression, press, religion, association, and access to information; (2) free, fair, and regular elections; (3) majority rule coupled with protection of individual and minority rights; and (4) subordination of government to the rule of law.

37 Patrick French, *India: A Portrait*, (London: Allen Lane, 2011).

38 The philosophy of Apple's founder Steve Jobs fit this outlook as well; he rejected the notion that individuals were rational, believing "consumers don't know what they want."

39 In China, for example, the One Child Policy prohibits a family from having more than a single child; a couple that has a second child may be fined the equivalent of $1,300—a steep penalty in rural areas where most annual incomes are a fraction of that sum.

40 "China's Future: Rising Power, Anxious State," *The Economist*, (June 25, 2011): 3; for example, bookstores in China stock works approved by the CCP.

41 Anne-Marie Brady, *Marketing Dictatorship: Propaganda and Thought Work in Contemporary China* (Lanham, MD: Rowman & Littlefield, 2007).

42 "Freedom in the World 2013: Middle East Gains Provoke Intensified Repression," *Freedom House*, retrieved January 20, 2013 from www.freedomhouse.org/article/freedom-world-2013-middle-east-gains-provoke-intensified-repression.

43 "China's Future: Rising Power, Anxious State," *The Economist*, Special Report: China (June 25, 2011): 3.

44 "Freedom in the World 2013: Middle East Gains Provoke Intensified Repression," *Freedom House.*

45 "The Long Arm of the State," *The Economist*, Special Report: China (June 25, 2011): 14.

46 Willy Lam,"China's State Giants too Big to Play with," *Asia Times Online*, retrieved May 26, 2011 from www.atimes.com/atimes/China_Business/MA22Cb01.html.

47 Keith Brasher,"Solar Panel Maker Moves Work to China," NYTimes.com, retrieved February 11, 2011 from www.nytimes.com/2011/01/15/business/energy-environment/15solar.html?pagewanted=2&hpw.

48 "Chinese Politics and the WTO: No Change," *The Economist*, (December 10, 2011): 46.

49 "China Squeezes Foreigners for Share of Global Riches," WSJ.com retrieved December 29, 2010 from online.wsj.com/article/SB10001424052970203731004576045684068308042.html?mod=rss_whats_news_us_business.

50 "Corporate Espionage: Who Needs Cyber-spying?," *The Economist,* (February 21, 2013):44.

51 Extracted from Mission Statement, Freedom House, retrieved June 28, 2009 from www.freedomhouse.org/template.cfm?page=2. For example, classical liberal philosophy holds that freedom is the absence of coercion of one person by others; jurisprudence holds that one has the right to determine one's own actions autonomously; environmentalism advocates constraints on the use of ecosystems in any definition of freedom. Others take a more abstract approach, discussing notions of positive versus negative freedom (the right to fulfill one's own potential vs. freedom from restraints).

52 Adrian Karatnycky, *Freedom in the World 2001–2002: The Democracy Gap* (New York: Freedom House, 2002), retrieved February 11, 2011 from www.freedom house.org.

53 Specifically, on December 10, 1948, the General Assembly of the United Nations adopted the Universal Declaration of Human Rights and has since called on all member countries to publicize the text and "to cause it to be disseminated, displayed, read, and expounded principally in schools and other educational institutions, without distinction based on the political status of countries or territories," For the full text of the Declaration, go to www.un.org/Overview/rights.html.

54 Samuel P. Huntington, *The Third Wave: Democratization in the Late Twentieth Century,* (Norman: University of Oklahoma Press, 1991).

55 Ibid.

56 Francis Fukuyama, *The End of History and the Last Man* (New York: Free Press, 1992).

57 "Sledge Hama," *The Economist,* (July 9, 2011):45.

58 "Angry Workers Push Back in Revolt over 2-minute Toilet Breaks," *CTV News,* retrieved January 22, 2013 from www.ctvnews.ca/business/angry-workers-push-back-in-revolt-over-2-minute-toilet-breaks-1.1124139.

59 *The Economist Intelligence Unit's Index of Democracy 2008,* retrieved June 24, 2009 from graphics.eiu.com/PDF/Democracy percent 20Index percent 202008.pdf.

60 Ronald Bailey, "Does Disease Cause Autocracy?" *Reason Magazine* (June 1, 2011).

61 Christian Haerpfer, Patrick Bernhagen, Ronald Inglehart, and Christian Welzel (eds.), *Democratization* (Oxford: Oxford University Press, 2009); "Two Billion More Bourgeois," *The Economist* (February 14, 2009): 18.

62 "Most Muslims Want Democracy, Personal Freedoms, and Islam in Political Life ⊠ Pew Global Attitudes Project," retrieved January 15, 2013 from www.pewglobal.org/2012/07/10/most-muslims-want-democracy-personal-freedoms-and-islam-in-political-life/; Tang Ming, "Chinese Want Democratic Reform First, Official Poll Shows," *Epoch Times,*" retrieved January 15, 2013 from www.theepochtimes.com/n2/china-news/chinese-want-democratic-reform-first-official-poll-shows-316896.html.

63 "Freedom in the World: The Annual Survey of Political Rights and Civil Liberties," *Freedom House,* retrieved February 11, 2011 from www.freedomhouse.org/template.cfm?

64 Arch Puddington, "Freedom in the World 2011: The Authoritarian Challenge to Democracy," *Freedom House,* freedomhouse.org: Freedom in the World 2011 Survey Release," retrieved April 21, 2011 from www.freedomhouse.org/template.cfm?page=594.

65 "Freedom in the World 2011," 48-49.

66 Arch Puddington, "Freedom in the World 2012," *Freedom House,* retrieved January 15, 2013 from www.freedomhouse.org/report/freedom-world/freedom-world-2012.

67 "*Democracy Index 2010: Democracy in Retreat,* "*Economist Intelligence Unit,*" retrieved February 7, 2011 from www.eiu.com/public/topical_report.aspx?campaignid=demo2010; Laza Kekic, "A Pause in Democracy's March," *The Economist,* The World in 2007 (Annual Review, 2007): 59–60.

68 Technically, the EIU evaluated 165 independent states and two territories.

69 Similarly, just over half the 70 seats in Hong Kong's Legislative Council are determined by popular vote; the remainder is decided by groups of industry and professional associations. Add it all up and you have what some see as "the most convoluted election system on the planet." "Streets, not seats", View of Suzanne Pepper, a fellow at the Chinese University of Hong Kong; *The Economist,* (September 15, 2012): 42; "Banyan: Post-merger integration," *The Economist,*" October 13, 2012; also "Monsoon of their Discontent," *The Economist,* (July 9, 2011): 40.

70 "World" population refers to the total population of the 167 countries covered by the index. Since this excludes only microstates, this is nearly equal to the entire actual estimated world population in 2010. *Economist Intelligence Unit.*

71 "Public Opinion in Eastern Europe: The Glow Fades," *The Economist,* retrieved January 31, 2011 from www.economist.com/research/articlesBySubject/displaystory.cfm?subjectid=7933596&story_id=14792427.

72 Paul Krugman, "Central European Shadows," *The New York Times,* retrieved January 16, 2013 from krugman.blogs.nytimes.com/2011/12/11/central-european-shadows/.

73 Amartya Sen, "The Crisis of European Democracy," *New York Times,* (May 22, 2012): A-8.

74 "*Democracy Index 2010: Democracy in Retreat,* "*Economist Intelligence Unit,*" retrieved February 7, 2011 from www.eiu.com/public/topical_report.aspx?campaignid=demo2010;

75 Julian Wucherpfennig, "Modernization and Democracy: Theories and Evidence Revisited, *Living Reviews in Democracy* (2009): 1.

76 "On The People's Democratic Dictatorship," Selected Works of Mao Tse-tung, retrieved January 15, 2013 from www.marxists.org/reference/archive/mao/selected-works/volume-4/mswv4_65.htm).

77 Pushkar, "India Waits for Democracy with Benefits," *Asia Times Online,* retrieved January 16, 2013 from www.atimes.com/atimes/South_Asia/NK03Df01.html.

78 "Countries at the Crossroads," freedomhouse.org, retrieved April 18, 2011 from www.freedomhouse.org/template.cfm?page=139&edition=9

79 Scott Shane, February 5, 2011 "America's Journeys with Strongmen," NYTimes.com," retrieved February 7, 2011 from www.nytimes.com/2011/02/06/weekinreview/06shane.html?_r=1&ref=us.

80 "Democracy Index 2011," *Economist Intelligence Unit*" retrieved January 20, 2013 from www.eiu.com/public/topical_report.aspx?campaignid=DemocracyIndex2011.

81 ILO, "World of Work Report 2010. From One Crisis to the Next?" retrieved February 7, 2011 from www.ilo.org/global/publications/books/WCMS_145259/lang–en/index.htm.

82 Richard Florida, "The Conservative States of America," *The Atlantic,* retrieved March 30, 2011 from www.theatlantic.com/politics/archive/2011/03/the-conservative-states-of-america/71827/.

83 "The Global Crisis and the Poor," *The Economist* (March 14, 2009): 62–64.

84 "Democracy? Hu Needs It," *The Economist* (June 28, 2007): 44; "A Warning for Reformers," *The Economist* (November 17, 2007): 67.

85 "'I am a True Democrat:' G-8 Interview with Vladimir Putin," *Spiegel Online,* retrieved June 4, 2007 from www.spiegel.de/international/world/0,1518,486345,00.html.

86 "Brazil's President Lula Says G7 Nations No Longer Speak for the World," *The Telegraph* (March 16, 2009): A-1.

87 Roger Cohen, November 11, 2006. "China vs. U.S.: Democracy Confronts Harmony. Stay Tuned." *New York Times,* retrieved February 7, 2011 from select.nytimes.com/iht/2006/11/22/world/IHT-22globalist.html.

88 "Freedom in the World-2011," 48-49.

89 "Military budget of the United States," *Wikipedia*, retrieved January 15, 2013 from en.wikipedia.org/wiki/Military_budget_of_the_United_States; "Military spending: Defence costs," *The Economist*, retrieved June 8, 2011 from www.economist.com/blogs/dailychart/2011/06/military-spending.

90 James Mann, *The China Fantasy: Why Capitalism Will Not Bring Democracy to China,* (London: Penguin 2007); Eamonn Fingleton, *In the Jaws of the Dragon: America's Fate in the Coming Era of Chinese Hegemony* (New York: Thomas Dunne Books, 2008); Martin Jacques, *When China Rules the World: The End of the Western World and the Birth of a New Global Order* (London: Penguin Press, 2009); Stefan Halper, *The Beijing Consensus: How China's Authoritarian Model Will Dominate the Twenty-First Century* (New York: Basic Books, 2010).

91 "Banyan: On the Defensive," *The Economist* (April 7, 2011): 49; Jacob Talmon, *The Origins of Totalitarian Democracy* (London: Secker & Warburg, 1952); "China: Democratic Dictatorship," *Time*, retrieved May 16, 2011 from www.time.com/time/magazine/article/0,9171,800834,00.html.

92 "Where do you live?" *The Economist*, Special Report: China (June 25, 2011): 12.

93 Roberto Tofani, "Business before Rights in Southeast Asia," Asia Times Online, retrieved January 16, 2013 from www.atimes.com/atimes/Southeast_Asia/NF01Ae02.html.

94 "China's Modern Authoritarianism," WSJ.com," retrieved February 10, 2011 from online.wsj.com/article/SB124319304482150525.html.

95 Matteo Cervellati, Piergiuseppe Fortunato, and Uwe Sunde, "Democratization and Civil Liberties: The Role of Violence during the Transition," IZA DP No. 5555 (March 2011).

96 Hassan Fattah, "Democracy in the Arab World, a U.S. Goal, Falters," *New York Times* (April 10, 2006): C-1.

97 Samuel Huntington, *The Clash of Civilizations and the Remaking of World Order* (New York: Simon & Schuster, 1996); Huntington, *Who Are We? The Challenges to America's National Identity* (New York: Simon & Schuster, 2004).

98 "US tells Egypt to Unblock Facebook, Twitter," retrieved January 31, 2011 from www.todayonline.com/World/EDC110128-0000197/US-tells-Egypt-to-unblock-Facebook,-Twitter; Edward Wong and David Barboza, "Wary of Egypt Unrest, China Censors Web," NYTimes.com, retrieved January 31, 2011 from www.nytimes.com/2011/02/01/world/asia/01beijing.html?_r=1&hp. For example, Iranian leaders in 2009 and Egyptian authorities in 2011 struggled to quash anti-government protests by blocking social networking sites that had been used to organize protests. Meanwhile, in the initial days of the Egyptian rebellion, wary Chinese officials instructed Sina.com and Netease.com — two of the country's biggest online portals — to block keyword searches of the word "Egypt"; Weibo, the Chinese equivalent of Twitter, did the same.

99 Category, Satisfaction with Country's Direction, Specific Query, "How satisfied are you with the country's direction?" Pew Global Attitudes Project, retrieved April 21, 2011 from pewglobal.org/database/?indicator=3&survey=12&response=Satisfied&mode=chart.

100 Aubrey Belford, 2011. "Indonesia's Political Landscape Offers Path for Egypt," *The New York Times*, retrieved February 16, 2011 from www.nytimes.com/2011/02/17/world/asia/17iht-indo17.html?partner=rss&emc=rss.

101 "Freedom in the World-2011," 48-49.

102 "Venezuelan Bluster? Hugo Chávez Threatens to Seize Banks and a Steel-Maker," *The Economist Intelligence Unit* (May 8, 2007): 57.

103 "Nigeria's Prospects: A Man and a Morass" *The Economist* (May 28, 2011): 24.

104 "Will Silver Surge Following the Nationalization of Bolivia's Silver Mines by Embattled President Evo Morales?" retrieved April 15, 2011 from www.zerohedge.com.

105 "Japan and China: Rattling the Supply Chains," *The Economist*, (October 20, 201):60.

106 Duff Wilson, "Cigarette Giants in Global Fight on Tighter Rules," NYTimes.com, retrieved February 1, 2011 from www.nytimes.com/2010/11/14/business/global/14smoke.html?_r=1.

107 "The 2010 Failed States Index," *Foreign Policy*, retrieved February 8, 2011 from.www.foreignpolicy.com/failedstates.

108 "Science: Getting in the Mood," *The Economist: The World in 2012*, (November 17, 2012):152.

109 Andrew Martin, "Turning Point for Suits over Chinese Drywall," *The New York Times*, (October 12, 2012): A-7.

110 For example, consider the legal concept of due diligence, which requires that the statements in a firm's security-registration forms be true and omit no material facts. Companies rely on due diligence to manage the risk of cross-border acquisitions; it enacts a legally binding process during which a potential buyer, say an Indian software designer, evaluates the assets and liabilities of a potential acquisition in say, Germany. Hence, due diligence is often the difference between success and failure—provided the local legal codes permit the full examination of operations and management and the verification of material facts. In the European Union, data protection rules can interfere with assessing important elements of a potential acquisition, such as managers' physical or mental health, patterns of trade union membership, and criminal histories. Hence, prudent companies considering cross-border acquisitions pinpoint issues, the country or countries involved, and the citizenship and identity of people involved from the pre-due-diligence phase to the close of the deal. These decisions inevitably reference aspects of constitutional law, (i.e., what philosophies anchor ownership rights?), criminal law, (i.e., what are the procedures and penalties for malfeasance?), and civil/commercial law, (i.e., do regulations promote disclosure and verification of information?). Similar situations arise with respect to discovery and with other aspects of the legal process. With respect to discovery, for example, language, culture, volume, and local law influence the right to demand documents relative to the case from the other party; "Translating and the law: Legal language," The Economist, (November 10, 2012): 66.

111 "Russia: The Long Life of Homo Sovieticus." *The Economist*" (December 10, 2011): 27-30.

112 "Russian Politics: Fear and Loathing," *The Economist*, (September 22, 2012): 60.

113 See Juriglobe World Legal Systems, www.juriglobe.ca/eng/.

114 *Stare Decisis:* Latin, "to stand by that which is decided."

115 Denis Wiechman, Jerry Kendall, and Mohammad Azarian, "Islamic Law: Myths and Realities," retrieved June 22, 2009 from muslimcanada.org/Islam_myths.htm.

116 Andorra and the Guernsey and Jersey Islands, both of which belong to the United Kingdom, apply customary law only. The codification of civil law developed out of legal customs that evolved in particular communities and, over time, were collected and recorded by local jurists.

117 "A Disorderly Heaven," *The Economist* (March 20, 2004): 75.

118 "Russian Politics: Fear and Loathing," *The Economist*.

119 Ian Morris, *Why the West Rules…For Now* (New York: Farrar, Strauss and Giroux, 2010).

120 "Revolution in the Arab World: The Twilight of the Dictators." *The Economist*, (August 4, 2012): 73.

121 Quote, He Weifang, p. 22. Ibid, 43.

122 Similarly, Thomas Paine wrote "in America, the law is king" in contrast to the view that the king was the law, *Common Sense*, retrieved March 26, 2011 from www.ushistory.org/paine/commonsense/singlehtml.htm.

123 "Rule of Law Index," *World Justice Project*," retrieved February 8, 2011 from worldjusticeproject.org/rule-of-law-index.

124 Paul Collier, *Wars, Guns, and Votes: Democracy in Dangerous Places* (New York: HarperCollins, 2009).

125 Hernando De Soto, *The Mystery of Capital: Why Capitalism Triumphs in the West and Fails Everywhere Else* (Basic Books, 2000).

126 See profile of the World Justice Project, reported in "The Paper Chase," *The Economist*, (June 25, 2011): 40.

127 "Business in Russia: Dancing with the Bear," 18.

128 "Belarus." *Freedom House*, retrieved January 16, 2013 from www.freedomhouse.org/country/belarus; "Kazakhstan" *Freedom House*, retrieved January 16, 2013 from www.freedomhouse.org/country/kazakhstan.

129 "Big US Firms Shift Hiring Abroad," *Wall Street Journal* (April 19, 2011): B1.

130 Louise Arbour, "The Rule of Law," *New York Times* (September 26, 2012): A-8; "Economics and the Rule of Law: Order in the Jungle," *The Economist* (March 13, 2008): 43-48.

131 Tom Friedman, "Our One-Party Democracy," *New York Times*, (September 8, 2009): A-8.

132 David Barstow and Alejandra Xanic Von Bertrab, "How Wal-Mart Used Payoffs to Get Its Way in Mexico" NYTimes.com, retrieved April 15, 2013 from ww.nytimes.com/2012/12/18/business/walmart-bribes-teotihuacan.html?pagewanted=all&_r=0.

133 Geoff Lewis, "Who in the World is Entrepreneurial?" *Fortune: Small Business* (June 1, 2007): 24.

134 Gardiner Harris, "India Backs Investment from Wal-Mart and Ikea," NYTimes.com, retrieved January 17, 2013 from www.nytimes.com/2012/09/15/business/global/india-backs-foreign-investment-in-retail-sector.html.

135 A contract is a binding legal agreement that formalizes promises between parties, the breach of which triggers legal action.

136 "Reform in Mexico: Labour pains," *The Economist*, (November 3, 2012): 37.

137 "Economics Focus: The Himalayas of Hiring," *The Economist* (August 7, 2010): 76.

138 "Improving the Investment Climate in India," South Asia Region and Investment Climate Unit," World Bank, Washington DC, 2005; Laura Alfaro and Anusha Chari, "India Transformed? Insights from the Firm Level 1988-2005," *Harvard Business School*, Working Paper 10-030, 2009.

139 "Doing Business – Measuring Business Regulations," *World Bank Group*, retrieved January 15, 2013 from www.doingbusiness.org.

140 "Lawmakers to U.S. Companies: Don't Buy Huawei, ZTE," *CNET News*, retrieved January 17, 2013 from news.cnet.com/8301-1035_3-57527782-94/lawmakers-to-u.s-companies-dont-buy-huawei-zte/.

141 "Brazil's Trade Policy: Seeking Protection," *The Economist*, (January 14, 2012):35.

142 Duncan Fairgrieve and Geraint Howells, "Is Product Liability Still a Global Problem?" *Managerial Law* 49:1/2 (2007): 6–9.

143 "Lego: Bricks and Flicks," *The Economist* (May 7, 2011): 70.

144 "Stephanie Clifford, "Recession? Knockoffs Go Down-market" NYTimes.com, retrieved February 14, 2011 from www.nytimes.com/2010/08/01/business/economy/01knockoff.html.

145 Veronica Weinstein and Dennis Fernandez, "Recent Developments in China's Intellectual Property Laws," *Chinese Journal of International Law* 3:1 (2004): 227.

146 "Gold from the Storm," *The Economist* (June 28, 2007): 65.

147 Personal Conversation, Daniel Sullivan and Mr. Patrick Hu, Shanghai (March 2, 2011).

148 Zhenmin Wang, "The Developing Rule of Law in China," *Harvard Asia Quarterly* (2000):4.

149 Robert Ostergard, "The Measurement of Intellectual Property Rights Protection," *Journal of International Business Studies*, 31 (Summer 2000): 349.

150 Stephanie Sanborn, "Protecting Intellectual Property on the Web—The Internet Age Is Making Digital Rights Management Even More Important," *InfoWorld* (June 19, 2000): 40.

151 "Executive Summary: Genetics, genomics and the patenting of DNA," World Health Organization, retrieved May 16, 2011 from www.who.int/genomics/publications/background/en/index.html.

152 Thomas W. Pearson "Life Is Not for Sale!: Confronting Free Trade and Intellectual Property in Costa Rica," *American Anthropologist*, March 2013, 115: 58–71; Lateef Mtima, "What's Mine is Mine but What's Yours is Ours: IP Imperialism, the Right of Publicity, and Intellectual Property Social Justice in the Digital Information Age," *SMU Science & Technology Law Review*, Fall, 2012; "Economists Say Copyright and Patent Laws Are Killing Innovation; Hurting Economy," Washington University, retrieved May 10, 2009 from www.newswise.com/articles/view/549822/sc=dwhn.

153 Jack Coats, "Intellectual Property: An Unnecessary Evil," CSMonitor.com, retrieved April 28, 2011 from www.csmonitor.com/Business/The-Adam-Smith-Institute-Blog/2011/0428/Intellectual-property-an-unnecessary-evil Stephan Kinsella, "Against Intellectual Property," Ludwig von Mises Institute, retrieved April 28, 2011 from mises.org/resources/3582/Against-Intellectual-Property.

154 "Going Up or Down?" *The Economist* (June 7, 2007): 45.

155 "A High Cost to Developing Countries," *New York Times* (October 5, 1986): D2.

156 Evans, Nathan, "India's New Patent Regime and its Impact on the Global Pharmaceutical Industry," *Pharmaceutical Law Insight*, (September 2007); "India: Cipla Launches 3-in-1 AIDS Pill," October 14, 2006, retrieved September 15, 2008 from www.medindia.net/news/view_news_main.asp?x=15038.

157 Gardiner Harris, "Top Court in India Rejects Novartis Drug Patent," *New York Times*, (April 1, 2013):A1.

158 "NBC Finds Formula for Fighting Piracy," CNET News, retrieved February 24, 2013 from news.cnet.com/8301-1023_3-10048949-93.html.

159 "A Gathering Storm," *The Economist* (June 7, 2007): 67.

160 Doron S. Ben-Atar, *Trade Secrets: Intellectual Piracy and the Origins of American Industrial Power* (New Haven, CT: Yale University Press, 2004).

161 Raja Murthy, "China on Patent Overdrive," *Asia Times Online*, retrieved March 24, 2011 from www.atimes.com/atimes/China_Business/MA07Cb01.html.

162 "U.S. Customs and Border Protection," *Trade*, retrieved February 14, 2011 from www.cbp.gov/xp/cgov/trade/priority_trade/ipr/pubs/seizure/.

163 "Battle of Ideas: Intellectual property in China," *The Economist* (April 25, 2009): 73; "China on Patent Overdrive," *Asia Times Online*, retrieved February 14, 2011 from www.atimes.com/atimes/China_Business/MA07Cb01.html.

164 Items commonly counterfeited include books, printer cartridges, music CDs, brake pads, DVDs, aircraft parts, cigarettes, wristwatches, razor blades, batteries, medicine, motorcycles, handbags, jewelry, automobiles, shampoo, pens, toys, wine, shoes, clothing, luggage, foods, beer, perfume, cleaning supplies, pharmaceuticals, and health-care supplies.

165 "Inside the Knockoff-Tennis-Shoe Factory," NYTimes.com, retrieved February 14, 2011 from www.nytimes.com/2010/08/22/magazine/22fake-t.html?_r=2&adxnnl=1&emc=eta1&adxnnlx=1282932069-1merRjlswb8WDMPz0lEG1w.

166 "Homepage | International Anti-Counterfeiting Coalition," retrieved February 14, 2011 from www.iacc.org/ ASIS International data reported in "Intellectual Property: Can You Keep a Secret?," *The Economist*, (March 16, 2013):67.

167 Stephanie Sutton, "EFCG: Counterfeit Medicines More Profitable than Heroin," retrieved February 16, 2011 from pharmtech.findpharma.com/pharmtech/Ingredients/EFCG-Counterfeit-Medicines-More-Profitable-than-He/ArticleStandard/Article/detail/635540.

168 Ibid.

169 William Booth,"Drug Cartels Muscle into Piracy Business," *The Washington Post* (June 1, 2011): A-1.

170 "Pirated Microsoft software funded Mexican drug cartel," retrieved February 16, 2011 from www.digitaltrends.com/computing/pirated-microsoft-software-funded-mexican-drug-cartel/.

171 Owen Fletcher and Jason Dean,"Ballmer Decries Huge China Sales Holes," *Wall Street Journal,* (May 27, 2011): A-1.

172 Ibid, Quote by Jonathan Erece, a trade enforcement coordinator for United States Protection.

173 "Fake Pharmaceuticals: Bad Medicine," *The Economist,* (October 13, 2012): 74.

174 "Fake drugs: Poison Pills," *The Economist,* retrieved February 14, 2011 from www.economist.com/node/16943895?story_id=16943895.

175 Ibid.

176 Benoit Godart,"IP Crime: The New Face of Organized Crime," *Journal of Intellectual Property Law & Practice,* retrieved February 14, 2011 from iplp.oxfordjournals.org/content/5/5/378.full.

177 "SPECIAL 301 Report, *Office of the United States Trade Representative,*" retrieved February 24, 2013 from www.ustr.gov/about-us/press-office/press-releases/archives/2007/april/special-301-report.

178 "Fake Pharmaceuticals: Bad Medicine," *The Economist,* (October 13, 2012): 74.

179 "Software Piracy Takes Toll on Global Scale," *Hack in the Box: Keeping Knowledge Free,* retrieved April 23, 2011 from www.hackinthebox.net/modules.php?op=modload&name=News&file=article&sid=2951.

180 "Microsoft Says Software Piracy Continues to Grow," *TG Daily,* retrieved February 14, 2011 from www.tgdaily.com/hardware-brief/13603-microsoft-says-software-piracy-continues-to-grow.

181 View of Mr. Orhii reported in "Fake Pharmaceuticals: Bad Medicine," *The Economist* (October 13, 2012): 74.

182 Microsoft Says Software Piracy Continues To Grow," *TG Daily.*

183 "Business in China and the West: A Tale of Two Expats," *The Economist* (December 29, 2010):73.

184 "Business Software Alliance - Global Software Piracy Study," retrieved February 16, 2013 from portal.bsa.org/globalpiracy2011/index.html.

CHAPTER 4

Economic Systems and Market Methods

OBJECTIVES

After studying this chapter, you should be able to

1. Communicate the importance of economic analysis
2. Discuss the idea of economic freedom
3. Profile the characteristics of the types of economic systems
4. Introduce the notion of state capitalism
5. Profile leading indicators of economic development, performance, and potential
6. Profile the benefits and drawbacks of economic growth
7. Profile leading global indices of economic performance

Source: © picadillu - Fotolia.com

A man is rich who owes nothing.

—French proverb

CASE The Comeback Accelerates[1]

In the world of globalization, one often struggles to separate the rhetoric from reality. Optimists view it as an unstoppable wave transforming everything. Realists see it as just the latest stage in the evolution of the market, improving transactional efficiencies and expanding market frontiers. Cynics see it as the final stage before forces of deglobalization usher in the inevitable return to local enterprise. Despite wide-ranging opinions, few doubt that the ongoing integration of national economies resets the scale and scope of the global market.

Discussions have taken a far more dramatic tone the past few years. Some commentators see the flattening of the world whereby advances in institutions, communications, and technology fundamentally change the economics of globalization. "Flatliners" speak of "distributed tools of innovation and connectivity empowering individuals from anywhere to connect, collaborate, and compete."[2] Powered by hardware and software innovations, anyone, anywhere, can trade anything, anytime.

Others emphasize the effect of the entry of billions of people into the global marketplace. Some reason that qualitative change in the magnitude of the market drives a two-part transformation. Notes a leading analysis, "Three billion new people—a billion and a half Chinese, a billion Indians, half a billion people from former Soviet bloc—have suddenly come into the global economy all at one time. Within these three billion people is a population as big as the United States, bigger than anybody in Europe or Japan, who are every bit as skilled and can do anything that could be done in the U.S. or Japan or any of the developed countries for ten cents on the dollar."[3] Perhaps once or twice a millennium do these sorts of revolutions occur. Inevitably, the supply shock of billions of low-wage skilled workers radically resets how we interpret capital and labor in the production of goods and services. Forecasts of an end state of "globality" see a world where everyone from everywhere competes for everything.[4]

Finally, the ongoing fallout of the global financial meltdown raises the specter of slowing markets triggering deglobalization. Growing debt burdens, deflationary dynamics, risk-averse companies, and nationalistic consumers slow the cross-national movement of information, people, products, capital, and jobs. Governments constrain the animal spirits of capitalism, regulating what had become hazardously free markets. Economic freedom, as we saw with political freedom in Chapter 3, is under siege from surging state intervention.

WHAT'S NEXT?

Provocative in their own right, these interpretations suggest that in the opening decades of the twenty-first century, globalization has reinforced long-running developments and initiated powerful trends. The combined effects challenge one's lifestyle, job, company, country, and future. The possibility that globalization has reached an inflection point—namely, a time when old strategic patterns give way to the new—signals the need for managers to rethink economic principles and practices.

Understanding where we are heading calls for highlighting where we have come from. Initially, attention turns to how the world economy evolved from 1950 through 2000. During this time, the diffusion of democracy and free market principles powered growing trade among the richer developed nations. It also spilled over to many poorer developing countries. Institutions such as the IMF, WTO, and World Bank stabilized the playing field. Companies from the United States, Western Europe, and Japan—the so-called "Triad"—ruled international business and globalized the world in their image.

The precedents from this era, however, increasingly fall short in helping managers interpret today's puzzles. Indeed, focusing on the tried-and-true indicators of the past distorts one's interpretation of the contemporary global economy. Unquestionably, measures of the performance and potential in developed countries matter. However, they no longer matter decisively. Unfolding trends direct attention toward an epochal shift in the center of gravity of the global economy.

THE EMERGENCE

By 2050, four of the six largest economies in the world—Japan, China, India, and Russia—will be in greater Asia. Their growth will create a second tier of robust economies among their Asian neighbors, such as Singapore, Philippines, South Korea, Indonesia, Taiwan, Kyrgyzstan, Vietnam, Thailand, and Australia. Countries in other, once sluggish, parts of the world—Brazil in South America, South Africa in Africa, and Israel and Saudi Arabia in the Middle East—will develop along with their Asian counterparts (see Map 4.1). All are inexorably moving from the periphery to the center of the global economy, though each at a different pace.

Extrapolating from 2013 out to 2050 is, unquestionably, more speculation than estimation. Still, these countries are implementing powerful pro-growth policies. Hard data

MAP 4.1 Leading Emerging Economies

There are various types of market designations, including advanced, industrial, postindustrial, and developing. Here, we highlight those markets that are commonly referred to as emerging economies. These countries earn this designation given the status of their market development and high rate of economic growth.

Source: Based on Morgan Stanley Emerging Market Index and the *Economist*.

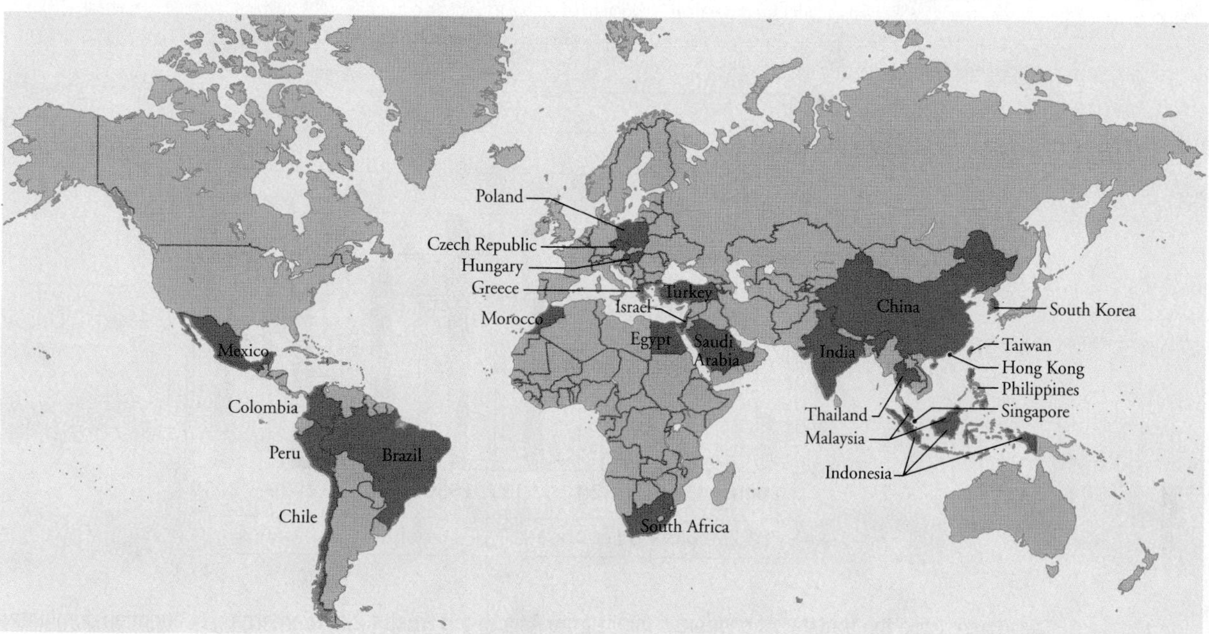

confirm their success so far. In 1980, the combined output of emerging economies accounted for 36 percent of global GDP. They crossed a milestone in 2009, accounting for more than half of total world GDP.[5] Similarly, emerging economies' share of world exports is nearly 50 percent (up from 20 percent in 1970). Their share of the world's foreign-exchange reserves is 70 percent (up from net deficits in the mid-1990s). China alone holds more than 28 percent of total reserves in the world. Elsewhere, the IMF reports that the ten fastest-growing economies during the years ahead will all be in emerging markets. Others suggest that 400 midsize emerging-market cities, many unfamiliar in the West (e.g., Sanaa, Ouagadougou, Chittagong, Kinshasa), will produce about 40 percent of global growth over the next 15 years.[6] Institutionally, the G-7, long a developed market stronghold, expanded into the G-20, thereby giving new members like China, India, Brazil, Mexico, and South Korea greater say in global governance. These new stakeholders advocate different views of trade promotion and investment regulation. Collectively, the accelerating rise of emerging economies signaled that the wealthy countries of the twentieth century would not dominate the global economy in the twenty-first century.[7]

The budding economics in emerging markets suggests the revolution has only begun. Ambition to improve infrastructure, increase productivity, create jobs, and alleviate poverty has put into motion what will likely be the biggest economic stimulus in history. The last transformation of similar magnitude—the Industrial Revolution—involved far fewer people in far fewer nations but still produced a century-and-a-half economic expansion that altered lives everywhere. Today's revolution spans the globe, includes far more people in far more countries, and represents the biggest opportunity in the history of capitalism. We are currently experiencing roughly ten times the economic acceleration of the Industrial Revolution, on more than 100 times the scale, resulting in an economic transformation that carries over 1,300 times the force of change. The transfer of the leadership baton from wealthy countries to emerging markets, for better and for worse, revolutionizes our interpretation of economic environments.

PRECEDENTS AND PREDICTIONS

Making sense of the situation moves some to review a broader span of history. Tracking the past millennium, they say, puts the current economic drama into perspective. Before the steam engine and the power

FIGURE 4.1 Emerging Markets Make a Comeback

Throughout most of the past millennium, today's emerging economies, most notably China and India, accounted for about 70 percent of global economic output. By the twentieth century, today's developed economies, such as the United States, Germany, and Japan, generated more than half of global economic output. Trends suggest that, by 2050, if not sooner, emerging economies will again account for more than 70 percent of global economic output, thereby culminating their comeback.

Source: Based on Development Centre Studies, *The World Economy:* A Millennial Perspective, OECD Publishing, 2006. Looking to 2060: *A Global Vision of Long-Term Growth,* OECD Economic Policy Papers, November 2012.

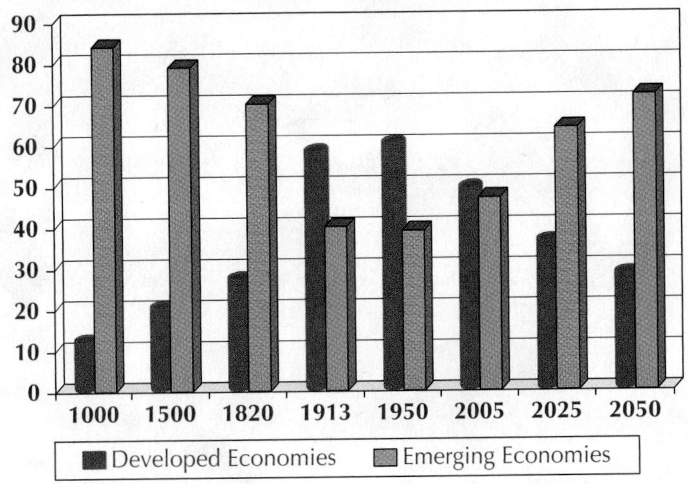

loom drove the transfer of economic might from Asia to the West, today's emerging economies dominated world output. From 1000 to the mid-1880s, they produced, on average, 70 to 80 percent of world output (see Figure 4.1). Over this span, China and India were the world's two biggest economies; China alone generated one-third of the world's gross domestic product in 1820. In 1850, China produced the highest percent of all the goods consumed in the world. Britain, riding the Industrial Revolution, soon claimed this title before ceding the top spot to the United States around the beginning of the 20th century. By 1950, emerging economies' share of global output had fallen to 40 percent, China's to 5 percent. They lost their lead (temporarily, trends now suggest) as internal political failure, aggravated by colonial exploitation and unfair trade agreements, spurred isolationism and xenophobia. Consequently, the Industrial Revolution benefited the West while bypassing today's emerging markets.

Today, their ambition is straightforward: Restore their historic stature as the engine of the global economy. Since 2001, annual growth in emerging markets has averaged 6.4 percent. While they expand, the global financial crisis slows and shrinks many developed economies, which on average have shown 1.6 percent annual average growth. Over the next decade, emerging economies will grow at an average of 6.8 percent a year. In addition, nearly 70 percent of the world growth over the next few years will come from emerging markets, with 40 percent coming from China and India and another 15 percent from Brazil, Indonesia, Russia, and South Korea.[8] In contrast, most developed economies will be fortunate just to grow. If these trends persist, in a couple of decades today's emerging economies will complete their comeback, again accounting for more than 70 percent of global output.[9] Symbolizing this process, China reclaimed the top spot it last held in 1850—producing 19.8 percent of all the goods consumed in the world in 2009; the United States, leader for the previous 110 years, produced 19.4 percent and fell to second.[10] Likewise, the IMF reported that by 2012 China had become the most "central" trading power in the world—the biggest or second-biggest trading partner for 78 countries.[11]

The diminishing role of today's rich economies, coupled with the accelerating scope of emerging ones, changes investment, trade, consumption, wealth, poverty, fiscal, and monetary patterns. For some, these shifts pose threats. For others, they create opportunities. Figure 4.2 suggests who sees which. Noted one observer, "No visitor to the emerging world can fail to be struck by its prevailing optimism, particularly if his starting point is the recession-wracked West. . . . [Emerging markets] see opportunities in every difficulty rather than difficulties in every opportunity."[12] In other words, strategic inflection points do not necessarily lead to disaster, as computers did to typewriters or the Internet to print-centric media.

FIGURE 4.2 Taking Stock of the Situation

Surveys regularly tap citizens' sense of their nation's economic situation. These results, the latest in a long-running series, suggest folks in emerging economies have greater confidence in their current economic situation than do their counterparts in developed markets.

Source: Based on Pew Global Attitudes Project: Country's Economic Situation, 2012, Retrieved April 15, 2013 from www.pewglobal.org/database/?indicator=5.

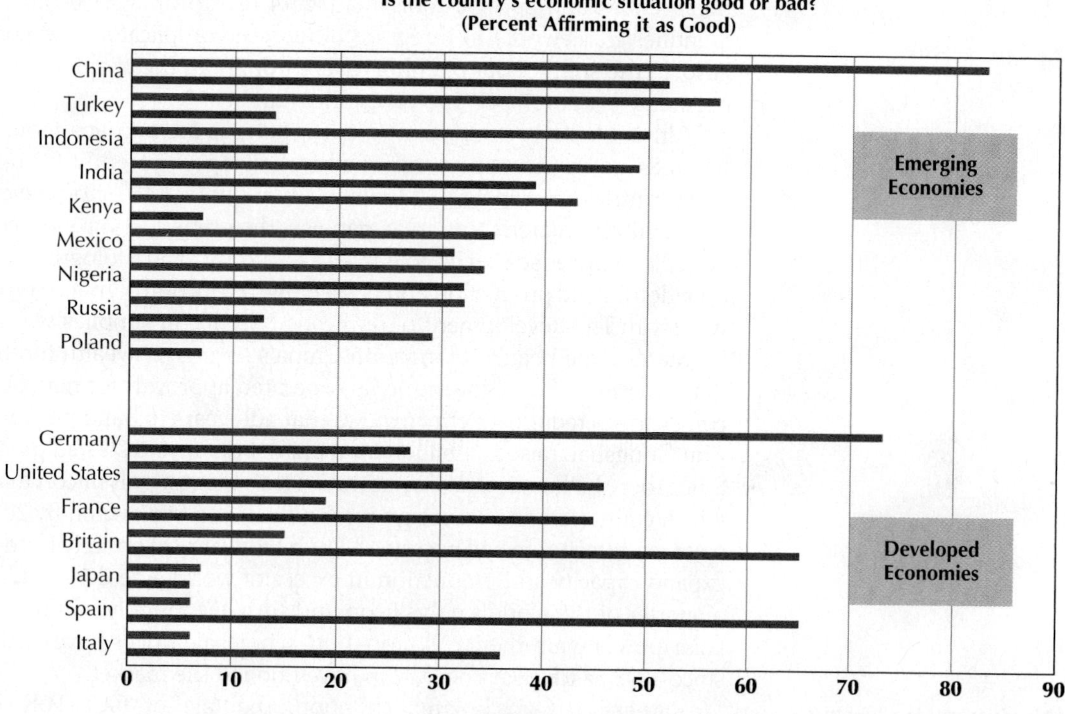

Change creates prospects for players, whether newcomers or incumbents, who are adept at operating in the new economy.

HERE AND NOW

Megatrends such as "The Comeback" are millennial events. And, unquestionably, trends often go awry. Still, at this point the odds are that policymakers, executives, workers, and investors will wrestle with the consequences of the Comeback. Against such a backdrop, this chapter profiles the frameworks they use to interpret the brave new world. Economic change, particularly the sort we have seen during the global financial crisis, seems unpredictable. Nevertheless, as this chapter shows, there is rhyme and reason that helps managers interpret the development, evaluate the performance, and assess the potential of economic environments. ■

QUESTIONS

4-1. Transformations such as the Comeback happen quite rarely. Their infrequency, however, only amplifies their revolutionary impact on our lives. Identify from the case how your life has changed, or will likely change, given the Comeback of the emerging economies. For a point of comparison, think about what you've learned through your studies about how the transition from the Agrarian to the Industrial Revolution changed the way people lived their lives.

4-2. Identify from the case the three most important factors that you believe drive the Comeback of emerging economies. Explain why you think they would have the greatest impact on the development, performance, and potential of the economic environment in a developed country such as Germany, Japan, or the United States.

INTRODUCTION

As our first three chapters have shown, cultural, political, and legal systems influence a company's decisions on where, when, and how to do business. Completing our profile of the key dimensions of the macro-business environment, this chapter presents the general perspectives and specific tools managers use to analyze economic systems. All along, it identifies frameworks to integrate otherwise complicated and confusing interpretations.[13] Also, in the spirit of our opening case, throughout the chapter we compare and contrast the economics of developed and emerging markets.

Although easily overdramatized, these tasks are perhaps more decisive than ever in our lifetimes given the opportunities and challenges currently facing individuals, companies, and countries. Consider the following situation: In 2007, shortage of polycrystalline silicon—the main raw material for solar panels—threatened China's nascent solar-energy industry. Polysilicon prices soared tenfold in a year, hitting $450 a kilogram in 2008. Foreign companies then dominated production and passed high costs onto Chinese producers. Beijing's response was swift: The development of domestic polysilicon supplies was declared a national priority. State-owned banks, along with China's sovereign-wealth fund, poured money into local manufacturers. Local governments expedited approvals for new plants. In the West, polysilicon factories require lengthy reviews that add years to building plans. In China, entrepreneur Zhu Gongshan raised $1 billion for a plant, built it, and started production within 15 months. Since then, he has created one of the world's biggest polysilicon makers, GCL-Poly Energy—which counts China's sovereign wealth fund as a key owner. By 2013, the 10 largest Chinese solar manufacturers had borrowed $18 billion, almost entirely from state-controlled banks, to expand capacity and production in excess of worldwide demand. Today, China makes about a quarter of the world's polysilicon and supplies roughly half the global market for finished solar-power equipment.[14] To top it off, wholesale prices have declined by nearly 75 percent since 2008 as Chinese companies have flooded the market.

Managers study a country's economic environment to assess its development, explain its performance, and estimate its potential.

Rather than an isolated situation, the tale of GCL-Poly Energy is becoming the norm. Emerging economies are reinventing systems of production and distribution and experimenting with entirely new business models. From mobile money in Kenya to frugal innovation in India, innovations change the business environment. As a result, Western MNEs increasingly rethink strategies and reposition assets. IBM India's headcount, for example, has grown from a few hundred in 1999 to more than 150,000 today. Likewise, Cisco combined all of its emerging-markets activities into a single unit: "Cisco East" in Bengaluru. To spearhead change, one of its highest-ranking executives moved to Cisco East with the title of chief globalization officer. All the while, policymakers worldwide watch the game, adding this or taking away that in order to boost performance.

NEW MARKETS, NEW PERSPECTIVES

Studying an economic environment helps managers make better investment choices and operating decisions.

Managers track changes, evaluating events and trends to spot opportunities and preempt difficulties. The scale and scope of new markets easily thwart analysis. Therefore, managers commensurately stress-test their interpretations by qualifying analysis with new perspectives. Key viewpoints include:

Countries Differ in Various Ways Countries have different levels of economic development, performance, and potential. For instance, in absolute terms, gross world output more than quintupled between 1970 and 2012, growing from $12 to $69 trillion. Thus, globalization seemingly expanded the economy for all. In relative terms, though, many countries prospered, some more than others, and a few not at all. Why? Different reasons explained different performances in different countries. Hence, dissimilar economic processes require anticipating new situations. Forecasting, say, China's response to polycrystalline silicon shortages would have encouraged some options while rejecting others. Estimating the attractiveness of a country as a place to do business and, once there, making prudent investment and operational decisions depends on how well managers understand, anticipate, and adapt to the peculiarities of its economic environment.

Economic and Political Changes Alter Market Circumstances Although the pace varies from country to country, economic environments continually change. Since the 1980s, companies came to enjoy opportunities as nations adopted the principles of capitalism and practices of free markets. China's fast-tracking its polysilicon factories, impossible in 1980, moved it from the periphery to the center of the solar power industry in 2013.[15] Indeed, Chinese businesses' eagerness to rush into attractive industries, such as wind turbines, solar power, and robotics, and swamp it with state-backed investment disrupts normal economic practices. In the West, the global financial crisis has reset the game, triggering market reforms and tighter regulation. In the East, it has endorsed growing government manipulation of market activities to achieve political goals.

In both worlds, changing economic policies reveal government ambitions and spotlight implications for economic freedom. Executives worldwide must determine if events are isolated or signal the start of a trend.[16] Consequently, managers study changes, both big and small, both here and there, that shape economic environments. And, in the back of their minds, managers realize that steps taken in Ireland, Thailand, Australia, or Mexico differ from those taken in China, Brazil, Estonia, or South Africa. Moving from good to great performance hinges on distinguishing common trends from unique events.

CONCEPT CHECK

"The Forces Driving Globalization" explained how an economic environment responds to technology, trade, competition, consumer attitudes, and cross-border relationships. The scope of the connections among these conditions spurs MNEs to examine them as both independent and interdependent factors.

Connections, Change, and Consequences Globalization connects countries. Choice in one has consequence in others. So companies monitor changes in countries where improving macro trends or revised policies open markets or strengthen competitors. For instance, the United Nations estimates there are approximately 22,000 multinationals based in the emerging world. Few of these existed 10 years ago. Many more will exist 10 years from now.[17] The number of companies from Brazil, India, China, or Russia on the *Financial Times 500* moved from 15 in 2006 to 55 in 2012. Going forward, 400 midsize emerging-market cities will generate about 40 percent of global growth over the next 15 years.[18] Figure 4.3 highlights this process, showing the changing center of economic gravity in our world. It has shifted over the past centuries, but, since the mid-1980s, the pace of change—from the West toward the East-has been increasing. Since this trend shows strong signs of continuing, executives and policy makers must respond.

Consider, for example, the consequence of this shift to Evergreen Solar. Aided by $43 million in public assistance, it became one of the largest makers of solar panels in the United States by 2009. In 2011, it shut its Massachusetts factory, fired 800 workers, and shifted production to a joint venture with a company in Wuhan, China, citing the superior location economics and higher government support.[19] Others fared far worse; more than a dozen solar panel makers in the United States, as well as in Europe, have shut factories or gone bankrupt since 2012.[20]

CONCEPT CHECK

A principle of the globalization doctrine is the broadening network of relationships among people, companies, countries, and institutions. Philosophically, the same principle applies to the emergence and evolution of economies.

Challenges of the Comeback The rise of emerging economies distort traditional economic indicators. Greater competition for scarce resources raises the prices of commodities but lowers the costs of manufactured goods; more people are working worldwide but poverty is increasing; growing political control of economic processes improves efficiencies in the East but lessens them in the West; and recycling massive foreign exchange reserves means capital is too cheap here, too expensive there.[21] More than 70 percent of the world's growth over the next few years will be in emerging markets. Managers' macroeconomic instincts, tried and tested for the past decades in the West, must adapt to the changing, sometimes contradictory, circumstances in emerging markets.

Choices of Citizens, Policymakers, and Institutions Economics is vital to citizens, policymakers, and institutions. By 2000, the apparent triumph of free markets over state-controlled economies had led many countries to launch bold liberalization programs.

FIGURE 4.3 Evolution of the Earth's Economic Center of Gravity: 1 CE to 2025

The world's center of economic gravity has changed over the past centuries. One sees here the big jump from Asia to Europe in the 1800s, due to the Industrial Revolution, and then onward to the United States in the 19th century. Since the mid-1980s, however, the direction and pace of shift has changed. Now, for a host of reasons, the center of economic gravity increasingly moves toward Asia.

Source: Based on Richard Dobbs, Jaana Remes, James Manyika, Charles Roxburgh, Sven Smit and Fabian Schaer, *Urban World: Cities and the Rise of the Consuming Class*, McKinsey Global Institute, June 2012.

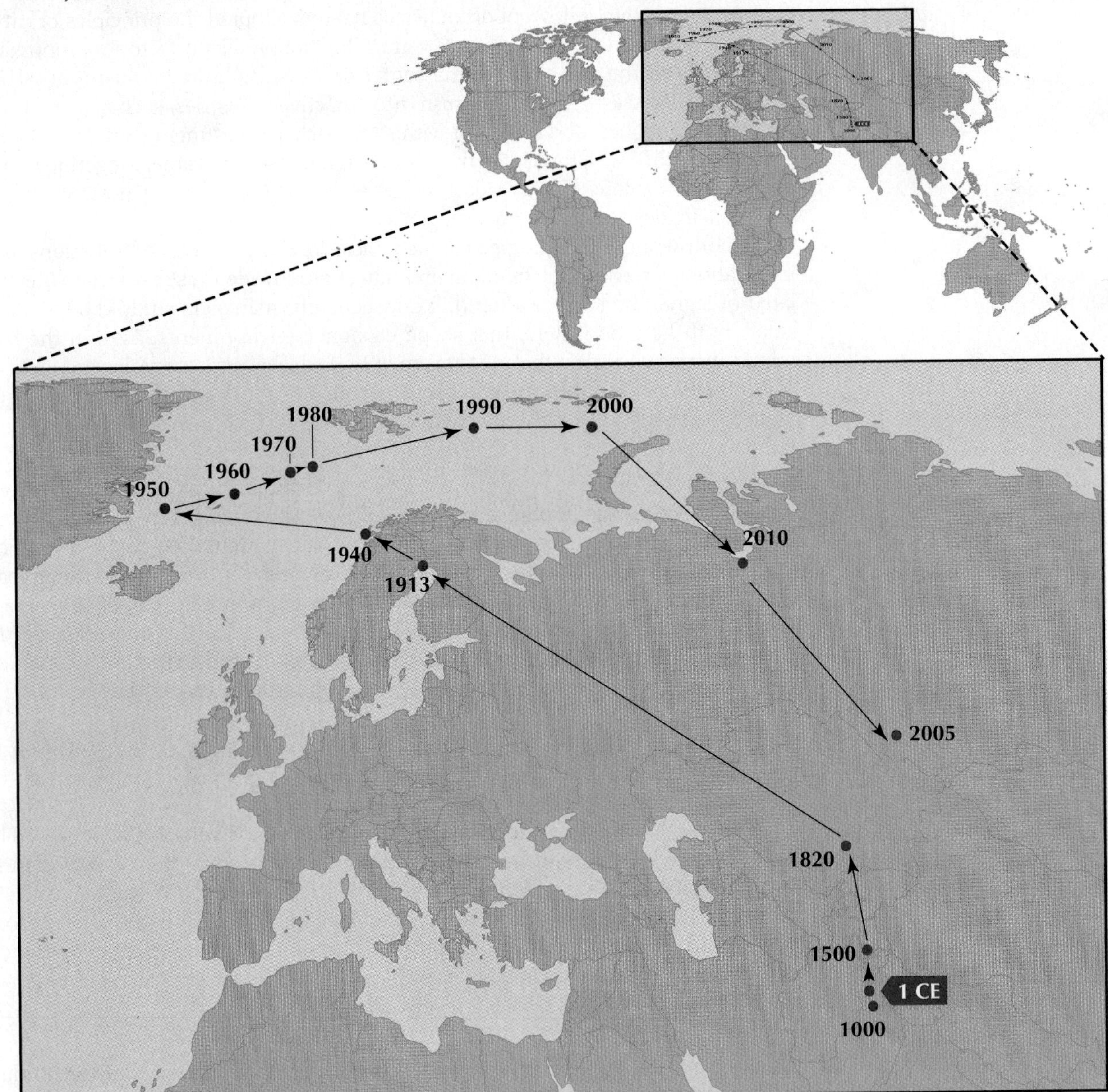

Pro-market reforms increased investment, consumption, employment, and wealth. The global financial crisis, however, contested the legitimacy and sustainability of market-led change. Free markets, the crisis showed, can also misallocate capital and fan opportunism. Governments, particularly those in the West, increasingly constrain the animal spirits of unbridled capitalism through stricter regulations. New market standards reset asset valuation and resource allocation, reshape trade and investment, and reconfigure industries. This perfect storm, as we saw unfold in the global solar power industry, changes efficiency frontiers, pricing patterns, competitive relationships, and government regulations. Hence, a fuller understanding of economic transitions and market evolution helps citizens, policymakers, and institutions make better decisions.

INTERNATIONAL ECONOMIC ANALYSIS

The World Bank identifies 214 discrete economic environments in the world today—188 countries and 26 economies with populations of more than 30,000.[22] Few MNEs can fund and run operations in all 214 markets. Resource constraints mean managers must prioritize their options, operating in countries that offer the greatest return with the least risk. Improving the odds of success depends on assessing the development, performance, and potential of an economy.

Given ever-present resource constraints, managers inevitably ask which countries in the world warrant investment as well as those they must avoid.

The study of economics has identified a host of objective measures that help systematize evaluation. However, although economics champions many scientific principles, it still relies on various behavioral assumptions to interpret activity.[23] As a result, the assessment of economic environments is often more conditional than universal because:

- *System Complexity* The complexity of even the simplest economic system defies straightforward classification. Stipulating indicators that definitively represent a country's economic performance and potential is difficult. Certainly, managers consult an ever-expanding set of indicators. The challenge is identifying those that matter, mapping them onto a market, and monitoring their performance.
- *Market Dynamism* Often, market changes make today's valid measures invalid tomorrow. In the wake of the global financial crisis, some indicators that worked in 2007 were flawed by 2009 and remained dubious in 2013. On a larger scale, analysis anchored in the market fundamentalism of the West poorly fits the state-sponsored capitalism at play in the East. Challenges arise in determining how to adjust trusted market analytics for new circumstances.
- *Market Interdependence* Just as no one is an island, no country is isolated. The consequence of connections is an integrated system in which actions in one market influence outcomes in others. Interdependencies complicate interpretations. Adjusting analysis for actions and reactions across a broad scope of markets is difficult.
- *Data Overload* Managers are flooded with more information, raw knowledge, and clever insights than ever before. Rather than improving market analysis, increasing data streams from workplace chats, mail, email, websites, voicemails, instant messaging, telephone and cellphone calls, memos, and onward complicates interpretation. If unchecked, analysis paralysis confounds decision-making.

Figure 4.4 shows how managers approach these issues. It identifies the macro-economic conditions that shape a country's development, performance, and potential. It also highlights

FIGURE 4.4 Economic Factors Affecting International Business Operations

Although economic environments vary from country to country, they share telltale principles. Managers often focus on universal characteristics, tors, notably the matters of economic freedom, type of economic system, and leading economic indicators, to organize analysis.

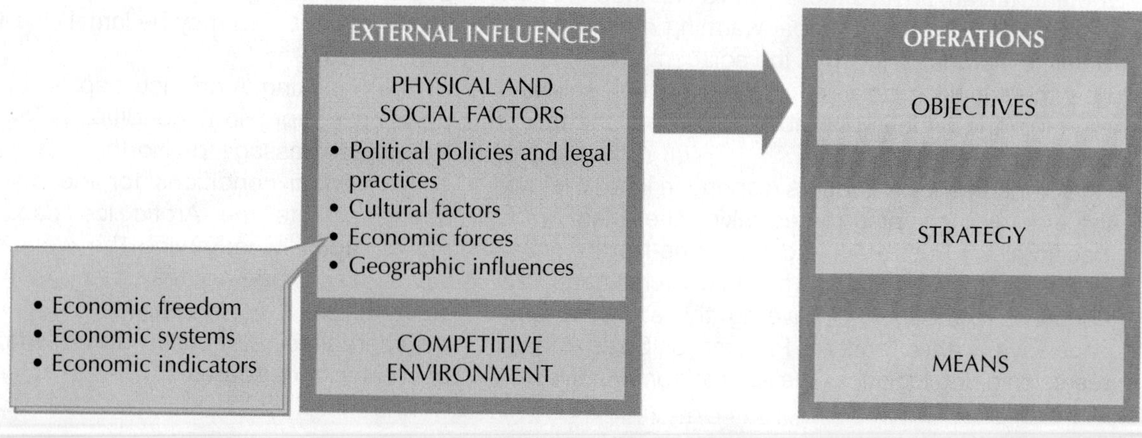

CONCEPT CHECK

Chapter 1 notes changing environmental conditions promote and constrain globalization, Chapter 2 notes changing cultural identities, and Chapter 3 notes changing political philosophies and legal outlooks. The same perspective applies here as well—namely, the changing economic environments of international business create opportunities and impose constraints.

the elements that guide assessment—namely, economic freedom and type of economic system—and suggests that linkages among them signify that a change in one causes change in others. Clarifying interactions among elements of an economy helps estimate its development path and performance potential. Therefore, managers typically integrate insights from company activities, analysts' reports, and news articles in developing a mosaic profile that represents an economy's features and estimates its interactions.

Figure 4.4 confirms the usefulness of applying a systems perspective.[24] It helps managers qualify their interpretation of economic conditions in terms of three criteria: (1) how much economic freedom they will have to make investments and run operations as they see fit; (2) the country's type of economic system and how current macro policies shape its development and performance; and (3) the drivers of economic change, particularly the micro-conditions that moderate economic freedom and the country's shifts in economic systems. Collectively, these insights pinpoint where investments should go and, more importantly, where they should not.

Does Geography Matter?

Consequence of Change in Arctic Sea Ice

Understanding economic environments moves managers to mind the world's changing dimensions, both physical as well as virtual. For example, economic geography is the study of the location, distribution, and spatial organization of economic activities across the earth. One would think, given the relentless expansion of trade and investment, that the terrain of our planet had been thoroughly mapped over the past millennium. However, for both good and bad reasons, we see intriguing developments in the geography of globalization.

Logistic Options: Canals and Passages Before the Panama and Suez Canals were built, shipping lanes circumnavigated the far reaches of the continents. Today, the bulk of goods moving between eastern United States, northern Europe, and Asia navigate the Panama Canal. Others, moving between Asia and southern Europe travel through the South China Sea, cut past Singapore, round the bottom of India, and pass through the Suez Canal to access the Mediterranean. Just as these canals changed the flow of trade, so too might global warming do the same. Satellite images, as seen in the adjacent photo, show how the shrinking polar ice cap has opened shipping routes in the once impassable "waters" at the top of the world.

Companies and countries respond in kind, evaluating emerging shipping routes linking the Atlantic and Pacific along Russia's Arctic coast (the Northern Sea Route) or through Canada's Arctic Archipelago (the Northwest Passage).[25] Traveling these fabled passageways, rather than via Panama or Suez Canals, resets shipping logistics. The voyage from Vladivostok in far east Russia to Rotterdam, Germany via the Northern Sea Route takes less than a month, compared to six to eight weeks through the Panama Canal. Shipping goods from Shanghai to Hamburg via the Northwest Passage shaves around 6,400 nautical miles (4,000 miles) and two to three weeks off the traditional journey through the Suez Canal.[26]

Ice Melts: Consequences and Choices Presently, ships can feasibly ply the northern routes at the end of the summer melt season.[27] Accelerating ice loss may largely free the Arctic Ocean of summer ice before 2050. Scientists tracking the annual maximum extent of the ice reported that 2011 was among the lowest ever measured. "For the first 20 years of the satellite record, the average annual maximum was basically uniform," reported NASA. "Then, in 2011, we see an abrupt decline."[28] Conditions continued deteriorating in 2012, with the total ice melt demolishing records. Satellite scans found that half of the ice went missing in September 2012, compared to the average September during 1979-2000. Current melt rates indicate the Arctic Sea may be largely ice-free as early as summer 2020.[29]

The shrinking Arctic ice cap is, at best, a mixed blessing. Improving conditions for traveling the Northwest Passage or Northern Sea Route depend on worsening conditions for the planet. As climate change resets the Arctic ice cap, to say nothing of radically redrawing the world's coastlines, it yields new trade routes, markets, and resources. Nevertheless, an increasingly hotter world poses innumerable side effects that may trump the benefits of shorter trade routes. ■

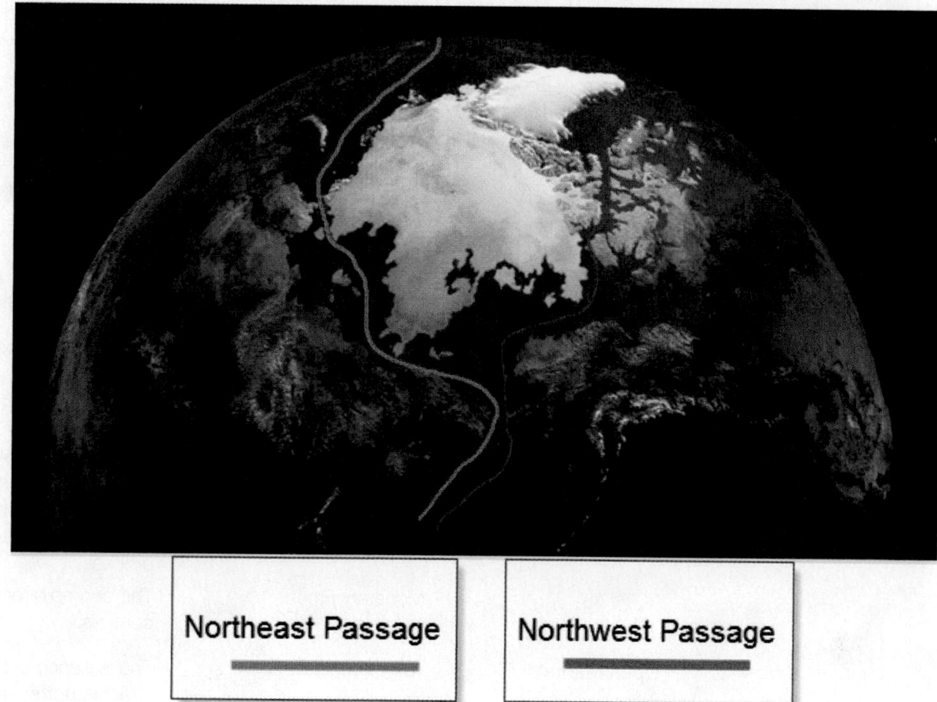

Passages through the Arctic Sea Ice

The shrinking Arctic ice cap is, at best, a very mixed blessing. If ice melt rates continue, they threaten to destabilize the environment. But, as less ice steadily opens the Northern Sea Route and Northwest Passage, it creates significant trade and logistic options.

Source: Based on NASA satellite image taken September 2010

ECONOMIC FREEDOM

Chapter 3 discussed political freedom for a simple reason: Any dialogue on politics, no matter the terminology, dimensions, or dynamics, ultimately addresses the issue of what one is free to do. We reapply the same logic here. Although managers monitor a range of economic issues, analysis ultimately centers on what they are free to do as economic agents: What investments can they make? How can they allocate resources? What property rights can they claim? How can they compete? Whom can they hire and fire? What forms of operations can they engage? In many countries, these sorts of freedoms are so taken for granted that they rarely cross one's mind. In many others, however, the freedoms are so repressed that they serve as ongoing points of fascination and recurring points of controversy.

Economic freedom holds that one has the right to work, produce, consume, save, and invest in the way that one prefers.

Against this backdrop, **economic freedom** is the "absolute right of property ownership, fully realized freedoms of movement for labor, capital, and goods, and an absolute absence of coercion or constraint of economic liberty beyond the extent necessary for citizens to protect and maintain liberty itself."[30] Put simply, the greater the degree of economic freedom, the greater freedom individuals have to decide how they wish to work, produce, consume, save, and invest. Economic freedom does not exist independent of the state. Rather, it is both protected and regulated by the state.

The **Economic Freedom Index** estimates the extent to which a government constrains free choice and free enterprise for reasons that go beyond the need to protect property, liberty, safety, and efficiency. The index rests on Adam Smith's notion that "basic institutions that protect the liberty of individuals to pursue their own economic interests result in greater prosperity for the larger society."[31] The Index of Economic Freedom analyzes 50 indicators that comprise 10 components organized into four categories (see Table 4.1). The Heritage Foundation annually applies this index to 177 countries, grading the performance of each. The higher the score on a factor, within the range of 0 to 100 percent, the higher the degree of economic freedom (or, conversely, the lower the level of government interference).

TABLE 4.1 Dimensions of the Index of Economic Freedom

The Index of Economic Freedom is constructed of 10 specific components of economic freedom. They are grouped into four broad categories.

Category	Component	Measure
Rule of Law	Property Rights	Ability of individuals to accumulate private property, secured by clear laws that are fully enforced by the state.
	Freedom From Corruption	Degree that corruption introduces insecurity and uncertainty into economic relationships
Limited Government	Fiscal Freedom	Tax burden imposed by government on its citizens.
	Government Spending	Government expenditures as a percentage of GDP.
Regulatory Efficiency	Labor Freedom	Aspects of the legal and policy framework that regulates the country's labor market.
	Business Freedom	The ability to start, operate, and close a business that represents the overall burden of regulation as well as the efficiency of government in the regulatory process.
	Monetary Freedom	The degree of price stability and the extent of price controls.
Open Markets	Trade Freedom	The absence of tariff and non-tariff barriers that affect imports and exports of goods and services.
	Investment Freedom	Ability of individuals and firms to move resources, without restriction, into and out of activities both internally and across the country's borders.
	Financial Freedom	Efficiency of banking as well as the independence of the financial sector from government control and interference.

Source: Based on information reported in "Methodology, 2013 Index of Economic Freedom Book," *The Heritage Foundation*, in partnership with the *Wall Street Journal*, retrieved February 6, 2013. www.heritage.org/index/book/methodology.

ECONOMIC FREEDOM TODAY

The aftermath of the great financial crisis and ensuing global recession has seen a decrease in economic freedom among countries worldwide. In 2011, economic freedom regained momentum, but by 2013 the global advance had ground to a halt.[32] Certainly, governments reiterated the importance of sound finances, open markets, regulatory reform, and property rights. And, among the 177 countries ranked in the 2013 Index, economic freedom scores improved for 91 of them while declining for 78. Nonetheless, the worldwide average freedom score was 59.6 percent in 2013, down from the pre-crisis high of 60.2 percent set in 2007.[33]

Asia-Pacific countries set the standard for both the best and the worst: Hong Kong, Singapore, Australia, and New Zealand are the world's freedom flagships, while North Korea, Uzbekistan, Turkmenistan, and Timor-Leste rank among the least economically free. Despite the United States' registering its fifth consecutive year of declining economic freedom, progress in Canada and Mexico supported North America as the world's freest region. Elsewhere, countries in South and Central America/Caribbean showed the sharpest drop in economic freedom; a continued decline held throughout the Middle East/North Africa; and the "mostly unfree" or "repressed" countries of sub-Saharan Africa struggled to gain traction. Europe shows progress with improvement in 32 countries and decline in just nine.

Worldwide, the expansion of economic freedom slowed in 2013; it remains below its pre-crisis high set in 2007.

Map 4.2 indicates that five countries have free economies, 30 are rated mostly free, 50 moderately free, 59 mostly unfree, and 33 repressed. The freest economies are Hong Kong, Singapore, Australia, New Zealand, and Switzerland; the least free include North Korea, Cuba, Zimbabwe, Eritrea, and Venezuela. The United States dropped to ninth place in 2013 largely due to increased government spending, debt, and regulations. Its score of 77.8

MAP 4.2 Global Distribution of Economic Freedom

The Index of Economic Freedom classifies a country as either: *free, mostly free, moderately free, mostly unfree*, and *repressed* given the degree to which its government regulates individual's economic choices. The greater the regulation, as indicated by a lower score, the less choice an individual commands.

Source: Terry Miller and Kim Holmes, 2013 Index of Economic Freedom, Washington, DC: The Heritage Foundation and Dow Jones & Co., Inc. 2013 (www.heritage.org/index/images/book/2013/region-web-map-WORLD-large.jpg, retrieved January 31, 2013).

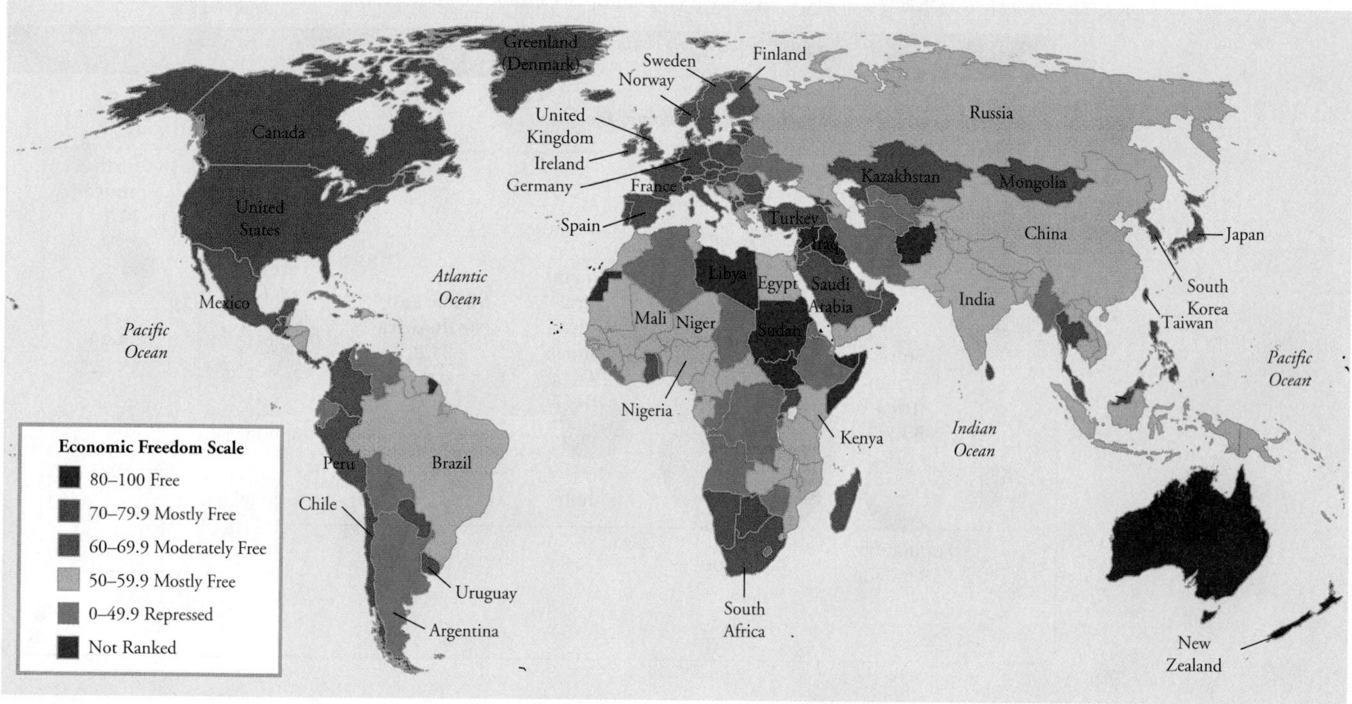

placed it in the "mostly free" category. In 2007, its score of 81.2 ranked it fifth worldwide and earned it a slot in the "Free" category. Lastly, qualifying the rankings by demographics refines analysis. Roughly 5.5 billion people reside in countries with somewhat to low degrees of economic freedom (see Figure 4.5), whereas approximately 1.3 billion live with moderate to high degrees.

THE VALUE OF ECONOMIC FREEDOM

Economic freedom helps explain a country's development, performance, and potential. Higher-rated countries generally outperform laggards on a variety of measures. They have higher rates of growth and productivity, and their average income is more than double the worldwide average and seven times higher than in mostly unfree and repressed economies (see Figure 4.6). Furthermore, inflation and employment rate better in economically free countries, as do life expectancy, literacy, poverty reduction, and environmental sustainability.[34] The message of economic freedom is unequivocal: liberating resources from government control improves financial performance, economic stability, and standards of living.

The track record of free markets around the world indicates that economic freedom is positively related to financial prosperity, economic stability, and standards of living.

TRENDS IN ECONOMIC FREEDOM

For the past few decades, managers had reasonably presumed that countries would reform their markets to increase economic freedom. Driving change was the fact that nations with free markets consistently outperformed unfree countries. The fall of the Berlin Wall in 1989, in punctuating the triumph of capitalism over communism, symbolized the supremacy of

FIGURE 4.5 Economic Freedom by Region, with Population

The relationship between economic freedom and population indicates that the vast majority of the world, approximately 5.5 billion people, lives in countries whose governments constrain their choices on how they wish to work, produce, consume, save, and invest.

Source: Terry Miller and Kim Holmes, 2013 Index of Economic Freedom, Washington, DC: The Heritage Foundation and Dow Jones & Co., Inc. 2013, retrieved January 31, 2013 from www.heritage.org/index/book/chapter-1, Chart 7.

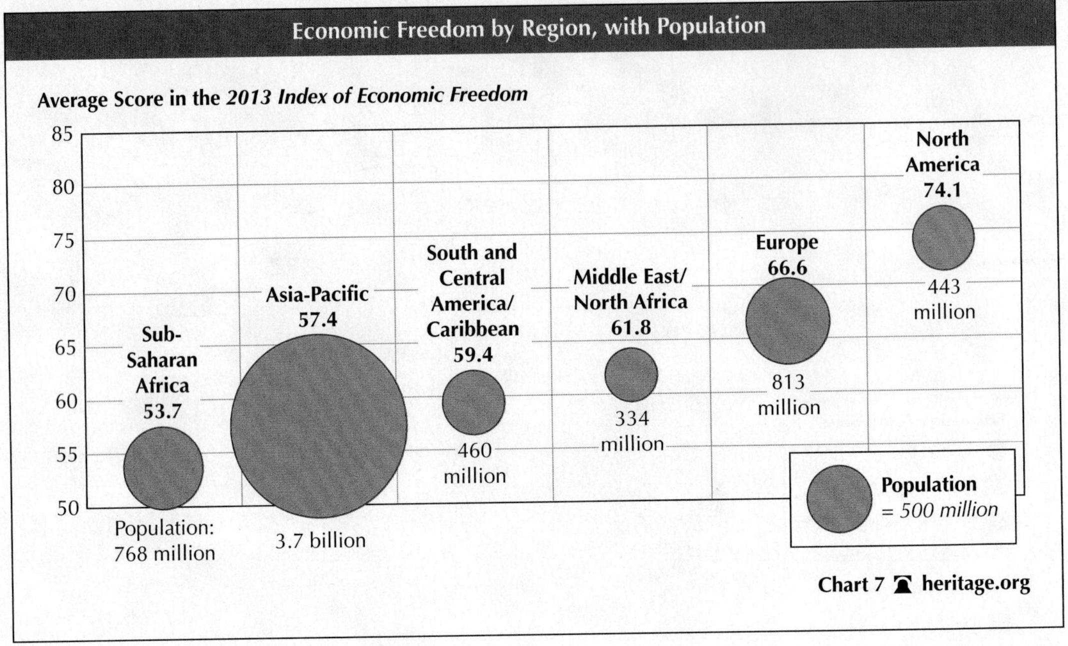

FIGURE 4.6 Economic Freedom and the Standard of Living

Economic freedom has powerful relationships with a variety of market, social, and political measures. Here, we see a strong positive correlation between economic freedom and a broad indicator of the standard of living.

Source: Terry Miller and Kim Holmes, 2013 Index of Economic Freedom, Washington, DC: The Heritage Foundation and Dow Jones & Co., Inc. 2013, retrieved January 31 from www.heritage.org/index/book/chapter-1, Chart 3, 2013.

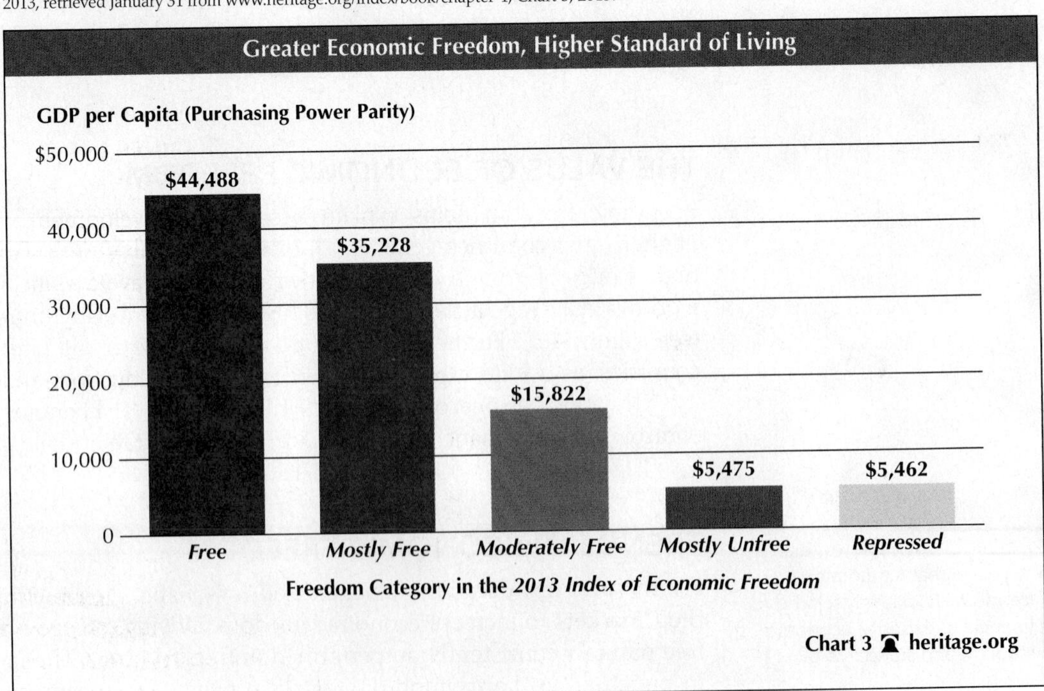

economic freedom over state tyranny. Large and growing majorities believed that people's lives benefit more, not less, with greater personal choice. Increasingly, countries abandoned the policies of state control and adopted the principles of economic freedom and practices of capitalism. Throughout the world, governments deferred to the laws of supply and demand—the invisible hand of the marketplace rather than the visible hand of politicians—to anchor the philosophy and regulate the practices of their economic environments.

The global financial crisis, by spurring a resurgence of state intervention, has interrupted the decades-long expansion of economic freedom.

Today, changing marketplace conditions and unfolding political trends threaten MNEs with increasingly uncertain economic circumstances. The global financial crisis has disrupted the expansion of economic freedoms. In the United States and elsewhere, the immediate aftermath of the crisis saw measures of consumption, investment, industrial production, exports, and equity valuations tracking or doing worse than trends seen during the Great Depression.[35] Stubborn downturns in many economies signaled the biggest global economic contraction since World War II.

The scale, scope, and swiftness of the global financial crisis highlighted the limits of a market economy, contested the usefulness of market fundamentalism, and spurred rethinking of government's role in the economy. To that end, declared former U.S. President George W. Bush during the height of the crisis, "I've abandoned free-market principles to save the free-market system."[36] States' neoliberal policies tightened controls in a rush to regulate the animal spirits of free markets. Stabilizing panics, safeguarding citizens, redistributing wealth, and sustaining demand took precedence; each objective inevitably diminished economic freedom.

Today, some seven years down the road from the start of the crisis, many economies have stabilized and begun recovering. Still, sovereign debt crises, deflationary dynamics, sluggish growth, and rising unemployment complicate projections. As the world regroups, managers struggle to pinpoint the implication of these trends.

Fear of Freer Markets The causes and consequences of the crisis challenge the legitimacy of the quest to maximize economic freedom. Many countries, especially those hit hardest and still experiencing anemic growth—such as Spain, Italy, Ireland, Portugal, Cyprus, Greece, France, and Japan—show weakening support for free markets. Rather than regarding economic freedom as an unconditional ideal, many fortify safeguards to prevent market disruptions. Consequently, state control of economic affairs escalates. Concurrently, dissatisfaction with neoliberal capitalism prevails across the globe. An average of 11 percent of respondents across 27 countries held the opinion that capitalism works well.[37] Some 23 percent saw it as fatally flawed. Many called for a new economic system—including 43 percent in France, 38 percent in Mexico, 35 percent in Brazil, and 31 percent in Ukraine. Only in two countries—United States (25 percent) and Pakistan (21 percent)—did more than one in five feel that capitalism works well as it stands.[38]

Our opening case cautions against qualifying attitudes in developed versus emerging economies. In 2002, 80 percent of Americans regarded the free market as the best economic system for the future—then the bellwether of support. By 2010, support had fallen to 59 percent. Conversely, emerging economies' enthusiasm for free markets exceed that now found in the United States. Nominally Communist China is one of the world's strongest supporters of free markets at 68 percent, up from 66 percent in 2002. Some 67 percent of Brazilians and 59 percent of Indians see free markets as the best option for the future, though they concede that its endemic flaws require reform and regulation.[39] Overall, about half of the "world" reasons that the free market is still the best option. However, as we will see below, standards of economic freedom differ between developed and emerging markets.

Managers watch key events to gauge the contest between economic freedom and state control. These include how the government

- regulates the economy
- protects property rights
- sets fiscal and monetary policies
- enforces antitrust regulation

The Market Test A first-order goal of an economic system is straightforward: apply sound macroeconomic policies that sustain productive enterprise. Low inflation, high employment, prudent public finances, and openness to trade and FDI are telltale signs. Meeting these standards powers performance and boosts potential. In situations like those we see today, the legitimacy of the prevailing economic outlook is ultimately tied to how people feel about their particular situation. Those whose lives improve support it; those whose lives deteriorate clamor for change. Dire circumstances spur calls for government intervention as citizens appeal to politicians to impose stability. Presently, if the legacies of the global financial crisis persist or worsen, we will see more people contest the legitimacy of free markets. Continuing skepticism will push for greater state control and, consequently, less economic freedom.

In summary, the question of whether free markets and their endorsement of maximum economic freedom create the superior economic system is no longer a straw man. The global financial crisis, besides disrupting markets, disrupts interpretations.[40] In many countries, notably those in the developed block, praise for the virtues of economic freedom has turned to criticism of its deficiencies. In others, notably emerging economies, we see the opposite. The evolution and interplay of these quite dissimilar perspectives alters the relationship between markets and governments. Managers watch trends evolve, resetting interpretations as needed.

TYPES OF ECONOMIC SYSTEMS

An economic system organizes the production, distribution, and consumption of goods and services.

Wherever they go, managers question how the host government might regulate the economy, authorize property rights, implement fiscal and monetary policies, and ultimately interpret economic freedom. Managers frame analysis by evaluating the particular type of **economic system** in a country. Despite variation here and there, throughout the world we see three types of economic systems: the *market*, *mixed*, and *command* economies (see Figure 4.7).

CONCEPT CHECK

Chapter 3 notes that the individual voter is the cornerstone of a democracy. Here we add that the individual, as a consumer, is the key factor in a free market. Whereas democracy recognizes the supremacy of voter sovereignty, the market economy recognizes the supremacy of consumer sovereignty.

MARKET ECONOMY

An economic system whereby individuals, rather than the government, make most decisions is a **market economy**. It is anchored in the doctrine of **capitalism** and the principle that private ownership confers inalienable property rights that legitimize the profits earned by one's initiative, investment, and risk. Optimal resource allocation follows from consumers exercising their freedom of choice and producers responding accordingly. A market economy of the sort seen in Hong Kong, Singapore, Australia, Switzerland, Canada, and the United States, for instance, grants people the economic freedom to decide where to work, what to do and for how long, how to spend or save money, and whether to consume now or later.[41]

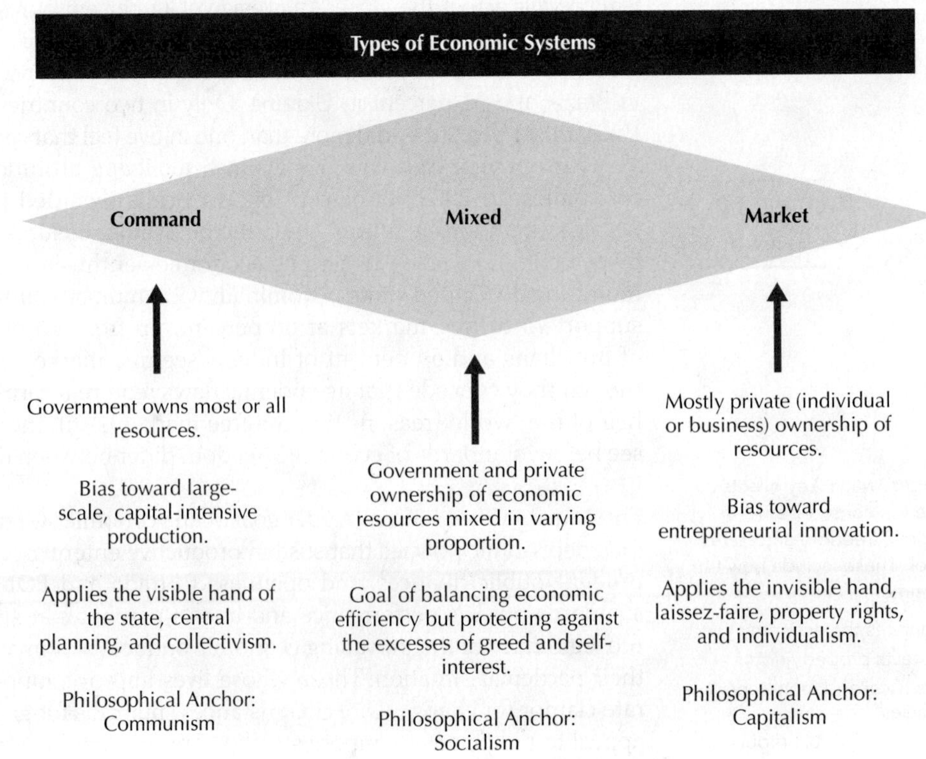

Types of Economic Systems
Command
Mixed
Market
Government owns most or all resources.
Bias toward large-scale, capital-intensive production.
Applies the visible hand of the state, central planning, and collectivism.
Philosophical Anchor: Communism
Government and private ownership of economic resources mixed in varying proportion.
Goal of balancing economic efficiency but protecting against the excesses of greed and self-interest.
Philosophical Anchor: Socialism
Mostly private (individual or business) ownership of resources.
Bias toward entrepreneurial innovation.
Applies the invisible hand, laissez-faire, property rights, and individualism.
Philosophical Anchor: Capitalism

FIGURE 4.7 Types of Economic Systems

The three predominant types of economic systems endorse different philosophies, advocate different principles, and apply different approaches.

TABLE 4.2 Means and Methods of a Market Economy

Telltale signs of a market economy endorse themes of individualism and principles of economic freedom. Here, we profile key means and methods of developing and sustaining a market economy.

Privatization	A necessary condition of a market economy is the state's sale and legal transfer of government-owned resources to private interests. Privatization, by letting the private sector regulate supply and demand, improves production and consumption decisions.
Deregulation	Government regulations reduce individual choice—i.e., "Government is not a solution to our problem. Government is the problem."[42] Deregulation helps markets optimize productivity.
Property Rights	Property rights give entrepreneurs ownership of their idea, effort, and risk. Protection boosts economic freedom by assuring individuals, not the government, will prosper from their ingenuity.
Antitrust Legislation	Antitrust laws encourage the formation of industries with as many competing businesses as the market can sustain. They prevent monopolies from exploiting consumers and restraining market growth.

Ultimately, individuals' free choice in a market economy powers a country's progress toward prosperity.

Capitalism is based on the principle of private ownership of capital.

The market economy champions the doctrine of **laissez-faire**, which can be literally translated as "Let do," and more broadly advises "Let it be" or "Leave it alone." Whatever the translation, it opposes governmental interference in economic affairs beyond the minimum necessary for the maintenance of peace, safety, and property rights. It sees the "invisible hand" of self-interested consumers as the foundation of efficient markets. Consumers, through their interactions with producers, optimally determine relationships among price, quantity, supply, and demand. As Adam Smith observed, a market economy pushes producers, spurred by the profit motive, to make products that consumers, spurred by their quest to maximize purchasing power, buy. Consequently, by virtue of what they buy—and, for that matter, do not buy—consumers direct the efficient allocation of resources and the optimal valuation of assets.

The doctrine of laissez-faire endorses governmental noninterference in economic affairs.

Less Is More An enduring bias toward minimal government intervention anchors market economies. The less visible the "hand" becomes due to government intervention, the more efficient the market. Still, the invisible hand is fallible. The need for public goods (e.g., traffic lights, flood control, national defense) and regulatory protections (e.g., minimum wage, product safeguards, environmental standards) requires some governmental involvement. Therefore, a market economy calls upon the state to enforce contracts, protect property rights, ensure fair and free competition, regulate certain activities, and provide general safety and security (see Table 4.2). Nevertheless, the anchor of the market economy remains the invisible hand of economically free agents driving growth and prosperity.

COMMAND ECONOMY

The invisible hand of a market economy, due to the need to provide public goods and protect society, is made visible by government involvement.

In theory, **communism** champions state ownership of resources and control of all economic activity. Nominally a political ideology, communism calls for an egalitarian, classless, and ultimately stateless society based on the government's command of the economy.[43] Implementing this socioeconomic structure imposes a **command economy** in which the government owns and controls resources, taking on the authority to decide what products to make, in what quantity, at what price, and in what way. For example, in a market economy, if the government wants computers, it collects taxes and buys computers at market prices from privately held companies. In a command economy, the visible hand of the government, with little if any regard for price, orders state-owned companies to make computers.[44]

In a command economy, the visible hand of the state supersedes the invisible hand of the market.

Making the invisible hand visible means that government officials—not consumers—determine the prices of goods and services. Often, product quality is erratic and typically deteriorates. Products are usually in short supply and there are few substitutes. State-owned companies, typically large-scale, capital-intensive, inefficient, and unprofitable, have few resources to upgrade or incentives to innovate. Indisputably, command economies can outperform for short periods. Controlling everything and everybody lets the state mobilize idle resources, usually labor, to generate high-growth spurts. High productivity continues as long as the state competently manages slack, low-cost resources. Improving performance often moves state officials to proclaim that a command economy is a productive alternative to capitalism. History, however, shows otherwise. Central planning often proves counterproductive, given that officials, no matter how clever, cannot consistently predict consumers' preferences. Far more typically, command economies crash in the face of growing inefficiency, inequality, cronyism, corruption, and, ultimately, disgruntlement.

CONCEPT CHECK

Totalitarianism subordinates people's day-today lives—including their market behavior and economic outlook—to the state. Government command of the economy supports this policy, enabling it to determine asset valuation and resource allocation.

Command economies have included the Soviet Union (which, at its height, was the world's second-largest economy), China during its Great Leap Forward era beginning in 1958, India prior to its economic reforms in 1991, and Afghanistan during the rule by Soviet occupation and the Taliban. Today, we see few pure examples, most notably North Korea and, to a lessening degree, Myanmar and Cuba. More often, managers operate in economies that exhibit many but not all methods of state control. These sorts of states, such as Iran, Venezuela, Turkmenistan, Belarus, Zimbabwe, Ethiopia, Vietnam, Saudi Arabia, Russia, and China, fall in the "mostly unfree" and "repressed" categories of the Economic Freedom Index. Their predominant bias toward political stability spurs the state to regulate individual choice extensively.

MIXED ECONOMY

A mixed economic system combines elements of the market and command economic systems; both government and private enterprise influence production, consumption, investment, and savings.

Most economies, broadly labeled **mixed economies**, fall between the market and command types. A mixed economy is a system in which economic decisions are principally market-driven and ownership is largely private, but the government intervenes, from a little to a lot, in allocating resources. For example, U.S. President Obama reasoned that it is the government's responsibility to make "strategic decisions about strategic industries."[45]

The mixed economy integrates elements of the command and market systems. On one hand, the state intermingles ownership of some resources, centralizes certain planning functions, and regulates the market. On the other hand, the interaction of supply and demand, signaled to producers through the price system, rather than public dictate, optimizes production.[46] For example, in a mixed economy the government may have partial ownership stakes in computer manufacturers. Rather than instructing these firms on the type, quantity, style, and price of computers to make, the government permits firms to decide given prevailing market conditions.

A market economy is anchored in capitalism, a command economy is anchored in communism, and a mixed economy is anchored in socialism.

Democracy, we saw, calls for a market economy. Communism calls for a command economy. Likewise, socialism calls for a mixed economy. Specifically, **socialism** advocates regulating economic activity with an eye toward social equality and fair distribution of wealth. It utilizes the market to allocate resources, as does capitalism, but it subjects investment to social controls that are directed by the government, as does communism. Socialism holds that a fair and just economy, besides optimizing efficiencies, defends the weak by supporting low unemployment, prevents the consolidation of wealth and privilege, helps the impoverished by fairly redistributing income, stabilizes the system by intervening in market failures, and protects society by limiting abuses of market power. Proponents argue that governments far more conscientiously promote an egalitarian ethos that deters opportunistic individualism than does a free market.

The aftermath of the global financial crisis supported many of these views. Countries that favored a strong state presence, higher taxes, heavier regulation, tougher job-protection laws, and generous social safety programs better navigated the economic upheaval than had their free market counterparts.[47] As the economically free United States regrouped and wondered "What next?" the socialism of Denmark supported its steady economic performance and citizens' status as the happiest people in the world.[48] As Britain's free market struggled, Sweden's mixed economy persevered, given its government's ownership of national companies.[49]

Advocates of the mixed economy do not unconditionally endorse state intervention as a panacea. Unchecked, the entanglement between politics and economics often makes it impossible to tell where the government ends and the corporation begins. Political agendas, the particular slate of officials, and social circumstances shape how the government balances economic freedom and state control.[50] Hence, the extent and nature of government intervention differs, depending on local circumstances, from country to country. At present, countries commonly classified as mixed economies include South Africa, Japan, South Korea, Sweden, Austria, France, Brazil, Germany, and India. They typically fall in the "mostly" and "moderately" free categories of the Economic Freedom Index.

Looking to the Future

State Capitalism: Detour or Destination?

Managers wonder: Will free markets prevail, protecting hard-won economic freedoms? Or will governments reclaim the commanding heights of the economy, taking control of development, regulating performance, and determining potential? For decades, economies had steadily adopted the free market model given the success of countries that had migrated from command and mixed to market economies. However, the financial crisis hurled markets into disarray. Now, buffeted by the choices and consequences, we see countries resorting to greater state economic control.

So, managers watch and wait as the contest between the siren call of free markets and the surge of state power determine the sort of economy that works best in the modern world. As they do, many reflect on a perplexing riddle: Notwithstanding its documented dividends, why do so few countries maximize economic freedom? Map 4.2 shows that five of 177 countries have "free economies" while another 30 are "mostly free." Put differently, 35 of 177 countries—just over 19 percent—grant their residents significant economic freedom. Worse still, just five of 177 countries—about 3 percent and home to less than one percent of the world's population—rank as "free."[51] The rest do not. Instead, many of these countries, such as China, Russia, United Arab Emirates, Mexico, Venezuela, and Saudi Arabia, practice forms of state capitalism.

State Capitalism

State capitalism is an economic system whereby political officials decide how assets are valued and when and where they are used.[52] The state nurtures national champions, manages trade relations and exchange rates to promote exports and discourage imports, leverages control of the financial system to provide low-cost capital to domestic industries, and runs nationalist legal and regulatory systems. Recall our earlier profile of GCL-Poly Energy of China. Zhu Gongshan, the owner, relied on quick approvals, cheap government loans, and state support to build a global-scale company in 15 months. China's ensuing disruption of the solar power industry prompted many firms to shut down; some, such as Evergreen Solar of the U.S., relocated to China.

Some may contend that state capitalism sounds a lot like a mixed or command economy. In some ways it is. But in important other ways, it is not. Foremost, state capitalism is a system whereby the government explicitly manipulates market outcomes for political purposes. Politics has a profound and pervasive impact on the performance of markets. The government uses markets to promote stability and growth, thereby creating the prosperity and wealth that maximize state power and legitimate its ongoing rule. State capitalism, unlike capitalism or communism, does not stipulate an ideological component; the government manages markets for long-term political survival and power projection, not to enforce an abstract ideal or promote the cult of personality. Instead of politicized revolutionaries promising a brave, new future, state capitalism relies on pragmatic technocrats who, applying sophisticated management ideas, develop a prosperous, productive economy. The payoff is plain: subverting political freedom with economic prosperity fortifies the authority of the state.

Visible Only as Needed

Absent an ideological agenda, the state prefers relative market anonymity. As long as a growing economy supports stability, it stays in the shadows, influencing activities and shaping outcomes. In the event plans go awry, the invisible hand quickly turns visible. The state steps in, revises policies, resets funding, and redirects activities. National, provincial, and local officials, by controlling resources, can direct operations and markets as needed.

State capitalism promotes the growth of particular industrial sectors and companies in order to speed economic development. Typically, the state attracts innovative foreign companies, using state-owned banks to provide cheap loans, favorable regulations, and stable industry settings. The state uses the tax code, for example, as a tool for economic, not social, engineering. Bolstering its solar power industry, for example, led China to recruit Evergreen Solar, a technology-rich U.S. company, by providing financial incentives and tax breaks.

Who Owns Whom

The state typically owns its national champions, using them to influence market activity as well as consolidate its authority. For instance, China is the majority owner of 99 of the 100 largest publicly listed Chinese companies, including all major banks, its three major oil companies, its three telecom carriers, and its major media firms. Collectively, 129 huge conglomerates in finance, media, mining, metals, transportation, communication, and so on answer directly to the Chinese central government.[53] Furthermore, China's provinces and cities own and run thousands of medium-sized and smaller ones. State officials, while discrete, are not shy. At all levels, "the tentacles of state-owned enterprises extend into every nook where profits can be made."[54] Similar situations in Saudi Arabia, Russia, and Brazil, for instance, spotlight the state's expanding economic clout.

Telltale Marks

State capitalist economies, whether in the Middle East, Asia, Eastern Europe, or South America, have telltale marks. Public investment, public wealth, and public enterprise prevail. Officials fan economic nationalism. The state promotes domestic markets as sanctuaries for national champions. The state favors local companies at the expense of their foreign rivals in order to nurture national companies into global leaders. State capitalism has little need for an independent judiciary; the state typically treats the legal system as an apparatus that legitimates its policies as needed. It games the system, capturing competitive advantages through whatever means necessary. Officials install barriers to trade and investment in order to generate local development and prosperity. Regulations require foreign investors to form joint ventures with local companies when entering strategic industries. Moreover, foreign companies receive scant protection and even weaker legal defense.

Gaining Momentum

The global financial crisis has expanded the scale and scope of state capitalism. On one hand, countries that favored a larger state presence, higher taxes, heavier regulation, tougher job-protection laws, and more generous social safety programs dealt more successfully with market disruptions than did their free-market counterparts. On the other, state capitalism professes to better protect social values, equalize income distribution, and prevent the accumulation of vast wealth and powerful self-interests that threaten social harmony. Allowed to run free, market economies encourage the psychology that greed is good. Only a strong state, goes the reasoning, stops it from devolving into psychosis.[55]

Presently, some 70 strategically important countries worldwide are at a critical crossroads in determining their political and economic futures.[56] Whether they advocate free markets or state capitalism remains to be seen. Many see China as the bellwether; where it goes, both good and bad, many will follow. China has used state capitalism to develop and direct the world's fastest growing economy, which has, in turn, powered the swiftest, most extensive rise out of poverty any nation has ever seen. Its success—not just surviving but also prospering during the crisis—convinced "Chinese leadership that state control of much of the country's economic development is the steadiest path toward prosperity—and, therefore, domestic tranquility."[57] Likewise, Brazil reasoned that the state succeeded where the private sector failed during the crisis; said its current president, state capitalism "prevented the economy from being shipwrecked."[58] Economic renaissance in these and many other countries suggests that Western-style economics is no longer the only viable route to modernization.[59] A generation ago, the state-controlled economy was seen as a way station on the path to a capitalism market. Now, many see state capitalism as a sustainable economic model.

Given economic circumstances in the world today, one should not be surprised if others, particularly authoritarian one-party political systems, find state capitalism attractive. Arcing through Asia, the Middle East, Africa, and Latin America, authoritarian governments emulate China's model.[60] Through this arc, state-backed companies grow and expand, having accounted for more than a third of the emerging world's FDI over the past decade. Democracy's retreat, covered in Chapter 3, along with the surging success of state capitalism, helps explain why, out of 177 countries, 147 significantly regulate, restrict, or repress economic freedom. ■

ASSESSING ECONOMIC DEVELOPMENT, PERFORMANCE, AND POTENTIAL

Given an understanding of the general types of economic systems, managers turn to evaluate their critical components. They tap a rich portfolio of macro and micro measures to assess a country's economic development, performance, and potential. Some measures may be informal or idiosyncratic, such as number of wireless subscriptions, amount of electrical power generated, internet searches for telltale terms, or military officers running companies.[61] Typically, convention dominates practice. Matters of income and wealth often anchor analysis. Managers elaborate their analyses with indicators of sustainability and stability.

Broad classes of countries include

- Developing countries
- Emerging economies
- Developed countries

Before reviewing each class, a brief note on how we classify countries is in order. We follow the lead of the United Nations and World Bank in labeling low- and middle-income nations as *developing countries.* Less commonly, some refer to them as "underdeveloped" or Third World Countries; the latter was in vogue during the Cold War Era when the First World referred to the Democratic West and the Second World designated the Communist East. The 150 or so developing countries, as a rule, have low per capita income—an average of $3,813 in 2012. The vast majority of their residents have low living standards, marked by limited access to few goods and services.[62] Virtually all future population growth will occur in today's developing countries.

CONCEPT CHECK

In discussing "Growing Consumer Pressures" among the drivers of globalization, Chapter 1 notes that worldwide consumption grew six-fold in the second half of the twentieth century. Such information improves managers' investment choices and operating decisions.

The faster-growing, relatively prosperous developing countries such as China, Brazil, and India are increasingly referred to as *emerging markets* or *emerging economies.* Currently, there are approximately 30 or so **emerging economies** in the world (see Map 4.1). Table 4.3 lists some of the acronyms used to sort them. When one speaks of the emerging economies, one usually speaks principally of Brazil, Russia, India, and China (**BRICs**). Although much larger in scale and scope than other emerging economies, the BRICs are the vanguard of the Comeback. Many presume that where the BRICs go, both good and bad, others will follow. Our closing case highlights trends afoot in the BRICs.

Developed countries are those with high per capita income—an average of $37,545 in 2012. Their citizens enjoy a high standard of living with access to a variety of goods

TABLE 4.3 The Alphabet of Emerging Economies

Commonly, one comes across acronyms that classify various sets of emerging economies. As different countries develop, observers have coined a variety of shorthand codes.

Acronym	Members
BRIC	B for Brazil, R for Russia, I for India, C for China
BIC	Remove R for Russia
BRICS	Add S for South Africa
BRICK	Add K for South Korea
BASIC	Add AS for South Africa, Removes R for Russia
BRIIC	Add I for Indonesia
BRICIT	Add I for Indonesia, T for Turkey
BRIMC	Add M for Mexico
BRICET	Add E for Eastern Europe, T for Turkey
BRICA	Add A for Arab countries—Saudi Arabia, Qatar, Kuwait, Bahrain, Oman, and the United Arab Emirates
MIST	Mexico, Indonesia, South Korea, Turkey
N-11 (The Next 11)	Bangladesh, Egypt, Indonesia, Iran, Mexico, Nigeria, Pakistan, Philippines, South Korea, Turkey, and Vietnam
CIVETS	C for Colombia, I for Indonesia, V for Vietnam, E for Egypt, T for Turkey, S for South Africa

FIGURE 4.8 If Only It Was All In the Name

Source: Lee Lorenz/New Yorker Cartoon Bank/www.cartoonbank.com

"No, no—we used to be an undeveloped country, but now we're a developing country."

and services. Developed countries include Japan, Australia, New Zealand, Canada, the United States, and most European nations. Less commonly, some refer to them as high-income countries, advanced markets, or industrial countries. In the future, we may see the developed countries relabeled Established Market Economies, given their high per capita income, high standard of living, and sophisticated institutional framework but comparatively slower growth.

MEASURES OF ECONOMIC PERFORMANCE

The expanding barrage of data spurs managers to streamline market evaluation. Many anchor analysis in comprehensive single-item measures that provide a quick indicator of whether an economy (1) is expanding or contracting, (2) needs a boost or should be constrained, and (3) is threatened by recession or inflation. Akin to taking the temperature of a patient, measures such as **gross national income (GNI)** or **gross national product (GNP)** efficiently summarize the economic activity of households, business, and government in terms of their consumption, investment, spending, and trading. Indeed, Paul Samuelson, a Nobel Laureate in economics, described the measure of gross domestic product as "truly among the great inventions of the 20th century, a beacon that helps policymakers steer the economy toward key economic objectives."[63]

GNI is the broadest measure of economic activity for a country.

Gross National Income (GNI) is the broadest measure of a country's economy. It measures the value of all production in the domestic economy together with the income that the country receives from other countries (mainly interest and dividends), less similar payments it has made to other countries. Thus, the value of a Samsung TV built in South Korea as well as the portion of the value of a Samsung TV made in Japan using Samsung's resources is

TABLE 4.4 The 10 Largest Economies by GNI, 2011[a]

Rank	Country	GNI ($, billions)[i]	% of World Total
1	United States	15,148	22.75
2	China	6,643	9.98
3	Japan	5,739	8.62
4	Germany	3,617	5.43
5	France	2,755	4.14
6	United Kingdom	2,370	3.56
7	Italy	2,114	3.18
8	Brazil	2,107	3.16
9	India	1,746	2.62
10	Canada	1,570	2.36
**	World	$66,577	

[i] Data calculated by the Atlas Method, which smoothes exchange rate fluctuations by applying a three-year moving average, price-adjusted conversion.

Source: Based on World Bank Development Indicators 2011. Copyright 2013 by the World Bank. Reproduced with permission of the World Bank.

counted in South Korea's GNI. Similarly, the portion of the value of a Sony TV built in South Korea using Sony's resources counts in the GNI of Japan. Last, if Samsung's Japanese subsidiary repatriates profits to headquarters in Seoul, it increases South Korea's GNI. Table 4.4 identifies the 10 largest economies in the world in terms of GNI. Recall that the World Bank identifies 214 discrete economic environments in the world today; the 10 countries listed in Table 4.4 account for 65.8 percent of world GNI.

GNP is the total value of all final goods and services produced within a nation in a particular year.

Gross National Product (GNP) is the value of all final goods and services produced within a nation in a given year, plus the income earned by its citizens abroad, minus the income earned by foreigners from domestic production. Conceptually, world GNP and world GNI are equal. However, their slightly different calculation can result in a small discrepancy at the country level.[64] Consequently, managers crosscheck their analyses, noting the assumptions of the measure and characteristics of a particular country.

GDP is the total market value of goods and services produced by workers and capital within a nation's borders; it provides the truest measure of national economic activity.

Gross Domestic Product (GDP) The total market value of all output produced within a nation's borders, no matter whether generated by a domestic or foreign-owned company, is reported as a nation's GDP.[65] It the most commonly used estimator of the true performance of an economy given that it measures income, not wealth. That is, GDP estimates the flow of economic activity within a country, not simply its stock of productive assets. It also assesses economic environments in which the output of the multinational sector is a significant share of total activity. For example, about 90 percent of Irish exports are made by foreign-owned firms; GDP, not GNI, more accurately measures Ireland's economic performance. Technically, GDP plus the income generated from exports, imports, and the international operations of a nation's companies equal GNI. Therefore, both Samsung and Sony TVs made in South Korea contribute to South Korea's GDP, but TVs made in Japan by Samsung do not.

ADJUSTING ANALYTICS

GNI and its offshoots estimate an economy's absolute performance. Despite their strengths, they can mislead managers when comparing countries. For example, economic powers like the United States, Japan, and Germany consistently claim the top rankings when sorted by GNI. Some may mistakenly presume that they are also more productive and faster growing than lower-ranked countries. Often, the opposite is true. Therefore, managers improve the usefulness of GNI, GNP, and GDP by adjusting each for the (1) rate of economic growth, (2) size of the population, and (3) purchasing power of the local currency.

Managers improve the usefulness of GNI by adjusting it for the

- Growth rate of the economy
- Number of people in a country
- Local cost of living

Rate of Economic Growth Gross aggregates give a static snapshot. They do not measure the rate of change in an indicator. Interpreting present and forecasting future performance require pinpointing an economy's growth rate. The growth rate of GNI indicates a country's economic potential: If it grows faster (or *slower*) than its population, the country's standards of living are rising (or *falling*).[66] Figure 4.9 reports the forecast for real GDP growth rates of various developed and emerging economies.

The growth rate of GNI also indicates business opportunities. Looking at countries in terms of their growth rate finds a wide range. For instance, GDP in approximately 80 developing economies is rising at twice the rate of per capita growth in the world's richest countries, thereby powering their "Comeback." More specifically, China has been one of the fastest growing economies over the past three decades; it has expanded by 9.8 percent

FIGURE 4.9 A Divided World

Nominal GDP increases from year to year partly because a country produces more goods and services and partly because prices increase. Real GDP strips out price effects in order to estimate the annual growth in the actual production of goods and services. This conversion shows that many emerging markets are forecast to grow faster than developed markets between now and 2030.

Source: Based on *Looking to 2060: A Global Vision of Long-Term Growth*, OECD Economic Policy Papers, November 2012.

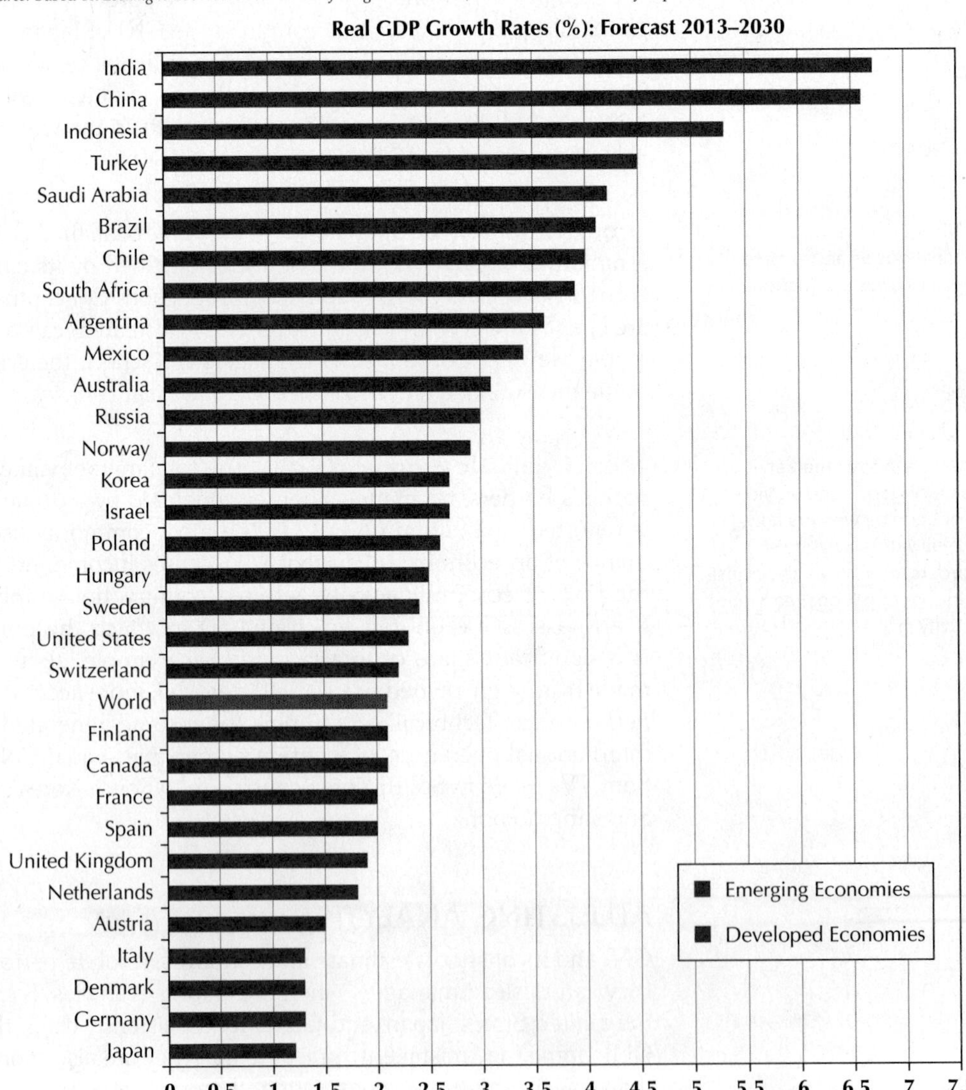

on average since 1995. Commensurately, its GDP has gone from about $600 billion then to $7.2 trillion in 2012. Rising income has fueled consumer demand, thereby attracting foreign investment.

Population Size Managers adjust GNI, like many other economic indicators, by the number of people who live in a country.[67] This conversion is common sense, given how unevenly the world's population of 7,174,530,636 (as of August 2013) is distributed—e.g., from a high of 1.34 billion in China to the low of 54 in the Pitcairn Islands.[68] Adjusting GNI by population, therefore, lets managers remove the effects of demography in assessing a country's relative performance.

For example, GNI may be low in absolute terms, such as is the case for Norway. However, Norway, with its 4.7 million residents, ranked first in the world by GNI per capita in 2012 at $98,860.[69] In comparison, the United States ranked 18th ($50,120), Japan 22nd ($47,870), Brazil 79th ($11,630), China 114th ($5,740), and India 164th ($1,530).

Map 4.3 shows that high-income countries are clustered in a few regions of the world. These countries account for about 15 percent of the world population but more than 70 percent of global GNI. On average, they report an average GNI per capita in the mid-tens of thousands ($). Lower-income countries are spread throughout the world and comprise a large share of the world population but a far smaller share of the world's GNI. They report GNI per capita from the mid-hundreds to low thousands ($).

Purchasing power parity provides a method of measuring the relative purchasing power of different countries' currencies for the same basket of goods and services.

Purchasing Power Parity GNI per capita does not account for the cost of living from one country to another. Instead, it presumes that a dollar of income in Minneapolis has the same purchasing power as a dollar of income in Mumbai, even though the cost of living differs between the United States and India. To state the obvious, costs of goods and services vary from country to country. Consequently, GNI per capita is unable to tell us much about

MAP 4.3 GNI Per Capita, 2011

A country's economic performance can change significantly when controlling for its demography. *GNI per capita* qualifies a country's economic performance in terms of the size of its population. For instance, China is the world's second largest economy when ranked by aggregate GNI. Adjusting its performance for its population of 1.344 billion people, however, moves it to the lower-middle income tier.

Source: Based on World Bank Indicators, The World Bank, http://data.worldbank.org/indicator/NY.GNP.PCAP.CD/countries?display=map

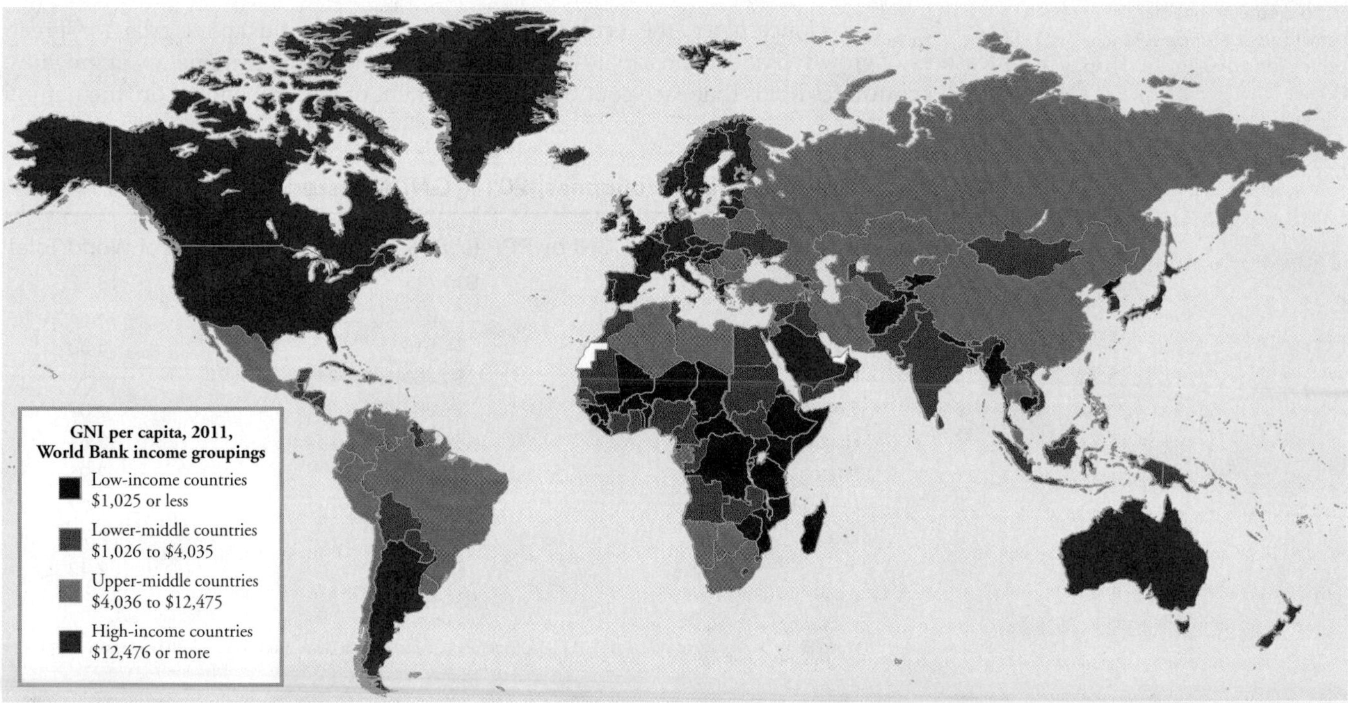

how many goods and services one can buy with a unit of income in one country relative to how much one can buy with a unit of income in another. Therefore, managers adjust GNI in terms of *purchasing power parity (PPP)*—namely, determining how much money is needed to purchase the same goods and services in two countries and using that information to calculate an implicit foreign exchange rate that reflects the same purchasing power, per unit of currency, in the different countries.[70] Adjusting income data for PPP essentially creates an international dollar that has the same purchasing power as a dollar has in the United States.

Table 4.5 shows the impact of adjusting national economic performance by PPP. Notably, the raw country rankings by GNI reported in Table 4.4 change. For instance, China, India, Russia, and Mexico move up while Japan, the United Kingdom, France, Italy, and Canada drop down or out. Second, PPP reduces some of the otherwise extreme variability in many country-to-country comparisons. Revisiting our comparison of the United States and India finds that India's GNI per capita in 2012 is $1,530 but rises to $3,840 when adjusted for local purchasing power.[71] The opposite occurs in the case of countries with expensive standards of living, such as Norway. Its GNI per capita falls from $98,860 to $64,030 when adjusted for the reduced purchasing power a unit of currency commands in that high-priced country. Map 4.4 profiles the countries of the world in terms of GNI per capita adjusted for PPP.[72]

PERFORMANCE AND POTENTIAL: ALTERNATIVE INTERPRETATIONS

Green measures gauge economic performance in terms of the effect of current choices on long-term sustainability.

Sustainability and stability perspectives hold that the objective of economic activity is to create an enabling environment for people to enjoy long, healthy, and happy lives.

Measures of gross national income emphasize monetary aggregates. As a result, GNI, GNP, and GDP, even after adjusting for growth rates, population size, and cost of living, only partially profile a country's performance and potential. Further complicating matters is the so-called "black" or "shadow" economy, namely legal and illegal business activities that fall beyond official measurement. In India, for example, the World Bank estimates the shadow economy was equivalent to a fifth of official GDP in 2010. Likewise, Europe's various shadow economies represent 22 percent of regional market activity—about $3.55 trillion and as large as Germany's entire economy.[73] In recourse, managers can improve analysis by estimating an economy's sustainability and stability.

Sustainability Concern for the ecological welfare of the world spurs calls for green measures of growth that expands analysis beyond narrow measures of monetary aggregates. **Green economics** holds that each country is a component of, and dependent on, the natural

TABLE 4.5 The 10 Largest Economies, 2011: GNI Adjusted for PPP

Rank	Country	GNI by PPP (U.S. $, 000 trillions)	% of World Total
1	United States	$15,211	18.82
2	China	$11,270	13.94
3	Japan	$4,516	5.59
4	India	$4,460	5.52
5	Germany	$3,287	4.07
6	Russian Federation	$2,917	3.61
7	France	$2,349	2.91
8	United Kingdom	$2,255	2.79
9	Brazil	$2,245	2.78
10	Italy	$1,968	2.43
**	World	$80,843	

Source: Based on World Bank Development Indicators 2011. Copyright 2013 by the World Bank. Reproduced with permission of the World Bank.

MAP 4.4 GNI Per Capita, 2011, Adjusted for Purchasing Parity

Adjusting raw income data in terms of purchasing power parity helps control for the relative costs of living and currency effects among countries. Doing so helps managers clarify a country's absolute economic performance in terms that reflect its particular living standards and market conditions.

Source: Based on World Bank Indicators, http://data.worldbank.org/indicator/NY.GNP.PCAP.PP.CD/countries?display=map

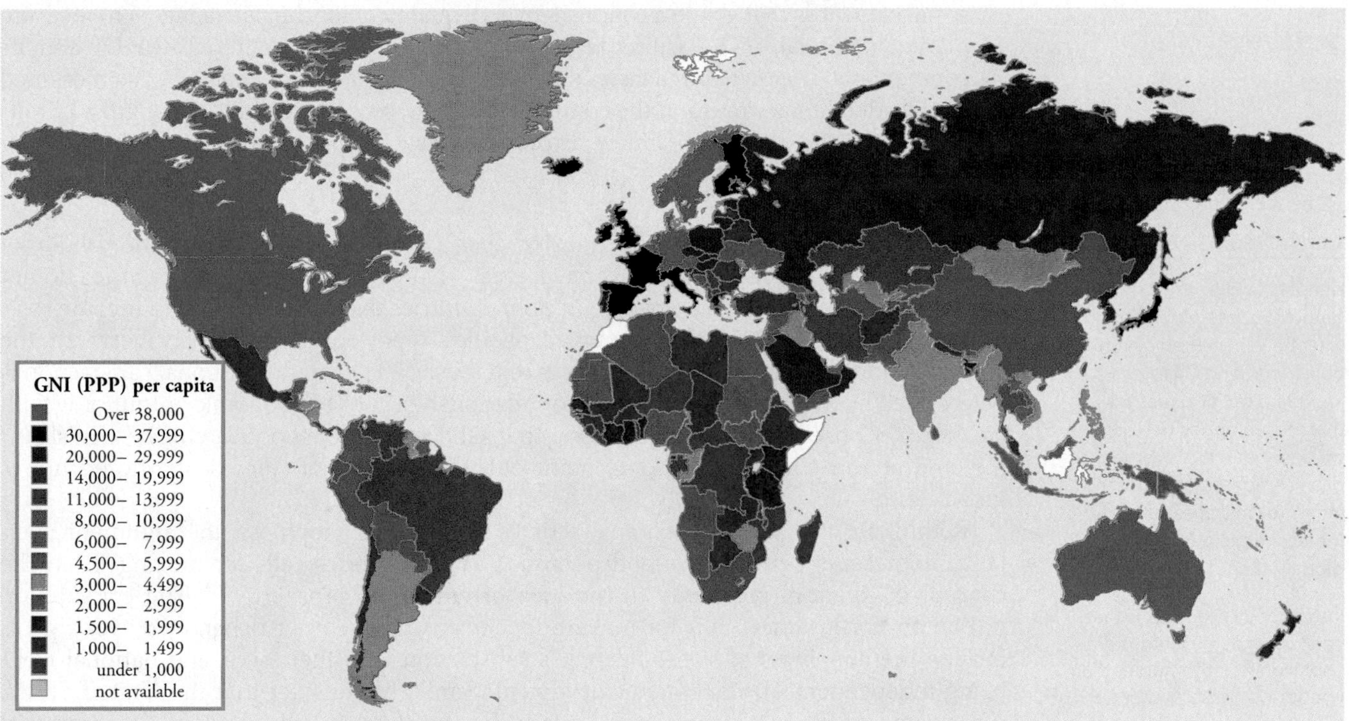

world. Measuring the monetary quantity of market activity through GNI, GNP, and GDP—without accounting for the associated social and ecological costs that result from the activity that generated economic growth—misrepresents performance and misinterprets potential. Instead, **sustainable development** proponents encourage interpreting economic activity in terms of its capacity to "meet the needs of the present without compromising the ability of future generations to meet their own needs."[74] As such, it endorses a broader accounting of the gains and costs of growth to better gauge an economy.

Presently, there is no consensus on how to greenify GNI, GNP, or GDP. Current candidates include:

- *Net National Product (NNP):* Measures the depletion of natural resources and degradation of the environment that result from generating GNI. As a company must depreciate its tangible and intangible assets when making a product, goes this reasoning, so too should countries. NNP does so by depreciating the country's assets commensurate with their use to generate growth.[75]
- *Genuine Progress Indicator (GPI):* Starts with the same accounting framework used to calculate GDP but then adjusts for values assigned to environmental quality, population health, livelihood security, equity, free time, and educational attainment. For example, unlike GDP, GPI values voluntary and unpaid household work as paid labor and subtracts the costs of crime, pollution, and family breakdown. Effectively, GDP versus GPI is analogous to the difference between the gross profits versus net profits—net is gross less the costs incurred. Accordingly, GPI will equal zero if the costs of pollution, crime, and family breakdown, holding all other factors constant, equal the monetary gains from the production of goods and services.

Fully understanding growth, progress, and prosperity calls for assessing the consequences of economic choice on sustainability and stability.

- *Human Development Index (HDI)* Matters of human development do not show up immediately in income or growth figures. Ultimately, the reasoning goes, they will, given that improving the human condition improves economic performance. So, estimating a country's degree of human development, in terms of the physical, intellectual, and social standards that shape a country's overall quality of life, helps managers to measure market potential.[76] The United Nations translates this view into the HDI and its components: *Longevity,* as measured by life expectancy at birth; *Knowledge,* as measured by the adult literacy rate and the combined primary, secondary, and tertiary gross enrollment ratio; and *Standard of Living,* as measured by GNI per capita expressed in PPP for U.S. dollars.

CONCEPT CHECK

Chapter 1 notes that some groups oppose globalization, Chapter 2 discussed cultural objections, and Chapter 3 identified political reasons that inspire opposition. Here, we add that critics charge that overly emphasizing monetary measures misrepresents the economic benefits of globalization.

An ongoing paradox is that people in rich countries are not significantly happier than people in poor countries.

Stability Policymakers have long puzzled over a paradox that questions the validity of monetary aggregates as performance measures.[77] Namely, people in rich countries do not appear to be any happier than people in poor countries. No matter how high income rose, little evidence indicated that it improved people's reported happiness. Furthermore, the emerging science of Happynomics reports that nearly 70 percent of personal satisfaction is determined by the quantity and quality of relationships, not by economic output or wealth creation.[78] Consequently, some contend that GNI and its offshoots are at best misleading, and at worst, flawed (as some point out, the expense of war boosts the economic growth rate).[79]

Rethinking the goal of economic activity in terms of happiness, the argument goes, better represents performance and potential. **Happynomics** calls for moving "from the concept of financial prosperity to the idea of emotional prosperity."[80] The constitution of Bhutan, for instance, calls for making its citizens happier, not richer, every year; goals include the happiness of society, people's satisfaction with their lives, and national well-being independent of monetary achievement. Similarly, consider that the United States, when rated on monetary measures, is far in front of France and Germany. Qualifying its performance in terms of life expectancy, leisure time, and income equality, however, moves living standards in France and Germany ahead of those in the United States.[81] Some may contend that mapping happiness unnecessarily confuses economic analysis. However, an unhappy citizenry may be a leading indicator of change in government policy that alters the economic environment.

Presently, estimation is difficult. Defining happiness, like beauty, is often in the eye of the beholder. Potential indicators, such as love, friendship, family relations, and actualization, are tough to pin down. In addition, how does one value goals, like safe streets and clean air, which can be measured? The intricacies of happiness capture increasing attention; insight should clarify measures. In the meantime, managers consider the following indices:

- *Your Better Life Index (YBLI)* This index measures well-being and perceptions of living conditions. Developed by the Organization for Economic Cooperation and Development (OECD), the YBLI advocates evaluating economic performance in terms of matters that people worldwide believe are important, such as housing, jobs, social relationships, health, security, work-family balance, and education, but that fall beyond the narrow scope of monetary measures. Explained the OECD, YBLI pushes the "boundaries of knowledge and understanding in a pioneering and innovative manner…It has extraordinary potential to help us deliver better policies for better lives."[82] The top ten countries, in terms of the YBLI and beginning with the leader, are Denmark, Canada, Norway, Australia, the Netherlands, Sweden, Switzerland, Finland, Israel, and Austria.[83]

Estimators of economic progress toward improving happiness include
- Your Better Life Index
- Gross National Happiness
- Happy Planet Index

- *Gross National Happiness (GNH):* Progressive society presumes that material and spiritual development occur side by side; one reinforces the other or both suffer. GNH measures a country's ability to promote equitable and sustainable socioeconomic development, preserving and promoting cultural values, conserving the natural environment, and establishing good governance.
- *Happy Planet Index (HPI):* Utilitarian views hold that people aspire to live long, healthy, happy lives. Therefore, a country's economic performance and potential is represented

by how well it helps its citizens do so while not infringing on the opportunity of future generations, and people in other countries, to do the same. HPI advocates measuring the environmental costs of growth while emphasizing that maximizing happiness and health, not monetary wealth, is the objective.

Point

Growth: Positive and Productive?

Point **Yes** Growth is not only good, it is a fundamental necessity. Growth is life, actualizing the productive potential of individuals, communities, institutions, and society. Growth provides long-term benefits to everyone in every country. It morally stabilizes society. It liberates those trapped in poverty. It reduces violent conflict. It raises living standards. It funds safety nets and government backstops. It creates material improvements that comfort life. It creates jobs, income, wealth, and prosperity for individuals and society. Let's take a closer look at each.

Moral Stability Growth affects social attitudes and political institutions, the keystone to the moral stability of society. People experiencing rising incomes and improving economies are commensurately tolerant of and benevolent toward each other. In a word, wealth engenders humanity. Growth creates the resources that promote transparency of authority, openness of opportunity, tolerance of diversity, pathways of social mobility, fair and just laws, and virtues of democracy.

Poverty Reduction Notwithstanding the kindness of strangers, growth is the only means to alleviate poverty for the billions struggling to sustain life. Growth in many impoverished countries has reduced the number of people living in abject poverty. Some 1.94 billion people, or 43 percent of the world population, lived below the extreme poverty line of $1.25 a day in 1981. Today, as freer markets fuel growth, it has dropped to 19 percent of the world—about 1.3 billion people.[84] Without growth, humanity loses the war against poverty. Billions, presuming they survive, suffer physically and psychologically.

Business Dividend Growth stimulates higher employment, capital investment, and profits. Rising asset valuations, stabilizing wealth effects, and resolute confidence in surviving tough times supports the prosperity of individuals and companies. Moreover, amidst the panic of the recent global crisis, people endorsed the virtue of growth. Some 76 percent of Americans agreed that U.S. strength is "mostly based on the success of American business" and that 90 percent admired people who "get rich by working hard."[85]

Fiscal Dividend Government finances are ultimately at the mercy of growth. A thriving economy boosts tax revenues, thereby providing local, state, regional, and national governments the monies to finance spending projects that support, enrich, and sustain society. Although appealing, history shows cheap government does not translate into good government.

Peace Dividend Growth creates more opportunities for more people in more places. People who see the potential for prosperity behave peacefully. Moving poor people into the middle class, for example, enables them to think and behave differently. Free from the tyranny of ceaselessly seeking sustenance and shelter, they become more open-minded, more concerned about their children's future, more influenced by abstract values than traditional norms, more inclined to settle conflicts peacefully, more supportive of free markets and democracy, and more inclined to have faith in the future.

Environmental Benefits Growth encourages innovations. People specialize in what they do best and, courtesy of pro-growth policies, outsource the rest. Together, these drive the efficient allocation of resources. The falling ratio of energy consumption per unit of GDP over the past 40 years, in the face of the growing abundance of goods and services, testifies to the benefits of growth. By making resources valuable, growth spurs us to consume them wisely.

Quest to Excel Growth incents people to bring to bear their ingenuity, their imagination, and their industriousness to find a better way, every day, to make a difference. Pushing back the frontier of human experience—whether it involves the trivial (e.g., forms of entertainment) or the substantive (e.g., alternative energy)—is powered by the quest to grow. Eliminating the pursuit of progress saps society's vibrancy.

Life Growth supports longer lives. In 1900, life expectancy at birth was 47 years in the United States; by 2013, after a century marked by an epic burst in economic growth, it was 78.2 years. Moreover, people now need to work just half the time they once had to, relying on new tools to boost productivity, finding comfort in rising quality-of-life standards, and taking solace in improving health care.

Progress or Decline Unquestionably, as the Counterpoint argues, growth imposes costs on individuals, humanity, and the planet. Moreover, we fully agree that these costs are striking. Still, our position is crystal clear: No matter the costs of growth, they pale in comparison to the unacceptable price of not growing. Put bluntly, when growth stops, decay starts.

Growth: Positive and Productive?

Counterpoint

No We accept the premise that growth supports life, fostering morality, transparency, tolerance, mobility, justice, and liberty. However, ignoring or, worse, denying the costs of these benefits—costs that seem to grow faster than growth itself—imperils civil society and, ultimately, the survival of humanity and the planet. Once you untangle the strands of half-truths, falsehoods, and self-interests that lace insidious pro-growth arguments, the promise of endless milk and honey for all devolves into a bitter delusion. The problems of growth span the immediate and the future; where one stops and the other starts is tough to pinpoint. Still, as this list shows, each hits society hard.

Growth Privileges Few The quintessential promise of growth is "a rising tide lifts all boats." In theory, as an economy grows, it generates higher wages, income, and wealth for all. In reality, the benefits of growth are unevenly distributed, creating extreme inequalities of income, wealth, and power. We agree that over the long run, increasing growth has lifted the tide for millions around the world. However, a share of the global population has seen their patchwork-rafts capsize, many struggle to keep their leaky boats afloat, and a tiny fraction upgraded to nicer yachts.

Growth Is Misleading Despite the hype and hoopla, growth does not deliver the benefits it promises. It rewards the financially strong but punishes the economically weak. It liberates people from old routines but enslaves them to new habits. It creates free time to spend with family and community but then demands mobility and migration that disrupt connections. It promises newer, cooler products to enable self-fulfillment but then restarts a never-ending cycle of hope and deception. In a phrase, economic growth oversells and under delivers, condemning people to "spiritual despair scarcely concealed by the frantic pace of life."[86] People, trapped on hedonic treadmills in the quest for newer, shinier, better, bigger, faster, or fancier, confuse consumption of the latest and greatest as the path toward actualization. Instead, the destination is alienation.

Growth Threatens Life Polluted air, poisoned water, and toxic land—let alone global warming, biodiversity collapse, and resource depletion—are the by-products of growth. Granted, we need some production and consumption. Overproduction and overconsumption, however, destabilize the basis of life. Ironically, when we measure the value created by an economy—say, in GNI—no costs are tallied. Rather, they are mysteriously called "externalities," understood to affect society but conveniently excluded while we praise the wondrous "benefits" of growth. Effectively,

Counterpoint

since "nobody" is responsible for the costs of externalities, "nobody" pays for them, and the growth engine chugs merrily along. Ultimately, "everybody" pays with a despoiled environment, warped society, and financial servitude.

Growth Destroys Individuality Growth's mandate to optimize efficiency requires massification—mass production, mass consumption, mass distribution, mass markets, mass media, and so on. Massification delivers great benefits, but at high cost. One observer noted that "a part of the price that people in the West pay for this unending procession of shiny assembly-line products is the concomitant loss of those now rarer things that once imparted zest and gratification—the loss of individuality, uniqueness and flavor; the loss of craftsmanship, local variety and richness; the loss of intimacy and atmosphere, of eccentricity and character."[87]

Current Growth Is Unsustainable Humanity plunders the earth at an unprecedented rate. Presently, human consumption is 30 percent larger than nature's capacity to regenerate. By 2050, at current trends, humanity will require three to five planets of natural resources just to keep the game going. "For more than 20 years we have exceeded the Earth's ability to support a consumptive lifestyle that is unsustainable and we cannot afford to continue down this path," warned the Worldwatch Institute.[88] Barring black-swan innovations in mining, agriculture, and manufacturing, no matter how hard we wish otherwise, Mother Earth is going to stop current growth patterns sooner than later.

Change the Game In summary, our position is straightforward. Epic poverty for billions, slow-motion death spiral of the ecosystem, false hope of actualization by consumption, binge-buying alienation, and the deterioration of nominal democracies into functional plutocracies puts the world at the proverbial fork in the road. We can remain blissfully ignorant of the price of growth, lost in the endless rush of apparent gains but continually surprised by inevitable and underestimated externalities. Alternatively, we can face the issue full on and radically reset the equation so that growth "meets the needs of the present without compromising the ability of future generations to meet their own needs."[89]

1. Put yourself in the following scenario: Tomorrow, while having lunch with your friends, the issue of economic growth pops up as a topic of discussion. Given your read of the information in the Point-Counterpoint, what three points of perspective would you use to communicate your understanding of economic growth?

ECONOMIC ANALYSIS

Narrow (e.g., GNI, GDP, and GNP) and broad (e.g., HDI, HPI, NPP) estimators profile absolute and relative economic conditions. They meaningfully indicate a country's performance and potential. Managers study other features to refine analyses and elaborate interpretation. Popular indicators include inflation, unemployment, debt, income distribution, poverty, and the balance of payments. Let's take a closer look at each.

INFLATION

Inflation measures the increase in the cost of living.

Inflation is the sustained rise in prices measured against a standard level of purchasing power. We estimate it by comparing two sets of products at two points in time and then computing the increase in cost that is not due to quality improvement. Mainstream economics holds that inflation results when aggregate demand grows faster than aggregate supply—essentially, too many people try to buy too few goods, thereby creating demand that exceeds supply that makes prices rise faster than incomes. Other theories, such as the Austrian School of Economics, hold that inflation results from an increasing supply of money by Central Banks.[90] Last, some define inflation as the continuous fall in the value of the currency.[91] No matter the explanation, managers watch inflation for its influence on interest rates, living costs, consumer confidence, political stability, and other factors.[92]

Inflation and the Cost of Living Consider how inflation affects the cost of living.[93] Unless incomes rise at the same pace or faster, consumers struggle to buy groceries, gas, and so forth. Sometimes just buying stuff is practically impossible. For example, during periods of rapid inflation, or "hyperinflation" as seen in Brazil, Yugoslavia, Turkmenistan, and Iran, consumers spent their money as fast as they got it or else watched it turn worthless.[94] More pointedly, in Zimbabwe over the past few years, prices rose up to 95 percent per day; by 2009, the annual inflation rate hit an astounding 79,600,000,000 percent, prices doubled every 25 hours and people used a hundred-trillion-dollar note to trade.[95] Noted one Zimbabwean, "There's a surrealism here that's hard to get across to people. If you need something and have cash, you buy it. If you have cash, you spend it today, because tomorrow it's going to be worth 5 percent less. Normal horizons don't exist here."[96] Even in normal circumstances, inflation significantly influences price. For example, in the United States, an item that cost $10.00 in 1950 would go for $95.27 in 2013.[97]

A country experiencing rising prices for a prolonged period suffers chronic inflation.

History shows that chronic inflation—high inflation over a prolonged period—erodes confidence in a country's currency and spurs people to seek other ways to store value. Chronic inflation has bleak implications for companies; neither they nor their customers can plan long-term investments. There is a disincentive to save. Ordinary investment instruments such as insurance policies and long-term bonds turn speculative. Inflation compels government response, often by raising interest rates, regulating wages and prices, or escalating protectionism. These measures slow performance and erode potential.

Measuring Inflation The measurement of inflation highlights a common difficulty: what a country measures when estimating an economic variable. Price indices are sensitive to decisions about their scope and the calculations applied.[98] For instance, the United States uses the Consumer Price Index (CPI). In the European Union, it is the Harmonized Index of Consumer Prices (HICP). Unlike the CPI, the HICP surveys the rural population and excludes owner-occupied housing. Consequently, managers mind the estimation process.[99]

Deflation, a decrease in the general price level of goods and services, is often caused by a reduction in the supply of money or credit.

If Not Inflation, Then Deflation A nagging consequence of the global financial crisis has been the movement of deflation from academic conjecture to practical concern. For the first time in generations, deflation, not just inflation, menaces economic performance and potential. Overcapacity, systematic deleveraging, shrinking credit, reduced corporate spending, declining real estate values, and falling consumer demand fan deflationary dynamics.

Deflation is the opposite of inflation—prices for products go down, not up. Technically, it occurs when the annual inflation rate is less than zero.

Deflation's rather ordinary circumstances create extraordinary pressures. Reduction in the supply of money or credit means a contraction in personal and investment spending. Declining demand and growing supply trigger increasing quantity and falling prices. Unchecked, economies fall into deflationary spirals wherein companies increasingly struggle to sell products. In recourse, they discount prices to appeal to consumers who delay purchases in order to exploit tomorrow's cheaper price. Japan, for example, has lost two decades of growth due to deflationary dynamics. Explained a Japanese analyst, "Profits fall, then wages come down, then consumers stop shopping. And because people aren't shopping, companies lower prices....It isn't easy to break out of."[100]

Deflation and unemployment are intricately linked. Lower demand slows the activity of a company, which then fires workers, who then scale back consumption, which then lowers demand, which leads companies to slow production further, and so on. At present, Central Banks and governments rely on **reflation**—increasing the money supply and reducing taxes to accelerate economic activity—to combat deflation. For example, the OECD urged the Bank of Japan to keep pumping cash into the economy until inflation turned positive.[101] This task is far easier said than done; from 1998 through mid-2013, Japan experienced falling prices and wages. Similarly, dealing with the consequences of the credit crisis has pushed the Federal Reserve of the United States to "quantitatively ease," essentially printing money to stimulate demand in order to preempt deflation.

UNEMPLOYMENT

Unemployment measures the number of workers who want to work but do not have paid jobs.

The **unemployment rate** is the share of out-of-work citizens seeking employment for pay relative to the total civilian labor force. Countries that cannot create jobs suffer sluggish growth, social pressures, and political instability. The proportion of employed workers in a country shows how well it productively uses its human resources. People gainfully employed testify to the competency of policymakers to sustain a productive economy. Persistent unemployment harshly spotlights government ineptitude.

Some economists advise tracking the **misery index** which is the sum of a country's inflation and unemployment rates. The higher the sum, the greater the economic misery, and the more likely consumers curtail spending, companies curb investment, and society confronts austerity. In addition, misery loves company; as the misery index increases, so do social costs, such as crime, despondency, and family stress.[102] In early 2013, Spain had the world's highest misery index score, at just under 30 percent; it was followed by South Africa, Croatia, Greece, Venezuela, Argentina, Egypt, Portugal, Slovakia, and Ireland. Recent work has expanded this idea in the form of the *Economic Security Index*; it assesses household economic instability in terms of the population that experiences at least a 25 percent decline in household wealth.[103]

Measuring Unemployment Change in unemployment over time may reflect change in the demand for and supply of labor; it may also reflect changes in reporting practices. Different assumptions (i.e., survey timing and seasonality effects) and exclusions (i.e., women tend to be undercounted) means that the unemployment rate often underestimates the scale and scope of the jobless. Technically, it measures how many people are not working for pay but seek paid employment. However, it excludes people who do not work at all, work without pay, or have stopped looking for work. Hence, unemployment measures often underestimate the true degree of joblessness.

Underemployment occurs when individuals work fewer hours a day than they would prefer or when individuals work below the level for which they have been trained.

Also, unemployment checks often underreport worker productivity. Countries in Asia, Africa, and South America commonly face economic, political, and social problems due to underemployment. That is, even though officially employed, people work only part time, thereby reducing productivity, lowering incomes, and decreasing social stability. Some propose an alternative measure to minimize these distortions, namely, the simple-to-calculate

Payroll to Population. This tracks the number of people employed full-time for an employer as a percentage of the nation's population, thereby eliminating the volatility of various adjustments.[104] Besides measurement issues, the unemployment rate means different things in different countries due to different social policies.[105] Some countries, such as France and Germany, provide generous unemployment protection, whereas countries like China, Kenya, or Jordan offer little to none.

DEBT

Internal debt: Portion of the government debt that is denominated in the country's own currency and held by domestic residents.

Debt, the total of a government's financial obligations, measures what the state borrows from its citizens, foreign organizations, foreign governments, and international institutions. The larger the total debt, the more uncertain an economy's performance and potential are. Interest expenses divert resources from more productive uses. More insidiously, future worries about the ability of coming generations to repay the debt saps consumer confidence and constrains government flexibility.

The national debt for many countries had been steadily, albeit slowly, increasing prior to 2007. This changed dramatically as governments responded to the global financial crisis. Company bailouts, unemployment benefits, fiscal resets, and macroeconomic stimulus led to unprecedented debt creation. The IMF estimates that the debt of the 10 wealthiest countries will have risen from 78 percent of their GDP in 2007 to nearly 115 percent by 2014; these governments, on average, will then owe approximately $50,000 for each citizen.[106]

External debt: Debt owed to foreign creditors and denominated in foreign currency.

A country's debt has two parts: internal and external. *Internal debt* results when the government spends more than it collects in revenues. Deficits occur for several reasons, such as when an imperfect tax system under-collects revenue, security and social programs exceed tax revenues, or state-owned enterprises run deficits.[107] Consequently, governments struggle with spending priorities, budget management, and tax policy. Growing internal debt, an early indicator of growing austerity and rising taxes, creates uncertainties for consumers, investors, and companies.

Growing public debt is a leading indicator of

- Tax increases
- Reduced growth
- Rising inflation
- Increasing austerity

External debt results when a government borrows money from lenders outside the country, such as private commercial banks, other governments, or international financial institutions (e.g., the IMF or World Bank). Interest on the debt, and eventually the debt itself, must be repaid in the currency in which the loan was made. Hence, the borrowing country may have to export its goods to the lender's country to earn that currency or to convert its currency into that of its creditor. Dreaded debt crises often occur when a weak economy can do so only at high political, economic, and social cost. In this situation, economic activity grinds to a halt. Stress and loss usually precede its reboot to an efficient, smaller-scale version.

INCOME DISTRIBUTION

Income distribution estimates the proportion of the population that earns various levels of income.

Income distribution often defines a market's performance and potential. GNI, even when adjusted for population size or purchasing power, can misestimate the relative wealth of a nation's citizens. That is, GNI per capita reports how much income the average person earns. However, because not everyone is average, we cannot determine what share of income goes to what segments of the population. For example, the GNI of the United States exceeds $15 trillion, a performance that ranks first among nations. Similarly, its GNI per capita was an impressive $50,120 in 2012.[108] However, its performance looks less awe-inspiring when qualified by its distribution of income among 314 million citizens. Presently, the richest 1 percent of Americans receive more income than the bottom 40 percent—the widest gap in 70 years. The top 1 percent own 37 percent of all privately held stock, 65 percent of financial securities, and 62 percent of business equity.[109] The top 10 percent own 85 to 90 percent of stocks, bonds, trust funds, and business equity, and over 75 percent of non-home real estate. Essentially, approximately 10 percent of U.S. citizens "own" the country.[110] The United States is not the exception; dozens of countries exhibit similar income distributions.

Across the world, inequality grows. In 1960, the richest 20 percent of the world's population had 30 times the income of the poorest 20 percent; by 2010 the number had grown to 85 times. Correspondingly, the richest 20 percent spent more than 75 percent of the world total, while the poorest 20 percent spent less than 2 percent.[111] The richest 1 percent claim as much income as the bottom 57 percent—in other words, the 70 million richest people in the world receive as much income as do the 4 billion poorest people. On average, the income of the richest 10 percent of the population is about nine times that of the poorest 10 percent in most countries; we see bigger multiples in Israel, Turkey, South Africa, the United States, Chile, and Mexico.[112]

There is a growing gap between the rich and poor in virtually every country in the world

Benefits and Costs Some income inequality is useful in rewarding effort, talent, and innovation. However, widening inequality threatens the stability that supports growth as it fuels conflicts that tear the social fabric.[113] Countries that are more unequal perform poorly on social indicators, have lower human-development records, and higher economic insecurity. Rising income disparities between booming cities and impoverished countrysides threaten social stability and economic performance.[114] China's steadfast commitment to a "harmonious society," for instance, reflects the CCP's fear of growing income inequality between the 800 million people living on its coastal plain and the 500 million who populate its interior.[115] Whereas Lexus, Lamborghini, and Bentley dealerships operate in Shanghai, many people in rural China rely on bicycles and animals for transportation.

Widening inequality eventually triggers destructive outcomes, including shrinking opportunity, resource inefficiencies, and excessive individualism.[116] Ultimately, income inequality erodes a country's sense of identity, in which unfair play and inequality of opportunity weaken performance and erode potential. For example, people with incomes below $20,000 in the United States have increasingly lost confidence in the free market; support dropped from 76 percent to 44 percent between 2009 and 2010.[117]

The Gini coefficient, the most commonly used measure of inequality, indicates the extent to which income shares deviate from a perfectly equal distribution.

Gini Coefficient Managers use the **Gini coefficient** to estimate the degree of inequality in a country's distribution of income. A score of zero implies perfect equality (everybody has the same income); a score of one implies perfect inequality (one person has all the income). Most countries range between 25 and 60 percent. Countries with lower inequality include Sweden (.23), Hungary (.24), Denmark (.24), and Austria (.26); those with higher inequality include South Africa (.65), Bolivia (.58), Guatemala (.55) China (.47), and the United States (.47).[118]

The Gini coefficient presumes that there is a reasonable degree of income within a country.[119] If not, then it partially represents income distribution. One controls for this error by assessing the scale and scope of poverty. Consider India. Although it reports a Gini coefficient of 33 percent, its performance does not reflect enlightened ideals of equality. Rather, it represents the cheerless reality that many Indians are poor: 80 percent of its population lives on less than $2 per day.[120] So income may be distributed evenly on a relative basis, but there is very little to distribute in absolute terms. India, although extreme, is not the exception.

CONCEPT CHECK

As we suggest in Chapters 1 and 3, both income inequality and poverty should diminish as international business improves the efficiency of resource allocation. The historic record of globalization, Chapter 1 suggested, showed that the productive use of liberated capital creates jobs and fosters income growth.

POVERTY

Poverty is the state of having little or no money, few or no material possessions, and limited access to education, health, and community.

Poverty prevails throughout the world. Managers fine-tune their study of income and wealth by considering its conditions and consequences. **Poverty** is a multidimensional condition whereby a person or community lacks the essentials for a minimum standard of well-being and life (See Table 4.6).[121] These essentials can be life-sustaining resources such as food, clean water, and shelter; they may be social resources such as access to information, education, and healthcare; they may be the opportunity to sustain extended families or connect with people to build communities.

Extreme poverty, according to the World Bank, is rated as living on less than $1.25 per day (PPP); moderate poverty is less than $2 per day (PPP). Approximately 1.3 billion people live

TABLE 4.6 The Multidimensional Poverty Index

Lack of income certainly indicates a state of poverty. Research increasingly assesses the broad mix of conditions that deprive people of sustenance, shelter, stability, and security. Technically, the index below rates a household poor if its sum deprivations exceed 33 percent.

Dimension of Poverty	Indicator	Deprived if…	Relative weight in index (%)
Education	Years of Schooling	No one has completed five years of schooling.	16.6
	Child School Attendance	A child is not attending school up to grade eight.	16.6
Health	Child Mortality	A child has died in the family.	16.6
	Nutrition	Anyone is malnourished.	16.6
	Electricity	The household had no electricity.	5.5
	Sanitation	No decent toilet or facilities are available but shared with other families.	5.5
	Drinking Water	No access to safe drinking water or it is more than a 30-minute roundtrip walk from home.	5.5
Living Standards	Flooring	Has a dirt, sand, or dung floor.	5.5
	Cooking fuel	Cooks with dung, wood, or charcoal.	5.5
	Asset ownership	The household does not own more than one radio, TV, telephone, bike, motorbike or refrigerator and does not own a car or truck.	5.5

Source: Based on *The Multidimensional Poverty Index*, The Oxford Poverty & Human Development Initiative, retrieved March 26, 2013 from www.ophi.org.uk/policy/multidimensional-poverty-index/.

in extreme poverty while some 2.5 billion live in modest poverty.[122] Today, the world population is roughly 80 percent poor, 10 percent middle income, and 10 percent rich. The historical record adds an important perspective. While dramatic income inequality is a recent phenomenon, widespread poverty is not.[123]

Prevalence of Poverty Poverty grows worldwide. Granted, estimates of the number of people in extreme poverty have fallen by approximately 300 million since 1990. However, this reduction has been concentrated in essentially one country. Removing China from the tally reveals that the number of the extreme poor in the developing world has changed little. The global financial crisis and resulting fiscal austerity has threatened many more; in 2013, global unemployment topped 200 million for the first time, pushing tens of millions more into poverty.[124] Presently, rising healthcare, education, and food costs imperil millions more.[125]

Consequences Poverty shapes economic environments. People struggle for food, shelter, clothing, clean water, and health services, to say nothing of safety, security, and education. Failure to find these results in malnutrition, mental illness, death, epidemics, famine, and war. For example, 100 percent of Canadians have access to clean water, compared to 13 percent of Afghans; the per capita dietary protein supply in the United States is 121 grams but 32 grams in Mozambique; the average life expectancy is 83 years in Japan yet 46 in the Central African Republic.[126]

The worldwide growth of business activity and economic progress ultimately depends on alleviating poverty.

The growth of business activity and economic progress ultimately depends on alleviating poverty. Markets experiencing extreme poverty mean MNEs must reassess many taken-for-granted aspects of an economy. Market systems may not exist, national infrastructures may not work, crime may be pervasive, and governments may struggle to regulate society consistently or adopt prudent economic policies.

The Potential of the Poor Managers monitor the buying potential of today's poor. For example, the number of mobile phone subscribers in India in 2002 was under 15 million; by 2006 it was 136 million; and in late 2012 it hit 930 million—even though more than 80 percent of Indians are poor, scraping by on less than $2 a day. Today, however, Indian companies offer the cheapest mobile services in the world while still earning profits. India and China (its mobile carriers report nearly 950 million subscribers) account for more than half the world's increase in wireless subscriptions over the past five years. Similar developments with computers (e.g., the XO-1 programs of low-cost systems for children), automobiles (the development of cheap, functional cars such as Tata's Nano), and housing (Idealab's program to provide functional homes for about $2,500) highlight finding opportunities in the face of dire circumstances. More dramatically, one manager noted, "A billion customers in the world are waiting for a $2 pair of eyeglasses, a $10 solar lantern, and a $100 house."[127]

The Base of the Pyramid is the largest, but poorest, socioeconomic group in the world.

This perspective alerts managers to the **Base of the Pyramid** phenomenon—the nearly four billion people that earn less than US$4 per day who live primarily in Asia, Africa, and South America. Largely excluded from formal markets, the Base represents a tremendous volume of consumption. Though long seen as inaccessible and unprofitable, the poor for some represent the next market frontier of the global economy.[128] Accelerating income growth in emerging economies will move many of today's poor into their expanding middle class.[129] Presently, the middle class includes about two billion people in a dozen emerging economies who collectively spend $6.9 trillion a year. During the next decade, their annual spending will rise to $20 trillion—twice current U.S. consumption.[130] The global middle class—or as some call them, "consumer class"—will include 4 billion people by 2025, up from a billion in 1990. They will inject almost $25 trillion into the global economy, thereby powering a surge unlike any we have ever seen.[131]

Frugal engineering takes the needs of poor consumers as a starting point in developing functional, cost-conscious products.

Success Standards As the world moves from being mostly poor to mostly middle class, the contours of the Pyramid will change. This multi-year process creates immense opportunities. Serving the Base has two preconditions. First, "seeing" opportunity calls for market pioneers that have a particular mindset. More pointedly, "When you look behind the success stories of leading globalizers, you find companies that have learned how to think differently from the herd. They seek out different information, process it in a different way, come to different conclusions, and make different decisions. Where others see threats and complexity, they see opportunity. Where others see a barren landscape, they see a cornucopia of choices."[132]

Second, the task at hand is developing affordable, easily used, eco-sensitive products that work in harsh environments. For example, Nokia, Samsung, and Motorola offer phones with sealed faceplates (for water and dirt resistance), 400 hours of standby time on one battery charge, and larger screens that work in reflected light, use no internal lamp, and are specially enabled for text messaging. Kenya's Safaricom takes these technologies to the next level, pioneering mobile money services in markets lacking efficient means of transaction. At the grassroots level, similar initiatives have built a refrigerator from clay (which uses no electricity yet keeps vegetables fresh for several days), a cheap crop duster (a sprayer mounted on a motorcycle), and smart phones with two SIM card slots (useful in countries with unreliable wireless services).[133]

CONCEPT CHECK

Although the Base of the Pyramid is attractive in terms of economic potential, managers heed the discussions of Chapters 2 and 3 concerning the different cultural, political, and legal environments found in developing countries. Still, Chapter 1 notes the drivers of globalization steadily narrow the gap between developed and developing countries.

Increasingly, these changes also benefit the rich. MNEs translate frugal innovations into new products that serve Western consumers. Chinese firms have introduced reusable sutures (versus the old approach of higher-cost disposable ones) as well as heart stents that run 40 percent cheaper than those in the West.[134] GE developed a low-cost electrocardiograph machine for rural India. Its efficiency and performance soon led to marketing these units in Germany and the United States.[135] A string of similar successes led GE to set India as its global center of "low-cost innovation."

The standards of the Base of the Pyramid—low-cost, high-performance, resource-minimizing, lifestyle-sensitive innovations—increasingly appeal to price-conscious consumers in Western markets. Declining affluence and slowing upward mobility in many rich countries results in a growing number of *nouveaux pauvres:* former middle-class folks who face tightening budgets. The dawning age of austerity in the United States, Ireland, Spain,

TABLE 4.7 Components of a Country's Balance of Payments

Current Account

- Value of exports and imports of physical goods, such as oil, grain, or computers (also referred to as *visible trade*)
- Receipts and payments for services, such as banking or advertising, and other intangible goods, such as copyrights and cross-border dividend and interest payments (also referred to as *invisible trade*)
- Private transfers, such as money sent home by expatriate workers
- Official transfers, such as international aid, on which the government expects no returns

Capital Account

- Long-term capital flows (i.e., money invested in foreign firms as well as profits made by selling those investments and returning the money home)
- Short-term capital flows (i.e., money invested in foreign currencies by international traders as well as funds moved around the world for business purposes by companies with international operations)

England, Greece, and fellow rich countries creates opportunities for frugal shops (notably Wal-Mart and Aldi), pre-paid service providers (Leap Wireless, TracFone), and new business designs such as "collaborative consumption" that lets people share or rent rather than own (as seen in Zipcar and Airbnb). In sum, the Base of the Pyramid is far wider and far more diffused than most realize. Frugal innovators like Tata and Haier see natural markets spanning Dresden, Delhi, Dongguan, and Detroit.[136]

THE BALANCE OF PAYMENTS

The BOP is a system of recording all of a country's economic transactions with the rest of the world.

A country's **balance of payments (BOP)** officially known as the *Statement of International Transactions,* reports its trade and financial transactions (as conducted by individuals, businesses, and government agencies) with the rest of the world.[137] The BOP tracks two different kinds of transactions: the *current account,* which tracks cross-border payments for goods and services (i.e., exports and imports) and the *capital account,* which tracks loans for cross-border payments for assets.

Table 4.7 lists the components of each account. Technically, exports generate positive sales abroad while imports generate negative sales domestically. Positive net sales, resulting when exports exceed imports, create a *current account surplus.* Conversely, importing more than exporting creates a *current account deficit.* Table 4.8 lists the five countries with the largest current account surpluses and those with the largest current account deficits.[138]

ELABORATING ECONOMIC ANALYSIS WITH GLOBAL INDICES

The study of individual dimensions of a nation's economic environment, much in the spirit of partial equilibrium analysis, is a productive approach. The complexity of modern market

TABLE 4.8 Current Account Balances: The Top and the Bottom Five

Top 5	Country	Current Account Surplus (in millions of US$)	Bottom 5	Country	Current Account Deficit (in millions of US$)
1	Germany	$208,100	159	Turkey	–$59,740
2	China	$170,800	160	Canada	–$59,920
3	Saudi Arabia	$150,000	161	Brazil	–$65,130
4	Russia	$85,060	162	India	–$80,150
5	Japan	$84,700	163	United States	–$487,200

Source: Based on Central Intelligence Agency, "Country Comparison—Current Account Balance," The World Factbook (2013), retrieved March 13, 2013 from www.cia.gov/library/publications/the-world-factbook/rankorder/2187rank.html

systems, however, both absolute and relative, means that the properties of a given system cannot be fully explained by evaluating a snapshot of disaggregated components. Studying the connections that link the parts of the systems improves analysis of its performance and potential. Let's take a look at various meta-models that guide managers.

Managers often consider meta-models to improve their understanding of the absolute and relative potential of an economic environment. Popular indices include:

- Global Competitiveness Index
- Global Innovation Index
- Where-To-Be-Born Index
- World Competitiveness Index

Global Competitiveness Index (GCI) The World Economic Forum assesses the basis of competitiveness in 144 economies.[139] Its analytics assume that providing prosperity to citizens hinges on how effectively a country develops institutions, applies policies, and employs resources to improve productivity. A country's skill in managing these responsibilities translates directly to its competitiveness among the world of nations. Operationally, the GCI summarizes the performance and relationship among 110 variables that comprise 12 so-called "pillars of competitiveness" within a nation. These pillars tap key dimensions, such as financial market development, macroeconomic environment, technological readiness, market efficiency, and innovation. The GCI links a broad set of economic indicators, effectively integrating macroeconomic and micro/business aspects of competitiveness into a single index. Continuing a long-running pattern, today's top 10 competitive economies are dominated by European countries. Switzerland sets the standard; Finland, Sweden, the Netherlands, Germany, and the United Kingdom also make the cut. The United States, along with three Asian economies—Singapore, Hong Kong, and Japan—complete the set. The United States, now ranked seventh, has dropped in the rankings for four consecutive years. Of the big emerging economies, China sets the pace, with Brazil moving up.

World Competitiveness Index (WCI) The World Competitiveness Project assesses a nation's ability to create and maintain an environment in which enterprises, private or state-owned, can compete, prosper, and create wealth. Four primary factors determine a nation's competitiveness index: economic performance, government efficiency, business efficiency, and infrastructure. These categories consist of various subfactors such as international trade, employment, prices, business legislation, productivity, and management practices. Ultimately, the WCI evaluates more than 300 criteria in developing its summary judgment about a nation's performance.

In 2012, Hong Kong topped the WCI scoreboard, followed by the United States, Switzerland, Singapore, Sweden, Canada, Taiwan, Norway, Germany, and Qatar. Again, U.S. performance has slipped over the past few years, forgoing the country's role as global pacesetter. Still, as the 2012 Report concludes, "despite all its setbacks, the U.S. remains at the center of world competitiveness because of its unique economic power, the dynamism of its enterprises and its capacity for innovation."[140]

Global Innovation Index (GII) Countries, as we noted in Chapter 3, increasingly look to their brainpower to create innovations that confer competitive advantage. The growing power of ideas and insights in the global market makes a country's ability to support innovation a critical facet of its economic environment. The GII measures a country's success in doing so, assessing its competency in promoting technologies, expanding human capacities, streamlining organizational capabilities, and improving institutional responsiveness that best leverages knowledge into market-changing innovation.[141] The GII anchors analysis in terms of five input pillars (Institutions and Policies, Human Capacity, Infrastructure, Technological Sophistication, Business Markets and Capital) and three output pillars (Knowledge, Competitiveness, Wealth). Combined, these measures estimate a nation's capacity to generate ideas, leverage them into innovative products, and improve knowledge, competitiveness, and wealth.

Presently, wealthy, developed countries claim the top spots in the GII standings: Switzerland is the global leader, followed by Sweden, Singapore, Finland, the United Kingdom, the Netherlands, Denmark, Hong Kong, Ireland, and the United States. Accelerating innovation in Asia sees India, Turkey, and China rising in rank. Collectively, Asia appears to be shifting from practices that optimized efficiency to policies that improve the environment for innovation.

Schoolchildren with their newly arrived laptops at a previously off-the-grid school in Ulaanbaatar, capital and largest city of Mongolia. The government is providing a laptop to every schoolchild with the goal of equipping the next generation of value creators with the tools to engage globalization. Similar programs are unfolding in countries throughout the world. The implications of this program to the division of labor, the trade of products, and the performance of markets will shape MNEs' strategies.

Source: VAN CAKENBERGHE TO/SIPA/Newscom

In general, smaller economies score higher in the lottery of life.

Where-To-Be-Born Index (WTBBI) Finally, looking a bit further into the future, the WTBBI holds that how well a country provides opportunities for a healthy, safe, and prosperous life helps explain both its current and future economic environment.[142] The WTBBI evaluates 11 indicators, such as geography, demography, quality of life, per capita income, and life expectancy. Today, the "lucky baby" league table, comprising 80 countries, is topped by Switzerland, followed by Australia, Norway, Sweden, and Denmark. Smaller nations dominate the top performers, accounting for the top 15 countries in the lottery of life. Large, wealthy countries—notably, United States (16), Japan (25), France (26), and Great Britain (27)—do not rank particularly well. Developing economies fall from the middle down to the bottom of the ranking—e.g., Brazil (37), China (49), India (66), and Russia (72).

CASE The BRICs: Vanguard of the Revolution[143]

Improving performance showcases the accelerating success of emerging economies. The focus of attention is now squarely on the vanguard of emerging economies, the so-called BRICs: Brazil, Russia, India, and China. Together, they are home to nearly 2.8 billion people (40 percent of the planet's population) and cover a quarter of the area of the world, spanning three continents. Combined, they presently account for about 18 percent of global GDP. That share will head to 25 percent over the next 10 years and about one-third by 2030. Adjusting for PPP turbocharges this performance: the BRICs currently generate about 30 percent of the world's GDP, with a projected 38 percent by 2020 and nearly 45 percent by 2030.

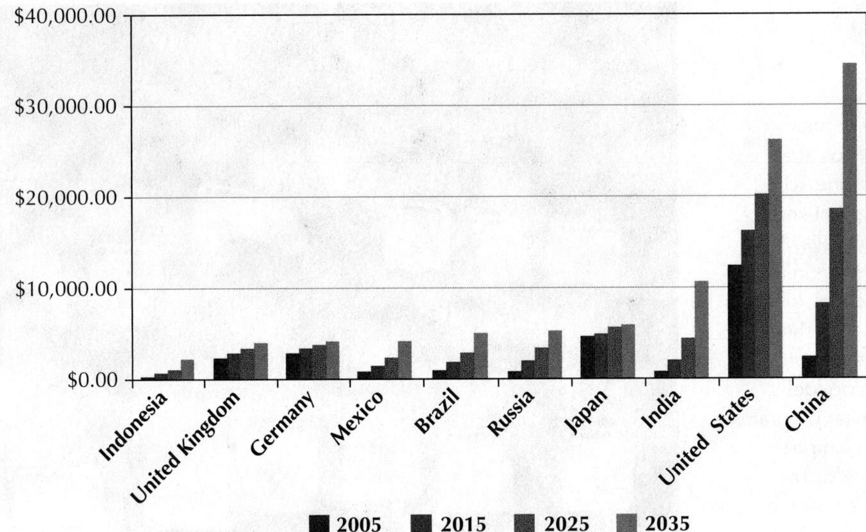

FIGURE 4.10 GDP of Top Ten Economies: 2005, 2015, 2025, 2035 ($ billions)

Here we see the trend in nominal GDP among the ten largest economies in the world, projected as of 2035. The baseline is set in terms of 2006 $ billions.

Source: Based on data in *Looking to 2060: A Global Vision of Long-Term Growth*, OECD Economic Policy Papers, November 2012; as well as assorted reports by the IMF World Bank, and McKinsey Global Institute."

Unquestionably, the BRICs are much larger in scale and scope than other emerging markets. Still, they are leading indicators of consumption patterns, investment policies, and social trends that are gaining momentum worldwide. Many see the BRICs as vanguards of the revolution: where they go, both good and bad, others will follow. We now profile their emergence, highlighting implications to the global marketplace and closing by identifying looming threats.

Changing of the Guard

First off, remind yourself where the BRICs were just 30 or so years ago. Brazil was an economic basket case suffering hyperinflation, Russia was in lockdown behind the Iron Curtain, India's aggressive socialism had led it to expel IBM and Coca-Cola, and China was recovering from the bedlam of the Cultural Revolution and struggling with the legacies of Mao Zedong. Today, conditions and circumstances have radically changed. At current trends and with reasonable projections, over the next few decades the four of them will become premier, powerful economies (see Figure 4.10).

Originally, some thought it would take until 2050 or so before the BRICs bypassed today's rich countries. The global financial crisis, however, has accelerated the schedule. Whereas the BRICs are growing, Germany, Japan, England, Italy, France, and the United States, among others in the West, struggle mightily. Wealthy countries also face a raft of other constraints: their aging workforces, overwhelming debt, and slowing productivity suggest growth will be hard-fought. Moreover, as shown in Figure 4.10, it will fall short of the growth in emerging markets. In the meantime, the speed of the BRICs' recovery paints the global financial crisis as a pivot point in the redistribution of economic power.

So, again, thinking of where the BRICs were 30 or so years ago, mapping their accomplishments, and projecting trend lines out 30 years from today makes for, depending on your perspective, an astonishing or worrisome outcome. Current circumstances make any timeline for the changing of the guard speculative. It does not, however, change secular trends that will culminate in the BRICs' converting demographic dividends, rising productivity, improving innovation, and increasing capital efficiency into the comeback of the emerging economies.

Changing Markets

The BRICs, like many fellow emerging markets, report rapidly growing economies. Historically, consumer demand takes off when GNI per capita is between US$3,000 and $10,000. Russia hit those levels first; China, India, and Brazil are steadily heading there. When adjusted for purchasing power, all have crossed the threshold.

The BRICs, save Russia, have growing middle classes. Forecasts see them expanding from 50 million to almost 600 million by 2025. More immediately, between 2005 and 2015, over 800 million people in the BRICs will cross the annual income threshold of US$3,000. By 2025, approximately 200 million people in the BRICs will have annual incomes above $15,000. Escape from poverty is a game changer; besides permitting more consumption, it often allows people to move from consuming generic necessities to preferring branded goods.

As income grows, so does demand for what once were unreachable luxuries. For example, there are roughly two cars for every 100 people in India and nine per 100 in China. In contrast, there are 63 and 82 cars per 100 people, respectively, in Germany and the United States. By 2030, India and China's car ownership will likely increase 5- to 25-fold. The total number of cars in the two countries combined could rise from around 150 million today to north of a billion by 2030, thereby accounting for more than half of all cars on the world's roads. Other countries show similar vehicle per capita rates: the Philippines' is 3.3 percent, Indonesia's 7 percent, and Turkey's 14 percent. Introduction of low-price autos like Tata's Nano—a frugally engineered rear-engine, four-passenger car targeting poorer folks—expand the global auto market. Similar trends in virtually every product class, many anchored in frugal innovation programs targeting the Base of the Pyramid, indicate market potentials last seen at the start of the Industrial Revolution.

Big Plans but Big Problems

Notwithstanding the spectacular performance and potential of the BRICs, there are skeptics. First, there is the problem of recency bias, which is the delusion that current trends will continue indefinitely and uninterrupted. History shows great mistakes made by many who extrapolated the present into the future. Invariably, economic growth rates slow as the base of activity expands. Moreover, advantages such as cheap labor or low-cost capital wane as growing demand increases marginal price pressures. And always on the horizon is a black-swan event—a large-impact, hard-to-predict, but rare event beyond the realm of normal expectations that resets the game, such as the collapse of the Soviet Union, the emergence of the Internet, or the global financial crisis.

Despite perils, people on the go need to move. Here we see Indian passengers catching a ride in ways that defy reason. The hazard of traveling this way, apparently, falls short of missing India's economic surge.

Source: © Terje Lillehaug / Alamy

Despite high-octane growth, the BRICs face futures of persistent poverty and distorted income distributions. By 2025, the income per capita in today's richer countries will exceed $35,000 for more than a billion people. In contrast, only 10 to 20 percent of the nearly 3 billion folks in the BRIC economies will hit that threshold. For the longer term, income per capita in the United States is projected to reach $80,000 by 2050, while China will likely be just over $31,000, Brazil about $26,600, and India just $17,400. With the possible exception of Russia, hundreds of millions of people in the BRICs will be far poorer on average than individuals in Germany, France, Japan, Italy, Canada, and the United States. Consequently, for the first time in history, the largest economies in the world will no longer be the richest when measured by GNI per capita.

National Challenges

Each of the BRICs struggles with its particular problems. Russia is particularly vulnerable. It depends on various energy and mineral exports for revenue. Erratic swings in commodity prices complicate setting budgets and planning programs. Additionally, Russia is considered riskier because of long-simmering tensions with the West and a legal and political infrastructure that imposes the rule of man. Going forward, besides its aging and declining population, Russia's oligarchic government and crumbling infrastructure confound growth projections. Hence, some advise replacing the BRIC notion with that of "BICs."

Brazil's economic potential has been anticipated for decades, but it has struggled to achieve expectations. Difficulties in income equality, productivity, and education have often snatched defeat from the jaws of victory. India, in addition to pressing economic and political challenges, has immense infrastructure shortfalls and hundreds of millions of poor people. Meeting current demands while building for the future poses immense resource demands. China's particular interpretation of the rule of law, rights of citizens, environmental sustainability, and principles of governance poses problems. China also faces a steadily closing window of opportunity; by 2020, it will have the largest number of old and very old people on earth. The IMF forecasted in 2013 that China's demographic dividend would end by 2020; its working age population would then go into precipitous decline. By 2030, China will face a labor shortage of almost 140 million workers, arguably the greatest jobs crunch in history.

Green Constraints

Wish as we might, the sad fact that there are only so many resources to go around shadows the bright futures of all. The emergence of the BRICs sorely challenges the sustainability of the global environment. Global warming, diminishing raw materials, and escalating pollution suggest that there is a limit to how much the BRICs, to say nothing of the 150 or so countries who seem intent on following in their footsteps, can develop before exceeding the capacity of the global economy to supply the necessary resources and of the environment to support them. More worrisomely, notes the *Worldwatch Institute*, if China and India were to consume resources and produce pollution at the current U.S. per capita level, we would need the resources of two additional Earths. Throwing everyone else into the mix ratchets up the pressure—estimates are that we are short approximately five planets of resources if the living standards found in today's wealthy countries prevailed worldwide.

Adding Mortar

BRIC leaders have not been idly sitting by, watching these threats thwart their future. Overlapping ambitions and agendas have led them to develop bilateral and multilateral agreements. India and China, the world's two most populous countries, formed a strategic partnership to end border disputes and boost trade. The agreement eased decades of mutual distrust between the two following a 1962 border war. "India and China can together reshape the world order," Indian Prime Minister Manmohan Singh proclaimed at a ceremony for then Chinese Premier, Wen Jiabao, at India's presidential palace.[144]

Similarly, indications show strengthening ties between Russia and China. Bilateral China-Russia trade was $84 billion in 2011, up from $20 billion in 2005, and is targeting $200 billion by

2020. In many people's eyes, Russia, by rolling back democracy and reviving its imperialist past, is now more politically aligned with the one-party state of China than the multiparty democracies in the West. Spearheading these efforts was then-President, now Prime Minister, Putin of Russia, with his goal to build "a new world economic architecture" that would reflect the rising power of emerging economies and the decline of the old heavyweights like the United States, Japan, and European countries.[145]

Dethroning the Dollar

The global financial crisis has accelerated these trends. Besides trade and economic relationships, the BRICs amplify their political, legal, and strategic influence in other ways. Attention often centers on the unit of exchange used to settle trade transactions. Since the Bretton Woods Agreement of 1944, the U.S. dollar has functioned as the world's reserve currency; as such, it is widely held by governments and institutions around the world and is used to finance every sort of international transaction. The BRICs increasingly try to erode the hegemony of the dollar. In 2009, China and Brazil agreed to no longer use it in doing business, instead adopting a yen-cruzeiro currency-swap agreement. China and Russia stopped using the dollar to settle bilateral trade in 2010, switching instead to the ruble or the yuan. By 2013, China had negotiated currency swaps with some 20 countries, including Australia, United Arab Emirates, Japan, France, and Turkey, to bypass the dollar in settling bilateral trade. We see similar moves elsewhere; notably, Turkey arranged with Russia and Iran to sidestep U.S. dollars and use their own currencies in bilateral transactions.

Stronger Ties

To cap matters, the BRIC leaders have begun holding BRIC-only summits to discuss ways to reset the global trade structure and champion a new supranational currency. In the backdrop is a sense, explained Prime Minister Putin, that the world "is changing before our very eyes. Countries that seemed hopelessly backward only yesterday are becoming the world's fastest-growing economies today." The BRICS, backed by fellow emerging economies, no longer merely want to be part of the world's outdated architecture—instead, they aim to go forward into a brave new world largely unencumbered by the past. Seeing their performance improve while that in the West stagnate has moved the BRICs to push farther ahead. Their 2011 summit increased the pressure on the West for a revamped global monetary system that relies less on the dollar as well as a louder voice in international financial institutions.

The Road Ahead

Inevitably, some speculate that the BRICs might turn into bricks in their march to miracle economies. Granted, their governments have developed economically sensible policies, opened trade and domestic markets, and begun building institutions that support economic freedom. The global financial crisis, however, brutally illustrated that economics can quickly move out of sync.

Despite ever-present gloom, reasonable optimism prevails. Research identifies four preconditions of consistent macro growth: sound macroeconomic policies; political institutions committed to transparency, fairness, and the rule of law; openness to trade and capital; and strong education systems. By and large, the BRICs, along with other emerging markets, steadily meet the general spirit of some of these standards. None, however, presently meets all. That said, the success of the BRICS questions whether, in fact, one needs to meet all. Their improving performance as their rich-country counterparts struggle suggests that conventional understanding of markets possibly mismaps the dynamics of economic environments. If so, perhaps Western markets, not the BRICs, must reform.

No matter what the future holds, few question that the ride will be captivating. The emergence of the BRICs signals that the next phase of the global economy has begun. And even if the BRICs fall short of their potential, their successes will redefine the structure of economic environments, patterns of growth, and dynamics of economic activity.

QUESTIONS

4-3. Estimate the likely market evolution of the BRICs over the next decade. What economic indicators might companies monitor to best guide their investments and actions?

4-4. Identify three implications of the emergence of the BRICs for careers and companies in your country.

4-5. Do you think recency bias has led to overestimating the potential of the BRICs? How would you, as a manager for a company assessing these markets, try to control this bias?

4-6. How might managers interpret the potential for their product in a market that is, in absolute economic terms, large but, on a per capita basis, characterized by a majority of poor consumers?

4-7. In the event that the BRICs fail to meet projected performance, what would be some of the implications for the international business environment?

4-8. Compare and contrast the merits of GNI, Net National Product, and Your Better Life Index as indicators of economic performance in Brazil, Russia, China, and India.

SUMMARY

- Economic freedom measures the absence of government coercion or constraint on the production, distribution, or consumption of goods and services beyond the extent necessary for citizens to protect and maintain liberty.
- Economically free countries tend to have higher per capita income, standards of living, and social stability than do less-free or repressed countries.
- The global financial crisis challenges the legitimacy of free markets. Governments in many countries have expanded their regulation of the economy to manage the consequences.
- In a market economy, private interests own resources while price and quantity, conveyed via the invisible hand, determine supply and demand.
- In a command economy, the government plans what goods and services a country produces, the quantity in which they are produced, and the price at which they are sold.
- A mixed economy includes some elements of market and command economies. Both influence investment activities and consumption behavior.
- A market economy endorses the doctrine of capitalism, its principles of the invisible hand and laissez-faire, and the goal of maximizing economic freedom.
- A command economy endorses the doctrine of communism, its principle of an activist government that commands and controls most if not all factors of production, and the goal of constraining economic freedom.
- A mixed economy endorses the doctrine of socialism, its principle of the partly visible hand of an activist government that commands and controls some factors of production, and the goal of regulating economic freedom.
- State capitalism is a system whereby the government manipulates market outcomes for political purposes.
- Managers assess markets in terms of size (GNI, GNP, GDP), income (GNI, GNP, or GDP per capita), stability (HDI, HPI), and sustainability (NNP, GPI, YBLI).
- Green measures of economic performance call for considering ecological aspects that support sustainable development.
- Concern that monetary measures misestimate economic performance leads to calls to expand the concept of prosperity to include aspects of happiness.
- Managers use several indicators to assess the performance and potential of an economy, including inflation, unemployment, debt, income distribution, poverty, and the balance of payments.
- The Base of the Pyramid is the largest but poorest socioeconomic group in the world. Although poor in terms of individual wealth, the aggregate income of the Base arguably makes it the next market frontier.
- Various global indices help managers develop a holistic profile of particular markets in terms of competitiveness, innovation, and the quality of life.

KEY TERMS

balance of payments (BOP) (p. 215)
Base of the Pyramid (p. 214)
BRICs (p. 199)
capitalism (p. 194)
command economy (p. 195)
communism (p. 195)
debt (p. 211)
deflation (p. 210)
economic freedom (p. 189)
Economic Freedom Index (p. 189)
economic system (p. 194)

emerging economies (p. 199)
Gini coefficient (p. 212)
green economics (p. 204)
gross national income (GNI) (p. 200)
gross national product (GNP) (p. 200)
happynomics (p. 206)
income distribution (p. 211)
inflation (p. 209)
laissez-faire (p. 195)
market economy (p. 194)
mixed economy (p. 196)
misery index (p. 210)
poverty (p. 212)
reflation (p. 210)
socialism (p. 196)
state capitalism (p. 197)
sustainable development (p. 205)
unemployment rate (p. 210)

ENDNOTES

1 ***Sources include the following:*** Thomas Friedman, *The World Is Flat: A Brief History of the Twenty-first Century"* (Farrar, Straus and Giroux, 2005); Clyde V. Prestowitz, *Three Billion New Capitalists: The Great Shift of Wealth and Power to the East* (New York: Basic Books, 2006); Clyde Prestowitz, "Three Billion New Capitalists," video transcript, *News Hour* (August 15, 2005), www.pbs.org/newshour/bb/economy/july-dec05/prestowitz_8-15.html; Kenneth Rogoff, "Betting with the House's Money," *Project Syndicate,* retrieved May 7, 2007 from www.project-syndicate.org/commentary/rogoff27; Anne O. Krueger, "Stability, Growth, and Prosperity: The Global Economy and the IMF," retrieved June 7, 2006 from www.imf.org/external/np/speeches/2006/060706.htm; Angus Maddison, *The World Economy, 1–2030 AD* (London: Oxford University Press, 2007); *The World Economy: Volume 1: A Millennial Perspective* (Paris: Development Centre, 2001); *Volume 2: Historical Statistics* (Paris: Development Centre, 2003); "BRICs, Emerging Markets and the World Economy: Not Just Straw Men," *The Economist* (June 18, 2009): 45; "Government v. Market in America: The Visible Hand," *The Economist* (May 28, 2009): 25–28, retrieved August 12, 2009 from www.economist.com/displaystory.cfm?story_id=13743310; "The Next Billions: Unleashing Business Potential in Untapped Markets," *World Economic Forum* (January 2009): 44; "A Special Report on Innovation in Emerging Markets: The World Turned Upside Down," *The Economist,* retrieved April 21, 2011 from www.economist.com/node/15879369; "China Claims #9 Rank In United States Patents!" retrieved April 23, 2011 from www.defence.pk/forums/china-defence/55892-china-claims-9-rank-united-states-patents.html; Ian Morris, *Why the West Rules... For Now* (New York, Farrar, Straus and Giroux, 2010).

2 Thomas Friedman, *The World Is Flat: A Brief History of the Twenty-first Century* (Farrar, Straus and Giroux, 2005).

3 Clyde V. Prestowitz, *Three Billion New Capitalists: The Great Shift of Wealth and Power to the East,* (New York: Basic Books, 2006).

4 Hal Sirkin, James W. Hemerling, Arindam Bhattacharya, *Globality: Competing with Everyone from Everywhere for Everything,* Grand Central Publishing, 2008.

5 "Global Economic Outlook,"The Conference Board," retrieved April 11, 2011 from www.conference-board.org/data/globalout look.cfm. They moved to 50.4 percent in 2010. "Global Development Horizons 2011—Multipolarity: The New Global Economy," *The World Bank* (retrieved May 19, 2011).

6 Martin Dewhurst, Jonathan Harris, and Suzanne Heywood, "The Global Company's Challenge," *McKinsey Quarterly,* December 31, 2012, from www.mckinseyquarterly.com/The_global_companys_challenge_2979.

7 So, for example, in May 2011, Chinese Central Bank governor Zhou Xiaochuan noted that "The new IMF leadership needs to reflect changes in the world economic order and be more representative of emerging market economies."

8 "A Special Report on Innovation in Emerging Markets: The World Turned Upside Down," *The Economist,* retrieved April 21, 2011 from www.economist.com/node/15879369; James Politi, "World Bank Sees End to Dollar's Hegemony," *Financial Times* (May 17, 2011).

9 Ibid.

10 Dustin Ensinger, "China Takes the Crown, Economy in Crisis," retrieved April 13, 2011 from www.economyincrisis.org/content/china-takes-crown.

11 People's Republic of China: Spillover Report." International Monetary Fund, retrieved January, 26, 2013 from www.imf.org/external/pubs/ft/scr/2011/cr11193.pdf.

12 Dustin Ensinger, "China Takes the Crown, Economy in Crisis," 5.

13 Clyde Prestowitz, "Three Billion New Capitalists," video transcript, *News Hour* (August 15, 2005), retrieved July 18, 2007 from www.pbs.org/newshour/bb/economy/july-dec05/prestowitz_815.html.

14 Jason Dean, Andrew Browne, and Shai Oster, "China's 'State Capitalism' Sparks a Global Backlash - WSJ.com" (November 16, 2010); Keith Bradsher, "In Trade Cases, Solar Panel Industry Follows Lead of Steel Industry," *New York Times* (October 12, 2012): B2.

15 Bradsher, Keith. "Strategy of Solar Dominance Now Poses a Threat to China," *New York Times* (October 5 2012): B1.

16 For example, in mid-2011, Bolivia dismantled its privatization model that governed the mining industry and expropriated all assets owned by private, largely foreign-owned mining companies. The fear was this action signaled rising resource nationalism worldwide.

17 "A Special Report On Innovation In Emerging Markets: The World Turned Upside Down."

18 Martin Dewhurst, Jonathan Harris, and Suzanne Heywood, "The Global Company's Challenge," *McKinsey Quarterly,* retrieved December 31, 2012 from www.mckinseyquarterly.com/The_global_companys_challenge_2979.

19 Jason Dean, Andrew Browne, and Shai Oster, "China's 'State Capitalism' Sparks a Global Backlash," WSJ.com, retrieved January 30, 2013 from online.wsj.com/article/SB10001424052748703514904575602731006315198.html.

20 Cardwell, Diane, and Keith Bradsher, "U.S. Will Place Tariffs on Chinese Solar Panels." *New York Times,* (October 11, 2012): B3.

21 Stephen King, *Losing Control: The Emerging Threats to Western Prosperity,* (New Haven, CT: Yale University Press, 2010).

22 "How We Classify Countries | Data," *The World Bank,* retrieved February 6, 2013 from data.worldbank.org/about/country-classifications.

23 See, for example, www.econlib.org/library/Enc/BehavioralEconomics.html.

24 Consider, for example, the consequences of a reduction in interest rates; a cut spurs more borrowing that fans greater demand that boosts inflation that erodes purchasing power that creates wage pressure that reduces profits that lowers savings and so on.

25 Kim Murphy, "Melting Ice Caps Open Up Shipping Routes," *Los Angeles Times* (October 13, 2009).

26 Simon Wilson, "Global Trade: The Opening of the Northeast Passage," *MoneyWeek* (September 25, 2009):45.

27 Ships attempting the Northern Sea Route or Northwest Passages face hundred-mile long swathes of shifting pack ice, even during the two months or so of each summer when safe passage is feasible.

28 "NASA—Arctic Ice Gets a Check Up," retrieved April 18, 2011 from www.nasa.gov/mission_pages/icebridge/multimedia/arcticseaice-max2011.html.

29 Arctic Sea Ice Volume Now One-fifth Its 1979 Level," *Weather Underground*, retrieved February 20, 2013 from www.wunderground.com/blog/JeffMasters/show.html; Justin Gillis, "Arctic Sea Ice Stops Melting, but Record Low Is Set," *New York Times*, (January 23, 2013): C4.

30 William W. Beach and Marc A. Miles, "Explaining the Factors of the Index of Economic Freedom," *2005 Index of Economic Freedom*, retrieved August 14, 2006 from www.heritage.org/research/features/index:33.

31 Quotation extracted from *The Wealth of Nations*. Reported in "Executive Summary," Index of Economic Freedom , retrieved February 4, 2008 from www.heritage.org/research/features/index/chapters/pdf/index2008_execsum.pdf.

32 "March Toward Economic Freedom Stalls With Only Two Regions Improving," The Heritage Foundation, retrieved January 23, 2013 from www.heritage.org/index/press-release-overview.

33 *The 2013 Index of Economic Freedom*, retrieved January 24, 2013 from www.heritage.org/Index.

34 E.g., Robert Lawson "Measuring Economic Freedom," Cato Institute, retrieved April 13, 2011 from www.cato.org/pub_display.php?pub_id=6101.

35 Barry Eichengreen and Kevin H. O'Rourke, "A Tale of Two Depressions," retrieved June 5, 2009 from www.voxeu.org/index.php?q=node/3421.

36 "Bush Says Sacrificed Free-market Principles to Save Economy," *Agence France-Presse*, retrieved January 28, 2013 from www.google.com/hostednews/afp/article/ALeqM5jyyKrPjYt7VhpS8G8DrRkr18B0hA.

37 Data drawn from 12,884 interviews across 25 countries. "Sharp Drop in American Enthusiasm for Free Market," *Globescan*, retrieved April 19, 2011 from www.globescan.com/news_archives/radar10w2_free_market; "Capitalism's waning popularity," *The Economist*, (April 7, 2011): 45.

38 Ibid.

39 Ibid.

40 Anatole Kaletsky, "*Capitalism 4.0: The Birth of a New Economy in the Aftermath of Crisis*, (New York: Public Affairs, 2010).

41 Strictly speaking, none of them is a "pure" market economy because their governments intervene in the marketplace. Still, their historic advocacy of economic freedom endorses the philosophy of capitalism and the principle of laissez-faire.

42 "Quote by Ronald Reagan: Government Is Not the Solution. . . ." retrieved February 24, 2013 from www.goodreads.com/quotes/179719-in-this-present-crisis-government-is-not-the-solution-to.

43 Only then, the thinking goes, are the proletariat (the social class that does manual labor or work for wages) protected from exploitation by the bourgeois (the social class that owns the factors of production).

44 Companies in centrally planned economies exhibited a particular quirk. The absence of competition and bankruptcy in this sort of economic system meant that once an enterprise was up and running, it survived indefinitely, irrespective of performance.

45 "The Global Revival Of Industrial Policy: Picking Winners, Saving Losers," *The Economist*, (April 27, 2011):55.

46 Michael Todaro, *Economic Development*, 6th edition (Reading, MA: Addison Wesley, 1996):705.

47 "The French Model: Vive la Différence!" *The Economist*, (May 7, 2009):37.

48 "Denmark 'happiest place on earth,'" BBC News, 28 July 2006. retrieved April 18, 2011 fromnews.bbc.co.uk/2/hi/health/5224306.stm; see also Russell Shorto, "Going Dutch: How I learned to love the welfare state," *New York Times*, retrieved April 17, 2011 from www.nytimes.com/2009/05/03/magazine/03european-.html.

49 For instance, the French government holds significance ownership stakes in several large companies, including Areva (15.88 percent stake), Renault (15 percent stake), Safran (30.2 percent stake), EDF (84.44 percent stake), and GDF Suez (36.36 percent stake).

50 Most worrisome to free market proponents is that, once a crisis passes, government control sometimes shrinks, but it never returns to its original size. Indeed, some argue that a mixed economy is essentially a move toward a socialist state.

51 Specifically, according to 2013 rankings, Hong Kong, Singapore, Australia, New Zealand, and Switzerland.

52 "Q&A with Ian Bremmer on State Capitalism," *Foreign Affairs*, retrieved April 13 2011 from www.foreignaffairs.com/discussions/interviews/qa-with-ian-bremmer-on-state-capitalism?page=show.

53 Michael Wines, "Make No Mistake: In China, State-run Firms Rule," *The New York Times* (August 31, 2010): B-4.

54 "China's Future: Rising Power, Anxious State," *The Economist*, Special Report: China (June 25, 2011): 14.

55 The state essentially prevents systemic distortions threatening the stability of the system and promoting societal welfare—or, as Marx prophesied, capitalism eventually is destroyed by its own contradictions.

56 "Countries at the Crossroads," retrieved April 18, 2011 from www.freedomhouse.org/template.cfm?page=139&edition=9.

57 Ian Bremmer, "State Capitalism and the Crisis," *McKinsey Quarterly*, (July, 2009): 4.

58 "Brazil's Presidential Campaign: Falling in Love Again with the State," *The Economist*, (August 18, 2012): 57.

59 Eric Li, "How China Broke The West's Monopoly On Modernization," CSMonitor.com, retrieved April 28, 2011 from www.csmonitor.com/Commentary/Global-Viewpoint/2011/0428/How-China-broke-the-West-s-monopoly-on-modernization.

60 Ian Bremmer, *The End of the Free Market: Who Wins the War Between States and Corporations?* (New York: Portfolio, 2010); Stefan Halper, *The Beijing Consensus: How China's Authoritarian Model Will Dominate the Twenty-First Century* (New York: Basic Books, 2010).

61 Regarding the informal, the *Economist* reported that "When Alan Greenspan was chairman of the Federal Reserve, he monitored several unusual measures. One favorite, supposedly, was sales of men's underwear, which are usually pretty constant, but drop in recessions when men replace them less often." See "Fast Food for Thought," *The Economist* (July 30, 2011): 12.

62 "Fact Sheet: World Population Trends 2012," *Population Reference Bureau*," retrieved January 24, 2013 from www.prb.org/Publications/Datasheets/2012/world-population-data-sheet/fact-sheet-world-population.aspx.

63 "GDP: One of the Great Inventions of the 20th Century," *Bureau of Economic Analysis*, retrieved from January 24, 2013 from www.bea.gov/scb/account_articles/general/0100od/maintext.htm.

64 For example, Indonesia's GNP is larger than its GNI—the former was \$706 billion in 2010, while the latter was \$599 billion. The same held for its neighbor, Thailand, with a GNI of \$286 billion versus GNP of \$318 billion the same year. In contrast, the GNI of the United States in 2010 was \$14.60 trillion, while its GNP was \$14.66 trillion. This discrepancy results from the fact that the net foreign factor income was negative for Indonesia and Thailand (i.e., a net outflow), but roughly balanced for the United States. Since GNI takes net flows into account, we have the resulting variance between GNI and GNP. As a rule, many developing countries produce more value than they receive as income, thereby leading to a higher GNP than GNI.

65 Historically, GNI was referred to as gross national product. The definition and measurement of GNI and GNP are analogous, but

institutions such as the World Bank and International Monetary Fund now use the term GNI.

66 For example, Latin America has seen income per capita drop five times since the 1980s. The current global credit crisis has triggered a sixth occurrence—population in the region is growing 1.3 percent a year but the economy "grew" –2.2 percent in 2009. As expected, consumer demand, public finances, financial reserves, and currency valuations tumbled. This calamity is not unique to Latin America; at least 60 developing markets suffered income drops in 2009, with especially hard times for Central and Eastern Europe and sub-Saharan Africa.

67 Technically, we compute per capita GNI by taking the GNI of a country and converting it into a standard currency—say, the U.S. dollar at prevailing exchange rates—and then dividing this sum by population size.

68 U.S. and World Population Clocks—POPClocks, retrieved January 30, 2013. Check www.census.gov/main/www/popclock.html for current statistic.

69 Technically, the World Bank estimates a higher per capita income level for Monaco. However, the 2011 report is an approximation and, moreover, there is no estimate for its purchasing power parity conversion. Hence, we use Norway given its complete data file for 2011.

70 We calculate PPP between countries by estimating the value of a universal "basket" of goods (e.g., soap and bread) and services (e.g., telephone and electricity) that can be purchased with one unit of a country's currency. For example, a loaf of bread that sells for 53.70 rupees in India should cost U.S. $1.00 in the United States given an exchange rate between India and the United States of 53.70 INR to U.S. $1. Exchange rates as of January 24, 2013.

71 World Bank, 2013 Survey (Atlas methodology for GNI per capita). Typically, the prices of many goods are considered and weighted according to their importance in the economy of the particular country.

72 The most common PPP exchange rate comes from comparing a basket of goods and services in a country with an equivalent basket in the United States.

73 "Europe's Shadow Economy: As Big As Germany," *Zero Hedge.*" Retrieved May 13, 2013 from www.zerohedge.com/news/2013-05-06/europes-shadow-economy-big-germany.

74 "Process of Preparation of the Environmental Perspective to the Year 2000 and Beyond," General Assembly Resolution 38/161," retrieved May 27, 2007 from www.un.org/documents/ga/res/38/a38r161htm.

75 Joseph Stiglitz, "Good Numbers Gone Bad: Why Relying on GDP as a Leading Economic Gauge Can Lead to Poor Decision-Making," *Fortune* (September 25, 2006):45-49.

76 Some maintain that the purpose of development is to enlarge people's choices. In principle, these choices can be infinite and can change over time. People often value achievements that do not show up at all, or not immediately, in income or growth figures: greater access to knowledge, better nutrition and health services, more secure livelihoods, security against crime and physical violence, satisfying leisure hours, political and cultural freedoms, and sense of participation in community activities. The objective of development is to create an enabling environment for people to enjoy long, healthy, and creative lives. Statement by Dr. Mahbub ul Haq, co-conceiver, with Amartya Sen of HDI.

77 Richard Easterlin, "Does Economic Growth Improve the Human Lot?" in Paul A. David and Melvin W. Reder, eds., *Nations and Households in Economic Growth: Essays in Honor of Moses Abramovitz* (New York: Academic Press, 1974); Richard Easterlin, "Income and Happiness: Towards a Unified Theory," *The Economic Journal* (2001): 465–84.

78 Eric Weiner, "The Happiest Places in the World," *Forbes* (April 23, 2008):55.

79 Mark Whitehouse, "GDP Can Be a Poor Measure of Success," WSJ.com, retrieved January 17, 2011 from online.wsj.com/article/SB10001424052748704064504576070343252409876.html; "Noreena Hertz: Even War Is Good for Economic Growth," *Spiegel Online,* retrieved January 28, 2013 from www.spiegel.de/international/world/globalization-critic-noreena-hertz-even-war-is-good-for-economic-growth-a-685491.html.

80 Roger Cohen, "The Happynomics of Life," NYTimes.com, retrieved April 27, 2011 from nytimes.com/2011/03/13/opinion/13cohen.html?_r=1.

81 Charles Jones and Peter Klenow, *Beyond GDP? Welfare across Countries and Time*, NBER Working Papers 16352, National Bureau of Economic Research (2010).

82 "OECD Launches Happiness Index, *AFP,* retrieved May 26, 2011 from www.google.com/hostednews/afp/article/ALeqM5jj15a9ZCL9ETVD9UAn18y7MlrG_g?docId=CNG.b86506f095cbf61164e88f98b0d5d21c.2a1.

83 The Happiest Countries in the World," *24/7 Wall St,* retrieved June 4, 2011 from 247wallst.com/2011/06/01/the-happiest-countries-in-the-world/2.

84 *World Bank Indicators, 2013,* The World Bank, data.worldbank.org/data-catalog/world-development-indicators.

85 "Government v. Market in America: The Visible Hand," *The Economist* (May 28, 2009): 25–28.

86 E. Mishan, *The Costs of Economic Growth* (New York: Praeger, 1967).

87 Ibid.

88 Jerome Glenn, Theodore Gordon, and Elizabeth Florescu, *2009 State of the Future, The Millennium Project,* retrieved May 15, 2011 from www.millenniumproject.org/millennium/sof2009.html; "Humans using Earth's Resources at Unsustainable Rate, Conservation Group Claims," retrieved June 2, 2011 from www.naturalnews.com/020873.html.

89 *Process of Preparation of the Environmental Perspective to the Year 2000 and Beyond,* General Assembly Resolution 38/161, retrieved May 27, 2007 from www.un.org/documents/ga/res/38/a38r161htm.

90 Murray Rothbard, "Ludwig von Mises (1881–1973)," retrieved May 27, 2009 from www.mises.org/content/mises.asp.

91 See www.usinflationcalculator.com/frequently-asked-questions-faqs.

92 For example, discontent with rising prices sparked China's Tiananmen Square protests of 1989. "China's Future: Rising Power, Anxious State," *The Economist,* Special Report: China (June 25, 2011): 9.

93 Economists use different types of indexes to measure inflation, but the one they use the most is the *Consumer Price Index (CPI).* The CPI measures a fixed basket of goods and compares its price from one period to the next. A rise in the index indicates inflation.

94 The Hanke-Krus hyperinflation table documents every known case of hyperinflation of the 20th century.

95 Steve H. Hanke and Alex K. F. Kwok, "On the Measurement of Zimbabwe's Hyperinflation," *Cato Journal,* (Spring/Summer 2009).

96 Steve H. Hanke and Alex K. F. Kwok, "On the Measurement of Zimbabwe's Hyperinflation," *Cato Journal,* (Spring/Summer 2009).

97 Analytics performed at www.usinflationcalculator.com/.

98 Kevin Phillips, "Numbers Racket: Why the Economy Is Worse than We Know," *Harper's,* retrieved April 26, 2001 from www.harpers.org/archive/2008/05/0082023; "Economics focus: Botox and bean counting," *The Economist* (April 30, 2011):84.

99 For instance, as of 2003, only three countries had annual inflation rates in excess of 40 percent, the level above which it is generally considered to be acutely damaging to an economy. All major industrial countries had inflation under 3 percent (and in Japan, deflation persisted). Moreover, inflation in many middle- and lower-income countries, once stuck with extreme inflation pressure, had fallen well into single digits in the early twenty-first century. Many credited the fall in inflation to a combination of the price pressures of globalization along with more vigilant central bankers and economic policymakers. See Ken Rogoff, "The IMF Strikes Back," *Foreign Policy* (January/February 2003): 39–48.

100 View of Junko Nishioka, Chief Japan economist at RBS Securities Japan Ltd. in Tokyo. From "Japan Succumbs to Deflation as Consumer

Prices Fall Record 1.1 percent," Bloomberg.com, retrieved June 29, 2009 from www.bloomberg.com/apps/news?pid=newsarchive&sid=aaQyqjERBorM.

101 Ibid.

102 Presently, the wealthier countries of the world are watching their working-age population shrink from approximately 740 to 690 million people between 2000 and 2025. However, over the same time, the working-age population will increase across poorer countries from about 3 to 4 billion people. In China alone, the population above the age of 16 will grow by 5.5 million annually on average in the next 20 years. The total population of working-age Chinese will reach 940 million by 2020. Presently, the youth of the world suffer the highest rates of unemployment in most countries, with rates twice that of adult (ages 25–65) unemployment. China, for example, sees the age structure of its population creating severe employment pressure within the next two decades.

103 "Economic Security Index: Putting a Face on American Economic Security," retrieved January 24, 2013, from economicsecurityindex.org/.

104 "In U.S., Employment Situation Deteriorates in January," *Gallup Economy,* retrieved January 28, 2013 from www.gallup.com/poll/159866/employment-situation-deteriorates-january.aspx.

105 See Constance Sorrentino, "International Unemployment Rates: How Comparable Are They?" *Monthly Labor Review* (June 2000): 3–20.

106 See U.S. National Debt Clock, www.brillig.com/debt_clock.

107 For example, arguably the U.S. fiscal system is plugged with many tax loopholes that cause inefficiencies, misallocation of resources, and lost revenues. Hence, eliminating the deficit requires eliminating these distortions.

108 GNI per capita data is adjusted by purchasing power parity (data as of February 2013).

109 Bob Herbert, "Losing Our Way," NYTimes.com, retrieved April 12, 2011 from www.nytimes.com/2011/03/26/opinion/26herbert.html?_r=1.

110 William Domhoff, "Wealth, Income, and Power," retrieved May 5, 2009 from sociology.ucsc.edu/whorulesamerica/power/wealth.html; see "Gap between Rich and Poor: World Income Inequality," retrieved July 4, 2009 from www.infoplease.com/ipa/A0908770.html.

111 *World Development Indicators 2012*, The World Bank.

112 "Growing Income Inequality in OECD Countries: What Drives It and How Can Policy Tackle It?" www.oecd.org/els/social/inequality (May 2010). Finally, income inequality is accelerating between top executives and the average employee. In 2010, the average CEO in the United States made 343 times more money than the average American did last year. In 2007, for example, CEOs of the 15 largest companies earned 520 times more than the average worker. This is up from 360 times more in 2003. We see similar patterns Australia, Germany, Hong Kong (China), the Netherlands, and South Africa.

113 "Inequality: Unbottled Gini," *The Economist,*" (January 20, 2011):45.

114 "Chinese Scholars Warn Growing Wealth Gap Likely to Trigger Social Instability," *Sina,* retrieved July 8, 2006 from english.sina.com/china/1/2005/0822/43237.html.

115 "China's Urban, Rural Income Gap Widens Despite Economic Recovery," *People's Daily Online,* retrieved April 19, 2011 from english.people.com.cn/90001/90778/90862/6875693.html

116 Joseph Stiglitz, "Of the 1 Percent, by the 1 Percent, for the 1 Percent," *Vanity Fair* (May 2011).

117 Ibid: 26.

118 Some controversy surrounds the Gini estimate with regards to China. China officially reported its Gini coefficient, for the first time in 12 years, in 2012 as .474. Skeptics argue otherwise. For example, a study based on the China Household Finance Survey reports a Gini coefficient of .58.

119 Others advocate refining analysis by calculating a "Global Gini" that measures the scale of income distribution among everyone in the world. Global inequality increased in the 19th and 20th centuries as richer countries, on average, consistently grew faster than poorer countries. Recently, the accelerating comeback of developing countries shows up in declining global inequality, indicating that the planet as a whole is increasingly fair.

120 "80 Percent of Indians Live on Less than $2 a day—World Bank," livemint.com, retrieved April 17, 2011 from www.livemint.com/articles/2007/10/16235421/80-of-Indians-live-on-less-th.htm.

121 "A Wealth of Data: A Useful New Way to Capture the Many Aspects of Poverty," *The Economist,* retrieved April 18, 2011 from www.economist.com/node/16693283.

122 "Impossible Architecture," *Social Watch Report 2006,* retrieved May 27, 2007 from www.socialwatch.org/en/portada.htm.

123 Noted Jeffery Sachs, "The world is more unequal than at any time in world history. There's a basic reason for that which is that 200 years ago everybody was poor. A relatively small part of the world achieved what the economists call a modern economic growth. Those countries represent only about one-sixth of humanity, and five-sixths of humanity is what we call the developing world. It's the vast majority of the world. The gap can be 100 to 1, maybe a gap of $30,000 per person and $300 per person. And that's absolutely astounding to be on the same planet and to have that extreme variation in material well-being." Transcript, Chapter 18, "Episode Three: The New Rules of the Game," *Commanding Heights: The Battle for the World Economy,* retrieved June 28, 2007 from www.pbs.org/wgbh/commanding-heights/lo/index.htm.

124 "Global Unemployment Expected to Surpass 200 Million," *Zero Hedge,* retrieved January 29, 2013 www.zerohedge.com/news/2013-01-22/global-unemployment-expected-surpass-200-million).

125 Sandrine Rastello and Wendy Pugh, "Food Surge Is Exacerbating Poverty, World Bank Says," Bloomberg.com, retrieved May 10, 2011 from www.bloomberg.com/news/2011-02-15/food-price-jump-pushes-44-million-into-extreme-poverty-world-bank-says.html.

126 The Food and Agriculture Organization of the United Nations translates the food commodities available for human consumption in a country into their protein equivalent. This measure compensates for differences in protein supplied by different foods across countries (go to www.fao.org).

127 Donald McNeil Jr., "Design That Solves Problems for the World's Poor," *New York Times* (May 29, 2007): B-2.

128 "The Next Billions: Unleashing Business Potential in Untapped Markets," *World Economic Forum* (January 2009): 44; C. K. Prahalad and S. L. Hart, "The Fortune at the Bottom of the Pyramid," *Strategy+Business* (2002) 26: 54–67.

129 Christa Case Bryant, "Surging BRIC Middle Classes Are Eclipsing Global Poverty," CSMonitor.com, retrieved May 25, 2011 from www.csmonitor.com/World/2011/0517/Surging-BRIC-middle-classes-are-eclipsing-global-poverty.

130 David Court and Laxman Narasimhan, "Capturing the World's Emerging Middle Class," *McKinsey Quarterly* (July 2010): 67.

131 "Chart Focus: The World's Economic Center of Gravity Shifts," *McKinsey Quarterly,* retrieved February 25, 2013 from www.mckinseyquarterly.com/newsletters/chartfocus/2013_02.html.

132 Jane Fraser and Jeremy Oppenheim, "What's New about Globalization," *The McKinsey Quarterly* (May 1997): 178. Erik Simanis, "When selling to poor consumers, companies first need to create the market," WSJ.com," retrieved January 29, 2013 from online.wsj.com/article/SB10001424052970203946904574301802684947732.html.

133 See, for example, www.nextbillion.net.

134 "Medical Technology: Frugal Healing," *The Economist,*" (January 11, 2011):45.

135 "Innovations to Create New Streams of Profitable Growth," *Accenture Outlook,* retrieved June 9, 2009 from www.accenture.com/in-en/outlook/Pages/outlook-journal-2010-less-is-new-more-innovation.aspx.

136 "The Tata Group: Out of India," *The Economist* (March 5, 2011):76–78; "The Bottom of the Pyramid," *The Economist* (June 25, 2011): 80.

137 The notion of *balance* means that all BOP transactions have an offsetting receipt. For instance, a country might have a surplus in merchandise trade (indicating that it is exporting more than it is importing) but may then report a deficit in another area, such as its investment income. In other words, because the current account and the capital account add up to the total account—which is necessarily balanced—a deficit in the current account is accompanied by an equal surplus in the capital account and vice versa. A deficit or surplus in the current account cannot be explained or evaluated without simultaneous explanation and evaluation of an equal surplus or deficit in the capital account.

138 Retrieved October 2, 2009 from www.cia.gov/library/publications/the-world-factbook/rankorder/2187rank.html.

139 "Global Competitiveness Index," *World Economic Forum,*" retrieved January 25, 2013 from www.weforum.org/issues/global-competitiveness.

140 "IMD Announces Its 2012 World Competitiveness Rankings," IMD, retrieved January 25, 2013 from www.imd.org/news/IMD-announces-its-2012-World-Competitiveness-Rankings.cfm.

141 "The Global Innovation Index 2012," retrieved January 25, 2013 from www.globalinnovationindex.org/gii/.

142 "The Lottery of Life," *The Economist: The World in 2013,* (November 21, 2012):91.

143 ***Sources include the following:*** Dominic Wilson and Roopa Purushothaman, "Global Economics Paper No. 99: Dreaming with BRICs: The Path to 2050," Goldman Sachs, at www.gs.com/insight/research/reports/report6.html; "The BRICs Are Coming—Fast," *Business Week* (October 27, 2003): 33; Daniel Gross, "The U.S. Is Losing Market Share. So What?" *New York Times* (January 28, 2007): A-2; Andrew Kramer, "Putin Wants New Economic 'Architecture,'" *International Herald Tribune* (June 10, 2007): 1; "Chilling Time," *The Economist* (June 14, 2007): 24; State of the World 2006: China and India Hold World in Balance, Worldwatch Institute; see www.worldwatch.org; N. Taleb, *The Black Swan: The Impact of the Highly Improbable* (New York: Random House, 2007); "Emerging Markets and the World Economy: Not Just Straw Men," *The Economist,* (June 18, 2009): 53. "What the West Doesn't Get About China - *Harvard Business Review,*" retrieved August 29, 2011 from hbr.org/2011/06/what-the-west-doesnt-get-about-china/ar/pr; *The World Economic Forum,* retrieved September 7, 2011 from www.reports.weforum.org/global-competitiveness-2011-2012/; Abhijit Neogy and Alexei Anishchuk, "BRICS demand global monetary shake-up, greater influence," *Reuters,* retrieved October 26, 2011 from www.reuters.com/article/2011/04/14/us-brics-idUSTRE73D18H20110414; Ambrose Evans-Pritchard, "IMF Sees 140m Jobs Shortage in Ageing China as 'Lewis Point' Hits," *Telegraph,* retrieved February 4, 2013 from www.telegraph.co.uk/finance/comment/9845959/IMF-sees-140m-jobs-shortage-in-ageing-China-as-Lewis-Point-hits.html; Arvind Subramanian, "BRICs Share of Global GDP Will Go up from 18% to 26% over the Next Decade," *Economic Times,* retrieved February 4, 2013, from articles.economictimes.indiatimes.com/2012-09-06/news/33650208_1_bric-countries-brics-share-punita-kumar-sinha; "Russia and China to Strengthen Trade Ties," FT.com, retrieved February 4, 2013 from www.ft.com/cms/s/0/d8999462-af27-11e1-a8a7-00144feabdc0.html.; "China Busy Signing Currency Deals," *Forbes,* retrieved February 4, 2013 from www.forbes.com/sites/jackperkowski/2012/06/26/china-busy-signing-currency-deals/.

144 India, China Hoping to 'Reshape the World Order' Together," Washingtonpost.com, retrieved February 24, 2013 from www.washingtonpost.com/wp-dyn/articles/A43053-2005Apr11.html.

145 Andrew E. Kramer, "Putin Wants New Economic 'Architecture'" *The New York Times,* (June 10, 2007): B-1.

CHAPTER 5

Trade and Factor Mobility Theory

OBJECTIVES

After studying this chapter, you should be able to

1. Understand how different approaches to international trade theories help policy makers achieve economic objectives
2. Comprehend the historical and current rationale for interventionist trade theories
3. Explain how free trade improves global efficiency
4. Distinguish factors affecting national trade patterns
5. Recognize why a country's export capabilities are dynamic
6. Detect why production factors, especially labor and capital, move internationally
7. Describe the relationship between foreign trade and international factor mobility
8. Grasp scenarios of possible changes in trade patterns

Source: © Edelweiss - Fotolia.com

A market is not held for the sake of one person.

—African (Fulani) proverb

CASE Costa Rica's Trade Evolution

Costa Rica is a Central American country of about 4.7 million people that borders the Pacific Ocean and the Caribbean arm of the Atlantic.[1] Bearing a name that means "Rich Coast," referring to its fertile soil and bountiful biodiversity, the country possesses attributes of both developed and developing countries. With a per capita GDP of $12,600 (based on purchasing price parity in 2012), Costa Rica depends on agricultural commodities—primarily bananas, pineapples, and coffee—for about 36 percent of its merchandise export earnings. However, its tourism earnings are higher than for those top three agricultural exports combined. (The opening photo is in a bio-diverse area that attracts ecotourism.) Costa Rica has a fairly high level of external debt, a literacy rate of about 95 percent, a life expectancy of 78 years, and a fairly even income distribution (the highest 10 percent of the population earns about 40 percent of its income). It has also enjoyed a long history of democracy and political stability. Map 5.1 shows Costa Rica's location and major export markets.

FOUR ERAS

Like all countries, Costa Rica relies on international trade and factor-mobility policies—strategies related to the movement of goods, services, and production factors across borders—to pursue its economic objectives. In any country, these two sets of policies evolve as domestic and foreign conditions change. They're also politically sensitive, especially when it comes to the economic priorities and judgments of the nation's leaders.

For Costa Rica, it's convenient to trace policy evolution through four historical periods, each characterized by particular strategies of international trade and factor mobility:

- *Late 1800s–1960: Liberal trade*—a policy calling for minimal government interference in trade and investment
- *1960–1982: Import substitution*—a policy calling for the local production of goods and services that would otherwise be imported
- *1983–early 1990s: Liberalization of imports,* export promotion, and incentives for most types of foreign investments
- *Early 1990s–present: Strategic trade policy* (or *industrial policy*) calling for the production of specific types of products and openness to imports

LATE 1800s–1960

In the latter part of the 1800s, most nations permitted goods, capital, and people to move with relative freedom from one country to another. Governments tended to interfere only minimally, and the general result was an economic environment in which individual producers determined what to produce and where to produce it. Trade flourished and countries tended to specialize in selling what they could best produce.

Most Latin American countries, including Costa Rica until the early 1960s, specialized in either a single or a few commodities (raw materials or agricultural products), which they exported in exchange for other commodities and manufactured goods. Costa Rican farmers specialized first in coffee and later, after the development of refrigerated ships, in bananas as well. For most of the period, the country was well served by this policy, primarily because commodity prices, especially coffee prices, remained high.

Eventually, however, three factors convinced Costa Rican leaders to encourage more diversified production and economic self-sufficiency:

- Two world wars disrupted the country's ability to export its commodities and import what it did not produce.
- Coffee and banana prices dropped relative to the prices of manufactured products, particularly as new commodity producers (especially in Africa) entered world markets.
- Latin American countries with less open international markets had insulated themselves more from adverse international conditions.

As a result of these developments, Costa Rica turned to policies centered on the idea of import substitution.

1960–1982

In the early 1960s, Costa Rican authorities reasoned that if they limited imports (say, by taxing them heavily), they'd give both home and foreign investors an incentive to produce and sell more things within the country; this policy is known as **import substitution**. They also realized that, unfortunately, the Costa Rican market was too small to support investments requiring large-scale production.

To address this problem, Costa Rica joined with four other countries—El Salvador, Guatemala, Honduras, and Nicaragua—to form the Central American Common Market

MAP 5.1 Costa Rica

In 2011, a bit more than 50 percent of Costa Rica's exports went to three countries. (Much of the exports shown for the Netherlands are transshipped to other European countries.)

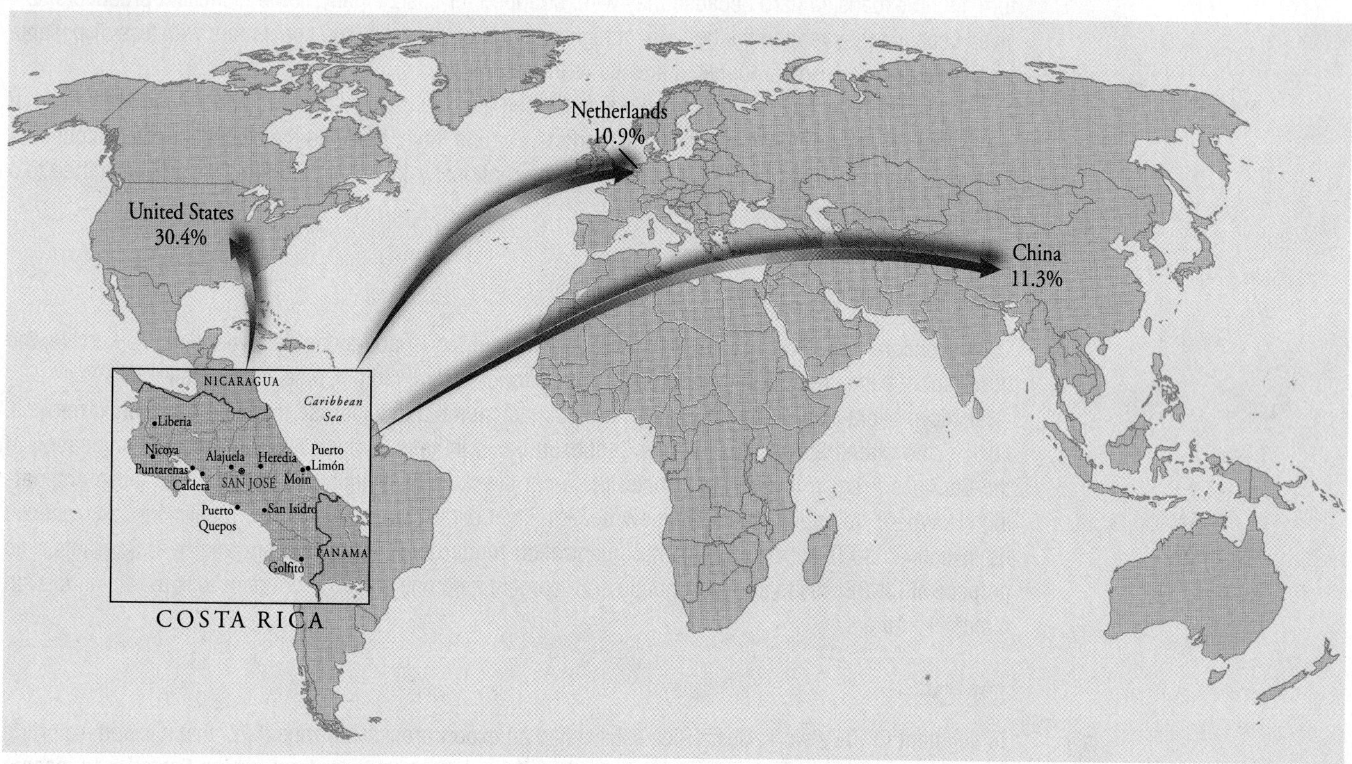

(CACM), which allowed goods produced in any member country to enter freely into the market of any other member. Thus, a company located in a member country could serve a five-country rather than a single-country market.

Miscalculations and Mixed Results

The results were mixed. Costa Rica's economic dependence on agriculture was already declining before the import substitution policy, from 40.9 percent to 25.2 percent of GDP between 1950 and 1960. Thus, the decline to 18 percent by 1980 could not be attributed completely to the policy change.

Likewise, most investors earmarked their new manufacturing to sell domestically and not in the larger CACM market. For example, import substitution helped attract pharmaceutical investment, but the availability of a larger market was not the primary reason; in this case, the strategy worked basically because small-scale packaging and processing are efficient within this industry.

So why was the strategy of import substitution, even coupled with a complementary regional trade agreement, less successful than CACM leaders had hoped? Quite simply, investors were convinced that CACM was destined for disruption—and, as it turned out, they were right. By the late 1970s, civil wars in both El Salvador and Guatemala stifled those economies, and a new regime in Nicaragua was ideologically committed to complete governmental control of all aspects of the economy, including trade.

In some cases, import substitution did lead to increased exports, such as for Costa Rican processed coffee and cottonseeds. Many economists and prospective investors, however, began to worry that policies designed to protect local production—including price controls, import bans, and subsidies—were channeling the country's resources toward inefficient production. For example, Costa Rica became nearly self-sufficient in rice production, but only because government policies kept lower-cost foreign-produced rice out of the market.

Moreover, the government held down consumer rice prices by subsidizing domestic rice producers. The money for these subsidies came largely from higher taxes on efficient industries—industries that, in turn, found expansion hard because they were strapped for cash. Finally, some inefficient producers survived because they reaped the benefits of high consumer prices, leaving consumers with less disposable income to spend on any products, domestic or foreign.

At this point, Costa Rican policymakers concluded that the country must emphasize the production of goods that could compete in international markets. For one thing, they had the example of Asian countries that were achieving rapid growth by competing internationally. In 1983, therefore, Costa Rica shifted to a policy of promoting exports.

1983–EARLY 1990s

To help ensure that only internationally competitive companies and industries were likely to survive, the government began removing import barriers. Rice imports, for example, rose substantially.

Policymakers also decided to seek more outside capital and expertise to support economic reforms. Luckily, the United States launched its Caribbean Basin Initiative, which allowed products originating in the Caribbean region to enter the United States at lower tariff (or import tax) rates than those originating elsewhere. To capitalize on this new opportunity, Costa Rica formed CINDE (Coalición Costarricense de Iniciativas de Desarrollo), a private organization funded by the government and by U.S. grants. The purpose of CINDE was to aid in economic development, and one of its top priorities was attracting foreign direct investment.

CINDE

To augment CINDE's work, Costa Rica established an export processing zone (EPZ) that allowed exporting companies to import all inputs and equipment tax free, exempted them from paying Costa Rican income tax for eight years and taxed them at only 50 percent for the next four. By 1989, 35 companies—mainly textile and footwear producers seeking to take advantage of the country's pool of inexpensive labor—had located in the EPZ.

By this time, however, CINDE's officials were beginning to worry about two potential problems facing its ambitious new initiatives:

1. Costa Rica could not remain cost-competitive in the type of products exported from the EPZ because other countries (mainly Mexico) were benefiting from even lower U.S. tariffs.
2. Costa Rica's highly skilled and educated workforce was being underutilized by the types of industries attracted to the EPZ.

CINDE decided to work with the Costa Rican government to identify and attract investors who matched up better with Costa Rican resources.

EARLY 1990s–PRESENT

Costa Rica targeted industries (a policy known as a **strategic trade policy**) for international competition (including medical instruments and appliances, electronics, and software) that promised high growth potential and could pay higher wages and salaries than most of those that had already invested in the EPZ.

The government also identified characteristics of developing countries that were attracting significant amounts of the type of foreign investment it wanted: a highly educated and largely English-speaking workforce (especially the availability of engineers and technical operators), political and social stability, a relatively high level of economic freedom, and a quality of life that would appeal to the managers and technical personnel that foreign investors would bring in to work in the facilities. The conclusion? In its targeted industries, Costa Rica should be able to compete internationally.

What CINDE Recommended

CINDE also hired the Foreign Investment Advisory Service (FIAS) of the World Banks' International Finance Corporation to study whether and how to attract companies in these industries. FIAS concluded that attracting the right number of the right companies was well within Costa Rica's reach, and suggested areas within this selection of targeted industries, such as power technologies, that best fit with the country's main advantage—a labor force that was well educated in relation to its cost. It also recommended that officials target companies that supported the electronics and computer industries, such as plastics and metalworking. Finally, FIAS noted that Costa Rica needed to improve the English proficiency of its technicians and engineers and the protection of intellectual property rights. In response, Costa Rica put English language skills in a revised curriculum for training mid-level technicians and set up Spanish-language training for the personnel brought in by foreign investors.

Progress Report

Setting out to attract investments in electronics and software, Costa Rica landed such high-tech investors as Reliability, Protek, Colorplast, and Sensortronics. By far, the largest investor was the computer-chip giant Intel. CINDE officials worked to attract Intel. They drew up a list of all the questions and concerns Intel might have and prepared knowledgeable responses to them. They also involved top government and corporate leaders in meetings with Intel executives, even enlisting the country's president, José Figueres, to pilot them on a helicopter survey of plant sites.

Since then, Costa Rica has turned its attention to medical devices, and attracted investments by such companies as Abbott Laboratories, Baxter, and Procter & Gamble. Although exports of coffee and bananas are still important to the nation's economy, about 60 percent of Costa Rica's merchandise exports are now manufactured goods, with high-tech products constituting the backbone of the economy and export earnings. ■

CRN Case Review Note

QUESTIONS

5-1. Using the framework in Table 5.1, explain which of the theories relate to Costa Rican trade policy during each of the four eras described in the case.

5-2. Map 5.1 shows that a bit over 50 percent of Costa Rican exports go to only three countries. Which trade theories may help to explain this concentration and why?

INTRODUCTION

The preceding case shows how Costa Rica has used trade and factor mobility (movement of capital, technology, and people) to help achieve its economic objectives. Figure 5.1 shows that countries are linked internationally by trade in goods and services and the movement of production factors. Like Costa Rica, other countries wrestle with the questions of what, how much, and with whom to trade. These questions are intertwined with considerations of what they can produce competitively by boosting the quality and quantity of capital, technical competence, and worker skills.

Trade theory helps managers and government policymakers focus on these questions:

- What products should we import and export?
- How much should we trade?
- With whom should we trade?

LAISSEZ-FAIRE VERSUS INTERVENTIONIST APPROACHES TO EXPORTS AND IMPORTS

Once countries set economic and political objectives, officials enact policies—including trade policies—to achieve desired results. This influences which countries can produce given products more efficiently and whether countries will permit imports to compete against their

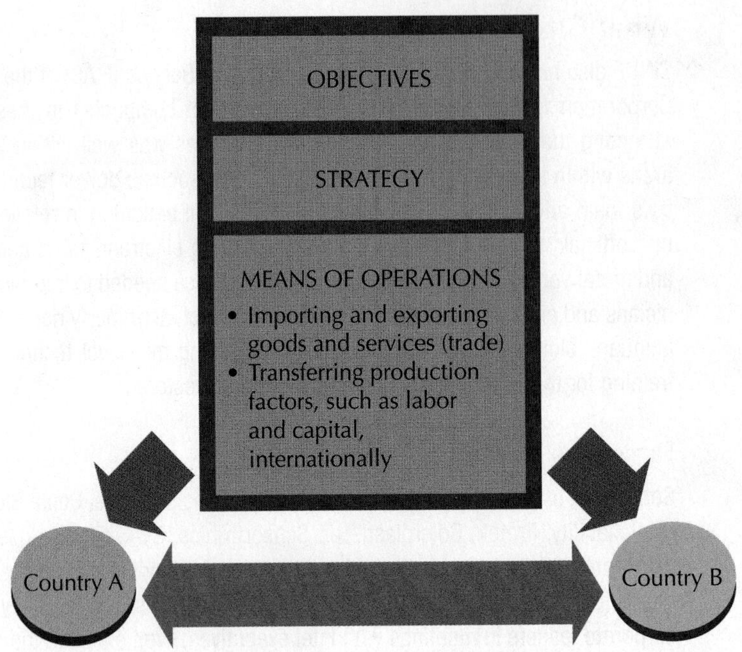

FIGURE 5.1 International Operations and Economic Connections

To meet its international objectives, a company must gear its strategy to trading and transferring its means of operation across borders—say, from (Home) Country A to (Host) Country B. Once this process has taken place, the two countries are connected economically.

CONCEPT CHECK

Compare Figure 5.1 with Figure 1.1, which outlines certain conditions that may affect a firm's operations when it decides to do business on an international scale. Here the graphic focuses in on operational adjustments that a company faces when it takes specific strategic actions to go international—namely, to trade and transfer means of production.

Some trade theories prescribe that governments should influence trade patterns; others propose a laissez-faire treatment of trade.

domestically produced goods and services. Some nations take a more *laissez-faire* approach, one that allows market forces to determine trading relations. *Free-trade theories* (absolute advantage and comparative advantage) take a complete laissez-faire approach because they prescribe that governments should not intervene directly to affect trade. At the other extreme are *mercantilism* and *neomercantilism,* which prescribe a great deal of government intervention in trade. Whether taking a laissez-faire or interventionist approach, countries rely on trade theories to guide policy development.

THEORIES OF TRADE PATTERNS

After taking a look at theories dealing with trade intervention, we examine those that help explain trade patterns (how much countries depend on trade, in what products, and with whom), including theories of *country size, factor proportions,* and *country similarity.* We then consider theories dealing with the dynamics of countries' trade competitiveness for particular products, which include the *product life cycle theory* and the *diamond of national competitive advantage theory.*

TRADE THEORIES AND BUSINESS

Table 5.1 summarizes the major trade theories and their emphases. These different theories expand our understanding of how government trade policies might affect business competitiveness. For instance, they provide insights on favorable locales and products for exports, thereby helping companies determine where to locate their production facilities when governments do or do not impose trade restrictions.

FACTOR-MOBILITY THEORY

Because the stability and dynamics of countries' competitive positions depend largely on the quantity and quality of their production factors (land, labor, capital, technology), we'll conclude this chapter with a discussion of factor mobility.

TABLE 5.1 What Major Trade Theories Do and Don't Discuss: A Checklist

A check mark indicates that a theory of trade concerns itself with the question asked at the head of the column; if there's a dash, it doesn't. In columns 4–7, you can see how each theory responds to the specific question; again, a dash indicates that the theory does not address the question.

	Description of Natural Trade			Prescription of Trade Relationships			
Theory	How Much Is Traded	What Products Are Traded?	With Whom Does Trade Take Place?	Should Government Control Trade?	How Much Should Be Traded?	What Products Should Be Traded?	With Whom Should Trade Take Place?
Mercantilism	—	—	—	yes	✓	✓	✓
Neomercantilism	—	—	—	yes	✓	—	—
Absolute advantage	—	✓	—	no	—	✓	—
Comparative advantage	—	✓	—	no	—	✓	—
Country size	✓	✓	—	—	—	—	—
Factor proportions	—	✓	✓	—	—	—	—
Country similarity	—	✓	✓	—	—	—	—
Product life cycle (PLC)	—	✓	✓	—	—	—	—
Diamond of national competitive advantage	—	✓	—	—	—	—	—

INTERVENTIONIST THEORIES

Let's begin with mercantilism because it is the oldest trade theory, out of which neomercantilism has more recently emerged. These theories are based on some of the reasons for governmental intervention, but there are other reasons as well that we discuss in the next chapter.

MERCANTILISM

According to mercantilism, countries should export more than they import.

Mercantilism holds that a country's wealth is measured by its holdings of "treasure," which usually means its gold. According to this theory, which formed the foundation of economic thought from about 1500 to 1800,[2] countries should export more than they import and, if successful, receive gold from countries that run deficits. Nation-states were emerging during this period, and gold empowered central governments to raise armies and invest in national institutions so as to solidify the people's primary allegiance to the new nations.

Governmental Policies To export more than they imported, governments restricted imports and subsidized production that otherwise could not compete in domestic or export markets. Some countries used their colonies to support this trade objective by having the colonies supply commodities that the colonial powers would otherwise have to purchase from nonassociated countries and by running trade surpluses as an additional way to obtain gold. They did this not only by monopolizing colonial trade but also by forcing their colonies to export less highly valued raw materials to them and import more highly valued manufactured products from them.

As the influence of the mercantilist philosophy weakened after 1800, the governments of colonial powers seldom directly intended to limit the development of industrial capabilities within their colonies. However, their home-based companies had technological leadership, ownership of raw material production abroad, and usually some degree of protection from foreign competition—a combination that continued to make colonies dependent on raw material production and tie their trade to their industrialized mother countries. We still see vestiges of these relationships, which we discuss in the next chapter.

The Concept of Balance of Trade Some terminology of the mercantilist era has endured. For example, a **favorable balance of trade** (also called a **trade surplus**) still indicates that a country is exporting more than it imports. An **unfavorable balance of trade** (also known as a **trade deficit**) indicates the opposite. Many of these terms are misnomers. For example, the word *favorable* implies "benefit," and the word *unfavorable* suggests "disadvantage." In fact, it is not necessarily beneficial to run a trade surplus or detrimental to run a trade deficit. A country with a favorable balance of trade is, for the time being, supplying people in foreign countries with more than it receives from them.[3]

Running a favorable balance of trade is not necessarily beneficial.

In the mercantilist period, the difference was made up by a transfer of gold; today it is made up by granting credit to the deficit country by holding its currency or investments denominated in that currency. If that credit cannot eventually buy sufficient goods and services, the so-called favorable trade balance actually may turn out to be disadvantageous for the country with the surplus.

NEOMERCANTILISM

The term **neomercantilism** describes the approach of countries that try to run favorable balances of trade in an attempt to achieve some social or political objective. A country may aim for increased employment by setting economic policies that encourage its companies to produce in excess of the demand at home and send the surplus abroad. Or it may attempt to maintain political influence in an area by sending more merchandise there than it receives from it, such as a government granting aid or loans to a foreign government to use to purchase the granting country's excess production.

A country that practices neomercantilism attempts to run an export surplus to achieve a social or political objective.

FREE-TRADE THEORIES

CONCEPT CHECK

In Chapter 1, we observe that nations are currently in the mood to reduce barriers to the movement of trade, capital, technology, and people; we also explain that this policy reflects a couple of key facts—namely, that consumers want a greater variety of goods and services at lower prices and that competition spurs efficiency.

Why do countries need to trade at all? Why can't Costa Rica (or any other country) be content with the goods and services it produces? In fact, many countries following mercantilist policy tried to become as self-sufficient as possible. In this section, we discuss two theories supporting free trade: *absolute advantage* and *comparative advantage.*

Both theories hold that nations should neither artificially limit imports nor promote exports.[4] The market will determine which producers survive as consumers buy those products that best serve their needs. Both free trade theories imply *specialization.* Just as individuals and families produce some things that they exchange for things that others produce, national specialization means producing some things for domestic consumption and export while using the export earnings to buy imports of products and services produced abroad.

THEORY OF ABSOLUTE ADVANTAGE

In 1776, Adam Smith questioned the mercantilists' assumptions by stating that the real wealth of a country consists of the goods and services available to its citizens rather than its holdings of gold. This theory of **absolute advantage** holds that different countries produce some goods more efficiently than others, and questions why the citizens of any country should have to buy domestically produced goods when they can buy them more cheaply from abroad. Smith reasoned that unrestricted trade would lead a country to specialize in those products that gave it a competitive advantage. Its resources would shift to the efficient industries because it could not compete in the inefficient ones. Through specialization, it could increase its efficiency for three reasons:

According to Adam Smith, a country's wealth is based on its available goods and services rather than on gold.

1. Labor could become more skilled by repeating the same tasks.
2. Labor would not lose time in switching production from one kind of product to another.
3. Long production runs would provide incentives for developing more effective working methods.

The country could then use its excess specialized production to buy more imports than it otherwise could have produced. But in what products should a country specialize? Although Smith believed the marketplace would make the determination, he thought that a country's advantage would be either *natural* or *acquired.*

Natural advantage considers climate, natural resources, and labor force availability.

Natural Advantage A country's **natural advantage** in creating a product or service comes from climatic conditions, access to certain natural resources, or availability of certain labor forces. As we saw in our opening case, Costa Rica's climate and soil support the production of bananas, pineapples, and coffee, while its biodiversity supports a thriving ecotourism industry. Costa Rica imports wheat. If it were to increase its wheat production, for which its climate and terrain are less suited, it would have to use land now devoted to the cultivation of bananas, pineapples, and coffee, or convert some of its biodiverse national park areas to agricultural production, thus reducing those earnings.

Conversely, the United States could produce coffee (perhaps in climate-controlled buildings), but at the cost of diverting resources away from products such as wheat, for which its climate and terrain are naturally suited. Trading coffee for wheat and vice versa is a goal more easily achieved than if these two countries were to try to become self-sufficient in the production of both. The more the two countries' natural advantages differ, the more likely they will favor trade with one another.

Variations among countries in natural advantages also help explain where certain manufactured or processed items might best be produced, particularly if a company can reduce transportation costs by processing an agricultural commodity or natural resource prior to exporting. Processing coffee beans into instant coffee reduces bulk and is likely to reduce transport costs on coffee exports; producing canned latte could add weight, lessening the industry's internationally competitive edge.

Acquired advantage consists of either product or process technology.

Acquired Advantage Most of today's world trade is of manufactured goods rather than agricultural goods and natural resources. Countries that are competitive in manufactured goods have an **acquired advantage**, usually in either product or process technology. An advantage of *product technology* is that it enables a country to produce a unique product or one that is easily distinguished from those of competitors. For example, Denmark exports silver tableware, not because there are rich Danish silver mines but because Danish companies have developed distinctive products.

An advantage in *process technology* is a country's ability to efficiently produce a homogeneous product (one not easily distinguished from that of competitors). Japan has exported steel despite having to import iron and coal to produce it because its steel mills have encompassed new labor- and material-saving processes. Thus, countries that develop distinctive or less expensive products have acquired advantages, at least until producers in another country emulate them successfully.

Acquired advantage through technology has created new products, displaced old ones, and altered trading-partner relationships. The most obvious examples of change are production and export of new products and services, such as software. Products that existed in earlier periods have increased their share of world trade because of technological changes in the production process. For example, early hand-tooled automobiles reached only elite markets, but a succession of manufacturing innovations, from assembly lines to robotics, has enabled automobiles to reach an ever-widening mass market.

In other cases, companies have developed new uses for old products, such as aloe in sunscreen. Other products, such as artificial fibers, have partially displaced traditional ones. Finally, technology may be used to overcome natural advantages. Iceland now exports tomatoes grown near the Arctic Circle, while Brazil exports quality wine produced near the equator—both of which were impossible until the development of fairly recent technology.[5]

Free trade will bring
- Specialization.
- Greater efficiency.
- Higher global output.

How Does Resource Efficiency Work? We can demonstrate absolute trade advantage here by examining two countries and two commodities. Because we are not yet

FIGURE 5.2 Production Possibilities under Conditions of Absolute Advantage

In short, specialization increases potential output.

ASSUMPTIONS for Costa Rica

1. 100 units of resources available
2. 10 units to produce a ton of wheat
3. 4 units to produce a ton of coffee
4. Uses half of total resources per product when there is no foreign trade

ASSUMPTIONS for United States

1. 100 units of resources available
2. 5 units to produce a ton of wheat
3. 20 units to produce a ton of coffee
4. Uses half of total resources per product when there is no foreign trade

PRODUCTION	Coffee (tons)	Wheat (tons)
Without Trade:		
Costa Rica (point *A*)	$12\frac{1}{2}$	5
United States (point *B*)	$2\frac{1}{2}$	10
Total	15	15
With Trade:		
Costa Rica (point *C*)	25	0
United States (point *D*)	0	20
Total	25	20

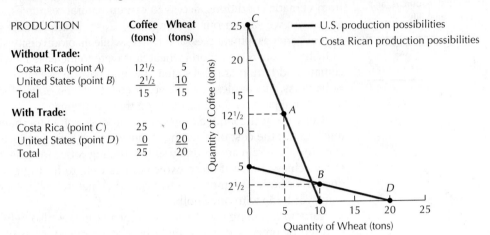

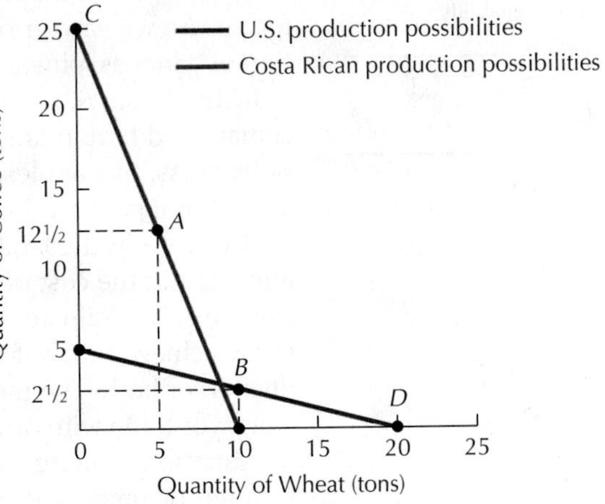

considering the concepts of money and exchange rates, we define the cost of production in terms of the resources needed to produce either commodity. This example is realistic because real income depends on the output of goods compared to the resources used to produce them.

Say that Costa Rica and the United States are the only two countries and each has the same amount of resources (land, labor, and capital) to produce either coffee or wheat. Using Figure 5.2, let's say that 100 units of resources are available in each country. In Costa Rica, assume that it takes four units to produce a ton of coffee and 10 units per ton of wheat. The purple Costa Rican production possibility line shows that Costa Rica can produce 25 tons of coffee and no wheat, 10 tons of wheat and no coffee, or some combination of the two.

In the United States, it takes 20 units per ton of coffee and five units per ton of wheat. The green U.S. production possibility line indicates that the country can produce five tons of coffee and no wheat, 20 tons of wheat and no coffee, or some combination of the two. Costa Rica is more efficient (that is, takes fewer resources to produce coffee), while the United States is more efficient in wheat production.

How can production be increased through specialization and trade? Let's say the two countries have no foreign trade. We could start from any place on each production possibility line; for convenience, let's assume that if each country devotes half of its 100 resources to production of each product, Costa Rica can produce 12.5 tons of coffee (divide 50 by 4) and five tons of wheat (divide 50 by 10), shown as point A in Figure 5.2, while the United States can produce 2.5 tons of coffee (divide 50 by 20) and 10 tons of wheat (divide 50 by 5), shown as point B in Figure 5.2.

Because each country has only 100 units of resources, neither can increase wheat production without decreasing coffee production, or vice versa. Without trade, the combined production is 15 tons of coffee (12.5 + 2.5) and 15 tons of wheat (5 + 10). If each country specialized in the commodity for which it had an absolute advantage, Costa Rica could then produce 25 tons of coffee and the United States 20 tons of wheat (points C and D in the figure).

You can see that specialization increases the production of both products. By trading, global efficiency is optimized, and the two countries can have more coffee and more wheat than they would without trade.

THEORY OF COMPARATIVE ADVANTAGE

Gains from trade will occur even in a country that has absolute advantage in all products, because the country must give up less efficient output to produce more efficient output.

We have just described absolute advantage, which is often confused with *comparative advantage.* In 1817, David Ricardo examined the question,"What happens when one country can produce all products at an absolute advantage?" His resulting theory of **comparative advantage** says that global efficiency gains may still result from trade if a country specializes in what it can produce most efficiently—regardless of other countries' absolute advantage.

Comparative Advantage by Analogy Although this theory may seem initially incongruous, an analogy should clarify its logic. Imagine that the best physician in town also happens to be the best medical administrator. It would not make economic sense for the physician to handle all the administrative duties of the office, because of earning more money by concentrating on medical duties, even though that means having to employ a less-skilled office administrator. In the same manner, a country gains if it concentrates its resources on the commodities it can produce most efficiently. It then trades some of those for commodities produced abroad. The following discussion clarifies this theory.

Production Possibility Assume the United States is more efficient in producing coffee and wheat than Costa Rica is, thus having an absolute advantage in the production of both.[6] Take a look at Figure 5.3. As in our earlier example, it assumes that there are only two countries, each with a total of 100 units of resources available, and half of each used in each product. It takes Costa Rica 10 units of resources to produce either a ton of coffee or a ton of wheat, whereas it takes the United States only five units to produce a ton of coffee and four for a ton of wheat. Costa Rica can produce five tons of coffee and five tons of wheat (point A on the purple line), and the United States can produce 10 tons of coffee and 12.5 tons of wheat (point B on the green line). Without trade, neither country can increase its coffee production without sacrificing some wheat production, or vice versa.

Although the United States has an absolute advantage in producing both commodities, its comparative advantage is only in wheat. This is because its wheat production is 2.5 times that of Costa Rica, whereas its coffee production is only twice as much. Although Costa Rica has an absolute disadvantage in the production of both products, it has a comparative

FIGURE 5.3 Production Possibilities under Conditions of Comparative Advantage

There are advantages to trade even if one country enjoys an absolute advantage in the production of all products.

ASSUMPTIONS
for Costa Rica

1. 100 units of resources available
2. 10 units to produce a ton of wheat
3. 10 units to produce a ton of coffee
4. Uses half of total resources per product when there is no foreign trade

ASSUMPTIONS
for United States

1. 100 units of resources available
2. 4 units to produce a ton of wheat
3. 5 units to produce a ton of coffee
4. Uses half of total resources per product when there is no foreign trade

PRODUCTION	Coffee (tons)	Wheat (tons)
Without Trade:		
Costa Rica (point *A*)	5	5
United States (point *B*)	10	12½
Total	15	17½
With Trade (increasing coffee production):		
Costa Rica (point *C*)	10	0
United States (point *D*)	6	17½
Total	16	17½
With Trade (increasing wheat production):		
Costa Rica (point *C*)	10	0
United States (point *E*)	5	18¾
Total	15	18¾

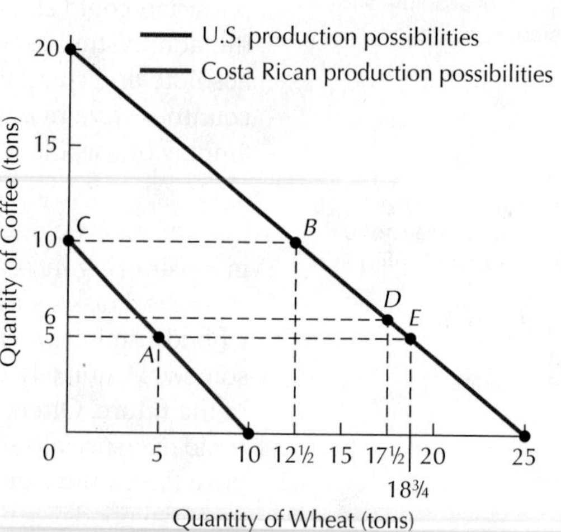

advantage (or less of a comparative disadvantage) in coffee. Why? Because its production is half as efficient in coffee and only 40 percent as efficient in wheat.

Without trade, the combined production is 15 tons of coffee (5 in Costa Rica plus 10 in the United States) and 17.5 tons of wheat (5 plus 12.5). Through trading, the combined production of the commodities within the two countries can be increased. For example, if the combined wheat production is unchanged from when there was no trade, the United States could produce all 17.5 tons by using 70 units of resources (17.5 tons times 4 units per ton). The remaining 30 units could be used for producing six tons of coffee (30 units divided by 5 units per ton), shown by point D in Figure 5.3. Costa Rica would use all its resources to produce 10 tons of coffee (point C). The combined wheat production has stayed at 17.5 tons, but the coffee production has increased from 15 to 16 tons.

If the combined coffee production is unchanged from the time before trade, Costa Rica could use all its resources to produce coffee, yielding 10 tons (point C in Figure 5.3). The United States could produce the remaining five tons of coffee by using 25 units, with its remaining 75 units being used to produce 18.75 tons of wheat (75 divided by 4). This production possibility is point E. Without sacrificing any of the coffee available before trade, wheat production has increased from 17.5 to 18.75 tons.

If the United States were to produce somewhere between points D and E, both coffee and wheat production would increase over what was possible before trade took place. Whether the production target is a rise in coffee or wheat or a combination of the two, both countries can gain by having Costa Rica trade some of its coffee production to the United States for some U.S. wheat output.

Don't Confuse Comparative and Absolute Advantage Most economists accept the comparative advantage theory and its influence in promoting policies for freer trade. Nevertheless, many government policymakers, journalists, managers, and workers confuse comparative advantage with absolute advantage and do not understand how a country can simultaneously have a comparative *advantage* and absolute *disadvantage* in the production of a given product.

THEORIES OF SPECIALIZATION: SOME ASSUMPTIONS AND LIMITATIONS

Both absolute and comparative advantage theories are based on increasing output and trade through specialization. However, these theories make assumptions, some of which are not always valid.

Full employment is not a valid assumption of absolute and comparative advantage.

Full Employment The physician/administrator analogy we used earlier assumed that the physician could stay busy full time practicing medicine. If not, the physician might perform the administrative work without sacrificing earnings from medical duties. The theories of absolute and comparative advantage both assume that resources are fully employed. When countries have many unemployed or unused resources, they may seek to restrict imports to employ or use idle resources.

Countries' goals may not be limited to economic efficiency.

Economic Efficiency Our analogy also assumes that the physician is interested primarily in maximizing income. Yet there are a number of reasons for choosing not to work full time at medical tasks, such as finding administrative work relaxing and self-fulfilling, fearing that a hired administrator would be unreliable, or wishing to maintain administrative skills in the somewhat unlikely event that administrators will command higher wages than physicians in the future. Often, countries also pursue objectives other than output efficiency. They may avoid overspecialization because of the vulnerability created by changes in technology and by price fluctuations or because they do not trust foreign countries to always supply them with essential goods.

CONCEPT CHECK

Recall from Chapter 2 our discussion of "Work Motivation," in which we explain that in cultures ranking high on so-called masculinity, people tend to value economic achievement over certain other values; we also observe, however, that in other cultures "work to live" is valued over economic performance.

Division of Gains Although specialization brings potential economic benefits to all trading countries, the earlier discussion did not indicate how countries will divide increased output. In the case of our wheat and coffee example, if both the United States and Costa Rica receive some share of the higher output, both will be better off economically through specialization and trade. However, many people are concerned with relative as well as absolute economic gains. If they perceive that a trading partner is gaining too large a share of benefits, they may prefer to forgo absolute gains for themselves so as to prevent others from gaining a relative economic advantage.[7]

Transport Costs If it costs more to transport the goods than is saved through specialization, the advantages of trade are negated. In other words, in our two-country scenario, some workers would need to forgo producing coffee or wheat in order to work in transporting the coffee and wheat abroad. However, as long as the diversion reduces output by less than what the two countries gain from specialization, there are still gains from trade.

Statics and Dynamics The theories of absolute and comparative advantage address countries statically—by looking at them at one point in time. However, the relative conditions that give countries production advantages and disadvantages change. For example, the resources needed to produce coffee or wheat in either Costa Rica or the United States could change because of advancements in and acceptance of genetically modified crops. In fact, most trade today is due to acquired advantage; thus, technical dynamics cause countries to gain or lose both absolutely and relatively.[8]

As we show in our opening case, when Costa Rica focused on goods that could compete in international markets, it developed and enhanced a competitive advantage in some promising high-tech industries. Thus, we should not assume that future absolute or comparative advantages will remain as they are today. We return to this theme later in the chapter as we examine theories to explain the dynamics of competitive production locations.

Services The theories of absolute and comparative advantage deal with products rather than services. However, with a growing portion of world trade made up of services, the theories apply because resources must also go into service production. For instance, the United States sells an excess of such services as education to foreign countries (many foreign students attend U.S. universities). At the same time, it buys an excess of foreign shipping services. To become more self-sufficient in international shipping, the United States might have to divert resources from its more efficient use in higher education or in the production of competitive products.

CONCEPT CHECK

As we point out in discussing the ramifications of globalization in Chapter 1, although any given product may carry a "made in" label (as in "Made in Taiwan"), such labels may actually obscure rather than clarify the origins of products, which nowadays often include components or ingredients from a surprising variety of countries.

Production Networks Both theories deal with trading one product for another. Increasingly, however, portions of a product may be made in different countries. A company might conduct R&D in Country A, secure components in Countries B and C, assemble final products in Country D, manage finances in Country E, and carry out call-center services in Country F. Although this type of development adds complexity to the analysis, it fits well with the concept of advantages through specialization. In other words, costs are saved by having activities take place in those countries where there is an absolute or comparative advantage for their production.

Mobility These theories assume that resources can move domestically from the production of one good to another—and at no cost. But this assumption is not completely valid. For example, steelworkers might not move easily into software development jobs because of different skill needs. Even if they do, they may be less productive than before.[9] The theories also assume that resources cannot move internationally. Increasingly, however, they do, and the movement affects countries' production capabilities. For instance, over 300 thousand Nicaraguans have moved to Costa Rica, mainly because of better job opportunities there.[10] Further, foreign companies have moved both personnel and capital to support their investments there, which has contributed to changing Costa Rican capabilities. Such movement is clearly an alternative to trade, a topic discussed later in the chapter. However, it is safe to say that resources are more mobile domestically than they are internationally.

TRADE PATTERN THEORIES

The free trade theories demonstrate how economic growth occurs through specialization and trade; however, they do not deal with trade patterns such as how much a country trades, what products it trades, or who will be its trading partners when following a free trade policy. In this section, we discuss the theories that help explain these patterns.

HOW MUCH DOES A COUNTRY TRADE?

Free-trade theories of specialization neither propose nor imply that only one country should or will produce a given product or service. **Nontradable goods**—products and services (haircuts, retail grocery distribution, etc.) that are seldom practical to export because of high transportation costs—are produced in every country. However, among tradable goods, some countries depend on imports and exports more than others. We will now examine theories that help explain country differences.

Bigger countries differ in several ways from smaller countries. They

- Tend to export a smaller portion of output and import a smaller part of consumption.
- Have higher transport costs for foreign trade.

Theory of Country Size Land area is an obvious way to measure a country's size and largely explains countries' relative dependence on trade. The **theory of country size** holds that large countries usually depend less on trade than small ones. Countries with large land areas are apt to have varied climates and an assortment of natural resources, making them more self-sufficient than smaller ones. Most large countries (such as Brazil, China, India, the United States, and Russia) import much less of their consumption needs and export much less of their production output than do small nations (such as Uruguay, Belgium, and Taiwan).

Furthermore, distance to foreign markets affects large and small countries differently. Normally, the farther the distance, the higher the transport costs, the longer the inventory carrying time, and the greater the uncertainty and unreliability of timely product delivery. The following example illustrates why distance is more pronounced for a large country than for a small one.

Assume that the normal maximum distance for transporting a given product is 100 miles because prices rise too much at greater distances. Although almost any location in tiny Belgium is within 100 miles of a foreign country, the same isn't true for its two largest neighbors, France and Germany. Thus, Belgium's dependence on trade as a percentage of its production and consumption is greater than the comparable figures in either France or Germany, a fact that can be partially explained by the distance factor due to country size.

Size of the Economy While land area helps explain the *relative* dependence on trade, countries' economic size helps explain differences in the *absolute* amount of trade. Nine of the world's top 10 exporters in 2012 were developed countries, and the only exception was China, which is the world's second largest economy. Similarly, developed countries account for well over half of the world's exports. Simply put, they produce so much that they have more to sell, both domestically and internationally. In addition, because they produce so much, incomes are high and people buy more from both domestic and foreign sources. At the same time, most of developing countries' trade is with developed countries, but there has been a recent upsurge of trade among developing countries mainly because of economic growth in China and India that has increased their demand for raw materials found mainly in developing countries.[11]

The United States offers a good example of the difference between relative and absolute dependence on trade because it is the third largest country in area and the largest economically. Although its dependence on either imports or exports is comparatively low, it is the world's largest trader (imports + exports). Map 5.2 illustrates the large U.S. economic size by showing how each of its states compares economically with countries.

MAP 5.2 U.S. States' Economies Compared to National Economies

The U.S. size, both geographically and economically, results in its being one of the world's largest traders while also depending relatively less than most countries on imports and exports.

Source: GDP figures for U.S. states based on "Gross Domestic Product by State," http://lwd.dol.state.nj.us/labor/lpa/industry/gsp/gsp_index.html (accessed June 26, 2013). Country GDP figures came from Wikipedia, "List of Countries by GDP (Nominal)" http://en.wikipedia.org/wiki/List_of_countries_by_GDP_%28nominal%29 (accessed June 26, 2013).

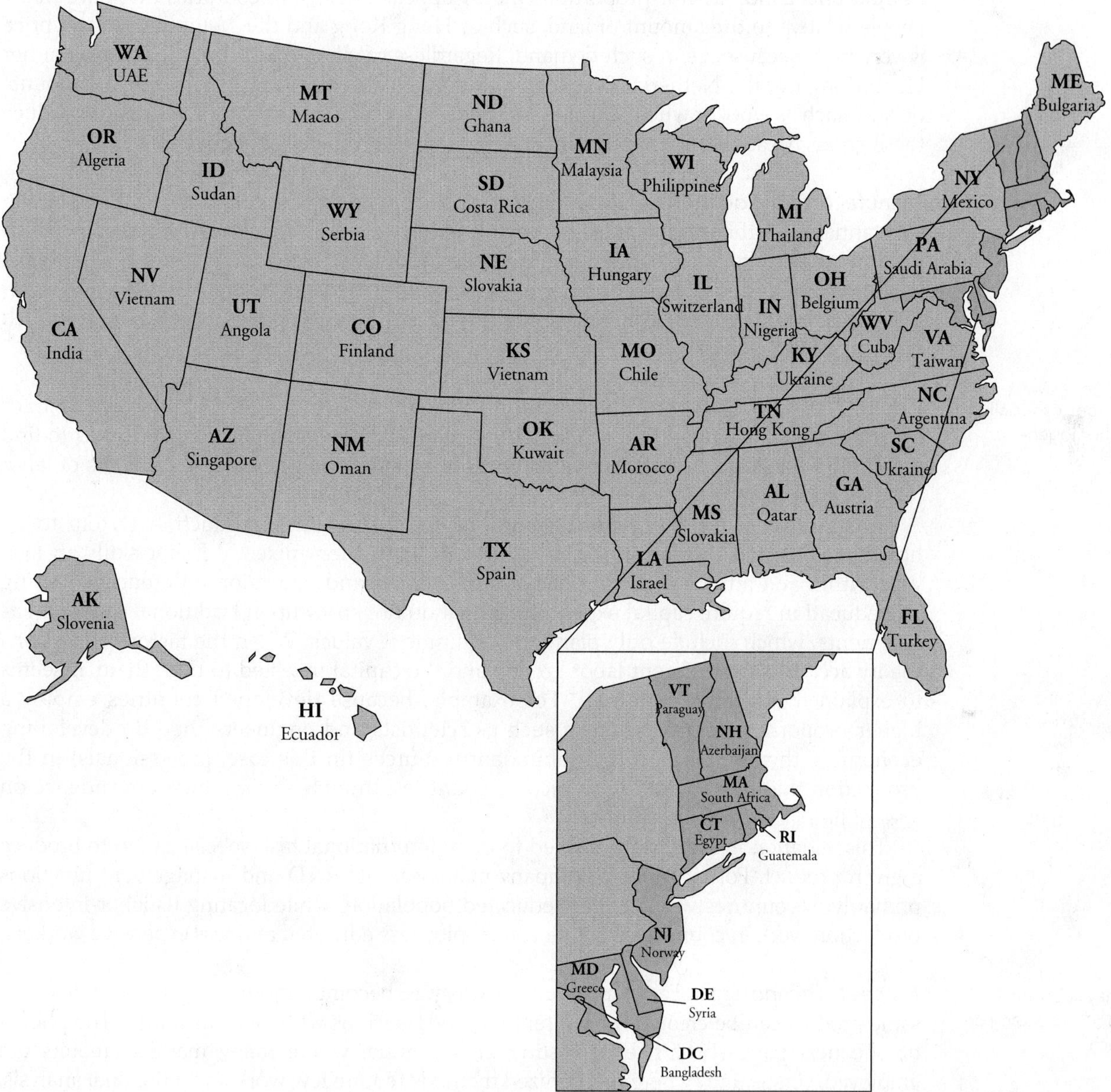

WHAT TYPES OF PRODUCTS DOES A COUNTRY TRADE?

In our discussion of absolute advantage, we indicated that this advantage might be either natural or acquired. Here, we discuss theories that help explain what types of products result from these natural and acquired advantages. We won't delve again into those factors we've already discussed (climate and natural resources) that give a country a natural advantage; however, we will examine the factor endowment theory of trade. For acquired advantage, we discuss the importance of production and product technology.

According to the factor-proportions theory, factors in relative abundance are cheaper than factors in relative scarcity.

Factor-Proportions Theory Eli Heckscher and Bertil Ohlin developed the **factor-proportions theory**, maintaining that differences in countries' endowments of labor compared to land or capital endowments explain differences in the cost of production factors. For instance, if labor were abundant in comparison to land and capital, labor costs would be low relative to land and capital costs; if scarce, the costs would be high. These relative factor costs would lead countries to excel in the production and export of products that used their abundant—and therefore cheaper—production factors.[12]

People and Land Factor-proportions theory appears logical. In countries that have many people relative to the amount of land, such as Hong Kong and the Netherlands, land price is very high because it's in such demand. Regardless of climate and soil conditions, neither Hong Kong nor the Netherlands excels in the production of goods requiring large amounts of land, such as wool or wheat. Businesses in countries such as Australia and Canada produce these goods because land is abundant compared to the number of people.

Manufacturing Locations Casual observation of manufacturing locations also seems to substantiate the theory. The most successful industries in Hong Kong are those in which technology permits the use of a minimum amount of land relative to the number of people employed. Its clothing production occurs in multistory factories where workers share minimal space, but it does not compete in the production of automobiles, which requires much more space per worker.

Production factors, especially labor, are not homogeneous.

Capital, Labor Rates, and Specialization In countries where little capital is available for investment and the amount of investment per worker is low, managers might expect to find cheap labor rates and export competitiveness in products that need large amounts of labor relative to capital.

However, because the factor-proportions theory assumes production factors to be homogeneous, tests to substantiate the theory have been mixed.[13] Labor skills, in fact, vary within and among countries because of training and education differences. Training and education require capital expenditures that do not show up in traditional capital measurements, which include only plant and equipment values. When the factor-proportions theory accounts for different labor groups and the capital invested to train them, it seems to explain many trade patterns.[14] For example, because developed countries employ a higher proportion of professionals such as scientists and engineers than do developing economies, they depend on their abundant resources (in this case, professionals) in the production that they export. Low-income countries, though, show a high dependence on less-skilled labor in their exports.[15]

This variation in labor skills has led to more international task specialization to produce a given product. For example, a company may locate its R&D and management functions primarily in countries with a highly educated population, while locating its labor-intensive production work in countries where it can employ less educated and less expensive workers.

Companies may substitute capital for labor, depending on the cost of each.

Process Technology Factor-proportions analysis becomes more complicated when the same product can be created by different methods, such as with labor or capital. The photos on the next page show rice harvesting in Indonesia, where many manual laborers are employed, versus Italy, where mechanized methods require few workers. In the final analysis, the optimum location of production depends on comparing the cost in each locale based on the type of production that minimizes costs there.

Bigger countries depend more on products requiring larger production runs.

Not all products lend themselves to such trade-offs in production methods. Some require huge amounts of fixed capital and long production runs to spread the fixed capital costs over more output units, usually resulting in development in large countries with large markets.[16] However, companies may locate long production runs in small countries if they expect to be able to export from them.[17] In industries where long production runs reduce unit costs substantially, companies tend to locate production in only a few countries, using these locations to export. Where long production runs are less important, we find a greater prevalence of multiple production units scattered around the world in different countries so as to minimize transportation costs through exporting.

In addition, high R&D expenditures create high up-front fixed costs. Therefore, a technologically intensive company from a small nation may need to sell more abroad than a

Source: Roberto Caucino/Shutterstock

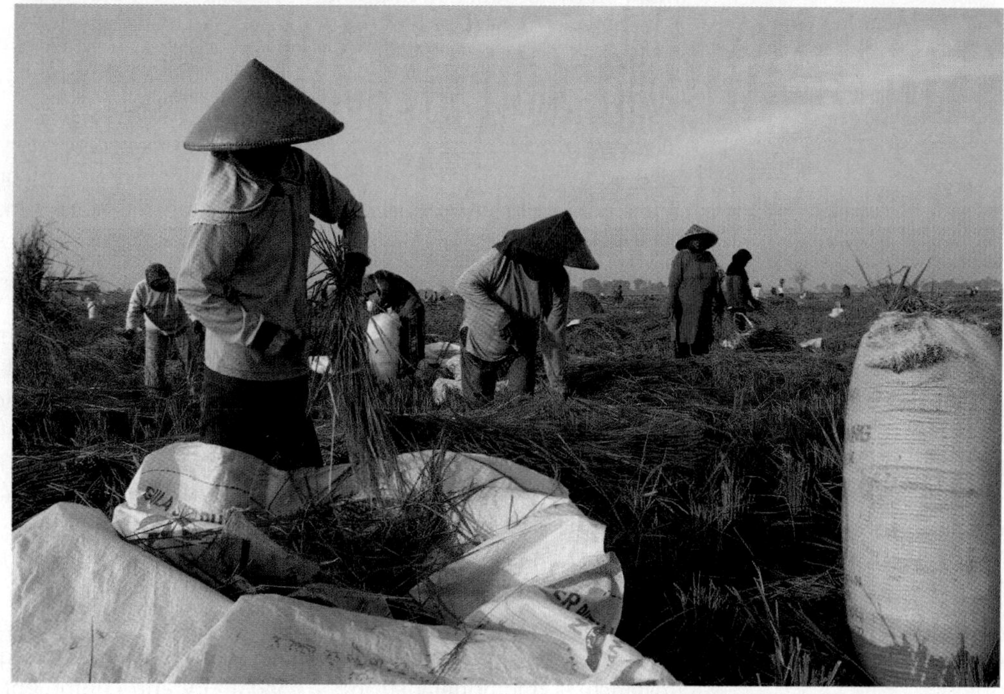
The rice harvesting is capital intensive in Italy, (top) where labor rates are high. It is labor intensive in Indonesia (bottom), where labor rates are low.
Source: mosista/Shutterstock

company in a large domestic market. It may, in turn, pull resources from other industries and companies within its domestic market, which means the country will have more national specialization than one finds in a larger country.[18]

Most new products originate in developed countries.

Product Technology Figure 5.4 shows the changing composition of world trade. Manufacturing is by far the largest sector, with commercial services the fastest-growing sector. Manufacturing competitiveness depends largely on technology to develop new products and processes. The technology depends, in turn, on a large number of highly educated people

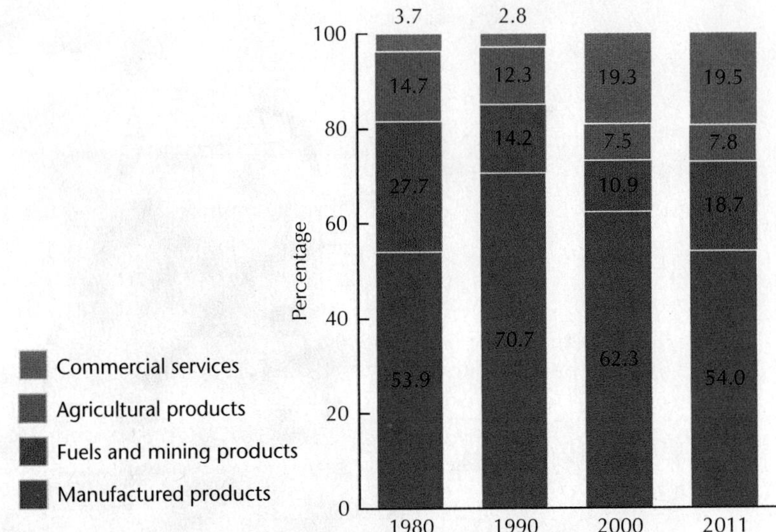

FIGURE 5.4 Worldwide Trade by Major Sectors

As a percentage of total world trade, manufactured products are more important than products in any other category. Services, however, constitute the fastest-growing category.

Source: Based on World Trade Organization, *Annual Report* (Geneva, various years).

(especially scientists and engineers) and a large amount of capital to invest in R&D. Because developed countries have an abundance of these features, they originate most new products and account for most manufacturing output and trade. Developing countries depend much more on the production of primary products; thus, they depend more on natural advantage.

WITH WHOM DO COUNTRIES TRADE?

We have already noted that developed countries account for the bulk of world trade. They also trade primarily with each other, whereas developing countries mainly export primary and labor-intensive products to developed countries in exchange for new and technologically advanced products. Below, we discuss the roles that country similarity and distance play in determining trading partners.

Developed countries trade primarily with each other because they

- Produce and consume more.
- Emphasize technical breakthroughs in different industrial sectors.
- Produce differentiated products and services.

Country-Similarity Theory The theories explaining why trade takes place have focused so far on the differences among countries in terms of natural conditions and factor endowment proportions. That most trade takes place among developed countries can be further explained by the **country-similarity theory**, which says that companies create new products in response to market conditions in their home market. They then turn to markets and consumer economic levels they see as most similar to what they are accustomed.[19]

Specialization and Acquired Advantage However, in order to export, a company must provide consumers abroad with an advantage over what they could buy from their domestic producers. Trade occurs because countries' producers spend more on R&D in some sectors than in others, thus leading to countries' specialization and acquired advantage. Germany, for instance, is traditionally strong in machinery and equipment, Switzerland in pharmaceutical products, and Denmark in food products.[20] Even developing countries gain advantages through specialization in very narrow product segments. Bangladesh has succeeded in exporting shirts, trousers, and hats, but not bed linens or footballs, which Pakistan has successfully exported.[21]

Product Differentiation Trade also occurs because *companies* differentiate products, thus creating two-way trade in seemingly similar products. The United States is both a major exporter and a major importer of tourist services, vehicles, and passenger aircraft because different firms from different countries have developed product variations with different appeals. For instance, both Boeing from the United States and Airbus from Europe produce large jet passenger aircraft that will fly from point A to point B, but U.S. and European airlines buy both companies' aircraft because their models differ in such features as capacity, flying range, fuel consumption, and perceived reliability.[22] As a result, Boeing and Airbus sell within their own and each other's home markets as well as within countries that produce no aircraft.

Trading partners are affected by
- Cultural similarity.
- Political relations between countries.
- Distance.

The Effects of Cultural Similarity Importers and exporters perceive greater ease in doing business in countries that are culturally similar to home, such as those that speak a common language. Likewise, historic colonial relationships explain much of the trade between specific developed and developing economies. For instance, France's colonial history in Africa has given Air France an edge in serving the continent's international air passenger markets.[23] Importers and exporters find it easier to continue business ties than to develop new distribution arrangements in countries where they are less experienced.

CONCEPT CHECK

In discussing "Cultural Distance" in Chapter 2, we show that "distance" is an index of similarities between countries based primarily on such shared cultural attributes as language, ethnicity, or values. We indicate that, by and large, a company from one country should expect fewer adjustments when moving to a country whose culture is close to that of its home base, but we also caution that even in these cases, executives should be aware of subtle cultural differences.

The Effects of Political Relationships and Economic Agreements Political relationships and economic agreements among countries may discourage or encourage trade between them. Witness the political animosity between the United States and Cuba that has diminished their mutual trade for about five decades. An example of trade encouragement is the agreement among many European countries to remove all trade barriers with each other, thereby causing a greater share of the countries' total trade to be conducted with each other.

The Effects of Distance Although no single factor fully explains specific pairs of trading partners, the geographic distance between two countries is important. In essence, greater distances usually mean higher transportation costs; that's why Intel's cost to ship semiconductors from Costa Rica to the United States is lower than if it had to bring them from, say, Argentina. However, distance is more important for homogeneous products than for differentiated products inasmuch as the former compete more on the basis of price.[24] In addition, analysis of cost differences must take into account the available transportation modes. Wine exports from Australia can reach the United Kingdom (UK) by container ship for about the same cost as wine exports shipped overland to the UK from southern France.[25]

Overcoming Distance Transport cost is not the only factor in trade partner choice. New Zealand competes with Chile, Argentina, and South Africa for out-of-season sales of apples to the Northern Hemisphere—but with a disadvantage in freight costs to the United States and Europe. It has countered this disadvantage by boosting yields, developing new premium varieties, bypassing intermediaries to sell directly to supermarkets abroad, and consolidating efforts through a national marketing board. However, such methods to overcome distance drawbacks are difficult to maintain. For example, rival orchardists have smuggled new strains of apple tree cuttings out of New Zealand.[26]

Does Geography Matter?

Variety Is the Spice of Life

As you study this chapter, you'll see that geography plays a role in many of the theories and questions on trade. We pull them together in this discussion.

Part of a country's trading advantage is explained by its natural advantage—climate, terrain, arable land, and natural resources. Thus, Saudi Arabia trades oil, a natural resource, for U.S. rice, which needs huge wet areas for production. Remember that technology (acquired advantage) may often negate natural advantage, as in the development of substitutes (synthetic nitrate for natural nitrate) and the development of different production methods (Chile not using traditional bogs for growing cranberries). Nevertheless, a country's geography—particularly the ease of moving goods to markets in other countries—may give it an advantage or disadvantage. For instance, landlocked countries have a considerable transport cost disadvantage relative to countries with seacoasts.[27]

Factor-proportions theory helps explain where certain goods may be more efficiently produced, such as labor-intensive goods where labor is plentiful in relation to capital and land. Bangladesh excels in producing clothing that requires lots of labor in relation to either capital or land. However, these factors can change in both quantity and quality. Singapore, with its very high population density, once excelled in the production of labor-intensive goods. But because it has accumulated capital and upgraded the education of its workforce, its competitive production and exports now encompass more capital intensity and skilled labor.

Usually, small countries need to trade more than large countries, primarily because they are apt to have fewer natural advantages. At the same time, small countries that also have low incomes tend to trade little because they produce and consume so little. Distance from foreign markets also plays a role. Geographically isolated countries such as Fiji trade less than would be expected from their size because transportation costs raise the price of traded goods substantially.[28]

Conversely, Canada is a large developed country whose dependence on trade and trade per capita are not only among the world's highest but also much higher than we would expect from the theory of country size. This may be explained largely by Canada's population dispersion. Ninety percent of its population is within 100 miles of the U.S. border, so shipping goods between, say, Vancouver and Seattle or Toronto and Cleveland is often more feasible than between Vancouver and Toronto.

Although we have discussed the effect of economic development on trade, this discussion raises the question of why some countries are developed and others are not—a very complex issue we cannot hope to answer. Nevertheless, some of the factors affecting income levels, and thus trade, are geographic. One study showed that 70 percent of countries' differences in per capita income can be accounted for by four factors: malaria, hydrocarbon endowments, coastal access, and transportation costs—all of which relate to geography.[29] ■

THE STATICS AND DYNAMICS OF TRADE

We've alluded to the fact that trading patterns change due to such factors as political and economic relations among countries and the development of new product capabilities. We now discuss two theories—the product life cycle theory and the diamond of national advantage—that help explain how countries develop, maintain, and lose their competitive advantages.

PRODUCT LIFE CYCLE (PLC) THEORY

According to the PLC theory of trade, the production location for many products moves from one country to another depending on the stage in the product's life cycle.

The international **product life cycle (PLC) theory** of trade states that the production location of certain manufactured products shifts as they go through their life cycle. The cycle consists of four stages: *introduction, growth, maturity,* and *decline.*[30] Table 5.2 highlights these stages.

Changes over the Cycle Companies develop new products primarily because they observe nearby needs for them; thus a U.S. company is most apt to create a new product for the U.S. market, a French company for the French market, and so on. At the same time, almost all new technology that results in new products and production methods originates in developed countries,[31] which have most of the resources to develop new products and most of the income to buy them.

The introduction stage is marked by

- Innovation in response to observed need.
- Exporting by the innovative country.
- Evolving product characteristics.

Introduction Once a company has created a new product, theoretically it can manufacture it anywhere in the world. In practice, however, the early-production stage, called the *introductory stage,* generally occurs in a domestic location so the company can obtain rapid market feedback and save on transport costs, since most sales are domestic. Any export sales are mainly to other developed countries because of more affluent customers there.

Production is apt to be more labor-intensive than in later stages because more labor-saving machinery may be introduced only when sales begin to expand rapidly and the product becomes highly standardized. Although production is in developed countries with high labor rates, their education and skills usually make this labor efficient in

TABLE 5.2 Life Cycle of the International Product

During the life cycle of a product, focus on its production and market locations often shifts from industrial to developing markets. The process is accompanied by changes in the competitive factors affecting both production and sales, as well as in the technology used to produce the product.

	Life Cycle Stage			
	1: Introduction	**2: Growth**	**3: Maturity**	**4: Decline**
Production location	• In innovating (usually industrial) country	• In innovating and other industrial countries	• Multiple countries	• Mainly in developing countries
Market location	• Mainly in innovating country, with some exports	• Mainly in industrial countries • Shift in export markets as foreign production replaces exports in some markets	• Growth in developing countries • Some decrease in industrial countries	• Mainly in developing countries • Some developing country exports
Competitive factors	• Near-monopoly position • Sales based on uniqueness rather than price • Evolving product characteristics	• Fast-growing demand • Number of competitors increases • Some competitors begin price cutting • Product becoming more standardized	• Overall stabilized demand • Number of competitors decreases • Price is very important, especially in developing countries	• Overall declining demand • Price is key weapon • Number of producers continues to decline
Production technology	• Short production runs • Evolving methods to coincide with product evolution • High labor input and labor skills relative to capital input	• Capital input increases • Methods more standardized	• Long production runs using high capital inputs • Highly standardized • Less labor skill needed	• Unskilled labor on mechanized long production runs

nonstandardized production. Even if production costs are high because of expensive labor, companies can often pass costs on to consumers who are unwilling to wait for possible price reductions later.

Growth is characterized by
- Increases in exports by the innovating country.
- More competition.
- Increased capital intensity.
- Some foreign production.

Growth Sales growth attracts competitors to the market, particularly in other developed countries. Let's say the innovator is in the United States and a competitor puts a manufacturing unit in Japan. The Japanese production is sold mainly in Japan for several reasons:

1. The growing demand there does not allow for much attention to other markets.
2. Producers there stay occupied in developing unique product variations for Japanese consumers.
3. Japanese costs may still be high because of production start-up problems.

Sales growth creates an incentive for companies to develop labor-saving process technology, but this incentive is partly offset because competitors are differentiating their products, especially to fit the needs of different countries. Thus the capital intensity, though growing, is less than will come later. The original producing country will increase its exports, especially to developing countries, but will lose certain key export markets in which local production commences.

Maturity is characterized by
- A decline in exports from the innovating country.
- More product standardization.
- More capital intensity.
- Increased competitiveness of price.
- Production start-ups in emerging economies.

Maturity In the *maturity stage,* worldwide demand begins to level off, although it may be growing in some countries and declining in others. Typically, there is a shakeout of producers, more standardized production, and increased importance of price as a competitive weapon. Capital-intensive production reduces per-unit cost, thus creating even more demand in developing economies. Because markets and technologies are widespread, the innovating country no longer commands a production advantage. Firms have incentives to shift production to developing economies where they can employ less skilled and less expensive labor efficiently for standardized (capital-intensive) production. Exports decrease from the innovating country as foreign production displaces it.

Decline is characterized by

- A concentration of production in developing countries.
- An innovating country becoming a net importer.

Decline As a product moves into the *decline stage,* those factors occurring during the maturity stage continue to evolve. The markets in developed countries decline more rapidly than those in developing economies as affluent customers demand ever newer products. By this time, market and cost factors have dictated that almost all production is in developing economies that export to the declining or small-niche markets in the developed world. In other words, the country in which the innovation first emerged—and was exported from—then becomes the importer.

Verification and Limitations of PLC Theory The PLC theory holds that the location of production facilities that serve world markets shifts as products move through their life cycle. Such items as ballpoint pens and hand calculators have followed this pattern. They were first produced in a single developed country and sold at a high price; then, production shifted to multiple developed country locations to serve those local markets. Today, most production has located in developing countries, and prices have declined.

Not all products conform to the dynamics of the PLC.

Types of products abound for which production locations usually do not shift. Such exceptions include the following:

- Products with high transport costs that may have to be produced close to the market, thus never becoming significant exports.
- Products that, because of very rapid innovation, have extremely short life cycles, making it impossible to reduce costs by moving production from one country to another. Some fashion items fit this category.
- Luxury products for which cost is of little concern to the consumer. In fact, production in a developing country may cause consumers to perceive the product as less luxurious.
- Products for which a company can use a differentiation strategy, perhaps through advertising, to maintain consumer demand without competing on the basis of price.
- Products that require specialized technical personnel to be located near production so as to move the products into their next generation of models. This seems to explain the long-term U.S. dominance of medical equipment production and German dominance in rotary printing presses.

Regardless of product, the trend is for international companies to introduce new products at home and abroad almost simultaneously. In other words, instead of merely observing needs within their domestic markets, companies develop products and services for observable worldwide market segments. In so doing, they eliminate delays as products are diffused internationally, and they choose an initial production location (which may or may not be in the innovating company's home market) that will minimize costs for serving markets in multiple countries.

According to the diamond of national competitive advantage theory, companies' development and maintenance of internationally competitive products depends on favorable

- Demand conditions.
- Factor conditions.
- Related and supporting industries.
- Firm strategy, structure, and rivalry.

THE DIAMOND OF NATIONAL COMPETITIVE ADVANTAGE

Why have countries developed and sustained different competitive advantages? The **diamond of national competitive advantage** is a theory showing four features as important for competitive superiority: demand conditions; factor conditions; related and supporting industries; and firm strategy, structure, and rivalry[32] (see Figure 5.5).

We have largely discussed these conditions in the context of other trade theories, but how they combine affects the development and continued existence of competitive advantages. The framework of the theory, therefore, is a useful tool for understanding how and where globally competitive companies develop and sustain themselves.

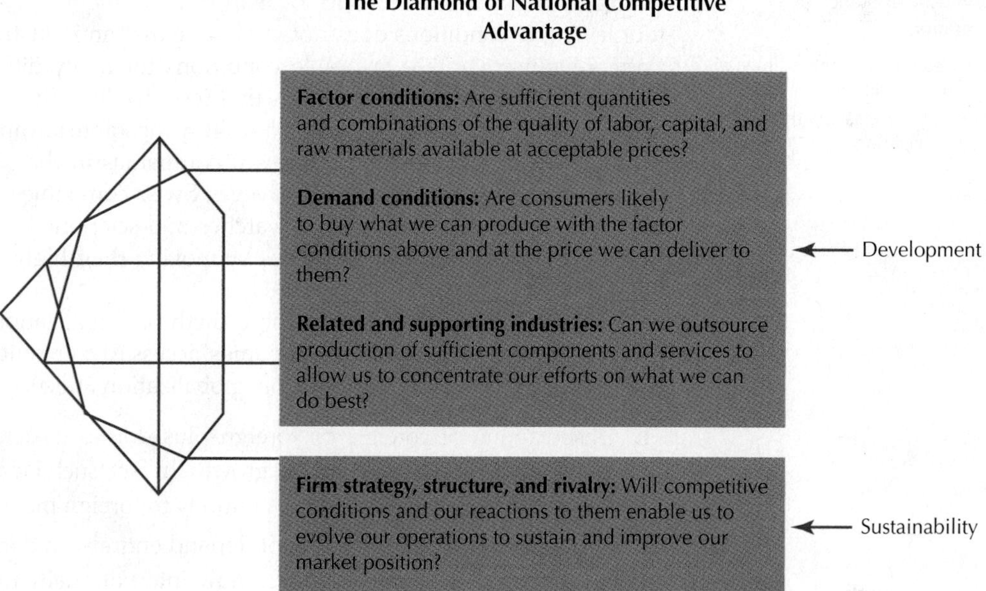

The Diamond of National Competitive Advantage
Factor conditions: Are sufficient quantities and combinations of the quality of labor, capital, and raw materials available at acceptable prices?
Demand conditions: Are consumers likely to buy what we can produce with the factor conditions above and at the price we can deliver to them?
Related and supporting industries: Can we outsource production of sufficient components and services to allow us to concentrate our efforts on what we can do best?
Development
Firm strategy, structure, and rivalry: Will competitive conditions and our reactions to them enable us to evolve our operations to sustain and improve our market position?
Sustainability

FIGURE 5.5 The Diamond of National Competitive Advantage

The interaction of these conditions must usually be favorable if an industry in a country is to develop and sustain itself. The theory was developed with domestic conditions in mind, but globalization results in favorable conditions that may come from anywhere.

Source: Based on Michael E. Porter, "The Competitive Advantage of Nations," Harvard Business Review, Vol. 68, No. 2, March-April 1990.

CONCEPT CHECK

In discussing the concept of the market economy in Chapter 4, we explain that such a system encourages an open exchange of goods and services among producers and consumers, both of which groups consist of "individuals" who make their own economic decisions; in this respect, then, the interaction among producers and consumers determines what products will be produced and in what quantities.

Facets of the Diamond Usually, all four conditions need to be favorable for an industry within a country to attain and maintain global supremacy.

Demand Conditions *Demand conditions* are the first feature in the theory. Both PLC theory and country-similarity theory show that new products (or industries) usually arise from companies' observation of need or demand, which has traditionally been in their home country, where they start up production. This was the case for the Italian ceramic tile industry after World War II: In a postwar housing boom, consumers wanted cool floors (which tile would provide) because of the hot Italian climate.

Factor Conditions Continuing our example, the second feature—*factor conditions* (recall natural advantage within the absolute advantage and factor-proportions theories)—influenced both the choice of tile to meet consumer demand and the choice of Italy as the production location. Wood was expensive, and most production factors (skilled labor, capital, technology, and equipment) were available within Italy on favorable terms.

Related and Supporting Industries The third feature—the existence of nearby *related and supporting industries* (enamels and glazes)—was also favorable. Recall, for instance, the importance of transport costs in the theory of country size, in assumptions of specialization, and in the limiting factors of the PLC theory.

Firm Strategy, Structure, and Rivalry The combination of three features—demand, factor conditions, and related and supporting industries—influenced companies' decisions to initiate production of ceramic tiles in postwar Italy. The ability of the companies to develop and sustain a competitive advantage required favorable circumstances for the fourth feature: *firm strategy, structure,* and *rivalry.*

Barriers to market entry were low in the tile industry (some companies started up with only three employees), and hundreds of companies initiated production. Rivalry became intense as companies tried to serve increasingly sophisticated Italian consumers. These circumstances forced breakthroughs in both product and process technologies, which gave the Italian producers advantages over foreign firms and enabled them to gain the largest global share of tile exports.

Domestic existence of all conditions

- Does not guarantee an industry will develop.
- Is not necessary with globalization.

Limitations of the Diamond of National Advantage Theory The existence of the four favorable conditions does not guarantee that an industry will develop in a given locale. Entrepreneurs may face favorable conditions for many different lines of business. In fact, comparative advantage theory holds that resource limitations may cause a country's firms to avoid competing in some industries despite an absolute advantage. Conditions in Switzerland would seem to have favored success if companies in that country had become players in the personal computer industry. However, Swiss companies preferred to protect their global positions in such product lines as watches and scientific instruments rather than downsize innovation efforts in those industries by moving their highly skilled people into developing a new industry.

A second limitation concerns the growth of globalization. The industries on which this theory is premised grew when companies' access to competitive capabilities was much more domestically focused. We can see how globalization affects each of the four conditions:

1. Observations of foreign or foreign-plus-domestic demand conditions have spurred much of the recent Asian export growth. In fact, such Japanese companies as Uniden and Fujitech target their sales almost entirely to foreign markets.[33]
2. Companies and countries do not depend entirely on domestic factor conditions. For example, capital and managers are now internationally mobile, and companies may depend on foreign locations for portions of their production.
3. If related and supporting industries are not available locally, materials and components are now more easily brought in from abroad because of transportation advancements and relaxed import restrictions. In fact, many MNEs now assemble products with parts supplied from a variety of countries.
4. Companies react not only to domestic rivals but also to foreign-based rivals they compete with at home and abroad. Thus the prior domestic absence of any of the four conditions from the diamond may not inhibit companies and industries from gaining these conditions and becoming globally competitive.

Using the Diamond for Transformation By expanding the diamond of national advantage theory to include changes brought about by globalization, we can see its validity for countries' economic policies. In our opening case, Costa Rica diversified its economy from agricultural products to modern high-tech products by satisfying the market entry conditions of the diamond. This transformation could not have occurred had Costa Rican authorities looked only at what was available within their own borders. In Costa Rica itself, there was (and still is) very little demand for the high-tech products it now produces, such as microchips and medical devices; good transportation, however, makes efficient export possible. Similarly, the country initially lacked some of the factor conditions necessary for producing high-tech products, especially trained personnel. Eventually, though, it altered its educational system to fit human resource development to production needs and allowed companies to bring in foreign managers and technicians to fill personnel gaps. Finally, it developed local factors, such as additional power and metalworking expertise, and attracted enough high-tech companies to ensure a vibrant competitive environment. Thus, understanding and having the necessary conditions to be globally competitive is important, but these conditions are neither static nor purely domestic.

FACTOR-MOBILITY THEORY

As both the quantity and quality of countries' factor conditions change, their relative capabilities change as well, possibly because of internal circumstances. For instance, if savings rates increase, countries have more capital relative to their factors of land and labor. If they spend relatively more on education, they improve the quality of the labor factor.

Point

Should Nations Use Strategic Trade Policies?

Point **Yes** What's so important about acquiring advantage in world trade? For one thing, if you're a country that wants to compete in today's globalized business environment (and you have to), you obviously must develop and maintain some industries that will be internationally competitive. But those industries also must grow and earn sufficient revenues to keep your domestic economy performing. What's the role of your government in the process of going global? It should be central to your whole effort; after all, we're talking about national economies here.

A government's role is rarely neutral. The government may claim that its economic policies don't affect the performance of specific domestic industries on the world stage, but a lot of those policies are bound to have precisely that effect. Who will argue that U.S. efforts to "improve agricultural productivity" and "enhance defense capabilities" have nothing to do with the fact that the United States does a healthy business in the export of farm and aerospace products?

Moreover, just about every government policy designed to help one industry will have a negative effect on another. European airlines complain (with some justification) that government support for high-speed rail traffic in Europe deprives them of the revenue they need to compete with U.S. overseas carriers, which don't have much to worry about from railroad passenger traffic at home. In other words, national policymakers everywhere face trade-offs. So if every government policy will help one party while hurting another, why shouldn't a country's practices call for taking special care of the industries that will likely give it its best competitive advantage?

Executing such a plan can be pretty simple. First, target a growth industry and figure out what factors make it competitive (or potentially competitive). Next, identify your country's likely competitive advantages (and make sure you know why you have them). Finally, develop a little synergy between the strong points you've uncovered during both processes: Target the resources needed to support the industries that fit best with your country's advantages.

This program—which comes under the general heading of strategic trade policy or industrial policy—is particularly effective if you're a developing country. Why? Because you've probably already decided that (1) you need to integrate yourself into the global economy and (2) you need to figure out the best way to excel in the international game. If your competitive countries support high-potential start-ups and you don't, your new industries will be disadvantaged.[34] So far, so good, but you need to remember that simply opening up your borders to foreign competition doesn't necessarily mean that domestic producers will have an easier time competing either abroad or at home.

When you throw open your borders, the first companies to take you up on the invitation will be foreign competitors with considerable advantages over the homegrown companies you're trying to develop. They've had a head start that's allowed them to develop not only certain internal efficiencies but cozy relations with everybody in the international distribution channel.

Moreover, no matter how promising your targeted industries may be, or how carefully you've tried to match up your industries with your competitive advantages, as a developing country your businesses probably lack the technology and marketing skills they'll need to compete. So, why not help them?[35]

This brings us back to why strategic trade policy is your optimal choice if you're a developing country: Your government must protect your local industries—say, by helping them get the skills and technology they'll need. You could also focus your efforts to attract foreign investment on companies that have the marketing and technical skills you need; that's one good way to bring in the kind of production you need. It also wouldn't hurt to extend incentives to the industries you're counting on.

Want some evidence that strategic trade policy is effective in helping developing nations go global? Look at South Korea, which not only managed to attract companies with experience in consumer-electronics production but eventually emerged as a global competitor because it built on imported technologies and targeted technical education to become both a competitive and technical leader.[36] By the same token, we have ample evidence that laissez-faire often doesn't work in developing countries. In sub-Saharan Africa, for example, government institutions are so deeply rooted that it's almost impossible for anyone—either individuals or multinationals—to make a move without getting entangled in the bureaucratic undergrowth.[37]

Moreover, because no single institution in developing countries has much in the way of resources, all are better off focusing their collective efforts on specific industries that have some potential for international competitiveness; otherwise, what you have is a bunch of under-resourced agencies and ministries aiming at markets scattered all over the economic landscape.[38]

Should Nations Use Strategic Trade Policies?

Counterpoint **No** Of course, countries should try to become most competitive in the industries that promise the best returns and have the most potential for going global. Obviously, they're the ones most likely to add value (in the form of high profits and good wages) to national production. However, strategic trade policy is not the best way to achieve these goals—about which nearly everybody agrees.

I'll make a concession: Under limited circumstances a targeting program will work, particularly for small countries such as Costa Rica. Because Costa Rica's GDP amounts to less than 10 percent of the value of Walmart's annual sales, parties involved can manageably work together to reach mutually beneficial agreements with minimal frustration. But in a large economy? Impossible.

However, it's debatable just how much Costa Rica's economic success is due to strategic trade policy and how much goes back to conditions that existed before the government started the whole process of targeting industries. Costa Rica already had a well-educated workforce, a relatively high level of economic freedom, a large population of English-speaking workers, a quality of life that had some appeal to foreign personnel, and a high level of political stability. Yes, Costa Rica landed Intel, but it's only fair to point out that Intel had already decided to put a plant somewhere in Latin America. Costa Rica's job, then, was basically convincing Intel it was a better choice than certain countries, such as Brazil and Chile, which were at a distance disadvantage when it came to sending output to the United States.

An alternative is for a country to focus on conditions affecting its attractiveness to profitable companies in general instead of targeted industries in particular. In other words, a government can alter conditions affecting, say, factor proportions, efficiency, and innovation by upgrading production factors—improving human skills, providing an adequate infrastructure, encouraging consumers to demand higher-quality products, and promoting an overall competitive environment—for any industry interested in doing business within its borders.

Let's turn to your comments about sub-Saharan Africa. I'll even make another concession: Institutional inertia is indeed a way of life in much of the area, and there's no reason to expect that it will go away any time soon.[39] But what if we looked at things from another perspective? Rather than trying to focus on a specific industry in, say, the global high-tech universe, wouldn't all these

Counterpoint

bureaucratic agencies and ministries find it easier to review (and enforce) their own laws, take steps to stabilize their populations, rectify their most glaring economic, social, and gender inequities, and support entrepreneurial activity in the informal sectors of their economies? Wouldn't they find it more productive to foster an environment of trust—one in which, say, the government helps cut transaction costs so local firms will be willing to work with other companies, domestic and foreign, to acquire a little of the knowledge and a few of the resources they need to compete?[40]

Again, instead of picking and haggling over special industries, wouldn't they be better advised to improve the investment environment in which, after all, everybody will ultimately have to operate anyway?

At this point, I might as well take the offensive in this debate. Strategic trade policies typically result in no more than small payoffs—primarily because most governments find difficulty in identifying and targeting the right industries.[41] What if a country targets an industry in which global demand never quite lives up to expectations? That's what happened to the United Kingdom and France when they got together to underwrite supersonic passenger planes. Or what if the domestic companies in a targeted industry simply fall short of being competitive? That's what happened when Thailand decided to get into the steel business.[42]

What if too many nations target the same global industries, thereby committing themselves to excessive competition and inadequate returns?[43] What if two countries compete to support the same industry, as happened when both Brazil and Canada decided to produce regional jets in the same hemisphere?[44] Finally, what if a country successfully targets an industry only to find unexpected conditions? Should it stay the course by reacting to various pressures, such as the pressure to support employment in a distressed industry?[45]

Finally, even if a government can identify a future growth industry in which a domestic firm is likely to succeed—a very big if—it doesn't follow that a company deserves public assistance. History recommends that nations permit their entrepreneurs to do what they do best: take risks that don't jeopardize whole sectors of the economy. The upshot will probably be the same as always: Some will fail, but the successful ones will survive and thrive competitively.

Currently, one of the biggest changes underway concerns relative population numbers. At present rates, 33 countries, including Japan and Italy, are projected to have smaller populations in 2050 than today, primarily because of low fertility rates. They are also encountering aging populations along with more people entering the workforce at a later age because of education, leaving fewer people to provide output and needing large immigration increases just to maintain the present ratios of employed people to retirees. Concomitantly, nine countries are expected to account for half of the world's population increase, with India, Pakistan, and Nigeria leading the pack.[46]

These changes, of course, are important in understanding and predicting changes in export production and import market locations. At the same time, the mobility of capital, technology, and people affect trade and relative competitive positions. Here we address the **factor-mobility theory**, which focuses on why production factors move, the effects of that movement on transforming factor endowments, and the impact of international factor mobility (especially people) on world trade.

WHY PRODUCTION FACTORS MOVE

CONCEPT CHECK

As we explain in Chapter 1, a foreign investment is an interest in a company or ownership of a loan made to another party in a foreign country. Companies typically use some form of portfolio investment for short-term financial gain as they routinely move funds from country to country to earn higher yields.

Capital Capital, especially short-term capital, is the most internationally mobile production factor. Companies and private individuals primarily transfer capital because of differences in expected return (accounting for risk). They find information on interest-rate differences readily available, and they can transfer capital by wire instantaneously at a low cost. Short-term capital is more mobile than long-term capital, such as direct investment, because there are more active markets to buy foreign holdings and sell them if investors want to transfer capital back home or to another country.

Political and economic conditions affect investors' perceptions of risk and where they prefer to put their capital. At the same time, companies invest abroad for the long term to tap markets, improve quality, and lower operating costs. However, businesses do not make all the international capital movements. Governments give foreign aid and loans. Not-for-profit organizations donate money abroad to relieve worrisome economic and social conditions. Individuals remit funds to help their families and friends in foreign countries. Regardless of the donor or motive, the result affects factor endowments.

Capital and labor move internationally to

- Gain more income.
- Flee adverse political situations.

People People are less mobile than capital. Some, of course, travel to other countries as tourists, students, and retirees; however, this does not affect factor endowments because these travelers do not work in the destination countries. Unlike funds that can be cheaply transferred by wire, people usually must incur high transportation costs to work abroad. Also, if they move legally they must get immigration papers, which most countries provide sparingly. Finally, they may have to learn another language and adjust to a different culture away from their customary support groups. Despite such barriers, people do endure hardships and risks to move to other countries.

Migration was the major engine of globalization during the late nineteenth and early twentieth centuries, and at present it is important again. About 3 percent of the world's population (over 200 million people) has migrated to another country. Because this 3 percent is spread unevenly, the percentage is much greater in some countries than in others; in Hong Kong and Singapore, it represents over 40 percent, and in Brazil and Mexico less than 1 percent of the population.[47]

Of the people who go abroad to work, some move permanently, some temporarily. Some might immigrate to another country, become citizens, and plan to reside there for the rest of their lives. In contrast, MNEs may assign some to work abroad for periods ranging from a few days to several years (usually to a place where they also transfer capital), while some countries allow workers to enter on temporary work permits, usually for short periods. For instance, most workers in the United Arab Emirates are there on temporary work permits.[48] In many cases, workers leave their families behind in the hopes of returning home after saving enough money working in the foreign country. Some move legally, others illegally

FIGURE 5.6 Some illegal or undocumented immigrants simply overstay their visas. Some sneak into a country.

Source: Alex Matthews/CartoonStock

(undocumented); that is to say they lack government permission to enter or work. Figure 5.6 shows an undocumented movement humorously.

Economic Motives People work in another country largely for economic reasons, such as Indonesian laborers working in Malaysia to earn more than at home. After the economic downturn of 2008, substantial numbers of immigrants worldwide returned to their native countries, such as an estimated 60,000 Indonesians who had been working in wealthier Asian nations.[49]

Political Motives People also move for political reasons—for example, because of persecution or war dangers, in which case they are known as refugees and usually become part of the labor pool where they live. It is not surprising that most refugees emanate from war-torn countries and go to a neighboring country; the largest recent movement has been from Afghanistan to Pakistan.[50] Sometimes it is difficult to distinguish between economic and political motives for international mobility because poor economic conditions often parallel poor political conditions. In the early twenty-first century, hundreds of thousands of Colombians left the country, fleeing both violence and unemployment. Map 5.3 highlights some major recent global migration.

Factor movements alter factor endowments.

EFFECTS OF FACTOR MOVEMENTS

Neither international capital nor population mobility is a new occurrence. For example, had it not been for historical mass immigration, Australia, Canada, and the United States would have greatly reduced populations today. Further, many immigrants brought human capital with them, thus adding to the base of skills that enabled those countries to be newly competitive in an array of products they might otherwise have imported. Finally, these same countries received foreign capital to develop infrastructure and natural resources, which further altered their competitive structures and international trade.

MAP 5.3 Major Net Migration, 2005–2010

The map shows net migration (immigration less emigration) for the 15 countries that had a figure of at least a million during the five-year period. (The figures are in thousands.)

Source: Based on data in United Nations Department of Economic and Social Affairs, Population Division, "World Population Prospects, the 2010 Revision," esa.un.org/wpp/Excel-Data/migration.htm (accessed February 1, 2013).

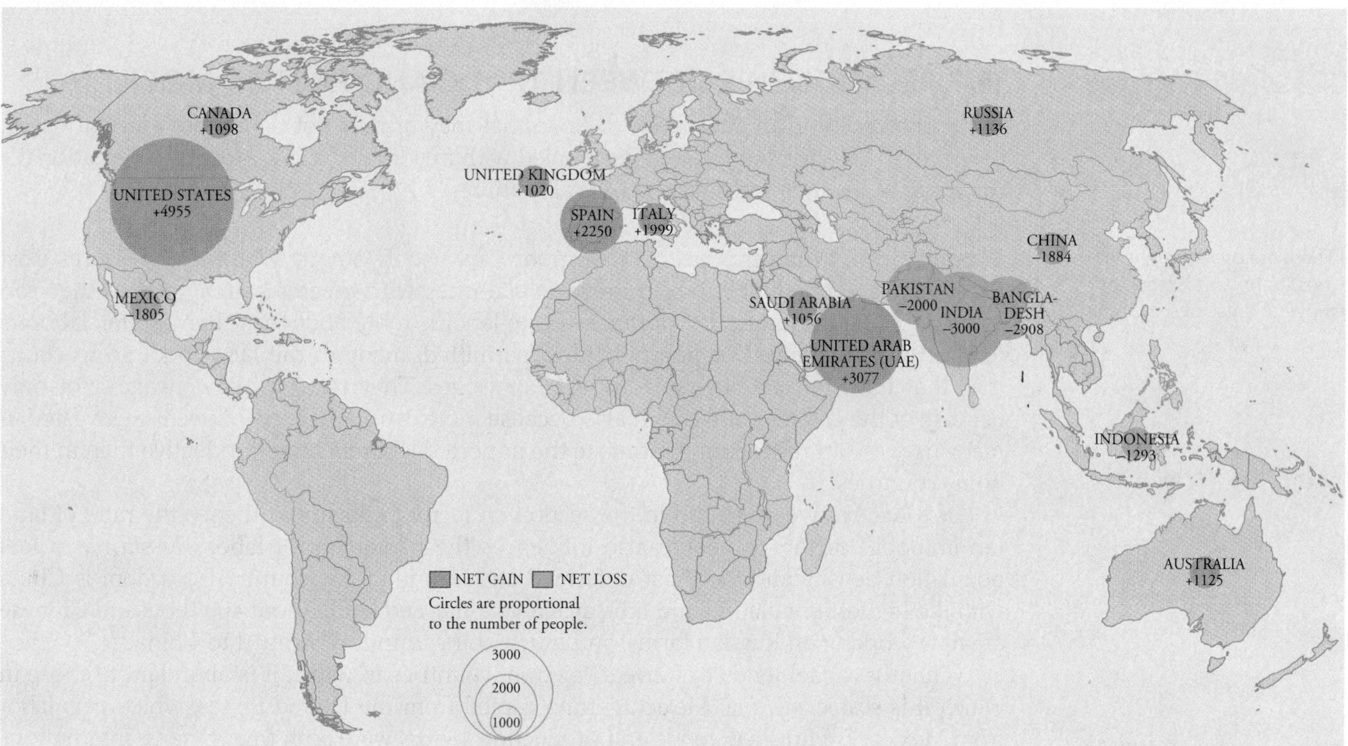

What Happens When People Move? Recent evidence is largely anecdotal. Nevertheless, we have indicated that immigration is substantial for many countries and insignificant for others.[51]

The United States is currently an example of a country whose recent immigration is largely concentrated at the high and low ends of human skills. Over a third of all people with doctoral degrees in the United States are foreign-born. At the other extreme, much recent U.S. immigration has been made up of low-skilled workers. At both extremes, the United States has had shortages of native-born workers, which has been partially alleviated through immigration.

A controversial issue is the effect of outward migration on countries. On the one hand, countries lose potentially productive resources when educated people leave—a situation known as a **brain drain**. On the other hand, they may receive money from those people. Developing countries have lost people with substantial work skills. However, many of these people are now sending remittances back. In fact, remittance flows to developing countries for 2011 were estimated at U.S. $372 billion.[52]

There is also evidence that the outward movement and remittances of people leads to an increase in start-up companies and capital in their home countries. Further, the emigrants learn abroad, transfer ideas back home, use remitted capital to start businesses with family members or on their own, and export to companies with which they had connections abroad.[53]

Finally, countries receiving productive human resources also incur costs by providing social services and acculturating people to a new language and society. Thus, on the one hand there is an employment need for the immigrants; on the other hand, there've been backlashes concerning the costs. The unskilled workers who take jobs that native-born workers don't want—dishwashing, maintaining grounds, picking agricultural produce—often have children who eventually enter the workforce. If these children are also unskilled, the country is perpetuating a long-term class of "have-nots." If the children attain skills, then there is a need to bring in even more unskilled workers from abroad.

THE RELATIONSHIP BETWEEN TRADE AND FACTOR MOBILITY

Factor movement is an alternative to trade that may or may not be a more efficient use of resources.[54] Let's see how free trade coupled with freedom of factor mobility internationally can result in the most efficient resource allocation.

There are pressures for the most abundant factors to move to areas of scarcity.

Substitution When the factor proportions vary widely among countries, pressures exist for the most abundant factors to move to countries with greater scarcity, where they can command a better return. In countries where labor is more abundant than capital, laborers tend to be unemployed or poorly paid. If permitted, many in the labor pool go to countries that have full employment and higher wages. They receive higher wages not only because of the greater scarcity, but also because more capital-rich countries have invested in machinery and infrastructure that make the imported laborers more productive than in their home countries.

Of course, as we discussed in the section on factor endowment theory, the ratio of land (an immobile factor) to people also influences the movement of labor. Russia has a low population density and the most unfarmed arable land of any country. Next door is China with the highest population and little available unfarmed land. About 400 thousand Chinese are now working on Russian farms, and much of the output is shipped to China.[55]

Similarly, capital tends to move away from countries in which it is abundant to those in which it is scarce, such as Mexico getting capital from the United States, which gets labor from Mexico.[56] If finished goods and production factors were both free to move internationally, the comparative costs of transferring goods and factors would determine production location.

However, as is true of trade, there are restrictions on factor movements that make them only partially mobile internationally—such as both U.S. immigration restrictions and Mexican foreign capital ownership restrictions in the petroleum industry.

A hypothetical example, shown in Figure 5.7, should illustrate the substitutability of trade and factor movements under different scenarios. Assume the following:

- The United States and Mexico have equally productive land available at the same cost for growing tomatoes.
- The cost of transporting tomatoes between the United States and Mexico is $0.75 per bushel.
- Workers from either country pick an average of two bushels per hour during a 30-day picking season.

The only differences in price between the two countries are due to variations in labor and capital cost. In the United States the labor rate is $20.00 per day, or $1.25 per bushel; in Mexico it is $4.00 per day, or $0.25 per bushel. The capital needed to buy seeds, fertilizers, and equipment costs the equivalent of $0.30 per bushel in the United States and $0.50 per bushel in Mexico.

If neither tomatoes nor production factors can move between the two countries (see Figure 5.7[a]), the cost of tomatoes produced in Mexico for that market is $0.75 per bushel ($0.25 of labor plus $0.50 of capital), whereas those produced in the United States for the U.S. market cost $1.55 per bushel ($1.25 of labor plus $0.30 of capital). If the two countries eliminate trade restrictions on tomatoes between them (Figure 5.7[b]), the U.S. will import from Mexico because the Mexican cost of $0.75 per bushel plus $0.75 for transporting the tomatoes will be $0.05 less than the $1.55-per-bushel cost of growing them in the United States.

FIGURE 5.7 Unrestricted Trade, Factor Mobility, and the Cost of Tomatoes

Costs are lowest when trade is unrestricted and production factors are mobile.

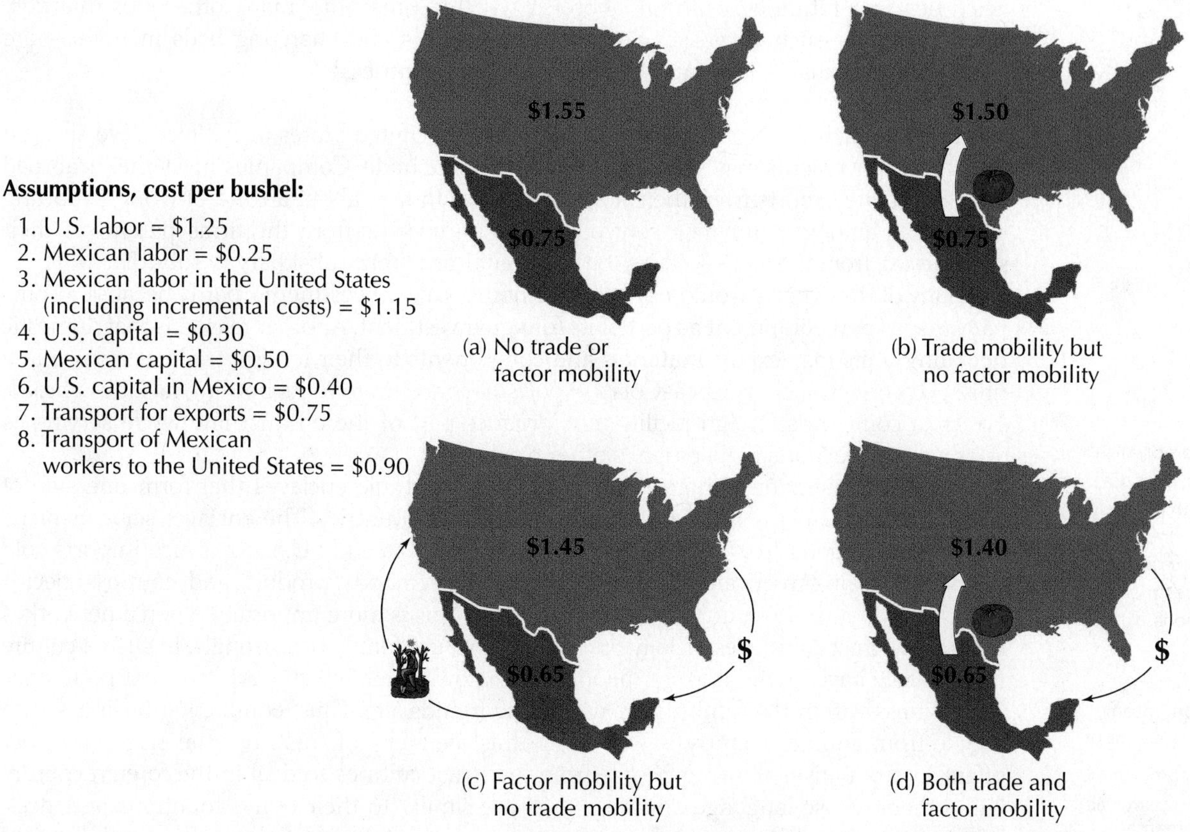

Consider another scenario in which neither country allows the importation of tomatoes but both allow certain movements of labor and capital (Figure 5.7[c]). Mexican workers can enter the United States on temporary work permits for an incremental travel and living expense of $14.40 per day per worker, or $0.90 per bushel. At the same time, U.S. companies will invest capital in Mexican tomato production, provided the capital earns more than it would earn in the United States—say, $0.40 per bushel, which is less than the Mexican going rate.

In this scenario, Mexican production costs per bushel will be $0.65 ($0.25 of Mexican labor plus $0.40 of U.S. capital), and U.S. production costs will be $1.45 ($0.25 of Mexican labor plus $0.90 of travel and incremental costs plus $0.30 of U.S. capital). Each country would reduce its production costs—from $0.75 to $0.65 in Mexico and from $1.55 to $1.45 in the United States—by bringing in abundant production factors from abroad.

The lowest costs occur when trade and production factors are both mobile.

With free trade *and* the free movement of production factors (Figure 5.7[d]), Mexico will produce for both markets by importing capital from the United States. According to the three assumptions just stated, doing this will be cheaper than sending labor to the United States. In reality, because neither production factors nor the finished goods they produce are completely free to move internationally, slight changes in the extent of restrictions can greatly alter how and where goods may be produced most cheaply.

In some cases, however, the inability to gain sufficient access to foreign production factors may stimulate efficient methods of substitution, such as the development of alternatives for traditional production methods.[57] For example, at one time U.S. tomato growers in California depended almost entirely on Mexican temporary workers under what was known as the *bracero program.* Since the termination of this program, the California tomato harvests have quadrupled, while mechanization has replaced 72 percent of the number of workers.

However, not all harvesting jobs can reasonably be mechanized at present. Because cantaloupes ripen at different times, pickers go through a cantaloupe field about 10 times. A robot would have to be able to distinguish colors so as to leave green cantaloupes behind.[58] However, advancement of robots using cameras that distinguish ripeness foretell the diminished need for future agricultural laborers.[59] At the same time, many other jobs that defy mechanization—such as bussing tables at restaurants and changing beds in hotels—are largely filled by unskilled immigrants in developed countries.

Complementarity In our tomato example for the United States and Mexico, we showed that factor movements may substitute for or stimulate trade. Companies' investments abroad often stimulate exports from their home countries. In fact, about a third of world exporting takes place among companies' controlled entities, such as from the firms' parents to their subsidiaries, from their subsidiaries to the parents, and from subsidiary to subsidiary.

Many of the exports would not occur without foreign investments, partly because a company may export equipment as part of its foreign investment. Another reason is that domestic operating units may export materials and components to their foreign facilities for use in a finished product, such as Coca-Cola's exports of concentrate to its bottling facilities abroad. Finally, a company's foreign facility may produce part of the product line while serving as sales agent for exports of its parent's other products.

CONCEPT CHECK

In Chapter 2, we emphasize societal differences in trust along with strength in family ties, especially as it affects trust. We also discussed that higher trust reduces the cost of business transactions.

Finally, immigration enhances trade by creating ethnic enclaves that form one side of ethnic networks linking immigrants with their native countries. The enclaves serve as niche markets for imports from their native countries, such as early U.S. soy sauce imports sold mainly to Asian-Americans. The ethnic networks embody product and country-specific knowledge that aid both importers and exporters. This is more important when a network is from a low-trust culture, especially one that also values family ties strongly. In such a culture most people have higher trust for people they know better, which leads to a first preference for business within the family, next with close friends, etc. Thus, conducting business with people from another country is well down this hierarchy of trust. But the ethnic network offers an alternative, allowing people from low-trust cultures to deal in the foreign country with others whose language and responses are similar to their home country experiences. Without this network, one needs much more time to overcome the perceived risk brought about by lack of knowledge and low trust of potential business partners. Thus potential importers and exporters are more willing to trade when they are part of the ethnic network.[60]

Factor mobility through foreign investment often stimulates trade because of

- The need for components.
- The parent company's ability to sell complementary products.
- The need for equipment for subsidiaries.

Looking to the Future

In What Direction Will Trade Winds Blow?

When countries have few restrictions on foreign trade and factor mobility, companies have greater latitude in reducing operating costs. For example, fewer trade restrictions give them opportunities to gain economies of scale by servicing markets in more than one country from a single base of production. Fewer restrictions on factor movements allow them to combine factors for more efficient production. However, government trade and immigration restrictions vary among countries, over time, and under different circumstances.

Nevertheless, it's probably safe to say that trade restrictions have been diminishing, primarily because of the economic gains that countries foresee through freer trade. Further, restrictions on the movement of capital and technology have become freer, but whether restrictions on the movement of people are freer is questionable.

There are uncertainties as to whether the trend toward the freer movement of trade and production factors will continue. Groups worldwide question whether the economic benefits of more open economies outweigh some of the costs, both economic and noneconomic. Although the next chapter discusses import restrictions (protectionism) in detail, it is useful at this point to understand the overall evolution of protectionist sentiment.

One key issue is the trade between developed and developing economies. As trade barriers are being lowered, some developing economies with very low wage rates are growing economically more rapidly than developed countries. Concomitantly, as companies shift production to developing economies, they displace jobs at home. These displaced workers need to find new jobs. But it is uncertain how fast new jobs will replace old ones and how much developed countries will tolerate employment displacement and job shifts. If they become intolerant, they may enact protectionist measures that would stifle trade.

Another key issue is the future of factor endowments. If present trends continue, relationships among land, labor, and capital will continue to evolve. For example, the population growth rate is expected to be much higher in developing economies than in developed ones. This could result in continued shifts of labor-intensive production to developing economies and pressures on the developed countries to accept more immigrants.

Urbanization will likely grow faster in developing than in developed countries, which are already heavily urbanized. Considerable evidence indicates that productivity rises with urbanization because firms can more likely find people with the exact skills they need, because there are economies in moving supplies and finished products, and because knowledge flows more easily from one company and industry to another. Thus we might expect higher growth in some developing countries due to their pace of urbanization. Such growth should also help them account for a larger share of world trade.

At the same time, on the one hand the finite supply of natural resources may lead to price increases for these resources, even though oversupplies have often depressed prices. The limited supply may work to the advantage of developing economies, because their supplies have been less fully exploited. On the other hand, technology to find and extract natural resources, such as fracking to secure natural gas from shale, may shift supply locations and lessen price rises.

We will probably see the continued trend toward a more finely tuned specialization of production among countries to take advantage of specific conditions. Although part of this will be due to wage and skill differences, other factors are important as well. For instance, country differences in property right protection may influence businesses to locate more of their technologically intensive activities within countries that offer more protection. Or they may disperse portions of production to different countries in order to hinder potential competitors from gaining the full picture needed to pirate their products and processes.

Four interrelated factors are worth monitoring because they could cause product trade to become relatively less significant in the future:

1. As economies grow, efficiencies of multiple production locations also grow because they can all gain sufficient economies of scale. This may allow country-by-country production to replace trade in many cases. For example, most automobile producers have moved into China and Thailand—or plan to do so—as a result of those countries' growing market size.
2. Flexible, small-scale production methods, especially those using robotics and digital technologies, may enable even small countries to produce many goods efficiently for their own consumption, thus eliminating the need to import those goods. For example, before the development of efficient minimills that can produce steel on a small scale, steel production took larger capital outlays that needed enormous markets. Similarly, consumers' demand for evermore differentiated products largely negates the cost advantages of long production runs, thus making smaller scale manufacturing close to markets more advantageous.[61]
3. Output from 3D printers has already reached the point at which 20 percent is of final products (e.g., medical implants, jewelry, lampshades, car parts, mobile phones); some predict that this figure will reach 50 percent by 2020. Basically, this permits a user to choose plans and use software for the printer to produce the product. It involves an additive technology (building a product up from raw materials) rather than a traditional subtractive technology (cutting, drilling, and bashing of raw materials). As this develops, products can be fabricated efficiently where they are used rather than traded from one country to another.[62] However, there will still be a need to trade production-grade metals and plastics as inputs to the computers.
4. Services are growing more rapidly than products as a portion of production and consumption within developed countries. Part of this change involves technology, such as the substitute of digitalized products like music and reading material, for traditionally manufactured products. Thus, one buys the right to copy (a service sale) from anywhere in the world with no need to ship products. Consequently, product trade may become a less important part of countries' total trade. Further, many of the rapid-growth service areas, such as retail gasoline distribution and dining out, are not easily traded, so trade in goods plus services could become a smaller part of total output and consumption. ■

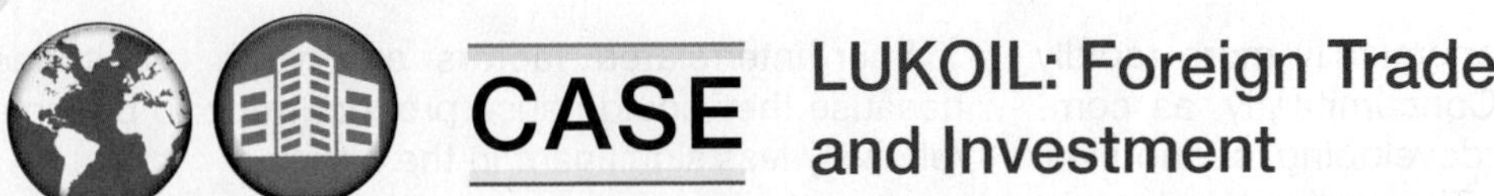

CASE LUKOIL: Foreign Trade and Investment

To keep a lamp burning, we have to keep putting oil in it – Mother Teresa.

To keep an economy growing, we also have to keep putting oil into energy expansion. A major oil and energy player is LUKOIL, which with 2012 sales of $139 billion, produces and distributes a wide range of petroleum and energy products such as gasoline, heating oil, crude petroleum, jet fuel, lubricants, natural gas, and petrochemicals. It is listed in both *Fortune's* and *Forbes'* world's 100 largest companies; in the former by sales, and the latter by valuation. It is not only Russia's second largest company, but also its largest privately-owned company. Many of the world's largest oil companies are government-owned, such as in Saudi Arabia, Iran, and Venezuela. Among privately owned oil firms, LUKOIL is the world's fourth largest, accounting for 17 percent of Russian crude oil production and refining.

The Russian Economy

LUKOIL's position is inexorably tied to conditions in Russia. Before the fall of the Berlin Wall in 1989 and the collapse of the Soviet Union, the Russian oil industry was government-owned within a command economy. In addition, the Soviet Union followed an inward-looking economic policy that depended minimally on foreign trade. In fact, a government monopoly handled all foreign trade and did not always relate prices to production costs. Russia privatized most industries in the 1990s; however, it has only partially privatized the energy sector because of its essentiality to national well-being. Russia faced abundant economic problems during the 1990s when it was transitioning to a market economy. Among other factors, many newly privatized companies lacked sufficient management and marketing skills, especially for selling abroad.

However, during the 10-year period from 1999 to 2008, Russia enjoyed significant GDP growth, led by the export of commodities. During this period, Russia became the world's largest natural gas and second largest oil exporter. The Russian economy was one of the hardest hit by the global economic crisis since 2008. Its GDP fell by 8 percent in 2009, but has since recovered by growing 4 percent, due largely to high oil prices in 2010. Russia's oil and gas sector accounts for about 25 percent of its GDP and a third of all its exports. Russia consumes about 5 percent of its oil and exports the rest.

On the downside, its dependence on petroleum exports makes Russia vulnerable to fluctuations in global petroleum markets, such as that caused by the 2009 economic downturn when global demand and prices for energy plummeted. Further, when the yearly average price per barrel of oil shifts by as much as $1, Russian revenues shift by about $2 billion in the same direction. In recent years, Russia has discovered so much oil that the country now has the world's eighth-highest level of proven reserves. In addition, Russia also controls petroleum exports from the former Central Asian Soviet republics of Azerbaijan and Kazakhstan, both of which, like Russia are oil rich.

Although some oil producing countries, especially members of the Organization of Petroleum Exporting Countries (OPEC), cut back production to maintain higher prices, Russia, which is not an OPEC member, is content to sell all the oil it can produce. This helps to explain the disparity between Russia's rank in exports versus proven reserves. However, its prices depend, of course, on world petroleum prices. Because of fierce competition in the global oil industry, even control of such vast supplies is no guarantee that Russia can sell its output at an acceptable margin. Additionally, Russia depends on oil exports to pay for imports (over half of which include machinery and transportation equipment), a top priority for the Russian government for three primary reasons:

1. At a purchasing price parity of $15,900 in 2010, Russian GDP per capita is still well below that of any other G8 country.

2. The oil sector—which is a capital- rather than labor-intensive industry—employs less than 1 percent of the country's population.
3. Natural disasters, such as the 2010 drought and fires, wreak havoc directly on the agricultural sector and indirectly on other economic sectors.

A Little History of LUKOIL

LUKOIL was formed in 1991 as a government-owned enterprise through a merger of three state-run companies in Siberia. LUK is an acronym for the names of the home cities of the three preexisting companies. At the time, the former Soviet deputy minister of oil production, Vagit Alekperov, believed the only way Russian oil companies could successfully compete against Western companies would be to vertically integrate the three main components of their business—exploration, refining, and distribution. In the old Soviet system, these components were strictly separate.

After its founding, LUKOIL moved quickly to establish this integration. In 1993, the government approved LUKOIL's privatization plan, and a little more than 9 percent of the ownership went private, mainly by giving shares to its employees. The following year LUKOIL sold its first private shares through an auction, which reduced government ownership to 80.59 percent. Government ownership fell to 33 percent in 1996, to 20 percent in 2000, and to 0 in 2004 when ConocoPhillips bought the last 7.59 percent of the company from the government. In the interim, LUKOIL began selling shares over the counter in New York and through several German exchanges. In 2002, LUKOIL became the first Russian company listed on the London Stock Exchange. The decrease in government ownership occurred partially by selling government shares and partially by issuing additional shares that diluted the government's ownership. Subsequent to being fully privatized, ConocoPhillips upped its ownership to 20 percent, but sold its holdings in 2010.

Although the Russian government is no longer a shareholder, it maintains close ties with LUKOIL because of its economic significance—LUKOIL controls about 19 percent of all Russian production and refining—and its political importance as a symbol of Russian prestige in foreign markets. An illustration of the latter was President Vladimir Putin's attendance to open a LUKOIL filling station in New York City. LUKOIL began its first foreign project in 1994, when it took a stake in an Azerbaijan oilfield. It has since expanded so that it now does business in 37 countries through a combination of exploration (10 countries), refining (5 countries), and distribution or transshipment (27 countries).

Map 5.4 identifies LUKOIL's foreign operations. Note that most of these countries are close to Russia. As of 2012, LUKOIL had almost 6000 filling stations worldwide. One of its farthest locations from Russia is the United States, where the company's expansion has occurred mainly through the acquisition of Getty Petroleum in 2000, and a string of gasoline stations owned by ConocoPhillips in 2004. Despite LUKOIL's foray into international business, it depends mainly on the Russian market for its sales and oil reserves.

Why Export?

As we've already seen, Russia and LUKOIL have a lot of oil reserves. When countries or companies have an abundant storable commodity, which is not easily spoiled, a number of factors may influence the quantity they try to sell in the short term, especially to export markets. One is the expectation of future prices compared with present ones (i.e., if future prices are expected to be higher than the net present value of investment earnings from immediate sale), one may be better off by limiting current sales. However, in the case of oil exports, projecting future prices is particularly problematic because they depend so much on derived demand, which in turn depends on uncertainties about industrial output, climatic and natural disaster conditions. Real natural and technical changes lead to hypothetical market changes for the future, (consider the future uncertainty of energy sources brought about by concern after a 2011 tsunami damaged a Japanese nuclear facility), and technological

MAP 5.4 LUKOIL's Global Oil and Gas Production and Sales

LUKOIL has expanded its operations internationally, not only by exporting (notably to the United States) but also by investing in foreign production, exploration, refining operations and marketing efforts. Note that the preponderance of the company's expansion has taken place in nearby countries. In addition to the information shown on the map, LUKOIL has petrochemical operations in Ukraine and Bulgaria and power production in Ukraine, Romania, and Bulgaria.

Source: Information to prepare the map is taken from LUKOIL *Annual Report* (2012).

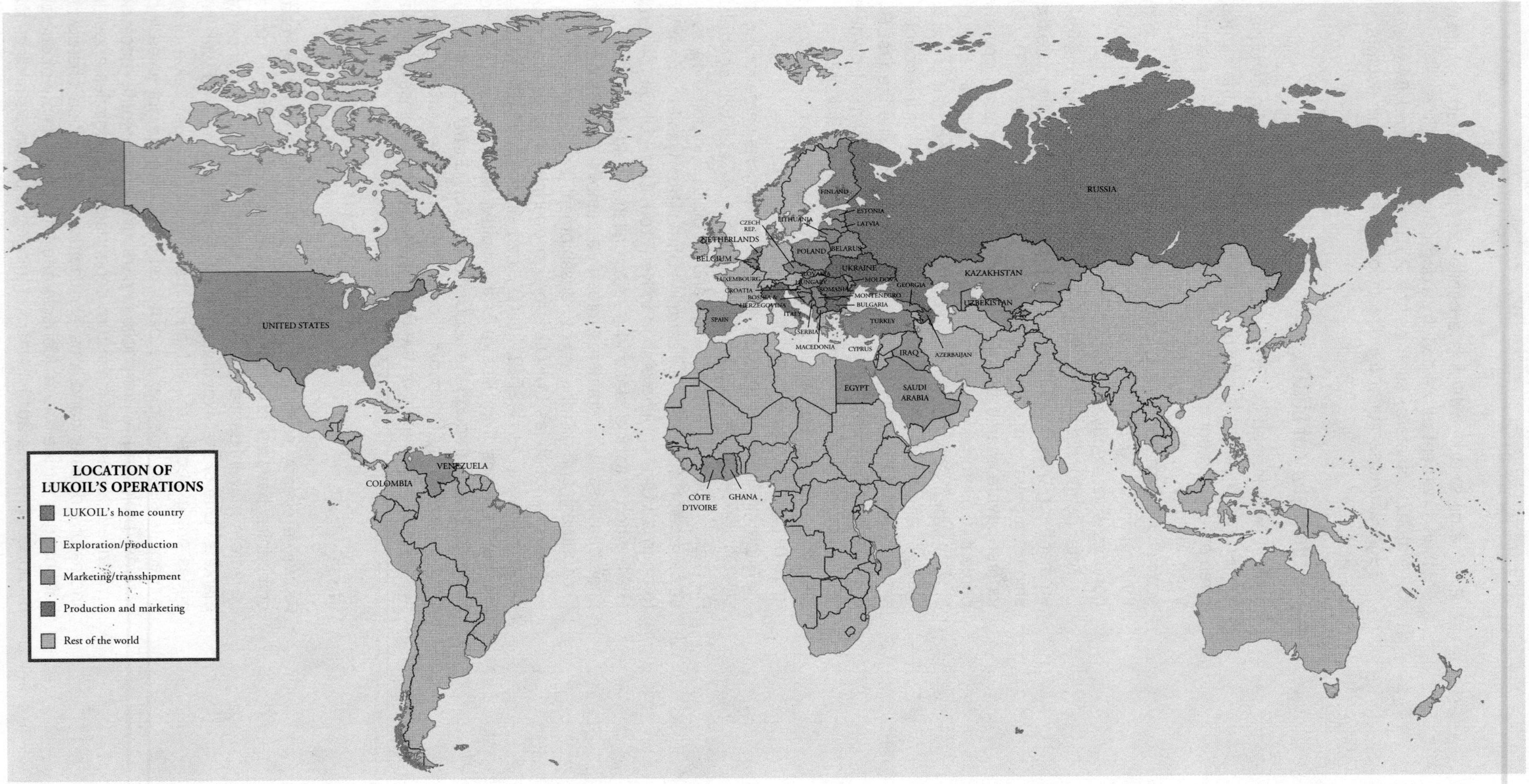

changes (consider, that the United States displaced Russia as the largest oil and gas producer in 2013 because of innovations in fracking technology). Likewise, prices depend on competition, and competitors never know what other producing countries and companies will do. At any rate, we have discussed reasons for the Russian policy of expanding current export oil sales, thus the decision is a "given" from the country's standpoint. We should point out that, since the beginning of the twenty-first century, the global price of oil has fluctuated substantially even though there has been a trend towards higher prices. For instance, the average monthly prices in 2008 were 42 percent higher than in 2007. Then they fell 41.5 percent in 2009. (If the highs and lows within particular years are compared rather than the yearly averages, the fluctuations are even greater.) Some of the factors influencing both price changes and price trends have been the uncertainty following 9/11, Chinese economic expansion, production cutbacks by OPEC, unsettlement in and trade embargoes in various oil-producing countries (e.g., Libya, Venezuela, and Iran), seasonal abnormal temperatures, and the global economic crisis that began in 2008. Nevertheless, Russia's export position has been generally quite good throughout the twenty-first century's first decade, with favorable balances of trade each year that have helped to pay for both imports and a high level of external credit.

But what about LUKOIL's dreams? Despite a growing domestic market, Russian demand is insufficient to absorb all of LUKOIL's capacity. Overall, it has been able to sell more oil at higher prices outside Russia than it could just a few years ago. Further, if LUKOIL were to curtail exporting, it might incur a political backlash of the Russian government as a result of economic policies deemed favorable for the entire economy. In addition to its increase in sales through exporting, the practice has enabled LUKOIL to amass a substantial store of capital that it has been able to channel into foreign investment.

Why LUKOIL Went the Foreign Investment Route

LUKOIL's management has long seen foreign expansion as a means both of earning bigger margins and ensuring more reliable, full, on-time payment than it can get in Russia. The question, however, remains: why doesn't LUKOIL simply export rather than risk foreign investment? The answer lies in a combination of factors.

Fluctuating World Markets

We have discussed how supply and demand changes have influenced prices, but they also affect the ability to sell. In the late 1990s, when a global oil glut impaired foreign sales, LUKOIL decided to emulate its larger Western competitors with a strategy of forward integration into the ownership of foreign distribution outlets. (Nevertheless, its plan for the 2012–2021 period is for over 80 percent of investment to be spent on exploration and production.) LUKOIL made its first foreign distribution investments not far from home in former Soviet satellite countries by buying long time retail customers in Bulgaria and Romania that were state-owned operations being privatized. Since then, LUKOIL has ventured farther afield, almost exclusively by means of purchasing existing operations. It's a sound strategy. When oil producers invest in distribution, they strengthen their ties to markets where they may be better able to sell crude oil in times of global oversupply. Moreover, integrating into distribution can potentially reduce operating costs, primarily because a producer doesn't have to rely on negotiating and enforcing a network of agreements by which it sells oil to intermediaries in other countries. Further, this vertical integration enables LUKOIL to smooth its profits by operating in the ever-changing portion going to production versus distribution. Concomitantly, LUKOIL has rebranded its acquisitions to gain uniformity in its image, which also helps to promote sales better.

Political Uncertainty

LUKOIL has been well aware of the fact that export sales are always subject to political disruptions. What if an importing country decides to reduce its purchases of Russian oil to protest some internal Russian political policy (or simply to diversify its own supply sources)? In turn, this risk has been a factor in LUKOIL's decision to expand into exploration and refining outside Russia. Or consider another problem that's more or less unique to LUKOIL's situation.

An oil rig in the North Sea. Thousands work around the clock to extract energy and natural gas along the coastline.
Source: © Simon Pedersen – Shutterstock

As it turns out, the Russian government owns the pipeline system through which virtually all Russian oil exports must pass, allocating access to the system by means of quotas among domestic oil companies. What if a competitor manages to gain sufficient influence with certain political decisionmakers to siphon off part of LUKOIL's quota? Although LUKOIL will never forget its own complete privatization, the Russian government still owns some of its domestic competitors, and has often bestowed on its firms preferential treatment in various matters. That is just one reason why LUKOIL is trying to increase foreign oil supplies to 20 percent of its total. However, moving internationally creates other political risks, such as ownership of assets in volatile environments such as Egypt and Venezuela. International sanctions caused LUKOIL to cease operating in Iraq when Saddam Hussein was in power. Some U.S. Congressmen have made scathing attacks against LUKOIL because some oil it shipped to China was then shipped to Iran despite a contract clause stating "not for supplies to the territory of Iran."

Efficiency Imperatives

To be a major global competitor, LUKOIL must become as efficient as its major Western competitors. Toward that end, it must not only achieve operating efficiencies but also acquire state-of-the-industry technology and marketing skills. For instance, it must adhere to ever-changing national product requirements concerning gasoline octane and cleanliness. In the past, LUKOIL's administrative expenses and cost of capital were high, compared with those of Western competitors. At home, such inefficiencies resulted in only minor problems because the competition consisted solely of other Russian oil companies hampered by the same operational inefficiencies inherited from the former state-owned oil monopoly. Even in Russia, however, new competitive threats are starting to emerge as Western oil firms have bought interests in Russian oil companies. LUKOIL, however, views foreign oil companies to be a stiffer threat than domestic competition: They are valuable sources of the technology and knowledge that must be competed with at home and abroad. With this strategy in mind, it has placed independent directors from Western oil companies on its board, used ConocoPhillips's management expertise when it owned 20 percent of the company, and has established several partnerships abroad, such as with Norway's Statoil. Meanwhile, foreign acquisitions, such as Getty in the United States, present another source of experienced personnel, technology, and competitive know-how.

QUESTIONS

5-3. What theories of trade help explain Russia's position as an oil exporter? Why? Which ones don't? Why not?

5-4. How do global political and economic conditions affect global oil markets and prices?

5-5. Discuss the following statement as it applies to Russia and LUKOIL: *Regardless of the advantages a country may gain by trading, international trade will begin only if companies within that country have competitive advantages that enable them to be viable traders—and they must foresee profits in exporting and importing.*

5-6. In LUKOIL's situation, what is the relationship between factor mobility and exports?

5-7. Why do you think LUKOIL's first foreign direct investments were in countries nearby to Russia (e.g. former Soviet republics and satellite countries)?

SUMMARY

- Some trade theories examine what will happen to international trade in the absence of government interference. Other theories prescribe how governments should affect trade flows to achieve certain national objectives.
- Trade theory is useful because it helps explain what might be produced competitively in a given locale, where a company might go to produce a given product efficiently, and whether government practices might interfere with the free flow of trade among countries. Other theories address the explanation of trade patterns.
- Mercantilist theory proposes that a country should try to achieve a favorable balance of trade (export more than it imports) to receive an influx of gold. Neomercantilist policy also seeks a favorable balance of trade, but its purpose is to achieve some social or political objective.
- The theory of absolute advantage proposes specialization through free trade because consumers will be better off if they can buy foreign-made products priced more cheaply than domestic ones.
- According to the theory of absolute advantage, a country may produce goods more efficiently because of a natural advantage (e.g., raw materials or climate) or because of an acquired advantage (e.g., technology or skill for a product or process advantage).
- Comparative advantage theory also proposes specialization through free trade because it says that trade can increase total global output even if one country has an absolute advantage in the production of all products.
- Policymakers have questioned some of the assumptions of the absolute and comparative advantage theories: that full employment exists, output efficiency is always a country's major objective, countries are satisfied with their relative gains, there are no transport costs among countries, advantages appear to be static, and resources move freely within countries but are immobile internationally.
- The theory of country size holds that because countries with large land areas are apt to have varied climates and natural resources, they are generally more self-sufficient than smaller countries. A second reason for this greater self-sufficiency is that large countries' production and market centers are more likely to be located at a greater distance from other countries, raising the transport costs of foreign trade.
- The factor-proportions theory holds that a country's relative endowments of land, labor, and capital will determine the relative costs of these factors. These factor costs, in turn, determine which goods the country can produce most efficiently.
- According to the country-similarity theory, most trade today occurs among developed countries because they share similar market characteristics and because they produce and consume so much more than developing economies.
- Much of the pattern of two-way trading partners may be explained by cultural similarity between the countries, political and economic agreements, and the distance between them.
- Manufactured products comprise the bulk of trade among high-income countries. This trade occurs because countries apportion their research and development differently among industrial sectors. It also occurs because consumers from high-income countries want and can afford to buy products with a greater variety of characteristics than are produced in their domestic markets.
- The international product life cycle (PLC) theory states that companies will manufacture products first in the countries in which they were researched and developed, which are almost always developed countries. Over the product's life cycle, production will shift to foreign locations, especially to developing economies, as the product reaches the stages of maturity and decline.
- The diamond of national competitive advantage theory shows that four conditions are important for gaining and maintaining

competitive superiority: demand conditions; factor conditions; related and supporting industries; and firm strategy, structure, and rivalry.

- Production factors and finished goods are only partially mobile internationally. The cost and feasibility of transferring production factors rather than exporting finished goods internationally will determine which alternative is better.
- Although international mobility of production factors may be a substitute for trade, the mobility may stimulate trade through sales of components, equipment, and complementary products.

KEY TERMS

absolute advantage (p. 236)
acquired advantage (p. 237)
brain drain (p. 257)
comparative advantage (p. 239)
country-similarity theory (p. 246)
diamond of national competitive advantage theory (p. 250)
factor-mobility theory (p. 255)
factor-proportions theory (p. 243)
favorable balance of trade (p. 236)
import substitution (p. 230)
mercantilism (p. 235)
natural advantage (p. 237)
neomercantilism (p. 236)
nontradable goods (p. 242)
product life cycle (PLC) theory (p. 248)
strategic trade policy (p. 232)
theory of country size (p. 242)
trade deficit (p. 236)
trade surplus (p. 236)
unfavorable balance of trade (p. 236)

ENDNOTES

1 ***Sources include the following:*** "Costa Rica Exports," www.tradingeconomics.com/costa-rica/exports, accessed January 31, 2013; World Trade Organization, "Trade Profiles: Costa Rica," retrieved January 31, 2013, from stat.wto.org/CountryProfile/WSDBCountryPFView.aspx?Language=E&Country=CR; Debora Spar, *Attracting High Technology Investment: Intel's Costa Rican Plant* (Washington, DC: The World Bank, Foreign Investment Advisory Service Occasional Paper No. 11, 1998); CIA Factbook, retrieved January 31, 2013, from CIA.GOV/CIA/publications/factbook/geos/cs.html; Gail D. Triner, "Recent Latin American History and Its Historiography," *Latin American Research Review* 38:1 (2003): 219–38; John Weeks, "Trade Liberalisation, Market Deregulation and Agricultural Performance in Central America," *The Journal of Development Studies* 35:5 (June 1999): 48–76; Niels W. Ketelhöhn and Michael E. Porter, "Building a Cluster: Electronics and Information Technology in Costa Rica," *Harvard Business School Case 9703422* (November 7, 2002); John Schellhas, "Peasants against Globalization: Rural Social Movements in Costa Rica," *American Anthropologist* 103:3 (2001):862–863; Jose Itzigsohn, *Developing Poverty: The State, Labor Market Deregulation, and the Informal Economy in Costa Rica and the Dominican Republic* (University Park, IL: Pennsylvania University Press, 2000); Roy Nelson, "Intel's Site Selection Decision in Latin America," *Thunderbird International Business Review* 42:2 (2001): 227–49; Andrés Rodríguez-Clare, "Costa Rica's Development Strategy Based on Human Capital and Technology: How It Got There, The Impact of Intel, and Lessons for Other Countries," *United Nations Human Development Report 2001* (New York: United Nations Development Programme, 2001).

2 For a good survey of mercantilism and the mercantilist era, see Gianni Vaggi, *A Concise History of Economic Thought: From Mercantilism to Monetarism* (New York: Palgrave Macmillan, 2002).

3 For reviews of the literature, see Jordan Shan and Fiona Sun, "On the Export-Led Growth Hypothesis for the Little Dragons: An Empirical Reinvestigation," *Atlantic Economic Review* 26:4 (1998): 353–71; George K. Zestos and Xiangnan Tao, "Trade and GDP Growth: Causal Relations in the United States and Canada," *Southern Economic Journal* 68:4 (2002): 859–74.

4 For a good discussion of the history of free trade thought, see Leonard Gomes, *The Economics and Ideology of Free Trade: A Historical Review* (Cheltenham, UK: Edward Elgar, 2003).

5 "Year Round Production of Tomatoes in Iceland," retrieved July 16, 2007, from www.freshplaza.com/news_detail.asp?id=3791; "The History of Wine Production in Brazil," retrieved July 16, 2007, from www.brazilianwines.com/en/brazilie_histoire.asp.

6 For simplicity's sake, both Smith and Ricardo originally assumed a simple world composed of only two countries and two commodities. Our example makes the same assumption. Now, although this simplification is unrealistic, it does not diminish the usefulness of either theory. Economists have applied the same reasoning to demonstrate efficiency advantages in multiproduct and multicountry trade relationships. Smith's seminal treatise remains abundantly in print; for a reliable recent edition, see *An Inquiry into the Nature and Causes of the Wealth of Nations* (Washington, DC: Regnery Publishing, 1998). Like Smith's *Wealth of Nations,* Ricardo's seminal work on comparative advantage, originally published in London in 1817, is continuously reprinted; see, for example, *On the Principles of Political Economy and Taxation* (Amherst, NY: Prometheus Books, 1996).

7 For a good discussion of this paradoxical thinking, see Paul R. Krugman, "What Do Undergraduates Need to Know about Trade?" *American Economic Review Papers and Proceedings* (May 1993):23–26. For a discussion of some developing countries' views that monopolistic conditions keep them from gaining a fair share of gains from international trade, see A. P. Thirwell, *Growth and Development,* 6th ed. (London: Macmillan, 1999).

8 Thomas I. Palley, "Institutionalism and New Trade Theory: Rethinking Comparative Advantage and Trade Theory," *Journal of Economic Issues* 42:1 (2008): 195–08.

9 Murray Kemp, "Non-Competing Factor Groups and the Normative Propositions of Trade Theory," *International Review of Economics and Finance* 17 (2008): 388–90.

10 Andrew Avery Herring, Roger Enrique Bonilla-Carríon, Rosilyne Mae Borland, and Kenneth Hailey Hill, "Differential Mortality Patterns Between Nicaraguan Immigrants and Native-born Residents of Costa Rica," *Immigrant Minority Health* 12 (2010): 33–42.

11 Gordon H. Hanson, "The Rise of Middle Kingdoms: Emerging Economies in Global Trade," *The Journal of Economic Perspectives* 26:2 (Spring 2012): 41–64.

12 Eli J. Heckscher, *Heckscher-Ohlin Trade Theory* (Cambridge, MA: MIT Press, 1991).

13 For a discussion of ways in which the theory does not fit the reality of trade, see Antoni Estevadeordal and Alan M. Taylor, "A Century of Missing Trade?" *The American Economic Review* 92:1 (2002): 383–93. For a study supporting the theory, see Yong-Seok Choi and Pravin Krishna, "The Factor Content of Bilateral Trade: An Empirical Test," *The Journal of Political Economy* 112:4 (2004): 887–915.

14 See, for example, Donald R. Davis and David E. Weinstein, "An Account of Global Factor Trade," *The American Economic Review* 91:5 (2001): 1423–53; Oner Guncavdi and Suat Kucukcifi, "Foreign Trade and Factor Intensity in an Open Developing Country: An Input-Output Analysis for Turkey," *Russian & East European Finance and Trade* 37:1 (2001): 75–88.

15 See, for example, P. Krugman and A. J. Venables, "Globalization and the Inequality of Nations," *Quarterly Journal of Economics* 110 (1995): 857–80.

16 See Paul Krugman, "Scale Economies, Product Differentiation, and the Patterns of Trade," *The American Economic Review* 70 (1980): 950–59; James Harrigan, "Estimation of Cross-Country Differences in Industry Production Functions," *Journal of International Economics* 47:2 (1999): 267–93.

17 Drusilla K. Brown and Robert M. Stern, "Measurement and Modeling of the Economic Effect of Trade and Investment Barriers in Services," *Title Review of International Economics* 9:2 (2001): 262–86, discuss the role of economies of scale and trade barriers.

18 See Gianmarco I. P. Ottaviano and Diego Puga, "Agglomeration in the Global Economy: A Survey of the 'New Economic Geography'," *The World Economy* 21:6 (1998): 707–31; Gianmarco I. P. Ottaviano, Takatoshi Tabuchi, and Jacques-François Thisse, "Agglomeration and Trade Revisited," *International Economic Review* 43:2 (2002): 409–35.

19 Stefan B. Linder, *An Essay on Trade Transformation* (New York: Wiley, 1961).

20 Dirk Pilat, "The Economic Impact of Technology," *The OECD Observer* 213 (August–September 1998): 5–8.

21 Anthony J. Venables, "Shifts in Economic Geography and Their Causes," *Economic Review—Federal Reserve Bank of Kansas City* 91:4 (2006): 61–85, referring to work by R. Hausmann and D. Rodrik, "Economic Development as Self Discovery" (2003), Harvard Kennedy School working paper.

22 Two discussions of intra-industry trade are: Don P. Clark, "Determinants of Intra-industry Trade between the United States and Industrial Nations," *The International Trade Journal* 12:3 (Fall 1998): 345–62; H. Peter Gray, "Free International Economic Policy in a World of Schumpeter Goods," *The International Trade Journal* 12:3 (Fall 1998): 323–44.

23 Daniel Michaels, "Landing Rights," *Wall Street Journal* (April 30, 2002): A1+.

24 Lars Håkanson and Douglas Dow, "Markets and Networks in International Trade: On the Role of Distances in Globalization," *Management International Review* 52:6 (2012): 761–90.

25 Christopher A. Bartlett, "Global Wine Wars: New World Challenges Old," Harvard Business School Case 9-303-056 (July 21, 2003).

26 Terry Hall, "NZ Finds Pirated Varieties in Chile," *Financial Times* (January 21, 1999): 24.

27 Anthony J. Venables, "Shifts in Economic Geography and Their Causes."

28 Jeffrey A. Frankel and David Romer, "Does Trade Cause Growth?" *The American Economic Review* 89:3 (June 1999): 379–99.

29 J. L. Gallup and J. Sachs, "Geography and Economic Development," in B. Pleskovic and J. E. Stiglitz, eds., *Annual World Bank Conference on Development Economics* (Washington, DC: The World Bank, 1998).

30 See Raymond Vernon, "International Investment and International Trade in the Product Life Cycle," *Quarterly Journal of Economics* 80 (May 1996): 190–207; David Dollar, "Technological Innovation, Capital Mobility, and the Product Cycle in North–South Trade," *American Economic Review* 76:1 (1986): 177–90.

31 This is true according to various indicators. See, for example, International Bank for Reconstruction and Development, "Science and Technology," *The World Development Indicators* (Washington, DC: International Bank for Reconstruction and Development, 2000): 300.

32 Michael E. Porter, "The Competitive Advantage of Nations," *Harvard Business Review* 68:4 (1990): 73–93.

33 Kiyohiko Ito and Vladimir Pucik, "R&D Spending, Domestic Competition, and Export Performance of Japanese Manufacturing Firms," *Strategic Management Journal* 14 (1993): 61–75.

34 Jeremy Wiesen, "The U.S. Needs Its Own Industrial Policy," *Wall Street Journal* (September 13, 2010): A19.

35 Hubert Schmitz, "Reducing Complexity in the Industrial Policy Debate," *Development Policy Review* 25:4 (2007): 417–28.

36 Liviu-George, Ion Ignat, and Andre Teofil Postolachi, "Theoretical Controversies on Strategic Trade Policy," *Economy Transdisciplinarity Cognition*15:1 (2012): 300–07.

37 Sonny Nwankwo and Darlington Richards, "Institutional Paradigm and the Management of Transitions: A Sub-Saharan African Perspective," *International Journal of Social Economics* 31:1/2 (2004): 111.

38 Jeffrey Sachs, "Institutions Matter, but Not Everything," *Finance and Development* (June 2003): 38–41.

39 Nwankwo and Richards, "Institutional Paradigm and the Management of Transitions," 111.

40 Andrés Rodríguez-Clare, "Clusters and Comparative Advantage: Implications for Industrial Policy," *Journal of Development Economics* 82 (2007): 43–57.

41 Paul Krugman and Alasdair M. Smith, eds., *Empirical Studies of Strategic Trade Policies* (Chicago: University of Chicago Press, 1993); Howard Pack and Kamal Saggi, "Is There a Case for Industrial Policy?" *The World Bank Research Observer* 21:2 (2006): 267.

42 Paul M. Sherer, "Thailand Trips in Reach for New Exports," *Wall Street Journal* (August 27, 1996): A8.

43 Richard Brahm, "National Targeting Policies, High-Technology Industries, and Excessive Competition," *Strategic Management Journal* 16 (1995): 71–91.

44 Andrea E. Goldstein and Steven M. McGuire, "The Political Economy of Strategic Trade Policy and the Brazil-Canada Export Subsidies Saga," *The World Economy* 27:4 (2004): 541.

45 Theresa M. Greaney, "Strategic Trade and Competition Policies to Assist Distressed Industries," *The Canadian Journal of Economics* 32:3 (1999): 767.

46 Department of Economic and Social Affairs, Population Division, *World Population Prospects: The 2008 Revision Highlights* (New York: United Nations, 2009): xi.

47 "List of Countries by Foreign-Born Population," en.wikipedia.org/wiki/List_of_countries_by_foreign-born_population_in_2005 (accessed February 1, 2013).

48 Sevil Sönmez, Yorghos Apostopoulos, Diane Tran, and Shantyana Rentrope, "Human Rights and Health Disparities for Migrant Workers in the UAE," *Health and Human Rights* Vol 13, No 2 (2011).

49 Patrick Barta and Joel Millman, "The Great U-Turn," *Wall Street Journal* (June 6–7, 2009): A1.

50 "Flight to Nowhere," *The Economist* (March 2, 2013): 58–59.

51 *Trends in International Migration,* retrieved March 18, 2005, from oecd.org/dataoecd/7/49/24994376.

52 Miriam Jordan, "Migrants' Cash Keeps Flowing Home," *Wall Street Journal (Online)* [New York, N.Y] 23 Sep 2012: n/a.," *Wall Street Journal (Online)* [New York, N.Y] 23 Sep 2012: n/a.

53 Paul M. Vaaler, "Immigrant Remittances and the Venture Investment Environment of Developing Countries," *Journal of International Business Studies* 42:9 (December 2011): 1121–49.

54 Keith Head and John Ries, "Exporting and FDI as Alternative Strategies," *Oxford Review of Economic Policy* 20:3 (2004): 409–29.

55 Andrew E. Kramer, Russian Farm, Chinese Farmer," *New York Times* (September 11, 2012): B1+.

56 See Frank D. Bean et al., "Circular, Invisible, and Ambiguous Migrants: Components of Differences in Estimates of the Number of Unauthorized Mexican Migrants in the United States," *Demography* 38:3 (2001): 411–22; United Nations Conference on Trade and Development, *World Investment Report 2000: Cross-Border Mergers and Acquisitions and Development* (New York and Geneva: United Nations, 2000): 312.

57 Paul Windrum, Andreas Reinstaller, and Christopher Bull, "The Outsourcing Productivity Paradox: Total Outsourcing, Organisational Innovation, and Long Run Productivity Growth," *Journal of Evolutionary Economics* 19:2 (2009): 197–229.

58 June Kronholtz, "Immigrant Labor or Machines?" *Wall Street Journal* (December 19, 2006): A4.

59 "March of the Lettuce Bot," *The Economist* (December 1, 2012): monitor 5.

60 ***Sources include the following:*** *LUKOIL Annual Report* 2012, retrieved October 14, 2013 from http://www.lukoil.com/materials/doc/Annual_Report_2012/Lukoil_GO_2012_eng.pdf; "Alliances, Acquisitions Key to LUKOIL Ambitions," International Petroleum Finance (June 8, 2007): 1; "World; LUKOIL to Boost Investment in 2011," Interfax: Ukraine Business Daily [Kiev], December 13, 2010; "Iran Claims Denied as LUKOIL Looks East," NEFT Compass, September 16, 2010; Sabrina Tavernise and Peter S. Green, "Oil Concerns in Russia Branch Out," *New York Times* (April 2, 2002): W1; Bhushan Bahree, "Western Oil Flirts with Russia Firms, Insider Says," Wall Street Journal (April 29, 2002): A13; Reuters, "Mobius and Chevron Exec Nominated for LUKOIL Board," (January 17, 2002), www.highbeam.com/doc/1G1-81866356.html; Paul Starobin, "LUKOIL Is Lonesome," Business Week Online, retrieved October 2, 2009, http://www.businessweek.com/stories/2000-04-23/lukoil-is-lonesome-intl-edition; www.lukoil.com; Vidya Ram, "A More Refined Lukoil," Forbes.com, retrieved October 2, 2009, www.forbes.com/2008/06/24/erg-lukoil-refining-markets-equity-cx_vr_0624markets11.html; "Focus, the Russians Are Coming," Petroleum Economist (December 31, 2000); Andrew Jack and Arkady Ostrovsky, "LUKOIL in U.S. Petro Deal," Financial Times (November 4, 2000): 8; David Ignatius, "The Russians Are Pumping," Pittsburgh Post-Gazette (December 28, 2001): A-21; Tina Obut, "Perspective on Russia's Oil Sector," Oil & Gas Journal (February 1, 1999): 20; LUKOIL Annual Report, various years; "Event Brief of September 30: ConocoPhillips and LUKOil," CCBN Wire Service (September 30, 2004); "LUKOIL Leading Peers in Adding to Production outside Russia," Platts Oilgram News (April 13, 2004): 1; "Russia," retrieved October 14, 2013, www.cia.gov/library/publications/the-world-factbook/geos/rs.html.

61 Paul Markillie, "Manufacturing the Future," *The Economist* (special issue, the world in 2013, no date): 128.

62 "Print Me a Stradivarius," *The Economist* (February 10, 2011), retrieved February 17, 2011, from www.economist.com/node/18114327?story_id=18114327&fsrc=nwl; J. M. Pearce, C. Morris Blair, K. J. Laciak, R. Andrews, R. Nosrat, and I. Zelenika-Zovko, "3-D Printing of Open Source Appropriate Technologies for Self-Directed Sustainable Development," *Journal of Sustainable Development* 3:4 (December 2010): 17–29.

CHAPTER 6
Trade Protectionism

OBJECTIVES

After studying this chapter, you should be able to

1. Explain why governments try to enhance and restrict trade
2. Show the effects of pressure groups on trade policies
3. Compare the potential and actual effects of government intervention on the free flow of trade
4. Illustrate the major means by which trade is restricted and regulated
5. Demonstrate the business uncertainties and opportunities created by governmental trade policies
6. Discern how businesses may respond to import competition
7. Fathom how the growing complexity of products and trade regulations may affect the future

MyManagementLab®
Improve Your Grade!
When you see this icon, visit **www.mymanagementlab.com** for activities that are applied, personalized, and offer immediate feedback.

Charity begins at home.

—English proverb

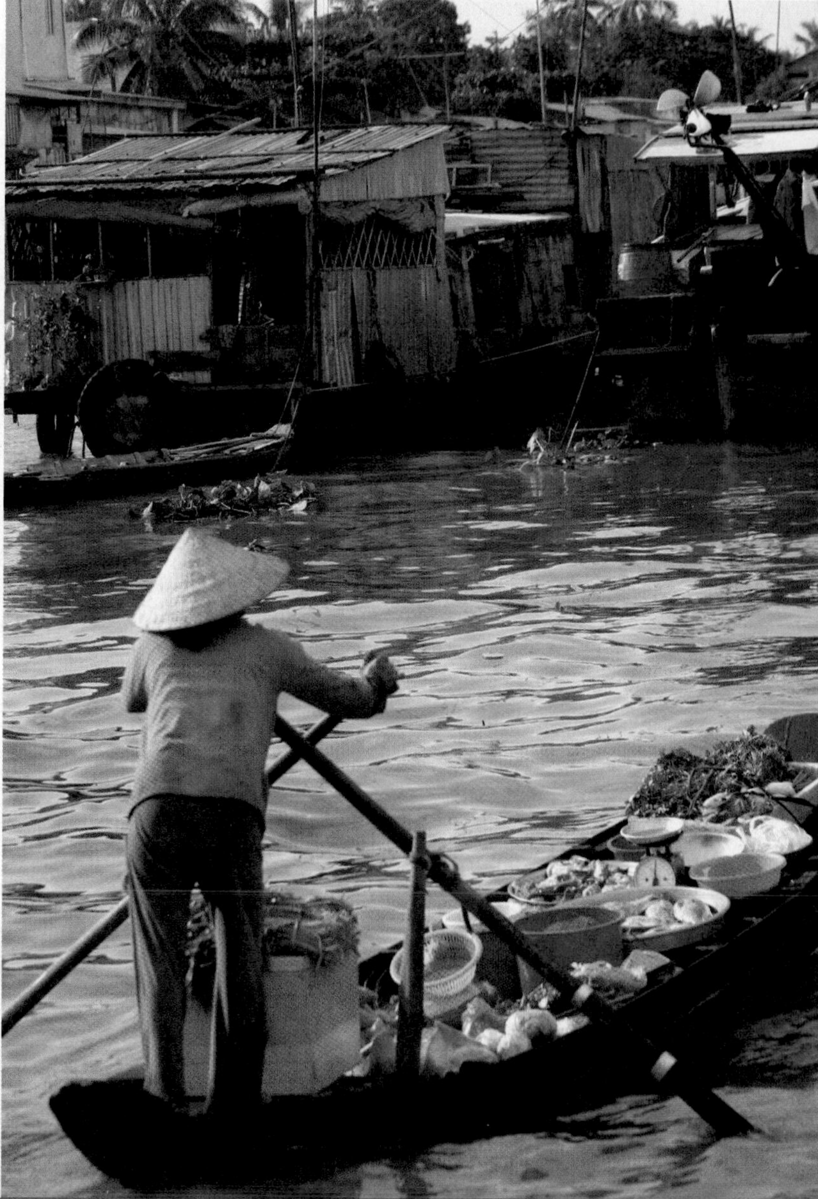

Source: © Arraial - Fotolia.com

CASE The U.S.–Vietnamese Catfish Dispute

Catfish are the sixth most consumed seafood or fish product in the United States and have long been part of the U.S. Deep South diet.[1] The U.S. industry is centered in poor areas of four states—Alabama, Arkansas, Louisiana, and Mississippi—which account for over 90 percent of U.S. production. At its height, it employed about 10,000 people. However, as imports (mainly from Vietnam) have increased and taken a larger share of the U.S. market (20 in 2005 versus 76 percent in 2011), U.S production has fallen. Meanwhile, the Vietnamese industry is also located in one of the poorer areas of the country, the Mekong Delta. (The opening photo shows small boats there.) It employs about 1 million people and accounts for about 2 percent of Vietnam's economy. The changing competitive situation has spurred a dispute between the two countries as the U.S. catfish industry has sought means to limit the importation of Vietnamese catfish. (Map 6.1 shows the production areas in the two countries.)

THE RISE OF AQUACULTURE

Humans have always depended on marine life for part of their food consumption, and during most of history this marine life grew faster than humans could consume it. However, the last half century has seen such an increase in marine catch (overfishing) that the numbers of many species are not being replenished. This increase has been due to a higher world population coupled with technology that enables fishing vessels to locate and land fish like never before. The boats must now go farther offshore, which increases fuel consumption at the same time that fuel prices are rising. One factor countering the overfishing has been the rise in aquaculture, or "fish farming." (The 2012 global revenue from commercial fishing and aquaculture combined was about $370 billion.) The catfish industry in both the United States and Vietnam has been part of the aquaculture revolution. In other words, rather than being caught in the wild in nets or hooked on fish line, catfish are grown in ponds and harvested when they grow to a certain size. As this change has taken place, the catfish have ceased to be traditional scavengers; instead, they are fed corn and soybean feed. Catfish growers in the United States, in turn, have publicized the feeding change to promote sales to consumers who do not want to eat scavenger fish.

THE VIETNAMESE ADVANTAGE

The U.S. catfish industry has been developed largely by converting unproductive cotton lands to fishponds. Much of that land is so high in clay content that, although it will no longer grow much cotton, it will hold pumped-in water very well. Meanwhile, the Vietnamese production has some competitive advantages that enable it to export. To begin with, the winterless Vietnamese climate permits the fish to grow faster. One Vietnamese catfish species, the *tra*, can go to the surface to breathe air; thus, fish can be grown in greater density. Further, U.S. governmental regulations limit the discharge of fishpond waters into rivers, whereas Vietnam has no restrictions. This difference also allows for a greater density of production in Vietnam. Finally, labor rates are lower in Vietnam than in the United States, an important factor in the cost of filleting and freezing the fish.

THE U.S. INDUSTRY FIGHTS BACK

Changing Names Alarmed by market losses, U.S. catfish growers' first defense was to convince their congressional representatives to push successfully in 2002 to disallow Vietnamese imports to be called "catfish." Thus, Shakespeare's "A rose by any other name would smell as sweet" was deemed not to be analogous for catfish. (Approximately 3,000 fish species fall into the overall family of catfish found mainly in freshwater places all over the world.) Because Vietnamese fish were of a different variety than those farmed in the United States, the Vietnamese varieties had to be imported as tra, basa, or pangasius. (The Maine lobster industry and European Union sardine fisheries were unsuccessful, respectively, in having Chilean langostino lobsters called crabs and Peruvian sardines called pilchards.) The U.S. producers reasoned that consumers, mainly in the Deep South, were not likely to buy some strange-sounding and unknown fish in lieu of the catfish that was part of their regular diet. Although the name change may have slowed the Vietnamese inroad, it did not prevent it. One of the problems the U.S. industry encountered was that few U.S. locales have truth-in-menu laws. Thus, the names for tra, basa, and pangasius were changed on menus to be "catfish," a more expensive grouper, or just plain "fish." Clearly, the U.S. catfish producers needed a different means to stifle the imports.

In the meantime, the U.S. industry was also facing a problem of diminished profit because of increased costs. In essence, the price of corn and soybean feed was rising faster than costs could be pushed onto consumers. The rising costs were due to a combination of harvest shortfalls, increased grain demands in Asia, and the use of corn and soybeans to produce ethanol. In order to raise prices and increase demand, an association representing catfish growers, the

MAP 6.1 Areas of Major U.S. and Vietnam Catfish Production

The catfish production for both the United States and Vietnam are near deltas of major rivers, the Mississippi and the Mekong respectively. Both areas have a great deal of poverty.

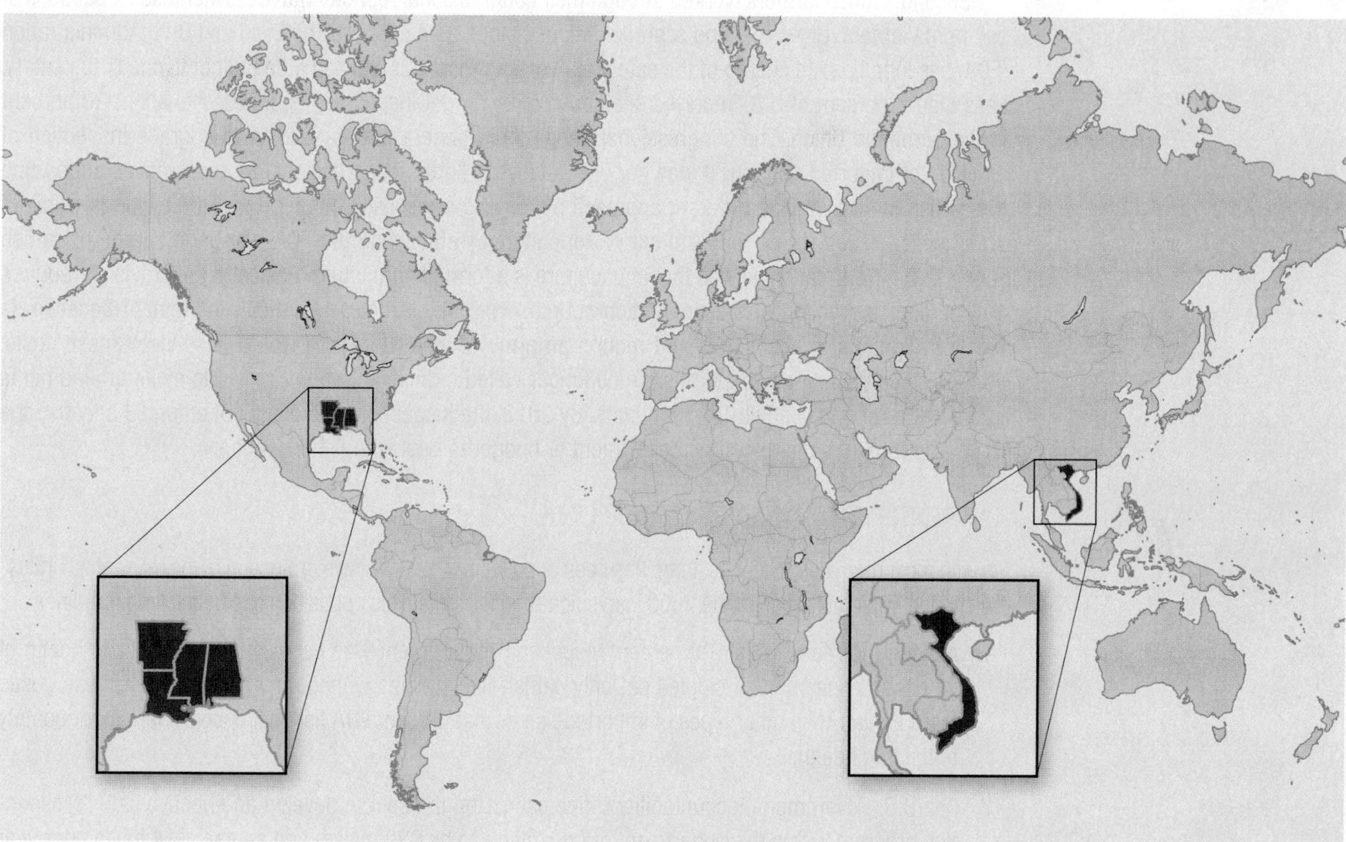

Catfish Institute, decided to change the fish's name. Basically, the name "catfish" has had a negative connotation for many people. (The catfish has been referred to in many ways over the years, including some ways that would be inappropriate in this textbook.) The Institute noted how name changing had recently helped sales of other previously unpopular fish, such as the slimehead becoming "orange roughy" and the Patagonian toothfish "Chilean sea bass." After market testing various names, the Institute has decided on "delacata" as a name for premium catfish. At this writing, it is too early to tell if the change-of-name strategy will work or not.

Unfair Competition: Dumping Let's get back to the import question. Because the U.S. industry was losing jobs and sales, it petitioned for increased taxes on the imported Vietnamese fish, claiming that they were being sold below the cost of production (dumping). Given that Vietnam is a command economy, it was difficult to establish what the true production costs were; however, these were estimated on the basis of Bangladesh production costs, and antidumping taxes (tariffs) of 64 percent were placed on the importation of the fish. In 2013 the industry succeeded in having estimates based on higher Indonesian costs.

Health Arguments Despite the higher prices, the Vietnamese fish have kept increasing their share of the U.S. market. Then, in 2007, the U.S. catfish industry seemed to have found salvation when about 39,000 U.S. dogs and cats were sickened or killed after consuming imported Chinese pet food. This led to an alert and negative attitude toward imported food products in general, especially seafood originating anywhere in Asia. The U.S. catfish farmers responded quickly with several initiatives. First, they publicly implied that imported fish may be contaminated, such as when the Catfish Institute put out publicity saying, "U.S. farm-raised catfish: Safety you can trust." The Institute has pushed for and gotten several states to require country-of-origin labeling on food and menus by advocating that consumers have the right to know whether the fish and seafood they buy could be contaminated. However, studies on changes in consumer purchases indicate that the labeling had no effect on demand.

Second, catfish farmers worked through their congressional representatives to increase inspections of fish from Vietnam. Given the food scare, emotions helped gain support. The Food and Drug Administration (FDA) has long been in charge of the safety of overseas food, but has had little budget to check the safety. Less than 2 percent of U.S. imported seafood shipments get inspected, as opposed to about 20 percent in the European Union. The congressional debates did generate a suggestion to upgrade inspection of all types of imported fish, but it was not well received. So the congressional representatives supporting the catfish industry took a different approach by burying a provision deep in the $300 billion farm bill of 2008, which called for the Department of Agriculture—rather than the FDA—to be in charge of catfish safety. Supporters' rationale was that aquaculture is a form of agriculture. Basically, the provision requires 100 percent inspection at the production source, which is particularly difficult in Vietnam because its highly fragmented production would require an army of inspectors that would raise Vietnamese costs. Further, since Vietnamese imports were no longer called catfish, enforcement had to await amendments in the bill to refer to "catfish-like" products. By 2012, the inspections were still not enforced because the Department of Agriculture had no department or budget to deal with fish inspections.

OPPOSITION AND THE FUTURE

As with most regulatory changes, there has been opposition to the effective protection of the U.S. catfish industry and the implementation of the 2008 inspection requirements. This opposition has been along four lines:

1. Although the farm bill's 100 percent inspection requirement was ostensibly to protect the health of American consumers, it singled out only catfish-like species without any evidence that these posed more danger than other types of imported fish or that present FDA fish inspections were inadequately protecting health.
2. The U.S. Government Accountability Office estimated the cost to develop an effective catfish inspection program within the Department of Agriculture to be $30 million and another $14 million per year to run it. Given budget deficit worries, there was little support to spend this money.
3. Vietnam is a fast growing economy with a large population. U.S. exports to Vietnam have been rising steeply. For instance, farm exports went from $215 million in 2006 to $1.3 billion in 2010. Additional U.S. catfish import restrictions could jeopardize U.S export sales to Vietnam because it has threatened to take retaliatory action, such as by buying less U.S. beef.
4. Finally, economic conflicts between the United States and Vietnam could deteriorate political relations between the two. Further, Vietnam said it would bring charges against the United States in the World Trade Organization (WTO), and there was a near-consensus that it would win. (Chapter 7 discusses the WTO's dispute mechanisms.) This would likely not only negate the protective catfish measures, but also weaken U.S. efforts to persuade other countries to reduce their trade barriers.

Based on these arguments, the United States Senate voted in 2012 to repeal the inspection requirements designed to burden Vietnamese producers with the high compliance costs.

An old adage says that if you give a man a fish, he will have food for a day. If you teach him to fish, he will have food for a lifetime. However, the U.S.–Vietnamese catfish controversy illustrates that knowing how to fish is insufficient, especially in international competition. One also needs to know how to influence and maneuver through a maze of government regulations that affect competition. ■

CRN
Case Review Note

QUESTIONS

✪6-1. List the advantages and disadvantages for the United States to protect its catfish industry.

✪6-2. As you read through the chapter, list the protective measures (instruments) the United States has *not* used to protect its catfish industry. Briefly explain why each would or would not be successful.

INTRODUCTION

At some point, you may work for or own stock in a company whose performance, or even survival, depends on governmental trade policies. These policies may affect the ability of foreign producers to compete in your home market. They may limit or enhance your company's ability to sell abroad or acquire needed foreign supplies. Collectively, governmental restrictions and support to influence international trade competitiveness are known as **protectionism**.

All countries seek to influence trade, and each has economic, social, and political objectives:

- Conflicting objectives
- Interest groups

The restrictions illustrated in the opening case are common; all countries regulate the flow of goods and services across their borders. Figure 6.1 illustrates the pressures on governments to regulate trade and the subsequent effect of regulation on business competitiveness. This chapter reviews the economic and noneconomic rationales for trade protectionism and explains the major forms of trade controls and their effects on companies' operating decisions.

CONFLICTING RESULTS OF TRADE POLICIES

CONCEPT CHECK

As we demonstrate in Chapter 5, specialization (coupled with trade) can increase a country's output of certain products; we also observe that the theories of both absolute and comparative advantage support the contention that free trade encourages specialization and more efficient output. Here we point out that protectionist policies though sometimes warranted, can impede the process that revolves around specialization.

Despite free-trade benefits, governments intervene in trade to attain economic, social, or political objectives. Officials apply trade policies that they reason will have the best chance to benefit their nation and its citizens—and, in some cases, their personal political longevity. Determining whether and how to influence trade is complicated by uncertain and conflicting policy outcomes. For example, catfish importing was restricted to help workers in depressed areas, but the restrictions forced consumers in those same areas to pay higher prices. In general, governments would also like to help their struggling companies and industries without penalizing those that are doing well. This goal is often impossible, however, especially if other countries retaliate by limiting their own imports.

THE ROLE OF STAKEHOLDERS

Proposals on trade regulations often spark fierce debate among people and groups that believe they will be affected—the so-called *stakeholders.* Of course, those most directly affected are most apt to speak out, such as the U.S. stakeholders (workers, owners, suppliers,

FIGURE 6.1 Physical and Social Factors Affecting the Flow of Goods and Service

In response to a variety of physical and social factors (i.e., political/legal, behavioral, economic, and geographic), governments enact measures designed to either enhance or restrict international trade flows. These measures invariably affect the competitive environment in which companies operate, either enhancing or hindering their capacity to compete on an international scale. To an extent, of course, the converse is also true: Companies influence government trade policies that affect their activities.

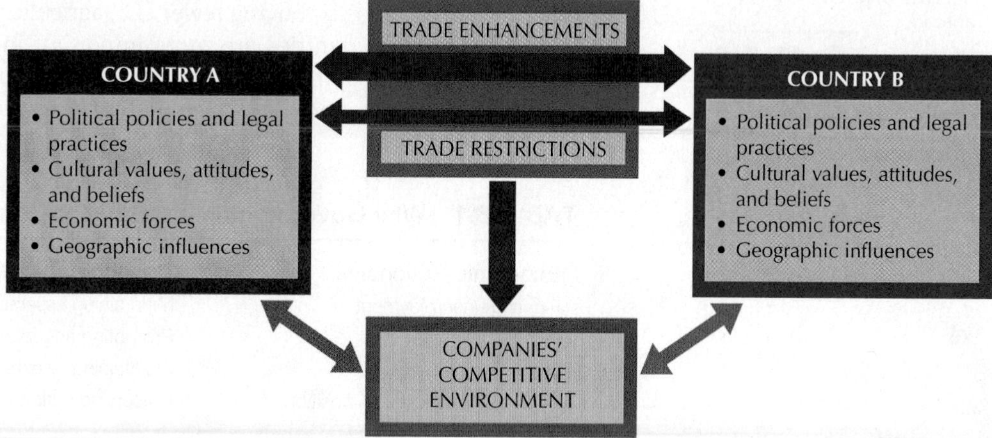

and local politicians) whose livelihoods depend on growing catfish. Displaced workers see themselves as being unemployed for the long term or forced to take new jobs in new industries, perhaps even in new towns at lower wages. People threatened in this way tend to object often and loudly.

The Role of Consumers In contrast, consumers (who are also stakeholders) typically buy the best product they can find for the price, often without knowing or caring about its origin. They often don't realize how much retail prices rise in aggregate because of import restrictions. Nor do they take much notice, since consumer costs are typically spread out among many people over time and entail a small price increase for individual purchases. For example, even if U.S. consumers knew how import restrictions on peanuts and sugar add to the domestic price of peanut butter and confectionary products, it likely would not spur them enough to band together and push government leaders to rectify the situation.

ECONOMIC RATIONALES FOR GOVERNMENTAL INTERVENTION

Governmental trade intervention may be classified as either economic or noneconomic, as shown in Table 6.1. Let's begin by analyzing some leading *economic rationales.*

FIGHTING UNEMPLOYMENT

The unemployed can form an effective pressure group for import restrictions.

There's probably no more effective pressure group than the unemployed; no other group has more time and incentive to protest publicly and contact government representatives. Workers displaced because of imports are often the least able to find alternative work, such as the fairly unskilled catfish workers in depressed regions. When they do, they generally earn less than before.[2] Moreover, they often need to spend their unemployment benefits to survive in the short term, and they put off retraining because they hope to be recalled to their old jobs. When they do seek retraining, many workers, especially older ones, lack the educational background needed to gain required skills, or they train for jobs that do not materialize.

Import restrictions to create domestic employment

- May lead to retaliation by other countries.
- Are less likely retaliated against effectively by small economies.
- Are less likely to be met with retaliation if implemented by small economies.
- May decrease export jobs because of price increases for components.
- May decrease export jobs because of lower incomes abroad.

What's Wrong with Full Employment as an Economic Objective? Although every country desires full employment, using trade policy to achieve it is problematic. From a practical standpoint, gaining jobs by limiting imports may not fully work as expected. Even if successful, the potentially high costs must be borne by someone.

The Prospect of Retaliation One difficulty with restricting imports to create jobs is that other countries, whose production may typically drop as a result, normally retaliate with their own restrictions. Our opening case addressed the concern that Vietnam would respond to U.S. catfish import restrictions by buying fewer U.S. agricultural products.

However, large trading countries are more important in the retaliation process. If the United States were to limit clothing imports in general, China would have more power to retaliate than, say, Mauritius. And the United States is less apt to retaliate against Mauritian

TABLE 6.1 Why Governments Intervene in Trade

Economic Rationales	Noneconomic Rationales
Fighting unemployment	Maintaining essential industries
Protecting infant industries	Promoting acceptable practices abroad
Promoting industrialization	Maintaining or extending spheres of influence
Improving comparative position	Preserving national culture

than Chinese trade restrictions because of the lesser effect on the U.S. economy. Even if no country retaliates, the restricting country may gain jobs in one sector only to lose them elsewhere. Why? Consider three factors:

1. Fewer imports of a product mean fewer import-handling jobs, such as those in the container-shipping industry.
2. Given the global complexity of production, import restrictions on one industry will likely cause lower sales in other industries because they must incur higher costs for inputs and components.[3] For example, U.S. import restrictions on steel raise automobile and farm equipment manufacturing costs.
3. Imports stimulate exports, though less directly, by increasing foreign income and foreign-exchange earnings, which foreign consumers then spend partially on new imports. Thus, restricting earnings abroad has some negative effect on domestic earnings and employment.

Possible costs of import restrictions include higher prices and higher taxes. Such costs should be compared with those of unemployment.

Analyzing Trade-Offs In deciding whether to restrict imports to create jobs, governments must face the difficult task of comparing the costs of limiting imports with the costs of unemployment from freer trade. It is hard to put a price on the distress suffered by people who lose their jobs due to import competition. It is also difficult for working people to understand that they may be better off financially because of lower prices even if they must pay higher taxes to support unemployment or welfare benefits for those who do lose their jobs.

In summary, persistent unemployment pushes many groups to call for protectionism. However, evidence suggests that efforts to reduce unemployment through import restrictions are usually ineffective. Unemployment in and of itself is better dealt with through fiscal and monetary policies.

PROTECTING "INFANT INDUSTRIES"

The infant-industry argument says that production becomes more competitive over time because of

- Increased economies of scale.
- Greater worker efficiency.

One of the oldest arguments for protectionism, the **infant-industry argument**, holds that a government should shield an emerging industry from foreign competition by guaranteeing it a large share of the domestic market until it can compete on its own. Many developing countries use this argument to justify their protectionist policies, especially if entry barriers are high and foreign competition is formidable.

Underlying Assumptions The infant-industry argument presumes that the initial operating costs for an industry in a given country may be so high as to make its output noncompetitive in world markets. Eventual competitiveness is the result of the efficiency gains that take time. Therefore, the industry's government needs to protect it long enough for its fledgling companies to gain economies of scale and their employees to translate experience into higher productivity, enabling efficient production and international competitiveness. The government can then recoup the costs of trade protection through benefits like higher domestic employment, lower social costs, and higher tax revenues.

Risks in Designating Industries Although it's reasonable to expect production costs to decrease over time, they may never fall enough to create internationally competitive products. This risk poses two problems.

CONCEPT CHECK

In Chapter 5 in the Point/Counterpoint section, we discuss the problems for a government to determine what industries to support when enacting a strategic trade policy and the difficulty of removing the support if the industries do not become globally competitive.

Determining Probability of Success First, governments must identify those industries that have a high probability of success. Some industries grow to be competitive because of governmental protection; automobile production in Brazil is a good example. However, in many other cases, such as automobile production in Malaysia, the protected industries remain inefficient even after years of government aid.

If infant-industry protection fails to reduce costs enough to compete against imports, chances are its owners, workers, and suppliers will constitute a formidable pressure group that may prevent the importation of competing lower-priced products. Also, the security of government protection against import competition may deter managers from adopting the innovations needed to compete globally and to provide their own consumers with high-quality products at a low price.

Who Should Bear the Cost? Second, even if policymakers can determine those infant industries likely to succeed, it does not necessarily follow that those companies therein should receive government assistance. Some segment of the economy must incur the higher cost when local production is still inefficient, such as consumers paying higher prices for the protected products or taxpayers paying for subsidies. Further, when taxes go to pay subsidies, governments can spend less elsewhere, such as on education and infrastructure, to improve overall competitiveness. There are many examples of entrepreneurs who endured early losses to achieve future benefits, without public help from consumers or taxpayers.

DEVELOPING AN INDUSTRIAL BASE

Countries seek protection to promote industrialization because that type of production

- Brings faster growth than agriculture.
- Brings in investment funds.
- Diversifies the economy.
- Brings more income than primary products do.
- Reduces imports and promotes exports.
- Helps the nation-building process.

Countries with a large manufacturing base generally have higher per capita GDPs than those that do not. Some, such as the United States and Japan, developed an industrial base while largely restricting imports. Many developing countries try to emulate this strategy, using trade protection to spur local industrialization. Specifically, they operate under the following set of assumptions:

1. Surplus workers can increase manufacturing output more easily than agricultural output.
2. Inflows of foreign investment in the industrial sector promote sustainable growth.
3. Prices and sales of agricultural products and raw materials fluctuate widely, which is a detriment to economies that depend heavily on just one or a few commodities.
4. Markets for industrial products grow faster than markets for commodities.
5. Industrial growth reduces imports and/or promotes exports.
6. Industrial activity helps the nation-building process.

In the sections that follow, we review each of these assumptions in some detail.

Surplus Workers Disguised unemployment is high in many developing countries' rural areas, where people are effectively contributing little, if anything, to the agricultural output. Consequently, many can move into the industrial sector without significantly reducing agricultural output. Like the infant-industry argument, the **industrialization argument** presumes that the unregulated importation of lower-priced manufactures prevents the development of a domestic industry. Although proponents of this argument explain they may be developing an inefficient industrial sector that does not become globally competitive, they nevertheless assert that there will be economic growth. In other words, growth occurs because the underemployed gain jobs.[4]

When a country shifts from agriculture to industry,

- Demands on social and political services in cities may increase.
- Output increases if the marginal productivity of agricultural workers is very low.
- Development possibilities in the agricultural sector may be overlooked.

Shifting people out of agriculture, however, can create at least two problems:

1. In rural areas, the underemployed may lose the safety net of their extended families, while many migrating to urban areas cannot find enough suitable jobs, housing, and social services. For example, although millions of Chinese have moved to cities to find jobs, many have not prospered through the move.[5]
2. Improved agriculture practices may be a better means of achieving economic success than a drastic shift to industry. Many developed countries continue to profit from exports of agricultural products and maintain high per capita income with a mix of industry and efficient agricultural production.

Investment Inflows Import restrictions, applied to spur industrialization, also may increase FDI, which provides capital, technology, and jobs. Barred from exporting to an attractive

If import restrictions keep out foreign-made goods, foreign companies may invest to produce in the restricted area.

foreign market, foreign companies may transfer manufacturing to that country to avoid the loss of a lucrative or potential market.

Diversification Export prices of many primary products, such as oil and coffee, fluctuate markedly. Price variations due to uncontrollable factors—such as weather affecting supply or business cycles abroad affecting demand—can wreak havoc on economies that depend on the export of primary products. This is especially true for many developing countries that must rely on only one or a few commodities. Frequently, they are caught in a feast-or-famine cycle, as it were: able to afford foreign luxuries one year but unable to find the funds for replacement parts for essential equipment the next. Contrary to expectations, a greater dependence on manufacturing does not guarantee diversification of export earnings. The population of many developing economies is small; a move to manufacturing may shift dependence from one or two agricultural commodities to one or two manufactured products, which face competitive risks and potential obsolescence.

Terms of trade for emerging economies may deteriorate because

- Demand for primary products grows more slowly.
- Production cost savings for primary products will be passed on to consumers.

Growth in Manufactured Goods The quantity of imports that a given quantity of a country's exports can buy—say, how many bananas Country A must sell to Country B to purchase one refrigerator from Country B—is referred to as **terms of trade**. Historically, the prices of raw materials and agricultural commodities have not risen as fast as those of finished products, although they have risen faster during short periods.[6] Over time, therefore, it takes more low-priced primary products to buy the same amount of high-priced manufactured goods.

In addition, the quantity of primary products demanded does not rise as rapidly as manufactured products and services, due partly to people spending a lower percentage of income on food as their incomes rise and partly to raw-material-saving technologies. Further, because commodities are hard to differentiate, producers must compete on price, whereas the prices of manufactured products can stay high because competition is based more on differentiation.

Industrialization emphasizes either

- Products to sell domestically or
- Products to export.

Import Substitution and Export-Led Development Traditionally, developing countries promoted industrialization by restricting imports in order to boost local production and consumption of products they would otherwise import. However, if the protected industries do not become efficient—an all-too-frequent outcome—local consumers may have to support them by paying higher prices or taxes. In contrast, some countries, such as Taiwan and South Korea, have achieved rapid economic growth by promoting the development of industries with export potential, an approach known as **export-led development**. In reality, it's not easy to distinguish between import substitution and export-led development. Industrialization may result initially in import substitution, yet export development of the same products may be feasible later.

CONCEPT CHECK

In the opening case of Chapter 5, we explain import substitution and demonstrate why this policy failed to achieve certain goals of Costa Rica's long-term trade strategy.

Nation Building There may be a strong relationship between industrialization and aspects of the nation-building process. Industrialization helps countries build infrastructure, advance rural development, and boost workforce skills. Ecuador and Vietnam maintain that industrialization has helped them move from feudal economies suffering chronic food shortages to nations with improved food security and budding export competitiveness.[7]

ECONOMIC RELATIONSHIPS WITH OTHER COUNTRIES

Every nation monitors its absolute economic welfare, compares its performance to that of other countries, and enacts practices aimed at improving its relative position. Among these many practices, four stand out: making balance-of-trade adjustments, gaining comparable access to foreign markets, using restrictions as a bargaining tool, and controlling prices.

Balance-of-Trade Adjustments A trade deficit creates problems for nations with low foreign exchange reserves—the funds that help finance the purchase of priority foreign goods

CONCEPT CHECK

In Chapter 4, we explain why a trade deficit usually indicates that a country's currency—along with its debt—is piling up around the world; we go on to explain why a country afflicted with a burgeoning trade deficit needs to reconsider key areas of its economic policy.

and maintain the trustworthiness of a currency. So if balance-of-trade difficulties arise and persist, a government may act to reduce imports or encourage exports to balance its trade account. Two options that can affect its competitive position broadly are:

1. Depreciating or devaluing its currency, which makes basically all of its products cheaper in relation to foreign products
2. Relying on fiscal and monetary policy to bring about lower price increases in general than those in other countries

Both of these options take time. Furthermore, they aren't selective; for instance, they make both foreign essentials and foreign luxury products more expensive. Thus, a country may use protection more effectively so as to affect only certain products. Doing so is really a stop-gap measure that gives the country time to address its fundamental economic situation—the perceived quality, characteristics, and prices of its products—that is causing its residents to buy more abroad than they are selling.

Domestic producers may be disadvantaged if their access to foreign markets is less than foreign producers' access to their market.

Comparable Access or "Fairness" Companies and industries often use the **comparable access argument**, which holds that they are entitled to the same access to foreign markets as foreign industries and companies have to theirs. Economic theory supports this idea for industries, such as semiconductors and chemicals, with substantial production cost decreases through economies of scale. Companies that lack equal access to a competitor's market will struggle to gain enough sales to be cost-competitive.[8]

The argument for comparable access is also presented as one of fairness. For instance, the U.S. government permits foreign financial service firms to operate in the United States, but only if their home governments allow U.S. financial service firms equivalent market access. There are, however, at least two practical reasons for rejecting the idea of fairness:

1. Tit-for-tat market access can lead to restrictions that may deny one's own consumers lower prices.
2. Governments would find it impractical to negotiate and monitor separate agreements for each of the many thousands of different products and services that might be traded.

Countries levy trade restrictions to coerce other countries to change their policies.

Restrictions as a Bargaining Tool The threat or imposition of import restrictions may be a retaliatory measure for persuading other countries to lower their import barriers. The danger is that each country then escalates its restrictions, creating, in effect, a trade war that has a negative impact on all their economies. To use restrictions successfully as a bargaining tool, you need to be very careful in targeting the products you threaten to restrict. In particular, you need to consider two criteria:

- *Believability:* Either you have access to alternative sources for the product or your consumers are willing to do without it. The EU successfully retaliated against U.S. import restrictions by threatening to impose trade restrictions on U.S.-grown soybeans when Brazil had a surplus.
- *Importance:* Exports of the product you're restricting are significant to certain parties in the producer country—parties influential enough to prompt changes in their own country's trade policy. This consideration was emphasized after the United States placed restrictions on the importation of steel. The EU threatened to restrict the importation of apples from the state of Washington and oranges from Florida. Given the importance of these two states in a close presidential election, the United States soon removed the steel import restrictions.

Export restrictions may

- Keep up world prices.
- Require more controls to prevent smuggling.
- Lead to substitution.
- Keep domestic prices down by increasing domestic supply.
- Give producers less incentive to increase output.
- Shift foreign production and sales.

Price-Control Objectives Countries sometimes withhold goods from international markets in an effort to raise prices abroad. This is most feasible when a few countries hold near-monopoly control of certain resources and can limit supply so consumers must pay a higher price. However, this policy often encourages smuggling (such as emeralds and diamonds), the development of technology (such as synthetic rubber in place of natural rubber), or different means to produce the same product (such as caviar from farm-grown rather than wild sturgeons).[9] Export controls are especially ineffective for digital products because they are so easily copied abroad. In addition, if prices are too high or supplies too limited, people will seek substitutes, such as ethanol for petroleum.

A country may also limit exports of a product that is in short supply worldwide to favor domestic consumers. Typically, a greater supply drops local prices beneath those in the intentionally undersupplied world market. Russia and Argentina have pursued this strategy by limiting exports of food products; India has limited cotton exports to increase supplies for its textile industry, and the United States is considering export limitations on natural gas to assist its chemical industry as new production comes on line.[10] Favoring domestic consumers usually disfavors domestic producers of the product, so they have less incentive to maintain production when prices are low.

There is also the fear that foreign producers will price their exports so artificially low that they will drive producers out of business in the importing country. If they succeed, there are two potential adverse consequences for the importing economy:

1. The foreign producers may be shifting their countries' unemployment abroad, but their own taxpayers are subsidizing the purchases by consumers abroad.
2. If there are high entry barriers, surviving foreign producers can charge exorbitant prices once their competitors go out of business. However, competition among producers from different countries usually limits anyone's ability to charge exorbitant prices. Low import prices have eliminated most U.S. production of consumer electronics; still, the U.S. has some of the lowest prices in the world for consumer electronics because so many companies make them in so many countries.

Import restrictions may
- Prevent dumping from being used to put domestic producers out of business.
- Get foreign producers to lower their prices.

Dumping Companies sometimes export below cost or below their home-country price—a practice called **dumping**. Most countries restrict imports of dumped products, but enforcement usually occurs only if the imported product disrupts domestic production. If there is no domestic production, then host-country consumers get the benefit of lower prices. Companies may dump products to introduce them and build a market abroad—essentially, a low price encourages consumers to sample the foreign brand—after which they can charge a high enough price to make a profit. However, the major motive from a national standpoint is to increase domestic employment. Recall in our opening case that the United States placed antidumping taxes on Vietnamese catfish.

Companies can afford to dump products if they can charge high prices in their home market or if their home-country government subsidizes them. Ironically, exporting-country consumers or taxpayers seldom realize that paying high prices or taxes can result in lower prices for foreign consumers. An industry that believes it's competing against dumped products may appeal to its government to restrict the imports. U.S. companies in such industries as carbon steel pipes, magnesium metal, and honey have done so recently. However, determining a foreign company's cost or domestic price is difficult because of limited access to the foreign producers' accounting records, fluctuations in exchange rates, and the passage of products through layers of distribution before reaching the end consumer. The result is that governments allegedly restrict imports arbitrarily through antidumping provisions of their trade legislation and are slow to dispose of the restrictions if pricing situations change. Companies caught by antidumping restrictions often lose the export market they labored to build.

Optimum-Tariff Theory The **optimum-tariff theory** states that a foreign producer will lower its prices if the importing country places a tax on its products. If this occurs, benefits shift to the importing country because the producer lowers its profits on the export sales.

Let's examine a hypothetical situation. Assume an exporter has costs of $500 per unit and is selling abroad for $700 per unit. With the imposition of a 10 percent tax on the imported price, the exporter may choose to lower its price to $636.36 per unit, which, with a 10 percent tax of $63.64, would keep the price at $700 in the foreign market. The exporter may feel that a price higher than $700 would result in lost sales and that a profit of $136.36 per unit instead of the previous $200 is better than no profit at all. Consequently, an amount of $63.64 per unit has shifted to the importing country.

As long as the foreign producer lowers its price by any amount, some shift in revenue goes to the importing country and the tariff is deemed an optimum one. There are many examples of products whose prices did not rise as much as the amount of the imposed tariff; however, it is difficult to predict when, where, and which exporters will voluntarily reduce their profit margins. In fact, a criticism of the optimum tariff is that developing country exporters reduce payment to their workers rather than absorbing the full impact through a lower profit margin, thus sometimes causing severe hardships.[11]

NONECONOMIC RATIONALES FOR GOVERNMENT INTERVENTION

Although noneconomic arguments are used to influence trade, many of these also have economic undertones and consequences. However, let's look at the major noneconomic rationales:

- Maintaining essential industries (especially defense)
- Promoting acceptable practices abroad
- Maintaining or extending spheres of influence
- Preserving national culture

MAINTAINING ESSENTIAL INDUSTRIES

Governments apply trade restrictions to protect essential domestic industries during peacetime so the country is not dependent on foreign supplies during war. (In some cases, they also prevent foreign companies from acquiring companies needed for national security; the United States does this through the Committee on Foreign Investment in the United States [CFIUS].) This is called the **essential-industry argument**. An example is the United States subsidizing the domestic production of silicon so domestic computer-chip makers won't need to depend on foreign suppliers. Because of nationalism, this argument has much appeal in rallying support for import barriers. However, in times of real (or perceived) crisis or military emergency, almost any product could be deemed essential.

In protecting essential industries, countries must

- Determine which ones are essential.
- Consider costs and alternatives.
- Consider political and economic consequences.

Because of the high cost of protecting an inefficient industry or a higher-cost domestic substitute, the essential-industry argument should not be (but frequently is) accepted without a careful evaluation of costs, real needs, and alternatives. It is difficult to remove protection, once given, because the protected companies and their employees support politicians who support their continued protection—even when the rationale for the subsidies has long since disappeared. This is why the United States continued to subsidize its mohair producers more than 20 years after mohair was deemed no longer essential for military uniforms.[12]

In addition, governments buy and stockpile supplies of essential raw materials that might be in future short supply. For example, the U.S. military needs weapons, jet engines, high-powered magnets, and other gear that require imported rare-earth elements, which it stockpiles because the production is primarily controlled by China.[13]

PROMOTING ACCEPTABLE PRACTICES ABROAD

Governments use national defense arguments to prevent the export, even to friendly countries, of strategic goods that might fall into the hands of potential enemies. They also limit

FIGURE 6.2

While using trade policies to influence acceptable political practices abroad, governments are also concerned about implications on their own countries' businesses.

Source: Joel -Mishon-/CartoonStock

trade to promote changes in a foreign country's policies or capabilities. The rationale is to weaken the foreign country's economy by decreasing its earnings from foreign sales or limiting its access to needed products so that it amends the externally unpopular policies. (Figure 6.2 shows this humorously.) A recent example is the effort to persuade Iran to abandon its nuclear capability program. Such constraints may be valid if the exporting country assumes there will be no retaliation that hurts itself even more than it hurts the trading partner. Even then, the latter may find alternative markets and supply sources. Or, it may develop a production capability of its own. Our ending case discusses some of the measures taken by the Singapore government to foster a business-friendly environment for foreign investors.

Trade controls are used to pressure foreign governments to alter their stances on a variety of other issues ranging from human rights to environmental protection to production of goods the importing country finds dangerous or immoral. Of course, import limitations on unacceptable products are obvious, but these limitations are often combined with other economic pressures—limiting other trade as well, restricting access to bank accounts, cutting off foreign aid, or giving it as an incentive. In effect, efforts to keep out unwanted products, such as narcotics, are often aimed at curtailing supply rather than demand for them. For instance, many countries restrict importation of ivory so that other (mainly African) countries will limit the supply of ivory by protecting elephants.[14] However, the adjacent photos show that, although restrictions may have slowed elephant slaughter, poaching still continues (about 25,000 elephants killed in 2011) because of high demand for ivory.

Economic sanctions may target specific companies because of their trading activities. In the case of sanctions on Iran, the United States not only penalizes U.S. companies that do business with Iran, but it also bars non-U.S. companies from the U.S. marketplace if they do business there.[15]

Source: David Keith Jones/Alamy

The photo of the slaughtered elephant is evidence that economic sanctions are insufficient to stop poaching as long as there is demand for ivory ornaments, such as those shown here.
Source: Thinkstock

Point — Should Governments Impose Trade Sanctions?

Point **Yes** Let's face it: We're now living in a global society where actions in one country can spill over and affect people all over the world. For instance, the development of a nuclear arsenal in one nation can escalate the damage that terrorists can do elsewhere. The failure of a country to protect endangered species can have long-term effects on the whole world's environment. We simply can't sit back and let things happen elsewhere that will come back to haunt us.

At the same time, some pretty dastardly things occur in some countries that most of the world community would like to see stopped: human trafficking for forced prostitution, child slaves to harvest crops, political prisoners given near-starvation diets, to name a few. Even if we can't stop such occurrences, we have a moral responsibility not to participate even if it costs us. I may get some economic benefits by buying from a criminal, and I may not stop his activity by withholding my business. However, I refuse to deal with him because, in effect, that makes me a criminal's associate.

Although not all trade sanctions have been successful, many have at least been influential in achieving their objectives. These included UN sanctions against Rhodesia (now Zimbabwe), U.K. and U.S. sanctions against the Amin government of Uganda, and Indian sanctions against Nepal.[16] U.S. sanctions against Cuba may have slowed that country's ability to create revolutions elsewhere. Sanctions against Myanmar helped bring the country to such economic disaster that its military leaders decided democracy was a better route to take.[17] There is evidence that trade sanctions against Iran may also lead to radical changes there.[18]

Finally, when a nation breaks international agreements or acts in unpopular ways, what courses of action can other nations take? Between 1827 and World War I, nations mounted 21 blockades, but these are now considered too dangerous. Military force has also been used, as for the overthrow of the Saddam regime in Iraq, but such measures have little global support. Thus, nations may take such punitive actions as withholding diplomatic recognition, boycotting athletic and cultural events, seizing the other country's foreign property, and eliminating foreign aid and loans. These may be ineffective in and of themselves without the addition of trade sanctions.

Should Governments Impose Trade Sanctions?

Counterpoint

No Every time I turn around, I see my government imposing a new sanction. Some of these cause law-abiding companies to lose revenue that took years to develop. MTN could not even repatriate a loan of almost $400 million that it had made to its Iranian joint venture, and it could not procure Iranian supplies needed for equipment to sell in other countries.[19] Thus, the trade sanctions aimed at hurting the government of Iran ended up hurting non-Iranian companies even though they'd never engaged in any objectionable behavior.

Besides, I really question whether these sanctions even work. When the United States was maintaining its 20-year trade embargo on Vietnam, Vietnamese consumers were still able to buy U.S. products such as Coca-Cola, Kodak film, and Apple computers through other countries that did not enforce the sanctions.[20] The U.S. trade embargo with Panama made Panama's Noriega government only more adamant in its opposition to the United States, requiring a military invasion to depose him. Oil embargoes against South Africa, because of its racial policies, merely spurred

Counterpoint

South African companies to become leaders in converting coal to oil.[21]

Even if trade sanctions succeed at weakening the targeted countries' economies, who really suffers? You can bet that the political leaders will still get whatever they need, so the costs of sanctions are borne by innocent people. This has occurred in Iran, where there have been widespread reports of deaths because of sanction-induced supply shortages of medicine.[22] Moreover, the people adversely affected usually blame their suffering not on their internal regime but on the countries carrying on the sanctions. Despots are very good at manipulating public opinion.[23]

Finally, governments sometimes seem to impose trade sanctions based on one issue rather than on a country's overall record. For instance, some critics have suggested using trade policies to press Brazil to restrict the cutting of Amazon forests, even though its overall environmental record—particularly its limiting of adverse exhaust emissions by converting automobile engines to use methanol instead of gasoline—is quite good.

MAINTAINING OR EXTENDING SPHERES OF INFLUENCE

Governments also use trade to support their spheres of influence—giving aid and credits to, and encouraging imports from, countries that join a political alliance or vote a preferred way within international bodies. The EU and the 77 members of the African, Caribbean, and Pacific Group of States signed the Cotonou Agreement to formalize preferential trade relationships that also strengthened political ties.[24] Venezuela has exported oil at low cost and with long-term financing to targeted Latin American countries to gain influence in the region.[25]

CONCEPT CHECK

We observe in Chapter 2 that a primary function of culture is to support a nation's sense of its uniqueness and integrity. We also explain that—especially in developing countries—many people fear that the escalation and influence of global business interaction is a prelude to another era of cultural imperialism in which weaker nation-states will be weakened even further. Finally, we note that similar concerns are raised by the prospect of cultural diffusion—a process by which elements of a foreign culture may infiltrate themselves into a local culture.

PRESERVING NATIONAL CULTURE

Countries are held together partly through a unifying sense of identity that sets their citizens apart from those in other nations. To sustain this collective identity, they prohibit exports of art and historical items that they deem to be part of their national heritage. In addition, they limit imports of certain foreign products and services that may either conflict with their dominant values, such as morality, or replace domestic sources of production that uphold these traditional values. The relevance of culture has been confirmed through several UNESCO conventions aimed at preserving cultural diversity, and the concern has been largely focused, but not entirely, on media (print, visual, and audio).[26] For many years, Japan, South Korea, and China maintained an almost total ban on rice imports, largely because rice farming has been a historically cohesive force in each nation.[27] Canada relies on a "cultural sovereignty" argument to prohibit foreign ownership or control of publishing, cable TV, and bookselling.[28]

INSTRUMENTS OF TRADE CONTROL

Governments use many rationales and seek a range of outcomes when they try to influence exports or imports. The choice of trade-control instrument is crucial because each type may incite different responses from domestic and foreign groups. One way to understand trade-control instruments is by distinguishing between two types that differ in their effects:

- Those that indirectly affect the amount traded by directly influencing export or import *prices*
- Those that directly limit the *amount* of a good that can be traded

Let's review these instruments.

TARIFFS

Tariffs may be levied
- On goods entering, leaving, or passing through a country.
- For protection or revenue.
- On a per unit, a value basis, or both.

Tariff barriers directly affect prices, and *nontariff barriers* may affect either price or quantity. A **tariff** (also called a **duty**), the most common type of trade control, is a tax levied on a good shipped internationally. That is, governments charge a tariff on a good when it crosses an official boundary—whether it be that of a nation or a group of nations that have agreed to impose a common tariff on goods crossing the boundary of their bloc.

Tariffs collected by the exporting country are called **export tariffs**; if they're collected by a country through which the goods pass, they're **transit tariffs**; if they're collected by importing countries, they're **import tariffs**. Because import tariffs are by far the most common, we discuss them in some detail.

Import Tariffs Unless they're *optimum tariffs* (discussed earlier in the chapter), import tariffs raise the price of imported goods by placing a tax on them, thereby giving domestically produced goods a relative price advantage. A tariff may be protective despite no domestic production in direct competition if it raises the price of some foreign production in order to curtail overall demand for imports.

Tariffs as Sources of Revenue Tariffs also serve as a source of governmental revenue. Import tariffs are of little importance to developed countries, usually costing more to collect than they yield.[29] However, in many developing countries they are a major source of revenue, potentially giving the governments more control over determining the amounts and types of goods crossing their borders and collecting a tax on them than they have over determining and collecting individual and corporate income taxes. Although revenue tariffs are most commonly collected on imports, some countries charge export tariffs on raw materials. Transit tariffs were once a major source of countries' revenue, but governmental treaties have nearly abolished them.

Criteria for Assessing Tariffs A government may assess a tariff on a per unit basis (a **specific duty**), as a percentage of the item's value (an **ad valorem duty**), or on both (a **compound duty**).

A tariff controversy concerns developed countries' treatment of manufactured exports from developing countries that seek to add manufactured value to their raw material exports. Raw materials frequently enter developed countries free of duty (say, coffee beans); however, if they are processed (instant coffee), developed countries then assign an import tariff. Because an ad valorem tariff is based on the total value of the product (say, $5 for a jar of instant coffee), meaning the raw materials and the processing combined ($2.50 for the coffee beans and $2.50 for the processing), developing countries argue that the **effective tariff** on the manufactured portion turns out to be higher than the published tariff rate. In other words, a tariff rate of 10 percent is effectively 20 percent on the manufactured portion. This anomaly further challenges developing countries to find markets for their manufactured products. At the same time, developed countries cannot easily remove barriers to imports of developing countries' manufactured products, largely because these imports are more likely to displace workers who are least equipped to change jobs.

NONTARIFF BARRIERS: DIRECT PRICE INFLUENCES

Now that we've shown how tariffs raise prices and limit trade, let's turn to a discussion of other ways that governments alter product prices to limit their trade.

Governmental subsidies may help companies be competitive,

- Especially to overcome market imperfections because they are least controversial.
- But there is little agreement on what a subsidy is.
- But agricultural subsidies are difficult to dismantle.

Subsidies **Subsidies** are a form of direct assistance to companies to boost competitiveness. Although this definition is straightforward, disagreement on what constitutes a subsidy causes trade frictions. In essence, not everyone agrees that companies are being subsidized just because they lose money, nor that all types of government loans or grants are subsidies. One long-running controversy involves commercial aircraft. Airbus Industrie and the EU claim that the U.S. national and state governments subsidize Boeing through R&D contracts for military aircraft that also have commercial applications and tax breaks to secure employment from Boeing's facilities. Meanwhile, Boeing and the U.S. government claim that the EU subsidizes Airbus Industrie through low-interest government loans.[30]

An area that may well raise future questions about subsidies is governmental support to shore up floundering companies and industries during the global recession. For instance, several governments have bailed out banks, granted generous consumer loans to support their auto companies, eliminated taxes on their companies' export earnings, and invested in an ownership share of key companies. In turn, these actions are altering international competitiveness.[31]

Agricultural Subsidies The one area in which everyone agrees that subsidies exist is agricultural products in developed countries. The official reason for granting subsidies to farmers is that food supplies are too critical to be left to chance. Although subsidies lead to surplus production, surpluses are argued to be preferable to the risk of food shortages. The question of food shortages came to the forefront during 2010 droughts when a number of countries limited or banned exports of such agricultural commodities as rice and wheat in order to maintain supplies for their own consumers.[32]

Although this official reason seems compelling, it does not explain agricultural subsidies for non-food products, such as U.S. subsidies for cotton that have disadvantaged Brazilian production.[33] There is an unofficial reason as well. Within the EU, Japan, and the United States, rural areas have a disproportionately high representation in government decision making. In the United States, for instance, there is one senator per 300,000 people in Vermont, a state with a 68 percent rural population, and one senator per 19 million in California, which is 93 percent urban. Agriculture accounts for 40 percent of the EU budget even though it comprises less than 2 percent of GDP and employs less than 5 percent of the workforce.[34] The result is that internal politics effectively prevent the dismantling of such instruments as price supports for farmers, government agencies to improve agricultural productivity, and low-interest loans to farmers.

What is the effect? Developing countries are disadvantaged in serving the developed markets with competitive agricultural products. Further, much of the surplus production from developed countries is exported at very low prices, thus distorting trade and disadvantaging production from developing countries.[35]

Overcoming Market Imperfections Another subsidization area is less contentious. Most countries offer potential exporters many business development services, such as market information, trade expositions, and foreign contacts. From the standpoint of market efficiency, these sorts of subsidies are more justifiable than tariffs because they seek to overcome, rather than create, market imperfections. There are also benefits to disseminating information widely because governments can spread the costs of collecting information among many users.

Aid and Loans Governments also give aid and loans to other countries. If the recipient is required to spend the funds in the donor country, which is known as *tied aid* or *tied loans,* some products can compete abroad that might otherwise be noncompetitive. For instance, tied aid helps win large contracts for infrastructure, such as telecommunications, railways, and electric power projects.

However, there is growing skepticism about the value of tied aid because it requires the recipient to use donor country suppliers that are shielded from competition and may not be the best. Tied aid can also slow the development of local suppliers in developing countries. These concerns led OECD members to untie financial aid to developing countries, no longer obliging aid-recipient countries to purchase equipment from suppliers in the donor country.[36] However, China is using tied aid for nearly all its foreign projects.[37]

Because it is difficult for customs officials to determine the honesty of import invoices,

- They may arbitrarily increase value.
- Valuation procedures have been developed.
- They may question the origin of and product-classification of imports.

Customs Valuation Tariffs for imported merchandise depend on the product, price, and origin—which tempts exporters and importers to declare these wrongly on invoices to pay less duty. Generally, most countries have agreed to use the invoice information unless customs officers doubt its authenticity. Agents must then assess on the basis of the value of identical goods. If not possible, agents must assess on the basis of similar goods arriving at or about the same time.[38]

For example, there is no sales invoice when imported goods enter for lease rather than purchase. Customs officials must then base the tariff on the value of identical or similar goods. If this basis cannot be used, officials may compute a value based on final sales value or on reasonable cost. Similarly, agents sometimes use their discretionary power to assess the value too high, thereby preventing the importation of foreign-made products such as occurred on Philippine cigarettes imported into Thailand.[39]

Valuation Problems The fact that so many different products are traded creates valuation problems, especially since new products are coming on the market all the time and must be classified within existing tariff categories. It is easy (by accident or intention) to misclassify a product and its corresponding tariff. Administering more than 13,000 categories of products means a customs agent must use professional discretion to determine, say, if silicon chips should be considered "integrated circuits for computers" or "a form of chemical silicon." In our opening case, we saw the controversy of whether the Vietnamese fish are catfish or whether they are basa, tra, or pangasius. The classification becomes even more complex as both U.S. and Vietnamese scientists develop fish hybrids that combine, for example, fast-growing with good-tasting fish. The differences among products in tariff schedules are also minute. For example, the United States has a different tariff on athletic footwear than on sports footwear, and these are further categorized by whether the sole overlaps the upper part of the shoe or not. Each type of accessory and reinforcement of the shoes' uppers has a different tariff.

Although classification differences may seem trivial, the disparity in duties may cost companies millions of dollars. Some contentious examples include whether the French company

Agatec's laser leveling device would be used primarily indoors or outdoors,[40] whether Marvel's X-Men Wolverines were toys or dolls, and whether sport utility vehicles—such as the Suzuki Samurai and the Land Rover—were cars or trucks. Because of a much higher U.S. tariff on trucks than on automobiles, Ford imported autos from Turkey and then removed the rear seats and replaced the rear windows with solid metal in order to turn them into trucks.[41]

Because countries treat products from different countries differently, customs must also determine products' origins. This is neither cheap nor easy either for customs or for traders. For example, red meat products may involve animals born in one country, raised in a second, and slaughtered in a third. U.S. Customs requires traders to provide details on these stages of production, thus adding documentation costs above those for meat products of a 100 percent U.S. origin.[42] Though difficult, officials have uncovered many instances of transshipping products or falsifying documents to avoid restrictions. For instance, U.S. Customs fined Staples, OfficeMax, and Target for mislabeling the country of origin of pencils in order to avoid paying anti-dumping duties assessed on Chinese imports.[43]

Other Direct-Price Influences Countries use other means to affect prices, including special fees (such as for consular and customs clearance and documentation), requirements that customs deposits be placed in advance of shipment, and minimum price levels at which goods can be sold after they have customs clearance.

NONTARIFF BARRIERS: QUANTITY CONTROLS

Governments use other nontariff regulations and practices to affect the quantity of imports and exports directly. Let's take a look at the various forms these typically take.

A quota may
- Set the total amount to be traded.
- Allocate amounts by country.

Quotas The **quota** is the most common type of quantitative import or export restriction, limiting the quantity of a product that can be imported or exported in a given time frame, typically per year. *Import quotas* normally raise prices for two reasons: (1) to limit supply and (2) to provide little incentive to use price competition to increase sales. A notable difference between tariffs and quotas is their effect on revenues. Tariffs generate revenue for the government. Quotas generate revenue only for those companies that are able to obtain and sell a portion of the intentionally limited supply of the product. (Sometimes governments allocate quotas among countries, based on political or market conditions.)

To circumvent quotas, companies sometimes convert the product into one for which there is no quota. For instance, the United States maintains sugar import quotas that result in its sugar prices averaging about double the world market price. As a result, many U.S. candy producers have moved plants to Mexico where they can buy lower-cost sugar (despite NAFTA) and import the candy duty-free to the United States.[44]

Import quotas are not necessarily imposed to protect domestic producers. Japan has maintained quotas on many agricultural products from outside the country, then allocated import rights to competing suppliers as a means of bargaining for sales of Japanese exports and preventing excess dependence on any one country for essential foods.

A country may establish *export quotas* to assure domestic consumers a sufficient supply of goods at a low price, to prevent depletion of natural resources, or to attempt to raise export prices by restricting supply in foreign markets. To restrict supply, some countries band together in various commodity agreements, such as OPEC for petroleum, which then restrict and regulate exports from the member countries.

Voluntary Export Restraint A variation of a quota is the so-called **voluntary export restraint (VER)**. Essentially, Country A asks Country B to voluntarily reduce its companies' exports to Country A. The term *voluntarily* is somewhat misleading; typically, either Country B volunteers to reduce its exports or else Country A may impose tougher trade regulations. Procedurally, VERs have unique advantages. They are much easier to switch off than an import quota, and the appearance of a "voluntary" choice by a particular country to constrain its shipments can do less damage to political relations than an import quota.

Embargoes A specific type of quota that prohibits all trade is an **embargo**. As with quotas, countries or groups of countries may place embargoes on either imports or exports, on whole categories of products regardless of origin or destination, on specific products with specific countries, or on all products with given countries. Governments impose embargoes in an effort to use economic means to achieve political goals. To the contrary, as we see in our closing case, Singapore's government seeks out business-driven strategic cooperation with China and other nations, by going out of its way to allow foreign operations to set up business operations in the country.

Through "buy local" laws
- Government purchases give preference to domestically made goods.
- Governments sometimes legislate a percentage of domestic content.

"Buy Local" Legislation Another form of quantitative trade control is so-called *buy local legislation.* Government purchases are a large part of total expenditures in many countries; typically, governments favor domestic producers. Sometimes they specify a domestic content restriction—that is, a certain percentage of the product must be of local origin. For example, the U.S. recession-driven economic stimulus package of 2009 required any funded project to use only U.S.-made steel, iron, and manufactured goods.[45] Sometimes governments favor domestic producers through price mechanisms, such as permitting an agency to buy a foreign-made product only if the price is at some predetermined margin below that of a domestic competitor. Sometimes governments favor domestic purchases indirectly, such as the U.S. prohibition of foreign Medicare payments for elderly Americans except in emergency situations—a regulation that limits U.S. foreign purchases in the fast-growing area of medical tourism.

Other types of trade barriers include
- Arbitrary standards.
- Licensing arrangements.
- Administrative delays.
- Reciprocal requirements.
- Service restrictions.

Standards and Labels Countries can devise classification, labeling, and testing standards to allow the sale of domestic products but obstruct foreign-made ones. Consider product labels. The requirement that companies indicate on a product where it is made informs consumers who may prefer to buy products from certain nations. In our opening case, we saw that the U.S. catfish industry sought country-of-origin labeling on fish. Countries also may dictate content information on packaging that is not required elsewhere. These technicalities add to a firm's production costs, particularly if the labels must be translated for different export markets. In addition, raw materials, components, design, and labor increasingly come from many countries, so most products today are of such mixed origin that they are difficult to sort out.

The professed purpose of standards is to protect the safety or health of the domestic population, but some companies argue they are just a means to protect domestic producers. For example, some U.S. and Canadian producers have contended that EU regulations and labeling requirements on genetically engineered corn and canola oil are merely means to keep out the products until their own technology catches up.[46] In another case, following U.S. publicity about contaminated Chinese foods, China upped its rejection of foodstuffs from the United States, citing contamination with drugs and salmonella.[47]

In reality, there's no way of knowing to what extent products are kept out of countries for legitimate safety and health reasons rather than arbitrarily to protect domestic production. Nevertheless, the U.S. FDA publishes a monthly summary of rejected import shipments, a list that is substantial. For example, in January 2013, it rejected over 1,700 shipments.[48] When developing country shipments are rejected for health and safety reasons, there may be a negative image for the country's other products that cause it to lose sales and lower its export prices.[49]

Specific Permission Requirements Some countries require that potential importers or exporters secure governmental permission (an **import or export license**) before transacting trade. A company may have to submit samples to government authorities to obtain such a license. The procedure can restrict imports or exports directly by denying permission or indirectly because of the cost, time, and uncertainty involved.

A **foreign-exchange control** is similar. It requires an importer to apply to a government agency to secure the foreign currency to pay for the product. As with an import license, failure to grant the exchange, not to mention the time and expense of completing forms and awaiting replies, obstructs foreign trade.

Administrative Delays Closely akin to specific permission requirements are intentional administrative customs delays or those caused by inefficiency, which create uncertainty and raise the cost of carrying inventory. Intentional delays may occur not only to protect domestic producers, but also for political reasons. Japanese companies reported such delays in China after Japan and China clashed over ownership of islands in the East China Sea.[50]

Reciprocal Requirements Because of government regulations in the importing countries, exporters sometimes must take merchandise or buy services in lieu of receiving cash payment. This requirement is common in the aerospace and defense industries—sometimes because the importer does not have enough foreign currency. For instance, Thailand has bought military equipment from China and Russia in exchange for dried fruit and frozen chickens.[51]

Countertrade **Countertrade** or **offsets** are government requirements in the importing country whereby the exporter, usually in sales (especially military ones) to a foreign government, must provide additional economic benefits such as jobs or technology as part of the transaction. When Lockheed Martin sold aircraft to the Polish government it had to use a number of Polish suppliers in its production as well as transfer much technology to Poland.[52] Countertrade has been criticized because large defense contractors usually keep sales of their own production intact while transferring their purchases from smaller domestic contractors to those in foreign countries, thus weakening domestic defense capabilities and hurting smaller domestic firms.[53]

Reciprocal requirements often mean that exporters must find markets for goods outside their lines of expertise, engage in complicated organizational arrangements that require them to relinquish some operating control, or undertake activities outside their expertise. Raytheon, which makes such defense products as missiles and radar systems, had to undertake shrimp farming to gain a Saudi Arabian contract.[54] All things being equal, companies avoid these transactions. However, some have developed competencies in these types of arrangements in order to gain competitive advantages.

Four main reasons why trade in services is restricted are

- Essentiality.
- Preference for not-for-profit operations.
- Standards.
- Immigration.

Restrictions on Services Service is the fastest-growing sector in international trade. In deciding whether to restrict service trade, countries typically consider four factors: *essentiality, not-for-profit preference, standards,* and *immigration.*

Essentiality Countries judge certain service industries to be essential because they serve strategic purposes or provide social assistance to citizens. Governments may prohibit private companies, foreign or domestic, in some sectors because they feel the services should not be sold for profit. In other cases, they set price controls or subsidize government-owned service organizations that create disincentives for foreign private participation. Some essential services in which foreign firms might be excluded are media, communications, banking, utilities, and domestic transport. India has also excluded foreign multi-brand retailers because of the disruption they might cause to local retail establishments.[55]

CONCEPT CHECK

In Chapter 1, we define service exports and imports and discuss the significance of services for some companies and countries. We also divide them into three categories: tourism and transportation, service performance, and asset use.

Not-for-Profit Services Mail, education, and hospital health services are often not-for-profit sectors in which few foreign firms compete. When a government privatizes these industries, it customarily prefers local ownership and control.

Standards Some services require face-to-face interaction between professionals and clients. At the same time, governments limit entry into many service professions to ensure practice by qualified personnel. The licensing standards for these personnel vary by country and include such professionals as accountants, actuaries, architects, electricians, engineers, gemologists, hairstylists, lawyers, medical personnel, real estate brokers, and teachers.

At present, there is little reciprocal recognition in licensing from one country to another because occupational standards and requirements differ substantially. This means that an accounting or legal firm from one country might face obstacles in another, even to serve its domestic clients' needs. The firm must hire professionals within each foreign country or else try to earn certification abroad. The latter option can be difficult because the professionals may have to take examinations in a foreign language and study materials different from those in their home country. There also may be lengthy prerequisites for taking an examination, such as internships, time in residency, and coursework at a local university.

Immigration Satisfying the standards of a particular country is no guarantee that a foreigner can then work there. In addition, governmental regulations often require an organization—domestic or foreign—to search extensively for qualified personnel locally before it can even apply for work permits for personnel it would like to bring in from abroad.[56]

DEALING WITH GOVERNMENTAL TRADE INFLUENCES

When facing import competition, companies can
- Move abroad.
- Seek other market niches.
- Make domestic output competitive.
- Try to get protection.

When companies face possible losses because of import competition, they have several options, four of which stand out:

1. Move operations to another country.
2. Concentrate on market niches that attract less international competition.
3. Adopt internal innovations, such as greater efficiency or superior products.
4. Try to get governmental protection.

CONCEPT CHECK

In discussing "Factor Mobility" in Chapter 5, we explain the effect of the increasing reliance on people as an internationally mobile production factor. In addition, we observe that most countries hand out immigration papers only sparingly and that many others allow workers to enter only for short periods of time.

Each option entails costs and risks. Nevertheless, companies undertake different ones. For example, competition from Japanese imports spurred the U.S. automobile industry to move some production abroad (such as subcontracting with foreign suppliers for cheaper parts), developing niche markets through the sale of minivan and sport utility vehicles (SUVs) that initially had less international competition, and adopting innovations such as lean production techniques to improve efficiency and product quality. General Motors and Chrysler eventually received substantial government funding to survive.

TACTICS FOR DEALING WITH IMPORT COMPETITION

Granted, these methods are not realistic for every industry or every business. Companies may lack the managerial, capital, or technological resources to shift their own production abroad, and finding qualified foreign suppliers may be problematic. They may not be able to identify more profitable product niches. Even if they do, foreign competitors may quickly copy their innovation. In such situations, companies often ask their governments to restrict imports or open export markets. As our opening case shows, U.S. catfish farmers have successfully gained government support to limit import competition, such as changing the name of and getting duties placed on the imported competitive fish.

CONVINCING DECISION MAKERS

Governments cannot try to help every company that faces tough international competition. Likewise, helping one industry may hurt another. Thus, as a manager, you may propose or oppose a particular protectionist measure. Inevitably, the burden falls on you and your company to convince officials that your situation warrants particular policies. You must identify the key decision makers and convince them by using the economic and noneconomic arguments presented in this chapter. In any situation, companies must convey to public officials that voters and stakeholders support their position.[57]

INVOLVING THE INDUSTRY AND STAKEHOLDERS

A company improves the odds of success if it can ally most, if not all, domestic companies in its industry. Otherwise, officials may feel that its problems are due to its specific inefficiencies rather than the general import challenges or difficulty in gaining export sales. Similarly, involving other stakeholders can help, such as the taxpayers and merchants in the communities where it operates. Finally, it can lobby decision makers and endorse the political candidates who are sympathetic to its situation.

PREPARING FOR CHANGES IN THE COMPETITIVE ENVIRONMENT

CONCEPT CHECK

As we point out in Chapter 3, although representative democracies tend to share many features, the process whereby citizens select representatives to make decisions on their behalf varies from country to country, especially when it comes to the centralization or decentralization of authority. Among other things, the task of locating decision makers for business purposes differs from one country to another.

Companies can take different approaches to deal with changes in the international competitive environment. Frequently, their attitudes toward protectionism are a function of the investments they have made to implement their international strategy. Those that depend on freer trade and/or have integrated their production and supply chains among countries tend to oppose protectionism. In contrast, those with single or multi-domestic production facilities, such as a plant in Japan to serve the Japanese market and a plant in Taiwan to serve the Taiwanese market, tend to support protectionism.

Companies also differ in their self-perception of being able to compete against imports. In nearly half the cases over a 60-year period in which U.S. firms proposed protecting a U.S. industry, one or more companies in that industry opposed it, typically commanding competitive advantages in terms of scale economies, supplier relationships, or differentiated products. Thus, they reasoned that not only could they successfully battle international rivals, they also stood to gain even more as their weaker domestic competitors failed to do so.[58]

Looking to the Future

Dynamics and Complexity

When trade restrictions change, there are winners and losers among countries, companies, and workers. So it's probably safe to say that we'll see mixtures of pushes for freer trade and greater protection.

In addition, gains to consumers from freer trade may be at the expense of some companies and workers—people who see themselves as big losers. They are not apt to lose without a struggle; they'll garner as much support for protection as they can, and they may win. The support may well come from alliances that cross national borders, such as clothing companies in various developing nations uniting to push governments to enact quota agreements to protect their export markets against Chinese and Indian competition. Thus, if you are a manager in an industry that may be affected by changes in governmental protection, you must watch closely to predict how the politics may affect your own economic situation.

Finally, the international regulatory situation is becoming more, rather than less, complex—a situation that challenges companies to find the best locations in which to produce. New products are coming onto the market regularly, thus making the task of tariff classification more difficult. Services available over the Internet, such as international online gambling, challenge governments to find means of regulation and tax collection. Heightened concerns about terrorism and product safety compound considerations of what should or should not be traded and with whom.

In Chapter 7, we discuss the trade agreements countries are reaching; nevertheless, it's useful at this point to mention the impact these have on decision making. Every time countries negotiate a trading agreement (and these agreements are proliferating), there is the possibility that a new optimum production location emerges. When the United States and Mexico negotiated a free trade pact, it caused some U.S. imports to shift from Taiwan to Mexico. However, with an additional free trade agreement between the United States and Central America, some of the production that developed in Mexico shifted to Central America. Another free trade agreement might cause another shift. All of this creates uncertainties and dynamics for companies' operations. ■

CASE Doing Business in Singapore

The Government of Singapore offers a pro-business environment and Singapore is placed 1st in the World Bank's global ranking index for "Ease of Doing Business" and "Trading Across Borders".[59] To achieve this, the Singapore government has created a robust ecosystem to promote international trade and investments through its various ministries and agencies or statutory boards. For instance, the mission of the Ministry Of Trade and Industry (MTI) of Singapore is to promote economic growth and create jobs, so as to achieve higher standards of living for its citizens, protecting Singapore's international trade interests, in particular, with a view to enhance access to global markets for goods, services and investments; and providing a good understanding of the current state of and outlook, for policy formulation and refinement.

These strategies are derived from Singapore's general philosophy of economic management—strong adherence to a free market economic system, and active pursuit of outward-oriented economic policies. Its vision is to develop a globalized, entrepreneurial and diversified economy to turn Singapore into a leading global city. MTI oversees ten statutory boards including the Singapore Economic Development Board (EDB).[60] The EDB is the lead government agency that plans and executes strategies to enhance Singapore's position as a global business center and grow its economy.[61] Its "Host to Home" strategy aims to move Singapore from being a host to companies to becoming a home where global business, innovation, and talent are nurtured. EDB's consistently result-oriented initiatives are testament to Singapore's governmental influence on trade.

The following are examples of some global companies that leveraged good government policy to expand their Asia wide presence in Singapore.

Siemens Medical Instruments

As one of the world's leading manufacturers of digital hearing instruments utilizing the latest microelectronic technology, Siemens established the operations of Siemens Medical Instruments (SMI) in Singapore in 1974. Ever since, their research department has grown into a full-fledged R&D center taking advantage of the robust growth and market opportunities in Asia that now homes a fast rising ageing population (presently 207 million, estimated to cross 850 million by 2050) and middle class. These factors prompted Siemens to boost its investments in research and development by 10 percent in 2013. Siemens' long term investment in and dedication to the region is testament to the Singapore government's growing role as a strategic partner with leading companies, to achieve visionary growth.

Trina Solar

Similarly in 2011, Trina Solar, one of the world's leading photovoltaic (PV) companies, established its Asia Pacific operating headquarters in Singapore to strengthen its growing presence and customer base in Asia after it sealed a research agreement with the Solar Energy Research Institute of Singapore to develop high efficiency solar cells using Trina Solar's mono-crystalline wafers.

The Singapore government through its energy agency Energy Innovation Programme Office (EIPO) created an investment environment that fostered the development of a skilled talent base and strong logistics infrastructures. These made it strategically advantageous for Trina Solar's regional R&D center as it developed new solar technologies and applications to meet the demands for clean energy expected to be fuelled by Asian markets.

Rolls-Royce

Since its entry into the country in the 1950s, Rolls-Royce has become a major player in Singapore's aerospace industry, accounting for over 15 percent of Singapore's aerospace output. A world leader of power systems and services, Rolls-Royce is anticipating strong growth in its operations in Asia achieved through joint ventures with key local industry partners including Singapore Airlines Engineering, and activities in the energy and marine sector.The Singapore government has been a strong partner of growth for Rolls-Royce and the country is a leader in aerospace maintenance, repair and overhaul, aviation manufacturing and R&D in Asia. According to Jonathan Asherson, Regional Director, Rolls-Royce, the company has also benefited from the valuable business opportunities, excellent talent pool, and solid infrastructure that Singapore offers.

Procter & Gamble

Procter & Gamble or P&G's market capitalization is more than the GDP of many countries and it markets its products in over 180 countries. It is the largest household and personal care company in the world, and its brands include some of the world's best-known names such as Gillette, Pampers, Pantene, Oral-B, and SK-II. The Asia Pacific headquarters for P&G's operations in Singapore carries out brand and business management activities like manufacturing, marketing, supply chain management, research and development, finance and talent development across the region. Singapore is also home to P&G's Asia Leadership Development Center.

P&G leveraged on the strong research capabilities in Singapore through an agreement with Singapore's government Agency for Science, Technology and Research (A*STAR). In 2011, P&G invested US$192 million to build a mega innovation center in Singapore. Deborah Henretta, Group President, Asia, P&G remarked that Singapore embodies the essence of what successful companies look for: commitment to innovation, world-class infrastructure, business-friendly environment, excellent local talent and an agility to work as partners in progress.

Unilever

Another leading global supplier of fast moving consumer goods (FMCG) with a presence in more than 150 countries is Unilever. Parent to the world's best-known brands such as Lipton, Wall's, and Dove, Unilever deals products in nutrition, hygiene and personal care reaching out to a wide range of consumers. Established in Singapore over 50 years ago, Unilever Singapore has since emerged as a strategic global hub for Unilever, and is home to several key members of its senior leadership team. Through Four Acres Singapore, its new global leadership development center, Unilever will access the Singapore EDB's LINK (Leadership Initiatives, Networks and Knowledge) ecosystem to provide executive talent development and leadership programmes with business schools and corporate partners. Paul Polman, CEO of Unilever recognizes that Singapore's evolved business infrastructure, excellent human capital, connectivity, and strong base for supporting industries combined with the support provided by the Singapore Government make it an ideal regional business hub.

Dell

Since 1984, Dell has pioneered technologies and innovations as the front-runner in the computer industry that sells custom-built computers directly to customers. Dell currently operates its Asia Pacific headquarters in Singapore using this cosmopolitan market and strategic location as a test bed for its services and solutions in Asia. Dell opened its first design center in Singapore in 2005 to boost the company's R&D capabilities in display and imaging products. It further added its Dell Singapore Solution Center (DSC) in 2011, tapping into the country's large pool of infocomm industry professionals and highly proactive government agency, the Infocomm Development Authority of Singapore (IDA). Amit Midha, President of Dell Asia Pacific and Japan, points to the fact that Singapore's robust ecosystem, pro-business environment, geo-political landscape and high-technology infrastructure enables Dell to bring the benefits of technology solutions to customers in the Asia Pacific region.

Mitsui Chemicals

Mitsui Chemicals (MCI) is one of the largest chemical companies in Japan. In Singapore, its business includes manufacturing plants, R&D facilities, and sales offices. MCI subsidiaries in Singapore are Mitsui Chemicals Asia Pacific Ltd, Mitsui Phenols Singapore Pte Ltd, and Mitsui Elastomers Singapore Pte Ltd. The company has invested over US$600 million to expand its operations in Singapore since the 1980s including phenol, bisphenol and Tafmer plants. MCI's Asia Pacific Headquarters in Singapore also provides support in sales and marketing, technical, logistics, and business planning functions. In 2011, it opened its R&D Center (MS-R&D) working closely with its Singapore government agency partner A*STAR and research institutes. Mr Yasushi Nawa, Managing Director of Mitsui Chemicals Asia Pacific, commented that Singapore's pro-business government policies, talented and hardworking workforce and top infrastructures have enabled Mitsui Chemicals to look to the country as a launch pad for its growth strategies in the Asia Pacific region.

China-Singapore Cooperation Initiatives

As part of an ongoing effort by Singapore's government to influence and facilitate international trade, the Monetary Authority of Singapore (MAS) has developed new initiatives to influence and support trade. Singapore and China have agreed on new initiatives to strengthen cooperation on financial sector development and regulation.[62] The new initiatives will further promote the international use of the Renminbi (RMB) through Singapore.

China will extend its Renminbi Qualified Foreign Institutional Investor (RQFII)[63] program to Singapore, with an aggregate quota of RMB 50 billion. This will allow qualified Singapore-based institutional investors to channel offshore RMB from Singapore into China's securities markets. RQFII licence holders may also issue RMB investment products to the broad pool of investors in Singapore, using the RQFII quota. The RQFII program will help to diversify the base of investors in China's capital markets and promote adoption of the RMB for investment.

Singapore will be given consideration as one of the investment destinations under the new Renminbi Qualified Domestic Institutional Investor (RQDII) scheme. This will allow qualified Chinese institutional investors to use RMB to invest in Singapore's capital markets. The measure will help to broaden the universe of assets available to Chinese investors as well as the investor base for Singapore's capital markets.

China and Singapore will introduce direct currency trading between the Chinese Yuan and Singapore Dollar. New measures will allow cross-border flows of RMB between Singapore and Suzhou Industrial Park (SIP) as well as Tianjin Eco-City (TEC).

In addition, Singapore and China have agreed on and announced measures to strengthen regulatory cooperation. Relevant agencies are in discussions to facilitate China-incorporated companies which have received regulatory approval to list directly in Singapore, instead of through entities incorporated outside China.

Furthermore, the Singapore Exchange and Shanghai Futures Exchange have signed an MOU to strengthen collaboration in the joint development of commodity derivatives.

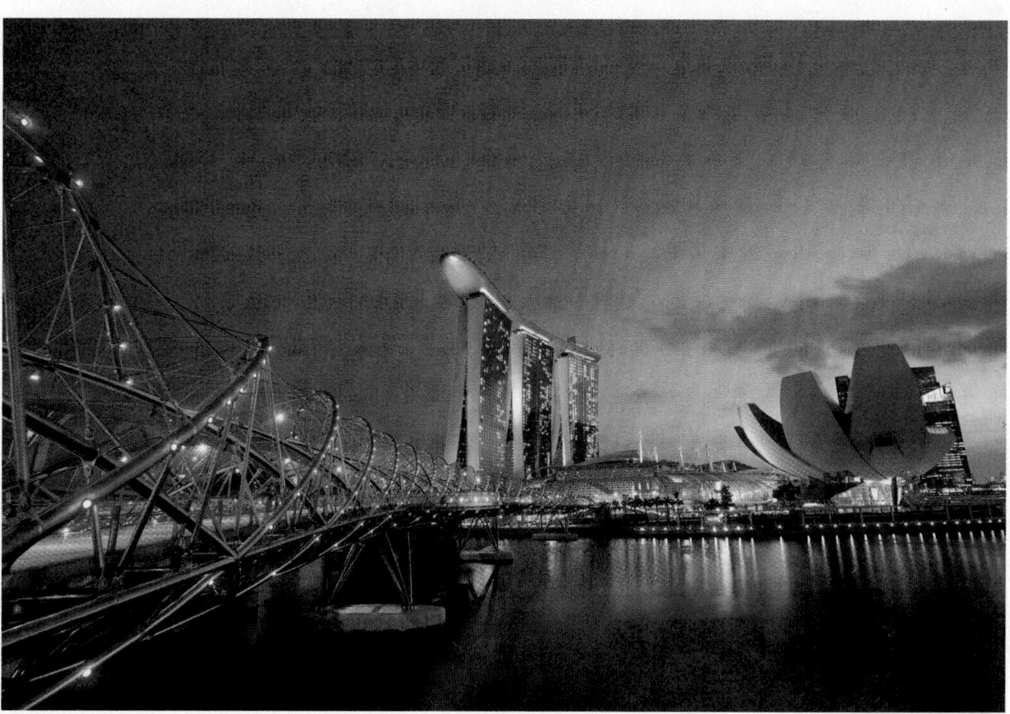

Singapore fosters a business-friendly environment and is one of the easiest places to conduct international business in.

Source: © tanatat - Fotolia.com

The Singapore and Chinese governments have also agreed to strengthen cooperation in banking regulatory issues, through exchanges and dialogs on topics of shared interest, and enhanced coordination on international regulatory issues. These new initiatives build on agreements concluded earlier this year, including the signing of the MOU on RMB Business Cooperation between the Monetary Authority of Singapore (MAS) and the People's Bank of China (PBC), and the enhancement of the bilateral swap agreement between the two central banks, which paved the way for the launch of RMB clearing functions in Singapore in May this year (2013).

MAS Managing Director, Mr. Ravi Menon, already declared that 2013 had been the productive year with lots of cooperation initiatives between Singapore and China. The excellent relations between MAS and the central bank and their regulatory counterparts in China only cemented ties between the two countries, putting Singapore in a position to promote RMB for long-term trade and investment in the future.

QUESTIONS

6-3. Discuss why and how the Singapore government promotes the international trade process.

6-4. Why is free trade so vital to Singapore's survival and growth?

6-5. Singapore has a highly developed trade-oriented market economy and its economy has been ranked as the most open in the world. What has been the government's role in achieving this feat?

6-6. Why do multinational corporations (MNCs) find Singapore an attractive place to do business?

SUMMARY

- Despite the documented benefits of free trade, no country permits an unregulated flow of goods and services across its borders.
- It is difficult to determine the effect on employment from protecting an industry due to the likelihood of retaliation and the fact that imports as well as exports create jobs.
- Policymakers continue to struggle with the problem of income redistribution due to changes in trade policy.
- The infant-industry argument for protection holds that governmental prevention of import competition is necessary to help certain industries evolve from high-cost to low-cost production.
- Government interference is often argued to be beneficial if it promotes industrialization, given the positive relationship between industrial activity and certain economic objectives.
- Trade controls to improve economic relations with other countries include objectives of improving the balance of payments, raising prices to foreign consumers, gaining comparable access to foreign markets, preventing foreign monopoly prices, assuring that domestic consumers get low prices, and shifting revenue from foreign producers to domestic tax receipts.
- Considerable government interference in international trade is motivated by political rather than economic concerns, including maintaining domestic supplies of essential goods and preventing potential enemies from gaining goods that would help them achieve their objectives.
- Trade controls that directly affect price and indirectly affect quantity include tariffs, subsidies, arbitrary customs valuation methods, and special fees.
- Trade controls that directly affect quantity and indirectly affect price include quotas, VERs, "buy local" legislation, arbitrary standards, licensing arrangements, foreign-exchange controls, administrative delays, and reciprocal requirements.
- A company's development of an international strategy will greatly determine whether it will benefit more from protectionism or from some other means for countering international competition.
- Changing trade agreements and the advent of new products create complexities for both companies and governments as they plan their policies.

KEY TERMS

ad valorem duty (p. 287)
comparable access argument (p. 280)
compound duty (p. 287)
countertrade (or offsets) (p. 291)
dumping (p. 281)
effective tariff (p. 287)
embargo (p. 290)
essential-industry argument (p. 282)
export-led development (p. 279)
export tariffs (p. 286)
foreign-exchange control (p. 291)
import (or export) license (p. 290)
import tariff (p. 286)
industrialization argument (p. 278)
infant-industry argument (p. 277)
optimum-tariff theory (p. 281)
protectionism (p. 275)
quota (p. 289)
specific duty (p. 287)
subsidy (p. 287)
tariff (or duty) (p. 286)
terms of trade (p. 279)
transit tariff (p. 286)
voluntary export restraint (VER) (p. 289)

ENDNOTES

1 ***Sources include the following:*** Melissa Martin, "New Tariff Could Protect Alabama's Catfish Industry," *Southeast Farm Press* (March 25, 2013): n.p.; "The Catfish Solution; U.S. Senators Drop Seafood Protectionism against Vietnam," *Wall Street Journal (Online)* (June 21, 2012): n/a; Roy Roberson, "Golden Opportunity for US Agriculture in Vietnam," *Western Farm Press* (October 10, 2012): n.p.; Terry Hanson and Dave Sites, "U.S. Farm-Related Catfish Industry 2009 Review and 2010 Outlook," Unpublished report, Department of Fisheries and Allied Aquacultures, Auburn University (March 2011); "Catfish Farmers Face Shifting Tides of Imports, Costs, *Southeast Farm Press* (August 14, 2012): n.p.; Fred Kuchler, Barry Krissoff, and David Harvey, "Do Consumers Respond to Country-of-Origin Labelling?" *Journal of Consumer Policy* 33:4 (December 2010): 323–37; "Catfish Industry Maintains Support for USDA," *The Mississippi Business Journal* 31:31 (August 3, 2009): 16; "Fishy Diplomacy with Hanoi," *Wall Street Journal (Online)* (September 21, 2010), accessed November 30, 2010; Bartholomew Sullivan, "Stakes High in Catfish Fight," *McClatchy – Tribune Business News* (October 31, 2010) accessed November 30, 2010; "Fishy Tales; Charlemagne," *The Economist* 387: 8584 (June 14, 2008): 53; Paul Greenberg, "A Catfish by Any Other Name," *New York Times* (October 12, 2008): 72; Ben Evans, "Catfish Plan Risks Trade War," *Miami Herald* (July 2, 2009): 4C; Jeffrey H. Birnbaum, "House Floats Idea for Fish Inspections, But No One Is Biting," *Washington Post* (March 11, 2008): A17; Taras Grescoe, "Catfish with a Side of Scombroid," *New York Times* (July 15, 2007): WK13.

2 Christopher J. O'Leary, Randall W. Eberts, and Brian M. Pittelko, "Effects of NAFTA on US Employment and Policy Responses," *OECD Trade Policy Working Papers* 131 (February 2012).

3 Michael Hart, "Breaking Free: A Post-mercantilist Trade and Productivity Agenda for Canada," *C.D. Howe Institute Commentary* 357 (August 2012): 1–27.

4 This argument is most associated with the writings of Raul Prebisch, Hans Singer, and Gunnar Myrdal in the 1950s and 1960s. For a recent discussion, see P. Sai-wing Ho, "Arguing for Policy Space to Promote Development: Prebisch, Myrdahl, and Singer," *Journal of Economic Issues* 42:2 (June 2008): 509–16.

5 Dorothy Solinger and Yiyang Hu, "Welfare, Wealth and Poverty in Urban China: The Dibao and Its Differential Disbursement," *The China Quarterly* 211 (September 2012): 741–64.

6 Benedict Ezema,"Effectiveness of Policy Responses to Terms of Trade Shocks in Selected African Countries,"*International Journal of Business and Management* 7:8 (April 2012): 88–101.

7 Hou Hexiang,"Vietnam to Accelerate Industrialization and Modernization of Rural Areas,"*Xinhua News Agency* [China] (June 2, 2002): 1008;"Pushing Ecuador into the 21st Century," *Latin Finance* (March 2002: 30), retrieved 17 July, 2002, from web.lexis-nexis.com/universe;"Is Inequality Decreasing? Debating the Wealth and Poverty of Nations,"*Foreign Affairs* (August 2002): 178.

8 Gerald K. Helleiner,"Markets, Politics, and Globalization: Can the Global Economy Be Civilized?"*Global Governance* (July–September 2001): 243; Marina Murphy,"EU Chemicals Need Flexibility: A Level Playing Field Should Be Established between the EU and U.S. Chemicals Industries,"*Chemistry and Industry* (July 1, 2002): 9; Lisa Schmidt,"How U.S. Sees Trade Rows,"*Calgary Herald* [Canada] (June 25, 2002): A2.

9 Annie Gowen,"U.S. Caviar with a Russian Accent,"*Washington Post* (December 31, 2004): Metro, B1.

10 Emiko Terazono,"UN Warns Over Volatility in Food Prices,"*Financial Times* (October 11, 2011): 20; Tennille Tracy,"Lawmaker Gets a Say on Gas Exports,"*Wall Street Journal* (December 26, 2012): A4; Keith Johnson,"Geopolitical Benefit Raised in Debate on Exporting Gas,"*Wall Street Journal* (May 6, 2013): A4.

11 Sanchita B. Saxena,"American Tariffs, Bangladeshi Deaths,"*New York Times* (December 12, 2012): A31.

12 Stephen Moore,"Tax Cut and Spend: The Profligate Ways of Congressional Republicans,"*National Review* (October 1, 2001): 19.

13 Liam Pleven,"Pentagon in Race for Raw Materials,"*Wall Street Journal* (May 3, 2010): A3+.

14 Andrew M. Lemieux and Ronald V. Clarke,"The International Ban on Ivory Sales and Its Effects on Elephant Poaching in Africa,"*The British Journal of Criminology* 49:4 (July 2009): 451–71; Bryan Christy,"Ivory Worship,"*National Geographic* (October 2012): 28-61.

15 Daniel Martin,"Tightening the Sanctions Noose,"*Petroleum Economist* (November 2012): n/a.

16 Lance Davis and Stanley Engerman,"Sanctions: Neither War nor Peace,"*Journal of Economic Perspectives* 17:2 (Spring 2003): 187–97.

17 Susie Sell,"Promise and Pitfalls in Myanmar,"*Asia's Newspaper for Media, Marketing and Advertising* (November 1, 2012): 42–43.

18 Farnaz Fassihi and Jay Soloman,"In Iran's Factories and Shops, Tighter Sanctions Exact Toll,"*Wall Street Journal (Online)* (January 4, 2013): n/a.

19 Devon Maylie,"Iran Sanctions Hinder MTN,"*Wall Street Journal* (April 19, 2013): B3.

20 Philip Shenon,"In Hanoi, U.S. Goods Sold but Not by U.S.,"*New York Times* (October 3, 1993): A1.

21 Patrick Barta,"Black Gold,"*Wall Street Journal* (August 16, 2006): A1+.

22 Thomas Erdbrink,"Iran Sanctions Take Unexpected Toll on Medical Imports,"*New York Times* (November 3, 2012): A4+.

23 Jacob Weisberg,"Sanctions Help to Sustain Rogue States,"*Financial Times* (August 3, 2006): 11.

24 "EU/Latin America/Caribbean: Leaders Aim to Revive Ties,"*European Report* (May 15, 2002): 501.

25 Vanessa Bauza,"In Struggle for Influence, It's Better to Give,"*Knight Ridder Tribune Business News* (March 24, 2007): 1.

26 Rostram J. Neuwirth,"The 'Culture and Trade Debate' Continues: The UNESCO convention in Light of the WTO Reports in China—Publications and Audiovisual Products: Between Amnesia or Déjà Vu?" *Journal of World Trade* 44:6 (December 2010): 1333–56.

27 Gail L. Cramer, James M. Hansen, and Eric J. Wailes,"Impact of Rice Tariffication on Japan and the World Rice Market,"*American Journal of Agricultural Economics* 81 (1999): 1149.

28 Matthew Fraser,"Foreign Ownership Rules Indefensible: And There Appears to Be Appetite for Change,"*Financial Post* (May 28, 2001): C2; and Hale E. Hedley,"Canadian Cultural Policy and the NAFTA: Problems Facing the U.S. Copyright Industries,"*The George Washington Journal of International Law and Economics* 28:3 (1995): 655–90.

29 "Futile Fortress,"*Financial Times* (August 26, 2003): 16.

30 "U.S.-EU Aircraft Subsidies Dispute Drags on, with No End in Sight in 2013,"*Inside US Trade* 31:1 (January 4, 2013): n.p.

31 John W. Miller,"WTO Warns Members Not to Undermine Trade,"*Wall Street Journal* (March 27, 2009): A8; Joseph Stiglitz,"The Global Crisis, Social Protection and Jobs,"*International Labour Review* 148:1/2 (June 2009): 1–13;"State Capitalism: Big Brother is Back,"*The Economist* (November 3, 2012): 63–64.

32 Andrew E. Kramer,"Russia, Crippled by Drought, Bans Exports of Grains,"*New York Times* (August 6, 2010): A1; Javier Blas,"Export Bans Prompt Reviews of Security of Supplies,"*Financial Times* (October 15, 2010): World Food, 1.

33 James Politi,"Brazil Moves Closer to Showdown over US Cotton Subsidies,"*Financial Times* (March 8, 2010): 4.

34 "Charlemagne: Milking the Budget,"*The Economist* (November 24, 2012): 62; For some data on the United States, see"At the Trough,"*The Economist* (June 1, 2013): 32.

35 G. Chandrashekhar,"Should India Demand Farm Subsidy Cuts by Developed Nations?"*Businessline* (January 4, 2006): 1; Carmen G. Gonzalez,"The Global Food System, Human Rights, and the Environment,"*GPSolo* 29:6 (November-December 2012): 72–73.

36 Chi-Chur Chao and Eden S. H. Yu,"Import Quotas, Tied Aid, Capital Accumulation, and Welfare,"*Canadian Journal of Economics* 34 (2001): 661; Mark Rice,"Australia Must Join Other Countries in Untying Overseas Aid,"*Australian Financial Review* (April 4, 2002): 59.

37 Falil M. Alsaaty and Granville Sawyer,"Competitive Advantage in the African Market: The United States versus China,"*The Business Review, Cambridge* 20:2 (December 2012): 209–15.

38 "An Opportunity to Support US Customs Valuations,"*International Tax Review* (June 2012): n.p.

39 "Philippines/Thailand: Philippines Urges Thailand to Fully Comply with WTO Customs Valuation Ruling,"*Asia News Monitor* [Bangkok] (May 19, 2012): n.p.

40 "National Import Specialist Addresses Outreach to the Public,"*U.S. Customs Border Protection Today* (October–November 2006), retrieved July 13, 2007, from www.customs.ustreas.gov/xp?CustomsToday/2006/october_nove mber/import_article; *Customs Bulletin and Decision* (June 27, 2007): 58.

41 Matthew Dolan,"To Outfox the Chicken Tax, Ford Strips Its Own Vans,"*Wall Street Journal* (September 22, 2009): A1+.

42 Alexander Moens and Amos Vivancos Leon,"Mandatory Country of Origin Labeling: The Case for a Harmonized Canada-US Beef and Pork Regulatory Regime,"*Fraser Forum* 4 (July-August 2012): 14–17.

43 "Target Corp., Staples Inc., and OfficeMax, Inc., Among Pencil Importers in the Subject of a False Claims Act Case Brought by The Cullen Law Firm, PLLC,"*PR Newswire* [New York] (May 17, 2012): n.p.

44 Christopher Swann,"Shielding Sugar Industry 'Costs Thousands of Jobs,'"*Financial Times* (February 15, 2006): 6; Douglas A. Irwin,"The Return of the Protectionist Illusion,"*Wall Street Journal* [New York, N.Y] (July 2, 2012): A11.

45 Sarah O'Connor,"Tug of War over Buy American,"*Financial Times* (June 24, 2009): 4.

46 Jeremy Grant and Ralph Minder,"Comment & Analysis: Agribusiness,"*Financial Times* (February 1, 2006): 11.

47 Anita Chang,"Food Safety,"*Miami Herald* (July 15, 2007): 18A.

48 U.S. Food and Drug Administration,"Import Refusal Report, January 2012,"retrieved February 13, 2013, from www.accessdata.fda.gov/scripts/importrefusals/ir_byProduct.cfm?DYear=2013&DMonth=1.

49 Marie-Agnés Jouanjean,"Standards, Reputation, and Trade: Evidence from US Horticultural Import Refusals,"*World Trade Review, suppl. Symposium Issue: Standards and Non-Tariff Barriers in Trade* 11:3 (July 2012): 438–61.

50 "Delays Reported in Customs-Clearance Procedures in China," *Jiji Press English News Service* [Tokyo] (September 20, 2012): n.p.

51 Jon Grevatt, "Thai Offset Plans Could Be Derailed By A Move to Reinstate Countertrade," *Jane's Defence Industry* 29:12 (December 1, 2012): n.p.

52 Carol Dawn Petersen, "Defense and Commercial Trade Offsets: Impacts on the U.S. Industrial Base Raise Economic and National Security Concerns," *Journal of Economic Issues* 45:2 (June 2011): 485–91.

53 Mark J. Nackman, "A Critical Examination of Offsets in International Defense Procurements: Policy Options for the United States," *Public Contract Law Journal* 40:2 (Winter 2011): 511–29.

54 "Guns and Sugar," *The Economist* (May 25, 2013): 63–65.

55 Vibhuti Agarwal and Megha Bahree, "India's Retreat Is Blow to Global Retailers," *Wall Street Journal* (December 8, 2011): B5.

56 Sara Robinson, "Workers Are Trapped in Limbo by I.N.S.," *New York Times* (February 29, 2000): A12.

57 Ralph G. Carter and Lorraine Eden, "Who Makes U.S. Trade Policy?" *International Trade Journal* 13:1 (1999): 53–100.

58 Eugene Salorio, "Trade Barriers and Corporate Strategies: Why Some Firms Oppose Import Protection for Their Own Industry," unpublished DBA dissertation, Harvard University, 1991.

59 See www.doingbusiness.org/rankings

60 See www.mti.gov.sg/Pages/home.aspx

61 See www.edb.gov.sg/content/edb/en.html

62 See www.mas.gov.sg/News-and-Publications/Press-Releases/2013/New-Initiatives-to-Strengthen-China-Singapore-Financial-Cooperation.aspx

63 The Qualified Foreign Institutional Investor (QFII; Chinese: 合格境外機構投资者) is a program that was launched in 2002 in People's Republic of China to allow licensed foreign investors to buy and sell yuan-denominated "A" shares in China's mainland stock exchanges (in Shanghai and Shenzhen). Chinese mainland stock exchanges were previously closed off to foreign investors due to China's exercise of tight capital controls which restrict the movement of assets in-and-out of the country.

The Qualified Foreign Institutional Investor (QFII) scheme enables specified types of foreigners to use their offshore foreign currency for investment in the Mainland's securities market. The Renminbi Qualified Foreign Institutional Investor (RQFII) scheme is a modified version of the QFII scheme which facilitates the use of Renminbi held outside the Mainland for investment in the Mainland's securities market. For further reading, please see www.kwm.com/hong-kong/documents/KWM_Connect_May_13_v8.pdf.

CHAPTER 7

Economic Integration and Cooperation

OBJECTIVES

After studying this chapter, you should be able to

1. Discuss the three major approaches to economic integration
2. Identify the major characteristics and challenges of the World Trade Organization
3. Discuss the pros and cons of global (the WTO), bilateral, and regional integration
4. Identify how the different approaches to economic integration can be a free trade agreement, a customs union, or a common market
5. Describe the static and dynamic impact of trade agreements on trade and investment flows
6. Compare and contrast different regional trading groups
7. Describe other forms of global cooperation such as the United Nations and OPEC

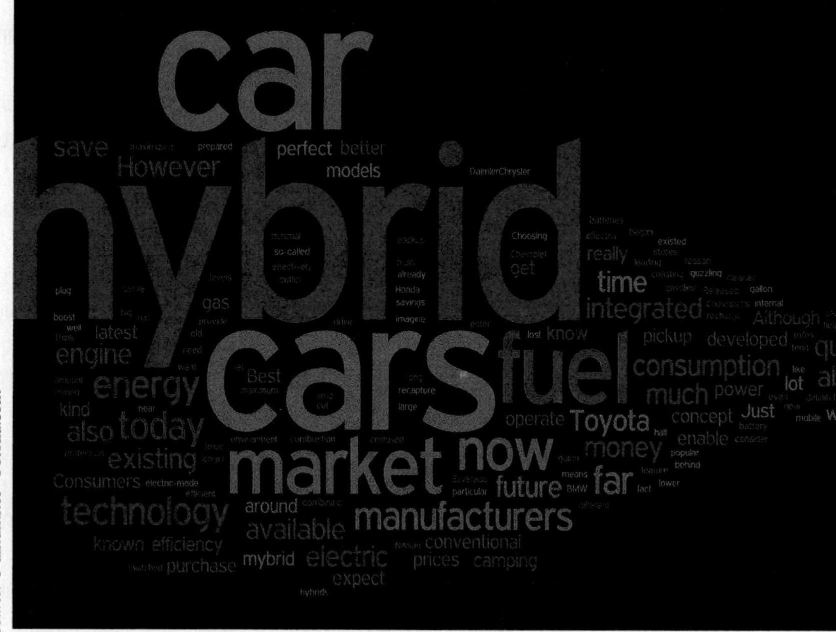

Source: © aihumnoi - Fotolia.com

MyManagementLab®
Improve Your Grade!
When you see this icon ✪, visit **www.mymanagementlab.com** for activities that are applied, personalized, and offer immediate feedback.

Marrying is easy, but housekeeping is hard.

—German proverb

CASE Toyota's European Drive

Anna Kessler put the key into the ignition of her brand-new Toyota Yaris, started the engine, and began to navigate her way home from work through the crowded streets of Berlin, Germany.[1] Having owned the car for just over a week, she was already satisfied with her decision. She liked the car's distinctive European look, the generous warranty it had come with, and its low fuel consumption.

Her decision the previous week marked the first time Anna had ever owned a vehicle manufactured by an Asian company; in fact, it was the first time she had considered one. When she had made her last car purchase, the thought of buying a car from Toyota—then known for its lackluster designs, limited options, and seven-month-long waiting lists—had not even entered her mind. However, as she was researching different vehicles, she found that Toyota had ranked the highest in several categories in a recent quality survey and that the Yaris had achieved an outstanding four-star Euro NCAP safety rating, which led her to investigate the car more thoroughly.

With her purchase, Anna became another one of the millions of Toyota vehicle owners located around the globe, contributing to the Japanese automaker's rapid growth over the past two decades. In 1990, the company possessed 20 production facilities in 14 countries. By 2012, it had 50 manufacturing facilities in 27 countries, including factories in the Czech Republic, France (where the Yaris is assembled), Poland, Portugal, the UK, and Russia. Known for its low-cost, efficient production operations, Toyota finally surpassed General Motors as the largest car manufacturer in the world in 2008 (although that only lasted until 2011 when GM and VW moved ahead). Given Toyota's steady increase in market share, it is hard to believe that before 2002, the company had not posted a profit for its European operations for three decades and had suffered from consistently low market share and growth in the region.

So why has it taken Toyota so long to crack into the competitive European market, and why are European companies only now beginning to feel the pressure from Asian manufacturers? Many analysts have pointed to an agreement between the Japanese government and the European Community (predecessor to the European Union) in which the two negotiated a quota each year for the number of Japanese cars imported into Europe. The quota amounts agreed upon each year depended on such factors as the level of consumer demand and sales growth in the region and were fixed at 11 percent of the European market.

The arrangement was set up to allow European carmakers to become more competitive as the EC made the transition to a common market; previously, several independent European nations had their own import and registration restrictions on Japanese cars. Italy, for example, limited the number of imported Japanese vehicles to 3,000, while France kept them at a 3 percent share of its market. Britain, Spain, and Portugal imposed similar restrictions. This policy goes back to the end of World War II when the Japanese government asked the European automakers to curtail exports to Japan to help the nation rebuild its industry. The Europeans reciprocated by limiting the access of Japanese autos to their market. At the time, that wasn't a problem. However, when the Japanese auto companies became export conscious, they wanted access to the European markets. The quota system helped protect the domestic industry.

Under the new system, these countries had to abandon their individual policies, but French carmakers fought to include an 80 percent local-content rule and an allowance to export 500,000 cars a year to Japan, five times the then-current level. In the end, the EC disregarded these additional requests, and in the first year of the agreement, 1.089 million Japanese cars were allowed to be imported.

The quota, however, also fixed separate caps for each participating country and then divided this amount among the Japanese automakers according to their historic market shares. The caps essentially prevented the Japanese from being able to transfer their excess imports from countries where their quotas weren't being met to ones where they were unable to meet demand due to having already reached the maximum limits. It was primarily for this reason that they never actually met their quota for the EC; during the seven years the quota system was in effect, Toyota was held to a 2 to 3 percent market share in most EU countries.

Although the system seemed to be having the desired effect, even some French auto officials admitted that the eventual opening of the market was inevitable. One noted, "Can we put off change for years? Officially, yes. But honestly, I don't think so." That statement proved prophetic when the EU lifted the import quota in 1999 and made it easier for the Japanese auto manufacturers to expand distribution and sign up dealers. Although this move did not necessarily cause the Japanese to flood the European market with their products, it did open the way for them to invest more heavily in design and manufacturing facilities in the EU, to broaden the range of products they marketed there, and to customize their offerings to better appeal to European tastes.

Toyota responded to the drop in barriers by introducing a new strategy of designing vehicles targeted specifically at European customers. This involved setting up a European Design and Development center in southern France and allowing design teams across the globe to compete for projects. The Yaris, Toyota's best-selling vehicle in the EU, was designed by a Greek and was the first to be developed within the region. It subsequently was named Car of the Year 2000 in both Europe and Japan. As another key element of its European strategy, Toyota has also set up additional production centers in the region and now manufactures all of its best European-selling vehicles in Europe, including the facility in France in the opening photo in the chapter. The new-generation Toyota Corolla, voted 2002 European Car of the Year, and the Avensis, the first Toyota vehicle to be exported from Europe to Japan, were both designed and built in Europe. In December 2006, Toyota celebrated its one millionth made-in-Europe Yaris. Manufacturing facilities in Eastern Europe allow the Japanese automaker to lower production costs due to lower wages.

The collapse of the auto industry in Europe has been hard on all manufacturers, which is one reason why Toyota's investment in Russia is so important, since that is one European country whose auto industry is growing. The situation seems even bleaker as Japanese competitors continue to open up facilities in the Eastern bloc countries recently admitted to the EU as well as in other low-wage areas such as China. As noted above, Toyota has already set up state-of-the-art production plants in the Czech Republic and Poland—the one in the Czech Republic being established in cooperation with France's PSA Peugeot Citroën to develop good relationships with PSA's local suppliers. Because of the elimination of internal tariffs in the EU, Toyota can manufacture automobiles anywhere within Europe and ship them to all markets duty-free. Before the reduction in tariff barriers, this would not have been possible.

Other recent trends in the EU have also favored Toyota since the quotas were eliminated. In light of a sluggish economy facing high unemployment and low growth, Europeans are becoming less loyal to European brands in their search for more economical, higher-quality vehicles. In recent J.D. Power customer surveys in the United Kingdom and Germany, Toyota ranked first overall and scored the highest in three of seven categories; Ford, Renault, and Volkswagen all ranked below average. In addition, Toyota's environmentally friendly hybrid vehicle, the Prius, was voted the 2005 European Car of the Year. In 2012, however, Toyota ranked just below Mercedes-Benz in terms of vehicle owner satisfaction, although the Yaris was best in class for the small car segment. In light of its growing presence in Europe, Toyota was accepted as a full member of the European Automobile Manufacturers' Association in 2008.

Riding on its success in Europe in the mid-2000's and its growth internationally, Toyota had ambitious goals for the future. However, the global financial crisis and the ongoing difficulties posed by international recalls of more than 9.5 million vehicles have put a crimp in those plans. In addition, the 2011 earthquake and tsunami in Japan severely disrupted Toyota's supply chain. However, Toyota began to recover sales and revenues in 2012, but the strong yen hampered the company's ability to export and depressed earnings from its foreign operations.

Toyota's European Division saw unit sales decrease by 19.2 percent in 2010 from 2009 levels, from 1,062,000 to 858,000 continuing a downward trend since 2007. Its market share in Europe has also been damaged by the financial crisis and its ongoing struggle to re-establish its quality image after the global recalls. In Europe, Toyota saw its market share fall to 4.4 percent in 2010, down from its peak of 5.9 percent in 2007. However, sales began to gradually improve in 2011 and 2012.

Despite difficulties posed by the present market conditions, and the necessity of having to lay off people worldwide, Toyota has so far resisted the move to shut down plants. Toyota is continuing its push to increase its share of the European market by restructuring its Brussels-based European division, including devolving more decision-making power from Japan, and focusing on the values of European consumers. This includes placing renewed focus on hybrid technology in Europe, in which the company still retains a comparative advantage over its global rivals. By the end of October 2012, Toyota Motor Company (TMC) was producing 19 hybrid passenger car models and one plug-in hybrid vehicle in 80 countries and regions, representing 14 percent of its global sales. TMC introduced a hybrid engine for the Yaris in 2012 which should add to the Yaris' popularity, given the strong interest in hybrid technology in Europe.

As the decade continues and many areas of the world begin to emerge from the financial crisis of the past several years, it will be interesting to see if Toyota can recapture the success it once enjoyed. Given all of the uncertainty of the last few years, you have to wonder if Anna Kessler is still driving her Yaris, or if she has traded it in for another Yaris, especially a hybrid version, or something else, such as the popular VW Golf or Ford Fiesta. ■

CRN Case Review Note

QUESTIONS

7-1. Why did the Europeans try to protect their auto industry from Japanese imports, and do you think this was fair to European consumers?

7-2. Toyota has established production facilities in Europe to service the European markets. Has Hyundai, Kia, or Honda followed the same strategy? If so, in which countries have they set up manufacturing, and are they the same ones where Toyota is manufacturing?

INTRODUCTION

CONCEPT CHECK

Recall from Chapter 5 our discussion of the ways in which the mobility of capital, technology, and people affects a country's trade and the relative competitive positions of domestic firms and industries. Imbalances in the mobility of factors of production are often addressed in strategies for cross-national integration.

In the mid- to late 1940s, many nations decided that if they were going to emerge from the wreckage of World War II and promote economic growth and stability within their borders, they would have to assist—and get assistance from—nearby countries. In some respects, the United States is the perfect example of such economic integration: the largest economy in the world comprising 50 states in continental North America and Hawaii, with a common currency and labor and capital mobility. However, it is just one country. What about the rest of the world? How do its nations and regions combine forces to give and gain the assistance they need to prosper together?

Economic integration is a term used to describe the political and monetary agreements among nations and world regions in which preference is given to member countries. There are three major ways to approach such agreements:

- **Global integration**—Countries from all over the world decide to cooperate through the World Trade Organization (WTO)
- **Bilateral integration**—Two countries decide to cooperate more closely together, usually in the form of tariff reductions
- **Regional integration**—A group of countries located in the same geographic proximity decide to cooperate, as with the European Union

Approaches to economic integration—political and economic agreements among countries in which preference is given to member countries—may be
- Bilateral,
- Regional,
- Global.

Why do you need to understand the nature of these agreements? Trade groups, whether global, bilateral, or regional, are an important influence on MNE strategies. They can define the size of the regional market and the rules under which a company must operate. In fact, an increase in market size is their single most important reason for existing.[2] A company in the initial stages of foreign expansion must be aware of how the groups encompass countries with good manufacturing locations or market opportunities. Recall from our opening case that Toyota has been able to find success in Europe by taking advantage of changes in EU policy that allow it to adjust its design and production strategies to meet the unique needs of European consumers. Similarly, in the ending case we'll see how Unilever has capitalized on the opportunities presented by emerging markets and strategized an East Asian Community in order to differentiate itself from its rivals. Thus, as a company expands internationally, it must change its organizational structure and operating strategies to continually benefit from these alliances.

MNEs are interested in regional trade groups because they tend to be regional as well. Although we often think of MNEs as companies that do business in all of the **triad** regions of the world—Europe, North America, and Asia—current research demonstrates that most generate most of their revenues in their home regions. In a sample of the top 500 companies in the world in terms of trade and FDI, it was found that 320 generate at least 50 percent of their revenues from their home region, 25 are biregional (at least 20 percent of their revenues from two regions but less than 50 percent from any single region), 11 are host-region oriented (more than half their revenue from a region outside their home region), and only 9 are truly global (at least 20 percent of their revenues from each of the three triad regions and with less than 50 percent of their sales from one region).[3] Additional research has shown that a 1% increase in physical distance results in a 1% decrease in trade and that a common border between two countries is likely to increase trade flows by 80%. This provides further evidence that firms are likely to generate a reasonably high percent of revenues from their home regions.[4] However, companies that sell in their own region are also interested in trade agreements with other regions. For example, although U.S. furniture, electronics, and appliances store RC Willey does not generate any foreign sales, it imports products from all over the world. Its managers are very interested in trade agreements because of their potential to affect the regions where they source their purchases and to reduce costs and improve quality.

CONCEPT CHECK

In Chapter 6, we explain that, in principle, no country allows an unregulated flow of goods and services across its borders; rather, governments routinely influence the flow of imports and exports. We also observe that governments directly or indirectly subsidize domestic industries to help them compete with foreign producers, whether at home or abroad. (In Chapter 1, we list the motivations for governments to engage in cross-national agreements—indeed, to cooperate at all.)

THE WORLD TRADE ORGANIZATION—GLOBAL INTEGRATION

Governments often actively cooperate with each other to remove trade barriers. The following discussion focuses on the **World Trade Organization (WTO)**, the successor to the **General Agreement on Tariffs and Trade (GATT)** and the major multilateral forum through which governments can come to agreements and settle trade disputes.

GATT: PREDECESSOR TO THE WTO

In 1947, 23 countries formed GATT under the auspices of the United Nations to abolish quotas and reduce tariffs. By the time the WTO replaced GATT in 1995, 125 nations had become members. Many believe that GATT's contribution to trade liberalization enabled the expansion of world trade in the second half of the twentieth century.

CONCEPT CHECK

In Chapter 6, we define a **tariff** as the most common type of trade control and describe it as a "tax" that governments levy on goods shipped internationally. Here we emphasize the fact that tariff barriers affect the prices of goods that cross national borders.

Trade Without Discrimination The fundamental principle of GATT was that each member nation must open its markets equally to every other member nation. This principle of "trade without discrimination" was embodied in GATT's **most-favored-nation (MFN) clause**—once a country and its trading partners had agreed to reduce a tariff, that tariff cut was automatically extended to every other member country, irrespective of whether the country was a signatory to the agreement.

Over time, GATT grappled with the issue of nontariff barriers in terms of industrial standards, government procurement, subsidies and countervailing duties (duties in response to another country's protectionist measures), licensing, and customs valuation. In each area, GATT members agreed to apply the same product standards for imports as for domestically produced goods, treat bids by foreign companies on a nondiscriminatory basis for most large contracts, prohibit export subsidies except on agricultural products, simplify licensing procedures that permit the importation of foreign-made goods, and use a uniform procedure to value imports when assessing duties on them.

CONCEPT CHECK

In discussing "Nontariff Barriers" as instruments of trade control in Chapter 6, we include **subsidies**, which we describe as direct government payments made to domestic companies, either to compensate them for losses incurred from selling abroad or to make it more profitable for them to sell overseas.

Then GATT slowly ran into problems. Its success led some governments to devise craftier methods of trade protection. World trade grew more complex, and trade in services—not covered by GATT rules—grew more important. Procedurally, GATT's institutional structure and its dispute-settlement system seemed increasingly overextended. Moreover, it could not enforce compliance with agreements. These market trends and organizational challenges made trade agreements harder to work out. Restoring an effective means for trade liberalization led officials to create the WTO in 1995.

WHAT DOES THE WTO DO?

The World Trade Organization is the major body for
- Reciprocal trade negotiations,
- Enforcement of trade agreements.

The WTO adopted the principles and trade agreements reached under the auspices of GATT but expanded its mission to include trade in services, investment, intellectual property, sanitary measures, plant health, agriculture, and textiles, as well as technical barriers to trade. Its 159 members collectively account for more than 97 percent of world trade and include the BRIC countries (Brazil, India, China, and Russia, which was finally admitted to membership in 2012). The entire membership makes significant decisions by consensus. However, there are provisions for a majority vote in the event of a non-decision by member countries. Agreements then must be ratified by the governments of the member nations.

CONCEPT CHECK

We explain TRIPS in Chapter 11 as an agreement that allows poor countries to either produce generic products for local consumption or import them from countries other than patent holders' home countries.

Most Favored Nation The WTO continued the MFN clause of GATT, which implies that member countries should trade without discrimination, basically giving foreign products "national treatment." Although the WTO restricts this privilege to official members, some exceptions are allowed, as follows:

1. Developing countries' manufactured products have been given preferential treatment over those from industrial countries.
2. Concessions granted to members within a regional trading alliance, such as the EU, have not been extended to countries outside the alliance. (Recall from our opening case, for instance, that although EU members can export and import cars from other EU nations without limitations, Japanese carmakers must comply with strict import tariffs.)
3. Countries can raise barriers against member countries who they feel are trading unfairly.

Exceptions are made in times of war or international tension.

CONCEPT CHECK

In Chapter 6, we show how the imposition of import restrictions can be used as a means of persuading other countries to lower import barriers. Here we point out that the same practice can also be used to punish nations whose policies fail to comply with provisions of the WTO or other agreements.

Dispute Settlement One function of the WTO that is garnering growing attention is the organization's dispute settlement mechanism, in which countries may bring charges of unfair trade practices to a WTO panel, and accused countries may appeal. There are time limits on all stages of deliberations, and the WTO's rulings are binding. If an offending country fails to comply with the panel's judgment, its trading partners have the right to compensation. If this penalty is ineffective, then the offending country's trading partners have the right to impose countervailing sanctions. However, the effectiveness of this system is under serious debate, given the ambiguity and time-consuming nature of certain cases.

One of the most interesting—and critical—disputes brought before the WTO is between the European company Airbus and its U.S. competitor Boeing, two of the world's largest aerospace companies and defense contractors. The case is critical because the market for aircraft is likely to top $3 trillion over the next several years. Since late 2004, the companies have traded charges of unfair subsidies from their respective supporting governments, the European Union and the United States, with each initially preferring to resolve the dispute outside of WTO jurisdiction, but then resorting to WTO arbitration. Boeing accused Airbus of receiving advantageous loans to offset a portion of its "launch" costs for its family of civilian aircraft; Airbus countered by accusing Boeing of gaining a competitive advantage from substantial U.S. government contracts and tax breaks in many of the regions of the U.S. in which the company operates. Negotiations to solve the dispute between the two companies and their representative governments outside of WTO arbitration broke down in 2004 and both parties elected to lodge formal complaints to the WTO, in order to receive a binding resolution.[5]

The latest panel report did conclude that some of Boeing's tax breaks and a number of government contracts acted as specific subsidies in violation of WTO conventions, providing Airbus with a victory in the case. On the other hand, however, the panel also agreed with Boeing that Airbus was guilty of receiving favorable capital loans from its sponsor governments to pay for launch costs incurred in developing new aircraft, as well as specific subsidies in the form of infrastructural loans and aid representing serious violations of WTO regulations.[6] As recently as 2013, the dispute had not been completely resolved.

An interesting dispute resolution between the United States and China involved trade in services. The U.S. maintained that China had established restrictions and requirements on foreign companies that wanted to process electronic services for the payment of credit card transactions. Although some of these allegations were denied by the WTO, it still found that Chinese practices needed to be altered to allow more competition in China and live up to the requirements of the General Agreement for Trade in Services, one of the three councils that make up the WTO, the other two being the Council for Trade in Goods and the Council for Trade-Related Aspects of Intellectual Property Rights. The issue was raised by the U.S. in September 2010: by the end of 2012, the U.S. and China had resolved the dispute and set up an implementation period to solve the problem[7]—a significantly better outcome than the clash between Boeing and Airbus.

Doha Round Most of the WTO's agenda was established by negotiations, or *rounds,* held by GATT—particularly the Uruguay Round, which took place from 1986 to 1994 and led up to the creation of the WTO. Perhaps the most complex issues the WTO currently faces, however, are those it is trying to address through the Doha Round, also called the Doha Ministerial Declaration, which commenced in Doha, Qatar, in 2001 with a focus on giving a boost to developing countries on the world scene. The largest of the disputes has essentially resulted in a split between developed members, such as the United States, Japan, and the EU, and developing countries, led by Brazil, China and India, over the large agricultural subsidies maintained by the richer nations and the industrial subsidies enforced by developing countries.

The initial deadline for completing the Doha agenda was January 1, 2005, but nothing happened when countries could not agree on key issues. By the third quarter of 2009, attempts to solve the problem of lowering tariffs on industrial goods (a demand by the United States and the EU) in return for reduced agricultural barriers (a demand of many developing countries) were not successful. In an interesting twist, Brazil sided with the U.S. and the EU, while India and China rejected the proposals because of their fear that imports would devastate their local economies in terms of both industrial and agricultural goods.[8]

The global financial crisis of 2008 got everyone's attention. Initially it put the Doha agenda temporarily on hold as governments struggled to bring their economies back to life and reignite global trade, which collapsed that year. The World Bank estimated that the global economy shrank by 1.9 percent in 2009 in terms of GDP and the WTO estimated that international trade in merchandise and services fell by 12 percent—the steepest decline in trade since World War II. Although world trade growth recovered in 2010, the level of growth fell to 5.2% in 2011 and 2.0% in 2012, largely due to a contraction in the European economies.

The WTO had hoped to scale back expectations on Doha by focusing on easier issues such as better coordinated exports rules and procedures and export incentive for developing countries. This new version, called "Doha Lite" or "Plan B" was approved by the WTO members in 2011, but it has not gained significant traction. Instead, many countries are setting up their own regional and bilateral arrangements, much to the dismay of the WTO.

THE RISE OF BILATERAL AGREEMENTS

Bilateral agreements can be between two individual countries or may involve one country dealing with a group of other countries.

As the negotiations over the Doha Round broke down, many countries began to shift to bilateral (or preferential) rather than multilateral free trade agreements. In 2012, for example, the U.S. signed free trade agreements with Colombia and South Korea, both of which reduced tariffs and other trade barriers for industrial products and agricultural products while strengthening intellectual property rights and trade in services. Even though bilateral trade is much simpler than trying to forge a deal in the WTO, neither deal was easy. And it is always difficult to measure the impact in the short run, especially during a time when the global economy is struggling. But the U.S. government was able to get support to pass the legislation by promising that improved trade would create more domestic jobs. In the case of Korea, the results appeared to be mixed in the short run. Even though U.S. exports to Korea rose in the first year of the agreement, Korean exports to the U.S. rose even more, resulting in a widening of the trade deficit.[9]

REGIONAL ECONOMIC INTEGRATION

Regional trade agreements—integration confined to a region and involving more than two countries.

Regional trade agreements are reciprocal pacts between two or more partners that lie somewhat between bilateral and global integration agreements. According to the World Trade Organization, 354 RTAs were in force as of mid-January 2013. Some of the best known RTAs are the European Union, the European Free Trade Association (EFTA), the North American Free Trade Agreement (NAFTA), the Southern Common Market (MERCOSUR), the ASEAN (Association of Southeast Asian Nations) Free Trade Area (AFTA), and the Common Market of Eastern and Southern Africa (COMESA).[10] As discussed below, however, other very significant regional agreements are being negotiated, especially in the Pacific Rim.

GEOGRAPHY MATTERS

Geographic proximity is an important reason for economic integration.

It's logical that most trade groups contain countries in the same area of the world. Neighboring nations tend to ally for several reasons:

- The distances that goods need to travel are short.
- Consumers' tastes are likely to be similar, and distribution channels can easily be established.

CONCEPT CHECK

In discussing geographic distance in Chapter 5, we observe that because greater distances ordinarily mean higher transportation costs, geographic proximity usually encourages trade cooperation. In the same chapter, we explain **country similarity theory** by showing that once a company has developed a new product in response to conditions in its home market, it will probably try to export it to those markets that it regards as most similar to its own.

Neighboring countries may have common histories and interests, and they may be more willing to coordinate their policies than non-neighbors.[11] Even though geographic proximity is a major factor leading to RTAs, this is not the case for all agreements. Armenia has RTAs in force with Kazahkstan, Moldova, the Russian Federation, Turkmenistan, and Ukraine; India has a number of trade agreements with most of the countries in its region; Germany exports and imports about 58 percent of its merchandise to other EU members; Switzerland, which is not a member of the EU but which has a trade agreement with it, shares more than half its exports and imports with EU countries; and NAFTA includes Canada and Mexico, both of which share a common border with the United States. The Canada-Israel RTA, on the other hand, is certainly not based on geographic proximity, nor is the U.S.-Korea FTA based on geographic proximity.

Geography matters for a number of reasons in the case of RTAs. Neighboring countries often share a common history, language, culture, and currency. Unless the countries are at war with each other, they have usually developed trading ties already. Close proximity reduces transportation costs, thereby making traded products cheaper in general. In fact, as physical distance between two countries increases by 1 percent, international trade drops by 1.1 percent. On the other hand, trade is likely to rise by 80 percent between countries with a common border, 200 percent with a common language (such as English between Canada and the United States), and 340 percent with a common currency (such as the euro for countries in the EU that have adopted it). Another strong incentive for geographically close countries to establish an RTA is that trade among bloc members is likely to rise by 330 percent once an agreement is established.[12]

The American Chamber of Commerce (AmCham) in Cairo has worked hard to sell Egypt as a regional trade hub for U.S. companies because of Egypt's trade agreements with the EU, the Greater Arab Free Trade Area, and the Common Market for Eastern and Southern Africa. The concern on the part of AMCHAM is that U.S. companies are losing market opportunities in the MENA (Middle East North Africa) region without a strong trade agreement with Egypt, which has the 15th largest population in the world. However, if U.S. companies locate in Egypt, they can penetrate all of the markets that Egypt is linked to in Europe, the Middle East, and North Africa. The challenge, of course, is political instability and security in Egypt.

Major types of economic integration:

- Free trade area—no internal tariffs.
- Customs union—no internal tariffs plus common external tariffs.
- Common market—customs union plus factor mobility.

As noted earlier, the major reason to establish a regional trade group is to increase market size. There are two basic types of RTAs from the standpoint of tariff policies; however, many agreements (especially agreements involving the United States) go beyond the liberalization of tariffs to include such issues as intellectual property, foreign direct investment, and services. From the standpoint of tariff reduction, the two main types of agreements are free trade agreements and customs unions.

- *Free Trade Agreement (FTA)* The goal of an FTA is to abolish all tariffs between member countries. It usually begins modestly by eliminating them on goods that already have low tariffs, and there is usually an implementation period during which all tariffs are eliminated on all products included in the agreement. Moreover, each member country maintains its own external tariffs against non-FTA countries. About 90 percent of the RTAs identified by the WTO are free trade agreements.
- *Customs Union* In addition to eliminating internal tariffs, member countries levy a common external tariff on goods being imported from nonmembers in order to establish a customs union. For example, when the EU was organized in 1957, it began to remove internal tariffs among member states, but in 1967 it eliminated the remaining internal tariffs and established a common external tariff, meaning that goods shipped into one member country from abroad are free from tariffs in the rest of the member countries. Now the EU negotiates as one region in the WTO and other regional and bilateral agreements rather than as separate countries. (Thus, as we observed in our opening case, when it came to import quotas on cars shipped to EU members, Japan had to negotiate with the EU as a whole, rather than with individual countries.) Customs unions account for less than 10 percent of the number of RTAs identified by the WTO, although the EU is a significant trade group. Most trade gains come from membership in an FTA, not a customs union, which is driven more by political than economic reasons.[13]

Common Market (or Economic Integration Agreement) Beyond the reduction of tariffs and nontariff barriers, countries can enhance their cooperation in a variety of other ways. The EU also allows free mobility of production factors such as labor and capital. This means that labor, for example, is generally free to work in any country in the common market without restriction. Adding free mobility of production factors to a customs union results in a **common market**. In addition, the EU has harmonized its monetary policies through the creation of a common currency, complete with a central bank. This level of cooperation creates a degree of political integration among member countries, which means they lose a bit of their sovereignty. The EU is formally listed by the WTO as a customs union and economic integration agreement.

THE EFFECTS OF INTEGRATION

Regional integration has social, cultural, political, and economic effects.

Regional economic integration can affect member countries in social, cultural, political, and economic ways. Initially, however, our focus is on its economic rationale. As we noted in Chapter 6, the imposition of tariff and nontariff barriers disrupts the free flow of goods, affecting resource allocation.

Static effects of integration—the shifting of resources from inefficient to efficient companies as trade barriers fall.

Dynamic effects of integration—the overall growth in the market and the impact on a company caused by expanding production and by the company's ability to achieve greater economies of scale.

Static and Dynamic Effects Regional economic integration reduces or eliminates those barriers for member countries, producing both *static* and *dynamic effects.* **Static effects** are the shifting of resources from inefficient to efficient companies as trade barriers fall. **Dynamic effects** are the overall growth in the market and the impact on a company caused by expanding production and by its ability to achieve greater economies of scale. Figure 7.1 shows how RTAs result in static and dynamic effects on trade and investment flows.

FIGURE 7.1 Impact of Free Trade Agreements

When economic integration reduces or eliminates trade barriers, the effects on the nations involved may be either *static* or *dynamic*. *Static effects* apply primarily to trade barriers themselves—for member countries they go down, and for nonmembers they go up. *Dynamic effects*, on the other hand, apply to economic changes affecting the newly structured market—not only does the market expand, but so do local companies, which take advantage of the larger market.

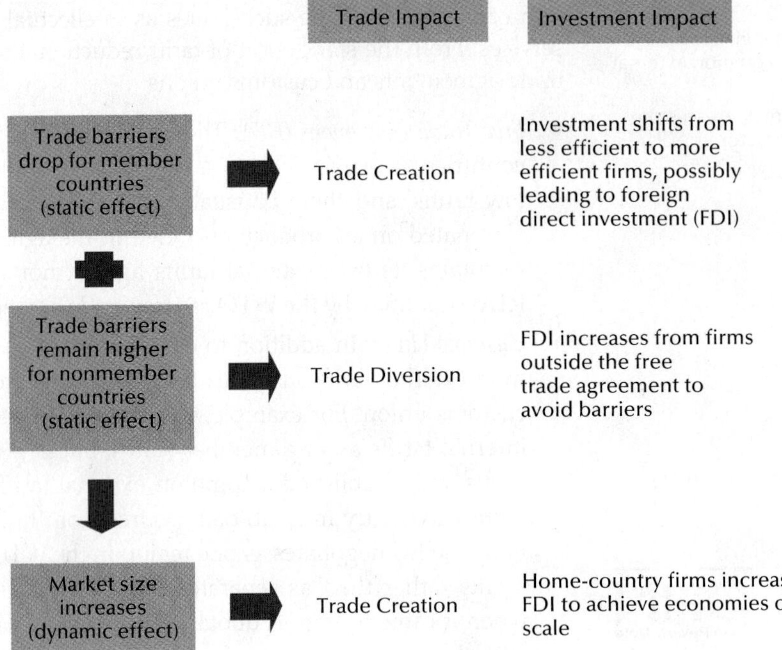

CONCEPT CHECK

In Chapter 6, we define **comparative advantage** as the theory that global efficiency gains may result from trade if a country specializes in those products it can produce more efficiently than other products (regardless of whether other countries can produce the same products even more efficiently).

Trade creation—production shifts to more efficient producers for reasons of comparative advantage.

Trade diversion—trade shifts to countries in the group at the expense of trade with countries not in the group.

Economies of scale—the average cost per unit falls as the number of units produced rises; occurs in regional integration because of the growth in the market size.

Static effects may develop when either of two conditions occurs:

1. *Trade Creation:* Production shifts to more efficient producers for reasons of comparative advantage, allowing consumers access to more goods at lower prices than would have been possible without integration. Companies protected in their domestic markets face real problems when the barriers are eliminated and they attempt to compete with more efficient producers. The strategic implication is that companies that were unable to export to another country—even though they might be more efficient than producers there—are now able to export when the barriers come down, creating more demand for their products and less for the protected ones. Investment also might shift to countries that are more efficient or that have a comparative advantage in one or more factors of production.
2. *Trade Diversion:* Trade shifts to countries in the group at the expense of trade with other countries, even though the nonmember companies might be more efficient in the absence of trade barriers.

Assume, for example, that U.S. companies are importing the same product from Country A and Country B. If the United States enters into an RTA with Country A, U.S. companies might be more likely to import goods from Country A than from Country B due to lower tariffs, other things being equal. Moreover, MNEs from countries outside the RTA might consider investing in the RTA countries to service the market more effectively. Trade diversion is a major criticism of RTAs because the agreements result in greater trade among a few WTO members but not among all. This undermines the multilateral process of the WTO.

Economies of Scale Dynamic effects of integration occur when trade barriers come down and markets grow. Because of that growth, companies can increase their production, which will result in lower costs per unit—a phenomenon we call **economies of scale**. Companies can produce more cheaply, which is good because they must become more efficient to survive. This could result in more trade between the member countries (trade creation) or an increase in investment in the region by local or foreign companies as the market grows.

Increased Competition Another important effect of an RTA is greater efficiency due to increased competition. Many MNEs in Europe have attempted to grow through mergers and acquisitions to achieve the size necessary to compete in the larger market. Companies in Mexico were forced to become more competitive with the passage of NAFTA due to competition from Canadian and U.S. companies. This could result in investment shifting from less efficient to more efficient companies, or it could result in existing companies becoming more efficient.

MAJOR REGIONAL TRADING GROUPS

The two ways to look at different regional trading groups are by location (such as the European Union) and by type (such as an FTA, customs union or common market). Major trading groups exist in every region of the world, and it is impossible to cover every group in every region, so we'll discuss a few of the major ones and examine the type of RTA they are.

Companies are interested in regional trading groups for their markets, sources of raw materials, and production locations. The larger and richer the new market, the more likely it is to attract the attention of the major investor countries and companies. In addition, it is important to understand how the reduction of tariffs and other barriers improves access to countries in the region.

The European Union:

- Changed from the European Economic Community to the European Community to the European Union
- The largest and most successful regional trade group
- Free trade of goods, services, capital, and people
- Common external tariff
- Common currency

THE EUROPEAN UNION

The largest and most comprehensive regional economic group is the **European Union (EU)**. It began by gradually abolishing internal tariffs but eventually established an external tariff while integrating in other ways such as facilitating the free movement of workers, establishing a common agricultural policy, and agreeing on a value-added tax system. The formation of the European Parliament and the establishment of a common currency, the euro, make the EU the most ambitious of all the regional trade groups.[14] Table 7.1 summarizes its key milestones, while Map 7.1 identifies its members and other key European groups.

CONCEPT CHECK

In Chapter 5, we discuss the **theory of country size**, which holds that large countries usually depend less on trade than small countries. The same principle tends to be true of economic blocs, and here we point out that **regional integration** is one way to achieve the size necessary to reduce members' dependence on trade.

Predecessors Because of the economic and human destruction left by World War II, European political leaders realized that greater cooperation among their countries would help speed up recovery. Many organizations were formed, including the European Economic Community (EEC), which eventually emerged as the organization that would bring together the countries of Europe into the most powerful trading bloc in the world. Several other countries, including the United Kingdom, formed the European Free Trade Association (EFTA) with the limited goal of eliminating internal tariffs. But most of those countries eventually became part of the EU, and those that have decided not to leave EFTA (Iceland, Liechtenstein, Norway, and Switzerland) still have a free trade agreement with each other and have established trade relations as a group with other entities outside the European continent, such as Peru. Iceland, Liechtenstein and Norway (but not Switzerland) are linked together with the EU in the European Economic Area, which provides them access to the "four freedoms" of the EU: the free movement of goods, services, persons, and capital. However, it does not include other areas of cooperation, such as a customs union and monetary union.[15]

European Free Trade Association—FTA involving Iceland, Liechtenstein, Norway, and Switzerland, with close ties to the EU.

The EEC, later called the European Community (EC) and finally the EU, set about to abolish internal tariffs to integrate European markets more closely and, ideally, to allow economic cooperation to help avoid further political conflict.

TABLE 7.1 A Few European Union Milestones

From its inception in 1957, the EU has been moving toward complete economic integration, starting with the initial six members: West Germany, France, Italy, Belgium, The Netherlands, and Luxembourg. However, it is doubtful that its initial adherents ever dreamed that European cooperation would result in a common currency.

1959	The first steps are taken in the progressive abolition of customs duties and quotas within the EEC (European Economic Community).
1960	The Stockholm Convention establishes the European Free Trade Association (EFTA) among seven European countries (Austria, Denmark, Norway, Portugal, Sweden, Switzerland, and the United Kingdom).
1961	The first regulation on free movement of workers within the EEC comes into force.
1962	The Common Agricultural Policy is adopted.
1966	Agreement is reached on a value-added tax (VAT) system; a treaty merging the Executives of the European Communities comes into force; and the EEC changes its name to European Community (EC).
1967	All remaining internal tariffs are eliminated, and a common external tariff is imposed.
1973	Denmark, Ireland, and the United Kingdom become members 7, 8 and 9 of the EC.
1981	Greece becomes the 10th member of the EC.
1986	Spain and Portugal become the 11th and the 12th members of the EC.
1990	East and West Germany unite.
1992	Agreement to change the EC to the European Union is adopted in 1992 and implemented in 1993.
1995	Austria, Finland, and Sweden become the 13th, 14th, and 15th members of the EU.
1996	An EU summit names the 11 countries that will join the European single currency with all EU countries joining except Britain, Sweden, Denmark (by their choice), and Greece (not ready).
1999	The euro, the single European currency, comes into effect (January 1, 1999).
2001	Greece becomes the 12th country to adopt the euro (January 1, 2001).
2002	The euro coins and notes enter circulation (January 1, 2002).
	All 15 member states ratify the Kyoto Protocol.
2004	Admission of Cyprus, the Czech Republic, Estonia, Hungary, Latvia, Lithuania, Malta, Poland, Slovakia, and Slovenia brings the number of member states to 25.
2007	Bulgaria and Romania join, bringing the number of member states to 27.
2012	A treaty is signed to create a European Stability Mechanism to help cope with economic challenges.
2013	Croatia joined on July 1, 2013 as 28th member; candidate countries are Iceland, Montenegro, Serbia, The Former Yugoslav Republic of Macedonia, and Turkey

Source: Based on Europa, "History" and "Countries" at http://europa.eu (accessed April 27, 2013).

Organizational Structure The EU encompasses many governing bodies, among which are the European Commission, European Council, European Parliament, European Court of Justice, and European Central Bank.[16]

In Chapter 3, we noted how important it is for MNE management to understand the political environment of every country in which it operates. The same is true for the EU. To be successful in Europe, MNEs need to understand the EU's governance process, just as they need to understand the governance process of each individual European country in which they invest or do business. These institutions set parameters within which companies must operate, so management needs to understand the institutions and how they make decisions that could affect corporate strategy. This is because even though all of the countries are a part of the same trade agreement, there are still individual differences that need to be understood and planned for. Recall from our opening case, for example, how EU policies shaped Toyota's corporate strategy in the region, inducing it to shift from limited exporting to the establishment of full design and manufacturing facilities.

The European Commission provides political leadership, drafts laws, and runs the various daily programs of the EU.

Key Governing Bodies The European Commission provides the EU's political leadership and direction. It is composed of commissioners nominated by each member government and approved by the European Parliament for five-year terms of office. The president of the commission is nominated by the member governments and approved by the European Parliament. The commissioners run the different programs of the EU on a day-to-day basis

MAP 7.1 European Trade and Economic Integration

Although the 27-member EU is easily the dominant trading bloc in Europe, it's not the only one. Founded in 1960, the four-member European Free Trade Association (EFTA) also maintains joint free trade agreements with several other countries. The European Economic Area (EEA) includes three members of the EFTA and all members of the EU. The Central European Free Trade Agreement (CEFTA) was originally formed to integrate Western practices into the economies of former Soviet bloc nations, two of whom have already been admitted into the EU.

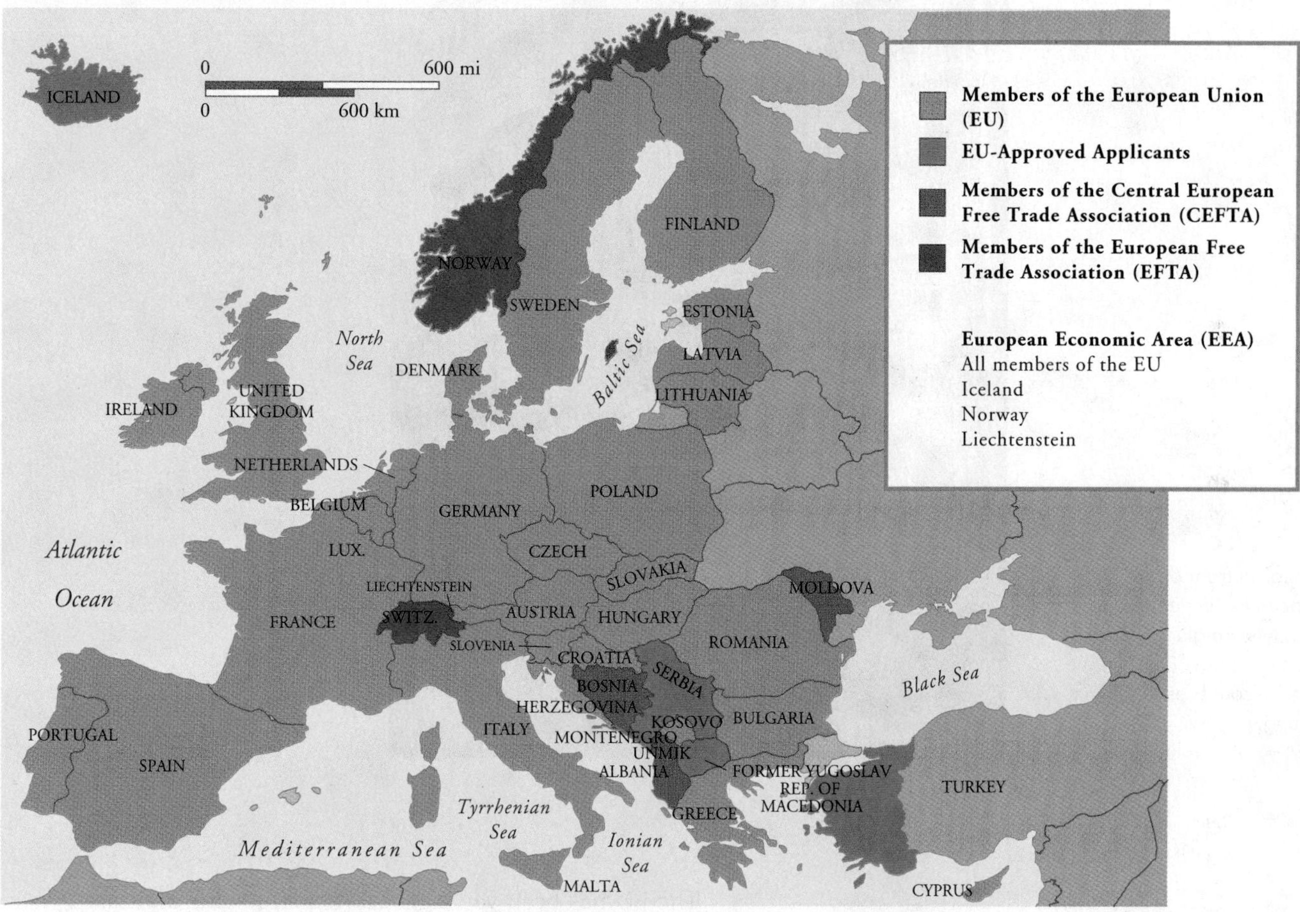

rather than serve as representatives of their respective governments. The commission drafts laws that it submits to the European Parliament and the Council of the European Union.

> The Council of the European Union, or European Summit, is composed of the heads of state of each member country.

The European Council is composed of representatives of each member country whose interests it represents. Along with the European Parliament, the council is responsible for passing laws and making and enacting major policies, including those in the areas of security and foreign policy. The respective ministers of each country meet periodically to discuss the issues facing those ministries (e.g., ministers of agriculture meet to discuss issues facing agriculture). The presidents and/or prime ministers meet up to four times a year to set broad policy.

> The three major responsibilities of the European Parliament are legislative power, control over the budget, and supervision of executive decisions.

The European Parliament is composed of 754 members from all member nations; they are elected every five years, and membership is based on country population. Its three major responsibilities are legislative power, control over the budget, and supervision of executive decisions. Members are grouped by political affiliation (such as Christian Democrats, greens, etc.) rather than by nationality. The commission presents community legislation to the Parliament, which must approve the legislation before it is submitted to the council for adoption.[17]

> The European Court of Justice ensures consistent interpretation and application of EU treaties.

The Court of Justice ensures consistent interpretation and application of EU treaties. Member states, EC institutions, and individuals and companies may bring cases to the Court, which serves as an appeals court for individuals, firms, and organizations fined by the commission for infringing treaty law.[18]

The flags in front of the European Parliament towers in Brussels, Belgium, signify the growth of the EU from the original 6 countries to 28 and counting.
Source: Sergey Kelin/Shutterstock

Antitrust Investigations The EU has been very aggressive in enforcing antitrust laws in the high-tech arena, where intellectual property is a very sensitive issue as countries move to protect their own industries from possible violations by foreign companies.

In 2009 Microsoft bowed to pressure from European antitrust regulators, agreeing to let European users of its Windows software have the option to choose which Web browsers they would like to use and be able to turn off Internet Explorer. Microsoft had already paid the equivalent of $2.4 billion in fines and penalties.[19] Antitrust investigations were also levied against Google based on complaints of other companies, including Microsoft, ironically, complaining that Google was using its market power to block competing search engines. Google has an 82 percent market share in internet searching in Europe.[20] Google finally agreed in 2013 to change how it displays search results in Europe, although as of this writing, concessions were still being studied by the EU and Google's competitors while Google conducted a market test of its new concessions.

The Single European Act was designed to eliminate the remaining nontariff barriers to trade in Europe.

The Single European Act and the Lisbon Treaty The passage of the Single European Act of 1987 was designed to eliminate the remaining barriers to a free market, such as customs posts and different certification procedures, rates of value-added tax, and excise duties. In addition, the Act resulted in closer cooperation in trade (the EU has one negotiator for the WTO who negotiates for all EU members), foreign policy, and the environment. However, barriers still remain, which is only natural given the diverse nature of the EU. One area has to do with labeling. The EU is considering mandating country-of-origin labels for products sold in the EU, even though that is standard practice in many countries (the U.S. has required such labels since the 1930s). One reason to encourage this policy is to protect companies that currently manufacture in Europe. When the controversy broke out in Europe over finding horse meat in foods thought to be primarily beef—such as IKEA's Swedish meatballs—the EU realized it did not have effective standards to guarantee the ingredients of processed meat products and a way to label the products effectively. Some critics maintained that it became an issue of public safety as well as product quality.[21]

The Lisbon Treaty, which went into effect on December 1, 2009, amends the earlier treaties that led to the creation of the EU. Some of the major objectives of the Lisbon Treaty are to strengthen the EU's governance process and improve its ability to make and implement decisions. However, some opponents view the new treaty as part of an agenda to create a stronger federalist union that reduces national sovereignty. It was difficult to pass, but finally all member countries voted to adopt the treaty.[22]

The Treaty of Maastricht sought to foster political union and monetary union.

The euro

- Is a common currency in Europe.
- Is administered by the European Central Bank.
- Was established on January 1, 1999.
- Resulted in new bank notes in 2002.
- Does not include the United Kingdom, Denmark, Sweden, or eight of the new entrants to the EU.

Monetary Union: The Euro In 1992, the members of the EU signed the Treaty of Maastricht in part to establish a monetary union. The decision to move to a common currency, the **euro**, in Europe has eliminated currency as a trade barrier for its adopters. As of 2013, 17 of the EU members had adopted the euro. Others are preparing to do so as well, while only Denmark, Sweden, and the United Kingdom have opted out of the common currency. Other European countries also use the euro, even though they are not EU members. We'll discuss the euro in more detail in Chapter 9 as well as the debt crisis that began with Ireland and then spread to Greece, Spain, Portugal, Italy, and Cyprus. The inability of these countries to meet their external debt obligations has threatened the banking system and forced other European countries to come to the rescue. As possibly the EU's single biggest challenge, this threatens the future of the euro, and there are many who wonder if the currency will survive.

The Schengen Area In order to facilitate the free flow of people from country to country within the EU, the Schengen Agreement was signed in 1990 with gradual implementation allowing citizens to cross internal borders without having to go through border checks. Not all members of the EU, such as the UK, Ireland, Romania, and Bulgaria, have opted to be in the Schengen Area, whereas some non-EU states, such as Iceland, Norway, and Switzerland, are part of it. Croatia, the newest member, intends to join in 2015. The UK has been especially vexed by the immigration issue. Although it must adhere to the freedom of movement within the member nations, it has been tougher on illegal immigrants from outside the EU.[23]

The EU expanded from 15 to 25 countries in 2004 with countries from mostly Central and Eastern Europe. Romania and Bulgaria were admitted in 2007 and Croatia in 2013, bringing the number to 28.

Expansion One of the EU's major challenges is expansion. The May 2004 expansion has been its largest and included Cyprus, the Czech Republic, Estonia, Hungary, Latvia, Lithuania, Malta, Poland, the Slovak Republic, and Slovenia. Bulgaria and Romania were admitted at the beginning of 2007, bringing the total to 27 countries, and in 2013, Croatia became the 28th member. Official candidates for future membership currently include Iceland, Turkey, Montenegro, Serbia, and the former Yugoslav Republic of Macedonia. Other potential candidates are Albania, Bosnia and Herzegovina, and Kosovo. Of the candidates and potential candidates, only Iceland is currently a member of the Schengen Area. Turkey is an interesting candidate since it straddles Europe and Asia, is 99.8 percent Muslim (mostly Sunni), and has a large population of 80.7million people, second only to Germany with 81.1 million people. It has a strong manufacturing base and already strong trade ties with Europe.

CONCEPT CHECK

In Chapter 5, we point out that in countries where labor is abundant compared to capital, many workers (not surprisingly) tend to be either unemployed or poorly paid. If permitted, they will migrate to countries that enjoy full employment and higher wages—a form of **factor mobility** that governments in the latter group of countries often restrict.

Despite the growth rates, which vary significantly from country to country in the EU, many people from the countries with higher unemployment and slower growth have been trying to immigrate to the higher-income nations, creating further challenges. The problem is that economic growth in Europe has been slow and unemployment high. In March 2013, the euro area unemployment rate was 12.1 percent and in the EU it was 10.9 percent: in Spain it was over 27 percent.[24] Export-oriented firms have been hampered by slow internal growth as well as slow growth in China and the United States. As one commentator noted, "The EU has made Europe a much more cohesive economy, which is good when things are going up. But when things are going down, the multiplier is very strong. An outgoing tide lowers all ships."[25]

Bilateral Agreements In addition to reducing trade barriers for member countries, the EU has signed numerous bilateral free trade agreements with other countries outside the region, including one with the Pan Arab Free Trade Area, discussed below. In 2013, the EU announced that it had agreed to start trade negotiations with Japan to form a new FTA.[26] Since the EU negotiates with other countries as one entity, its trade talks are considered bilateral, even though all member states benefit from the results of the talks.

The Transatlantic Trade and Investment Partnership One of the more intriguing potential agreements involves the U.S. and the EU. Even though tariffs between the two super powers are already low (the U.S. and EU have the world's largest trading relationship and account for nearly half of the world's economic output), the new agreement would eliminate the remaining tariffs and boost trade between the regions and aid in harmonizing product standards between them. U.S. labor unions would be more willing to support such an agreement because of the region's similar labor and environmental standards and because an agreement could result in billions of dollars in yearly growth and thousands of jobs.[27]

As the U.S. and EU began negotiations in 2013, however, a number of challenges began to arise. The French, backed by the European Parliament, want to continue providing subsidies and quotas to support its film and music industries and thus exclude the cultural industries from any future trade talks. On the other side, U.S. farmers are very upset about European agricultural safety standards and view them as protectionist. Obviously, any agreement will be difficult to reach, in spite of the hope for expanding economic growth in the regions.[28]

Implications of the EU for corporate strategy:

- Companies need to determine where to produce products.
- Companies need to determine what their entry strategy will be.
- Companies need to balance the commonness of the EU with national differences.

How to Do Business with the EU: Implications for Corporate Strategy The EU is a tremendous market in terms of both population and income—one that companies cannot ignore. It is also a good example of how geographic proximity and the removal of trade barriers can influence trade. As noted earlier, more than half the merchandise exports and imports of EU countries are considered to be intrazonal trade.

Doing business in the EU can influence corporate strategy, especially for outside MNEs, in three ways:

1. *Determining where to produce.* One strategy is to produce in a central location in Europe to minimize transportation costs and the time it takes to move products from one country to another. However, the highest costs are in central Europe. As we saw in our opening case, for instance, manufacturing wages in the German auto industry were much higher than the lower wages among Eastern European members. That's why Toyota opted to set up operations in lower-wage countries such as the Czech Republic and Poland.

2. *Determining whether to grow through new investments, through expanding existing investments, or through joint ventures and mergers.* As we've seen, Toyota has entered into a joint venture with PSA Peugeot-Citroën to build a new factory in the Czech Republic in order to take advantage of the European carmaker's supplier network. The market is still considered fragmented and inefficient compared with the United States, so most experts feel that mergers, takeovers, and spinoffs must continue in Europe, and U.S. companies are buying European companies to gain a market presence and to get rid of competition.
3. *Balancing "common" denominators with national differences.* There are wider national differences in the EU than in various U.S. states, mostly due to language and history. But there are also widely different growth rates as mentioned above. Many smaller nations, such as Ireland and Belgium, are experiencing unprecedented growth because their membership has increased their attractiveness for FDI, helped them develop global perspectives, and sheltered them from economic risks.

A good example of adapting business strategies to Europe is Toyota. In terms of products, Toyota is busy designing a European car, but for which Europe? Tastes and preferences—not to mention climate—vary greatly between northern and southern Europe. Toyota, however, is attempting to use production location and design to facilitate a pan-European strategy.

Companies will always struggle with the degree to which they develop a European strategy versus different national strategies inside Europe. In spite of the challenges, there are many opportunities for companies to expand their markets and sources of supply as the EU grows and encompasses more of Europe.

THE NORTH AMERICAN FREE TRADE AGREEMENT (NAFTA)

The North American Free Trade Agreement

- Includes Canada, the United States, and Mexico.
- Went into effect on January 1, 1994.
- Involves free trade in goods, services, and investment.
- Is a large trading bloc but includes countries of different sizes and wealth.

Various forms of mutual economic cooperation have historically existed between the United States and Canada, such as the Canada-U.S. Free Trade Agreement of 1989, which eliminated all tariffs on bilateral trade by 1998. In February 1991, Mexico approached the United States to establish a free trade agreement. Canada was included in the formal negotiations and the resulting **North American Free Trade Agreement (NAFTA)** became effective on January 1, 1994.

NAFTA rationale:

- U.S.-Canadian trade is the largest bilateral trade in the world.
- The United States is Mexico's and Canada's largest trading partner.

Why NAFTA? NAFTA has a logical rationale in terms of both geographic location and trading importance. Although Canadian-Mexican trade was not significant when the agreement was signed, the U.S. had key trade relationships with each of them. In fact, the one between the United States and Canada is the largest in the world, not including the 28-member EU. As Table 7.2 indicates, NAFTA is a powerful trading bloc with a combined population and GDP slightly less than the 28-member EU. What is significant, especially when compared with the EU, is the tremendous size of the U.S. economy compared to those of its neighbors. In addition, Canada has a much richer economy than that of Mexico, even though its population is about a third of Mexico's. However, the EU has its own disparities. Compare Germany and its nearly 82 million people to Malta, the smallest country, with a population of 411,277. Meanwhile, the average population in the EU is only 18.6 million people.

NAFTA is a free trade agreement in goods and services rather than a customs union or a common market, and there is no common currency. However, its cooperation extends far beyond reductions in tariff and nontariff barriers to include provisions for services, investment, and intellectual property.

NAFTA calls for the elimination of tariff and nontariff barriers, the harmonization of trade rules, the liberalization of restrictions on services and foreign investment, the enforcement of intellectual property rights, and a dispute settlement process.

Mexico made significant strides in tariff reduction after joining GATT in 1986, when its tariffs averaged 100 percent. As of January 1, 2008, all tariffs and quotas were eliminated on U.S. exports to Canada and Mexico.

Static and Dynamic Effects NAFTA provides the static and dynamic effects of economic integration. For example, Canadian and U.S. consumers benefit from lower-cost agricultural products from Mexico, a *static* effect of economic liberalization. U.S. producers also benefit

TABLE 7.2 Comparative Statistics by Trade Group

	Population in Millions (2012)	GDP Billions of $ (2012)	Per Capita GDP in $ (2012)
European Union (EU)	507.4	16,138	31,805
North American Free Trade Agreement (NAFTA)	463	18,874	40,765
Southern Common Market (MECOSUR)	279	3,606	12,924
ASEAN Free Trade Area (AFTA)	623.4	3582	5,746
Common Market of Eastern and Southern Africa (COMESA)	455.6	1086.4	2,385
Pan Arab Free Trade Area (PAFTA)*	290	2,890	9,966

*Also known as the Greater Arab Free Trade Area (GAFTA). The population and income numbers do not include Palestine because that information is not available; data for the EU was collected before Coatia became a member.

Source: Based on information from the CIA World Fact Book.

from the large and growing Mexican market, which has a huge appetite for U.S. products—a *dynamic* effect.

NAFTA is a good example of trade diversion; some U.S. trade with and investment in Asia have been diverted to Mexico.

Trade Diversion NAFTA is also a good example of trade diversion. Prior to the agreement, many U.S. and Canadian companies had established manufacturing facilities in Asia to take advantage of low-cost labor. IBM, for example, was making computer parts in Singapore. After NAFTA, Mexico became a good option for those companies, and in five years IBM boosted exports from Mexico to the United States from $350 million to $2 billion.

Non-NAFTA companies are also investing in Mexico to take advantage of its FTA with Canada and the United States. Sony has huge manufacturing facilities there, especially in Tijuana, just over the border from Southern California. In 2009, Sony closed five factories worldwide and expanded its workforce in Tijuana, adding 1,500 new jobs to take up the slack.[29] The company is able to take advantage of NAFTA free trade provisions to ship products to the United States and save on time and transportation costs. Sony, Samsung, Sanyo, Panasonic, LG and Sharp manufacture television sets in their facilities in Tijuana, most of which are exported to the U.S., Europe, and elsewhere.

Rules of Origin and Regional Content An important component of NAFTA is the concept of rules of origin and regional content. Because it is a free trade agreement and not a customs union, each country sets its own tariffs to the rest of the world. That's why a product entering the United States from Canada must have a commercial or customs invoice that identifies the product's ultimate origin. Otherwise, an exporter from a third country could always ship the product to the NAFTA country with the lowest tariff and then re-export it to the other two countries duty-free. A major criticism of RTAs like NAFTA is that the rules of origin are complex and detract from the spirit of multilateral tariff reductions in the WTO.

Rules of origin—goods and services must originate in North America to get access to lower tariffs.

Rules of Origin "Rules of origin" ensure that only goods that have been the subject of substantial economic activity within the free trade area are eligible for the more liberal tariff conditions created by NAFTA. This is a major contrast with the EU, which is a customs union rather than just an FTA. When a product enters France, for example, it can be shipped anywhere in the EU without worrying about rules of origin because tariffs are the same for all member countries. If NAFTA were a customs union instead of a free trade agreement, a product entering Mexico from, say, Japan and shipped to the United States would enter the U.S. duty-free because both countries would have the same duty on imports.[30]

Regional content:

- The percentage of value that must be from North America for the product to be considered North American in terms of country of origin
- 50 percent for most products, 62.5 percent for autos

Regional Value Content Requirement One aspect of rules of origin in NAFTA refers to the Regional Value Content requirement. According to regional content rules, at least 50 percent of the net cost of components, raw materials, and labor of most products must come from the NAFTA region to qualify for the FTA. As long as a company meets the standard—and the regional content rules may vary depending on the nature of the product—a company may manufacture or assemble products in the NAFTA region and ship the goods to other members duty-free.

Additional NAFTA provisions:

- Workers' rights
- The environment
- Dispute resolution mechanism

Special Provisions Because of U.S. labor unions' and environmentalists' strong objections, two auxiliary agreements covering their concerns were included in the NAFTA agreement. Opponents to the agreement worried about the potential loss of jobs in Canada and the United States to Mexico as a result of its cheaper wages, poor working conditions, and lax environmental enforcement. U.S. union organizers, in particular, thought companies would close down factories in the north and set them up in Mexico. As a result, the labor lobby in the United States forced the inclusion of labor standards such as the right to unionize, while the environmental lobby pushed for an upgrade of environmental standards in Mexico and the strengthening of compliance. This is a challenge internationally because not all countries are as concerned about labor and environmental standards.

The Impact of NAFTA There are pros and cons to any trade agreement, and NAFTA is no exception. It is obvious that trade and investment have increased significantly since the agreement was signed in 1994. U.S. goods and services trade with NAFTA totaled $1.6 trillion in 2009 (according to the latest data available). U.S. goods trade with the two partners totaled $918 billion in 2010, with the U.S. recording a trade deficit in goods. [31] Canada is the largest export market for U.S. goods, and Mexico is number two. And Canada and Mexico are the second and third largest suppliers of goods to the U.S.

Because of its size, the U.S. is very important to Canada and Mexico for both exports and imports. Canada exports 75 percent of its merchandise to the U.S. and receives 51.2 percent of its imports from U.S. For Mexico, the numbers are 80.7 percent and 48.1 percent, respectively. Although trade between Canada and Mexico has grown since the implementation of NAFTA, the U.S, because of its size, is still the most significant market for their firms.

A major challenge to NAFTA is illegal immigration.

Immigration A major challenge to NAFTA is immigration. As trade in agriculture increased with the advent of NAFTA, more than a million farm jobs disappeared in Mexico due to U.S. competition. Many of these farmers ended up as undocumented workers in the United States, sending home more money in wire transfers (see the opening case in Chapter 8) than Mexico receives in FDI. This has become a major political issue in both countries, especially as the United States tries to figure out how to stop the flow of illegal immigrants and what to do with those already in the United States. In 2013, the presidents of the two countries met to discuss economic, immigration, and security challenges, especially in light of estimates of around 11 million illegal immigrants in the United States, most of whom come from Mexico. A strong Mexican economy and a more secure border will help, but until the U.S. comes up with comprehensive immigration reform, there will be political and economic challenges between the two.

CONCEPT CHECK

As you'll recall from Chapter 5, trade restrictions may diminish export capabilities and induce companies to locate some production in countries imposing the restrictions; the absence of trade barriers gives them more flexibility not only in deciding where to locate production but also in determining how to service different markets.

How to Do Business with NAFTA: Implications for Corporate Strategy Although NAFTA has not expanded beyond the original three countries due to political obstacles, each member has entered into bilateral agreements with other countries. However, when U.S. companies invest in Mexico, for example, they have an opportunity to penetrate markets in countries where Mexico has FTAs. The situation is somewhat similar to that in the ASEAN region. The closing case shows how Unilever has been successful in its expansion in that region. That allows them to add additional scale as the market broadens, even though Mexico's other trading partners are not members of NAFTA.

Rationalization of Production One of the predictions made when NAFTA was signed was that companies would look at it as one big regional market, allowing them to rationalize production, products, financing, and the like. That has largely happened in a number of industries, especially in automotive products and electronics. Each NAFTA member ships more automotive products, based on specialized production, to the other two countries than any other manufactured goods. Rationalization of automotive production has taken place for years in the United States and Canada, but Mexico is a recent entrant, attracting auto manufacturing from all over the world, not just the United States. NAFTA's rules of origin have forced European and Asian automakers to bring in parts suppliers and set up assembly operations in Mexico.

The Volkswagen Group is an excellent example of a European company with a strong NAFTA strategy. In 2013, VW opened an engine production facility in Mexico, adding capacity to its production network in North America with facilities in Tennessee (U.S.) and Silao, Puebla, Queretaro, and San José Chiapa (Mexico). VW used to assemble the old-style Beetle in Mexico for export to the U.S., but the old-style Beetle was eventually replaced with a newer style which began production in Puebla in 2012. Volkswagen of Mexico employs over 15,000 workers in the country, highlighting Mexico's importance as a manufacturing hub that supplies autos for the domestic and export markets. In addition, VW announced in 2013 that it was going to produce its next-generation Golf in Puebla. With its new facilities, VW hopes to build more than 75 percent of the cars it sells in the NAFTA region, thus insulating VW from currency risk and allowing it to take advantage of NAFTA provisions.[32]

Another prediction was that sophisticated U.S. companies would run Canadian and Mexican companies out of business once the markets opened up. That has not happened. In fact, U.S. firms along the Canadian border are finding that Canadian companies are generating more competition for them than low-wage Mexican companies are. Also, many Mexican companies have restructured to compete with U.S. and Canadian firms. The lack of protection has resulted in much more competitive Mexican companies And the closing case shows how a company, Unilever, has successfully taken its subsidiaries to markets in the ASEAN and established itself as a distinguished, fast-growing FMCG firm in the region.

Mexico as a Consumer Market An additional benefit is that Canadian and U.S. companies have realized that Mexico is a consumer market rather than just a production location. Initially, the excitement over the country for U.S. and Canadian firms was the low-wage environment. However, as Mexican income continues to rise—which it must do as more investment enters and more of its companies export production—demand is rising for foreign products.

REGIONAL ECONOMIC INTEGRATION IN THE AMERICAS

If you look at Maps 7.2 and 7.3, you'll see six major regional economic groups in the Americas, divided into Central American and South American. Central America (excluding Mexico) has the Caribbean Community (CARICOM), the Central American Common Market (CACM), and the Central American Free Trade Agreement (CAFTA-DR)—which includes the members of CACM but also Honduras and the Dominican Republic, along with the United States. The two major groups in South America are the Andean Community (CAN) and the Southern Common Market (MERCOSUR). The Andean Community is a customs union, whereas MERCOSUR is set up to be a common market.

In 2008, the Union of South American Nations (UNASUR), was created with the goal in mind of merging CAN and MERCOSUR, which are both customs unions, into a larger

MAP 7.2 Economic Integration in Central America and the Caribbean

Throughout Central America and the Caribbean, the focus on economic integration has shifted from the concept of the *free trade agreement* (whose goal is the abolition of trade barriers among members) to that of the *common market* (which calls for internal factor mobility as well as the abolition of internal trade barriers). The proposed structure of the Caribbean Community and Common Market (CARICOM) is modeled on that of the EU.

MAP 7.3 Latin American Economic Integration
There are only two key RTAs in South America: the Andean Group and MERCOSUR. The Latin American Integration Association, which was established in 1980, has failed to establish a free trade agreement or a dispute resolution mechanism.

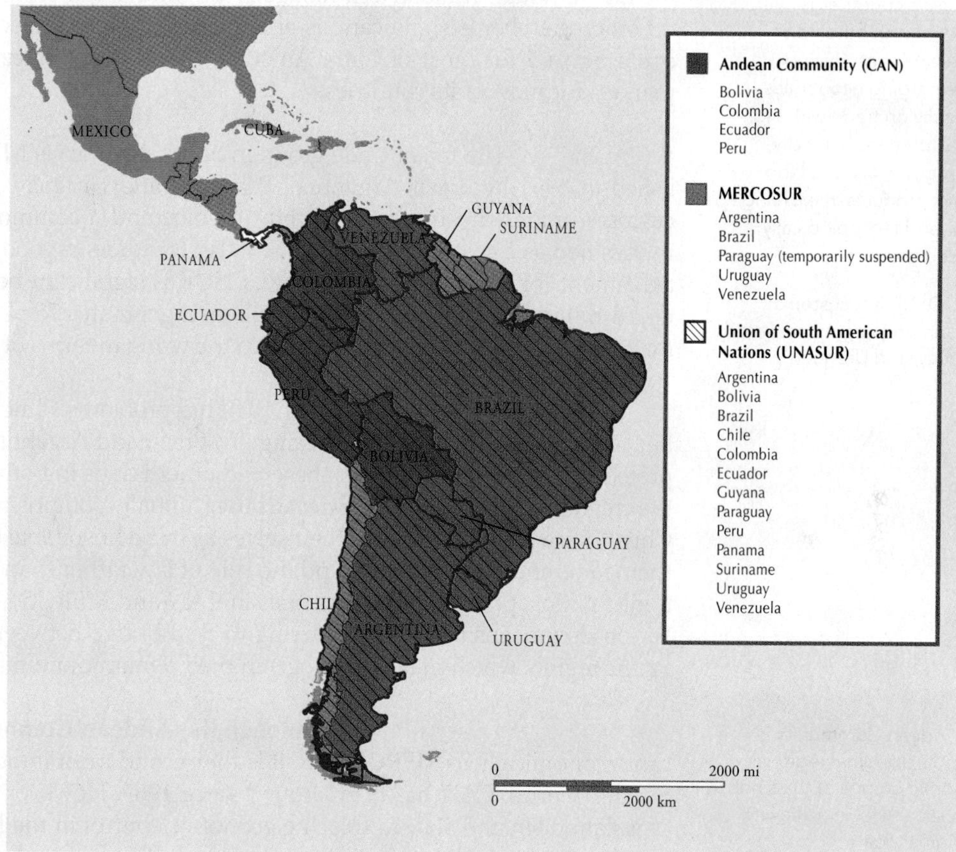

group modeled after the European Union. Brazil helped initiate UNASUR (or UNASUL in Portuguese) to foster political cooperation and to replace a U.S. initiative to create a 34-nation Free Trade of the Americas. However, UNASUR is in its initial phases.

The major reason for these different collaborative groups was market size. The post–World War II strategy of import substitution to resolve balance-of-payments problems in much of Latin America was doomed because of the region's small national markets. Therefore, some form of economic cooperation was needed to enlarge the potential market size so that Latin American companies could achieve economies of scale and be more competitive worldwide.

CARICOM The **Caribbean Community (CARICOM)** is working hard to establish an EU-style form of collaboration, complete with full movement of goods and services, the right of establishment, a common external tariff, free movement of capital and labor, a common trade policy, and so on. It is officially classified by the WTO as an Economic Integration Agreement. Many of these initiatives have come about through an initiative called the CARICOM Single Market and Economy (CSME).

In some ways, the changes in the Caribbean Community mirror what has happened in the EU, though on a smaller scale. The entire population is only 6.5 million people, 60 percent of whom live in only two countries: Jamaica and Trinidad and Tobago. That would put it on the level of EU member Bulgaria in terms of population. However, it is important for CARICOM to succeed in order to expand market size and attract more investment and jobs.

CONCEPT CHECK

In Chapter 5, we observe that little of the trade of low-income countries is conducted with other low-income countries. By and large, emerging economies rely heavily on trade with high-income countries, typically exporting primary and labor-intensive products in exchange for new and technologically advanced products.

The Challenge of Export Reliance Countries in Latin America and the Caribbean rely heavily on countries outside the region for trade. For example, Jamaica, a member of CARICOM, exports 49.3 percent of its merchandise to the United States and 18 percent to the EU. Although Trinidad and Tobago is the third major exporter of merchandise to Jamaica, no other member is significant as either a destination or a source for its exports. The same could be said for most of Latin America. The United States and EU represent significant markets for most of its countries.

MERCOSUR is a customs union among Argentina, Brazil, Paraguay, and Uruguay.

MERCOSUR The major trade group in South America is **MERCOSUR**, which was established in 1991 by Brazil, Argentina, Paraguay, and Uruguay. Its major goal is to become a customs union with free trade within the bloc and a common external tariff. MERCOSUR is classified as a customs union by the WTO for trade in goods and an economic integration agreement for trade in services. MERCOSUR is significant because of its size: a population of 251 million and a GDP of $2.457 trillion. It generates 75 percent of South America's GDP, making it the third largest trading bloc in the world in terms of GDP after the EU and NAFTA.

Pacific Alliance However, MERCOSUR has problems. It included Venezuela as a full member, and temporarily suspended Paraguay. Brazil and Argentina have serious problems with protectionism. Frustration over these and other issues in both CAN and MERCOSUR led to the creation in 2012 of the **Pacific Alliance**, initially comprising Mexico, Colombia, Peru, and Chile. These countries refer to themselves as more hospitable to trade and investment due to their adherence to democracy and the rule of law rather than the more populist and protectionist philosophies of other countries in CAN and MERCOSUR.[33] Having borders with the Pacific also means that they are trying to be a bridge between Latin America and the Asia-Pacific region, which makes sense given their dynamic and market-oriented economies.[34]

The Andean Community is one of the original regional economic groups but has not been successful in achieving its original goals.

Andean Community (CAN) Although the **Andean Community (CAN)** is not as significant economically as MERCOSUR, it is the second most important official regional group in South America. CAN has been around since 1969. However, its focus has shifted from one of isolationism and statism (placing economic control in the hands of the state—the central government) to being open to foreign trade and investment. Colombia, one of the founding members of CAN, has changed significantly in recent years and entered into a bilateral trade agreement with the U.S., solidifying its move to greater openness in comparison with other members of CAN. As noted above, Colombia and Peru, both members of CAN, have decided to join the Pacific Alliance.

Is CAFTA-DR a Good Idea?

Point

Point **Yes** The Dominican Republic-Central American Free Trade Agreement is a *great* idea. Linking the United States together with six other countries—Costa Rica, Dominican Republic, El Salvador, Guatemala, Honduras, and Nicaragua—the FTA holds enormous benefits for its signatories: opening the door for increased trade between the United States and the region; stimulating economic growth in the region by encouraging FDI and offering shorter international supply chains; and encouraging economic and political reform in an area historically plagued by Marxism, dictatorships, and civil wars.

As of 2013, the U.S. has 15 FTAs in force with 20 countries, including new agreements with South Korea, Panama, and Colombia. CAFTA-DR is an FTA that is regional in scope but which is between the U.S. on one side and CAFTA-DR on the other. One of the biggest benefits for the United States is reciprocal tariff treatment from the other nations. Due to temporary trade-preference programs and other regional agreements, 80 percent of the products from at least five Central American nations already enter the United States duty-free. Prior to signing the agreement, U.S. manufactured exports were subject to tariffs that averaged 30 to 100 percent higher than those faced by Central American exports when entering the United States.[35] CAFTA-DR allows the Central American nations to maintain these favorable gains, but it also leaves the playing field for the U.S. to benefit similarly by reducing restrictions on 80 percent of U.S. consumer and industrial exports to the region, with the rest to be phased out over 10 years. Since the agreement is not a customs union, products eligible for the benefits must meet relevant rules of origin, similar to the provisions of NAFTA.

There's fear that the freer inflow of Central American agricultural products will undercut U.S. prices. But again, the United States is already largely open to these products, and although the heavily subsidized U.S. sugar industry adamantly opposed CAFTA-DR, the sugar deal will set a quota that will amount to only 1.7 percent of U.S. production in 15 years.

Although many critics argue that the benefits certain CAFTA-DR countries gain will come at the expense of other participating countries, in truth the gains will be mutual. For example, the growth that CAFTA-DR will foster in Central American industries, particularly its apparel industry, will also benefit exporters in the United States whose products are used in their manufacturing processes. Fifty-six percent of the apparel exports from the Central American region are produced from textiles exported from the United States; 40 percent of U.S. yarn exports and about 25 percent of its fabric exports are purchased by these nations. By working together through CAFTA-DR, the United States and Central America will prevent the loss of Central American apparel jobs to China, whose products contain little or no input from the United States. The National Council of Textile Organizations, which represents more than 88 textile companies, strongly supports CAFTA-DR because U.S. exports of yarns and fabric can be turned into garments in the region and re-exported back to the U.S. duty-free. As the CAFTA-DR Free Trade Commission continues to adapt rules to strengthen the textile/apparel supply chain, U.S. textile and apparel exports increased, resulting in CAFTA-DR taking third place behind Mexico and Canada, whereas exports from the region to the U.S. trailed only China as a textile and apparel supplier to the United States.[36]

Another argument critics make is that CAFTA-DR will create job market shifts that will lead to thousands of job losses in the manufacturing and agricultural sectors. However, predictions from the U.S. Chamber of Commerce don't bear out this claim. For example, in North Carolina alone, CAFTA-DR should increase industrial output by $3.9 billion and create some 29,000 jobs over nine years. Other sources have stated that 250,000 jobs in Central America depend on CAFTA-DR being approved. And although labor organizations have decried the lack of worker-protection clauses in the agreement, a report from the International Labor Organization actually praises Central American labor laws and standards.[37]

Is CAFTA-DR a Good Idea?

Counterpoint

No CAFTA-DR is not a good idea at all—not for the United States or for the impoverished nations it allegedly helps. Much has been said about how the accord will boost trade between the two regions, support constructive economic and political reforms in Central America, create thousands of jobs, and demonstrate the benefits of free trade and open competition. However, there is neither the evidence to bear out these claims nor consideration for any consequences. CAFTA-DR undermines the efforts of the WTO to liberalize trade worldwide rather than region by region. In addition, it excludes trade negotiations with other countries in the region, such as Argentina and Brazil, who have proved to be more difficult countries to negotiate with.

The agreement will open the participating Central American countries to more duty-free exportation on behalf of U.S. manufacturers and farmers, but will this really translate into benefits for either side? The U.S. agricultural industry already can sell pretty much all the

Counterpoint

products it wants on the worldwide market; what it really needs is an increase in the worldwide market prices, but Central America's economies are too small to even affect world prices. Plus, the increased flow of U.S. corn and rice into Central America will devastate the region's own farm economies.

The idea that it will benefit the region by allowing increased exports to the United States is also faulty. Due to its giant trade deficit, the United States really cannot afford to tolerate a major increase in imports from the CAFTA-DR countries.

In addition, CAFTA-DR will actually be increasing some barriers to free trade. For example, the accord may make it harder for countries such as Guatemala to obtain access to affordable lifesaving medicines because of stringent intellectual property clauses included in the agreement.

CAFTA-DR is also a bad move for labor and workers' rights. It will most likely trigger the loss of manufacturing jobs in the United States and agricultural jobs in Central

America. Although proponents of the deal assert that it will stem illegal immigration from these poorer nations, the shift in jobs will most likely increase immigration, as it did with NAFTA.

Furthermore, it will trigger a "race to the bottom" when it comes to wages. The accord will open up U.S. labor markets to competition from a low-wage area, which could drive down the current wage level.

Because the accord involves developing countries with vastly different interests than the United States, it will be hard to please all parties. For example, Costa Rica faced opposition from trade unions, farm groups, and even businesses, as well as fears about the accord's stringent intellectual-property clauses and the chance that it might force the country to privatize its free universal healthcare system.

In spite of all the concerns, the agreement has been implemented by all of the parties. U.S. exports to CAFTA-DR increased by 43 percent in the first five years that the agreement was in force, compared with an increase of only 25 percent in the five years prior to the agreement. It seems to have helped U.S. exports to the region, but have the CAFTA-DR countries benefited as well?

1. Why do you think it was so important for the members of CAFTA-DR to sign an agreement with the United States given that tariffs on goods entering the U.S. were already so low?

REGIONAL ECONOMIC INTEGRATION IN ASIA

There are several RTAs in Asia as recognized by the WTO and a few significant trade initiatives in process. Of the officially approved RTAs, the most important is the Association of Southeast Asian Nations/ASEAN Free Trade Area. As is the case in Latin America, regional integration in Asia has not been as successful as in Europe or North America because most of the countries in the region have relied on U.S. and EU markets for as much as 20 to 30 percent of their exports—not as extensive as in Latin America but still significant. In addition, China and Japan, which are not members of ASEAN/AFTA, are significant players in the region in terms of trade and investment.

Association of Southeast Asian Nations (ASEAN) Organized in 1967, **ASEAN** is a comprehensive association that includes preferential trade as one of its many goals. This preferential trade agreement comprises Brunei Darussalam, Cambodia, Indonesia, Laos, Malaysia, Myanmar, the Philippines, Singapore, Thailand, and Vietnam (see Map 7.4). With a combined GDP of $2.28 trillion and an estimated population of 622.5 million people[38]—it is a significant organization.

The ASEAN Free Trade Area is a successful trade agreement among countries in Southeast Asia.

ASEAN Free Trade Area On January 1, 1993, ASEAN officially formed the ASEAN Free Trade Area (AFTA) with the goal of cutting tariffs on all intrazonal trade to a maximum of 5 percent by January 1, 2008. The weaker ASEAN countries would be allowed to phase in their tariff reductions over a longer period. By 2005, most products traded among the AFTA countries were subject to duties from 0 to 5 percent, so AFTA has been successful in its objectives. Free trade is crucial to the member countries because their ratio of exports to GDP is almost 70 percent. The best achievement of AFTA is that is has reduced tariffs, attracted FDI, and turned the region into a huge network of production, leading to what some call "factory Asia."[39]

Although China is not a part of ASEAN, it is essential to ASEAN's future. China's working-age population is 795.4 million people, compared with 298 million for the ASEAN countries. Although the average monthly wage for manufacturing workers is much higher in Singapore ($2,832) and Malaysia ($666.10) than in China ($412.50), it is much lower in the other ASEAN countries. As wages continue to rise in China, there are opportunities for ASEAN countries to attract more FDI, but those countries need to work hard to improve their infrastructure, especially supply chain and manufacturing infrastructure.[40] These opportunities combined with China's competitive position are forcing ASEAN to work harder to strengthen the ties among member countries. In addition to the FTA, ASEAN has a goal of

MAP 7.4 The Association of Southeast Asian Nations

Although the total population of ASEAN countries (as of 2013) is larger than that of either the EU or NAFTA, per capita GDP is considerably lower. Economic growth rates among ASEAN members, however, are among the highest in the world.

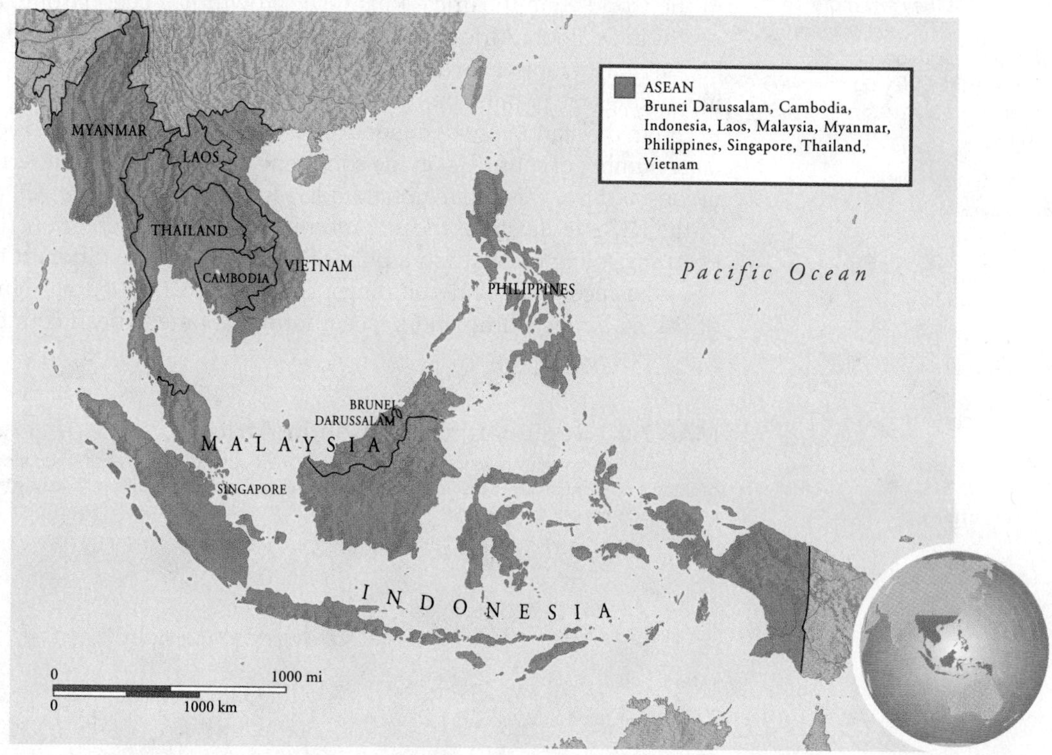

establishing the ASEAN Economic Community (AEC) by 2015, which the member countries hope will go beyond trade liberalization and help establish the region as a single market and production base.

APEC comprises 21 countries that border the Pacific Rim; progress toward free trade is hampered by size and geographic distance between member countries and by the lack of a treaty.

Asia Pacific Economic Cooperation (APEC) Formed in November 1989 to promote multilateral economic cooperation in trade and investment in the Pacific Rim,[41] **Asia Pacific Economic Cooperation (APEC)** is composed of 21 countries that border both Asia and the Americas. All but three members of AFTA are members of APEC, plus Canada, the U.S., Mexico, Peru, and Chile in the Americas; Australia and New Zealand; and China, Japan, Korea, Russia, and Chinese Taipei. It is a large and powerful organization that is focused on a wide range of activities related to trade and investment, security, energy, sustainability, anti-corruption, and transparency, among other things. However, it is not an RTA as defined by the WTO and does not show up on that list of RTAs. The sheer size of APEC is what sets it apart: 55 percent of global GDP and 43 percent of world trade. The U.S. hosted APEC in 2011 for the first time since 1993, and its meetings rotate among the 21 member nations.

Trans-Pacific Partnership (TPP) The TPP was initiated by the U.S. to spur economic growth and create jobs, and it involves Australia, Brunei, Canada, Chile, Japan, Malaysia, Mexico, New Zealand, Peru, Singapore, the United States, and Vietnam. The formation of the initiative was announced in 2011, and Japan was added as a member in 2013. A main goal of the TPP is to enhance trade and investment. Interestingly, the TPP does not include all members of APEC but it provides a more limited scope of negotiations in the Pacific region for the U.S. in the same way that U.S. negotiations with Europe provide an Atlantic initiative. The latest movement is the goal of establishing a Free Trade Area of the Pacific.

REGIONAL ECONOMIC INTEGRATION IN AFRICA

There are several African trade groups, but they rely more on their former colonial powers and other developed markets for trade than they do on each other.

Africa is truly the new frontier. Between 2001–2010, six of the fastest growing economies in the world were in Africa. Real GDP growth has been strong, and FDI has risen significantly. In addition, Africa has the fastest-expanding labor force in the world with more than 500 million people of working age (15–64), and is expected to surpass China and India in working-age population by 2040.[42]

From the standpoint of regional integration, however, Africa is complicated because of the large number of countries on the continent and the fact that there are three regional monetary unions and five existing regional trade associations. On Map 7.5, we have selected only four of the RTAs to illustrate the situation in Africa. The problem is that African countries have been struggling to establish a political identity, and the different trade groups have political as well as economic underpinnings. The key to continued growth in Africa is the reduction of risk as conflicts drop and peace improves. Some African countries are members of more

MAP 7.5 Regional Integration in Africa

Although African nations have joined to form several groups for the purpose of economic integration, the total amount of trade among members remains relatively small. African nations tend to rely heavily on trading relationships with countries elsewhere in the world—notably with industrialized nations.

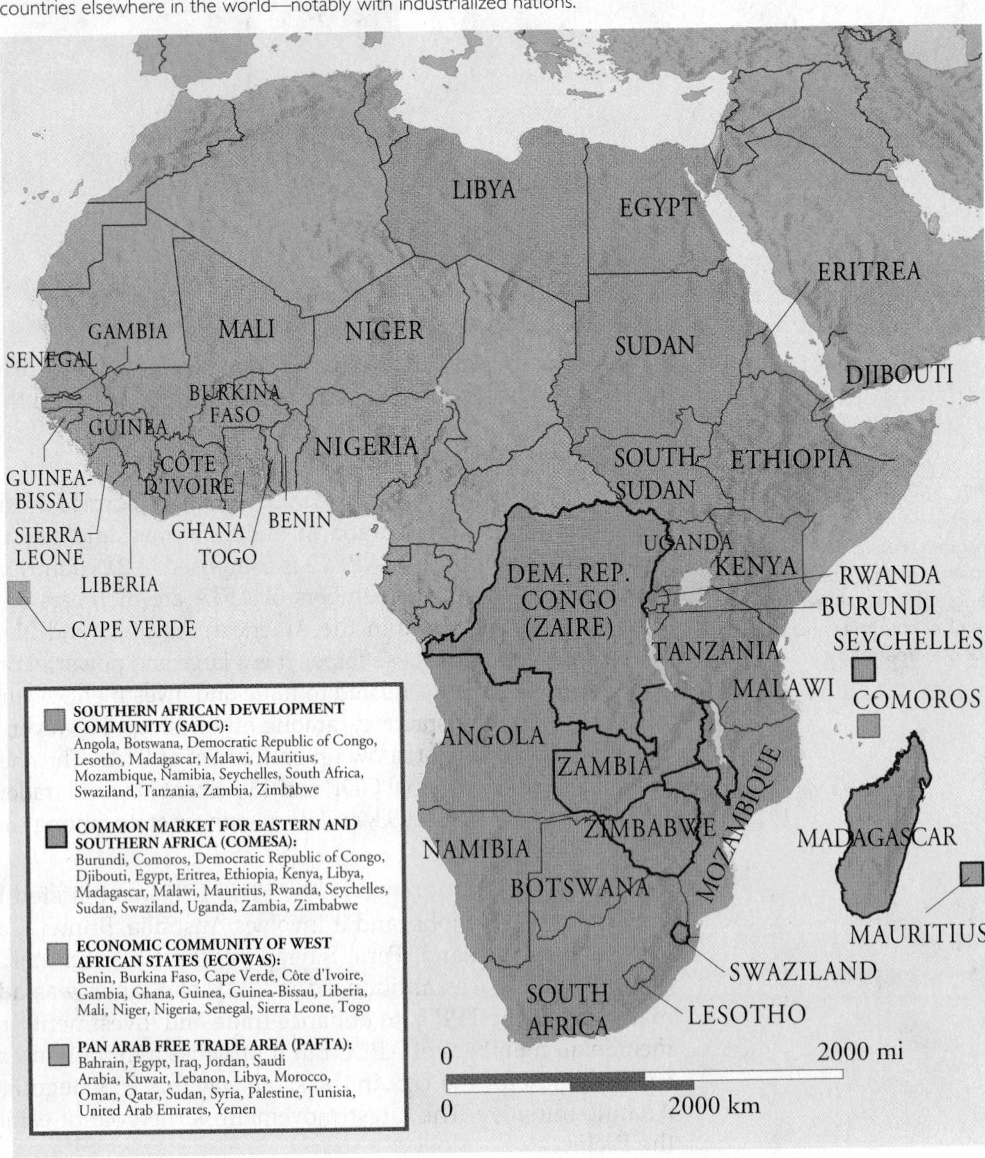

than one RTA. An example is Zambia, which is a member of both SADC and COMESA. That makes sense in one respect since Zambia borders COMESA on the North and SADC on the South. Another example is Egypt which is a member of the Pan Arab Free Trade Area (also called the Greater Arab Free Trade Area) and COMESA. In addition, Egypt has access to Europe through free trade agreements with the EU and EFTA. Former colonial links are also important. Most but not all of the members of ECOWAS are former French colonies and thus still have economic ties with France.

The **Pan Arab Free Trade Area (PAFTA)** is an interesting group because its members span North Africa (Egypt, Tunisia, Sudan, Libya, and Morocco) and the Middle East (UAE, Bahrain, Jordan, Saudi Arabia, Syria, Iraq, Oman, Palestine, Qatar, Kuwait, Lebanon, and Yemen). Officially recognized by the WTO as an RTA, its goal is to reduce trade barriers among its member countries. In addition to PAFTA, the **Arab League** represents more countries but with political rather than economic objectives. Subsets of Arab League countries, such as the **Gulf Cooperation Council** are more effective than the larger Arab League and PAFTA because of the smaller number of countries involved. The GCC basically includes Bahrain, Saudi Arabia, Kuwait, Oman, Qatar, and the UAE. Whereas the African countries have large populations and a variety of natural resources in high demand, PAFTA and the GCC have smaller populations but huge oil and natural gas reserves. Political instability, especially the repercussions of the Arab Spring of 2011 and the overthrow in 2013 of the government in Egypt, makes economic collaboration a huge challenge, at least in the short run.

The African Union (AU) One group not shown on Map 7.5 is the African Union, created by 53 countries in 2002 to focus on political issues in Africa, notably colonialism and racism. It has gotten involved in civilian conflicts throughout Africa and is not the organization pushing for trade liberalization. Civil war, corruption, diseases such as AIDS, and poor government infrastructures have hampered African countries and their ability to progress economically. The AU now includes every country in Africa except Morocco, and it is pushing aggressively to promote peace and security through openness and democracy. Eventually, the AU wants to push for economic integration, but it is not formally negotiating trade deals, but rather letting the various regional trade groups do that.[43]

Because most African countries rely more on trade links with former colonial powers than with each other, intrazonal trade is not significant. The markets, with the notable exception of South Africa, are relatively small and undeveloped, making trade liberalization a relatively minor contributor to economic growth in the region. However, any type of market expansion through regional integration will help these small countries.

OTHER FORMS OF INTERNATIONAL COOPERATION

Up to now, this chapter has focused on treaties between nations designed to reduce trade and investment barriers and increase trade and investment among member nations. We have moved from the global—the WTO—to the bilateral and the regional. However, there are other forms of cooperation worth mentioning that could have an influence on MNE strategies.

The United Nations The first form of cooperation worth exploring is the United Nations, which was established in 1945 in response to the devastation of World War II to promote international peace and security and to help solve global problems in such diverse areas as economic development, antiterrorism, and humanitarian actions. If the UN performs its responsibilities, it should improve the environment in which MNEs operate around the world, reducing risk and providing greater opportunities.

The UN was established in 1945 following World War II to promote international peace and security. It deals with economic development, antiterrorism, and humanitarian movements.

Organization and Membership The UN family of organizations is too large to list, but it includes the WTO, the International Monetary Fund, and the World Bank (the latter two discussed in subsequent chapters). These organizations are all part of the Economic and

Social Council, one of six principal organs of the UN System, which also includes the General Assembly, the Security Council, and the International Court of Justice.

The UN has 193 member states represented in the General Assembly, including 15 that comprise the Security Council. There are five permanent members of the Security Council—China, France, the Russian Federation, the United Kingdom, and the United States—and 10 other members elected by the General Assembly to serve two-year terms.[44]

UNCTAD was established to help developing countries participate in international trade.

UNCTAD The UN Conference on Trade and Development, or **UNCTAD**, was established in 1964 to integrate developing countries into the global economy. UNCTAD's main activities include globalization and development strategies, trade in goods and services, commodities, investment and enterprise development, and trade logistics and human resource development. In particular, UNCTAD has been active in contributing to the debate on issues related to developing countries and the global economy.[45]

NGOs: Private nonprofit institutions that are independent of the government.

Nongovernmental Organizations (NGOs) Nongovernmental, nonprofit voluntary organizations are all lumped under the category of NGOs: private institutions that are independent of any government. Some NGOs operate only within the confines of a specific country, whereas others are international in scope. An example of the latter is the International Red Cross, which is concerned with humanitarian issues around the world, not just in one country. One of the functions of UNCTAD is to work with NGOs in helping shape policies and activities related to concerns of developing countries.

Many NGOs, such as Doctors without Borders, are like the Red Cross in that they are concerned about humanitarian issues. Others came about as a response to what is perceived as the negative side of globalization. Many NGOs that deal with the environment and labor issues will be discussed in Chapter 11. NGOs perform an important role in bringing potential abuses to light and tend to be very narrowly focused, usually on a specific issue. In addition to UNCTAD, there is a Committee on Non-Governmental Organizations that is a part of the Economic and Social Council (ECOSOC) of the UN that meets to discuss issues of importance to general and specific NGOs.

COMMODITY AGREEMENTS

Commodities refer to raw materials or primary products that enter into trade, such as metals or agricultural products. Primary commodity exports—such as crude petroleum, natural gas, copper, tobacco, coffee, cocoa, tea, and sugar—are still important to developing countries. Out of 151 developing countries, 100, two-thirds of the total, derive more than 50 percent of their export value from commodities.[46]

The attempts of countries to stabilize commodity prices through producer alliances and commodity agreements have been largely unsuccessful.

COMMODITIES AND THE WORLD ECONOMY

Both long-term trends and short-term fluctuations in commodity prices have important consequences for the world economy. On the demand side, commodity markets play an important role in industrial countries, transmitting business cycle disturbances to the rest of the economy and affecting the growth rate of prices. On the supply side, as noted above, primary products account for a significant portion of the GDP and exports of many commodity-producing countries.

CONCEPT CHECK

Commodities often represent natural advantages, which we define in Chapter 5 as advantages in producing products resulting from climatic conditions, access to certain natural resources, or availability of certain labor forces.

CONSUMERS AND PRODUCERS

For many years, countries tried to band together as producer alliances or joint producer/consumer alliances to try to stabilize commodity prices. However, these efforts—with the exception of OPEC, which we discuss below—have not been very successful. UNCTAD

CONCEPT CHECK

Remember from Chapter 5 the fact that lower-income countries depend much more on the production of primary products than do wealthier nations; consequently, they depend more heavily on **natural advantage** as opposed to the kinds of **acquired advantage** that involve more advanced technologies and processes.

established a Special Unit on Commodities to attempt to deal with the issues facing developing countries because of high dependence on commodities, especially agricultural commodities, for export revenues. Given such reliance, UNCTAD is concerned that it will be impossible to resolve poverty issues, especially in Africa, without dealing with fluctuating commodity prices.

The most important international commodity organizations and bodies, such as the International Cocoa Organization and the International Copper Study Group, take part in UN-led discussions to help commodity-dependent countries establish effective policies and strategies. However, each one, such as the International Coffee Organization (ICO), has its own organizational structure independent of the UN. The ICO is composed of 38 coffee-exporting nations—all of them developing countries—and 32 importing nations, most of which are developed countries. ICO members are responsible for over 97 percent of the world's coffee exports and 80 percent of the world's coffee consumption.[47]

Many commodity agreements now exist for the purpose of

- Discussing issues,
- Disseminating information,
- Improving product safety.

Whereas many of the original commodity agreements were designed to influence price through a variety of market-interfering mechanisms, most of the existing ones have been established to discuss issues, disseminate information, improve product safety, and so on. Very little can be done outside of market forces to influence price. The ICO, for example, helps fund projects for coffee growing nations to combat pests and diseases and to expand coffee consumption through promotion efforts. Coffee consumption varies a lot from country to country, so the promotion efforts supported by ICO are designed to increase per capita consumption in low-consuming countries.

Because commodities are the raw materials used in the production process, it is important for managers of companies that use them to understand the factors that influence their prices. Investment and pricing decisions must be based on the cost of inputs, and it is difficult to forecast those costs when the commodities markets are highly volatile.

For many years, commodity prices fluctuated but did not increase dramatically. In the decade of the 2000s, however, global economic growth pulled them up. China, in particular, was growing so fast that it was pulling up most of them, leading to trade agreements between China and many commodity-producing countries, as well as substantial foreign investment. The global economic crisis, however, caused a significant contraction in commodity prices of nearly 17 percent in 2009, which had a very negative impact on the economies of the commodity-producing countries. The prices increased by 23 percent from January 1, 2010 to January 2011 as the global economy began to recover.[48] However, as the Chinese economy began to contract in 2013, commodity prices dropped again.

THE ORGANIZATION OF THE PETROLEUM EXPORTING COUNTRIES (OPEC)

OPEC is a producers' alliance in oil that has been successful in using quotas to keep oil prices high.

The **Organization of the Petroleum Exporting Countries (OPEC)** is an example of a producer cartel that relies on quotas to influence prices. It is a group of 12 oil-producing countries that have significant control over supply and band together to control output and price. Its members include Algeria, Angola, Ecuador, Iran, Iraq, Kuwait, Libya, Nigeria, Qatar, Saudi Arabia, the United Arab Emirates, and Venezuela. Indonesia suspended its membership in January 2009, and several of the largest oil exporting countries, including the Russia, Norway, Canada, the U.S., and Mexico, are not members of OPEC.

Price Controls and Politics OPEC controls prices by establishing production quotas on member countries. Saudi Arabia has historically performed the role of the dominant supplier in influencing supply and price. Periodically OPEC oil ministers gather together to determine the quota for each country based on estimates of supply and demand. Politics is also an important dimension of the deliberations. OPEC member countries with large populations need large oil revenues to fund government programs. As a result, they are tempted to exceed their export quotas to generate more revenues.

Output and Exports OPEC member countries produce about 33.6 percent of the world's crude oil and 19 percent of its natural gas. However, its oil exports represent about 60.4 percent of the oil traded internationally.[49] In addition, OPEC has 81 percent of the world's oil reserves, with the Middle East containing 66.4 percent of OPEC's total reserves. Therefore, OPEC can have a strong influence on the oil market, especially if it decides to reduce or increase its level of production. However, the biggest producer of crude oil is Russia, followed by Saudi Arabia, the U.S., China, and Iran. In 2007, Brazil, which is not a member of OPEC, announced a deep-sea oil discovery that was supposed to launch Petrobras into one of the biggest oil companies in the world and help Brazil to become a major oil exporter. However, Brazilian economic policies have forced state-owned Petrobras to buy ships, oil platforms, and other equipment from Brazilian companies not well-positioned to compete in the global economy, and oil production in Brazil has fallen. Petrobras' stock price has fallen, pushing down the market value of the company below that of many smaller countries, including Colombia.[50]

Sometimes OPEC policies work; sometimes they don't. In addition, events beyond its control can influence prices. The rapidly escalating price of crude oil prior to the global economic crisis was a mixture of rising demand worldwide (especially in China), political instability in the Middle East, and a shortage of refining capacity, caused in part by environmental rules in some countries that preclude the building of new refineries. At the height of the global economic growth and strong demand for all commodities, oil prices spiked to $145 a barrel in July 2008 and then dropped to $33 a barrel that December. Prices have continued to rise and fall in recent years due to fluctuations in the global economy as well as political instability.

The downside of high oil prices for OPEC:

- Producers investing in countries outside of OPEC
- Complication of balancing social, political, and economic objectives

The Downside of High Prices Keeping oil prices high has some downside for OPEC. Competition from non-OPEC countries rises because the revenues accruing to the competitors are higher. Because some OPEC countries are putting up roadblocks to production, major producers like BP, ExxonMobil, and Shell are investing heavily in areas like the Caspian Basin, the Gulf of Mexico, and Angola and are trying to enter areas like the Russian Federation. Production in these areas is expected to grow significantly. High prices also attract competition to conventional oil, including nonconventional oil (such as oil shale and biofuels) and

An offshore oil rig at the Campos Basin by Rio de Janeiro, Brazil. Brazil, though not a member of OPEC, has the potential to be a major producer and exporter of oil as its deep water wells are tapped.
Source: Leo Francini/Shutterstock

FIGURE 7.2

Source: Norman Jung/CartoonStock, Ltd.

nuclear energy, although the damage to the nuclear reactors in Japan as a result of the earthquake and tsunami in 2011 had a chilling effect on nuclear energy.

Political and social forces also affect oil prices. The civil war in Libya impacted oil markets in 2011, causing oil prices to spike due to the fear that the unrest could spread to other big Middle East oil producers.

Looking to the Future:

Will the WTO Overcome Bilateral and Regional Integration Efforts?

Will regional integration be the wave of the future, or will the World Trade Organization become the focus of global economic integration? The WTO's objective is to reduce barriers to trade in goods, services, and investment. Regional groups attempt to do that and more. Although the EU has introduced a common currency and is increasing the degree of cooperation in areas such as security and foreign policy, the WTO will likely never engage in those issues. Regional integration deals with the specific problems facing member countries, whereas the WTO needs to be concerned about all countries in the world.

However, regional integration might actually help the WTO achieve its objectives in three major ways:

1. Regionalism can lead to liberalization of issues not covered by the WTO.
2. Regionalism is more flexible, given that it typically involves fewer countries with similar conditions and objectives.
3. Regional deals lock in liberalization, especially in developing countries.

As we have seen in this chapter, no trade agreement is easy or perfect. The WTO has serious challenges due to its size. Regional agreements like NAFTA, the EU, Mercosur, and others have many different challenges as well. In cases of NAFTA and Mercosur, one dominant country in each (the U.S. and Brazil, respectively) implies that the balance of power among the member countries is not equal. The EU has its own challenges due to enlargement and the debt crises of several member countries, especially Greece.

Regional integration in Africa will continue at a slow pace due to the vast size of the continent and that fact that so many countries have common borders with countries that are involved in different regional economic groups. However, Africa is flush with natural resources and will be a favorite trading partner of resource-hungry China for a long time to come. That will help fill the foreign exchange coffers of the African countries and possibly help them resolve some of their long-standing problems. In addition, greater peace and stability in Africa and the rise in working-age population will make the continent an interesting place in which to invest and a potential source for consumer growth.

Asian integration, primarily in AFTA, APEC and possibly the Trans Pacific Partnership, will pick up steam as the economies of East and Southeast continue to open up and as they collaborate to meet the challenge of China. Since the beginning of the decade, Asian countries have signed over 70 trade agreements among themselves. Japan, which is not a member of AFTA, has signed a number of bilateral agreements with other countries in Asia, including an FTA with the members of ASEAN. It became a member of the Trans Pacific Partnership in 2013 and is in the process of implementing new agreements with Australia, the Gulf Cooperation Council, India, and Korea. However, the key to the growth of most countries in Southeast Asia may be China and its rapidly growing influence in Asia and the rest of the world. ■

CASE Unilever Goes East[51]

The creation of ASEAN, one of the oldest regional blocs, dates back to 1967, when the five main economies of Southeast Asia—Thailand, Malaysia, Singapore, Philippines, and Indonesia—signed an association agreement. The other five members (Myanmar, Laos, Cambodia, Vietnam, and Brunei) have aggregated over time, until the last one, Cambodia, joined in 1999.

The importance of ASEAN has been growing over time, linked to the progressive growth of the economies of Southeast Asia since the early 80s, and only temporarily slowed down by the Asian crisis in the 90s. Increasingly, a number of multinationals with a steady interest in Asia Pacific have been selecting the region as their manufacturing base, also serving as a hub for their operations. The list of reasons for this choice is long and substantial.

The area is currently a market of 617 million people (about 10 percent of the world population), with a global GDP projected to reach US$4.7 trillion in 2020 (approximately Japan's level of today) and a share of world trade of about 7 percent. ASEAN has been working towards creating an East Asian Community (EAC) by the end of 2015, by integrating into a single and coherent market the 10 economies that up to now have been functioning at different speeds.

Whilst there are still a lot of differences among member states, the main economies of the region share a long tradition in manufacturing, and some of them enjoy excellent facilities in terms of infrastructure, ports, and technology (Singapore is the best example, but not the only one), which makes them an excellent choice for offshoring.

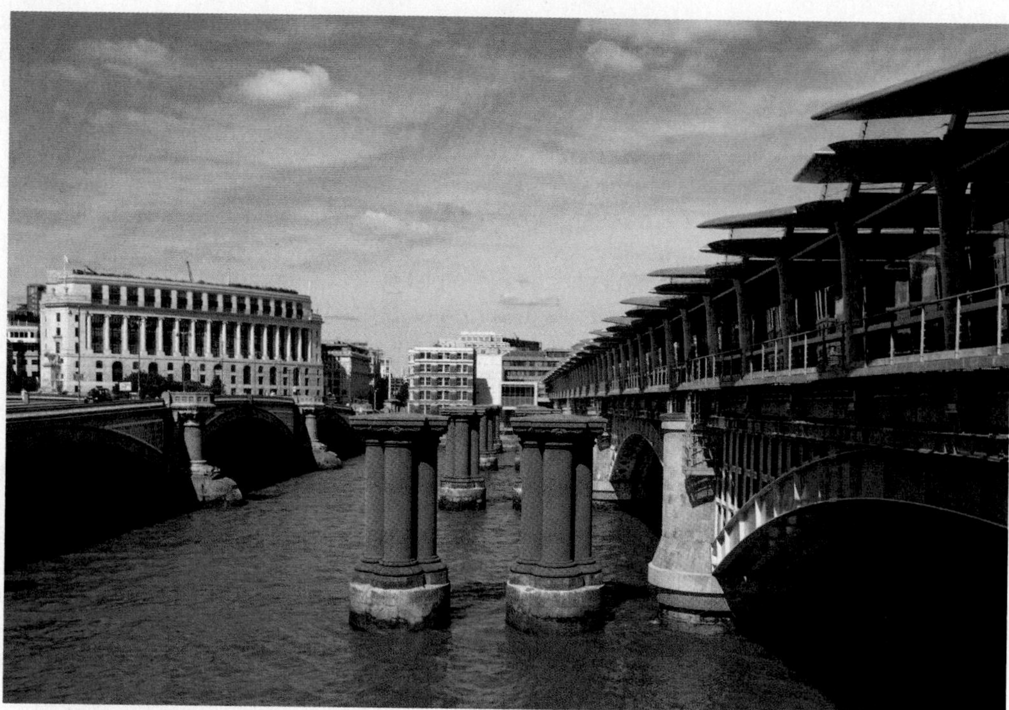

The Unilever Building in Albert Embankment, London, overlooking the Thames. The business has a diversified worldwide presence.
Source: © starekase - Fotolia.com

Unilever and the ASEAN countries: a success story

The world's third largest FMCG company, with 173,000 employees in 190 countries and an established presence in food and personal care, Unilever features in its vast portfolio some of the world's most famous food and household products, including Dove, Lipton, Rexona, Vaseline, Magnum, Omo, Cif, Ponds, P&G, and Knorr. Founded in 1930—even though some of the companies that later on joined forces to create it were already existing since 1885—the Anglo-Dutch giant was one of the first to enter Southeast Asian markets and has certainly been one of the most successful worldwide.

In 2011, Paul Polman, the newly appointed CEO, decided to make the corporation more dynamic and even further oriented to emerging markets. At the same time, he created the post of COO, with the directive of concentrating on these new regions and elaborating a unique strategy for them. This meant instead of replicating what Unilever was doing in first-world markets—where food represents half their business—the Asian subsidiaries were going to heavily invest in personal and health care, allotting food products a more marginal space in their business plans. This winning strategy has yielded remarkable results.

Albeit the global slowdown and problems in some of its core markets (namely Europe), Unilever's 2012 operative results were remarkably good, with an increase in turnover of 10.5 percent which brought it to € 51.3 billion overall.

Moreover, during the 2012 World Economic Forum at Davos, Harish Manwani, Unilever's COO allegedly declared that the company's diversified portfolio and its presence in Asia has helped it offset its weakness in Europe. Unlike competitors P&G and Nestle, who were more focused on mature markets, Unilever, whose business comprises 56 percent emerging markets, has been less affected by challenging global economic conditions than some of its rivals because of its extensive portfolio of brands and its emphasis on emerging markets. Preliminary results for 2013 confirmed this trend of a shifting importance towards extra-Europe markets, still growing in contrast with the slowing sales in the EU. The company has an established presence in Southeast Asia, going back to the end of World War II, and has been steadily growing since.

From the regional HQ in Kuala Lampur, Unilever has been active in Malaysia since 1947. As recently as 2013, Unilever Malaysia, also responsible for Singapore, has opened up Four Acres Singapore, a huge training facility of 2.3 hectares for its management, the only center of its kind outside the UK—a clear indication of the importance the Anglo-Dutch multinational attaches to the region.

Unilever Thailand is another rapidly expanding subsidiary. Currently Thailand's largest FMCG firm, the corporation is going to spend B$2.8 billion (US$ 90 million) on building additional facilities to support its growth. Among them is the projected manufacturing plant for homecare products due for completion by the end of 2013.

Indonesia currently represents for Unilever, one of the largest emerging markets where it had invested more than US $625.9 million over the period 2007-2012. Unilever Indonesia's turnover had reached US$ 2.3 billion in 2011 (around 5 percent of Unilever's global turnover for that year), and registered an internal growth of almost twice the worldwide equivalent.

Unilever Vietnam has achieved a strong and sustained growth over the last 14 years, with an astounding average of over 30 percent making it one of the fastest growing companies within Unilever Asia, as well as in Vietnam's FMCG sector. In 2008, the company's total sales represented around 1 percent of Vietnam's GDP, with a network of about 200 distributors and over 400,000 retail outlets. A case study conducted by the Central Institute for Economic Management (CIEM), a think tank under the Vietnamese Ministry of Planning & Investment with an advisory role, has investigated the reasons for its exceptional performance. According to its findings, a substantial part of its success was due to the fact that the company is a long-term investor, representing a model of constructive partnership and efficient collaboration between an MNC and local business. Also, its positive spillover is not only linked to capacity building and technology transfer, but also involves a global socioeconomic development for the country.

Unilever Philippines aims to source all of its peanut, tamarind, and tuber supplies from local farmers as part of its strategy to support indigenous business growth in the regions it operates. The Unilever Sustainable Living Plan, in fact, targets to halve the environmental footprint of the multinational's products and source 100 percent of the agricultural raw materials by local farmers in a sustainable fashion.

Future developments

More is to come from Unilever in the near future, as the company enlarges its operations, reaching out to countries outside its area of recent interest. Investments into China are going to keep their pace, even if moving inward, in the so-called fourth pole of China's socio-economic development after the Yangtze River Delta, the Pearl River Delta and the Beijing-Tianjin-Hebei region. This is the Sichuan Province, geographically and logistically connected to Yunnan and the Mekong area, and therefore nearer to the ASEAN countries.

Other bases are being developed as well. The most remarkable case in point being Myanmar, where Unilever was present since the 1960s and then left when the junta seized power to institute a dictatorship. Following news of the country's reopening and its democratic elections, the company returned in 2010 as one of the first to invest. Furthermore, to strengthen the relevance and standing of Unilever in Myanmar and the whole region on 30th May 2012, Aung San Suu Kyi, General Secretary of Myanmar's National League for Democracy, paid a visit to Unilever Thailand's Minburi factory, during her first overseas visit in over 24 years.

What lies ahead?

Unilever represents the clear success story of a multinational that has been able to diversify its portfolios of countries and products, showing no sign of slowing down. Its focus on emerging

Unilever is home to some of the world's best known brands in FMCG including products like Vaseline, Dove and Lipton.
Source: © Irina Brinza - Fotolia.com

markets, primarily ASEAN, seems to have reaped good dividends. More companies are going to follow this approach, especially at the completion of the EAC in 2015.

The future will most likely witness additional foreign investments pouring into the regions both as M&A and as greenfield investments, especially since even more multinationals will aim at cutting their operation costs and pursuing a more aggressive integration with China and India's consumer markets. Furthermore, consumer spending in Asia-Pacific will keep rising, making the whole region even more attractive to investors. Corporations will certainly profit from Singapore's centrality as a hub its highly sophisticated facilities, technology infrastructures and deep-sea container port. Unsurprisingly, 75 percent of the companies also run their regional operations from there, followed by a 10 percent in the nearby Kuala Lumpur (Malaysia).

It is no mystery that China's labor costs have been steadily rising over the years, becoming almost aligned with U.S. costs (even if, by hourly measure, China's is still substantially lower. The difference here is clearly in productivity). ASEAN is therefore becoming increasingly popular as a manufacturing center and a constant presence in the global supply chain of multinationals, using countries like Indonesia and Vietnam—with a labor cost only 37 percent of the U.S. level—as favorite production bases. Analysts observed that this offshoring process toward the region is only beginning.

However, challenges loom ahead. Southeast Asia faces a series of obstacles on its road to achieving full economic integration, comparable to the EU—which nonetheless remains, since the beginning the model ASEAN is constantly striving towards.

Protectionism in the region keeps running high, even in the framework of free-trade areas, which yet allow for sensitivity lists for particular products, without even mentioning non-tariff barriers like industrial standards and red tape.

Other problematic issues include the implementation of AFTA (ASEAN Free Trade Area). While AFTA has been a success, together with the one-to-one preferential trade agreements linking each one of the ASEAN countries to the rest of East Asia, a more cautious evaluation has to be done of the complex regional trade agreements of the Asia Pacific region. More often than not, its hurdles have outweighed its advantages, and it has been reported that its implementation is sometimes costly and complex, making it impossible for Small and Medium Enterprises (SMEs) to benefit from this. An abundance of academic literature on this aspect, together with some firm surveys, seems to confirm this problematic point.

Another issue is the lack of infrastructure. Transportation costs can represent a formidable obstacle in some of the most promising countries for offshoring. For example, for Unilever Indonesia the cost of transportation, warehousing, and logistics accounts to about 4 percent sales revenue. And the whole system is often slow and unresponsive—with documented cases of containers waiting up to three weeks in the port of arrival. Without optimizing the supply chain, further progress is going to be challenging.

Finally, amazing diversity in the countries of the region constitute a threat as well as an opportunity. Consumer purchasing power is a good example, since the ten states present a whole range of cases, between Singapore, with almost US$ 50,000 GDP per capita and Myanmar, the poorest member of ASEAN, with only US$ 896 GDP per capita. Furthermore, there are huge differences in terms of political systems, religions and languages, making agreements difficult to reach. For this reason, it's often impossible for multinationals to adopt a single market approach and they are often obliged to resort to a variety of strategies. The coming years and the implementation of the EAC, will probably make or break the region as one of the new powerhouses of global growth, and significantly affect market results of Unilever and the other MNEs in the region.

QUESTIONS

✪7-3. Why is Unilever investing so much in emerging markets, especially Southeast Asia?

✪7-4. Myanmar is a country opening up after decades of having been closed to business due to political issues. Based on further data collection, explain Unilever's investment strategy in the country.

7-5. Why does ASEAN represent an area of growing interest for multinationals, to the point that some of them use it as an operations management hub? Cite clearly reasons that make the region an attractive place for manufacturers to set up their bases.

7-6. What are the challenges for a real regional integration among ASEAN countries? Mention some of the main issues that make it a difficult and lengthy process and their impact on companies like Unilever.

SUMMARY

- The General Agreement on Tariffs and Trade (GATT), begun in 1947, created a continuing means for countries to negotiate the reduction and elimination of trade barriers and to agree on simplified mechanisms for the conduct of international trade.
- The World Trade Organization (WTO) replaced GATT in 1995 as a continuing means of trade negotiations that aspires to foster the principle of trade without discrimination and to provide a better means of mediating trade disputes and of enforcing agreements.
- Efforts at regional economic integration began to emerge after World War II as countries saw benefits of cooperation and larger market sizes. The major types of economic integration are the free trade area and the customs union, followed by broader economic and political integration in the common market.
- Free trade agreements result in trade creation and diversion as barriers drop for member countries but remain higher for nonmembers. There are static effects of the reduction of trade barriers. The static effects of economic integration improve the efficiency of resource allocation and affect both production and consumption. The dynamic effects are internal and external efficiencies that arise because of changes in market size.
- Once protection is eliminated among member countries, trade creation allows MNEs to specialize and trade based on comparative advantage.
- Trade diversion occurs when the supply of products shifts from countries that are not members of an economic bloc to those that are.
- Regional, as opposed to global, economic integration occurs because of the greater ease of promoting cooperation on a smaller scale.
- The European Union (EU) is an effective common market that has abolished most restrictions on factor mobility and is

harmonizing national political, economic, and social policies. It comprises 28 countries, including 13 from mostly Central and Eastern Europe that have joined since 2004. The EU has abolished trade barriers on intrazonal trade, instituted a common external tariff, and created a common currency, the euro.

- The North American Free Trade Agreement (NAFTA) is designed to eliminate tariff barriers and liberalize investment opportunities and trade in services. Key provisions in NAFTA are labor and environmental agreements.
- There are key trade groups in other parts of the world, including Latin America, Asia, and Africa, but the U.S. has pursued a variety of targeted trade agreements in Asia and the EU to expand exports and create jobs.
- The United Nations is composed of representatives of most of the countries in the world and influences international trade and development in a number of significant ways.
- Many developing countries rely on commodity exports to supply the hard currency they need for economic development. Instability in commodity prices has resulted in fluctuations in export earnings. OPEC is an effective commodity agreement in terms of attempting to stabilize supply and price.

KEY TERMS

Andean Community (CAN) (p. 322)
Asia Pacific Economic Cooperation (APEC) (p. 325)
Association of Southeast Asian Nations (ASEAN) (p. 324)
Arab League (p. 327)
bilateral integration (p. 304)
Caribbean Community (CARICOM) (p. 321)
common market (p. 309)
dynamic effect (p. 309)
economic integration (p. 304)
economies of scale (p. 311)
euro (p. 315)
European Union (EU) (p. 311)
General Agreement on Tariffs and Trade (GATT) (p. 305)
global integration (p. 304)
Gulf Cooperation Council (p. 327)
MERCOSUR (p. 322)
most-favored-nation (MFN) clause (p. 305)
North American Free Trade Agreement (NAFTA) (p. 317)
Organization of the Petroleum Exporting Countries (OPEC) (p. 329)
Pacific Alliance (p. 322)
Pan Arab Free Trade Area (PAFTA) (p. 327)
regional integration (p. 304)
static effect (p. 309)
Treaty of Lisbon (p. 315)
triad (p. 304)
UNCTAD (p. 328)
World Trade Organization (WTO) (p. 305)

ENDNOTES

1 ***Sources include the following:*** Stephen Power, "EU Auto Industry Faces Overhaul as Japanese Gain in Market Share," *Wall Street Journal* (October 14, 2004): A1; Jathon Sapsford, "Toyota Aims to Rival GM Production," *Wall Street Journal* (November 2, 2004): A3; Mari Koseki, "Quota on Auto Exports to EC Curbed at 1.089 Million in '93," *Japan Times* (April 12–18, 1993): 14; Nick Maling, "Japan Poised for EU Lift of Export Ceiling," *Marketing Week* (May 6, 1999): 26; Todd Zaun and Beth Demain, "Leading the News: Ambitious Toyota, Buoyed by Europe, Sets Global Goals," *Wall Street Journal* (October 22, 2002): A3; Mark M. Nelson, Thomas F. O'Boyle, and E. S. Browning, "International—The Road to European Unity—1992: EC's Auto Plan Would Keep Japan at Bay—1992 Unification Effort Smacks of Protectionism," *Wall Street Journal* (October 27, 1988): A1; Sapsford, "Toyota Posts 3.5% Profit Rise, Boosts Sales Forecast for Year," *Wall Street Journal* (February 4, 2005): A3; Gail Edmondson and Chester Dawson, "Revved Up for Battle," *Businessweek* (January 10, 2005): 30; Joe Guy Collier, "Toyota Posts Record $14-Billion Profit," *Knight Ridder Tribune Business News* (May 9, 2007): 1; "ACEA Board of Directors Recommends Accepting Toyota Motor Europe Membership Application," *PR Newswire Europe Including UK Disclose* (May 4, 2007); Toyota home page, "Toyota—Joining Europe," at www.toyota-europe.com/experience/the_company/toyota-ineurope.aspx (accessed May 10, 2007); Toyota home page, "Toyota: Company Profile," at www.toyota.co.jp/en/about_toyota/outline/index.html (accessed May 10, 2007); Christoph Rauwald, "Leading the News: Toyota Sales in Europe Jump as Market Stalls," *Wall Street Journal* (March 16, 2007): 2; "World Business Briefing Europe: Germany: Sale of Unit Helps VW," *New York Times* (February 21, 2007): C10; Mark Milner, "Financial: Car Boss Calls on EU to Tackle Yen," *UK Guardian* (March 30, 2007): 32; Toyota Annual Report 2010: Toyota Motor Corporation, April, 2010 (accessed March 23, 2011).

2 Peter J. Buckley, Jeremy Clagg, Nicolas Forsans, and Kevin T. Reilly, "Increasing the Size of the 'Country': Regional Economic Integration and Foreign Direct Investment in a Globalised World Economy," *Management International Review* 41:3 (2001): 251–75.

3 Alan M. Rugman and Alain Verbeke, "A Perspective on Regional and Global Strategies of Multinational Enterprises," *Journal of International Business Studies* 35 (2004): 7.

4 Pankaj Ghemawat, "Distance Still Matters: The Hard Reality of Global Expansion," *Harvard Business Review*, September 2001, 3–11.

5 "Airbus wins WTO subsidy dispute, but Boeing says it's the winner," *New Europe*, 28 March, 2010. www.neurope.eu/articles/99919.php (accessed 15 April 2011); John Miller and Daniel Michaels, "Boeing Set for Victory Over Airbus in Illegal Subsidy Case," *Wall Street Journal* (September 3, 2009): A1, A14.

6 World Trade Organization, Dispute Settlement; DS316 Panel Report (June 30, 2010): "European Communities—Measures Affecting Trade in Large Civil Aircraft" (accessed April 8, 2011).

7 "China – Certain Measures Affecting Electronic Payment Services," www.wto.org/english/tratop_e/dispu_e/cases_e/ds413_e.htm.

8 John W. Miller, "Global Trade Talks Fail as New Giants Flex Muscle," *Wall Street Journal* (July 30, 2008): A1.

9 Josh Mitchell, "U.S. Gains Mixed in Seoul Trade Deal," *The Wall Street Journal*, April 15, 2013, A13.

10 "Regional Trade Agreements,"World Trade Organization, Facts and Figures, www.wto.org/english/tratop_e/region_e/region_e.htm (accessed April 15, 2013).

11 Bela Balassa, *The Theory of Economic Integration* (Homewood, IL: Richard D. Irwin, 1961): 40.

12 Op cit.,Ghemawat.

13 Buckley et al.,"Increasing the Size of the 'Country.'"

14 For more information on the EU, check out its Web site at europa.eu (accessed April 27, 2013).

15 "About EFTA" in www.efta.int (accessed May 6, 2013).

16 "EU Institutions and Other Bodies," europa.eu (accessed April 27, 2013)

17 "The European Parliament" at europa.eu (accessed on April 27, 2013).

18 "The European Court of Justice" in "Institutions and Bodies," at europa.eu (accessed April 29, 2013).

19 Charles Forelle,"Microsoft Yields to EU on Browsers," *Wall Street Journal* (July 25/26, 2009): B1; Kevin J. Obrien,"Europe Drops Microsoft Antitrust Case," *The New York Times (online)* (December 16, 2009), accessed June 7, 2011.

20 James Kanter,"Google Makes Offer in 3-Year European Antitrust Case," *The New York Times* (February 1, 2013); Juergen Baetz,"Google Agrees to Change How It Displays Search Results in Europe," *Tech Time* (April 25, 2013); Carol Matlack and Stephanie Bodoni,"Google's EU Antitrust Proposal Will Likely Be Tweaked," *Businessweek* (April 15, 2013).

21 Stephen Castle,"Europe Says Tests Show Horse Meat Scandal Is 'Food Fraud,'" *The New York Times* (April 16, 2013).

22 "The Treaty of Lisbon," in europa.edu/lisbon_treaty/index_en.htm (accessed May 6, 2013).

23 Stephen Castle,"British Government Moves to Toughen Rules on Immigrants," *The New York Times* (May 9, 2013), A7.

24 Eurostat News Release, reference: Stat/13/70, April 30, 2013, europa.eu/rapid/press-release_STAT-13-70_en.htm, accessed May 7, 2013; Jack Ewing,"The Downturn in Southern Europe May Be Spreading North," *The New York Times* (April 26, 2013), B1.

25 Carl B. Weinberg, chief economist of High Frequency Economics in Valhalla, NY, as quoted by Jack Ewing in "The Downturn in Southern Europe May Be Spreading North," *The New York Times* (April 26, 2013), B1.

26 Mitsuru Obe and Toko Sekiguchi,"Japan, EU to Start Trade Talks," *The Wall Street Journal* (March 25, 2013).

27 Sudeep Reddy, Mathew Dalton, and Joann S. Lubin,"Broad Trade Deal on the Table," *The Wall Street Journal* (February 13, 2013).; Annie Lowrey, "Sore Feelings on U.S. and Europe Begin Trade Talks," *The New York Times* (July 9, 2013, p. B8).

28 Joshua Chaffin and James Politi,"Fractures Appear on Trade Pact," *Financial Times* (May 24, 2013), 2.

29 Sandra Dibble,"Sony Will Increase Work Force in Tijuana," *The San Diego Union-Tribune* (June 26, 2009), E1.

30 Text of the North American Free Trade Agreement,"Chapter 4: Rules of Origin," at www.ustr.gov/trade-agreements/free-trade-agreements/north-american-free-trade-agreement-nafta (accessed May 8, 2013).

31 Office of the United States Trade Representative,"North American Free Trade Agreement," www.ustr.gov/trade-agreements/free-trade-agreements/north-american-free-trade-agreement-nafta, (accessed May 27, 2013).

32 "Volkswagen Announces Production of the Golf in Mexico," January 25, 2013, media.vw.com/newsrelease.do;jsessionid=E9B24BF58F0B-6D174CB7A7C5628417F3?&id=1352&allImage=1&teaser=volkswagen-announces-production-golf-mexico&mid=125 (accessed May 27, 2013).

33 Andres Oppenheimer,"While Pacific Alliance Thrives, Mercosur Withers," *The Miami Herald* (May 27, 2013).

34 Sebastian Sermiento-Saher,"The Pacific Alliance: The Americas' Bridge to Asia?" *Pacific Money: Economics and Business* (May 25, 2013), thediplomat.com/pacific-money/2013/05/25/the-pacific-alliance-the-americas-bridge-to-asia/ (accessed May 27, 2013).

35 Alan M. Field,"Showdown for CAFTA-DR," *Journal of Commerce* (April 11, 2005): 1.

36 "CAFTA-DR Partners Agree to Fix Technical Errors in Agreement," *Textile World* 161:2 (Mar/Apr 2011), 10.

37 Field,"Showdown for CAFTA-DR,"1.

38 The CIA World Factbook, (accessed May 8, 2013).

39 "AFTA Doha," *The Economist* (September 6, 2008): 85.

40 Patrick Barta and Alex Frangos,"Southeast Asia Linking Up to Compete with China," *The Wall Street Journal* (August 23, 2010), A2.

41 Paul Cashin, Hong Liang, and C. John McDermott,"Do Commodity Price Shocks Last Too Long for Stabilization Schemes to Work?" *Finance & Development* 36:3 (Summer 1999); Asia-Pacific Economic Cooperation, "About APEC," at www.apecsec.org.sg, (accessed October 1, 2009).

42 "Foreign Direct Investment in Africa," KPMG (June 1, 2012), www.kpmg.com/africa/en/issuesandinsights/articles-publications/pages/foreign-direct-investment-in-africa.aspx (accessed on May 27, 2013).

43 "The African Union: Short of Cash and Teeth," *The Economist* (January 29, 2011), 46.

44 The United Nations, at www.un.org/en/mainbodies/index.shtml (accessed May 27, 2013).

45 "About UNCTAD," unctad.org.

46 United Nations Conference on Trade and Development,"The State of Commodity Dependence 2012,"11.

47 International Coffee Organization, www.ico.org (accessed May 27, 2013).

48 UNCTAD, Commodities at a Glance,"9.

49 OPEC,"Annual Statistical Bulletin," www.opec.org/opec_web/static_files_project/media/downloads/publications/ASB2012.pdf (accessed May 27, 2013).

50 Simon Romero,"Petrobras, Once Symbol of Brazil's Oil Hopes, Strives to Regain Lost Swagger," *The New York Times* (March 26, 2013).

51 ***Sources include the following:*** *Asean Business News* (2013), Unilever spends B$ 28bn on growth, available at: http://asean-business-news.com/thailand/uncategorized/unilever-spends-b28bn-on-growth/; Baldwin, R. (2006), "Multilateralizing Regionalism: Spaghetti Bowls as Building Blocks on the Pathto Global Free Trade." *World Economy* 29(11): 1451–518; *The Economist* (2013)"Riding the ASEAN elephant. How business is responding to an unusual animal."Available at: http://ftp01.economist.com.hk/ECN_papers/ridingASEAN.pdf; *The Jakarta Post* (2012) Executive column: Indonesia promises bullish prospects for Unilever, available at: www.thejakartapost.com/news/2012/05/28/executive-column-indonesia-promises-bullish-prospects-unilever.html; *South China Morning Post* (2013),"US companies see delay on Asean single market" www.scmp.com/news/asia/article/1298442/american-firms-doubt-aseans-single-market-will-launch-2015; Paladini, S. (2009) "Outlook of ASEAN's Free Trade Areas", in *Italian Foreign Trade Report 2008–2009*, Italian Trade Commission Rome; CIEM (2009), Unilever in Vietnam: a case study, available at: www.unilever.com/images/sd_Exploring_the_Links_between_International_Businesses_and_Socio-economic_Development_of_Vietnam_A_Case_Study_of_Unilever_Vietnam_Executive_Summary_tcm13-212702.pdf; Unilever's corporate website and news, at www.unilever.com; EDB(2013), Unilever opens global leadership development centre – Four Acres Singapore www.eco-business.com/news/unilever-launches-leadership-centre-Singapore/; *Interaksyon* (2013) Unilever expects sales to grow faster than Philippine economy available at: www.interaksyon.com/business/62293/unilever-expects-sales-to-grow-faster-than-philippine-economy; *The Economist* (2011)"Unilever looks East", available at: www.economist.com/blogs/schumpeter/2011/06/consumer-goods?zid=293&ah=e50f63

CHAPTER 8
Markets for Foreign Exchange

OBJECTIVES

After studying this chapter, you should be able to

1. Learn the fundamentals of foreign exchange
2. Identify the major characteristics of the foreign-exchange market and how governments control the flow of currencies across national borders
3. Describe how the foreign-exchange market works
4. Examine the different institutions that deal in foreign exchange
5. Understand why companies deal in foreign exchange

MyManagementLab®
Improve Your Grade!
When you see this icon, visit **www.mymanagementlab.com** for activities that are applied, personalized, and offer immediate feedback.

Another man's trade costs money.

—Portuguese Proverb

Source: © albertocc311 - Fotolia.com

CASE Going Down to the Wire in the Money-Transfer Market

Long known as "the fastest way to send money," U.S.-based Western Union controls nearly 80 percent of the money-transfer market and is widely acknowledged as the world leader in wire transfers—electronic transfers of funds from one financial institution to another.[1] In this case, it's a transfer from one Western Union office to another. Now, however, Western Union is facing stiff competition from banks threatening to encroach on its market share of the electronic money-transfer business.

Western Union was started in 1851 when a group of businessmen in Rochester, New York, formed the New York and Mississippi Valley Printing Telegraph Company. The name was changed to Western Union in 1861 when the first transcontinental telegraph line was completed. Western Union introduced its money-transfer service in 1871; in 1989 it began offering it outside North America. Today, more than half a million Western Union agent locations are found in over 200 countries and territories around the world. Money transfers make up 85 percent of Western Union's revenues, with the company transferring about $80 billion annually.

Customers have many different options when sending money through Western Union: in person, at an agent location, over the phone, or online; via cash, debit cards, or credit cards. And they can use the service at a variety of locations: an actual Western Union office, a grocery store, a post office—just about anywhere people go to transact business. To send money to, say, India or Mexico using a Western Union agent location, the customer fills out a "Send Money" form and gets a receipt, which includes a Money Transfer Control number to give to the person receiving the funds. To retrieve the funds, the receiver then fills out a "Receive Money" form and presents the Money Transfer Control number along with valid identification at a Western Union agent location.

CONVERTING CURRENCY

Transfer funds are converted into the foreign currency using an exchange rate set by Western Union. The fees for sending money are determined based on how much is sent, in what form (cash or debit/credit card), and where it is going. For example, sending $500 to Mexico from Utah costs $12. Part of Western Union's attractiveness is its speed and anonymity—it can move cash from one location of the world to another in just minutes. Money can be sent through an agent by cash, debit card, credit card, or a Western Union Gold Card, and senders are required to fill out a form and show a proper ID.

SOURCES AND DESTINATIONS OF MIGRATION

Migration is based on supply and demand. People work in other countries because of better economic opportunities. A country accepts migrant workers because it is short on labor. Each situation is different. The top five countries in terms of the number of immigrants recently were the United States (42.8 million), Russia (12.3 million), Germany (10.8 million), Saudi Arabia (7.3 million), and Canada (7.2 million). In terms of percentage of the total population, however, three of the top five destinations for migrant workers were from the Gulf Cooperation Council, with Qatar at #1 (86.5 percent of the total population) and the United Arab Emirates, including Dubai, at #3 (70 percent of the population). Of the top five emigration countries, Mexico was #1 with 11.9 million people working abroad, and India was #2 with 11.4 million. The top migration corridor in 2010 was from Mexico to the United States, with 11.6 million workers. India sent 2.2 million workers to the UAE, which ranked as the #9 migration corridor. Excluding the former Soviet Union, the India-UAE corridor ranked #5 in the world.

In spite of the economic crisis, remittances from international immigrants were expected to total $534 billion in 2012, of which $406 billion went to families in developing countries. Remittances were projected by the World Bank to continue to expand, possibly hitting $685 billion by 2015. In 2012, the top remittance-receiving country was India at $70 billion, followed by China at $66 billion and the Philippines and Mexico at $24 billion each. High oil prices were driving migrant workers to the Gulf Cooperation Council Countries, whereas remittances to Latin America and the Caribbean suffered due to weak economies in Europe and the United States. The U.S. was by far the top remittance-sending country.

The Mexican Connection (I)

Most of the migrant workers in the United States come from Latin America and the Caribbean. Most of Western Union's wire transfer business in the U.S. comes from Mexican immigrants who send part of their paychecks home to support their families. Mexico has historically ranked as the largest host country in Latin America for remittances, followed by Brazil. Remittances already exceed foreign direct investment and overseas aid as sources of foreign exchange. Annual remittance income has passed tourism to become the second-largest source of foreign-exchange income in Mexico, after oil revenues.

EXCHANGE RATES AND COMPETITION

A class-action lawsuit was filed against Western Union in 1997, charging that it offered its customers lower exchange rates than the market without informing them of the difference. The lawsuit was settled in 2000, and Western Union is now required to state on its receipts and advertisements that it uses its own exchange rate on transactions and that any difference between the company rate and the market rate is kept by the company. For example, the market exchange rate on April 18, 2013, for Mexican pesos was 12.26 pesos/US \$ (US \$500 = 6,100 pesos), whereas Western Union's offered exchange rate was 11.896 pesos/US \$ (US \$500 = 5,948 pesos). One reason for the difference is that the market rate is typically for very large commercial transactions, whereas the normal Western Union transaction is much smaller—the smaller the transaction, the less favorable the exchange rate. Compare that with buying products in bulk rather than a few at a time.

Financial institutions such as banks have pressured Western Union to use better exchange rates. Profit margins in the money-transfer business can reach 30 percent, and many banks have started to offer their own money-transfer services in an attempt to take advantage of the continued expected growth of the foreign money-transfer industry. For example, in 2001 Wells Fargo agreed to accept consular identification cards from Mexican immigrants who want to open bank accounts but lack U.S. driver's licenses. These cards verify Mexicans' identities without revealing their immigration status. After Wells Fargo began accepting the consular identification card, the number of bank accounts opened with a consular ID jumped by over 500 percent within three years.

The Mexican Connection (II)

Wells Fargo and other U.S. banks, including Citi and Bank of America, have established alliances with Mexican banks to offer remittance accounts to the immigrant workers in the United States. Workers can now open U.S. bank accounts with their consular IDs and each ask for two ATM cards. They can then deposit remittance money in the U.S. account, and their family members at home can withdraw the money from the associated Mexican bank.

In 2005, the Federal Reserve teamed up with Mexico's central bank to create a new program that facilitates remittances made from the U.S. to Mexico. The program allows U.S. commercial banks to make money transfers for Mexican workers through the Fed's own automated clearinghouse, which is linked to Banco de México, the Mexican central bank.

Even the wire transfer fees at banks are cheaper than Western Union's. For example, Wells Fargo charges a \$6 fee to send \$500 to Mexico, while Western Union charges \$12 for the same transaction. Many banks are moving toward eliminating exchange-rate spreads (the difference between the market rate and the rate they use for the wire transfer) and transfer fees to Mexico to provide more attractive alternatives to immigrant workers.

This new onslaught of competition by banks has forced Western Union to cut its fees and offer new services, including a home-delivery service, where money is delivered directly to the recipient's door. Western Union is also moving into countries such as China and India to boost its market share. The increased competition has driven down remittance fees around the world.

The Mexican Connection (III)

Immigrant workers complain about the high transfer fees and exchange-rate spread associated with Western Union, but many continue to use this service instead of the lower-cost method of remitting money through banks. Mexico has a history of unstable currencies and widespread inflation, resulting in a traditional mistrust of banks. Other immigrants base their choice on word of mouth or convenience and location. Many are simply unaware of the variety of choices available for sending money and do not know how to get the best deal.

Another reason why many continue to use Western Union is its worldwide availability. For thousands of tiny villages, Western Union is the main link to the outside world. Look at Coatetelco, a small village south of Mexico City with no bank. A few people grow maize, chiles, and fruit there, but it is remittances—mostly from agricultural or construction workers in Georgia and the Carolinas—that account for 90 percent of the villagers' incomes. Patricio, 49, says that at the end of each month he gets a call from his two sons, who are working illegally in Georgia. They give him a code number, and he drives or rides his horse four miles to the nearest Western Union office, located in a government telegraph office, to pick up the $600 they spent $40 to wire to him. Less expensive remittance services are available at the nearby Banamex bank in Mazatepec, but so far Patricio and his neighbors are not willing to travel the eight miles to get there. Besides, he says, "we do not trust the banks, and they make everything more difficult."

The Dubai Connection

Dubai, one of the seven states in the United Arab Emirates (UAE), is an interesting point of comparison with Mexico. Although workers from India and Pakistan go to Dubai to work because of higher wages, they are actually recruited by companies in Dubai. Because of Dubai's relatively small local Emirati population (only 19 percent of the total population), there is no way the country could develop without foreign workers—skilled, semi-skilled, and unskilled. India is the natural source of workers, with Mumbai only about 1,200 miles (1,900 km) away. Employees must have a permit to work in Dubai, typically for three years at a time, and they are not allowed to become citizens. In addition, there is no illegal immigration, and workers can be sent home whenever their employers decide they are no longer needed. But these workers are critical for the growth of the local economies. They have increased the speed of urbanization, fast-tracked infrastructure and economic development, helped the GCC countries diversify from oil by helping construct hotels and tourist attractions, and contributed to solid economic growth.

Given that the migrant workforce in Dubai cannot own property or invest in business ventures, workers need to send the money back home. Western Union, with a deep understanding of the remittance markets, its ethnic marketing expertise, diversified presence and resulting closeness to customers, and its rapid growth in Dubai, has developed high and growing brand awareness there and has worked hard to develop products and messages that appeal to the customers. Dubai and the United States are different in terms of size and the demand for labor, while India and Mexico are different in terms of how and why they supply labor, but there is one constant: people need to move money, and that is where Western Union comes in. ■

CRN
Case Review Note

QUESTIONS

8-1. The United Emirates, of which Dubai is a member, is one of the Gulf Cooperation Council members. How does it compare with the other GCC countries in terms of total population and the non-immigrant population as a percentage of total population? How important do you think migration and therefore capital remittances are for each of the countries in the GCC?

8-2. Should the U.S. government regulate the exchange rate that financial institutions charge Mexican migrant workers for sending money back to Mexico? Why or why not?

CONCEPT CHECK

When we introduced the idea of a **multinational enterprise (MNE)** in Chapter 1, we emphasized that MNEs are firms that take a global approach to production and markets. Here we add that the need to deal with **foreign exchange** is one of the important factors in the environment in which MNEs must conduct business.

INTRODUCTION

Changing money from one currency to another and moving it around to different parts of the world is serious business, on both a personal and a company level. To survive, MNEs and small import and export companies alike must understand foreign exchange and exchange rates. In a business setting, there is a fundamental difference between making a payment in the domestic market and making one abroad. In a domestic transaction, companies use only one currency; in a foreign transaction, they can use two or more. A

U.S. firm that exports, say, skis to a French distributor may ask the distributor to remit payment in dollars, unless the U.S. firm has some specific use for euros, such as paying a French supplier.

Assume you're a U.S. importer who has agreed to purchase a certain quantity of French perfume and pay the French exporter €4,000 for it. Assuming you had the money, how would you go about paying? First, you would go to the international department of your local bank to buy €4,000 at the going market rate. If the euro/dollar exchange rate is, say, €0.6974 per dollar, your bank would then charge your account $5,736 ($4,000/€0.6974) plus the transaction costs and transfer the funds to the exporter's bank through a wire transfer to complete the transaction.

WHAT IS FOREIGN EXCHANGE?

Foreign exchange—money denominated in the currency of another nation or group of nations.

Exchange rate—the price of a currency.

Foreign exchange is money denominated in the currency of another nation or group of nations.[2] The market in which such transactions take place is the **foreign-exchange market**. Foreign exchange can be in the form of cash, funds available on credit and debit cards, traveler's checks, bank deposits, or other short-term claims.[3] As an example, our opening case illustrates how Mexican immigrant workers in the United States often use Western Union to convert dollars to pesos and then wire the pesos to offices in Mexico where relatives can retrieve the cash.

An **exchange rate** is the price of a currency—specifically, the number of units of one currency that buy one unit of another currency. The number can change daily. On May 1, 2013, €1 could purchase US $1.3181 (or $1 could purchase €0.7587). Exchange rates make international price and cost comparisons possible.

PLAYERS ON THE FOREIGN-EXCHANGE MARKET

The Bank for International Settlements divides the foreign-exchange market into reporting dealers (also known as dealer banks or money center banks), other financial institutions, and nonfinancial institutions.

The foreign-exchange market is made up of many different players. The **Bank for International Settlements (BIS)**, a central banking institution in Basel, Switzerland, owned and controlled by 60 member central banks, divides the market into three major categories: *reporting dealers,* other *financial institutions,* and *nonfinancial institutions.*[4]

Reporting dealers, also known as *money center banks,* are financial institutions that actively participate in local and global foreign exchange and **derivative** markets. Comprising mainly the large commercial and investment bank, they are widely assumed to include the 10 largest banks and financial institutions in terms of overall market share in foreign-exchange trading: Deutsche Bank, Barclays Capital, UBS, Citi, JP Morgan, HSBC, RBS, Credit Suisse, Goldman Sachs, and Morgan Stanley. (In our closing case, we show how one money center bank, HSBC, was involved in the gradual internationalization of the Chinese yuan.) Because of the volume of transactions that the money center banks engage in, reporting dealers influence price-setting and are the market makers.

The other financial institutions are not classified as reporting dealers. They include smaller commercial banks, investment banks and securities houses, hedge funds, pension funds, money market funds, currency funds, mutual funds, specialized foreign-exchange trading companies, and so forth. Western Union, whose current activities are detailed in our opening case, is a good example of a nonbanking financial institution that deals in foreign exchange. As for nonfinancial customers, they comprise any counterparty other than those described above and include any non-financial end user, such as governments and companies (MNEs as well as small- and medium-size corporations and firms).

Figure 8.1 shows the percentage of the counterparties—reporting dealers, financial institutions, and nonfinancial customers—represented in foreign currency transactions.

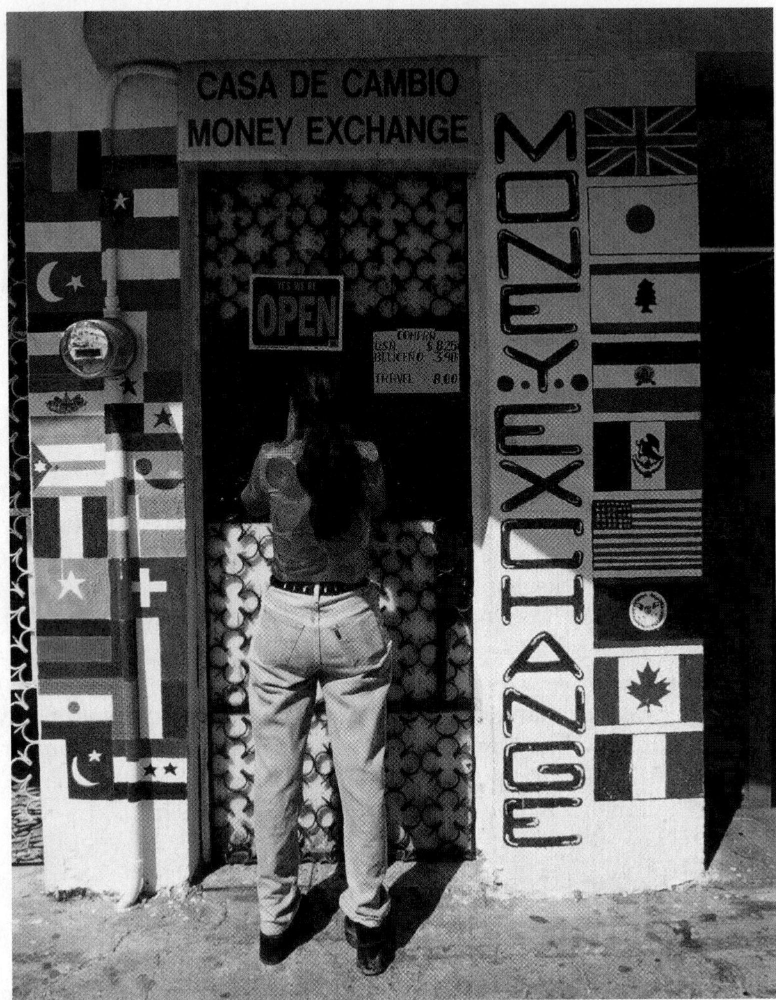

A woman standing in front of a counter at a money exchange booth in Mexico. The flags represent the wide range of countries whose currencies are traded at the money exchange.

Source: Linda Whitwam, Dorling Kindersley

FIGURE 8.1 Foreign-Exchange Markets: Turnover by Counterparty, September 2013

The counterparty segment that contributed the most to growth in global FX turnover between 2010 and 2013 was other financial institutions, which surpassed reporting dealers for the first time in the 2010 survey.

Source: Based on Bank for International Settlements, *Central Bank Survey Report on Foreign Exchange Turnover in April 2013: Preliminary Global Results, September 2013* (Basel, Switzerland: BIS, September 2013, 6).

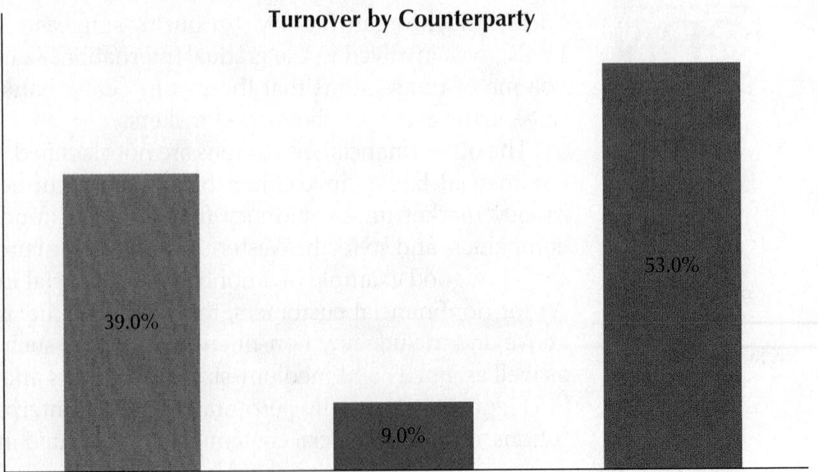

Dealers can trade foreign exchange

- Directly with customers,
- Through voice brokers,
- Through electronic brokerage systems,
- Directly through interbanks.

HOW TO TRADE FOREIGN EXCHANGE

Foreign exchange is traded using electronic methods (41.3 percent of all trades), customer direct (24.3 percent), interbank direct (18.5 percent), or voice broker (15.9 percent).[5] Different kinds of electronic methods are involved. One is an electronic broking system in which trades are matched up for foreign exchange dealers using electronic systems such as EBS, Thomson Reuters, and Bloomberg. Another is an electronic trading system that is executed on a single-bank proprietary system or a multibank dealing system. One example of this type of system is FXConnect, a Boston-based U.S. company that provides trading and settlement options for its clients. Customer direct refers to trades between a reporting dealer and either a non-reporting dealer or customer, without a third party being involved. Usually trades are executed by telephone or direct electronic trading. Interbank direct refers to trades between dealer banks via telephone or direct electronic trading. Voice broker is a trade via telephone communication with a foreign exchange voice broker.[6] Electronic methods are pretty evenly split among three options: broking systems, multibank trading systems, and single-bank trading systems.

CONCEPT CHECK

In discussing "The Political Environment" in Chapter 3, we observe that the relationships comprising a country's political system—relationships among its institutions, organizations, and interest groups—depend on the "political norms and rules" over which its government exercises control. As we'll see in Chapter 10, these structures include rules for trading currency; moreover, governments are active traders of foreign currency through money center banks.

The electronic services provided for customers by EBS, Thomson Reuters, and Bloomberg also furnish a great deal of market data, news, quotes, and statistics about different markets around the world. It is not uncommon for a trading room to have more than one electronic service and for traders to have different preferences within the same office. Bloomberg and Reuters provide market quotes from a large number of banks, so their quotes are close to the market consensus. EBS provides live trades through their system. Deutsche Bank, UBS, and Barclays Capital are moving to dominate e-trading of foreign exchange on their proprietary platforms. If you are accepted to trade on their platforms, you have to trade at the rates they quote. However, a quick check of the market consensus on Bloomberg or Reuters will let you know how good those quotes are.

Reuters, EBS, and Bloomberg provide electronic services for their customers. These services include market data, news, quotes, and statistics about different markets around the world.

SOME ASPECTS OF THE FOREIGN-EXCHANGE MARKET

Foreign-exchange market:

- Over-the-counter (OTC) commercial and investment banks
- Securities exchanges

The foreign-exchange market has two major segments: the over-the-counter market (OTC) and the exchange-traded market. The OTC market is composed of commercial banks as just described, investment banks, and other financial institutions. The exchange-traded market comprises securities exchanges, such as the CME Group, NASDAQ OMX, and NYSE Liffe, where certain types of foreign-exchange instruments, such as futures and options, are traded.

Global OTC foreign exchange instruments:

- Spot
- Outright forward
- FX swap
- Currency swaps
- Currency options
- Other foreign exchange products

GLOBAL OTC FOREIGN EXCHANGE INSTRUMENTS

The phrase "global OTC foreign exchange instruments" refers to *spot transactions, outright forwards, FX swaps, currency swaps, currency options,* and other foreign exchange products. These instruments are all traded in the markets mentioned above.

The spot rate is the exchange rate quoted for transactions that require delivery within two days.

- **Spot transactions** involve the exchange of currency at an agreed-upon rate for delivery within two business days. For example, a bank would quote an exchange rate for a transaction on May 1, but the transaction would actually be settled two days later, on May 3. The rate at which the transaction is settled is the **spot rate**. (Our opening case, which discusses Western Union's policies on currency conversion, gives a good idea of how individuals can trade foreign exchange on the spot market.)

Outright forwards involve the exchange of currency beyond three days at a fixed exchange rate, known as the forward rate.

- **Outright forward transactions** involve the exchange of currency on a future date beyond two business days. It is the single purchase or sale of a currency for future delivery. The rate at which the transaction is settled is the forward rate and is a contract rate between the two parties. The forward transaction will be settled at the forward rate no matter what the actual spot rate is at the time of settlement.

An FX swap is a simultaneous spot and forward transaction.

- In an **FX swap**, one currency is traded for another on one date and then swapped back later. Most often, the first or short leg of an FX swap is a spot transaction and the second or long leg a forward transaction. Let's say IBM receives a dividend in British pounds from its subsidiary in the United Kingdom but has no use for British pounds until it has to pay a U.K. supplier in 30 days. It would rather have dollars now than hold on to the pounds for a month. IBM could enter into an FX swap in which it sells the pounds for dollars to a dealer in the spot market at the spot rate and agrees to buy pounds for dollars from the dealer in 30 days at the forward rate. Although an FX swap is both a spot and a forward transaction, it is counted as a single transaction.

Currency swaps, options, and futures contracts are other forms of transactions in foreign exchange.

- **Currency swaps** deal more with interest-bearing financial instruments (such as a bond) and involve the exchange of principal and interest payments. **Options** are the right, but not the obligation, to trade foreign currency in the future.
- A **futures contract** is an agreement between two parties to buy or sell a particular currency at a particular price on a particular future date, as specified in a standardized contract to all participants in a currency futures exchange rather than in the over-the-counter market.

Figure 8.2 illustrates the turnover in foreign exchange by each of the instruments above in the OTC market. Outright forwards and FX swaps remain the dominant category of instruments, closely followed by spot transactions.

SIZE, COMPOSITION, AND LOCATION OF THE FOREIGN-EXCHANGE MARKET

Estimated daily foreign exchange turnover in 2010 was $5.3 trillion, up 32.5 percent from the 2010 survey.

Before we examine the market instruments in more detail, let's look at the size, composition, and geographic location of the market. Every three years, the BIS conducts a triennial survey of foreign-exchange activity in the world. The ninth triennial survey was conducted in April 2013, and preliminary data was released in September 2013. As noted in Figure 8.3, in 2013 the BIS estimated daily foreign exchange turnover to be $5.3 trillion. This reflects an increase of 32.5 percent over the 2010 survey, driven largely by increases in spot market transactions. However, the rise in activity was much smaller than the 71 percent increase in trades from 2004 to 2007. The global economic crisis clearly slowed down the volume of foreign exchange transactions from 2007–2010, but global recovery from the crisis, though still a little slow,

FIGURE 8.2 Foreign-Exchange Markets: Turnover by Instrument, September 2013

The spot market turnover increased by 38 percent since the 2020 survey. This is largely due to other financial institutions participating in more active trading. The rest of the markets grew as well but at more moderate paces.

Source: Based on Bank for International Settlements, *Triennial Central Bank Survey Report on Foreign Exchange Turnover in April 2013* (Basel, Switzerland: BIS, September 2013): 8.

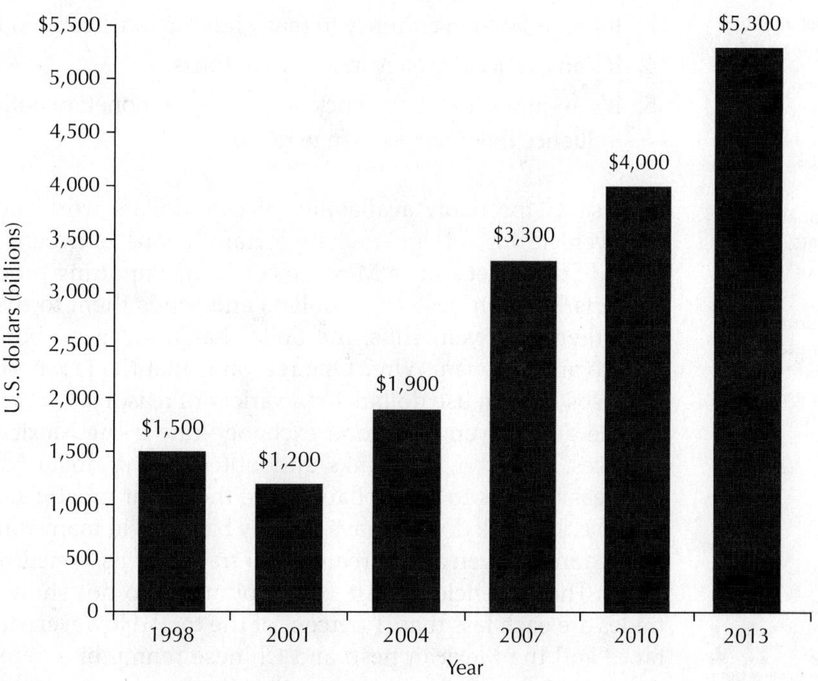

FIGURE 8.3 Foreign-Exchange Markets: Average Daily Volume, 1998–2013

The data compiled by the BIS include traditional foreign-exchange activity (such as spots, outright forwards, and FX swaps), as well as the volume of derivatives (such as hedge funds) traded in the OTC.

Source: Based on Bank for International Settlements, *Central Bank Survey Report on Foreign Exchange Turnover in April 2013: Preliminary Global Results (Basel, Switzerland, BIS, September 2013), p. 3.* (Basel, Switzerland: BIS, December 2010): 7.

CONCEPT CHECK

It's interesting (though not necessarily surprising) to note that the most widely traded currencies in the world are those issued by countries that enjoy high levels of political freedom (see Chapter 3) and economic freedom (see Chapter 4).

allowed foreign exchange activity to pick up even more. As noted above, by 2013, the daily turnover was reported to be $5.3 trillion.

Some of the reasons for the increase in trading activity are the growing importance of foreign exchange as an alternative asset and a larger emphasis on **hedge funds**—funds typically used by wealthy individuals and institutions that are allowed to use aggressive strategies unavailable to mutual funds.

Using the U.S. Dollar on the Foreign-Exchange Market The U.S. dollar is the most important currency on the foreign-exchange market; in 2013, it was one side (buy or sell) of 87 percent of all foreign currency transactions worldwide, as Table 8.1 shows. (Numbers in the table are percentages and add up to 200 percent because there are two sides to each transaction.) There are five major reasons why the dollar is so widely traded:[7]

1. It's an investment currency in many capital markets.
2. It's a reserve currency held by many central banks.

TABLE 8.1 Global Foreign Exchange: Currency Distribution

The U.S. dollar is involved in 87 percent of all worldwide foreign-exchange transactions. Because it's so readily available, it's a popular choice for exchanges between two countries other than the United States, and it's involved in four of the seven most frequently traded currency pairs (the $/€ is number one, the $/¥ number two).

Currency	April 2001	April 2004	April 2007	April 2010	April 2013
U.S. dollar	89.9	88.0	85.6	84.9	87.0
Euro	37.9	37.4	37.0	39.1	33.4
Japanese yen	23.5	20.8	17.2	19.0	23.0
Pound sterling	13.0	16.5	14.9	12.9	11.8
Australian dollar	4.3	6.0	6.6	7.6	8.6
Swiss franc	6.0	6.0	6.8	6.4	5.2
All others	25.4	25.3	31.9	30.1	31.0

Source: Based on Bank for International Settlements, *Central Bank Survey Report on Foreign Exchange Turnover in April 2013* (Basel, Switzerland: BIS, September 2013), p. 10.

The dollar is the most widely traded currency in the world:

- An investment currency in many capital markets,
- A reserve currency held by many central banks,
- A transaction currency in many international commodity markets,
- An invoice currency in many contracts,
- An intervention currency employed by monetary authorities in market operations to influence their own exchange rates.

3. It's a transaction currency in many international commodity markets.
4. It's an invoice currency in many contracts.
5. It's an intervention currency employed by monetary authorities in market operations to influence their own exchange rates.

Because of the ready availability of U.S. dollars worldwide, this currency is important as a vehicle for foreign-exchange transactions between two countries other than the United States. Let's say a Mexican company importing products from a Japanese exporter converts Mexican pesos into dollars and sends them to the Japanese exporter, who converts them into yen. Thus, the dollar has one leg on both sides of the transaction—in Mexico and in Japan. Why? One reason is that the Japanese exporter might have no need for pesos but can use dollars for a variety of reasons. Or the Mexican importer might have trouble getting yen at a good exchange rate if the Mexican banks are not carrying yen balances. However, the banks undoubtedly carry dollar balances, so the importer might have easy access to the dollars. Thus, the dollar greatly simplifies life for a foreign bank because the bank doesn't have to carry balances in many different currencies. Note the rise in the euro and yen as a percentage of transactions, concurrent with a slight fall in the U.S. dollar. The currencies of the BRIC countries do not show up on Table 8.1 because their trades are each less than 1 percent of the total. However, they are steadily rising in importance and the Mexican peso and Chinese renminbi entered the top 10 for the first time in the 2013 Survey. We'll explore the situation involving the renminbi in the ending case.

The dollar is part of four of the top seven currency pairs traded:

- The dollar/euro is number one,
- The dollar/yen is number two.

Frequently Traded Currency Pairs Another way to consider foreign currency trades is to look at the most frequently traded currency pairs. The top seven pairs in the 2013 BIS Survey involved the U.S. dollar, with the top two being euro/dollar (EUR/USD)—24.1 percent of the total—and dollar/yen (USD/JPY).[8] Because of the importance of the U.S. dollar in foreign-exchange trade, the exchange rate between two currencies other than the dollar—for example, the exchange rate between the Swiss franc and the Brazilian real—is known as a **cross rate**.

The trade between the dollar and yen is very sensitive politically because the exchange rate is often a function of trade negotiations between Japan and the United States.[9] The yen is an important currency in Asia because its value reflects the competitive positions of other countries in the region and because it is freely traded—unlike the Chinese yuan, which is more tightly controlled by the government but is moving to become more of a regional and eventually a global currency (as discussed in the ending case). The yen is also affected by what is called **carry trade**. With interest rates being so low in Japan, investors will borrow in yen and invest the proceeds in other countries, such as Brazil. However, at the slightest concern over a risky global economic environment, the investors will liquidate their investments in Brazil and "carry" the proceeds back to Japan. This also occurs at the end of the fiscal year in Japan (March 31), when companies may need Japanese yen. Other carry trades often followed by the market are the U.S. dollar against the South African Rand and the Hong Kong dollar, the Australian dollar against the Japanese yen, and the New Zealand dollar against the Japanese yen.

The biggest market for foreign exchange is London, followed by New York, Tokyo, and Singapore.

The Euro The euro is also in four of the top ten currency pairs. Although the dollar is still more popular in most emerging markets, the euro is gaining ground, particularly in Eastern European countries. Moreover, it is slowly rising in importance as a trading currency, even outside of Europe.

Given that the dollar is clearly the most widely traded currency in the world, you'd expect the biggest market for foreign-exchange trading to be in the United States. As Figure 8.4

FIGURE 8.4 Foreign-Exchange Markets: Geographical Distribution, September 2013

The United Kingdom handles 40.9 percent of all world foreign-exchange activity (compared to just 18.9 percent by the United States). Location is a big factor in the United Kingdom's popularity: London is close to all the capital markets of Europe, and its time zone makes it convenient for making trades in both the U.S. and Asian markets.

Source: Based on Bank for International Settlements, *Central Bank Survey Report on Foreign Exchange Turnover in April 2013: Preliminary Global Results* (Basel, Switzerland: BIS, September 2013: 14): 1

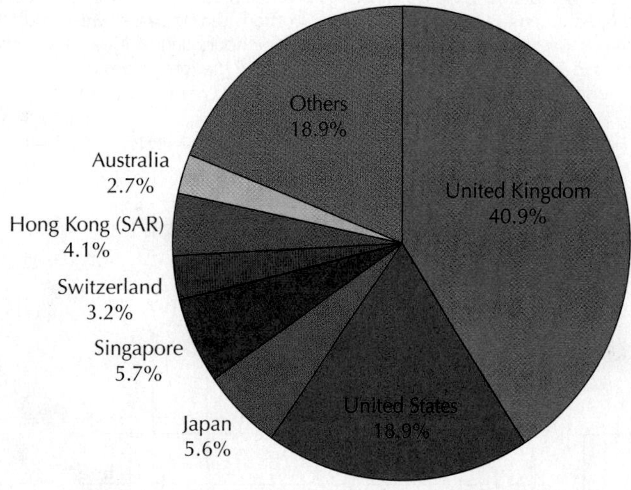

illustrates, however, the biggest by far is in the United Kingdom. The four largest centers for foreign-exchange trading (the United Kingdom, the United States, Japan, and Singapore) account for 71.1 percent of the total average daily turnover. The U.K. market is so dominant that more dollars are traded in London than in New York.[10]

Does Geography Matter?

Foreign-Exchange Trades and Time Zones

If the U.S. dollar is the most widely traded currency in the world, why is London so important as a trading center? There are two major reasons. First, London, which is close to the major capital markets in Europe, is a strong international financial center where many domestic and foreign financial institutions operate. Thus, its geographic location relative to significant global economic activity is key.

Second, London is positioned in a unique way because of its time zone. As Map 8.1 shows, noon in London is 7:00 a.m. in New York and evening in Asia. The London market opens toward the end of the trading day in Asia and is going strong as the New York foreign-exchange market opens up. Thus, the city straddles both of the other major world markets.

Another way to illustrate the importance of geography is to note the daily volume of market activity that takes place in different markets around the world, especially in North America and Europe. Figure 8.5 shows the how the time overlaps when foreign exchange markets are open. The time on the horizontal axis is set according to EST to correspond with when the U.S. markets are open, because at 5:00 P.M. on Friday when the New York market closes, foreign exchange trades shut down until Sunday afternoon (U.S. time) when the markets open in Wellington, NZ (Monday morning NZ time). The times of greatest foreign exchange activity are when Tokyo and London are both open, a period of about two hours. The next period of greatest foreign exchange activity is when New York opens and London is still in full swing, from 8:00 A.M. until noon New York time. However, London has already been open and active for four hours before New York opens, so New York foreign exchange traders usually start early so as not to miss the activity in London. ■

MAP 8.1 International Trade Zones and The Single World Market

The world's communication networks are now so good that we can talk of a single world market. It starts in a small way in New Zealand at around 9:00 a.m. (local time), just in time to catch the tail end of the previous night's market in New York (where it's about 4:00 p.m. local time). Two or three hours later, Tokyo opens, followed an hour later by Hong Kong and Manila, then half an hour later by Singapore. By now, with the Far East market in full swing, the focus moves to the Near and Middle East. Mumbai (formerly Bombay) opens two hours after Singapore, followed after an hour and a half by Abu Dhabi and Athens. At this stage, trading in the Far and Middle East is usually thin as dealers wait to see how Europe will trade. Paris and Frankfurt open an hour ahead of London, and by this time Tokyo is starting to close down, so the European market can judge the Japanese market. By lunchtime in London, New York is starting to open up, and as Europe closes down, positions can be passed westward. Midday in New York, trading tends to be quiet because there is nowhere to pass a position to. The San Francisco market, three hours behind New York, is effectively a satellite of the New York market, although very small positions can be passed on to New Zealand banks. (Note that in the former Soviet Union, standard time zones are advanced an hour. Also note that some countries and territories have adopted half-hour time zones, as shown by hatched lines.)

Source: Based on Julian Walmsley, *The Foreign Exchange Handbook* (New York: John Wiley, 1983): 7–8. Reprinted by permission of John Wiley & Sons, Inc. Some information taken from *The Cambridge Factfinders*, 3rd ed., David Crystal (ed.) (New York: Cambridge University Press, 1998): 440.

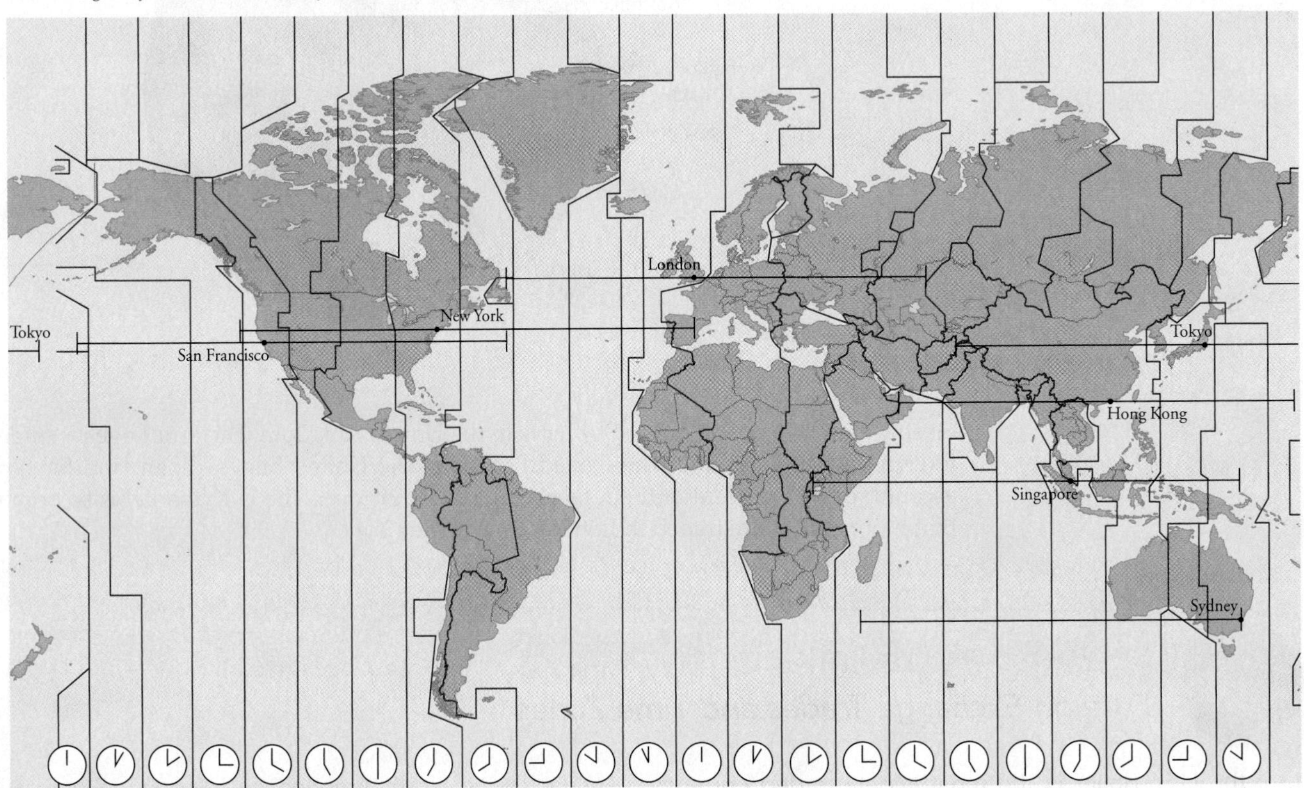

FIGURE 8.5 Overlapping Time Zones and Foreign Exchange Trades

Although foreign exchange is traded 24 hours a day, most of the trading activity occurs when the major foreign exchange markets, especially London and New York, are open.

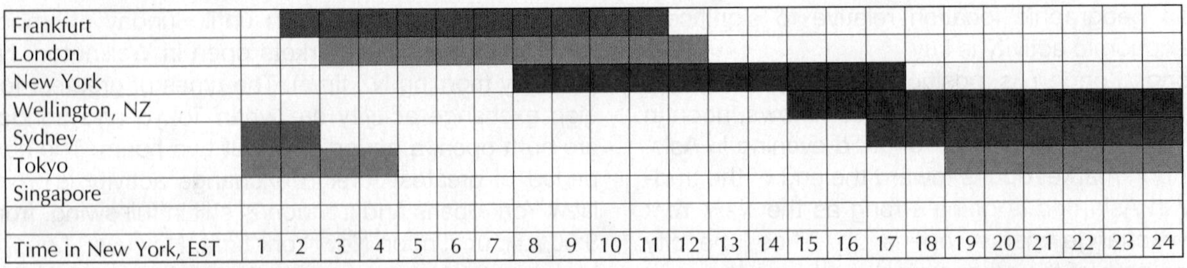

Frankfurt																								
London																								
New York																								
Wellington, NZ																								
Sydney																								
Tokyo																								
Singapore																								
Time in New York, EST	1	2	3	4	5	6	7	8	9	10	11	12	13	14	15	16	17	18	19	20	21	22	23	24

MAJOR FOREIGN-EXCHANGE MARKETS

THE SPOT MARKET

Foreign-exchange dealers are the ones who quote the rates. The **bid (buy) rate** is the price at which the dealer is willing to buy foreign currency; the **offer (sell)** is the price at which the dealer is willing to sell foreign currency. In the spot market, the **spread** is the difference between the bid and offer rates, as well as the dealer's profit margin. In our opening case, we explain how Western Union quotes exchange rates for the purpose of trading dollars for pesos. Its rates are often different from those quoted by commercial banks, but some people prefer to use Western Union, pay higher fees, and get lower exchange rates. Why? In part, because of a lack of trust in the banking system.

Key foreign-exchange terms:

- Bid—the rate at which traders buy foreign exchange
- Offer—the rate at which traders sell foreign exchange
- Spread—the difference between bid and offer rates
- American terms, or direct quote—the number of dollars per unit of foreign currency
- European terms, or indirect quote—the number of units of foreign currency per dollar

Direct and Indirect Quotes Let's look at an example of how a bid and offer might work. Assume that the rate a U.S.-based dealer quotes for the British pound is $1.5556/58. This means the dealer is willing to buy pounds at $1.5556 each and sell them for $1.5558 each—i.e., buying low and selling high. In this example, the dealer quotes the foreign currency as the number of U.S. dollars for one unit of that currency. This method of quoting exchange rates is called the **direct quote**, which is the number of units of the domestic currency (the U.S. dollar in this case) for one unit of the foreign currency. It is also known as **American terms**.

The other convention for quoting foreign exchange is known as the **indirect quote**, or **European terms**. It is the number of units of the foreign currency for one unit of the domestic currency. On May 1, 3013, the direct quote for the U.K. pound was $1.5556, and the indirect quote was £0.6429.[11]

Base and Term Currencies When dealers quote currencies to their customers, they always quote the **base currency** (the denominator) first, followed by the **terms currency** (the numerator). A quote for USD/JPY (also shown as USDJPY = X) means the dollar is the base currency and the yen is the terms currency (the number of Japanese yen for one U.S. dollar). If you know the dollar/yen quote, you can divide that rate into 1 to get the yen/dollar quote. In other words, the exchange rate in American terms (the direct quote) is the reciprocal or inverse of the exchange rate in European terms (the indirect quote). For example, on May 1, 2013, the indirect quote for Japanese yen (USD/JPY) was ¥97.39 for one dollar. The reciprocal would be 1/¥97.39 = $0.010268.[12]

In a dollar/yen quote, the dollar is the denominator, the yen the numerator. By tracking changes in the exchange rate, managers can determine whether the base currency is strengthening or weakening. For example, on May 1, 2012, the dollar/yen rate was ¥80.08/$1.00; on May 1, 2013, it was ¥97.39/$1.00. As the numerator increases, the base currency (the dollar) is strengthening. Conversely, the terms currency (the yen) is weakening.

There are many ways to get exchange rate quotes, including online and print media. Because most currencies constantly fluctuate in value, many managers check the values daily. For example, *The Wall Street Journal* provides spot rate quotes in American terms (US $ equivalent) and European terms (currency per US $) for several currencies. In addition, if provides one-month, three-month, and six-month forward rates for a few currencies.

Interbank Transactions The spot rates provided by *The Wall Street Journal* are the selling rates for **interbank transactions** of $1 million and more. Retail transactions—those between banks and companies or individuals—provide fewer foreign currency units per dollar than interbank transactions. Similar quotes can be found in other business publications and online. However, these are only approximations; exact quotes are available through the dealers.

Traders at GPS Capital Markets, a leading corporate foreign exchange brokerage firm, scan current exchange rate trends on the electronic services they subscribe to.
Source: GPS Capital Markets, Inc.

THE FORWARD MARKET

The forward rate is the rate quoted for transactions that call for delivery after two business days.

As noted earlier, the spot market is for foreign-exchange transactions that occur within two business days. But in some transactions, a seller extends credit to the buyer for a period longer than that. For example, a Japanese exporter of consumer electronics might sell television sets to a U.S. importer with immediate delivery but payment due in 30 days. The U.S. importer is obligated to pay in yen in 30 days and may enter into a contract with a currency dealer to deliver the yen at a forward rate—the rate quoted today for future delivery.

In addition to the spot rates for each currency, *The Wall Street Journal* provides the forward rates for the Australian dollar, Japanese yen, Swiss franc, and British pound —the most widely traded currencies in the forward market. However, forward contracts are available from dealers in many other currencies as well. Electronic services such as Bloomberg provide forward rates for most currencies for different maturity dates in the future. The more exotic the currency, the more difficult it is to get a forward quote out too far in the future, and the greater the difference is likely to be between the forward rate and the spot rate.

A forward discount exists when the forward rate is less than the spot rate.

Forward Discounts and Premiums Building on what we said earlier, we now can say that the difference between the spot and forward rates is either the **forward discount** or the **forward premium**. In order to explain how to compute and interpret the premium or discount, let's use the direct rate between the U.S. dollar and the Swiss franc—in this case, the number of dollars per franc. If the forward rate for the Swiss franc is greater than the spot rate, the franc would get more dollars in the future, so it would be trading at a premium. If the forward rate is less than the spot rate, the franc would be selling at a discount since it would get you less dollars in the future. Using the May 1, 2013 direct quote for the Swiss franc for a six-month forward contract[13], the premium or discount would be computed as follows:

$$\frac{\$1.0808 - 1.0784}{1.0784} \times \frac{12}{6} = .00445 \times 100 \text{ or } 0.45\%$$

A premium exists when the forward rate is greater than the spot rate.

The premium is annualized by multiplying the difference between the spot and forward rates by 12 months divided by the number of months forward—six months, in this example. Then you multiply the results by 100 to put them in percentage terms. Because the forward rate is greater than the spot rate, the Swiss franc is selling at a premium in the forward market by 0.45 percent above the spot rate. During this particular period of time, interest rates in the major economies were quite low because of the global economic slowdown and the desire to keep interest rates low in order to speed up economic growth. Thus the premium is also quite low. During periods of greater divergence in interest rates, the premium or discount could be much larger. In 2007, for example, the franc was selling at a 2.5 percent premium in the six-month forward market.

OPTIONS

An option is the right, but not the obligation, to trade a foreign currency at a specific exchange rate.

An option is the *right,* but not the *obligation,* to buy or sell a foreign currency within a certain time period or on a specific date at a specific exchange rate. It can be purchased OTC from a commercial or investment bank or on an exchange. For example, a U.S. company purchases an OTC option from a commercial or investment bank to buy 1,000,000 Japanese yen at ¥85 per US $ ($0.011765 per yen)—or $11,765. The writer of the option will charge the company a fee for writing it. The more likely the option is to benefit the company, the higher the fee. The rate of ¥85 is called the *strike price* for the option; the fee or cost is called the *premium.* On the date when the option is set to expire, the company can look at the spot rate and compare it with the strike price to see what the better exchange rate is. If the spot rate were ¥90 per US $ ($0.01111 per yen)—or $11,000—it would not exercise the option because buying yen at the spot rate would cost less than buying them at the option rate. However, if the spot rate at that time were ¥80 per US $ ($0.0125 per yen)—or $12,500—the company would exercise the option because buying at the option rate would cost less than at the spot rate. The option gives the company flexibility because it can walk away from the option if the strike price is not a good price. In the case of a forward contract, the cost is usually cheaper than the cost for an option, but the company cannot walk away from the contract. So a forward contract is cheaper but less flexible.

The above example is for a simple, or *vanilla,* option. However, exotic or structured options are used more widely to hedge exposure, especially by European companies. The idea behind them is to provide an option product that meets a company's risk profile and tolerance and results in a premium that is as close to zero as possible. The writer of the option can still make money on the structured option, but if the option is set up effectively, the company buying it won't have to write out a big check for the premium.

FUTURES

A futures contract specifies an exchange rate in advance of the actual exchange of currency, but it is not as flexible as a forward contract.

A foreign currency futures contract resembles a forward contract insofar as it specifies an exchange rate some time in advance of the actual exchange of currency. However, a future is traded on an exchange, not OTC. Instead of working with a bank or other financial institution, companies work with exchange brokers when purchasing futures contracts. A forward contract is tailored to the amount and time frame the company needs, whereas a futures contract is for a specific amount and maturity date. It is less valuable to a company than a forward contract. However, it may be useful to speculators and small companies that cannot enter into the latter.

THE FOREIGN-EXCHANGE TRADING PROCESS

Large MNEs go through their money center banks to settle foreign-exchange balances, but smaller firms use local banks or other financial institutions.

When a company sells goods or services to a foreign customer and receives foreign currency, it needs to convert it into the domestic currency. When importing, the company needs to convert domestic to foreign currency to pay the foreign supplier. This conversion usually takes place between the company and its bank.

Originally, the commercial banks provided foreign-exchange services for their customers. Eventually, some in New York and other U.S. money centers, such as Chicago and San

FIGURE 8.6 The Foreign-Exchange Trading Process

Let's say that you're U.S. Company A, that you've received euros in payment for goods, and that you want to sell your euros in return for dollars. To make the exchange, you may contact your local bank or go directly to a money center bank.
On the other hand, perhaps you're U.S. Company B and you expect to receive euros as a future payment. To protect yourself against fluctuations in the exchange rate, you want to buy euros that you can subsequently trade back for dollars. You could choose, say, a forward or a swap, and your path would be essentially a mirror image of Company A's. Finally, either Company A or Company B could choose to convert by such means as an option or a futures contract—in which case the trade could be made by an options and/or futures exchange, either directly or through a broker.

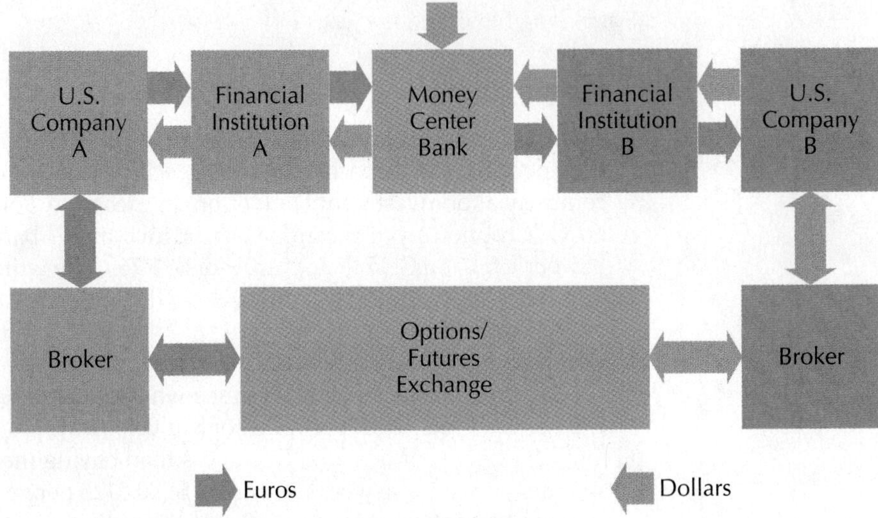

Francisco, began to look at foreign-exchange trading as a major business activity instead of just a service. They became intermediaries for smaller banks by establishing correspondent relationships with them. They also became major dealers in foreign exchange.

The left side of Figure 8.6 shows what happens when U.S. Company A needs to sell euros for dollars. This situation could arise when A receives payment in euros from a German importer. The right side of the figure shows what happens when B needs to buy euros with dollars, which could happen when a company has to pay euros to a German supplier. In either case, the U.S. company would contact its bank for help in converting the currency. If it is a large MNE, such as a Fortune 500 firm in the United States or a Global Fortune 500 company, it will probably deal directly with a money center bank (as shown on the top arrow in Figure 8.6) and not worry about another financial institution. Generally, because the MNE already has a strong banking relationship with its money center bank (or several different money center banks), the bank trades foreign exchange for the client as one of the services it offers. Companies below the Fortune 500 level operate through other financial institutions, such as local or regional banks or other banking institutions that can facilitate foreign-exchange trades. In that case, Financial Institution A and Financial Institution B still operate through a money center bank to make the trade because they may be too small to trade on their own. They typically have correspondent relationships with money center banks to allow them to make the trades.

Assume that U.S. Company B is going to receive euros in the future. Because it cannot convert in the spot market until it receives the euros, it can consider a forward, swap, options, or futures contract to protect itself until the currency is finally delivered. Financial Institution B can do a forward, swap, or options contract for Company B. However, Company B can also consider an options or futures contract on one of the exchanges, such as the CME Group. The same is true for Company A, which will need euros in the future.

CONCEPT CHECK

In explaining "The Forces Driving Globalization" in Chapter 1, we observe that although many barriers to the cross-border movement of commercial resources—including capital—are being removed, they have by no means completely disappeared. One reason for maintaining cordial relations with one's banker is the fact that these barriers make conducting international business more expensive than conducting domestic business. As we also explain in Chapter 5, conducting international business, especially on a large scale, requires high levels of capital mobility.

BANKS AND EXCHANGES

At one time, only the big money center banks could deal directly in foreign exchange. Regional banks had to rely on them to execute trades on behalf of their clients. The emergence of electronic trading has changed that. Now even the regional banks can hook up to Bloomberg, Thomson Reuters, or EBS and deal directly in the interbank market or through brokers. Despite this, the greatest volume of foreign-exchange activity takes place with the big money center banks. Because of their reach and volume, they are the ones that set the prices in global trading of foreign exchange.

The top banks in the interbank market in foreign exchange are so ranked because of their ability to

- Trade in specific market locations,
- Engage in major currencies and cross-trades,
- Deal in specific currencies,
- Handle derivatives (forwards, options, futures, swaps),
- Conduct key market research.

Top Foreign-Exchange Dealers There is more to servicing customers in the foreign-exchange market than size alone. Each year, *Euromoney* magazine surveys treasurers, traders, and investors worldwide to identify their favorite banks and the leading dealers in the interbank market. In addition to examining transaction volumes and quality of services, the criteria for selecting the top foreign-exchange dealers include:

- Ranking of banks by corporations and other banks in specific locations, such as London, Singapore, and New York
- Capability of handling major currencies, such as the U.S. dollar and the euro
- Capability of handling major cross-trades, such as those between the euro and pound or the euro and yen
- Capability of handling specific currencies
- Capability of handling derivatives (forwards, swaps, futures, and options)
- Capability of engaging in research and analytics.[14]

Given the differing capabilities, large companies may use several banks to deal in foreign exchange, selecting those that specialize in specific geographic areas, instruments, or currencies. In the past, for example, AT&T used Citibank for its broad geographic spread and wide coverage of different currencies, but it also used Deutsche Bank for euros, Swiss Bank Corporation for Swiss francs, NatWest Bank for British pounds, and Goldman Sachs for derivatives.

Table 8.2 identifies the top banks in the world in terms of foreign-exchange trading. They are the key players in the OTC market and include commercial banks (such as Deutsche Bank and Citi) as well as investment banks (such as UBS, the London-based investment banking division of Union Bank of Switzerland and Swiss Bank Corporation). Whether one is looking at overall market share of foreign-exchange trading or the best banks in the trading of specific currency pairs, these top 10 banks are usually at or near the top in every category. It is also interesting to note that consolidation in the banking industry worldwide has resulted

TABLE 8.2 Foreign-Exchange Trades: Top Commercial and Investment Banks, 2012 as Ranked by Overall Market Share

Trading Bank	Estimated Market Share%	Market Share in Western Europe	Market Share in North America	Market Share in Asia	Market Share in Australasia
1. Deutsche Bank	14.57%	12.40%	13.16%	20.66%	20.83%
2. Citi	12.26%	11.03%	12.31%	14.87%	8.13%
3. Barclays	10.95%	10.08%	12.89%	11.26%	
4. UBS	10.48%	13.21%	9.39%	5.76%	7.76%
5. HSBC	6.72%	7.26%	4.16%	9.69%	
6. JPMorgan	6.60%	5.53%	9.21%	5.07%	
7. RBS	5.86%	7.92%	4.67%	4.12%	
8. Credit Suisse	4.68%	5.67%	4.18%	4.22%	
9. Morgan Stanley	3.52%	2.74%	5.72%		
10. Goldman Sachs	3.12%		4.94%	2.07%	

Source: Based on Estimated Market Share source: "FX Survey 2012: Overall results," *Euromoney* (May 2012) - Estimated Market Share source; and Market Share by Region source: "FX Survey 2012: Market Share by Region," *Euromoney* (May 2012).

in a concentration of foreign exchange activity. For example, in 1998, 177 banks were responsible for 75 percent of the foreign exchange turnover worldwide, whereas that number had dropped to only 93 banks in 2010. In the United States, that number had dropped from 20 to 7; in the United Kingdom, it went from 24 to 9.[15]

TOP EXCHANGES FOR TRADING FOREIGN EXCHANGE

CONCEPT CHECK

In Chapter 12, we explain why companies work so hard to establish and maintain effective value chains—frameworks for dividing value-creating activities into separate processes. For one thing, a reliable value chain permits a firm to focus on its core competencies—the unique skills or knowledge that make it better at something than its competitors. Because managing currencies and cross-trades is typically not among a firm's core competencies, its bankers are key components of its value chain.

Major exchanges that deal in foreign currency derivatives are the CME Group, NASDAQ OMX, and NYSE Liffe.

In addition to the OTC market, foreign-exchange instruments, mostly options and futures, are traded on commodities exchanges. Three of the best-known exchanges are the **CME Group**, **NASDAQ OMX**, and **NYSE Liffe**.

CME Group The CME Group was formed on July 9, 2007, as a merger between the Chicago Mercantile Exchange and the Chicago Board of Trade. The CME operates according to so-called open outcry: Traders stand in a pit and call out prices and quantities. The platform is also linked to an electronic trading platform, which is growing in popularity. The CME Group trades many different commodities. In terms of foreign exchange, it trades a suite of 60 futures and 31 options contracts, with a liquidity of over $105 billion daily[16]. Futures and options are traded in G10 and emerging market currencies. Contracts are available for the dollar against a variety of currencies as well as cross-trades, such as the euro against the Australian dollar. CME uses two electronic trading platforms to trade different commodities, including currencies: CME Globex and CME Clearport. Technology is the key to opening access to trades and expanding their reach worldwide.

NASDAQ OMX Prior to 2008, the Philadelphia Stock Exchange was one of the pioneers in trading currency options. In July 2008, PHLX merged with NASDAQ OMX and it now operates two U.S. options markets—PHLX and the NASDAQ Options Market—that represent 20 percent of the total U.S. equity options trading. They also formed a new hybrid of trading, which involves both traditional floor and online trading. Options were being offered by PHLX in the Australian dollar, the British pound, the Canadian dollar, the euro, the Japanese yen, and the Swiss franc. Futures were offered in British pounds and the euro.[17] These activities have now been absorbed by NASDAQ OMX.

NYSE Liffe NYSE Liffe Futures and Options is the global derivatives business of the NYSE Euronext Group. It is Europe's largest exchange by value of business traded and the second largest in the world. The London International Financial Futures and Options Exchange (LIFFE) was founded in 1992 to trade a variety of futures contracts and options. It was bought ten years later by Euronext, at the time a European stock exchange based in Paris but with subsidiaries in other European countries. Beginning in 2003, the electronic platform where its derivatives products traded on member exchanges was known as LIFFE CONNECT. In 2007, Euronext merged with the New York Stock Exchange to create NYSE Euronext. The international derivatives business of NYSE Euronext is now handled by NYSE Liffe, using the LIFFE CONNECT platform developed before the merger between NYSE and Euronext. Euro/Dollar futures and options are traded on LIFFE CONNECT. When the purchase by ICE (InternationalExchange) of the NYSE Euronext is finally approved by regulators, the combined enterprise will have a significantly bigger footprint in many products, including derivatives like futures.

CONCEPT CHECK

In Chapters 10 and 19, we discuss the functions of a company's CFO, not only in managing its cash flows, but in managing its foreign-exchange exposure—the extent to which fluctuations in currencies can affect the costs of its international transactions.

HOW COMPANIES USE FOREIGN EXCHANGE

Companies enter the foreign-exchange market to facilitate their regular business transactions and/or to speculate. Their treasury departments are responsible for establishing policies for trading currency and for managing banking relationships to make the trades. From a business standpoint, a company, first of all, trades foreign exchange for exports/imports and the buying or selling of goods and services.

When Boeing sells the new 787 Dreamliner commercial airplane to LAN, the largest airline in South America, it has to be concerned about the currency in which it will be paid and how it will receive payment. In this case, the sale is probably denominated in dollars, so Boeing will not have to worry about the foreign-exchange market (nor, in theory, will its employees). However, LAN will have to worry about the market. Where will it come up with the dollars, and how will it pay Boeing?

BUSINESS PURPOSES (I): CASH FLOW ASPECTS OF IMPORTS AND EXPORTS

When a company must move money to pay for purchases, or receives money from sales, it has options as to the documents it can use, the currency of denomination, and the degree of protection it can ask for. Obviously, if Boeing wanted the greatest security possible, it could ask LAN to pay for the Dreamliner before LAN takes title to the aircraft. That is not very practical in this case, but sometimes it happens when the seller has all the control in the transaction. More common is the use of commercial bills of exchange and letters of credit.

With a draft or commercial bill of exchange, one party directs another party to make payment.

Commercial Bills of Exchange An individual or a company that pays a bill in a domestic setting can pay cash, but checks are typically used—often electronically transmitted. The check is also known as a **draft** or a **commercial bill of exchange**. A draft is an instrument in which one party (the *drawer*) directs another party (the *drawee*) to make a payment. The drawee can be either a company, like the importer, or a bank. In the latter case, the draft would be considered a bank draft.

A sight draft requires payment to be made when it is presented. A time draft permits payment to be made after the date when it is presented.

Documentary drafts and documentary letters of credit are often used to protect both the buyer and the seller. They require that payment be made based on the presentation of documents conveying the title, and they leave an audit trail identifying the parties to the transactions. If the exporter requests payment to be made immediately, the draft is called a **sight draft**. If the payment is to be made later—say, 30 days after delivery—the instrument is called a **time draft**.

A letter of credit obligates the buyer's bank to honor a draft presented to it and assume payment; a credit relationship exists between the importer and the importer's bank.

Letters of Credit With a bill of exchange, it is always possible that the importer will not be able to make payment to the exporter at the agreed-upon time. A **letter of credit (L/C)**, however, obligates the buyer's bank in the importing country to honor a draft presented to it, provided the draft is accompanied by the prescribed documents. Of course, the exporter still needs to be sure the bank's credit is valid as well, since the L/C could be a forgery issued by a nonexistent bank. Even with the bank's added security, the exporter still needs to rely on the importer's credit because of possible discrepancies that could arise in the transaction. The L/C could be denominated in the currency of either party. If it is in the importer's currency, the exporter will still have to convert the foreign exchange into its currency through its commercial bank.

Although a letter of credit is more secure than a documentary draft alone, there are still risks. For the L/C to be valid, all of the conditions described in the documents must be adhered to. For example, if the L/C states that the goods will be shipped in five packages, it will not be valid if they are shipped in four or six packages. It is important to understand the conditions of the documents, as well as counterparty risk. Although a forged L/C is an obvious danger, the global financial crisis has exposed counterparty risk when banks did not have sufficient capital to stand behind their L/Cs. Prior to 2008, the risk was not so significant; afterward, businesses were hesitant to trust their banks because they might not be able to deliver on an L/C. In addition, letters of credit are irrevocable, which means they cannot be canceled or changed in any way without the consent of all parties to the transaction.

A key issue related to this chapter is that the L/C needs to specify the currency of the contract. If the L/C is not in the exporter's currency, the exporter will have to convert the foreign exchange into that currency as soon as it is received.

Confirmed Letter of Credit A letter of credit transaction may include a confirming bank in addition to the parties mentioned previously. With a **confirmed letter of credit**, the exporter has the guarantee of an additional bank—sometimes in the exporter's home country, sometimes in a third country. It rarely happens that the exporter establishes the confirming relationship. Usually, the opening bank seeks the confirmation of the L/C with a bank with which it already has a credit relationship. For an irrevocable L/C, none of the conditions can be changed unless all four parties agree in advance.[18]

BUSINESS PURPOSES (II): OTHER FINANCIAL FLOWS

Companies also deal in foreign exchange for other transactions, such as the receipt or payment of dividends or the receipt or payment of loans and interest.

Companies may have to deal in foreign exchange for other reasons. For example, if a U.S. company has a subsidiary in the United Kingdom that sends a dividend to the parent company in British pounds, the parent company has to enter into the foreign-exchange market to convert pounds to dollars. If it lends dollars to the British subsidiary, the subsidiary has to convert them into pounds. When paying principal and interest back to the parent company, it has to convert pounds into dollars.

Speculation Companies sometimes deal in foreign exchange for profit. This is especially true for some banks and all hedge funds. But sometimes corporate treasury departments see their foreign-exchange operations as profit centers and also buy and sell foreign exchange with the objective of earning profits.

Speculators take positions in foreign-exchange markets and other capital markets to earn a profit.

Investors can use foreign-exchange transactions to speculate for profit or to protect against risk. **Speculation** is the buying or selling of a commodity—in this case, foreign currency—that has both an element of risk and a chance of great profit. Assume that a hedge fund buys euros in anticipation that the euro will strengthen against other currencies. If it does, the investor earns a profit; if it weakens, the investor incurs a loss. Speculators are important in the foreign-exchange market because they spot trends and try to take advantage of them. They can create demand for a currency by purchasing it in the market, or they can create a supply by selling. However, speculation is also a very risky business. In recent years, the advent of e-trading has attracted a lot of day traders in foreign exchange. The problem is that day traders rarely make money speculating in exchange rates. As we will show in Chapter 10, forecasting currency movements is indeed a risky business.

Arbitrage is the buying and selling of foreign currencies at a profit due to price discrepancies.

Arbitrage One type of profit-seeking activity is **arbitrage**, which is the purchase of foreign currency on one market for immediate resale on another market (in a different country) to profit from a price discrepancy. For example, a dealer might sell U.S. dollars for Swiss francs in the United States, then Swiss francs for British pounds in Switzerland, then the British pounds for U.S. dollars back in the United States, with the goal of ending up with more dollars.

Here's how the process might work: Assume the dealer converts 100 dollars into 150 Swiss francs when the exchange rate is 1.2 francs per dollar. The dealer then converts the 150 francs into 70 British pounds at an exchange rate of 0.467 pounds per franc and finally converts the pounds into 125 dollars at an exchange rate of 0.56 pounds per dollar. In this case, arbitrage yields $125 from the initial sale of $100. Given the transparency of exchange rate quotes globally, it is difficult to make a lot of money on arbitrage, but it is possible for an investor who has a lot of money and can move quickly.

Interest arbitrage involves investing in interest-bearing instruments in foreign exchange in an effort to earn a profit due to interest rate differentials.

Interest arbitrage is the investing in debt instruments, such as bonds, in different countries. A dealer might invest $1,000 in the United States for 90 days, or convert $1,000 into British pounds, invest the money in the United Kingdom for 90 days, then convert the pounds back into dollars. The investor would try to pick the alternative that would yield the highest return at the end of 90 days.

Point

Is It OK to Speculate on Currency?

Point **Yes** People trade in foreign exchange for a number of reasons, and one of them is speculation, which is not illegal or necessarily bad. Just as stockbrokers invest people's money to try to earn a return higher than the market average, foreign currency traders invest people's money in foreign exchange to make a profit for the investors. Or individuals can become day traders and try to make a profit trading online on their own. Speculation is merely taking a position on a currency in order to profit from market trends.

Electronic trading has made it easier for a variety of investors to speculate in foreign exchange. Hedge funds are an important source of this foreign-exchange speculation. There is no one specific strategy that hedge fund managers follow. However, the transparency in trading has driven the smaller players out of the market and allowed the large institutions and traders to earn profits on small margins that require large volumes of transactions. Hedge funds generally deal in minimum investments that are quite large, so the hedge fund managers that trade in foreign exchange trade in very large volumes. They might make long-term bets on a currency based on macroeconomic conditions, or they might try to balance off buy-and-sell strategies in currencies so that one side offers protection against the other. In either case, the hedge fund manager is betting on the future position of a currency to earn money for the investors in the fund.

Speculation is not for the faint of heart. Political and economic conditions outside the speculators' control can quickly turn profits to losses—probably quicker than in the stock market. Currencies are inherently unstable. Consider the problems of the U.S. dollar in 2007 and 2008, when it was quite weak against the euro and the yen. What should hedge fund managers do? They might expect the dollar to continue to weaken. But what if it strengthens? Or they might think the dollar has reached its floor and is ready for a rise, which would argue that the managers should buy dollars. But when will it rise and by how much? By mid-March 2008, the dollar had declined by 15 percent in the prior 12 months; two months later, many experts felt it had reached a low point and expected it to rise. This was based on the market expectations that interest cuts by the Fed were expected to stop and that the credit crisis was beginning to soften. Now the speculators have to decide what to do with those expectations. Similar trends occurred in 2010-2011 when the dollar fell from a mid-2010 high of \$1.2187 per euro to a low of \$1.4546 by early May 2011. However, uncertainty over the Greek debt crisis pushed the euro down, leaving speculators wondering what would happen next.

Sometimes speculators can buy a currency on the basis of good economic fundamentals, or they can buy or sell currency because they feel that governments are following poor economic policies. In late 2012, the Japanese economy was very weak, but the yen was strong. As the new Japanese government announced that it was considering policies to weaken the yen, many hedge funds jumped into the market and sold yen, helping to push down the value. At what point do they feel that the yen has fallen enough and that it is in their best interests to be on a rise in the value of the yen? It is always tough to figure out the right timing of a movement and how far it will rise (or fall). As long as markets are free and information is available, traders ought to be able to make some money on their predictions of the future. There is even a good argument that speculators help keep governments honest by betting in directions they feel reflect political and economic fundamentals. Either governments must adjust to reality or suffer the consequences. Of course, if governments close their markets to speculation, as is the case with China, it's tough for the speculators to trade and make money.

The key is that currency speculation is a different way to invest money and allows investors to diversify their portfolios from traditional stocks and bonds. Just as foreign exchange can be traded for speculative purposes, trading in shares is also speculation. Even though we call such trades "investments," they are just another form of speculation hoping to gain a return that is higher than the market average and certainly higher than what a CD can yield.

Is It OK to Speculate on Currency?

Counterpoint

No There are plenty of opportunities for a trader, whether in foreign exchange or securities, to make money illegally or contrary to company policy. The culture of individual traders trying to make money off trading foreign exchange or other securities, combined with lax controls in financial institutions, contributes greatly to these scandals.

One of the most publicized events in the derivatives markets in recent years involved 28-year-old Nicholas Leeson and the 233-year-old British bank Barings PLC. Leeson, a dealer for Barings, went to Singapore in the early 1990s to help resolve some of the bank's problems. Within a year, he was promoted to chief dealer, with responsibility for trading securities and booking the settlements. This meant that there were no checks and balances on his trading actions, thus opening the door to fraud.

When two different people are assigned to trade securities and book settlements, the person booking the settlements can confirm independently whether the trades were accurate and legitimate. In 1994, Leeson bought stock index futures on the Singapore International Monetary Exchange, or SIMEX, on the assumption that the Tokyo stock market would rise. Most dealers watching his feverish trading activity assumed Barings had a large client that he was trading for. It turns out, however, that he was using the bank's money to speculate. Because the Japanese economy was recovering, it made sense to assume the market would continue to rise, thus generating more profits for Leeson and Barings. Unfortunately, something happened that nobody could predict—the January 17, 1995, earthquake that hit the port city of Kobe.

As a result of the devastation and uncertainty, the market fell, and Leeson had to come up with cash to cover the margin call on the futures contract. A margin is a deposit made as security for a financial transaction that is otherwise financed on credit. When the price of an instrument changes and the margin rises, the exchange "calls" the increased margin from the other party—in this case, Leeson.[19]

However, Leeson soon ran out of cash from Barings and had to come up with more. One approach he used was to write options contracts and use the premium he collected on the contracts to cover his margin call. Unfortunately, he was using Barings' funds to cover positions he was taking for himself, not for clients, and he also forged documents to cover his transactions.

As the Tokyo stock market continued to plunge, Leeson fell further and further behind and eventually fled the country, later to be caught and returned to Singapore for trial and prison. Barings estimated that Leeson generated losses in excess of $1 billion, and the bank eventually was purchased by Dutch bank ING.[20]

Since the collapse of Barings, measures have been put into place in banks to prohibit such consequences. However, negative outcomes of rogue trading continue to happen. Leeson's record losses were surpassed in 2008 by Jérôme Kerviel of French bank Société Générale. A onetime employee in the back office (the part of the bank that processes transactions), Kerviel became a trader in 2005 in the relatively unimportant Delta One trading unit. In his new position, he began trading futures on the bank's own account. His role was to take opposite positions on the direction of the market in order to earn money on the spread. However, he began to take one-way positions to earn even more money for the bank and hopefully a bigger bonus. The problem is that he bet the European markets would rise—and in early 2008 they fell rather sharply. Through a variety of actions that went against the internal controls of the banks as well as outright lies about what he was doing, he was able to fool bank insiders while hoping to cover his positions. The bank eventually found out what Kerviel was doing and discovered that he had exposed it to a €50 billion risk. By the time the bank had unwound all of its trading positions, it had lost €1.5 billion, or $2.22 billion. Unlike Leeson, Kerviel was not using his bank's money to trade on his own account, but like Leeson, he created serious problems for the bank, which lost a lot of money.[21]

1. Is any kind of speculation wrong? How can companies establish policies that forbid speculation by their foreign exchange traders as a way to protect corporate assets?

Looking to the Future

Where Are Foreign-Exchange Markets Headed?

Significant strides have been made and will continue to be made in the development of foreign-exchange markets. The speed at which transactions are processed and information transmitted globally will certainly lead to greater efficiencies and more opportunities for foreign-exchange trading. The impact on companies is that trading costs should come down and companies should have faster access to more currencies.

In addition, exchange restrictions that hamper the free flow of goods and services should diminish as governments gain greater control over their economies and liberalize currency markets. Capital controls still affect foreign investment, but they will continue to become less of a factor for trade in goods and services. The introduction of the euro has allowed cross-border transactions in Europe to progress more smoothly. As the euro solidifies its position in Europe, it will reduce exchange-rate volatility and the euro should be able to take some of the pressure off the dollar. However, financial crises in Europe have threatened the very existence of the euro and its role in global currency markets. The UK still has not adopted the euro and is even threatening to leave the EU. Many of the countries in southern Europe which are under severe economic pressure are wondering if it is in their best interests to keep using the euro. However, as the global economy recovers, these pressures to leave the euro or the EU will probably dissipate.

The real wild card in global foreign exchange is the Chinese yuan. As we will discuss in the following case, the Chinese government continues to liberalize trading in foreign exchange, but the yuan is not a freely traded currency. Given that China has the largest foreign exchange reserves in the world and is investing all over the world, especially in the emerging markets that have large deposits of natural resources, the RMB has the potential of becoming a major traded currency. Even the Brazilian real, the currency of another BRIC country, is poised to make an impact on currency markets. However, that depends on what happens to commodity prices since Brazil is so dependent on commodity exports, especially to China. One trend that could be the wave of the future is currencies settling with each other rather than through the dollar. That is now occurring between the RMB and Brazilian real due to strong trading relationships between the two countries as Brazil exports commodities to China, and China exports manufactured goods to Brazil.

Technological Developments

Technological developments may not cause the foreign-exchange broker to disappear entirely, but they will certainly cause foreign-exchange trades to be executed more quickly and cheaply. The advent of technology clearly has caused the market to shift from phone trades to electronic trades.[22]

It is hard to know how extensive online trading will become. Numerous companies now advertise it for investors, but that is not where most of the trades take place. The growth of Internet trades in currency will take away some of the market share of dealers and allow more entrants into the foreign-exchange market. Internet trade will also increase currency price transparency and improve the ease of trading, thus allowing more investors into the market. It is interesting to note that Barclays Capital, the third largest bank in foreign-exchange trades, is trying to build its online trading portal by offering automated exchange tools to financial and nonfinancial clients. One idea is to offer the system to their correspondent banks, who can then offer it to their corporate clients. This is a response to the fact that foreign-exchange trading is shifting from telephone to online,[23] forcing the banks to offer more services to clients. Deutsche Bank and UBS, the top two foreign-exchange traders, are also expected to expand their proprietary platforms for e-trading. ■

CASE Do Yuan to Buy Some Renminbi?

In mid-2011, the Chinese government was trying to decide when was the right time to allow its currency, the renminbi (RMB), to float freely on global currency markets and permit its free flow from China to anywhere in the world—the final steps to allowing it to take its place as one of the world's major currencies. The renminbi, also known as the *yuan*, is the official name of the currency, and the yuan is the basic unit of account. In the currency markets, the sign for the currency is ¥ (the same symbol used for the Japanese yen) and the code is CNY. Since the terms are used interchangeably, we'll use "yuan" in this Case. Although the yuan has been relatively fixed and controlled by the Chinese government, there are signs that it is getting close to being unleashed. What does this mean for currency traders and the future balance of power in global currency markets currently dominated by the U.S. dollar, the euro, and the yen?

A Little History

On January 7, 1994, the Chinese government, after debating what to do with its currency, decided to fix the value to the U.S. dollar at a rate of ¥8.690 per dollar.[24] This was easy to do, given that currency trading was controlled by the Chinese government and not allowed offshore. In 2004, Hong Kong residents were allowed to exchange local Hong Kong dollars for yuan in a first move to allow some limited trading offshore. By early 2005, the yuan was trading at a fixed rate of ¥8.2665 per dollar. But pressure began to build in 2005 as both the

FIGURE 8.7

Source: Harley Schwadron/ CartoonStock, Ltd.

"Of course I know the value of the dollar. That's why I'd like my allowance in Chinese Yuan."

European Union and the United States faced strong competition from imports from China as well as from Chinese exports to developing markets.

When China fixed the value of its currency in 1994, the country was not considered a major economic powerhouse. Then things began to change. By 1999, China was the largest country in the world in population, and in 2003 it was the seventh largest in the world in GNI, exceeded only by the United States, Japan, Germany, the United Kingdom, France, and Italy. It was also growing faster than any of the top six countries. In the decade of the 1990s, China grew by an annual average of 9.5 percent and was above 8 percent every year in the first half of the 2000s.

Because of China's low manufacturing wages, it was exporting far more to the United States than it was importing. In 2004, it had a trade surplus of $155 billion with the U.S., compared with a surplus of only $86 billion with the EU. However, between 2002 and 2004 China's surplus with the EU doubled, while growing by a little over a half with the U.S. The major problem with the EU is that, during that time period, the euro had grown by 45 percent against the dollar, which meant it had also grown by 45 percent against the yuan, which was fixed against the dollar. In effect, Chinese exports had gotten cheaper against European products both in the euro zone as well as in Europe's export markets. Also during that time, there were capital controls on the flow of yuan in and out of China, so there was a tremendous inflow of yuan into the banking sector in China with no real way to move the money offshore. That meant that banks could lend money at very low interest rates, fueling a real estate boom. Also, China had to do something with its building reserves. Initially it invested huge sums of money in U.S. treasury bills, helping to fund the growing U.S. budget deficit. Then it began encouraging foreign direct investment, especially in natural resources around the world.

However, the competitive pressure of China in Asia was not the same. Because most Asian currencies were also locked onto the dollar, the yuan traded in a narrow range against those currencies. Most of the Asian countries were using China as a new market for their products, and they were not anxious to have anything upset the Chinese economy and reduce demand for their products.

Critics from the United States and EU argued that the yuan was undervalued by 15 to 40 percent and the Chinese government needed to free the currency and allow it to seek a market level. The pressures for and against change were both political and economic. The U.S. government had been working with the Chinese for an extended period of time to get them to revalue their currency, but the Chinese government had found plenty of excuses not to do that.

Political Pressures in China

China had its own political pressures. For one thing, a lot of people had been moving currency there in anticipation of a revaluation of the yuan, which was creating inflationary pressures. The Chinese government was forced to buy the dollars and issue yuan-denominated bonds as a way of "sterilizing" the currency—taking it off the market to reduce the pressures. The government was not very excited about revaluing the yuan and rewarding the speculators, so it kept saying it would not announce if, when, or how much the revaluation would be. It also did not want to revalue under pressure from foreign governments lest it appear to be bowing under pressure from abroad.

Finally, China has serious problems with employment. Even though its billion-plus population grows at only 1 percent annually, it adds the equivalent of a new country the size of Ecuador or Guatemala every year. China needs to add enough jobs to keep up with its population growth and displaced workers from its agricultural sector and state-owned firms. That means adding 15 to 20 million new jobs per year, or about 1.25 million per month. In comparison, the United States created 275,000 new jobs in April 2005. If China slows down its economy to keep inflation in check, it needs a strong export sector to keep creating jobs. If that sector cools because of a revalued currency, political and social chaos could ensue.

The Advent of the Currency Basket

Given these pressures, China took an historic step on July 21, 2005, and de-linked the yuan from its decade-old peg to the U.S. dollar in favor of a currency basket because, though the dollar has been the dominant currency in determining the value of the yuan, there are periods of time when some Asian currencies have also shown themselves to be influential. So the currency basket was largely denominated by the dollar, the euro, the yen, and the South Korean won—currencies that were selected because of their impact on China's foreign trade, investment, and foreign debt. Even when the basket grew to 11 currencies, these four dominated.

The People's Bank of China (PBOC, the country's central bank) decides a central parity rate daily and then allows a trading band on either side of the decided point. The move to the currency basket increased the yuan-to-dollar rate by 2.1 percent. Before the peg was de-linked, the yuan was kept around ¥8.2665; immediately afterward, it rose to ¥8.1011, an increase of 2 percent. The United States, Europe, and Japan thought the change was too small and continued to assert that the yuan was undervalued.

By the end of 2006, the yuan had appreciated by 5.68 percent. The effect on the U.S. trade deficit was minimal because the first quarter 2007 deficit reached $56.9 billion, a 36 percent increase over the $41.9 billion deficit in first quarter 2005. The international community continued to heap pressures on China.

The PBOC responded to the pressures by widening the trading band of the yuan on May 18, 2007, from 0.3 percent to 0.5 percent on either side of the fixed rate. Obviously, that small difference allowed little room for traders. The move came a week before the Chinese delegation was to meet for a second round of strategic economic talks with senior U.S. officials, while the Treasury Department was preparing its semiannual report on the currency market. Many believed China would be cited as a currency manipulator in the Treasury Department report.

Baby Steps

Until the yuan began its ascent against the U.S. dollar, it was very easy to deal in foreign exchange in China because the rate was fixed against the dollar. It doesn't take a lot of judgment for a trader to operate in a fixed-rate world. The exchange rate is managed by the State Administration of Foreign Exchange (SAFE), which is closely linked to the PBOC. SAFE is responsible for establishing the new foreign-exchange trading guidelines as well as for managing China's foreign-exchange reserves. A major concern of the PBOC is that China's financial infrastructure might be capable of trading foreign exchange in a free market. In the Triennial Central Bank Survey on foreign exchange market activity conducted by the Bank for International Statements in 2010, the Chinese yuan did not show up as an important currency in terms of turnover, and the Chinese banks were not represented in the 2011 *Euromoney* survey of top foreign exchange-trading banks. This is because most of the yuan was deposited in China, and Chinese banks were not permitted to set up operations in Hong Kong to trade their massive deposits in yuan in global capital markets.

SAFE was moving to change that. When the PBOC made the decision to loosen up the value of the yuan in 2005, it opted to allow banks in Shanghai to trade and quote prices in eight currency pairs, including the dollar-sterling and euro-yen. Prior to that, licensed banks were only allowed to trade the yuan against four currencies: the U.S. dollar, the Hong Kong dollar, the euro, and the yen. Shanghai was being positioned as the financial center of China, hopefully by 2020. However, all the trades were at fixed rates, and they did not involve trades in non-yuan currency pairs. SAFE also decided to open up trading to seven international banks (HSBC, Citigroup, Deutsche Bank, ABN AMRO, ING, Royal Bank of Scotland, and Bank of Montreal) and two domestic banks (Bank of China and CITIC Industrial Bank). Several of these international banks are among the most sophisticated foreign exchange traders in the world. For example, HSBC, which got its start in Hong Kong in 1865, has offices around the world, and its stock is listed on exchanges in London, Hong Kong, New York, and Bermuda. It has strong geographic reach that could easily expand the trading in yuan once controls are lifted.

The Bank of China Tower in Hong Kong is on the left, and the HSBC Main Building is on the right. Both are prime real estate assets as Hong Kong was ranked as the most expensive office market by total occupancy cost in 2013.
Source: Bloomberg via Getty Images

Fast Forward

However, the global financial crisis forced the Chinese government to return the yuan to a peg against the U.S. dollar that lasted from July 2008 until June 2010, during which time the U.S. and China were embroiled in a war of words over the value of the currency. The U.S. wanted the Chinese to allow their currency to continue to rise to help solve the trade imbalance, and the Chinese wanted the U.S. to get its economy under control and stabilize the value of the dollar, which had been falling in value against most other currencies. China was even calling for the creation of a new reserve asset to take the place of the dollar in the global economy. Why was China so worried about the dollar's value? Because most of its reserves—the largest in the world at more than $3 trillion, fed largely by its huge trade surplus—are in U.S. dollars. The last thing China wanted was to have all of its dollar reserves losing value in the global economy.

China's Economic Challenges

By the end of 2010, not only had China replaced Japan as the #2 country in the world in terms of GDP, it was closing fast on the United States. In addition, China surpassed Germany and the U.S. as the largest exporter in the world, which meant that it was continuing to generate large foreign exchange assets that were exposed to losses in value as the dollar fell against other world currencies.

China, however, had its own set of problems, irrespective of what was going on in the West. When it decided to let the yuan gradually rise against the dollar in June 2010, the result was a 3.6 percent rise in the yuan's value against the dollar by the end of 2010. However, inflation was rising in China faster than in the U.S., so Chinese exports were becoming increasingly expensive. The rise in the currency compounded the loss in competitive position brought on by the rise in inflation. Powerful Chinese exporters were very upset with the idea that the government might free up the currency and speed up their competitive challenges. Because of inflation, Chinese workers were increasingly unhappy with their working conditions, and they began to demonstrate, sometimes violently. As workers pushed for higher wages, manufacturers faced even greater cost pressures. With general inflation, higher wages, and the possibility of an even more expensive yuan, manufacturers were being forced to move further inland to find cheaper labor, or even move abroad. Many U.S. manufacturers began moving manufacturing back to the U.S. or to cheaper Asian countries.

Between July 2005 and April 2013, China's real effective change rate had appreciated 33.8 percent. Since June 2010, the yuan had appreciated by 10 percent against the dollar, so some movement in the exchange rate between the two had taken place; However, many experts felt the yuan was still significantly undervalued against the dollar and unlikely to solve the trade problems with the rest of the world.

Improvement of the Trading Infrastructure

In the meantime, the PBOC announced in 2009 that it was going to allow companies in Shanghai and four other major cities to settle foreign trade in yuan instead of dollars. Remember that 84.9 percent of all foreign exchange transactions worldwide take place in dollars. If Chinese companies can get more exporters and importers to settle their obligations in yuan instead of dollars, they can save a lot of transaction fees and the yuan will gradually increase in importance.

Even though China wants to make Shanghai its future financial center, a lot of yuan transactions occur in Hong Kong, which generates 5 percent of the foreign exchange trades in the world. It is the only place outside of mainland China that is allowed to set up yuan bank accounts. Hong Kong is China's testing ground for the liberalization of currency trading. However, Singapore is also being considered as a place for yuan transactions, and it also trades about the same as Hong Kong in foreign exchange.

The PBOC permitted HSBC and the Bank of East Asia to issue yuan-denominated bonds in Hong Kong in 2007, allowing Hong Kong to increase in importance as an offshore financial center for yuan trading. As banks and companies issue bonds and securities in yuan, the amount of yuan in circulation outside China will steadily grow. From the standpoint of traditional foreign exchange trading, yuan trades in foreign currency swaps and forwards increased dramatically in 2010, by 60 percent and 235 percent, respectively. Although still small, the trades are growing. And SAFE decided in April 2011 to allow options to be traded among banks and for banks to sell options to companies.

In October 2010, ICAP PLC and Thomson Reuters began to trade yuan on their electronic-trading platforms and announced that they were working with banks in the U.S. and Europe to use their platforms to trade yuan. Before this, banks in Hong Kong were trading yuan with each other OTC or through brokers. The use of the electronic platform promises to increase transparency and traffic. Deutsche Bank AG and others can now use ICAP and Reuters platforms to trade yuan. In spite of these moves, the onshore market in mainland China still dwarfs the offshore trading, and the fixed exchange rate set by SAFE will be the most important rate. Even though Hong Kong is a special administrative region (SAR) with its own laws and administrative structure, it still works closely with China when it comes to things like currency trading in yuan.

In the second half of 2010, the Chinese government loosened some of the restrictions on how banks could use yuan in Hong Kong. Banks and individuals could freely trade yuan outside the mainland, and the number of companies allowed to settle trades in yuan grew, but the government still controlled the inflow and outflow of capital between China and the rest of the world lest it lose control over inflation and interest rates. It also still kept close control on the currency trades. Banks wanting to participate in currency trades in Hong Kong needed a clearing and settlement arrangement with a financial institution supervised by the Hong Kong Monetary Authority.

Not every world currency is being traded against the yuan in Hong Kong. Initially, Thomson Reuters permitted trades against the dollar, euro and yen, whereas ICAP started only with trades against the dollar. However, both services are expected to expand the currencies available for trades. The U.S. dollar is essential since the Hong Kong dollar is fixed against it, and most China trades have been going through U.S. dollars. Offshore yuan is quoted as CNH, whereas the standard symbol is CNY. As the rules changed in 2010, daily foreign exchange trading in yuan went from zero to $400 million in just a few months. Banks like HSBC and Citi began to offer options and interest-rate derivatives in yuan.

The onshore market in mainland China is far more tightly controlled. Even though major money center banks such as HSBC are allowed to trade currency in China, their volume dwarfs that of the large Chinese banks. As those banks gain greater expertise in global trades, they will become even more significant outside of China. And as China and Singapore explore the possibility of Singapore joining Hong Kong as another location for yuan trades, the international banks will ramp up their yuan trading competencies in both locations. As capital controls in China are loosened, the international banks will also have to ramp up their presence there to compete with the huge Chinese banks that are now starting to get involved in the global foreign exchange trading game.

QUESTIONS

8-3. Why is it important for the Chinese yuan to become a major world currency?

✪**8-4.** What needs to take place for the yuan to be listed right along with the U.S. dollar and the euro as global currencies?

8-5. Why is the Chinese government so hesitant to open up the yuan to market forces to determine its value inside and outside of China?

8-6. What role do foreign banks like HSBC and electronic platforms like Thomson Reuters and ICAP play in helping the yuan move closer to becoming a global currency?

✪**8-7.** By the end of 2013, the Bank for International Settlements will have issued its next triennial survey on foreign exchange. Look up the report on the bis.com website. What are the major differences in that survey from what is reported in the 2010 Survey in the chapter?

SUMMARY

- Foreign exchange is money denominated in the currency of another nation or group of nations. The exchange rate is the price of a currency.
- The foreign-exchange market is dominated by the money center banks, but other financial institutions (such as local and regional banks) and nonfinancial institutions (such as corporations and governments) are also players in the foreign-exchange market.
- Dealers can trade currency by telephone or electronically, especially through Reuters, EBS, or Bloomberg.
- The foreign-exchange market is divided into the over-the-counter (OTC) market and the exchange-traded market.
- The traditional foreign-exchange market is composed of the spot, forward, and foreign-exchange swap markets. Other key foreign-exchange instruments are currency swaps, options, and futures.
- Spot transactions involve the exchange of currency on the second day after the date on which the two dealers agree to the transaction.
- Outright forward transactions involve the exchange of currency three or more days after the date on which the dealers agree to the transaction. A foreign-exchange swap is a simultaneous spot and forward transaction.
- Approximately $5.3 trillion in foreign exchange is traded every day. The dollar is the most widely traded currency in the world (on one side of about 85 percent of all transactions), and London is the main foreign-exchange market in the world.
- Foreign-exchange dealers quote bid (buy) and offer (sell) rates on foreign exchange. If the quote is in American terms, the dealer quotes the foreign currency as the number of dollars and cents per unit of the foreign currency. If the quote is in European terms, the dealer quotes the number of units of the foreign currency per dollar. The numerator is called the *terms currency* and the denominator the *base currency*.
- If the foreign currency in a forward contract is expected to strengthen in the future (the dollar equivalent of the foreign currency is higher in the forward market than in the spot market), the currency is selling at a premium. If the opposite is true, it is selling at a discount.

- An option is the right, but not the obligation, to trade foreign currency in the future. Options can be traded OTC or on an exchange.
- A foreign currency future is an exchange-traded instrument that guarantees a future price for the trading of foreign exchange, but the contracts are for a specific amount and specific maturity date.
- Companies work with foreign-exchange dealers to trade currency. Dealers also work with each other and can trade currency through voice brokers, electronic brokerage services, or directly with other bank dealers. Internet trades of foreign exchange are becoming more significant.
- The major institutions that trade foreign exchange are the large commercial and investment banks and securities exchanges. Commercial and investment banks deal in a variety of different currencies all over the world. The CME Group and the Philadelphia Stock Exchange trade currency futures and options.
- Companies use foreign exchange to settle transactions involving the imports and exports of goods and services, for foreign investments, and to earn money through *arbitrage* or *speculation*.

KEY TERMS

American terms (p. 351)
arbitrage (p. 358)
Bank for International Settlements (BIS) (p. 343)
base currency (p. 351)
bid (buy) rate (p. 351)
carry trade (p. 348)
Chicago Mercantile Exchange (CME) Group (p. 356)
confirmed letter of credit (p. 358)
cross rate (p. 348)
currency swap (p. 346)
derivative (p. 343)
direct quote (p. 351)
draft (or commercial bill of exchange) (p. 357)
European terms (p. 351)
exchange rate (p. 343)
foreign exchange (p. 343)
foreign-exchange market (p. 343)
forward discount (p. 352)
forward premium (p. 352)
futures contract (p. 346)
FX swap (p. 346)
hedge fund (p. 347)
indirect quote (p. 351)
interbank transaction (p. 351)
interest arbitrage (p. 358)
letter of credit (L/C) (p. 357)
NASDAQ OMX (p. 356)
NYSE Liffe (p. 356)
offer (sell) (p. 351)
option (p. 353)
outright forward transactions (p. 345)
sight draft (p. 357)
speculation (p. 358)
spot rate (p. 345)
spot transaction (p. 345)
spread (p. 351)
terms currency (p. 351)
time draft (p. 357)

ENDNOTES

1 ***Sources include the following:*** World Bank, *Migration and Remittances Factbook 2011* (The International Bank for Reconstruction and Development/World Bank: Washington, D.C., 2011);"Topics in Development: Migration & Remittances,"worldbank.org (accessed May 3, 2013);"The GCC in 2020: The Gulf and its People,"Economist Intelligence Unit, 2009;"Immigrants Sent 3.7 Billion Euros from Spain to Latin America in 2006, Says IDB Fund,"press release, Inter-American Development Bank (June 5, 2007);"Remittances to Latin America and the Caribbean to Top $100 Billion a Year by 2010, IDB Fund Says,"press release, Inter-American Development Bank (March 18, 2007); Marla Dickerson,"Cash Going to Mexico Likely to Start at a Bank,"*Los Angeles Times* (February 14, 2007): 21; Miriam Jordan,"U.S. Banks Woo Migrants, Legal or Otherwise,"*Wall Street Journal* (Eastern Edition) (October 11, 2006): B1; Ioan Grillo,"Wired Cash,"*Business Mexico* 12:12/13:1 (2003): 44; Julie Rawe,"The Fastest Way to Make Money,"*Time* (June 23, 2003): A6; Rosa Salter Rodriguez,"Money Transfers to Mexico Peak as Mother's Day Nears,"*Fort Wayne* (IN) *Journal Gazette* (May 1, 2005): 1D; Deborah Kong,"Mexicans Win Back Fee on Money They Wired,"*Grand Rapids* (MI) *Press* (December 19, 2002): A9; Karen Krebsbach,"Following the Money,"*USBanker* (September 2002): 62; Tyche Hendricks,"Wiring Cash Costly for Immigrants,"*San Francisco Chronicle* (March 24, 2002): A23; Nancy Cleeland,"Firms Are Wired into Profits,"*Los Angeles Times* (November 7, 1997): 1; David Fairlamb, Geri Smith, and Frederik Blafour,"Can Western Union Keep On Delivering?"*Businessweek* (December 29, 2003): 57; Heather Timmons,"Western Union: Where the Money Is—In Small Bills,"*Businessweek* (November 26, 2001): 40.

2 Sam Y. Cross, *All about the Foreign Exchange Market in the United States* (New York: Federal Reserve Bank of New York, 1998): 9.

3 Cross, *All about the Foreign Exchange Market,* 9.

4 Bank for International Settlements,"Triennial Central Bank Survey: Foreign Exchange Turnover in 2013: Preliminary Global Results (Basel: BIS, September 2013, 6.

5 Bank for International Settlements,"Triennial Central Bank Survey: Report on Global Foreign Exchange Market Activity in 2010," (Basel: BIS, December 2010): 16.

6 Ibid., 35.

7 Cross, *All about the Foreign Exchange Market,* 19.

8 Bank for International Settlements,"Triennial Central Bank Survey, (2013), 6."

9 Brian Dolan,"Tailoring Your Technical Approach to Currency Personalities," www.forex.com/currency_pairs.html (accessed October 8, 2009).

10 Cross, *All about the Foreign Exchange Market,* 12.

11 Source: wsj.com/mdc/public/page/2_3021-forex.html

12 Ibid.

13 Ibid.

14 See"Foreign Exchange Poll 2009: Methodology,"*Euromoney* (May 2009), 76.

15 Bank for International Settlements (2010 Survey), *op cit.*, 9.

16 CM Group 2013"FX Products: Product Guide & Calendar"at www.cmegroup.com/trading/fx/files/2013-product-guide-and-calendar-fx-products.pdf (accessed March 28, 2013).

17 PHLX News Release,"The Philadelphia Stock Exchange and the Philadelphia Board of Trade to Expand World Currency Product Line with Launch of Options and Futures on Major Currencies,"phlx.com/news/pr2007/07pr042707.htm (accessed April 27, 2007).

18 A confirmed letter of credit adds the obligation of the exporter's bank to pay the exporter.

19 More specifically, Leeson did not actually buy the contracts outright, but rather paid a certain percentage of the value of the contract, known as the *margin*. When the stock market fell, the index futures contract became riskier, and the broker who sold the contract required Leeson to increase the amount of the margin.

20 "The Collapse of Barings: A Fallen Star," *The Economist* (March 4, 1995): 19–21; Glen Whitney, "ING Puts Itself on the Map by Acquiring Barings," *Wall Street Journal* (March 8, 1995): B4; John S. Bowdidge and Kurt E. Chaloupecky, "Nicholas Leeson and Barings Bank Have Vividly Taught Some Internal Control Issues," *American Business Review* (January 1997): 71–77; "Trader in Barings Scandal Is Released from Prison," *Wall Street Journal* (July 6, 1999): A12; Ben Dolven, "Bearing Up," *Far Eastern Economic Review* (July 15, 1999): 47; "Nick Leeson and Barings Bank," *bbc.co.uk*, at www.bbc.co.uk/crime/caseclosed/nickleeson.shtml (accessed May 19, 2005); Nick Leeson and Edward Whitley, *Rogue Trader* (London: Little, Brown, 1996): 272.

21 David Gauthier-Villars and Carrick Mollenkamp, "Société Générale Blew Chances to Nab Trader," *Wall Street Journal* (January 29, 2008): 1; Gauthier-Villars, Mollenkamp, and Alistair MacDonald, "French Bank Rocked by Rogue Trader," *Wall Street Journal* (January 25, 2008): A1; Gauthier-Villars and Mollenkamp, "Portrait Emerges of Rogue Trader at French Bank," *Wall Street Journal* (February 2, 2008), A1.

22 Steve Bills, "State St.'s Forex Deal a Lure for Hedge Funds," *American Banker* (January 23, 2007): 10.

23 Steve Bills, "Barclays Seeking Forex Boost via Online Offerings," *American Banker* (October 10, 2006): 17.

24 ***Sources include the following:*** Ying Fang, Shicheng Huang and Linlin Nie, "De Facto Currency Baskets of China and East Asian Economies: The Rising Weights," BOFIT Discussion Papers, vol. 2/2012; U.S. Department of the Treasury, "Report to Congress on International Economic and Exchange Rate Policies" (Washington D.C., Office of International Affairs, U.S. Department of Commerce, April 12, 2013); Tom Orlick, "Get Ready: Here Comes the Yuan," *The Wall Street Journal* (June 2, 2011): C7; Peter Stein, "The Chinese Test Kitchen," *The Wall Street Journal* (June 2, 2011): C8; Peter Stein and Shai Oster, "China Speeds Yuan Push," *The Wall Street Journal* (April 20, 2011); Lingling Wei, "Beijing Considers New Hub for Yuan," *The Wall Street Journal* (April 9–10, 2011), B1; Wynne Wang and Jean Yung, "China Allows More Options for Trading in Yuan," *The Wall Street Journal* (February 17, 2011): C2; "The Rise of the Redback," *The Economist* (January 22, 2011): 14; Shai Oster, Dinny McMahon, and Tom Lauricella, "Offshore Trading in Yuan Takes Off, *The Wall Street Journal* (December 14, 2010) A1; Dinny McMahon, "Yuan Goes Electronic in Global Market Bid, *The Wall Street Journal* (October 8, 2010): C1.

CHAPTER 9

Factors that Influence Exchange Rates

OBJECTIVES

After studying this chapter, you should be able to

1. Describe the International Monetary Fund and its role in determining exchange rates
2. Discuss the major exchange-rate arrangements that countries use
3. Explain the European Monetary System and how the euro became the currency of the euro zone
4. Identify the major determinants of exchange rates
5. Show how managers try to forecast exchange-rate movements
6. Explain how exchange-rate movements influence business decisions

Source: © Sergey Nivens - Fotolia.com

He that has no money has no friends.

—Arabian proverb

CASE El Salvador Adopts the U.S. Dollar

El Salvador, a country of 6.1 million people, is the smallest and most densely populated country in Central America—about the same size in area as the state of Massachusetts.[1] It has been a member of the Central American Common Market (CACM), along with Guatemala, Honduras, and Nicaragua, since the organization's inception in 1960 (Costa Rica joined two years later). El Salvador was also the first of the Central American countries to sign on to the CAFTA-DR Agreement as of March 1, 2006, bringing the country closer to trade relations with the United States.

In 1994, the government of El Salvador decided to peg its currency, the colón, to the U.S. dollar. In 2001, it decided to do away with the peg and the colón altogether and adopt the dollar as the national currency, thus completing the transition to dollarization (although it took a couple of years to withdraw colones from circulation). El Salvador is now one of ten countries that have entered into an exchange arrangement in which they do not have their own currency; seven of those ten use the U.S. dollar.

Two other countries in Latin America have adopted the dollar as their currency: Panama did so when it gained independence from Colombia over a century ago, and Ecuador dollarized its economy in 2000 as a means of eliminating hyperinflation.

WHY THE DOLLAR?

Why did El Salvador adopt the dollar? The country's economy is closely tied to that of the United States; in fact, at the time of the adoption, the U.S. imported more than two-thirds of El Salvador's exports. In addition, more than 2 million Salvadorans lived in the U.S. and remitted their earnings to their families back home, generating about the same amount of currency as El Salvador earned in exports. By switching to the dollar, Salvadoran companies and the government gained access to cheaper interest rates because the move eliminated, or at least reduced, the risk of devaluation, thereby infusing more confidence in foreign banks to lend to the country. Corporate borrowing rates in El Salvador are among the lowest in Latin America, and consumer credit rose as the lower rates made it more attractive to borrow. Research on the impact of dollarization has borne out that reducing currency risk lowers interest rates 4–5 percent, generating savings to both the public and private sectors.

ECUADOR: THE TEST CASE

Ecuador tied its currency to the dollar in 2000, though its situation was a little different. Ecuador has a population double the size, and a GNI a little less than double the size, of El Salvador's. Moreover, it doesn't rely on the U.S. market as much as El Salvador does. When Ecuador decided to dollarize its economy, the president was in the midst of a political crisis and the announcement was totally unexpected. In 1999, the country's consumer price inflation was 52.2 percent, the highest in Latin America. Until February 1999, the central bank had maintained a crawling peg exchange-rate system. However, pressure on the currency forced the central bank to leave the peg and allow the currency to float freely, upon which it promptly devalued by 65 percent.

At that time, Panama was the only country in Latin America that had dollarized, although Argentina had officially linked its currency to the dollar, so Ecuador was seen as a test case that many thought would spread to other countries in Latin America, especially El Salvador. A World Bank official, discussing the rationale for Ecuador's decision, noted that "most countries have a large amount of their debt in dollars, maintain a large percent of their reserves abroad in dollars, and write contracts indexed to the dollar." Moreover, Ecuador, a member of OPEC, generates most of its foreign-exchange earnings from oil, which is also priced in dollars. One difference between Ecuador and El Salvador is that Ecuador maintains its currency, the sucre (ESC), but it pegs it to the dollar at ESC25,000/US$. El Salvador, on the other hand, no longer uses its currency, only the dollar.

Test Results

Ecuador's experiment with dollarization has been successful, but it has not been easy. When dollarization became official in 2000, inflation rose to 96.1 percent. Then it dropped back to 29.2 percent in 2001, less than 20 percent in 2002, under 7 percent in 2003, and to an estimated 3.4 percent in 2006. However, with 70 percent of the population living below the poverty level, Ecuador still has political and economic problems that dollarization alone will not cure. In particular, the rise of the U.S. dollar against Ecuador's neighboring trading partners has created problems in the country's trade balance. Added to those problems are the decline of both oil prices and remittances from Ecuadorians working abroad.

THE DOWNSIDE OF DOLLARIZATION

As we noted, there are many advantages to dollarization, but what are the disadvantages? Consider El Salvador's neighbors. When the country dollarized, over two-thirds of its exports went to the United States. By 2003, that had changed: only 19 percent of them went to the United States, putting the latter in the number-two spot after Guatemala. As of 2013, 46.1 percent of El Salvador's merchandise exports went to the U.S., followed by 13.9 percent to Guatemala, 13.2 percent to Honduras, 6.0 percent to the 27-member EU, and 5.6 percent to Nicaragua. Thus, four of the top five destinations for Salvadoran products were CACM countries. On the import side, the United States was the country's largest supplier, with 38.2 percent of the market, followed by Guatemala, Mexico, the EU, and China.

CONCEPT CHECK

In Chapter 7 we introduce the Central American Free Trade Agreement–Dominican Republic (CAFTA-DR) as a free trade agreement designed to reduce tariffs between the United States on the one hand and six Latin American countries on the other. We also note that, despite a membership of seven, it's actually a bilateral agreement.

Crawling Pegs and Crawling Bands

El Salvador's other neighbors in Central America had different exchange-rate regimes. Costa Rica and Nicaragua had crawling pegs, which means that their currencies were adjusted periodically in response to selected indicators. In their cases, the U.S. dollar was the key exchange-rate anchor boon upon which they based their currency values. However, their currencies were more flexible than those of El Salvador and Honduras, both of which had a currency more firmly pegged to the value of the dollar. Guatemala's currency was considered to be a managed floating currency, and its value was based on inflation. During the global financial crisis in 2008, the value of the currencies did not stray very far from each other—unlike earlier in the decade, when the Costa Rican colón fell 43.9 percent and the Nicaraguan cordoba 26.5 percent against the dollar. During that same period, the Honduran lempira fell about 15 percent against the dollar, but its currency regime is now officially pegged to the dollar. The Guatemalan quetzal has a managed floating currency, but its value remains relatively close to the U.S. dollar.

CONCEPT CHECK

In Chapter 4 we discuss the importance of the role of government in influencing the economic environment in which companies, both domestic and foreign, must operate. Here, we cite an instance of unforeseeable change in a country's economic environment: Although a government usually tries to build a consensus to support important political decisions, unexpected policy shifts are also a significant fact of life in the international business environment.

SURVIVING DOLLARIZATION

On one hand, the problem for Salvadoran companies is that their prices and competitiveness are closely tied to the dollar's value. In the early 2000s, companies from El Salvador were having a difficult time in export markets due to the strength of their currency against those of their Central American neighbors. How could they possibly compete against companies from Nicaragua and Honduras, which were reaping a huge cost advantage in export markets, when those currencies had fallen against the dollar? El Salvador has had to move into new sources of growth, such as shipping, tourism, and communications, to avoid having its economy hollowed out due to higher costs relative to its neighbors.

Fresco Group S.A. and Grupo Hilasal

Many Salvadoran companies have had to change the way they do business. Fresco Group S.A., a family-owned textile company in El Salvador, has struggled to compete. Although it was able to get low-cost loans to fund an expansion of facilities, it has had to move away from simple stitching of garments to creating designs, procuring materials, and manufacturing clothing based on a single sketch.

Basically, Fresco Group had to move upscale and leave the lower-end manufacturing to other Central American companies that benefited from weak currencies. It was also concerned about its ability to compete with textile companies from India and China because textile and garment quotas were eliminated in 2005.

Fresco Group may have disappeared in the onslaught of Chinese textile and garment exports since 2005, but Grupo Hilasal is an example of a vertically integrated textile company that has survived and thrived. Established in 1942 as a family-owned textile firm, Grupo Hilasal is currently one of the largest manufacturers of fiber-reactive printed beach towels in the world and the largest towel manufacturer in North America. It owns Export Salva Free Zone, a duty-free service & business park near San Salvador. In the zone, the company has six apparel plants and a logistics center employing approximately 2,500 workers. It attributes its success in part to economic and political stability in El Salvador and the adoption of the U.S. dollar as the official currency in 2001, which adds to the economic stability and attracts foreign investment.

THE FUTURE OF DOLLARIZATION IN EL SALVADOR

El Salvador is hoping that remittances by Salvadorans living abroad, increased FDI, and the reduction of trade barriers with other countries will help stimulate the economy and offset any downsides to dollarization. As explained above, however, it does not appear that dollarization has hurt El Salvador's economy. Of course, the global financial crisis sharply reduced remittances from Salvadorans living abroad, and FDI dropped dramatically. But the currencies of its neighbors remained relatively close to the value of the dollar, thus reducing the impact of currency in El Salvador's ability to compete. The initial strengthening of the dollar in fall 2008 really hurt El Salvador's export competitiveness, but the subsequent weakening of the dollar has helped the country. ■

CRN
Case Review Note

QUESTIONS

9-1. Given the success in El Salvador, do you think the other countries in CAFTA-DR should adopt the U.S. dollar as their currency? Why or why not?

9-2. In Chapter 7, we mentioned that Mexico and Canada have kept their own currency, even though they are partnered with the U.S. in NAFTA. Why do you think they have decided not to adopt the U.S. dollar as their currency, even though El Salvador and Ecuador, who are not members of NAFTA, have adopted the dollar as their currency?

INTRODUCTION

As we learned in Chapter 9, an exchange rate represents the number of units of one currency needed to acquire one unit of another. Although this definition seems simple, managers must understand how governments set an exchange rate and what causes it to change. Such understanding can help them anticipate exchange-rate changes and make decisions about business factors that are sensitive to those changes, such as the sourcing of raw materials and components, the placement of manufacturing and assembly, and the choice of final markets.

CONCEPT CHECK

Recall that we devote Chapter 8 to discussions of the **foreign-exchange market**, the ways in which currencies are quoted and traded, and the various instruments through which foreign exchange may be traded. In this chapter, we shift our focus to the ways in which currency values are determined, considering especially the roles of governments and the vagaries of the market.

THE INTERNATIONAL MONETARY FUND

In 1944, toward the close of World War II, the major Allied governments met in Bretton Woods, New Hampshire, to determine what was needed to bring economic stability and growth to the postwar world. As a result of those meetings, the **International Monetary Fund (IMF)** came into official existence on December 27, 1945, with the goal of promoting exchange-rate stability and facilitating the international flow of currencies. The IMF began financial operations on March 1, 1947.[2]

CONCEPT CHECK

In Chapter 7, we report on the establishment of the United Nations and the subsequent creation of a number of UN satellite organizations, including the **IMF**. Today, the IMF is in a position to influence economic policy among UN-member nations.

ORIGIN AND OBJECTIVES

Twenty-nine countries initially signed the IMF agreement; there were 187 member countries as of July 1, 2011.[3] The fundamental mission of the IMF is to:

- promote international monetary cooperation and exchange-rate stability,
- facilitate the balanced growth of international trade,
- provide resources to help members in balance-of-payments difficulties or to assist with poverty reduction.[4]

Through a process of surveillance, the IMF monitors the global economy as well as the economies of individual countries and advises on needed policy adjustments. In addition to surveillance, it provides technical assistance—mainly to low- and middle-income countries—and makes loans to countries with balance-of-payments problems.

The Bretton Woods Agreement established a par value, or benchmark value, for each currency initially quoted in terms of gold and the U.S. dollar.

Bretton Woods and the Principle of Par Value The **Bretton Woods Agreement** established a system of fixed exchange rates under which each IMF member country set a **par value** for its currency based on gold and the U.S. dollar. Because the value of the dollar was fixed at $35 per ounce of gold, the par value would be the same whether gold or the dollar was used as the basis. This par value became a benchmark by which each country's currency was valued against others. Currencies were allowed to vary within 1 percent of their par value (extended to 2.25 percent in December 1971), depending on supply and demand. Additional moves from, and formal changes in, par value were possible with IMF approval. As we see later, par values were done away with when the IMF moved to greater exchange-rate flexibility.

Because of the U.S. dollar's strength during the 1940s and 1950s and its large reserves in monetary gold, currencies of IMF member countries were denominated in terms of gold and U.S. dollars. By 1947, the United States held 70 percent of the world's official gold reserves, so governments bought and sold dollars rather than gold. The understanding, though not set in stone, was that the United States would redeem dollars for gold. The dollar became the world benchmark for trading currency and has remained so, in spite of the move away from fixed rates to flexible exchange rates.

THE IMF TODAY

The IMF quota—the sum of the total assessment to each country—becomes a pool of money that the IMF can draw on to lend to other countries. It forms the basis for the voting power of each country—the higher its individual quota, the more votes a country has.

The Quota System When a country joins the IMF, it contributes a certain sum of money, called a **quota**, broadly based on its relative size in the global economy. The IMF can draw on this pool of money to lend to countries, and it uses the quota as the basis of how much a country can borrow from the Fund. It is also the basis on which the IMF allocates special drawing rights (SDRs), discussed later.

Moreover, the quota determines the voting rights of the individual members. On December 15, 2010, the Board of Governors of the IMF approved a package of reforms that would double the total quotas to SDR 476.8 (about $750 billion at current exchange rates at the time) and shift more of the quota shares to dynamic emerging market and developing countries (EMDCs). According to the realignment, the U.S. would still have the largest quota, but China would be #3, and the four BRIC countries would be among the 10 largest shareholders in the Fund.[5]

The IMF lends money to countries to help ease balance-of-payments difficulties.

Assistance Programs In addition to identifying exchange-rate regimes, the IMF offers a great deal of aid to member countries, negotiating with them to provide financial assistance if they agree to adopt certain economic stabilization policies. This arrangement is presented in a letter of intent to the executive board of the Fund, which, upon accepting it, releases the funds in phases so it can monitor progress.

The SDR is

- An international reserve asset given to each country to help increase its reserves.
- The unit of account in which the IMF keeps its financial records.

Special Drawing Rights (SDRs) To help increase international reserves, the IMF created the **special drawing right (SDR)** in 1969 to help reinforce the fixed exchange-rate system that existed at that time. To support its currency in foreign-exchange markets, a country could use only U.S. dollars or gold to buy currency. However, the collapse of the Bretton Woods system, the move to floating exchange rates by most of the major currencies, and the growth of global capital markets as a source of funds for governments lessened the need for SDRs. Thus, the SDR is an international reserve asset created to supplement members' official holdings of gold, foreign exchange, and IMF reserve positions. In addition, the SDR serves as the IMF's *unit of account*—the unit in which the IMF keeps its records—and can be used for IMF transactions and operations.

Currencies making up the SDR basket are the U.S. dollar, the euro, the Japanese yen, and the British pound.

On January 1, 1981, the IMF began to use a simplified basket of four currencies for determining valuation. As of January 1, 2011, the U.S. dollar made up 41.9 percent of the value of the SDR, the euro 37.4 percent, the British pound sterling 11.3 percent, and the Japanese yen 9.4 percent.[6] These weights were chosen because they broadly reflect the importance of each particular currency in international trade and payments. The next review will take place in 2015.

THE GLOBAL FINANCIAL CRISIS AND THE IMF

Because of the global financial crisis, the G20 voted to significantly increase reserves available to the IMF to help countries in distress.

One fallout of the global crisis that began in 2008–09 was the concern over global liquidity, especially in the emerging markets. The G8 countries injected hundreds of billions of dollars into their financial systems and implemented large stimulus packages to get their economies moving. They also injected huge amounts of cash into the IMF. In April 2009, the G20 (the G8 expanded to include the central bank governors of 19 countries and the EU) voted to give approval to the IMF to raise $250 billion by issuing SDRs and to put another $500 billion into the IMF for them to use in case of a systemic crisis, thereby bringing the IMF's available resources to $1 trillion. As the IMF is trying to help countries with serious deficits, such as Greece, implement austerity measures, it is trying to encourage richer countries to back off on austerity measures so they can be the engine for growth and create markets for counties that need to export to earn more foreign exchange and create jobs.[7]

The IMF has played an important role in the Greek financial crisis that unfolded in 2010 and carried into 2013 (and probably beyond). Greece, a member of the European Union, has adopted the euro as its currency and thus has no control over monetary policy. Interest rates are set by the European Central Bank. But Greece has piled up huge sovereign debt that exceeds 160 percent of GDP, largely to other banks in Europe. The Greek economy has been in recession, the public sector generates 40 percent of the economy and 25 percent of the workforce, and the government keeps piling up budget deficits. In order to keep the government from defaulting on its debt, the IMF partnered with the European Union and the European Central Bank to provide loans to Greece on the condition that it would take severe austerity measures to solve its budget crisis, including raising taxes, cutting spending, and selling off state-owned assets. However, the recession has reduced tax revenues and severe austerity measures only increase unemployment, which has led to social unrest. In addition, its privatization efforts, which are necessary to raise revenues, have not been successful. Greece has few options. It can continue to try to follow the austerity measures suggested by the ECB and IMF, it can try to restructure its debt, it could default on its debt like Argentina did in 2002, or it could leave the euro and bring back its own currency, the drachma, which would lead to severe devaluation relative to the euro. It is not likely that Greece will leave the euro zone, but the need to support Greece financially has created strains in the EU. The IMF has worked hard to create a crisis firewall by increasing its lending capability and by improving its analysis and policy advice.[8] It is interesting to note that whereas the IMF has traditionally taken the lead in providing technical assistance to countries in distress, in this case the ECB has taken the lead in negotiating with Greece to help resolve its debt crisis.

EVOLUTION TO FLOATING EXCHANGE RATES

The IMF's system was initially one of fixed exchange rates. Because the U.S. dollar was the cornerstone of the international monetary system, its value remained constant with respect to the value of gold. Other countries could change the value of their currency against gold and the dollar, but the value of the dollar remained fixed.

On August 15, 1971, as the U.S. balance-of-trade deficit continued to worsen, U.S. president Richard Nixon announced that the United States would no longer trade dollars for gold unless other industrial countries agreed to support a restructuring of the international monetary system. He was afraid that the United States would lose its large gold reserves if countries, worried about holding so many dollars resulting from the large U.S. trade deficit, turned in their dollars to the U.S. government and demanded gold in return.

Exchange-rate flexibility was widened in 1971 from 1 percent to 2.25 percent from par value.

The Smithsonian Agreement The resulting **Smithsonian Agreement** of December 1971 had several important aspects:

- An 8 percent devaluation of the dollar (an official drop in the value of the dollar against gold)
- A revaluation of some other currencies (an official increase in the value of each currency against gold)
- A widening of exchange-rate flexibility (from 1 to 2.25 percent on either side of par value)

This effort did not last, however. World currency markets remained unsteady during 1972, and the dollar was devalued again by 10 percent in early 1973 (the year of the Arab oil embargo and the start of fast-rising oil prices and global inflation). Major currencies began to float against each other, relying on the market to determine their value. The period from 1972–1981 led to the end of the Bretton Woods system and the move to flexible exchange rates.

The Jamaica Agreement of 1976 resulted in greater exchange-rate flexibility and eliminated the use of par values.

The Jamaica Agreement Because the Bretton Woods Agreement was based on a system of fixed exchange rates and par values, the IMF had to change its rules to accommodate floating exchange rates. The **Jamaica Agreement** of 1976 amended the original rules to eliminate the concept of par values and permit greater exchange-rate flexibility. The move toward greater flexibility can occur on an individual country basis as well as on an overall system basis. Let's see how this works.

EXCHANGE-RATE ARRANGEMENTS

The IMF surveillance and consultation programs are designed to monitor exchange-rate policies of countries and to see if they are acting openly and responsibly in exchange-rate policies.

The Jamaica Agreement formalized the break from fixed exchange rates. As part of this move, the IMF began to permit countries to select and maintain an exchange-rate arrangement of their choice, provided they communicated their decision to the IMF. The formal decision of a country to adopt a particular exchange-rate mechanism is called a *de jure* system. In addition, the IMF surveillance program determines the *de facto* exchange-rate system that a country uses.

The IMF also consults annually with countries to see if they are acting openly and responsibly in their exchange-rate policies. Each year, each country notifies the IMF of the arrangement it will use, and the IMF uses information provided by the country and evidence of how the country acts in the market to place it in a specific category. Table 9.1 identifies

TABLE 9.1 Exchange Rate Arrangements and Anchors

		Exchange Rate Anchor				Monetary Policy Framework			
Exchange Rate Agreement	Total	US dollar	Euro	Composite	Other	Monetary aggregate target	Inflation-targeting	Other	
Hard Peg	25								
No separate legal tender	13	8	3		2				
Currency board	12	8	3		1				
Soft Peg	99								
Conventional peg	43	14	18	5	5				
Stabilized arrangement	16	7	1	1		2	1	4	
Pegged exchange rate within horizontal bands	1		1						
Crawling peg	3	1		1				1	
Crawl-like arrangement	12	4	1	1		4	1	2	
Other managed arrangements	24	1		5		9		9	
Floating Arrangements	66								
Floating	35					14	19	2	
Free floating	31						11	20	
Total	190	43	27	13	8	29	32	38	
Percent of Total IMF Members		22.6	14.2	6.8	4.2	15.3	16.8	20	99.9

Source: Based on International Monetary Fund, *Annual Report on Exchange Arrangements and Exchange Restrictions, 2012 (Washington, D.C., IMF, October 2012), Table 1, p. 5-7.*

MAP 9.1 Exchange-Rate Arrangements, 2012

34.7% of the nations in the world have opted for floating exchange rates; the rest are either hard-peg (13.2%), soft-peg (39.5%), or residual (12.6%) arrangements.

Source: Based on data from "Annual Report on Exchange Arrangements and Exchange Restrictions, 2012," (Washington, D.C., IMF, October 2012), Table 1, pp. 5-7 and Table 2, p. 9.

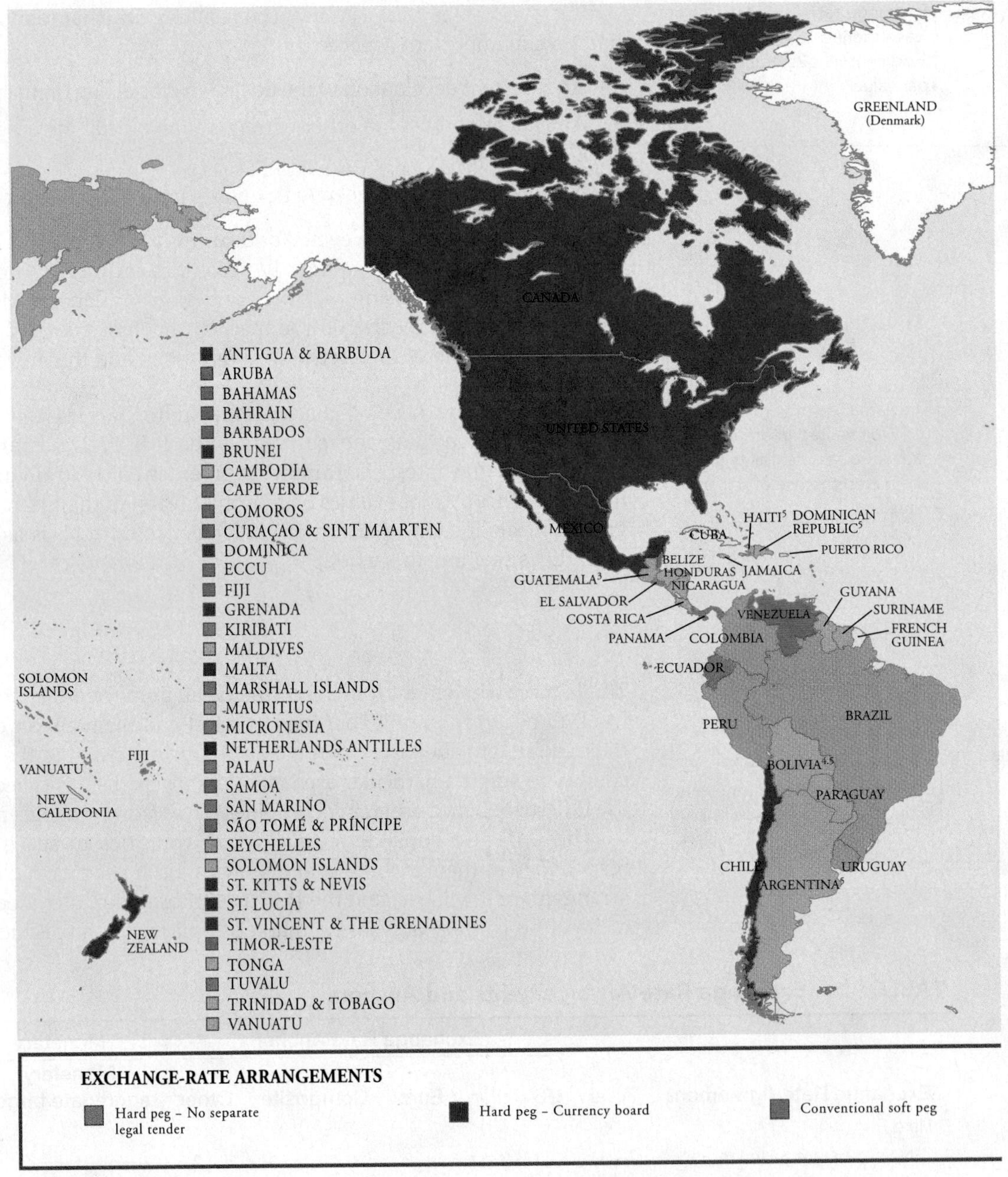

the different exchange-rate arrangements that countries have adopted. The arrangements are ranked primarily on their degree of flexibility, from least to most.

The IMF requires countries to identify how they base their exchange rate mechanism.

In addition, the IMF requires countries to identify how they base their exchange rate mechanism—whether they use a specific anchor or a monetary framework. Some use an exchange rate such as the U.S. dollar as their anchor. Others use either monetary aggregate targets (such as M1 money supply—which usually comprises cash and assets that can be converted quickly to currency) or inflation targets. Table 9.1 identifies the most recent exchange-rate arrangements and the monetary-policy framework used by each. The actual countries that fit in each cell can be found on the IMF website, as cited at the bottom of the table and in Map 9.1.

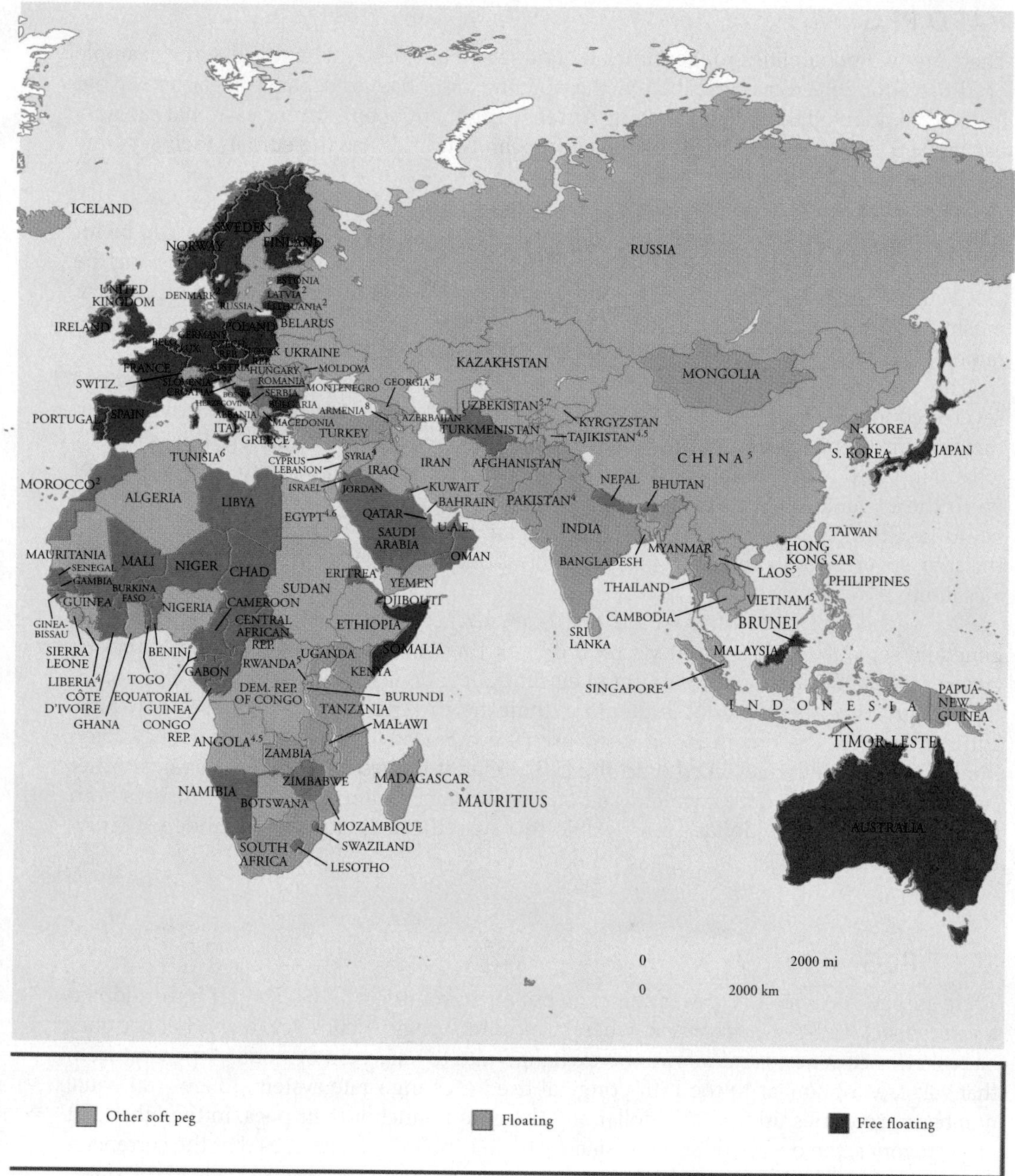

THREE CHOICES: HARD PEG, SOFT PEG, OR FLOATING ARRANGEMENT

The IMF classifies currencies into one of three broad categories, moving from the least to the most flexible. If they have adopted a hard peg (13.2 percent of the total), they lock their value onto something and don't change. If they have adopted a soft peg (39.5 percent), they are pretty rigid but not as rigid as the hard peg. If they have adopted a floating arrangement (34.6 percent), their value is based on supply and demand. Some countries are not classified.[9]

HARD PEG

There are two possibilities for countries that adopt a hard peg. The first is like the example of El Salvador, which, as described in the opening case, has no separate legal tender but instead has adopted the U.S. dollar as its currency. Eight out of ten currencies in that category use the U.S. dollar as their anchor. A few European countries use the euro as their separate legal tender.

Using the dollar as an exchange arrangement with no separate legal tender is also called *dollarization* of the currency, as illustrated in our opening case. The idea would be for a country to take all of its currency out of circulation and replace it with dollars, allowing the U.S. Federal Reserve Bank (the Fed), rather than the government of the dollarizing country, greater control over monetary decisions. Prices and wages would be established in dollars rather than in the local currency, which would disappear.

Countries can adopt another currency in place of their own, as is the case with El Salvador.

The concern is that this would result in a loss of sovereignty and potentially lead to severe economic problems if the United States decided to tighten monetary policy when those countries needed to loosen policy to stimulate growth. Unfortunately, this is exactly what happened in Argentina in 2002. Although Argentina's exchange-rate regime did not go to the extreme of dollarization, its currency board regime was just a step away. The board tied the peso closely enough to the dollar and to the decisions made by the Fed that the government's ability to use monetary policy to strengthen its stalling economy was limited.[10]

Another form of a hard peg is a currency board.

The second example of the hard peg is a *currency board,* which is an organization generally separate from a country's central bank that is responsible for issuing domestic currency typically anchored to a foreign currency. If it does not have deposits on hand in the foreign currency, it cannot issue more domestic currency. Twelve countries now have currency boards. The one in Hong Kong uses the U.S. dollar as its anchor currency. Even though the HK dollar is locked onto the U.S. dollar, it moves up and down against other currencies as the U.S. dollar, which is a floating currency, changes in value. Thus it is both fixed (against the U.S. dollar) and flexible (because the U.S. dollar is an independently floating currency).

SOFT PEG

There are many different kinds of soft pegs but the most common is a conventional fixed-peg arrangement.

There are several different types of soft pegs, but most countries in this category have adopted a *conventional fixed-peg arrangement,* whereby a country pegs its currency to another currency or basket of currencies and allows the exchange rate to vary plus or minus 1 percent from that value. Most similar to the IMF's original fixed exchange-rate system, roughly an equal number of countries use the U.S. dollar and the euro to anchor their pegs. In the other soft peg categories, the degree of flexibility increases, but the IMF determines that the currencies are not floating. The Chinese yuan fits in the soft peg category, more specifically in the stabilized arrangement, which means that the exchange rate remains within a margin of 2 percent against its anchor as explained in the case in Chapter 8. However, the Chinese government is gradually increasing the margin of flexibility of the yuan. We note in our opening case that, whereas El Salvador has adopted a hard peg strategy by using the dollar as its currency, Costa Rica and Nicaragua, two of the countries with which it competes in CAFTA-DR, have adopted a soft peg strategy with greater flexibility than El Salvador but still linked to the U.S. dollar as an anchor.

FLOATING ARRANGEMENT

Currencies considered to be in a floating arrangement are either floating (35 countries) or free floating (31 countries). Floating currencies are those that generally change according to market forces but may be subject to market intervention. However, the intervention serves to moderate the rate of change or prevent undue fluctuations in the exchange rate, with the intention of not deviating too far from market forces. Freely floating currencies are subject to intervention only in exceptional circumstances. The major trading currencies, including the U.S. dollar, the Japanese yen, the British pound, and the euro, are freely floating currencies. Brazil and India, two of the BRIC countries, are considered to have floating currencies.

Floating exchange-rate regimes include floating and freely floating.

Countries may change the exchange-rate regime they use, so managers need to monitor country policies carefully.

Anyone involved in international business needs to understand how the exchange rates of countries with which they do business are determined because exchange rates affect marketing, production, and financial decisions (as discussed at the end of the chapter). Note that countries sometimes change their approach to managing or not managing their currency, as Argentina did in 2002 when it moved from a currency board to a floating currency. Chile was listed in a prior IMF survey as a country that kept its exchange rate within a crawling band, adjusting the rate periodically according to inflation. But in late 1999, Chile suspended the trading bands it had established around the peso and moved to a floating-rate regime in an effort to stimulate export-led economic growth—and is now considered to have a freely floating currency. Likewise, in 2001 Iceland moved from a pegged regime, within a horizontal band, to a free-floating regime, as did Brazil in early 1999 and Turkey in 2001.[11]

It is important for MNEs to understand the exchange-rate arrangements for the currencies of countries where they are doing business so they can forecast trends more accurately. It is much easier to forecast a future exchange rate for a relatively stable currency pegged to the U.S. dollar, such as the Hong Kong dollar, than for a currency that is freely floating, such as the Japanese yen.

CONCEPT CHECK

Each of these commitments to greater economic cooperation represents a step in the direction of regional integration, a form of economic integration that we defined in Chapter 8 as the elimination of economic discrimination among geographically related nations. Here we emphasize that the EU has introduced a common currency to its already-existing internal free trade agreement and common external tariff policy.

THE EURO

One of the most ambitious examples of a freely floating arrangement that resulted in countries giving up their own currency to create a new one is the euro. Not content with the economic integration envisaged in the Single European Act, the EU nations signed the Treaty of Maastricht in 1992, which set steps to accomplish two goals: political union and monetary union. The decision to move to a common currency in Europe has eliminated currency as a trade barrier. To replace each national currency with a single European currency, the countries first had to converge their economic policies.

FIGURE 9.1

The EU has sprung several leaks. Will it stay afloat?

Source: Ed Fischer/CartoonStock, Ltd.

The European Monetary System and the European Monetary Union Monetary unity in Europe did not occur overnight. The roots of the system began in 1979, when the **European Monetary System (EMS)** was set up as a means of creating exchange-rate stability within the European Community (EC). A series of exchange-rate relationships linked the currencies of most members through a parity grid. As the countries narrowed the fluctuations in their exchange rates, the stage was set for replacing the EMS with the Exchange Rate Mechanism (ERM) and full monetary union.

The criteria that are part of the Growth and Stability Pact include measures of deficits, debt, inflation, interest rates, and exchange rate stability.

According to the Treaty of Maastricht, countries had to meet certain criteria to comply with the ERM and be part of the **European Monetary Union (EMU).** Termed the "Stability and Growth Pact," the criteria outlined in the treaty—which continue for euro applicants today—are:

- Annual government deficit must not exceed 3 percent of GDP,
- Total outstanding government debt must not exceed 60 percent of GDP,
- Rate of inflation must remain within 1.5 percent of the three best-performing EU countries,
- Average nominal long-term interest rate must be within 2 percent of the average rate in the three countries with the lowest inflation rates,
- Exchange-rate stability must be maintained, meaning that for at least two years the country concerned has kept within the "normal" fluctuation margins of the European Exchange Rate Mechanism.[12]

The United Kingdom, Sweden, and Denmark are the only members of the original 15 EU countries that opted not to adopt the euro.

After a great deal of effort, 11 of the 15 EU countries joined the EMU on January 1, 1999, while Greece joined on January 1, 2001. Those of the original 15 countries not yet participating in the euro are the United Kingdom, Sweden, and Denmark. Sweden announced in July 2002 that it had met all the criteria for joining the EMU,[13] but voters' rejection of the euro in 2003 placed its entry on hold for the time being.[14] Denmark's currency is pegged to the euro as a conventional peg (soft peg category), whereas the currencies of the United Kingdom and Sweden are free-floating.

With the exception of those three countries, the other members of the EU that do not use the euro as their currency are new member states. Cyprus, Malta, Slovenia, and Slovakia adopted the euro as of 2009, so 16 of the 28 EU countries have now done so. (Croatia joined the EU on July 1, 2013, but the data was collected by the IMF before this happened.) Table 9.1 identifies 27 countries using the euro as their exchange-rate anchor, four of which are non-adopting EU members and the rest nations in Africa or Eastern Europe. Most of the remaining non-adopting EU countries have freely floating currencies and use inflation as the framework to target the value of their currencies. This is consistent with the role of the European Central Bank in closely monitoring inflation as a means of setting interest-rate policy.

The European Central Bank sets monetary policy for the adopters of the euro.

The euro is administered by the **European Central Bank (ECB)**. Established on July 1, 1998, the ECB has been responsible for setting monetary policy and for managing the exchange-rate system for all of Europe since January 1, 1999. The ERM is important in converging the EU economies. Because the ECB is an independent organization like the U.S. Fed, it can focus on its mandate of controlling inflation. Of course, different economies are growing at different rates in Europe, and it is difficult to have one monetary policy that fits all. Countries might be tempted to use an expansion fiscal policy to stimulate economic growth, but the deficit requirements of the ERM keep countries from stimulating too much.

PLUSES AND MINUSES OF THE CONVERSION TO THE EURO

From the standpoint of companies rather than countries, the initial move to the euro was smoother than predicted. Companies have been affected in a variety of ways. Banks have had to update their electronic networks to handle all aspects of monetary exchange, such as systems that trade global currencies, buy and sell stocks, transfer money between banks, manage customer accounts, or printed bank statements. Deutsche Bank estimates that the conversion process cost several hundred million dollars.[15]

However, many companies also believe the euro will increase price transparency (the ability to compare prices in different countries) and eliminate foreign-exchange costs and risks. Foreign-exchange costs are narrowing as companies operate in only one currency in Europe, while foreign-exchange risks between member states are disappearing, though they still exist between the euro and nonmember currencies (the U.S. dollar, British pound, Swiss franc, and so on).

CONCEPT CHECK

When we get to Chapter 12, we'll point out that when a country initiates a comprehensive policy change over which businesses (whether domestic or foreign) have no control, they should re-examine each link in their value chains—the collective activities required to move products from materials purchasing through operations to final distribution. Here we observe that a change in a nation's exchange-rate regime is just one of the changes in economic conditions that foreign firms can't control.

The Euro and the Global Financial Crisis Since the initial introduction of the euro, the currency has steadily grown in strength and importance. In mid-2008 it was trading at around $1.59. However, after Lehman Brothers filed for bankruptcy in September 2008, the U.S. stock markets dropped in value. At the same time, the euro fell because investors were pulling money out of stocks and putting it into safe-haven currencies such as the Japanese yen and the U.S. dollar. When the stock markets recovered, the dollar fell in value and the euro rose. At the time, interest rates were higher in Europe than in the U.S., so the euro was perceived to be an investment asset whose value was greater than the dollar. As interest rates fell in the major industrial countries to help stimulate their economies, the interest rate differential disappeared, and currency values began to reflect other factors, such as the perceived strength in their relative economies. This was not helpful to the euro since the European economies were in serious financial trouble.

During the global financial crisis, investors fled to dollars as a safe-haven currency and returned to euros when their appetite for risk increased.

The role of the European Central Bank is to protect the euro against the ravages of inflation. There are still problems with the euro, however. An ongoing challenge is the lack of uniform standards of fiscal regulation among member nations, which allows countries like Greece or Portugal to spend well beyond their budgets to support their welfare systems with few actual checks from the European Central Bank. As we've seen from the worldwide financial crisis beginning in 2007, this has consequences for the entire euro zone, dragging down the currency's value and hurting countries relying on exports—particularly the euro's primary benefactor, Germany. Without stronger regulations and the adoption of austerity measures in the bubble countries of Europe, the unequal distribution of the recession hinders the entire economy.

The lack of uniform standards of fiscal regulation, the inability countries have to adjust their own interest rates, as well as cultural differences are all problems that those countries using the euro experience.

Another challenge to the euro zone's countries is their inability to adjust their own interest rates to counter inflation and stymie the depth of the recession. If interest rates are changed for the entire euro zone to help the few hardest-hit countries, some countries for whom the recession is not so profound could be harmed. There are few ways to address the economic problems of the country without access to these levers of control, and fiscal responses in bankrupt countries require expensive bailouts.

In addition to these challenges, cultural differences within the euro zone itself create conflict on issues such as labor reform and social welfare systems, especially in light of the recent financial downturn. These extremes of economic culture in Europe are perhaps best represented by the differences in retirement policy in Greece and Germany. Prior to the financial crisis of 2008, Germany had already approved measures that raised the age of receiving a state pension to 67. In Greece, however, workers can begin to collect a state pension at age 58 if they have worked for 35 years, despite the legal retirement age being 65.

These discrepancies in the internal workings of the various euro constituents can cause a great deal of instability, given the right circumstances. Not only can they decrease the currency's economic value to large stable economies like Germany's, but social inequalities can arise that could be exploited by individual citizens within the euro zone.

As the economic crisis has deepened in Europe, the contagion has spread from Ireland and Greece to Spain, Portugal, and Cyprus. Most of the governments had issued sovereign debt to fund their deficits, but the default risk on the bonds was so high that many of the European banks that held the debt were in danger of default themselves. As a result, the European Central Bank teamed up with the IMF and the European Commission, nicknamed the "troika," to help increase financial liquidity and to pressure the countries to solve their budget problems. The ECB's main mandate to control inflation expanded to include increasing liquidity when they approved a European stability mechanism that would enable them to lend to struggling countries that met certain conditions. The idea was to allow the fund to buy bonds from troubled euro-zone governments that would keep interest rates low. The fear in Europe is that if the ECB purchases bonds that default, the individual governments would be stuck with the bill, which means that German taxpayers, for example, could be the ones to pay for Greek debt. Obviously, that is not a politically popular situation.

Point

Should Africa Develop a Common Currency?

Point **Yes** So far, we've looked at the potential formation of currency blocks in NAFTA and CAFTA-DR to model the success in Europe. But what about Africa, the continent of some of the world's fastest-growing frontier economies? The success of the euro and the deep economic and political problems in Africa have caused many experts to wonder whether the continent should attempt to develop one common currency with a central bank to set monetary policy.[16] In 2003, the Association of African Central Bank Governors of the African Union (AU) announced it would work to create a common currency by 2021. This would benefit Africa by hastening economic integration in a continent that desperately needs to increase market size to achieve more trade and greater economies of scale. A common currency would lower transaction costs and make it easier to engage in intra-country trade.

Africa has several degrees of economic cooperation already, including two forms of currency cooperation that are classified by the IMF as conventional pegs tied to the euro:

1. The Economic and Monetary Community for Central Africa (CAEMC), including Cameroon, Central African Republic, Chad, Republic of Congo, Equatorial Guinea, and Gabon
2. The West African Economic and Monetary Union (WAEMU), including Benin, Burkina Faso, Côte d'Ivoire, Guinea-Bissau, Mali, Niger, Senegal, and Togo

Both monetary unions are part of the CFA franc zone, designated by the IMF as "other conventional fixed-peg arrangements" pegged to the euro,[17] and each has a central bank that monitors the value of the CFA franc. Though successful in delivering low inflation, the CFA franc zone has not necessarily delivered high growth.

In addition to the two regional monetary unions, Africa has five existing regional economic communities: Arab Monetary Union, Common Market for Eastern and Southern Africa, Economic Community of Central African States, Economic Community of West African States, and Southern African Development Community. These groups are working hard to reduce trade barriers and increase trade among member countries, so all they would have to do is combine into one large African economic union, form a central bank, and establish a common monetary policy like the EU has.

A major advantage of establishing a central bank and common currency is that institutions in each African nation will have to improve, and the central bank may be able to insulate the monetary policy from political pressures, which often create inflationary pressures and subsequent devaluations. The East African Council of Ministers announced in 2013 that it planned to establish an East African Bank to facilitate the development of a common currency within 10 years, but that assumes the countries can resolve issues of differences in GDP, currencies, and institutions.[18]

Should Africa Develop a Common Currency?

Counterpoint

Counterpoint **No** There is no way the countries of Africa will ever establish a common currency, even though the African Union hopes to do so by 2021 and the East African Council even sooner. The institutional framework in the individual African nations is simply not ready. Few of the individual central banks are independent of the political process, so they often have to stimulate the economy to respond to political pressures. If the process is not managed properly and the currency is subject to frequent devaluation, there will be no pride in the region or clout on the international stage.

Further, each country will have to give up monetary sovereignty and rely on other measures—such as labor mobility, wage and price flexibility, and fiscal transfers—to weather the shocks. Even though there is good labor mobility in Africa, it is difficult to imagine that the African countries will be able to transfer tax revenues from country to country to help stimulate growth. In addition, it is difficult to transfer goods among the different countries in Africa because of transportation problems, which is not an issue in the EU.

The establishment of the euro in the EU was a monumental task that took years, following a successful customs union and a gradual tightening of the ERM in Europe.

For Africa to establish a common currency, there must first be closer economic integration. Thus, it is important to be patient and give Africa a chance to move forward. Maybe one way to move to a common currency is to strengthen the existing regional monetary unions, then gradually open them up to neighboring countries until there are a few huge monetary unions. These can then discuss ways to link together into a common African currency.

DETERMINING EXCHANGE RATES

A lot of different factors cause exchange rates to adjust. The exchange-rate regimes described earlier in the chapter are either fixed (hard peg or soft peg) or floating, with fixed rates varying in terms of how fixed they are and floating rates varying in terms of how much they actually float. However, currencies change in different ways depending on the type of regime. Here we examine how supply and demand determine currency values in a floating world in the absence of government intervention, and how governments can intervene in markets to help control the value of a currency.

NONINTERVENTION: CURRENCY IN A FLOATING-RATE WORLD

Currencies that float freely respond to supply and demand conditions uncontrolled by government intervention. This concept can be illustrated using a two-country model involving the United States and Japan. Figure 9.2 shows the equilibrium exchange rate in the market and then a movement to a new equilibrium level as the market changes. The demand for yen in this example is a function of U.S. demand for Japanese goods and services, such as automobiles, and yen-denominated financial assets, such as securities.

The supply of yen is a function of Japanese demand for U.S. goods and services and dollar-denominated financial assets. Initially, this supply of and demand for yen meet at the equilibrium exchange rate e_0 (for example, 0.00926 dollar per yen, or 108 yen per dollar) and the quantity of yen Q_1.

Demand for a country's currency is a function of the demand for that country's goods and services and financial assets.

Assume that Japanese consumers' demand for U.S. goods and services drops because of, say, high U.S. inflation. This lessening demand would result in a reduced supply of yen in the

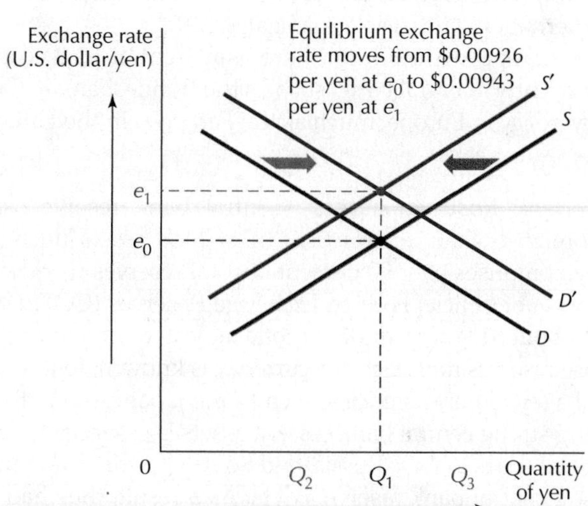

FIGURE 9.2
The Equilibrium Exchange Rate and How It Moves

Let's say that inflation in the United States is comparatively higher than in Japan. In that case (and assuming that Japanese consumers are buying U.S. goods and services), the demand for the Japanese yen will go up, but the supply will go down. What if Japan wants to keep the dollar-to-yen exchange rate at e_0? IT can increase the supply of yen in the market—and therefore lower the exchange rate—by selling yen for dollars.

foreign-exchange market, causing the supply curve to shift to S'. Simultaneously, the rising prices of U.S. goods might lead to an increase in American consumers' demand for Japanese goods and services, which in turn would lead to an increase in demand for yen in the market, causing the demand curve to shift to D', and finally to an increase in the quantity of yen and in the exchange rate.

The new equilibrium exchange rate would be at e_1 (for example, 0.00943 dollar per yen, or 106 yen per dollar). From a dollar standpoint, the higher demand for Japanese goods would increase the supply of dollars as more consumers tried to trade their dollars for yen, and the reduced demand for U.S. goods would result in a drop in demand for dollars, causing a reduction in the dollar's value against the yen.

INTERVENTION: CURRENCY IN A FIXED-RATE OR MANAGED FLOATING-RATE WORLD

In the preceding example, Japanese and U.S. authorities allowed supply and demand to determine the values of the yen and dollar. That doesn't happen for currencies that fix their exchange rates and then don't allow them to move according to market forces. There can be times when one or both countries might not want exchange rates to change.

Assume, for example, that the United States and Japan decide to manage their exchange rates. Although both currencies are independently floating, their respective governments could intervene in the market. The U.S. government might not want its currency to weaken because its companies and consumers would have to pay more for Japanese products, which would lead to more inflationary pressure in the United States. Or the Japanese government might not want the yen to strengthen because it would mean unemployment in its export industries.

But how can the governments keep the values from changing when the U.S. is earning too few yen? Somehow yen supply and demand must be equalized. To understand this process, let's first examine the role of central banks in foreign-exchange markets.

Central banks control policies that affect the value of currencies; the Federal Reserve Bank of New York is the central bank in the United States.

The Role of Central Banks Each country has a central bank responsible for the policies affecting the value of its currency, although countries with independent currency boards use them to control the currency value. In the United States, the New York Federal Reserve Bank, in close coordination with and representing the Federal Reserve System of 12 regional banks and the U.S. Treasury, is responsible for intervening in foreign-exchange markets to achieve dollar exchange-rate policy objectives and counter disorderly conditions in foreign-exchange markets. The U.S. Treasury is responsible for setting exchange-rate policy, whereas the Fed is the Central Bank and is responsible for executing foreign-exchange intervention. Further, the New York Fed serves as a fiscal agent in the United States for foreign central banks and official international financial organizations.[19]

In the European Union, the European Central Bank coordinates the activities of each member country's central bank, such as the Bundesbank in Germany, to establish a common monetary policy in Europe, much as the Fed does in the United States.

Central bank reserve assets are kept in three major forms: gold, foreign-exchange reserves, and IMF-related assets. Foreign exchange is 90 percent of reserve assets worldwide.

Central Bank Reserve Assets Central bank reserve assets are kept in three major forms: foreign-exchange reserves, IMF-related assets (including SDRs), and gold. Foreign exchange comprises over 90 percent of total reserves worldwide. In fourth quarter 2012, the Composition of Official Foreign Exchange Reserves (COFER) reported that U.S. dollars represented about 61.9 percent of the total allocated foreign-exchange reserves (which includes only those reserves for which the currency is known), followed by the euro at about 23.9 percent, and a few other currencies, such as the Japanese yen, British pound, and Swiss franc.[20]

Having strong central bank reserve assets is essential to a country's fiscal strength. When the financial crises in Asia, Russia, and South America hit in the late 1990s, very few countries had strong central bank reserve assets. As a result, they had to borrow a lot of U.S. dollars, which turned out to be devastating when they finally had to devalue their currencies. Since 2000, however, the picture has changed. Due to strong commodity prices, expanding exports, and restraint in incurring dollar debt, many of those same countries have strengthened their financial position by increasing their reserves.

Take Brazil. Its foreign-exchange reserves were $371.1 billion as of late March 2013, leading the way for the rest of Latin America, where reserves have increased fourfold since 2000.[21] However, this is relatively small compared to China, which had $3.5 trillion in reserves. The top countries in the world in terms of total reserves are China, Japan, Saudi Arabia, Russia, Taiwan, Brazil, Switzerland, South Korea, Hong Kong, and India.[22]

Central banks intervene in currency markets by buying and selling currency to affect its price.

How Central Banks Intervene in the Market A central bank can intervene in currency markets in several ways. The U.S. Fed, for example, commonly uses foreign currencies to buy dollars when the dollar is weak, or sells dollars for foreign currency when the dollar is strong. Depending on the market conditions, a central bank may do any of the following:

- Coordinate its action with other central banks or go it alone,
- Enter the market aggressively to change attitudes about its views and policies,
- Call for reassuring action to calm markets,
- Intervene to reverse, resist, or support a market trend,
- Announce or not announce its operations—be very visible or very discreet,
- Operate openly or indirectly through brokers.[23]

CASE The U.S. Dollar and the Japanese Yen

Although the U.S. dollar is an independently floating currency, let's continue with the example illustrated in Figure 9.2 and show how a central bank could intervene. In a managed fixed-exchange-rate system, the New York Fed would hold foreign-exchange reserves, which it would have built up through the years for this type of contingency. It could sell enough of its yen reserves (make up the difference between Q_1 and Q_3 in Figure 9.2) at the fixed exchange rate to maintain that rate. Or the Japanese central bank might be willing to accept dollars so that U.S. consumers can continue to buy Japanese goods. These dollars would then become part of Japan's foreign-exchange reserves. Although this is a two-country example, sometimes several central banks coordinate their intervention to support a currency. On March 18, 2011, for example, the New York Fed intervened in the foreign exchange markets by purchasing $1 billion against the yen in an effort to push down the value of the yen. The action was coordinated with the Central Bank of Japan, the European Central Bank, and the Central Banks of Canada and the U.K. The fixed rate could continue as long as the United States had reserves or as long as the Japanese were willing to add dollars to their holdings. Sometimes governments use monetary policy such as raising interest rates to create a demand for their currency and keep the value from falling. However, interest rate policy is usually a function of inflationary expectations and/or concerns about economic growth rather than just to influence exchange rates.

In 2012, the Japanese yen was very strong against the dollar, which was hurting Japan's export industries and keeping the domestic economy from growing. So the Central Bank engaged in quantitative easing, something that other Central Banks were utilizing as well to stimulate their economies. In the case of Japan, the Central Bank government purchased bonds, corporate debt, and stocks to pump more money into the economy. This had the effect of not only stimulating the economy but also reducing the value of the yen from its high point in 2012.[24]

If a country determines that intervention will not work, it must adjust its currency's value. If the currency is freely floating, the exchange rate will seek the correct level according to the laws of supply and demand. However, a currency pegged to another currency or to a basket of currencies usually is changed on a formal basis—in other words, through a devaluation or revaluation, depending on the direction of the change.

Different Attitudes Toward Intervention Government policies change over time, depending on economic conditions and the attitude of the prevailing administration in power, irrespective of whether the currency is considered to be freely floating.

Governments vary in their intervention policies.

The global financial crisis has roiled foreign-exchange markets and forced many central banks to intervene to support their currencies. Consider Hungary. Though a member of the European Union, it has not yet adopted the euro. However, the EU is its most important market, with 79 percent of its exports going to, and 70 percent of its imports coming from, EU members. The rising value of the euro against the U.S. dollar created serious economic problems for Hungary. Its currency, the forint, fell 22 percent against the euro in the first few months of 2009, forcing the Hungarian central bank to intervene in foreign-exchange markets.[25]

In 2012, the Hong Kong dollar was strengthening against the U.S. dollar due to stimulus measures by the U.S. government and the EU, so foreign exchange was pouring into Hong Kong, raising the value of the HK dollar and creating problems for Hong Kong exporters. So the Currency Board sold HK dollars in order to push down its value. Hong Kong is a special case because its currency is fixed against the U.S. dollar and only allowed to trade within a narrow band. Since the trading value had reached the upper end of the band, the Currency Board had to step in and push down the value of the currency.

Challenges with Intervention In general, the U.S. Fed disapproves of foreign-currency intervention because it is very difficult, if not impossible, for intervention to have a lasting effect on the value of a currency. Given the daily volume of foreign-exchange transactions, no one government can move the market unless its movements can change market psychology. Intervention may temporarily halt a slide, but the country cannot force the market to move in a direction it doesn't want to go, at least for the long run. For that reason, it is important for countries to focus on correcting economic fundamentals instead of spending a lot of time and money on intervention.

CONCEPT CHECK

In Chapter 8, we discuss the importance of the BIS in collecting information about the massive volume of activity on the global foreign-exchange market. Here we add that the BIS may also help coordinate the policies of central banks in matters of foreign-exchange intervention.

Nevertheless, countries still intervene, and the above examples illustrate different approaches to intervention, from raising interest rates to using foreign-exchange reserves to buying and selling currencies. When daily foreign-exchange trades are about $4.4 trillion, it is hard to intervene enough to move the markets very much. Any intervention can be construed as a central bank signal, but the long-term policies will eventually make the big difference.

Revisiting the BIS Coordination of central bank intervention can take place bilaterally or multilaterally. The Bank for International Settlements (BIS) in Basel, Switzerland, links together the central banks of the world. As we noted in Chapter 8, the BIS was founded in 1930 and is owned and controlled by the major central banks of the world. Its main objective is to promote the cooperation of central banks to facilitate international financial stability. The BIS has 60 member central banks, and it serves as a central bank hub.[26]

The Bank for International Settlements in Basel, Switzerland, is owned by and promotes cooperation among a group of central banks.

The BIS acts as a central banker's bank. It gets involved in swaps and other currency transactions between the central banks in other countries. It is also a gathering place where central bankers can discuss monetary cooperation, and it is increasingly getting involved with other multilateral agencies, such as the IMF, in providing support during international financial crises. In addition, the BIS conducts the triennial central bank survey of foreign-exchange and derivatives market activity that is the basis for much of the trading data provided in Chapter 8.

BLACK MARKETS

A black market closely approximates a price based on supply and demand for a currency instead of a government-controlled price.

In many of the countries that do not allow their currencies to float according to market forces, a **black market** can parallel the official market and yet be aligned more closely with the forces of supply and demand. The less flexible a country's exchange-rate arrangement, the more likely there will be a thriving black (or parallel) market, which exists when people are willing to pay more for dollars than the official rate. In order for such a market to work, the government must control access to foreign exchange so it can control the price of its currency.

Zimbabwe's terrible financial problems are manifest in the currency markets. Its official currency regime is a soft-peg arrangement and used to be pegged to the U.S. dollar, but that doesn't seem to have helped much. In 2007, with inflation hitting around 4,500 percent—the highest in the world—the currency was plunging. A loaf of bread cost 44,000 Zimbabwean dollars, which was only 18 cents at black-market rates but $176 at the official exchange rate.[27] By early 2009, the economy was still a disaster, and the country was suffering from a cholera epidemic and political turmoil. Hyperinflation was so bad that the central bank issued a $100 trillion banknote that was worth about US$5 on the black market. Prices were doubling every day, and food and fuel were in short supply. The currency was so worthless that most trades in Zimbabwe were in U.S. dollars or the South African rand. However, demand began to pick up because collectors from outside of Zimbabwe wanted one of $100 trillion banknotes to remind them of what inflation can do to the value of a currency.[28]

FOREIGN-EXCHANGE CONVERTIBILITY AND CONTROLS

Some countries with fixed exchange rates control access to their currencies. *Fully convertible currencies* are those that the government allows both residents and nonresidents to purchase in unlimited amounts.

Rampant inflation in Zimbabwe drove down the value of the currency so much that it was practically worthless.

Source: Trevor Kelly/Shutterstock

A hard currency is a currency that is usually fully convertible and strong or relatively stable in value in comparison with other currencies.

A soft currency is one that is usually not fully convertible and is also called a weak currency.

Hard and Soft Currencies **Hard currencies**—such as the U.S. dollar, euro, British pound, and Japanese yen—are those that are fully convertible. Highly liquid and relatively stable in value over a short period of time, they are generally accepted worldwide as payment for goods and services. They are also desirable assets. Currencies that are not fully convertible, or **soft currencies,** have just the opposite characteristics: they are very unstable in value, not very liquid, and not widely accepted as payment for goods and services. A major reason why countries restrict convertibility of their currencies is that they are short on foreign-exchange reserves and try to use them for essential transactions. That's why soft currencies tend to be from developing countries, where foreign-exchange reserves are low. The higher the reserves, the less a country has to resort to restricting convertibility. It is interesting to note that many developing countries dominate the list of nations with the highest foreign-exchange reserves. In spite of that, when paying for exports and imports they need to go through hard currencies such as the dollar, euro, and yen.

Most countries today have *nonresident* (or *external*) *convertibility,* meaning that foreigners can convert their currency into the local currency and back into theirs as well. Tourists generally have no problems doing this, although sometimes countries put restrictions or conditions on trade from the local currency back to the hard currency when tourists leave the country.

Controlling Convertibility To conserve scarce foreign exchange, some governments impose exchange restrictions on companies or individuals who want to exchange money. The devices they use include *import licensing, multiple exchange rates, import deposit requirements,* and *quantity controls.*

Sri Lanka is a country with lots of currency controls. In June 2013, however, the government relaxed foreign exchange controls for travel, migration, sale of residential property by non-residents, and maintaining foreign exchange accounts. The macroeconomic situation in Sri Lanka had improved so much that foreign exchange for travel, for example, was raised from $2,500 to $5,000.[29]

Licensing occurs when a government requires regulation and control of all foreign-exchange transactions.

Licenses Government licenses fix the exchange rate by requiring all recipients, exporters, and others who receive foreign currency to sell it to its central bank at the official buying rate. The bank then rations the foreign currency it acquires by selling it at fixed rates to those needing to make payment abroad for essential goods. An importer may purchase foreign exchange only if it has obtained an import license for the goods in question.

In a multiple exchange-rate system, a government sets different exchange rates for different types of transactions.

Multiple Exchange Rates Another way governments control foreign-exchange convertibility is by establishing more than one exchange rate. This restrictive measure is called a **multiple-exchange-rate system**. The government determines which kinds of transactions are to be conducted at which exchange rates. Countries with multiple rates often have a floating rate for luxury goods and financial flows, such as dividends, and a fixed, usually lower rate for other trade transactions such as imports of essential commodities and semi-manufactured goods. Venezuela used a multiple exchange rate restriction until 2011. Under the system, essential imports—such as capital goods, food, and medicine—converted at 2.6 bolívars to the dollar, whereas such non-essential goods as cars, appliances, and alcohol were fixed at 4.3 bolívars to the dollar. At the time, the black market rate was nearly 8 bolívars to the dollar. However, the black market put too much pressure on the official rate, so the government devalued the currency by 32 percent and then established a parallel exchange rate to combat the black market which was worth four times the official rate.[30]

Advance import deposit—a government-required deposit of money prior to the release of foreign exchange to pay for imports—varies by as long as a year in advance.

Import Deposits Another form of foreign-exchange convertibility control is the **advance import deposit**. In this case, the government tightens the issue of import licenses and requires importers to make a deposit with the central bank—often for as long as one year and interest-free—covering the full price of manufactured goods they would purchase from abroad.

Quantity controls—government limits on the amount of foreign currency that can be used in a specific transaction.

Quantity Controls Governments may also limit the amount of exchange through quantity controls, which often apply to tourism. A quantity control limits the amount of currency a local resident can purchase from the bank for foreign travel, which was illustrated above in the Sri Lanka example.

In the past, currency controls have significantly added to the cost of doing business internationally, resulting in the overall reduction of trade. However, trade liberalization in recent years has eliminated a lot of these controls to the point that they are considered a minor impediment to trade.[31] In addition, the move from fixed to flexible exchange rates has also eliminated the need for controls in many countries.

EXCHANGE RATES AND PURCHASING POWER PARITY

The next three sections examine three interconnected issues: the relationship between inflation and exchange rates, the relationship between interest rates and exchange rates, and the factors you can use to forecast (or at least attempt to forecast) future exchange rates.

Purchasing power parity (PPP) is a well-known theory that, from the standpoint of exchange rates, seeks to define the relationships between currencies based on relative inflation. In essence, it claims that a change in relative inflation between two countries (meaning a comparison of the countries' rates of inflation) must cause a change in exchange rates to keep

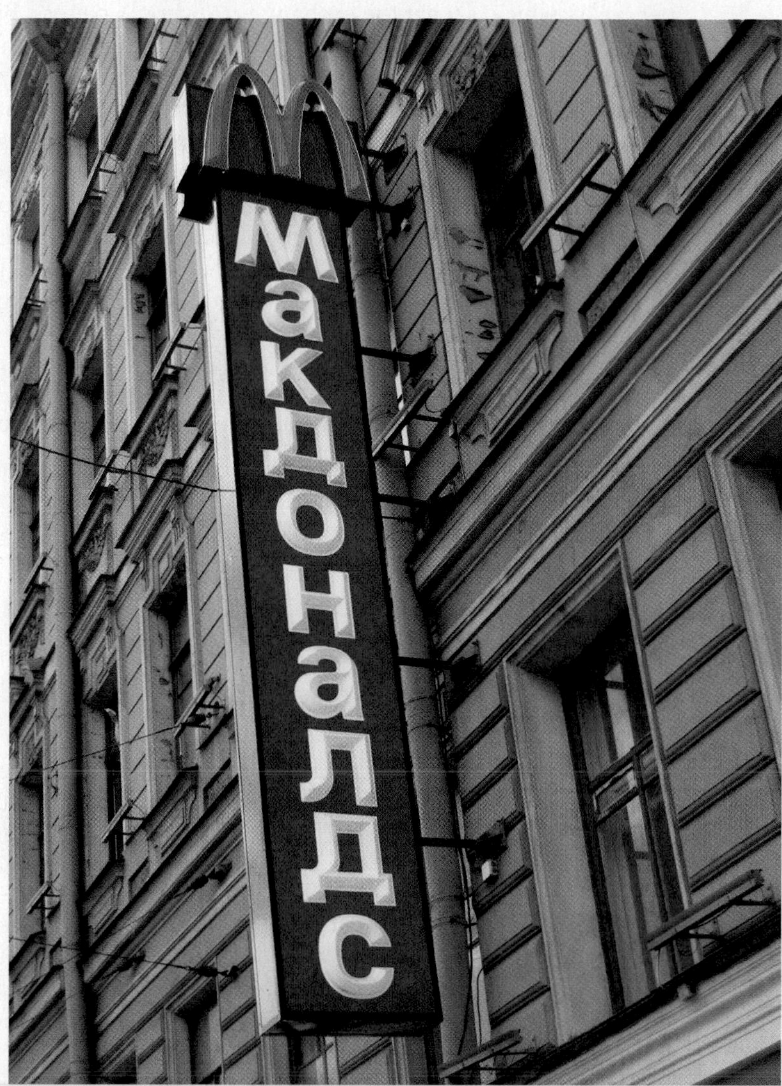

McDonald's in St. Petersburg, Russia is a popular place to eat, and a Big Mac there costs less in U.S. dollar terms than it would in the U.S.

Source: Jonathan Smith, Dorling Kindersley

the prices of goods in the countries fairly similar. According to the PPP theory, if, say, Japanese inflation were 2 percent and U.S. inflation were 3.5 percent, the dollar would be expected to fall by the difference in inflation rates. The dollar would then be worth fewer yen than before the adjustment, and the yen would be worth more dollars than before the adjustment.

The "Big Mac Index" An interesting illustration of the PPP theory for estimating exchange rates is the "Big Mac index" of currencies used by *The Economist* each year. Since 1986, the British periodical *The Economist* has used the price of a Big Mac to estimate the exchange rate between the dollar and another currency (see Table 9.2). Because the Big Mac is sold in more than 34,000 McDonald's restaurants serving more than 69 million people in 118 countries every day, it is easy to use it to compare prices. PPP would suggest that the exchange rate should leave hamburgers costing the same in the United States as abroad. However, the Big Mac sometimes costs more and sometimes less, demonstrating how far currencies are under- or over-valued against the dollar.

If the domestic inflation rate is lower than that in a particular foreign country, the domestic currency should be stronger than the foreign currency.

The Big Mac price in U.S. dollars is found by converting the price in the local currency into dollars at the current exchange rate. For example, in Table 9.2, the dollar equivalent of a Big Mac in China is US$2.57 which is the price of the Big Mac in China (¥16.0) converted into dollars at the actual exchange rate (which was CNY6.2200). Column 3, the implied PPP of the dollar, shows what the exchange rate should be if the price in dollars equals the price in the local currency. Continuing with China as the example, if you divide ¥16.0 by US$4.37 (the prices of the Big Mac in China and in the United States), you get ¥3.66 per dollar, which is what the exchange rate should be for a Big Mac to cost the same in the two countries. Column 4 shows the actual exchange rate, and column 5 shows how much the currency is under- or overvalued. For the Chinese yuan, you take (3.66 – 6.22)/6.22 = –0.41157, which shows that the yuan is undervalued against the dollar by 41.1 percent.

As you can see from Table 9.2, the euro and the currencies of European countries tied to it, such as Switzerland, Denmark, and Sweden, were overvalued against the dollar, whereas those of many countries in Latin America and Asia were undervalued. That makes it easier for U.S. companies to export to Europe and harder for European companies to export to the United States.[32]

The Big Mac index, also known as "McParity," has both supporters and detractors. Even though McParity may hold up in the long run, as some studies have shown, there are short-term problems that affect PPP:

- The theory of PPP falsely assumes there are no barriers to trade and that transportation costs are zero.
- Prices of the Big Mac in different countries are distorted by taxes. European countries with high value-added taxes are more likely to have higher prices than countries with low taxes.
- The Big Mac is not just a basket of commodities; its price also includes nontraded costs, such as rent, insurance, and so on, which tend to be lower in developing countries.
- Profit margins vary by the strength of competition: The higher the competition, the lower the profit margin and, therefore, the price.[33]

The value of the Big Mac index is in understanding that price differences are not sustainable in the long run. Exchange rates will eventually have to equalize price differences more closely, or the law of supply and demand will take over. Of course, nobody is going to import Big Macs from China to the United States because they are so cheap. But if Big Macs are cheap, so are other products, and trade flows could be influenced by price differences.

The Starbucks Index A similar study of PPP has been done using Starbucks' lattes around the world. Generally, when European latte prices are converted into U.S. dollars, they tend to be more expensive than lattes in America. This illustrates, as with the Big Mac Index, that the dollar doesn't go as far in Europe, providing an example of how the euro is overvalued. On the other hand, prices of lattes in many Latin American and Asian countries are cheaper than in the U.S., illustrating that their currencies are undervalued against the dollar. The Starbucks

TABLE 9.2 The Big Mac Index

Country	Big Mac Prices: In Local Currency	Big Mac Prices: In dollars	Implied PPP* of the dollar	Actual Exchange Rate: Jan 30, 2013	Under (-)/Over (+) Valuation against the dollar, %
United States	4.37	4.37	–	1.00	0.00
Argentina	19.00	3.82	4.35	4.98	−12.58
Australia	4.70	4.90	1.08	0.96	12.21
Brazil	11.25	5.64	2.58	1.99	29.22
Britain	2.69	4.25	0.62	0.63	−2.73
Canada	5.41	5.39	1.24	1.00	23.51
Chile	2050.00	4.35	469.39	471.75	−0.50
China	16.00	2.57	3.66	6.22	−41.10
Colombia	8600.00	4.85	1969.14	1773.18	11.05
Costa Rica	2200.00	4.39	503.73	500.83	0.58
Czech Republic	70.33	3.72	16.10	18.89	−14.77
Denmark	28.50	5.18	6.53	5.50	18.69
Egypt	16.00	2.39	3.66	6.69	−45.20
Euro area	3.59	4.88	0.82	0.74	11.69
Hong Kong	17.00	2.19	3.89	7.76	−49.83
Hungary	830.00	3.82	190.04	217.47	−12.61
India	89.00	1.67	20.38	53.40	−61.83
Indonesia	27939.00	2.86	6397.18	9767.50	−34.51
Israel	14.90	4.00	3.41	3.72	−8.40
Japan	320.00	3.51	73.27	91.07	−19.54
Latvia	1.69	3.28	0.39	0.52	−24.90
Lithuania	7.80	3.07	1.79	2.54	−29.81
Malaysia	7.95	2.58	1.82	3.08	−40.96
Mexico	37.00	2.90	8.47	12.74	−33.49
New Zealand	5.20	4.32	1.19	1.20	−0.98
Norway	43.00	7.84	9.85	5.48	79.56
Pakistan	290.00	2.97	66.40	97.67	−32.01
Peru	10.00	3.91	2.29	2.56	−10.54
Philippines	118.00	2.91	27.02	40.60	−33.45
Poland	9.10	2.94	2.08	3.09	−32.61
Russia	72.88	2.43	16.69	30.05	−44.46
Saudi Arabia	11.00	2.93	2.52	3.75	−32.84
Singapore	4.50	3.64	1.03	1.23	−16.56
South Africa	18.33	2.03	4.20	9.05	−53.61
South Korea	3700.00	3.41	847.19	1085.48	−21.95
Sri Lanka	350.00	2.77	80.14	126.45	−36.62
Sweden	48.40	7.62	11.08	6.35	74.54
Switzerland	6.50	7.12	1.49	0.91	63.14
Taiwan	75.00	2.54	17.17	29.50	−41.79
Thailand	87.00	2.92	19.92	29.76	−33.05
Turkey	8.45	4.78	1.93	1.77	9.39
UAE	12.00	3.27	2.75	3.67	−25.19
Ukraine	19.00	2.33	4.35	8.14	−46.58
Uruguay	105.00	5.45	24.04	19.28	24.70
Venezuela	39.00	9.08	8.93	4.29	107.93
Austria	3.39	4.60	0.78	0.74	5.33
Belgium	3.80	5.16	0.87	0.74	18.07
Estonia	2.70	3.66	0.62	0.74	−16.11
Finland	3.75	5.09	0.86	0.74	16.51
France	3.60	4.89	0.82	0.74	11.85
Germany	3.64	4.94	0.83	0.74	13.09
Greece	3.30	4.48	0.76	0.74	2.53
Ireland	3.49	4.74	0.80	0.74	8.43
Italy	3.85	5.22	0.88	0.74	19.62
Netherlands	3.45	4.68	0.79	0.74	7.19
Portugal	2.95	4.00	0.68	0.74	−8.34
Spain	3.50	4.75	0.80	0.74	8.75

Source: Based on The Big Mac Index, www.economist.com/content/big-mac-index (accessed January 31, 2013).

A Latte at Starbucks in Berlin is more expensive than one in the U.S., confirming the basic idea with the Big Mac Index that the Euro is overvalued against the U.S. dollar.
Source: U. Baumgarten via Getty Images

measure provides prices for lattes in various parts of the U.S., showing that there are regional differences in prices, whereas the Big Mac index uses an average price for New York City, Chicago, Atlanta, and San Francisco.[34]

EXCHANGE RATES AND INTEREST RATES

Although inflation is the most important medium-term influence on exchange rates, interest rates are also important. Interest rate differentials, however, have both short-term and long-term components to them. In the short term, exchange rates are strongly influenced by interest rates. One factor keeping the euro strong against the dollar in late 2008/early 2009 was that the European Central Bank was keeping interest rates relatively high compared to those in the United States. Once the appetite for risk returned to the market, investors looked at the euro as a good place to invest, so money flowed to the euro, increasing its value against the U.S. dollar. When the European Central Bank reduced interest rates to help stimulate economic growth, the difference between U.S. and European interest rates narrowed, so money stopped flowing to the euro and it fell in value.

In the long term, however, there is a strong relationship between inflation, interest rates, and exchange rates. To understand this, we need to examine two key finance theories: the *Fisher Effect* and the *International Fisher Effect.* The first links inflation and interest rates, while the second links interest rates and exchange rates.

The nominal interest rate is the real interest rate plus inflation. Because the real interest rate should be the same in every country, the country with the higher interest rate should have higher inflation.

The Fisher Effect The **Fisher Effect** is the theory that the nominal interest rate in a country (r, the actual monetary interest rate earned on an investment) is determined by the real interest rate (R, the nominal rate less inflation) and the inflation rate (i) as follows:

$$(1 + r) = (1 + R)(1 + i) \text{ or } r = (1 + R)(1 + i) - 1$$

According to this theory, if the real interest rate is 5 percent, the U.S. inflation rate 2.9 percent, and the Japanese inflation rate 1.5 percent, then the nominal interest rates for the United States and Japan are computed as follows:

$$r_{US} = (1.05)(1.029) - 1 = 0.08045, \text{ or } 8.045\%$$
$$r_j = (1.05)(1.015) - 1 = 0.06575, \text{ or } 6.575\%$$

Thus, the difference between U.S. and Japanese interest rates is a function of the difference between their inflation rates. If inflation rates were the same (zero differential) but interest rates were 10 percent in the U.S. and 6.575 percent in Japan, investors would place their money in the U.S., where they could get the higher real return.

The IFE implies that the currency of the country with the lower interest rate will strengthen in the future.

The International Fisher Effect The bridge from interest rates to exchange rates can be explained by the **International Fisher Effect (IFE)**, the theory that the interest-rate differential is an unbiased predictor of future changes in the spot exchange rate. For example, if the IFE predicts that nominal interest rates in the United States are higher than those in Japan, the dollar's value should fall in the future by that interest-rate differential, which would be an indication of a weakening, or depreciation, of the dollar. That is because the interest-rate differential is based on differences in inflation rates, as we discussed earlier. The previous discussion on PPP also demonstrates that the country with the higher inflation should have the weaker currency. Thus, the country with the higher interest rate (and the higher inflation) should have the weaker currency.

Of course, these issues cover the long run, but anything can happen in the short run. During periods of general price stability, a country that raises its interest rates is likely to attract capital and see its currency rise in value due to the increased demand. However, if the reason for the increase in interest rates is that inflation is higher than that of its major trading partners, and if the country's central bank is trying to reduce inflation, the currency will eventually weaken until inflation cools down.

OTHER FACTORS IN EXCHANGE-RATE DETERMINATION

Other key factors affecting exchange-rate movements are confidence and technical factors, such as the release of economic statistics.

Confidence: Flight to Risk vs. Flight to Safety Various other factors can affect currency values. One not to be dismissed lightly is confidence: In times of turmoil, people prefer to hold currencies that are considered safe. When the banking crisis in Cyprus unfolded in March of 2013, investors moved money out of euros and invested in U.S. dollars because of concerns over the effect of the crisis on the rest of Europe, which was already very fragile in the banking sector. During last quarter 2008, the dollar rose dramatically in value due to its status as a safe-haven currency and because investors withdrew capital from emerging markets and deposited in "safe" dollars and yen. (The Swiss franc is also considered a safe-haven currency.)

On the other hand, sometimes the appetite for risk is more important than safety. In 2008–09, as soon as the markets began to recover and the restructuring of the banking system and auto industries took hold in the U.S., money began to flow into euros and back into the emerging markets, reducing the dollar value: the flight to safety was replaced by a flight to risk, where investors could earn a higher return.

Information It is interesting how the release of information can influence currency values. Services such as Bloomberg are so important because they carry up-to-date financial news that traders can follow as they try to figure out what will happen to exchange rates. Consider what happened on May 22, 2013 when the Chairman of the U.S. Federal Reserve testified before Congress and intimated that the Fed might stop its bond-buying program sooner than anticipated. That announcement caused many investors to leave the dollar and move to Japanese yen and Swiss francs as safe-haven investments.[35]

FORECASTING EXCHANGE-RATE MOVEMENTS

Because various factors influence exchange-rate movements, managers must be able to analyze these factors to formulate a general idea of the timing, magnitude, and direction of an exchange-rate movement. However, prediction is not a precise science, and many things can cause the best of predictions to differ significantly from reality.

Reasons vary widely as to why companies try to forecast exchange rates. A country manager establishing a budget for the coming year must estimate factors like the exchange rate over the time horizon. Companies involved in buying or selling goods and services need to forecast future exchange rates as part of their pricing decisions, choice of currency, and hedging strategies. Others may try to forecast exchange rates as an investment strategy and hope that their forecasts can beat the market.

FUNDAMENTAL AND TECHNICAL FORECASTING

Fundamental forecasting uses trends in economic variables to predict future exchange rates. Technical forecasting uses past trends in exchange-rate movements to spot future trends.

Managers can forecast exchange rates by using either of two approaches: fundamental or technical. **Fundamental forecasting** uses trends in economic variables to predict future rates. The data can be plugged into an econometric model or evaluated on a more subjective basis. **Technical forecasting** uses past trends in exchange rates themselves to spot future rate trends. Technical forecasters, or *chartists,* assume that if current exchange rates reflect all facts in the market, then under similar circumstances future rates will follow the same patterns.[36] However, research has shown that, except in the very short run, past exchange rates are not an accurate predictor of future ones. According to this theory, then, exchange rate movements are a random walk, implying they cannot be predicted.[37]

Dealing with Biases Some biases exist that can skew forecasts:

- Overreaction to unexpected and dramatic news events;
- Illusory correlation—that is, the tendency to see correlations or associations in data that are not statistically present but are expected to occur on the basis of prior beliefs;
- Focusing on a particular subset of information at the expense of the overall set of information;
- Insufficient adjustment for subjective matters, such as market volatility;
- The inability to learn from one's past mistakes, such as poor trading decisions;
- Overconfidence in one's ability to forecast currencies accurately.[38]

Good treasurers and bankers develop their own forecasts of what will happen to a particular currency and use fundamental or technical predictions of outside forecasters to corroborate them. Doing this helps them determine whether they are considering important factors and whether they need to revise their forecasts in light of outside analysis.

Managers need to be concerned with the timing, magnitude, and direction of an exchange-rate movement.

Timing, Direction, and Magnitude Forecasting includes predicting the timing, direction, and magnitude of an exchange-rate change or movement. For countries whose currencies are not freely floating, the timing is often a political decision and not easy to predict. And though the direction of a change can probably be predicted, the magnitude is difficult to forecast. So, not only is it difficult to predict what will happen to currencies, it is equally difficult to use those predictions to forecast profits and establish operating strategies.

FUNDAMENTAL FACTORS TO MONITOR

Key factors to monitor—the institutional setting, fundamental analysis, confidence factors, events, and technical analysis.

For freely fluctuating currencies, the law of supply and demand determines market value. Your ability to forecast exchange rates depends on your time horizon. In general, the best predictors of future exchange rates are interest rates for short-term movements, inflation for medium-term movements, and current account balances for long-term movements.[39] Given that even those countries whose currencies are freely floating are concerned about the value of their currencies, managers can monitor the same factors the governments follow to try to make a prediction:

- *Institutional Setting*
  - Does the currency float, or is it managed—and if so, is it pegged to another currency, to a basket, or to some other standard?
  - What are the intervention practices? Are they credible? Sustainable?

- *Fundamental Analysis*
  - Does the currency appear undervalued or overvalued in terms of PPP, balance of payments, foreign-exchange reserves, or other factors?
  - What is the cyclical situation in terms of employment, growth, savings, investment, and inflation?
  - What are the prospects for government monetary, fiscal, and debt policy?
- *Confidence Factors*
  - What are market views and expectations with respect to the political environment, as well as to the credibility of the government and central bank?
- *Circumstances*
  - Are there national or international incidents in the news, the possibility of crises or emergencies, or governmental or other important meetings coming up?
- *Technical Analysis*
  - What trends do the charts show? Are there signs of trend reversals?
  - At what rates do there appear to be important buy and sell orders? Are they balanced? Is the market overbought? Oversold?
  - What is the thinking and what are the expectations of other market players and analysts?[40]

We have already discussed interest rates and inflation, but what about current account balances? A current account surplus means that a country exports more than it imports and is building foreign-exchange reserves from the countries that are buying its goods and services. For the long term, the expectation is that the currency of that country will strengthen vis-à-vis its trading partners. Conversely, a current account deficit means that a country imports more than it exports and is building up debt abroad as it struggles to find the foreign exchange to pay for its imports. In that case, the long-term expectation is that the currency will weaken vis-à-vis its trading partners.

BUSINESS IMPLICATIONS OF EXCHANGE-RATE CHANGES

Why do we need to bother with predicting exchange-rate changes? As we will see in the closing case, they can dramatically affect operating strategies as well as translated overseas profits. We now look briefly at how exchange-rate changes can affect companies' marketing, production, and financial decisions.

MARKETING DECISIONS

Strengthening of a country's currency value could create problems for exporters.

Marketing managers watch exchange rates because they can affect demand for a company's products at home and abroad. In 2013, as the Indian rupee plunged in value against the U.S. dollar, Indian small importers were in trouble because they didn't have the financial strength to deal with the currency fluctuations. In most cases, they had to pay their suppliers in U.S. dollars, and when the rupee fell, they had to come up with more rupees to convert into dollars to pay the suppliers, and they were struggling to do so.[41] On the other hand, India's agricultural exports were expected to rise due to the fall in the value of the rupee. On the export side, Chinese exporters were struggling to continue strong exports as the yuan rose in value against the yen and dollar. In a survey of 1,000 exporters, 73.4 percent expected the stronger yuan to adversely affect their exports.[42]

Companies might locate production in a weak-currency country because

- Initial investment there is relatively cheap.
- Such a country is a good base for inexpensive exportation.

PRODUCTION DECISIONS

Exchange-rate changes can also affect production decisions. A manufacturer in a country where wages and operating expenses are high might be tempted to relocate production to a country with a currency that is rapidly losing value. The company's home currency would buy lots of the weak currency, making the company's initial investment cheap.

Further, goods manufactured in that country would be relatively low-cost in world markets. For example, BMW decided to invest in production facilities in South Carolina because of the unfavorable exchange rate between the Deutsche mark (now the euro) and the dollar. However, the company announced plans to use the facilities not only to serve the U.S. market but also to export to Europe and other markets.[43] Another example is the devaluation of the Mexican peso, which came shortly after the introduction of NAFTA. Although companies had already begun to establish operations in Mexico to service North America, the cheaper peso certainly helped their manufacturing strategies.

FINANCIAL DECISIONS

Exchange rates can influence the sourcing of financial resources, the cross-border remittance of funds, and the reporting of financial results.

Exchange rates can affect financial decisions primarily in sourcing financial resources, remitting funds across national borders, and reporting financial results. In the first area, a company might be tempted to borrow money in places where interest rates are lowest. However, recall that interest-rate differentials often are compensated for in money markets through exchange-rate changes.

In deciding about cross-border financial flows, a company would want to convert local currency into its own home-country currency when exchange rates are most favorable so it can maximize its return. However, countries with weak currencies often have currency controls, making it difficult for MNEs to do so.

CONCEPT CHECK

In Chapter 19, we'll explain how companies factor in foreign exchange in preparing financial statements, we'll show how exchange rates influence financial flows, and describe some of the strategies that companies enlist to protect themselves against exchange-rate risk.

Finally, exchange-rate changes can influence the reporting of financial results. A simple example illustrates their impact on income: If a U.S. company's Mexican subsidiary earns 2 million pesos when the exchange rate is 9.5 pesos per dollar, the dollar equivalent of its income is $210,526. If the peso depreciates to 10.2 pesos per dollar, the dollar equivalent of that income falls to $196,078. The opposite will occur if the local currency appreciates against that of the company's home country. In 2013, GM announced that its profits fell by $300 million in the first quarter due to the devaluation of the Venezuelan bolivar and because of the weakening of the British pound against the dollar.[44]

It is important to learn about exchange rates and the forces that affect their change. Several years ago, a manager in a large U.S.-based telephone company was preparing a bid for a major telecommunications project in Turkey. Knowing nothing about the Turkish lira, and without consulting with the company's foreign-exchange specialists, he figured out the bid in dollars, then turned to the foreign-exchange table in the *Wall Street Journal* to see what rate he should use to convert the bid into lira. What he didn't realize was that the lira at that time was weakening against the dollar. By the time he was awarded the project, he had lost all of his profit to the change in the value of the lira against the dollar; by the time he finished the project, he had lost a lot of money. If he had talked to someone who knew anything about the lira, he could have forecast (or at least tried to forecast) the future value and maybe entered into a hedging strategy to protect his receivables in lira. Managers who don't understand how currency values are determined can make serious, costly mistakes.

Looking to the Future

Determination of Exchange Rates–Exploring the Case of Singapore's Monetary Policy as a Model for Sustainable Economic Growth

The exchange rate (the price of a currency) in a free market situation is influenced by economic growth, interest rates and inflation, market behavior, and government action. Advanced economies generally use the floating exchange rate system without government intervention. However, some developing economies use the fixed exchange rate system where its national currency is pegged to another more stable and widely used currency;[45] while others manage their currency against the value of a basket of currencies (that is, a managed float system).[46]

The Monetary Authority of Singapore (MAS) uses an exchange rate system in the form of an adjustable crawling peg with a band, referred to as BBC (basket, band, crawl), as the currency is pegged against a basket of currencies in order to minimize misalignment with its major trading partners.[47] MAS also uses the exchange rate as a monetary policy to stabilize the business cycle,[48] with the primary objective of promoting medium term price stability as a basis for sustainable economic growth.

Singapore's exchange rate system has the following characteristics[49]:

Firstly, the Singapore dollar is managed against a basket of currencies of its major trading partners and competitors. The composition of the basket (of currencies) is reviewed and revised periodically taking into account changes in the global economy. Different weightages are given to each currency within this basket.

Second, the trade-weighted exchange rate is allowed to fluctuate within an undisclosed policy band which provides flexibility to accommodate short-term fluctuations in the foreign exchange markets. When the exchange rate moves out of the band range MAS will intervene to steer the exchange rate back within the band.The band is reviewed quarterly and adjusted as necessary to keep in line with the economic fundamentals affecting the Singapore economy so as to avoid any misalignment of the value of the Singapore dollar. This review gives MAS the flexibility to take into account any short-term volatility in financial markets.

Finally, adopting the BBC exchange rate policy means MAS does not control domestic interest rates and money supply. Interest rates in Singapore are largely determined by foreign interest rates and investor expectations of the future movements in the Singapore dollar.

MAS chose a "managed float" exchange rate regime to allow it to deal with unpredictable swings and short-term volatility while at the same time maintaining the purchasing power of the Singapore dollar so as to maintain confidence in the currency and preserve the value of workers' savings. It also serves as an effective anti-inflation tool for the Singapore economy.

In summary, Singapore's exchange rate (and monetary policy) is determined by two strategic factors: first, the small and open nature of the Singapore economy means that the exchange rate is the most effective policy instrument for maintaining domestic price stability; second, the country's obviously sound macroeconomic fundamentals and prudent fiscal policy. ■

CASE Welcome to the World of Sony—Unless the Falling Yen Rises Again[50]

The year 2010 was pretty tough for Sony, and 2011 didn't seem to be getting much better. Revenues fell by 500 million yen in 2012 and conditions worldwide continued to deteriorate while the yen remained strong. The global economic crisis not only resulted in a huge drop in demand worldwide, it also roiled the foreign currency markets. As if the crisis weren't enough, on March 14, 2011, Japan was devastated by a 9.0 earthquake and resulting tsunami on the Pacific Coast near Tohoku. By the end of Sony's fiscal year 2010 and the release of its annual report (like most Japanese companies, Sony's fiscal year ends on March 31), the yen was trading at ¥84.1184 per dollar—a significant increase in value from just five years earlier, when it was trading at ¥110.5583 on August 15, 2008, shortly before the global

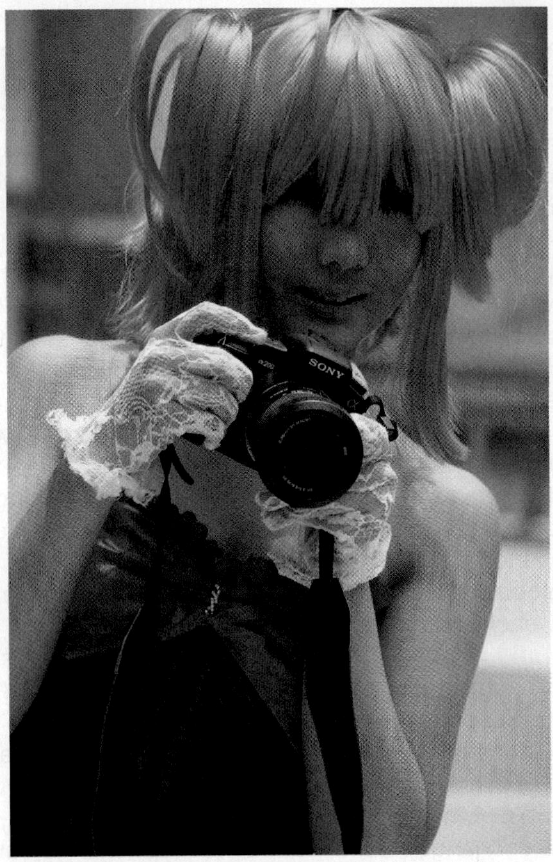

A model is using a Sony camera at a Japanese Cosplay festival in Bangkok, Thailand, bringing a unique aspect of Japanese youth culture to the costume convention where cosplayers dress up in their favorite costumes and wigs. As Sony says about its cameras, "believe that anything you imagine, you can make real."
Source: © dave stamboulis/Alamy

economic crash. The crazy currency swings had a devastating impact on Sony and all other major MNCs in Japan. What will the future bring now?

The Past

Before attacking the future, let's look at the past, especially from the perspective of the Japanese yen. In the post–World War II years, the yen was extremely weak against the dollar, trading at ¥357.65 in 1970. At that time, in 1946, the Tokyo Tsushin Kogyo Corporation was founded, officially becoming known as Sony Corporation in 1958, the year its stock was first listed on the Tokyo Stock Exchange. It also became the first Japanese company to list American Depositary Receipts (ADRs) on the New York Stock Exchange in 1961, finally listing its own shares in September 1970.

In those early years of operation, Sony had the luxury of operating in a currency that was not only weak against the dollar, but also highly controlled by the government. Japanese foreign-exchange policies favored companies and industries that the government wanted to succeed, especially in export markets. With a cheap yen, it was easy for companies to expand exports rapidly.

The First Endaka

From its 1970 high, the yen steadily strengthened until 1985, when it *really* shot up in value. Due to economic problems in the United States, the dollar began to fall during the latter part of 1985, and the yen ended the year at ¥200 per dollar. By the latter part of 1986, it was trading at ¥150, a steep rise from its historical highs. The Japanese called this strengthening of the yen *endaka,* which literally translates "high yen." *Endaka* resulted in serious problems for Japanese exporters and potential pain for the entire Japanese economy, which depended heavily on international trade. However, one advantage of *endaka* was that imports were cheaper, and Japan relied heavily on imports of virtually all commodities. Thus its input costs fell, even as it found its export prices rising.

The strong yen was due primarily to a strong Japanese economy, large trade surpluses, and the largest foreign-exchange reserves in the world. In addition, Japan had low unemployment, low interest rates, and low inflation. But cracks began to show in its economy. A combination of a drop in the stock market, a rise in inflation, and a real estate bubble hurt the economy and confidence in the yen. The governor of the Bank of Japan raised interest rates in December 1989, but the resulting furor forced him to stop. Since the interest rates in the United States were higher, investors pulled money out of Japan and put it into U.S. dollars to take advantage of higher returns. This drop in demand for yen and rise in demand for dollars pushed up the value of the dollar against the yen, and the yen closed out 1989 at ¥143.45, from ¥125.85 only a year earlier.

Both the United States and Japan were worried about inflation in the early 1990s, and they tried to coordinate exchange-rate policies, but the United States didn't want to push down the value of the dollar too much and lose its own fight against inflation. The two nations tried to get the central banks of Germany, the United Kingdom, and other countries to intervene in the markets and sell their currencies for yen in order to strengthen it. But there wasn't much they could do to move the market given that interest rates were driving market psychology.

In the ensuing years, many factors influenced the yen/dollar exchange rate, including a weak U.S. economy (favoring a drop in interest rates), the Persian Gulf War (which favored the dollar as a safe-haven currency), a rise in Japanese interest rates relative to U.S. interest rates, and a lack of agreement among G8 countries in 1993 about whether the yen was too weak or about right.

A Second Endaka

As if one *endaka* were not enough, a second one hit in 1995, when the yen rose to ¥80.63 per dollar. Toyota announced that a one-point increase in the yen eliminated $111 million in dollar-denominated profits from their U.S. operations, and exporters were having a difficult time figuring out how to remain competitive in export markets. As they did with the first *endaka,* Japanese companies looked for ways to cut costs and remain competitive. During that period, the Japanese economy was in a recession, so the Bank of Japan dropped interest rates to stimulate demand, and the yen fell against the dollar, favoring exporters once again.

Competitive Pressures

During these decades of currency swings, Sony kept moving along as one of the premier companies in the world in consumer electronics, games, music, and movies. Its wide array of product innovations earned it a premium in the market; then competition began to step in. Korean companies like Samsung began to produce cheaper products that rose in quality as each year went by, and Samsung began to develop its own reputation for innovation in electronics. In addition, Samsung and other foreign competitors began setting up plants offshore, especially in China, to improve their cost advantage even more. Some of Sony's Japanese competitors, including Toshiba and Panasonic, reduced their exposure to a strong yen by moving plants overseas to countries like Indonesia and the Philippines and by increasing the dollar-based imports of parts.

From the beginning of 2003 until the end of 2004, the dollar continued to weaken against both the euro and the yen. In an attempt to strengthen the dollar, the Japanese central bank spent a record 20 trillion yen in 2003 and 10 trillion yen in the first two months of 2004. Despite such efforts, the yen rose 11 percent against the dollar in 2003 and continued to strengthen through 2004. The Japanese finance ministry stopped its foreign-exchange intervention in

March 2004, but the dollar's continued weakening against both the euro and the yen at the end of 2004 sparked new threats of intervention by the Japanese and Europeans.

Fast-Forward to 2008

The collapse in the housing market in the United States and the ensuing credit crisis in 2007, followed by the bankruptcy of Lehman Brothers and the U.S. government takeover of global insurer AIG in September 2008, had a devastating effect on the global economy. The U.S. stock market crashed, followed by similar crashes around the world, and investors pulled funds out of risky emerging markets and placed them in safe-haven assets. As a result, the euro dropped against the two major beneficiaries: The U.S. dollar and the Japanese yen. The Chinese yuan wasn't a factor because its currency is fixed against the dollar rather than flexible and subject to normal market forces.

Why did this happen? In the case of the U.S. dollar, the market reaction was a standard flight to safety—which often happens when global events get scary—even though the U.S. markets started the collapse. Political stability and the size of the economy tend to make the United States an attractive place for investment. Thus, the fear factor seemed to be a critical vote for the dollar during the crisis. This was a short-term phenomenon, however, and was eventually be replaced by economic fundamentals.

During the crisis, the dollar went up and down depending on what news was most important. When the crisis was the news, the dollar was strong. When the news favored a recovery of the U.S. economy, money flowed into equity markets in the United States and abroad, seeking higher returns and causing the dollar to drop in value. With the slowdown in the U.S. economy, export-dominated countries, especially emerging markets, were expected to suffer. Also, the credit crisis the U.S. was going through was expected to expand to other countries. One interesting effect of the crisis was that the euro tended to be very sensitive to the U.S. stock market. When the market was falling, so was the euro. When the market began to recover, so did the euro. The euro is obviously a strong and important currency, but it lacks a strong central government that can coordinate a response to economic crisis. The European Central Bank can influence interest rates, but that's about all.

What about the yen? Interestingly enough, the yen also became a safe-haven currency during the crisis, along with the dollar. Obviously, the yen is Asia's most important currency because Japan has the second-highest foreign-exchange reserves in the region and the world, just after China, and because it is a freely convertible currency with high market liquidity, as well as an important trading currency. Also, with Japanese interest rates so low, many investors were borrowing in yen and investing their proceeds abroad to get access to higher returns. When the crisis hit, the money quickly left the emerging markets and returned to Japan, a practice called *carry trade.* Whenever volatility in currency markets goes up, investors unwind (reverse) their trades; this gave strength to the yen.

The markets also demonstrated that the yen and U.S. stock market were inversely related. When markets are less risk-averse, stocks gain in value and the yen drops in value. When markets are more risk-averse, stock prices fall and the yen trades higher.

2011: The Year of Tragedy

The earthquake and tsunami that struck Japan on March 11, 2011 were devastating in terms of lives lost and overall human tragedy. In addition, there was a great deal of uncertainty over damage to nuclear reactors and disruption to the global supply chain. (Consider that Japanese factories produce about 25 percent of the world's semiconductors and 40 percent of electronic components, while Sony makes 10 percent of the world's laptop computer batteries.) Plants in affected areas were shut down due to property damage, power outages, and a transportation infrastructure that ground to a halt.

What happened to the Japanese yen during this crisis? Conventional wisdom would say that the yen fell against the dollar, but it actually rose in value. After the quake, there was a massive inflow of capital from the Japanese as they liquidated investments made with cheap Japanese money and invested in emerging markets where returns are high. In addition, many Japanese companies brought money back to the country at the end of the fiscal year (March 31), so the need for capital resulted in a tremendous inflow of it, causing the yen to rise in value.

What Does All This Mean to Sony?

In 2012, Sony generated 32.4 percent of its sales in Japan, 18.7 percent in the United States, 19.5 percent in Europe, and 29.4 percent elsewhere. Thus, the company was well diversified geographically, operating in some countries where the local currency was weaker and others where the local currency was stronger than the yen. Sony was also targeting the BRIC countries for future growth.

In addition to targeting global markets for sales, Sony was taking advantage of production outside of Japan. In the television division, for instance, the majority of LCD TVs for the Americas and Europe are produced in the factories in Tijuana, Mexico and Nitra, Slovakia. In the digital imaging division, Sony is moving some of its production of the DSLR camera from Japan to Thailand, where the photo of the cosplayer taking the picture with the Sony camera was shot.

One major effect of the strong yen and the global slowdown was the sharp drop in exports from Japan. In January 2009, for example, exports dropped 49 percent compared to a year earlier. As exporters found their sales falling, they cut orders from their suppliers, so there was a ripple effect in the Japanese economy, affecting both production and employment. These events caused a sharp contraction in Japan as GDP fell 12.1 percent in the fourth quarter of 2008 compared to a year earlier, and many experts felt that Japan was going through its worst recession since World War II. Deflation was also affecting the Japanese economy again, and consumers were delaying purchases hoping that prices would continue to fall, while companies were hesitant to invest more.

The strong yen was also hurting Sony's financial statements. As Sony translates U.S. dollar or euro financial statements into yen, net assets and earnings are worth less in yen, dragging down Sony's consolidated results. The only way to offset this drop is to sell more and improve profit margins, both of which are hard to do in a slow global economy. From a cash-flow point of view, Sony's operations abroad are remitting dividends back to Japan, but they are worth less yen as the dollar and euro weaken against it. One silver lining is that the purchasing power of the yen rises as it strengthens compared to other currencies, so everything Sony imports into Japan for its manufacturing is cheaper. The same would be true for anything manufactured outside Japan, thus reducing costs and hopefully increasing margins. As long as Sony is invoicing its exports in dollars to customers worldwide, it needs to match the dollar revenues with dollar expenses through investing more in the United States or in other countries in Asia, like Taiwan, where components such as flat panel displays are cheaper and where Sony can invoice its purchases in dollars.

The 2011 earthquake and tsunami also affected Sony's results. The company announced that the devastation probably helped push them to a $3.2 billion loss for the March 31 fiscal year—just one of many Japanese manufacturers that reported substantial losses from the disaster. Nine of Sony's plants in northeastern Japan were damaged, supply chains were disrupted, and a drop in domestic demand did not bode well for Sony that year. Coupled with the overall slowdown in the global economy, especially in the U.S. and debt-ridden Europe, demand for Sony products was not forecast to grow.

A Reversal of Fortunes - Abenomics Just when things looked bleak due to the strong yen and weak demand in Europe and China, Japan elected a new Prime Minister in November 2012, Shinzo Abe, who decided to fight deflation at home and a weak domestic economy through loose monetary, fiscal, and structural policies. For most of 2012, the yen had been trading below ¥80/US $, but by the end of 2012 it was trading at 85.96; by May 6, 2013, it was at 99.10 and falling. At the end of the first quarter of 2013, Sony doubled its annual profit estimates due partly to the falling yen.

If the strong yen made it difficult for exporters to sell abroad and weakened foreign earnings, the weak yen was just the opposite. Exporters like Sony, Toyota, and Panasonic were ecstatic about the weaker yen (which had fallen by more than 20 percent since Abe took office) and the opportunity to expand their sales abroad. The full extent of their ability to take advantage of the weaker yen still depended on economic recovery in the U.S., Europe, and China, but at least the currency wasn't an additional weight on their competitive position.

QUESTIONS

9-3. What were the major factors that led to the drop in Sony's exports from Japan?

9-4. In what other ways has the strong yen affected Sony's bottom line? What would be the effect of a weak yen?

9-5. Why do you think it is important for Sony to manufacture more products in the United States and Europe and to also buy more from suppliers in other countries in Asia?

9-6. What are the major forces that affected the Japanese yen over the years? What factors do you think are important to monitor as you try to forecast what will happen to the value of the yen in the future?

SUMMARY

- The International Monetary Fund (IMF) was organized in 1945 to promote international monetary cooperation, facilitate the expansion and balanced growth of international trade, promote exchange-rate stability, establish a multilateral system of payments, and make its resources available to those members who are experiencing balance-of-payments difficulties.
- The special drawing right (SDR) is a special asset the IMF created to increase international reserves.
- The IMF started out with fixed exchange rates but now allows countries to choose how fixed or flexible they want their exchange rates to be.
- The euro is a common currency in Europe that has been adopted by 12 of the first 15 members of the EU, and was adopted by 16 total countries by mid-2013, with other new EU members working to meet the convergence criteria.
- The Chinese yuan is poised to be one of the most influential currencies in the world as China strengthens its institutions and the regulatory structure and trading capacity of its banks and other financial institutions.
- African countries are committed to establishing a common currency by 2021, but many obstacles may prevent them from accomplishing this objective.
- Currencies that float freely respond to supply and demand conditions free from government intervention. The demand for a country's currency is a function of the demand for its goods and services and for financial assets denominated in its currency.
- Fixed exchange rates do not automatically change in value due to supply and demand conditions, but are regulated by their central banks.
- Central banks are the key institutions in countries that intervene in foreign-exchange markets to influence currency values.
- The Bank for International Settlements (BIS) in Switzerland acts as a central banker's bank. It facilitates communication and transactions among the world's central banks.
- A central bank intervenes in money markets by increasing a supply of its country's currency when it wants to push down the value and by stimulating demand for the currency when it wants the value to rise.
- Many countries that strictly control and regulate the convertibility of their currencies have a black market that maintains an exchange rate more indicative of supply and demand than the official rate.
- Fully convertible currencies, often called *hard currencies,* are those that the government allows both residents and nonresidents to purchase in unlimited amounts.
- Currencies that are not fully convertible are often called *soft* or *weak currencies.* They tend to be the currencies of developing countries.
- To conserve scarce foreign exchange, some governments impose exchange restrictions—such as import licensing, multiple exchange rates, import deposit requirements, and quantity controls—on companies or individuals who want to exchange money.
- Some factors that determine exchange rates are purchasing power parity (relative rates of inflation), differences in real interest rates (nominal interest rates reduced by the amount of inflation), confidence in the government's ability to manage the political and economic environment, and certain technical factors that result from trading.

KEY TERMS

advance import deposit (p. 390)
black market (p. 389)
Bretton Woods Agreement (p. 375)
European Central Bank (ECB) (p. 382)
European Monetary System (EMS) (p. 382)
European Monetary Union (EMU) (p. 382)
Fisher Effect (p. 394)
fundamental forecasting (p. 396)
hard currency (p. 390)
International Fisher Effect (IFE) (p. 395)
International Monetary Fund (IMF) (p. 374)
Jamaica Agreement (p. 377)
multiple exchange-rate system (p. 390)
par value (p. 375)
purchasing power parity (PPP) (p. 391)
quota (p. 375)
Smithsonian Agreement (p. 377)
soft (or weak) currency (p. 390)
special drawing right (SDR) (p. 375)
technical forecasting (p. 396)

ENDNOTES

1 ***Sources include the following:*** Andrew Swiston, "Official Dollarization as a Monetary Regime: Its Effects on El Salvador," *IMF Working Paper* (June 2011): 22-23; "El Salvador Learns to Love the Greenback," *The Economist* (September 26, 2002): 62; John Lyons, "Squeezed by Dollarization," *Wall Street Journal* (March 8, 2005): A18; Bureau of Economic and Business Affairs, U.S. Department of State, "2001 Country Reports on Economic Policy and Trade Practices" (February 2002), at www.state.gov/documents/ organization/8202.pdf (accessed May 30, 2005); U.S. Department of State, "Background Note—El Salvador," at www.state.gov/r/pa/ei/bgn/2033.htm (accessed May 30, 2005); U.S. Department of State, "Background Note—Ecuador," www.state.gov/r/pa/ei/bgn/35761.htm (accessed May 30, 2005); Juan Forero, "Ecuador's President Vows to Ride Out Crisis over Judges," *New York Times* (April 18, 2005): A12. "El Salvador Trade Profile," at www.wto.org (accessed May 6, 2013).

2 International Monetary Fund, "IMF Chronology," at imf.org/external/np/exr/chron/chron.asp (accessed August 22, 2007).

3 IMF, "History" at www.imf.org/external/about/history.htm (accessed June 17, 2013).

4 IMF, "Overview: What Do We Do?" at imforg/external/about/overview.htm (accessed June 17, 2013).

5 IMF, "International Monetary Fund Factsheet: IMF Quotas," www.imf.org/external/np/exr/facts/quotas.htm (accessed June 17, 2013).

6 IMF, "Currency Amounts in New Special Drawing Rights (SDR) Basket," www.imf.org/external/np/tre/sdr/sdrbasket.htm (accessed June 17, 2013).

7 Thomas Catan and Ian Talley, "IMF Renews Push Against Austerity," *The Wall Street Journal,* (April 16, 2013), online edition.

8 International Monetary Fund, " IMF's Response to the Global Economic Crisis," March 29, 2013, www.imf.org/external/np/exr/facts/changing.htm (accessed June 17, 2013).

9 International Monetary Fund, *Annual Report on Exchange Arrangements and Exchange Restrictions* (Washington, D.C., IMF, 2012): Appendix 1.

10 See Mercedes Garcia-Escribano and Sebastián Sosa, "What is Driving Financial De-dollarization in Latin America," *IMF Working Paper* (January 2011): 1–23; Guillermo A. Calvo and Carmen M. Reinhart, "Capital Flow Reversals, the Exchange Rate Debate, and Dollarization," *Finance & Development* 36:3 (1999): 13; "No More Peso?" *The Economist* (January 23, 1999): 69; Steve H. Hanke, "How to Make the Dollar Argentina's Currency," *Wall Street Journal* (February 19, 1999): A19; Michael M. Phillips, "U.S. Officials Urge Cautious Approach to Dollarization by Foreign Countries," *Wall Street Journal* (April 23, 1999): A4; "A Decline without Parallel," *The Economist* (February 28, 2002), www.economist.com.

11 Craig Torres, "Chile Suspends Trading Band on Its Peso," *Wall Street Journal* (September 7, 1999): A21; "IMF Welcomes Flotation of Iceland's Krona," *IMF News Brief,* www.imf.org/external/np/sec/nb/2001/nb0129.htm (accessed March 28, 2001).

12 "Convergence Criteria for European Monetary Union," *Bloomberg News,* www.bloomberg.com (accessed August 9, 2002).

13 "Prime Minister Says Sweden Fulfills Criteria to Adopt Euro," *Dow Jones Newswires* (August 19, 2002), www.wsj.com (accessed August 19, 2002).

14 Christopher Rhoads and G. Thomas Sims, "Rising Deficits in Europe Give Euro Its Toughest Challenge Yet," *Wall Street Journal* (September 15, 2003): A1.

15 Edmund L. Andrews, "On Euro Weekend, Financial Institutions in Vast Reprogramming," *New York Times* (January 2, 1999), www.nytimes.com (accessed October 12, 2009).

16 Paul Masson and Catherine Patillo, "A Single Currency for Africa?" *Finance & Development* (December 2004): 9–15; "History of the CFA Franc," at www.bceao.int/internet/bcweb.nsf/pages/umuse1 (accessed May 30, 2005); IMF, "The Fabric of Reform—An IMF Video," at www.imf.org/external/pubs/ft/fabric/ backgrnd.htm (accessed May 30, 2005).

17 Though initially pegged to the French franc, the peg shifted to the euro in 1999 when France adopted it as its currency. All of the countries in the CFA franc zone are former colonies of France and maintain French as the official language, except for Guinea-Bissau and Equatorial Guinea, which were ruled by Portugal and Spain, respectively.

18 Isaac Imaka, "East Africans to Wait for 10 Years to Get Common Currency, Officials Say," (June 18, 2013), www.monitor.co.ug/News/National/East-Africans-to-wait-for-10-years--to-get-common/-/688334/1864310/-/sg6wfrz/-/index.html (accessed June 18, 2013).

19 "Operating Policy," at www.ny.frb.org/markets/foreignex.html (accessed July 1, 2011).

20 International Monetary Fund, "Currency Composition of Official Foreign Exchange Reserves (COFER)," www.imf.org/external/np/sta/cofer/eng/cofer.pdf (accessed March 29, 2013).

21 Joanna Slater and John Lyons, "Emerging Markets Lose a Little of Their Resilience—Now Face Stress Test," *Wall Street Journal* (July 17, 2007): C1.

22 www.cia.gov/library/publications/the-world-factbook/rankorder/2188rank.html (accessed March 29, 2013).

23 Sam Y. Cross, *All about the Foreign Exchange Market in the United States* (New York: Federal Bank of New York, 2002): 92–93.

24 Jon Hilsenbrath and Brian Blackstone, "Inside the Risky Bets of Central Banks," *The Wall Street Journal* (December 12, 2012): A1.

25 Paul Evans, "Dollar Climbs Back on Rivals," *Wall Street Journal* (March 11, 2009): C14.

26 Bank for International Settlements, "About BIS: Organisation and Governance," at www.bis.org/about/orggov.htm (updated 19 December 2011 and accessed May 17, 2013).

27 Sheridan Prasso, "Zimbabwe's Disposable Currency," *Fortune* (August 6, 2007), CNNMoney.com (accessed August 25, 2007).

28 Patrick McGroarty and Farai Mutsaka, "How to Turn 100 Trillion Dollars into Five and Feel Good About It," *The Wall Street Journal* (May 11, 2011), online edition.

29 "Sri Lanka Relaxes Foreign Exchange Controls," *Lanka Business Online* (June 18, 2013).

30 Benedict Mander,"Exchange Rate Irks Venezuela," *Financial Times* (April 30, 2010): 20; Corina Pons and Charlie Devereaux,"Venezuela to Create new Parallel Exchange Rate, Ramirez Says," Bloomberg.com (accessed March 13, 2013).

31 Natalia T. Tamirisa,"Exchange and Capital Controls as Barriers to Trade," *IMF Staff Papers* 46:1 (1999): 69.

32 "The Big Mac Index," *The Economist* (January 31, 2013), economist.com/bigmac; "The Big Mac Index: Bunfight," *The Economist* (February 2, 2013): 60.

33 "The Big Mac Index: Food for Thought," *The Economist* (May 27, 2004): 75; quoting Michael Pakko and Patricia Polland, "For Here or to Go? Purchasing Power Parity and the Big Mac" (St. Louis, MO: Federal Reserve Bank of St. Louis, January 1996).

34 "The Big Mac Index (an interactive currency-comparison tool)," www.economist.com/content/big-mac-index (accessed May 28, 2013); Ira Iosebashvili,"Countries' Heated Rhetoric Points Out Lack of a Universal Measuring Stick," *The New York Times* (February 22, 2013): A12.

35 Clare Connaghan, "Flight to Safety Gathers Pace in Bond, Currency Markets After Bernanke," *The Wall Street Journal* (May 23, 2013), online edition.

36 "Forecasting Currencies: Technical or Fundamental?" *Business International Money Report* (October 15, 1990): 401–02.

37 See Ian H. Giddy and Gunter Dufey,"The Random Behavior of Flexible Exchange Rates: Implications for Forecasting," *Journal of International Business Studies* 6:1 (1975): 1–32; Christopher J. Neely and Lucio Sarno, "How Well Do Monetary Fundamentals Forecast Exchange Rates?" *St. Louis Fed* (September/October 2002), 51–74, on www.research.stlouisfed.org/publications/review/ 02/09/51-74Neely.pdf (accessed October 8, 2009).

38 Andrew C. Pollock and Mary E. Wilkie,"Briefing," *Euromoney* (June 1991): 123–24.

39 David A. Moss, *A Concise Guide to Macro Economics* (Boston: Harvard Business School Press, 2007): 131.

40 Cross, *All about the Foreign Exchange Market*, 114.

41 Sudeep Jain and Debiprasasd Nayak,"Rupee Fall Hits India's Small Importers," *The Wall Street Journal* [India] (June 18, 2013), online edition.

42 Yajun Zhang,"Stronger Yuan to Hit China Exports – Commerce Ministry," *The Wall Street Journal* (June 18, 2013).

43 Oscar Suris,"BMW Expects U.S.-Made Cars to Have 80% Level of North American Content," *Wall Street Journal* (August 5, 1993): A2.

44 "GM Hit by Foreign Exchange," *CFO Journal* (May 2, 2013).

45 Wild, J.J. and Wild, K.L. (2013), *International Business: The Challenges of Globalization*, 7th Edition, Global Edition, Pearson Education.

46 Cavusgil, S.T., Knight, G. and Riesenberger, J.R. (2014), *International Business: The New Realities*, 3rd Edition, Global Edition, Pearson Education.

47 Williamson, J. (1998),"Crawling Bands or MonitoringBands: How to Manage Exchange Rates in a World of Capital Mobility", *International Finance*, Vol. 1(1), pp. 59–79.

48 Mihov, I. (2013),"The Exchange Rate as an Instrument of Monetary Policy", Special Feature A, *Macroeconomic Review April 2013*, Monetary Authority of Singapore.

49 See, MAS (2001)"Singapore's Exchange Rate Policy" on www.mas.gov.sg/about-mas/monographs-and-information-papers/monographs/2001/singapore-exchange-rate-policy.aspx

50 ***Sources include the following:*** Hiroko Tabuchi,"Weaker Yen Helps Sony Raise Its Profit Outlook," *The Wall Street Journal* (April 26, 2013): B6; Mayumi Negishi and Daniel Inman,"Falling Yen Sets Stage for Windfall," *The Wall Street Journal* (April 24, 2013): B6; Thomas Black, "Now, A Weak Link in The Global Supply Chain," *Businessweek* (March 21-27, 2011): 18; Hiroko Tabuchi,"Sony Warns of a Loss From Quake," *The Wall Street Journal* (May 24, 2011) online edition; Jamie McGeever, "Dollar Gets Battered across the Board," *Wall Street Journal* (December 9, 2003): C17; Sebastian Moffett,"Japan's Yen Strategy Offers Economic Relief," *Wall Street Journal* (January 12, 2004): A2; Miyako Takebe, "Japan Plans to Keep Intervening in Markets to Hold Down the Yen," *Wall Street Journal* (March 17, 2004): B4E; Alan Beattie,"Japan and ECB Consider Joint Currency Move as Dollar Falls," *Financial Times* (December 2, 2004): 11; Sony 2008 Annual Report; Robert Flint,"Yen Gains on Dollar, Europe in Flight from Risk," *Wall Street Journal* (January 13, 2009): C2; Joanna Slater, Yuka Hayashi, and Peter Stein,"Move to Stem Yen's Rise Is Likely," *Wall Street Journal* (October 28, 2008): C1; Stanley Reed,"What's Driving Up the Dollar," *Businessweek* (December 8, 2008): 38; John Murphy and Hiroko Tabuchi,"Japan's Companies, Consumers, React to New Reality," *Wall Street Journal* (October 29, 2008): A13; John Murphy,"Toyota's Global Woes Start to Hit Home in Japan," *Wall Street Journal* (November 4, 2008): A10; Yumiko Ono and Andrew Monahan,"Japan Exports Fall 49% as U.S. Trade Plunges," *Wall Street Journal* (March 26, 2009): A7; John Murphy, Peter Stein, and Neil Shah,"Dollar Vexes Asian Central Banks," *Wall Street Journal* (May 26, 2009): C1.

CHAPTER 10
Global Debt and Equity Markets

OBJECTIVES

After studying this chapter, you should be able to

1. Describe the finance function and how it fits in the MNE's organizational structure
2. Show how capital structure varies internationally
3. Describe the different ways to access debt internationally
4. Show how companies can raise capital on stock markets outside their home countries
5. Highlight tax issues facing MNEs

MyManagementLab®
Improve Your Grade!
When you see this icon ✪, visit **www.mymanagementlab.com** for activities that are applied, personalized, and offer immediate feedback.

Source: © sergey_p - Fotolia.com

To have money is a good thing; to have a say over the money is even better.

—Yiddish proverb

CASE

GPS: In the Market for an Effective Hedging Strategy?

On April 10, 2000, U.S.-based firms Wells Fargo & Company and First Security Corporation announced that they had signed a merger agreement involving their banks in San Francisco and Salt Lake City, respectively.[1] Both banks, located in the West, were clearly positioning themselves to compete with each other, especially in the Utah market, which is composed of individuals, small businesses, middle-market businesses, farmers, ranchers, and a few large corporate customers. Wells Fargo was operating in 22 states, First Security in seven. Given the overlapping markets and client demographics, it was clear that services were to be consolidated over the next several months.

First Security Bank had three key personnel in the international banking area: Ryan Gibbons, VP and manager of the Foreign Exchange Department; Jason Langston, who had recently been promoted to VP and foreign-exchange trader; and Ali Manbeian, who had become VP and trade products manager in the International Banking Division. All three had significant experience in international banking, and First Security had a trading room where they could provide foreign exchange services and trade-related collections and payments for clients. With the merger, however, many of the more interesting businesses shifted to San Francisco, and the three could see the writing on the wall.

THE START-UP OF GPS

In 2002, with the help of some key investors, Manbeian, Langston, and Gibbons formed GPS Capital Markets Inc. Realizing there was a niche market in foreign exchange that was no longer being served in the Intermountain West, they struck out on their own with a business model they believed could be successful.

Bringing investors on board, particularly their large clients and brokers, was essential to their success because they needed the necessary credit backing and reputation to enter the wholesale market. Jason Langston noted that "90 percent of the transactions [we've] done in the past wouldn't have happened without these credible investors." However, GPS has been able to move beyond the help of its initial investors due to a strong working capital position.

TARGET MARKET AND CLIENT STRATEGY

To compete effectively in the market, GPS initially decided to target small and medium-sized companies (SMEs) and focus on serving those that had significant foreign-exchange needs, but not their own foreign-exchange team. With this in mind, they started out by providing the regular services that

GPS Capital Markets, Inc. headquartered near Salt Lake City, Utah, uses global capital markets to provide foreign exchange services to clients ranging from small to Fortune 500. It also recently opened an office in London to service clients in Europe as well as help its U.S.-based clients operate more effectively in Europe.

Source: GPS Capital Markets, Inc.

commercial banks offer, believing that their expertise and low overhead would help them outbid the larger banks for their business. At first, they offered traditional inbound and outbound payments—areas in which they excelled at First Security Bank. Such payments are the basic needs of firms that are going to receive or are required to pay invoices in a different currency.

GPS, however, was finding it difficult to obtain clients. The first choice for most companies when it comes to foreign exchange is to use their commercial bank with which they already have a good relationship and which provides traditional banking services, including inbound and outbound payments. GPS financial advisers have overcome this obstacle with their competitors by visiting potential clients personally and building an open and transparent relationship. Travel to New York, Los Angeles, and other cities outside the Rocky Mountain region makes this more expensive, of course, but it has paid off because the advisers have developed relationships and obtained new clients. Some competitive advantages GPS has over the commercial banks are lower transaction costs, 100 percent transparency, and customizing solutions to satisfy customer needs.

Commercial banks have so many different departments and services that the foreign-exchange transactions tend to be more expensive in order to meet the overhead. Also, the banks look at foreign exchange as a potential area for earning a lot of money, so they price aggressively to build their profits. GPS is smaller and more specialized in the foreign-exchange market, so it can keep its costs low and pass on lower prices to companies.

Until the Internet brought more transparency to foreign-exchange markets, companies often didn't know how much banks or brokers were making on foreign-exchange transactions. GPS has adopted complete transparency with its clients, disclosing to them how much it will make on the deal (something the commercial banks hesitate to do). By showing clients the value-added services it is providing, GPS can justify its profits and not hesitate to disclose its model.

While big banks tend to want to sell standardized services—one size fits all—GPS tries to focus on satisfying the foreign-exchange needs of its clients individually. Its managers sit down with the clients to discuss needs and strategies and come up with innovative solutions that result in more satisfactory foreign-exchange transactions. These strategies appear to be working because GPS has grown significantly since its inception.

Thomson Reuters and Bloomberg play an important role in the business of GPS, with their powerful analytical tools, market information, real-time pricing, and a trading platform. In addition, the services are essential for trying to price more complex foreign-exchange products such as options. Despite the high cost of subscribing to these services, GPS decided to go with both. In fact, the three partners have different preferences as to which service they like the best, which has generated a friendly rivalry over the merits of Reuters versus Bloomberg.

CONCEPT CHECK

We're concerned in this chapter with the *financial* aspects of MNE operations—in particular, with the ways in which MNEs gain access to *capital* in both local and global markets. Recall, however, our introduction of such global information providers as Reuters and Bloomberg in Chapter 8 where we refer to their role in furnishing *money center banks* with the data about **foreign exchange** that the banks pass on to client MNEs. Here, we hasten to reaffirm the importance of information and information flows in making not only **exchange-rate** transactions but a vast range of other decisions as well.

FUTURE CHALLENGES

Although GPS has never lost a client to another competitor, the future holds a number of challenges. The first is services. If GPS had stuck with its initial goal of providing traditional foreign-exchange services, it would have opened itself up to significant competition with the banks and other market entrants, such as boutique firms that can focus only on the payments side in the SME market. So the key was to find ways to move clientele upstream with other value-added services, while the problem was to decide what areas to enter and where to find the expertise.

A second risk has to do with its target market. Given the merger and acquisition activity in the United States, could GPS continue to maintain its client base, or would its clients get bought out by larger firms, just as Wells Fargo snapped up First Security? If that were to happen, GPS would have to figure out how to sell its expertise to larger clients who had no experience or track record with them.

A third risk is the potential of unfavorable new regulations. The regulatory environment of the foreign-exchange trade is intense and changes frequently, both in the U.S and abroad. The Dodd-Frank Wall Street Reform and Consumer Protection Act was signed into law in the U.S. on July 21, 2010, with potentially significant ramifications to GPS's business in the foreign currency derivatives market. Among other things, the Dodd-Frank Act established a Financial Stability Oversight Council with the power to regulate non-bank financial companies in areas such as improved transparency and accountability for trading in derivatives. Although Dodd-Frank affects who can engage in the business, a key issue is the onerous reporting requirements.

THE GLOBAL FINANCIAL CRISIS: CHALLENGES AND OPPORTUNITIES

When the global economic crisis hit in 2008, it became obvious that *counterparty risk* was a real issue: the risk that the other party to an agreement—in this case, a money center bank entering into a foreign-exchange agreement—might default. Many of GPS's clients or potential clients became nervous as one major money center bank after another ran into problems in late 2008. Because GPS was on sound financial footing, many companies flocked to it to handle their foreign-exchange transactions, which caused a large spike in activity. In addition, GPS's lower rates were more attractive. As the global economy began to contract, investors realized how important it was to squeeze out any savings they could, which played right into the hands of GPS.

Just as the crisis dropped a lot of business in GPS's lap, the government bailout took it right back. As soon as the U.S. Fed decided to bail out the banks and reduce the counterparty risk, many of GPS's new clients realized that they needed to go back to the banks, given how tight credit was. GPS was, however, able to retain some of them.

EXPANDED SERVICES: A KEY TO FUTURE GROWTH

As Langston, Gibbons, and Manbeian looked at their business, they realized that the key to their future was to develop a broader base of services to their clients. So they decided to focus on their strength—corporate foreign exchange—and provide expanded services in global business risk management. The general idea of trading currencies to satisfy their initial core business of import and export transactions was simple. Some transactions went beyond exports and imports and involved derivatives to protect against future risks. With their connection to Bloomberg and Reuters, they had the capabilities necessary to enter into any transaction the client needed.

Then, as they began to work with SME companies with operations around the world, they realized that many of these companies were spending a lot of money making trades. Analyzing the cash flows in different currencies, it was easy to see that as their clients' markets and the currencies in which they operated increased, they had to enter into more and more foreign-exchange transactions.

One client, a large technology firm, was expanding internationally so rapidly that the growth was straining the capabilities of its finances to keep up. With hundreds of currency pairs and financial statements being generated in many different currencies and using several different functional currencies, the client was having a difficult time keeping on top of the complexities. GPS realized it could save its client a lot of money by netting its transactions. Instead of having each entity around the world settle its transactions with every other entity, GPS helped the firm set up a system that could reduce the number of times it had to exchange currency. By doing that, it reduced the costs of each transaction—an important source of revenue to the client's bank.

FXpert

GPS developed proprietary software called FXpert to help its clients monitor foreign-exchange flows and determine how to save money on transactions. After identifying the timing and nature of the cash flows through a specialized audit, a GPS financial adviser proposes an effective hedging solution that GPS can provide. The solution might be as simple as reducing the number of foreign-currency transactions or as complex as hedging some of the exposures using forwards, options, or futures contracts.

The global risk-management business also offers foreign accounts receivable reviews, worldwide business consultation on finance methods, dispute resolution in solving payment disputes, international loan packaging, and letters of credit. As it has developed these services, GPS has had to expand its expertise base to include an understanding of complex accounting rules on derivatives, complex financial hedging strategies, and software development.

ADDITIONAL STRATEGIC MOVES

Given the risky foreign-exchange environment, GPS has shifted some of its efforts to work as an agent or broker with clients' banks instead of being the direct counterparty in foreign-exchange transactions. This allows it to do what it does best: use its proprietary software to find business solutions for clients to reduce foreign-exchange risks and lower the costs of trading foreign exchange. With its knowledge of the markets, GPS is able to negotiate with clients' banks to get the best possible exchange rate on a transaction and earn a little in the process.

In addition to technical expertise, GPS has developed a solid marketing strategy, continuing to focus on SMEs while expanding its client base by setting up regional offices in Los Angeles, Phoenix, Dallas, and Boston. Recently, it opened an office in London and received regulatory approval to operate there. That has opened up significant opportunities for GPS in the UK and the rest of Europe. Not only can it pick up new customers in Europe, it can also represent U.S. clients in Europe more effectively.

As GPS expands in the United States and London, it must constantly refine its message. From a sales point of view, its managers need to make sure they understand what CFOs and treasurers need to know about the firm and what it has to offer. And they need to figure that out for the different regulatory environments in which GPS operates. In London they face competition that only offers traditional payments clearance, but it is nevertheless difficult even to get an audience with CFOs to explain how they can help in ways that go way beyond payments clearances and involve risk management in global capital markets.

Finally, a key aspect of GPS's success is its proprietary software. Given the rapidly changing market and the need to constantly upgrade the quality of its offerings, GPS needs to bring its software development in-house. That involves higher costs but also results in a better product, and it is essential to control the speed and quality of innovation. Foreign-exchange exposure has provided lots of opportunities, and now GPS needs to keep pushing ahead with its competitive advantage in global capital markets. ■

QUESTIONS

10-1. What is the unique market niche for GPS, and what does it have to offer compared to larger banks and other financial institutions?

10-2. What do you think are the major obstacles to success for GPS in Europe?

INTRODUCTION

To succeed internationally, MNEs must have access to capital markets in different countries to finance expansion. Indeed, finance is integral to firms' international strategies. The small company involved in international business only tangentially may not be concerned about global capital markets, but it will probably still have to deal in foreign exchange through its commercial bank to settle payments for exports and imports. However, the MNE investing and operating abroad is usually concerned about access to capital in local markets as well as in large global markets.

This chapter examines external sources of debt and equity capital available to MNEs as well as how companies use tax haven countries to minimize tax liabilities and provide more internally generated cash to fund innovation and expansion, much to the chagrin of governments worldwide.

THE FINANCE FUNCTION

In order to give some strategic context to global capital markets and how companies can use them to access capital, let's discuss who in the company is responsible for acquiring and managing capital. A key member of the management team is the chief financial officer (CFO)—the one with the most important global finance-related responsibilities. Figure 10.1 illustrates how the responsibilities of the CFO, controller, and treasurer fit into a firm's organizational structure and especially how global financial management fits into the overall finance function, which focuses on short- and long-term cash flows. The role of financial management is to maintain and create economic value or wealth by maximizing shareholder wealth—the market value of existing shareholders' common stock.[2] The management activities related to cash flows can be divided into four major areas:

The corporate finance function acquires and allocates financial resources among the company's activities and projects. The key functions are

- Make financing decisions,
- Make investment decisions,
- Manage short-term capital needs.

- Make financing decisions—especially regarding capital structure (the proper mix of debt and equity) and long-term financing (selecting, issuing, and managing long-term debt and equity capital, including location—home country or elsewhere—and currency—home or foreign)
- Make investment decisions—typically in the context of capital budgeting, which will be discussed in Chapter 19
- Manage short-term capital needs (which will be discussed in Chapter 19)—managing the MNE's currency assets and liabilities (cash, receivables, marketable securities, inventory, trade receivables and payables, and short-term bank debt)

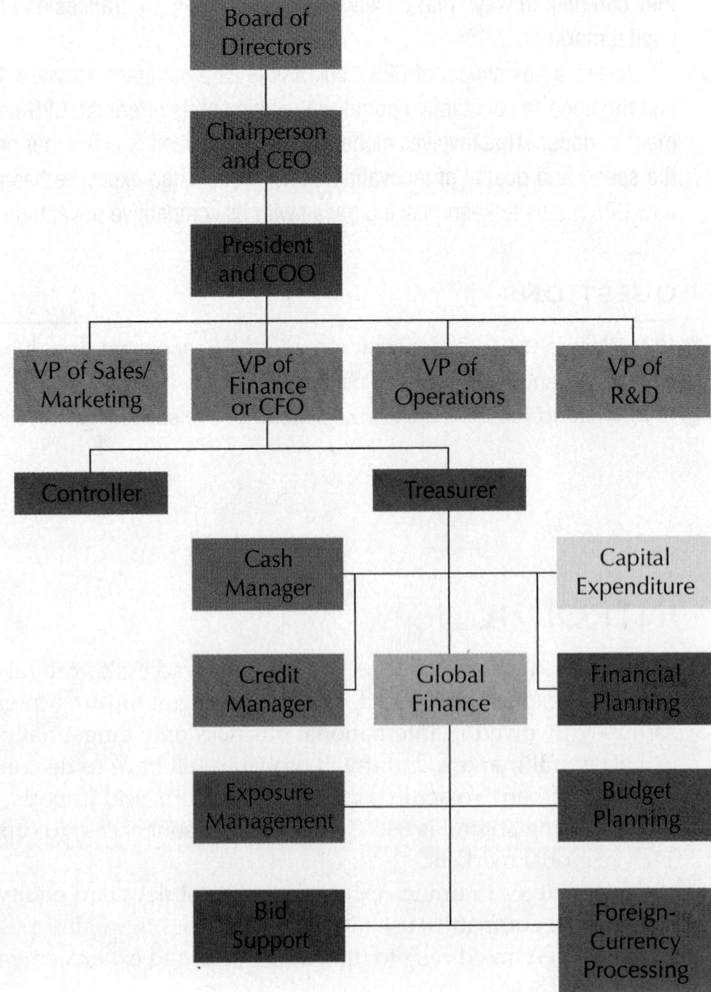

FIGURE 10.1 The Role of Treasurer in the Financial Function

As a chief accounting officer, the *controller* evaluates the financial results of business operations (see Chapter 19). The *treasurer* writes the checks—or, more precisely, controls the company's cash payments. The treasurer's department handles both domestic and foreign financial functions, including cash and exposure management, capital expenditure, and foreign-currency processing.

In addition, we will examine how taxes affect the flow of capital and give rise to offshore financial centers or tax haven countries.

THE ROLE OF THE CFO

The CFO acquires financial resources—that is, he or she generates funds either internally or from external sources at the lowest possible cost—and allocates them among the company's activities and projects. For instance, when GPS began, the founders needed outside investors with significant resources to fund the start-up as well as lend credibility to potential clients. Then it shifted to internally generated cash to fund operations. Allocating resources (investing) means increasing stockholders' wealth through the allocation of funds to different projects and investment opportunities.

CONCEPT CHECK

It's worthwhile to make a quick comparison between Figure 10.1 and Figure 19.2, which focuses on the twofold responsibility of the company *controller*—overseeing activities in both accounting and financial management. Here we focus on the responsibilities of the *treasurer*—controlling the company's cash payments and the related financial functions, both domestic and foreign. As both figures show, the functions of the two offices fall under the overall responsibility of the CFO (or VP of Finance).

The CFO's Global Perspective The CFO's job is more complex in a global environment than in the domestic setting because of such forces as foreign-exchange risk, currency flows and restrictions, political risk, different tax rates and laws determining taxable income, and regulations on access to capital in different markets. The rest of this chapter examines the following areas:

1. Overall capital structure
2. Global capital markets
3. Taxation of foreign-source income and influence on capital markets
4. Offshore financing, offshore financial centers, and tax havens

CAPITAL STRUCTURE

A CFO must determine the company's proper mix between long-term debt and equity—in other words, its *capital structure*. Many companies start off with an initial investment and then grow through internally generated funds. However, when those sources are inadequate to fund continued growth into new markets, the CFO's office must decide the proper debt/equity mix.

LEVERAGING DEBT FINANCING

Leverage—the degree to which a firm funds the growth of business by debt.

The degree to which a firm funds the growth of business by debt is known as **leverage**. The degree to which companies use leverage instead of *equity capital*—known as stocks or shares—varies throughout the world. Country-specific factors are a more essential determinant of a firm's capital structure than any others because a firm tends to follow the financing trends in its own country and within its particular industry there. Leveraging is often perceived as the most cost-effective route to capitalization because the interest that companies pay on debt is a tax-deductible expense in most countries, whereas the dividends paid to investors are not.

When Is Leveraging *Not* the Best Option? Leveraging is not always the best approach in all countries, for two major reasons. First, excessive reliance on long-term debt raises financial risk and thus requires a higher return for investors. This was very evident in Europe during the global financial crisis as companies and governments tried to raise capital through bond issues, and they either had to offer high interest rates to attract investors, or they had difficulty getting any investors at all. Second, foreign subsidiaries of an MNE may have limited access to local capital markets, making it difficult for the MNE to rely on debt to fund asset acquisition.[3]

TABLE 10.1 Selected Capital Structures, FY 2012

	2010		2012	
Country	**Debt-Asset (%)**	**Equity-Asset (%)**	**Debt-Asset (%)**	**Equity-Asset (%)**
Brazil	58.3	41.7	0.80	0.20
Japan	42.4	57.6	0.56	0.44
UK	49.9	50.1	0.54	0.46
USA	57.4	42.6	0.55	0.45
France	58.6	41.4	0.58	0.42
Germany	54.5	45.5	0.53	0.47
Mexico	51.7	48.3	0.57	0.43

Source: Based on data collected by Compustat Global; available at www.wrds.wharton.upenn.edu (accessed June 10, 2013).

Table 10.1 shows the debt-to-asset and equity-to-asset ratios for a large sample of firms in a selected group of countries. Data for 2010 and 2012 are included for the purposes of comparison. Note the relatively higher reliance on debt financing by Brazilian, Japanese, and, to a lesser extent, British and Mexican companies in 2012 relative to 2010. But Brazilian companies had much higher reliance on debt than the other countries in the sample. In many emerging markets, wealth is usually concentrated in families, so even though there appears to be a heavy reliance on equity, there may be only a few shareholders. In contrast, shares of stock are broadly held in countries such as the United States and the United Kingdom. Although research has confirmed that country-specific factors are important determinants of firms' capital structure,[4] broader macroeconomic forces can influence the mix of debt to equity in funding the business. This occurred from 2007 to 2012 when companies that had been highly leveraged tried to reduce the amount of leverage and focus more on equity funding than debt funding due to the financial risks of the period.

FACTORS AFFECTING THE CHOICE OF CAPITAL STRUCTURE

Choice of capital structure depends on tax rates, degree of development of local equity markets, and creditor rights.

Many factors influence the choice of an MNE's capital structure, both within a country and with affiliates in different countries. These include local tax rates, the degree of development of local equity markets, and creditor rights. One study of the capital structure of U.S.-based MNEs' foreign affiliates found that local tax rates influenced the debt-to-equity ratios. Although the firm as a whole might have a debt-to-equity ratio based on U.S. capital-market expectations, its foreign affiliates have to be sensitive to local conditions. The study noted:

> Ten percent higher local tax rates are associated with 2.8 percent higher debt/asset ratios, with internal borrowing particularly sensitive to taxes. Multinational affiliates are financed with less external debt in countries with underdeveloped capital markets or weak creditor rights, reflecting significantly higher local borrowing costs. Instrumental variable analysis indicates that greater borrowing from parent companies substitutes for three-quarters of reduced external borrowing induced by capital market conditions. Multinational firms appear to employ internal capital markets opportunistically to overcome imperfections in external capital markets.[5]

In addition, different tax rates, dividend remission policies, and exchange controls may cause a company to rely more on debt in some situations and more on equity in others. Understand that the different debt and equity markets discussed in this chapter have different levels of importance for companies worldwide.

A major cause of the Asian financial crisis of 1997 was excessive dollar bank debt. The crisis of 2010 and 2011 was due more to sovereign liquidity than exchange rate risk.

Debt and Exchange Rates As with the Asian financial crisis of 1997, the global crisis of 2007–2009 highlighted foreign-exchange risk. Leading up to the crisis, many individuals, banks, and companies borrowed in dollars or euros because of the relatively lower interest rates in the United States and Europe. Although this phenomenon happened around the world, it was especially problematic in Eastern Europe and Iceland.

In Iceland, a country with its own currency (the krona), the Central Bank kept interest rates high, attracting lots of foreign investment and keeping the krona strong. People's standards of living, among the highest in the world, were supported by the strong currency and the ability to import products. They sustained their high consumption by financing houses and other purchases through borrowing in cheaper currencies. When the crisis hit, however, the krona plunged in value, the banks failed, and consumers could not afford to service their debts. The lower foreign interest rates were replaced by exchange-rate risk.[6]

A major cause of the 1997 Asian crisis was that the lack of development of bond and equity markets forced Asian firms to rely too much on debt, especially bank debt, for growth. Many Asian banks borrowed dollars from international banks and lent the money to local companies in local currencies, not dollars. At the time, many of the countries pegged their currencies to the U.S. dollar, so the assumption was that if you borrow in dollars it is the same as borrowing in the local currency. When the currencies fell against the dollar, many banks could not service their loans and went into bankruptcy. Firms that borrowed directly in dollars suffered the same fate.

The economic crisis in Europe in 2010–2011 occurred for different reasons. The slowdown in the global economy meant that many countries in Europe could not generate enough revenue to service their sovereign debt. Initially, the European Central Bank kept interest rates relatively higher than U.S. rates due to fears of inflation, so the euro did not fall in value. Since much of the debt was denominated in euros, the banks and countries did not necessarily have exchange rate risk, as with Iceland in 2008, but there was simply not enough cash being generated to pay off loan obligations. As noted in Chapter 9, other problems arose in the banking sector in Europe, which complicated the ability of companies to access capital there.

By 2012 and 2013, the financial crisis in Europe escalated, the ECB dropped interest rates to stimulate economic growth, and the euro fell in value against the dollar. However, the banking crisis meant that even though companies wanted to borrow money, the banks were hesitant to lend. This was true all over the world. With a shortage of bank financing, the only other source of debt was issuing bonds, but instability and fear in the bond markets made it difficult for companies (and countries) to issue bonds without having to pay a higher interest rate to reflect the risk premium.

Another interest case is Thailand. During the Asian financial crisis of 1997, excessive borrowing in U.S. dollars coupled with a plunging Thai baht created a real cash crisis for Thai companies since they weren't generating enough baht to pay off their U.S. dollar debts. In 2013, however, the situation was very different because the availability of capital was a function of economic growth, interest rates, and exchange rates. The Thai economy wasn't growing much internally, interest rates were high relative to interest rates in other Asian countries, and there were significant capital inflows to take advantage of the yield on government bonds, a strong currency, and a relatively robust stock market. Any growth in the economy was due to exports, which make up about 60 percent of Thailand's economy. However, the strong Thai baht was starting to affect exports, a major source of cash for Thai companies. The stock market was robust enough that the companies that had listed on the market could raise cash there if they needed to. But the high borrowing costs were starting to create problems, so companies were encouraging the government to take measures that would reduce interest rates, thereby lowering borrowing costs and weakening the baht. A weaker baht would certainly promote exports, and there didn't seem to be as much exposure to U.S. dollar debt as there was in 1997. However, the government was worried about doing anything that could fuel inflation and possibly pull money out of the stock market, one of the really bright things about the Thai economy. Companies found themselves in the difficult position of how to get cash to fund their operations—borrow, raise equity capital, or hope that they could generate enough cash from exports.[7]

Regulatory Risk As pointed out in the opening case, regulatory reform has complicated access to debt financing. As noted below, bonds are a great way for companies to raise capital for operations. However, companies also rely heavily on bank financing, and the failure of banks during the global financial crisis and resulting impact on the global economy has made countries very nervous about the financial stability of banks. The Basel Committee on Global Banking Supervision, which is a part of the Bank for International Settlements and is comprised of some of the world's top regulators and central bankers, has worked hard to put together rules to ensure that banks will be able to withstand future economic crises. The basic idea is to set standards for stronger capital positions and increased liquidity. The most recent agreement is called Basel III.[8] On the one hand, the world should be better off as banks comply with Basel III and increase their capital positions, but on the other hand, higher capital requirements also mean lower funds available to lend to companies that might not be able to raise capital through an IPO (discussed below) or by floating a bond issues. However, new requirements should make the banking system more secure and less prone to financial collapse.

DEBT MARKETS AS A MEANS OF EXPANSION

CONCEPT CHECK

In discussing "Players on the Foreign-Exchange Market" in Chapter 8, we describe the role of *money center banks* (or *reporting dealers*) in making **foreign-exchange** transactions. Here we point out that, as significant players in the *interbank market*—the market for exchanges between dealer banks—money center banks either deal directly with each other or operate through foreign-exchange brokers. They are, in other words, well placed to provide services in **offshore financing**.

Companies can use local international debt markets to raise funds.

In the early 1990s, Nu Skin, a direct seller of skin treatments and personal-care products, embarked on a program of expansion into Japan and borrowed capital in yen in order to fund a portion of that expansion and to act as a hedge against their yen revenues. As a result, its long-term debt ultimately included the long-term portion of Japanese-yen-denominated 10-year notes issued to the Prudential Insurance Company of America in 2000. The notes bore interest at an effective rate of 3 percent per annum and were due October 2010, with annual principal payments that began in October 2004.[9] In their 2012 annual report, Nu Skin disclosed that it had issued additional debt in U.S. dollars and Japanese yen. The yen debt had much lower interest rates—ranging from 1.7 to 3.3 percent—than the U.S. dollar debt at 6.2 percent. The lower-cost Japanese debt is okay as long as the yen remains stable against the dollar. When the yen strengthens against the dollar, as it did throughout much of 2012, the dollar equivalent of the debt rises and wipes out any gains on the lower interest rates. As the yen began to fall at the end of 2012 and into 2013, the dollar equivalent of the debt also fell, making the debt look even less expensive. In addition, Nu Skin raised yen debt in Japan because it had large operations in Japan generating yen revenues, so the yen debt acted as a hedge against the yen revenues.

MNEs have an advantage because they can tap local and foreign debt and equity markets (such as the Eurodollar, Eurobond, and Euroequity markets). Most local firms are locked into local or possibly foreign debt markets, but they may not have the ability to raise funds as extensively as the local affiliates of MNEs do—unless they are MNEs themselves, such as Toyota or Nissan.

GLOBAL CAPITAL MARKETS

Two major sources of funds external to the MNE's normal operations are debt markets and equity markets.

Companies have many ways of raising capital to fund operations, and their home countries have debt and equity markets. However, we take a look here at the role of foreign debt and equity markets as sources of funds for MNEs. First, we'll examine foreign debt markets, especially the Eurocurrency and international bond markets. Then we'll examine the role of equity capital, including global stock markets, as an alternative to funding operations with internally generated funds and debt.

EUROCURRENCIES AND THE EUROCURRENCY MARKET

A Eurocurrency is any currency outside its country of origin, but it is primarily dollars banked outside the United States.

The **Eurocurrency market** is an important source of debt financing to complement what MNEs can find in their domestic markets. A **Eurocurrency** or *offshore currency,* is any currency banked outside its country of origin.

The Eurodollar market is the most significant eurocurrency market. A **Eurodollar** is a certificate of deposit in U.S. dollars in a bank outside the United States. Most Eurodollar CDs are held in London, but they could be held anywhere outside the U.S., including the Bahamas, the Cayman Islands, Hong Kong, Japan, the Netherlands Antilles, and so on. A major advantage of the Eurodollar market is that it is not regulated by the U.S. Federal Reserve Bank. The same is true for other eurocurrencies and their major regulators. The Eurodollar market started with the deposit of U.S. dollars in London banks during the Cold War by the Soviet Union to avoid the possibility that their accounts could be frozen in the United States. As other currencies entered the offshore market, the broader "Eurocurrency" name was adopted for market use, although the market tends to use the name of the specific currency, such as *Euroyen* or *Eurosterling*. Eurodollars constitute a majority of the Eurocurrency market. Dollars held by foreigners on deposit in the United States are not Eurodollars, but dollars held at branches of U.S. or other banks outside the United States are.

Major Sources of Eurocurrencies There are four major sources of Eurocurrencies:

- Foreign governments or individuals who want to hold dollars outside the United States
- Multinational enterprises that have cash in excess of current needs
- European banks with foreign currency in excess of current needs
- Countries such as China, Japan, the EU, Saudi Arabia, Russia, and Taiwan that have large foreign exchange reserves

The demand for Eurocurrencies comes from sovereign governments, supranational agencies such as the World Bank, companies, and individuals. Eurocurrencies exist partly for the convenience and security of the user and partly because of cheaper lending rates for the borrower and better yield for the lender.

Characteristics of the Eurocurrency Market Because the Eurocurrency market is a wholesale (companies and other institutions) rather than a retail (individuals) market, transactions are very large. Public borrowers such as governments, central banks, and public-sector corporations are the major players. MNEs are involved in the Eurodollar market, but it has historically been an interbank market. Since the late 1990s, however, London banks have shifted to using nonbank customers for Eurodollar transactions, partly because of the introduction of the euro, the subsequent fall in foreign transactions, and consolidation in the banking sector.[10]

The Eurocurrency market is both short- and medium-term. Short-term borrowing is composed of maturities of less than one year. Anything from one to five years is considered a **Eurocredit**, which may be a loan, a line of credit, or another form of medium- and long-term credit. This would include **syndication**, in which several banks pool resources to extend credit to a borrower and spread the risk. Short-term borrowings, called eurocommercial paper, are unsecured loans issued by a bank or corporation in the offshore money market and typically in the currency that is different from the corporation's domestic currency. For example, a German company can issue eurocommercial paper in London and denominated in U.S. dollars. Maturities are less than one year.

Interest Rates in the Eurocurrency Market A major attraction of the Eurocurrency market is the difference in interest rates compared to those in domestic markets. Domestic rates are a function of the monetary policies adopted by the Central Banks of each country. The rate a company must pay to get loans or issue bonds depends not only on benchmark rates but also its creditworthiness. The better the creditworthiness, the lower the rate compared to other borrowers.

LIBOR is a short-term interest rate for dollars held in the Eurodollar market.

London Inter-Bank Offered Rate Because of the large transactions and the lack of controls and their attendant costs, Eurocurrency deposits tend to yield more than domestic deposits do, and loans tend to be cheaper than in domestic markets. Traditionally, loans are made at a certain percentage above the **London Inter-Bank Offered Rate (LIBOR)**, which is a short-term interest rate for loans priced in London. Each day since 1986, the British Bankers' Association has been publishing LIBOR rates in 10 currencies and 15 different maturities. This is an average rate submitted by 18 different banks, and it reflects the rate at which banks can borrow from each other. The rates are calculated by Thomson Reuters, who drops the four highest and four lowest, averages the rest, and publishes them about 11:30 AM London time. This rate is extremely important because it is the basis for computing trillions of dollars of loans worldwide.[11]

For example, the LIBOR rates quoted on May 15, 2013 for Eurodollars were 0.19820 percent for one month, 0.27410 percent for three months, 0.41990 percent for six months, and 0.68989 percent for one year.[12] The amount of the interest rate above LIBOR that a borrower is charged depends on the creditworthiness of the customer and must be large enough to cover expenses and build reserves against possible losses. Most loans have a variable rate, and the rate-fixing period is generally six months, although it may be one or three months.

The LIBOR Scandal In 2012, a scandal broke out in London over how LIBOR was set. Rumors had it that LIBOR was lower than the market should be, and investigations by both the U.S. and UK regulators found that several banks tried to manipulate the rates. The chairman of Barclays, who was also on the board of the BBA, was forced to resign, while Barclay's had to pay a steep fine for rate manipulation. Royal Bank of Scotland (RBS) and UBS have also been fined by the BBA, and more banks are being investigated. The U.K.'s Serious Fraud Office brought eight counts of"conspiracy to defraud"against a former trader at UBS AG and Citigroup who was at the center of efforts to rig LIBOR on a daily basis over several years so that he could improve profits in his trading portfolio. Not only is he wanted in the U.K. but also the U.S. The Hong Kong Monetary Authority was also looking at manipulation of Hibor, the Hong Kong Interbank offered rate, so the scandal truly is worldwide. In addition to going after the perpetrators, efforts are now are being made to determine how to solve the problem so that everyone has confidence in the rate again.[13]

INTERNATIONAL BONDS

Many countries have active bond markets available to domestic and foreign investors. The United States is the largest market in the world for domestic bonds, accounting for 38 percent of all those issued in 2010. Bonds are used by governments, financial institutions, and corporations, with corporate issues being the smallest segment.[14] Just to give you an idea of the size of the global bond market, amounts outstanding on it were $100 trillion in March 2012, of which domestic bonds were 70 percent and international bonds 30 percent. In 2012, the global bond market was almost twice the size of the global equity market as defined by market capitalization. The U.S. was the largest bond market in the world with 33 percent of the total, followed by Japan with only 14 percent, and the UK and France.

One reason the bond (and stock) markets in the United States are so influential is because the companies of continental Europe still rely disproportionately on banks for finance. However, that began to change due to the economic crisis in Europe and the drop in available bank funding. Emerging markets are increasingly turning to the bond market for funding and now constitute about 10 percent of the market worldwide.[15]

There are two types of international bonds: foreign bonds and Eurobonds. The international bond market is primarily a wholesale market in which bond holders are usually institutional investors while issuers are large companies, governments, and international organizations.

A foreign bond is one sold outside the country of the borrower but denominated in the currency of issue. A Eurobond is a bond issue sold in a currency other than that of the country of issue.

Foreign Bonds **Foreign bonds** are sold outside the borrower's country but denominated in the currency of the country of issue. A French company floating a bond issue in the United States in U.S. dollars, say, would be issuing a foreign bond. These also have creative names, such as Yankee bond (issued in the United States), Samurai bond (Japan), Bulldog bond (England), and Panda bond (China).

Eurobonds A **Eurobond** is usually underwritten (placed in the market for the borrower) by a syndicate of banks from different countries and sold in a currency other than that of the country of issue. A bond issue in dollars floated by a U.S. company in London, Luxembourg, or Switzerland is a Eurobond. In 2011, two-thirds of the international bonds issued (both foreign and Eurobond) were in U.S. dollars. International bonds issued in euros were the next biggest group of bonds, representing 26 percent of Eurobonds issued. However, these amounts fluctuate a lot from one year to the next. London and New York are the two largest centers for the issuance of international bonds.

Rising in importance are "dim sum" bonds, which are offshore bonds denominated in Chinese yuan. In 2012, the dim sum bond market was fairly quiet, but in the first half of 2013 more dim sum bonds were issued than in all of 2012. In spite of such growth, many MNCs are slow to enter the market due to its limited size and depth.[16] However, the bonds' popularity rises as China looks for a way to capitalize on its immense foreign exchange reserves. Foreign investors who want to buy debt denominated in Chinese yuan usually face strict capital controls. However, these obstacles do not exist when it comes to dim sum bonds, which are typically issued in Hong Kong.[17]

What's So Attractive About the International Bond Market? The international bond market is a desirable place to borrow money. For one thing, it allows a company to diversify its funding sources from the local banks and the domestic bond market and borrow in maturities that might not be available in the domestic markets. It also tends to be less expensive than local bond markets and attracts investors from around the world, as evidenced in the Alliance Oil Company example described below.

Not all companies are interested in global bonds or Eurobonds. Before the Asian financial crisis hit, Asian firms relied on their domestic banks more because of the ready availability of cheap loans, as well as a cozier relationship than that between Western companies and banks.[18] However, the crisis demonstrated the fundamental flaws in this strategy as banks went under and companies were forced to face the fact that they couldn't generate enough funds to pay back the loans. The same story was repeated with the global financial crisis in the late 2000s.

Although the Eurobond market is centered in Europe, it has no national boundaries. In contrast to most conventional bonds, Eurobonds are sold simultaneously in several financial centers through multinational underwriting syndicates and are purchased by an international investing public that extends far beyond the confines of the countries of issue. U.S. firms first issued Eurobonds in 1963 as a means of avoiding U.S. tax and disclosure regulations. They're typically issued in denominations of $5,000 or $10,000, pay interest annually, are held in bearer form, and are traded over the counter (OTC), most frequently in London.[19] Any investor who holds a bearer bond is entitled to receive the principal and interest payments. In contrast, for a registered bond, which is more typical in the United States, the investor is required to be registered as the bond's owner to receive payments. An OTC bond is traded with or through an investment bank rather than on a securities exchange, such as the London Stock Exchange.

How Corporations Use Eurobonds to Fund Expansion Eurobond issues are very popular with companies in Russia and the former Soviet Union as a way to get access to international capital. As a result, Russian companies on average had a relatively high debt-to-asset ratio during the period of 2006–2010 compared to that of other countries. For example, Gazprom, Russia's largest company and the world's largest extractor of natural gas, raised about $1 billion in Eurobonds in 2010, with JP Morgan and Calyon (which became the Crédit Agricole Corporate and Investment Bank) as the organizers of the issue. The capital-intensive nature of the extractive industry means that they need capital for expansion, and the Eurobond market is a natural for raising capital. Although Gazprom is a joint stock company, more than 50 percent of the shares are owned by the Russian government. Private sector corporations use Eurobonds as well. In 2011, Amcor, the large Australian packaging solutions company, announced a ¢550 million Eurobond issue with a maturity of April 16, 2019. The Eurobond was listed on the Singapore Stock Exchange with BNP Paribas and Deutsche Bank as the lead banks. The proceeds of the bonds were in euros and will be used to refinance maturing bond and existing floating rate debt.[20] This is a good example of a Eurobond: issued in euros, outside of Australia, and in Singapore where the currency is not the euro.

In 2013, Alliance Oil Company, a leading oil and gas company with vertically integrated operations in Russia and Kazakhstan, issued a 7-year USD 500 million Eurobond that will mature in 2020 and pay a fixed coupon of 7 percent per annum. The offering was placed on the Irish Stock Exchange for investors from around the world. Alliance Oil, a Bermuda-based company, aggressively raises capital internationally and trades Swedish depository receipts on NASDAQ OMX Nordic in Stockholm.[21]

Occasionally, Eurobonds may provide currency options, which enable the creditor to demand repayment in one of several currencies, thus reducing the exchange risk inherent in single-currency foreign bonds. More often, however, both interest and principal on Eurobonds are payable to the creditor in U.S. dollars (or in the currency of issue, such as euros in the example of Amcor). It is also possible to issue a Eurobond in one currency—say, the U.S. dollar—and then swap the obligation to another. For example, a U.S. company with a subsidiary in Britain would generate large quantities of British pounds through normal operations, then use them to pay off a British-pound bond. If the U.S. company had issued Eurobonds in dollars in London, it could enter into a swap agreement through an investment bank to exchange its future dollar obligations with a British-pound obligation and use the pound revenues to pay off the swapped obligation.

EQUITY SECURITIES

Another source of financing is *equity securities,* whereby an investor takes an ownership position in return for shares of stock in the company and the promises of capital gains and dividends. A company that wants to raise equity capital to fund operations, especially a start-up, may work with private investors who want to take an equity interest in the company rather than just loan money to the company. Or it might raise equity capital through an Initial Public Offering where it goes directly to a stock market. If the company wants to issue an IPO, it has to decide if it wants to raise capital in its domestic market or abroad.

Access to Equity Capital A company can easily and cheaply gain access to capital through a private placement with an angel investor (a wealthy individual who wants to invest in a small private firm), a venture capital firm (which invests funds of a group of private investors), or institutional investors (a pension fund, insurance company, and so on). An example of a venture capital investment in a global context was the acquisition in 2001 of Tokyo Sowa Bank by Lone Star Funds, a Dallas, Texas-based private equity firm that specializes in acquiring distressed bank stocks. The bank was renamed Tokyo Star Bank and was listed on the Tokyo Stock Exchange in 2005. As the venture became profitable, Lone Star decided it was time to list shares on the Tokyo Stock Exchange while still retaining an ownership interest. After the investment had returned an acceptable profit, Lone Star Funds cashed out its position and moved on to other investments.

Sovereign wealth funds (SWFs) are also an important source of capital. An SWF is a state-owned investment fund that generates its resources from a variety of places, including revenues from the exports of natural resources such as oil.[22] The top five SWFs in terms of assets are Government Pension Fund (Norway), the Abu Dhabi Investment Authority, the SAFE Investment Company (China), SAMA Foreign Holdings (Saudi Arabia), and the China Investment Corporation. Six of the top ten funds and twelve of the top twenty are based on oil revenues.[23] The funds, which are professionally managed, can invest in specific projects or stock markets. For example, Invest AD (the Abu Dhabi Investment Company) is one of the SWFs in the UAE, with a primary role of investing in the Middle East and Emerging Africa and providing investment opportunities to third-party clients. Its officers scour the capital markets in the region to find stocks to invest in, and it has developed several funds, including the Emerging Africa Fund, the GCC Focus Fund, the Iraq Opportunity Fund, and the

Middle East and Africa Bond Fund. When SWFs invest in specific projects, they operate more like a venture capital firm. When they invest in stock markets, one of the strategies of Invest AD, they are not providing new capital but are taking advantage of shares already listed on stock markets. Even though this is not the same as providing new capital, it opens up many markets, especially the emerging markets of the Middle East North Africa (MENA) region, to demand for shares. This will help lift the markets and increase the price of the shares of companies they invest in.

In addition to private placements, companies can access the *equity-capital market*, more commonly known as the *stock market.* They can raise new capital—known as an Initial Public Offering, or IPO—by listing their shares on a stock exchange, either home-country or foreign. For example, Beijing-based LightInTheBox, which sells inexpensive Chinese-made products like fishing rods, raised $79 million by issuing an IPO on the New York Stock Exchange. The major underwriters are Credit Suisse and Stifel Financial, and it is the first Chinese company to list an IPO in the U.S. in 2013. Chinese companies have been plagued with corporate governance and accounting problems, so the CEO of LightInTheBox, a former Google China executive, traveled to London and several U.S. cities to answer questions and raise interest in the IPO. Although the IPO had been priced at $9.50, its stock price jumped by 17.5 percent in its first trade on the NYSE.[24]

Another example of an international IPO was the listing of Prada on the Hong Kong Stock Exchange in 2011, which will be discussed in more detail in the ending case for the chapter. It's natural for companies to list on their home stock markets first, due to their better name recognition, though the size of the U.S. stock market attracts many firms, such as LightInTheBox, to list there. But as we'll see in the Prada case, there are other reasons to pick a place to list an IPO.

The IPO market is not only important for start-ups in big economies such as the United States, but also for emerging markets like Brazil that are turning away from family wealth and bank financing to a more balanced source of capital, which includes equity capital. Remember from Table 10.1 that in 2012, a large sample of Brazilian companies had a debt-asset ratio of 80 percent, up from 58.3 percent in 2010 and much higher than any other country in the table. Even Mexico, another emerging market, had a ratio of only 57 percent. Unfortunately, debt is still a large source of capital for Brazilian companies.

Brazil's first IPO was issued in 2002, so the market is relatively new, and most of the investors were foreign investors. From an investor point of view, Brazil was growing rapidly and the currency was relatively strong, so foreign investors could enter the market and earn higher returns than in safer, more stable markets. From the standpoint of local investors, the reduction of inflation and interest rates meant that bond investments weren't giving good returns, so they were better off seeking higher returns in the stock market. In 2012, the main Brazilian stock exchange forecasted that 40–45 Brazilian companies would list IPOs, but only three did. There were several reasons: the slowdown in the Brazilian and global economies (leading to a flight to safety instead of to risk), pressure on several economic sectors to reduce consumer prices (which also held down profits), tax and regulatory measures to weaken the Brazilian real, and uncertainty in the minds of foreign investors over the future of Brazil.[25] After the Brazilian government realized it had instituted a number of measures that had a chilling impact on the ability of new Brazilian ventures to raise capital through IPOs, it instituted some reforms to attempt to be more investment-friendly and jump start the IPO market in 2013. However, massive demonstrations against the Brazilian government and widespread corruption in mid-2013 is likely to have a chilling effect on both domestic and international investors because of the ensuing political and economic instability.

THE SIZE OF GLOBAL STOCK MARKETS

Map 10.1 identifies the 20 largest stock markets in the world (of which nine are from emerging economies) in terms of the December 31, 2012 **market capitalization**—the total number of shares of stock listed times the market price per share. The global financial crisis has really

MAP 10.1 Global Markets: Market Capitalization, 2012

Data reflects domestic market capitalization—total number of shares of stock listed multiplied by market price per share.

Source: Based on World Federation of Exchanges, Statistics (www.world-exchanges.org/statistics/monthly-reports). Accessed June 19, 2013.

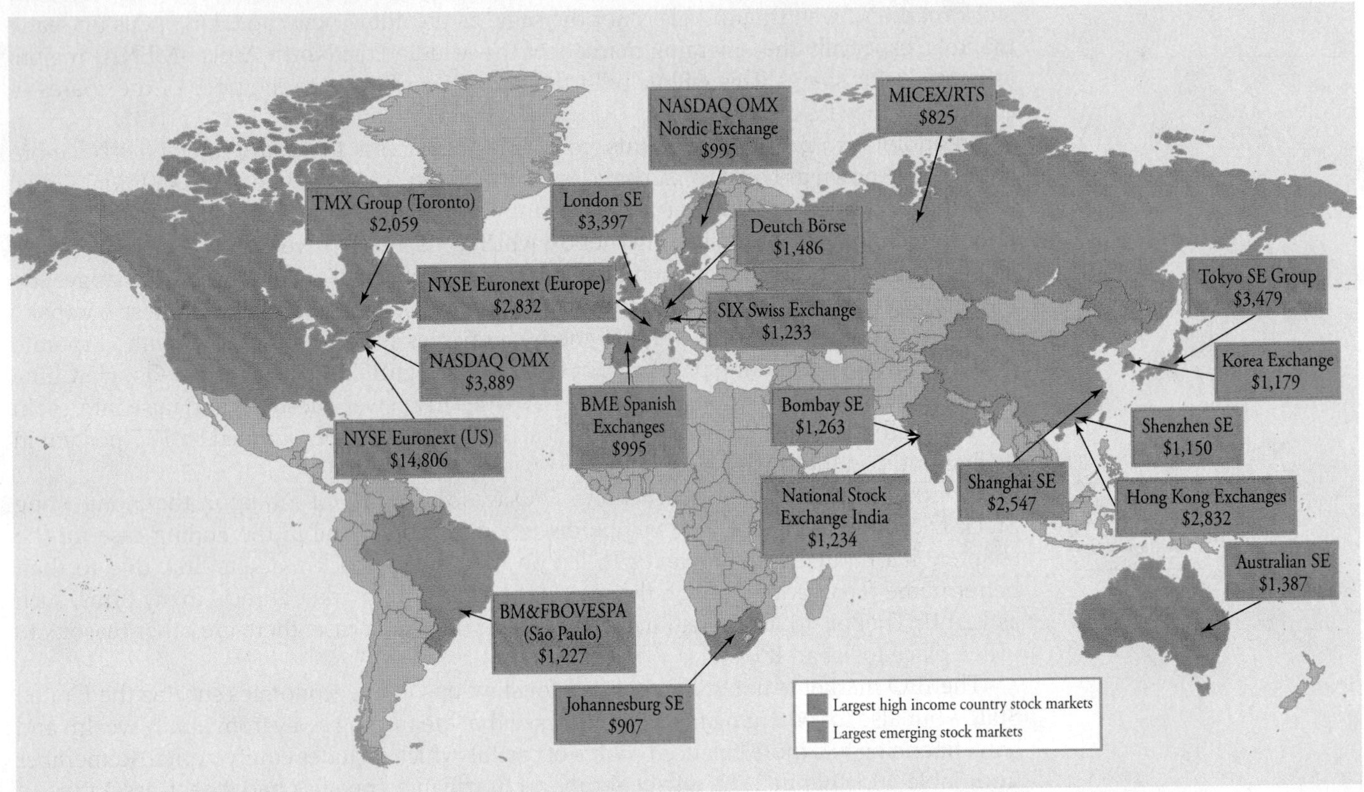

taken a toll on stock markets: Stock market capitalization worldwide dropped by 46.5 percent between the end of 2007 and the end of 2008. There was a slow recovery as market capitalization grew to $47.7 trillion in 2009 and reached $54.9 trillion in 2010.[26] The progress halted in 2011 but continued the next year; in fact, about $22 trillion of the $28 trillion in market cap lost in 2008 had been recovered by the end of 2012.[27]

The numbers in Map 10.1 represent each specific stock market rather than all of the markets in the country. For example, NYSE Euronext (U.S.) includes market capitalization in that specific market, not all of the markets in the United States.

The three largest stock markets in the world are in New York, Tokyo, and London, with the U.S. markets controlling nearly half of the world's stock market capitalization.

Trends in Global Stock Market One interesting trend is the rise in importance of the stock markets in emerging economies, especially China. The Hong Kong Exchanges were number six, followed by the Shanghai Stock Exchange at #7 and the Shenzhen SE at #16. All of the BRICs had stock exchanges in the top 20.

With the introduction of electronic platforms and high frequency trading, coupled with the decrease in economic activity around the world, the major stock exchanges have seen a drop in their trading volume. In 2012, trading volumes in equity transactions on stock exchanges worldwide were down by 22.5 percent, having fallen in every region of the world. As a result, global stock markets have begun talking about merging.[28] For example, the shareholders of Deutsche Börse (Germany) announced on July 15, 2011, that they had approved a proposed combination with NYSE Euronext. In 2012, the European Union blocked the planned merger due to concerns over potential antitrust issues and the fear that the new enterprise would result in a quasi-monopoly over the trading of European financial derivatives.

However, that didn't stop moves to consolidate stock exchanges worldwide. By the end of 2012, Intercontinental Exchange (ICE), a U.S.-based commodity exchange, had purchased

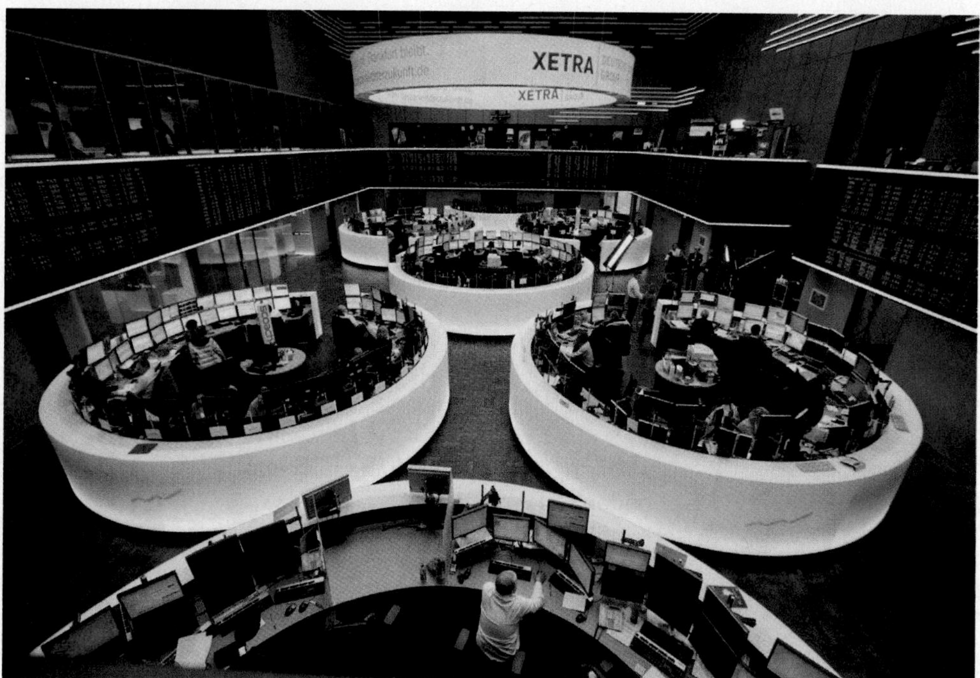

Stock traders work at the Deutsche Bourse in Frankfurt am Main. The EU Commission vetoed a transatlantic tie-up of the Frankfurt and New York Stock Exchanges in 2012 which would have given a huge boost to the Deutsche Bourse.
Source: AFP/Stringer/Getty Images

NYSE Euronext for $8.2 billion, bringing together trading in stocks, derivatives, and commodities. The deal was overwhelmingly approved by NYSE Euronext's shareholders and is subject to approval by competition and regulatory authorities in the U.S. and Europe. At the time of the merger, NYSE Euronext's equities markets represented about one-third of the world's equities trading.[29]

The United Arab Emirates, which has the second largest economy in the Arab world, has two stock exchanges: the Dubai Financial Market and the Abu Dhabi Securities Exchange. They are looking at the possibility of merging the two exchanges in order to deepen the equity market in the UAE rather than competing with each other for potential listings. The Kuwait Stock Exchange, which is shown in the opening photo, is not one of the largest in the world, but like the stock markets in the United Arab Emirates, it represents the growing equity market in the Gulf states.

Emerging Stock Markets It's been interesting to track the development of the emerging stock markets. For many years, they were growing fairly rapidly. By 1998, however, the Asian financial crisis had clobbered them, and they plunged to only 6.9 percent of the total. That was followed by economic crises in Russia and Latin America. As the global economy recovered from the Asian financial crisis, the emerging markets rose in importance as investors looked for higher returns. The flight to safety in 2008 pulled money out of the markets, but the funds started flowing back in as they began to recover.

The emerging markets seem to benefit from a flight to risk seeking higher returns and a rise in commodities prices. However, the markets also fall fairly quickly if there is a flight to safety. As noted above, market capitalization rose in 2012 even though trading volumes fell. In the Asia-Pacific region, the fastest growth in the stock markets occurred in Thailand, the Philippines, Singapore, Hong Kong and India. The markets in China and Japan rose at a much slower rate than the other countries mentioned above.

Euroequities are shares listed on stock exchanges in countries other than the home country of the issuing company.

The Rise of the Euroequity Market Another significant event in the past decade is the creation of the **Euroequity market**, the market for shares sold outside the boundaries of the issuing firm's home country. Euroequity describes an IPO occurring simultaneously in two different countries different from the one where the company is based.[30] Another way to look at euroequity is when a company's shares are made available internationally rather than just in the country where the company is based.[31] Prior to 1980, few companies thought about offering stock beyond the national borders of their headquarters country. Since then, hundreds of firms worldwide have issued stock simultaneously in two or more countries to attract more capital from a wider variety of shareholders. For example, when Daimler and Chrysler merged, the company issued global shares on 21 different markets in eight different countries: Germany, the United States, Austria, Canada, France, Britain, Japan, and Switzerland. As noted above, Alliance Oil Company is a Russian company which is domiciled in Bermuda and which lists its shares on NASDAQ OMX Nordic Exchange in Stockholm. Another example of a euroequity issue involves Gucci, the luxury goods company. Gucci is interesting because it is an Italian company that sells French fashion and is based in the Netherlands due to favorable tax laws. In 1995, InvestCorp, a global private equity firm that had gained control of Gucci, decided to take advantage of Gucci's return to profitability by floating an IPO simultaneously on the New York and Amsterdam Stock Exchanges and London's SEAQ International market.

The Trend Toward Delisting The trend of listing on more than one exchange began to reverse somewhat as more and more companies reduced the number of exchanges on which their stocks were listed. In Chapter 7, we noted in the case on Walmart that Comerci, a Mexican company, had listed on the NYSE but decided to delist and just raise capital on the Mexican Stock Exchange. In 2013, Tata Communications, an Indian company, announced that it was going to delist from the NYSE due to low trading volumes and liquidity.[32] Investors are finding that the best price for stocks is usually in the home market of the company in which they are investing.

Furthermore, companies pay annual fees to list on exchanges, so if trading is light on a certain exchange, as was the case with Tata Communications, they can save money by listing on an exchange with heavier trading volume. Other reasons for delisting shares include weak market returns (fewer investors are putting their money into stocks) and increased regulation (such as the U.S. Sarbanes-Oxley Act).

The problem is that the U.S. market is important for American and foreign companies looking for equity capital and is popular for Euroequity issues, partly because of the market size and the speed with which offerings are completed. The large pension funds in the United States can buy big blocks of stock at low transaction costs, and pension fund managers regard foreign stocks as a good form of portfolio diversification.

Most foreign companies that list on the U.S. stock exchanges do so through American Depositary Receipts, which are financial documents that represent a share or part of a share of stock in the foreign company.

American Depositary Receipt The most popular way for a Euroequity to get a listing in the United States is to issue an **American Depositary Receipt (ADR)**, a negotiable certificate issued by a U.S. bank in the United States to represent the underlying shares of a foreign corporation's stock held in trust at a custodian bank in the foreign country. ADRs are traded like stock shares, with each one representing some number of shares of the underlying stock. For example, Toyota has listed ADRs on the NYSE since 1999 at a rate of two per common Toyota share. They issue through a sponsored ADR facility operated by the Bank of New York. In addition to the NYSE and the Tokyo Stock Exchange, Toyota also lists its ADRs on the London Stock Exchange.

Many foreign corporations try to raise capital in the United States but don't want to list on an exchange because they don't want to comply with the onerous reporting requirements of the SEC. Still, those that do so gain access to a large percentage of the world's market capitalization, a fact that is a significant advantage to those with a U.S. listing. Companies generally list on their home country's exchange first and then venture into the international exchanges with depositary receipts. One important change in ADR regulations is that non-U.S. companies that have adopted International Financial Reporting Standards (IFRS) can list in the U.S. without having to reconcile their financial statements to U.S. GAAP, which eliminates a major reporting requirement.

TAXATION OF FOREIGN-SOURCE INCOME

Gaining access to capital is about more than interest rates and stock exchange listing requirements. Tax planning is a crucial responsibility for a CFO because taxes can profoundly affect profitability and cash flow. This is especially true in international business. As complex as domestic taxation seems, it is child's play compared to the intricacies of international taxation. The international tax specialist must be familiar with both the home country's tax policy on foreign operations and the tax laws of each country in which the MNE operates.

Taxation has a strong impact on several choices:

- Location of operations
- Choice of operating form, such as export or import, licensing agreement, or overseas investment
- Legal form of the new enterprise, such as branch or subsidiary
- Possible facilities in tax-haven countries to raise capital and manage cash
- Method of financing, such as internal or external sourcing, and debt or equity
- Capital budgeting decisions
- Method of setting transfer prices

CONCEPT CHECK

We introduce the OECD in discussing the OECD Anti-Bribery Convention in Chapter 11. In addition, the OECD is concerned about a broader range of activities that involve cross-border operations. We also mention the OECD's earlier Guidelines for MNEs, which came out in 1976 includes a code of conduct for MNEs engaged in cross-border operations. Here we observe that, because **offshore financing** has proved conducive to such misbehavior as tax avoidance, the OECD and several other multilateral organizations have made efforts to strengthen ethical practices in offshore transactions.

Tax planning influences profitability and cash flow.

INTERNATIONAL TAX PRACTICES

Differences in tax practices around the world often cause headaches for MNEs. Lack of familiarity with laws and customs can create confusion. In some countries, tax laws are loosely enforced. In others, taxes may generally be negotiated between the tax collector and the taxpayer—if they are ever paid at all. In still others, they must be rigidly followed.

Problems with different countries' tax practices arise from

- Lack of familiarity with laws.
- Loose enforcement.

Differences in Types of Taxes Countries differ in terms of the types of taxes they have (income versus excise), the tax rates applied to income, the determination of taxable income, and the treatment of foreign-source income. Although we focus in this section on corporate income taxes, excise taxes are another important source of income to governments. The value-added tax (VAT) is an example of an excise tax used in Europe as well as other parts of the world. It is a percentage levied on products at the point of sale in every stage of the value chain, and is included in the final price of the product rather than added to the price at the final point of sale, as is the case with the sales tax in the United States. There are many other excise taxes, and the large number of taxes in some countries, like Brazil, is very confusing to both local and foreign investors.

With a value-added tax, each company pays a percentage of the value added to a product at each stage of the business process.

Differences in Generally Accepted Accounting Principles (GAAP) Variations among countries in GAAP can lead to differences in determining taxable income. In countries where tax laws allow firms to depreciate assets faster than accounting standards allow but where the firms must use the same standards for tax and book accounting, higher depreciation expenses result in lower income and therefore lower taxes. Revenue recognition is also an important issue. Some countries tax income from worldwide revenues of MNEs, whereas others only recognize income from revenues generated in the domestic environment.

Corporate tax rates vary from country to country.

Differences in Tax Rates Corporate tax rates also vary from country to country. OECD central-government corporate income-tax rates range from a low of 8.5 percent in Switzerland to a high of 35 percent in the United States. However, the total corporate income tax burden includes sub-central government taxes (such as provincial or state and local taxes) as well as the central-government corporate income tax. In this case, the combined rate ranges from a low of 12.5 percent in Ireland to a high of over 37 percent in Japan and 39.1 percent in the United States.[33]

Two Approaches to Corporate Taxation Taxation of corporate income is accomplished through one of two approaches in most countries: the *separate entity approach* (also known as the *classical approach*) or the *integrated system approach.*

In the separate entity approach, governments tax each taxable entity when it earns income.

Separate Entity Approach In the separate entity approach, which the United States uses, each separate unit—company or individual—is taxed when it earns income. For example, a corporation is taxed on its earnings, while stockholders are taxed on the distribution of earnings (dividends). The result can be double taxation.

An integrated system tries to avoid double taxation of corporate income through split tax rates or tax credits.

Integrated System Approach Many other developed countries use an integrated system to eliminate double taxation. Australia and New Zealand, for example, give a dividend credit to shareholders to shelter them from double taxation. This means that when shareholders report the dividends in their taxable income, they also get a credit for taxes paid on that income by the company that issued the dividend. That keeps the shareholders from paying tax on the dividend because the company has already done so.

Germany used to have a split-rate system with two different tax rates on corporate earnings: one on retained earnings and one on distributed earnings. However, they abolished it in 2001 and adopted a classical system with an overall lower corporate tax rate on earnings of 15 percent plus a 5.5 percent solidarity surcharge (to help in the reunification with East Germany), resulting in a combined rate of 15.8 percent.[34] Taxation of foreign-source income depends on the country where the parent company is domiciled. It is common for most developed countries to tax MNEs on their worldwide income and give them a credit for foreign corporate income taxes paid. That is not true everywhere, however. Hong Kong companies, for example, pay tax only on Hong Kong-source income, even if remitted to Hong Kong, and their corporate tax rate is only 16.5 percent.[35]

TAXING BRANCHES AND SUBSIDIARIES

In order to innovate and expand, companies need to gain access to capital, both debt and equity, from home country capital markets or markets abroad. However, companies can also raise capital through minimizing their tax liability worldwide so that they can use internally generated cash to expand. To illustrate how this is done, let's look at how U.S.-based companies tax earnings from a *foreign branch* and a *foreign subsidiary.*

Foreign branch income (or loss) is directly included in the parent's taxable income.

The Foreign Branch A foreign branch is an extension of the parent company rather than an enterprise incorporated in a foreign country. Any income the branch generates is taxable immediately to the parent, whether or not cash is remitted by the branch to the parent as a distribution of earnings. However, if the branch suffers a loss, the parent is allowed to deduct that loss from its taxable income, reducing its overall tax liability.

Tax deferral means that income is not taxed until it is remitted to the parent company as a dividend.

The Foreign Subsidiary Whereas a branch is a legal extension of a parent company, a foreign corporation is an independent legal entity set up in a country (incorporated) according to that country's laws of incorporation. When an MNE purchases a foreign corporation or sets up a new one in a foreign country, it is called a *subsidiary* of the parent. Income earned by the subsidiary is either reinvested in the subsidiary or remitted as a dividend to the parent company.

Subsidiary income is either taxable to the parent or tax-deferred—that is, it is not taxed until it is remitted as a dividend to the parent. Which tax status applies depends on whether the foreign subsidiary is a *controlled foreign corporation (CFC)*—a technical term in the U.S. tax code—and whether the income is active or passive. This is a relatively unique concept for U.S. companies.

In a CFC, U.S. shareholders hold more than 50 percent of the voting stock.

The Controlled Foreign Corporation A **controlled foreign corporation (CFC)**, from the standpoint of the U.S. tax code, is any foreign company in which more than 50 percent of its voting stock is held by "U.S. shareholders," which are U.S. citizens or companies that each hold 10 percent or more of the CFC's voting stock. Any foreign subsidiary of an MNE would

TABLE 10.2 Controlled Foreign Corporations

To qualify as a *controlled foreign corporation (CFC)*, more than 50 percent of a company's voting shares must be held by U.S. shareholders. A *U.S. shareholder* must be a U.S. person or company holding at least 10 percent of the corporation's voting shares. Foreign Corporation B qualifies as a CFC, because the combined shares of U.S. Persons V, W, and X (each consisting of at least 10 percent) add up to 75 percent of the total.

	Percentages of the Voting Stock		
Shareholder	**Foreign Corporation A**	**Foreign Corporation B**	**Foreign Corporation C**
U.S. Person V	100%	45%	30%
U.S. Person W		10%	10%
U.S. Person X		20%	8%
U.S. Person Y		25%	8%
Foreign Person Z			44%
Total	**100%**	**100%**	**100%**

automatically be considered a CFC from the standpoint of the tax code. However, a JV company abroad that is partly owned by the U.S.-based MNE and partly by local investors might not be a CFC if the U.S. MNE does not own more than 50 percent of the JV's stock.

Table 10.2 shows how this might work. Foreign Corporation A is a CFC because it is a wholly owned subsidiary of a U.S. parent company (U.S. Person V). Foreign Corporation B also is a CFC because U.S. Persons V, W, and X each own 10 percent or more of the voting stock, which means they qualify as U.S. shareholders and their combined voting stock is more than 50 percent of the total. This situation might exist if three U.S. companies partnered together with a foreign firm to establish a JV overseas.

Such collaborative arrangements are not uncommon, especially in telecommunications and high-tech industries. Foreign Corporation C is not a CFC because even though U.S. Persons V and W qualify as U.S. shareholders, their combined stock ownership is only 40 percent. U.S. Persons X and Y do not qualify as U.S. shareholders because their individual ownership shares are only 8 percent each. When Enron set up its shell companies in tax-haven countries, it was careful not to own more than 50 percent of the stock so that it could avoid having to include the debt in those operations in its consolidated income.[36]

Active income is derived from the direct conduct of a trade or business. Passive income (also called Subpart F income) is usually derived from operations in a tax-haven country.

Active Versus Passive Income If a foreign subsidiary qualifies as a CFC, the U.S. tax law requires the U.S. investor to classify the foreign-source income as *active* or *Subpart F (passive) income.* **Active income** is derived from the direct conduct of a trade or business, such as from sales of products manufactured in the foreign country. **Subpart F or passive income**, which is specifically defined in Subpart F of the U.S. Internal Revenue Code, comes from sources other than those connected with the direct conduct of a trade or business, generally in tax-haven countries, and includes the following:

- *Holding company income*—income primarily from dividends, interest, rents, royalties, and gains on sale of stocks.
- *Sales income*—income from foreign sales corporations that are separately incorporated from their manufacturing operations. The product of such entities is manufactured and sold for use outside the CFC's country of incorporation, and the CFC has not performed significant operations on the product.
- *Service income*—income from the performance of technical, managerial, or similar services for a company in the same corporate family as the CFC and outside the country in which the CFC resides.

Subpart F income usually derives from the activities of subsidiaries in tax-haven countries such as the Bahamas, the Netherlands Antilles, Panama, and Switzerland. The tax-haven subsidiary may act as an investment company, a sales agent or distributor, an agent for the parent in licensing agreements, or a holding company of stock in other foreign subsidiaries

FIGURE 10.2 The Tax-Haven Subsidiary as Holding Company

A U.S. company has established a *tax-haven subsidiary* as a *holding company* in an offshore location. As such, the offshore subsidiary owns shares in three foreign subsidiaries called *grandchild subsidiaries*. The offshore holding company generates *holding company income*, which is recorded by the U.S. parent company as *Subpart F income*.

Parent Company in the United States

Tax-Haven Subsidiary

Grandchild Subsidiary | Grandchild Subsidiary | Grandchild Subsidiary

that are called *grandchild—or second-tier—subsidiaries.* This setup is illustrated in Figure 10.2. In the role of a holding company, its purpose is to concentrate cash from the parent's foreign operations into the low-tax country and use the cash for global expansion.

Different rules regarding the tax status and deferability of income are in effect for non-CFCs, CFCs, and foreign branches.

Determining a Subsidiary's Income Figure 10.3 illustrates how the tax status of a subsidiary's income is determined. All non-CFC income—active and Subpart F—earned by the foreign corporation is deferred until remitted as a dividend to the U.S. shareholder (the parent company, in this example). In contrast, a CFC's active income is tax-deferred to the parent, but its Subpart F income is taxable immediately to the parent as soon as the CFC earns it, subject to some limitations and exceptions. If a foreign branch earns income, it is immediately taxable to the parent company, whether it is active or Subpart F income.

TRANSFER PRICES

A transfer price is a price on goods and services one member of a corporate family sells to another.

A major tax challenge as well as an impediment to performance evaluation is the extensive use of transfer pricing in international operations. Because the price is between related entities, it is not necessarily an **arm's-length price**—that is, a price between two companies that do not have an ownership interest in each other. The assumption is that an arm's-length price is more likely than a transfer price to reflect the market accurately.

Transfer Prices and Taxation Companies establish arbitrary transfer prices primarily because of differences in taxation between countries. For example, if the corporate tax rate is higher in the parent company's country than in the subsidiary's country, the parent could set a low transfer price on products it sells to the subsidiary to keep taxable profits low in its

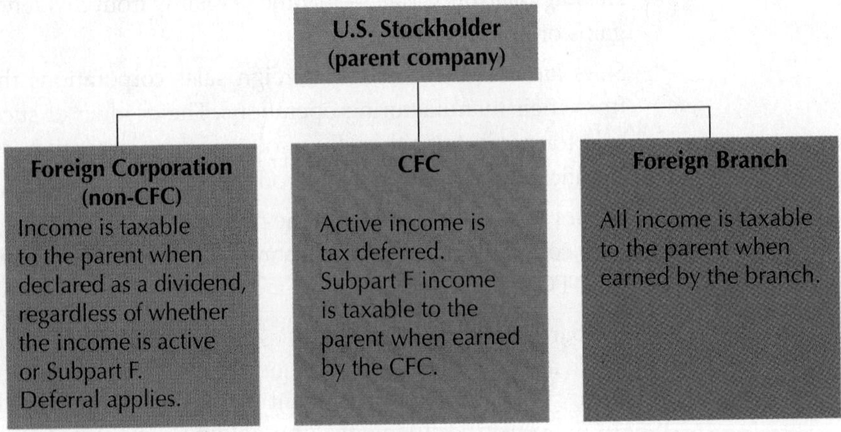

U.S. Stockholder (parent company)
Foreign Corporation (non-CFC)
Income is taxable to the parent when declared as a dividend, regardless of whether the income is active or Subpart F. Deferral applies.
CFC
Active income is tax deferred. Subpart F income is taxable to the parent when earned by the CFC.
Foreign Branch
All income is taxable to the parent when earned by the branch.

FIGURE 10.3 The Tax Status of U.S.-Owned Foreign Subsidiaries

Both CFC and Subpart F provisions are designed to prevent U.S. firms from establishing tax-haven subsidiaries for the purpose of investing *passive income* indefinitely, thus earning tax-free income. Basically, these provisions treat tax income just as if it had been remitted to the U.S. parent at the time when it was earned.

country and high in the subsidiary's country. The parent could also set a high transfer price on products sold to it by the subsidiary.

The OECD is very concerned about the ways in which companies manipulate transfer prices to minimize their tax liability worldwide. For this reason, the OECD Center for Tax Policy and Administration meets periodically to discuss the adoption of sound transfer pricing policies (along with a wide range of other tax issues). The OECD issued guidelines on transfer pricing in 1979 and updated the policies in 1995 to provide guidance on how to tell if a transfer between independent firms is similar to a transfer within a group and on different transfer pricing methods that could be used. To avoid transfer-price manipulation, it recommends determining the tax liability in each country by applying an arm's-length price, and it has issued guidelines on the matter. Additional OECD policy revisions have been published since 1995 and continue to be published periodically.[37]

Companies can get into disputes with different tax jurisdictions over transfer pricing policies. GlaxoSmithKline (GSK), the British pharmaceutical company, settled a transfer pricing dispute with the U.S. Internal Revenue Service in 2006 by paying $3.1 billion in federal, state, and local taxes and interest—slightly less than the $5 billion the IRS was seeking and nearly half of GSK's operating cash flow. The IRS contends that GSK charged its U.S. affiliate too little for marketing services provided by the affiliate, which meant that U.S. earnings were low, resulting in lower taxes collected in the United States. The dispute arose over whether GSK should have paid for the marketing services at cost or at the price it would have paid an independent third party. These are complex issues that leave companies open to significant financial risks if they don't price services or products correctly.[38]

DOUBLE TAXATION AND TAX CREDIT

The IRS allows a tax credit for corporate income tax U.S. companies pay to another country. A tax credit is a dollar-for-dollar reduction of tax liability and must coincide with the recognition of income.

Every country has a sovereign right to levy taxes on all income which could result in double taxation if both the home and host country tax the income.

In U.S. tax law, a U.S. MNE gets a credit for income taxes paid to a foreign government. For example, when a U.S. parent recognizes foreign-source income (such as a dividend from a foreign subsidiary) in its taxable income, it must pay U.S. tax on that income. However, the IRS allows the parent company to reduce its tax liability by the amount of foreign income tax already paid. It is limited by the amount it would have had to pay in the United States on that income.

Assume, for example, that U.S. Company A earns $100,000 of foreign-source income on which it paid $40,000 (40 percent tax rate) on that income in the foreign jurisdiction. If that income is considered taxable in the United States, Company A would have to pay $35,000 in income taxes (35 percent tax rate). In the absence of a tax credit, Company A would have paid a total of $75,000 in income tax on the $100,000 of income, a 75 percent tax rate.

The IRS, however, allows Company A to reduce its U.S. tax liability by a maximum of $35,000—what it would have paid in the United States if the income had been earned there. If Company A's subsidiary had paid $20,000 in foreign income tax (a 20 percent tax rate), it would be able to claim the entire $20,000 as a credit because it was less than the U.S. liability of $35,000. Company A will pay a total of $35,000 in corporate income tax on its foreign-source income—$20,000 to the foreign government and $15,000 to the U.S. government.

Tax Treaties: Eliminating Double Taxation The primary purpose of tax treaties is to prevent international double taxation or to provide remedies when it occurs. The United States is an active participant in 75 different tax treaties involving 58 different countries.[39] The general pattern between two treaty countries is to grant reciprocal deductions on dividend withholding and to exempt royalties—and sometimes interest payments—from any withholding tax.

The purpose of tax treaties is to prevent double taxation or to provide remedies when it occurs.

The United States has a withholding tax of 30 percent for owners (individuals and corporations) of U.S. securities issued in countries with which it has no tax treaty. However, interest on portfolio obligations and on bank deposits is normally exempted from withholding. When a tax treaty is in effect, the U.S. rate on dividends is generally reduced to 5 to 15 percent, and the tax on interest and royalties is either eliminated or reduced to 5 to 10 percent.

DODGING TAXES

Two things will always be true: governments will always try to figure out how to collect as much in taxes as they can and companies (and individuals) will try to avoid paying as much in taxes as they can. Since the economic crisis began in 2008, governments have been scrambling to generate as much tax revenue as they possibly can, not only to reduce massive budget deficits but also to fund special programs, such as the Affordable Care Act in the United States. Unfortunately, there are only so many sources of revenue, and it is politically easier to try to collect more taxes from companies than from individuals. This can happen through raising tax rates, closing loopholes, and eliminating exemptions and deductions, or all of the above.

On the other hand, companies will always hire the best and the brightest to figure out how to pay as little in taxes as possible because that reduces their need to borrow money and gives them a larger pot of cash to use to invest in innovation. One advantage that companies, especially MNCs, have is that it may be hard for a country to figure out its own tax policy, but it is almost impossible for countries to come up with one global tax policy that everyone can agree on. As a result, companies do the best they can to exploit the differences.

Take Google, for example, an internet company headquartered in the United States but operating worldwide. Google established its European headquarters in Ireland where the corporate tax rate is 12.5 percent and has its customers who buy advertising on Google's search engine sign contracts with its Irish subsidiary rather than in the country where they reside. Thus Google generates revenues across Europe but pays taxes in Ireland rather than in the other countries whose tax rates are substantially higher. To reduce their tax liability even more, Google runs some of its royalty payments through a subsidiary in Bermuda, where there are no corporate income or withholding taxes.[40]

There are many reasons why companies set up operations abroad: to be closer to customers, or to get access to intellectual property, raw materials, or labor. But another reason to locate abroad is to minimize taxes as described above. Eaton, a U.S.-based manufacturer of components and electrical equipment, acquired Cooper Industries PLC and moved its place of incorporation to Dublin from Cleveland. In doing so, the company expects to save $160 million a year in U.S. taxes. Eaton's management is very open about complaining that the relatively high corporate tax rate in the U.S. is placing it at a disadvantage against its competitors. In addition, it doesn't see the environment getting any better as the U.S. government looks for ways to reform the tax code to generate more revenue.

OFFSHORE FINANCING AND OFFSHORE FINANCIAL CENTERS

Offshore financing—the provision for financial services by banks and other agents to nonresidents

Companies are partly able to be successful in reducing their tax liabilities because of tax haven countries and the ability to use them for a variety of offshore activities. **Offshore financing** is the provision of financial services by banks and other agents to nonresidents. In its simplest form, this involves borrowing money from and lending to the nonresidents.[41] A good example of legitimate offshore financing is the use of the Eurodollar market. A U.S. company can raise Eurodollars in London by working with a bank to issue bonds or syndicate a loan. Or it could float Eurobonds in Bermuda where there are no withholding taxes on interest, which is more beneficial to the investor.

WHAT IS AN OFC?

Offshore financial centers (OFCs)—cities or countries that provide large amounts of funds in currencies other than their own

Offshore financial centers (OFCs) are cities or countries that provide large amounts of funds in currencies other than their own and are used as locations in which to raise and accumulate cash. Usually, the financial transactions are conducted in currencies other than that of the country and are thus the centers for the Eurocurrency market. An OFC could be defined as any financial center where offshore activity takes place, but a more practical definition is a center where the bulk of financial activity is offshore on both sides of the balance sheet, the transactions are initiated elsewhere, and the majority of the institutions involved are controlled by nonresidents.[42]

OFCs offer low or zero taxation, moderate or light financial regulation, and banking secrecy and anonymity.

Offshore financial centers can be operational centers or booking centers.

Key offshore financial centers are in the Bahamas, Bahrain, the Caribbean, Hong Kong, Ireland, London, New York, Singapore, and Switzerland, among other locations.

Characteristics of OFCs The markets in these centers tend to be regulated differently—and usually more flexibly—than domestic markets. The centers provide an alternative, (usually) cheaper source of funding for MNEs so the latter don't have to rely strictly on their own national markets. Offshore financial centers have one or more of the following characteristics:

- A large foreign-currency (Eurocurrency) market for deposits and loans (in London, say)
- A market that functions as a large net supplier of funds to the world financial markets (such as in Switzerland)
- A market that functions as an intermediary or pass-through for international loan funds (e.g., the Bahamas and the Cayman Islands)
- Economic and political stability
- An efficient and experienced financial community
- Good communications and support services
- An official regulatory climate favorable to the financial industry, in the sense that it protects investors without unduly restricting financial institutions[43]

However, the OECD prefers to differentiate between well and poorly regulated financial centers rather than offshore and onshore.[44]

CONCEPT CHECK

In the section on "Forecasting Exchange-Rate Movements" in Chapter 9 we point out the importance to MNEs of formulating general ideas of the timing, magnitude, and direction of exchange-rate movements. We also describe two approaches that companies can take to forecast exchange rates: **fundamental forecasting** (which bases external or internal decisions on a range of economic variables) and **technical forecasting** (which depends on specialists to analyze trends in exchange rates themselves).

Operational Versus Booking Centers *Operational centers* have extensive banking activities involving short-term financial transactions; *booking centers* have little actual banking activity taking place but transactions are recorded to take advantage of secrecy and low (or no) tax rates. In the latter case, individuals may deposit money offshore to hide it from their home-country tax authorities, either because the money is earned and/or to be used illegally—such as in the drug trade or to finance terrorist activities—or because the individual or company does not want to pay tax. London is an example of an operational center; the Cayman Islands is an example of a booking center.

OFCs as "Tax Havens" A major concern with OFCs is the tax avoidance dimension of their activities. The OECD has been working closely with the major OFCs to ensure that they are engaged in legal activity. It uses the following key factors in identifying tax havens: (1) no or only nominal taxes, (2) lack of effective exchange of information (especially bank secrecy), (3) lack of transparency, and (4) no substantial activities.[45] Although not trying to tell the sovereign countries what their tax rates should be, the OECD is trying to eliminate harmful tax practices in these four areas:

The OECD is trying to eliminate the harmful tax practices in tax-haven countries.

1. The regime imposes low or no taxes on the relevant income (from geographically mobile financial and other service activities).
2. The regime is ring fenced (i.e., separated) from the domestic economy.
3. The regime lacks transparency; for example, the details of it or its application are not apparent, or there is inadequate regulatory supervision or financial disclosure.
4. There is no effective exchange of information with respect to the regime.[46]

Obviously, there is a lot of overlap in these definitions. In a 2009 report, the OECD identified 28 tax-haven countries and 10 other financial centers that were moving to adopt their standards for good tax behavior, while no national jurisdictions were reported that had not committed to the internationally accepted tax standard. That is pretty significant progress.[47] The OECD is trying to reduce harmful tax practices through improved translation and disclosure. Putting the spotlight on countries seems to be the best approach.

Point

Should Offshore Financial Centers and Aggressive Tax Practices Be Eliminated?

Point **Yes** The problem with OFCs is that they operate in a shroud of secrecy that allows companies to establish operations there for illegal and unethical purposes. In December 2001, U.S. energy giant Enron filed for bankruptcy—one of the largest in corporate history. Contributing to Enron's problems was the creation of hundreds of subsidiaries in tax havens—including 662 in the Cayman Islands, 119 in Turks and Caicos, 43 in Mauritius, and 8 in Bermuda—that were used to pass off corporate debts, losses, and executive compensation.[48] The fondness of unscrupulous MNEs for OFCs only serves to underscore the unqualified truth voiced in Figure 10.4.

As we'll point out in Chapter 19, Parmalat set up three shell companies based in the Caribbean to capture cash. The companies allegedly sold Parmalat products, and Parmalat sent them fake invoices and charged costs and fees to make the sales look legitimate. It would then write out a credit note for the amount the subsidiaries supposedly owed and take that to banks to raise money. Given the location of the subsidiaries, you would think the banks would have been suspicious, but Parmalat got away with these activities.

Off-balance-sheet financing was also used to hide debts. The company transferred over half of its liabilities to the books of small subsidiaries based in offshore tax havens such as the Cayman Islands. This allowed it to present a healthy balance sheet and a profitable income statement to investors and creditors by hiding large amounts of debt, understating interest expenses (thus overstating income), and overstating revenues for false bookings. Parmalat's actual debt was nearly double the amount disclosed to outsiders.

Terrorists and drug dealers also use OFCs to launder money. When the U.S. government went after the money of Osama bin Laden, it went after OFCs notorious for their secrecy. When a bank in the Bahamas refused to open its books to U.S. government investigators, the United States cut the bank off from the world's wire transfer systems. Within two hours, the bank changed policies.[49] Standard Chartered PLC, a British bank, was fined $340 million for violating U.S. money-laundering laws involving an illegal scheme to hide more than 60,000 transactions worth $250 billion for Iranian clients.[50] These kinds of activities must stop.

FIGURE 10.4

Source: Harley Schwadron/Cartoon Bank

SCHWADRON
" RON CHOATE, OFFSHORE TAX HAVEN CONSULTANT, SPEAKING..."

Should Offshore Financial Centers and Aggressive Tax Practices Be Eliminated?

Counterpoint **No** OFCs are an efficient way for companies to use their financial resources more effectively. They are good locations for establishing finance subsidiaries that can raise capital for the parent company or its subsidiaries. And they allow the finance subsidiaries to take advantage of lower borrowing costs and tax rates.

Not all types of tax-minimization activities are illegal because the companies are still subject to home- and host-country laws and tax regulations. It is true that some transactions may be illegal, but most are not. The key to policing truly illegal activities, such as hiding drug money or engaging in corporate fraud like the Parmalat case, is to improve transparency and reporting.

Why shouldn't countries have the opportunity to attract business by offering tax-haven status to MNEs? Many don't have other visible means of generating resources. They are too small to set up manufacturing operations, have too small a population base to offer low-cost labor, and don't have natural resources they can sell. So what can they do? Companies and individuals need places to bank their wealth or raise capital, so the OFCs have decided to use the theory of factor proportions (discussed in Chapter 5) and develop the banking and financial infrastructure necessary to attract wealth. As long as they establish banking, privacy, and taxation laws that attract money, they should be allowed to do so. The Cayman Islands attract a lot of tourism, but the territory is also one of the world's biggest

Counterpoint

financial centers, and one of the most secretive as well. It has worked hard to crack down on money laundering so it can use its financial expertise in legal ways to help companies and individuals.[51]

OFCs don't rely on taxation to fund huge government expenditures because they don't have a large military budget or significant welfare costs. Is there anything wrong with not collecting large amounts of taxes? Some countries are upset that OFC's offer a tax-free environment for revenues generated offshore, but that's their business. Nobody should force them to collect higher taxes just because the high-tax countries are at a disadvantage in attracting banking and finance. If countries want to charge high taxes on financial transactions, let them do so, but don't force the OFCs to play their game.

Even the Chairwoman of the British Public Accounts Committee, in complaining about the tax policies of MNEs like Google, Amazon, and Starbucks, admitted that they are probably not doing anything illegal; she was accusing them of being immoral.[52]

1. You can order a book from Amazon in the UK using a British website (amazon.co.uk) and receive it from a British warehouse through the British Royal Mail. However, you will be paying an Amazon subsidiary set up in Luxembourg, which offers more favorable tax conditions than the UK. Is Amazon illegal, immoral, both, or neither for having a subsidiary in Luxembourg to minimize its tax bill?

Looking to the Future

The Growth of Capital Markets and the Drive by Governments to Capture More Tax Revenues by MNEs

The competition for global capital will be fierce as companies are forced to shift funding from banks that are under great financial stress to issuing stocks and bonds as a way to grow and expand. In addition, stock markets will continue to compete with each other to attract companies that are looking for a place to raise capital. Mergers of stock markets to reduce costs and expand their market potential will continue to be the wave of the future, barring regulatory concerns.

Emerging stock markets will continue to grow in importance as their economies grow and companies look for more capital to expand both domestically and internationally. As companies drive down costs to boost their profitability and market value, they will need to reduce borrowing costs. Greater emphasis will be placed on moving corporate cash worldwide to take advantage of differing rates of return. In addition, they will need to perfect their strategies for issuing bonds at the cheapest price possible and minimizing their tax bills worldwide.

However, the United States has been clamping down on tax minimization schemes and attacking those that provide them (such as law firms and public accounting firms), as well as going after the corporate clients that are adopting them. In addition, the U.S. and other OECD countries are going after tax-haven countries and trying to break down the barriers to bank secrecy so they can access the records of individuals and companies they suspect are illegally avoiding taxes. As companies establish strategies to take advantage of tax havens, they must be very careful to avoid strategies that will turn them into the next Enron or Parmalat. The move to drive down costs can't come at the expense of the future viability of the company.

The OECD, the IMF, and the EU are three institutions that will help countries narrow their tax differences and crack down on the transfer of money for illegal purposes. Although illegal financial transfers have occurred for years, especially due to drug trafficking, the attacks on 9/11, and subsequent moves to track down money laundering by terrorists have created a more urgent need to reform the global financial system. As governments attempt to institute tax reform to collect more tax revenues from companies, they will have to perform a delicate balancing act of increasing revenues without stifling innovation and forcing companies to search for the next best tax haven country. ■

CASE Does The Devil Really Wear Prada?

Probably not, but the Italian Prada Group, clearly one of the top luxury businesses in the world, is designing, producing, and distributing luxury handbags, leather goods, footwear, ready-to-wear apparel, accessories, eyewear, and fragrances all over the world.[53] It operates in 70 countries through 461 directly operated stores, 25 franchise stores, and high-end multi-brand stores and luxury department stores.

Prada is a closely held firm in which the Prada family—led by Miuccia Prada, president and head designer, and her husband, CEO Patrizio Bertelli—holds 80 percent of the shares,

A Chinese woman walks past the Prada store in Beijing China. According to the Beijing-based World Luxury Association, the Chinese luxury market is the largest in the world, replacing the Japanese, and Chinese consumers will account for about 1/3 of the global market by 2015.
Source: Feng Li/Getty Images

with Italian bank Intesa Sanpaolo holding the rest. When Bertelli and Prada realized that the future of luxury consumption would be in Asia, they had to decide how they were going to fund their expansion. Due to a string of debt-financed acquisitions in the early 2000s, Prada ran into liquidity problems and had to turn to Intesa for funding. Intesa purchased the 5 percent interest in the company in 2006 for ¢100 million, which put a valuation on Prada of ¢2 billion at the time. They had considered an IPO in 2001 and 2008, but the collapse in global stock markets both times forced them to pull back. However, 2011 seemed like a good time. Issuing stock to outside investors would bring in new money, but it would also force Prada to deal with non-family shareholders and the financial discipline of the market. Also, they had to figure out where to issue the IPO and how much of the company they should sell. Should they list on the Milan Stock Exchange, as they were being advised by nearly everyone in Italy? Or should they become the first Italian company to list in Hong Kong, where they could be closer to the future growth markets in China?

Who Is Prada?

Prada began in 1913 when Mario Prada opened a luxury store in the Galleria Vittorio Emanuele II in Milan. Prada quickly built a strong reputation in luxury goods due to its exclusive designs, superior manufacturing techniques, and high-quality materials. By 1919, Prada had become an official supplier to the Italian Royal Family and a benchmark for fashion throughout Europe.

At the end of the 1970s, Mario's great-granddaughter, Miuccia Prada, entered into a partnership with Patrizio Bertelli, a Tuscan businessman who was involved in high-quality leather goods. Initially, Bertelli's company, I.P.I. spa, had an exclusive license to produce and distribute leather goods using the Prada name, but in 2003 I.P.I. spa and Prada merged into Prada SpA. (SpA—Società per Anzioni—is the same as "corporation" in the U.S. or plc in the U.K.).

In the 1990s and early 2000s, Prada began to expand by launching new brands (such as Miu Miu), acquiring new businesses (such as Church's Group and Car Shoe), and entering into licensing and joint venture agreements with Italian eyewear manufacturer Luxottica and Spanish cosmetic manufacturer PUIG Beauty & Fashion Group. With these acquisitions, Prada expanded its product lines and opened new stores. It even launched a new phone by LG of South Korea.

In 2010, Prada was basically a European company, generating nearly half of its revenues from Europe, including 19.5 percent from Italy. However, the importance of Asia was expanding. By 2012, European revenues were 22.7 percent, including 16.2 percent from Italy, but Asia Pacific (excluding Japan) rose to 35.6 of total revenues. In spite of its acquisitions, the Prada brand still counted for nearly 80 percent of the company's global revenues. The Asia-Pacific area had the highest growth rate of all geographic areas in which Prada was operating, benefitting from organic growth rather than acquisitions. Prada opened 17 new stores in the region and did a lot of work upgrading existing stores.

Why China?

The luxury goods market, of which Prada is a member, is hard to define. It is typically composed of goods that are high-priced, high-quality, and high-status. Some of the other largest luxury goods firms in the world are French-based LVMH, Christian Dior (which holds 42 percent of LVMH), PPR (which includes Gucci and Yves Saint Laurent), and Richemont (which includes Cartier, Chloé, and Alfred Dunhil, and has a JV with Polo Ralph Lauren). Of course, there are also luxury goods firms in many industries, such as fashion, automobiles, watches and jewelry, and drinks. It is clear, however, that Asia, especially China, is rapidly becoming the future of the luxury goods industry.

In addition to having the largest population in the world, China is now the world's second largest economy and growing at a faster rate than any of the advanced countries and the rest of the BRICs. There are several reasons why China is becoming the target of the luxury goods markets. The country is expected to be the largest luxury market in the world by 2020, catering to both men and women. Until recently, the market in China was driven by men, but women are becoming increasingly important. Maserati SpA and Bulgari SpA have been successful in China because they have positioned themselves as the ultimate male status symbols. Much of the luxury goods purchases were by men for women, but now women are starting to assert themselves as consumers. In 2009, for example, 30 percent of Maserati's sales were to women, up from 7 percent in 2005. In the broader luxury market sales, women accounted for over half of the $15 billion in sales, compared with 45 percent in 2008. Also, the average female luxury consumer spent 22 percent more in 2010 than in 2008.

The upshot of the emerging female luxury goods consumer is that brands that have catered more to women are putting even greater emphasis on China. Chloé, for example, predicts that China will be its biggest market by 2013. Female luxury consumers in China are a result of more women achieving success in business.

This is not lost on Prada, but it is interested in China for other reasons as well. As the head designer for the company, Ms. Prada is especially drawn to Chinese influences on fashion, which she feels are more contemporary than conservative Europe. Her company has a design team of 60 designers that she feels are curious, excited, fresh, and innovative. To take advantage of this talent, Prada is opening a design center in Hong Kong and hopes to expand its stores by 10–12 per year from 14 stores in 2011. Not only is China its market of the future, as it is for many other luxury goods companies, but it is also the location of ideas. It makes sense that Prada would need to set up a team to design products for the Chinese market, as well as get innovative ideas that it can use for its products worldwide.

Where to Issue the IPO?

As Prada considered how to expand, it looked at several options. It could borrow from banks, issue bonds in the domestic and international bond markets, and bring in outside investors. In 2010, 51 percent of Prada's assets were funded by equity and 49 percent by debt; compare that to a sample of Italian companies, whose average debt/asset ratio in 2009–2010 was much higher at 57.4 percent. Of the debt, 57 percent was in current liabilities and 43 percent in long-term debt. Prada's long-term debt is primarily bank debt, sometimes to a syndicate of banks. Although its largest exposure in long-term debt is in euros, it also has long-term debt in U.S. dollars, Chinese renminbi, Japanese yen, and British pounds. Apparently, Prada's strategy in debt markets has been to work with banks instead of relying on the Eurobond or Foreign Bond markets.

The decision to raise capital in the form of equity is complicated. As noted earlier, Prada is a closely held family company, so raising capital through an IPO is a major departure from the past. Would the Prada family be willing to give up a say in the future of the company? If so, where would be the best place to list the IPO? As an Italian company based in Milan, it would seem logical to list on the Milan stock exchange. But being the rebel she is, Ms. Prada had other ideas. Her feeling was that Hong Kong would be a better choice for several reasons. First, brand name companies feel that having an important presence in the region is the best way to get your brand out to the consumer. Road shows attract a lot of press and attention from consumers as well as the financial community. Given the projected growth of China, Hong Kong makes sense. Second, Hong Kong was the world's biggest IPO market in 2010, with US $57.7 billion raised from 87 listings.

Timing is everything, of course. Prada has tried to raise capital before, but the timing just wasn't right, mostly due to factors out of their control. After the Japanese earthquake on March 11, 2011, there was a lull in market activity, but sales began to pick up again once markets quieted down. For instance, Glencore International PLC raised more than $10 billion in a London-Hong Kong listing—the largest in 2011—which made the IPO market in general seem promising. And the rapid influx of capital into Hong Kong from China coincided with Prada's decision to go to the markets.

The IPO

Finally, Prada decided to move forward with the IPO in Hong Kong, not Milan. The feeling was that since the proceeds would be used to fund expansion in China, why not bring in investors from Hong Kong, the gateway to China? Prada decided to sell a 20 percent stake in the company, significantly changing its ownership structure. But Ms. Prada knew it was the right move. Friends and advisors convinced her that in some respects the stock market and the discipline it imposes would help ensure the future of Prada and help with the succession. Prada hoped to raise 20 billion HK$ in the offering (about US $2.6 billion), a significant amount of money. The goal was to sell about 423 million shares at HK$36.50 to HK$48.00. If the demand were strong, Prada could sell an additional 63 million shares, or 15 percent of the offer on an over-allotment option. That goal was to list on the stock exchange on June 24, 2011, after beginning the process with institutional investors and then the wider investing public. As Prada got closer to the listing date, prices began to move down a little due to uncertainty in global markets from the European debt crisis, the U.S. debt crisis, and inflation in China. Prada adjusted its target price to consumers to a range of HK$39.50 to HK$42.25 per share (US $5.07 to US $5.42). This would put its value at 22.8 to 24.4 times 2011 expected earnings, which is still higher than LVMH, which trades at 20.1 times earnings. Pricing is clearly better in Hong Kong than elsewhere.

When the stock finally hit the exchange, retail investors didn't come into the market as much as anticipated, and Prada wasn't able to sell all of the shares allotted to investors. In addition, prices didn't really jump all that much initially. Within about two weeks, however, prices were up 13 percent over their HK$39.50 IPO price, or HK$44.64.

Now we'll see how this move affects Prada in the future, as well as other companies preparing to jump into Hong Kong to take advantage of rising expectations in China. If this is a successful move, will Prada issue more stock in the future and further dilute the ownership of the Prada family? Only time will tell.

QUESTIONS

10-3. Why does Prada need to raise additional funds?

✪ **10-4.** Do you agree with the decision to list an IPO, or should Prada have borrowed more money, possibly floating a dim sum bond or a Eurobond in London or elsewhere?

10-5. What do you feel are the best justifications for Prada to issue the IPO in Hong Kong? Are there any downsides to their decision to list in Hong Kong?

✪ **10-6.** Many of the other luxury fashion companies are also largely family owned. What is the impact to Prada of diluting the family ownership, and is this a model that other companies can be expected to follow?

10-7. What types of foreign exchange risk does Prada face, and what advice would you give them to hedge against their risks?

SUMMARY

- The corporate finance function deals with the acquisition of financial resources and their allocation among the company's present and potential activities and projects.
- CFOs need to be concerned with the international dimensions of the company's capital structure, capital budgeting decisions, long-term financing, and working capital management.
- Country-specific factors are the most important determination of a company's capital structure.
- Two major sources of funds external to the MNE's normal operations are debt markets and equity markets.
- A Eurocurrency is any currency banked outside its country of origin, but it is primarily dollars banked outside the United States.
- A foreign bond is one sold outside the country of the borrower but denominated in the currency of the country of issue. A Eurobond is a bond issue sold in a currency other than that of the country of issue.

- Euroequities are shares listed on stock exchanges in countries other than the home country of the issuing company. Most foreign companies that list on the U.S. stock exchanges do so through American Depositary Receipts (ADRs), which are financial documents that represent a share or part of a share of stock in the foreign company. ADRs are easier to trade on the U.S. exchanges than are foreign shares.
- Offshore financial centers such as Bahrain, the Caribbean, Hong Kong, London, New York, Singapore, and Switzerland deal in large amounts of foreign currency and enable companies to take advantage of favorable tax rates.
- International tax planning has a strong impact on the choice of location for the initial investment, the legal form of the new enterprise, the method of financing, and the method of setting transfer prices.
- Countries differ in terms of the types of taxes they have (income versus excise), the tax rates applied to income, the determination of taxable income, and the treatment of foreign-source income.
- Tax deferral means that the income a foreign subsidiary earns is taxed only when it is remitted to the parent as a dividend, not when it is earned.
- A controlled foreign corporation (CFC) must declare its Subpart F income as taxable to the parent in the year it is earned, whether or not it is remitted as a dividend.
- A tax credit allows a parent company to reduce its tax liability by the direct amount its subsidiary pays a foreign government on income that must be taxed by the parent company's government.
- The purpose of tax treaties is to prevent international double taxation or to provide remedies when it occurs.

KEY TERMS

active income (p. 427)
American Depositary Receipt (ADR) (p. 424)
arm's-length price (p. 428)
controlled foreign corporation (CFC) (p. 426)
Eurobond (p. 419)
Eurocredit (p. 417)
Eurocurrency (p. 416)
Eurocurrency market (p. 416)
Eurodollar (p. 417)
Euroequity market (p. 423)
foreign bonds (p. 418)
leverage (p. 413)
London Inter-Bank Offered Rate (LIBOR) (p. 418)
market (p. 421)
market capitalization (p. 421)
offshore financial centers (OFCs) (p. 430)
offshore financing (p. 430)
sovereign wealth fund (SWF) (p. 420)
Subpart F (or passive) income (p. 427)
syndication (p. 417)

ENDNOTES

1 ***Sources include the following:*** "People on the Move," *Deseret News* (January 31, 1999): M02; Wells Fargo News Release, "Wells Fargo & Company and First Security Corporation Agree to Merge" (April 10, 2000), at www.wellsfargo.com/press/firstsec20000410?year= 2000 (accessed November 20, 2007); interviews with Ali Manbeian and Jason Langston; Wells Fargo company literature.

2 Jonathan Berk, Peter De Marzo and Jarrad Harford, *Fundamentals of Corporate Finance*, second edition (Pearson Prentice-Hall, Upper Saddle Ridge, NJ: 2012), 9–10.

3 "Theory versus the Real World," *Finance & Treasury* (April 26, 1993): 1.

4 Abe de Jong, Rezaul Kabir, and Thuy Thu Nguyen, "Capital Structure around the World: The Roles of Firm- and Country-Specific Determinants," *Journal of Banking & Finance* 32 (2008), pp. 1954–1969.

5 De Jong et al., "Capital Structure around the World, op. cit.

6 Charles Forelle, "The Isle That Rattled the World—Tiny Iceland Created a Vast Bubble, Leaving Wreckage Everywhere When It Popped," *Wall Street Journal* (December 27, 2008): A1.

7 James Hookway and Nopparat Chaichalearmmongkol, "Thailand Wrestles with Currency Woes," *The Wall Street Journal* (May 28, 2013).

8 David Enrich, Geoffrey T. Smith and Andrew Morse, ""Rules for Lenders Relaxed," *The Wall Street Journal*, January 7, 2013, C1.

9 Nu Skin Enterprises Inc., *Nu Skin Annual Report* (2010): 62.

10 Patrick McGuire, "A Shift in London's Eurodollar Market," *BIS Quarterly Review* (September 2004): 67.

11 Michael J. de La Merced, "Understanding LIBOR," *The Wall Street Journal* (July 11, 2012): B3; David Enrich and Max Colchester, "Before Scandal, Clash Over Control of LIBOR, *The Wall Street Journal* (September 11, 2012): A1.

12 Global-rates.com (accessed on May 15, 2013).

13 Op. cit., Enrich and Colchester; David Enrich, "Former Trader is Charged in U.K. Libor Probe," *The Wall Street Journal* (June 19, 2013, C3).

14 Financial Market Series, *Bond Markets* (October 2012): 3, (accessed June 3, 2013).

15 "IMF Global Stability Report, 2009": 177.

16 Fiona Law, "Dim-Sum Bond Issuance Climbs," *The Wall Street Journal*, online edition (accessed March 25, 2013).

17 Peter Stein, "'Dim Sum Bonds' on the Menu For Foreign Investors," *The Wall Street Journal* (October 31, 2010), retrieved July 13, 2011, from http://wsj.com.

18 "An Offer They Can Refuse," *Euromoney* (February 1995): 76.

19 Anant Sundaram, "International Financial Markets," in Dennis E. Logue (ed.), *Handbook of Modern Finance* (New York: Warren, Gorham, Lamont, 1994): F3–F4.

20 "Amcor Announces Successful ¢550 Million Benchmark Bond Issue," AMCOR News Release (accessed July 18, 2011).

21 "Alliance Oil Company Issues 7-Year Eurobond," *The Wall Street Journal*, online edition (accessed April 25, 2013).

22 The Sovereign Wealth Fund Institute, (accessed on June 3, 2013).

23 Ibid.

24 Telis Demos, "First Chinese IPO of 2013 Delivers Decent Pop," *The Wall Street Journal, Money Beat*, blogs.wsj.com/moneybeat/2013/06/06.

25 Dan Horch, "After IPO Drought, Brazil Is More Hospitable to Investors," *The New York Times* (January 9, 2013): B5.

26 World Federation of Exchanges, "2010 WFE Market Highlights" (January 26, 2011), at http://world-exchanges.org/files/file/stats%20and%20

charts/2010%20WFE%20Market%20Highlights.pdf, (accessed June 4, 2013).

27 Mark J. Perry,"World Stock Market Capitalization closes year at $54.6 Trillion,"AEIdeas (January 18, 2013) at www.aei-ideas.org/2013/01/world-stock-market-capitalization-at-54-6-trillion/ (accessed June 4, 2013).

28 Maggie Lake,"Stock Marker Merger Mania: Marriage of Necessity?" *CNN* (February 10, 2011), at http://business.blogs.cnn.com/2011/02/10/stock-market-merger-mania/ (accessed July 14, 2011).

29 Michael J. de la Madrid,"From Old and New, a Powerhouse,"*The New York Times* (December 21, 2012): B1;"NYSE Euronext Shareholders Approve Acquisition by IntercontinentalExchange,"June 3, 2013 (accessed June 4, 2013).

30 "Definition of Euroequity"in Investopedia, (accessed on June 19, 2013).

31 Financial Times, http://lexicon.ft.com/Term?term=euro_equity-issue, accessed June 10, 2013.

32 Vinod Kumar,"Tata Communications Says to Delist from NYSE,"*The Economic Times* (accessed June 4, 2013).

33 OECD,"Taxation of Corporate and Capital Income, Table II.1,"*OECD Tax Database* (2013), www.oecd.org/tax/taxdatabase.htm (accessed June 19, 2013).

34 Deloitte,"International Tax and Business Guide: Germany"(2023), at www.deloitte.com/taxguides.

35 Deloitte,"International Tax and Business Guide: Hong Kong"(2013).

36 Johnston,"Enron Avoided Income Taxes in 4 of 5 Years."

37 OECD, *Transfer Pricing Guidelines for Multinational Enterprises and Tax Administrations*, Paris: OECD Publishing, August 11, 2009, www.oecd.org/document/34/0,3343,en_2649_33753_1915490_1_1_1_1,00.html (accessed October 23, 2009).

38 Ronald Fink,"Haven or Hell,"*CFO Magazine* (March 2004), www.cfo.com/article.cfm/3012017 (accessed October 23, 2009); Helen Shaw, "Transfer Students,"*CFO Magazine* (April 2007), at www.cfo.com/article.cfm/8885626/c_8910395?f=insidecfo (accessed August 30, 2007).

39 IRS Publication 901, *U.S. Tax Treaties*, Revised April 2013, at www.irs.gov/pub/irs-pdf/p901.pdf.

40 Eric Pfanner,"European Countries Seek More Taxes from U.S. Multinational Companies,"*The New York Times* (November 19, 2012): B1.

41 IMF Monetary and Exchange Affairs Department,"IMF Background Paper: Offshore Financial Centers"(www.imf.org/external/np/mae/oshore/2000/eng/back.htm#1). June 23, 2000

42 Ibid.

43 "How the Heavyweights Shape Up,"*Euromoney* (May 1990): 56.

44 "On or Off? It's a Matter of Degree,"in"Places in the Sun: A Special Report on Offshore Finance,"*The Economist* (February 24, 2007): 7.

45 OECD, *Harmful Tax Competition: An Emerging Global Issue* (Paris: OECD, 1998): 23.

46 OECD, *Harmful Tax Competition: An Emerging Global Issue* (Paris: OECD, 1998): 27.

47 OECD, *Overview or the OECD's Work on Countering International Tax Evasion* (Paris: OECD, August 11, 2009): 8; www.oecd.org/dataoecd/32/45/42356522.pdf (accessed October 23, 2009).

48 David Cay Johnston,"Enron Avoided Income Taxes in 4 of 5 Years,"*New York Times (Late Edition [East Coast])* (January 17, 2002): A1.

49 Lucy Komisar,"Funny Money,"*Metroactive News & Issues*, January 24, 2002, at www.metroactive.com/papers/sonoma/01.24.02/offshorebanking-0204.html (accessed June 7, 2005).

50 Liz Rappaort,"Bank Settles Iran Money Case,"*The Wall Street Journal* (August 15, 2012): A1.

51 Nick Davis,"Tax Spotlight Worries Cayman Islands,"*BBC News* (March 31, 2009) at news.bbc.co.uk/go/pr/fr/-/2/hi/americas/7972695.stm (accessed October 23, 2009).

52 Pfanner, ibid.

53 ***Sources include the following:*** "Hong Kong's Fickle IPO Investors," *The Wall Street Journal* (July 11, 2011); Kelvin Chan,"Prada Says Hong Kong IPO Roadshow Going Well,"*Businessweek* (June 12, 2011); George Stalk and David Michael,"What the West Doesn't Get About China," *Harvard Business Review* (June 2011): 25–27; Prudence Ho,"Hong Kong's IPO Engine Sputters,"*The Wall Street Journal* (online.wsj.com, June 17, 2011); Nisha Gopolan and Prudence Ho,"Prada's Promising IPO,"*The Wall Street Journal* (June 7, 2011): C3; Laurie Burkett,"In China, Women Begin Splurging,"*The Wall Street Journal* (June 13, 2011): B11; Prudence Ho and Yvonne Lee,"Hong Kong IPOs Back in Fashion," *The Wall Street Journal* (May 23, 2011): B2; Alison Tudor,"Prada Sees Future in Asia,"*The Wall Street Journal* (June 13, 2011): C3.

CHAPTER 11
Ethics and Social Responsibility

OBJECTIVES

After studying this chapter, you should be able to

1. Examine the broad foundations of ethical behavior
2. Demonstrate the cultural and legal foundations of ethical behavior
3. Discuss the importance of social responsibility when operating internationally, especially in the areas of sustainability
4. Discuss key issues in the social activities and consequences of globalized business
5. Examine corporate responses to globalization in the form of codes of conduct, among other things

MyManagementLab®

Improve Your Grade!

When you see this icon ✪, visit **www.mymanagementlab.com** for activities that are applied, personalized, and offer immediate feedback.

When the last tree has been cut down, the last river has been polluted and the last fish has been caught—only then do you realize that money can't buy everything.

—Native American proverb

Source: © siamphoto - Fotolia.com

CASE Ecomagination and the Global Greening of GE

As noted on Map 11.1, a recent TV ad invites viewers to "accompany" a small green frog as it does a little globe hopping from one exotic location to another.[1] The frog, however, doesn't seem intent on hitting the usual tourist spots, instead preferring stopovers at such places as a solar farm in South Korea, a water-purification plant in Kuwait, and a wind farm in Germany. To begin the second leg of his tour, he hops on a GE90 Aircraft engine flying over China and takes viewers to a "clean" coal-powered facility somewhere in Florida. Then he boards a GE Evolution locomotive in the Canadian Rockies as a voiceover explains the point of all this seemingly ordinary sightseeing: "At GE, we're combining imagination with advanced technology around the world to make it a better place to live for everyone." The journey's end finds our frog in the midst of a lush—and very green—tropical rain forest.

"GREEN IS GREEN"

The ad is part of a major promotional campaign by General Electric Company (GE) for its Ecomagination Initiative. Announced in 2005 by CEO Jeffrey Immelt, Ecomagination is an ambitious strategy designed to demonstrate that an ecologically conscious conglomerate can cultivate the bottom line while doing its duty toward the global environment—hence, the campaign motto "Green Is Green." The clever promotional campaign has highlighted several interesting Ecomagination initiatives, such as the 2011 Super Bowl ad on Biogas Technology featuring cows at a rock concert (the accompanying endnote provides links to the YouTube ads).

The world's second largest corporation (in terms of market capitalization), GE is based in Fairfield, Connecticut and operates in more than 100 countries through six core businesses: commercial finance, consumer finance, industrial manufacturing, infrastructure, healthcare, and communications. It sells, among other things, appliances, aircraft engines, consumer electronics, energy-related products such as solar panels and wind generators, locomotive engines, and nuclear products and services through a venture with GE Hitachi. The company's media division also includes 49 percent ownership of NBC Universal, following the completion of its sale of the majority ownership to Comcast Corporation in the first quarter of 2011.

When the company announced its plan to launch an internal green revolution, GE surprised both investors and industrial customers who had long seen the firm as an ally in the struggle against environmental activists and lobbyists. But as more and more evidence piles up to support the claim that carbon dioxide emitted from human-made sources is heating up average global temperatures, GE has decided to take a more conciliatory stance, allying itself with a growing number of companies that regard investor and environmental interests as intrinsically interlocked, rather than diametrically opposed.

Commitments and Goals

GE's new initiative represents five basic commitments on its part: (1) to reduce greenhouse emissions and improve the energy efficiency of operations; (2) to double investment in the research and development of "clean" technologies; (3) to increase revenues from those same technologies; (4) to reduce its global water use by 20 percent; and (5) to keep the public informed. It now evaluates business unit managers not only on profitability and return on capital but also on success in reducing carbon dioxide emissions, the chief greenhouse gas (GHG) attributed to global warming. Energy-intensive divisions, such as those catering to the power and industrial sectors, are responsible for the largest cuts, but even the financial services and communications units are required to reduce whatever emissions they produce.

The company's overall target was a 1 percent reduction from 2004 levels by 2012. At first glance, the goal doesn't seem to have been overly ambitious, but that number represents a significant improvement if you account for the fact that, given GE's projected growth, levels would otherwise soar to 40 percent above 2004 levels. Immelt also committed the company to reducing the intensity of GHG emissions—its level of emissions in relation to the company's economic activity—30 percent by 2008 and to improving energy efficiency 30 percent by 2012. To ensure that these goals were met, Immelt assembled a cross-business, cross-functional team to oversee planning and monitor progress. By 2011, the company had reduced GHG emissions by 29 percent, had improved energy intensity by 32 percent from 2004 levels.

A Little Consensus Seeking

In addition to instituting the internal changes necessary to curb GHG emissions, Immelt has taken a close look at GE's global political environment. He has enlisted the Belgian and Japanese governments in the global ecological discussion and has allied GE with other green-minded corporations to lobby American lawmakers on such matters as mandatory GHG reductions. Working with the Environmental and Natural Resources Defense Council and the Pew Center on Global

MAP 11.1 Global Travels of GE's "Green Frog," Its Symbol of Commitment to the Environment

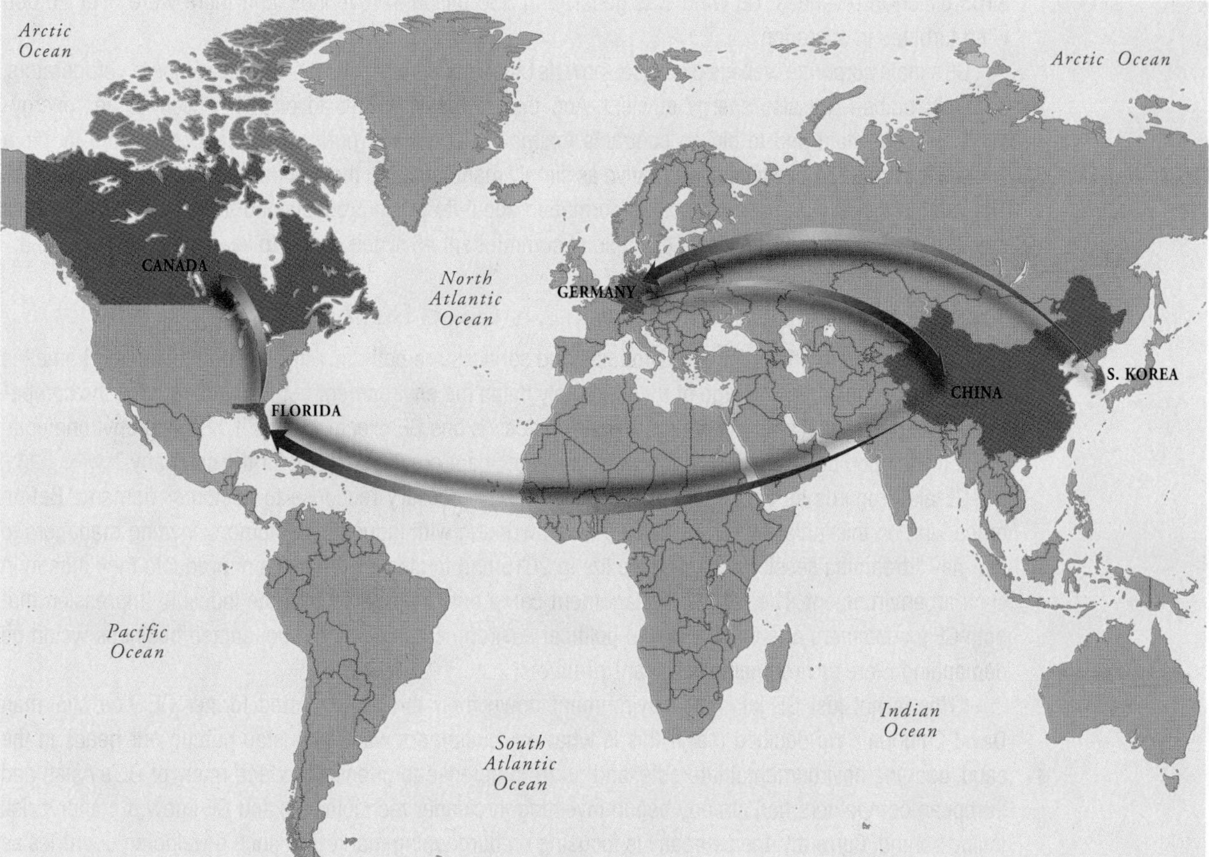

Climate Change, GE has also joined the likes of BP, DuPont, and Duke Energy to form the U.S. Climate Action Partnership, which seeks to help shape the international political debate over global warming.

Bear in mind that neither GE nor its corporate allies claim to be acting strictly from civic-minded motives. As to be expected, they're pursuing their own best interests, particularly the idea that ecologically proactive firms are fashioning a strategic advantage over companies that are still dragging their feet. With other countries already enforcing limits stipulated by the Kyoto Protocol, and with other jurisdictions (such as the state of California) beginning to set their own limits, global corporations have much more to consider when it comes to developing forward-looking strategies and making long-term investments in an increasingly fragmented regulatory environment. With half of its markets located outside the United States, GE is already under the jurisdiction of foreign governments that are more active than the U.S. in addressing environmental issues.

TECHNOLOGICAL TACTICS AND ECO-FRIENDLY PRODUCTS

Under Immelt's direction, GE has also been gearing up to double R&D investment in clean technologies, including renewable-energy, water-purification processes, and fuel-efficient products, from $700 million in 2005 to $1.5 billion in 2010, and $2.3 billion in 2011. In turn, GE expects significant revenue growth. Its Ecomagination products earned $6 billion in 2004, $12 billion in 2006, $18 billion in 2009, and $21 billion in 2011.

Back in 2005, when the Ecomagination initiative was first launched, GE marketed only 17 products that met its own Ecomagination criteria; by 2009, there were 90 such products, including the Jenbacher Biogas Engine, which converts biological waste into electricity and heat, as well as all of GE's

EnergyStar-approved consumer products. By 2011, there were 140 products and solutions generating $105 billion in revenues. GE wind was generating $30 billion in revenues, and there were over 20,000 wind turbines in operation.

GE's main corporate website discusses how its other standard products—clothes washers, refrigerators, and light bulbs—are also energy efficient. And the company intends to establish itself as an "energy-services" consultant and to bid on contracts for maintaining water-purification plants and wind farms, a venture that could be five times as lucrative as simply manufacturing the products needed for such projects. The use of its website to communicate information about its green products and the efforts to improve its own GHG emissions reduction is an example of commitment #5, listed above: to keep the public informed.

"Solving Environmental Problems Is Good Business"

GE insists that the markets for such products and services are both growing and profitable, and Immelt is convinced that taking advantage of them not only helps the environment but also strengthens the company's strategic position with major profit opportunities. As one GE executive puts it, "Solving environmental problems is good business ... and constitutes a significant growth strategy for the company."

GE also regards its Ecomagination strategy as a necessary response to customer demand. Before embarking on this initiative, GE spent 18 months working with industrial customers, inviting managers to two-day "dreaming sessions" to imagine life in 2015 and to discuss the kinds of products they'd need in such an environment. The result? Management came out of the talks with the indelible impression that both GE's customers and the social and political environments in which it conducted business would be demanding more environmentally "clean" products.

"This is not just GE jamming environment down their throats," insisted former GE vice chairman David Calhoun. "We decided that if this is what our customers want, let's stop putting our heads in the sand, dodging environmental interests, and go from defense to offense." In fact, many of GE's Asian and European competitors had already begun investing in cleaner technologies, and GE knew it couldn't risk falling behind. Currently, the company is focusing on burgeoning markets in such developing countries as China and India, where rapid economic growth has spurred the need for expanded infrastructures, such as water and sewage systems, and for means of curbing appallingly high levels of pollution. China alone, which is home to no fewer than 16 of the world's 20 most polluted cities, has earmarked at least $85 billion for environmental spending.

MIXED REACTIONS

Not surprisingly, GE has been praised for its efforts to go green. It reached the eleventh spot on *Fortune* magazine's list of the "Most Admired Companies" for 2013, and it earned a place on the Dow Jones Sustainability Index, which identifies the 300 firms that perform best according to combined environmental, social, and financial criteria.

At the same time, however, the company has generated a certain amount of skepticism. What happens, for example, if the markets it's betting on don't materialize fast enough (or at all)? Back in the 1980s and 1990s, for instance, a number of firms—including DuPont and the French water company Suez—predicted double-digit growth in clean-technology markets and invested heavily in the area, only to be forced to scale back considerably when demand didn't take off as expected.

Another potential risk revolves around the participation of developing nations in the clean-technology push. In particular, will they be willing to pay prices that developed countries pay for the technology that reaches the market? Even GE's Calhoun admitted that, at least in the key Chinese market, margins were already tight. And GE still faces the challenge of implementing the internal changes entailed by its fledgling green strategy. Traditionally, the firm's culture has been accustomed to strategies of incremental change in time-tested products and services. In fact, its highly touted Six Sigma program, championed by ex-CEO Jack Welch, inherently discourages radical deviation and unnecessary risk taking. Management may have its work cut out when it comes to persuading marketing, sales, and production teams that untested, early-stage Ecomagination products are worth the risk.

Then, of course, there are clients and shareholders. Many of GE's customers work out of the utility sector, which has assumed a leadership role in disregarding warnings of climatic change and opposing ecofriendly regulation. In 2007, GE was presented with a shareowner resolution calling for top management to document the projected costs, benefits, and profits of the Ecomagination initiative. Some investors seemed particularly concerned about the company's newfound activism and the potential of newly instituted greening initiatives to alienate industrial customers. Given the enormous growth in revenue from the Ecomagination product line, generating more than $105 billion in revenue since 2005, it seems that GE's management made both a wise and profitable decision. ■

CRN
Case Review Note

QUESTIONS

11-1. What are the major challenges GE faces in adopting a green strategy while keeping all of its stakeholders happy?

11-2. From the standpoint of environmental impact, do you think it's more important for GE to reduce its carbon footprint or to develop products that fit their Ecomagination strategy of being energy efficient?

INTRODUCTION

As we transition from the environments of international business to operations, let's look at how globalization affects society and managers' judgments as they interact with different laws and cultures. As we learned in Chapter 1, the globalization of business has not been only positive, but has also resulted in three major criticisms: threats to national sovereignty, growth and environmental stress, and rising income inequality and personal stress. Doing business abroad is not easy. The greater the "distance" from one's home country, the more complicated it is to do business. Distance can be described in many different ways, but one way to identify it is the acronym CAGE: cultural (also known as psychic distance), administrative (such as political and institutional policies), geographic, and economic.[2] Given the criticisms of globalization and the challenge of companies and individuals doing business in areas of the world that are quite distant, as defined above, how can companies and individuals be successful, or at least not create serious mistakes?

This chapter examines globalization and society from the standpoint of ethics and social responsibility. Initially, we'll examine ethics in a global context, especially in issues surrounding bribery and corruption, the environment, and corporate codes of conduct. Then we'll look at corporate social responsibility more broadly and examine how individuals as well as companies are trying to improve the human condition.

STAKEHOLDER TRADE-OFFS

Companies must satisfy
- Shareholders,
- Employees,
- Customers,
- Society.

To prosper—indeed, to survive—a company must satisfy different groups of **stakeholders**, including shareholders, employees, customers, suppliers, and society at large. Obviously, this juggling act can be quite tricky. The shareholder (or stockholder)-versus-stakeholder dilemma pits the demands of one stakeholder against all the others. The basic idea of focusing on stakeholders more broadly is that companies can consider various socially important groups when making decisions.[3] In the short term, for example, group aims often conflict. *Shareholders* want additional sales and increased productivity (which result in higher profits and returns). *Employees* want safer workplaces and higher compensation. *Customers* want higher-quality products at lower prices. *Society* would like to see more jobs, increased corporate taxes, more corporate support for social services, and more trustworthy behavior on the part of corporate executives.

In the *long* term, all of these aims must be adequately met. If they aren't, there's a good chance that none of them will be, especially if each stakeholder group is powerful enough to bring operations to a standstill. In addition, pressure groups—which may reflect the interests of any stakeholder group—lobby governments to regulate MNE activities both at home and abroad.

As we noted in our opening case, for example, GE's Ecomagination initiative has generated pressure from various constituencies, including clients and shareholders concerned about profitability, various governments concerned with drafting regulations, employees wondering about changes in the company's strategies and goals, and environmental lobbyists, NGOs, and fellow businesses trying to preserve the environment. Each group has a powerful influence on how GE does business and on how successful it is in the marketplace.

THE FOUNDATIONS OF ETHICAL BEHAVIOR

Many actions elicit universal agreement on what is right or wrong, but other situations are less clear.

Companies and those who work for them must act *responsibly* wherever they go. However, a look at ethical behavior tends to focus on individuals—those who finally make the decision of how to behave. Top management can determine the values a company espouses and to which employees must adhere. Such values are generally included in a Code of Conduct (discussed at the end of the chapter) and in the behavior of other individuals in the organization, especially peers and superiors. In order to ensure adherence to those values, management will try to hire individuals who are willing to work in the type of ethical environment it is trying to create. However, people still must make the decision about how they are going to act in any given situation.

There are three levels of moral development

- Preconventional
- Conventional
- Postconventional, autonomous, or principled

The sections below will examine the cultural and legal dimensions of ethical behavior in a global context. First, though, let's briefly examine the broad foundations of ethical behavior. There are three levels of moral development:[4]

- Level 1, the *preconventional* level, where children learn what is right and wrong but don't necessarily understand *why* their behavior is right or wrong.
- Level 2, the *conventional* level, where we learn role conformity, first from our peers (including parents), then from societal laws. One could argue that company codes of conduct are also part of the *conventional* level of behavior in the narrow context of a company rather than a society. However, it is likely that these codes also reflect the values of the company's home country.
- Level 3, the *postconventional, autonomous, or principled* level, where individuals internalize moral behavior, not because they are afraid of sanctions, but because they truly believe such behavior is right.

It is possible that behaviors under Level 2 and Level 3 are the same as long as individuals accept the laws where they live, or the codes of conduct of the companies they work for, as consistent with what they believe is correct.[5]

Teleological Approach: Decisions are based on the consequences of the action.

Utilitarianism: An action if right if it produces the greatest amount of good.

Deontological Approach: Moral judgments are made and moral reasoning occurs independent of consequences.

When individuals confronted with ethical decisions enter the realm of moral reasoning, they examine their moral values, especially as related to levels 2 and 3 above, and decide what to do. One method of doing so, the **teleological approach**, holds to the idea that decisions are based on the consequences of the action. **Utilitarianism**, a consequences-based theory of moral reasoning, means that "an action is right if it produces, or if it tends to produce, the greatest amount of good for the greatest number of people affected by the action. Otherwise, the action is wrong."[6] A second method, the **deontological approach**, asserts that we make moral judgments or engage in moral reasoning independent of consequences. It implies that actions are right or wrong *per se.*[7] In other words, ethics teaches that "people have a responsibility to do what is right and to avoid doing what is wrong."[8] When individuals engage in moral reasoning, they use one or the other of these methods, or possibly some mixture of the two.

When an individual moves abroad, moral reasoning becomes very complicated. Consequences may vary due to legal differences, and what is right or wrong may depend to an extent on local values. People need to figure out how make moral decisions—and so do the companies they work for. Two questions arise here: Why should companies and individuals care about ethical behavior? And what are the cultural and legal foundations of ethical behavior when it comes to adapting to a foreign environment?

WHY DO COMPANIES CARE ABOUT ETHICAL BEHAVIOR?

First, let's take a brief look at a preliminary but fairly important question: Why should companies worry about ethical behavior at all? As we discuss later, there are cultural and legal reasons to behave ethically. Also, individuals may have high standards of ethical behavior that can be translated into company policy and often company policy is influenced by a leader, often the founder of a company or a new CEO. From a business standpoint, ethical behavior can be instrumental in achieving one or both of two possible objectives:

1. To develop competitive advantage
2. To avoid being perceived as irresponsible

As for the first objective, some analysts argue that responsible behavior contributes to strategic and financial success because it fosters trust, which in turn encourages commitment.[9] For instance, GE's Ecomagination program reflects top managers' belief that by actively responding to social concerns about global warming, GE can gain a strategic advantage over competitors, perhaps developing an edge in emerging markets that are facing severe environmental problems.

NGOs are active in prodding companies to comply with certain standards of ethical behavior.

As for the second objective, companies are aware that more and more NGOs are becoming active in monitoring—and publicizing—international corporate practices. The Interfaith Center on Corporate Responsibility (ICCR), for example, is an NGO that represents nearly 300 faith-based institutional investors, including national denominations, religious communities, pension funds, foundations, hospital corporations, economic development funds, asset management companies, colleges, and unions.[10] Initially organized to protest the policies of apartheid in South Africa, ICCR has become involved in a number of different projects, such as ranking companies in different industry sectors according to their carbon emissions, or introducing a resolution at the annual shareholders' meeting to adopt principles for healthcare reform. This is just one of many examples of NGOs that focus on country and industry issues. NGOs are not the only institutions that monitor the behavior of companies and their employees. Governments want to ensure that individual and corporate behavior is consistent with the best interests of the broader community and that laws are being duly followed.

THE CULTURAL FOUNDATIONS OF ETHICAL BEHAVIOR

Values differ from country to country and between employees and companies.

In the early 2000s, many companies around the world faced severe financial problems and even went out of business because of their managers' unethical or illegal actions. Enron, a U.S.-based energy company with operations worldwide, was one of the first MNEs forced into bankruptcy because of illegal employee acts. Other U.S. companies followed suit, while similar problems occurred outside the United States; one example, Parmalat, will be discussed in greater detail in Chapter 19. Some of these companies had hidden their actions for a number of years through their international operations.

The results of these revelations included public outrage, investor anxiety, and a generally heightened interest in the activities of companies and those who run them. Thus a big question arose: Is this type of behavior universal, or is it more likely to occur in some countries or cultures than others?

RELATIVISM VERSUS NORMATIVISM

CONCEPT CHECK

Recall from Chapter 2 our discussion of "Cultural Awareness" and the various ways in which social and cultural distinctions can characterize a country's population. We also observed that companies doing business overseas need to be sensitive to internal diversity: They should remember that people in most nations are often members of multiple **cultures** and in some cases have more in common with certain foreign groups than with domestic groups.

Despite the cultural differences found among countries, as discussed in Chapter 2, it is tempting to assume that there is almost universal agreement on what's right and what's wrong when it comes to ethical and socially responsible behavior in business—especially for those who follow the deontological approach described above.[11] In the real world, however, managers face situations in which the whys and hows of applying cultural values are less than crystal clear. For example, people's differing ideas about right and wrong are influenced by family and religious values, laws and social pressures, their own observations and experiences, and even economic circumstances. Because ethical convictions tend to be deep-seated, people can be avid in defending their views.

Even within a given country there are starkly contrasting views on ethical matters. To complicate things even more, our own personal values may differ from our employers' policies, prevalent social norms, or both. Finally, everything that complicates dilemmas in the domestic business environment tends to complicate them even further in the international arena. So, does ethical behavior vary by country, or are there uniform values that everyone should share?

Relativism: Ethical truths depend on the groups holding them.

Relativism One point of view is to accept that there are significant differences from country to country that might affect our behavior. "When in Rome, do as the Romans do" is an oft-quoted expression that dates to the fourth century AD in a letter to St. Augustine from St. Ambrose, the bishop of Milan. It really had nothing to do with ethical behavior; in fact, it meant, "When I go to Rome, I fast on Sunday, but here in Milan I do not"[12]—in other words, adjust to what makes sense in different environments, adapt to local customs out of respect for them. A more aggressive application of the phrase is, "If it's okay to bribe in country X, I guess I need to bribe when I'm in country X." But the phrase need not be an excuse for ethical lapses.

FIGURE 11.1 What's Right and What's Wrong

Source: Leo Cullum/The New Yorker Collection/www.cartoonbank.com

"Honesty is the best policy, Fernbaugh, but it's not company policy."

Applying this expression in an international environment may depend on whether we assume that decisions are based on the consequences of our actions or on a strongly held view of right and wrong. **Relativism** holds that ethical truths depend on the values of a particular society and may vary from one society or country to another.[13] The implication is that it would not be appropriate to inject or enforce one's ethical values on another, or that a foreigner must adopt local values or morals whether or not they are consistent with the foreigner's own home values and beliefs.

CONCEPT CHECK

In discussing ways of "Dealing with Cultural Differences" in Chapter 2, we demonstrate that successful accommodation to a host country's culture depends not only on that culture's willingness to accept anything foreign but also on the extent to which foreign firms and their employees are able to adjust to the **culture** in which they find themselves.

Normativism: There are universal standards of behavior that all cultures should follow.

Normativism In contrast, **normativism** holds that there are indeed universal standards of behavior that, although influenced by different cultural values, should be accepted by people everywhere. Even a pluralistic society such as the United States has a large core of commonly held values and norms.[14] However, people do tend to adopt other values and norms as their own. The key is to distinguish between what is common to all and what is unique to the individual. As suggested in Chapter 2, these commonly held values and norms are part of what distinguishes one culture (or country) from another. From this perspective, *nonintervention* is unethical.

Walking the Fine Line Between Relative and Normative Companies and their employees are always struggling with the problem of how to implement their own ethical principles in foreign business environments: Do those principles reflect universally valid "truths" (the normative approach)? Or must they adapt to local conditions on the assumption that every place has its own "truths" and needs to be treated differently (the relative approach)? A company may be pressured to comply with local norms, such as laws that permit—or even require—only certain practices that grant competitive advantages to firms accepting local norms while throwing up roadblocks in front of those that try to impose home-country practices in the local arena. Conversely, it may face certain pressures from its home-country government *not* to comply, or even from constituencies that threaten retaliatory action if it submits to objectionable foreign practices.

Managers need to exhibit ordinary decency—principles of honesty and fairness.

Many individuals and organizations have laid out minimum levels of business practices that they say a company (domestic or foreign) must follow regardless of the legal requirements or ethical norms prevalent where it operates.[15] One could consider this as behavior based on principles of honesty and fairness, or what can be called "ordinary decency."[16] The argument is that legal permission for some action may be given by uneducated or corrupt leaders who do not understand or care about the consequences, and that MNEs are obligated to set good examples that may become the standard for responsible behavior.

Managers need to create competitive advantages through ethical behavior and avoid being perceived as irresponsible.

Negotiating Between Evils Another potential complication is that both societies and companies must often choose between the lesser of two evils. Consider the use of the pesticide DDT. In the 1950s and 1960s, the U.S. Department of Agriculture began to prohibit many of the uses of DDT because of evidence of its declining benefits, environmental and toxicological effects, and evidence that it is a probable human carcinogen. Now the use of DDT has been discontinued in the U.S. The Stockholm Convention on Persistent Organic Pollutants (under the auspices of the United Nations) has banned the use of DDT with limited exceptions for malaria control. In 2006, the World Health Organization gave its support to the use of DDT in African countries where malaria is a major problem, citing that the benefits outweigh the costs.[17]

CONCEPT CHECK

As we point out in Chapter 2, **international business** on any scale increases interactions among countries, and any level of interaction is apt to introduce cultural change. We list a couple of types of cultural influence—namely, creolization and cultural diffusion—that, although introducing only certain elements of a foreign culture, have been known to cause concern about cultural identity in the host country.

THE LEGAL FOUNDATIONS OF ETHICAL BEHAVIOR

Social responsibility requires human judgment, which is subjective and ambiguous.

Dealing with *ethical dilemmas* is often a balancing act between *means* (the actions we take, which may be right or wrong) and *ends* (the consequences of our actions, which may also be right or wrong). Legal foundations for ethical behavior can provide guidance here, but legal justification is more rooted in the teleological approach to moral reasoning and moral behavior (consequences) than in the deontological approach (right vs. wrong behavior). However, there are good reasons to consider the law as a foundation of ethical behavior, just as there are limitations to using the law.

LEGAL JUSTIFICATION: PRO AND CON

CONCEPT CHECK

Note that in Chapter 3 we define a country's legal system as the fundamental institution that creates a comprehensive legal network to regulate social interaction; its purpose is to stabilize political and social environments as well as to ensure a fair, safe, and efficient business environment.

Indeed, some experts suggest that legal justification for ethical behavior is the only important standard. According to this theory, an individual or company can do anything that isn't illegal. Opponents respond that there are five good reasons why this is inadequate:

1. Some things that are *unethical* are not *illegal*, so the law is not an appropriate standard for regulating *all* business activity. Some forms of interpersonal behavior, for example, can clearly be wrong even if they're not against the law.
2. The law is slow to develop in emerging areas, and it takes time to pass and test laws in the courts. Moreover, because laws essentially respond to issues that have already surfaced, they can't always anticipate dilemmas that will arise in the future. Countries with well-developed systems of civil law rely on specificity, and it isn't feasible to enact laws dealing with every possible ethical issue.
3. The law is often based on imprecisely defined moral concepts that can't be separated from the legal concepts they underpin. In other words, we must in any case consider moral concepts whenever we're considering legal ones.
4. The law often needs to undergo scrutiny by the courts. This is especially true of case law, in which the courts create law by establishing precedent.
5. The law simply isn't very efficient. "Efficiency" in this case implies achieving ethical behavior at a very low cost, and it would be impossible to solve every ethical behavioral problem with an applicable law.[18]

CONCEPT CHECK

Recall our explanation in Chapter 3 of a civil law system as one based on a systematic and extensive codification of laws.

In contrast, there are also several good reasons for using the law to justify ethical behavior:

1. The law embodies many of a country's moral principles, making it an adequate guide for proper conduct.
2. The law provides a clearly defined set of rules, and following it at least establishes a good precedent for acceptable behavior.
3. The law contains enforceable rules that apply to everyone.
4. Because the law represents a consensus derived from widely shared experience and deliberation, it reflects careful and wide-ranging discussions.[19]

Legal justification for ethical behavior may not be sufficient because not everything that is unethical is illegal.

The law is a good basis for ethical behavior because it embodies local cultural values.

As countries tackle similar ethical issues, laws will become more similar.

EXTRATERRITORIALITY

When trying to use the law to govern behavior in different countries, we soon run into a very basic problem—laws can vary from country to country. Recall the challenges GE faces in its efforts to deal with international variations in environmental laws. GE has actually lobbied the U.S. government to enact legislation more closely aligned to Europe's, reasoning that having to deal with a shifting array of regulations and limitations will not only impede its strategy but also become unnecessarily costly.

In addition, strong home-country governments may adopt a practice known as **extraterritoriality**: imposing domestic legal and ethical practices on the foreign subsidiaries of companies headquartered in their jurisdictions. This has become very controversial and, as argued by some, inconsistent with increased globalization and the need to collaborate across national boundaries.[20] An perfect example of extraterritoriality involves the requirement by the U.S. government that foreign companies that list on U.S. stock exchanges, sell securities in the U.S., or do business in the U.S. must follow the Foreign Corrupt Practices Act wherever they do business, not just in the U.S.[21]

ETHICS AND CORPORATE BRIBERY

CONCEPT CHECK

As we explain in Chapter 3, the continued democratization of countries has led to the diffusion of the rule of law in place of the rule of man, which is more symbolic of totalitarian regimes. However, the global economic crisis may have slowed that process for a while.

Granted, we've gone from con to pro and back again in introducing the relationship between ethics and the law. Nevertheless, let's return once more to a pro-law argument for certain types of behavior. Why? Because despite all the problems that arise, considering the law is still a good place to start when studying ethics. The reason shouldn't be surprising: As countries find themselves searching for common solutions to common problems—problems like those discussed in the following sections—they find themselves taking common legal steps.

CORRUPTION AND BRIBERY

The first issue is *bribery,* which is actually one facet of the much bigger issue of *corruption.* The multifaceted determinants of corruption include cultural, legal, and political forces.[22] As defined by Transparency International, corruption is "the abuse of entrusted power for private gain."[23] There are some variations on this basic definition, but it is as good as any. Here we'll focus more on bribery because it is at the heart of corrupt behavior.

There are many examples of corruption and bribery that could be described in detail, but let's just mention a few. The clothing retailer Ralph Lauren agreed to pay about $1.6 million in fines for making nearly $600,000 in illegal payments to foreign government officials in Argentina from 2005–2009 to allow them to avoid customs inspections and related paperwork. They have since closed operations in Argentina.[24] There are other high-profile cases involving well-known companies, such as Walmart in Mexico, Microsoft in China, and Panasonic in a variety of countries, allegedly bribing foreign government officials. However, allegations often hit the press without ever leading to prosecution, but it is obvious that no company is immune from being tainted by bribery and corruption. Even Greek politicians make the news. In April 2013, a former Greek defense minister was put on trial for collaborating with his wife, daughter and 16 associates to launder money offshore that came from receiving bribes and kickbacks for defense contracts, including the purchase of a Russian missile-defense system and German submarines.[25]

Bribery of public officials takes place to obtain government contracts or to get officials to do what they should be doing anyway.

Congressional investigations of U.S. MNEs in the 1970s yielded anecdotal information that questionable payments to foreign government officials had long been business as usual in both industrial and developing countries. The reports indicated that 400 corporations had admitted making questionable or illegal payments in excess of $300 million. In comparison with the large amounts of bribes paid today, this seems like a small sum of money. However, it was the beginning of collecting and reporting the extent of bribes being paid.[26]

Figure 11.2 provides information on the Corruption Perceptions Index for 2012 by identifying the perceived levels of public-sector corruption for a small sample of countries.

FIGURE 11.2 Where Bribes Are (and Are Not) Business as Usual

Transparency International asked country experts, nonresidents, and residents about the overall extent of corruption (frequency and/or size of bribes) in the public and private sectors. The scale runs from 0 to 100, where 0 means that a country is perceived as highly corrupt and 100 means it is perceived as very clean. The figures include a sample of countries.

Source: Based on Transparency International, "TI Corruption Perceptions Index" (2012), at transparency.org (accessed June 1, 2013).

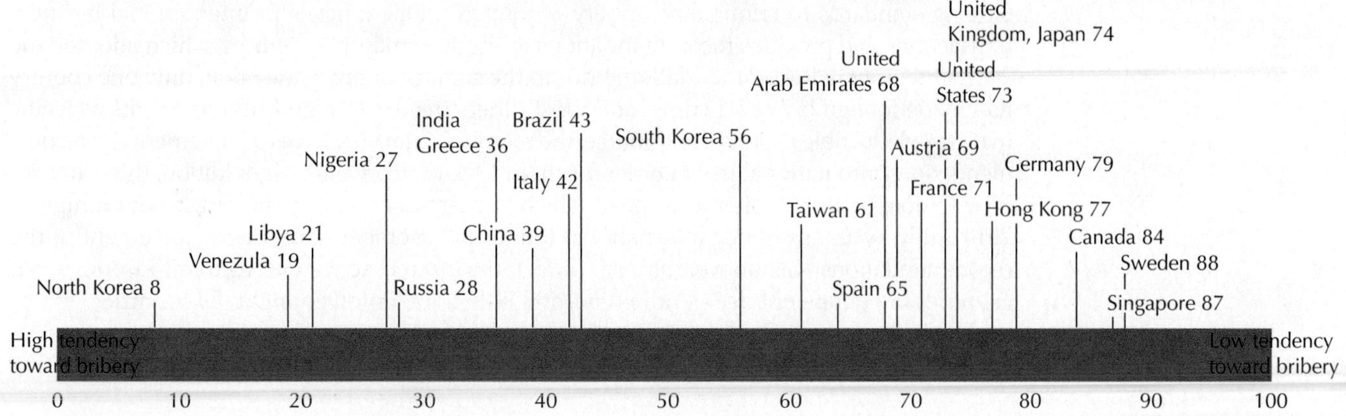

Although no country is free of corruption, it is depressing to note that two-thirds of the countries surveyed score below 50, and the lower the score (meaning the public sector is perceived to be corrupt), the more likely the countries are to be from Africa and Latin America. Clearly poverty is an issue, although there are some high income countries like Italy and Greece that fall below 50, as do all of the BRIC countries. Transparency International says public corruption generates "popular anger that threatens to destabilize societies and exacerbate violent conflicts."[27] That was demonstrated in June 2013 when millions of Brazilians took to the streets to demonstrate their fury over an increase in bus fares. However, the grievances escalated to include many things, including corrupt politicians. Their CPI may have only been 43 out of 100, but that was enough for Brazilians to take to the streets.

Transparency International not only publishes a Corruption Perceptions Index but also a Bribe Payers Index. In a recent survey, they reported that individuals from the Netherlands, Switzerland, Belgium, and Germany were least likely to pay bribes, while individuals from Russia, China, and Mexico were most likely to pay bribes. The United States fit somewhere in between.[28]

THE CONSEQUENCES OF CORRUPTION

Bribes are payments or promises to pay cash or anything of value.

There are a number of problems with bribery. First, it affects both company performance and country economies. Higher levels of corruption, for instance, correlate strongly with lower national growth rates and lower levels of per capita income.[29] Corruption can also erode the authority of governments that condone it. Over the years, bribery-based scandals have led to the downfall of numerous heads of state, with many government officials and business executives being imprisoned, fined, or forced to resign. In an extreme case, China's former head of the State Food and Drug Administration, convicted of accepting bribes in return for approving certain medicines, was executed.[30] Moreover, disclosures of corruption not only damage the reputations of companies and whole countries, they also compromise the legitimacy of MNEs in the eyes of local and global communities.[31] Finally, corruption is expensive, inflating a company's costs and bloating its prices. Nevertheless, it persists as one of the most challenging concerns in international business and politics in the world today.

WHAT'S BEING DONE ABOUT CORRUPTION?

Many efforts are underway to slow the pace of bribery as an international business practice at global, regional, and national levels. International multilateral accords for combating bribery at the global rather than regional level include those established by the OECD (Organization for Economic Cooperation and Development), the ICC (International Chamber of Commerce), and the United Nations through UNCAC (United Nations Convention against Corruption).

The OECD comprises 34 mostly high-income countries from around the world. Its Anti-Bribery Convention, signed in 1997 by the 34 member countries plus six non-member countries (Argentina, Brazil, Bulgaria, Colombia, Russia, and South Africa), establishes legally binding standards to criminalize bribery of foreign public officials in international business transactions and provides recommendations to the 40 signatory countries, which adopted the 2009 Anti-Bribery Recommendation. Prior to the signing of the convention, only one country had made foreign bribery a crime, and most others treated foreign bribe payments as legitimate tax-deductible expenses. Of course, the member countries have to implement the recommendations into national law in order for them to have any weight. In addition, the countries have to do a better job of enforcement, which appears to be uneven at best.[32] For example, a 2010 study by Transparency International found that member countries' enforcement of the recommendations was uneven at best. In fact, they found active enforcement in only seven countries, moderate enforcement in nine, and little or no enforcement in 20 countries.[33]

The International Chamber of Commerce issued a code of rules against corrupt practices in 1999 and has since been active in supporting other multilateral approaches to combating bribery, including codes of conduct issued by the OECD and the United Nations. Whereas the OECD Convention targets the supply side of companies' bribing officials in the public sector, the ICC is particularly interested in the private sector and the demand side of cross-border economics, where extortion of companies by public officials is a favorite criminal practice.[34] Due to the lack of an enforcement mechanism, the rules are viewed as self-regulation by companies and a roadmap for governments to follow to fight extortion and bribery.

The United Nations Office on Drugs and Crime (UNCAC) covers a broad range of corruption issues and does not focus solely on bribery. In November 2009, representatives of the 148 member governments that ratified UNCAC met in Doha, Qatar, to discuss a review mechanism to see if member governments were applying UNCAC standards to combat corruption. The conference concluded with the creation of a more specific review mechanism to measure the implementation of UNCAC initiatives in ratifying member states over successive four-year periods. In 2010, implementation progress reviews were conducted for 28 UNCAC-ratifying members by both regional and international peers. The second session of the Implementation Review Group on Prevention took place in the spring of 2011 for another 42 members of the convention, the third session in Vienna in 2012, the fourth session in Vienna in 2013. Once again, enforcement is a major issue because the UN has no power to enforce its provisions—this must be done by member governments.[35]

In addition to the broader global efforts to combat corruption, efforts in Africa and Latin America are addressing specific regional issues there. However, the key is national legislation and enforcement. Changes in behavior take time.

Regional Initiative: The European Union The European Commission confirmed its support for strong anti-corruption measures within the EU in a 2007 communication to the European Council, Parliament, and Economic and Social Committee. This included the adoption of the UN's official definition of corruption and support for many of the policies contained within international agreements. The communication also sanctions the work of the Commission's office of antifraud (OLAF), which conducts the affairs of the EU relevant to corporate and individual corruption, as well as an internal auditing service that monitors the activities of all of the Commission's departments. Starting in 2013, the Commission will publish an anticorruption report every two years as a way to evaluate and monitor the enforcement efforts of member countries given the uneven nature of the implementation of existing laws. The EU does not have specific anti-corruption legislation, but it encourages member nations to adopt high standards and follow them. One of the purposes of the anticorruption report is to spotlight what countries are doing and encourage the sharing of best practices.

The Foreign Corrupt Practices Act is U.S. legislation that makes bribery illegal. It applies to domestic or foreign operations and to company employees as well as their agents overseas.

National Initiative: The U.S. Foreign Corrupt Practices Act An example of a national approach is the **Foreign Corrupt Practices Act (FCPA)** in the United States, which outlaws bribery payments by U.S. firms to foreign officials, political parties, party officials, and political candidates. As noted above in the discussion on extraterritoriality, the coverage of the FCPA was extended in 1998 to include bribery by foreign firms operating in any U.S. territory. The FCPA applies not only to companies registered in the United States but also to any foreign company quoted on any U.S. stock exchange.

There is an apparent inconsistency in the FCPA's provisions: although it is legal to make payments to officials to expedite otherwise legitimate transactions (officially called *facilitating payments* but sometimes referred to as *speed money* or *grease money*), payments can't be made to officials who aren't directly responsible for the transactions in question. In 1988, an amendment to the FCPA actually excluded facilitating payments from the definition of *bribery.* Now, for example, payment to a customs official to clear legitimate merchandise is legal, whereas paying a government minister to influence a customs official is not. What's the difference? In the former case the FCPA recognizes that officials can delay legal transactions indefinitely or until they receive payments. However, sometimes behaviors that might be considered inappropriate by individuals in one country would be acceptable in another. A survey of Chinese managers found that gift giving is considered a normal part of the high-context Chinese culture and not a bribe, unless the gift is perceived as being so big that it results in contracts and favors in a business transaction.[36] The problem is in establishing the size of the gift. In 2007, the U.S. Justice Department levied a $2.5 million fine against Lucent Technologies Inc. for improperly recording millions of dollars in travel to Disney World and Las Vegas for about 1,000 Chinese employees of state-owned telecom companies.[37] Apparently, the Justice Department didn't consider the trips mere gifts.

An interesting twist to the FCPA is that the Justice Department is aggressively pursuing U.S. companies that make payments to executives at government-owned companies, especially Chinese state-owned enterprises, under the assumption that they are really government employees. This goes beyond the intent of the law, which was to pursue payments made to government officials to abuse their power.[38]

The U.S. government continues to step up anticorruption efforts both at home and abroad. As of December 2010, the Justice Department had filed at least 140 cases at various stages of investigation for FCPA violations, compared to only 43 in 2007.[39] Additional legislation has been enacted since the FCPA that indirectly affects the crackdown on corporate bribery. Most notable, perhaps, is the Sarbanes-Oxley Act (SOX), which was passed in 2002 as a response to an epidemic of well-known corporate scandals involving such companies as Enron and Tyco International. SOX toughened standards with regard to corporate governance, financial disclosure, and oversight of accounting and auditing practices. With its passage, the Justice Department began to use the FCPA more aggressively to combat bribery.

However, companies have always been nervous about which activities constitute a violation of the FCPA and which do not. As a result, the Justice Department and the Securities and Exchange Commission issued "A Resource Guide to the U.S. Foreign Corrupt Practices Act" on November 14, 2012, which gives pragmatic advice on how to do business abroad without violating provisions of the FCPA. Although not perfect, it gives guidance and provides examples of common situations and how they might rule on them.[40]

Sarbanes-Oxley legislation in the United States is helpful in combating corruption through more effective corporate governance, financial disclosure, and public accounting oversight.

In addition to the United States, other governments worldwide are starting to crack down harder on bribery. In 2010, the UK Bribery Act received Royal Assent, and it went into force on July 1, 2011. The Act gives guidance to UK companies on how they can put into place procedures to prevent bribery. The Serious Fraud Office is an independent government department in the UK that works under the supervision of the Attorney General and pursues and prosecutes those who commit, among other things, bribery and corruption.[41] On their website, the SFO provides a lot of good information for companies on bribery and corruption: what it is, what some of the indicators are of bribery, etc.

A zero-tolerance pact against bribery was signed by companies at the 2005 World Economic Forum.

Industry Initiatives Finally, various industries have recently stepped up their own efforts against bribery and corruption. In 2005, for example, in conjunction with the World Economic Forum, nearly 50 multinational construction and natural-resource companies, representing at least $300 billion in annual revenues, signed a "zero-tolerance" pact against extortion by bribery. By 2010, the number of signatory companies had risen to 150. This voluntary effort, called the Partnering Against Corruption Initiative (PACI), calls for member firms to set up "extensive internal programs to educate and oversee company officials and business partners and also [to] prohibit political contributions and charitable gifts designed to curry favor."[42] Although many firms still adhere to their own anti-bribery standards, participants hope that PACI will encourage companies within the industry to monitor each other.

CONCEPT CHECK

In Chapter 3, we explain how important it is for a nation's political process to generate rational laws that companies and individuals can follow. We also explain that, unfortunately, laws are based on cultural values that are bound to vary from country to country. Finally, we point out that laws, rational or otherwise, aren't necessarily enforced with the same rigor in every country.

Relativism, the Rule of Law, and Responsibility Obviously, avoiding bribe payments when they're regarded as business-as-usual is a challenge, especially when business is being held up by foreign government officials. Although it might be easier to fall back on the standard of cultural *relativism* (and, for example, simply pay bribes where they're accepted and/or expected), the international initiatives described here have made some headway in introducing the rule of law into more and more international business activity. Companies are now freer to establish policies and procedures that are consistent with high standards of ethical behavior. As the principles laid down by the OECD and the UN are incorporated into national statutes, companies are finding that laws and practices that once varied radically from country to country have become more uniform and easier to implement.

Point

Are Top Managers Responsible When Corruption Is Afoot?

Point **Yes** In November 2006, German police raided the offices of the giant electrical engineering and electronics company Siemens AG. They netted nearly 36,000 documents to support allegations that Siemens regularly diverted funds filed under bogus consulting contracts into a network of "black accounts" for bribing officials in countries like Italy, Greece, Argentina, and Saudi Arabia, where it was seeking lucrative public-sector contracts. Following the raid, the company itself announced it had uncovered over €420 million (US $570 million) in suspicious payments going back as far as the early 1990s. Several managers caught up in the probe insisted that corruption was endemic to the company's culture and that they had acted with the knowledge—even the approval—of CEO Klaus Kleinfeld and board chief (and former CEO) Heinrich von Pierer.[43]

Now, nobody will deny that what Siemens employees did was misguided and wrongheaded, but let's be realistic: Step 1 in every textbook on foiling fraud is to follow the money, and in this case you can follow the money back to a culture that condones financial shenanigans. That means the real blame for the company's mess rests with top management.

Here's a little background on the business world in which Siemens is a leading corporate citizen. Compared to some other countries, Germany was slow to enact laws prohibiting bribery. In fact, up until 1999, German law allowed executives to write off overseas bribes as legitimate business expenses. Until 2002, it was still legal to bribe employees of foreign companies for anyone willing to absorb the cost without the tax break.[44]

The point? Like a lot of other German companies, Siemens was hanging on to a corporate culture that was perfectly comfortable with bribery and other forms of corrupt behavior. One senior executive says it even had an encryption code for itemizing bribe payments. The same exec says that he himself got a call from a Saudi contractor demanding $910 million in commission payments or else they'd send incriminating documents to certain U.S. authorities. When the exec alerted his superiors—including Kleinfeld and von Pierer—they replied that $910 million was perhaps a little high but suggested that a deal for $17 million in "past obligations" and $33 million in "hush money" wasn't beyond reason. According to this insider, most of his colleagues tossed off bribe payments as mere "peccadilloes" because, after all, "it was all for the good of the company."[45]

All of this transpired on von Pierer's and Kleinfeld's watch. To say the goings-on completely escaped their notice is unrealistic. It's top management's responsibility to lay out the ethical boundaries at a company and see that no one crosses them. Siemens management wasn't guarding its own ethical borders.

On top of everything else, Kleinfeld's management style of "fix, sell, or close"[46] was hardly the right approach for a company with a dirty-tricks chapter in its playbook. Once he became CEO, Kleinfeld immediately set high profit targets and began spinning off divisions that apparently weren't sufficiently inspired by the profit motive. His motto was "Go for profit and growth," and when a team of managers failed to deliver, he just took an axe to the whole division.[47] Under top-down pressure like that, what other choice did employees really have? If the answer is "none," you have to admit that ultimate responsibility for company-wide behavior rests in the executive suite.

Are Top Managers Responsible When Corruption Is Afoot?

Counterpoint

Counterpoint **No** Granted, Siemens was up to its corporate neck in a culture of corruption. But is that supposed to excuse the actions of the individuals directly involved in the present case? Or, to put it in more legal-sounding terms: Does it mitigate their culpability? At the end of the business day, the actions of individuals, more than the official codes and theoretical due diligence of top managers, actually shape a company's culture.

Even so, back when he was CEO, von Pierer not only authorized a strict company-wide code of conduct, he also hired a few hundred compliance officers to enforce it.[48] When Kleinfeld's turn came, he instituted a "zero-tolerance" policy toward corruption.[49] But more importantly, for a far-flung, highly decentralized conglomeration with 11 business units run by separate boards as virtually independent operating entities, it's hardly reasonable to expect top executives back home in Munich to know everything that's going on from Siemens Turkey to Siemens Taiwan. Former CEO von Pierer is absolutely right in arguing that under such circumstances, "deducing a political responsibility" would be absurd. As most of us learned in business school, the job of senior executives is strategic planning; it doesn't involve auditing the books and double-checking every suspicious double entry.[50]

And while we're on the subject of top-level managers, it's true that a bunch of former employees who are in trouble with the law claim that top Siemens managers knew all about the bribery and other underhanded activities. So far, however, no one, including an independent law firm that's looking into the matter, has found any solid evidence that they're telling the truth. Plus, neither Kleinfeld nor von Pierer has been officially accused of any wrongdoing.

As for the question of whether dragging its governmental feet on anti-bribery legislation has anything to do with the resilience of corruption in Germany, there's little question that adapting to or passing new laws may take quite some time. But that doesn't justify breaking them until you're good and ready to obey them. Regardless of the company's approach to adapting to a new legal environment, those of its employees who perpetuated the practice of paying bribes fully understood what the law said and that they were violating it. Besides, creating false consulting contracts and diverting company money into slush funds has come under the heading of legally dubious behavior for a long time just about everywhere. And no matter when a law goes into effect, it always comes with a pretty clear list of "do's and don'ts." It's obvious that certain individuals at Siemens took it upon themselves to ignore those guidelines.

Finally, what about the argument that employees had no choice but to violate the law because they had to protect their jobs? The fact that many of them faced criminal charges and jail time with no hope of continuing their careers at Siemens or anywhere else attests to the faulty logic of that claim. Meanwhile, their former employer, which is still responsible for nearly half a million paychecks worldwide, has already paid out €63 million (US $85.7 million) to outside auditors and investigators and still faces a court-ordered fine of €38 million (US $51.4 million) following the conviction of just one finance officer and one consultant.[51] By the end of 2008, U.S. and German authorities had levied $1.6 billion in fines against Siemens. Why the United States? Because Siemens lists its stock there and is therefore subject to the FCPA. Siemens also risks being banned from contract bidding in any one of the 190 countries where it does business and generates wealth.

1. What are the major reasons why Siemens was so heavily involved in bribery and corruption, and what are a few key things that would have prevented or at least minimized this behavior?

ETHICS AND THE ENVIRONMENT

If for no other reason, environmental problems are important because they're a matter of life or death, either now or in the future. As we saw in our opening case, GE has come to see eco-responsibility as a matter of protecting not only the future of the environment but also its own future. Like GE, companies contribute to environmental damage in a variety of ways. Some, for example, contaminate the air, soil, or water during manufacturing, or make products such as automobiles or electricity that release fossil-fuel contaminants into the atmosphere.

Companies that extract natural resources, generate air or water waste, or manufacture products such as autos that generate pollution need to be concerned with their environmental impact.

In extracting natural resources, other companies also have a direct and unmistakable effect on the environment. But even in these cases the issue isn't necessarily clear-cut. Granted, although some resources (such as minerals, gas, and oil) may not be renewable, others (such as timber) are, and some observers even suggest that resources can never really become scarce. Why? Because as they become less available, prices go up and technology or substitutes compensate.

WHAT IS "SUSTAINABILITY"?

Sustainability involves meeting the needs of the present without compromising the ability of future generations to meet their own needs while taking into account what is best for the people and the environment.

Despite confusion and disagreement over the term, we assume here that **sustainability** means meeting the needs of the present without compromising the ability of future generations to meet their own needs. In this respect, we are using sustainability from the perspective of environmental sustainability. Proponents of the concept argue that sustainability considers what's best for both people and the environment. Nevertheless, it remains a controversial concept—one whose definition is subject to different interpretations, from environmentalists to businesspeople.[52] It is important that, regardless of how they feel about the principle of sustainability, businesses that affect the environment establish policies for responsible behavior toward the earth—a responsibility that has both cultural and legal ramifications.

But is it possible that sustainability is not only a good business practice, but also good business? GE has demonstrated that it makes good business sense to adopt a strong policy of sustainability, but it also has vast resources at its disposal. However, even born-global companies can adopt a sustainable strategy and generate export revenues at the same time.

Sustainability is no longer just good business practice. New businesses are emerging that are combining the idea of environmental responsibility and profitability.

One such company, based in Shepherd, Montana, is called Floating Island International (FII), which was founded by Bruce Kania in 2000 when a combined concern for the environment and a clever concept formed the opportunity for a valuable business venture. After several years of R&D, Kania and a team of engineers and scientists created their primary product, BioHaven Islands, made from post-consumer recycled materials and native plants and soils. The islands have more than 30 identified applications for use—including wetland treatment and preservation, erosion control, and habitat creation—and are designed to mimic natural biological processes that encourage the restoration of food chains and maintain a clean environment.[53] Within the first five years of operation, FII produced and sold over 4,000 of its floating islands around the world, including the United States, Canada, Australia, United Kingdom, Korea, Singapore, and New Zealand. The company licenses its products to regional dealers across the U.S., but also has licensees in China, New Zealand, and South Africa. Clearly, this is an example of a firm making its mark internationally by focusing exclusively on filling the demand for environmentally oriented products that are profitable as well.[54]

GLOBAL WARMING AND THE KYOTO PROTOCOL

Global warming results from the release of greenhouse gases that trap heat in the atmosphere rather than allowing it to escape.

In illustrating some of the challenges faced by these companies, we start by examining the issue of *global warming,* including the role of the Kyoto Protocol and its potential impact on corporate behavior.

The Kyoto Protocol At the core of the international treaty known as the **Kyoto Protocol** is the theory that global climate change results from an increase in carbon dioxide and other gases that act like the roof of a greenhouse, trapping heat that would normally radiate into space, and thereby warming the planet. If carbon dioxide emissions aren't reduced and controlled, rising temperatures could have catastrophic consequences, including melting the polar ice cap, flooding coastal regions, shifting storm patterns, reducing farm output, causing drought, and even killing off plant and animal species.[55] Most observers agree that the world is warming; however, there's no clear consensus on the cause or scope of the problem, much less the solution.[56]

The Kyoto Protocol was signed in 1997 to require countries to cut their greenhouse gas emissions to 5.2 percent below 1990 levels between 2008 and 2012. Some countries have adopted stricter requirements, and others, such as the United States, China, and India, have not ratified the Protocol.

The Kyoto Protocol, an extension of the UN Framework Convention on Climate Change of 1994, was born of the need to reduce greenhouse gas (GHG) emissions from burning fossil fuels and methane. Signed in 1997, the Protocol committed signatory countries to reducing the emissions to 5.2 percent below 1990 levels between 2008 and 2012. As of March 2013, the Protocol had been ratified by 192 nations and regional economic organizations.[57] The United States, which generated 19 percent of the world's greenhouse gases in 2008, initially signed the agreement in 1998 but withdrew in 2001, citing concerns about domestic economic growth and exemptions for rapidly growing developing countries like China and India.[58] Canada announced at the end of 2011 that it was going to withdraw from the Kyoto Protocol, largely because the Conservative Party in Canada had never been in favor of joining Kyoto, which had been pushed by the Liberal Party when it was in power. Another contributing factor was that talks to extend the Protocol at the end of 2011 didn't come to anything conclusive.[59]

The United States' reluctance to continue with Kyoto stems from a desire to develop low-carbon technologies to solve the problem, rather than attempt to meet mandatory reductions, for fear that reduced economic growth would create domestic employment problems. Although the U.S. government has moved aggressively to implement new policies to reduce GHG emissions, the preference has been to defer signing the existing Protocol and work instead on the new framework for climate control that was adopted in December 2012. Even though the U.S. didn't sign the agreement, it inadvertently met the goal of reducing

GHG emissions due to the economic slowdown. Typically when the G8 meetings are held, climate change is on the top of the agenda, and efforts to reduce the global carbon footprint are still of great importance. In the G8 meetings held in Northern Island in June 2013, however, climate change wasn't even on the agenda, in spite of the demands of France and Germany to the contrary. Instead, there was more interest in discussing trade, transparency, and tax reform.[60]

One approach favored by many is to invest more in alternative and renewable energy, such as nuclear, wind, and solar technologies. The dramatic rise in oil prices in 2007–08 spurred a lot of interest in renewable energy, but enthusiasm waned when prices fell. Renewable energy still has a bright future, and suppliers are truly global. Germany, for example, produces more energy from wind than any other country, and its companies have a head start in penetrating global markets. However, suppliers from India, Spain, and Denmark are also major contributors of wind turbines and other parts.[61]

Nuclear energy is an important source of electricity in many countries. In France, for example, it makes up 75 percent of domestic energy production, compared to 29 percent in Japan and 20 percent in the United States. However, the future of nuclear energy suffered a setback on March 11, 2011, when a 9.0 earthquake and a resulting massive tsunami hit Japan, which caused serious damage to the Fukushima Dai-ichi nuclear power station. The initial disruption to the country's power was serious enough that the long-term effects on nuclear energy as an alternative to carbon fuels is uncertain. However, it is obvious that the nuclear option will be an important dimension to electricity generation for the foreseeable future as countries struggle with environmental and safety issues.

National and Regional Initiatives Meanwhile, firms operating in countries that have adopted the Kyoto Protocol are under pressure to take one of two steps: reduce emissions or buy credits from companies that have reduced emissions below target levels. The choice isn't terribly attractive because the firms will have to invest in new technologies, change the way they do business, or pay for others to clean up their acts. In addition, MNEs (such as GE) are now forced to reconsider their global strategies, particularly because firms with operations in countries that have adopted the Protocol are required to adhere to the same standards as local companies, which may be more aggressive than Protocol standards. The European Union, for instance, has set a target of an 8 percent reduction of GHG from 1990 levels. The Germans have gone one step further, setting a target of 21 percent (based on the assumption that they'd be able to close down coal-fired power plants still operating in the former East Germany).[62]

U.S.-based MNEs must comply with the Kyoto Protocol in compliance countries where they may have operations.

Company-specific Initiatives As a result, of course, U.S. companies operating in Europe share the same stringent requirements with European-based firms. Not surprisingly, many U.S.-based MNEs, though not bound by Protocol targets at home, are preparing for what they believe is inevitable. Between 2000 and 2005, for example, GM took part in a voluntary emissions-reduction program and achieved a 10 percent reduction in North American plant emissions. It is now trying to determine what it needs to do to make its 11 European plants comply with EU standards.[63] DuPont has cut emissions by 65 percent since 1990,[64] and Alcoa exceeded its 2010 goal of a 25 percent reduction of 1990 levels by some 11 percent.[65] Thus, companies are clearly changing the way they do business, whether or not they're bound by Protocol standards. Our opening case provides a good example: Recall that GE set a target of reducing GHG emissions at all operational levels to 1 percent below 2004 levels.

Finally, bear in mind that many MNEs, based in the United States or elsewhere, also have the task of adapting to different standards in different countries. A European-based MNE with operations in, say, the United States, Germany, and China, and a U.S.-based MNE with plants in the same countries are faced with a smorgasbord of regulatory environments. On the one hand, the *legal* approach to responsible corporate behavior says an MNE can settle for operating in accord with local laws. The *ethical* approach, on the other hand, urges companies to go beyond the law to do whatever is necessary and economically feasible to reduce GHG emissions, given that they still have multiple stakeholders to satisfy.

Does Geography Matter?

Where Small Carbon Footprints Mean Big Business

Countries of the Arabian Gulf are among those with the highest rates of greenhouse gas emissions alongside Kuwait, Qatar, and the United Arab Emirates (UAE).[66] What worsens their carbon footprints is their populations' high rate of energy consumption. The per capita consumption of energy in Qatar is 12,799 kgoe (kilograms of oil equivalent) per annum, whereas in Kuwait the figure is 12,204 kgoe, and in the UAE it is 8,271 kgoe. In the UK and USA the figures are 3,254 kgoe and 7,164 kgoe respectively. In striking contrast, India's average rate of energy consumption is 566 kgoe.[67] The growing consciousness among consumers, governments, and corporations of the impact of unrestrained use of natural resources has thrown open a valuable business opportunity for corporations to develop environmentally sustainable practices to deliver to more ecologically sophisticated consumers against a backdrop of government support.

The Gulf Region's high consumption of fossil fuels is enabled by the exceptionally high per capita incomes of these countries[68] and also by government subsidies of petrol. These facts along with the ecological damage by the vast petrochemical sector in the region have caused governments to strategize how to curb environmental damage and excessive reliance on fossil fuels. The UAE was one of the first major oil-producing countries to ratify the Kyoto Protocol and urged for its renewal when its first commitment period expired in 2012.[69] The UAE government has been dedicated to implementing the protocol's Clean Development Mechanism (CDM), a section of the protocol which encourages developing countries to reduce their carbon dioxide emissions in return for a Certified Emission Reduction (CER), a 'carbon credit' against every ton of carbon dioxide equivalent reduced. Playing a significant role in this drive is Masdar City.[70] Located near the country's capital Abu Dhabi, Masdar is a major undertaking in the advancement of renewable energy acting as an alliance between government and corporations to develop projects that commercialize green-friendly technologies. The city has been designed to generate low carbon emissions and rely solely on renewable energy sources and is home to 50,000 residents living in environmental friendly housing and a further 600,000 workers commuting each day to their

Masdar's mission is to invest, incubate, and establish the new energy industry in Abu Dhabi and around the world. By adopting an integrated, holistic business model – merging higher education, R&D, investment and sustainable living – Masdar can meet the changing needs of the evolving industry.
Source: © graphicsdunia4u - Fotolia.com

respective places of work/business, many employed in the ecology sector. It incorporates a free zone targeted at companies with environment-focused operations and attracts foreign companies to setup by offering 100 percent foreign ownership, no restrictions on movement of capital, and no corporate or personal taxation.[71] Companies which have established operations there include eCullet (USA), an advanced glass recycling company, and Europlasma (France) specializing in waste destruction and renewable energy production.[72] Masdar's involvement in renewable energy goes beyond the UAE through the Masdar Clean Technology Fund, which is developing an investment portfolio in companies around the globe devoted to clean energy production, conserving environmental resources, and material efficiency sectors.[73]

The Masdar City project provides a highly ambitious case of how an ecological platform is harnessing international business opportunities within a framework of intense environmental awareness to increasingly eco-savvy consumers to secure market leadership and sustainable profits. ■

ETHICAL DILEMMAS AND THE PHARMACEUTICAL INDUSTRY

In addition to the ethical challenges of bribery and reactions to global warming, we examine two other examples of ethical dilemmas and socially responsible behavior. Sometimes these dilemmas are industry-specific, such as pharmaceuticals; other times they deal with cross-industry issues, such as labor conditions in developing countries. We have chosen these two examples to demonstrate how companies must examine their ethical conduct as they spread internationally. Because the pharmaceutical industry and developing country labor conditions are prominent in the news, they should give you an idea of what you might face and how you can resolve the conflicts satisfactorily. We then finish this section and the chapter by discussing the importance of corporate codes of conduct. GlaxoSmithKline (GSK), one of the largest research-based pharmaceutical companies in the world, focuses on two lines of business: pharmaceuticals (prescription drugs and vaccines) and consumer healthcare products. With annual revenues in 2012 of GBP 26.4 billion, the U.K.-based company operates in over 100 countries, and employs nearly 100,000 people working at 87 manufacturing sites worldwide and significant R&D facilities in the UK, U.S., Spain, Belgium, and China.

To continue developing new products, GSK spent 15.2 percent of its revenues (also called group turnover) on R&D.[74] And like most research-based pharmaceutical firms, it is involved in the R&D, manufacturing, and sales ends of the patented-pharmaceuticals industry. In order to fund their large R&D budgets, and because so many of the drugs they try to develop take so long to get to market (or never make it there), these companies sell their successful drugs at high prices as long as the drugs are covered by patents. After a patent expires (after 17 years, in the U.S.), the proven drug becomes generic and is manufactured at lower costs and sold at a much lower price.

TIERED PRICING AND OTHER PRICE-RELATED ISSUES

Tiered pricing for pharmaceuticals means that companies charge a market price for products sold in industrialized countries and a discounted price for products sold in developing countries.

There are some exceptions to this pricing structure. Only 18 percent of GSK's revenues, for instance, come from the Emerging Markets and Asia Pacific region, but 80 percent of the vaccines GSK manufactures go to developing countries where the company offers preferential prices for vaccines. This practice is known as *tiered pricing,* in which consumers in developed countries pay higher prices and those in developing countries—especially low-income ones—pay lower, subsidized prices. If a government buyer is still unsatisfied with the high cost of patented drugs, it may resort to substituting generics, which are legitimate *if* the countries in which they're produced extend patent protection to patent holders. (One more point about generics: often they're simply pirated versions of the real thing, and pirated versions—about 10 percent of medicines sold worldwide, according to the World Health Organization [WHO]—often lack key ingredients.[75])

Recently, however, GSK was accused of bribery and tax evasion as it tried to increase sales in the small but rapidly growing pharmaceuticals market in China. A major problem is that because bribes and kickbacks were being paid to doctors and hospitals in the government-run healthcare system, GSK is basically bribing foreign government officials and therefore is in violation of the Foreign Corrupt Practices Act since it is listed on the New York Stock Exchange.[76]

Here's an example of the kinds of problems that can arise when the cost of pharmaceuticals becomes a point of contention in the marketplace. AIDS is a major health problem in Brazil, where the government, at substantial cost, distributes AIDS drugs to anyone who needs them. In 2007, when drug maker Merck offered to provide an AIDS drug at a 30 percent discount, the Brazilian government said thanks but no thanks, and instead made it lawful for Brazilian firms to manufacture or buy generic versions of the drug while paying Merck only nominal royalty fees.[77] Brazil has also resorted to the tactic of *reverse engineering* certain key drugs so they can be produced at lower prices.

Our closing case includes a similar illustration, which involves the efforts of GSK to offer steep discounts on AIDS drugs to an MNE attempting to provide free treatment to workers in South Africa.

TAKING TRIPS FOR WHAT IT'S WORTH

CONCEPT CHECK

In Chapter 3, we define *intellectual property rights (IPRs)* as intangible property rights resulting from intellectual effort. Note, however, that an IPR registered in one country doesn't necessarily confer protection in another.

The WTO Agreement on Trade-Related Aspects of Intellectual Property Rights (TRIPS) allows poor countries to counter the high cost of patented drugs by doing either of two things: (1) producing generic products *for local consumption* or (2) importing generic products from other countries *if they themselves don't have the capacity to produce them.* In both cases, the developing nation is compelled to license patented drugs from legal patent holders, rather than buy them from pirated sources, so that the patent holders generate revenue on the drugs they developed. However, in claiming that health problems such as HIV/AIDS and heart disease are "national emergencies," Brazil and Thailand have permitted local companies to make *unlicensed* generics and thus take advantage of a TRIPS clause that allows them to avoid paying the royalties, even though some companies and countries dispute that decision.[78]

Legal generic products allow countries to purchase drugs at lower costs and comply with drug patents, whereas illegal generic products are fakes that may or may not be of high quality.

Not surprisingly, this tactic is a major concern for pharmaceutical companies. For one thing, they worry that these generic products will find their way back into the developed countries that generate the majority of patent holders' revenues. They also worry about fakes for the same reason.

R&D AND THE BOTTOM LINE

Drugs are *very* expensive to develop, and much more so in high-income countries. The cost of developing a new drug can be close to $1 billion in the United States but as little as $100 million in a country like India. In addition, it can take as much as 15 years to take a product from the start of R&D through the approval process to the consumer.

Countries with health crises, such as African countries with high rates of AIDS, are allowed by TRIPS to manufacture or import generic drugs.

As it happens, India is now home to a thriving industry in generic drugs. It is the world's third largest drug producer in terms of volume and is the largest exporter of generic drugs (exporting about $10 billion in generic drugs a year). As a producer of *unlicensed* generic drugs as well, India once enjoyed hefty FDI in pharmaceuticals. But when it refused to secure patents on drugs made there by foreign companies, those companies chose to leave the country rather than give away all their secrets to local competitors. However, a new patent-protection law passed in 2005 has brought India into line with WTO guidelines and fostered a whole new environment for pharmaceuticals. Many Indian R&D facilities have sprung up to develop drugs that can be legitimately produced and sold by Indian companies, and foreign pharmaceutical firms are now looking at different strategies for penetrating the Indian market—from FDI to licensing agreements with generic manufacturers. One provision of the

2005 legislation is that reverse engineering will not be allowed as of 2015, which will have a big impact on the generic drug business in India. Most Indian companies got their start by reverse engineering drugs and selling them as unlicensed generic drugs.

India is a major manufacturer of generic drugs and is now moving to R&D of new drugs.

In this arena, then, the issue of social responsibility comes down to cultivating ways in which pharmaceutical companies can generate enough revenues to create new products (which is, after all, their major source of competitive advantage) while responding to the needs of developing countries that are long on diseases and short on funds. For example, Novartis developed a drug called Gleevec that is effective in treating a form of leukemia that is slow-growing but fatal. The drug can cost $70,000 a year in the United States, but the Indian generic version costs only $2,500 a year. In spite of the high cost, 90 percent of the cancer patients in India who need the drug can get it for free. However, Novartis had hoped to get patent protection for the drug in India for fear that it would lose out on sales from the generic before its patent protection in other countries expired.[79]

ETHICAL DILEMMAS OF LABOR CONDITIONS

A major challenge facing MNEs today is the twofold problem of globalized supply chains and the labor conditions of foreign workers. Labor issues—which involve companies, governments, trade unions, and NGOs alike—include wages, child labor, working conditions, working hours, and freedom of association. They're especially critical in retail, clothing, footwear, and agriculture—industries in which MNEs typically outsource huge portions of production to independent companies abroad. There have always been concerns about offshoring production or supply chaining (utilizing third parties to manufacture products such as clothing), but in 2013 a factory collapsed in Bangladesh and over 1,000 workers died. Although we'll discuss that case in more detail in Chapter 18, we mention it here due to the ethical issues surrounding the provision of safe and hygienic working conditions. Stakeholders will certainly question the care in which companies work with their supply chain: for instance, was the accident the fault of the companies that subcontracted manufacturing to the company in Bangladesh, or was it the fault of the government agencies that did not implement the law on occupational safety and health and the building code?

Major labor issues that MNEs get involved in through FDI or purchasing from independent manufacturers in developing countries are fair wages, child labor, working conditions, working hours, and freedom of association.

Figure 11.3 highlights the multiple pressures external stakeholders place on companies to force them to adopt responsible employment practices in their overseas operations. A more specific listing of worker issues was developed by the Ethical Trading Initiative (ETI),

FIGURE 11.3 Sources of Worker-Related Pressures in the Global Supply Chain

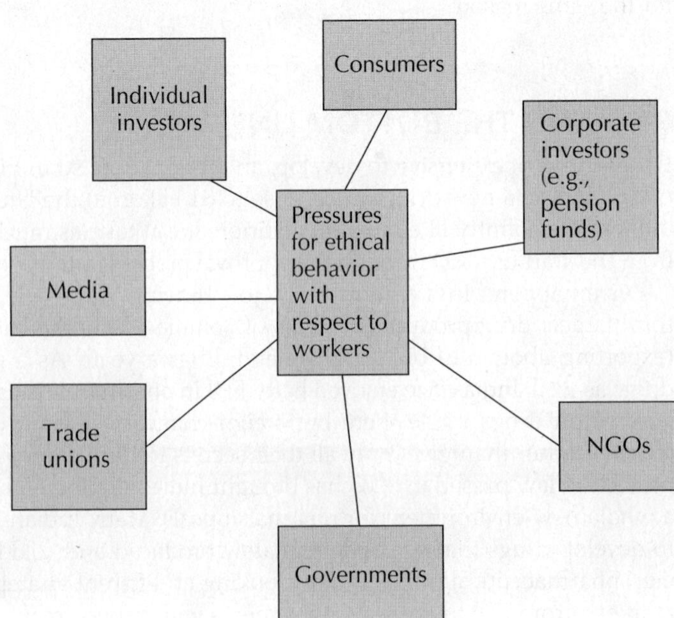

a British-based organization that focuses on MNEs' employment practices. Its members include representatives from Gap Inc., Levi Strauss & Co., Marks & Spencer, The Body Shop International, and other companies, as well as from trade union organizations, NGOs, and governments. The objective of ETI is to get companies to adopt ethical employment policies and then monitor compliance with their overseas suppliers. ETI's trading initiative base code identifies the following issues:

1. Employment is freely chosen.
2. Freedom of association and the right to collective bargaining are respected.
3. Working conditions are safe and hygienic.
4. Child labor shall not be used.
5. Living wages are paid.
6. Working hours are not excessive.
7. No discrimination is practiced.
8. Regular employment is provided.
9. No harsh or inhumane treatment is allowed.[80]

Although all issues identified by ETI are important, we focus on the one that, for a variety of good reasons, receives significant attention: *child labor.*

THE PROBLEM OF CHILD LABOR

Let's start by considering a couple of very brief cases:

- There are two arguments for the use of children in the Indian carpet industry: (1) they're better suited than adults to perform certain tasks, and (2) if they weren't employed, they'd be even worse off. In fact, children in India are often put to work because parents don't earn enough to support families; if parents can't pay off debts, their children are often *indentured* to creditors.
- In the 1990s, the impoverished Asian nation of Bangladesh was pressured to stop employing thousands of child workers or face U.S. trade sanctions. In this case, the plight of the children did in fact go from bad to worse. Between 5,000 and 7,000 young girls, for example, went from factory work to prostitution.[81]

An estimated 250 million children between 5 and 17 years old are working, but only about 5 percent of child labor is involved in export industries.

Some companies avoid operating in countries where child labor is employed, whereas others try to establish responsible policies in those same countries.

MNEs may not be willing to hire local workers who want to work long hours, due to concerns about exploitation.

According to the International Labor Organization (ILO), a UN institution, 215 million children between the ages of 5 and 17 are working worldwide, many of them full-time. The challenge is that much of this data is not current or is difficult to get. However, the ILO has very specific guidelines over what it considers child labor to be and what the worst forms of child labor are. In particular, the worst forms involve slavery and prostitution, illicit activities that are a danger to the health, safety and morals of a child.[82] ILO guidelines state that children who are at least 13–15 years old (12–14 as possible exceptions for developing countries) may be employed in "light" work that's not harmful to their health and doesn't interfere with school. All children under the age of 18 (16 under strict guidelines) should be protected against the most abusive labor conditions.[83]

For MNEs, the basic challenge is negotiating a global labyrinth of business environments with different cultural, legal, and political rules than those they're used to at home. In addition, they typically rely on local suppliers who are subject to specifically local pressures. Under these conditions, MNEs clearly can't solve all the problems revolving around child labor, especially given the fact that only about 5 percent of working children worldwide are in industries supported by MNEs.[84] Most underage workers can be found in the informal sectors of an economy—especially agriculture—where it's difficult to protect them.

Filipino child laborers work in the charcoal dump in Manila. The use of child labor in the Philippines has been highlighted recently in a report by the International Labor Organization, which estimated over 5 million children, or 18.9 percent of children aged 5–17 are working.
Source: Dondi Tawatao/Getty Images

WHAT MNES CAN AND CAN'T DO

This doesn't mean that MNEs are powerless when it comes to labor-related matters in overseas facilities. When the Swedish retailer IKEA ran into trouble in India for buying carpets from local companies that relied heavily on extensive child labor, it identified and tackled two different problems rather than try to force suppliers to stop exploiting the children. First, it helped working mothers increase family earning power so they could escape the clutches of the loan sharks to whom they were putting up their children as collateral. Second, it set up "bridge schools" to enable working children to enter mainstream education channels within a year.[85]

CONCEPT CHECK

In discussing "Legal Issues in International Business" in Chapter 3, we enumerate certain "operational concerns" of which overseas managers should be conscious. In particular, they need to accept three facts: (1) they may need to jettison any plan to directly transfer principles and practices that work in the domestic business environment; (2) political and legal systems differ among countries; (3) these differences affect the ways in which firms can exploit opportunities and deflect threats.

Frequently, MNEs operating in countries with very different labor policies succumb to the pressure to simply leave the market. Usually, this turns out to be a shortsighted decision. Research shows, for instance, that companies like Nike have substantially improved the conditions of workers in overseas facilities. Granted, MNEs are in no position to revolutionize the employment practices of the countries in which they operate, but they can improve conditions at subcontract facilities and even influence the guidelines set by other foreign investors. In the case of IKEA, carpets make up a small percentage of sales, and it would have been easy to simply give up the product line and move out of India. But officials at IKEA felt a responsibility to the children and decided to do as much as possible to make a difference. As the company got more involved in India, it set up the IKEA Foundation and partnered with UNICEF, contributing over $200 million in cash and in-kind donations to UNICEF programs to help children and their families. IKEA's work with UNICEF went beyond the issues of the supply chain and moved more into the humanitarian aspect of how to help the children. The IKEA Foundation targets South Asia, especially India, because of its supply chain issues, but it also targets that region because of the tremendous need for child aid.[86] By the end of 2012, funding from the IKEA Foundation will have enabled IKEA to help over 74 million children in India.

CORPORATE CODES OF ETHICS: HOW SHOULD A COMPANY BEHAVE?

After discussing numerous issues related to the impact of globalization on business, the role of businesses in the globalization process, and the impact of MNEs on society, we now come to a qualitatively different question: How *should* a company behave? The United

Nations Global Compact is a good start, since it identifies ten broad principles in the areas of human rights, labor, environment, and anti-corruption—all of which we've described in this chapter.[87] The Global Compact is not legally binding, but it is a helpful guide for companies in establishing a code of conduct. Launched in 2000, the initiative has more than 10,000 participants, of which more than 7,000 are businesses representing 145 countries. The UN Global Compact Web site allows you to search participating companies by country. It is interesting to note that on June 20, 2013, there were 824 French companies actively participating in the initiative, compared to 302 from the United States, 211 from the United Kingdom, and 241 from Germany. Brazil leads the BRIC countries with 342 active business participants, more than the U.S., UK, and Germany, and Russia has the least among the BRICs with only 28 participants.[88]

MOTIVATIONS FOR CORPORATE RESPONSIBILITY

Companies generally experience four strong motivations for acting responsibly:

1. Unethical and irresponsible behavior can result in *legal headaches,* especially in such areas as financial mismanagement, bribery, and product safety.
2. Such behavior could also result in *consumer action* such as a boycott.
3. Unethical behavior can affect *employee morale.* Conversely, responsible behavior can have a positive influence on a workforce, both at corporate headquarters and in overseas facilities.
4. You never know when *bad publicity* is going to cost you sales. Perhaps this concern is one reason why Nike and other apparel and clothing companies responded so quickly to criticism about allegedly unfair employment practices in developing countries.

DEVELOPING A CODE OF CONDUCT

Companies need to act responsibly because unethical and irresponsible behavior

- Could result in legal sanctions.
- Could result in consumer boycotts.
- Could lower employee morale.
- Could cost sales because of bad publicity.

A major component in a company's strategy for ethical and socially responsible behavior is a code of conduct.

Codes of conduct involve four dimensions:

- Setting a global policy that must be complied with wherever the company operates,
- Communicating the code to employees, suppliers, and subcontractors,
- Ensuring that policies are carried out,
- Reporting results to external stakeholders.

A code of conduct is a major component of most companies' strategies for ethical and socially responsible behavior. In the context of international operations, it can take the form of two perspectives: external and internal. Bear in mind, though, that external **codes of conduct** are useful insofar as they give companies some general guidance on how to operate. The practical challenge for the company is familiarizing itself with the codes of many different organizations and using them to fashion its own *internal code of conduct.*

What makes a good internal code of conduct? Here are four criteria:

1. *It sets global policies with which everyone working anywhere for the company must comply.* A good example is the code promulgated by the Finnish cell-phone company Nokia, which discusses how its code was set, who approved it, how it is communicated to its employees, and what its foundation values are.
2. *It communicates company policies not only to all employees but to all suppliers and subcontractors as well.* Gap, for example, maintains an education program to help subcontractors develop their own compliance programs that meet the objectives of Gap's code.[89]
3. *It ensures that the policies laid out in the code are carried out.* There are a variety of ways to approach this task:
   - GSK requires employees to confirm in writing that they've read and understand the company's code of conduct, then sign off that they understand and will follow the policies.
4. *It reports the results to external stakeholders.* This can be a complicated and sometimes tricky process, as Nike found out. Up until a few years ago, Nike was willing to provide a lot of information about its labor practices. In 1998, however, when a lawsuit charged that the report constituted false advertising, Nike was forced to pay $1.5 million to the

Fair Labor Association. Ever since the ruling came down in 2001, the giant shoe and apparel company has been less forthcoming about labor-related activities. Gap, however, has begun providing *more* information about its worldwide monitoring activities, including details about its code of conduct and practices; the Gap report also discusses its challenges—and failures—in getting subcontractors to act in accord with company policies.[90]

Most public companies provide a lot of information about their codes of conduct. The codes may be fairly general, or they may be specific. GE, for example, provides among other things a general statement of integrity, and then gives specific information about its code of conduct, who has to follow it, how to raise an integrity concern, how to work with customers, suppliers, and with governments, how to compete globally, and how to operate in the community. Some companies even provide reports, separate from their annual reports, that deal with sustainability and include codes of conduct. The important thing is to be aware of what a company's code of conduct is and how it applies to you, whether you are an employee, a customer, a supplier, or a member of the local community.

Looking to the Future

Dealing with Ethical Dilemmas in the Global Economy

This chapter has continued the discussion from Chapter 1 on the effects of globalization, but with more focus on the ethical issues and how companies can be more responsible as they operate abroad. Chapter 1 identified three scenarios on the future of globalization:

- Further globalization is inevitable.
- International business will grow primarily along regional rather than global lines.
- Forces working against further globalization and international business will slow down the growth of both.

Regardless of what happens, the more companies expand abroad, the greater the likelihood they will encounter ethical dilemmas that will make life challenging for them and for the people who work for them. However, two things will have an impact on future ethical behavior. First, as countries confront common problems, such as corruption and bribery, and try to work together to solve those problems, there will be a greater convergence of proper ethical conduct. Second, as individuals and companies gain more experience abroad, they will develop skills in ethical behavior. Sometimes you need experience in a country to learn how to make ethical decisions. The more companies encourage management to gain international experience, the more likely they are to figure out how to behave ethically.

In addition, social media will have a greater impact on ethical behavior in the future. Historically, we have always thought that one of the keys to transparency is an independent press willing to investigate and report on wrong-doings. But now social media such as Facebook, Twitter, YouTube, and so on have added an important new dimension to transparency. Even in countries where the press is controlled, news can go viral through the use of social media, as we have learned ever since the Arab Spring in 2011. Practically no event goes unnoticed. Social media will be an important source of influence on future behavior, and companies need to be aware that whatever they do is likely to show up somewhere.

However, there is more to responsible behavior than just not doing bad things. An important part of the impact of globalization on society is doing good things. Today's students, who will be tomorrow's business and government leaders, are very interested in helping to solve some of the world's greatest problems though social innovation, microfranchising, volunteering, and other activities. They are willing to go around the world to build homes and schools in areas devastated by natural disasters, or help the poor learn how to be effective entrepreneurs. Although some of these individuals will go on to work for NGOs or other not-for-profit ventures, others will work in the for-profit sector but with a different attitude toward the problems of the world than their predecessors. They are more likely to help initiate and get involved in humanitarian ventures sponsored by their companies. These activities will continue to grow, in spite of or maybe because of difficult economic times, and employees who support and get involved in them will be changed through what they do. ■

CASE Anglo American PLC in South Africa: What Do You Do When Costs Reach Epidemic Proportions?

By now it should be obvious that, regardless of where it chooses to do business, an MNE is going to face quite a variety of threats and disruptions to its plans and operations, ranging from bureaucratic corruption and political instability to terrorism and war. In 2007, Anglo American PLC, at that time one of the world's largest gold miners, found itself facing a threat that, although by no means new, defies most traditional categories of things that complicate business overseas—an HIV/AIDS epidemic in South Africa, the world's largest gold producer.[91]

In 2002, Anglo American made a landmark decision to provide free antiretroviral therapy (ART) to HIV-infected employees there. Surprisingly, however, this commitment met with mixed reactions from various stakeholders and achieved only controversial results. Now the U.K.-based company is asking itself, "Where do we go from here?"

AIDS in South Africa

How bad must a disease be to be accorded the status of an "epidemic"? Here's some background information. Sub-Saharan Africa is home to just over 10 percent of the world's population and 60 percent of all people infected with HIV, the virus that causes AIDS. Located at the southernmost tip of the African continent, the nation of South Africa has the highest number of people living with HIV/AIDS and suffers one of the world's highest rates of HIV infection—approximately 5.5 million people live with the virus in a population of 49 million. Every day, almost 1,000 South Africans die from AIDS-related diseases. Moreover, the UN and the World Health Organization say the epidemic has a long way to go before it reaches its peak.

Thus, over the past decade the spread of HIV/AIDS has had a profound impact on both the people of South Africa and their economy. Life expectancy is 48.98 years compared to, say, 75.63 years in Poland, a country with a similar population size and per capita GDP.

A group of Boy Scouts in Uganda hold up placards with the slogan "Be wise Immunize." The Ministry of Health in Uganda not only is fighting the scourge of HIV/AIDS, but it also is doing its best to eradicate childhood diseases that can be prevented with vaccines.

Source: © Mike Goldwater/Alamy

AIDS has also devastated the country's economy. Between 1992 and 2002, South Africa lost $7 billion annually—around 2 percent of GDP—as a result of AIDS-related worker deaths. Experts predict that, as AIDS spreads throughout sub-Saharan Africa, it will continue to reduce per capita growth by 1 to 2 percent per year and, in the worst-affected countries, cut annual GDP growth by as much as 0.6 percent by 2010. The consequences include both diminishing populations and shrinking economies, with GDPs deflating anywhere from 20 to 40 percent of the sizes they would have reached in the absence of AIDS.

Anglo American Operations in South Africa

Anglo American PLC is a diversified mining conglomerate operating in 45 countries and employing 107,000 permanent employees to produce precious metals (platinum and diamonds), base metals (copper, nickel, zinc, and phosphates), and bulk metals (for ferrous metals and coal). Founded in 1917 as the Anglo American Corporation of South Africa, it was South Africa's first home-based public limited company. Now a multinational firm headquartered in London, Anglo American has its primary listing in London, its secondary listing in Johannesburg, and a presence in Europe, Africa, Asia, North America, and South America.

In spite of its global spread, the company dominates South Africa's domestic economy through direct employment, contractors, and its supply chain. Through majority-share ownership of subsidiaries and associate companies, it controls over 25 percent of all shares traded on the South African stock market.

Anglo American and ART

With such a huge investment in South Africa, Anglo American has been hit hard by the HIV/AIDS epidemic. Having recognized the threat as far back as the early 1990s, Anglo was one of the first corporations to develop a comprehensive, proactive strategy to combat the ravages of the disease on its workforce and the repercussions for its operations.

Originally, the program consisted of prevention initiatives aimed at education and awareness, the distribution of condoms, financial and skill-related training to alleviate poverty, and a survey system to monitor the prevalence of the infection. Eventually, these policies were expanded to include voluntary counseling, testing, and care-and-wellness programs, and the services of all programs were extended to cover not only the families of employees but also the populations of surrounding communities. Anglo also became a member of the Global Business Council on HIV/AIDS, an organization of multinational companies that focuses on alleviating the effects of AIDS throughout the world and on protecting the rights of infected workers.

By adopting these strategies so early, Anglo American became a de facto leader in the private-sector fight against HIV/AIDS in Africa. Many other MNEs—including Coca-Cola, Ford, Colgate-Palmolive, and Chevron Texaco—soon followed Anglo's example and initiated prevention, education, and wellness programs of their own. Even then, however, the majority of companies operating in South Africa still hesitated, which is why Anglo's 2002 announcement that it would provide ART to its South African workforce (at company expense) was met with a good deal of excited approval from such interested parties as the WHO, the Global Business Council on HIV/AIDS, and a host of other NGOs.

The Costs of Operating in an Epidemic

The incentive for Anglo American's ART program largely came from the failure of its AIDS-prevention efforts to make much headway in stemming the spread of the disease. By 2001, according to Brian Brink, senior VP of the firm's medical division, the prevalence of HIV-positive workers had risen to an average of 21 percent across all operations—a figure that was climbing steadily at a rate of 2 percent annually. Bobby Godsell, CEO and chairman of the subsidiary AngloGold, reported that HIV/AIDS was adding as much as $5 to the cost of producing one ounce of gold, thereby tacking on $11 million a year to the company's production costs. Then there was the $7 million it was spending annually to combat such AIDS-related illnesses as tuberculosis (which was five times as prevalent as it had been just a decade earlier).

Finally, in addition to losses in productivity, the company had to bear the costs entailed by high levels of absenteeism, the constant retraining of replacement workers, and burgeoning payouts in health, hospitalization, and death benefits. Studies conducted at the time indicated not only that the costs of AIDS could reach as much as 7.2 percent of the company's total wage bill but also that the costs of leaving employees untreated would be even higher than the cost of providing ART.

Nine years after it rolled out its ART program, Anglo now finds itself struggling to please various stakeholders and determine whether all of its efforts are making a difference in the underlying problem or merely masking its effects. By the end of 2009, for instance, although 3,211 employees—approximately 27% of the HIV-infected workforce—were receiving ART, the company still struggled with high rates of non-adherence and dropout from treatment regimens. However, in 2012, Anglo tested 95,000 employees for HIV and provided ART to more than 5,000 employees. In addition, 25 percent fewer infections were recorded, and an increasing proportion (45%) of estimated HIV-positive employees were receiving treatment.

Anglo also faces the problem of spiraling costs for the program itself. Even though the prices of most of the necessary drugs have been decreasing, the cost of distributing them remains high, and the treatment regimen costs the company an estimated $4,000 per year per employee—quite expensive, especially compared to the wages and benefits that Anglo typically offers mineworkers. (Average monthly wages in the South African mining industry are about 5,100 rand, or US $830.) Meanwhile, as Anglo officials continue to remind investors that treating workers ultimately serves the bottom line, recent estimates project a total cost to the company of $1 billion or more over 10 years.

On the upside, cost per patient should decrease as the number of workers participating in the program increases. Unfortunately, one of the biggest challenges facing Anglo is encouraging participation among a migrant and largely uneducated workforce laboring under harsh conditions in an unstable environment. In South Africa, HIV/AIDS still carries a severe stigma, and many South Africans refuse to be tested or to admit they've been infected for fear of discrimination by managers, fellow employees, and even society at large. Moreover, many of those who agreed to participate have been confused by rumors and misinformation into assuming that they could stop using condoms once they were on the drugs—a situation, of course, that only exacerbated the prevalence of unsafe behavior.

ART is in fact a lifelong regimen that can lead to various side effects and needs to be administered under strict supervision. Anglo American, however, continues to struggle with high levels of non-adherence, even though that seems to be improving. The concern is that extensive patterns of non-adherence pose a risk of fostering new drug-resistant strains of the virus.

In addition, harsh working conditions often make it hard for workers to take medications on time or to deal with certain side effects. Finally, migrant workers—about four-fifths of the total workforce—who come from isolated villages hundreds of miles away are 2.5 times more likely to contract the disease, which they take with them back to their villages.

Constituencies and Critics

Anglo American also faces the problem of pressure from various stakeholders. The National Union of Mineworkers has been hesitant to voice its support, citing the company's limitations on health-insurance benefits and lack of cooperation with national agencies. The union has also accused the company of helping to foster working conditions that exacerbate the problem. Even Brian Gilbertson, former CEO of BHP Billiton, another large mining concern operating in South Africa, charged Anglo with merely trying to contain the problem instead of attacking its underlying causes, saying, "You don't approach the problem by just throwing drugs at it."

Anglo has countered many of these criticisms, insisting that it's beyond the resources and capacity of a single company to combat the overall problem, and it has called for more involvement on the part of the South African government. Instead of cooperation, however, the company has encountered outright opposition from political leaders. Indeed, South Africa has proved to be one of the African countries least committed to a program of effective intervention. Over the course of two years, the government diverted only 0.6 percent of the national budget to the HIV/AIDS crisis and has even resisted the wide distribution of ART drugs on the grounds that it's too expensive and too difficult to implement.

Matters weren't helped any when former President Thabo Mbeki publicly questioned the link between the HIV virus and the onset of AIDS. Then the country's health minister decried the Anglo American initiative as a "vigilante" move designed to place unreasonable burdens on the government, which would, after all, have to pick up the tab for treatments once workers had retired or left the company's employment.

In addition, dealing with pharmaceutical companies has proved a tricky proposition. On the one hand, Anglo has a deal with GlaxoSmithKline allowing it to purchase ART drugs at a tenth of the market price in the industrialized world (the same that GSK charges not-for-profit organizations). At the same time, however, other pharmaceutical companies have been hesitant and unreliable at best, promising price cuts and then reneging over fears of violating intellectual property rights. As a matter of fact, several of these companies, complaining that cheap generic drugs made available in Africa will eventually be resold by profiteers on higher-priced Western markets, have put their energies into suing the South African government for what they claim to be generally poor enforcement of their patent rights.

Given the many challenges Anglo has faced, not to mention the opposition from unexpected quarters, some observers have gone so far as to suggest that the company would be better off by simply pulling back on its HIV/AIDS treatment program rather than pouring more resources into the effort to make it work. In the long run, however, Anglo must consider the continued pressure it will get from ethically minded shareholders as well as its own sense of moral responsibility.

There are also indications that the future may not be as bleak as it often appears. Of the workers who faithfully adhere to the drug regimen, more than 90 percent have responded well to treatment and are working productively. The South African government may also be undergoing a gradual change of heart, having recently launched a National Strategic Plan for combating HIV/AIDS, which included the aggressive goal of cutting the number of HIV infections in half by 2011. And in June 2009, the company's subsidiary, Anglo-Coal South Africa, was recognized by the Global Business Coalition on HIV/AIDS, Tuberculosis, and Malaria as best-in-class for the private sector for the success of its VCT (Voluntary Counseling and Testing) programs, with 94 percent of employees having undergone testing.

Anglo American's strategy for HIV/AIDS intervention has in some ways become a model closely followed by other companies with operations in regions heavily affected by the disease, including its industry rival, Rio Tinto PLC. Rio introduced a community intervention plan for HIV/AIDS as early as 2003 for all of its Sub-Saharan operations, which included similar objectives of providing outreach activities and treatment options to employees, as well as to family and community members.[92] For their efforts, the Global Business Coalition on HIV/AIDS, Tuberculosis, and Malaria recognized Rio Tinto's program in the Limpopo region of South Africa in 2008 as "Best in Business Action."[93] So, perhaps the criticism for such interventions is waning as companies continue to adopt responsible and effective initiatives for HIV/AIDS treatment.

QUESTIONS

11-3. Who are the various stakeholders that Anglo American needs to consider as it adopts an effective HIV/AIDS strategy?

✪ **11-4.** What are the pros and cons of Anglo's adoption of an aggressive strategy in combating HIV/AIDS among its South African workforce? What recommendations would you give the company concerning its HIV/AIDS policy?

11-5. Because such a large percentage of its workforce consists of migrant workers who are more likely to acquire and spread HIV/AIDS, should Anglo adopt the policy of not hiring migrant workers? Should the South African government close the doors to migrant workers?

✪**11-6.** What role do pharmaceutical companies play in responding to the HIV/AIDS epidemic in South Africa? Given that India can manufacture and export HIV/AIDS drugs much cheaper than they cost from the pharmaceutical companies themselves, should Anglo just import the drugs to be used for their employees?

SUMMARY

- MNEs must balance the interests of different constituencies that have different objectives.
- Companies create Codes of Conduct to help their employees understand how they are expected to act. Ultimately, however, individuals are the ones that make decisions, so companies must be sure to hire ethical employees.
- Behaving ethically can help a company develop competitive advantage and avoid being seen as irresponsible.
- Relative behavior implies that we act according to the norms of the countries in which we operate. Normative behavior implies that there are universal standards for ethical conduct that should be followed everywhere.
- The law is an important basis for ethical behavior, but not all unethical behavior is illegal. Thus, ethical behavior must go beyond the law to include common decency.
- Bribery is a form of unethical behavior being addressed at the multilateral level, such as at the UN and the OECD, and at the national level, such as with the Foreign Corrupt Practices Act in the United States.
- Environmental concerns are raised over extractive industries and those that generate air and water pollution or that make products such as automobiles that use fossil fuels.
- The Kyoto Protocol, which requires the reduction of the emission of greenhouse gases, has not been adopted by all countries and is therefore still limited in its total global impact. However, companies must adapt to countries that have implemented the Protocol.
- Pharmaceutical companies face challenges on how to make enough money to fund R&D into new drugs and how to help provide critical drugs to developing countries at lower prices.
- A major challenge facing MNEs is the globalization of the supply chain and the impact on workers, especially in the areas of fair wages, child labor, working conditions, working hours, and freedom of association.
- Companies respond to the pressures for greater corporate social responsibility by establishing codes of conduct, distributing them to suppliers and subcontractors internationally, and ensuring compliance with the codes through effective training and auditing programs.

KEY TERMS

code of conduct (p. 465)
deontological approach (p. 446)
extraterritoriality (p. 450)
Foreign Corrupt Practices Act (FCPA) (p. 453)
Kyoto Protocol (p. 457)
normativism (p. 449)
relativism (p. 448)
stakeholders (p. 445)
sustainability (p. 456)
teleological approach (p. 446)
utilitarianism (p. 446)

ENDNOTES

1 *Sources include the following:* General Electric Co. home page, at www.ge.com/en/company (accessed May 16, 2013); GE Ecomagination home page, at ge.ecomagination.com/site/index.html (accessed May 16, 2013); "A Lean, Clean Electric Machine," *The Economist* (December 10, 2005): 77–79; *GE 2010 Annual Report*, General Electric Co. (2007); Alan Murray, "Business: Why Key Executives Are Warming to Legislation on Climate Change," *Wall Street Journal* (February 7, 2007): A10; Rachel Pulfer, "Gambling on Green," *Canadian Business* (April 24, 2006): 35; Kara Sissell, "Major Corporations Form Advocacy Group to Curb Climate Change," *Chemical Week* (January 31, 2007): 12; "Safety, Health & the Environment at GE," *Professional Safety* 51:12 (Des Plaines: Dec 2006):18; Anne Fisher, "America's Most Admired Companies," *Fortune* (March 19, 2007): 88–94; Neal St. Anthony, "'Green' Strategy Has GE Investor Seeing Red," *Minneapolis-St. Paul Star Tribune* (February 3, 2006): 1; Brendan Murray and Kim Chipman, "Bush Opposes Limits on Pollution Linked to Global Warming," *Pittsburgh Post-Gazette* (January 23, 2007): A5; John Teresko, "Technology of the Year: Connection Profits and Preservation," Industryweek.com (December 2005); "Press Release: GEs 2008 ecomagination revenues to rise 21%, cross $17 bn," (www.meed.com/sectors/industry/

manufacturing/ges-2008-ecomagination-revenues-to-rise-21-cross-17bn/3067016.article, October 29, 2008); *Indexes Update March 2009*, pages 5, 9, 10, at www.sustainability-index.com.

2 Pankaj Ghemawat, "Distance Still Matters: The Hard Reality of Global Expansion," *Harvard Business Review* (September 2001): 137–47.

3 Bradley R. Agle, Thomas Donaldson, R. Edward Freeman, Michael C. Jensen, Ronald K. Mitchell, and Donna J. Wood, "Dialogue toward Superior Stakeholder Theory," *Business Ethics Quarterly* 18:2 (2008): 153–90.

4 Lawrence Kohlberg, "The Claim to Moral Adequacy of a Highest Stage of Moral Judgment," *Journal of Philosophy* 70 (1973): 630–46.

5 Richard T. DeGeorge, *Business Ethics*, 7th edition (Upper Saddle River, NJ, 2010): 22–24.

6 De George (2010): 39, 44.

7 Op. cit.

8 Alfred Marcus, *Business & Society: Ethics, Government, and the World Economy* (Homewood, IL: Irwin, 1996)

9 David J. Vidal, *The Link between Corporate Citizenship and Financial Performance* (New York: Conference Board, 1999).

10 "Interfaith Center on Corporation Responsibility," www.iccr.org/ (accessed March 28, 2013).

11 Ronald Berenbeim, "The Search for Global Ethics," *Vital Speeches of the Day* 65:6 (1999): 177–78.

12 Trivia-Library.com, "Origins of Sayings – When in Rome, Do As the Romans Do" (accessed March 30, 2011), reproduced with permission from the People's Almanac series of books, 1975–1981 by David Wallechinsky & Irving Wallace.

13 See John M. Kline, *Ethics for International Business: Decision Making in a Global Political Economy* (London and New York: Routledge, 2005).

14 DeGeorge (2010): 33.

15 S. Prakash Sethi, "Standards for Corporate Conduct in the International Arena: Challenges and Opportunities for Multinational Corporations," *Business and Society Review* (Spring 2002): 20–39.

16 "The Ethics of Business," in "A Survey of Corporate Social Responsibility," *The Economist* (January 22, 2005): 20.

17 U.S. Environmental Protection Agency, "DDT-A Brief History and Status," www.epa.gov/pesticides/factsheets/chemicals/ddt-brief-history-status.htm (accessed June 1, 2013).

18 John R. Boatright, *Ethics and the Conduct of Business* (Upper Saddle River, NJ: Prentice Hall, 1993): 13–16.

19 Boatright, *Ethics and the Conduct of Business*, 16–18.

20 Austen L. Parrish, "The Effects Test: Extraterritoriality's Fifth Business," *Vanderbilt Law Review* 61:5 (October 2008): 1453+.

21 Leslie Wayne, "Foreign Firms Most Affected By a Law Barring Bribes," *The New York Times* (September 4, 2012): B1.

22 See A. M. Ali and I. H. Saiad, "Determinants of Economic Corruption," *Cato Journal* 22:3 (2003): 449–66; H. Park, "Determinants of Corruption: A Cross-National Analysis," *Multinational Business Review* 11:2 (2003): 29–48.

23 Transparency International, "How Do You Define Corruption? in *Frequently Asked Questions about Corruption*, www.transparency.org/whoweare (accessed June 1, 2013).

24 Peter Lattman, "Ralph Lauren Corp. Agrees to Pay Fine in Bribery Case," *The New York Times* (April 23, 2013): B2.

25 Niki Kitsantonis, "Greek Ex-Minister is Tried in Bribery Cover-Up Case," *The New York Times* (April 23, 2013): A8.

26 "The Short Arm of the Law—Bribery and Business," *The Economist* (March 2, 2002): 78.

27 Transparency International, "Corruption Perceptions Index," cpi.transparency.org/cpi2012/results/ (accessed May 13, 2013).

28 Transparency International, "Bribe Payers Index 2011," bpi.transparency.org/bpi2011/results/ (accessed May 13, 2013).

29 See The World Bank, *World Development Report 2002: Building Institutions for Markets;* M. Habib and L. Zurawicki, "Country-Level Investments and the Effect of Corruption—Some Empirical Evidence," *International Business Review* 10:6 (2001): 687–700.

30 "China Execution Warning to Others," Aljazeera.net (July 11, 2007), at english.aljazeera.net (accessed August 20, 2007).

31 S. Ghoshal and P. Moran, "Towards a Good Theory of Management," in J. Birkinshaw and G. Piramal, eds., *Sumantra Ghoshal on Management: A Force for Good* (Upper Saddle River, NJ: Financial Times/Prentice Hall, 2005): 1–27.

32 Mark Pieth and Huguette Labelle, "Bribery in International Business: Making Sure That Bribes Don't Pay," www.oecd.org/daf/anti-bribery/makingsurethatbribesdontpay.htm (accessed June 20, 2013).

33 Fritz Heimann and Gillian Dell, *Progress Report 20010: Enforcement of the OECD Convention on Combating Bribery of Foreign Public Officials in International Business Transactions* (Transparency International, July 28, 2010): 12.

34 International Chamber of Commerce, "ICC Rules on Combating Corruption," (2011 Edition) www.iccwbo.org/Advocacy-Codes-and-Rules/Document-centre/2011/ICC-Rules-on-Combating-Corruption/ (accessed June 20, 2013).

35 UN Convention Against Corruption (UNCAC) www.unodc.org/unodc/en/treaties/CAC/index.html (accessed March 9, 2011).

36 Qing Tian, "Perception of Business Bribery in China: The Impact of Moral Philosophy," *Journal of Business Ethics* 80 (2008): 437–45.

37 Dionne Searcey, "U.S. Cracks Down on Corporate Bribes," *Wall Street Journal* (May 26, 2009): 1, 4.

38 Stuart Pfeifer, "Bribes to Foreign Firms are Targeted; Federal Authorities Step Up Prosecution of Businesses That Make Payments to Officials to Win Deals," *Los Angeles Times* (March 11, 2011): B1.

39 U.S. Department of Justice: Foreign Corrupt Practices Act: www.justice.gov/criminal/fraud/fcpa/cases/a.html (accessed March 9, 2011); Dionne Searcey, "U.S. Cracks Down on Corporate Bribes," *Wall Street Journal* (May 26, 2009): 1, 4.

40 Joe Pallazolo and Christopher M. Matthews, "Bribery Law Dos and Don'ts," *The Wall Street Journal* (November 15, 2012): B1.

41 "Bribery Act 2010," The UK Serious Fraud Office (at legislation.gov.uk and www.sfo.gov.uk), accessed June 1, 2013.

42 Glenn R. Simpson, *Wall Street Journal [Eastern edition]* (Jan 27, 2005): A2.

43 Colleen Taylor, "U.S., Japan Authorities Join in Siemens "Black Money' Probe," *Electronic News* (February 12, 2007): 7; David Crawford and Mike Esterl, "Room at the Top: German Giant Siemens Faces Leadership Crisis," *Wall Street Journal* (http://online.wsj.com, April 26, 2007); Crawford and Esterl, "Widening Scandal: At Siemens, Witnesses Cite Pattern of Bribery," *Wall Street Journal* (January 31, 2007): A1.

44 "The Hollow Men," *The Economist* (March 17, 2007): 71.

45 Crawford and Esterl, "Widening Scandal,"

46 Konstantin Richter, "The House of Siemens," *Wall Street Journal* (April 27, 2007): 13.

47 Jack Ewing, "Siemens' Culture Clash: CEO Kleinfeld Is Making Changes, and Enemies," *Businessweek* (January 29, 2007): 42–46.

48 Richter, "The House of Siemens," 13.

49 David Crawford and Mike Esterl, "Siemens to Decide if New Leader Is Needed amid Widening Probes," *Wall Street Journal* (April 25, 2007): A3.

50 Ewing, "Siemens' Culture Clash," 42–46; Richter, "The House of Siemens," 13.

51 G. Thomas Sims, "Siemens Struggles to Regain Equilibrium," *New York Times*, online edition (April 27, 2007); Sims, "Two Former Siemens Officials Convicted for Bribery," *New York Times*, online edition (May 15, 2007).

52 Josef Jabareen, "A New Conceptual Framework for Sustainable Development," *Environment, Development and Sustainability* 10:5 (April 2008): 29.

53 Floating Island International, "Products" and "Applications," www.floatingislandinternational.com (accessed March 10, 2011).

54 Floating Island International, "Company Profile" and "Licensing Opportunities," www.floatingislandinternational.com (accessed May 13, 2013).

55 John Carey, "Global Warming," *Businessweek* (August 16, 2004): 60–69.

56 "Hotting Up," *The Economist* (February 5, 2005): 73–74; Richard S. Lindzen, "The Climate Science Isn't Settled," *The Wall Street Journal* (December 1, 2009): A19.

57 UNFCC home page, at unfccc.int/kyoto_protocol/status_of_ratification/items/2613.php (accessed June 6, 2013).

58 Alison Graab, "Greenhouse Gas Market to Slow Global Warming," CNN.com (accessed April 12, 2005).

59 Ian Austen, "Canada Announces Exit from Kyoto Climate Treaty," *The New York Times* (December 13, 2011): A9.

60 Ed King, "Key Cameron Advisor Blocks Climate Change from G8 Agenda," *The Guardian* (March 26, 2013), www.guardian.co.uk/environment/2013/mar/26/cameron-adviser-blocks-climate-change-g8 (accessed March 26, 2013).

61 Jack Ewing, "The Wind at Germany's Back," *Businessweek* (February 11, 2008): 68.

62 Mark Lander, "Mixed Feelings as Kyoto Pact Takes Effect," *New York Times*, www.nytimes.com/2005/02/16/business/worldbusiness/16kyoto.html?pagewanted=2&_r=0 (February 16, 2005).

63 Lander, "Mixed Feelings as Kyoto Pact Takes Effect."

64 Carey, "Global Warming," 62.

65 "Alcoa Inc.; Alcoa Volunteers Set to Contribute to a More Sustainable Future," *Biotech Week* (May 13, 2009): 2792.

66 *National Geographic.* "Ten Countries with the biggest footprints" <http://environment.nationalgeographic.com/environment/sustainableearth/> pictures-ten-countries-with-the-biggest-footprints/#/rio-20-united-nations-country-footprints-uae_" (September, 2013).

67 Saifur Rahman, "UAE's per capita energy consumption among the highest" (April 16, 2013),<http://gulfnews.com/business/economy/uae-s-per-capita-energyconsumption-among-the-highest-1.1171313> (accessed September 2013).

68 www.photius.com/rankings/economy/gdp_per_capita_2013_0.html

69 Vesela Todorova, "UAE wants world governments to extend KYOTO Protocol" *The National* <http://www.thenational.ae/news/uae-news/environment/uae-wants-world-governments-to-extend-kyoto-prootocol> (accessed September 2013).

70 MASDAR, <http://www.masdar.ae/en/#masdar> (accessed September 2013).

71 Ibid., "What are the benefits of setting up in a Free Zone?" (accessed September 2013).

72 Ibid., "Past and Present Companies," (accessed September 2013).

73 Ibid., "DB MASDAR Clean Tech Fund" (accessed September 2013).

74 *GlaxoSmithKline 2012 Annual Report*p. 8 , www.gsk.com/content/dam/gsk/globals/documents/pdf/GSK-Annual-Report-2012.pdf, accessed June 1, 2013.

75 WHO, "Medicines: Spurious/Falsely-Labelled/Falsified/Counterfeit (SFFC) Medicines," WHO Media Centre Fact Sheets, Fact Sheet No. 275 (May 2012), www.who.int/mediacentre/factsheets/fs275/en/index.html (accessed June 15, 2013).

76 David Barboza, "GlaxoSmithKline Accused of Corruption by China," *The New York Times*, July 12, 2013, p. B1.

77 Miriam Jorda, "Brazil to Stir Up AIDS-Drug Battle," *Wall Street Journal* (September 5, 2003): A3; "Brazil to Break Merck AIDS Drug Patent," *Associated Press* story on MSNBC Web site (May 4, 2007).

78 "A Gathering Storm: Pharmaceuticals," *The Economist* (June 9, 2007): 73.

79 Vikas Bajaj and Andrew Pollack, "A Case in India Pits Drug Makers Against Advocates for the Poor," *The New York Times* (March 7, 2012): B1; Jessica Wapner, "Indian Court rules in Favor of Generic Gleevec," *PLOS Blogs* (April 2, 2013), blogs.plos.org/workinprogress/2013/04/02/indian-court-rules-in-favor-of-generic-gleevec/ (accessed on June 21, 2013).

80 Ethical Trading Initiative, www.ethicaltrade.org (accessed June 1, 2013).

81 Ans Kolk and Rob van Tulder, "Child Labor and Multinational Conduct: A Comparison of International Business and Stakeholder Codes," *Journal of Business Ethics* 36:3 (March 2002): 291–301.

82 ILO, "Worst Forms of Child Labor," www.ilo.org/ipec/facts/WorstFormsofChildLabour/lang--en/index.htm (accessed June 1, 2013).

83 ILO, "ILO Convention No. 138 on the Minimum Age for Admission to Employment and Work," www.ilo.org/ipec/facts/ILOconventionsonchildlabour/lang--en/index.htm

84 Kolk and van Tulder, "Child Labor and Multinational Conduct."

85 Edward Luce, "Ikea's Grown-Up Plan to Tackle Child Labour," *Financial Times* (September 15, 2004): 7.

86 UNICEF's Corporate Partnerships: IKEA, www.unicef.org/corporate_partners/index_25092.html, (accessed May 13, 2013).

87 United Nations, *United Nations Global Compact*, www.unglobalcompact.org/AboutTheGC/ (accessed June 20, 2013).

88 Ibid., "Participants & Stakeholders," *United Nations Global Compact*, www.unglobalcompact.org/ParticipantsAndStakeholders/ (accessed on June 20, 2013).

89 Amy Merrick, "Gap Offers Unusual Look at Factory Conditions," *Wall Street Journal* (May 12, 2004): A1.

90 Sarah Murray and Alison Maitland, "The Trouble with Transparent Clothing," *Financial Times* (May 12, 2004): 8.

91 ***Sources include the following:*** *UNAIDS 2008 Report on the Global AIDS Epidemic; HIV and AIDS in South Africa*, available for download at www.unaids.org/en/media/unaids/contentassets/dataimport/pub/globalreport/2008/jc1510_2008globalreport_en.pdf; *Delivering Real Excellence: Annual Report* 2010, Anglo American; *Making a Difference Report to Society 2008*, Anglo American; *Delivering Real Excellence: Annual Report 2010*, Anglo American; "HIV/AIDS Co-Infection: Anglo American's Coal Division in South Africa Wins Global Business Coalition Award for Top International Workplace HIV and AIDS Programme," *Law & Health Weekly* (July 11, 2009): 849; Alec Russell, "Answers to an AIDS Epidemic: New Initiatives to Help Infected Workers Mark a Big Shift in Attitude and Approach at Some of South Africa's Largest Companies," *Financial Times* (October 4, 2007): 14; Mark Schoofs, "Anglo American Drops Noted Plan on AIDS Drugs," *Wall Street Journal* (April 16, 2002): A19; World Health Organization/AFRO, "Southern African Health Challenges Intensify," press release (September 13, 2004): 1–2; Mark Schoofs, "New Challenges in Fighting AIDS—Enlisting Multinationals in Battle," *Wall Street Journal* (November 30, 2001): B1; "AIDS in the Workplace," *Business Africa* (July 1, 2001): 1–2; "The Corporate Response," *Business Africa* (September 1, 2001): 4; Mark Schoofs, "South Africa Reverses Course on AIDS Drugs," *Wall Street Journal* (November 20, 2003): B1; "Anglo American to Provide HIV/AIDS Help for Workers," *American Metal Market* (August 7, 2002): 4; Bruce Einhorn and Catherine Arnst, "Why Business Should Make AIDS Its Business—Multinationals Are Taking Baby Steps to Control the Disease in Their Workforce," *Businessweek* (August 9, 2004): 83; "Digging Deep," *The Economist* (August 10, 2002): 55; James Lamont, "Anglo's Initiative," *Financial Times* (August 8, 2002): 10; "Anglo American to Give Mineworkers AIDS Drugs Free," *Wall Street Journal* (August 7, 2002): A13; Matthew Newmann, Scott Hensley, and Scott Miller, "U.S. Reaches Patent Compromise to Provide Drugs to Poor Nations," *Wall Street Journal* (August 28, 2003): A3; Statistics South Africa, "Labour Statistics Survey of Average Monthly Earnings," *Statistical Release P0272* (February 2002): 3; Central Intelligence Agency, *The World Factbook*, www.cia.gov/library/publications/the-world-factbook/ index.html (June 1, 2013); Julia Werdigier "Xstrata Ends Bid for Rival in London," *NY Times* (October 16, 2009): B8; *Delivering Sustainable Value Report to Society 2009*, Anglo American.

92 Rio Tinto, "Rio Tinto HIV/AIDS strategy," www.riotinto.com/ (accessed March 1, 2011).

93 Global Business Coalition on HIV/AIDS, TB, and Malaria, "Member Profiles: Rio Tinto," www.gbcimpact.org/ (accessed March 1, 2011).

CHAPTER 12
Strategies for International Business

OBJECTIVES

After studying this chapter, you should be able to

1. Evaluate industry structure, firm strategy, and value creation
2. Profile the features, functions, configuration, and coordination of the value chain
3. Describe how and why companies choose to cluster in close geographic proximity
4. Describe how robots in specific and automation in general change how managers interpret the value chain
5. Discuss the industry change affects the effectiveness of a value chain
6. Compare and contrast the strengths and drawbacks of a reality versus virtuality in designing the value chain
7. Explain the ideas of global integration and local responsiveness
8. Profile the types of strategies used by MNEs

Source: © koya979 - Fotolia.com

Vision without action is a daydream. Action without vision is a nightmare.

—Japanese proverb

CASE Zara's Strategy for Value Creation in the Global Apparel Industry[1]

Traditionally, national retailers outsource apparel production via global brokers to thousands of small apparel makers. The typical manufacturer, usually located in a low-wage country, is a small-scale operation that employs a few to a few dozen workers. In a labor-intensive process, workers make specific pieces of clothing, often in a narrow range of sizes and colors, which are then integrated with the output of hundreds of other such companies spread across dozens of countries. As more companies in more countries make more specialized products—i.e., one factory makes zippers, one makes linings, one makes buttons, and so on—multinational trading companies perform as cross-border intermediaries and supervise the assembly of component pieces into finished goods, which are then shipped to apparel retailers.

Responding to market shifts relentlessly pressures apparel retailers. In turn, they push multinational trading companies to improve coordination among themselves and apparel makers. By planning collections closer to the selling season, testing the market, placing smaller initial orders, and reordering more frequently, retailers can reduce forecasting errors and inventory risks. The final links are markets and customers. Although tastes overlap among countries, local customers' preferences traditionally vary. For example, the British seek stores based on class sensitivities, Germans are value-conscious, Chinese shoppers are brand-aware, and shoppers in the United States look for a mix of variety, quality, and price. Collectively, these conditions create a buyer-driven chain that links fragmented factories, global brokers, dispersed retailers, and local customers.

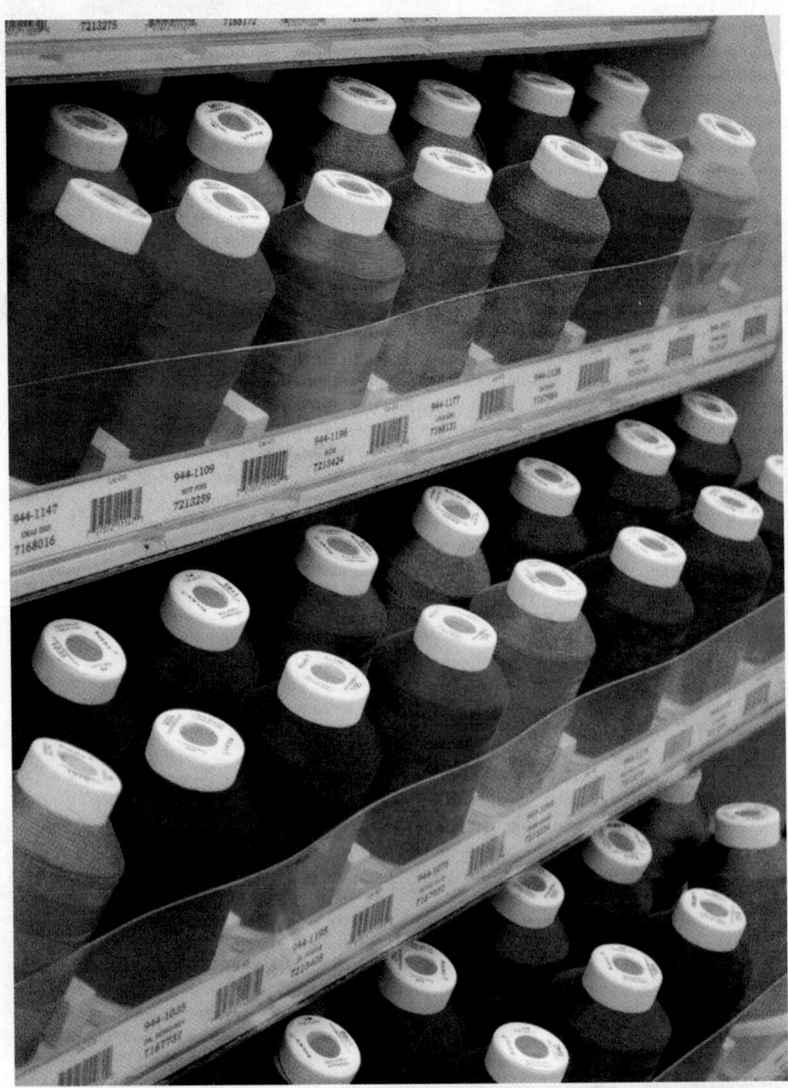

From simple spools of thread, Zara weaves a far-flung empire.

Source: JJAVA/Fotolia

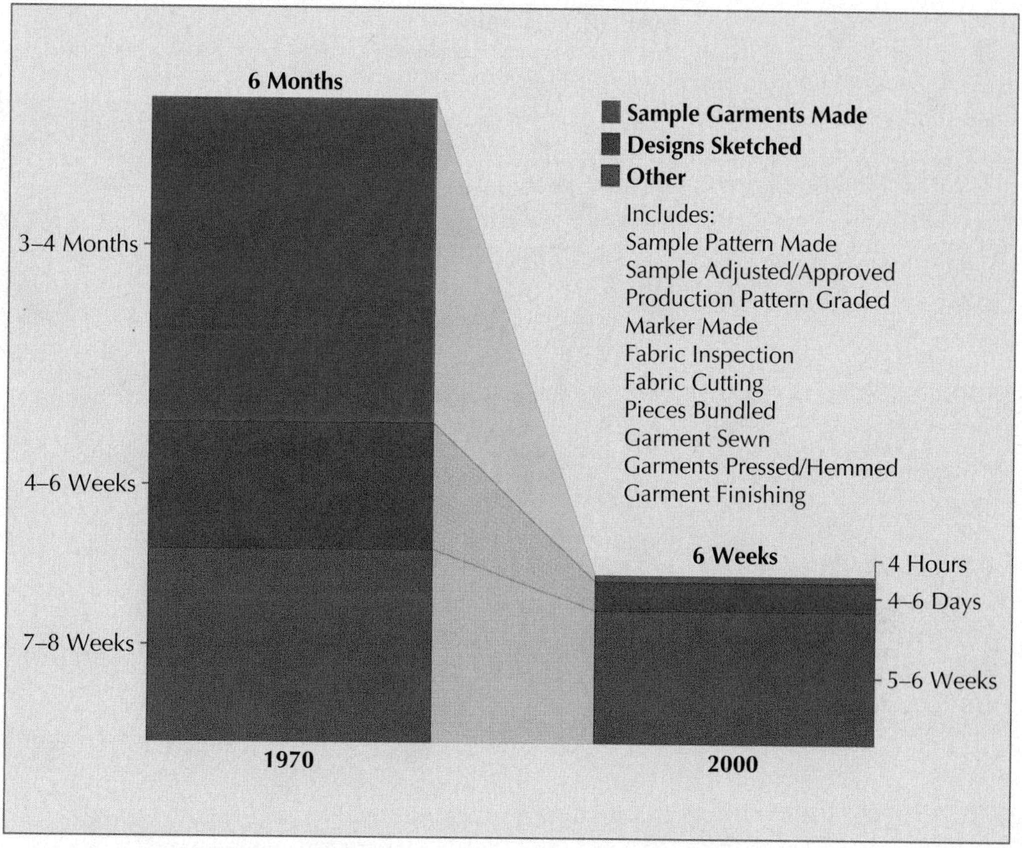

FIGURE 12.1 Cycle Time in the Global Apparel Industry

Globalization creates options for countries and companies in the apparel industry. Improving technology, sourcing, and production systems let innovative apparel makers compress cycle time. Shortening cycle time increases efficiencies and boosts profits. This chart highlights how Zara applied its innovative strategy to reset the standards of operational efficiency in the global apparel industry.

Industry wisdom spurred firms to choose a "sliver" of a particular activity—make zippers, manage logistics, focus on store design, cater to customer segments—instead of creating value across multiple slivers. Effectively, "Do what you do best and outsource the rest" drove strategy. Globalization reset the game board. Fewer barriers, better logistics, and improving communications created new industry standards and strategic choices.

A compelling example is the compression of cycle times in the apparel-buyer chain (see Figure 12.1). In the 1970s, getting a garment from factory to customer took approximately nine months—six to design the collection and another three to make and ship it. Now, it takes the typical company from six months down to six weeks to run this cycle. For a firm named Zara, it takes between two to four weeks. By rejecting conventional standards, Zara implemented disruptive innovations that reset the relationship among industry structure, company strategy, and value creation. In the process, it became the world's leading apparel company and its founder, Amancio Ortega, one of the world's wealthiest people.

ZARA WHO?

The Inditex Group, a Spanish apparel MNE, is the parent corporation of eight global retail chains, including Zara, Bershka, Massimo Dutti, Stradivarius, and Oysho. No matter the brand, the all-trendy, reasonably priced products are sold in attractive stores worldwide. Zara is the flagship of Inditex, generating the bulk of total sales. Inditex runs operations from "The Cube," its gleaming, futuristic headquarters in Artexio, near La Coruña, a small, seaside town in northwest Spain about 300 miles from Madrid (see Map 12.1). Inditex employed more than 111,000 in 2012, up from 90,000 in 2010. The company workforce is young (average age: 26) and female (besides representing more than 80 percent of employees, women hold more than half of the executive, technical, and managerial positions).

MAP 12.1 Spain

Zara is headquartered in La Coruña, a small town of 250,000 in the northwest corner of Spain. Since 1975, Zara has expanded from its original outlet in La Coruña to a network of thousands of stores spanning the globe.

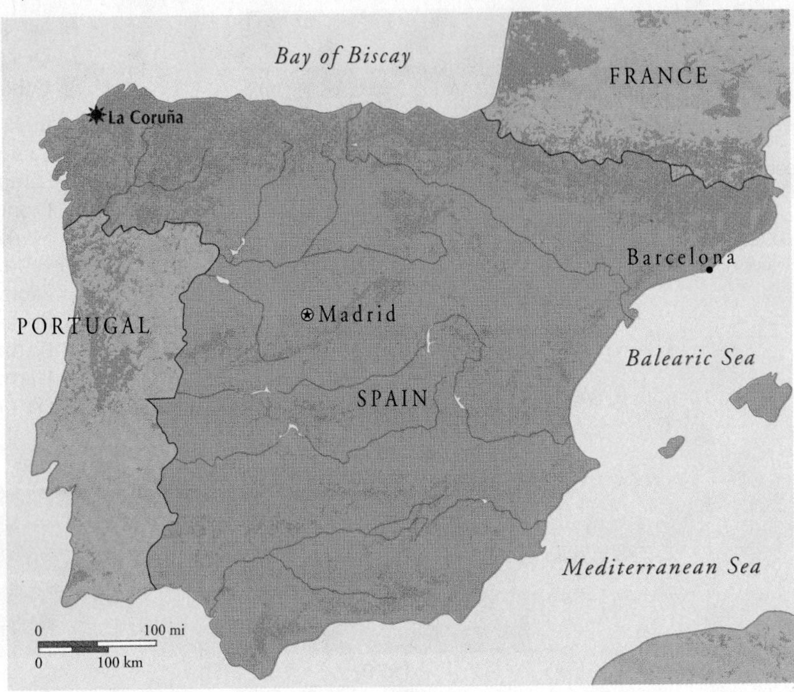

Inditex's revenue approached $21 billion in 2012, far ahead of Sweden's Hennes & Mauritz (H&M) at $18.8 billion and long-time worldwide leader Gap's $15.6 billion. Spain, Inditex's home market, accounted for about a quarter of sales, while Asia's and the Americas' continued growth accounted for more than a third of 2012 sales. Its nearly 6,000 storefronts spanning 85 countries collectively sold the 840 million garments Inditex made that year.

The first Zara shop opened its doors in 1975 in La Coruña. Today, there are nearly 1700 outlets and, on average, a new one opening every day. Zara uses an innovative strategy to power its global performance, integrating fashion and information technology to make and move sophisticated clothing at compelling costs. One analyst calls it "Armani at moderate prices," while another characterizes its fashions as "Banana Republic priced like Old Navy." No matter the portrayal, all agree that Zara's strategy has challenged historic ideas of value creation in the global apparel industry. Understanding its success requires understanding its competency in configuring and coordinating value-creating activities.

Design

Zara rejects the idea of conventional spring and fall clothing collections in favor of "live collections" that are designed, manufactured, and sold almost as quickly as customers' fleeting tastes—no style lasts more than four weeks. The company's 300 or so designers monitor market events, fashion trends, and customer preferences in designing about 11,000 distinct items per year. Compare that to 2,000 to 4,000 items made by rivals. Zara translates the latest fashion trend from a catwalk in Paris to its store shelves in Shanghai in as little as two weeks, versus the industry standard of several months.

Zara's designers get ideas from store managers, industry publications, TV, Internet, and films. Its trend spotters focus on university campuses and nightclubs. Its so-called slaves-to-fashion staff snap shots at couture shows and post them to designers who quickly reproduce the look for the mass market. For example, when Madonna played a series of concerts in Spain, teenage girls arrived at her final show sporting a Zara knock-off of the outfit she had worn during her first show. Nevertheless, though Zara pushes the edge, its fashions are never too far out there.

Zara does not adapt products to a particular country's preferences. The convergence of fashion and taste across national boundaries endorses management's bias toward standardization. Some product designs cater to physical, cultural, or climate differences—smaller sizes in Japan, special women's clothing in Arab countries, different seasonal weights in South America. Still, Zara has standardized about 85 percent of its designs for the global market, believing that fashion trends are global.

Sourcing

Zara's headquarters staff and purchasing offices in Barcelona, Beijing, and Hong Kong acquire fabric, components, and finished products from suppliers in Spain, Portugal, India, Turkey, Morocco, and China. Linked into Zara's network, suppliers coordinate their production with its projections. Zara buys about half of its fabric "gray" (not yet dyed) in order to update designs quickly. José Maria Castellano, Inditex's former CEO, explains, "We have the ability to scrap an entire production line if it is not selling. We can dye collections in new colors, and we can create a new fashion line in days."[2]

Production

Like its rivals, notably H&M and Gap, Zara sources finished garments from suppliers in Europe, North Africa, and Asia. Unlike its rivals, Zara employs nearly 20,000 people, distributed across 23 factories, to make more than half of its finished garments. This odd situation stems from Ortega's original intent to run his manufacturing business in La Coruña. Exploiting short-lived fashion trends, he reasoned, obliges making those items close to home. Hence, Zara makes its most time- and fashion-sensitive products in its 20 factories clustered in La Coruña. Inditex outsources about a third of its remaining manufacturing to China, Bangladesh, Vietnam, and Brazil, and 15 percent or so to factories in Portugal, Morocco, and Turkey. These suppliers make staple items with longer shelf lives, such as t-shirts and jeans. Inditex's factories are highly automated, specialize by garment type, and focus on the capital-intensive parts of the production process—i.e., pattern design and cutting—as well as finishing and inspection.

Zara spent 20 to 40 percent more to make garments in Spain and Portugal than rivals spent in Asia, mainly due to higher labor costs. It compensates for costlier production by minimizing advertising, cutting inventory expenses, and quickly adjusting to fashion trends. Inditex's gross margins in 2010 were 56.8 percent—half again the 37.5 percent claimed by the Gap.

Making high-end garments requires a human touch, so Zara has organized a network of some 500 workshops in Galicia, the home state of La Coruña, as well as across the border in northern Portugal. These workshops are small operations, averaging about 20 to 30 workers who specialize by product type and hand-sew garment pieces that have been cut at Zara's factories. Zara accounts for most, if not all, of the shops' business and provides tools, technology, logistics, and working capital while paying standard rates per finished garment. Many local cooperatives have worked with Inditex so long they no longer operate with written contracts.

Logistics

Most of Zara's garments, both internally made and externally contracted, flow through its massive distribution center in La Coruña—about the size of 90 football fields—or smaller satellite centers in Brazil and Mexico. A state-of-the-art tracking system moves hanging garments to appropriate bar-coded areas. As goods travel along 125 miles of underground rails that link production sites, they are sorted in carousels capable of handling 45,000 folded garments per hour. Once garments are completed, Zara ships about two-and-a-half million items per week to stores worldwide. Third-party delivery services manage the transfer of preprogrammed lots to stores; they deliver customized orders within 24 hours for stores in Europe, the Middle East, and much of the U.S., and 48 hours for Asia and Latin America. Such fancy footwork has dropped Zara's inventory to 7 percent of annual revenues, compared with the mid-to-high teens for its rivals.

Marketing

Zara's trailblazing strategy challenges age-old retail marketing practices. Its product policy emphasizes goods of reasonable quality, adaptability, and high fashion. The company uses little advertising or promotion. Its founder, Armancio Ortega, long regarded advertising as a "pointless distraction;" indeed, he has never given an interview and rarely allows his picture to be taken.[3] Zara spends just 0.3 percent of sales on advertising, compared with 3 to 4 percent for most fashion retailers. Its bare-bones marketing department avoids flashy campaigns, relying instead on word of mouth among its legions of loyal shoppers. Like its founder, it does not promote itself; it leaves that to satisfied customers.

Zara specializes in lightning-quick turnarounds of the latest designer trends—many items you see in stores didn't exist three weeks earlier. Explains Marcos Lopez of Inditex, "The key driver in our stores is the right fashion. Price is important, but it comes second."[4] Zara aggressively prices its products, and adjusts pricing for the international market, making customers in foreign markets bear the costs of shipping products from Spain. On average, its prices are 10 percent higher in other European countries, 40 percent higher in northern European countries, 70 percent higher in the Americas, and 100 percent higher in Japan.

Zara's stores present the company's face to the world and function as grassroots marketing research agents. Indeed, if there is marketing at Zara, it's done via high-profile real estate. The stores command high-profile slots in historically appealing, premier shopping venues such as the Champs-Elysées in Paris, Regent Street in London, Fifth Avenue in New York, and Nanjing Road in Shanghai. Its location strategy has created interesting tensions. Noted a consultant, "Prada wants to be next to Gucci, Gucci wants to be next to Prada. The retail strategy for luxury brands is to try to keep as far away from the likes of Zara. Zara's strategy is to get as close to them as possible."

Operations

Fitting in with fancy neighbors requires that Zara put its best face forward. Traveling teams of window dressers and interior coordinators visit each Zara store every three weeks, ensuring that window displays and interior presentations convey the targeted message.

Back at headquarters, designers wander the mock store, testing possible design themes, lighting schemes, and product presentation. Its "Fashion Street" in the basement of "The Cube" houses a Potemkin row of storefronts meant to mimic some of its locations. Store employees don Zara's fashions while working; store managers and staff suggest merchandise to order, discontinue, and recommend. Networked stores transfer data on merchandise sales, along with customer requests, to Zara's design teams, factories, and logistics center in La Coruña. Relaying color fabric preferences straight from its shoppers enables the retail staff to localize otherwise globally standardized products. Finding store managers capable of handling these responsibilities, executives believe, is the main constraint on Zara's expansion.

Infrastructure

A key competency is the infrastructure that Zara uses to coordinates its value chain. Two features stand out: managers' sense of customers and their ability to coordinate worldwide activities. The allure of Zara is the freshness of its offerings, the creation of a sense of exclusiveness, attractive in-store ambience, and positive word of mouth. These ideas drive rapid product turnover, with new designs arriving in twice-weekly shipments. Fans learn which days of the week goods are delivered—so-called "Z-days"—and shop accordingly. About three-quarters of the merchandise on display changes every three to four weeks, which corresponds to the average time between Zara customers' visits: 17 times a year, versus three to four visits per year for competitors.

Attractive stores, both inside and out, are vital. Explains Luis Blanc, a director at Inditex, "We invest in prime locations. We place great care in the presentation of our storefronts. That is how we project our image. We want our clients to enter a beautiful store where they are offered the latest fashions. But most important, we want our customers to understand that if they like something, they must buy it now because it won't be in the shops the following week. It is all about creating a climate of scarcity and opportunity."[5]

Zara feeds scarcity with small shipments—say, three or four dresses in a particular style—to a store. Small shipments make for sparsely stocked shelves and products have a display limit of one month. Rapid turnover does the rest: even though consumers visit Zara frequently, when they return, things look different. The CEO of the National Retail Federation, reflecting on Z-days and "fast fashion," marveled, "It's like you walk into a new store every two weeks."[6] Besides keeping its stores looking fresh, these policies reduce price markdowns: Zara books some 85 percent of its unit sales at full price against the industry average markdown ratio of about 50 percent. The number of items Zara puts on clearance sale is about half the industry average.

Challenge and Change

Despite its aura of strategic excellence, not all is picture-perfect in the land of Zara. Some wonder how long Zara can charge different prices in different countries. Others question how much longer it can continue running global operations from its centralized base in Spain—especially given the rise of the U.S. and Chinese markets, which accounted for a third of total sales in 2012 despite few stores (China has about 400, the U.S. 50 or so). Does it still make sense to keep product design, manufacturing, and logistics activities in Spain with Asian sales set to soar? In its concentrated value chain, some clothes that Zara makes in China are shipped to Spain for finishing and, amazingly enough, then sent to stores in China. Despite this quirk, the chief executive of Inditex, Pablo Isla, sees no need for a second product base: "We're not thinking of replicating the brain in Asia" he maintains, though he concedes that they may adjust logistics.[7]

Ultimately, Zara's adept coordination of the overlapping activities among its designers, plants, storefronts, and salespeople testifies to the power of its strategy. No other company can design, make, ship, and sell fashion as speedily as Zara. Its business design leaves rivals with less time to figure out how to configure and coordinate operations better. Some believe companies have little option but to follow Zara's strategic lead. If they don't, warns a leading retail analyst, they "won't be in business in 10 years."[8] ■

QUESTIONS

12-1. Zara believes that finding store managers capable of effectively running its retail properties is the primary constraint on its global expansion. What skills do you think Zara seeks in its ideal candidates? Why would they be difficult to find?

12-2. From the beginning, Zara's business model differed from the norm. Today its strategy depends on managing the connections between its various activities, notably design, sourcing production, logistics, and store operations. What do Zara's managers, working out of "The Cube," see as the most effective way to manage the relationships among these activities?

INTRODUCTION

In the first half of this text we explained that MNEs operate in environments shaped by cultural, political, legal, economic, trade, monetary, governmental, ethical, capital, and institutional forces. Individually and combined, these forces influence managers' strategic decisions and operating actions (see Figure 12.2). What managers do to make their companies competitive, given conditions and trends in the international business environment, anchors this chapter's goal: to profile how managers devise strategies to engage customers in multiple markets that drive current performance and sustain long-term growth.

Global integration standardizes worldwide activities to maximize efficiency, whereas national responsiveness adapts local activities to optimize effectiveness.

Cross-national commonalities in institutional contexts, market structures, and customer preferences create opportunities for MNEs; their differences constrain the choices. Making sense of this trade-off anchors strategy-making. This chapter profiles the factors that influence managers' strategic analyses, including their evaluations of the idea of strategy, the perspectives that integrate their insights, and the tools that develop their choices. We apply

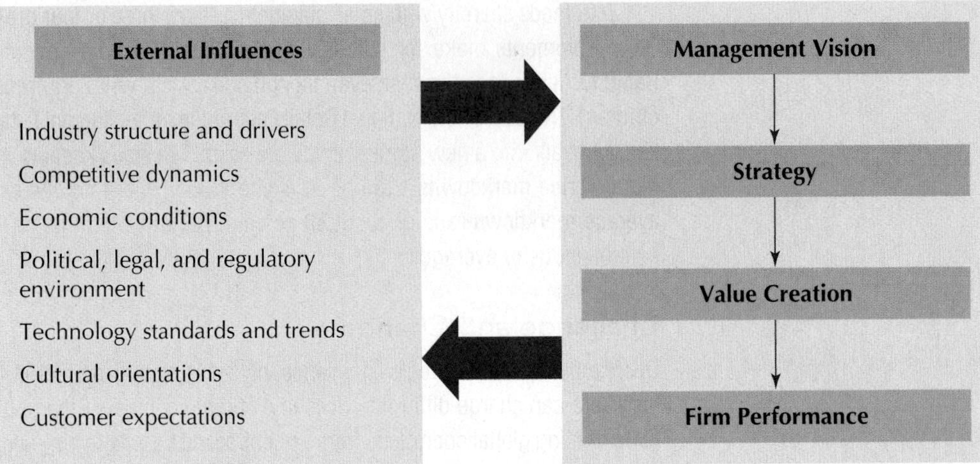

FIGURE 12.2 The Role of Strategy in International Business

Chapter 1 showed that that the MNE's operating environment includes physical, cultural, market, and competitive factors. Chapters 2 through 11 developed key features of each. This chapter discusses these features in relation to an MNE's strategy. It highlights how managers configure resources and coordinate operations to respond to opportunities and threats. These ideas anchor our discussions in Chapter 13 through 20.

the framework we build here in subsequent chapters, using it to assess a range of issues. Specifically, we consider how MNEs enter foreign markets, form alliances, and organize activities, to name just a few, based upon their choice of strategy. In the final section of the book, ideas from this chapter similarly anchor discussions of how MNEs design and implement their marketing, manufacturing, supply, accounting, finance, and human resource activities.

Our opening profile of Zara previews many of these issues. When Zara began its global expansion, strategy in the apparel business was dictated by the structure of the industry—a structure that was inefficient (too much time to design and deliver clothing) and ineffective (apparel makers and sellers plagued by forecasting and inventory problems). Rejecting the conventions dictated by this structure, Zara's founder spent a decade developing an innovative strategy that reset industry standards of operational efficiency and market effectiveness. Zara's success, to say the least, disrupted the global apparel industry. It changed how a company creates value in design, manufacturing, logistics, and marketing. It changed standards for coordinating functions to support value creation. Ultimately, these changes highlight the purpose of strategy in the MNE: to create value by standardizing activities to maximize global efficiency while simultaneously adapting activities to optimize local effectiveness.

CONCEPT CHECK

In Chapter 3, we used the dichotomy between **democracy** and **totalitarianism** to build a framework to assess political freedom. In Chapter 4, the differences among **market**, **mixed**, and **command economies** built a similar framework that assessed resource allocation. A key framework in this chapter is the different ways managers think of **strategy** within the context of industry structure.

INDUSTRY STRUCTURE

MNEs face a diversity of forces that shape how they devise strategy. For example, German carmaker BMW monitors how technology developments, interest rate trends, and political leadership changes affect its quest for profits. However, forces in its immediate industry setting exert the greatest influence. BMW is far more sensitive to the actions of fellow industry members like Mercedes-Benz, Toyota, Michelin, Goodyear, and Bosch because they directly affect its performance. Understanding strategy, therefore, begins by understanding **industry structure**.

An industry is composed of those companies engaged in a particular type of enterprise.

The idea of industry structure represents the interdependent relationships among

- Suppliers of inputs,
- Buyers of outputs,
- Substitute products,
- Potential new entrants,
- Rivalry among competing firms.

Interpretation often relies on the concepts and tools represented in the **five-forces model**.[9] It holds that firm performance is a function of its strategy, which is determined by factors that shape the nature of competition within its industry. As such, it directs managers' attention to the dimensions and their interaction that influence the potential profitability of a particular strategy within a particular industry. Technically, the five-forces model maps the relationship among companies within an industry, highlighting how competitors, new entrants, suppliers, buyers, and substitute products affect potential profitability.

Consider how an industry with few entry barriers, many accessible buyers, and an expanding supply of low-cost technologies tends to have many firms aggressively competing for profits. Think of, say, cell phones, e-commerce, financial services, or entertainment. Conversely, an industry with high entry barriers, steep capital requirements, and tough R&D

standards—say, the pharmaceutical, aircraft, or automobile industries—tends to have few firms competing for profits. In both types, the prevailing industry structure shapes an MNE's strategic choices regarding matters such as research and innovation, product positioning, plant investment, logistic networks, and price policies. Choices on these sorts of big issues define a strategy that, in turn, shapes company performance.[10]

INDUSTRY CHANGE

Firm conduct refers to the choices a company makes regarding research, manufacturing, marketing, distribution, and the like that influence its profitability.

Industry structure is dynamic. New products, new firms, new markets, and new managers trigger new developments in rivalry, pricing, substitutes, buyers, and suppliers. These developments often change a minor feature of the industry, such as the expansion of an existing distribution channel or availability of higher quality inputs. Minor changes leave managers the freedom to tweak their strategy.

Generally, industry structure naturally evolves. Disruptive innovations accelerate the rate of change.

Occasionally, an extraordinary change redefines one or more of the five forces, thereby disrupting the industry's structure.[11] MNEs must assess the impact of such significant changes on the likely reset among the five forces and the resulting implication to their profitability. Often, big changes involve competitors, products, processes, and politics. Let's take a closer look.

Product Disruptions Disruptive innovations drive industry change. New products, for example, make alternatives obsolete. Likewise, new processes reset the way they are made, delivered, and serviced.[12] For example, out of nowhere, netbooks—small, cheap, light computers optimized for basic tasks such as Web browsing and email—disrupted the global PC industry in 2009. Traditional personal computers and the many companies that make their components, like Samsung, Intel, and Microsoft, faced the biggest upheaval in industry structure since the rise of the laptop. Noted an analyst, "A broad shift in the consumer market toward low-cost PCs clearly put pressure on the revenues of nearly every player in the value chain, from component suppliers to retailers."[13]

Then, once the netbook dust settled, the innovativeness of Apple's iPad disrupted the PC industry in 2010. Again, competitors had to adjust several elements of their strategies, rethinking chip architecture, performance-to-weight ratios, software platforms, and design ergonomics. By 2011, a slew of ever more powerful tablet devices decimated the traditional PC market far faster than was forecast. By 2013, worldwide PC shipments were falling faster than they ever had while tablet sales accelerated.[14] HP, Dell, and Acer, the world's largest makers of desktop PCs, hailed just a few years earlier as brilliant strategists, scrambled to reposition in the face of falling sales, collapsing margins, and the dread of the "Post-PC era."

CONCEPT CHECK

Fast-rising MNEs from emerging economies use product and process innovations to disrupt industry structures. In particular, their application of frugal engineering, a logical response given the prevalence of the Base of the Pyramid phenomenon in their home markets, pushes companies in the West to rethink value creation.

Process Disruptions Innovations in management processes drive industry change. Look at the MNEs from emerging markets that are reinventing systems of production and distribution, experimenting with new business models, and resetting the standards of executive effectiveness. Managers take the needs of poor consumers at the Base of the Pyramid as a starting point, applying processes of *frugal innovation* to develop products that eliminate all but the most essential features in order to more economically fit existing needs. Frugal innovation pushes managers to rethink entire production processes and business models so that they can use existing technologies in imaginative new ways or apply mass production techniques to new and unexpected areas. Presently, Indians see frugal innovation as perhaps their distinctive contribution to management thinking. By no means is this competency found only there. Frugal innovation processes in Africa (i.e., Safaricom with mobile money) and Asia (i.e., reusable sutures from Chinese suppliers) similarly disrupt industry economics.[15]

Political Disruptions Changes in the political arena continually concern managers. A powerful example is the recent global financial crisis.[16] Its fallout crisis continues resetting the structure of many industries. Dislocations in financial markets altered credit terms and financing options, thereby changing the cost of capital and return thresholds. Growing sovereign debt problems impose fiscal discipline on governments. Consequential falls in consumer, industrial, and public demand have changed the power of buyers and suppliers. Pushback against economic freedom and growing state capitalism resets competitive rivalry. The potential for profitability in industries is in flux. Managers react in kind, questioning their strategy, rethinking their value proposition, reorienting operations to faster growing product markets, and repositioning resources to preserve efficiencies.[17]

Industry structure changes because of events like

- Competitors' moves,
- Government policies,
- Shifting consumer preferences,
- Technological developments.

Telltale Signals The nature of disruptive innovations varies. Past precedents include the following:

- Significant change in the long-term growth rate
- Breakthrough technologies that realign efficiency frontiers, like containerization, wireless communications, or smart phones
- New consumer purchase and usage patterns, such as streaming movies online or replacing landlines with VoIP systems
- Manufacturing innovations, like *Six Sigma* or *Lean Production*, which revolutionize productivity potentials
- Rapid diffusion of business, executive, and technical expertise across countries, such as the transfer of Eastern management approaches to Western companies, which intensifies rivalry
- Abrupt change in government regulation, such as escalating government involvement in capital markets that resets economic freedom
- New forms of rivalry, such as the emergence of state-owned companies altering competitive dynamics
- Improbable black swan events, such as the Internet or the global financial crisis, which radically reset business principles

PERSPECTIVES ON STRATEGY

The importance of understanding industries and how they change spurs researchers to study how companies move from successful short-term enterprises to standard-setting giants that are "built to last." In other words, how good companies develop strategies that help them achieve greatness.[18] Analysis finds that such firms apply a down-to-earth, pragmatic, "committed-to-excellence framework." Besides keeping their leaders and workers on track for the long haul, it separates short-term good performers from long-term great ones. The trick, of course, is where to launch this quest. As a search of the Internet quickly shows, there are thousands of theoretically credible approaches. Two prominent models of strategy—the **Industry Organization Paradigm** and **Great by Choice**—can help managers make the transition from confusion to clarity. Let's take a look at each.

Perfect competition presumes

- Many buyers and sellers, such that no individual agent determines price or quantity.
- Perfect information for both producers and consumers.
- Few, if any, barriers to market entry and exit.
- Full mobility of resources.
- Perfect knowledge among firms and buyers.

The Industry Organization (IO) Paradigm The IO Paradigm emphasizes the determinism of industry structure in the belief that it decisively sets a firm's profitability. It begins by presuming that markets tend toward perfect competition: Many firms with small market shares are price-takers that sell identical products and freely enter and exit the industry; buyers understand product features and competitors' prices; risk-adjusted rates of return are constant; in situations of high profits, new companies enter and create competition that lowers prices and profits; in situations of low profits, firms exit or markets close. Put differently, over time, no firm or industry consistently outperforms others, no matter the innovativeness of a particular executive or company.[19] As a rule, an unattractive industry is one in which perfect competition drives down overall profitability.

In reality, many industries are far from perfectly competitive.[20] Various firms sustain different levels of profitability in ways that are shaped, but not determined, by the structure of their industry. Many industries exhibit situations in which entry barriers deter potential rivals, or a few large sellers behave as oligarchs. Such imperfect industries include firms that consistently earn above-average, risk-adjusted returns: Intel in integrated circuits, Apple in technology, Infosys in business services, Safaricom in mobile money, LVMH in luxury products, Baidu in Internet search, Johnson & Johnson in healthcare, and Nestlé in food services are examples. An attractive industry is one in which far-from-perfect competition lets companies consistently earn above-average profitability.

Bright executives exploit market imperfections to outperform rivals.

Great by Choice If markets are not always perfectly competitive, industry structure does not entirely determine performance, and some firms consistently outperform rivals, then what explains performance? This question spotlights the power of bright, motivated managers and their keen sense of innovative products or processes to devise a strategy that is difficult, if not impossible, to copy—think of Apple's technology platform, or Google's search expertise. In doing so, they consistently outperform industry rivals. Essentially, industry structure matters, but some companies thrive because of their executives' choice to be great and, we hasten to add, their distinctive competency in achieving their ambitions.[21]

More pointedly, Zara's strategy of making and moving sophisticated, moderately priced fashions required management to come up with the process innovations that enabled the company to integrate design talent, customer responsiveness, and information technology. At the time, the structure of the global apparel industry opposed this strategy. As a result, Zara's managers developed a repertory of competencies spanning design, production, logistics, and retailing that converted its innovative strategy into action. A key decision was its founder's intent to maintain manufacturing in La Coruña. Since then, this business model has successfully rejected industry norms. Its standout performance highlights the idea that great managers make great strategies that make great companies that outperform their rivals over the long haul.

Strategy helps managers assess the company's present situation, identify the direction it should go, and determine how it will get there.

Strategy's Hallmarks The overlapping assumptions of the IO paradigm and Great by Choice model testify to the hallmarks of effective strategy. Both define the perspectives and tools an MNE applies to deal with industry structure, allocate resources optimally, and conceive ingenious innovations that steadfastly support growing profitability. Combined, they show that strategy builds and sustains the "committed to excellence framework" that separates great firms from good ones. Difficult for all, these issues are especially tough for the MNE. Besides dealing with domestic issues, it must operate in different countries, which puts it in a more challenging mix of consumers, industries, and institutions.

Value is the measure of a firm's capability of selling what it makes for more than the costs incurred in making it.

Managerial practices highlight a variety of tactical solutions. Common to all, however, is their contribution to an MNE's ability to generate value above industry benchmarks over the long term. Essentially, they confirm that the goal of strategy is to create **value**—the measure of a firm's capability to sell what it makes for more than the costs incurred to make it.[22] As such, **strategy** is the committed-to-excellence framework that exploits industry conditions and leverages executive quality to create superior value.

APPROACHES TO VALUE CREATION

To create value, an MNE must develop a compelling value proposition (why a customer should buy its goods or use its services) that specifies its targeted markets (those customers for whom it creates goods or services). This analysis, whether done on a nation-by-nation, region-by-region, or worldwide basis, requires managers to make and sell products that exceed customers' value expectations. The MNE translates this mandate into a committed-to-excellence framework that, subject to industry conditions, builds value by making products for lower costs than competitors (the strategy of *cost leadership*) or making products for which consumers willingly pay a premium price (the strategy of *differentiation*).

CONCEPT CHECK

In Chapter 2, we explain how **globalization** spurs a variety of managerial approaches. Similarly, in Chapters 3 and 4, we emphasize how companies operating internationally encounter a variety of **political**, **legal**, and **economic environments**. Here, we engage the notion that globalization imperatives and local constraints bound an MNE's strategy.

The cost leadership strategy aims to make a product at a given level of quality for a cost below those of competitors.

COST LEADERSHIP

The MNE implementing a **cost leadership** strategy aims to be the industry's low-cost producer for a given level of quality. Offering standardized products to the biggest possible market at the lowest competitive price, it reduces its costs relative to rivals by streamlining product design, investing in state-of-the-art technologies and processes, running operations smoothly, applying rigorous controls, and leveraging its distinctive competencies.

No matter the program or proposal, the cost leadership strategy evaluates usefulness in terms of its contribution to improving overall efficiency. The absoluteness of efficient operations follows from the fact that costs typically differ across different companies within the same industry. Companies invariably incur different costs because of disparities in executive quality, input prices, wage rates, employee productivity, production scale, and distribution expenses. In the realm of the cost leadership strategy, costs lower than those of rivals translates superior efficiency into strategic success.

A cost-leadership strategy is a vital advantage in highly competitive industries, such as the airline, steel, mortgage, white goods, and package delivery markets. Companies such as Southwest Airlines, UPS, Haier, Thai Union Frozen, Citigroup, ArcelorMittal, Cemex, Ranbaxy Laboratories, Virgin Mobile, and Foxconn practice it. Industries marked by intense rivalry push MNEs to offset high capital requirements by exploiting the economies of large-scale standardization. In the brutal game of low-cost competition, increasing volume puts pressure on less efficient competitors. In the event of a price war, for example, the low-cost leader can cut prices, thereby imposing losses on rivals while still earning some profits. Even without a price war, as the industry matures and prices decline, the MNE that makes the lowest-cost products outlasts rivals.

Today, many Chinese companies apply the cost leadership strategy, outperforming rivals by combining efficient manufacturing operations, inexpensive labor, global distribution, state support, and growing scientific and technological sophistication.[23] Take a look at Chinese pearl farmers, who have begun flooding the world with low-cost, high-quality pearls. By late 2011, a Chinese half-inch pearl sold for $4 to $8 at wholesale; a Tahitian pearl of similar size rang in at $25 to $35. The influx from China, noted one observer, "has made pearls affordable for the average working woman."[24] Not content to rest on their current price advantage, Chinese pearl farmers are investing in automation and sequencing the genome of the mussels that produce freshwater pearls. If successful, the price of higher-quality Chinese pearls will fall further.

This situation spans a broad range of product markets. Consequently, Chinese companies' successful implementation of cost leadership strategies leaves rivals a stark choice. Advised one analyst, "If you still make anything labor-intensive, get out now rather than bleed to death. Shaving 5 percent here and there won't work. Chinese producers can make the same adjustments. You need an entirely new business model to compete."[25] The Director of Nalco China concurred, noting that "once you compete on price here, the game's over."[26]

DIFFERENTIATION

Industries marked by a continuous stream of branded product innovations—as we see in consumer electronics, software, entertainment, wealth management, or fashion markets—typically do not emphasize cost leadership. Instead, they opt for **differentiation**, creating value by generating insights into consumer behavior, developing cutting-edge products, designing high-profile marketing programs, and quickly moving products to market. Think of our opening profile of Zara, particularly its belief that "The key driver in our stores is the right fashion. Price is important, but it comes second." Identifying, designing, and delivering the "right fashion," however, requires a range of process skills, built atop a tech-intensive infrastructure, that quickly turns cool ideas into hot fashions.

Differentiation dynamics play in every industry; even commodities like milk, aspirin, or DRAM chips, seemingly an exception, can be differentiated based on ancillary services or product tie-ins.[27] Still, the differentiation strategy is especially evident with high-profile products in high-margin markets. The differentiation strategy fixates on accelerating innovation, not relentlessly reducing costs, as the basis for sustainable value creation. Its goal is to develop products that offer unique attributes to customers who perceive them as superior to alternatives and thus willingly pay a premium price. Differentiation requires developing competencies that rivals find hard, if not impossible, to match or copy. The sleek design of an Apple iPad, engineering sophistication of a Lexus sedan, customer service at a Ritz-Carlton, premium real estate slots for Zara shops, or efficiency of Google's search algorithm, besides generating profits, sets high standards that rivals struggle to outdo.

Differentiation champions developing products that customers value and that rivals find hard, if not impossible, to match or copy.

Typically, companies differentiate offensively, using it as a tool to project competitiveness. Starbucks, which began internationalizing operations in 1996 and had more than 17,000 stores in 57 countries around the world by 2013, has anchored expansion on a proprietary blend of coffee, aesthetics, and aura. Its product quality along with unique customer experience supports charging premium prices.[28] Along the way, Starbucks has improved its differentiation strategy. Boosting performance in Europe, for example, has led it to rely on edgy architecture, including chandeliers and stages for poetry readings, in order to lure customers socialized on a high-touch café culture. In late 2012, Starbucks opened its first outlet in Mumbai, India, in a 50-50 joint venture with Tata Global Beverages. Several false starts had pushed it to fine-tune its differentiation strategy for the Indian consumer. Now, Starbucks sells coffee from beans grown and roasted in-country, brewing a distinct Indian blend.[29] Its beverages sell for less in India than elsewhere in the world—a latte that cost \$4.30 in New York, \$4.81 in Beijing, or \$3.81 in London goes for \$1.70 in New Delhi.[30] The company also alters its menu to Indian tastes, notably offering a unique dish in the Indian cities that host franchises."[31]

The differentiation strategy calls for continual innovation, whereas cost leadership champions sustainable efficiency.

The fact that today's innovation is often tomorrow's obsolescence is an ongoing threat to the differentiation strategy. The presence of strong rivals worldwide, in both advanced and emerging economies, makes identifying the basis of differentiation a never-ending challenge. Innovations conceived in Germany quickly diffuse to rivals in Brazil, the United States, or China. Companies that battle on product features must, as the CEO of IBM notes, tirelessly determine "what will cause work to move to me? On what basis will I differentiate and compete?"[32]

THE FIRM AS VALUE CHAIN

In principle, an MNE can opt for cost leadership or differentiation. In practice, the asymmetric demands of each make it quite difficult to pursue both simultaneously. Consider, for example, of the handful, if that many, of MNEs that successfully sell low-cost, cutting-edge products. Whatever its choice, the potential profitability of a MNE's strategy is a function of the value that customers see in its product relative to its corresponding costs. Put simply, a MNE outperforms its rivals when it offers more value, relative to price, to its customers. Understanding this relationship and translating it into a committed-to-excellence framework is the hallmark of superior strategy.[33]

The value chain is the set of linked activities the company performs to design, produce, market, distribute, and support a product.

Cost leadership or differentiation ambitions reflect industry structure as well as executives' analytics. For example, implementing Zara's "Armani at moderate prices" strategy triggers a series of questions: Where do we find design ideas? How should we set global standards? When does local responsiveness makes sense? Where should we make products? Can our suppliers support our plans? How do we distribute worldwide? What are our most effective marketing tools? What kind of people should we hire to run operations? How might rivals respond?

These questions shape how Zara, like other MNEs, organizes its operations to design, make, move, and sell products; how it finds efficiencies in various countries in doing so; and how it coordinates decisions in one part of the business with those made in others.[34] Effectively managing them separates the great MNEs from the good. Making sense of this challenge, by following the best practices of successful MNEs, directs attention to interpreting the activities as elements of the firm's value chain.

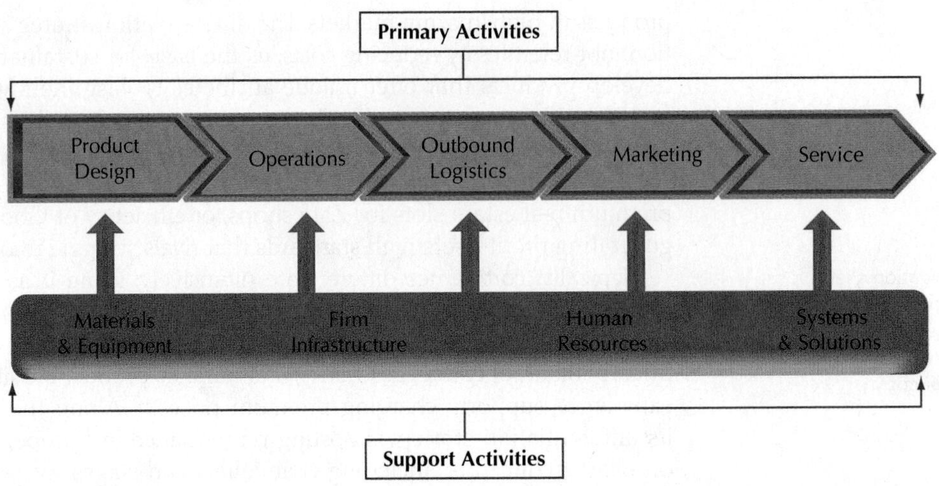

FIGURE 12.3 Visualizing the Value Chain

The value chain is made up of generic primary activities that reflect classical business functions and managerial orientations. The value chain also specifies support activities, representing day-to-day tasks, which help implement the primary activities. Each support activity helps all primary activities, as we see in their run along the breath of the value chain.

A value chain disaggregates a firm into

- Primary activities that design, make, sell, and deliver the product.
- Support activities that implement the primary activities.

The **value chain** follows from the principle that "every firm is a collection of discrete activities performed to do business that occur within the scope of the firm."[35] The value chain specifies the system of activity the firm sets to implement its strategy. Fundamentally, its analytical framework lets managers deconstruct the abstraction of creating value into a step-by-step model that outlines how products move from conception in R&D through sourcing materials, organizing manufacturing, supervising logistics, applying marketing, and setting up service options. Figure 12.3 maps this flow, identifying the sequence of functions that comprise a company's value chain. Figure 12.4 profiles the characteristic of each dimension.

Primary activities define the core business functions: from developing a product and building the operations that make it onward through logistics, marketing, distributing, and servicing. Because they reflect classic business activities and managerial orientations, primary

FIGURE 12.4 Specifying the Value Chain

The generic primary and support activities of the value chain identify the steps an MNE takes to create value. By disaggregating activities into discrete responsibilities, as we see here, the value chain provides managers a powerful tool to plan strategically

The Value Chain	Category	Activity	Description
The Value Chain	Primary Activities	Product Design	Designing the functions, features, and aesthetics of the product or process.
		Operations	Converting inputs into a finished product in terms of sourcing components, arranging supply chains, configuring plant location, and optimizing manufacturing processes.
		Outbound Logistics	Moving finished product from operations to wholesalers, retailers, or end-consumers. Deals with distribution channels, inventory management, warehousing, and transportation logistics.
		Marketing	Informing buyers and consumers about products and services, developing a sales force, devising packaging schemes, defining the brand, and devising promotions.
		Service	Servicing customers with installation support, after-sales service, and training.
	Support Activities	Materials and Equipment	Managing the procurement, transportation, storage, and distribution of materials and equipment necessary to conduct the primary activities.
		Human Resource Management	Recruiting, developing, motivating, and rewarding the workforce.
		Systems and Solutions	Managing information processing, overseeing information systems, and integrating technologies platforms.
		Infrastructure	Classic overhead functions, like accounting, finance, legal, safety and security, and quality control, which all firms perform.

activities carry functional labels such as operations or marketing. Figure 12.3 also identifies secondary processes called **support activities** that apply to each primary activity. Human resources, for example, are needed at each value activity, from supervising the arrival of raw materials, to running production processes, to shipping products and filling orders, to serving customers. Support activities, besides defining the infrastructure of the firm, anchor the day-to-day performance of the primary activities.

MANAGING THE VALUE CHAIN

A value chain identifies the format and interactions between its various activities.

An MNE's competitiveness depends on efficiently distributing value activities and effectively linking them so that the different parts become a single whole. Distributing value activities around the world involves **configuration.** Linking them involves **coordination.** Configuration and coordination, flip sides of the value chain coin, are intrinsically related. Still, each has unique characteristics.

CONFIGURATION

The worldwide distribution of value activities is the matter of configuration.

What and how much of its value chain to move to foreign markets is one of the most important choices a company makes. Insightful choices turbocharge performance, while ill-advised choices prove disastrous. The option to go anywhere in the world to do any part of their business gives MNEs tremendous choice in configuring their value activities. Choice has consequences, and many MNEs get it right. Still, many struggle to choose the ideal location given changing configuration options.

No matter how big or small, every MNE looks to put value activities in the highest productivity spot in the world. In theory, configuration ranges from **concentrated** (performing all value-chain activities in one location) to **dispersed** (performing different value-chain activities in different locations). The tension between which activities to concentrate and which to disperse follows from the fact that different activities impose different costs in different locations. Recall that value creation is a function of an MNE's selling what it makes for more than it costs to make it. Therefore, MNEs configure value activities to exploit **location economies,** specifically the efficiencies one captures by performing a value activity in the most productive location given prevailing economic, political, legal, and cultural conditions.

CONCEPT CHECK

In discussing "Elements of the Economic Environment" in Chapter 4, we note labor costs and productivity are key elements of an MNE's strategy. In Chapter 6, we discuss methods of interpreting the relative economic performance of different countries. Here, we reiterate that location economics determine how MNEs configure value activities.

Say a single market provides the lowest-cost, highest-productivity environment for all activities. An MNE would concentrate its value chain there and serve its global market through exports. Conversely, a dispersed value chain makes sense when some activities cost less in country X, others cost less in country Y, and still others less than country Z. So if the best industrial designers are in Taiwan, the company bases design operations there. If the most productive labor force for assembly is in China, that's where it builds its plants. If the most imaginative minds are in Denmark, it develops its advertising campaign there.

Location economics influence an MNE's decision to concentrate or disperse value activities.

Today, conflicting pressures for global integration and national responsiveness means fewer MNEs have the option to concentrate their value chain in a single location. Our opening case highlighted this dilemma as Zara's key challenge: Should it continue concentrating its value chain in Spain, thereby maximizing global efficiencies, or disperse some value activities to its fastest-growing markets in Asia, thereby adapting activities to optimize local effectiveness? Its decision to reject industry practice, preferring to stay close to home, has been an anchor of its competitiveness. Changing industry trends pressure it to change its configuration strategy.

Where to Go Location decisions are subject to the unpredictability of the prevailing economic, legal, political, and cultural conditions. This constraint frustrates configuration choices. Abrupt change can turn a low-cost location into a prohibitively expensive one. Following yet another gyration in the business environment, Jack Welch, former chair and CEO of General Electric (GE), thought the best location for GE factories was a mobile platform, explaining,

"Ideally, you'd have every plant you own on a barge, to move with currencies and changes in the economy."[36] The impracticality of an armada of barges ferrying factories throughout the seven seas requires that managers monitor how market, legal, political, and cultural conditions moderate location economics. MNEs must pay particular attention to *business environment quality, innovation context, economies of scale,* and *resource costs* to set configuration parameters. They then qualify analysis by considering the moderating influences of *logistics, digitization,* and increasingly, *robotics.*

Factors that influence the configuration of a value-chain include

- Business environment,
- Innovation context,
- Scale efficiencies,
- Resource costs,
- Robotics,
- Logistics,
- Digitization.

Business Environment Quality The impracticality of Jack Welch's factory-on-a-barge wish pushes MNEs to configure value chains to enter, or avoid, a country given its business environment.[37] Countries recognize MNEs' sensitivity and take steps to improve their location economics. Techniques include reducing capital requirements for startups, streamlining property registration, expediting regulatory review, and liberalizing labor regulations. Often, opportunistic governments recruit foreign investors, promising business-friendly markets that offer flexible operating requirements, lower tax rates, cheap financing, and responsive public policies.[38] Evergreen Solar, a leading manufacturer of solar panels in the United States in 2010, shut its Massachusetts factory, laid off 800 workers, and shifted production to a joint venture with a Chinese company in Wuhan. It cited China's superior location economics given the low-cost loans, stronger government support, and cheaper labor.[39]

CONCEPT CHECK

A theme of our text is the variability of business environments from country to country. Chapters 1 through 11 highlight the range of factors that vary, spanning the dimensions of people, products, processes, and perspectives.

At present, doing business remains easiest in high-income countries such as Singapore, Denmark, Hong Kong, New Zealand, Canada, Sweden, and the United States.[40] Their combination of stable public institutions, extensive infrastructure, expansive financial systems, flexible labor markets, and economic outlook support business development. Likewise, there are risky environments. Countries whose governments condone the rule of man, for instance, often deter firms fearful of intellectual property theft. Venezuela, Zimbabwe, Chad, Burundi, Cameroon, Bolivia, and Tajikistan are currently rated among the worst business environments. Generally, circumstances are improving worldwide. The importance of business activity to economic growth spurs many countries to reform the local environment.

Innovation Context The application of new ideas benefits consumers, companies, and countries.[41] Consumers enjoy rising living standards. Companies fortify competitiveness. Governments fuel economic growth. Looking forward, the dominant engine of innovation—technology—accelerates. The *Singularity Principle* holds that in the next 30 years the "pace of technological change will be so rapid, its impact so deep… that technology appears to be expanding at infinite speed."[42] Developments in genetics, robotics, nanotechnology, and computing will overturn many mainstream practices. Predictions are that 2013 will see the construction of a supercomputer that exceeds the computational capability of the human brain. More radically, a $1,000 computer will exceed the capabilities of humanity by 2050.[43] Standard-setting companies in these and related industries will generate vast wealth and many jobs. The rush to lead the race pushes MNEs to locate value activities in countries whose innovation contexts support progress.

Host governments race to build knowledge-intensive, technology-enabled business environments. Promoting technologies, expanding human capacities, streamlining organizational capabilities, and improving institutional responsiveness determine those locations seen as best leveraging knowledge into market-changing innovation.[44] Presently, developed countries claim the highest spots in the innovation rankings, with Switzerland, Sweden, Singapore, Finland, and United Kingdom grabbing the top five spots.[45] But rising innovation in Asia is boosting South Korea, India, Turkey, and China up league tables. Collectively, Asian countries appear to be moving from practices that optimize production efficiencies to policies that improve the environment for innovation.[46] MNEs respond and redeploy accordingly. Specifically, GE opened a research center in Brazil in 2010 following openings of centers in China and India; each aims to benefit from the host countries' improving innovation contexts. Farther down the road, MNEs anticipate adjusting configuration choices toward markets with increasing numbers of knowledge workers. Table 12.1 profiles a leading indicator.

TABLE 12.1 Global Distribution of University Students: Top 10 Countries

Knowledge and innovation have an inalienable relationship. Building the cool products of tomorrow requires developing bright minds today. Better estimating a local environment's potential for innovative performance moves MNEs to monitor the the pipeline of knowledge workers worldwide.

Rank	Country	Total University Student Count	% of Global Pool of University Students, 2011[1]
1	**China**	26,692	16.8%
2	**United States**	18,248	11.5%
3	**India**	14,863	9.4%
4	**Russia**	9,446	6.0%
5	**Brazil**	5,958	3.8%
6	**Indonesia**	4,420	2.8%
7	**Japan**	3,939	2.5%
8	**South Korea**	3,204	2.0%
9	**Ukraine**	2,848	1.8%
10	**Egypt**	2,594	1.6%
—	**World**	158,713	100%

Source: Based on UNESCO Global Education Digest 2011, retrieved from www.uis.unesco.org/Education/Pages/default.aspx.

Does Geography Matter?

Clusters and Configuring Value Chains

Quite expectedly, geography fundamentally shapes how MNEs configure their value chains. Of course there are the obvious determinants, such as where one finds raw materials or productive labor. Increasingly, MNEs configure value chains to tap **cluster effects**. Basically, just as birds of a feather flock together, so too with MNEs in particular industries—New York City for global finance, Baden-Württemberg for cars and electrical engineering, Dhahran Techno-Valley for energy, Holland for cut flowers, Silicon Valley for technology, Silicon Wadi for wireless telecom, Belluno for eyewear products, Mumbai and Hollywood for entertainment, and so on. The geographic mechanics of a business cluster are straightforward: competing, complementary, interdependent firms and industries that do business with each other and share overlapping needs for talent, technology, and infrastructure increasingly operate in close proximity. Vibrant clusters then attract related vendors, service providers, investors, analysts, skilled workers, trade association members, and consultants.[47]

Geographic proximity turbocharges knowledge exchange. The firms may be direct competitors or alliance partners that typically purchase inputs from and rely on services provided by others in the cluster. Thus, clustering supports collaboration, intensifies competition, and creates unique location economics that let MNEs optimize the coordination of value chains. Watching and working with "neighbors" drives knowledge spillovers and productivity innovations.

Arguably, the key driver of business clusters is its reinforcing dynamic: As buyers and sellers of a product cluster, they convince others to follow suit, and the expanding congregation creates a critical mass of companies, rivals, suppliers, and buyers. Their collective efforts improve the cluster's performance, thereby attracting more firms and repowering the cycle. Eventually, as noted economist Alfred Marshall observed in 1890, "the mysteries of the trade become no mysteries; but are as it were in the air. . . ."[48] More practically, a manager in Warsaw, Indiana, home to a cluster of medical-implant makers, relates how an engineer can phone a subcontractor to propose an idea and then "five minutes later he can call round to show how the product should be made. It's a lot easier to do that kind of thing here than if the businesses were thousands of miles apart."[49]

Countries actively promote clusters, hoping to influence how MNEs configure their value chains. Knowledge exchange and spillover among members of the cluster stimulate national economic development and promote local innovation. The Taiwanese government, for example, developed Hsinchu Science and Industrial Park outside Taipei into a high-tech cluster. Today, it is the hub of Taiwan's IT industry and home to about 400 high-tech companies that make more than 50 percent of integrated circuits, nearly 70 percent of computer displays, and more than 90 percent of portable computers used in the world. ■

Economies of Scale The improved efficiency that comes with larger operations and increased usage of inputs systematically reduces per-unit cost. The source of efficiency gains varies, including acquiring materials (bulk buying of resources through long-term contracts), production (distributing fixed costs across a large number of units), finance (access to a greater range of capital instruments in a wider range of countries), and advertising (spreading the expense of a promotion concept over more markets). The phenomenon whereby increasing size of operations enables a firm to improve the efficiency of doing things is referred to as **economies of scale**.

The high potential for scale economies encourages MNEs to concentrate value activities.

The benefits of scale economies explain patterns of value chain configurations. Steep upfront capital costs create high potential for scale economies. Long production runs lower per-unit costs as marginal production cost decreases while cumulative output increases. The MNE facing steep scale economies, particularly one following a cost leadership strategy, concentrates its value activities to capture the efficiencies provided by a few large-scale plants.

For example, a minimum efficient-sized factory for making integrated circuits costs roughly US $3 to $5 billion. As a result, Intel, the world's largest semiconductor chipmaker, supplies customers from 12 fabrication plants located in four countries—seven in the United States, three in Ireland, one in Israel, and one in China. Certainly, Intel could opt for many smaller plants in more countries, but the reduced efficiency of widely dispersed, small-scale manufacturing activities would diminish its competitiveness.

Labor Costs Cost differentials shape how MNEs configure value activities. Differences in wage rates, worker productivity, and government regulations mean that the cost of doing the same thing varies from country to country. Expectedly, MNEs scrutinize where it makes the most sense to locate activities, configuring and reconfiguring operations as situations change. For example, North American footwear makers once made shoes in the United States, but over a 30-year span, they moved production from subcontractors in Taiwan to the Philippines, Thailand, South Korea, Vietnam, and China in the quest for low costs.

Likewise, the immense pools of productive, low-cost labor have led thousands of MNEs to open operations in China. For example, in 2003, the average hourly compensation for production workers in China was $0.80 versus $25.34 in the United States.[50] By 2007, average weekly wages in China for unskilled labor were about 3 to 5 percent of those in the United States. Even after China raised minimum wages several times, by 2012 its wage rates were

Here, we see a skyline vista of the epicenter's of the global capital market, the Financial District of New York City. This cluster is home to the New York Stock Exchange, Federal Reserve Bank of New York, NASDAQ, World Financial Center, New York Mercantile Exchange, and New York Board of Trade, as well as the headquarters or subsidiaries of many financial MNEs.
Source: Dobresum/Shutterstock

15 to 20 percent of the U.S. standard. Shanghai, for instance, ranked first in the nation with a monthly minimum wage of ¥1,450 ($232) versus ¥7,656 ($1,160) in New York.[51]

Currently, average weekly wage rates vary dramatically from country to country. Present and projected wage differences shape how MNEs configure their value chains. Providing a sense of the range in wages worldwide, Table 12.2 reports the hourly compensation costs in manufacturing across 32 countries, ranging from $64.15 in Norway to an average of $2.01 per hour in the Philippines.[52] Difficulty hampers estimating labor costs in India and China; indicators suggest that unskilled labor in both countries costs just 3 to 5 percent of American wages—approximately a dollar per hour. Skilled labor is another matter entirely. Infosys, a

TABLE 12.2 The Cost of Labor Across the World

Northern and Western Europe nations set the pace in paying workers. High hourly compensation costs are consistently found in Australia, Canada, Italy, Japan, and the United States. Countries with lower hourly compensation costs were primarily in Southern and Eastern Europe, Asia, and Latin America.

	Hourly Compensation Costs ($US)		Percent
	1997	2011	Change
Norway	25.84	64.15	148.2%
Switzerland	30.42	60.40	98.55%
Belgium	28.92	54.77	89.38%
Denmark	23.70	51.67	118.02%
Sweden	25.02	49.12	96.32%
Germany	29.16	47.38	62.48%
Australia	18.93	46.29	144.53%
Finland	22.36	44.14	97.41%
Austria	24.91	43.16	73.26%
Netherlands	22.45	42.26	88.24%
France	24.86	42.12	69.43%
Ireland	16.69	39.83	138.65%
Canada	18.49	36.56	97.73%
Italy	19.76	36.17	83.05%
Japan	21.99	35.71	62.39%
United States	23.04	35.53	54.21%
United Kingdom	19.30	30.77	59.43%
Spain	13.95	28.44	103.87%
New Zealand	12.06	23.38	93.86%
Singapore	12.15	22.60	86.01%
Greece	11.61	21.78	87.60%
Israel	12.28	21.42	74.43%
South Korea	9.22	18.91	105.10%
Argentina	7.55	15.91	110.73%
Czech Republic	3.25	13.13	304.00%
Portugal	6.45	12.91	100.16%
Slovakia	2.84	11.77	314.44%
Brazil	7.07	11.65	64.78%
Taiwan	7.04	9.34	32.67%
Hungary	3.05	9.17	200.66%
Poland	3.15	8.83	180.32%
Mexico	3.47	6.48	86.74%
Philippines	1.28	2.01	57.03%

Source: Based on "International Comparisons of Hourly Compensation Costs in Manufacturing, 2011" United States Bureau of Labor Statistics, Released December 19, 2012.

CONCEPT CHECK

Chapter 4 discusses features of emerging markets, notably the appearance of new companies looking to expand internationally, the influence of the tens of millions of consumers who are experiencing rising incomes, and the emergence of the Base of the Pyramid. All indicate changing customer needs. These developments spur MNEs to rethink the configuration of value chains.

Costs vary among countries because of wage rates, worker productivity, resource availability, and fiscal and monetary policies.

The demography of labor influences location economics and, thus, MNEs' configuration choices.

leading Indian information technology company, reported that the total cost of its professional employees in India used to run about 80 percent less than those in the United States. By 2013, the gap had shrunk to 30 to 40 percent and was steadily narrowing.[53]

Granted, high-wage employees could work harder, generating higher productivity to offset wage disadvantages. Still, it's difficult for relative productivity performances to neutralize differences between high and low wage markets. Excluding capital structures and technology differentials, a worker in the United States must be roughly seven times more productive than counterparts in China to equalize the per unit labor rate. For the record, in 2010, productivity in China grew by 8.2 percent compared with a rise of 1 percent in the United States.[54] Between 2005 and 2010, China averaged 17 percent productivity growth versus 4, 2, and 1 percent, respectively, in the U.S., Japan, and Germany.[55]

Consider the implications of Wonder Auto of China. A maker of automobile parts, it spent US $4 million to set up an assembly line employing 20 workers in Jinzhou, a city of 800,000 in northeastern China. The combined wages of these 20 workers were a bit more than $40,000 a year—roughly the annual base pay for one unionized auto-parts worker or two nonunion auto-parts workers in the United States.[56] Similarly, moving from Massachusetts to China let Evergreen Solar reduce weekly wages for its factory workers from $1,350 to $75.[57] These effects are not limited to the manufacturing sector. Relocating service activities, such as call-center operations from the United States to India, results in similar cost differentials.[58]

Going forward, how might labor influence MNEs' configuration choices? Auguste Comte reasoned, "Demography is destiny"; so it is, in large degree, with the configuration of value chains vis-à-vis labor. The demography of labor spurs MNEs whose activities are sensitive to labor cost differentials—such as those implementing a cost leadership strategy—to exploit favorable wage rates, labor supply, and worker productivity by operating in lower-cost, higher-productivity locations. GM, for example, is going great guns in China, although it struggles in the United States. After China overtook the United States as the world's biggest auto market in 2009, GM's 2010 China sales surpassed those in the United States for the first time in the carmaker's 102-year history; thus, as GM streamlines its value-chain in the United States, it expands it throughout Asia.[59] Meanwhile, 2012 saw Ford Motor launch its largest factory expansion program in a half century, expanding its existing plants in Chongqing as well as breaking ground on new assembly plants in Chongqing and Hangzhou.[60]

These trends will accelerate. The McKinsey Global Institute suggests that 400 mid-size emerging-market cities, many unfamiliar in the West, will generate about 40 percent of global growth over the next 15 years.[61] MNEs like GM, Ford, and IBM, by choice or by force, respond and redeploy. PwC China's headcount went from under a thousand at the start of the millennium to 14,000 in 2011, and expects to hit 30,000 by 2020. Even more dramatically, IBM is making India its center of gravity, with a headcount there that has grown from a few hundred in 1999 to more than 150,000 (about one in three IBM employees).[62] Straight-line projection of current trends shows that IBM will employ more in India than in the United States within the next decade. In a twist, some propose renaming IBM—officially, International Business Machines—to "India-Beijing Machines."

Given that higher supply results in lower wages, countries with the largest labor forces indicate where MNEs will seek inexpensive workers and thus reset the labor characteristics of their value chains. Table 12.3 signals the likely direction of job migration as Western MNEs move operations to labor-rich countries in Southeast Asia, Central and Eastern Europe, and South America. Already, we see powerful effects. Between 2000 and 2010, U.S. companies cut their workforces in the United States by nearly 3 million while concurrently boosting employment overseas by 2.4 million. In contrast, during the 1990s U.S. companies added 4.4 million workers at home while hiring 2.7 million abroad.

Asked about this big shift, GE's CEO replied, "Today we go to Brazil, we go to China, we go to India."[63] In fact, China and India account for 38 percent of total labor in the world. In the longer term, many MNEs will look past China to opportunities in India. While China's population will have risen about 79 million and the United States' about 100 million by 2050, India will have grown by more than half a billion. Over the coming decade its workforce will increase by at least 80 million. This demographic dividend girds optimism in India today.

TABLE 12.3 Global Distribution of Labor: Top 10 Countries

MNEs routinely configure value chains given the supply of resources such as land, capital, technology, and labor. Regarding the latter, China and India are attractive sources of abundant, productive, low-cost labor. Expectedly, many MNEs from many countries configure their value chains to develop Chinese and Indian operations.

Rank	Country	Total Labor Force	Percent Share of Global Labor Pool, 2011[1]
1	**China**	795,500,000	22.7%
2	**India**	487,600,000	13.9%
3	**European Union**	228,300,000	6.5%
4	**United States**	153,600,000	4.4%
5	**Indonesia**	117,400,000	3.3%
6	**Brazil**	104,700,000	3.0%
7	**Bangladesh**	75,420,000	2.1%
8	**Russia**	75,330,000	2.1%
9	**Japan**	65,910,000	1.8%
10	**Pakistan**	58,640,000	1.6%
—	**World**	3,492,935,876	100%

Source: Based on Central Intelligence Agency, "Country Comparisons: Labor Force," *The World Factbook*, at www.cia.gov (retrieved January 25, 2013).

Wage differences are steadily shrinking worldwide. Rising wages in emerging markets signal smaller cross-national gaps. Wages in China and India, particularly for skilled labor, have increased by 10 to 20 percent over the past decade. The ILO reports that between 2000 and 2008, real wages in Asia rose about 8 percent a year. Complicating the wage factor are various secular trends. Growing automation reduces labor's share of the total cost of manufacturing; relative to wage costs, average robot prices since 1990 have fallen 40 to 50 percent in many advanced markets. Local market scale, infrastructural efficiency, and supply chain supports can make a higher wage country outperform its low-wage competitor. Too, the rising cost and persistent delays of shipping goods halfway around the world increasingly sensitizes companies to the disadvantages of the distance between factory and customer. In so doing, these trends expand the lexicon of location decisions (See Table 12.4). Going

TABLE 12.4 The Expanding Lexicon of Locations

The placement of jobs has taken increasing paths the past few years. Once, discussion revolved around the issue of offshoring. Now, developments in automation, sensitivity to national economic growth, concerns for intellectual property protection, and the growing link between responsiveness and competitiveness expand interpretation—as we see below in the range of modifiers that qualify our notion of "shoring."

Form of Shoring	Characteristic
offshoring	A company relocates a primary or support value activity to a different country. The offshored activity can either remain within or go outside the formal boundaries of the company.
Homeshoring	The act of relying on home-based staff to handle particular value activities that had previously been offshored to overseas centers and performed by foreign workers. Now, companies ignore the offshore option and look first to homeshore the activities in the domestic market.
Onshoring	The act of relocating a business process or work unit to a more productive, lower-cost section of the home country.
Re-shoring	The opposite of offshoring; an organization repatriates the value activity from the foreign location to a work site in the original country.
Nearshoring	A less-aggressive form of off shoring whereby the company transfers a value activity to a neighboring or "near" country.

forward, then, local wage rates will shape, but no longer determine, configuration. MNEs will configure value activities more selectively, heeding a wider range of considerations than merely local labor rates.

LOGISTICS

Running a value chain generates exchanges among primary and support activities. For instance, to produce lithium ion batteries, an MNE must mine the lithium in Bolivia, move it to a manufacturing plant in Guangzhou, then ship the finished goods to its distributor in France, who supplies market channels in the European Union. Each transaction generates an exchange between different stages of the chain. The management of these transactions is the matter of **logistics**. MNEs configure the location of value activities to minimize logistics expenses; given that transport adds nothing to the final value of a good, cost minimization is crucial.[64]

Logistics, important to any company, is oftentimes vital to others. Consider Zara, where the logistics department—"the essence of the company"—powers the machine.[65] Giving customers what they want and getting it to them faster than anyone else, Zara's twin organizing principles, can only happen through efficient logistics. Alternatively, consider logistics at Apple. While many praise it for its innovative designs and cool products, others point to its supply chain logistics as its true advantage. Noted one analyst, "Apple has put a ton of work into building a supply chain and technological prowess that is second to none. This has made competing with it an incredibly difficult proposition."[66] Incidentally, the current CEO of Apple, Tim Cook, replaced legendary Steve Jobs based on his performance configuring Apple's logistics network.[67]

Logistics involves how companies obtain, produce, and exchange material and services in the proper place and in proper quantities for the proper activity.

In some situations, the value-to-weight ratio of transactions shapes configuration decisions. The greater the value of a product to its weight, the less transportation costs matter. Logistics costs are relevant, yet not decisive in this scenario. In deciding where to make computer chips, software, or aircraft, unlike tractor axles or carpeting, the distance between the factory and the consumer does not matter.

Presently, ongoing advancement in container ships makes transport costs less important. Containerization continues revolutionizing cargo shipping, powering tremendous efficiencies in loading, cargo volume, and unloading. First-generation ships, introduced in the late 1950s, carried 480 twenty-foot equivalent (TEU) containers—those ubiquitous 20'×8'×8' boxes. Today, the biggest ships carry up to 15,000 TEUs; the next generation will stack 18,000. Presently, more than 90 percent of non-bulk cargo worldwide moves by TEU containers stacked on transport ships of the sort seen in the adjacent photo. The reduced costs and improved efficiencies of containerization continues reshaping global trade; some say it has proven more important for globalization than freer trade.[68] Long term, the rise of robotics, as we discussed in our *Looking to the Future* insert, will likely reset our interpretation of global logistics. Locating factories based not on the availability of people, but of robots, will let MNEs reshore foreign factories.

Digitization The process of **digitization** converts an analog product into a string of zeros and ones. Increasingly, MNEs digitize products like software, music, and books, as well as services like application processing, financial consolidation, and legal assistance. Plugged into the network, a firm can move goods and services anywhere in the world at negligible cost and complication. The potential to locate digital activities virtually anywhere, particularly as the Internet cloud expands, influences how an MNE configures its value chain. Digitization changes location economics, creating options that did not exist a decade ago—say, X-rays taken in Boston but read in Bangkok. Distance, historically measured in terms of geographic space, is now measured in terms of electronic time.

Digitization influences location economics by resetting the relative productivity of competing sources.

Ongoing improvements in digitization signals continuing disruption. Once, many activities could be done only in a few specialized places, such as due diligence processes in mergers and acquisitions that largely took place in New York City or London, where corresponding

Here we see a "Panamax" container ship, one of the world's largest, at sea. This leviathan can carry up to 14,500 20-foot containers. In comparison, a train carrying that load would stretch more than 60 miles (96 km). Every day, international trade sets in motion millions of containers, using them to transport products among plants, ports, and consumers worldwide.
Source: il-fede/Fotolia

value activities such as regulatory registration or evaluation were concentrated. Digitization enables dispersion of these activities. Indeed, it has created a new global model for financial services, unleashing disruptive innovations that change the rules of the game. One analyst maintains that"there has never been an economic discontinuity of this magnitude in the history of the world....These powerful forces are allowing companies to rethink their sourcing strategies across the entire value chain."[69] Indeed, some have projected digitization as "creating a second economy that's vast, automatic, and invisible—thereby bringing the biggest change since the Industrial Revolution."[70]

Similar trends have begun to disrupt configuration strategies in the legal field. India's legal outsourcing industry is growing from an experimental enterprise to a mainstream part of the global business of law. At Pangea3, Office Tiger, and Lexadigm, Indian lawyers do the routine work traditionally assigned to enterprising junior lawyers in the United States at a fraction of the cost. Moreover, amendments to the U.S. Federal Rules of Civil Procedure expand the scope of discovery to include electronic documents, such as emails, instant messages, and voicemails. E-Discovery further incents offshoring legal work to productive providers. Add it all up, says a director of Harvard Law School, and legal outsourcing"is not a blip...it is a big historical movement."[71]

Going forward, the narrowing *digital divide*—the gap between those with regular access to digital technologies and those without—plugs more people into the global network. Accordingly, MNEs' location economics change and their configuration choices evolve. The diffusion of lower-priced tablets and netbooks to people worldwide means that fewer and fewer spots in the world remain off the grid. As newly wired folk connect with their counterparts throughout the world, they develop proficiencies with various technology platforms. Consequently, MNEs rethink configuration options in order to tap new sources of competencies.[72]

COORDINATION

Configuring activities arranges the architecture of the value chain. Making it perform requires coordinating how activities transact with each other. One way to engage this idea is to think of the configuration process as placing pieces atop the global game board. Given location

Looking to the Future
The Rise of Robots

Advances in robotics threaten to disrupt much of what we know about configuring value activities. Configuration decisions, originally made based on hand labor, later based on factory assembly lines manned by humans, increasingly follow the promise of digital manufacturing done by robots.

In your daily life, think of the implications of ATMs, self-checkout tills, and remotely guided trains. More pointedly, consider that at the Philips Electronics factory in Zhuhai, China, hundreds of workers go old-school and use hand tools to assemble electric shavers. Meanwhile, 128 robot arms do the same work at a sister factory in the Netherlands. The Dutch factory has several dozen workers per shift, about a tenth as many as the Zhuhai plant, yet it out-produces its counterpart.[73] Elsewhere, fear of rising wages drives others to do the same. Foxconn, the maker of "all things Apple," has factories filled with tens of thousands of workers but looks to install more than a million robots within a few years.

Change is not limited to manufacturing. In distribution facilities, companies like Amazon look to robots to store, retrieve, and pack goods far more efficiently than people. Indeed, robot manufacturers contend that robots are already more cost-effective than humans in many applications. Says the founder of robot builder Industrial Perception, "We're on the cusp of completely changing manufacturing and distribution. I think it's not as a singular event, but it will ultimately have as big an impact as the Internet."[74]

In the longer term, the improving performance of three-dimensional printing means that big factories may be unnecessary to achieve efficient production—the falling cost of making much smaller batches of a much wider variety moves MNEs to scenarios where they make each product tailored precisely to a customer's request. So, three-dimensional printing, ingenious software, and novel materials signal situations that fundamentally reset location economics.[75] Moving factories to low-cost labor markets to mass-produce goods, long a deterministic driver of plant location, may eventually become secondary. Instead, robotic platforms will support small-scale factories, located anywhere and everywhere in the world, as they efficiently focus on mass customization.

The increasing need to be closer to customers, supported by small-scale facilities "manned" by robots, radically reshuffles production analytics. Indeed, the day may soon arrive when MNEs cast aside the long-sacred rules of configuration, such as "You must seek economies of scale," "You must reduce unit-labor costs," and "You must exploit location effects."[76] Already, we see production activities that have routinely been moved to low-cost labor locations re-shoring to rich countries. The Boston Consulting Group, for instance, reports that nearly half of U.S.-based manufacturing executives at companies with sales greater than $10 billion are planning to or are actively considering bringing production back to the United States from China.[77] Further, it estimates that in the transport, computer fabricated metals, and machinery industries nearly a third of the goods the U.S. imports from China could be made in the States by 2020. Inevitably, changes here will reset how a MNE configures its value chain. On a larger scale, they could move the world to the cusp of a robot-led industrial revolution.[78] ■

economics, an MNE moves its R&D piece to Brazil, factory piece to Vietnam, logistics piece to the United States, marketing piece to Italy, and the service piece to Japan. Once configured, executives specify how these pieces link to and relate with each other. Therefore, **coordination** sets links that integrate and animate value activities.

Coordination specifies how value activities interact with each other.

Coordination ranges from not at all (each piece is independent) to extensive (each piece is interdependent). Managing activities spanning the globe, one would think, requires extensive coordination connections. Consider the coordination demands imposed by Zara's strategy of rapid response to fashion trends. Headquarters coordinates reports from salespeople who, acting as grassroots market researchers, interpret buying trends, capture customers' comments, and propose improvements. Indeed, Zara coaches its sales staff to solicit input from customers. Real-time data on customer preferences is uploaded to headquarters where managers take the "fashion pulse of the world." Explained Inditex, "The store manager will

say, 'My customers are asking for red trousers,' and if it's the same demand in Istanbul, New York and Tokyo, that means it's a global trend, so they know to produce more red pants."[79] Fed fresh data, the machine responds; product designers, materials managers, production supervisors, and logistics controllers go into action. In a matter of days, new designs turn into new clothes that are sent worldwide—essentially, some say, creating custom orders for global, mass-made products.

The task is tough; managers coordinate information flows from 1,000-plus storefronts spanning the globe, oversee its translation into innovative products, organize material flows from suppliers, forward orders to factories, and orchestrate delivery to the same storefronts—all within two weeks. Adding another level of complexity is the fact that linkages exist between primary and support activities. Executives synchronize the company's infrastructure, develop human resources to staff operations, update technologies to expedite transactions, manage capital processes, and consolidate accounts.

CONCEPT CHECK

In discussing the worldwide "Increase and Expansion of Technology" in Chapter 1, we note that technology fosters new ways of communicating among worldwide operations. New technologies enable MNEs to experiment with options, many of them unprecedented, to coordinate dispersed value activities.

Hence, coordinating activities requires adeptly moving ideas, materials, people, and capital. Done well, the MNE improves its performance. For example, IBM, GE, Microsoft, and Accenture opened R&D facilities in India, reasoning that the productivity of the local scientific community and its unique philosophy of frugal innovation offered new points of value creation. Breakthroughs at GE's Technology Center in Bengaluru, owing to adroit coordination processes, spread to GE's operations in Hungary, Brazil, China, the United States, and onward. In one instance, GE's Indian technology center helped develop a small, low-cost electrocardiograph machine for doctors and hospitals in rural communities. Its price and performance soon led to marketing units in Germany and the United States.[80]

Managers configure value chains with an eye to how they will coordinate activities—recall the aphorism that any chain is only as strong as its weakest link. As several factors moderated managers' configuration choices, so too with the approaches to coordination. Specifically, managers coordinate activities mindful of *core competency, subsidiary networks,* and *operational obstacles.*

Factors that influence the coordination of a value-chain include

- Operational obstacles,
- Core competency,
- Subsidiary networks.

Core Competency The competitive imperative of leveraging core competencies throughout the value chain intensifies the importance of skillfully coordinating activities.[81] Like beauty, the idea of a core competency defies precise specification—it is an almost ethereal concept that many see as the basis of an MNE's distinctive success. Popular examples of core competencies include Apple's eye for design, Walmart's sophisticated information-management and product-distribution systems, Tata's legacy of product innovation, Honda's understanding of engine mechanics, and Nestlé's marketing finesse. Against this profile, a **core competency** is the special outlook, skill, capability, or technology that runs through the firm's operations, threading discrete activities into an integrated value chain.[82]

A core competency can emerge from various activities, including

- Product development,
- Employee productivity,
- Manufacturing expertise,
- Marketing imagination,
- Executive leadership.

Operationally, then, an MNE's core competency gives everyone in the company a principle that helps them coordinate transactions among value activities. Framing exchanges in the context of core competencies help managers see particular activities, not as ends unto themselves but as parts of the larger, integrated scheme of creating value. Google, for instance, has configured its value chain to make information universally accessible; coordinating these activities follows Google's core competency in organizing the world's information. Google's capability of associating its various activities, assets, costs, and revenues with its core competency helps its managers better coordinate its value chain.

CONCEPT CHECK

Fast-growing emerging economies spur big changes in global strategies. Here, we observe that one of these shifts moves companies to assess operating in different environments with a keen eye toward leveraging innovations across subsidiaries.

Subsidiary Networks Globalization and technology trends have built a world marked by real-time connectivity with anyone, anywhere. The Internet, some argue, is the most powerful force for globalization, democratization, education, and economic growth in history.[83] MNEs respond in kind, expanding operations to fortify their relationships with existing customers and connecting with the remaining billions joining the nervous system of civilization. Commensurately, the number of MNEs worldwide has grown from 30,000 in 1990 to more than 70,000 in 2010; these 70,000-plus operate almost a million subsidiaries worldwide. Hence, the average MNE has a subsidiary network of about 13 units, with a range of a few to several hundred.[84] Expanding connections among expanding subsidiary networks influences how managers coordinate value activities.

The perspectives of social networks help an MNE analyze the interaction among its subsidiaries.

Managers are keen to use their subsidiary networks to support efficient transactions and fortify core competencies. The advent of social networks, like LinkedIn, Orkut, or Facebook, increasingly influences how managers achieve these goals.[85] Rather than transactions based on traditional business directives, social networking shows that information flows more efficiently in a collaborative, peer-to-peer format. Workers are more inclined to communicate and collaborate while simultaneously contributing and participating in coordinating the value chain. In the case of Zara, interactions between store managers around the world and designers stationed in Spain helps localize what otherwise would be standardized global products. Retail input on particular colors or fabrics that sell better in certain locales versus others makes for easy product adaptations. Absent the real-time coordination between the field and headquarters, these adaptations would follow hunches.

By diffusing knowledge among value activities, coordination systems help an MNE to localize operations.

Operational Obstacles MNEs often struggle to get the links of their global value chain to engage each other. Granted, improving communications systems, made faster by cheaper voice, video, and data options, help workers coordinate activities. Still, MNEs run into problems because of time zones, differing languages, and ambiguous meanings. Picture a company whose value chain spans the globe. Parts and products flow from South Africa and Chile to their ultimate destination in Malaysia, Germany, Canada, the United States, and China. Each transfer, from mines to plants to ships to warehouses to storefronts, creates links that require coordination. Toss into the mix multiple time zones and multiple languages, and the potential for misalignment escalates.

Most MNEs apply browser-based communication tools to coordinate handoffs. Electronic transactions boost efficiency by streamlining exchanges among links in the chain. In larger markets, this interface is prevalent among manufacturers and their first-tier suppliers, such as the relationship between Costco and Procter & Gamble. Many MNEs set the open-source language protocol of the Internet—specifically, hypertext markup language (HTML) or XML—as the global standard. So far, though, there is slight consensus on interface standards, as evidenced in the proliferation of Web service composition standards.[86] However, the increasing simplicity, generality, and usability of information exchange over the Internet spurs global standards.

CHANGE AND THE VALUE CHAIN

Once it is configured, executives resist seeing the value chain set in stone. Product features and functions continually change, as we see in electronics, financial services, apparel, and entertainment. Consequently, the basis of value creation in an industry evolves. Certainly, some firms, like Zara and Google, appear distinctively able to anticipate market situations and then keenly adapt activities. Far more common are those companies that struggle.

In the United States, for instance, the average time a company spends in the S&P 500 capitalize index has declined from 75 years in the 1930s to about 15 years today. Up to 90 percent of start-ups fail shortly after being founded; venture-capital firms see more than 80 percent of their investments fail; more than 80 percent of equity mutual funds consistently underperform the S&P 500; and more than 75 percent of mergers and acquisitions never pay off.[87] Companies, rather than maximizing success, far more commonly struggle to survive.

A CASE IN POINT

The configuration and coordination of a value chain responds to changes in customers, industries, institutions, and environments.

In 1997, Sony Corporation, Japan's premier electronics giant, took slight notice of the Samsung Electronics Company, a South Korean television maker then snared in a life-or-death struggle to survive the Asian currency crisis. Today, Samsung has nearly twice the market capitalization of Sony and commands the role Sony once claimed: the competitor with a portfolio of trend-setting products, world-class manufacturing, and premium brand appeal.

A back-of-the-store brand with bulky, low-quality televisions in 1997, Samsung powered its rise by radically rethinking its value chain. In terms of R&D, it has been one of the world's "top 10" in U.S. patents for several years, relying on 60,000-plus staff members working in 34 research centers across the globe to invent tomorrow's products.[88] Its quest to become "world's best" drives its massive capital spending (some $10.5 billion, or 5.7 percent of revenue, in 2012) in plants that make components for its many products, like memory chips and display panels, at some of the lowest costs in the world.[89] Similarly, it has annually invested billions of dollars in advertising to burnish its image. By 2005, for the first time, Samsung's brand value exceeded that of Sony. It has since maintained this lead; by 2012, Samsung ranked 12th in the world for brand value whereas Sony ranked 38th.[90]

Interesting in its own right, the Sony–Samsung contest spotlights an intrinsic risk of strategy. The strategy literature holds that a decisive sense of purpose anchors short-term competitiveness and long-term sustainability. However, this outlook can also stifle creativity and erode the effectiveness of decision-making.[91] As Samsung encroached on Sony's territory, Sony did not idly rest on its laurels; its management improved products, served customers, anticipated new markets, and invested billions to improve its value chain. However, it saw little gain in market share and profits. Growing anxiety about its fading competitiveness led to shock therapy—it took the unprecedented step, for a major Japanese MNE, of naming an American as its chairperson.[92] It again reconfigured its value chain, reorganizing product and market divisions, and invested in promising ventures. Ultimately, though, these efforts fell short and problems persist. Sony had net losses of nearly $5 billion in 2012. Meanwhile, Samsung reported profits of $6 billion.[93]

Designing and delivering a strategy is an ongoing challenge. While some succeed, others fall short.

The upshot is that no matter how sensitive their strategic compass, executives' cognitive limitations, along with marketplace uncertainty, can turn a superbly configured and coordinated value chain into a liability.[94] Faced with such adversity, managers often return to basics, retry tired methods, and persuade themselves that "doing the same things, but better" will prevail. Compounding these limitations are large-scale changes in the environment, whether owing to industry disruptions, or, as we see in our Point/Counterpoint feature, adjusting the value creation tools of the twentieth century to the opportunities and challenges of the twenty-first.

Point

Building a Better Value Chain: The Superiority of Convention

Point **Yes** Analysts conceived the value chain in the 1960s and 1970s to chart the step-by-step development strategy for mineral-exporting economies in developing countries—in essence, mapping an integrated system of production where none existed. It was then depicted in French planning literature as a *filière* (literally, a "thread") to describe the need for French industrial capability to build a competitive economic infrastructure based on a fully specified strategic framework. According to this reasoning, the idea of *filière*, or what we now call "core competency," argues that the full chain of activities that go into a product should take place within national boundaries. A country intent on developing capabilities in, say, TVs, would set industry policies to create the infrastructure needed to develop expertise in display technology, to support circuit board design and manufacturing, and to enable design and production of electronic components and metal- and plastic-forming technologies. Specifying the optimal *filière*, the thinking was, gave governments and companies a holistic view of developing the location economics that optimally configure and coordinate value chains.

A Foundation Tool Value chain analysis has since become a widespread management tool. It frames the evaluation of an MNE's strengths and weaknesses and interprets the determinants of its internal cost structure. It represents its core competency, emphasizing activities that support a cost leadership or differentiation strategy. In the case of cost leadership, it spurs management to understand costs and identify the potential for streamlining value activities. In the case of differentiation, it emphasizes activities that support outperforming rivals on providing the latest, greatest products. It links a firm's competencies to its marketplace strategy and frames interpreting industry structure. Value-chain analysis, in summary, helps managers leverage core competencies, set configuration and coordination policies, and stress-test scenarios against industry structure. Such discipline boosts the effectiveness of strategic analysis in MNEs.

The Discipline of Boundaries The value chain, however, imposes analytical boundaries. It obliges managers to follow the model's template in data collection and interpretation, emphasizing the activities, functions, and business processes that move a product through its design, production, marketing, and distribution stages. It imposes an analytical discipline that stipulates how managers assess markets. Acceptable for similar markets (say, moving from the United States to Canada), this perspective struggles to adjust analytics for dissimilar markets (say, moving from Australia to Venezuela). In theory, anchoring analysis in terms of the orderly progression of value-chain activities lets managers formulate optimal strategies. Still, as with any systematic model, we recognize that the template can misinterpret markets and misdirect strategic responses.

The Siren Call of Virtuality What, then, of this notion, raised in the counterpoint, that the newfangled world of virtuality trumps reality? We disagree. Despite its limits, the tried-and-true value chain framework superbly equips managers to deal with what it is best suited to deal with: the realities of international business. Expanding into familiar markets or heading to different territories share commonalities that the value chain has proven it can manage. Granted, the idea of virtual companies operating in cyberspace, free of physical constraints, may happen. And we agree that the counterpoint does offer interesting arguments. However, the false promise of networked cyberspace ultimately mismaps global operations.

Unchecked, the dazzle of virtuality may lead some to underestimate the difficulties of configuring and coordinating value activities. MNEs must not sacrifice the proven benefits of hard analysis with the promise of cool conjecture. Ultimately, international business takes place in the real world marked by real geographic borders, regulated by real national governments, and populated by real companies running real value chains. Good MNEs move toward great when their value chain reflects this reality.

Building a Better Value Chain: The Superiority of Convention

Counterpoint

No The value chain has a beguiling yet flawed assumption: that management is a science with immutable laws that predictably configure and coordinate activities. In disruptive times, the static, sequential depiction of classic business functions no longer transcends time and place. The dynamism of the global marketplace signals the necessity of a different perspective that helps managers commensurately reset their "committed to excellence" framework. As reality gives way to virtuality in more facets of our lives, courtesy of the Internet and its many offshoots, so too must traditional principles of the value chain give way to emergent practices of virtuality.

The Intersection Already, companies in agrochemical, business services, biotech, social networking, information, entertainment, and furniture industries see the intersection of Internet perspectives and management practices heralding the advent of the virtual value chain. MNEs in emerging markets are reinventing systems of production and distribution and experimenting with entirely new business models that move beyond the conventional formats found in Western MNEs. Products and processes once locked into traditional value chains evolve in unprecedented ways. The global financial crisis has ratcheted up the pressure on firms to accept this inevitability. Tough times require rethinking traditional cost-cutting. Rebooting a company requires taking a hard look at getting things done.

Counterpoint

The Power of the Net Insightful analysis, we argue, calls for abandoning reality for virtuality. Principles of virtuality tap into the Internet's capacity to support new architectures that challenge the Industrial-Age view of the value chain as sequential steps organized by classic business functions. Managers must abandon static, internally focused "chains" commanded and controlled by analytically detached executives. Instead, the task is configuring activities as dynamic networks that apply principles of agent-based models. Such virtual value networks, as seen at Alibaba, Li & Fung, eBay, Facebook, and Cisco, form open, interconnected systems that support dynamic configurations. By trumping the rigidities of conventional value chains, dynamic configurations support potent coordination methods.

Collecting and coordinating information flows among the members of an organization is the heart of virtuality. Leveraging ideas and insights lets companies generate new products to serve new markets, much the same way Google has evolved from a single-product search engine to a diversified information-management and media company that liberates information in whatever form it takes. Virtuality also pioneers paths for value creation, allowing managers to capture lower costs for searching, coordination, contracting, and collaboration. Streamlining information flows supports new methods of coordinating value activities, a competency that then supports new methods of configuring value activities.

Do What You Do Best Virtuality has provocative implications for how managers decide what to do and where to do it. Reebok owns no plants, instead relying on contract manufacturers to manufacture, inspect, and distribute its products to retailers. Similarly, Nike, Apple, Cisco, and Qualcomm outsource production to manufacturers in low-cost labor countries in order to do what each does best: maximizing value creation through R&D and marketing. Though nominally independent, extensive coordination systems integrate agents into the network, thereby creating virtual production capabilities. Nike, for example, focuses on increasing value creation by leveraging its core competencies in design and marketing, confident in manufacturers' expertise to change product mixes as consumer preferences evolve.

Granted, it is easy to overhype the virtues of virtuality. Prudent management acknowledges that the relative importance of a real versus virtual value chain depends on product features as well as dealing with the imperatives imposed by industry structure. As such, the potential of virtuality has transformational implications for Google's global expansion of its geography-free network but middling implications for Nestlé's physical situations in different geographies. Therefore, while virtuality may be far-fetched for some MNEs, it is future-defining for others. In any case, just asking the question "Real or virtual?" sparks useful debate that clarifies configuration and coordination choices.

1. Value measures a firm's capability to sell what it makes for more than the costs incurred to make it. Given that straightforward stipulation, do you believe the MNE that continues applying conventional methods will outperform those that implement virtual approaches? Please identify three factors to support your interpretation.

GLOBAL INTEGRATION VERSUS LOCAL RESPONSIVENESS

MNEs face asymmetric forces: pressures for the efficiency of **global integration** versus those for the effectiveness of **local responsiveness**. The constant tug-of-war between globalism and localism puts contradictory demands on how managers configure and coordinate value chains. Research suggests straightforward relationships: The higher the pressure for global integration, the greater the need to concentrate configuration and standardize coordination. Conversely, the higher the pressure for local responsiveness, the greater the need to disperse configuration and adapt coordination. Few MNEs operate in an industry where one perspective dominates. Rather, the common scenario is an industry setting where the MNE must strike some sort of balance, reconciling the competing imperatives given the demands of its strategy.

PRESSURES FOR GLOBAL INTEGRATION

Global integration is the process of combining differentiated parts into a standardized whole. Local responsiveness is the process of disaggregating a standardized whole into differentiated parts.

Global markets produce and consume more than 20 percent of world output and are projected to approach 80 percent by 2025. Similarly, more cross-national economic integration will take place in the next 30 years than occurred in the previous 10,000. Again, think of the agents promoting globalization: from 30,000 MNEs in 1990 to more than 70,000 today, operating more than 900,000 subsidiaries spread around the world. Managers, companies, and industries react accordingly, as seen in the ongoing formation of global markets in chemicals, credit cards, financial services, accounting, food, healthcare, mass media, forest products, information technology, automobiles, telecommunications, and so on. Moreover, emerging economies intensify these processes. The United Nations estimates there are approximately 22,000 multinationals based in the emerging world; few of these existed 10 years ago. More will exist in a decade given that the ten fastest-growing economies during the years ahead will all be in emerging markets.[95] Combined, nearly 70 percent of the world growth over the next few years will come from emerging markets, with 40 percent in just China and India.[96]

The convergence of national markets, standardization of business, and efficiency imperatives push MNEs to integrate activities.

Earlier chapters indicate that many factors encourage global integration. Here, we highlight two significant drivers: the *globalization of markets* and the *efficiency gains of standardization.*

Globalization of Markets Global buying patterns indicate that consumers worldwide seek global products—think of, for example, the global appeal of Apple iPhones, Starbucks lattes, Samsung LED screens, Huawei routers, Nokia cell phones, American Express charge cards, or Zara blouses. Effectively, consumer behavior in many product areas transcends geography, moving national markets to the global standard. The quest to maximize individual purchasing power, coupled with the increasing availability of increasingly standardized goods at increasingly lower prices, drives this trend. In other words, two dynamics—demand-pull and supply-push—power the globalization of markets.

Money has three inalienable features: It is
- Difficult to acquire,
- Transient,
- Scarce.

The intrinsic functions of money power the demand-pull conditions. No matter the society, money exhibits inalienable features: it is hard to acquire (one typically must work for it), transient (it is quickly used), and scarce in supply (no matter the amount, it often seems not enough). Consequently, consumers worldwide pursue a common quest: maximize purchasing power by buying the highest-quality product for the lowest possible price. Ultimately, goes this reasoning, economically rational consumers will disregard a product's national origin, buying a foreign-made product rather than the local substitute, as long as it delivers superior value.[97] The sweep and scope of technology intensifies this tendency. Consumer preferences converge as connections across countries proliferate. The shrinking digital divide exposes more people to common media, thereby promoting universal consumption ideals, and, in turn, standardizing consumer behaviors.

Technology, by shrinking the globe, powers the globalization of markets.

Supply-push conditions feed the globalization machine. Earlier discussion of digitization and logistics highlighted the increasing availability of the same product worldwide. The expanding trading network of globalization, regulated by institutions such as the World Trade Organization, sanctioned by governments committed to free trade, and driven by companies intent on expanding operations, make it increasingly easy to supply the same products everywhere.

MNEs exploit these circumstances, configuring value chains with a keen sensitivity to standardization imperatives. Our opening case chronicles the unique, but increasingly common, response. Zara realized that offering standardized fashion styles at reasonable prices neutralized stubborn local preferences. Its global network, supported by state-of-the-art logistics, gave customers worldwide real-time access to the newest, coolest fashion trends. Global markets let Zara leverage its global scale investment in design, manufacturing, distribution, and retail activities. The resulting efficiencies, in turn, supported making high quality, low-cost products that, by offering compelling value, repowered the cycle. Similar circumstances in high-tech (think of the performance potential of the latest, greatest Apple iPhone) and high-touch (think of the personalized service involved in purchasing a Starbucks latte) markets highlight the intricate relationship between global integration and value creation.

Efficiency Gains of Standardization Globalization is the "process by which the experience of everyday life is becoming standardized around the world."[98] So put, the consequence of globalization is people worldwide doing the same thing, the same way. This imperative drives MNEs to produce low-cost, high-quality products that differ little, if any, in features and functionality, confident that customers will find their value proposition compelling. So charged, MNEs eye the efficiency gains of standardization as the foundation for competitive advantage.

CONCEPT CHECK

Movements in national markets toward regional trade agreements along with the globalization of capital markets support the standardization of products and processes. Increasing standardization supports configuring concentrated value chains.

The logic of standardization is straightforward. Repeatedly doing the same task the same way, by capturing location, scale, and learning effects, creates efficiencies that enable reducing costs without sacrificing quality. Efficiencies emerge across the value chain. The MNE, for example, can streamline product processes in order to standardize production equipment, negotiate quantity discounts on material purchases, rationalize materials management, and optimize outbound logistics. The MNE also realizes efficiencies in other value activities: R&D benefits by leveraging a common design platform, advertising benefits by communicating a universal message, and distribution benefits by improving channel performance.

Standardization drives improving the efficiency of effort, which, in turn, supports charging lower prices.

Strategic implications of international business is that MNEs prefer a seamless operating environment that enables the straightforward transfer of standardized practices, products, and processes throughout global operations. The globalization of markets supports this quest, developing an increasingly consistent environment. This outcome, in turn, creates greater potential for scale economies, thereby promoting increasing degrees of standardization. Several trends reinforce this scenario. Presently, 157 nations are members of the World Trade Organization, the regulator of the rules of world trade.[99] Membership requires replacing differentiated national regulations with global standards that support trade liberalization. Standardizing the rules of the globalization game, so to speak, supports standardizing the methods of play. Progressive trade liberalization permits MNEs to configure value activities in optimal locations without forsaking access to markets worldwide. Hence, business-process outsourcing firms in India, robot builders in Germany, solar-panel makers in China, or chip designers in Taiwan can design value chains that maximize standardization without sacrificing access to consumers in other countries.

PRESSURES FOR LOCAL RESPONSIVENESS

CONCEPT CHECK

Globalization, though a powerful force, is not inevitable. Chapters 3 and 4 developed this thesis by noting that political and economic freedoms are in flux. Here we add that, for similar sorts of reasons, both consumer needs and host-government pressures prompt companies to adapt their value chains to local conditions.

Culture, politics, law, and markets differ across countries. Besides shaping the general business environment, they set the myriad factors that determine location economics. As a result, MNEs face a diversity of principles, practices, and agents as they operate from country to country. Some differences are superficial distractions that surrender to the allure of higher-quality, lower-cost products—think of worldwide demand for an Apple iPad, Starbucks latte, Facebook wall, or Twitter feed. Others, however, press MNEs to tailor the configuration and coordination of value chains. For instance, just 329 brands are recognized by consumers in eight or more countries; only 16 percent of all brands are recognized in two or more countries. What then of increasing communication across borders? Presently, about 1 percent of the world's physical mail crosses borders, less than 2 percent of calling minutes are international, and a quarter of Internet traffic crosses national borders.[100] Lastly, most people live their entire lives within one country, supporting local production and consumption of goods and sustaining local politics, history, culture, and identity. Localism, not globalism, is the lifestyle context for many people in virtually every country.

Given that adaptation reduces the potential efficiency gains of standardization, MNEs are understandably reluctant to adjust operations unnecessarily. Local imperatives, most notably those posed by *divergent consumer behaviors* and *host-government policies,* often compel them to do so.

Divergent Consumer Behaviors Rejecting the globalization of markets thesis, others argue that stubborn divergences in consumer preferences across countries necessitate adapting products and processes to local circumstances.[101] Certainly, money and technology encourage consumer behavior that privileges purchasing power over national allegiance. Nevertheless, differences in local consumers' preferences endure due to cultural predisposition, historical legacy, and latent nationalism (i.e., buy-local campaigns).[102] Also, consumers prefer products that are sensitive to their distinctive, everyday idiosyncrasies. Examples include designing and making products that local customers prefer (e.g., large cars in the United States, smaller cars in Europe, still smaller cars in emerging markets), tailoring channel structures to buyer preferences (e.g., Web-based and 4G-driven content in South Korea, print and media promotion in France, personal selling in Brazil), modifying product features for local tastes (e.g., light coffee roasts in Germany and Scandinavia, dark coffee roasts in Italy and Spain), and adapting marketing practices to consumption patterns (e.g., large package sizes in Australia, smaller sizes in Japan, single-unit sizes in poorer countries). These sorts of cross-national divergences press MNEs to optimize, rather than maximize, the standardization of products and processes.

Differences in local consumers' preferences endure due to cultural predisposition, historical legacy, and endemic nationalism.

It's important to note that local responsiveness, in some industries, is a powerful strategy. Look at Nestlé, with its slight incentive to standardize many activities across countries. Local habits, cultural traditions, and social norms shape the standards of preferred, palatable food. Food inputs are generally commodities, production has limited potential for scale economies, widespread distribution faces high costs given low value-to-weight ratios, and marketing is

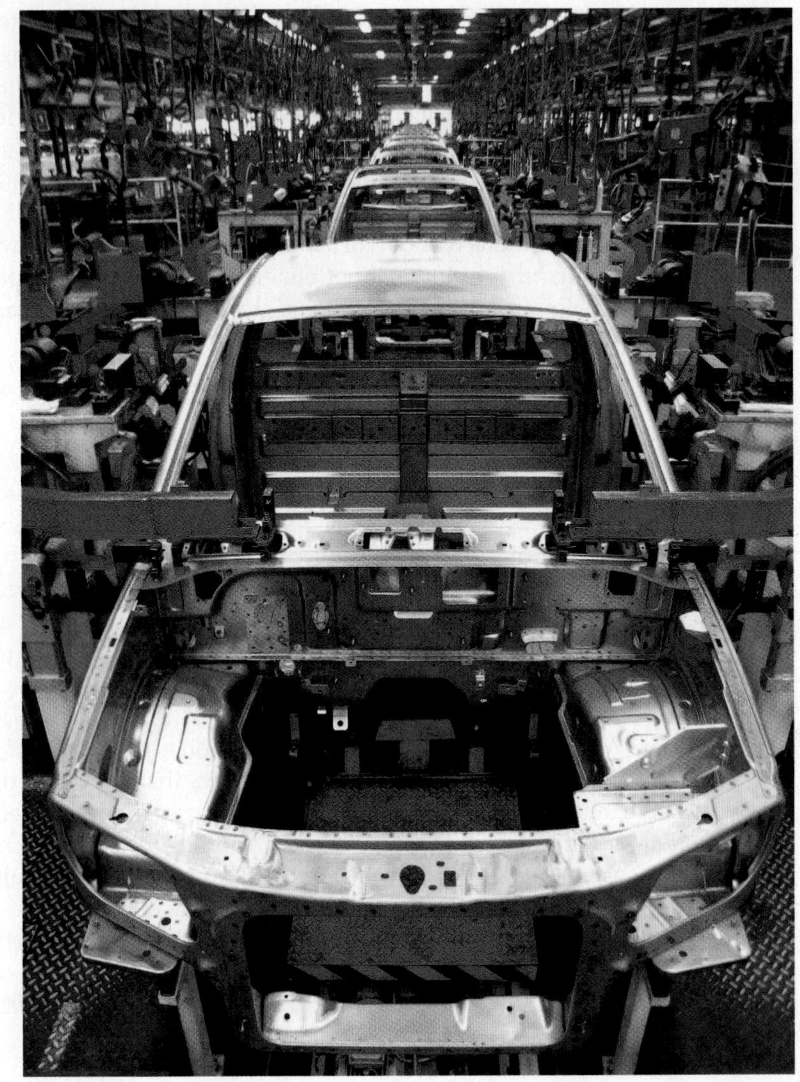

The sequential layout of an assembly line compels standardizing components, processes, and products. Standardization, in turn, drives efficiencies that improve productivity and decrease costs. MNEs translate these outcomes into competitive advantages.
Source: gjeerawut/Fotolia

best done locally given differentiated tastes, regulations, competitors, and retail channels. Certainly, Nestlé can standardize some global activities such as information systems, brand names, advertising message, and packaging processes. Ultimately, though, many activities of its value chain are intrinsically suited to local adaptation.

Host-Government Policies A recurring theme of our text is the variability of political, legal, cultural, and economic environments. The source of many variations is the policies, or the lack thereof, instituted by the national government. Prior to the recent global financial crisis, MNEs had steadily confronted fewer differences as free market principles shaped politics in more countries. Market fundamentalism encouraged countries to adopt freer trade, greater privatization, and less regulation. Now, skepticism of capitalism spurs governments to tighten the rules of the game. The CEO of IKEA, speaking of expanding operations, noted, "What some years ago took two to three years, now takes four to six years. And we also see that there's a lot of hidden obstacles in different markets and also within the European Union that's holding us back."[103]

Aggravating matters for MNEs is the fact that different countries have taken different paths to reset fiscal, monetary, and business regulations. Collectively, these actions install regulations that oblige MNEs to localize value activities.[104]

The ongoing financial crisis spurs governments to strongly encourage MNEs to improve their local responsiveness.

A Case in Point The pharmaceutical industry likely foreshadows this scenario. In theory, industry conditions in pharmaceuticals call for hard economics to drive value chain configuration. Competitiveness hinges on achieving the efficiency gains of standardization where and when possible. Many companies, for example, sell low-margin, generic products such as aspirin; profitability demands efficient production. Alternatively, companies offering branded, proprietary products incur steep R&D costs; profitability requires high-volume sales to a global market.

Responsiveness pressures, however, require the pharmaceutical MNE to trade global efficiency for local access. Specifically, drug makers commonly disperse value activities to meet a national government's mandates that clinical testing, registration procedures, pricing restrictions, and marketing regulations comply with local regulations. As a result, firms adapt manufacturing and marketing to local market circumstances.

Arguably, an enterprising pharmaceutical firm could reject industry practices, as Zara did in the global apparel industry, and concentrate its value chain in superior locations. Public regulation of the healthcare industry largely nullifies this option. Besides funding big chunks of the healthcare budget, governments regulate its delivery. Qualifying companies must show sensitivity to the national healthcare system, standards of care for citizens, and local stakeholders. Antagonizing political officials by deemphasizing local responsiveness is rife with risks.

CONCEPT CHECK

The unfolding consequences of the global financial crisis hit many facets of the business environment. Growing state intervention into the market reduces the freedom companies have to pursue the efficiencies of global integration. It also benefits those companies that improve their local responsiveness.

A few years ago, the sweep of free markets and market fundamentalism meant fewer and fewer industries fell into this situation. The fallout of the global financial crisis suggests that in a few years, more and more will do so. Banks, energy providers, media, miners, insurance carriers, healthcare management, carmakers, and airlines, to name the most obvious, increasingly fall under the policy purview of national governments. Meeting growing public demands for transparency prods MNEs to improve the local responsiveness of their value chains. Those that protest will likely face stern rebuke. Governments have forceful tools to make MNEs adapt activities: protectionism to encourage local production, regulations to constrain market moves, or, ultimately, the command to divest and depart.

WHEN PRESSURES INTERACT

No global industry exists in which either complete standardization or full adaptation is an option. Those in salient national sectors, such as pharmaceutical companies, concentrate some activities while their counterparts in global scale-sensitive industries, such as computer chips, disperse some activities. Hence, no matter the industrial setting, operating internationally requires configuring and coordinating operations in ways that reconcile the competing demands of global integration and local responsiveness—not, as we see in Figure 12.5, foolishly ignoring one for the other. The **Integration-Responsiveness (IR) Grid** provides executives a framework to begin managing this challenge. (See Figure 12.6.)

The IR Grid relates the global and local pressures that influence an MNE's strategy.

The IR Grid positions an industry in the quadrant that represents its sensitivity to the dual imperatives. For instance, it indicates that strong pressures to respond locally but low pressures to integrate globally encourage adapting value activities to host country conditions. In this scenario, MNEs like Procter & Gamble, Shiseido, or Unilever that operate in industries with strong cultural sensitivities, see few benefits from global integration but high returns from local responsiveness. Alternatively, high pressure to integrate globally along with slight pressure for local responsiveness encourages standardization. Flat-panel displays, for instance, are vital components for a range of products; few consumers, if any, care where they are made. Thus, firms like LG Philips, Chi Mie Optoelectronics, Beijing Orient Electronics, and Samsung respond to competitive pressures by concentrating value activities in economically superior locations.

A third class includes MNEs in industries such as telecommunications, information technology, automobiles, pharmaceuticals, and financial services. These industries fall in the

a.bacall
"I think the reason our international unit is performing poorly is because our mission statement says 'Think Locally and Act Locally'."

FIGURE 12.5 How Not to Reconcile the Dual Imperative
Source: Aaron Bacall/CartoonStock

center zone of the IR grid—essentially trapped, shall we say, on the horns of a dilemma. They face strong pressures for global integration while simultaneously dealing with powerful demands for local responsiveness. Configuring and coordinating value activities to resolve this dilemma pose enduring challenges. For companies like McKinsey & Company, Dentsu, Citibank, Panasonic, Johnson & Johnson, or Infosys, this situation requires more complex configuration formats and coordination systems.

In summary, the IR Grid helps managers map their strategic options given prevailing pressures for standardization and adaptation in their particular industry.[105] In so doing, it clarifies how industry structure sets the context, strategy specifies the end, and the value chain defines the best means in building a company to last.

TYPES OF STRATEGY

Recurring patterns in the marketplace identify generic strategies among MNEs, namely, *international, multidomestic, global,* or *transnational.* We now profile each type, emphasizing its implications to configuring and coordinating value chains. Table 12.5 summarizes these discussions.

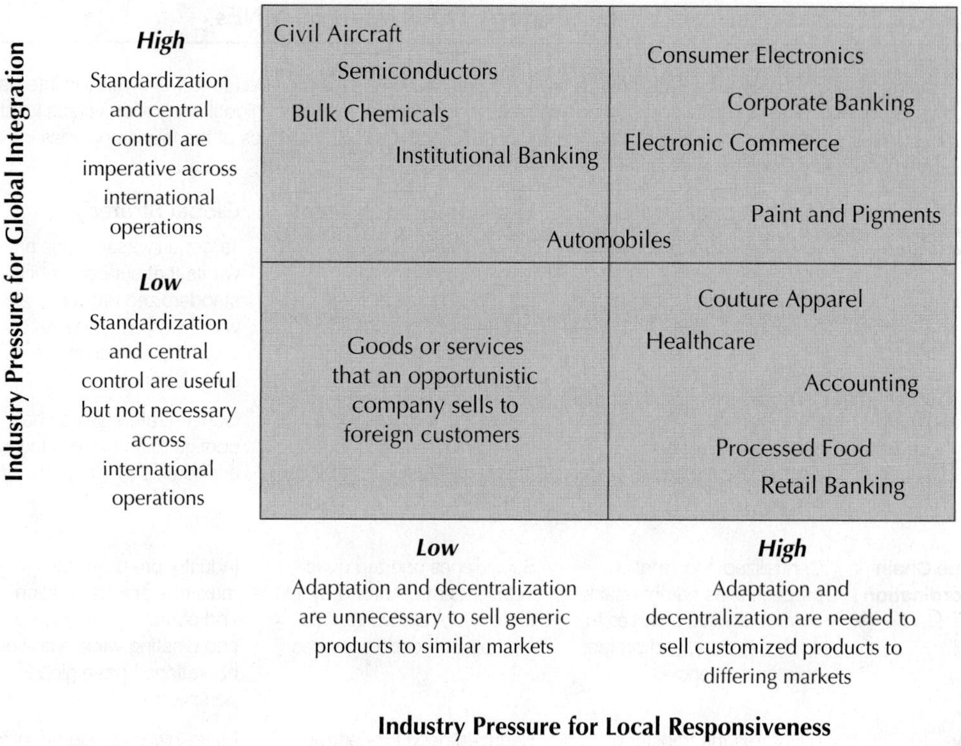

FIGURE 12.6 The Integration-Responsiveness Grid: By Industry

Each strategy archetype embodies a unique concept of value creation that reflects its resolution of the asymmetric pressure for global integration versus local responsiveness. The Integration-Responsiveness Grid maps this response, highlighting the interaction between each pressure that faces the MNE operating within a particular industry. As such, it helps managers map their strategies to reconcile the competing imperatives of standardization and adaptation.

INTERNATIONAL STRATEGY

Companies implement an **international strategy** when they leverage core competencies around the globe in an industry marked by low pressure for global integration and local responsiveness (the lower left quadrant of the IR Grid). This approach emphasizes replicating home-country-based competencies, such as production expertise, design skills, or brand power, in foreign markets. The primacy of replication requires that foreign units operate activities that are configured and coordinated by the home-country headquarters. Ultimate control resides with executives there, given their reasoning that they best understand the application, protection, and extension of the company's core competencies. The testing ground of new ideas, goes such thinking, is the home market, not foreign countries; hence, subsidiaries have limited autonomy to adapt products or processes. MNEs implementing an international strategy include Apple, Airbus, and Google.

The international strategy leverages a company's core competencies into foreign markets.

Headquarters is the decisive driver of the international strategy. Google, for example, develops the core architecture of its Web products at the Googleplex, its corporate headquarters complex in Mountain View, California. It allows national subsidiaries to customize aspects of its Web pages to deal with local differences in language and alphabet. Executives in the Googleplex safeguard the search algorithms that create its competitive advantage; they then direct product development and set business processes for overseas operations. Hence, headquarters transfers principles, practices, and processes to foreign operations. It does not, however, transfer control.

Benefits of the International Strategy An international strategy creates value by transferring core competencies to units in foreign markets where rivals lack a competitive alternative. The international strategy works well when industry conditions do not demand high degrees of global integration or local responsiveness and the firm business practices, either in minimizing costs or leveraging its brand, set market standards. The superior

TABLE 12.5 Characteristics of the Strategy Types Used by MNEs

The strategy gamut of "international-multidomestic-global-transnational" has prevailed for several years in international business theory. Each archetype speaks directly and differently to how the MNE reconciles the tension of global integration versus local responsiveness. Managers, mindful of industry structure and drivers of value creation, trade off the characteristics of the four archetypes in making their strategic choice. This table summarizes key points of concern and comparison.

	International Strategy	Multidomestic Strategy	Global Strategy	Transnational Strategy
Orientation	Leverage core competencies and home country innovations into competitive positions abroad.	Differentiate products to respond to national differences in customer preferences, industry characteristics, or government regulation.	Target universal needs or wants that support selling standardized products worldwide. Emphasize volume, cost minimization, and efficiency.	Simultaneously manage the tensions of global integration and local differentiation in ways that leverage specialized knowledge and promote worldwide learning.
Value Chain Configuration	Concentrated; value activities are set and directed by the home office.	Dispersed; subsidiaries command discretion to adapt value activities to local conditions.	Concentrated; value chain configuration exploits location economics.	Concentrated to tap location economies. Dispersed, subject to minimum efficiency standards, to meet local preferences.
Value Chain Coordination	Centralized coordination processes as parent retains control of value activities to apply, regulate, and protect core competencies.	Subsidiaries operate quasi-independently. Autonomy lets them adapt activity to local marketplace circumstances.	Industry pressures to maximize standardization and contain costs require coordinating value activities operations from a global perspective.	Simultaneous goal of integration and responsiveness calls for sharing coordination between headquarters or subsidiaries.
Key Advantage	Facilitates the transfer of skills and expertise from the parent company to international units.	Reduced need for central support to manage local activities. Greater sensitivity to local preferences.	Make low-cost, high-quality products that differ little, but appeal to consumers worldwide.	Supports efficiency, compels effectiveness, and leverages learning that drives innovations through units worldwide.
Key Disadvantage	Centralizing the value chain in the home country often weakens configuration efficiency and coordination flexibility.	Encourages "mini-me" phenomenon that replicates value activities across subsidiaries.	Reduced learning opportunities given the dominance of global standard. Requires rigorous coordination to regulate global matrix of inputs and outputs.	Requires elaborate mechanisms to integrate dispersed operations. Difficult to configure, tough to coordinate, and prone to performance shortfalls.
IR Grid Positioning	Pressure for global integration: low. Pressure for national responsiveness: low.	Pressure for global integration: low. Pressure for national responsiveness: high.	Pressure for global integration: high. Pressure for national responsiveness: low.	Pressure for global integration: high. Pressure for national responsiveness: high.
Examples	Kraft, Google, P&G, Nucor, Harley Davidson, Baidu, Apple, Carrefour	Unilever, Nestle, Heinz, The Body Shop, McDonald's, Johnson & Johnson, Pfizer, Embraer, Ranbaxy	Toyota, Canon, Haier, Texas Instruments, Caterpillar, Cemex, Infosys, Walmart, Huawei, Haier, LVMH, American Express, Nokia, Cisco.	GE, Tata, Zara, IBM

competitiveness of these advantages means that expanding to foreign markets incurs moderate operational costs (the expenses of product extension and oversight) yet earns high profits (the yield of international leverage). The international strategy, relative to the multidomestic, global, and transnational options, is particularly straightforward. These benefits make it usually the first strategy adopted when firms venture abroad.

An international strategy fits an MNE that (1) has a core competency that foreign rivals lack and (2) does not face strong demands for global integration or local responsiveness.

Limitations of the International Strategy Headquarters' one-way view from the home office to the rest of the world may misread opportunities and threats in foreign markets. Applying the firm's core competency, as prescribed by headquarters, constrains local responsiveness. Initially, this inflexibility does not impose a high cost. But as the firm gains greater success in overseas markets and aims to expand its operations, perspectives anchored in the international strategy can misinterpret local circumstances. Moreover, the strategy may sustain superior competitiveness as long as foreign rivals scramble futilely. Companies in many foreign markets, especially those in emerging economies, are reinventing systems of production and distribution, experimenting with new business models, and resetting the standards of innovation. An unexpectedly enterprising competitor may disrupt industry structure. Google, for example, faces increasingly adept local rivals in South Korea and China—Naver and Baidu, respectively—whose native sensitivities to local search tendencies strongly position them in fast-growing Asian markets.[106]

MULTIDOMESTIC STRATEGY

Some MNE faces high pressure for local responsiveness and a low need to reduce costs via global integration (the lower right quadrant of the IR Grid). In these industries, unique local cultural, legal-political, and economic conditions spur the MNE to adapt value activities. This approach represents the **multidomestic strategy**. Value-chain design follows the lead of foreign operations, not the home office's direction. That is, the company's subsidiaries in their respective local markets design, make, and market products that respond to local preferences. So the managers of, say, a backpack factory in Singapore decide the size, shape, and style of product to make given their understanding that local customers see greater appeal in their preferred design—even if their choices differ from those made by fellow operations in Turkey, Kenya, and Colombia.[107]

The multidomestic strategy adjusts value activities to local circumstances.

Johnson & Johnson (J&J) exemplifies this strategy. Company leaders reason that inalienable differences among countries preclude universal direction from one. Optimizing performance calls for allowing its 250 business units worldwide to behave like small, innovative, entrepreneurial firms, configuring and coordinating key activities to meet local imperatives.[108] Headquarters' role, in turn, is to do what it does best—configure and coordinate global activities that support local units leveraging the company's research, executive, financial, marketing, and logistic resources.

Benefits of the Multidomestic Strategy The multidomestic strategy superbly speaks to the unique features of consumer preferences, market tendencies, and institutional expectations found in national markets. Localizing value activities also helps the MNE reduce political risk given its company's local standing, lower exchange-rate risks given less need to repatriate funds, and translate local performance into national prominence. The strategy also gives the MNE a distinctive advantage against local competitors who lack the benefits provided by the parent's global operations. Industries of the sort found in the lower right corner of the IR Grid, such as clothing, food, and retail banking, typically have local companies that only operate nationally. The multidomestic strategy enables MNEs, such as McDonald's Nestlé, or HSBC, to build superior competitive positions in local markets on the strength of their global advantages.

The multidomestic strategy, by encouraging operational overlap, increases overhead expenses.

Limitations of the Multidomestic Strategy This strategy requires replicating value activities from subsidiary to subsidiary. Essentially, the MNE operates"mini-me"units around the world. Customizing a product or process to a particular market situation increases costs along the value chain. Different product designs require different materials, smaller markets make for shorter production runs, different channel structures call for dissimilar distribution formats, and divergent technology platforms complicate information exchange. Hence, the multidomestic strategy is impractical in cost-sensitive situations. Carrefour, for instance, found difficulties in the United States when, to deal with local preferences, it shifted from its successful international strategy to a multidomestic approach. Costly problems ultimately forced Carrefour to close its failing U.S. operations. Similar troubles hit Tesco, the British supermarket MNE. After six years of struggling to understand American consumer behavior, Tesco surrendered. It announced its withdrawal from the United States at a direct cost of $1.8 billion, atop of the many hundreds of millions it had already spent trying to respond to the local marketplace.[109]

The multidomestic MNE often faces coordination complications. Local adaptation promotes management styles and value-chain designs that differ from unit to unit. Allocating authority to local decision makers can, over time, create powerful subsidiaries. On any given configuration or coordination matter, they may opt not to follow headquarters' policy, instead maintaining that their situation warrants a different approach. If the subsidiary is a virtual stand-alone operation, as often happens in the multidomestic strategy, headquarters must resort to persuasion in lieu of command. The difficulty of this task escalates as the number of subsidiaries rises. Ensuing power struggles blunt the MNE's competitiveness. For instance, J&J launched Tylenol in 1960 as an over-the-counter pain reliever in the United States. The product was available to foreign units shortly thereafter. The quasi-independent Japanese unit, despite duress from headquarters, did not begin selling it until 2000.

GLOBAL STRATEGY

The **global strategy** drives worldwide performance by making and selling common products that vary little from country to country. Effectively, managers face high pressures for global integration yet low pressures for local responsiveness. Industries of this sort are found in the upper left quadrant of the IR Grid. MNEs in this situation implement absolute production and marketing standards to achieve the maximum efficiency gains of global integration.

A global strategy champions worldwide standardization of value activities.

The global strategy pushes companies to create products for a world market, manufacturing them on a global scale in a few highly efficient plants, and marketing them through a few focused distribution channels. It requires that MNEs aggressively exploit location economies to maximize the scale effects of making a standardized product for a global market segment; using resources for anything other than improving efficiency erodes competitiveness. Likewise, the strategy calls for selling globally standardized products that require little to no local adaptation. Hence, the global strategy sees the world as a single market.

The so-called China Price phenomenon profiles the stakes of the global strategy.[110] The China Price refers to situations in which Chinese firms make something for significantly less than can be done in Western countries. In the extreme case, it means Chinese rivals sell products for less than the cost of materials in the West. Many Chinese companies apply the China Price approach within the context of the global strategy. Rival MNEs implementing a global strategy must ingeniously configure and coordinate value activities. If not, the alternative is dire.[111]

For some products, notably commodities, the global strategy is essentially the only option. Commodities serve a universal need (think gasoline, steel, aspirin, memory chips, sugar, and so on). Consumer preferences in different countries, if not identical, are highly similar. Choosing between essentially identical products (i.e., Company X gasoline versus Company Y gasoline) makes price a key point of competitiveness.

The global strategy is not restricted to commodity markets. Market globalization encourages companies like Hennes & Mauritz (H&M) in apparel or LVMH in luxury goods to standardize historically differentiated products, manufacture them on a global scale, and market them through focused distribution channels. Unquestionably, cross-national differences in consumer preferences exist. The global strategy, however, assumes that there are no differences among countries with regard to consumer preferences or, if there are, that consumers will willingly sacrifice them to buy a high-quality, low-priced substitute. Ultimately, consumers' disposition to discount nationalism girds the global strategy.

Firms that choose the global strategy face strong pressure for cost reductions but weak pressure for local responsiveness.

The efficiency standards of the global strategy push the MNE to achieve cost leadership in its industry; if not the leader, then it must be competitive with the industry's pacesetter. Cost leadership has stark implications to value chain design. Units operate only in superior locations that support maximizing the efficiency of global scale production—e.g., a shoe factory in Vietnam, an auto-parts maker in China, a service call center in India. Value activities need not be in the same country; a fully optimized global value chain will locate an activity in the best possible place. IBM, for instance, supports its Asian value chain with HR specialists in Manila, accounts receivable experts in Shanghai, accountants in Kuala Lumpur, and procurement officers in Shenzhen.[112] Once configured, headquarters coordinates activities by standardizing practices and processes.

Benefits of the Global Strategy The supreme advantage of the global strategy is leveraging economies of scale. Configuring and coordinating activities to capture scale effects drives the global efficiencies needed to compete with like-minded rivals and to convince consumers to forsake national preference for global products. The global strategy also benefits from the ongoing integration of global markets. Institutional developments progressively reduce the trade frictions and investment restrictions that had historically constrained location economics. Now, MNEs have tremendous flexibility to move anything, anywhere in the pursuit of maximizing efficiency; the globalization of markets, quite simply, expands opportunities for integration. Lastly, the global strategy clarifies decision-making. Single-minded focus on improving efficiency imposes an absolute logic on strategic analysis: when push comes to shove, global integration trumps local differentiation.

Limitations of the Global Strategy The cost-sensitivity of a global strategy leaves MNEs little latitude to adapt value activities to local conditions. Hence, the MNE's success is a function of the validity of the one-size-fits-all approach. Similarly, making a single bet on a single approach for a single global market is operationally risky. Change of all sorts, as we have seen throughout our text, is an intrinsic feature of international business. A disruptive innovation turns the single-minded focus of a globally tuned value chain into a maladapted delusion. The fallout of the global financial crisis, for example, saw big banks such as Citibank, Royal Bank of Scotland, and Fortis foiled by their previously high-performance global strategies. Despite leadership in global capital markets, the disruptive change of the crisis and ensuing demand for local responsiveness turned many of their strengths into liabilities.

TRANSNATIONAL STRATEGY

Today's environment of interconnected consumers, industries, and markets requires that an MNE, of the sort we see in the upper right quadrant of the IR Grid, configure a different type of value chain. It must exploit location economies while also applying coordination methods that leverage core competencies and, throughout it all, reconcile a complex mix of global and local pressures. Managing this feat enables the MNE to implement a **transnational strategy**, thereby differentiating capabilities and contributions from country to country, finding ways to learn systematically from its various environments, and diffusing this knowledge throughout its global operations.

The transnational strategy reconciles global integration and local responsiveness in ways that leverage the MNE's core competency throughout worldwide operations.

The transnational strategy requires a sophisticated value chain that simultaneously implements integration, responsiveness, and learning. It configures its value activities, subject to satisfying minimum efficiency standards, from country to country given prevailing cultural, political, legal, and economic conditions. But, in a critical break from the multidomestic strategy, the transnational strategy champions the cause of interactive "global learning." It uses its insights to upgrade its core competencies and then determinedly spreads its proprietary innovations worldwide. Rather than top-down (headquarters to a foreign subsidiary) or bottom-up (foreign subsidiary to the headquarters) coordination, the transnational strategy promotes knowledge flows from idea generators to idea adopters, no matter where one or the other resides. Headquarters applies systems to motivate communication and collaboration.

Transnational Strategy: A Case in Point Some question the feasibility of the transnational strategy. But the record of GE affirms its practicality. In the 1980s, growing threats from low-cost competitors in Asia pushed GE to look to global markets to sell products. Managers reasoned that expanding sales globally would boost scale economies. At the time, CEO Jack Welch declared, "the idea of a company being global is nonsense. Businesses are global,

The transnational strategy endorses the efficiency of global integration, the effectiveness of local responsiveness, and the systematic diffusion of innovations.

not companies."[113] As such, divisions, no matter where located, were held to a straightforward performance standard: "be either number 1 or 2" in its domestic industry or else face divestment.

In the late 1980s, GE's sense of globalization moved from finding new markets to finding new worldwide sources that supplied higher-quality inputs at lower cost. As integration efforts increasingly linked national markets, GE redefined its outlook toward globalization, elevating it to a dominant strategic theme. Commensurately, Welch raised the performance standard for each business unit from its position in its domestic to its global industry.

Around this time, Welch articulated his vision of the *boundaryless company,* namely, an "open, anti-parochial environment, friendly toward the seeking and sharing of new ideas, regardless of their origins" (suggestive of the transnational organization). He explained that the "boundaryless company we envision will remove the barriers among engineering, manufacturing, marketing, sales, and customer service; it will recognize no distinctions between domestic and foreign operations—we'll be as comfortable doing business in Budapest and Seoul as we are in Louisville and Schenectady."[114]

Success stories emerged along GE's value chain: increased efficiency in its appliance business, productivity breakthroughs in lighting, improved transaction effectiveness in GE capital, cost reductions in aircraft engines, and better global account management in plastics. Lessons learned spread to other GE businesses. Indeed, careers ended if managers refused to share ideas with others; as Welch explained, "We take people who aren't boundaryless out of jobs. If you're turf-oriented, self-centered, don't share with people, and aren't searching for ideas, you don't belong here." Soon thereafter, GE began phase three of its globalization evolution. Besides emphasizing global markets and global sources, Welch pushed managers to "globalize the intellect of the company," seeking best practices from anyone, anywhere, and spreading them throughout GE's global operations.[115]

By 1999, at the end of Welch's tenure, GE was named the most respected company in the world by the *Financial Times,* and Jack Welch was judged the CEO of the twentieth century. His successor, Jeffrey Immelt, continues these efforts, explaining that success in international business is "truly about people, not about where the buildings are. You've got to develop people so they are prepared for leadership jobs and then promote. That's the most effective way to become more global."[116]

GE's performance speaks to the key principle of the transnational strategy: the mindset of global learning that uses best practices to set configuration and coordination. Ideas, constantly tested, enhanced, and exchanged across units, improve the value chain. As managers translated ideas into better designs, production methods, and business processes, they made more profitable decisions. Ultimately, integration happened more efficiently, responsiveness happened more effectively, and innovations spread more systematically.

The transnational strategy encourages sophisticated coordination methods in order to diffuse the lessons learned at one unit to other units.

Benefits of the Transnational Strategy The learning principle of the transnational strategy reconciles the dual imperatives of global integration and local responsiveness. The vitality of learning enables managers to respond to changing environments, reorienting activities without imposing additional bureaucracy. Ultimately, these capabilities support standardizing activities to generate global efficiencies without overly discounting the demands of responsiveness.

The transnational strategy, admittedly difficult to specify in theory, is difficult to implement in practice. Limitations arise from complicated agendas, high costs, and cognitive limits.

Limitations of the Transnational Strategy The transnational strategy is difficult to configure, tough to coordinate, and prone to shortfalls. Reconciling integration and responsiveness pressures, further complicated by the mission to upgrade knowledge worldwide, can overwhelm the best-intentioned MNEs. For every GE, there are ABBs, Philips, Panasonics, and Acers that struggled to engage the strategy. Furthermore, developing a network mindset among employees, installing the requisite communication network, and navigating the ambiguity of multi-criteria decision making is expensive. Such costs are especially burdensome when slowing economies call for streamlining activities.

The Mobile Money Revolution: A Look at Safaricom's M-Pesa[117]

The diffusion of work and technology from established countries to emerging markets changes the game of globalization. Companies throughout the world respond in kind, rethinking their strategies and resetting their value chains. Many increasingly find that the improving sophistication of information systems and supply-chain logistics supports radical change. New frontiers have opened for products (solar cell panels manufactured in Shanghai but sold in Stockholm) as well as previously non-tradable services (X-rays taken in Boston, but interpreted in Bangkok). The changing standards for configuring and coordinating value activities, both by companies in established markets as well as their counterparts in emerging economies, spur executives to question how they interpret strategy and manage value chains.

Big Changes Here, There, and Everywhere

Accelerating a century-long trend, IBM continues redefining how it creates value. IBM is reconfiguring activities to support a "globally integrated enterprise" that places people, jobs, and investments anywhere in the world "based on the right cost, the right skills and the right business environment." Operationally, IBM does cutting-edge research and development, compiles next generation software, and runs call centers in locations that a decade earlier were far removed from the global economy.

Others point to like-minded trendsetters. Li & Fung, an MNE few have heard about yet, is a key player in the global apparel industry. It directs logistics for many high-profile storefronts such as Macy's, Khol's, or Nordstrom. Headquartered in Hong Kong, Li & Fung owns no sewing machines, employs no tailors, makes no buttons, zippers, or hooks, and owns not a single clothing factory. Rather, it owns the knowledge to organize a specialized network of more than 15,000 apparel manufacturers spread across 60-plus countries. From Hong Kong, Li & Fung's global apparel hyperarchy commands tremendous purchasing power, market knowledge, and competitiveness.

Mobile money is transforming the design and delivery of banking in developing countries, while empowering those at the bottom of the pyramid with its revolutionary reach and benefits.

Source: © Idprod - Fotolia.com

Others go to even more extreme measures, playing up the interaction of technological trends and creative disruptions to organize pioneering value chains. For example, AirTel, the Indian market leader in mobile telephony, and Safaricom, the market leader in Kenya, charge some of the lowest prices in the world for nationwide calls, yet generate growing profits. More significantly, Safaricom is revolutionizing mobile payments through M-Pesa (M for mobile, Pesa is Swahili for money). This system effectively moves historically disenfranchised people from rudimentary barter systems to state-of-the-art financial practices. In doing so, M-Pesa, along with similar sorts of mobile payments in other countries, catapults people worldwide into increasingly sophisticated financial systems. Let's take a closer look at market trends and industry conditions in the brave new world of mobile money.

Market Trends

Mobile money, also referred to as mobile payments, mobile money transfer, and mobile wallet, refers to payment services performed via a mobile device such as a smartphone. Earlier, one relied on old-school mediums such as cash, checks, or credit cards. Now, a connected consumer uses a cellular device, for which there are nearly 7 billion mobile cellular subscriptions worldwide, to deposit and withdraw money, transfer money to other users and non-users, settle bills, and pay for all sorts of services as well as digital or hard goods. It has for long been predicted that mobile banking technologies will replace paper and plastic currencies. The technologies enabling mobile money are increasingly available and progressively affordable.

Anchoring estimates of mobile payments' potential is the sense that whatever technology touches, it transforms. Already, the Internet has proven to be the most powerful force for globalization, democratization, economic growth, and education, to name just a few, in the history of humanity. So too, industry watchers noted, the Internet steadily reset the idea and use of money. Evidence that ongoing innovations spark dramatic change in how people conduct financial transactions suggested to some that, "If cash is king, then the king is dead."

Not surprisingly, mobile money has grown by leaps and bounds. Worldwide mobile payment transaction values were about $235 billion in 2013, a 120 percent jump from 2011's $106 billion. The number of mobile payment users hit 245 million in 2013, up from 160 million in 2011. Forecasts saw global mobile transaction volumes averaging 35 percent plus annual growth through 2017. At that point it was pegged that nearly 450 million worldwide users would drive total transaction value past $725 billion.

Beyond that, the scale and scope of mobile money could only be left to the imagination. Safe, secure, and an efficient means of storing and transferring money, especially involving micro-payments, holds universal appeal. The growing ease with which it enables people to collect payments from customers, buy goods, pay for services, and send money to family and friends, fuels tremendous optimism.

Expectedly, mobile money gains momentum worldwide. Perhaps most dramatically, it is transforming the design and delivery of banking in developing countries. Historically, these countries suffered infrastructure shortfalls that limited their citizens' ability to access basic services. Indeed, estimates of the so-called "unbanked" or "underbanked" portion of the world routinely includes nearly half of the world's adult population.

Moreover, the particular needs of the billions of people who populate the "Base Of The Pyramid" market drives increasing ingenuity. In countries throughout Africa and South Asia, for example, users buy bus and railway tickets through a mobile payment service. Earlier, people often faced long journeys to the station, always running the risk of not securing a seat upon arrival, given non-existent reservation systems and tickets typically in short supply. Now, they conveniently secure tickets via mobile payment systems before traveling to the station. Longer term market trends signalled the potent intersection of mobile money, mobile health, and mobile agriculture solutions.

Industry Structure

Money and its many applications through financial services, is a universal feature of our lives. However, the industry structure that supports it varies from country to country. In absolute terms, key moderators include local physical infrastructure, such as branch/ATM networks, sophistication of the buyers and sellers of financial services, and the effectiveness of regulatory institutions. The interplay among these dimensions, as well as others, directly shapes the structure of an industry and the conduct of companies within it.

In wealthier developed countries, extensive access, diverse options, high sophistication, and far-reaching regulations make for a different industry context than typically found in poorer developing countries. For example, in places such as Denmark, Japan, Germany, and Sweden, virtually all adults report having a formal bank account.

The opposite is true elsewhere. In several African countries, such as the Democratic Republic of Congo, Guinea, and Niger, less than 5 percent of the adult population reports owning a bank account. Consequently, the vast majority of people in developed countries, have little need for mobile money—correspondingly, its use is trivial there.

In contrast, the World Bank, Gates Foundation, and Gallup World Poll studied how adults in 148 economies save, borrow, and make payments. They found 20 countries in which more than 10 percent of the adult population say they used mobile money. Of those, 15 are African. The standout success story has been Sub-Saharan Africa, particularly Kenya, Sudan and Gabon, where half or more of the adult population uses mobile money.

The use of mobile money in developing markets differs dramatically from developed markets. First, mobile money can operate outside the structure of the formal financial sector. For example, in Somalia, a country that mightily struggles to sustain a legitimate government, a third of adults used mobile money in 2012. More generally, more than a third of mobile money users in the 10 economies with the highest reported use of mobile payments are not part of the formal financial system. Operating beyond the purview of regulatory agencies and authorities reduces barriers to entry and mobility in the mobile payment industry.

Second, mobile money is a powerful substitute for conventional alternatives. M-Pesa, for example, is the mobile-phone based money transfer and microfinancing service run by Kenya-based Safaricom. Many regard M-Pesa as the best performing mobile payment system in the world. It enables users with a national ID card or passport to deposit, withdraw, and transfer money through a mobile device via a network of agents; the latter are extraordinarily diverse, with some operating out of a makeshift street stall, others running from a small retail outlet, but all functioning as de facto banks. M-Pesa, by enabling people who cannot visit a branch or ATM to access an expanding range of financial services, encourages the idea of branchless banking and endorses its disruptive implications to the historic structure of financial services.

In Kenya, for example, M-PESA is the default bank account and debit card—more than 90 percent of Kenya's 19 million adults have an M-Pesa account and nearly 70 percent regularly use mobile money. Consequently, the cash equivalent of about one-third of Kenya's GDP passes through the circuits of M-Pesa. Safaricom charges users a small fee for each transaction. Safaricom is a mobile network operator. It is neither registered as a deposit-taking institution nor, put differently, a bank. In 2008, a group of traditional Kenyan banks lobbied the Kenyan finance minister to audit M-Pesa, in an effort to slow, if not stop, it. Instead, the ploy backfired as the audit confirmed M-Pesa's robustness. Still, the growing use of mobile money attracts increasing government attention; concern about potential criminality calls for vigilant regulators.

Looking Forward

One sees similar market industry trends elsewhere. Since 2009, there have been more than 100 mobile-money deployments in emerging markets; nearly 90 percent of them began operating as recently as three years ago: M-Paisa (the paisa being the largely unused subunit of the Indian rupee) underway in India. Likewise, as we observe the moves of MTN Uganda, Vodacom Tanzania, FNB in South Africa, and GCASH and Smart Money in the Philippines to mobilize money, we find that despite this newfound ubiquity of mobile money in emerging markets, it is hard to ignore the fact that more than half the world's adults do not use basic—to say nothing of sophisticated—financial services. To top that, more than a billion people in emerging and developing markets have cellphones, but no formal bank accounts.

QUESTIONS

12-3. Dynamism creates opportunity as well as constraints. Identify the most promising opportunities as well as constraints for mobile money service providers in developed markets. Then, do the same for firms in developing markets. How are they similar? How do they differ?

12-4. Looking out over the next decade, forecast the likely standards of value creation in the mobile money industry. How would you advise a company like Deutsche Bank or Visa to configure and coordinate its value chain to prosper in this environment? Would you advise the same to companies like IBM, Google, or Safaricom?

12-5. What sort of executive perspectives do you see as critical to identify and understand the opportunity of mobile money in emerging markets? Will the same set apply to executives working in established countries?

12-6. In the long run, do you anticipate a few global players applying an integrated strategy across multi-markets or many national companies emphasizing local adaptation to create more value in the mobile money industry? Identify technology trends, business practices, and regulatory conditions that support your choice.

SUMMARY

- Managers devise strategies to engage international markets in ways that that fortify their companies' competiveness, boost their profitability, and sustain their growth.
- Industry structure influences a company's profitability, especially in situations of perfect competition, less in situations of imperfect competition.
- Bright managers convert innovative strategies into above-average, risk-adjusted profitability, especially in situations of imperfect competition, less in situations of perfect competition.
- Managers anchor analysis of industry structure in the context of the five-forces model and its representation of competitive rivalry, threat of new entrants, substitutes, supplier power, and buyer power.
- Competitive rivalry refers to the moves of rivals battling for market share. Threat of new entrants refers to entry of new rivals seeking market share. A substitute refers to a complementary product that gives the consumer an appealing alternative. Supplier power refers to the push by input suppliers to charge more for the product. Buyer power is the push by output buyers to pay less for the product.
- Value measures a firm's ability to sell what it makes for more than the cost incurred to make it.
- MNEs create value through a cost leadership or a differentiation strategy. The former drives a firm to reduce its costs, for a given level of quality, below its competitors. The latter drives a firm it to increase the perceived value of its products relative to that of rivals.
- The value chain lets managers deconstruct the general idea of "create value" into a series of discrete, sequential activities.
- Managers configure value activities to reflect location economics; factors that moderate it include cluster effects, logistics, digitization, robotics, scale economies, and business environments. Importantly, as location economics change, so too do configuration choices.
- Managers coordinate value activities to reflect core competencies, operational obstacles, and subsidiary networks.
- Global integration aims to standardize worldwide activities in order to maximize efficiency whereas national responsiveness adapts local activities in order to optimize effectiveness.
- Drivers of globalization include the integration of national markets and the efficiency gains of standardization.
- Drivers of local responsiveness include cross-national consumer divergences and host-government intervention.

- The higher the pressure for global integration, the greater the need to concentrate configuration and standardize coordination.
- The higher the pressure for local responsiveness, the greater the need to disperse configuration and adapt coordination.
- The firm entering and competing in foreign markets can adopt an international, multidomestic, global, or transnational strategy.
- An international strategy transfers core competencies to foreign markets where local rivals lack an alternative and industry conditions impose low pressures for global integration and national responsiveness.
- A multidomestic strategy emphasizes locally adapting processes and products to the unique circumstances in a country's market.
- A global strategy drives performance by making standardized products that are marketed with minimum adaptation to local conditions.
- A transnational strategy simultaneously leverages core competencies worldwide, reduces costs by exploiting location economics, and adapts, mindful of efficiency standards, to local conditions.
- The company implementing a transnational strategy aims not to work harder or work smarter than competitors but rather work differently based on diffusing the lessons it has learned and the knowledge it has earned throughout its worldwide operations.

KEY TERMS

cluster effect (p. 491)
concentrated configuration (p. 489)
configuration (p. 489)
coordination (p. 498)
core competency (p. 499)
cost leadership (p. 486)
differentiation (p. 486)
digitization (p. 496)
dispersed configuration (p. 489)
economies of scale (p. 492)
five-forces model (p. 482)
global integration (p. 503)
global strategy (p. 512)
great by choice (p. 484)
industry organization (IO) paradigm (p. 484)
industry structure (p. 482)
Integration-Responsiveness (IR) Grid (p. 507)
international strategy (p. 509)
local responsiveness (p. 503)
location economies (p. 489)
logistics (p. 496)
multidomestic strategy (p. 511)
primary activities (p. 488)
strategy (p. 485)
support activities (p. 489)
transnational strategy (p. 513)
value (p. 485)
value chain (p. 488)

ENDNOTES

1 ***Sources include the following:*** A. Bonnin,"The Fashion Industry in Galicia: Understanding the 'Zara' Phenomenon," *European Planning Studies* 10 (2002): 519; "Inditex: The Future of Fast Fashion" *The Economist,* retrieved May 31, 2011, from www.economist.com/node/4086117?story_id=4086117; "The Stars of Europe—Armancio Ortega, Chairman, Inditex," *Businessweek,* (June 11, 2001): 65; Richard Heller, "Galician Beauty," *Forbes* (May 28, 2001): 28; Rachel Tiplady, "Zara: Taking the Lead in Fast-Fashion," *Businessweek* (June 4, 2006): 19; "Shining Examples," *The Economist* (June 15, 2006): 54; "Zara Grows as Retail Rivals Struggle," *Wall Street Journal* (March 26, 2009): C1; "Zara, the Lead in Fast Fashion," *Fashion Muse,* retrieved May 31, 2011, from www.fashionmuse.com/women-fashion/zara-lead-fast-fashion; Lauren Cochrane," The Winning and Losing Brands In Fashion Right Now," *The Guardian,* (September, 21, 2012).

2 "The Fashion Industry in Galicia: Understanding the 'Zara' Phenomenon," *European Planning Studies* 10 (2002).

3 Vivienne Walt, "Meet Amancio Ortega: The Third-richest Man in the World," *Fortune* (January 14, 2013): 56–59.

4 "The Stars of Europe—Armancio Ortega, Chairman, Inditex," *Businessweek,* (June 11, 2001): 65.

5 Ibid, Pankaj Ghemawat and Jose Luis Nueno; Also, another analyst added, "When you went to Gucci or Chanel in October, you knew the chances were good that clothes would still be there in February." Adds another manager, "With Zara, you know that if you don't buy it, right then and there, within 11 days the entire stock will change. You buy it now or never. And because the prices are so low, you buy it now." Suzy Hansen, "How Zara Grew into the World's Largest Fashion Retailer," *New York Times,* (November 9, 2012).

6 Patrick Byrne, "Closing the Gap between Strategy and Results," *Logistics Management* (March 2004): 13.

7 "Fashion for the Masses: Global Stretch," *The Economist* (March 10, 2011): 88.

8 R. Carruthers, "Rapid Response Retail," *Marketing* (April 3, 2003): 43.

9 Michael Porter, *Competitive Advantage* (New York: Free Press, 1985).

10 Research reports that industry effects explain 75 percent of the difference in average returns for companies in an industry. Jens Boyd, "Intra-Industry Structure and Performance: Strategic Groups and Strategic Blocks in the Worldwide Airline Industry," *European Management Review* 1 (2004): 132–45; Schmalensee, "Do Markets Differ Much?" *American Economic Review* 75: 3 (1985): 341–51.

11 Clayton Christensen, *The Innovator's Solution: Creating and Sustaining Successful Growth,* Harvard Business Press, (2003).

12 Joseph Bower and Clayton Christensen, "Disruptive Technologies: Catching the Wave" *Harvard Business Review* (January–February 1995).

13 Ashlee Vance and Matt Richtel, "Light and Cheap, Netbooks Are Poised to Reshape PC Industry," *New York Times* (April 1, 2009): C1.

14 Chad Brooks, "PC Is Dead. Cloud Computing, Mobile Devices Taking Over," CSMonitor.com, retrieved June 9, 2011, from www.csmonitor.com/Business/Latest-News-Wires/2011/0608/PC-is-dead.-Cloud-computing-mobile-devices-taking-over; Nick Wingfield, "PC Sales Still in a Slump, Despite New Offerings," *New York Times* (April 10, 2013): A1.

15 "A Special Report on Innovation in Emerging Markets: The World Turned Upside Down," *The Economist,* retrieved May 2, 2011, from www.economist.com/node/15879369.

16 Consider that two of the five top-rated business environments in summer 2008—Ireland and the United Kingdom—were seeing shaky financial markets, spiraling unemployment, collapsing currencies, and shaken consumer confidence by that winter. By mid-2009, similar, albeit less drastic, trends were evident in the United States, Taiwan, Japan, Spain, France, Germany, and Australia. By 2010 and onward, escalating political economic tension in Greece, Spain, and elsewhere severely disrupted market routines; See Jack Gage, "The Best Countries for Business," *Forbes* (June 26, 2008): 55.

17 Martin Dewhurst, Jonathan Harris, and Suzanne Heywood, "The Global Company's Challenge," *McKinsey Quarterly*, retrieved December 31, 2012, from www.mckinseyquarterly.com/The_global_companys_challenge_2979.

18 Jim Collins, "Good to Great," retrieved April 26, 2011, from www.jim-collins.com/article_topics/articles/good-to-great.html

19 In general, the higher the risk, the higher the return. Therefore, riskier projects and investments must be evaluated differently from their riskless counterparts. By discounting risky cash flows against less-risky cash flows, risk-adjusted rates account for changes in the profile of the investment.

20 See B. Wernerfelt, "A Resource-Based View of the Firm," *Strategic Management Journal* (1984): 171–80; In addition, Rumelt found that corporate-parent effects contributed to the variance in firm performance; Richard Rumelt, "How Much Does Industry Matter?" *Strategic Management Journal* (1985): 167–86; McGahan and Porter (2002) found similar evidence of corporate-parent effects: see "What Do We Know about Variance in Accounting Profitability?" *Management Science* (2002): 834–51.

21 See Wyn Jenkins, "Competing in Times of Evolution and Revolution: An Essay on Long-Term Firm Survival," *Management Decisions* 43 (January 1, 2005): 26; Belen Villalonga, "Intangible Resources, Tobin's Q, and Sustainability of Performance Differences," *Journal of Economic Behavior & Organization* 54 (June 2004): 205. Determining whether a money manager outperforms a market index relies on separating the returns available from market movements (*beta* in the jargon) and managerial skill (*alpha*). Like great product managers, great money managers find innovative ways to earn in excess of what would be predicted by an equilibrium model like the *capital asset pricing model* (CAPM). More specifically, we can compare the performance of investment managers by allowing for portfolio risk with the so-called Jensen index, also called Alpha. This measure uses the CAPM as its basis for determining whether a money manager outperformed a market index. The sum of the outperformance is known as alpha.

22 The idea of value can be defined in a variety of ways, including but by no means limited, to economic, market, pro forma, social, book, insurance, use, par, or replacement. We can also define value from different perspectives, such as those of customers, employees, stakeholders, or shareholders.

23 "Special Report: The China Price," *Businessweek* (December 6, 2004), retrieved June 25, 2005, from www.businessweek.com/magazine/content/04_49/b3911401.htm.

24 Keith Bradsher, "China's High-Quality Pearls Enter the Mass Market," NYTimes.com, retrieved August 16, 2011 from www.nytimes.com/2011/08/02/business/global/chinas-high-quality-pearls-enter-the-mass-market.html. For example, a strand of perfectly round, blemish-free, half-inch pearls from China ran $1,800 whereas the same sort from Tahiti, although displaying a richer luster, cost $14,000.

25 Oded Shenkar, *The Chinese Century: The Rising Chinese Economy and Its Impact on the Global Economy, the Balance of Power, and Your Job* (Upper Saddle River, NJ: Pearson Prentice Hall, 2006).

26 Personal Conversation, Daniel Sullivan and Peter Leung, Director Nalco China, Beijing, March 1, 2011.

27 Similarly, Sony began selling its first netbook computer in the fall of 2009, finally entering the only sector of the PC market then showing significant growth.[27] Its netbook used the same processor found in competing products and, like other netbooks, had a 10-inch screen. However, its display resolution was 1,366 × 768 pixels rather than the standard 1,024 × 600 pixels, meaning that more of a website would fit onto the screen. For scrolling, Sony's machine provided a touch panel of the same size as the larger one found on laptops. Hence, Sony used the higher resolution and larger touch pad as key differentiators between its product and competing netbooks. Granted, improving screen resolution or touchpad size are not revolutionary design innovations. However, they supported Sony's claim that its products are different, better, and therefore justifiably more expensive than those offered by rivals.

28 Interestingly, a 150 pound bag of coffee beans might earn a farmer approximately $50. The "street value" of that same bag, once processed into approximately 10,000 cups of coffee and depending upon the particular outlet, is anywhere between $10,000 to $40,000.

29 Vikas Bajaj, "Starbucks Opens in India With Pomp and Tempered Ambition," *New York Times* (October 19, 2012); Anita Sharan, "Starbucks Come Lately," *Hindustan Times*," (January 5, 2013).

30 "The Starbucks Index—Coffee Price Parity," *Zero Hedge*, retrieved March 4, 2013 from www.zerohedge.com/news/2013-02-27/starbucks-index-coffee-price-parity.

31 Neha Thirani, "Starbucks makes long-awaited India entry in South Mumbai," *New York Times* (September 28, 2012).

32 "Hungry Tiger, Dancing Elephant: How India Is Changing IBM's World," *The Economist* (April 4, 2007): 58–61.

33 Michael Porter, "What Is Strategy?" *Harvard Business Review* (November–December 1996): 61–79.

34 Managers may make decisions that they strongly reason support the firm's strategy but, in actuality, more often do not support it. Challenges emerge because often few managers understand the full demands of the company's strategy and its implications for international operations. More worrisome, managers are far more likely to make the wrong than right decision. See Dan Lovallo and Daniel Kahneman, "Delusions of Success: How Optimism Undermines Executives' Decisions," *Harvard Business Review* (July 2003): 56.

35 Michael Porter, "Competition in Global Industries: A Conceptual Framework," in M. Porter (ed.), *Competition in Global Industries*, (Boston: Harvard Business School Press, 1986).

36 Janet C. Lowe, *Welch: An American Icon* (New York: Wiley and Sons, 2002).

37 Shenkar, *The Chinese Century*, 16.

38 Keith Bradsher, "Solar Panel Maker Moves Work to China," NYTimes.com, retrieved March 9, 2011 from www.nytimes.com/2011/01/15/business/energy-environment/15solar.html?pagewanted=2&_r=1&hpw.

39 Personal Conversation, Daniel Sullivan and Peter Leung, Director Nalco China, Beijing, March 1, 2011.

40 Kurt Badenhausen, "Best Countries for Business," Forbes.com, retrieved March 10, 2011, from www.forbes.com/lists/2010/6/best-countries-10_Best-Countries-for-Business_Rank.html.

41 Christine Greenhalgh and Mark Rogers, *Innovation, Intellectual Property, and Economic Growth* (Princeton: Princeton University Press, 2010).

42 Jerome Glenn, Theodore Gordon, and Elizabeth Florescu, "2009 State of the Future." The Millennium Project defines singularity as the "time in which technological change is so fast and significant that we today are incapable of conceiving what life might be like beyond the year 2025," (p. 22), from www.millennium-project.org/millennium/sof2009.html.

43 "Futurology: The New Overlords," *The Economist* (May 12, 2011): 98.

44 Soumitra Dutta and Simon Caulki, "The World's Top Innovators," *The World Business/INSEAD Global Innovation Index* (2007), retrieved June 18, 2007, from www.worldbusinesslive.com/article/625441/the-worlds-topinnovators.

45 "Global Innovation Index, 2012," retrieved January 7, 2013 from www.globalinnovationindex.org/gii/.

46 Ibid.

47 See the Cluster Profiles Project of the Institute for Strategy and Competitiveness at Harvard Business School, data.isc.hbs.edu/cp/index.jsp.

48 "Free Exchange: Concrete Gains," *The Economist* (October 13, 2012): 90.

49 Peter Marsh, *The New Industrial Revolution: Consumers, Globalisation and the End of Mass Production,* Yale University Press, 2012.

50 See Arindam Bhattacharya et al., *Capturing Global Advantage: How Leading Industrial Companies Are Transforming Their Industries by Sourcing and Selling in China, India, and Other Low-Cost Countries* (Boston: Boston Consulting Group Publications, April 9, 2004), esp. Exhibit 7.

51 "Salary threshold for living comfortably in big cities," *People's Daily Online,* retrieved January 7, 2013 from english.peopledaily.com.cn/90882/7986614.html; Currency conversions made Jan 7, 2012, rate of ¥6.23 to $1; Monthly wage rate for New York City calculated at $7.25 per hour for 160-hour work month, "Minimum Wages," *New York State Department of Labor,* retrieved January 7, 2013, www.labor.state.ny.us/workerprotection/laborstandards/workprot/minwage.shtm); Paul Krugman, "Divided over Trade," *New York Times* (May 14, 2007): A18; "Most of China Raises Minimum Wage," China.org.cn, retrieved March 11, 2011, from www.china.org.cn/business/2010-08/19/content_20744153.htm.

52 "International Comparisons of Hourly Compensation Costs in Manufacturing, 2011," *U.S. Bureau of Labor Statistics,* retrieved January 7, 2013 from www.bls.gov/news.release/ichcc.toc.htm;" International Comparisons of Hourly Compensation Costs in Manufacturing, 2011" United States Bureau of Labor Statistics, released December 19, 2012;. "Manufacturing in India: The Masala Mittelstand," *The Economist* (August 11, 2012): 55.

53 "Here, There and Everywhere: Outsourcing and Off Shoring," *The Economist,* Special Report (January 19, 2013): 1–20.

54 Bower and Christensen, "Disruptive Technologies."

55 "Labour productivity," *The Economist,*" retrieved January 7, 2013 from www.economist.com/node/17966988.

56 Keith Bradsher, "Chinese Auto Parts Enter the Global Market," *New York Times* (June 7, 2007): B8. Calculated at the exchange rate of 7.65 yuan to the dollar, as of June 12, 2009.

57 Shenkar, *The Chinese Century.*

58 Diana Farrell, Noshi Kaka, and Sascha Sturze, "Ensuring India's Offshoring Future," *McKinsey Quarterly* (2005): 92–103.

59 "GM Sales Up 22.3% in China," retrieved March 17, 2011, from www.industryweek.com/articles/gm_sales_up_22-3_in_china_23846.aspx; "GM's First-Half China Sales Surge Past the U.S," *Businessweek,* retrieved March 17, 2011, from www.businessweek.com/news/2010-07-02/gm-s-first-half-china-sales-surge-past-the-u-s-.html.

60 Keith Bradsher, "Ford plans extensive factory expansion in China," *New York Times* (April 20, 2012): B7.

61 Martin Dewhurst, Jonathan Harris, and Suzanne Heywood, "The Global Company's Challenge," *McKinsey Quarterly,* retrieved December 31, 2012, from www.mckinseyquarterly.com/The_global_companys_challenge_2979.

62 Symbolizing the growing primacy of its Indian operations was IBM's historic decision to hold its annual Investors Day in 2007 on the grounds of the Bangalore Palace—an event that had never before been held outside the United States. The change made perfect sense given that "India is at the epicenter of the flat world." "India Is Epicenter at the Flat World," *BPO Tiger,* retrieved May 10, 2011, from www.bpotiger.com/2007/04/india_is_epicenter_at_the_flat.html.

63 "Big US Firms Shift Hiring Abroad," *Wall Street Journal* (April 19, 2011): B1.

64 Problems with moving a company's stuff can threaten its success. Walmart relies on a sophisticated inbound and outbound truck system to move goods among its stores; without that system, it could not compete. In India, bad roads, many middlemen, government red tape, and tough thugs slow, if not stop, the flow of goods. Goods that make it through, after all the various charges, can see their price, set that morning by the farmer, shoot up 500 percent by delivery that evening. "Bad Roads, Red Tape, Burly Thugs Slow Wal-Mart's Passage in India," WSJ.com, retrieved January 12, 2013, from /online.wsj.com/article/SB10001424127887323622904578129294224588914.html?mod=WSJ_hpp_LEFTTopStories.

65 Vivienne Walt, "Meet Amancio Ortega: The Third-richest Man in the World," *Fortune* (January 14, 2013): 56–59.

66 "Apple Supply Chain Strength Weakens Competition," *Supply Chain Digital,* retrieved January 10, 2013, from www.supplychaindigital.com/global_logistics/apple-supply-chain-strength-weakens-competition.

67 "Tim Cook Is One of the Three People Who Saved Apple," *Business Insider,* retrieved January 10, 2013, from www.businessinsider.com/tim-cook-is-one-of-the-three-people-that-saved-apple-2012-11.

68 "The Humble Hero: Containers have been more important for Globalisation than Freer Trade," *The Economist* (May 18, 2012): 56.

69 Quote from Bain's Mark Gottfredson, reported in "Financial Firms Hasten Their Move to Outsourcing," *New York Times* (August 18, 2004): C1.

70 W. Brian Arthur, "The Second Economy," *McKinsey Quarterly,* retrieved January 8, 2013, from www.mckinseyquarterly.com/The_second_economy_2853.

71 Heather Timmons, "Outsourcing to India Draws Western Lawyers," NYTimes.com, retrieved April 26, 2011, from www.nytimes.com/2010/08/05/business/global/05legal.html?_r=1. Presently, Pangea3 is "getting more résumés from United States lawyers than we know what to do with," said the managing director of its litigation services group.

72 The consolidation of existing communication technologies, to say nothing of the construction of Internet bases with wireless transmissions in increasingly remote locations, supports "new business models to connect the poorest two billion people to the evolving nervous system of civilization." See "2009 State of the Future," The Millennium Project, 22.

73 John Markoff, "New Wave of Deft Robots Is Changing Global Industry," *New York Times* (August 18, 2012).

74 John Markoff, "New Wave of Deft Robots Is Changing Global Industry," NYTimes.com, retrieved February 25, 2013, from www.nytimes.com/2012/08/19/business/new-wave-of-adept-robots-is-changing-global-industry.html?pagewanted=all.

75 "The Digitization of Manufacturing Will Transform the Way Goods are Made—And Change the Politics of Jobs too," *The Economist* (April 21 2012): 56.

76 "Manufacturing the Future: The Next Era of Global Growth and Innovation," *McKinsey Global Institute,* retrieved January 13, 2013 from www.mckinsey.com/insights/mgi/research/productivity_competitiveness_and_growth/the_future_of_manufacturing; "Manufacturing: The New Maker Rules," *The Economist,* (November 12, 2012): 73.

77 "More Than a Third of Large Manufacturers Are Considering Reshoring from China to the U.S.," Boston Consulting Group, retrieved January 8, 2013 from www.bcg.com/media/PressReleaseDetails.aspx?id=tcm:12-104216.

78 Peter Marsh, *The New Industrial Revolution: Consumers, Globalisation and the End of Mass Production.*

79 Vivienne Walt, "Meet Amancio Ortega: The Third-richest Man in the World," *Fortune* (January 14, 2013): 56–59.

80 "Innovations to Create New Streams of Profitable Growth," *Accenture Outlook,* retrieved June 9, 2011, from www.accenture.com/in-en/outlook/Pages/outlook-journal-2010-less-is-new-more-innovation.aspx.

81 *Synergy* is defined as the combination of parts of a business such that the sum is worth more than the individual parts. It is often expressed in the equation *2 + 2 = 5,* with the additional unit of value the result of synergy. Research reports a relationship between a firm's performance and a manager's sophistication in diffusing core competencies throughout the value chain.

82 Technically, a core competency satisfies three conditions: It provides consumer benefits, it is difficult for competitors to imitate, and it is leveraged to different products and markets. The fact that rivals cannot easily match or replicate a firm's core competency serves as a powerful competitive advantage.

83 Jerome Glenn, Theodore Gordon, and Elizabeth Florescu,"2009 State of the Future."

84 Medard Gabel and Henry Bruner, *An Atlas of the Multinational Corporation Globalinc,* New York: The New Press, 2003.

85 Adam Bryant,"Google's 8-Point Plan to Help Managers Improve," NYTimes.com, retrieved March 13, 2011, from www.nytimes.com/2011/03/13/business/13hire.html?hp; Christopher A. Bartlett and Meg Wozny,"GE's Two-Decade Transformation: Jack Welch's Leadership," Harvard Business School Case 399-150 (Boston: HBSP, 2001).

86 Platforms include ebXML Business Process Specification Schema, Web Services Business Process Execution Language, and so on. See lsdis.cs.uga.edu/proj/meteor/mwscf/standards.html for a fuller profile.

87 "Schumpeter: Fail often, fail well," *The Economist,* retrieved April 28, 2011, from www.economist.com/node/18557776?story_id=18557776&fsrc=rss.

88 Samsung,"2012_Facts_and_Figuresm, retrieved January 7, 2013 from www.samsung.com/us/aboutsamsung/sustainability/sustainabilityreports/download/2012/2012_Facts_and_Figures_FINAL.pdf).

89 "Samsung Challenges Apple's Cool Factor," *New York Times* (February 11, 2013): C1.

90 "The World's Most Powerful Brands, 2012," *Forbes,* retrieved January 7, 2013 from www.forbes.com/powerful-brands/#page:1_sort:0_direction:asc_search:.

91 Lovallo and Kahneman,"Delusions of Success,"56.

92 James Brooke and Saul Hansel,"Samsung Is Now What Sony Once Was," *New York Times* (March 9, 2004): A1.

93 "Samsung Profit Beats Estimates on Surging Sales of Phones," *Businessweek* (October 26, 2012).

94 Lovallo and Kahneman,"Delusions of Success,"56. Often, analysis of these sorts of prescient management tends toward halo effects, whereby a positive impression in one area, say the ease of Google's search algorithm, influences assessment of others, say Google's executive leadership. Moreover, the often anecdotal"lessons learned"are not easily distilled into objective principles or useful to companies in dissimilar industries and countries.

95 Martin Dewhurst, Jonathan Harris, and Suzanne Heywood, "The Global Company's Challenge," *McKinsey Quarterly,* retrieved December 31, 2012, from www.mckinseyquarterly.com/The_global_companys_challenge_2979.

96 "A Special Report on Innovation in Emerging Markets: The World Turned Upside Down," *The Economist,* retrieved April 21, 2011 from www.economist.com/node/15879369.

97 Theodore Levitt,"The Globalization of Markets," *Harvard Business Review* 61 (1983): 92–102.

98 Encyclopedia Britannica, www.britannica.com/EBchecked/topic/1357503/cultural-globalization.

99 "What Is the WTO?"retrieved January 8, 2013 from www.wto.org/english/thewto_e/whatis_e/whatis_e.htm.

100 Adrian Wooldridge. *Masters of Management: How the Business Gurus and Their Ideas Have Changed the World—for Better and for Worse,* (HarperCollins, 2011): 273.

101 Lui Hebron and John F. Stack, *Globalization: Debunking The Myths,* Pearson Prentice Hall, January 18, 2008; Jan Nederveen Pieterse, *Globalization & Culture: Global Mélange,* Rowman & Littlefield Publishers (2009); Michael Veseth, *Globaloney: Unraveling the Myths of Globalization,* Rowman & Littlefield (2006).

102 Regarding cultural predisposition, Japanese doctors disfavor the American-style, high-pressure sales force. Pharmaceutical sales representatives, therefore, adapt their marketing practices in that country. Regarding historical legacy, people drive on the left side of the road in England, thereby creating demand for right-hand-drive cars, whereas people in Italy drive on the right side of the road, thereby creating demand for left-hand-drive cars. Similarly, consumer electrical systems are based on 110 volts in the United States, whereas many European countries use a 240-volt standard.

103 Anna Molin,"IKEA Chief Ohlsson Says Red Tape Is Hobbling Growth," WSJ.com, retrieved January 25, 2013 from online.wsj.com/article/SB10001424127887323301104578257873705189676.html.

104 "IMD World Competitiveness Yearbook,"retrieved January 24, 2013 from www.imd.org/research/publications/wcy/.

105 C. Prahalad and Y. Doz, *The Multinational Mission: Balancing Local Demands and Global Vision* (New York: Free Press, 1987).

106 "Google in Asia: Seeking Success," *The Economist,* retrieved March 15, 2011, from www.economist.com/node/13185891?story_id=13185891.

107 Similarly, if the host government offers incentives for local manufacturing, the subsidiary can build its own plant; if local consumers prefer dealing directly with salespeople rather than relying on mass media, the subsidiary can build a sales force; if the country changes labor laws, the subsidiary can adjust human resource policies.

108 "A Special Report on Entrepreneurship: Global Heroes," *The Economist,* retrieved March 15, 2011, from www.economist.com/node/13216025.

109 Julia Werdigier,"Tesco to Pay Dearly to Leave United States," *New York Times* (April 17, 2013): C2.

110 Alexandra Harney, *The China Price: The True Cost of Chinese Competitive Advantage* (New York: Penguin, 2008);"The China Price," *Businessweek,* retrieved March 30, 2011, from www.businessweek.com/magazine/content/04_49/b3911401.htm;"The China Price,"retrieved January 10, 2013 from thechinaprice.blogspot.com/.

111 Shenkar, *The Chinese Century.*

112 Toby Gibbs, Suzanne Heywood, and Leigh Weiss,"Organizing for an Emerging World," *McKinsey Quarterly,* June 2012.

113 Noel Tichy and Stratford Sherman, *Control Your Destiny or Someone Else Will* (New York: HarperCollins, 2005).

114 Ibid.

115 Quotations from the following: Jack Welch and John A. Byrne, *Jack: Straight from the Gut* (New York: Warner Business Books, 2001); Lovallo and Kahneman,"Delusions of Success," 56.

116 Ibid. Jack Welch and John A. Byrne.

117 ***Sources include the following:*** "Gartner Says Worldwide Mobile Payment Transaction Value to surpass $171.5 Billion,"accessed October 23, 2013, www.gartner.com/newsroom/id/2028315;"Gartner Says Worldwide Mobile Payment Transaction Value to Surpass $235 Billion in 2013,"accessed October 28, 2013 www.gartner.com/newsroom/id/2504915;"Mobile Money in Africa: Press 1 for Modernity." *The Economist* (April 28, 2012):64; Beth Cobert, Brigit Helms, and Doug Parker,"Mobile Money: Getting to Scale in Emerging Markets," *The McKinsey Quarterly* (May, 2012)22–29; Ian Urbina and Keith Bradsher,"Linking Factories to the Malls, Middleman Pushes Low Costs," *The New York Times* (August 7, 2013):A-1;"AFRICA: Mobile Banking Prospects Remain Positive," *The New York Times,"* Accessed October 23, 2013, www.nytimes.com/2008/10/03/world/

africa/03iht-03oxan-Mobbank.16671846.html; "Charging the Mobile," *The Economist* (June 22, 2013):58; "Half Of The World Is 'Unbanked'– New Global Estimate Reveals 2.5 Billion Adults Worldwide Lack Savings or Credit Account," accessed October 23, 2013, www.financialaccess.org/newsroom/press-releases/2012/05/half-world-%E2%80%9Cunbanked%E2%80%9D-%E2%80%93-new-global-estimate-reveals-25-billion; "Hungry Tiger, Dancing Elephant: How India Is Changing IBM's World," *The Economist*, (April 4, 2007): 58–61; Global mobile statistics 2013 Part A: Mobile Subscribers; Handset Market Share; Mobile Operators," accessed October 28, 2013, mobithinking.com/mobile-marketing-tools/latest-mobile-stats/a#subscribers; "Ministry of Finance Audit Findings on M-Pesa Money Transfer Services," accessed January 6, 2014, http://kenyapolitical.blogspot.com/2009/01/ministry-of-finance-audit-findings-on-m.html.

CHAPTER 13
Evaluation of Countries for Operations

OBJECTIVES

After studying this chapter, you should be able to

1. Grasp company strategies for sequencing the penetration of countries
2. See how scanning techniques can help managers limit geographic alternatives and consider otherwise overlooked areas
3. Discern the major opportunity and risk variables to consider in deciding whether and where to expand abroad
4. Know the methods and problems of collecting and comparing international information
5. Understand some simplifying tools for helping decide where to operate
6. Consider how companies allocate emphasis among the countries where they operate
7. Comprehend why location decisions do not necessarily compare different countries' possibilities
8. Fathom the conditions that may cause prime business locations to change in the future

MyManagementLab®
Improve Your Grade!
When you see this icon ✪, visit **www.mymanagementlab.com** for activities that are applied, personalized, and offer immediate feedback.

The place to get top speed out of a horse is not the place where you can get top speed out of a canoe.

—African (Hausa) proverb

Source: © Nitr - Fotolia.com

CASE Burger King®

As of 2013, Burger King was the world's largest flame-broiled fast food hamburger chain, with 12,997 restaurants in 84 countries and two U.S. territories (Guam and Puerto Rico).[1] Only Yum Brands, Subway, McDonald's, and Starbucks had more. Its regional distribution of restaurants was North America (Canada and the United States), 57 percent; Europe, Middle East, and Africa, 24 percent; Latin America and Caribbean, 11 percent; and Asia-Pacific, 8 percent. It plans to have 17,000 restaurants by 2016, with most growth occurring internationally. Despite such a widespread global presence, 60 percent of its foreign restaurants were in only eight countries. Map 13.1 shows the countries with the largest number of restaurants.

Two major ways Burger King differentiates itself from competitors are the way it cooks hamburgers—flame-broiling rather than grilling or frying—and the options it offers customers as to how they want their burgers prepared. The company began in 1954 by offering a menu of beef burgers, fries, milk shakes, and sodas; that menu now includes breakfast as well as turkey burgers, wraps, smoothies, desserts, a variety of coffees, and various chicken, fish, and salad offerings. Many of these additions have come since 2011 as the company has sought to fill menu gaps and broaden its target market. Nevertheless, hamburgers remain the company's mainstay, and 2007 marked the 50th anniversary of the Whopper® sandwich, its signature product.

Burger King has also differentiated itself with some inventive advertising campaigns, such as its use of *HAVE IT YOUR WAY*® ads and the figure of a man who was the Burger "King" for a long time. The company logo has changed slightly through the years, yet it has always been displayed and recognizable globally, as illustrated in the chapter opener photo of a sign advertising a restaurant in Thailand.

A BIT OF HISTORY

Starting out as Insta-Burger King in 1954, the corporation opened five restaurants during its first five years—all in the Miami, Florida area. In 1959, with its name shortened to Burger King, it began domestic franchising and grew to 274 restaurants. Pillsbury, owner of several other retail food groups, purchased the corporation in 1967 and franchising increased substantially over the next few years. When Pillsbury shed its restaurant business in 1989, it sold Burger King to the British company Grand Metropolitan, which then converted most of its Wimpy restaurants in the United Kingdom to Burger King restaurants. Grand Metropolitan merged with Guinness in 1997 to form Diageo, and when Diageo divested itself of restaurant operations in 2002, it sold Burger King to a consortium of private equity firms controlled by TPG Capital, Bain Capital Partners, and the Goldman Sachs Funds. In May 2006, Burger King consummated its initial public offering, becoming a publicly traded company on the New York Stock Exchange. In 2010, however, 3G Capital, backed by Brazilian investors, took the company private again with the prospect that management could concentrate on medium- and long-term operations rather than being subject to shareholder responses to short-term performance. Two years later, the company once again went public and changed its name to Burger King Worldwide, Inc. to convey its interest in future global expansion. The years of transformed ownership have caused changes in emphasis for Burger King, and its interests have sometimes been secondary to those of its parent company.

Despite the evolving ownership, Burger King did expand internationally: to the Bahamas and Puerto Rico in the early 1960s, and Europe, Asia, and Latin America in the 1970s. Some of these moves turned out to be highly successful, a few did not. It entered and then retreated from operations in such countries as Colombia, France, Israel, Japan, and Oman. (It has reentered some of these markets.) Much of Burger King's early international forays came about either because someone in another country approached someone in the corporation or because someone in the corporation was familiar with a particular country and thought it would offer opportunities. Two reasons have been prevalent in the company's decisions to leave markets: (1) the franchisee not performing adequately, such as not making royalty payments or investing sufficiently in the business; and (2) the market being too small to support the necessary infrastructure, such as slaughterhouse and beef-grinding facilities.

Over time, Burger King has taken a more systematic approach toward restaurant expansion. It still sees substantial growth opportunities within the United States but considers that a more mature market for fast food, especially hamburgers, than other countries. In seeking new places to enter, Burger King looks most favorably at countries with large populations (especially young people), high consumption of beef, availability of capital to franchisees for growth, a safe pro-business environment, growth in shopping centers, and availability of a potential franchisee with experience and resources. Recently its model has been to grant exclusive franchisee rights for a

MAP 13.1 Burger King's Major Restaurant Locations by Country
Although Burger King had restaurants in 84 countries plus two U.S. territories at the start of 2013, 85 percent of those restaurants were located in only nine countries. These nine countries, along with the number of restaurants, are shown on the map. (In Australia, the restaurants use the Jack in the Box name rather than the Burger King name.)

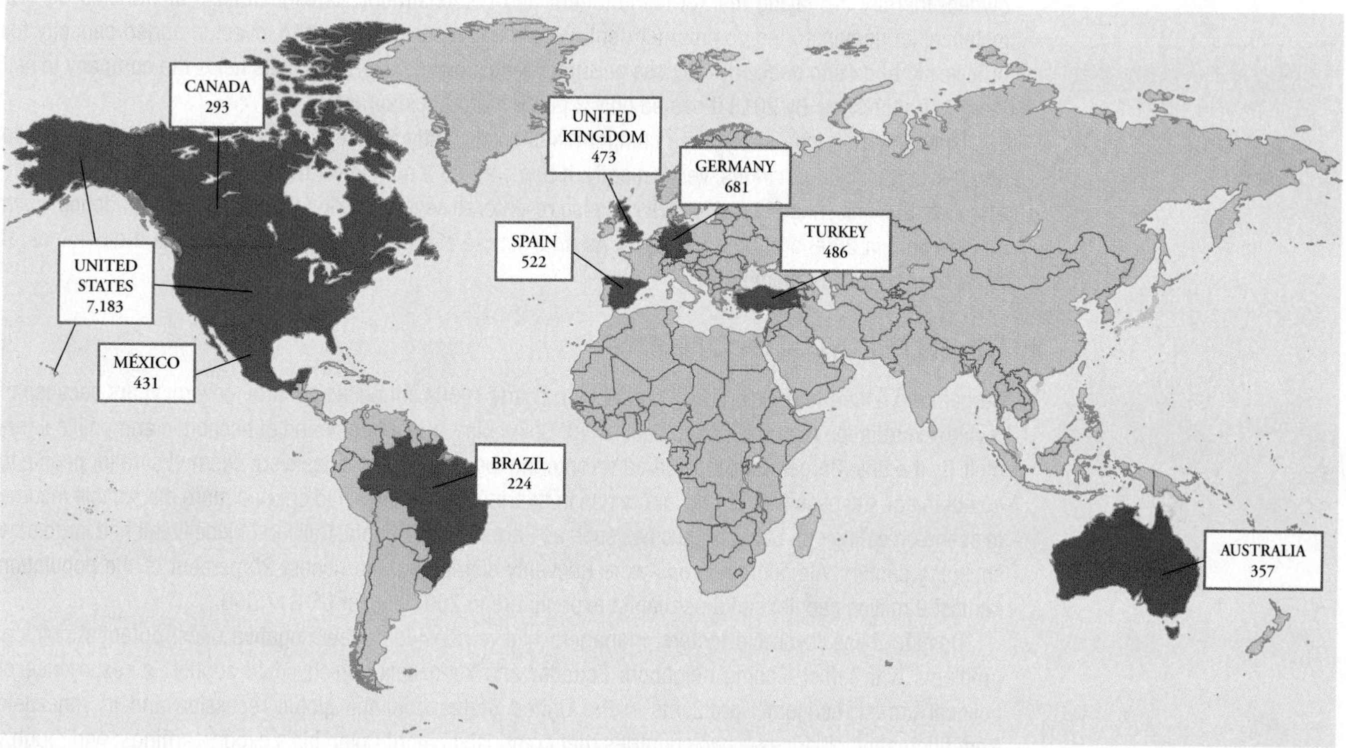

country or group of countries by pairing a private equity firm with an experienced restaurant operator in a joint venture (JV). In some cases, Burger King has become the third party in the JV without committing capital to it.

Overall, Burger King has expanded abroad later than its primary rival, McDonald's, resulting in both advantages and disadvantages. On the one hand, later entry is a drawback in very small markets due to an inadequate number of suppliers, such as only one slaughterhouse whose owners may be unwilling to work with more than one customer. On the other hand, a late entry in larger markets may benefit from the product demand and supply infrastructure created by earlier entrants. In some later-entry markets, Burger King has been able to concentrate almost entirely on emphasizing its product (*HAVE IT YOUR WAY®*, good taste of flame-broiled burgers) without incurring early development costs. For instance, in Latin America and the Caribbean, McDonald's and Burger King compete in almost all countries and territories, with Burger King currently leading in the number of restaurants in about half of those markets.

Keep in mind that local firms also learn from the successes of foreign fast-food companies, sometimes altering their menus and flavorings to appeal to local tastes. Some notable examples are Bembos in Peru, Mr. Bigg's in Nigeria, Pollo Campero in Guatemala, and Quick in Belgium.

The Latin America and Caribbean group has many countries with very small populations, such as the Cayman Islands, Aruba, and Saint Lucia. So why did Burger King develop a presence in these markets long before entering places with much bigger populations, such as China, Russia, and South Africa? The answer is largely due to location—it remains headquartered in Miami, which is often called "the capital of Latin America." Because so many people from that region come to or through Miami, the Burger King reputation spilled over there early on, which simplified gaining brand recognition and acceptance. Further, the nearness of the Latin American and Caribbean countries to Miami enhances the ability of Burger King managers to visit these countries and for franchisees to visit headquarters.

Although Burger King prefers to operate in markets through franchising, doing so has sometimes been initially difficult because suppliers and prospective franchisees did not know the company well enough. When such a market looked attractive enough, Burger King would enter with the operations it owned, thereby displaying market commitment and demonstrating its expectations of franchisees. For instance, its demonstrated commitment entices a meat-processing plant to invest in added capacity for processing of ground beef. The success of Burger King's owned operating units helps the company to sell them to franchisees. By 2013 it owned only 3 percent of its restaurants.

Throughout its long history, the company has consistently focused on expanding its global portfolio into new and existing markets. Very recently, it has entered a number of them for the first time, including Morocco, Slovenia, and South Africa. It has also re-entered several markets it had earlier abandoned, such as Colombia in 2008 and Oman in 2010. As an example of country evaluation, let's take a quick look at decisions regarding Colombia.

RE-ENTERING COLOMBIA

Burger King entered the Colombian market in the early 1980s but pulled out after several years because of royalty expatriation restrictions and because of Colombia's prolonged period of economic and political turmoil. By the time Burger King considered re-entering the country, the cities were deemed safe for people to go out to eat, the peso was strong, and a rise in two-income families had created more disposable income to spend on eating out. Some large cities such as Barranquilla, Bogotá, Cali, and Medellin all had large new shopping centers. Although incomes were unevenly distributed, the richest 20 percent of the population (almost 9 million people) had a per capita expenditure in 2007 of over US $17,000.

Despite these favorable factors, managers had to consider a few negative ones: potential political problems with leftist-leaning neighbors Ecuador and Venezuela, which could support a resurgence of political unrest; economic problems in the United States from the global recession and in Venezuela from fluctuating oil prices—two countries that comprised half of Colombia's export earnings; and roughly 2 percent of Colombian GDP in 2007 coming from remittances of expatriates working abroad, mainly in Spain, which was hard hit by the global recession. In effect, economic downturns could ravage fast-food sales—a lesson Burger King learned in Mexico and Germany that caused it to tactically develop a more relevant value proposition, including value meals.

Overall, the Colombian situation has been bright. Burger King signed an agreement with KINCO, a well-established Colombian company with restaurant experience, for franchise rights to Medellin, Cali, and northern Colombia, then signed a second franchise agreement with Alsea, a Mexican firm, for rights to Bogotá. Alsea owned 75 percent of the Colombian operation of Domino's Pizza and operated Burger King restaurants in Mexico.

THE BRICS

In Chapter 4 we explored why so many companies have been emphasizing the BRIC countries: Brazil, Russia, India, and China. Burger King is no exception. The possibilities are simply too great to ignore.

Burger King opened its first Brazilian and Chinese restaurants in 2004. By then, many foreign fast-food franchisors had entered the markets, some successfully, some not. For the most part, failure occurred because of underestimating what it would take to succeed there. While Burger King has had success in both these countries, it was able to expand much faster in Brazil than in China. By 2013, it had 221 restaurants in the former and 86 in the latter.

Two factors largely explain the rapid Brazilian expansion. First, the company has had much more of a recognition advantage there than in China because a half million Brazilians fly into Florida each year, where Burger King restaurants abound. In addition, about 300,000 Brazilians live in the South Florida area, most of whom have relatives back home. Second, Burger King forged a location strategy that emphasized development in major cities and adjacent geographies with established shopping mall locations. By focusing initially on São Paulo, Brazil's largest city, Burger King developed economies in its marketing and distribution, with subsequent expansion focusing on nearby cities and states.

In China, Burger King encountered laws requiring that it either form a joint venture with a Chinese firm or own and operate two or more stores for at least a year before starting franchise operations. The company chose the latter alternative, which delayed its start of franchising. Later, finding potential franchisees with sufficient financial and restaurant capabilities was difficult, particularly since the franchise concept was rather new to China. (Some of its competitors, mainly Yum Brands and McDonald's, made joint venture investments and expanded with owned stores.) In 2012 Burger King announced the formation of a three-partner JV to serve the Chinese market. One partner, the Carpesian Capital Group, is a global private equity company specializing in developing country investments. The other is the Korduglu family from Turkey, which is Burger King's largest franchisee outside the United States. Its plan is to open 1,000 restaurants in China within five to seven years.

In 2010 Burger King opened its first restaurants in Russia, a country it has found attractive not only because of the population and growth factors affecting all BRICs but also because it can serve as a contiguous area for further expansion into Eastern Europe. Indeed, Burger King's 2011 entry into Slovenia has benefitted from supply integration with the Russian operation. In addition, concluding that finding the right franchisee was essential for the Russian market, Burger King's managers spent over a year getting to know the eventual franchisee, Alex Kolobov, who owns Shokolanitsa, a chain of about 200 Russian coffee shops. Although the formation of the franchise known as Burger Rus has resulted in growth in Moscow and St. Petersburg, more capital has been necessary to expand outside those cities. In 2013 Burger King announced the formation of a joint venture between Burger Rus and Russia's VTB Capital in order to open several hundred new restaurants in the country within the next few years.

India is the one BRIC country Burger King has not yet entered. However, 2013 reports indicate the company is in discussions with Everstone Capital, which is both a private equity firm and the holder of controlling interest in India's largest restaurant group.

THE FUTURE

Recent experience indicates that Burger King's locational emphasis can affect its performance considerably. For the first quarter of 2011, same-store sales fell 6 percent in North America. However, the drop was largely offset by gains in the rest of the world, so the global decline was only 3.6 percent. During 2012, Wendy's overtook Burger King as the second largest burger chain in the United States. To counter this loss of position, Burger King has been augmenting its menu with new items, changing its advertising focus, and getting franchisees to modernize their stores. At the same time, as the case indicates, the company is planning unprecedented international expansion. In fact, some of its competitors have expanded abroad much more than Burger King, which may indicate that it has untapped potential. This raises a number of questions for management regarding location priorities: Should primary emphasis be on bolstering its domestic presence or on expanding internationally? If the former, should the company concentrate on adding more restaurants or on boosting sales within existing ones? If the latter, should it concentrate on entering new markets? (It is presently in only about 40 percent of countries.) If so, which look most promising? Or should it concentrate on sales within existing markets? Are there markets in which Burger King is under-performing? Should it work on bolstering that performance? Or should it pull out of those markets to use its resources more effectively elsewhere? These are all location questions that dog managers in any company with international operations. ■

CRN
Case Review Note

QUESTIONS

✪13-1. Discuss the risks that an international restaurant company such as Burger King would have by operating abroad rather than just domestically.

✪13-2. How has the Burger King headquarters location influenced its international expansion? Has this location strengthened or weakened its global competitive position?

INTRODUCTION

Companies lack resources to take advantage of all international opportunities.

The old adage that "location, location, and location" are the three most important factors for business success rings quite true for international business. The world offers different locales, opportunities, and risks as companies try to create value from increasing sales or acquiring competitively useful assets. Because all companies have limited resources, they must be careful in making the following decisions:

1. The location of sales, production, and administrative and auxiliary services
2. The sequence for entering different countries
3. The portion of resources and efforts to allocate to each country where they operate

Companies need to

- Determine the order of country entry.
- Set the rates of resource allocation among countries.

Committing human, technical, and financial resources to one locale may mean forgoing or delaying projects elsewhere. In actuality, a company may first set a strategy of domestic versus international emphasis. For instance, General Electric set an objective of having international operations account for 60 percent of its total sales.[2] Afterward, a company sequences entry by country or region and then chooses where to operate within a country of choice. However, our emphasis in this chapter is in the selection of countries. Even after a firm is well established in most countries, it still needs to allocate resources by emphasizing some locations more than others. Further, when companies add new products they must decide the sequence of countries to sell them and how fast to spread the introduction into different countries.[3] Thus, taking time to pick the right place affects a firm's ability to gain and sustain competitive advantage.[4]

Figure 13.1 highlights the importance of MNEs' location decisions. By examining the external environment and comparing it with a company's objectives and capabilities, managers might ask: Where can we best leverage our existing competencies? And where can we go to best sustain, improve, or extend our competencies?

FIGURE 13.1 Location Decisions Affecting International Operations

In choosing locations for international operations, a company should begin by analyzing three factors: its *objectives*, its *strategies*, and its comparative *environmental fit* with conditions in the countries under consideration.

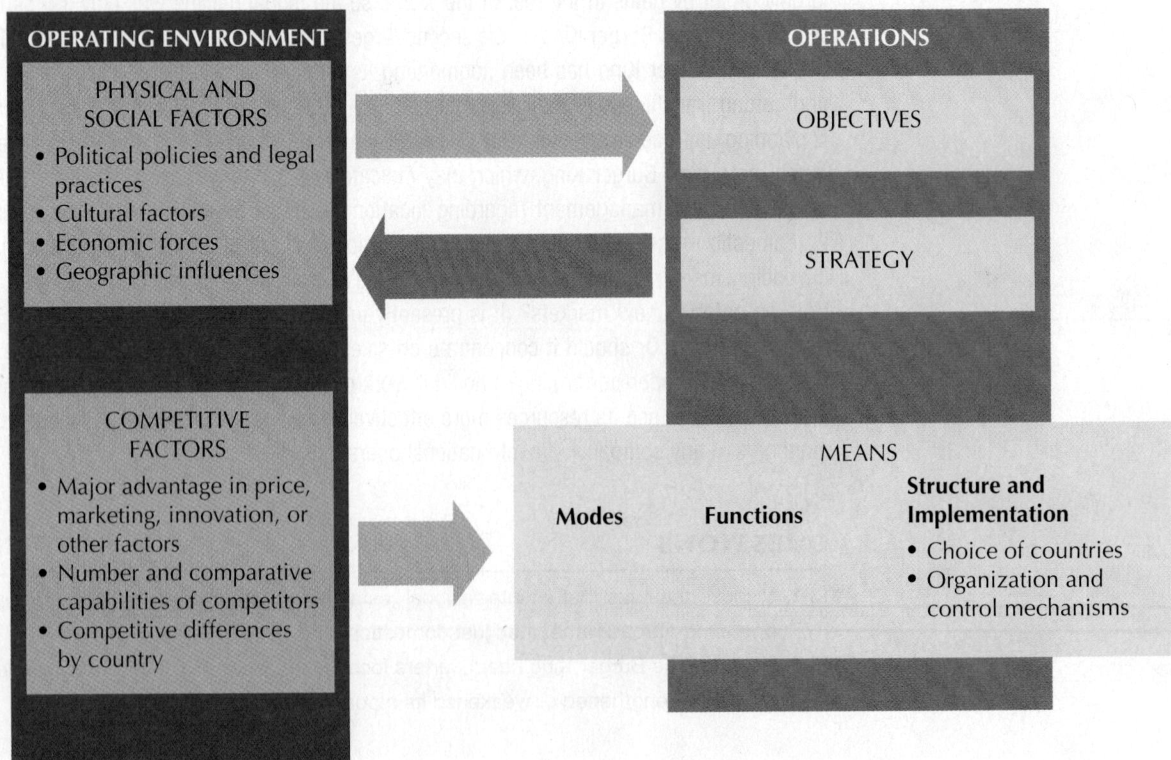

In choosing geographic sites, a company must decide

- Where to sell.
- Where to produce.

To answer those questions, managers need to answer two more: Which markets should we serve? And where should we place production to serve them? On one hand, the answers can be the same, particularly if transport costs or government regulations mean producing in the countries where you sell. Many service industries, such as restaurants, construction, and retailing (like Burger King), must locate facilities near their foreign customers.

On the other hand, large-scale production technology may favor producing in only a few countries and exporting to others, such as with companies in the capital-intensive automobile and steel industries. Finally, location decisions may be more complex, such as using multiple countries for sourcing raw materials and components that go into one finished product. Or a company may divide operating functions—locate headquarters in the United States, a call center for handling service in the Philippines, an R&D facility in Switzerland, and so on.

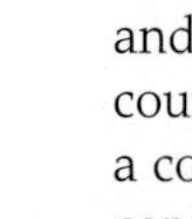

Flexibility in locations is important because country and competitive conditions change. A company needs to respond to new opportunities and withdraw from less profitable ones. Recall in the opening case that Burger King withdrew from Colombia because of prolonged economic and political problems along with difficulty in remitting earnings from royalties. There is no one-size-fits-all theory for picking operating locations because product lines, competitive positions, resources, and strategies make each company unique—a situation that, in turn, will be better realized in some countries than in others.[5] Moreover, hiring the right people to analyze country differences and implement company operations is critical. Highly skilled managers can sometimes compensate for location deficiencies, and poor managers can sometimes cause poor performance in the best locations. However, having skilled managers in the most appropriate locations is the best possible combination. Figure 13.2 shows the major steps international business managers should take in making location decisions. The following discussion examines those steps in depth.

FIGURE 13.2 The Location Decision Process

Location, location, location: Committing resources to a foreign location may entail risky trade-offs—say, forgoing or abandoning projects elsewhere. The decision-making process is essentially twofold: examining the external environments of proposed locations and comparing each of them with the company's objectives and capabilities.

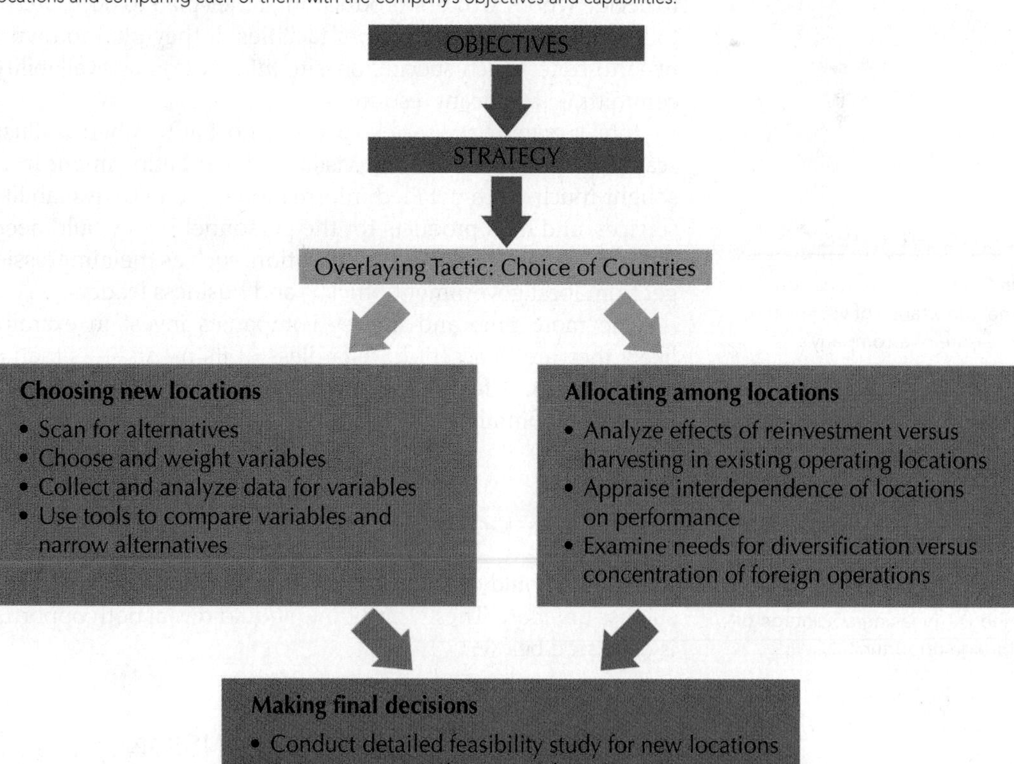

HOW DOES SCANNING WORK?

Without scanning, a company may
- Overlook opportunities and risks.
- Examine too many or too few possibilities.

Managers use scanning techniques to examine and compare countries on broad indicators of opportunities and risks.[6] Scanning is like seeding widely and then weeding out; it is useful insofar as a company might otherwise consider too few or too many possibilities. Given that there are approximately 200 countries, managers might easily overlook some good opportunities without first looking very broadly. Instead, they might zero in on those that come to mind first.

SCANNING VERSUS DETAILED ANALYSIS

Step 1: Scanning **Scanning** is the process by which managers examine many countries broadly and then narrow them down to the most promising ones. That is, they compare country information that is readily available, inexpensive, and fairly comparable—usually without having to incur traveling expenses. They analyze publicly available information, such as from the Internet, and communicate with experienced people. They compare countries on a few conditions that could significantly affect the success or failure of their business and that fit with its resources and objectives. Because of using fairly easy-to-find information, they may consider a large group of countries at this point, such as all those within a global region.

On-site visits follow scanning and are part of the final location decision process.

Step 2: Detailed Analysis Once managers narrow their consideration to the most promising countries, they need to compare the feasibility and desirability of each. At this point, unless they are satisfied enough to outsource all their production and sales, they almost always need to go on location to analyze and collect more specific information.

Take a situation in which managers need to decide where to place their sales efforts. They will likely need to visit the countries shortlisted through scanning in order to conduct market research and visit with distributors before making a final decision. Or let's say managers need to decide where to locate production. If they plan to outsource the production, they may want to inspect potential contractors' facilities. If they plan to own facilities themselves, they will need to collect such specific on-site information as availability of land and suppliers before committing significant resources.

Intel's manufacturing expansion into Latin America illustrates an example. Intel used scanning techniques to limit visits to a few Latin American countries. The follow-up visits sought much more detailed information—even the availability of suitable housing, medical services, and food products for the personnel Intel would need to transfer. The visitors were also able to gain qualitative information, such as their impressions of the welcome they might get from local government officials and business leaders.

The more time and money companies invest in examining an alternative, the more likely they are to accept it, regardless of its merits—a situation known as an **escalation of commitment.** A feasibility study should have clear-cut decision points, whereby managers can cut the commitment before they invest too much.

CONCEPT CHECK

In Chapter 12, we focus on the importance of value—the measure of a company's ability to sell products for more than it costs to make them—in a firm's strategy, adding that "creating value" is primarily a matter of meeting (indeed, exceeding) customer expectations. Here we point out the importance of both factors—cost and customer needs—in taking advantage of foreign opportunities.

WHAT INFORMATION IS IMPORTANT IN SCANNING?

Managers should consider country conditions that could significantly affect their company's success or failure. These conditions should reveal both opportunities and risks, each of which is discussed below.

OPPORTUNITIES: SALES EXPANSION

Expectation of a large market and sales growth is probably a potential location's major attraction.

Expansion of sales is probably the most important factor motivating companies to engage in international business because of the assumption that more sales will lead to more profits. Thus, it is vital to decide where best to make those sales.

Of course, managers would like to have sales figures for the type of product they want to sell, but such information may not be available, especially if the product is a new one. In such instances, they could make rough estimates of sales potential by basing projections on what has happened to sales for a similar or complementary product. For instance, they might project the potential sales of flat-screen televisions based on figures for DVD equipment sales. If complementary figures are unavailable, management can use economic and demographic data to project sales potential.

Of course, you should examine indicators related directly to your products. If you're trying to sell, say, luxury products, GDP per capita may tell you very little. Instead, you need to know how many people have income above a certain level. Take India: Its GDP per capita is low, but it has enough millionaires to support the sale of high-end luxury products.

Moreover, although your product or service may not appeal to the average customer, you may seek out niches within that market. Pollo Campero, a Guatemalan-based fast-food chain, and Gigante, a Mexican supermarket chain, have both entered the United States by going to cities with large Central American and Mexican populations.[7]

Companies must consider variables other than income and population when estimating potential demand for their products in different countries.

Examining Economic and Demographic Variables Primary considerations when examining economic and demographic variables are listed below, with some examples:

- *Obsolescence and leapfrogging of products.* Consumers in developing economies do not necessarily follow the same patterns as those in higher-income countries. In China, consumers have leapfrogged the use of landline telephones by going from having no phones to using cell phones almost exclusively.[8]
- *Prices.* If prices of essential products are high, consumers may spend more on them than what would be expected based on per capita GDP and thus have less to spend on discretionary purchases. The expenditures on food in Japan are higher than would be predicted by either population or income level because food is expensive and work habits promote eating out.
- *Income elasticity.* A common tool for predicting total market potential is to divide the percentage of change in product demand by the percentage of change in income in a given country. The more demand shifts in relation to income changes, the more elastic it is. Demand for necessities such as food is usually less elastic than for discretionary products such as flat-screen TVs.
- *Substitution.* Consumers in a given country may more conveniently substitute certain products or services than those in other countries. There are fewer automobiles in Hong Kong than one would expect based on income and population because the crowded conditions make the efficient mass transit system a desirable substitute for automobiles. Gasoline- and diesel-powered cars are also substitutes. Indian demand for the former fell and the latter increased when government regulations led to high fuel-cost disparities, thus forcing companies such as Suzuki, Toyota, and General Motors to alter their mix of vehicle production.[9]
- *Income inequality.* Where income inequality is high, the per capita GDP figures are less meaningful. Many people have little to spend, while many others have substantial spending money, as noted by Mercedes-Benz sales in India.[10]
- *Cultural factors and taste.* Countries with similar per capita GDPs may have different preferences for products and services because of values or tastes. The same is true for consumer sub-segments within countries. The existence of a large Hindu population in India reduces per capita meat consumption there as compared with some countries with similar per capita GDPs, yet there is a large niche market of Indians who are neither Hindu nor vegetarian.

CONCEPT CHECK

Recall our discussion of "Regional Economic Integration" in Chapter 7, where we explain the dynamic effects of integration. As we point out, when trade barriers come down within a regional bloc, the size of the market available to small member nations typically increases quite dramatically.

- *Existence of trading blocs.* Although a country may have a small population and GDP, its presence in a regional trading bloc gives its output access to a much larger market. Uruguay has a small domestic market, but its production has duty-free access to other countries in MERCOSUR.

Given all these factors, managers cannot project potential demand perfectly. However, by considering factors that may influence the sale of their products, they can make workable estimates that help them narrow detailed studies to a reasonable number.

OPPORTUNITIES: RESOURCE ACQUISITION

Companies undertake international business to secure resources that are either too expensive or not readily available in their home countries. They may purchase them from another organization, or they may establish foreign investments to exploit them. In either case, they must prioritize where they can best secure what they're after.

If they want to acquire a scarce resource, they are obviously limited to those locales that have it, such as securing petroleum only in those countries that have reserves. When resources are very limited, such as prime areas for building beach resorts, land owners and governments are likely in a strong bargaining position when ceding rights to a foreign firm.[11] However, even when the resource is limited to a few countries, some offer better opportunities than others. In the case of petroleum reserves, there are cost differences in extraction, transportation, and taxes. When considering cost differences, a particular resource may be overriding for specific industries or companies, such as sugar for candy companies or low-cost water power for aluminum companies.

Costs—especially labor costs—are an important factor in companies' production-location decisions.

Cost Considerations A company's total cost is made up of numerous subcosts, many of which are industry- or company-specific. Nevertheless, several of the factors affecting these subcosts—*labor, infrastructure, ease of transportation and communications,* and *government incentives*—apply to a large-cross section of companies.

Labor Although capital intensity is growing in most industries, labor compensation remains an important cost for most companies. The scanning process allows examination of such factors as labor market size, labor compensation, minimum wages, customary and required fringe benefits, education levels, and unemployment rates in order to compare labor cost, skills, and availability. The process should also examine trends and likely changes. For example, many companies have recently been shifting production dependence away from China and toward such countries as Myanmar and Mexico because of rising Chinese costs.[12]

Labor, however, is not homogeneous. Neither are companies' labor needs. The desire to establish a low-cost call center has led many U.S. companies to locate in the Philippines, with its many English speakers, but not in Senegal, where many French companies locate call centers to serve French-language markets. South Africa has been a favorite location for MNEs' African regional offices because of available skilled office personnel there.[13] Or you may wish to establish an R&D facility where figures on the number of science and engineering graduates give you a rough idea that needed skills are available. In fact, many companies have set up R&D facilities in China, Hungary, India, and Israel because of the availability of technical talent at low cost.[14]

If a country's labor force lacks the specific skill levels required, an MNE might have to train, redesign production, or add supervision—all of which are expensive. Keep in mind also that there may be sector and geographic differences in wage rates within countries. In Mexico, tire wages are much higher than the average industrial wage, while wages in the capital and other large cities are higher than elsewhere.[15] In addition, you should look for conditions that can cause changes in labor availability and cost. For example, the HIV rate is very high in southern African countries, a problem that may drastically reduce their future labor forces.

When companies move into developing countries because of labor-cost differences, their advantages may be short-lived for one or more of three reasons:

- Competitors follow leaders into low-wage areas.
- There is little first-mover advantage for this type of production migration.
- The costs rise quickly as a result of pressure on wage or exchange rates.

Infrastructure problems add to operating costs.

Infrastructure Poor internal infrastructure may easily negate cost differences in labor rates. In many developing countries, infrastructure is both substandard and unreliable, which adds to companies' costs of operating. Consider Cadbury in Nigeria. Its workers spend extra hours getting to and from work on congested roads, which decreases their productivity. It uses its own power generators at two and a half times the cost of the unreliable publicly provided power to prevent assembly line stoppages that could cause food products to spoil. Because phone reception is often unreliable, Cadbury must send people out to visit customers and suppliers. When goods are ready for delivery, they must again face the slow roads and congestion.[16] (The adjacent photo shows a congested street in Mexico.)

The need to coordinate product, process, production, and sales influences location decisions.

Ease of Transportation and Communications Related to infrastructure is the advantage of locating near customers and suppliers. However, firms with rapidly evolving technologies need to tightly coordinate product and production technologies to speed new products' introduction and diminish competitors' opportunity to copy them.[17] This tends to push more production into developed countries, where such firms conduct most of their R&D.

Other factors also affect the efficient flow of goods. One is distance, which roughly correlates with time and cost of shipments; thus, a geographically isolated country like New

Although Mexico City has an extensive metro system along with some double-decker expressways, it remains one of the world's most congested cities, as the photo shows. Such congestion delays shipments and raises the cost of distribution.
Source: Paul Franklin/dkimages

Zealand does not fit as easily into a company's global integration strategy because supplies to and production from there may be untimely and costly.[18] Second, countries with few trade restrictions and efficient customs operations offer advantages such as reduced tariff costs and shorter clearance times, leading to a more continuous flow of components when and where they are needed.[19]

When entrepreneurs set up firms, they generally headquarter them where the founders reside to take advantage of personal networks that ease their operations; however, as companies become international, they may also find advantages in being near specialized private and public institutions handling international functions, such as banks, financing firms, insurance groups, public accountants, freight forwarders, customs brokers, and consular offices. Once they shift the geographic center of their sales and operations, they may even move their headquarters to another country.[20] Halliburton relocated its CEO and corporate headquarters from the United States to Dubai to be closer to customers and employees. If a company is looking for a production location that will serve sales in more than one country, the ease of moving goods into and out of the country is very important, so managers should consider the efficiency of port facilities along with the country's trade liberalization agreements.[21]

Government practices may increase or decrease companies' costs.

Governmental Incentives and Disincentives Most countries seek foreign investment because of the jobs it will create, the competitiveness it will enhance, and the impact it will have on their trade balance. It is common to see ads in business newspapers enticing foreign firms to consider a particular country as an investment location.

Because countries compete to attract investors, many offer incentives through regulations or negotiations that cut operating costs. These include such things as lower taxes, employee training, loan guarantees, low-interest loans, exemption of import duties, and subsidized energy and transportation. For example, the European structural funds program aimed at preventing European deindustrialization has helped fund projects for such companies as Coca-Cola, Fiat, and GlaxoSmithKline.[22] Differences in tax rates are particularly important when deciding where to produce within a regional trading bloc, inasmuch as companies can serve the entire region from any country within the bloc.[23]

At the same time, World Bank studies show that companies may begin operating more quickly and with fewer steps in some countries than in others because of differences in the ease or difficulty of starting a business, entering and enforcing contracts, hiring and firing workers, getting credit, and closing a business.[24] Government actions may delay or prevent companies from bringing in expatriate personnel and from getting needed imports cleared through customs in good time.

Countries also differ in corruption and in both legal transparency and enforcement. Too often managers must spend excessive time in satisfying government agencies on taxes, labor conditions, environmental compliance, and other matters when they are unsure of the legal consequences of their actions and competitive consequences of government corruption.[25] A particular thorny question concerns the poor protection of intellectual property rights; some firms prefer to avoid these locations and some others feel they can best protect their rights by operating in those markets. At the same time, poor protection is a double-edged sword. Although companies may relinquish technology to other companies, they may more easily gain access to other companies' technologies as well.[26] Nevertheless, companies appear to prefer operating in countries where both corporate social responsibility and environmental regulation are high, as long as rules and expectations are transparent.[27]

CONCEPT CHECK

We show in Chapter 5 that, in applying factor-proportions theory to determine the best place to locate a manufacturing facility, a company may compare the amount (and cost) of machinery that it will need in one place to the number (and cost) of people that it will need in another. We also show that new technologies, such as 3D printing, can change optimal production locations.

A Caveat The continuous development of new production technologies makes cost comparisons among countries more difficult. With more and more ways to make a product, a company might have to compare the cost of labor-intensive production in a low-wage country with that of capital-intensive production in a high-wage country. A company should also compare the cost from large-scale production that reduces fixed costs per unit by serving multi-country markets with the cost from multiple smaller-scale production units that reduce transport and inventory costs.

RISKS

Any company decision involves weighing opportunity against risk. For example, a sales-seeking company may not necessarily go to the country showing the highest sales potential. Nor will an asset-seeking company necessarily go where the assets are cheapest. In both cases, this is because decision makers may perceive that the risks in those locales are too high.

Factors to Consider in Analyzing Risk Keep in mind several factors as we discuss specific types of risk:

1. *Companies and their managers differ in their perceptions of what is risky,* how tolerant they are of taking risk, the returns they expect, and the portion of their assets they are willing to put at risk.[28]
2. *One company's risk may be another's opportunity.* For example, companies offering security solutions (e.g., alarm systems, guard services, insurance, weapons) may find their biggest sales opportunities where other companies find only operating risks. (This is shown humorously in Figure 13.3.)
3. *Companies may reduce their risks by means other than avoiding locations,* such as by insuring. But all these options incur costs that decision makers should take into account.
4. *There are trade-offs among risks.* Avoiding a country where, say, political risk is high may leave a company more vulnerable to competitive risk if another one earns good profits there. And returns are usually higher where risk is higher.

Besides considering the individual nature of risk assessment, companies should consider several important factors, grouped into three categories: political, foreign exchange, and competitive. It is important to examine risks throughout complex supply chains because your suppliers, although located in low-risk countries, may depend, in turn, on suppliers in high-risk countries, who in turn depend on suppliers elsewhere.[29]

"Don't think of them as terrorist states. Think of them as terrorist markets."

FIGURE 13.3 One company's risk may be an opportunity for another.

Source: Mick Stevens/New Yorker Cartoon Bank/www.cartoonbank.com

CONCEPT CHECK

Recall from Chapter 3 our definition of political risk as the possibility that political decisions, events, or conditions will affect a country's business environment in ways that will cost investors some or all of the value of their investment or force them to accept lower-than-projected rates of return.

Political Risk Changes in political leaders' opinions and policies, civil disorder, and animosity between the host and other countries, particularly the firm's home country, may be politically risky for a company due to lost or damaged property, disrupted operations, and the need to adjust to changes in the rules governing business. Unilever encountered difficulty in attracting foreign executives to work in Pakistan because of security concerns; Chiquita Brands paid money to terrorists in Colombia to protect its employees there; Holcim had its cement investments nationalized in Venezuela; Marriott had a hotel bombed in Indonesia; and Coca-Cola had interrupted services requiring police protection of its trucks and telephone connections in Angola.

Managers use three approaches to predict political risk: *analyzing past patterns, analyzing opinions,* and *examining potentially risky social and economic conditions.*

Analyzing Past Patterns Predicting risk on the basis of past political occurrences is problematic because situations may change for better or worse. Moreover, examining a country's overall situation masks political risk differences within countries and among MNEs. For example, unrest that leads to property damage and disruption of supplies or sales may be limited geographically, such as when companies in Slovenia escaped the damage that others incurred elsewhere during the civil war that led to the breakup of Yugoslavia. With few exceptions, government takeovers of companies have been highly selective, primarily affecting operations that have a visible widespread effect on the country because of their size or monopoly position.

When a company does incur property damage or asset takeover, it is not necessarily a full loss to investors. First, damage may be covered by insurance. Second, governments have preceded most takeovers with formal declarations of intent and have followed with legal processes to determine the foreign investor's compensation, such as the settlement between Venezuela and Holcim.[30] In addition to the investment's book value, other factors may determine the adequacy (or not) of compensation. It may earn a lower return elsewhere, or other agreements (such as purchase and management contracts) may create additional benefits for the former investor. Past settlements may serve as indicators in predicting the likely loss if political problems occur.

Companies should
- Examine views of government decision makers.
- Get a cross-section of opinions.
- Use expert analysts.

Analyzing Opinions Because influential people may sway future political events affecting business, managers should access statements by political leaders both in and out of office to determine their private business philosophies, foreign business relations, the means of effecting economic changes, and their feelings toward given foreign countries. They should also access polls showing different leaders' likelihood of gaining political office. Modern technology has improved access to global media so that reports can be retrieved quickly. When considering a country for the first time, managers should visit to listen to a cross section of opinions from, say, embassy officials, foreign and local businesspeople, journalists, academicians, middle-level local government authorities, and labor leaders. These people usually reveal their own attitudes, which often reflect political conditions that may change and affect the business sector. If already operating within a country, the managers working therein can offer evaluations of changing situations.

Companies have been relying more on commercial-risk assessment services rather than generating their own risk analyses because the services offer concise reports they view as credible. Nevertheless, determining what type of information goes into these reports, how it is collected, and what the track record has been for predictions is certainly useful.

Examining Social and Economic Conditions Countries' social and economic conditions may lead to unrest if population segments have unmet aspirations. Frustrated groups may disrupt business by calling general strikes and destroying property and supply lines, such as in the Niger Delta region of Nigeria, where groups have attacked foreign oil companies' property and kidnapped their employees. Frustrated groups might also replace government leaders, such as in response to the violent 2010–2013 demonstrations in Egypt and Tunisia. And political leaders sometimes harness support by blaming problems on foreigners and foreign companies, which could lead to boycotts or rule changes for MNEs or even expropriation of their properties. However, there is no general consensus as to what constitutes dangerous conditions or how such instability can be predicted. The lack of consensus is illustrated by the diverse reactions of companies to the same political situations.

Rather than political stability itself, the direction of governmental change seems to be very important. But even if a company accurately predicts changes that will affect business, how long the government will take to enact new practices is still uncertain.

CONCEPT CHECK

As we explain in Chapter 8, an exchange rate is the price of a currency; in Chapter 9, we discuss some of the causes of exchange-rate changes (including interest rates and those in floating rate regimes) and explain various methods of forecasting exchange-rate movements (such as focusing on trends in economic variables or trends in the rates themselves).

Foreign Exchange Risk Changes in exchange rates or the ability to move funds out of a country may also affect an MNE. Let's examine these two types of risks.

Exchange-Rate Changes The change in foreign currency value is a two-edged sword, depending on whether you are going abroad to seek sales or resources. Let's say a U.S. company is doing business in India. If it is exporting to India, then a deterioration in the value of the Indian rupee will make it less competitive because it will cost more rupees to buy the U.S. products or services. If it is producing within India to serve the Indian market, its competitiveness in India will not change, but its rupee profits will buy fewer U.S. dollars to bring back to the United States. If, however, it is seeking assets from India, such as Indian personnel to staff a call center, a fall in the rupee value lowers the dollar cost of the personnel.

Companies may accept a lower return in order to move their financial resources more easily.

Mobility of Funds If a company is to invest abroad, then the ability to get funds out of the country is a factor in country comparison. A theory that helps explain this is **liquidity preference,** which is much like option theory in that it relates to investors' desire for some of their holdings to be in highly liquid assets on which they are willing to take a lower return. They need liquidity to make near-term payments, such as paying out dividends; to cover unexpected contingencies, such as stockpiling materials if a strike threatens supply; and to be able to shift funds to even more profitable opportunities, such as purchasing materials at a discount during a temporary price depression.[31]

The comparative liquidity among countries varies because of capital market activity and government exchange control. An active capital market, particularly a stock market, helps a company sell its assets, especially if it wishes to sell shares on a local exchange or sell the entire operation. In the opening case, Burger King moved from being privately held to being publicly held, which was facilitated by its U.S. location with a huge capital market. Thus, when comparing countries you may wish to include the existence of an active stock market as a favorable variable.

If the government restricts the conversion of funds (several countries have various degrees of exchange control), the foreign investor will be forced to spend some profits or proceeds from share sale in the host country. Thus, it's not surprising that, if other things are equal, investors prefer projects in strong-currency countries with little likelihood of exchange controls.

Competitive Risk The comparison of likely success among countries is largely contingent on competitors' actions. We now examine four competitive factors to be considered in choice of location: *making operations compatible, spreading risk, following competitors or customers,* and *heading off competitors.*

Companies are highly attracted to countries that

- Are located nearby.
- Share the same language.
- Have conditions similar to those in their home countries.

Making Operations Compatible Because companies operating abroad encounter less-familiar environments, they have more or different operating risks than local firms. Thus, managers initially prefer to operate where they perceive conditions to be more similar to their home country—provided, of course, that the location also offers sufficient opportunities in terms of sales or resource acquisition.[32] (The major types of attributes of similarity versus dissimilarity are shown in Table 13.1.) As they gain experience, they improve their assessments of consumer, competitor, and government actions, thereby reducing their uncertainty. In fact, MNEs have a lower survival rate than local companies for many years after they begin operations—a situation known as the **liability of foreignness.** However, those that learn about their new environments and manage to overcome their early problems eventually have survival rates comparable to those of local firms.[33]

Does Geography Matter?

Don't Fool with Mother Nature

In the past few years, major earthquakes hit Chile, Haiti, and New Zealand, torrential floods inundated parts of northeast Australia, and a deadly flu pandemic spread from Mexico. These events have publicized global vulnerability to natural disasters and communicable diseases. Each year, about 130 million people are exposed to earthquake risk, 119 million to tropical cyclone hazards, 196 million to catastrophic flooding, and 220 million to drought. Natural disasters, on average, claim 184 deaths per day and cause physical damage to factories, crops, inventories, and infrastructure.

These natural disasters are spread unevenly around the world. Parts of Asia are heavily exposed to earthquakes; some African countries are most vulnerable to drought. The United Nations Development Programme has used 450 variables to analyze and publish a disaster risk index (DRI) that compares physical exposure to hazards by country.[34]

Although only 11 percent of those exposed to such disasters are in the world's poorest nations, those nations account for 55 percent of the deaths because so many of their people live in poor housing and lack adequate medical assistance. Likewise, the rural-to-urban migration in developing countries is largely to dangerous mountainsides, ravines, and low-elevation areas ill-equipped to deal with earthquakes and cyclones.

Catastrophic events upset markets, infrastructure, and production while damaging companies' property and injuring their personnel. Who can forget the heartbreaking 2011 telecasts of Japanese houses, cars, and trains being tossed around like toys in a toddler's bath? The earthquake-induced tsunami played havoc with global supplies as well, such as upsetting the world's auto industry production by creating auto parts shortages.[35] Four months later, heavy rains in Thailand hit first-tier auto parts suppliers as well as second- and third-tier suppliers of small parts for bigger suppliers of components abroad.[36]

Thus, natural events create additional operating risks and insurance costs. In turn, insurance companies are challenged to estimate the likelihood and cost of these events. The World Health Organization has, for instance, developed global atlases of infectious diseases,[37] many of which occur where medical facilities are weakest because of the diseases' association with poverty. They are also associated with natural disaster, such as cholera and malaria outbreaks after flooding, and tend to follow geographic patterns. For example, malaria kills about 2 million people a year, mainly in Africa.

The debilitating effects of disease have an impact on labor force participation and life expectancy and are costly to companies, such as Sasol Petroleum's need to set up a clinic in Mozambique to treat its workers for malaria.[38] Companies also hesitate to send their personnel to epidemic areas. During the Asian severe acute respiratory syndrome (SARS) outbreak, Walmart, Gap, Liz Claiborne, and other companies banned employee travel to affected countries, thus hindering their buying and quality-assurance programs.[39] ■

CONCEPT CHECK

In discussing "Cultural Distance" in Chapter 2, we observe that when two countries are culturally close, a company usually expects fewer differences—and must make fewer adjustments— when moving operations from one to the other. Here we point out that economic similarity often fosters the same conditions of compatibility.

This concept helps explain why, for instance, U.S. companies put earlier and greater emphasis on Canada and the United Kingdom than would be indicated by the opportunity and risk variables discussed so far. In short, managers feel more comfortable doing business in a similar language, culture, and legal system.[40] These similarities may also keep operating costs and risks low because of easier communications. Following early entries, companies also find it useful to create an expansion pattern that will allow management within a portfolio of countries to work interdependently with each other.[41] The opening case shows that Burger King had a strong early emphasis on Latin America and the Caribbean, largely because of distance and communications advantages between that area and the Miami headquarters.

Economic similarity is an important consideration. Both Canada and the United Kingdom have high per capita GDPs, similar to those in the United States, which indicate a likely demand for products first created for the U.S. market. If you first develop products for your domestic market, you might consider other countries' similarity to yours in terms of economic level.

TABLE 13.1 The Distance Sensitivity of Industries: Indicators

Cultural Distance	Administrative Distance	Geographic Distance	Economic Distance
High linguistic content	Government involved in funding, procurement, regulating standard-setting, before international bodies, etc.	Low value-to-weight or bulk	High intensity of labor, other factors prone to absolute cost differences
Strong country of origin effects (vertical distance)	Strategic industry status (votes, money, staples, state control, national champions)	Hazards in transportation	Potential for international scale/scope/experience economies
Significant differences in preferences/standards (horizontal distance)	Specialized, durable sunk capital (and holdup potential)	Perishability/ time-sensitivity	High income-related increases in willingness-to-pay
Entrenched tastes/ traditions	Restraints on trade/FDI (e.g., agriculture)	Need to perform key activities locally (favors FDI over trade)	Differences in customers/channels/ business systems

Source: Based on Pankaj Ghemawat, *World 3.0: World Prosperity and How to Achieve It*, (Boston: Harvard Business Review Press, 2011): 299, which is based on his earlier framework in "Distance Still Matters: The Hard Reality of Global Expansion," *Harvard Business Review*, 79:8 (September 2001): 140.

CONCEPT CHECK

Recall from Chapter 5 that a factor helping to explain trade patterns—why a country trades more with certain countries than with others—is the historical relationship between them, especially continued trade between a former colonizer with its former colonies.

In addition, historical ties between pairs of countries help explain companies' geographic preferences for foreign operations.[42] While many of these ties relate to common culture and ethnicity, others have a history of positive exchanges that reduce the perception of operating risk for companies in home countries and for stakeholders in host countries.

You should also try to ensure that a country's policies and norms are compatible with your company's competitive advantages. Blockbuster failed in Germany because the laws prevented it from operating on evenings, Sundays, and holidays—popular times in the United States and for last-minute impulse decisions to rent videos anywhere.[43]

Companies may also prefer locales that will permit them to operate with product types, plant sizes, and operating practices familiar to their managers. When examining locales, teams that include personnel with backgrounds in each functional area—marketing, finance, human resources, engineering, and production—will more likely uncover the best fits with their companies' resources and objectives.

Finally, companies should consider local availability of resources in relation to their needs. Many foreign operations require local resources, which may severely restrict the feasibility of given locales. A company may need to find local personnel or a viable local partner with an understanding of its type of business and technology. Or it may need to add local capital to what it is willing to bring in.

Geographic Diversification By operating in diverse localities, companies may be able to smooth their sales and profits, which, in turn, gains them a competitive advantage in raising funds.[44] They may further guard against the effects of currency value changes by locating in countries whose exchange rates are not closely correlated with each other.[45] Such a strategy is in many ways opposite to what we just discussed about preferring countries similar to the home country. This is because the best smoothing of sales and profits will likely occur from operating in economies that are the least correlated; however, the downside is that operating in these dissimilar economies may give rise to greater competitive risk because management is less familiar with operating conditions.

Given growing product complexity, companies cannot easily find all needed resources within a single country, especially those based on knowledge. At the same time, such resources are very country-specific because of long-term specialization. Although knowledge flows internationally and from one organization to another, MNEs enhance their access to it by having foreign subsidiaries in source countries. Because pieces of the knowledge emanate from different places, companies need multiple access points to gain a speedy

In terms of competition, some different strategies are to go

- First where other firms are most apt to enter the market as competitors.
- Into markets that competitors have not entered.
- Where there are clusters of competitors.

and comprehensive picture. In fact, evidence indicates that in industries where technology changes rapidly, MNEs with a high breadth of foreign subsidiaries improve their performance more than those concentrating their foreign operations in only a few countries.[46]

Following Competitors or Customers Managers may purposely crowd a market to prevent competitors from gaining advantages there that they can use to improve their competitive positions elsewhere—a situation known as **oligopolistic reaction.**[47] This helps explain why China now has over 170 automobile producers, which is more than any other country and far more than market analysts believe it can sustain.[48]

At the same time, companies may gain advantages by locating where competitors are. To begin with, the competitors may have performed the costly task of evaluating locations and building market acceptance for a particular type of product, so followers may get a so-called free ride. Recall that Burger King profited in some markets from McDonald's development of meat suppliers and demand for hamburgers. Moreover, there are clusters of competitors (sometimes called agglomeration) in various locations—think of all the computer firms in California's Silicon Valley. The adjacent photo shows Europe's largest technology park. These clusters attract multiple suppliers and personnel with specialized skills, as well as buyers who want to compare product and service options but don't want to travel great distances among suppliers. A company also gains better access to information about new developments by coming in frequent contact with personnel from the other firms.[49]

There are also advantages of following customers into a market. Bridgestone Tires was a major supplier to Japanese auto companies in Japan, and it followed them when they established U.S. manufacturing facilities. First, Bridgestone's track record with Japanese auto companies, such as Toyota, gave it an advantage over other tire manufacturers in the United States. Second, if another tire manufacturer were to develop a strong relationship with Toyota in the United States, it might use this experience as a successful springboard to undermine Bridgestone's position elsewhere.

Heading Off Competition A company may try to reduce competitive risk by getting a strong foothold in markets before competitors do, by avoiding strong competitors altogether, or, when its innovative advantage may be short-lived, by moving quickly into markets before competitors can copy the innovation. Of course, this strategy implies ample market where one locates.

The aerial photo shows Sophia Antipolis in the south of France, which is Europe's largest technology park. As of January 2011, there were 1,260 companies with facilities there.
Source: Marcel Jolibos/Getty Images

By being first into a market, a firm may more easily gain the best partners, best locations, and best suppliers—a strategy to gain **first-mover advantage.** Another first-mover advantage is the potential of gaining strong relations with the government, such as Volkswagen in China and Lockheed with Russia.[50]

Companies may also develop location strategies to avoid significant competition. PriceSmart, a discount operator, has all its warehouse stores outside its home country (the United States) and has succeeded by targeting locations in Central America, the Caribbean, and Asia that are considered too small to attract early entry of warehouse stores from competitors like Walmart and Carrefour.[51]

COLLECTING AND ANALYZING DATA

Information is needed at all levels of control.

- Companies should compare the cost of information with its value.

Companies undertake business research to reduce outcome uncertainties from their decisions and to assess their operating performance. The research includes finding answers to questions such as: Can we hire qualified personnel? Will the economic and political climate allow us to reasonably foresee our future? Are our distributors servicing sufficient accounts? What is our market share?

Clearly, information helps managers improve corporate performance. However, they can seldom get all the information they want, due to time and cost constraints. So managers should compare the estimated costs of information with the probable payoff it will generate in revenue gains or cost savings.

SOME PROBLEMS WITH RESEARCH RESULTS AND DATA

Because of the lack, obsolescence, and inaccuracy of data on many countries, research can be difficult and expensive to undertake. Such problems are most acute in developing countries. Let's discuss the two basic problems: inaccuracy and non-comparability.

Information inaccuracies result from

- Difficulty in collecting and analyzing data.
- Purposefully misleading data.
- Exclusion of nonmarket and illegal activity.

Inaccuracy For the most part, we can list five basic reasons why reported information may be inaccurate:

1. *Governmental resources may limit accurate data collection.* Countries may have such limited resources that other projects necessarily receive budget priority, such as spending to improve health and literacy rather than to measure them. Even if governments emphasize data collection, funds may be short for buying the latest computer hardware, software, and training programs. The result may be gaps in reliable and timely information.
2. *Governments may purposely publish misleading information.* Of equal concern to researchers is the publication of false or purposely deceptive information designed to mislead government superiors, the country's rank and file, or companies and institutions abroad. For instance, the European Commission rebuked Greece in 2010 for falsifying public finance data.[52]
3. *Respondents may give false information to data collectors.* Mistrust of how the data will be used may lead respondents to answer questions incorrectly, particularly if they probe financial details or anything else that respondents may consider private. For example, many government figures are collected through questionnaires, such as those in the United States to estimate international travel and tourism expenditures. People may misstate their actual expenditures, particularly if they did not report the true value of foreign purchases on incoming customs forms.
4. *Official data may include only legal and reported market activities.* Further distortions may occur because nationally reported income figures don't include illegal income from such activities as the drug trade, theft, bribery, and prostitution. Such income may appear in other economic sectors because of money laundering. Contraband figures do not appear

in official trade statistics and may be substantial, such as an estimated $7 billion per year of Nigerian oil exports.[53] Finally, many economic activities are unreported and substantial, such as payments in cash to avoid tax payments on income.

5. *Poor methodology may be used.* Inaccuracies are also due to questionable collection and analysis by researchers both within and outside the government. Many statistics are based on estimates and sampling. By using two different means for estimating Chinese consumption in 2012, there was a difference of $1.6 trillion, which was more than the entire GDP of Australia.[54]

In addition, too often broad generalizations are drawn from too few observations on non-representative samples and poorly designed questionnaires.

Problems in information comparability arise from
- Differences in definitions and base years.
- Distortions in currency conversions.

Non-Comparability Countries do not necessarily publish reports such as censuses, output figures, and trade statistics for the same time periods or at the same time as each other. So a company must extrapolate in order to estimate how countries compare. Countries also differ in how they define items, such as family income, literacy, and FDI. Activities taking place outside the market economy, such as within the home, do not show up in income figures. Thus, the different extent among countries in terms of people producing for their own consumption (growing vegetables, preparing meals at home, sewing clothes, cutting hair, and so on) distorts country comparisons.

Accounting rules such as depreciation also differ, resulting in non-comparable net national product figures. Another problem concerns exchange rates, which must be used to convert countries' financial data to some common currency. A 10 percent appreciation of the Japanese yen in relation to the U.S. dollar results in a 10 percent increase in the per capita GDP of Japanese residents when figures are reported in dollars. Does this mean the Japanese are suddenly 10 percent richer? Obviously not, because they use about 85 percent of their yen income to make purchases in yen in their economy; thus, they have little additional purchasing power for 85 percent of what they buy.

EXTERNAL SOURCES OF INFORMATION

Although information is needed for making good location decisions, there are simply too many sources for us to include a comprehensive list. Chances are, at least for scanning purposes, that you will use the Internet to collect most of your information. Some searches will lead you to free information, others to services for which you must pay. The following discussion highlights the major types of information sources in terms of their completeness, reliability, and cost.

Individualized Reports Market research and business consulting companies conduct studies for a fee. They generally are the most costly information source because their individualized nature restricts prorating among a number of companies. However, the fact that a company can specify what information it wants often makes the expense worthwhile.

Specialized Studies Research organizations prepare and sell fairly specific studies at costs much lower than those for individualized reports. These specialized studies are sometimes directories of companies that operate in a given locale, perhaps containing financial or other information about the companies. They may also be about business in certain locales, forms of business, or specific products.

Service Companies Most companies providing services to international clients—such as banks, transportation agencies, and accounting firms—publish reports that are usually geared toward either the conduct of business in a given area or some specific subject of general interest, such as tax or trademark legislation. Because the service firms intend to reach a wide market of companies, their reports tend to be fairly general. Some also offer informal opinions about such things as the reputations of possible business associates and the names of people to contact in a company.

Government Agencies When a government wants to stimulate foreign business activity, the amount and type of information it makes available may be substantial. The U.S. Department of Commerce compiles news and regulations about individual foreign countries, disseminates specific information on product sales locations in the National Trade Data Bank, and can also help set up appointments with businesspeople abroad.

International Organizations and Agencies Numerous organizations and agencies are supported by more than one country, including the UN, the WTO, the IMF, the OECD, and the EU. All of them have large research staffs that compile basic statistics and prepare reports and recommendations concerning common trends and problems. Many international development banks even help finance investment-feasibility studies.

Trade Associations Trade associations connected to various product lines collect, evaluate, and disseminate a wide variety of data dealing with technical and competitive factors in their industries. Many of these data are available in the trade journals published by such associations; others may or may not be available to nonmembers.

INTERNALLY GENERATED DATA

MNEs may have to collect much information themselves, sometimes simply by observing keenly and asking many questions. Investigators can see what kind of merchandise is available, determine who is buying and where, and uncover the hidden distribution points and competition. Hidden competition for ready-made clothing may be seamstresses working in private homes; for vacuum cleaners, it may be servants who clean with mops. Surreptitiously sold contraband may compete with locally produced goods. Traditional analysis methods would not reveal such facts.

Companies already operating within a market offer another source of information. Limited Brands has used this source, such as meeting with Apple's management in China, to ascertain experiences encountered during entry.[55]

COUNTRY COMPARISON TOOLS

Once companies scan for information, they need to analyze it. Two common tools for this are *grids* and *matrices.* In preparing either, it is useful to have a team made up of people from different functions so that various perspectives are considered. However, once companies commit to locations, they need continuous updates.

Should Companies Operate in and Send Employees to Violent Areas?

Point

Point **Yes** Where there's risk, there are usually rewards. Companies should not shun areas with violence. Businesspeople have always taken risks, and employees have always gone to dangerous areas. As far back as the seventeenth century, immigrants to what are now the United States, India, and Australia encountered disease and hostile native populations. Had companies and immigrants not taken chances, the world would be far less developed today.

You can't look at the risk from violence apart from others. Although we don't have historical data, most situations are probably safer today. Disease is still a bigger danger than violence, but medical advances against a number of historical killers (polio, measles, smallpox, tuberculosis, etc.)

have reduced that risk, while evacuation in case of a *real* emergency situation is much faster.

But let's assume for a moment that we decide to avoid countries with the potential for violence against our facilities and employees. Is there any such place? To answer this question, you need to consider an array of indicators that include overall crime rate, murder rate, terrorism, kidnapping, and political violence. Because so many occurrences go unreported, the statistics are unreliable. Further, situations can change quickly, as witnessed by the sudden outbreak of violence in Syria. The opinions from so-called risk experts are certainly conflicting. Finally, countries that we think of as safe—Norway, United Kingdom, United States—have had such recent violence as mass shootings, bombings, and street riots. In fact, the deputy assistant director of the FBI said, "We are dealing every single day with a variety of domestic terrorism threats that are alive and well and in this country [United States]."[56] Now about the only place that everyone agrees is low-risk is Greenland.

Some industries don't have the luxury of avoiding violent countries. Take the petroleum industry. Oil companies have to go where there is a high likelihood of finding oil. It would be great to find it all in places like Switzerland, but this is not the reality. Most of the credible alternatives are in areas that have had recent bombings, kidnappings, or organized crime—the Middle East, West Africa, the Central Asian former Soviet republics, and Venezuela. If companies didn't go to these places, they'd be out of business.

In effect, we'll keep operating anywhere there are opportunities. If a place seems physically risky, we'll take whatever precautions we can. We'll share intelligence reports, put people through safety training courses (there are plenty of these available now), and take security actions abroad. And perhaps we won't transfer spouses and children to the "risky" areas so we don't have to be on top of what is happening with as many people.

Should Companies Operate in and Send Employees to Violent Areas?

Counterpoint

No We're no longer concerned simply with being caught in the crossfire between opposing military factions. Antiglobalization groups want to harm our personnel and facilities so that we'll leave, or so that they gain international publicity. Groups see us as easy marks for extortion by threatening harm or kidnapping our personnel. Still others are against foreigners, regardless of their aims. Such a group in Afghanistan killed staff members from Médecins sans Frontières and the Red Cross who were there to treat sick and injured people.[57]

At the same time, getting caught in the crossfire has become a bigger risk. Arms trafficking has risen and has lowered prices not only to revolutionaries but also to drug and alien smugglers and money launderers.[58] As MNEs, we can't help being visible, and thus vulnerable.

In essence, if we operate where risk of violence is great, we put our personnel in danger. Even if no violence comes to them, they endure stress that negatively affects their performance.[59] Although local personnel may be at a lesser risk of, say, kidnapping, experience shows that they too are not immune. Furthermore, we have to send foreign personnel there. Some go as managers or technicians on long assignments; others must go on business trips to do such things as audit books, ensure quality control, and offer staff advice through on-site visits. The dangers are not inconsequential.

Counterpoint

There are thousands of reported kidnappings per year, many targeting foreign workers and their families. Nigeria has been the site of recent kidnappings of foreign oil workers, ship crew members, and even a visiting priest.[60]

It's simply unethical to put our employees in such situations. Of course, we don't force them to go to dangerous places, and we can get enough people to work there, especially during a global recession. However, our experience is that there are three types of people who want or are willing to work in such areas, and none are ideal. First are those who simply want the high compensation and big insurance policies, some of whom are experienced in military or undercover activities. They tend to be highly independent and hard to control. Second are the naïve who don't understand the danger and are difficult to safeguard through training and security activities. Third are the thrill seekers, who find that adrenaline is like an addictive drug; they are most at risk because of the thrill of danger and their reluctance to leave when situations worsen.[61]

High risk to individuals is indicative of a political situation out of control—a harbinger of additional risks that may occur through governmental changes, falls in consumer confidence, and a general malaise that damages revenues and operating regulations. This is not the kind of country in which to conduct operations.

GRIDS

Grids are tools that

- May depict acceptable or unacceptable conditions.
- Rank countries by important variables.

Managers may use a grid to compare countries on whatever factors they deem important. Table 13.2 is an example of a grid with information placed into three categories. The managers may immediately eliminate certain countries from consideration because of characteristics they find unacceptable (companies vary in this). These factors are in the first category of variables, by which Country I is eliminated. The managers assign values and weights to other variables so that they rank each country according to attributes of relative importance to the company. In this hypothetical example, we've attached more weight to the size of investment needed than to the tax rate. For instance, the table graphically pinpoints Country II as high return–low risk, Country III as low return–low risk, Country IV as high return–high risk, and Country V as low return–high risk.

Both the variables and the weights differ by product and company depending on the company's internal situation and its objectives. For instance, managers in a company selling a low-priced consumer product might weigh population size heavily as an indicator of market opportunity, whereas those in a company selling tires might weigh heavily the number of vehicles registered. The grid technique is useful even when a company does not compare countries because it can set the minimum score needed for either investing additional resources or committing more funds to a more detailed feasibility study.

Grids do tend to get cumbersome, however, as the number of variables increases. Although they are useful in ranking countries, they often obscure interrelationships among them.

TABLE 13.2 Simplified Market-Penetration Grid

This table is simply an example: In the real world, a company chooses the variables that it regards as most important and may weight some as more important than others. Here managers rate Country II the most attractive because it's regarded as high return–low risk. Country IV also promises a high return and Country III low risk. Note that Country I is eliminated immediately because the company will go only where 100 percent ownership is permitted.

		Country				
Variable	**Weight**	**I**	**II**	**III**	**IV**	**V**
1. Acceptable (A), Unacceptable (U) factors						
a. Allows 100 percent ownership	—	U	A	A	A	A
b. Allows licensing to majority-owned subsidiary	—	A	A	A	A	A
2. Return (higher number = preferred rating)						
a. Size of investment needed	0–5	—	4	3	3	3
b. Direct costs	0–3	—	3	1	2	2
c. Tax rate	0–2	—	2	1	2	2
d. Market size, present	0–4	—	3	2	4	1
e. Market size, 3–10 years	0–3	—	2	1	3	1
f. Market share, immediate potential, 0–2 years	0–2	—	2	1	2	1
g. Market share, 3–10 years	0–2	—	2	1	2	0
Total			18	10	18	10
3. Risk (lower number = preferred rating)						
a. Market loss, 3–10 years (if no present penetration)	0–4	—	2	1	3	2
b. Exchange problems	0–3	—	0	0	3	3
c. Political-unrest potential	0–3	—	0	1	2	3
d. Business laws, present	0–4	—	1	0	4	3
e. Business laws, 3–10 years	0–2	—	0	1	2	2
Total			3	3	14	13

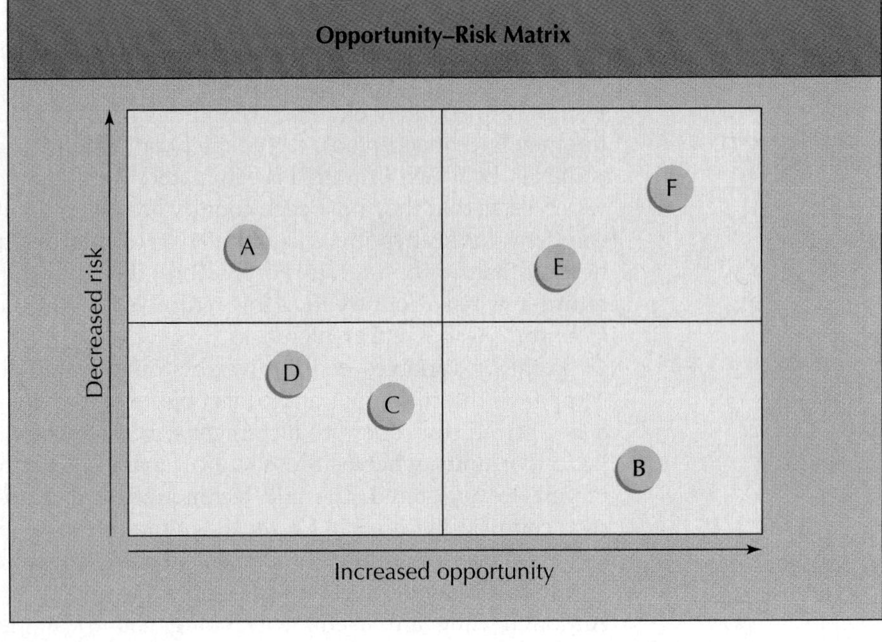

FIGURE 13.4 Opportunity–Risk Matrix

Countries E and F are the most desirable because they boast a combination of a high level of opportunity and a low level of risk. But what if the decision came down to Countries A and B? The level of opportunity in Country A may not be as high as a company would like, but the low level of risk may be attractive. Country B, however, promises a high level of opportunities but also threatens a high level of risk. A decision between Countries A and B will probably take the firm's risk tolerance into consideration.

With an opportunity-risk matrix, a company can

- Decide on indicators and weigh them.
- Evaluate each country on the weighted indicators.

MATRICES

To more clearly show the opportunity/risk relationship, managers can plot values on a matrix such as the one shown in Figure 13.4. In this particular example, Countries E and F are high-opportunity and low-risk countries compared to Countries A, B, C, and D, making them better candidates for detailed analysis.

In reality, however, managers may sometimes have to choose between a country with high risk and high opportunity and another with low risk and low opportunity, thus making a decision based on their tolerance for risk and on the portfolio of countries where the company is already operating. Further, although A, B, C, and D are less appealing than E and F, the company may nevertheless find opportunities in A, B, C, and D—perhaps licensing or shared-ownership arrangements—without necessarily making a large commitment.

But how can managers plot values on such a matrix? They must determine which factors are good indicators of their companies' risk and opportunity and weight them to reflect their importance. For instance, on the risk axis they might give 20 percent (0.2) of the weight to expropriation risk, 25 percent (0.25) to foreign-exchange controls, 20 percent (0.2) to civil disturbances and terrorism, 20 percent (0.2) to natural disasters, and 15 percent (0.15) to exchange-rate change, for a total allocation of 100 percent. They would then rate each country on a scale, such as from 1 to 10 for each variable (with 10 indicating the best score), and multiply each variable by the weight they allocate to it. If they give Country A a rating of 8 on the expropriation-risk variable, they would multiply 8 by 0.2 (the weight they assign to expropriation) for a score of 1.6. They would then sum all of Country A's risk-variable scores to place it on the risk axis, and similarly plot the location of Country A on the opportunity axis.

A key element of this kind of matrix, and one that managers do not always include in practice, is the projection of where countries will be in the future, or at least the direction in which they *should* move. Such a projection is obviously useful, but the farther one forecasts into the future, the less certain the projection.

ALLOCATING AMONG LOCATIONS

The scanning tools just described are useful for narrowing country alternatives and allocating operational emphasis among countries. We now examine three complementary strategies for international expansion: alternative gradual commitments, geographic diversification versus concentration, and reinvestment versus harvesting.

ALTERNATIVE GRADUAL COMMITMENTS

Companies may reduce risks from the liability of foreignness by

- Going first to countries with characteristics similar to those of their home countries.
- Having experienced intermediaries handle operations for them.
- Operating in formats requiring commitment of fewer resources abroad.
- Moving initially to one or a few, rather than many, foreign countries.

As we've discussed, because of liability of foreignness, companies favor operations in areas similar to their home countries. Nevertheless, there are alternative means of risk-minimization expansion patterns they can undertake, as shown in Figure 13.5. As you examine this figure, note that the farther a company moves from the center on any axis, the deeper its international commitment becomes.

However, a company does not necessarily move at the same speed along each axis. In fact, it may jump over some of the steps. A slow movement along one axis may free up resources that allow faster expansion along another.

Let's examine Figure 13.5 more closely. Axis A shows that companies tend to move gradually from a purely domestic focus to one that encompasses operations in countries similar and then dissimilar to one's own country. However, an alternative when moving quickly along the A axis (and even jumping the intermediate step) is to move slowly along the B axis. The B axis shows that a company may use intermediaries to handle foreign operations during early stages of international expansion because this minimizes the resources it puts at risk and its liability of foreignness. It can then commit fewer resources to both international endeavors, relying instead on the intermediaries that already know how to operate in the foreign market. A related example is the foreign expansion of some high-tech companies from developing countries. Rather than first targeting nearby countries with characteristics similar

FIGURE 13.5 The Usual Pattern of Internationalization

The farther a company moves outward along any of the axes (A, B, C, D), the deeper its international commitment. Most companies move at different speeds along different axes.

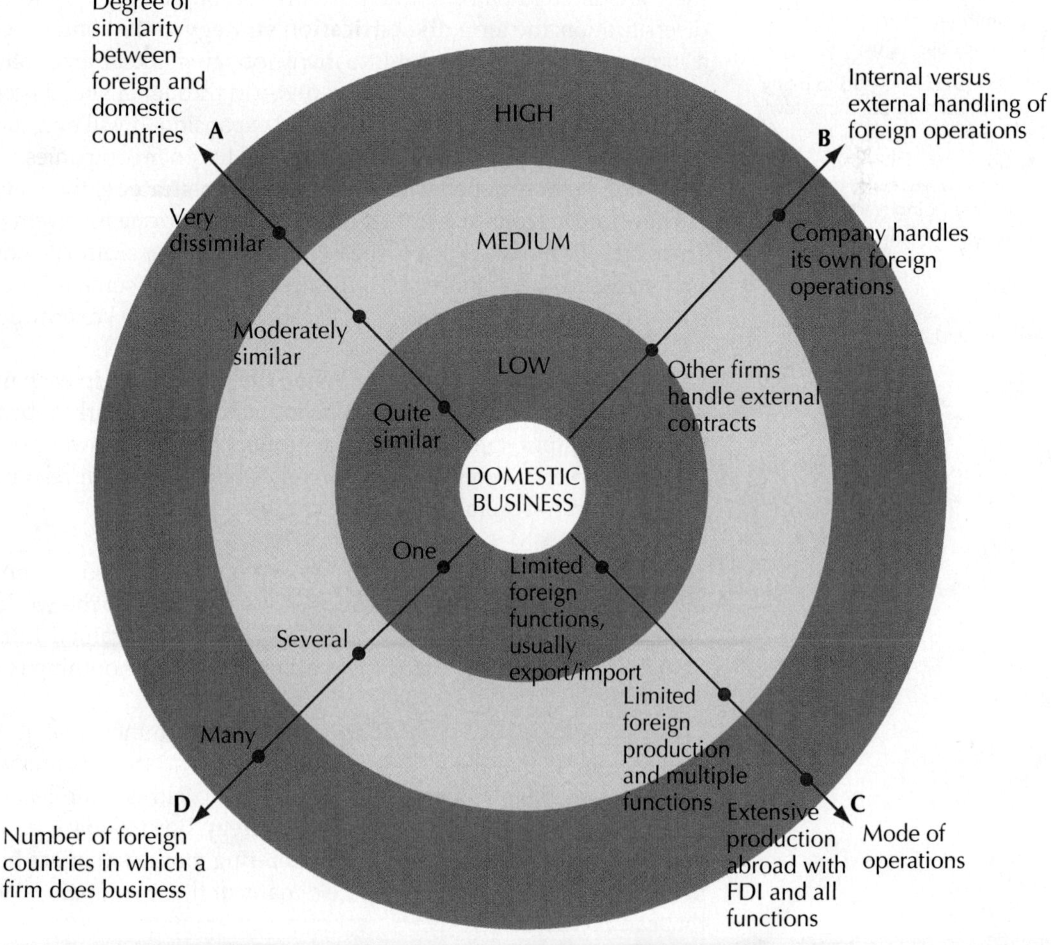

to their home markets, they have gone to high-income countries where short-term market potentials are higher. However, they have relied heavily on intermediaries and have made foreign acquisitions that include the personnel who know the markets they are targeting.

However, if the business grows successfully, the company may want to handle the operations with its own staff. This is because by learning more about foreign operations it perceives them less risky than at the onset, and it realizes that the volume of business may justify the development of internal capabilities such as hiring trained personnel to maintain a department for foreign sales or purchases.

Axis C shows that importing or exporting is usually the first international mode a company undertakes. At an early stage of international involvement, importing and exporting require the placement of few company resources abroad. In fact, it may involve investing few additional resources if the company can use excess production capacity to produce more goods, which it would then export. Thus, moving along the C axis is a means to minimize the risk of the liability of foreignness because of first forgoing such functions as managing a foreign workforce for production.

Later, the company might, in addition to exporting, make an even higher commitment through FDI to produce abroad. Its infusion of capital, personnel, and technology is highest for these operations. Axis D shows that companies can move internationally one country at a time, which keeps them from being overwhelmed by learning about many countries all at once. However, as we discuss in the next section, there may be a competitive drive to move to a number of countries almost simultaneously.

GEOGRAPHIC DIVERSIFICATION VERSUS CONCENTRATION

Strategies for ultimately reaching a high level of commitment in many countries are

- Diversification—go to many fast and then build up slowly in each.
- Concentration—go to one or a few and build up fast before going to others.
- A hybrid of the two.

Ultimately, a company may gain a sizable presence and commitment in most countries; however, there are different paths to that position. Although any move abroad means some geographic diversification, the term **diversification strategy** in the context of location decisions describes a company's rapid movement into many foreign markets, gradually increasing its commitment within each one. A company can do this, say, through a liberal licensing policy to ensure sufficient resources for the initial widespread expansion. It will eventually increase its involvement by taking on activities that it first contracted to other companies.

At the other extreme, with a **concentration strategy,** the company will move to only one or a few foreign countries until it develops a very strong involvement and competitive position. There are, of course, hybrids of the two strategies—for example, moving rapidly to most markets but increasing commitment in only a few. Table 13.3 sums up the major variables a company should consider when deciding which strategy to use.[62] We now discuss each of these.

Growth Rate in Each Market When the growth rate in each market is high or needs to be high, a company should usually concentrate on a few markets because it will cost a great deal to expand output sufficiently for each one. However, slower growth or the need for growth in each market may result in a company's having enough resources to build and maintain a market share in several different countries.[63]

Sales Stability in Each Market As we have discussed, a company may smooth its earnings and sales because of operations in various parts of the world. The more stable the sales and profits within each market, the less advantage gained from a diversification strategy. Similarly, the more correlated the markets, the less smoothing is achieved by selling in each.

Competitive Lead Time If a company determines that it has a long lead time over competitors, it may be able to follow a concentration strategy and still beat competitors into other markets. Otherwise, it may need to either cede leadership in some countries to competitors or follow a diversification strategy. Born global companies are particularly prone to follow diversification strategies by entering markets that are both similar and dissimilar to those in their home markets because many of these companies depend on new technologies that can obsolesce quickly.[64]

TABLE 13.3 To Diversify or to Concentrate: The Role of Product and Market Factors

If a company determines that "Product or Market Factors" satisfy the conditions in the column headed "Prefer Diversification," it may benefit from moving quickly into several markets simultaneously. If the same factors satisfy the conditions under "Prefer Concentration," it may decide to enter and work initially to develop a substantial presence in just one or a few markets.

Product or Market Factor	Prefer Diversification If:	Prefer Concentration If:
1. Growth rate of each market	Low	High
2. Sales stability in each market	Low	High
3. Competitive lead time	Short	Long
4. Spillover effects	High	Low
5. Need for product, communication, and distribution adaptation	Low	High
6. Program control requirements	Low	High

Source: "Marketing Expansion Strategies in Multinational Marketing," *Journal of Marketing* 43 (Spring 1979): 89. Reprinted by permission of the American Marketing Association © 1979.

Spillover Effects Situations in which the marketing program in one country results in awareness of the product in other countries are known as **spillover effects.** These are advantageous because additional customers may be reached with little additional cost, which can happen if the product is advertised through media sent cross-nationally, such as U.S. television ads that reach Canadians. When marketing programs reach many countries, such as by satellite television or the Internet, a diversification strategy has advantages.

Need for Product, Communication, and Distribution Adaptation Companies may have to alter products and methods of operating abroad—a process that, because of cost, favors a concentration strategy. The adaptation cost may limit the resources the company has for expanding in many different markets. Further, if the adaptations are unique to each country, the company cannot easily spread the costs over sales in more than one country to reduce total unit costs.

Program Control Requirements The more a company needs to control its operations in a foreign country, the more favorable a concentration strategy is. This is because the company will need to use more of its resources to maintain that control, such as by taking a larger percentage of ownership in the operation. Its need for more control could be for various reasons, including the fear that collaboration with a partner will create a competitor.

Subsequent Product Diversification The above discussion centers on initial movements into different countries. In addition, companies add new products to their portfolios and must decide where and how quickly to introduce them abroad. The more related the new products are to their existing products, especially those they are already selling abroad, the quicker they can move them into other markets. This is because the companies have experience that is more applicable to their products' introduction.[65]

REINVESTMENT AND HARVESTING

So far, we've discussed the sequencing of country entry. Then, once a company is operating abroad, it must evaluate how much effort to allocate to each location. With FDI, the company transfers financial capital and has physical and human capital in place. If the investment is successful, the company will earn money that it may remit back to headquarters or reinvest to increase the investment value. Over time, most of the value of a company's foreign investment, if successful, comes from reinvesting. If the investment is unsuccessful, the company may consider transferring capital elsewhere.

A company may have to make new commitments to maintain competitiveness abroad.

Reinvestment Decisions Companies treat decisions to replace depreciated assets or to add to the existing stock of capital from retained earnings abroad somewhat differently from original investment decisions. Once committed to a given locale, a company may find no option to move a substantial portion of the earnings elsewhere; to do so would endanger the continued successful operation of the given foreign facility. The failure to expand might result in a falling market share and a higher unit cost than that of competitors.

Aside from competitive factors, a company may need several years of almost total reinvestment and allocation of new funds in one area to attain its objectives, such as meeting target growth. Moreover, a company may treat reinvestment decisions differently because experienced personnel in a given country may be the best judges of what is needed there, so headquarters may delegate certain investment decisions to them.

Companies must decide how to get out of operations if

- They no longer fit the overall strategy.
- There are better alternative opportunities.

Harvesting Companies commonly reduce commitments in some countries because those countries have poorer performance prospects than do others—a process known as **harvesting (or divesting).** Burger King, for example, sold off underperforming operations in Korea and Slovakia so as to have funds for more promising ventures in the Chinese and Russian markets. There are other reasons as well. J. Sainsbury withdrew from the Egyptian market because its management did not expect a turnaround in its poorly performing operation there.[66] Dana sold its U.K. facility to use funds to concentrate on developing different automotive technologies.[67] Goodyear sold its Indonesian rubber plantation because of its decision to stop producing rubber.[68]

Some indications suggest that companies might benefit by planning divestments better and by developing divestment specialists. Companies have tended to wait too long before divesting, instead trying expensive means of improving performance, such as those proposed by local managers who fear losing their positions if the company abandons the operation Ideas for investment projects typically originate with middle managers or managers in foreign subsidiaries who are enthusiastic about collecting information to accompany a proposal as it moves upward in the organization. After all, the evaluation and employment of these people depend on growth. They have no such incentive to propose divestments. These proposals typically originate at the top of the organization after upper management has tried most remedies for improving operational performance.[69]

Companies may divest by a sale or closure of facilities, usually preferring a sale because they receive some compensation. A company that considers divesting because of a country's well-publicized political or economic situation may find few potential buyers except at very low prices. In such situations, it may try to delay divestment, hoping that the situation will improve. If it does, the firm that waits out the situation generally is in a better position to regain markets and profits than one that forsakes its operation.

A company cannot always simply abandon an investment either. Governments frequently require performance contracts, such as substantial severance packages to employees that make a loss from divestment greater than the direct investment's net value. Further, the length of time to go through insolvency (up to 10 years in some countries) alters the percentage of value recovered from a divestment. In Japan, investors recover an average of 93 percent of the value, whereas in Madagascar they typically recover only 13 percent.[70] Finally, many MNEs fear adverse international publicity and difficulty in reentering a market if they do not sever relations with a foreign government on amicable terms.

NONCOMPARATIVE DECISION MAKING

Most companies examine proposals one at a time and accept them if they meet minimum-threshold criteria.

Because companies have limited resources at their disposal, it might seem that they maintain a storehouse of foreign operating proposals that they can rank by some predetermined criteria. If this were so, managers could simply start allocating resources to the top-ranked proposal and continue down the list until they could make no further commitments. This is often not the case, however. They make **go-no-go decisions** by examining one opportunity at a time and pursuing it if it meets some threshold criteria.

To begin with, companies sometimes need to respond quickly to prospects they had not anticipated. Many might need to respond to unsolicited proposals to sell abroad or sign joint venture or licensing contracts. Many might initiate export activity passively—that is, foreign companies or export intermediaries approach them to be suppliers. Similarly, undertakings may be onetime possibilities because a government or another company solicits requests. For example, Tasmanian development offices (Australia) proposed that Malaysia's Ta Ann Holdings use its veneer peeling technology by investing in Tasmania. For Ta Ann, it was a one-time opportunity to say "yes" or "no."[71] Or a government may change rules to allow foreign acquisitions, such as Nigeria did for banking.[72] Further, there may be a chance to buy properties that another company divests. When Enron faced bankruptcy, it needed to sell many of its foreign facilities, so companies such as Tractebel from Belgium and Royal Dutch/Shell bid on its Korean facilities.[73] Having discussed the competitive advantages of following customers' and competitors' moves into foreign markets, we know we cannot always foresee when the customers and competitors will move.

Another factor inhibiting the comparison of country operations is that their interdependence can keep them from being meaningfully evaluated separately. Profit figures from individual operations may obscure the real impact on overall company profits. If a U.S. company were to establish an assembly operation in Australia, the operation could either increase or reduce exports from the United States, thus affecting U.S. profit figures. Moreover, headquarters may have to incur additional costs to oversee the Australian operation and coordinate the movement of components into Australia. These costs are difficult to estimate and will likely not show up in the Australian income figures.

Or perhaps by building a plant in Brazil to supply components to Volkswagen of Brazil, the company may increase the possibility of selling to Volkswagen in other countries. As a result of the Australian or Brazilian projects, management would have to make assumptions about the changed profits for the company's total global operations. Finally, interdependence occurs because much of the sales and purchases of foreign subsidiaries are among units of the same parent company. The prices the company charges on these transactions will affect the relative profitability of one unit compared to another.

Clearly, companies cannot afford to conduct very many feasibility studies simultaneously. Even if they can, the studies are apt to be in various stages of completion at any given time. Suppose a company completes its study for an Australian project while continuing studies on New Zealand, Japan, and Indonesia. Can the company afford to hold off on making a decision about Australia? Probably not. Waiting would likely invalidate much of the Australian study, thus necessitating added expense and further delays to update it. In sum, three factors inhibit companies from comparing investment opportunities: cost, time, and the interrelation of operations on global performance.

Looking to the Future

Will Prime Locations Change?

Future sales- and resource-seeking opportunities and risks may shift among countries because of a variety of demographic, sociocultural, political-legal, technological, and economic conditions. We will concentrate here on population changes and where populations can and will prefer to work. In Chapter 5, we discussed how demographers expect a slowing in the growth of global population through 2050, with some countries experiencing declining populations. At the same time, growth should remain robust in many developing economies, particularly those in sub-Saharan Africa. The projection is that the percentage of people living in currently developed countries is expected to fall to 13.7 percent from a 2000 figure of 19.7 percent. The least developed countries will have the biggest population increase.

Further, because the world's population will continue to age, the share of what we now consider the working-age population should fall for developed countries and increase in many developing ones.

Because there is a positive relationship between the proportional size of the working-age population and per capita GDP, the growth in per capita GDP should be higher in today's developing economies than in today's developed countries unless we redefine working age.[74] These demographic changes, if they materialize, will have implications for the location of both markets and labor forces.

An intriguing possibility is the near-officeless headquarters for international companies. Technology may permit more people to work from anywhere as they email and teleconference with their colleagues, customers, and suppliers. In fact, they can live anywhere in the world and work from their homes, as is already occurring at least part-time within some professions. However, if people can work from home, they may move those homes where they want to live rather than living where their employers are now located. Highly creative, innovative, self-motivated people can usually get permission to live in almost any country of the world.

A leading researcher on urbanization and planning has shown that beginning at least as early as the Roman Empire these types of people have been drawn to certain cities that were the centers of innovation. He maintains that this attraction is due to people's improvement through interchange with others like themselves—like "a very bright class in a school or a college. They all try to score off each other and do better." Thus, if he's correct, the brightest minds may work more at home but still need the face-to-face interaction with their colleagues.[75] The continued attraction of young technical people to places like Silicon Valley seems to confirm this viewpoint.[76]

These arguments are provocative, particularly because we now have technology to allow people to communicate without traveling as much. Yet the continued increase in business travel shows that there is still a need for face-to-face interaction. The researcher further suggests that these people will be drawn to the same places that attract tourists.

Concomitantly, another view is that in leading Western societies, the elite made up of intellectuals and highly educated people is increasingly using its capability to delay and block new technologies. If successful, their efforts will result in the emergence of different countries at the forefront of technological development and acceptance.[77] ■

CASE The LEGO® Group[78]

The LEGO® Group is a family business founded in 1932, making wooden toys in the city of Billund, Denmark. In 1958, Godtfred Kirk Christiansen, son of the company founder Ole Kirk Christiansen, created the LEGO© brick, widely praised and acclaimed as the "Toy of the Century," by both *Fortune* magazine and the British Association of Toy Retailers (LEGO, Annual Report, 2011). Today, LEGO is Europe's largest and the world's second-largest toy manufacturer in terms of sales volume. It had a turnover of €2,511 million in 2012, and employed more than 9,000 worldwide. LEGO's sales during the first half of 2013 increased by 13 percent with its strongest growth in Asia. The company has been a pioneer in breaking convention at the cost of failing and almost going bankrupt by 2003, with its adventurous forays and building what it believed was a diverse portfolio that boasted of video and other games, apparel, and theme parks. Riding high on the success of its *Harry Potter* and *Star Wars* themed series, LEGO's road to self-realization was in understanding that the brick was at its core.

The diversification was a direct response to developments and challenges in the industry. In the 1990s, the segment for construction toys was shrinking. The competition for kids' time and their parents' money was getting sharper. LEGO is part of the market called "edutainment," including products with the ability to entertain and educate at the same time. First of all, computer games "stole" a lot of potential LEGO users. Little virtual playgrounds and computer games like SimCity or Civilization soon presented themselves as a threat to

A girl plays with LEGO toys in Thailand
Source: © panitanjohn - Fotolia.com

traditional toymakers like LEGO. Who needed toy bricks, with the deluge of computer and other simulation games flooding the market!

Simultaneously, the power of retailers grew. Especially in the United States, the buyers of LEGO products were reduced to only a few companies like Toys"R"Us, Walmart, and Kmart. LEGO's business model was very dependent on retailers, who now started demanding larger discounts and specially adjusted products. LEGO was caught in a dilemma, between the decision to adopt a flexible price strategy that would cater to lower budgets or to continue with its existing price structures that promised standardized products across the board. To protect its brand in the market, LEGO wanted customers to be able to buy the same products at almost the same price everywhere. If these customers knew that there was only one price and quality level for a certain LEGO product, they would see the company as a lot more trustworthy, as opposed to a situation where all LEGO products were available at a low cost and, possibly, low-quality at some retailers. The company's CEO reached out to LEGO's fanbase who responded with threats to leave their favorite brand if it steered from quality in an attempt to offer their toys for cheaper prices. It was decided that LEGO's overall reputation for reliability was best left untouched with its promise of upholding a single high standard for its corresponding quality and price; conversely LEGO's consumer image would have suffered had it compromised over price.

To become more independent, the company slowly began to look for different platforms and new ways of selling its existing products and building on innovation from within. The internet provided that opportunity. In the early 2000s, LEGO launched LEGO Direct, which was the successor of the not-so-successful LEGO World Shop. With LEGO Direct, it became possible for customers to invent or assemble their own LEGO (virtual) constructions on their personal computers like in video games. When finished, they could order the specific LEGO products required for their dream constructions. This option gave the company some valuable advantages: They became more independent of the retailers and enjoyed a direct communication channel with their customers on their Web site, where they could quickly realize new demands from their consumers. LEGO.com has been very successful and has had over a million visitors per month, with the average visitor staying for 8–9 minutes.

Moreover, LEGO is the only major traditional toy maker that targeted the adult market, and has a strong following in the Adult Fans of Legos or AFOL communities worldwide. LEGO's Architecture Series directly targets this market of adult Lego fans, a solid example of LEGO's attempts to return to its core strength. Seoul's Sungnyemun gate and Tokyo's Imperial Hotel featured in LEGO's Architecture series, further establish the company's hunger for new markets across not just age segments but also different geographies. More recently, LEGO adapted an existing dinosaur set and repackaged it as a commemorative Year of the Snake special edition, sold only in China.

Meanwhile, the global toy industry has been growing at a Compound Annual Growth Rate (CAGR) of 2.9 percent from 2008 to 2012, while the global economy has grown by only 2.6 percent. The industry growth is not equally divided; neither by region, nor by country. While some countries, especially emerging markets, are experiencing relevant growth such as France, Germany, Australia, Brazil, and China, others like USA and Canada are experiencing negative growth in their market shares. To reach its global customer base, LEGO currently has offices in 29 countries. Because its products don't need local adaptation, the company has reduced its office base over time. The company only needs to accommodate the products to local laws, which can be done initially for each product line in a centralized setting. Initially, LEGO moved many production sites to international locations, to lower its costs as with the Czech Republic and Mexico plants, and also the outsourcing of production of Flextronics to Poland.[79]

Over the past two decades, LEGO has made several production location decisions, with its underlying purpose being the accumulation of cost savings. However, this time a growing demand and an effort to reduce lead time between order and delivery are the main drivers behind the company's decision to invest hundreds of millions of euros in the new in-region manufacturing facilities in China. According to the global research firm Companies and Markets, by 2016, the Asia-Pacific region is expected to become the world's largest toy market. In the words of LEGO's spokesperson Roar Rude Trangbaek, the strategy was to shift production closer to its core markets. Factories in the Asia-Pacific region would thus, not supply to Europe or North America. The stated goal is for the LEGO factory in China to be able to supply 70 to 80 percent of the LEGO bricks sold in Asia in 2017.

Although Asia is LEGO's smallest market, contributing less than 10 percent of its revenue, annual sales in the region have peaked by more than 50 percent as millions of Asian consumers are buying educational toys amidst improved wage scenarios and better living standards. In the first half of 2013, the company experienced their strongest performance in Asia with consumer sales growing by about 35 percent. In fact, LEGO's CEO Jørgen Vig Knudstorp, expects higher growth rates in Asia. LEGO's revenue of nearly two billion dollars in the first half of 2013—compared with $1.43 billion for Hasbro, its close competitor—was boosted heavily by its growth of seventy per cent in China. China has become the world's second-largest toy market. It is predicted that the Asia-Pacific region will overtake North America as the largest regional toy market in 2014. The LEGO group also aims for the European, African and the Middle Eastern region, Asian, and American markets to contribute equally to sales and fuel further expansions.

The decision to choose China as the destination for setting up their production facility might have raised eyebrows within the industry. Previously, toy makers faced continuous struggles in China, where parents would rather see their children reading books than playing. In fact, playing has often been considered a dirty word in a culture where formal education is prioritized. However, many toy companies are already discovering that they can influence Chinese parents by positioning their toys as 'educational items.' In this regard, LEGO has already struck a chord with affluent Chinese parents, with toys that are being branded as educational tools to help children with developing dexterity and creativity. In an initiative to make itself known to the Chinese public, LEGO is spearheading several projects including mobilizing a group of students from Tsinghua University to build a low-cost atomic force microscope with LEGO's 3D parts and electronics.

A challenging issue for LEGO in China is consumers get lured by similar products by other manufacturers who build identical looking LEGO bricks, commonly known as "LEGO clones." Already swamped in a history of court battles over its copyright, LEGO is presently also locked in a legal spat with Hong Kong's Best-Lock Construction Toys, accused of ripping off LEGO's signature mini-figures. Although LEGO has been relatively successful in its copyright battles so far, several copies and clones abound in the market either claiming to be LEGO products or stating compatibility/association with the world's leading toy bricks. Blocks marketed by Chinese companies Ligao and Banbao are often direct copies of LEGO designs.

One potential strategy to keep these pirates at bay is to increase LEGO's already high manufacturing standards as most Chinese toy factories are focused on producing and exporting low-cost inferior products rather than high-quality ones for domestic consumption. LEGO has invested in creating customized products for Chinese or Asian markets. Judging by precedent, this is a risky strategy to adopt, with products destined to share the fate of the highly local but now defunct 'Orient Expedition' set which did not sustain the popularity or subscription it was pegged to capture.

LEGO painstakingly researched comparatively new markets in the Asia-Pacific that it wants to turn into a stronghold and came up with two brand new ranges of toys. LEGO Legends of China, with plenty of models and buildable figures of warriors and beasts; and the more controversial LEGO friends, targeted at young girls. LEGO has achieved a complete turnaround in the span of a few years and stands to gain from a host of company decisions that include maintaining its focus on the brick, creatively building on its own patents and storywriters to bolster its theme of unlimited play, and more crucially, shifting part of its production facility to China.

QUESTIONS

✪13-3. LEGO has placed an emerging country such as China ahead of developed economies of Japan and South Korea in its location decision. Discuss the pros and cons of this strategy.

✪13-4. LEGO's product portfolio is quite large. Discuss the advantages and disadvantages of product concentration versus diversification in such a context.

13-5. LEGO is a latecomer in the Chinese market. Discuss how it may overcome this barrier to achieve the expected rates of sales growth.

13-6. LEGO is heavily investing in the Chinese consumer first. Discuss the pros and cons of this strategy.

13-7. China is considered the land of knock-offs and imitation products. What are the measures major multinationals could take to stem the spread of clones or pirated products, in their decision to locate to China?

SUMMARY

- Because companies seldom have sufficient resources to exploit all opportunities, two major considerations facing managers are which markets to serve and where to locate the production to serve those markets.
- Companies' decisions on market and production location are highly interdependent because they often need to serve markets from local production and want to use existing production capacity.
- Scanning techniques aid managers in considering alternatives that might otherwise be overlooked. They also help limit the final detailed feasibility studies to a manageable number of those that appear most promising.
- Because each company has unique competitive capabilities and objectives, the factors affecting the choice of operating location will be different for each. Nevertheless, many consider similar-country comparative indicators when seeking advantages from foreign sales or foreign assets.
- Four broad categories of risk that companies may consider are political, foreign exchange, natural disaster, and competitive.

- The amount, accuracy, and timeliness of published data vary substantially among countries. Managers should be particularly aware of different definitions of terms, different collection methods, and different base years for reports, as well as misleading responses.
- Companies frequently use several tools to compare opportunities and risk in various countries, such as grids that rate country projects by a number of separate dimensions and matrices on which companies plot opportunity on one axis and risk on another.
- When allocating resources among countries, companies need to consider how to treat reinvestments and divestments, the interdependence of operations in different countries, and whether they should follow diversification versus concentration strategies.
- Companies may reduce the risk of liability of foreignness by moving first to countries more like their home countries. Alternatively, they may contract with experienced firms to handle operations for them, limit the resources they commit to foreign operations, and delay entry to many countries until they are operating successfully in one or a few.
- Companies must develop location strategies for new investments and devise means of deemphasizing certain areas and divesting if necessary.
- Companies often evaluate entry to a country without comparing it with other countries. This is because they may need to react quickly to proposals or respond to competitive threats, and because multiple feasibility studies seldom are finished simultaneously.
- Optimal future locations are most apt to change because of relative population growth and changes in types of technology.

KEY TERMS

concentration strategy (p. 550)
diversification strategy (p. 550)
escalation of commitment (p. 532)
first-mover advantage (p. 543)
go-no-go decision (p. 552)
harvesting (or divesting) (p. 552)
liability of foreignness (p. 539)
liquidity preference (p. 539)
oligopolistic reaction (p. 542)
scanning (p. 532)
spillover effects (p. 551)

ENDNOTES

1 ***Sources include the following:*** We'd like to acknowledge the invaluable assistance of Jonathan Fitzpatrick, former Executive V.P. and Chief Brand Operations Officer; Julio A. Ramirez, former Executive Vice President Global Operations; Arianne Cento, Senior Analyst, Global Communications; and Ana Miranda, Senior Manager Investor Relations, all with Burger King Corporation. Additional information came from *Form 10-K: Burger King, 2012* (Filed February 22, 2012); Elaine Walker, "BK Plans 1,000 Restaurants in China," *Miami Herald* (June 16, 2012): H1; "Burger King Worldwide Inc at ICR XChange Conference," *Fair Disclosure Wire* (January 16, 2013): n.p.; "Burger King Scouting for Locations in Major Siberian Cities," *Interfax: Russia & CIS Business and Financial Newswire* (January 22, 2013): n.p.; Samidha Sharma and Boby Kurian, "Burger King in Talks to Revive India Plans," *The Economic Times (Online)* [New Delhi] (February 1, 2013): n.p.; Elaine Walker, "Burger King Goes for New Look," *Miami Herald* (May 31, 2011): 1A–2A; Rebecca Ordish, "Testing the Franchising Waters in China," *The China Business Review* 33:6 (November–December 2006): 30–33; "Burger King Plans to Double Restaurant Count in Russia in 2011," *Interfax, Ukraine Business Daily* (Kiev) (November 17, 2010); "Negocio de Resturantes Aumenta 8% en Colombia," *Noticieras Financieras* (December 22, 2010); Business Monitor International, *Colombia Food & Drink Report Q1 2009* (London: Business Monitor International, 2009); Gemma Charles, "Burger King Adds First 'Value Meal' to Menu," *Marketing* (February 11, 2009): 3; "The Burger King's Brand Enters Colombia," *Business Wire* (December 13, 2007): n.p.

2 Paul Glader, "GE Is Reassigning Veteran Rice to Job Focusing on Overseas Sales," *Wall Street Journal* (November 9, 2010): B2.

3 Thomas Hutzschenreuter and Martin Hommes, "What Determines the Speed of New Product Area International Rollout?" Proceedings of the 54th Annual Meeting of the Academy of International Business (June 30–July 3, 2012).

4 Shige Makino, Takehiko Isobe, and Christine M. Chan, "Does Country Matter?" *Strategic Management Journal* 25 (2004): 1027–43.

5 Tony W. Tong, Todd M. Alessandri, Jeffrey J. Reuer, and Asda Chintakananda, "How Much Does Country Matter? An Analysis of Firms' Growth Options," *Journal of International Business Studies* 39:3 (2008): 387–405.

6 Peter Enderwick, "The Imperative of Global Environmental Scanning," *AIB Insights* 11:1 (2011): 12–15.

7 David Gonzalez, "Fried Chicken Takes Flight, Happily Nesting in U.S.," *New York Times* (September 20, 2002): A4; Joel Millman, "California City Fends Off Arrival of Mexican Supermarket," *Wall Street Journal* (August 7, 2002): B1+.

8 Don E. Schultz, "China May Leapfrog the West in Marketing," *Marketing News* (August 19, 2002): 8–9.

9 Amol Sharma, "In India, Subsidies Upend Car Sales," *Wall Street Journal* (July 1, 2012): B1+.

10 Anjjli Raval, "Mercedes-Benz Turns to India," *Financial Times* (July 19, 2010): 20.

11 Nicholas James Bailey, "MNE Bargaining Power Under Constrained Location Choices: Evidence from the Tourism Industry," Proceedings of the 54th Annual Meeting of the Academy of International Business (June 30–July 3, 2012).

12 Nicholas Casey, "In Mexico, Auto Plants Hit the Gas," *Wall Street Journal* (November 20, 2012): A1+; "The Rise of Mexico," *The Economist* (November 24, 2012): 14; Keith Bradsher, "Hello, Cambodia," *New York Times* (April 9, 2013): Business 1+.

13 John Manuel Luiz and Busi Radebe, "The Strategic Location of Regional Headquarters for Multinationals in Africa," Proceedings of the 54th Annual Meeting of the Academy of International Business (June 30–July 3, 2012).

14 Anil Khurana, "Strategies for Global R&D," *Research Technology Management* (March/April 2006): 48–59.

15 David Luchnow, "Missing Piece of the Mexican Success Story," *Wall Street Journal* (March 4, 2002): A11+.

16 Michael Peel, "Bitter-Sweet Confections of Business in Nigeria," *Financial Times* (November 20, 2002): 10.

17 Andrew Bartmess and Keith Cerny, "Building Competitive Advantage through a Global Network of Capabilities," *California Management Review* 35: 2 (Winter 1993): 78–103; Emanuela Delbufalo and Corrado Cerruti, "Configuration and the Capability of Firms to Innovate: A Theoretical Framework," *International Journal of Management* 29: 3 Part 1 (September 2012): 16–28.

18 G. Bruce Knecht, "Going the Wrong Way down a One-Way Street," *Wall Street Journal* (March 18, 2002): A1.

19 Alfredo J. Mauri and Arvind V. Phatak, "Global Integration as Inter-Area Product Flows: The Internationalization of Ownership and Location Factors Influencing Product Flows across MNC Units," *Management International Review* 41 (2001): 233–49.

20 Julian Birkinshaw, Pontus Braunerhjelm, and Ulf Holm, "Why Do Some Multinational Corporations Relocate Their Headquarters Overseas?" *Strategic Management Journal* 27 (2006): 681–700; Erik Stam, "Why Butterflies Don't Leave: Locational Behavior of Entrepreneurial Firms," 83: 1 *Economic Geography* (January 2007): 27–50.

21 Nagesh Kumar, "Multinational Enterprises, Regional Economic Integration, and Export-Platform Production in the Host Countries: An Empirical Analysis for the U.S. and Japanese Corporations," *Weltwirtschaftliches Archive* 134:3 (1998): 450–83.

22 Cynthia O'Murchu and Jan Cienski, "Multinationals Reap the Rewards," *Financial Times* (December 2, 2010): 9.

23 C. Denbour, "Competition for Business Location: A Survey," *Journal of Industry, Competition and Trade,"* 8:2 (June 2008): 89–111.

24 World Bank, International Finance Corporation, *Doing Business in 2013, 10th edition* (Washington, DC: The International Bank for Reconstruction and Development, 2013).

25 Hoon Park, "Determinants of Corruption: A Cross-National Analysis," *Multinational Business Review* 11:2 (2003): 29–48.

26 Mario I. Kafouros, Peter J. Buckley, and Jeremy Clegg, "The Effects of Global Knowledge Reservoirs on the Productivity of Multinational Enterprises: The Role of International Depth and Breadth," *Research Policy* 41:5 (June 2012): 848–61.

27 Colin Kirkpatrick and Kenichi Shimamoto, "The Effect of Environmental Regulation on the Locational Choice of Japanese Direct Investment," 40:11 *Applied Economics* (June 2008): 1399; and George Z. Peng and Paul W. Beamish, "The Effect of National Corporate Responsibility Environment on Japanese Foreign Direct Investment," 80:4 (July 2008): 677–95.

28 John D. Daniels and James A. Schweikart, "Political Risk, Assessment and Management of," in Rosalie L. Tung (ed.), *IEBM Handbook of International Business* (London: International Thomson Business Press, 1999): 502–14.

29 Robert Wright, "Continuity Planning is Strengthened," *Financial Times* (March 20, 2012): Risk Management/Supply Chain 1.

30 Haig Simonian, "Venezuela to Pay Holcim $650M Compensation for Seized Assets," *Financial Times* (September 14, 2010): 17.

31 Much like options theory, theory of liquidity preference is associated with the work of Robert C. Merton, Myron S. Scholes, and Fisher Black. For good, succinct coverage, see John Krainer, "The 1997 Nobel Prize in Economics," FRBSF Economic Letter No. 98–05 (February 13, 1998).

32 Paul D. Ellis, "Does Psychic Distance Moderate the Market Size-Entry Sequence Relationship?" *Journal of International Business Studies* 39:3 (2008): 351–69.

33 See Srilata Zaheer and Elaine Mosakowski, "The Dynamics of the Liability of Foreignness: A Global Study of Survival in Financial Services," *Strategic Management Journal* 18 (1997): 439–64; Stewart R. Miller and Arvind Parkhe, "Is There a Liability of Foreignness in Global Banking? An Empirical Test of Banks' X-Efficiency," *Strategic Management Journal* 23 (2002): 55–75.

34 United Nations Environment Programme, *Reducing Disaster Risk: A Challenge for Development* (New York: United Nations, 2004).

35 Sharon Terlep and Mike Ramsey, "Disaster in Japan: Supply Shortages Stall Auto Makers," *Wall Street Journal* (March 19, 2011): 9.

36 Alistair Gray, "Disasters Expose Flaws in Assumptions," *Financial Times* (March 20, 2012): Risk Management/Supply Chain 1.

37 WHO, Public Health Mapping and GIS, Map Library, retrieved June 11, 2007, from gamapserver.who.int/mapLibrary/default.aspx. Also see World Health Organization, *World Health Statistics 2012* (Geneva: World Health Organization, 2012) for statistics on communicable and non-communicable diseases by country.

38 "A Threat Deadlier than a Landmine," *Financial Times* (December 2, 2002): 10.

39 Amy Merrick and Ann Zimmerman, "Wal-Mart Bans Some Work Travel Due to SARS," *Wall Street Journal* (April 10, 2003): 36.

40 Mikhail V. Gratchev, "Making the Most of Cultural Differences," *Harvard Business Review* (October 2001): 28–30.

41 John Cantwell, "Location and the Multinational Company," *Journal of International Business Studies* 40:1 (January 2009): 35–41; Nandini Lahiri, "Geographic Distribution of R&D Activity: How Does It Affect Innovation Quality?" *Academy of Management Journal* 53:5 (2010): 1194–1209; and Lilach Nachum and Sangyoung Song, "The MNE as a Portfolio: Interdependencies in MNE Growth Trajectory," *Journal of International Business Studies* 42:3 (April 2011): 381–405.

42 Shige Makino and Eric W.K. Tsang, "Historical Ties and Foreign Direct Investment: An Exploratory Study," *Journal of International Business Studies* 42:4 (May 2011): 545–57.

43 Khanh T. L. Tran, "Blockbuster Finds Success in Japan," *Wall Street Journal* (August 19, 1998): A14; Cecile Rohwedder, "Blockbuster Hits Eject Button as Stores in Germany See Video-Rental Sales Sag," *Wall Street Journal* (January 16, 1998): B9A.

44 Jon A. Doukas and Ozgur B. Kan, "Does Global Diversification Destroy Firm Values?" *Journal of International Business Studies* 37 (2006): 352–71.

45 B. Kazaz, M. Dada, and H. Moskowitz, "Global Production Planning under Exchange-Rate Uncertainty," *Management Science* 51 (2005): 1101–09.

46 Mario I. Kafouros, Peter J. Buckley, and Jeremy Clegg, loc.cit.

47 Edward B. Flowers, "Oligopolistic Reactions in European and Canadian Direct Investment in the United States," *Journal of International Business Studies* 7:2 (Fall–Winter 1976): 43–55; Frederick Knickerbocker, *Oligopolistic Reaction and Multinational Enterprise* (Cambridge, MA: Harvard University, Graduate School of Business, Division of Research, 1973).

48 Rose Yu, "Chinese Dilemma: 170 Auto Makers," *Wall Street Journal* (April 10, 2013): B10.

49 See J. Myles Shaver and Fredrick Flyer, "Agglomeration Economies, Firm Heterogeneity, and Foreign Direct Investment in the United States," *Strategic Management Journal* 21 (2000): 1175–93; Philippe Martin and Gianmarco I. P. Ottaviano, "Growth and Agglomeration," *International Economic Review* 42 (2001): 947–68; Edward E. Leamer and Michael Storper, "The Economic Geography of the Internet Age," *Journal of International Business Studies* 32 (2001): 641–65.

50 Jedrzej George Frynas, Kamel Mellah, and Geoffrey Allen Pigman, "First Mover Advantages in International Business and Firm-Specific Political Resources," *Strategic Management Journal* 27 (2006): 321–45; Makino, Isobe, and Chan, "Does Country Matter?"

51 Joel Millman, "PriceSmart to Restate Results Due to an Accounting Error," *Wall Street Journal* (November 11, 2003): B9.

52 Tony Barber and Kerin Hope, "Brussels Attacks Greece over False Data," *Financial Times* (January 13, 2010): 8.

53 Benoît Faucon, "Oil Thefts Plague Nigeria," *Wall Street Journal* (April 12, 2013): B1–2.

54 "China: Bottoms Up," *The Economist* (March 30, 2013): 43–44.

55 Andrea Cheng, "Limited Brands Defends Its International Plan," *Market Watch* (October 19, 2011): n.p.

56 Andrew Ward, "Terror Threat from Within Keeps America on High Alert," *Financial Times* (April 19, 2005): 3, quoting John Lewis.

57 Azam Ahmed, "Suicide Bombers Attack a Red Cross Compound in Eastern Afghanistan," *New York Times* (May 30, 2014): A6.

58 Moisés Naím, "The Five Wars of Globalization," *Foreign Policy* (January–February 2003): 29–36.

59 Benjamin Bader and Nicola Berg, "An Empirical Investigation of Terrorism-Induced Stress on Expatriate Performance," Proceedings of the 54th Annual Meeting of the Academy of International Business (June 30–July 3, 2012).

60 A good history of violence and kidnapping in Nigeria appears in Soye Peniel Asawo, "Corporate Integrity and Company-Community Conflict Management in the Niger Delta Region of Nigeria," *Journal of Leadership, Accountability and Ethics* 8:3 (March 2011): 77–88.

61 "Doing Business in Dangerous Places," *The Economist* (August 14, 2004): 11.

62 Igal Ayal and Jehiel Zif, "Marketing Expansion Strategies in Multinational Marketing," *Journal of Marketing* (Spring 1979): 84–94.

63 Makino, Isobe, and Chan, "Does Country Matter?"

64 Susan Freeman, Kate Hutchings, and Sylvie Chetty, "Born-Global and Culturally Proximate Markets," *Management International Review* 52 (2012): 425–60.

65 Hutzschenreuter and Hommes, op. cit.

66 Susanna Voyle and James Drummond, "J. Sainsbury to Withdraw from Egypt," *Financial Times* (April 10, 2001): 23.

67 Nikki Tait, "Dana Set to Sell UK-Based Components Arm," *Financial Times* (November 29, 2000): 22.

68 Makino, Isobe, and Chan, "Does Country Matter?"; Bernard Simon, "Goodyear Sells Its Last Plantation," *Financial Times* (December 1, 2004): 18.

69 See Jean J. Boddewyn, "Foreign and Domestic Divestment and Investment Decisions: Like or Unlike?" *Journal of International Business Studies* 14:3 (Winter 1983): 28; Michelle Haynes, Steve Thompson, and Mike Wright, "The Determinants of Corporate Divestment in the U.K.," *Journal of Industrial Organization* 18 (2000): 1201–22; Jose Mata and Pedro Portugal, "Closure and Divestiture by Foreign Entrants: The Impact of Entry and Post-Entry Strategies," *Strategic Management Journal* 21 (2000): 549–62.

70 World Bank and International Finance Corporation, *Doing Business 2013* (Washington, DC: The International Bank for Reconstruction and Development, 2013).

71 Ricardo Gabriel Flores and Victoria Jordan-Jones, "Inexperienced Firms and Foreign Operation Success," Proceedings of the 54th Annua Meeting of the Academy of International Business (June 30–July 3, 2012).

72 Matthew Green, "Nigeria Set to Lift Decades-Old Ban on Foreign Takeovers of Its Banks," *Financial Times* (June 22, 2009): 1.

73 "Enron Assets Outside U.S. Go Up for Sale; Activity Seen in South Korea and India," *Wall Street Journal* (January 22, 2002): A6.

74 International Monetary Fund, *World Economic Outlook, September 2004* (Washington, DC: International Monetary Fund, 2004): 143–49.

75 Peter Hall, *Cities in Civilization: Culture, Technology, and Urban Order* (London: Weidenfeld & Nicholson, 1998).

76 "A Sense of Place," *The Economist* (October 27, 2012): Special Report on Technology and Geography, 6.

77 David Aviel, "The Causes and Consequences of Public Attitudes to Technology: A United States Analysis," *International Journal of Management* 18 (2001): 166.

78 ***Sources include the following:*** "*The Year of the Lego*", retrieved November 12, 2013, from www.newyorker.com/online/blogs; Pooja Thakur, "Lego to Boost China Sales With Local Factories Supplying to Asia," *Bloomberg* (October 2, 2013): n.p.; JENS HANSEGARD and LAURIE BURKITT, "Lego Ramps Up Production for Asia," *Wall Street Journal Online* (March 18, 2013): n.p.; Fugazi, "LEGO Group to build factory in China," *Eurobricks Online* (March 18, 2013): n.p.; Lego Annual Report, retrieved November 12, 2013, from http://aboutus.lego.com/en-gb/lego-group/annual-report, n.p; Christian Wienberg, "Lego Beats Hasbro as World's No. 2 Toymaker Amid Asia Sales Jump," <www.bloomberg.com/news/2013-09-05/lego-beats-hasbro-as-world-s-no-2-toymaker-amid-asia-sales-jump.html> *Bloomberg* (September 5, 2013): n.p.; <www.bbc.co.uk/news/business-23968860> "Lego becomes world's second-biggest toy maker" (September 5, 2013): n.p. LEGO Annual Report <http://aboutus.lego.com/en-us/lego-group/annual-report> LEGO website (September 2013):n.p.; Jens Hansegard and Laurie Burkitt, "Lego to Build Plant in China With Eye on Asia Sales," *Wall Street Journal Online* (March 19, 2013): n.p.; (retrieved September2013); online.wsj.com

79 www.bloomberg.com/news/2013-10-02/lego-to-boost-chinasales-with-local-factories-supplying-to-asia.html; LEGO: Lythke-Jørgensen, Skjøtt-Larsen and Svendsen (2001): "SCM: Supply Chain Management i et ledelsesperspektiv". Børsen

CHAPTER 14
Modes of Trading Internationally

OBJECTIVES

After studying this chapter, you should be able to

1. Explain the idea of exporting and profile its elements
2. Explain the idea of importing and profile its elements
3. Evaluate the relative benefits and drawbacks of the export and import of e-waste
4. Describe the problems and pitfalls that challenge international traders
5. Describe the resources and assistance for international traders
6. Define the idea of an export plan
7. Discuss the practice of countertrade
8. Describe the resources and assistance for international traders
9. Identify and discuss the platforms that support expanding international trade

Source: © RealPhotoItaly - Fotolia.com

When one is prepared, difficulties do not come.

—Ethiopian proverb

CASE SpinCent: The Decision to Export[1]

Big exporters such as General Electric, Caterpillar, and Boeing generate about 60 percent of total exports from the United States. Their smaller shipments are usually much larger than the largest shipments of smaller companies. Still, small and medium-size enterprises (SMEs)—specifically, companies with fewer than 500 workers—account for nearly 98 percent of all U.S. exporters. One such SME is SpinCent of Pennsylvania.

SpinCent manufactures laboratory and industrial centrifuges—machines that spin a substance into high-speed rotation around a fixed axis—that provide separation solutions for firms in the chemical, pharmaceutical, food, environmental, and mining industries. Centripetal acceleration causes the substance to separate, moving heavy elements to the bottom, lighter objects toward the top, and liquid in between. SpinCent's 54 employees—45 workers, four product engineers, and five managers—operate out of its 60,000-square-foot facility in suburban Philadelphia.

SpinCent began operations in 2000 with one goal in mind: to create a line of centrifuges in which customers would have absolute confidence. Its patented technology anchors a full line of automatic and manual centrifuges recognized for quality, high performance, and value. It also offers custom-engineering design and tools that serve the most demanding industries. To this day, management believes it builds "centrifuges for which there simply are no equals."

TO EXPORT OR NOT TO EXPORT: THAT IS THE QUESTION

From its start, SpinCent approached export passively. Its international sales often resulted from other U.S. firms' orders destined for export, occasional sale leads received at trade shows, or an unsolicited order through the Web or the mail. Results were mixed, with exports generating reasonable returns; they would have been higher but for unexpected problems and pitfalls. Consequently, SpinCent's net margins for its export sales were about 20 percent less than for its domestic sales.

Paul Knepper, CEO and founder, explained that recurring problems had deterred his interest in exporting. First, he and his colleagues were skeptical about the likelihood of international success. Previous efforts, they felt, had spent more time on unfocused searching than on purposefully growing export sales. Moreover, serving customers in the domestic market kept them busy. Developing international operations always seemed to overstretch their thin management structure. Going international, they knew, would not be a cakewalk, especially heading into direct competition with seasoned exporters from Germany and Japan.

Finally, Knepper knew the day of reckoning was at hand: SpinCent had to make its decision. Concerns about productivity, profitability, and diversification had bubbled for years. The struggling U.S. economy had slowed SpinCent's growth and pushed some of its customers to import cheaper, lower-end centrifuges from foreign suppliers. Increasing price competition from both domestic and international rivals seemed inevitable. Adding it all up, management realized it could either focus fully on the domestic market and exploit every possible efficiency, or expand aggressively into export. Ultimately, Knepper conceded, market trends forced his hand. The slow-moving deindustrialization of the United States, forecast to continue for years, would systematically reduce domestic demand for centrifuges. Meanwhile, quickly industrializing emerging economies, particularly in Asia, signaled rich opportunities. Hence, Knepper grudgingly accepted that SpinCent had to export to find more promising markets.

ASIA CALLS

Key market trends signaled potential selling opportunities in Asia. "Industries were coming online everywhere and seemingly overnight," Knepper said. Pro-market reform, economic development, and globalization were industrializing activities in several countries. Moreover, the volume of goods moving through Asia's seaports indicated something big was happening. Increasingly, building industries in emerging markets required the sophisticated sorts of centrifuges that SpinCent made. And unlike the United States, which was in the mature part of the product lifecycle, these emerging economies looked set to grow for years.

GETTING STARTED

New to the idea of the Asian market, SpinCent sought help on how best to access the large, diverse region. Knepper feared wasting resources going solo. Moreover, he was not looking to generate a burst of export sales but to develop relationships that would drive long-term growth. Hence, the primary challenge was finding competent and trustworthy distributors who would take responsibility for local sales. "We were looking for a long-term partner and not a quick export sale," said Knepper. "The right partner for SpinCent needed to be as confident and competent about the product as we are, and able to promote, educate, and serve consumers in the respective territories." The key, he added, was partnering with a respected firm in the target country. On the flip side, SpinCent had to assure potential partners that it was a good long-term fit for them.

To that end, Knepper sought background information on potential distributors, making sure possible agents were who they said they were. A few of the company's earlier export transactions, for instance, had run into problems with buyers who wouldn't pay or couldn't arrange letters of credit. As Knepper warned, "Getting paid is a huge part of running a business, and unless a company has the right payment policies in place, it will get scammed."

Mindful of these issues, Knepper attended a trade seminar sponsored by the U.S. Commercial Service's Export Assistance Center of Philadelphia that featured market analysis and trade reports on the fast-growing, emerging economies of Asia. Taking his seat, he couldn't help but wonder about the opportunities. Sure, they sounded great. However, he had seen hype like this come back to bite, not to mention the horror stories he'd heard at trade shows about the inevitable problems and evolving pitfalls of exports. Indeed, he reflected, a key reason for attending the seminar was to reconcile his vague sense of the opportunities and threats.

GETTING HELP

Since exports promote economic growth, policymakers and government agencies offer extensive assistance, such as trade seminars, market research, training programs, financial planning, and many other services. Trade officials especially encourage SMEs like SpinCent, seeing them as the primary beneficiaries of initiatives to improve and accelerate international trade activity. U.S. trade officials, for instance, reason that since 60 percent or so of all SME exporters posted sales to only one foreign market, many could boost performance by entering just one or two new markets. Expanding SMEs' market horizons through trade seminars and such could bolster their confidence.

After a full morning of profiles and presentations, Knepper increasingly believed the Asian markets held more opportunities than risk. He learned quite a bit about Asia, as well as some technicalities of exporting. Still, his unfamiliarity with the region, compounded by the company's lack of local sales representatives, bothered him. He believed that grassroots research was necessary before committing SpinCent. Before leaving that day, he spoke to Commercial Service agents and arranged to tag along on a 12-day trade mission that was heading to Hong Kong, Philippines, Vietnam, and Taiwan the following month.

GOAL SETTING

The goals of his trip were straightforward: assess market potential, identify competitors, get a sense of reasonable price points, and recruit local sales representatives. Although he had never traveled to Asia before, he believed he had prepared well. His time with the trade experts in Philadelphia had educated him on the general characteristics and industry conditions in Asian markets. Also, SpinCent had at some time past received inquiries from Asian distributors asking to represent the company; depending on how busy the company was with its domestic customers, SpinCent had tried to respond. These contacts had been saved, thereby giving Knepper a start on potential distributors and likely customers. In addition, he tapped the Commercial Services' Gold Key program to prescreen potential distributors. This program helps SMEs enlist Commercial Services agents overseas to scan local markets for qualified agents, distributors, and representatives. Exporters report that it ensures that when a firm adds a partner to its network, it is a respected company in the target country.

Thinking back to his days as a Boy Scout, Knepper took comfort in the fact that he believed he had met the sacred command: "Be prepared." With a briefcase full of brochures, a laptop loaded with profiles of his product line, and the sense of doing something potentially great, he headed to Asia. Over the next two weeks, he interviewed potential agents, chatted with likely customers, scouted competitors' offerings, test called their service support, spoke to freight forwarders and logistics companies, and visited local government officials and customs agencies.

ASIA CALLS, SPINCENT ANSWERS

On the flight home, tired but charged, Knepper realized that his misgivings about exporting had been unfounded. There were indeed risks, but they were outweighed by the numerous opportunities he had come across. Exporting was no longer an option for SpinCent; it was an imperative. Perhaps more important, Knepper had a new sense of commitment. He also had a bit more confidence, given the newly signed distributors in the Philippines and Taiwan as well as sales leads there and in Hong Kong.

Back in the office, Knepper tested the Asian market a bit more, sampling potential interest by advertising in trade publications as well as running banner ads on relevant trade sites in tandem with his newly signed distributors (he handled the English ads, they the Mandarin versions). In addition, he began working with an agent from Commercial Services on an export plan. This work helped SpinCent secure its largest overseas partner to date, a distributor in Hong Kong who served the booming Chinese market. Commercial Services also arranged meetings with others, eventually signing a distributor in Singapore and generating leads in Australia.

Having found strong partners, SpinCent continues tapping the counseling and market intelligence provided by various government agencies. Indeed, the more he has dealt with them, the more Knepper appreciates a friend's advice: "Let the government do it for you. This is their niche and they're the best at it." Now, with the export plan in hand, Knepper has begun working with the Export-Import Bank to secure financing options for overseas distributors and customers.[2]

GOING FORWARD

Steadily, as SpinCent gains experience in Taiwan, Philippines, Hong Kong, and Singapore, it looks onward. Although exporting has created challenges, it has helped SpinCent improve its performance. Indeed, overseas sales provided the firm with a growing stream of business during the economic downturn in the United States, while rivals who had not diversified via exports struggled. More important, exporting has given SpinCent a low-cost, high-return opportunity to leverage its core competency in centrifuge technology.

This experience, reflects Knepper, has had straightforward lessons: If you are thinking about exporting internationally, do it. Get going, do your homework, utilize low-cost resources, participate in trade missions, learn about cultures, and build international relationships. Always check on your potential business partners. Gather as much information as you can. Don't assume; the wrong choice costs your business time and money. Above all, no matter the problems you run into, stay committed to the goal. All of these seem tough, but they only cost pennies on the dollar and the returns can be substantial. ■

CRN
Case Review Note

QUESTIONS

14-1. List the three challenges that SpinCent overcame in developing its export activity. Describe and evaluate the processes it followed to overcome each challenge.

INTRODUCTION

Exporting and importing are among the fastest-growing economic activities in the world.

Exports and imports have always been an important facet of the global economy. As globalization, free trade agreements, and institutional development open the economies of more and more countries, the importance of international trade increases. Figure 14.1 shows that the value of trade as a share of world GDP has steadily risen over the past 50 years. This trend, while hitting air pockets now and then, has been relentless. Even the most recent drop in world trade, the consequence of the global financial crisis and sharp fall in consumer confidence in 2008 and 2009, has begun fading. World merchandise exports increased 5 percent in volume in 2011, while exports of commercial services grew by 11 percent in value.[3]

FIGURE 14.1 World Trade, 1960–2010

Despite periodic ups and downs, for the past 50 years the dominant trend in international trade, as a share of global business activity, has been strong, steady expansion. By the way, these trade data combine imports and exports—i.e., a bit of double counting. Still, the upward trend continues.

Source: Based on Assembled from data reported in the WorldBank's World Development Indicators, in particular *Trade* (% of *GDP*) (Series NE_TRD_GNFS_ZS), retrieved February 13, 2013, from data.worldbank.org/data-catalog/world-development-indicators.

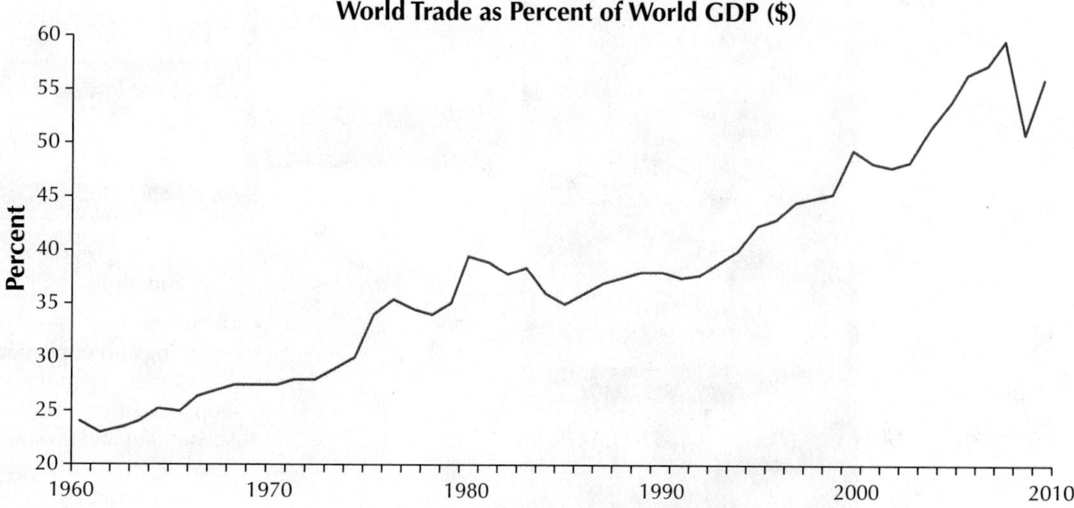

Besides general trends, the composition and direction of trade flows continue changing. Export and import flows reflect the ongoing transformation of developing economies into industrializing versions, emerging markets tapping developed countries for tools to continue doing so, and developed countries looking to their developing counterparts for competitively priced goods and services. For instance, emerging markets increasingly drive the growth of Irish food and drink exports: during 2011, Ireland's exports to China rose by 47 percent, South Africa by 43 percent, Nigeria by 38 percent, and Russia by 30 percent.[4] Likewise, U.S. companies continued expanding markets and now trade with 233 countries and territories.[5] Also, as Ireland has experienced, the United States saw increasing trade involving companies in Brazil, Chile, Australia, Columbia, Saudi Arabia, and Nigeria.[6]

Companies worldwide respond accordingly, using exporting and importing to go international. Granted, earlier chapters report that companies engage in international business through a variety of modes. The choice a company makes, say, in choosing exporting rather than licensing, joint ventures, or FDI, follows its analysis of external factors as well as its core competencies (see Figure 14.2).

Exporting sends products to another country; importing brings products in from another country.

Export and import are the most common modes of international business. The number of firms that engage in both have seen steady and substantial growth. Indeed, the United States saw the value of its total exports grow 21 percent and total imports 22.7 percent in 2010. The headcount for identified exporters rose 6 percent that year compared to 2009, climbing to 293,000. The roll of importers also expanded, from 179,800 to 181,600.

CONCEPT CHECK

"Why Companies Engage in International Business" emphasized three operating objectives: expanding sales, acquiring resources, and minimizing risk. To achieve one or more of these objectives, companies choose from various "Modes of International Business." Among these modes, **exporting** and **importing** are the most prevalent, especially among small and medium-sized enterprises (SMEs).

These statistics underestimate the number of exporters and importers; the complexity of trade means that we cannot link all international shipments to specific firms. Many products, for example, are indirectly exported—embedded in other products that are exported via other firms—and tracking them is tough. The key takeaway, though, is straightforward: Exports and imports are a major part of the global economy, a critical feature of the nations' economic performance, and a big strategic choice for companies of all sizes in countries worldwide.

The popularity of export and import follows their key advantages. Both are relatively easy, low cost, and quick means to engage foreign markets; they impose minimum business risk, require relatively low resource commitment, and improve marketplace flexibility. Moreover, whether large or small, international trade helps companies increase sales and profits, tap points of innovation, and stabilize seasonal fluctuations. Then there is the seemingly minor

FIGURE 14.2 Factors Influencing Export and Import Operations

Our interpretation of export and import highlight the environmental and operational factors that influence its practice and performance. This means of international business is a key functional operation in small, medium, and large-sized MNEs.

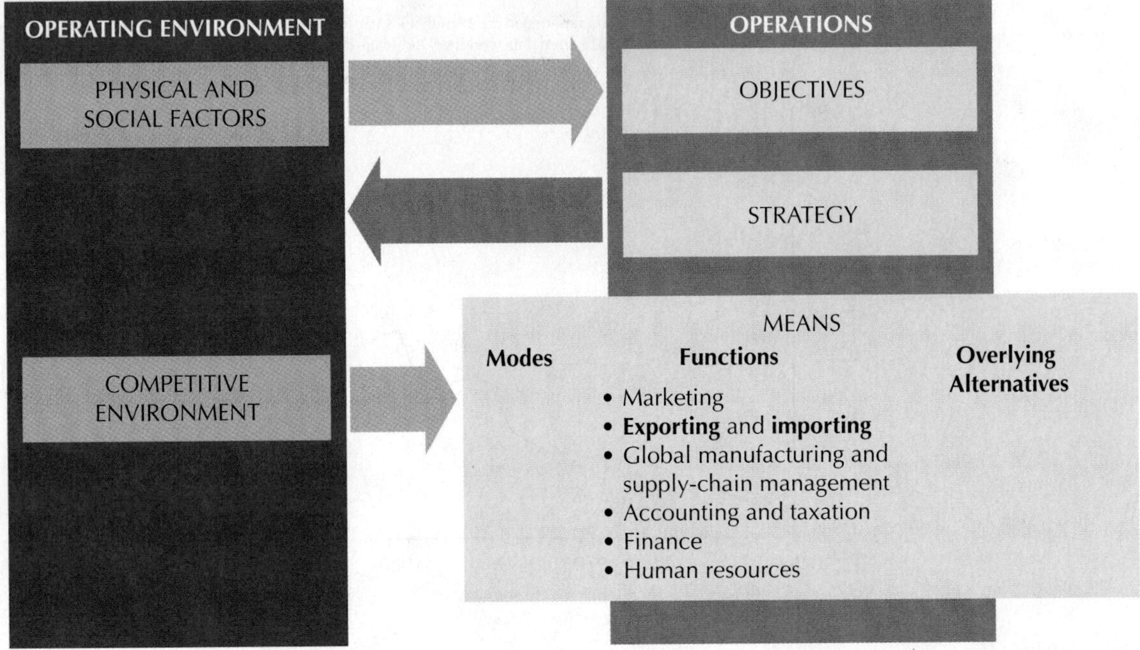

detail that most people live elsewhere in the world than in any one country. In the case of Germany, for example, nearly 99 percent of consumers live outside it and command more than 95 percent of the world's purchasing power. Therefore, a German company selling domestically can reach a maximum of some 81 million consumers. Conversely, a local competitor selling internationally can potentially reach nearly 7 billion more.

Consequently, international trade presents many opportunities to enterprising companies. Perhaps as expected, it also exposes them to a range of problems and pitfalls. Still, as this chapter shows, there are powerful approaches and proven solutions to help them.

EXPORTING

Exporting is the sale of goods or services produced by a firm based in one country to customers that reside in another country. The idea of exporting manufactured goods presents a clear situation, as in the case of Indian carmaker Tata Motors shipping (exporting) automobiles made in Pune to customers (importers) in Bangladesh. Hence, exports involve any good or service that is traded from sellers in one country to buyers in another country.

Technically, a product need not physically leave a country to qualify as an export. Rather, it need only earn foreign currency. For example, you may not normally think of the foreign national students sitting alongside you in class as part of your country's export strategy. However, higher education ranks among the top 10 service exports for several Western nations. In fact, tuition, fees, and living expenses paid by some 765,000 international students and their families contributed more than $22 billion to the U.S. economy during the 2011–2012 academic year.[7] In Canada, the total amount spent by international students—more than $8 billion in 2010—exceeded the country's export of helicopters, airplanes, and spacecraft.[8] Besides education, leading types of service exports include financial, information, professional, scientific, and technical services, travel and tourism, transportation, insurance, and entertainment.

The trade of services, such as we see with higher education, makes it a bit tougher to define what qualifies as an export. Still, service exports occur across a range of industry sectors. Engineering contractors—such as Bechtel, Skanska AB, or Kajima—export services when they construct buildings, roads, utilities, airports, or seaports in a foreign country. Management consultants such as McKinsey & Company export when they perform advisory services for foreign clients. Investment banks, such as Goldman Sachs and UBS, export when they help a foreign client arrange financing or navigate capital markets. Similarly, services are exported indirectly when the Japanese advertising firm Dentsu, the world's largest single-brand agency, creates a marketing campaign for Sony that then uses that campaign outside Japan. Hydraulx Visual Effects, designers of digital monsters and such, exports its services when it helps overseas clients add visual effects to feature films, commercials, and music videos. In these examples, the seller is the exporter while the buyer is the importer.

Conversely, it clarifies matters to define what some mistakenly classify as a service export. Opening a Starbucks in Argentina, which we commonly regard as a service enterprise, does not qualify as a service export. Rather, the foreign ownership of some or all of the productive assets of the local operation qualifies it as a foreign direct investment. Furthermore, a royalty fee paid to Starbucks in the face of no foreign ownership would qualify the Argentina activity as a licensing agreement.

WHO ARE EXPORTERS?

Many companies claim the intention to export, anticipating it will accelerate growth and boost profits. In reality, not all companies export, and among those that do, some do far more than others. Company practices identify three types of exporters.

Types of exporters include
- Non-exporter
- Occasional exporter
- Regular exporter

Non-Exporters Such a company commands little to no knowledge about exporting and often professes no intention to engage in international trade at any time. Although this may sound like a deficiency, many firms grow in their domestic market without exporting simply because they make goods or provide services that do not travel well to foreign markets. Still, many firms whose products appeal to customers elsewhere prefer disregarding exporting. This latter population is a primary target of export promotion programs.

Occasional Exporters This type of company fills unsolicited orders from foreign buyers but investigates international trade options passively, if at all. Think of SpinCent's international activities prior to Knepper's realization of the need to export. It would try to fill export orders as they arrived, depending on activity in the domestic market. Generally, though, it regarded them as anomalies. Occasional exporters understand the basics of the export process, but, for any number of reasons, they assign it low priority.

Regular Exporters A company that aggressively pursues export sales as a productive, profitable, strategic activity is regarded as a regular exporter. It has experience along with an improving understanding of the routines and technicalities of international trade. Again, think of SpinCent's activities following Knepper's realization, corroborated by his chats with Commercial Service agents and travels to Asia, of the importance of exporting. Each step demystified aspects of the experience, thereby fortifying Knepper's commitment. And just as success feeds upon success, so it is with exporting.

THE MATTER OF ADVANTAGES

The question of who is likely to start and sustain exporting directs us toward a broader conception of a company's choice of how best to go international. Earlier materials identified several options that firms consider, most notably export, licensing, joint venture, alliance, or FDI. They also profiled the influence of ownership, location, and internalization advantages on a firm's preferred entry mode into foreign markets.[9] Here, we apply these discussions to the export decision.

Ownership advantages of the company, location advantages of the market, and internalization advantages from controlling transactions shape how firms enter foreign markets.

Ownership Advantages A firm's core competencies—the special outlook, skills, capabilities, or technologies that run through its operations—are the basis of its competitive advantage. These proprietary advantages anchor how a firm enters foreign markets. For instance, SpinCent capitalized on its ownership advantages by leveraging its core competency in designing, manufacturing, and servicing centrifugal equipment. These advantages, "owned" by SpinCent due to its proprietary technology and expertise, support its international expansion. Companies that command weak ownership advantages, anticipating fierce struggles with foreign rivals, typically disregard export.

CRN
Case Review Note

Resource-constrained or risk-averse companies that have strong ownership advantages often enter foreign markets through export.

Location Advantages The combination of sales opportunity and investment risk in foreign markets creates favorable locations. In other words, stable markets with many consumers increase the odds that someone will demand your product. As expected, favorable business environments such as Canada, Japan, or Germany attract exporters, though high-potential markets in far corners of the world increasingly attract aspiring and experienced traders. Again, SpinCent saw trends in Asia creating favorable locations marked by strong industrial demand, supportive business policies, and attractive industry structures. Because the industrialization of emerging economies spurs local firms to make the sorts of products that require high-performance centrifuges, targeting these fast-developing markets taps location advantages that support SpinCent's international expansion.

Internalization Advantages Companies often respond to market imperfections—namely, the sorts of circumstances that create uncertainties—by internalizing market processes. Directly controlling and managing market activities inside the company reduces the risks and exploits gaps resulting from market imperfections. Internalizing activities enables executives to retain their core competency within the company rather than licensing or selling it. Again, SpinCent could have opted to license its technology to Asian manufacturers. This likely proves cheap in the short term but costly over the long haul as it helps local licensees evolve into local competitors. Indeed, our earlier discussion of the rule of man as the basis of law, such as that found in several Asian markets, highlighted its poor record of protecting intellectual property. This sort of market imperfection leads companies, such as we see with SpinCent, to retain control of their core competencies through internalization. Granted, SpinCent could have served its Asian customers by directly investing in a local manufacturing facility rather than exporting to local distributors. However, management reasoned that its resource situation and risk tolerance better fit an export strategy than FDI.

CONCEPT CHECK

The complexity posed by differing cultural, political, legal, and economic environments, many of which we covered in the first half of the text, imposes a so-called "liability of foreignness." This idea holds that foreign companies, by virtue of their spotty familiarity, incur additional economic and social costs of doing business when operating overseas. Companies offset this liability by capitalizing on advantages as well as selecting the mode of international business that best reflects their resource profile and risk tolerance.

CHARACTERISTICS OF EXPORTERS

The effort to promote international trade spurs identifying the characteristics of successful exporters. Pinpointing important attributes, the reasoning goes, will help companies develop the necessary competencies and governments to design better forms of assistance. Analysis often starts with firm size, comparing and contrasting the trading activities of big and small companies.

In exporting, company size matters in interesting ways. Naturally, large MNEs like Samsung, Boeing, and Hon Hai are big exporters. Their ownership, location, and internalization advantages help them identify markets, leverage organizational capabilities, and manage international risks. Thus, many presume that export is an option best left to large companies. In fact, there is some truth to this inference. The largest companies routinely account for the lion's share of exporting throughout countries worldwide. In the United States, the 500 biggest firms accounted for nearly 60 percent of total export value, the 250 biggest accounted for more than half, and the 100 biggest contributed just under one-third.[10] We see the same shares for big importers in the United States.

The largest companies are the biggest exporters. SMEs, however, are steadily expanding export activity.

Nevertheless, many see great potential in **small and medium-sized enterprises (SMEs)**—those firms that, by definition, have fewer than 500 employees. In the United States, SMEs account for 97.8 of all identified exporters and 97.2 percent of all identified importers, while claiming 33.7 percent and 31.6 percent of total export and import value, respectively.[11] This situation is not unique to the United States. Worldwide, more than two-thirds of exporters have fewer than 20 employees. More than 98 percent of companies in the Asia-Pacific region are SMEs. China has more than 42 million SMEs, defined as enterprises with annual revenues of less than $250 million. They account for about 99 percent of all companies and contribute approximately 60 percent of China's GDP, more than 70 percent of the country's employment, and more than 80 percent of its exports.[12]

CRN
Case Review Note

Unquestionably, firm size helps explain who exports. It does not, however, determine who exports. SpinCent, a typical SME, marshaled the resources and made export an important part of its strategy. Its size moderated its decision to seek assistance from federal and state agencies, but did not determine its decision to export. Instead, research directs our attention to the importance of other factors. Specific characteristics, such as core competencies, competitive prices, efficient production, executive leadership, and effective marketing techniques better predict export activity than does the size of the firm.[13] Production efficiency, rather than size, was a better predictor of Swedish companies' export activity; those firms with higher productivity targeted foreign markets while those with lower productivity focused on domestic customers.[14] Chinese SMEs' labor costs, R&D advantages, and state ownership better predicted their export activity than did their size.[15] Likewise, higher-performing Taiwanese firms, no matter how large or small, were more likely to become exporters than lower-performing firms.[16] Similarly, firm competencies, not size, had more to do with Canadian companies' propensity to export, the number of countries they exported to, and their export intensity (the ratio of a firm's revenue from its export sales to its total revenue). Finally, top management's favorable perception of exports, based on their anticipated contribution to growth and profits, fueled the commitment that powered exporting in British companies.[17]

A firm's characteristics moderate its export activity. Size matters, but often management commitment, efficiency, and cost structure matter more.

In summary, firm size can influence a company's inclination to initiate or escalate exporting, but other features matter more. More pointedly, Texas-based Coffee & More, a small company selling premium coffees and related products, looked to boost growth through export. Its CEO's reasoning captures many common themes: "People thought we were cutting our throats by exporting, and I admit we had our own doubts. However, we knew the customer base for our product outside the United States was large, and so was the potential for success. Perseverance and commitment paid off. Now international exporting has become an integral part of the company. Our international exports went from 2 percent of annual income in 2005 to 60 percent of annual income in 2009."[18]

WHY EXPORT?

Several factors motivate export. Companies that are capital- and research-intensive, such as those making pharmaceuticals or avionics equipment, export products to amortize the steep costs of development and production. Many, such as advertisers, lawyers, and consultants, export their services to meet the needs of clients working abroad; they either follow their clients there or risk losing them to the rival that does. Smaller firms in their domestic markets may export as an indirect way to counter the production volume advantage commanded by the industry leader. Finally, some companies export rather than invest abroad because alternate modes such as licensing, joint ventures, and FDI carry higher risks. Serving foreign markets from the home office imposes far fewer operational requirements than other modes.

Exporting helps companies
- Increase profitability,
- Improve productivity,
- Diversify activities

From this diverse set of scenarios, we can derive the three dimensions that drive export: profitability, productivity, and diversification.

PROFITABILITY

Point blank, the key advantage of exporting is the potential to become more profitable. Companies often sell their products for higher prices abroad than at home. Foreign markets may lack competitive alternatives, or they may be in different stages of the product's life cycle. Mature products at home may trigger price competition, whereas growth stages in foreign markets allow premium prices. Also, exports enable a firm to expand its sales frontier. Though not quite decisive for firms in large markets, such as the United States, accessing bigger markets is a make-or-break factor for firms in small markets, such as Switzerland. "By not exporting, we were not tapping our full sales potential—sort of like leaving money on the table," said the Director of Business Development for Certified Worldwide.[19] And, given the link between profitability and sustainability, evidence indicates that exporters have significantly lower bankruptcy rates than nonexporters with similar characteristics.[20]

CONCEPT CHECK

The attractiveness of **trade** as a means of internationalization has been enhanced by the improving efficiencies of import and export. The liberalization of the cross-border movement of resources and the development of services that support trade make these modes more attractive to a broader range of companies.

PRODUCTIVITY

Exporting helps companies improve productivity, which is often tied to increasing economies of scale. Exploiting unused capacity or spreading research costs over more customers, helps companies improve their operational efficiency. Hence, selling more products in more markets drives productivity gains, while the knowledge flows between international buyers and foreign competitors spurs exporters to innovate. Participating in export markets promotes a firm's learning, thereby enhancing the potential for innovation. Research reports a "dynamic virtuous cycle" between export and innovation in which each positively reinforces the other.[21] More precisely, exporters often have access to knowledge that is absent in their domestic market. Exposure prepares them to use this knowledge to generate higher-quality innovations, which in turn powers their entry into new geographic markets with higher-quality products, thereby boosting the benefits of exporting.

When Mississippi-based Domes International, maker of inexpensive housing, decided to expand internationally, it headed to India. Early experiences, though difficult, spurred innovations that improved its productivity and fortified its competitiveness. Its CEO explained, "There's no doubt that Domes International is a better company as a result of our experience in India. We are much more flexible and innovative. The client wanted a less expensive structure, so we went back to our labs and came up with an insulation solution that met their needs. Now we use these discoveries to improve core products and to offer more variations. We are much more confident going into new situations—listening, adapting, and finding the best solution."[22]

The U.S. International Trade Commission reports that despite facing trade barriers and other impediments, SMEs that export outperform those that do not.[23] Beside more than doubling the total revenue of their nonexporting counterparts, their revenue per employee, a rough measure of labor productivity, was over 70 percent greater than that of the nonexporters.

DIVERSIFICATION

Exporting enables companies to diversify their activities, thereby fortifying their adaptability to market trends and disruptive innovations. In the least, developing customers in different markets reduces a firm's vulnerability to the loss of a local buyer while improving its bargaining power with existing suppliers. Moreover, different growth rates in different markets enables it to use strong sales in one country to offset weak sales in another. SpinCent, for example, looked to develop export markets in faster growing Asia to reduce its overdependence on the slowing U.S. economy.

In the aftermath of the recent global financial crisis, national unemployment hit a high of 10.6 percent in the United States. In Greene County, Tennessee, it soared to 17.9 percent. Jarden Zinc Products, headquartered there, makes solid zinc strips and zinc-based products used in coinage, automotive and electronic applications, building materials, rain goods, plumbing hardware, and cathodic protection products. Anxiety about sustaining sales moved managers to look to exporting. Scanning global markets identified an opportunity in a call for bids by the Bangko Sentral ng Pilipinas (BSP), the central bank of the Philippines. After several months of effort, BSP awarded the coinage contract to Jarden Zinc, which enabled the SME to retain jobs that had been at risk, recall over twenty employees from earlier layoffs, and create fifteen new jobs. Explained its Vice President of Coinage Sales, "Having a global presence has been essential in Jarden's growth. The diversity of the opportunities abroad has provided us with the ability to prosper even during challenging economic times in the U.S. domestic market."[24]

Keeping the global trade game going requires accurately storing, stacking, sorting, and shipping cargo. The logistic flow of the game is astounding–from 1990 through 2011, the global stock of 20-foot equivalent units (TEUs) containers, the most common means of transporting goods, grew from 28.7 million to more than 200 million. In 2011, port container traffic saw those TEUs make nearly 600 million "trips" among trading partners. Here, we see TEUs in transit at a Hong Kong terminal.
Source: Lee Yiu Tung/Shutterstock

The shift in economic power from the West to the East is often portrayed as a threat to developed countries. Alternatively, it likely signals that companies will increasingly look to diversify through export. The industrial and infrastructure ambitions of emerging economies push them to import machinery from rich countries. In fact, imports into emerging markets have grown twice as fast as those into richer nations over the past decade.[25] The U.S., for instance, saw 30 percent of its export go to emerging markets in 1990; by 2012, almost 60 percent did. As SpinCent and Jarden Zinc show, it represents an opportunity for companies in such Western markets as the United States, Italy, and the United Kingdom to diversify sales by exporting to faster-growing, increasingly wealthy emerging countries.[26]

EXPORT: INITIATION AND DEVELOPMENT

Two views of export shape interpretation: the deliberate, sequential dynamic of incremental internationalization and the instant internationalization of the born global.

Research assesses how, when, and why companies initiate and develop exporting. Reports cover a lot of territory, evaluating the influence of managerial attitudes, product features, organizational resources, firm strategy, market trends, technology tools, disruptive innovations, public policy, and so on. Although there is some consensus, divergence persists. Indeed, as far back as 1991, research compiled more than 700 explanatory variables as plausible drivers of export initiation and expansion.[27] Today, two perspectives anchor interpretation: the incremental internationalization and the born global.

SEQUENCES AND INCREMENTS

Incremental internationalization sees physical distance, cultural ties, and market similarities fundamentally shaping how companies approach export. Specifically, exporting follows a sequential process that leads a company to sell initially from its home market to the most geographically and psychologically proximate countries. From there, it deliberately expands exports to more and more dissimilar and distant countries.

Initially, companies find it easier and less risky to trade with customers in countries that share geographic, cultural, linguistic, political, and legal commonalities. As one would expect, trading with folks in similar markets who speak the same or similar languages and share historical legacies puts less stress on managers' competencies. Trade data indicate strong effects: countries will engage in 42 percent more trade if they share a common language than if they do not, 47 percent more if both countries belong to a trading bloc such as the European Union or NAFTA, 114 percent more if they share a common currency, and 188 percent more if they have a common colonial past.[28]

Progressively gaining experience in successfully dealing with dissimilarity encourages managers to expand their international horizon to include increasingly different markets.

The dynamic of incremental internationalization is straightforward: Initial success trading with similar foreign customers, by developing managers' outlook and competencies, moderates ensuing export activity. That is, the firm's country-by-country export expansion follows a learning process through which managers' growing experience with and knowledge of increasingly dissimilar foreign markets creates the confidence to export to countries that share even fewer commonalities and are farther afield. Essentially, as the company exports more, managers' perception of the severity of problems and pitfalls declines. At the same time, their courage and confidence to expand further abroad increases.

Consider the experiences of Analytical Graphics of Pennsylvania, a manufacturer of software applications that support cost-effective development and deployment of space, defense, and intelligence missions. It began exporting in the late 1990s, targeting opportunities in Europe. Gradually, success there encouraged management to pursue export opportunities in Japan and South Korea. Its growing experience with the various business cultures in the Asian region, particularly regarding language customization and local training requirements, led it to open an office in Singapore to coordinate its increasing Asian sales.[29]

The interaction of managers' experiential learning and the market features of various countries often results in common export expansion scenarios. SMEs in the United States, for example, typically export first to Canada or the United Kingdom, then move on to Mexico, Europe, and eventually countries in South America, Asia, Africa, and the Middle East.[30] Conversely, an SME in Vietnam, Thailand, or Malaysia would typically follow a different path, exporting first to countries in Southeast Asia, moving on to greater Asia, and then, as business practices improved based on lessons learned, head to the United States, Europe, and Africa.

BORN GLOBALS

Born globals, owing to their executives' international orientation and improving technological options, begin trading internationally at inception.

The second perspective, derived from the international entrepreneurship literature, holds that some firms initiate exporting as a **born global** (also known as an "instant international" or "international new venture"). Rather than methodically engaging a sequence of increasingly dissimilar foreign markets, born globals step onto the world stage immediately upon their founding or soon after. The born global does not regard international markets as a refuge when sales slow in the home market. Rather, it begins with the belief that the domestic market is one of many opportunities in the world.[31] Granted, Figure 14.3 overly dramatizes the appeal of international business. Still, going global is an increasingly common scenario for an increasing number of companies worldwide.

We find born globals worldwide. In big markets, the choice to go global initially is still a choice, since the scale of the domestic market provides many business opportunities. But startups in smaller countries, such as Israel, Estonia, Djibouti, or Macau, must look beyond their borders from the get-go. No matter the scale of the local market, a key characteristic of born globals is that their executives have an international focus from the outset and pursue rapid globalization. Logitech, the Swiss-based maker of such computer devices as mice, keyboards, and speakers, was founded by a Swiss and an Italian who met while studying at Stanford University in the United States and was exporting products worldwide soon after startup.[32] Similar examples indicate that folks who establish born globals have a strong international orientation due to the insights gained from living or studying abroad. Often, too, we see a seasoned executive who leaves an MNE and launches a firm that goes global at the outset.[33]

Perhaps most critically, managers of born globals can do so because environmental circumstances enable it. Technological advances and the growing openness of countries to international trade enable them to implement their global visions quickly and cheaply. The born global phenomenon largely follows the ongoing globalization of markets, falling

FIGURE 14.3

Source: Robert Weber/New Yorker Cartoon Bank/www.cartoonbank.com

"Grab some lederhosen, Sutfin. We're about to climb aboard the globalization bandwagon."

trade barriers, growing demand for specialized products, and improving communication technologies. The enterprising firm exploits these circumstances, building a powerful business platform to develop and deliver innovations in niche markets that, although specialized, span the world.

Take the case of Evertek Computer, a U.S. SME, which started up in 1990 and quickly began to export. By 2009, it was exporting to customers in 105 countries, 30 percent of which were in South America, 20 percent in Europe, and 20 percent in the Middle East and North Africa. Its success comes from selling refurbished computers and parts, for which worldwide demand is booming because buyers, particularly poorer ones, don't need the latest and most expensive equipment. "They want cheap," says Evertek's international sales manager, John Ortley. "The firm's business model," he adds, "matches these folks with those who want to sell their used personal computer equipment."[34]

At first glance, liquidating obsolete pieces and parts seems an unlikely basis for successful exporting. And Evertek does not command the intimidating ownership advantage that usually supports exporting. However, the international orientation of its top management creates a powerful driver. Mr. Oxley's enthusiasm for international business, for example, fortifies the firm's belief that a big part of its business is found abroad: "For me," he says, "it started with being curious about the world. I enjoy learning about other cultures and respecting people who have a different background than mine."[35] Then, speaking like a true born global, he adds, "We're thriving. The world is shrinking, and it's getting easier and less expensive to do business on a global basis."[36]

CONCEPT CHECK

Change in the structure and dynamics of world business has taken a significant turn to new and novel standards. A flat world, billions of new capitalists, emerging economies, the global financial crisis, and so on, challenge many of our conventional theories. Consequently, scholars study trends, such as those dealing with incremental internationalization and the born-global phenomenon, to assess the direction and momentum of change.

INTERACTION: TIME AND PLACE

Neither the incremental nor the born global perspective definitively represents how companies initiate and escalate exporting. Research as well as company practices confirm that each credibly interprets the export process. For instance, recall that U.S. exports travel to 233 countries and territories. Many reflect long-running trade relationships, such as that between the United States and Canada. Others reflect more recent relationships, such as the United States and Kyrgyzstan. The scale and scope of this export universe supports scenarios in which companies have developed the competencies to service more markets (the incremental internationalization perspective) and can reach faraway markets with greater ease and immediacy (the born global view).

Table 14.1, by indicating an interaction between the two perspectives, proposes a useful way to interpret the export process. Among the top 15 countries that the United States both exports to and imports from, nine overlap. Its top four international trade partners—Canada, China, Mexico, and Japan—account for 45 percent of its total exports and 52 percent of its total imports. Most notably, the past two decades have seen trade with China and Mexico grow significantly. In 1992, for example, about 12 percent of total U.S. imports came from China and Mexico; by 2011, their combined share was 31 percent. Regarding trends, Mexico's import share rose from 4.3 percent in 1992 to 12.3 percent in 2011. Likewise, China's share of total U.S. imports grew from 4.8 to 18.5 percent over the same span.[37] Hence, on one hand we have the steady rise of Mexico while on the other we see the accelerating emergence of China.

Mexico's performance fits well with the incremental expansion thesis. Its geographic proximity, cultural overlap, similar institutional set-up, and membership in NAFTA present few problems and pitfalls to the occasional or regular exporter in the United States. China, as we saw in Chapters 2, 3, and 4, is culturally, politically, legally, and economically dissimilar to the United States. Still, Table 14.1 highlights its consequence to U.S. trade activity.

Firm-level data elaborate the trade relationship between China and the United States.[38] In 1992, 4,092 U.S. firms exported to China; by 2010, this number had increased more than 700 percent to 32,213 firms. This trend is particularly dramatic for SMEs in absolute terms

TABLE 14.1 Top Trade Partners of the United States: Exports and Imports

While the United States trades with 233 different countries and territories, its top 15 trade partners dominate total volume. On the export side, its top trade partner is Canada. On the import side, its leading supplier of goods and services is China.

Rank	Country	Exports	%, Total Exports	Rank	Country	Imports	%, Total Imports
1	Canada	245.2	19.1	1	China	351.3	18.5
2	Mexico	181.1	14.1	2	Canada	270.8	14.2
3	China	89.6	7.0	3	Mexico	233.7	12.3
4	Japan	58.4	4.5	4	Japan	122.8	6.4
5	United Kingdom	46.4	3.6	5	Germany	89.2	4.7
6	Germany	41.1	3.2	6	South Korea	49.4	2.6
7	Brazil	36.3	2.8	7	Saudi Arabia	47.7	2.5
8	South Korea	35.8	2.8	8	United Kingdom	45.9	2.4
9	The Netherlands	33.5	2.6	9	France	34.5	1.8
10	Hong Kong	29.7	2.3	10	India	34.5	1.8
11	Australia	26.1	2.0	11	Taiwan	32.6	1.7
12	France	25.8	2.0	12	Venezuela	32.1	1.7
13	Singapore	25.1	2.0	13	Italy	30.7	1.6
14	Belgium	24.6	1.9	14	Ireland	28.3	1.5
15	Switzerland	22.6	1.8	15	Brazil	27.6	1.5
-	Total, Top 15 Countries	921.2	71.6	-	Total, Top 15 Countries	1431	75.2
-	Total, All Countries	1286	100	-	Total, All Countries	1903.6	100

Source: U.S. Census Bureau, Foreign Trade, U.S. International Trade Data, 2012. Data: Year-to-Date October 2012.

as well as relative to large exporters. From 1992 to 2009, the number of SMEs exporting to China surged 776 percent versus 167 percent for large-company exporters. This effect is far more pronounced on the import side; SMEs accounted for 96 percent of the 87,910 U.S. firms that imported merchandise from China in 2009. The scale and scope of U.S.-China trade by a growing variety of SMEs speaks to the born global phenomenon.

Trade data suggest increasing interaction between the incremental international and born global perspectives.

Going forward, we anticipate stronger interaction effects between the incremental internationalization and born global perspectives. First, e-commerce continues turbo charging the latter. A generation ago, going global involved slow-acting trade officials directing slow-moving flows between tough-to-understand markets that differed on countless regulations and routines. Hence, incremental, market-by-market export expansion was not only feasible, it was arguably the only practical option.[39] Now e-commerce, fortified by social media, immediately gives small startups global reach, providing a platform that efficiently overcomes historic barriers to internationalization. Our closing case profiles a leading intermediary, Alibaba.com, which facilitates this process. Second, for those exporters more inclined toward incremental expansion, the Internet provides cheap, easy, and effective means to analyze and access dissimilar markets. Hence, their expansion to far more such markets fits the incremental view, whereas the acceleration of this process fits the born global perspective.

THE WILDCARD ROLE OF SERENDIPITY

Exporters are often proactive decision makers. Sometimes, however, serendipity—making fortunate discoveries by accident—initiates exports.

It is appealing to depict export initiation and development, whether done incrementally or immediately, as a purposeful strategy designed and delivered by proactive executives. However, research tells of accidental exporters who, responding to happenstance or odd circumstances, successfully enter foreign markets. Essentially, some companies start exporting because of fortuitous events rather than purposeful intent. Perhaps the most common trigger is the arrival of an unsolicited order in the mail, either postal or electronic. Others include a new hire that has connections to foreign buyers, an international contact made at an industry conference, personal travel abroad that alerts one to new options, and so on. Thus, **serendipity**—making fortunate discoveries by accident—is not an uncommon export trigger.

Edward Cutler is such a case. He is the owner and founder of Pennsylvania-based Squigle, a unique brand of toothpaste for people who cannot tolerate mass-produced varieties.[40] Upon launching Squigle, Mr. Cutler exclusively focused on the U.S. market. Internet posters spread the news of his product, and Squigle soon received inquiries from Taiwan, Turkey, and elsewhere. One customer, a canker-sore sufferer in Britain, was so enthusiastic about it that he began importing Squigle into England for local sale. That was good news for Mr. Cutler because it let him expand abroad at little cost and low risk. Now he is eager to export more, explaining, "We're looking to sell overseas for the same reason the big companies do: Most of the world's population lies outside the United States."[41]

Similarly, Vellus, a small Ohio-based company that makes a line of high-end pet grooming products, began its export odyssey when a Taiwanese businessperson, after trying its customized shampoos, bought $25,000 worth of the company's products to sell in Taiwan. Soon, word spread from show to show on the global canine circuit. Recounted Vellus's CEO, "I started receiving calls from people around the world who would hear of our products at dog shows and ask organizers how they could get in touch with me to buy our products."[42] Today, Vellus exports its products to about 30 countries.

CONCEPT CHECK

The Internet influences political change, improves the operations of **foreign-exchange markets,** and changes the location economies that drive **value chain** configurations. Similarly, the Internet reshapes export and import activity by opening new markets, supporting new strategies, and providing new tools.

APPROACHES TO EXPORTING

Granted, export sounds straightforward—make it, sell it, pack it, and ship it.[43] To some degree, this holds true for many trades. Generally, the ease of exporting reflects how a company chooses to do so. As we explain below, there are several options.

Exporting directly involves independent representatives, distributors, or retailers outside of the exporter's home country.

Direct Exporting In this scenario, the company directly sells its products to an independent intermediary, such as an agent, distributor, or retailer outside its home country, who then sells the product to the local consumer. **Direct exporting** is an ambitious approach. It requires that the company manage the export process, minding the many aspects of making and marketing the product for foreign buyers. *Ceteris paribus*, most direct exporters are larger-scale enterprises. They are efficient, low-cost suppliers leveraging economies of scale, able to spread high fixed costs of storage, processing, marketing, and transportation over large sales volumes.

Still, SMEs can develop successful approaches to direct exporting. Recall that as of 2010 SMEs comprised 97.8 percent of all identified exporters and accounted for 33.7 percent of the known exports of the United States. SpinCent highlights this situation. Its CEO analyzed markets, assessed industries, prepped his company, traveled overseas, and sought, screened, and hired trustworthy distributors to supervise sales in Asian markets. As needed, he called upon federal and local agencies for assistance in developing his export strategy. Consequently, direct exporting requires executive commitment and company resources to get the show started and then to sustain activity. Once up and running, exporting directly through trustworthy distributors is often administered efficiently.

Indirect exports are products sold to an intermediary in the home market, which then exports those products to other countries.

Indirect Exporting A company can use distributors, agents, or export management companies to export its products. Alternatively, it can supply inputs to other companies for incorporation into their products that are then exported. In the former scenario, the company sells its products to an independent intermediary in the domestic market, which then exports the product to its foreign agents, who then sell it to the end consumer. In this case, **indirect exporting** results because the exporter makes its product but relies on an intermediary—say, a global retailer—to supervise marketing, terms of sale, packaging, distribution, and credit and collection procedures. The approach is often relatively stress-free. Edward Cutler, maker of Squigle toothpaste, explained,"It is just easier to deal with distributors. We prefer to deal in master shippers of 144 tubes. We don't have to do anything then but slap a label on it."[44] In the other scenario—the firm selling inputs into other products that are then exported—the fact that the ultimate destination may be several transactions beyond its final sale, often leaves the SME unaware if its product was exported.

The intersection of retail and globalization trends makes indirect selling increasingly practical. Global retail chains such as Walmart, Carrefour, and Ahold facilitate the movement of products from exporters to storefronts. Think of, for example, a DVD manufacturer in China who supplies Walmart International with a product that Walmart then sells in its retail locations worldwide. Though not as lucrative as direct exporting, indirect exporting makes far fewer demands. Too, it is often a transition phase whereby the neophyte can gain familiarity with foreign consumers and competitors.

Many service companies export their product indirectly rather than directly. An indirect service export results when a nonexporting firm provides services to another company that ultimately exports its products abroad. We commonly associate indirect services exports with professional and business services such as accounting, advertising, consulting, and legal services. An indirect service export on the part of, say, a Swedish accounting firm occurs when it prepares the books of a Swedish company that exports to foreign markets. Indirect services exports occur across many industries, including audiovisual providers to film and television studios whose media are viewed overseas, or a hedge fund that sells shares to foreign investors through a wealth management advisory firm.

Passively Filling Orders from Domestic Buyers Who Then Export the Product From the perspective of the seller, these sorts of international sales are indistinguishable from domestic sales. Essentially, a buyer contacts the company, submits an order, takes delivery, and exports the product. Again, the company may be unaware that its product has been shipped abroad.

Oddly suggestive of a Potemkin village, this exhibition hall hosts the International Business Intelligence and Information Technology trade fair. The meeting and greeting that goes on here creates connections that often sparks export and import activity.

Source: © Robert Harding Picture Library Ltd/Alamy

Selling to Domestic Buyers Who Represent Foreign End Users or Customers MNEs, general contractors, foreign trading companies, foreign governments, and foreign distributors and retailers purchase goods for export. These buyers either need a product or see demand for it in foreign markets, so they buy it here and ship it there. Again, the company that makes the product may not know of its export.

WHICH APPROACH WHEN?

No one approach is intrinsically superior. At the broadest level, the company's particular ownership, location, and internalization advantages moderate its optimal approach. Considering firm size, large MNEs generally serve foreign customers through their foreign affiliates, while SMEs typically export directly or indirectly.[45] There is no hard and fast rule that one option is superior—approximately half of SMEs' exports are direct (i.e., produced by the exporting SME immediately before export) while the other half are indirect (i.e., supplied by the SME to other companies that then ultimately export it).[46]

CRN Case Review Note

Several factors shape an SME's preferred approach. Protecting ownership advantages endorses exporting directly. SpinCent, for example, saw direct selling as the best means to retain control of its core competency. Similarly, top management's outlook and company resources endorse some choices while discouraging others. A regular exporter is more likely to export directly. Firms new to exporting or those who are unable to commit staff and funds will likely prefer indirect methods.

Internet marketing helps companies—large and small—engage in international trade quickly, easily, and cheaply.

Technology's Role Technology influences the relative merits of the different approaches. The Internet makes direct exporting increasingly efficient and effective by providing immediate, low-cost access that lets regular exporters, particularly born globals, more easily access more markets.[47] In addition, e-commerce helps companies, both big and small, overcome capital and infrastructure limitations.[48] For example, exporters in Chile use extranets to communicate with importers around the world, while exporters in Costa Rica have used online shops to export directly.[49] Our closing case looks at how a little electronic magic at Alibaba.com, the world's largest business-to-business online marketplace, helps SMEs engage buyers and sellers worldwide. Twenty years ago, firm resources, communication channels, and trade logistics mattered immensely if you were a SME in Patagonia trying to reach markets in Europe. Today, due to Alibaba.com and like-minded Internet platforms, they matter far less.

The four approaches to exporting are not mutually exclusive; company and market circumstances moderate whether managers opt to apply one or a mix.

Mix-and-Match The four approaches to exporting are not mutually exclusive. A firm can engage different methods to trade different products to serve different markets. A Canadian company may export directly to similar markets such as the United States, Australia, and Britain while using indirect methods to handle exports to dissimilar markets in Asia or Africa. Recall that Analytical Graphics, which began exporting in the late 1990s, had expanded sales into 13 countries by 2011, serving them through a mix of methods: a direct selling strategy in Canada and United Kingdom, reseller partners in dissimilar countries such as Japan, South Korea, India, Russia, and Brazil.[50] So while there are general rules about which approach when, the ideal choice fits the firm's competencies, its executives' commitment, and the market features of the targeted countries.

IMPORTING

Importing is the purchase of a good or service by a buyer in one country—the importer—from a seller in another—the exporter. Samsung's shipment of a smart phone made in Seoul to a buyer in Belgium registers as an import for Belgium and an export for South Korea. Service imports, given their intangibility, take various forms. Foreign banks, like Royal Bank of Canada, that provide financial services to U.S. customers qualify as service imports. Similarly, when Lloyd's of London writes an insurance policy for a client in Brazil, trade authorities in Brazil record an import.

A service import is a service transaction that does not result in ownership and is rendered by non-residents to local residents.

The import of services has subtle characteristics. For example, the installation of nuclear power equipment in Sweden by French firm Areva, even though it is a hard good, qualifies as a service import for Sweden. The standard to keep in mind is that the import of a service consists of any transaction that (1) does not result in ownership and (2) is rendered by nonresidents to residents.

WHO ARE IMPORTERS?

Our earlier classification of exporters—non-, occasional, and regular—has broad analogues in the import sector. Although terminology can differ, we commonly see three types:

INPUT OPTIMIZERS

There are three general types of importers:

- Input optimizers
- Opportunistic
- Arbitrageurs

This type uses foreign sourcing to optimize, in terms of price or quality, the inputs fed into its supply chain. Essentially, a company scours the globe for optimal inputs, then directs them to its various production points that it has configured worldwide. Its various factories assemble them into finished goods that are then imported by markets worldwide. Logically, the flow of inputs and finished goods from country to country, besides representing imports, also qualifies as exports.

OPPORTUNISTIC

These importers looks for products around the world that they can import and profitably sell to local citizens. They see a gap in the local marketplace, whether real (customers cannot find what they want) or perceived (the presumption that products from some countries are intrinsically superior to local substitutes). They then opportunistically exploit it by finding, buying, transporting, and distributing products available only from foreign suppliers to local customers. The product is secondary; rather, the game is using import channels to fill gaps in the local marketplace profitably. For example, the release of the latest, greatest iPad typically triggers consumer frenzy, including scalpers aiming to exploit a temporary market gap given that it is only available in the United States for the first several weeks. Demand in other countries creates compelling opportunities. Buyers in China, for instance, hired shoppers in New York to buy whatever quantity they could and overnight it to Shanghai, where it is then marked up twice or thrice more.[51] Eventually, as Apple stores begin selling the iPad in China, the gap closed.

ARBITRAGEURS

Arbitrageurs look to foreign sourcing to get the highest-quality product at the lowest possible price. This motivation is timeless—an agent takes advantage of a price or quality difference between two or more markets, transacting deals that exploit the imbalance, and profiting from the difference. For instance, after Utah-based SME ForEveryBody began making bath and body products locally, it became an importer once it discovered low-cost home decorations available from Asian manufacturers that were competitive with premium products in the United States.

CHARACTERISTICS OF IMPORTERS

Extensive research has investigated the characteristics of exporters; for any number of reasons, however, importers have received far less investigation. Data do indicate that importers are also likely to be exporters, and that these firms account for the bulk of the world's exports and imports.[52] In the United States, for instance, 2010 data indicated that 212,491 companies only exported goods, and 101,008 companies only imported goods, while 80,640 companies handled both. Moreover, the latter companies accounted for 94.1 percent of total export value and 85.1 percent of the total import value.[53] In fundamental ways, then, our discussion of the characteristics of exporters applies to importers. For instance, importers tailor international activity to reflect their ownership, localization, and internalization advantages, exhibit incremental and born global characteristics, and indicate that firm size, along with efficiency, innovation, and commitment, explain their activity.

Several points qualify the degree of overlap. Historically, importers traded relatively few products with a relatively few developing countries.[54] Essentially, the bulk of imports tended toward opportunism or arbitrage—i.e., cheap oil in Saudi Arabia became expensive oil in the United States. The emergence of fast-growing economies accelerates and alters this relationship. These countries increasingly produce more goods and services that outperform, in price and function, local choices in advanced markets. They also increasingly provide higher-end products that once were the province of advanced markets—recall U.S. companies importing business process services from India-based firms. Finally, globalization supports far more differentiated supply chains that are longer, have more links, and cross more markets. Their growth has commensurately increased the import of inputs.

Several reasons motivate importing:

- Specialization of labor
- Global rivalry
- Local unavailability
- Diversification
- Top management's outlook

WHY IMPORT?

Various factors spur a firm to begin importing and motivate that firm's ongoing activity. Research emphasizes high product quality, satisfactory order processing, reliable delivery, lower prices, and domestic shortages. These factors, singly and collectively, push importers to scan world markets in search of lower-priced, better-quality, or locally unavailable products. This supposition raises the question: Why do these market anomalies exist? Absent these gaps, there is little need for import or, for that matter, export. Other parts of our text, particularly Chapters 6 and 12, speak to this issue. For our purposes, we highlight the following import drivers.

SPECIALIZATION OF LABOR

Managers commonly divide a production process into a sequence of stages and assign workers to particular stages so that one worker does one task, another does another task, and so on. This specialization of labor enables the organization of production to exploit location economics, especially different wage rates and factor costs, across countries. Improved efficiencies reduce costs that encourage companies to import cheaper products. For instance, Nike buys shoes manufactured by companies in several Asian countries, where local companies make higher quality shoes for lower cost. Nike finds it impossible to manufacture the same products in its home market, sell them at a reasonable price, and still make a profit; as a result, it imports shoes made in Asian factories into markets worldwide.

The same logic applies to the production of the iPad. Specifically, Apple contracts with Foxconn to make the iPad in China, which is then imported into the United States and other markets. Foxconn reportedly pays employees 1,200 yuan per month, or about $185.[55] Generously assuming an average 8-hour-per-day, 250-day-per-year schedule, that works out to about $1.11 per hour.[56] In contrast, the average U.S. manufacturing/mining/construction hourly compensation was officially $32.53 as of December 2010.[57] Reportedly, making the iPad requires about nine hours of direct labor. So, in this admittedly simple scenario, making the 32 GB Wi-Fi 3g iPad in China results in a retail price of $729 in the United States. Making it in the United States would have resulted in a retail price of $1,144.[58] Consequently, Apple imports iPads.

GLOBAL RIVALRY

Industries with a high degree of global competitive rivalry, such as we see in telecommunications, automobiles, and business services, impose relentless cost pressures. Many products, such as aircraft or cars, rely on thousands of parts produced in factories around the world. Companies use foreign suppliers in order to lower input costs or boost the quality of finished products.

LOCAL UNAVAILABILITY

Companies import products they cannot obtain locally for geographic, regulatory, or developmental reasons. Canada imports bananas from tropical climates because of its unsuitable climate; absent imports, Canadians would not enjoy fresh bananas. The same goes for eating seasonal fruits and vegetables out-of-season: e.g., grapes from Chile grace Christmas dinner in Denmark. Food is a rather obvious sector, but the same logic applies to an endless range of products, including tablet computers, medical technology, and financial services.

DIVERSIFICATION

Importers, like exporters, diversify operating risks by tapping international markets. Developing alternative suppliers makes a company less vulnerable to the dictates of a local supplier. For example, customers of U.S. steelmakers, such as automobile companies, have diversified their purchases to include European, Indian, and South Korean suppliers. This strategy reduces the risk of supply shortages or unilateral price hikes by U.S. steelmakers.

Point — Exporting E-waste: A Useful Solution?

Point **Yes** Exporting is a win-win situation: The more companies and countries export, the more they improve their performance. Exporting enables companies to increase sales, improve productivity, and diversify activities. Likewise, exporting helps countries generate jobs, accelerate innovation, and improve living standards. In broader terms, it promotes connections among countries that improve foreign relations and stabilize international affairs.

Despite these virtues, some contend there is a dark side of exporting, namely the trade of hazardous waste in the form of obsolete computer equipment. E-waste—trash composed of computers, monitors, electronics, game consoles, smartphones, and other items—inexorably increases as the Information Era rolls on. In 2006, nearly 66 million used electronic components were collected for reuse or recycling in the United States; most were exported.[59] By 2011, e-waste was pushing several hundred million pieces, with the U.S generating about 400 million and China 160 million units. Ongoing trends crank out newer, cooler, faster, smaller, fancier devices that, in replacing their predecessors and then eventually being replaced themselves, will increase e-waste nearly 500 percent over the next decade.

Where Should E-waste Go? Where to put all this e-trash is a tough question. Many counties and municipalities in the United States, for example, ban outright dumping of e-waste in local landfills. This legislation means that disposing of e-waste products, when possible, in any given industrialized country costs from $2,500 to $4,000 a ton. In contrast, selling untreated waste to countries in Africa and Asia, where it will be recycled, reused, or dumped, reportedly goes as low as $50 a ton.[60] Low costs follow from cheap labor, different environmental regulations, and growing processing capacity. Plus, the absence of public opposition reduces processing expenses and desperate folks seeking work dampens public objections. As might be expected, major e-waste shipping routes show that the industrial nations export the bulk of their e-waste to developing countries, notably China, Malaysia, India, Nigeria, and Bangladesh (see Map 14.1).[61]

Benefits for All Exporting e-waste to recycling centers throughout the world is an efficient solution to an escalating problem. First and foremost, recycling sustains our resources and helps us protect the environment. In developing countries, industries have sprung up to recycle old computers, monitors, circuit boards, scanners, printers, routers, cell phones, and

MAP 14.1 The Patterns of Trade of Electronic Waste

When computers, cell phones, and other electronic equipment become obsolete, they are no longer worth much in rich countries. E-waste, however, has some value in developing countries. That is exactly where, as exports, it usually ends up. Proponents note it promotes productive recycling as well as local economic development. Critics charge it is viciously hazardous and callously exploits cheap labor and lax regulations.

Source: Basel on Action Network; Silicon Valley Toxics Condition, www.ban.org/about/.

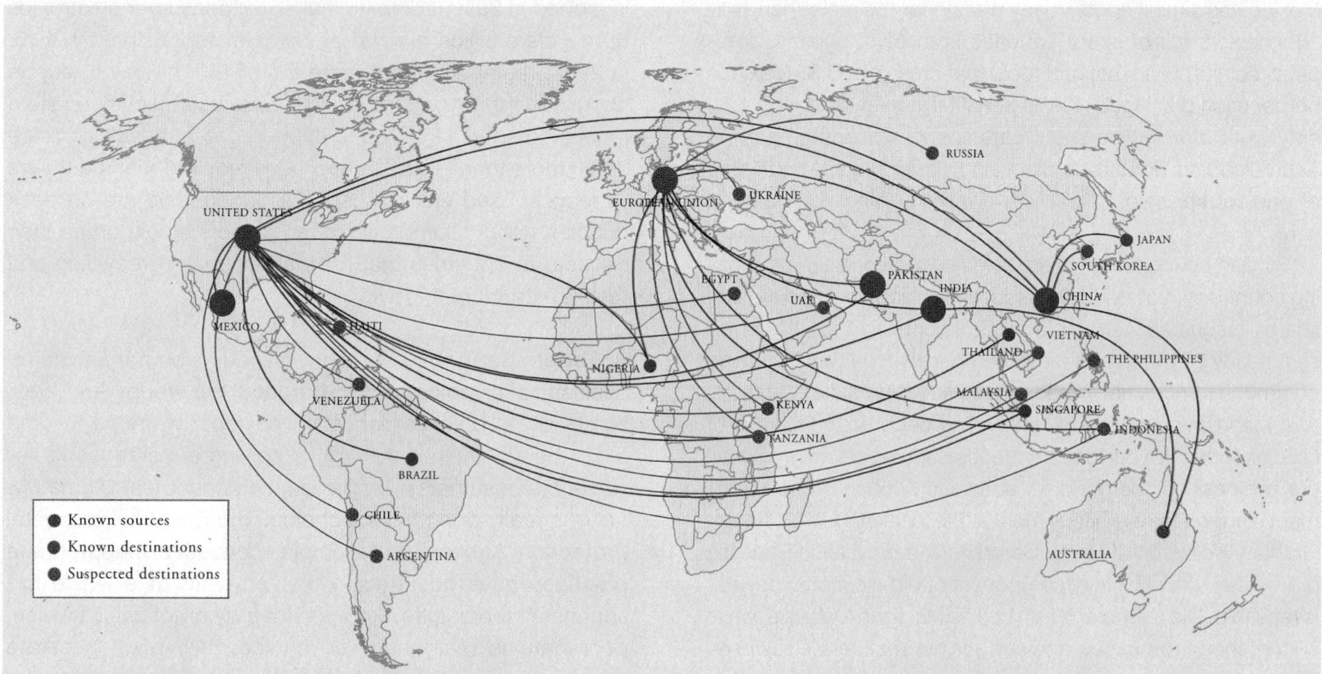

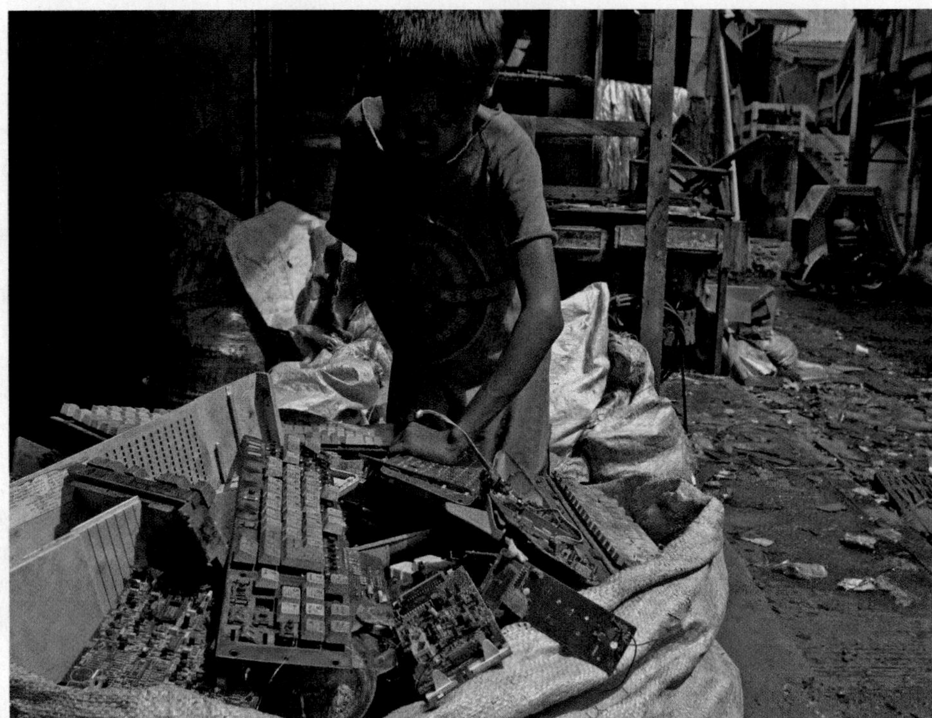

Here we see an enterprising ▶ Nigerian child running a grassroots e-recycling facility. Although junk to many, scavenging and selling useful parts creates value for him, his community, and the world.

Source: Enrique Soriano-Silverlens/ ZUMA Press/Newscom

network cards. While rudimentary, these industries create jobs in places where jobs are hard to find and difficult to sustain. To their credit, developing countries have converted their superior location economics into vital jobs, income, and markets. There are more than 5,500 businesses employing 100,000 workers at ground zero of the e-waste trade: Guiyu, China. Previously subsistence farmers and fishermen, they now process more than 100 truckloads of e-waste that arrive daily.[62] Mexico has similar spots, many waiting for the more than sixty 18-wheelers full of spent batteries from cars, phones, computer, solar appliances, and tools that cross the U.S.-Mexican border each day. Again, locals benefit. Despite the dangerous, dirty work of recycling spent batteries, people living near the Acumuladores de Jalisco plant find opportunity. As the wife of one worker said, "There are not many other jobs around here."[63]

Similarly, exporting e-waste helps entrepreneurs in developing countries create value by recovering, recycling, and reusing scarce resources. Copper, a valuable commodity, can represent nearly 20 percent of a mobile phone's total weight. Rising commodity prices have made these activities quite profitable. Atul Maheshwar, owner of a recycling depot in India, says of U.S. exports, "If your country keeps sending us the material, our business will be good."[64] In addition, much of the equipment shipped to Asia helps improve the local standard of living. Graham Wollaston of Scrap Computers, a recycler in Phoenix, claims that virtually every component of old electronic devices is reusable. Old televisions turn into fish tanks in Malaysia, while silicon shortage creates demand for old monitors elsewhere. "There's no such thing as a third-world landfill," Mr. Wollaston explains. "If you were to put an old computer on the street, it would be taken apart for the parts."[65] Similarly, Luc Lateille of the Canadian firm BMP Recycling says, "We don't send junk—we only send the materials that they are looking for."[66]

Exporting hazardous waste also helps MNEs improve their social responsibility. Samsung, Mitsubishi, and Nokia, among others, increasingly assume cradle-to-grave responsibility for their products. The eCycling Leadership Initiative, launched in 2010, commits makers of consumer electronics to recycle a billion pounds of e-waste responsibly by 2016; in 2011, members spent more than $100 million to recycle about 500 million pounds of old electronics. Elsewhere, state regulation spurs laggards to support green recycling. Since 2004, more than 20 U.S. states have required manufacturers to recycle used electronics. Likeminded laws are on deck in other states. Companies often comply by exporting their e-waste to countries that have an interest in recycling and the infrastructure to do it.

A Tough Solution Certainly, callous companies dump useless, often toxic e-waste around the world. And, yes, some of it pollutes landfills, poisons waterways, and fouls the air. Overall, though, exporting e-waste works for citizens, consumers, companies, and countries. Ultimately, nations really don't have a choice. The U.S. Environmental Protection Agency, for example, concedes inappropriate practices have occurred in the recycling of e-waste but suggests stopping its export is not truly practical. Likewise, poor nations really have no choice; they must generate income some way or condemn themselves to poverty.

Exporting E-waste: A Useful Solution?

Counterpoint

No In theory, recycling is beneficial. Recycling your e-waste, however, does not always mean you're doing the right thing. Explained the director of the Basel Action Network, "The dirty little secret is that when you take [your electronic waste] to a recycler, instead of throwing it in a trashcan, about 80 percent of that material, very quickly, finds itself on a container ship going to a country like China, Nigeria, India, Vietnam, Pakistan—where very dirty things happen to it."[67] Added the chief executive of RSR, a Dallas-based lead recycler that operates solely in the United States, "We're shipping hazardous waste to a neighbor ill-equipped to process it, and we're doing it legally, turning our heads, and pretending it's not a problem."[68] Growing exports of hazardous waste have created dangerous recycling industries in many developing countries. Going forward, exports will accelerate as e-waste increases far faster than other sorts of rubbish. Collectively, the tsunami of e-trash imposes far more costs than the pittance recycling it generates.

A Witch's Brew Most developing countries lack the regulatory codes or disposal infrastructure to safeguard against such dangers. Locals often use crude methods that, besides being illegal in the United States, expose workers and residents to a witch's brew of toxins. For example, some e-waste contains trace amounts of precious metals like copper and silver. Extracting them encourages cash-strapped, loosely regulated recyclers to use unsafe, antiquated open-air incineration methods. Burning electronic parts to separate copper, solder, or other metals from plastic coatings releases dioxins and other hazardous chemicals. Indeed, snagging that sliver of silver unleashes a mixture of more than a thousand chemicals, including toxic metals (e.g., lead, barium, and mercury), flame-retardants, cadmium, acids, plastics, and chlorinated and brominated compounds. Local air quality suffers as "circuit boards are burned after acid washing, spewing deadly smoke and exposing workers and people living around these facilities."[69] Once local scrap shops finish disassembling equipment, the trash goes into public landfills, the acid runoff flows into groundwater, and the noxious fumes follow air currents—all mercilessly contaminating the environment.

Casual Inhumanity Madhumita Dutta of Toxics-Link Delhi argues that these problems are less disturbing than the "appalling" working conditions in recycling facilities: "Everything from dismantling the computer to pulling out parts of the circuit boards to acid-washing boards to recover copper is done with bare hands without any protective gear or face protection." Rare is the worksite that uses proper disposal practices. Workers and society, to say nothing of environmental sustainability, suffer.

What, then, of the premise of charity—that is, sending computer equipment from countries where it has little use to countries where it can make a difference? Critics shred this straw man, asserting that wealthier countries and powerful companies conveniently donate obsolete equipment to dodge high recycling expenses. "Too often, justifications of 'building bridges over the digital divide' are used as excuses to obscure and ignore the fact that these

Here we see a frightful wasteland near Lagos, Nigeria. Notwithstanding the toxic threats of this witches' brew, desperation spurs people to scavenge for anything of value.
Source: n86/ZUMA Press/Newscom

bridges double as toxic waste pipelines," said one critic.[70] Moreover, most of the computer equipment sent is worthless trash—waste that can be neither repaired nor resold.[71]

Institutional Gaps Some argue that manufacturers need to step up and take full responsibility for the hazardous materials they used to build products that had earned them profits.[72] Companies have moved in this direction, sponsoring green campaigns to recycle e-waste. Substantive progress has been slow, however. Environmentalists recommend that countries set tougher standards to monitor, control, and certify cross-border shipments of e-waste. That has proven disappointing. Inspections of e-waste cargo at 18 European seaports awaiting export, for example, found that nearly half was illegal.[73]

Then again, presumed solutions can lead to unintended problems. The fact that many U.S. states require companies to take responsibility for recycling electronic equipment has curtailed the export of e-waste to developing countries—but only of the more valuable components. Processors cherry-pick parts that can be refurbished for reuse. The remainder is disassembled, with urban miners targeting silver, gold, and palladium. The final patch of trash, the worst of the worst, has no reuse market and is shipped to developing countries for disposal.[74]

Who to Turn To? Others endorse stronger enforcement of the Basel Convention on the Transboundary Movement of Hazardous Wastes and their Disposal, a United Nations treaty that regulates the generation, management, movements, and disposal of hazardous waste. It proposes aggressive measures, including an international ban on the export of all toxic waste, no matter whether for recovery, recycling, reuse, or final disposal. As of 2013, 172 countries had ratified the Basel Convention. The United States, which generates more than half of the world's e-waste, has signed the treaty but not ratified it.[75]

1. The export of e-waste to recycling facilities worldwide seems like a win for the world given that recycling is always considered a beneficial activity. However, there are serious costs. Identify three benefits as well as three costs of recycling the U.S.'s e-waste in other countries. Then state whether you believe the benefits exceed the costs or vice versa.

IMPORTING AND EXPORTING: PROBLEMS AND PITFALLS

CONCEPT CHECK

As straightforward as the concept of **exporting** may seem on the surface, whether you are a born-global entrepreneur or an established **MNE**, it is fraught with challenges. *Behavioral barriers* complicate international operations. Political and legal codes pose pitfalls, *government regulation* impacts trade relationships, and *foreign-exchange instruments* necessitate financial sophistication.

Companies, both big and small, identify problems and pitfalls that complicate international trade. Moreover, trade veterans explain that exporting and importing are fraught with ongoing complexities and evolving barriers. Presently, there is considerable variation regarding the type, characteristics, and impact of obstacles. The United States International Trade Commission polled the managers of a stratified random sample of more than 8,400 U.S. firms—both big companies and SMEs from the manufacturing and service sectors—about the influence of 19 potential barriers to trade.[76] Table 14.2 shows the range of opinions. The ratings confirm that international traders deal with a battery of problems and pitfalls. Data indicate that different types of firms differently interpreted different impediments.

Related survey data indicate that as SMEs export more, their perception of the severity of impediments declines—much as we would expect, given our earlier discussion of the internationalization process.[77] Indeed, international experience matters greatly; newer SMEs, particularly those in services versus manufacturing who export less intensively and to fewer regions, regarded barriers as disproportionately more severe than did their experienced counterparts. However, practice was not a panacea. Experienced companies exporting to multiple regions of the world still struggle with impediments to trade. So, as in the past, we anticipate exporters and importers will face recurring difficulties that test the resolve of the most committed internationalist. Let's take a closer look at key areas of concern.

FINANCIAL RISKS

SMEs regularly rate financial constraints as the most daunting barrier to international trade.

Financial constraints are arguably the greatest impediment to international traders. In a survey of 978 SMEs that asked their perceptions of trade barriers, the top-ranked factor was the shortage of working capital to finance export.[78] Likewise, financial concerns consistently rank high in Table 14.2. Traders often reason that export or import offers low profitability given unexpected costs and unknown financial constraints, both of which are aggravated

TABLE 14.2 The Relative Influence of Leading Barriers to Export

International trade presents a range of difficulties. Here we see how managers of both SMEs and large companies, operating in either making a good or providing a service, rate the challenge of leading types of trade impediments.

Note: The higher the percentage, the greater the perceived severity of the particular impediment to trade.

Barrier to Export	SME Manufacturer	Large Manufacturer	SME Services	Large Services Firm
Transportation/shipping costs	88.5	93.6	53.6	35.1
Language/cultural barriers	82.2	86.8	53.4	42.2
Difficulty locating sales prospects	79.1	83.2	55.8	45.2
Foreign regulations	78.0	90.0	51.1	48.3
U.S. regulations	73.4	86.8	45.4	37.8
Foreign sales not sufficiently profitable	72.5	84.4	58.7	46.2
Customs procedures	71.9	87.4	44.6	35.5
Difficulty receiving or processing payments	67.9	87.9	39.3	41.1
U.S. taxation issues	62.8	80.7	37.4	39.2
Lack of trained staff	62.6	85.7	36.7	46.5
Insufficient intellectual property protection	61.8	71.6	43.6	27.3
Foreign taxation issues	60.4	80.5	36.1	40.6
Preference for local goods/services in foreign market	57.4	81.7	37.8	35.8
Difficulty establishing affiliates in foreign markets	57.2	76.9	29.8	33.8
High tariffs	56.6	81.6	36.8	28.8
Lack of government support programs	56.4	70.3	29.2	29.4
Obtaining financing	51.6	63.8	38.5	31.9
Unable to find foreign partners	50.5	66.6	33.0	36.0
Visa issues	30.1	67.8	34.9	33.5

Source: The *United States International Trade Commission* asked 3,500 U.S. big and SME in manufacturing and service industries firms if they had ever exported or considered exporting (the latter point was included to account for the possibility that firms had faced perceived insurmountable barriers). These firms were then asked to report whether they had encountered the various impediments and, if yes, assess the impediment's severity on a scale of 1 to 5, with 1 representing no impediment, 3 a moderate impediment, and 5 a major impediment. See "Small and Medium-Sized Enterprises: Characteristics and Performance," United States International Trade Commission, Investigation No. 332-510, USITC Publication 4189, November 2010.

by fluctuating exchange rates. Managing these risks involves currency and credit processes that call for sophisticated financial expertise. Moreover, completing international sales often requires helping foreign customers obtain credit, whether in the form of trade credits, government-financed support, or bank guarantees.[79] Firms accustomed to offering financing in terms of the traditional 30- or 60-day trade-credit cycle at home regard the need for different arrangements denominated in different currencies as excessively escalating risk.

CUSTOMER MANAGEMENT

An enduring barrier to exporting is misunderstanding the difficulty of profitably serving consumers in foreign markets.

Historically, exports and imports were arm's-length, ship-it-and-forget-it transactions. Contact with customers relied on documents either faxed or posted overnight. This situation created useful time lags with which to deal with questions and complaints. Now, contacting vendors via email or voice-over-Internet-protocol (VoIP) gives customers, no matter how far away, real-time access. The resulting boost of customers' service expectations reduces the appeal of international trade. "The new notch in the bar for us is the requests from our customers for additional services beyond the port of delivery," said the materials manager of Seco/Warwick, a manufacturer of heat-treating equipment. "In previous years, I would be responsible for cost, insurance, and freight (CIF) to the port of import, but now I'm often tasked with all aspects of delivery to the customer's plant location. Now we're often involved in the installation and startup of the equipment, so we have service engineers and cranes waiting for the on-time delivery."[80]

Customer management concerns particularly challenge SMEs. Their orientation toward specialized opportunities and narrow gaps in the market often prompt them to apply niche strategies. Doing so pushes them to customize services and marketing support to fit overseas segments in ways that often exceed those offered in the home market. Recurring resource constraints as well as the preference to avoid head-on competition with larger companies reinforce these tendencies.[81]

INTERNATIONAL BUSINESS EXPERTISE

The problems and pitfalls of international trade consistently frustrate the occasional and regular exporter.

International traders note the difficulties of understanding foreign business practices. Ordinary as well as idiosyncratic problems include limited knowledge of foreign competitors, unfamiliarity with local customs regulations, uncertainty about the prevailing price-to-quality standards, difficulty optimizing transportation and insurance options, and confusion about market channels and consumer behavior. Certainly, there are solutions, as we saw with our opening profile of SpinCent. Fear of misunderstanding local markets led it to hire local distributors. Firms that struggle with interpreting export markets typically exit international trade.

MARKETING CHALLENGES

Traders regularly complain of high shipment costs and logistic demands; difficulties in matching foreign rivals' prices, effectively promoting products, and establishing distribution networks; and weak foreign market connections. In addition, providing after-sales service imposes the aggravation of translating warranties as well as navigating ambiguous cultural differences. Non-exporters express greater anxiety about these marketing uncertainties, particularly when they benchmark them against the comparatively lower demands in their home markets. In addition, the decidedly more complex demands of market structures and consumer behaviors in emerging markets amplify problems. Going from the United States to Canada is one thing; going from the United States to Turkmenistan is entirely another.

TOP MANAGEMENT COMMITMENT

Persevering in the face of problems and pitfalls requires executives committed to internationalization.

Management characteristics, especially senior executives' international outlook and risk orientation, influence import activity. Most companies, particularly SMEs, focus on domestic rather than foreign markets. In the United States, for instance, SMEs comprise 97 percent of all exporters, yet less than 1 percent of all SMEs export. Of those that do export, nearly two-thirds export to just one foreign market.[82] Asked about their export-shyness, managers cite familiarity with the home market along with equivocal top management commitment. Even when top management acknowledges the benefit of trade, its riskiness and resource demands dissuade most from internationalizing operations.

Exporting and importing put tough demands on management. Rare is the firm that eagerly adjusts its customary practices for foreign business standards. As a result, top management often emphasizes the domestic market and duly notes the intention to export down the road. Recall Knepper's original export outlook at SpinCent; at best, he was an occasional exporter who felt the risks outweighed rewards. Eventually, profitability and diversification concerns forced him to reconsider. From then on, his company's core competency, support from public agencies, and trustworthy distributors fortified his export commitment.

GOVERNMENT REGULATION

Export and import inefficiencies persist due to delays, documents, and administrative fees. The rules and regulations governing trade, notwithstanding the success of the WTO, endure. New Jersey–based Spectra Colors, manufacturer and distributor of high-quality customized dyes and colorants, runs into problems because import regulations differ from one country to the next. "In Europe, REACH regulations (Registration, Evaluation, and Authorization of Chemicals) have caused us lengthy delays and expense," said Spectra's business manager.[83]

Occasionally, shipments to various markets require government clearance. Refusals come easily to officials facing product constraints at home or political tension abroad. REACH disproportionately affects SME exporters, given staff and resource constraints to ensure compliance. Worse still, Canada, China, Japan, Switzerland, Taiwan, and Turkey are developing regulations like those of REACH. [84]

CONCEPT CHECK

"Legal Issues in International Business," profiled in Chapter 3, note how a country's legal system influences operating decisions. Chapter 7 shows how governments influence import flows with instruments of trade control. Here, we add revenue collection and homeland security to the list of moderators.

Similar regulatory situations are emerging in other industries. Exporters of medical devices face complex regulations and lengthy approval times that require extensive test data. Many countries, including Australia, Canada, China, certain EU member states, Japan, and the United States (and the list is growing), impose approval procedures that require firms to implement an ISO-certified production quality management system. Firms intent on complying must pay various fees and related charges to gain and maintain certification. Many exporters, particularly SMEs, struggle to fund such efforts.

Table 14.2 shows that service exporters also run into other problems. Professional service providers, such as the sort found in engineering, legal, finance, and entertainment services, regularly send employees abroad to perform contracted services. In Malaysia, for example, foreign engineers cannot work on building projects unless the hiring company demonstrates to the Malaysian Board of Engineers that a Malaysian engineer cannot do the job.[85] It's harsher in Thailand—its Alien Occupation Act reserves architecture and engineering services jobs for Thai nationals.[86] Morocco likewise prohibits foreign architects registering with its National Association of Architects, then mandates that only members of this Association can legally practice architecture. The Philippines goes even farther, reserving the practice of most licensed professions to Philippine citizens.[87] Finally, India restricts the right to practice law to natural persons who are both Indian citizens and on the advocates' roll in the particular Indian state where legal services will be provided. Furthermore, to qualify as an advocate, candidates must be either an Indian citizen or a citizen of a country that allows Indian nationals to practice law on a reciprocal basis, hold a degree from a university recognized by the Bar Council of India, and be at least 21 years of age.[88] Similar situations in Brazil, Bahrain, and Hong Kong, to name just a few, challenge the legal firm with international ambitions.

E-commerce, while a powerful export platform, does not let companies circumvent barriers. Government regulations may lag company actions, given the speed by which e-commerce occurs, but they eventually regain their authority. For example, Chinese law holds that an enterprise seeking to operate in the digital publishing field of China must obtain at least one of the four licenses for publishing, copying, distributing, or importing e-books in order to operate legally. Within a day of Amazon announcing its Kindle store launch in China, for instance, the Chinese authorities began investigating its legality, claiming its licensing agreement with its Chinese partner, Chineseall.com, was insufficient.[89]

In the United States, homeland security issues constrain trade. The logistics manager at Schott North America notes that the real danger to international trade these days is not tariffs; rather, it's "that your containers are stuck down at the terminal in New York [harbor] waiting for inspection" by radiation detection instruments before being allowed to enter the United States.[90] Likewise, moving goods across borders takes far longer today than it did a dozen years ago given security procedures: processing a truckload of goods across the Canadian–American border takes three times as long as it did pre-September 11, 2001.[91] The United Kingdom, likewise, replaced its "account consignor scheme" that had allowed logistics groups to accept goods for cargo planes from self-certified businesses in order to improve its air cargo safety. As a result, importers and exporters must have all shipments scanned by the freight firms, such as FedEx, TNT, and UPS, or establish high-security sites.[92] Governments work toward common standards, adopting similar screening methods, and harmonizing security measures. The sensitivity of these issues, particularly security, slows progress.[93] Consequently, national, regional, and global trade regulations impose persistent barriers.

TRADE DOCUMENTATION

Governments require international traders to thoroughly document transactions.

A battery of documents regulates international trade. Duty rates, customs clearance, and entry processes, though overlapping, invariably differ across countries. Tariff classifications, value declarations, and duty management spawn confusion and boost costs. Customs and

TABLE 14.3 Types of Export Documents

Many concerns motivate the government to monitor export activities, ranging from tracking transactions to defending national security. Here we see a subset of the forms that exporters commonly complete.

Type	Specification
Pro Forma Invoice	A document from the exporter to the importer that outlines the selling terms, price, and delivery as if the goods had actually shipped. If the importer accepts the terms and conditions, it sends a purchase order and arranges for payment, at which point the exporter issues a commercial invoice.
Shipper's Export Declaration	The most common of all export documents, used by the exporter's government to monitor exports and compile trade statistics.
Bill of Lading	A receipt for goods delivered to the common carrier for transportation, a contract for services rendered by the carrier, and a document of title. The customer usually needs an original as proof of ownership before assuming title.
Consular Invoice	Sometimes required by countries to monitor imports, it is used by governments to track import prices and generate revenue.
Certificate of Origin	Indicates the product's origination and is usually validated by an external source, such as the Chamber of Commerce. It helps countries determine the tariff schedule for imports.
Export-Packing List	Itemizes the material in each individual package, indicates the type of package, and is attached to the outside of the package. Used by the shipper and sometimes customs officials to verify the cargo.
Commercial Invoice	A bill for the goods from buyer to seller listing a description of the goods, buyer/seller addresses, and delivery and payment terms. Governments use it to determine the value of goods when assessing customs duties. Figure 14.4 shows a sample of this form, identifying the various data an exporter must report to comply with current U.S. trade policy.

security initiatives impose various regulations. Navigating these obstacles requires that traders manage the paper trail that documents, certifies, and legalizes transactions. Table 14.3 profiles key customs documents. For many companies, completing these and many others is unacceptably burdensome. A look at Figure 14.4 gives one a sense of this task—and, keep in mind that this is just one of the many required forms.

Mistakes can arise in any number of slots. For example, many loss-and-damage challenges stem in part from the sizable percentage of exporters that use incorrect International Commercial Terms, or Incoterms.[94] Sometimes, exporters fail to classify their products accurately in terms of the tariff schedule of the country of destination. Goods that arrive with commercial invoice descriptions not matching those of the importing country's tariff classification are registered under a catchall description, such as "machinery, other." Besides slowing the transaction, imprecise descriptions often incur higher duty charges.

Importers typically receive products without purchasing them. That is, they take the title of ownership without laying out any money. The arrival of the shipment in-country requires filing documents with various offices and agencies in order to pay up, take title, settle duty charges, and arrange delivery. Required documents vary by country. Typically, customs agencies require an entry manifest, commercial invoice, and packing list.[95]

IMPORTING AND EXPORTING: RESOURCES AND ASSISTANCE

The problems and pitfalls of international trade, besides discouraging potential exporters and importers, complicate the activities of committed internationalists and born globals. SMEs are particularly vulnerable. Many could boost profits and improve productivity by entering new markets.[96] In 2010, 60 percent of U.S. SME exporters sold to customers in only one foreign market, whereas more than half of big exporters recorded sales to five or more foreign

FIGURE 14.4 Sample Commercial Invoice

Here we see a sample of the sorts of forms that U.S. exporters routinely face. In this case, the form is a commercial invoice, a bill for the goods from the foreign buyer to the U.S. seller. Completing this form correctly makes for efficient transfers. Completing it incorrectly results in costly delays and often higher duty charges.

Source: Based on data reported in the WorldBank's World Development Indicators, in particular *Trade* (percent of *GDP*) (Series NE_TRD_GNFS_ZS), retrieved June 15, 2013, from data.worldbank.org/data-catalog/world-development-indicators.

COMMERCIAL INVOICE

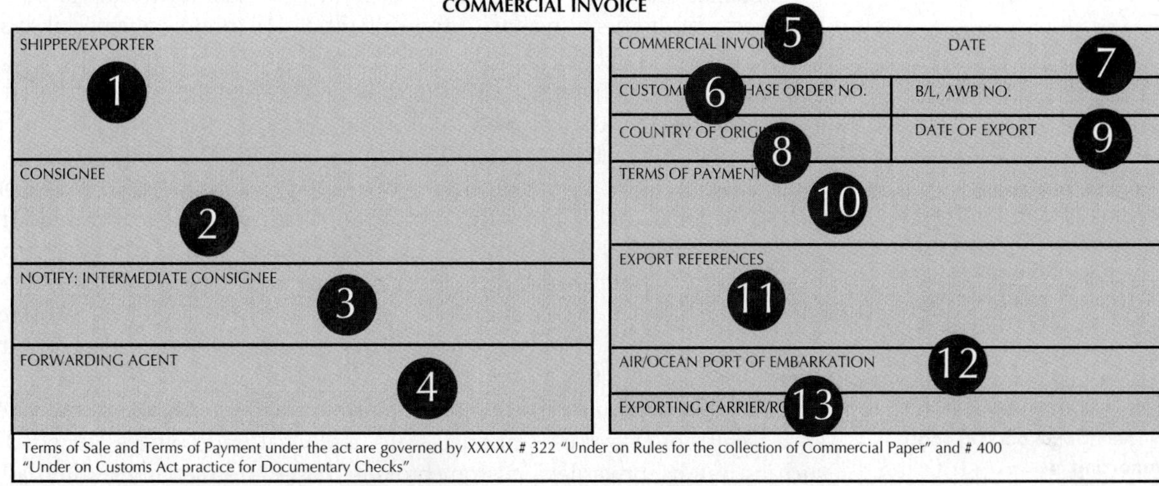

SHIPPER/EXPORTER (1)	COMMERCIAL INVOICE NO. (5) / DATE (7)
	CUSTOMER PURCHASE ORDER NO. (6) / B/L, AWB NO.
	COUNTRY OF ORIGIN (8) / DATE OF EXPORT (9)
CONSIGNEE (2)	TERMS OF PAYMENT (10)
NOTIFY: INTERMEDIATE CONSIGNEE (3)	EXPORT REFERENCES (11)
FORWARDING AGENT (4)	AIR/OCEAN PORT OF EMBARKATION (12)
	EXPORTING CARRIER/ROUTE (13)

Terms of Sale and Terms of Payment under the act are governed by XXXXX # 322 "Under on Rules for the collection of Commercial Paper" and # 400 "Under on Customs Act practice for Documentary Checks"

PKGS	QUANTITY	NET WT (Kilos)	GROSS WT (Kilos)	DESCRIPTION OF MERCHANDISE	UNIT PRICE	TOTAL VALUE
14	15	16	16	17		18

PACKAGE MARKS (19)	MISC. CHARGES (packings, insurance, etc.) (20)	
	INVOICE TOTAL	

CERTIFICATIONS (21)

AUTHORIZED SIGNATURE

1. EXPORTER	The name and address of the principal party responsible for effecting export from the United States. The exporter as named on the Export License.
2. CONSIGNEE	The name and address of the person/company to whom the goods are shipped for the designated end use, or the party so designated on the Export License
3. INTERMEDIATE CONSIGNEE	The name and address of the party who effects delivery of the merchandise to the ultimate consignee, or the party so named on the Export License.
4. FORWARDING AGENT	The name and address of the duly authorized forwarder acting as agent for the exporter.
5. COMMERCIAL INVOICE NO.	Commercial Invoice number assigned by the exporter
6. CUSTOMER PURCHASE ORDER NO	Overseas customer's reference of order number
7. B/L, AWB NO.	Bill of Lading, or Air Waybill number, if known
8. COUNTRY OF ORIGIN	Country of origin of shipment
9. DATE OF EXPORT	Actual date of export of merchandise
10. TERMS OF PAYMENT	Describe the terms, conditions, and currency of settlement as agreed upon by the vendor and purchaser per the Pro Forma Invoice, customer Purchase Order, and/or Letter of Credit
11. EXPORT REFERENCES	May be used to record other useful information, e.g. - other reference numbers, special handling requirements, routing requirements, etc.
12. AIR/OCEAN PORT OF EMBARKATION	Ocean port/pier, or airport to be used for embarkation of merchandise
13. EXPORTING CARRIER/ROUTE	Record airline carrier/flight number or vessel name/shipping line to be used for the shipment of merchandise
14. PACKAGES	Record number of packages, cartons, or containers per description line
15. QUANTITY	Record total number of units per description line.
16. NET WEIGHT/GROSS WEIGHT	Record total net weight and total gross weight (includes weight of container) in kilograms per description line.
17. DESCRIPTION OF MERCHANDISE	Provide a full description of items shipped, the type of container (carton, box, pack, etc.), the gross weight per container, and the quantity and unit of measure of the merchandise.
18. UNIT PRICE/TOTAL VALUE	Record the unit price of the merchandise per the unit of measure, compute the extended total value of the line.
19. PACKAGE MARKS	Record in this Field, as well as on each package, the package number (e.g. - 1 of 7, 3 of 7, etc.), shippers company name, country of origin (e.g. - made in USA), destination port of entry, package weight in kilograms, package size (length x width x height), and shipper's control number (e.g. - C/I number; optional).
20. MISC. CHARGES	Record any miscellaneous charges which are to be paid for by the customer - export transportation, insurance, export packaging, inland freight to pier, etc.
21. CERTIFICATIONS	Any certifications or declarations required of the shipper regarding any information recorded on the commercial invoice.

Source: www.unzco.com/basicguide/figure2.html Accessed March 19, 2009.

markets. A tiny share of exporters, just 0.4 percent, shipped goods to 50 or more countries. We see similar characteristics on the import side. Sixty-one percent of U.S. SMEs imported from one foreign market, while 57 percent of large firms imported from five or more foreign markets.[97] Likewise, fewer than 0.1 percent of importing companies brought in goods from 50 or more countries.

Globalization spurs companies to expand their market frontiers. Liberalizing markets and opening borders increases the potential for trade—again, take a quick look at Table 14.1. Generally, big companies outperform their smaller counterparts pursuing these opportunities; ownership and internalization advantages as well as superior resources better position them. In contrast, most SMEs lack the competencies and connections to pursue trade opportunities. For example, 92 percent of all U.S. SME exporters do business from a single location, and only 15 percent of SME exports go to related affiliates abroad. In contrast, just 11 percent of large firms that export are single-location companies and 38 percent of their exports go to foreign affiliates—essentially, MNEs "export" their products to their foreign subsidiaries who then distribute to local buyers.[98] Furthermore, SMEs' typically tight resource constraints hamper developing international expertise. Consequently, many SMEs find themselves in situations where public resources and assistance can meaningfully influence their international activities.

CONCEPT CHECK

In Parts I and II of the text, we note that **international business** creates jobs, generates income, and raises living standards. Parts II and III show how governments shape trade relationships through pro-trade policies. Here, we observe that governments provide a variety of programs to improve the ease and efficiency of **exporting and importing.**

Public agencies and private intermediaries provide non-, occasional, and regular exporters a wealth of resources. National, state, and local trade offices along with private parties such as freight forwarders, custom brokers, trade intermediaries, international banks, and consultants are a few of the many resources that help companies navigate international trade (see Table 14.4). Our opening look at SpinCent highlighted the assistance provided by the U.S. Commercial Service's Export Assistance Center of Philadelphia. It helped Knepper assess the Asian markets, supported his tag-along on the Asia trade mission, helped prescreen distributors, and arranged visits with local officials.

GOVERNMENT AGENCIES

Public officials champion export given its macroeconomic and microeconomic benefits. From a macroeconomic perspective, it helps countries generate jobs, build foreign exchange reserves, improve the balance of trade, develop foreign relationships, and raise living standards. In the United States, for example, exports support more than 10 million jobs. In the manufacturing sector, export-related jobs accounted for 22 percent or more of total employment in ten U.S. manufacturing industries.[99] Overall, manufacturing exports support more than one of every five jobs in the United States. From a microeconomic perspective, exporting helps firms leverage core competencies, improve financial performance, fortify competitive positioning, and sustain the enterprise. New markets open paths to higher productivity and profitability. Consequently, governments in virtually every country assist potential and active exporters. To a lesser degree, they also protect the interests of their struggling importers.

In the United States, as in most countries, public agencies help firms initiate and develop exports and imports.

In the United States, SMEs often start at the nearest Commercial Service office, the trade promotion arm of the U.S. Department of Commerce's International Trade Administration. Its representatives in more than 100 U.S. cities and 75 countries help U.S. companies to start exporting or to seek sales in new markets. Its global network helps SMEs target markets, organize operations, and overcome barriers. For Analytical Graphics, Commercial Service supports its Asian market expansion, setting up meetings with potential resellers in Japan and South Korea.[100] Other units of the International Trade Administration resolve related trade complications, such as helping Garmine Marine clear its navigational GPS through Turkish customs by informing Turkish government officials that the units can be self-certified by an accredited independent lab, in compliance with the relevant EU standard.[101]

The U.S. government, through these and other resources, provides information and advice on the practicalities and technicalities of exporting. Its official gateway, www.export.gov, offers a variety of support services. Personal help is also available at export centers run by various branches of the Commerce Department, International Trade Administration, and the Small Business Administration. These and related agencies strengthen the competitiveness of U.S.

TABLE 14.4 Trade Assistance by Type and Source

If your company is thinking about initiating or escalating international trade activity, the following organizations and agencies offer assistance on a host of issues.

Source	Nature of Assistance
Government Agencies	Market demographics, product demand, and competition
	Complying with domestic and foreign trade regulations
	Customs, regulatory, and tax issues
	Sales financing, credit, and insurance
	Trade data analysis
	Licenses and regulations
	International financing
	International sales and marketing
	Trade events, partners, and trade leads
	Shipping documentation and requirements
	Pricing, quotes, and negotiations
Trade Associations	Market demographics, product demand, and competition
	Export training seminars online and on-site
	Advertising and sales promotion alternatives
	Profile distribution channels and logistics networks
	Customs regulations and tax issues; compliance with global trade laws
	Navigating homeland security programs
	Standardizing and streamlining trade processes
Trade Intermediaries	Customs management system and tariff classification
	Online trade infrastructures and virtual trade shows
	Legal, accounting, security, and tax compliance
	Secure electronic procurement and automated supply chain processes
	Trade finance, credit-scoring, and insurance
	Exporting training and trade strategies
	Transport and logistics management

industry, promote trade and investment, help U.S. companies compete at home and abroad, and ensure fair trade through the rigorous enforcement of trade laws and agreements.[102]

Similarly, most states and many cities run export financing programs, including pre- and post-shipment working-capital loans and guarantees, accounts receivable financing, and export insurance. The limited reserves of some agencies requires proof of adequate safeguards from the exporter. For instance, authorities usually require a letter of credit or sufficient credit insurance. Often, states and cities stipulate that exporters transact part of the funded activity within their jurisdiction.

CONCEPT CHECK

In Chapter 1, we suggest that **international business** is challenging for people who like to operate solo. Collecting information about foreign markets, navigating export regulations, mastering foreign-exchange procedures, or complying with homeland security policies can prove overwhelming. Consequently, some companies prefer to get help in finding information about potential markers. International trade intermediaries often command sophisticated knowledge of international trade.

EXPORT INTERMEDIARIES

Third-party firms that market products and services abroad on behalf of domestic companies qualify as **export intermediaries.** For many companies, particularly SMEs, they offer an operationally easier and relatively risk-free approach to managing export intricacies.[103] Their expertise and experience provide management skills and economies of scale that are beyond the reach of the typical SME, while their experience with regulations, taxes, duties, insurance, and transportation makes them productive resources. The export management company and the export trading company are prominent types.

Export Management Company (EMC) An EMC, by acting as the international trade arm of a company, helps firms establish overseas markets. An EMC can significantly simplify SMEs' efforts to identify and penetrate foreign markets, thereby reducing key impediments of

Export.gov is the official gateway to a range of resources for international traders in the United States. Here, both the aspiring and experienced exporter finds information, opportunities, and solutions on a host of international trade topics.
Source: export.gov

exporting. Maintaining a close relationship with its clients, it can act as an unofficial marketing department: generating orders, organizing distribution channels, developing promotions, verifying credit information, advising on foreign accounts and payment terms, and even using the firm's letterhead in communicating with foreign sales representatives and distributors. It can also oversee trade documents, schedule transportation, and arrange patent and trademark protection.[104] Finally, it can expedite resolutions and, as needed, represent the client at customs investigations.

Trade intermediaries are third parties that provide exporters a variety of services.

EMCs operate on a contractual basis, providing exclusive representation in a formally defined market. Their contract with a company specifies pricing, credit, and financial policies, promotional services, and method of payment. An EMC might operate on a commission basis (unless it takes title to the merchandise) and charge fees for other services. It usually concentrates on complementary and noncompetitive products from various companies in order to market a full product line.

Many EMCs are entrepreneurial ventures that specialize by product, function, or market area.

In the United States, most EMCs are entrepreneurial firms that specialize by product, function, or market area. Some are large concerns, handling lines from many manufacturers that cut across several industries. Others are smaller and work with fewer clients. Some specialize in certain products or focus on particular places, while others are generalists. The Federation of International Trade Associations (FITA) estimates that more than 1,000 EMCs operate in the United States, each representing, on average, about 10 suppliers. Although few U.S. companies use them, FITA reasons that many would benefit.[105] Still, though versatile, EMCs are not a panacea. Typically small, stand-alone firms with limited resources, some EMCs may struggle to warehouse a company's product or offer extended in-house financing. In addition, they focus on products that bring them the most profit, avoiding those with sketchy prospects.

The United States exempts ETCs from antitrust provisions, thereby permitting competitors to combine forces in foreign markets.

Export Trading Company (ETC) In 1982, the U.S. enacted the Export Trading Company Act, which relaxed some antitrust regulations that had restricted some foreign market behaviors. Groups of direct competitors, once prohibited, were now allowed to form ETCs to develop exports jointly without fear of antitrust action. Dutch, Japanese, and British competitors had long done so profitably.[106] Free of legal barriers that had prevented joining forces with rivals, ETCs boost the export competitiveness of U.S. companies.

ETCs operate based on demand rather than supply. They identify suppliers who can fill orders in overseas markets.

ETCs differ from EMCs in that they operate based on demand rather than supply. An ETC brings buyers and sellers together, functioning as a trade matchmaker. It creates value by determining foreign customers' preferences, identifying domestic suppliers, and expediting transactions between the two parties. Rather than representing a single manufacturer, an ETC works with many. Operating as independent distributors, they avoid carrying inventory in their own name or performing post-sales service.

Fees Trade intermediaries charge for their expertise and services. Commonly, they operate on (1) a commission rate ranging from 10 percent for consumer goods to 15 percent or more for industrial products, (2) a buy-sell basis that asks for a firm's best home country discount plus an extra discount for a product that is marked up when sold abroad, and/or (3) contributions for special events such as exhibiting products in a foreign trade show or an advance payment for advertising and promotion.

Besides payments, hiring a trade intermediary requires that an exporter relinquish some to considerable business control in the matters of buyer segments, price policies, quality of promotion materials, flexibility of delivery schedules, or standards of customer service; these matters are determined by the intermediary. Some companies discover that if an intermediary promotes their products feebly they struggle to generate international sales. To retain control, a company can employ intermediaries less comprehensively. As in any make-vs.-buy situation, companies trade off their preference for control versus the cost of directly managing export activity.[107]

Finally, some feel the fees imposed by EMCs and ETCs reduces their appeal, particularly as language barriers lessen, international communication improves, and trade finance practices harmonize. In response, more intermediaries focus on exporting high-value products within the context of a single industry to select markets, rather than exporting bulk and commodity products. Improving industry expertise boosts effectiveness, whereas offering multiple product lines through foreign distributors improves efficiency. These innovations reduce the time it takes to move SMEs into enter foreign markets, a benefit some see as justifying the corresponding fees.

CUSTOMS BROKERS

Customs agents enforce the rules of trade for a particular country by controlling the flow of goods moving in and out of it. In the United States, for example, the Bureau of Customs and Border Protection (CBP, formerly the U.S. Customs Service) of the Department of Homeland Security monitors imports and exports. The CBP assesses and collects duties, taxes, and fees on imported merchandise, enforces customs and related laws, and administers certain navigation laws and treaties. It also polices smuggling threats and protects the United States from threatening imports.[108]

Countries vary to the degree to which their customs agencies help or hinder international traders (see Table 14.5). Several of the top ten countries on the ease-of-trading list are European. In fact, trading across Europe has become increasingly seamless due to the ongoing market integration efforts of the European Union. Free trade pacts in other parts of the world have similar effects, such as NAFTA expediting trade among Canada, Mexico, and the United States.

In contrast, irregular customs practices in African and South Asian markets routinely hamper exports and imports. Moving from port to port in these markets finds a hodgepodge of arbitrary and often contradictory regulations that can veer toward illegality. One Zambian trader noted, "My cargo of copper wire was held up in Durban, South Africa, for a week. The port authorities required proof that the wooden pallets on which the wire was loaded were free of pests. After a few days, the Ministry of Agriculture's inspector checked that the wood was fumigated—for a \$100 fee.[109] No matter the locale, importing requires understanding relevant customs regulations and policies, knowing how to clear goods through customs, assigning the appropriate customs duties, and complying with special procedures.

TABLE 14.5 Where the Trading Is Easy—and Where It's Not

There is wide variability in the ease of exporting and importing among countries. Here, we see those countries that lead and lag the world in increasing the ease of export and import. These rankings reflect the average of a country's performance in terms of the time and cost (excluding tariffs) involved in exporting and importing a standardized cargo of goods by sea transport. Key indicators include the number of documents customs requires traders to complete and the length of time and overall cost required to complete an import or export transaction.

Easiest	Rank	Hardest	Rank
Singapore	1	Burundi	177
Hong Kong, China	2	Afghanistan	178
South Korea	3	Iraq	179
Denmark	4	Chad	180
United Arab Emirates	5	Congo, Republic	181
Finland	6	Tajikistan	182
Estonia	7	Kazakhstan	182
Sweden	8	Central African Republic	183
Panama	9	Tajikistan	184
Israel	10	Uzbekistan	185

Source: Based on The International Bank for Reconstruction and Development/The World Bank, "Doing Business in 2012: Doing Business in a More Transparent World."

A customs broker helps an importer navigate the regulations imposed by customs agencies.

Finding Help In terms of procedures, when merchandise reaches its port of entry, the importer files documents with customs officials, who then assign a provisional value and tariff classification. The United States has nearly 10,000 classifications in its Harmonized Tariff Schedule, approximately 60 percent of which are open to interpretation—that is, a particular product fits more than one classification. Often, it is an art form to determine the tariff classification that minimizes duty assessment. Importing requires considerable expertise to manage this and other processes. Trade paperwork is extensive, involving document preparation and/or electronic submissions, calculating and paying taxes, duties and excises, and overseeing communications between government authorities and traders. Not every company commands these proficiencies, especially SMEs. Consequently, some hire a **customs broker** to clear products through customs agencies. The broker helps through many means, including:

- *Qualifying for duty refunds through drawback provisions.* Some exporters use imported inputs, for which they paid a custom duty, in their manufacturing process. In the United States, drawback provisions allow domestic exporters to apply for a 99 percent refund of the duty paid on the imported goods as long as the goods become inputs into the firm's exports.
- *Deferring duties by using bonded warehouses and foreign trade zones.* Companies need not pay duties on imports stored in bonded warehouses and foreign trade zones until the goods are removed for sale or used in a manufacturing process. A broker oversees compliance with pertinent provisions.
- *Valuing products so they qualify for favorable duty treatment.* Different products incur different duties, or assessed taxes, when crossing borders, such as finished goods typically having a higher duty than components. Customs brokers' expertise helps determine the optimal classification.
- *Managing trade documentation.* Paperwork goes hand in hand with international trade, particularly that which falls under the auspices of homeland security. A customs broker obtains government permissions before forwarding paperwork to the carrier-overseen delivery.

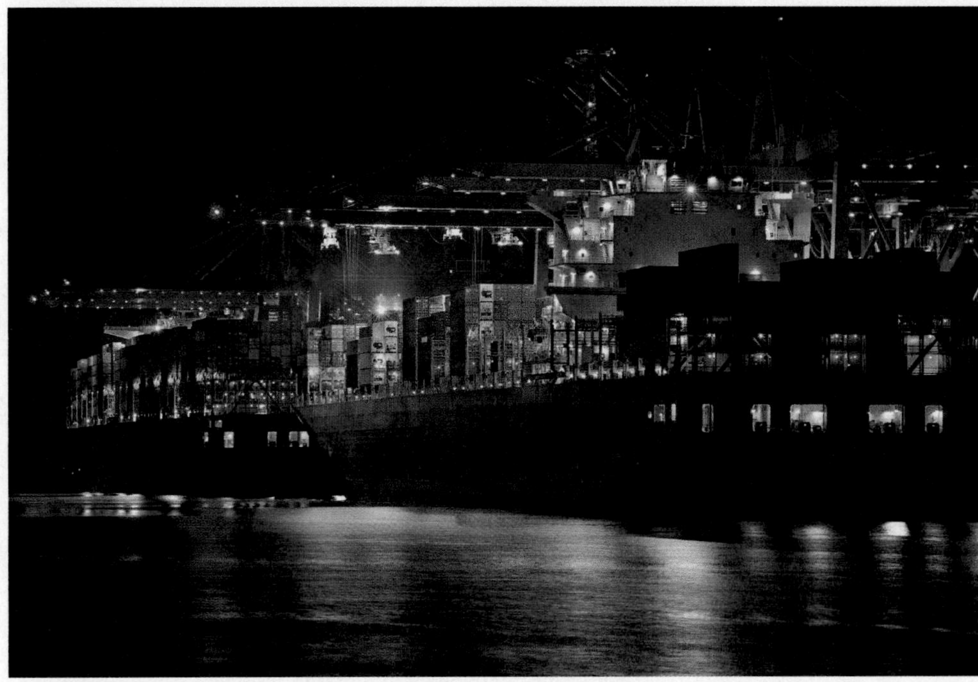

Container ships are the sure-sailing movers of imports and exports. Pound for pound, they are the most efficient means of transporting goods between countries. Here, we see two container ships being unloaded at the Rotterdam Harbor; 24/7/365 activities like this take place in seaports worldwide.
Source: keller/Fotolia

- *Limiting liability by properly marking an import's country of origin.* Governments assess duties on imports based in part on the country of origin. A mistake in marking the country may increase the import duty. In the United States, if a product or its container is improperly marked when it enters the country, the product may be assigned a marking duty equal to 10 percent of the declared customs value. This charge is tacked onto the normal tariff.[110]

A customs broker helps importers in terms of
- Valuation
- Qualification
- Deferment
- Liability

FREIGHT FORWARDERS

Freight forwarders, popularly known as the "travel agent of cargo," are the largest export/import intermediary in terms of value and weight of products shipped internationally.[111] Operationally, upon finalizing a foreign sale, an exporter hires a freight forwarder to arrange the fastest, cheapest transportation method. Balancing the constraints of space, speed, and cost, it identifies the optimal path to move the shipment from the manufacturer to an air, land, or ocean terminal, supervises clearing customs, and schedules delivery to the foreign buyer.

A freight forwarder specializes in moving goods from sellers to buyers.

In the same process, the freight forwarder arranges storage prior to shipment, verifies letters of credit, obtains export licenses, pays consular fees, processes special documentation, and prepares shipping manifests. It may also advise on packing and labeling, transportation insurance, repacking of shipments damaged en route, and warehousing products. It does not take ownership title or act as a sales representative—that falls in the realm of an EMC or ETC. As a rule, freight forwarders offer fewer services than those agents.

Freight forwarders are particularly important when the cost or timing of freight can make or break a deal. One straightforward solution, advises the director of business development of Certified Worldwide, is "seek out your local Commercial Service office and find a freight forwarder, interview different freight forwarders, and remember that the company chosen will be responsible for shipping your product."[112]

The freight forwarder usually charges the exporter a percentage of the shipment value, plus a minimum charge depending on the number of services provided. It also receives a brokerage fee from the carrier. Most companies, especially SMEs, find it costly to deal with logistics. Freight forwarders' expertise enables them to secure shipping space at better rates and provides the flexibility to consolidate shipments.

THIRD-PARTY LOGISTICS

A 3PL is a trade intermediary that applies sophisticated technologies and systems to supervise trade logistics.

Third-party logistics (3PLs) are a growing force in international trade. Like freight forwarders, they move cargo and provide logistic options across virtually every market in the world. Unlike freight forwarders, they collaborate with manufacturers, shippers, and retailers to relieve them of logistics responsibilities. FedEx, for example, represents a one-stop shop that helps traders deal with transportation, warehousing, cross-docking, inventory management, packaging, and freight forwarding. Think of, on a very small scale, your last UPS experience; just as you did, an SME relies on UPS to track and transport the product, all the while providing access to real-time information to chart its progress. 3PLs also consolidate billing inclusive of all transportation, customs brokerage, duties, taxes, and package delivery services. Finally, they handle product returns, warranty claims, parts exchanges, and reverse logistics.

Expanding globalization and trade liberalization are accelerating the growth of 3PLs. Their U.S. gross revenues steadily grow at double-digit rates.[113] They are particularly helpful to the born global company; rather than building its own logistics operation, the born global need only tap the state-of-the-art sophistication of a 3PL. Big companies also benefit: nearly 80 percent of Fortune 500 companies use 3PLs to manage logistics and supply chains. Procter & Gamble, Walmart, PepsiCo, and Ford, for example, use the services of 30 or more of them. Overall, 3PLs have been growing their business at the expense of freight forwarders. In response, the latter are expanding their historic role as the travel agents of cargo to offer some of the services provided by 3PLs.

RECONCILING OPPORTUNITY AND CHALLENGE: AN EXPORT PLAN

From negotiating an international sale to shipping and receiving products, the exporter/importer manages an array of financial, logistic, and legal responsibilities. Each activity represents a link in the international transaction chain (see Figure 14.5). At times, some activities press more than others, such as finance concerns prior to shipment, delivery concerns post-shipment, and so on. Ultimately, all influence the process.

An export plan defines a company's intent to leverage resources and manage constraints in initiating and developing export activity.

The decision to engage or escalate international trade is one that few companies take lightly. It is one thing to consider exporting and quite another to take the first steps in doing so. Going international, as depicted in the transaction chain, imposes many demands that, collectively, influence resource allocation, executive effectiveness, operational flexibility, and financial stability. Successful exporters report that developing an **export plan** manages these demands—think of the notion, for example, that "companies don't plan to fail, they fail to plan."

An export plan prioritizes export markets, formalizes top management export buy-in, organizes international activities, and forecasts future resource needs as foreign sales increase. The process of defining objectives, sequencing tactics, and setting timelines pushes the firm to assess resources, assign responsibilities, and stipulate controls. A rigorous plan helps executives track the performance of an export strategy in the face of the ongoing, if not seemingly endless, decisions along the many steps of the transaction chain. Table 14.6 outlines an export-planning framework. At first glance, it may appear daunting. Remember, though, an export plan need only be just a few pages to start. It will steadily expand as it evolves.

Importantly, managers report that developing an export plan in an open process improves its effectiveness. By no means does that guarantee success. Strategic planning in any context is challenging, especially when one must abandon the familiarity of domestic routines for the anomalies of international trade. External validation goes a long way toward preempting blind spots as well as potential delusions about the likely success of export ventures. More practically, a well-specified plan is a precondition for export financing assistance from public agencies.

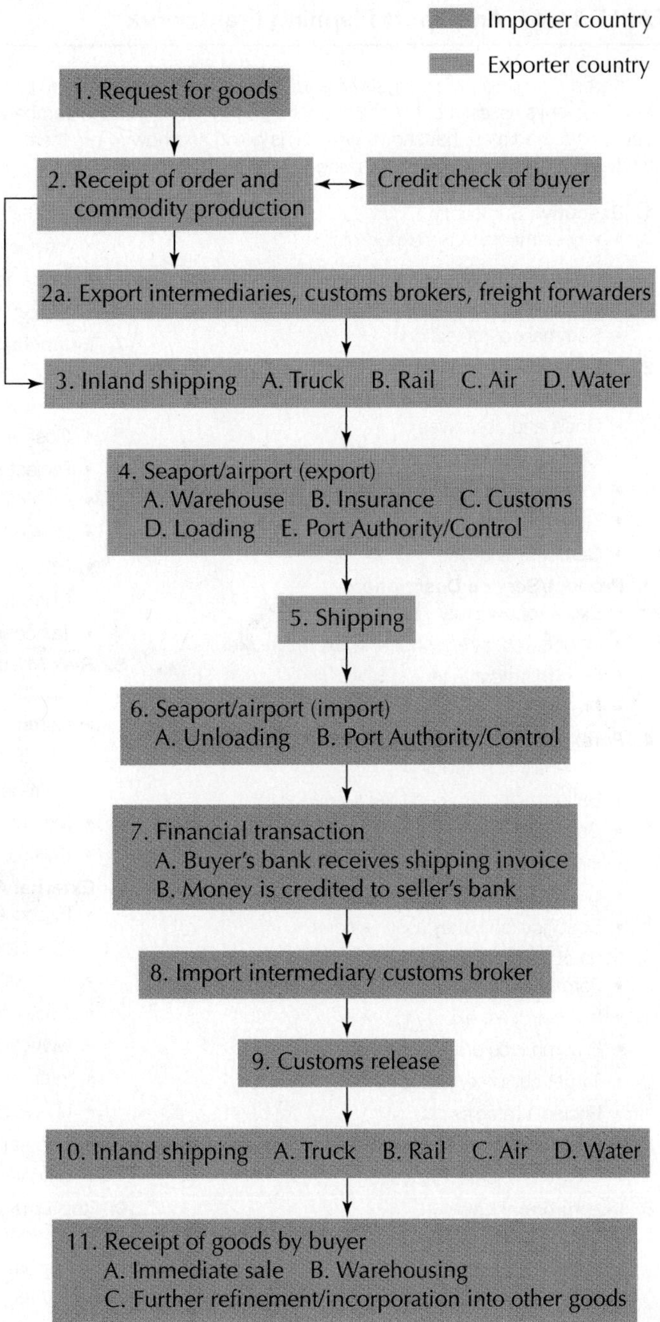

FIGURE 14.5 The International Transaction Chain

Between the point at which they negotiate an international sale and the point at which products have been delivered, both the exporter and the importer manage a complex array of financial, logistics, and legal tasks. Each of these tasks defines a link in the transaction chain that reflects the particular elements of each firm's strategy.

Source: Export America 1 (November 1999): 17. Magazine published by the International Trade Administration of the U.S. Dept. of Commerce.

Managers stress test an export plan by consulting trade specialists and public agencies.

Successful exporters note that consulting government agencies and third-party intermediates helps clarify opportunities and preempt problems. Noted the CEO of Coffee & More, "My advice to other companies considering exporting is to go for it, but be smart and do your homework first. Educate yourself and use your local U.S. Commercial Service office."[114] Added the Manager of International Operations at Analytical Graphics, "Don't just strike out on your own; take advantage of the U.S. Commercial Service. They are familiar with the ways of doing business in your market destination and know how U.S. companies can succeed there. It's saved us valuable time and resources."[115]

The element of an export plan that routinely stymies companies, particularly SMEs, is selecting the "right" foreign market. SMEs are often discouraged when their first foray fails. Instead of applying the standards of sound strategy that made them successful in the first

TABLE 14.6 An Export Planning Framework

An export plan organizes analysis of issues that influence the initiation and escalation of export. Management's assessment of the changing marketplace and the company competencies and culture develops a road map that shows where it is going and how to get there. Companies evaluating international frontiers commonly study the following issues:

1. **Executive Summary**
   - Key elements of the export plan
   - Description of business and target markets
   - Specification of management team
   - Summary of projections
2. **Company Description**
   - History
   - Goals and objectives
   - Core competency
   - Management
   - The export team
   - Company finances
3. **Product/Service Description**
   - Export opportunity
   - Fit of company's products in export market
   - Growth potential
   - Product strategy
4. **Foreign Marketplace Analysis**
   - Rationale for exporting
   - Rationale for targeted foreign market
   - Country profile
   - Industry profile
   - Competitor analysis
   - Specification of key assumptions
5. **Market Entry Strategies**
   - Form of operation
   - Indirect/direct exporting
   - E-commerce options
   - Target customer profile
   - Pricing strategies
   - Sales and promotion strategies
   - Logistics and transportation
6. **International Law**
   - Dispute resolution
   - Language consideration
   - Contract terms and conditions
   - Product liability considerations
   - Intellectual property protection
   - Sales agent and/or distributor agreements
   - Export/import regulations
7. **Financial Analysis**
   - Facility and equipment requirements
   - Sales forecast
   - Cost of goods sold
   - Projected international income statement
   - Projected international cash flow
   - Breakdown analysis
   - Financing requirements
   - Current financing sources
   - Tax consequences
8. **Risk Management**
   - Country risk
   - Commercial risk
   - Credit risk
   - Currency risk
   - Market risk
   - Political risk
9. **External Assistance**
   - Export America
   - U.S. Commerce Department
   - Census Bureau
   - Customs and Border Protection
   - www.export.gov
   - International Trade Administration
   - U.S. Export-Import Bank
   - National, regional, and local organizations
   - Cross-border trade consultancies
10. **Implementation Schedule**
    - Operational time line
    - Performance milestones
    - Contingency plans

place, many follow hunches about foreign markets—i.e.,"China is growing so fast that there must be many people there who want my product." Likewise, it is tough to try to conquer customers from Bonn to Beijing to Benares in a day. A useful rule is to look at a few markets where the odds favor success rather than trying to sell to the world.[116] Useful questions to debate during the development of an export plan include:

- Am I committed to exporting?
- Would our resources be better utilized developing our domestic businesses?
- What do we want to gain from exporting?

- Is exporting consistent with our long-term goals?
- What need does my product or service fill in the targeted foreign market?
- Are there competitive products?
- How much will it cost to get the product to the foreign market?
- Will exporting put undue demands on management, production, finance, and marketing?
- Does exporting leverage our core competency?
- Does exporting fit our value chain configuration?
- Do our coordination and control systems support exporting?
- Do the financial and strategic benefits of exporting exceed its direct and indirect costs?

Last, like yin and yang, import and export are complementary opposites within the greater whole of international trade. Strategic and practical aspects of the import process mirror those of the export process. So, just as the international transaction chain includes a sensitivity to those export and import issues, so too with the export plan. Changing the terminology from "export" to "import" does not require changing the contents of the plan. Rather, companies adjust their analytics, interpreting events from the analogous perspective of importing.

Looking to the Future

Technology and International Trade

The transaction costs of international trade steadily decrease. Advances in transportation and communications systems, by making it easier and cheaper to trade, accelerate export and import activity. The Internet helps individuals throughout the world engage each other easily and quickly. Online filing of cargo manifests, customs documents, and transit forms expedites shipments. Customs software that works in Hamburg or Sydney is also used in Hong Kong and Long Beach. Also, more parties track the shipment than not; the originating shipper, transit depots, and other suppliers and customs agents, along with the buyer and seller, monitor the flow. All in all, greater flexibility and improving efficiency let companies engage an expanding range of export and import options.

Synchronizing import or export activities redefines the way companies, both big and small, connect with foreign buyers and sellers. Historically, big companies reaped the biggest rewards. Their superior resources and organizational competencies positioned them to capture advances in moving goods, funds, and information. Now, the technology of trade seems to offer bigger benefits to smaller companies. Improving technologies create online, software, and logistics platforms that blur the distinction between the big, global giant and the small, neighborhood startup. In fact, it has become harder to tell the difference between an SME operating on a shoestring budget and its larger counterpart.

Online Platforms

Increasingly, companies look to online technologies to start or expand exporting. They rely on the Internet as their primary channel for getting information, sourcing products, finding suppliers, marketing products, and tapping new markets. In many cases, companies build a virtual value chain online, running export transactions from start to finish without ever leaving their hometowns. The inexorable expansion of the Internet gives potential and practicing international traders nearly infinite resources. They can browse through catalog archives, business-to-business exchanges, electronic trade boards, consumer surveys, online trade journals, and virtual trade shows to find a product to import or a market for their export.

Increasingly, as SMEs throughout the world gain Internet access for the first time, they use online platforms to build their export businesses. Besides introducing mom-and-pop shops from around the world to each other, websites open a vast and largely uncharted small-business hinterland in markets from Tibet to Patagonia. Long the unseen production sites for many pieces of the global economy, these small companies had to trade within the context of global supply chains directed by large MNEs. Now, going online lets them go straight to buyers or sellers.

Software Platforms

A burst of business software in the past few years has "created a total revolution in what small businesses are able to accomplish overseas."[117] Collaborative software lets entrepreneurial exporters with single-digit head counts track foreign vendors without traveling the world. For example, U.S.-based Edgar Blazona used to log 100,000 miles of travel annually, visiting factories in the Far East. Now he uses two factories—one in Thailand and one in India—to manufacture his furniture designs that he then imports into the United States. A meeting and document-sharing program lets him work in real time with his overseas factories. Costing less than $100 per month, this software coordinates workflows, expedites exchanges, and eases communications.

Similarly, Evertek Computer Corporation, a U.S. SME, has capitalized on software innovations to build e-commerce Web sites and portals that expand its market frontier. In 1990, Evertek began selling new and refurbished computers and parts; by 2008, it had become the world's largest closeout computer wholesaler, clearance computer supplier, and closeout electronics wholesaler. Within a year of purchasing BuyUSA.com, an Internet-based program from the U.S. Commerce Department that identifies buyers around the world, Evertek began selling in 10 new countries, with single purchases reaching up to $75,000. In 2010, international sales zoomed to $34 million, an increase of 84 percent from the previous year, on exports to 105 countries.

Other companies use similarly innovative programs to manage overseas factories with tools that once were reserved for big MNEs. China Manufacturing Network, for instance, relies on its 10-person staff in California to coordinate production of industrial devices among more than 90 independent factories in China, Malaysia, and Singapore. It uses on-demand, scalable enterprise software to track activity orders, monitor build rates, and manage inventory across its manufacturing network.

Logistics Platforms

Improving logistics helps SMEs move products more cheaply and easily to more places. High-tech, low-cost shipping services rob big firms of a long-running competitive advantage. Now, the no-name, one-person exporter down the street from you, because of its big-name shipping partners spanning the globe, has many of the same logistics capabilities commanded by a large MNE but at a fraction of the cost. In fact, SMEs increasingly have as much, if not a bit more, logistic flexibility. Unlike big companies that rely on their in-house systems, SMEs pick and choose solutions from freight forwarders and 3PLs—think of the ease of using FedEx, for example. The small international trader can hire any of these sorts of intermediaries to warehouse, truck, sail, fly, and deliver goods from factories in Asia to customers in Europe—all the while never taking physical possession of the goods.

South West Trading in Arizona, a family-owned startup, imports yarns made from bamboo, corn, and soy fibers by fabric plants in China. When South West Trading suffered recurring logistics problems as it imported products from China, UPS provided an efficient solution. Its Shanghai facility consolidated orders from various Chinese factories into one transport container, supervised customs paperwork, shipped it, and trucked the goods to South West Trading's warehouse in Phoenix. The company's bottom line immediately benefited. Where it once paid $9,400 to run four China-to-Arizona shipments per month, its once-a-month UPS shipment costs about $3,600 and reliably takes 21 days to travel.

The Great Leveling

Improving online, software, and logistics platforms, by improving the technology of trade, levels the playing field of international trade.[118] The combination of ubiquitous, fast Internet connections and cheap, plentiful, cloud-based computing power make it easier to export and import. Big and small companies respond to these trends, confident that technology will create tools that let them jump hurdles and capture opportunities. SMEs, in particular, stand to prosper from the improving technology of trade. Perhaps most significantly, technology decouples the issues of size and capability. Observed the CEO of China Manufacturing, "Our customers can't really tell how big we are. In a way, it's irrelevant. What matters is that we can get the job done."[119] ■

CONCEPT CHECK

Recall our discussions of poverty in Chapters 4 and 5. Here, we point out that shortages of resources impoverish nations as well as individuals. Some countries struggle to acquire the foreign reserves they need to purchase goods from other nations. If unsuccessful, they may resort to countertrade.

COUNTERTRADE

Currency or credit—easy, fast, and straightforward—are the preferred payment options for export or import transactions. Sometimes, though, companies face the harsh reality that buyers cannot pay in cash because the home country's currency is nonconvertible or the nation holds scant reserves or has insufficient credit. Consequently, if they wish to trade, they must resort to other means.

Consider the following transactions. Coca-Cola has traded its syrup for cheese from the Soviet Union, oranges from Egypt, tomato paste from Turkey, Polish beer, and soft drink bottles from Hungary. Malaysia swapped palm oil for fertilizer and machinery with North Korea, Cuba, and Russia and was negotiating deals with Morocco, Jordan, Syria, and Iran. Thailand, the world's largest exporter of rice, has been negotiating rice-for-oil deals with Middle Eastern countries, whereas the Philippines, the world's largest importer of rice, secured rice supplies through an agreement with Vietnam.[120] Boeing exchanged ten 747s for 34 million barrels of Saudi Arabian oil. Argentina awarded a fertilizer factory to Czechoslovakian firms with the stipulation that suppliers buy vegetables and other agricultural goods produced with fertilizer.[121]

These sorts of trades fall under the umbrella term **countertrade.** Any one of several different arrangements that parties use to trade products via transactions that use limited or no currency or credit qualify as a countertrade. Table 14.7 identifies its principal forms.[122]

Countertrade is an umbrella term for several sorts of trade, such as barter or offset, in which the seller accepts goods or services, rather than currency or credit, as payment.

Inconsistent disclosure hinders estimating the volume of countertrade. Secretive government-to-government deals and disguised transactions are not unusual. Roughly, more than 80 countries nowadays use or require countertrade. These transactions comprise anywhere between 5 to 15 percent of the world trade.[123] Countertrade generally increases in economies that are experiencing economic problems. Since the latter is a seeming inevitability, given the boom-bust market dynamics in many countries, countertrade is likely an enduring feature of international trade.

Countertrade has several disadvantages:

- Inefficiency
- Risk
- Complicated

COSTS

Countertrade, put simply, is an inefficient way of doing business. Companies prefer the efficiency of cash or credit to settle a transaction—all it requires is consulting foreign-exchange tables to set exchange rates. Countertrade, instead, requires buyers and sellers to rely on

TABLE 14.7 Common Forms of Countertrade

The unusual circumstances that surround countertrade transactions leads agents to use different forms in different situations. Here, we see commonly used forms.

Form	Description
Barter	Products are exchanged directly for products of equal value without the use of money as a means of purchase or payment.
Buyback	A supplier of capital or equipment agrees to accept future output generated by the investment as payment. For example: The exporter of equipment to a chemical plant may be repaid with output from the factory to whose owner it "sold" the equipment.
Offset	An exporter sells products for cash and then helps the importer find opportunities to earn hard currency for payment. Offsets are most common when big-ticket products (e.g., military equipment) are involved.
Switch or Swap Trading	One company sells to another its obligation to purchase something in a foreign country. They carry this label because the arrangement often involves switching the documentation and destination of merchandise while it's in transit.
Counter purchase	A company that sells products to a foreign country promises to make a future purchase of a specific product made in that country. A supplier agrees to purchase products from a foreign buyer as a condition of getting the buyer's order.

nonmarket forces to set the value of the trade, negotiating some standards such as how many tons of rice for how many farm tractors. Agreeing to "payment" is not the only hurdle. The traded goods may be of poor quality, packaged unattractively, or difficult to sell and service. Consequently, countertrade deals are prone to price, financial, and quality distortion. Ultimately, countertrade and its variations threaten free market forces with protectionism and price-fixing. Unchecked, trade relations tend toward inefficiency.

BENEFITS

Companies and countries often use countertrade to build mutually beneficial relationships.

The reality of international trade means that countertrade is often unavoidable for companies that want to do business with buyers who have limited or no access to cash or credit. Although some dislike it, companies and countries in tough binds use it to generate jobs, preserve foreign exchange holdings, and develop trade relationships. Countertrade helps countries reduce their need to borrow working capital and gives them access to companies' technological skills and marketing expertise. Companies also benefit; they can resolve bad debts, repatriate blocked funds, or build customer relationships. In addition, accepting countertrade signals a seller's good faith and flexibility. Such sensitivities can position a firm to gain preferential market access in the future.

CASE A Little Electronic Magic at Alibaba.com

E-commerce, by changing the way companies around the world do business, makes trade easier and cheaper.[124] Before the Internet, tracking down a product to import, or finding foreign customers to export to, was daunting for the typical SME. Most relied on occasional trade shows and expensive, time-consuming foreign travel to identify possible products or assess potential suppliers. Certainly, traders could tap local embassies or consulates to support export promotion or provide import assistance. Although sounding straightforward, in practice they typically proved cumbersome. Consequently, international trade was largely limited to big companies that could afford to attend trade shows, translate brochures, travel internationally, hire intermediaries, and supervise the many activities that comprise the export transaction chain (see Figure 14.5).

Today, the Internet gives SMEs cost-effective means to manage these demands. It makes information on any conceivable product from virtually any market readily and inexpensively accessible. Falling trade barriers, courtesy of the WTO, and more efficient logistics from 3PLs like FedEx, DHL, and UPS offer an array of trade possibilities.[125] The Internet, simply put, transforms whatever it touches. It is already the most powerful force for globalization, democratization, economic growth, and education in history. The same, we see, applies to the game of international trade.

The emergence of country-specific portals and Web exchanges accelerates this trend. Replicating what eBay has done for consumer-to-consumer e-commerce, several sites offer online bazaars for international traders. Here, exporters can lay out their wares on the digital carpet and haggle with potential buyers from the far corners of the world. For instance, potential importers looking for products from South Korea can access www.koreatradeworld.

com; those targeting India can check out www.trade-india.com; those focusing on Europe need only visit www.bizeurope.com to tap into high-quality trade boards. One can also shop the world at www.tradekey.com.

These and similar sites promote the commercial potential of a country or region. They provide direct services to large and small international traders, such as export training, cyber trade infrastructures, international special exhibitions, virtual trade shows, and trade strategies. Conceptually, their mission is direct: connect sellers in one place to buyers in another. Operationally, they provide powerful business-to-business tools that improve the mechanics of trade, creating flexible and dynamic platforms that let buyers and sellers of everything from bamboo toothpicks to industrial equipment find each other, negotiate the terms of trade, and seal the deal.

Alibaba: Opening Global Markets

Spearheading these changes is Alibaba, a Chinese Internet company that specializes in introducing Chinese manufacturers to buyers worldwide. Founded in 1999 by Jack Ma, who has been dubbed "the Father of the Chinese Internet," Alibaba makes international trade cheaper, faster, and easier. Based in Hangzhou, about a two-hour drive south of Shanghai, it began operations with the goal of getting big by staying small. Jack Ma believes that his target customers are SMEs, not MNEs—or, in his words, "shrimps," not "whales."

The Framework

Making this happen is the call of www.alibaba.com, an English-language global trade website that connects international buyers with Chinese sellers. Today, it is the world's largest online business-to-business marketplace, reaching Internet users in more than 240 countries and territories. The site supports an interactive community of millions of buyers and sellers who meet, greet, chat, and trade online. Running an online global trade fair, Alibaba enables "shrimps" with import and export ambition but tight budgets to reach the global market. Alibaba also provides an array of business management software, Internet infrastructure services, payment processing, and export-related services.

Many Alibaba users are SMEs in developing countries around the world, from rural areas to large cities, in countries such as Kyrgyzstan, Sierra Leone, and Peru. Few are glamorous and high-tech; most are low-tech firms making labor-intensive, scale-insensitive products. However, Alibaba provides tools to expand their market reach and grow their businesses. An SME, working from the smallest apartment anywhere in the world, yet on the grid, can conceivably create a global business.

Operations

The mechanics of Alibaba are straightforward: Importers around the world shop the site, looking for potential products from a mind-boggling array of goods—as hinted by the adjacent image of Alibaba's home page. Alibaba has organized more than a thousand product categories, each with many subcategories, and offers new channels to trade services. The classic garage inventor in Caracas or Chicago has the option to design a product and then use Alibaba to find Chinese factories that will make, package, and ship it to customers worldwide.

Operationally, buyers use Alibaba to find potential suppliers, thereby eliminating the need to hire a local representative to negotiate with Chinese manufacturers. For example, an enterprising company in Argentina looking to buy 500 DVD players can visit Alibaba.com, search among the dozens of potential suppliers, learn their terms of trade, contact the preferred vendor, negotiate the specifics, and set the deal in motion. Said the cofounder of www.meetchina.com, a similar e-commerce site, "We want to make buying 1,000 bicycles from China as easy as buying a book from Amazon.com."[126]

Trust and Transparency

As a rule, importers worry about being defrauded by unknown suppliers. More practically, how does an importer in Buenos Aires find a trustworthy supplier in Guangzhou? As sites like Alibaba inject more transparency into trade, buyers worry less about fraud. Alibaba users, like those on similar e-commerce sites, post information about their companies and review information about a vendor's reliability from other users. Buyers access Alibaba's profiles of its registered users, as well as the seller's posted references, to verify their status. These data let the importer in Argentina crosscheck the credibility of potential trade partners.

This system of checks and balances is how Alibaba makes money. It offers a basic service of listing a company and its products on its site free of charge, then generates revenue from more than 100,000 members who pay a few hundred to several thousand dollars annually for services such as personalized Web pages, high-quality online introduction, and priority listing of products. It has also increasingly generates revenue from online advertising.

Crisis and Change

The global financial crisis, Jack Ma reasoned, created an opportunity to transform Alibaba from a China-focused e-commerce provider into a global Web marketplace. "Before this financial crisis, we were helping China's products abroad," Ma says. "Now we are thinking about helping small and medium-sized enterprises in other parts of the world." Ma also saw the chance to expand China's historic outward flow of products to the world to include flows throughout the world. "We want to help them sell across the nations, help them sell to China," he explains. "I believe in the next three years, China will be one of the world's largest buying markets. China needs to buy these things."[127]

As the crisis diminished, Alibaba set its sights higher. It now plans to build a network of warehouses across China to transform the country's logistics business. Ma explains, "Hopefully within 10 years' time, anyone placing an order online from anywhere in China will receive their goods within eight hours, allowing for the virtual urbanization of every village across China.... In order to achieve this, we will need to establish a modern, 21st-century logistics network." In addition, Alibaba expanded AliExpress to offer traders warehousing, shipping, and logistics options. Essentially, noted an analyst, Alibaba "wants to be Amazon."[128] Steadily, it has done so; in late 2012, Jack Ma suggested, "It's very likely that next year, our transaction volume will be bigger than all the American e-commerce companies combined."[129]

QUESTIONS

14-2. Do you think most international trade might eventually take place through websites like Alibaba.com? How might that influence your interest in importing and exporting?

14-3. Identify a product you would like to import. Visit www.alibaba.com, go to the advanced search field, and enter it. Select required criteria and click on "Search." Review the list of companies that qualify. Find a suitable seller. Analyze this process for ease, usefulness, and potential value.

✪**14-4.** Identify and describe three benefits and three costs of using websites like Alibaba to export and import.

14-5. Visit www.alibaba.com, www.trade-india.com, and www.europages.com. Compare and contrast these Web sites from the view of the seller to the buyer.

✪**14-6.** Provide three recommendations that you would offer a SME, based on the opportunities and constraints of electronic websites like Alibaba, as it considers engaging exporting or importing.

14-7. How transparent do sites like Alibaba.com make import-export transactions? To what degree would you worry about fraud? What safeguards would you seek?

SUMMARY

- Exporting refers to the sale of goods or services produced by a company based in one country to customers that reside in another. Importing is the opposite: the purchase of a product by a buyer in one country from a seller in another.
- A company's export activity is (1) related to but not determined by its size and (2) related to and often determined by a range of firm-specific characteristics, such as management interest, production efficiency, labor costs, and R&D advantages that are independent of its size.
- The incremental internationalization view holds that exporting begins as a sequential process of deliberate trial and reasonable error that leads a company to expand from its home market to the most geographically and psychologically proximate markets. It then progressively expands to customers in more distant and dissimilar countries.
- The born-global perspective holds that companies step straight onto the world stage, engaging international trade from inception.
- The idea of serendipity refers to so-called accidental traders who, responding to happenstance or odd circumstances, successfully begin exporting or importing.
- A service import does not result in ownership and is rendered by nonresidents to the local residents in a country.
- The macro and micro benefits of international trade spur governments to help potential and active exporters.
- Exporters may deal directly with agents or distributors in a foreign country or indirectly through third-party intermediaries, such as export management firms or other types of trading companies.
- Trading companies perform many functions that regularly pose problems for clients that lack export and import expertise.
- Freight forwarders act as agents for international traders in supervising the movement of goods to foreign buyers.
- Third-party logistics (3PLs) help traders understand their current practices, identify opportunities and risks, and improve the efficiency of logistics.
- Countertrade is any one of several different arrangements by which products are traded in transactions that do not involve cash or credit.

KEY TERMS

born global (p. 572)
countertrade (p. 601)
customs broker (p. 594)
direct exporting (p. 576)
exporting (p. 566)
export intermediaries (p. 591)
export plan (p. 596)
freight forwarder (p. 595)
importing (p. 578)
incremental internationalization (p. 571)
indirect exporting (p. 576)
serendipity (p. 575)
small and medium-sized enterprise (SME) (p. 568)
third-party logistics (p. 596)

ENDNOTES

1 ***Sources include the following:*** Case developed based on profiles of company management, company activities, and country profiles reported at www.export.gov; United States International Trade Administration; United States Census Bureau, *Profile of U.S. Exporting Companies,* at www.census.gov/foreign-trade/aip/edbrel-0203.pdf; *Small & Medium-Sized Exporting Companies: Statistical Overview,* tse.export.gov/EDB/SelectReports.aspx?DATA=ExporterDB. SpinCent represents the reported experiences of active exporters as well as the observations expressed by their management. In particular, please visit www.export.gov/articles/successstories/eg_success_story_021417.asp for an overview of the source documents.

2 The Ex-Im Bank is the official export-credit agency of the United States. It help create and maintain U.S. jobs by financing the sales of U.S. exports, primarily to emerging markets, providing loan guarantees, export-credit insurance, and direct loans.

3 "WTO Releases 2011 Trade and Tariff Data," retrieved December 18, 2012 from www.wto.org/english/news_e/news12_e/stat_23oct12_e.htm.

4 Joe Dermody, "Emerging Markets Play Growing Role in Exports Growth," *Irish Examiner,* December 4, 2012.

5 "A Profile of U.S. Importing and Exporting Companies, 2009 – 2010," U.S. Department of Commerce, retrieved April 24, 2013, from www.census.gov/foreign-trade/Press-Release/edb/2010/edbrel.pdf.

6 Ibid.

7 Francisco Sánchez, "No Better Export: Higher Education - Commentary - The Chronicle of Higher Education," retrieved May 3, 2011, from chronicle.com/article/No-Better-Export-Higher/126989; John Siegmund, "Higher Education Shows a Big Trade Surplus for the United States, International Trade Administration," retrieved May 15, 2013, from trade.gov/press/publications/newsletters/ita_0909/higher_0909.asp.

8 Tamara Baluja, "Canada Must Attract Foreign Students to Fuel Innovation, Drive Economy," *The Globe and Mail,* August 14, 2012.

9 John H. Dunning, "The Eclectic Paradigm of International Production: Some Empirical Tests," *Journal of International Business Studies* (Spring 1988): 1–31.

10 "A Profile of U.S. Importing and Exporting Companies, 2009–2010."

11 "A Profile of U.S. Importing and Exporting Companies, 2009–2010"; USITC, "Small and Medium-Sized Enterprises: Overview of Participation in U.S. Exports," January 2010; USITC, "Small and

Medium-Sized Enterprises: U.S. and EU Export Activities, and Barriers and Opportunities Experienced by U.S. Firms," July 2010.

12 Hernan Roxas, Vai Lindsay, Nicholas Ashill, and Antong Victorio, "Institutional Analysis of Strategic Choice of Micro, Small, and Medium Enterprises: Development of a Conceptual Framework," *Singapore Management Review* 30.2 (July–Dec 2008): 47; Nancy Ku, "SMEs Look to Non-traditional Lenders," *China Brief*, American Chamber of Commerce in China (March 2009).

13 S. Cavusgil and S. Zou, "Marketing Strategic Performance Relationship," *Journal of Marketing* (1994); J. Meran and A. Moini, "Firm's Export Behavior," *American Business Review* (1999): 86.

14 D. Greenway, J. Gullstrand, and R. Kneller, "Exporting May Not Always Boost Firm Productivity," *Review of World Economics*, 4 (December 1, 2005): 561–82.

15 L. Yun, "Determinants of Export Intensity and FDI Presence: Case of Manufacturing Industries of Guangdong Province, the People's Republic of China," *International Journal of Logistics Systems and Management* (2006): 230–54.

16 B. Aw, M. Roberts, D. Xu, "R&D Investment, Exporting, and Productivity Dynamics," retrieved December 18, 2012, from www.econ.psu.edu/~mroberts/arxmarch2010.pdf.

17 D. Crick, "UK SMEs' Motives for Internationalizing: Differences between Firms Employing Particular Overseas Market Servicing Strategies," *Journal of International Entrepreneurship* (2007): 11–23, retrieved May 15, 2011.

18 Coffee & More, LLC, retrieved May 15, 2011, from www.export.gov/articles/successstories/eg_success_story_022775.asp.

19 Certified Worldwide LLC, retrieved May 15, 2011, from www.export.gov/articles/successstories/eg_success_story_020902.asp.

20 A. Bernard and B. Jensen, "Exceptional Exporter Performance: Cause, Effect, or Both?" retrieved December 18, 2012, from www.nber.org/papers/w6272.

21 Elena Golovko and Giovanni Valentini, "Exploring the Complementarity Between Innovation and Export for SME's Growth," *Journal of International Business Studies*, 42: 362–80, 2011.

22 Domes International, retrieved May 15, 2011, from www.export.gov/articles/successstories/eg_success_story_021027.asp.

23 USITC, "Small and Medium-Sized Enterprises: Overview of Participation in U.S. Exports," January 2010; USITC, "Small and Medium-Sized Enterprises: U.S. and EU Export Activities, and Barriers and Opportunities Experienced by U.S. Firms," July 2010.

24 "Jarden Zinc Products of Tennessee," retrieved December 17, 2012, from export.gov/articles/successstories/eg_main_035140.asp.

25 "Hey Big Spenders," *The World in 2012, The Economist,* retrieved December 22, 2012 from www.economist.com/theworldin/2012.

26 "Global Development Horizons 2011—Multipolarity: The New Global Economy," *The World Bank,* retrieved May 30, 2011, from web.worldbank.org/wbsite/external/extdec/extdecprospects/extgdh/0,,menupk:7933477~pagepk:64167702~pipk:64167676~thesitepk:7933464,00.html.

27 Hans Gemunden, "Success Factors of Export Marketing: A Meta-Analytic Critique of the Empirical Studies," in *New Perspectives on International Marketing,* (Ed.) S. Paliwoda (London: Routledge, 1991): 33–62; Julia Armario, David Ruiz, and Enrique Armario, "Market Orientation and Internationalization in Small and Medium-Sized Enterprises," *Journal of Small Business Management* (October 2008): 485.

28 "Schumpeter: The Case against Globaloney," *The Economist* (April 23, 2011): 72.

29 Analytical Graphics, Inc., Profile at export.gov, retrieved December 15, 2012, from export.gov/articles/successstories/eg_main_033668.asp.

30 Paul Westhead, Mike Wright, and Deniz Ucbasaran, "International Market Selection Strategies Selected by 'Micro' and 'Small' Firms," *Omega* (February 2002): 51.

31 McKinsey & Co. (1993), "Emerging Exporters: Australia's High Value-added Manufacturing Exporters," Melbourne: Australian Manufacturing Council, retrieved May 17, 2011, from catalogue.nla.gov.au/Record/2621131.

32 Examples cited in T. Koed Madsen and P. Servais, "The Internationalization of Born Globals: An Evolutionary Process?" *International Business Review* (1997): 561–83.

33 O. Moen, R. Sorbeim, and T. Erikson. "Born Global Firms and Informal Investors: Examining Investor Characteristics," *Journal of Small Business Management* (October 2008): 536.

34 Evertek Computer Corp., retrieved May 15, 2011, from www.export.gov/articles/successstories/eg_success_story_021490.asp.

35 Ibid.

36 Ibid.

37 Country percentages calculated from data reported at: U.S. International Trade In Goods and Services (www.census.gov/foreign-trade/statistics/historical/), 1992: U.S. trade in goods with China, (www.census.gov/foreign-trade/balance/c5700.html#1992), and 1992: U.S. trade in goods with Mexico (www.census.gov/foreign-trade/balance/c2010.html).

38 Small & Medium-Sized Exporting Companies: Statistical Overview, 2010, International Trade Administration, retrieved December 15, 2012, from www.trade.gov/mas/ian/smeoutlook/index.asp#P44_5045; USITC, "Small and Medium-Sized Enterprises: Overview of Participation in U.S. Exports," January 2010; USITC, "Small and Medium-Sized Enterprises: U.S. and EU Export Activities, and Barriers and Opportunities Experienced by U.S. Firms," July 2010.

39 Daniel Sullivan and Alan Bauerschmidt, "Incremental Internationalization: A Test of Johanson and Vahlne's Thesis," *Management International Review* (1990): 19–30.

40 Some folks object to the abrasives, flavors, tartar-control agents, and bleaches found in mass-market toothpaste.

41 Mark Stein, "Export Opportunities Aren't Just for the Big Guys," *New York Times* (March 24, 2005): C1.

42 Vellus Products, retrieved May 15, 2011, from www.export.gov/articles/successstories/eg_main_020763.asp.

43 Adapted from *A Basic Guide to Exporting*, 10th edition (Washington, D.C.: Commerce Dept., International Trade Administration, 2011).

44 Mark Stein, "Export Opportunities Aren't Just for the Big Guys," *New York Times* (March 24, 2005): C1.

45 In 2007, for example, an estimated 85 percent of foreign sales by large firms were conducted through foreign affiliates of U.S. firms, versus approximately 16 percent of foreign sales conducted via direct exports; Source: "Small and Medium-Sized Enterprises: Overview of Participation in U.S. Exports."

46 "Small and Medium-Sized Enterprises: Characteristics and Performance," United States International Trade Commission, Investigation No. 332-510, USITC Publication 4189, November 2010.

47 Jiang Jingjing, "Walmart's China Inventory to Hit US $18B this Year," *China Business Weekly,* retrieved November 29, 2004, from www.chinadaily.com.cn/english/doc/2004–11/29/content_395728.htm.

48 Anna Thomas and Susan Bridgewater, "Internet and Exporting: Determinants of Success in Virtual Export Channels," *International Marketing Review* 21:4 (2004): 393.

49 Merlin Bettina, "Internet Marketing in Exports—A Useful Tool for Small Businesses," *Small Enterprise Development* (December 2004): 38.

50 Analytical Graphics, Inc., Profile at export.gov, retrieved Saturday, December 15, 2012 from export.gov/articles/successstories/eg_main_033668.asp.

51 Pascal-Emmanuel Gobry, "Asian Scalpers Are Wiping Out Apple's Supply Of iPad 2s In New York," retrieved May 31, 2011, from www.businessinsider.com/ipad-scalpers-new-york-2011-3.

52 Andrew Bernard, Bradford Jensen, and Peter Schott, "Importers, Exporters, and Multinationals: A Portrait of Firms in the U.S. that Trade Goods," NBER Working Paper No. 11404, June 2005.

53 "A Profile of U.S. Importing and Exporting Companies, 2009–2010," U.S. Department of Commerce, retrieved April 24, 2013, from www.census.gov/foreign-trade/Press-Release/edb/2010/edbrel.pdf; Statistical Overview, 2009, U.S. International Trade Administration, retrieved May 12, 2011 from www.trade.gov/mas/ian/smeoutlook/tg_ian_001925.asp.

54 Andrew Bernard, Bradford Jensen, and Peter Schott, "Importers, Exporters, and Multinationals: A Portrait of Firms in the U.S. that Trade Goods," NBER Working Paper No. 11404, June 2005.

55 Based on exchange rates of yuan to dollar of 0.154/$1 as of May 6, 2011.

56 Arguably, an unrealistic assumption but one that we make for the sake of convenience.

57 "Table 1: Civilian workers, by Major Occupational and Industry Group," *U.S. Bureau of Labor Statistics,* retrieved May 9, 2011, from www.bls.gov/news.release/ecec.t01.htm.

58 "How much would the iPad 2 Cost if it was made in the U.S.A?" Stone Street Advisors, retrieved May 9, 2011, from stonestreetadvisors.com/2011/05/06/how-much-would-the-ipad-2-cost-if-it-was-made-in-the-u-s-a; Andrew Rassweiler, "iPad 2 Carries Bill of Materials of $326.60, IHS iSuppli Teardown Analysis Shows," retrieved May 9, 2011, from www.isuppli.com/teardowns/news/pages/ipad-2-carries-bill-of-materials-of-$326-60-ihs-isuppli-teardown-analysis-shows.aspx.

59 J. Laurie Flynn, "Poor Nations Are Littered with Old PC's, Report Says," *New York Times* (October 24, 2005): C2.

60 "Africa Waste Trade," retrieved May 4, 2011, from www1.american.edu/TED/oauwaste.htm; Estimates for developed economies taken from Hazardous Waste Disposal, www.uos.harvard.edu/ehs/environmental/hw_faq_answers.shtml; Leslie Kaufman, "A Green Way to Dump Low-Tech Electronics," *New York Times* (June 30, 2009).

61 Helen Baulch, "Error: Dumping Does Not Compute," *Alternatives Journal* (Summer 2002): 2.

62 "Electronic Waste in Guiyu" *Wikipedia,* retrieved December 22, 2012 from en.wikipedia.org/wiki/Electronic_waste_in_Guiyu.

63 Elisabeth Rosenthal, "Recycled Battery Lead Puts Mexicans in Danger," NYTimes.com, retrieved December 23, 2012 from www.nytimes.com/2011/12/09/science/earth/recycled-battery-lead-puts-mexicans-in-danger.html?pagewanted=all&_r=0.

64 Reported by Karl Schoenberger, "E-Waste Ignored in India," *Mercury News,* retrieved May 4, 2011, from www.ban.org/ban_news/ ewaste_ignored_031228.html.

65 Matthew Khan, "Environmental and Urban Economics: October 2005," retrieved February 25, 2013, from greeneconomics.blogspot.com/2005_10_01_archive.html.

66 "After Dump, What Happens to Electronic Waste?" *NPR,* retrieved April 19, 2011, from www.npr.org/2010/12/21/132204954/after-dump-what-happens-to-electronic-waste.

67 Michelle Castillo, "Electronic Waste: Where Does It Go and What Happens To It?" TIME.com, retrieved February 25, 2013, from techland.time.com/2011/01/14/electronic-waste-where-does-it-go-and-what-happens-to-it/.

68 Elisabeth Rosenthal, "Recycled Battery Lead Puts Mexicans in Danger," *NYTimes.com,* retrieved February 25, 2013 from www.nytimes.com/2011/12/09/science/earth/recycled-battery-lead-puts-mexicans-in-danger.html?pagewanted=all&_r=0.

69 Helen Baulch, "Error: Dumping Does Not Compute," *Alternatives Journal* (Summer 2002): 2.

70 "The Digital Dump: Exporting Reuse and Abuse to Africa," *Basel Action Network,* retrieved May 4, 2011, from www.ban.org/banreports/10-24-05/index.htm.

71 Basel Action Network, retrieved May 5, 2007, from www.ban.org/index.html; Flynn, "Poor Nations Littered with Old PCs."

72 "E-Waste Importers," *Hazardous Waste Superfund Week* (December 23, 2002).

73 "Where Does E-Waste End Up?" retrieved May 4, 2011, from www.greenpeace.org/international/campaigns/toxics/electronics/where-does-e-waste-end-up.

74 Kaufman, "A Green Way to Dump Low-Tech Electronics"; "The Politics of E-waste: A Cadmium Lining," *The Economist,* (January 26, 2013): 56.

75 See "Secretariat of the Basel Convention, Competent Authorities," retrieved March 26, 2009, from www.basel.int. By definition, a "Competent Authority" means one governmental authority designated by a Party to be responsible within such geographic areas as the Party may think fit, for receiving the notification of a transboundary movement of hazardous wastes or other wastes, and any information related to it, and for responding to such a notification. Also, see en.wikipedia.org/wiki/Basel_Convention.

76 *Small & Medium-Sized Exporting Companies: Statistical Overview,* tse.export.gov/EDB/SelectReports.aspx?DATA=ExporterDB.

77 L. Leonidou, "An Analysis of the Export Barriers Hindering Small Business Export Development," *Journal of Small Business Management* (2004): 279–302; Martina Battisti and Martin Perry, "Creating Opportunity for Small-firm Exporters through Regional Free Trade Agreements: A Strategic Perspective from New Zealand," *Australasian Journal of Regional Studies* (2008): 275–86.

78 OECD, OECD-APEC paper on removing barriers to SME access to international market (2006). See also Alan Bauerschmidt, Daniel Sullivan, and Kate Gillespie, "Common Factors Underlying Barriers to Export Studies in the U.S. Paper Industry," *Journal of International Business Studies,* 16:3 (1985): 111–23.

79 "Congress Pushes More Export Financing for Small Business," *Associated Press* (September 5, 2006).

80 John Kerr, "Exporters Need to Connect with Customers," *Logistics Management* (March 1, 2006): 41.

81 O'Gorman, C. (2000), "Strategy and the Small Firm," In S. Carter and D. Jones-Evans (Eds.), *Enterprise and Small Business: Principles, Practice, and Policy* (Harlow: Prentice Hall, FT Pearson).

82 "A Profile of U.S. Importing and Exporting Companies, 2009–2010."

83 Spectra Colors of NJ, retrieved May 15, 2011, from www.export.gov/articles/successstories/eg_success_story_023038.asp.

84 Banerjee, "REACH-Like Regulations Enacted Globally: A Regulatory World Tour," ICIS Chemical Business, May 26, 2010 (accessed June 25, 2010). For a more detailed information about REACH, see European Chemicals Agency Helsinki, "About Reach," (accessed June 25, 2010); European Commission, Enterprise and Industry, Chemicals, "REACH: Registration, Evaluation, Authorization and Restriction of Chemicals," (accessed June 25, 2010).

85 U.S. Trade Representative, 2010 National Trade Estimate Report on Foreign Trade Barriers, 2010.

86 U.S. Department of Commerce, International Trade Administration, "Country Commercial Guide: Thailand," February 18, 2008, 64.

87 U.S. Trade Representative, 2010 National Trade Estimate Report on Foreign Trade Barriers, 2010.

88 WTO, Trade Policy Review: India, April 18, 2007, 147.

89 "China to Amazon Re: Kindle Store: Not So Fast," DBW, retrieved December 17, 2012, from www.digitalbookworld.com/2012/china-to-amazon-re-kindle-store-not-so-fast/.

90 Kerr, "Exporters Need to Connect with Customers."

91 "Schumpeter: The Case against Globaloney," *The Economist* (April 20, 2011): 52.

92 "Exporters Hit by Air Freight Restrictions" *Telegraph*, retrieved December 21, 2012 from www.telegraph.co.uk/finance/yourbusiness/8860814/Exporters-hit-by-air-freight-restrictions.html.

93 "A 'Green Zone' for Firms in Ciudad Juárez: Business on the Bloody Border," *The Economist*, retrieved December 22, 2012 from www.economist.com/node/21540262; "Canada and the United States: The Border Two-step," *The Economist*, retrieved December 22, 2012 from www.economist.com/node/21541421.

94 Incoterms are the rules for the division of cost and risk in international sales transactions. They set three-letter standard trade terms that are commonly used in international sales contracts that help exporters avoid disputes with customers by specifying each party's responsibilities.

95 The commercial invoice, for instance, contains information such as the country of origin, the port of entry to which the merchandise is destined, information on the importer and exporter, a detailed description of the merchandise, including its purchase price, and the currency used for the sale.

96 "A Profile of U.S. Importing and Exporting Companies, 2009–2010."

97 Ibid.

98 Ibid.

99 Ibid.

100 Analytical Graphics, retrieved January 15, 2013, from export.gov/articles/successstories/eg_main_033668.asp.

101 "Garmin Marine Navigation GPS Units Navigate Turkish Customs," retrieved January 15, 2013, from export.gov/articles/successstories/eg_main_046466.asp.

102 Japan, for instance, relies on several offices, such as the Small and Medium Enterprise Agency, the Agency of Industrial Science and Technology, and the Ministry of International Trade and Industry. The latter, often referred to as MITI, develops policies and provides assistance to help Japanese companies trade.

103 Lee Li, "Joint Effects of Factors Affecting Exchanges Between Exporters and Their Foreign Intermediaries: An Exploratory Study," *Journal of Business & Industrial Marketing* (February–March 2003): 162–78. Trade intermediaries help navigate complex homeland security concerns. Increasing government regulation regarding what can be shipped where and to whom has prolonged border delays.

104 See U.S. Department of Commerce, *Guide to Exporting, 1998*, p. 20; Philip MacDonald, Practical Exporting and Importing, 2nd edition (New York: Ronald Press, 1959): 30–40.

105 Courtney Fingar, "ABCs of EMCs," The Federation of International Trade Associations (July 2001); Nelson T. Joyner, "How to Find and Use an Export Management Company," retrieved May 9, 2007, from www.fita.org/aotm/0499.html.

106 Geoffrey G Jones, *The Multinational Trader* (Routledge International Studies in Business History, 1998).

107 "Basic Question: To Export Yourself or to Hire Someone to Do It for You?" *Business America* (April 27, 1987): 14–17.

108 Because a practical discussion of importing procedures in every trading country of the world is impossible within this chapter, we focus on the matter of importing to the United States. We note that although U.S. import requirements and procedures provide a sufficient base for judging situations in other countries, a company must assess the importing regulations at play in those countries that it plans to engage. For an organizational chart of the U.S. Customs Bureau, including a roster of specific responsibilities, go to the home page of the U.S. Bureau of Customs and Border Protection, www.customs.ustreas.gov.

109 International Bank/World Bank, "Doing Business in 2007."

110 U.S. Department of the Treasury, U.S. Customs Service, *Importing into the United States* (Washington, DC: U.S. Government Printing Office, September 1991).

111 U.S. Department of Commerce, *Guide to Exporting* (Washington, DC: U.S. Government Printing Office, 1998): 63.

112 Certified Worldwide LLC, retrieved May 4, 2011, from www.export.gov/articles/successstories/eg_success_story_020902.asp.

113 Richard Armstrong, "The Top 40 3PLs 2010," *Logistics Quarterly Magazine* (2011).

114 Quote from CEO Robert Allen, Coffee & More, LLC, retrieved May 15, 2011, from www.export.gov/articles/successstories/eg_success_story_022775.asp.

115 Analytical Graphics, Inc., Profile at export.gov, retrieved December 15, 2012 from export.gov/articles/successstories/eg_main_033668.asp.

116 Benson Smith and Tony Rutigliano, *Discover Your Sales Strengths* (New York: Warner Business Books, 2003).

117 Julie Sloane, Justin Martin, and Alessandra Bianchi, "Small Companies That Play Big," *FSB Magazine* (November 1, 2006), quoting Ram Iyer.

118 Justin Lahart, "For Small Businesses, Big World Beckons," *WSJ.com*, retrieved January 27, 2011, from online.wsj.com/article/SB10001424052748703951704576092010276714424.html?mod=WSJ_hp_MIDDLENexttoWhatsNewsFifth.

119 Gary Hamel, "*What Matters Now: How to Win in a World of Relentless Change, Ferocious Competition, and Unstoppable Innovation* (Wiley, 2012).

120 Javier Blas, "Nations Turn to Barter Deals to Secure Food," *Financial Times*, retrieved March 11, 2009, from www.ft.com/cms/s/0/3e5c633c-ebdc-11dd-8838-0000779fd2ac.html; Dan West, "Countertrade—An Innovative Approach to Marketing," retrieved May 15, 2007, from www.barternews.com/approach_marketing.htm. On a more exotic note, Pepsi-Cola, which has the marketing rights for all Stolichnaya Vodka in the United States, delivers syrup that is paid for with Stolichnaya Vodka. In addition, early on, Pepsi took delivery of 17 submarines, a cruiser, a frigate, and a destroyer from the Russian government in payment for Pepsi products. In turn, Pepsi sold its "fleet" of 20 naval vessels for scrap steel, thereby paying for the Pepsi products sent to the Soviet Union.

121 V. S. Rama Rao, "Counter Trade," retrieved May 23, 2011, from www.citeman.com/2390-counter-trade.

122 One can divide countertrade into two classes: barter, based on clearing arrangements used to avoid money-based exchange; and buybacks, offsets, and counter purchases, which are used to impose reciprocal commitments between the various parties.

123 Dan West, "Countertrade—An Innovative Approach to Marketing," retrieved March 12, 2009, from BarterNews.com; "Counter trade," Wikipedia, retrieved December 20, 2012 from en.wikipedia.org/wiki/Counter_trade.

124 ***Sources include the following:*** Various sources at www.Alibaba.com; Forbes Global (April 25, 2005): 30; TradeStats Express, retrieved July 1, 2009, from tse.export.gov; John Heilemann, "Jack Ma Aims to Unlock the Middle Kingdom," *Business 2.0 Magazine*, (July 31, 2006); Jack Ma, "China Discovers Its Future," *International Herald Tribune* (December 17, 2008); "Alibaba Prepares for Global Expansion," *Financial Times* (January 19, 2009); "News on Alibaba.com, Business, Price Watch, Finance, Industry, Trade," retrieved December 21, 2012 from news.alibaba.com/; "China's Alibaba Group Q2 Net Profit Doubles: SEC Filing, Yahoo!, accessed December 21, 2012, ca.news.yahoo.com/chinas-alibaba-group-q2-net-profit-doubles-sec-043933703--sector.html; "Alibaba reaches 1 trillion RMB ($157B) in sales to become

biggest e-commerce company in the world, VentureBeat, accessed December 24, 2012, venturebeat.com/company/alibaba/.

125 The U.S. Small Business Administration estimates that the number of small companies exporting products tripled from 1994 through 2004. In terms of monetary flows, the value of exports from the United States grew from $731 billion in 2001 to $1.03 trillion in 2006, while imports grew from $1.14 trillion to $1.9 trillion.

126 "Fast as a Rabbit, Patient as a Turtle," *Forbes.com*, retrieved February 25, 2013 from www.forbes.com/forbes/2000/0717/6602074a_print.html.

127 "Alibaba Prepares for Global Expansion," *Financial Times*, retrieved February 25, 2013 from news.alibaba.com/article/detail/alibaba/100057556-1-alibaba-prepares-global-expansion.html.

128 "Alibaba wields its pricing power," *Asia Times Online*, retrieved February 17, 2011, from www.atimes.com/atimes/China_Business/MB18Cb01.html.

129 "Jack Ma," *Times of India*, retrieved December 21, 2012 from timesofindia.indiatimes.com/topic/Jack-Ma/quotes/.

CHAPTER 15

Forms and Ownership of Foreign Production

OBJECTIVES

After studying this chapter, you should be able to

1. Clarify why companies may use modes other than exporting to operate effectively in international business
2. Comprehend why and how companies make foreign direct investments
3. Understand the major motives that guide managers to choose a collaborative arrangement for international business
4. Compare the major types of collaborative arrangements
5. Describe what to consider when entering into international arrangements with other companies
6. Grasp why collaborative arrangements succeed or fail
7. See how companies can manage diverse collaborative arrangements
8. Appreciate how growth in project size and complexity will require more future collaboration

Source: © FM2 - Fotolia.com

If you can't beat them, join them.

—American proverb

CASE Meliá Hotels International

—Fidel León-Darder and Cristina Villar

"God bless the inventor of sleep."
(Miguel de Cervantes Saavedra, *Don Quijote de la Mancha*)

Li Feng arrived in London after a 13-hour flight from Beijing, her first company trip since completing her MBA and her first time outside China.[1] Upon entering her room at the Meliá White House, she felt too exhausted to do much more than shower and enjoy the comfort and amenities in her room. (The quote from Don Quijote was certainly applicable.) However, the excitement of being abroad for the first time kept her from sleeping right away. So she perused the attractive hotel directory on her bedside table and was surprised to read that her hotel belonged to a Spanish company with more than 350 hotels all over the world. (The country locations are shown on Map 15.1.) The photos showed an array of attractive hotels, ranging from those in big cities (primarily to serve businesspeople) to others on pristine beaches surrounded by palm trees and large areas of lush vegetation (primarily to serve vacationers). (The chapter's opening photo shows a Meliá hotel in Morocco.)

She was also intrigued by a small black and white picture of Gabriel Escarré, who founded the chain in 1956. At only 21, he had leased his first hotel in Majorca (Mallorca), Spain with only the savings he had earned and the expertise he had gained from his job at a travel agency. Li Feng was curious to learn how Meliá had reached its position in the global hospitality industry. She fell asleep and dreamt of holidaying in a Meliá beach resort, but she awoke curious as to how Mr. Escarré had built the business. For the next five days, she worked long hours, squeezed in a little sightseeing, and then returned to Beijing. Despite jet-lag, she went to work the next day and began catching up with the pile of papers that had accumulated on her desk. In her spare time she did some research on Meliá. What she learned is described below.

GROWTH IN SPAIN

That Gabriel Escarré's first hotel was in Majorca is not surprising because most entrepreneurs begin in familiar surroundings. His timing was good—European incomes were rising and package tours for sun-loving tourists were gaining popularity. Most important, Escarré exhibited both a knack for hotel management and a motivation to expand. He grew by acquiring other properties in Spain's Balearic and Canary Islands, branding them first as Hoteles Mallorquines and later as Hoteles Sol, then still later to Sol-Meliá, which many people still call it, and finally to Meliá Hotels International in 2011. The early hotels aimed their sales at beach-seeking tourists. In 1982, three years before its first foreign entry, the company began diversifying by adding urban hotels that targeted business travelers.

In 1984, while still known as Hoteles Sol, the company bought 32 hotel properties of Hotasa, a Spanish chain taken over by the government because its holding company was involved in a massive fraud. Sol acquired the properties but neither Hotasa nor its brand name. Thus, the hotels were re-branded as Sol and entered more Spanish cities. Three years later, Sol acquired Meliá from Paretti, an Italian group, which led to further diversification of the client base because most Sol Hotels were three- and four-star beach properties, whereas most Meliá's were four- or five-star urban hotels. In 2000, Meliá merged with another Spanish hotel chain, TRYP, thus adding 45 hotels in Spain. Meliá is now the largest hotel operator in Spain, and Spain is the largest location for Meliá.

INTERNATIONAL EXPANSION

Despite the importance of Spain to Meliá, 80 percent of its current income is from international operations. Some international expansion came from the acquisitions we've discussed, such as Meliá bringing operations in the Americas and Europe into Sol's portfolio. The TRYP agreement included eight leased agreements in Tunisia and three management contracts in Cuba. Meliá has used its 1999 purchase of the White House in London and the 2007 acquisition of the Inside Inns in Germany to bolster its urban presence in Europe.

Having acquired experience and expertise within Spain, the firm's first hotel venture with a start-up abroad was the Meliá Bali in Indonesia. This resulted from a long and complicated process, in which the firm had difficulty finding local suppliers, then encountered logistics and import problems in sending materials from Majorca. Soon after, the company focused on Latin America and eventually on other areas. (Figure 15.1 shows expansion by regions.) Let's examine some major international forays that demonstrate different modes of operations.

MAP 15.1 Location of Meliá Hotels Operations

The identified countries indicate where Mélia operates. It will soon be adding Austria and Denmark to its portfolio.

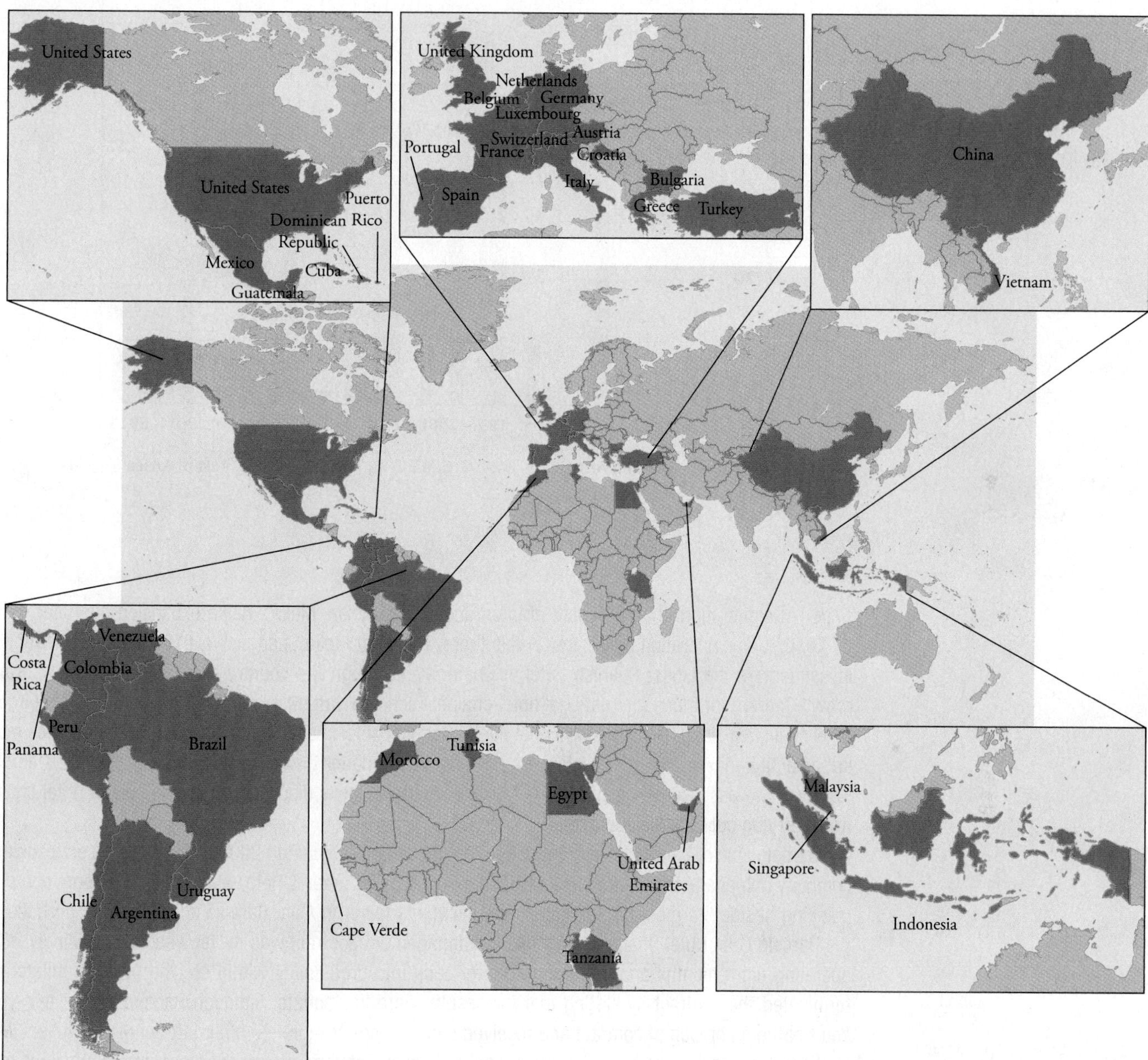

Cuba In terms of the number of hotels, Cuba's 26 make up Meliá's largest foreign presence. Yet the company has no ownership in hotels there because Cuba's centralized economy disallows foreign hotel groups to take full ownership. Thus, Meliá, like other foreign hotel chains, had to establish an agreement with a public agency, which usually owns the properties. Meliá's agreements are to manage those owned by Cubanacán.

Operating in Cuba slowed Meliá's access to the U.S. market because the U.S. government maintains restrictions on companies doing business with Cuba, such as on those managing expropriated assets once owned by U.S. citizens. (Recall the ending case in Chapter 6.) Meliá had to prove that the hotels under its management were not expropriated from U.S. citizens before it could enter the U.S. market, where it currently operates two hotels.

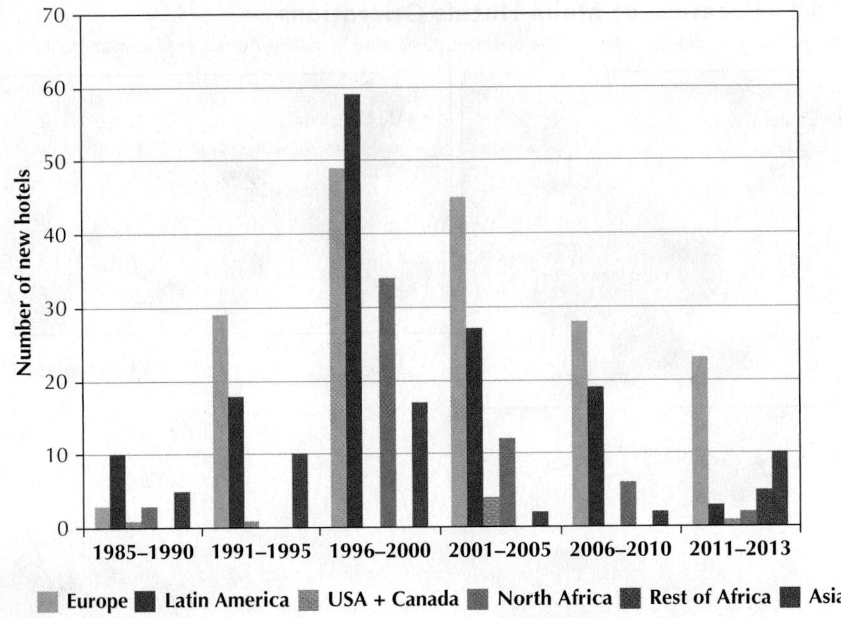

FIGURE 15.1 Meliá's New Foreign Operations by Region and Years

China Despite more than 25 years of international expansion, Meliá's Asian expansion has been slow. By 2010, it was operating only a few hotels there. The Gran Meliá Shanghai, a €180 million construction investment, is the oldest Spanish hotel in China, even though the country has long been an important growth market for many international hotel chains, such as Hyatt, Marriott, Radisson, and China's largest hotel chain, Jin Jiang. This anomaly is not due to Spanish hotel chains' being unaware of the Chinese market potential; indeed, many projects were developed to conquer the market as much as ten years earlier. However, the unsuccessful experience of Spain's Barceló Hotels discouraged other Spanish hotel chains from carrying out Chinese operations.

Barceló, one of Meliá's main competitors, reached an agreement in 2000 with a Chinese state-owned company to manage the Shanghai International Convention Center & Hotel, a five-star, 270-room complex standing beside the most famous telecommunications tower in Asia. Barceló added it to its portfolio as the Barceló Gran Hotel Shanghai because its management contract was for ten years. Surprisingly, after operating eight months and bringing the hotel back into profitability within six, the owners unilaterally terminated the contract by stating that the results were inadequate. Although Barceló won a two-year court battle on breach of contract and received some compensation, the affair left Spanish hoteliers with a bitter aftertaste and the suspicion that Chinese government partners would break agreements once they learned enough from their foreign partners.

Sol Meliá broke the Spanish hotel curse in 2009 by reaching a ten-year management contract agreement, renewable for another ten. Meliá's entry was facilitated by its favorable 20-year relationship with Cubanacán, which shares the Shanghai hotel ownership with the Chinese company Xintian (Suntime). Still, getting the deal was not easy; it took more than five years from the time talks began to the hotel's opening.

Subsequently, Meliá announced co-management plans with Jin Jiang and Greenland, a Chinese real estate company. The plans provide for management sharing in six hotels previously managed separately. This will allow the Chinese partners to extend their operations into three hotels—one each in Germany, Spain, and France—in exchange for Meliá's co-management of hotels in three Chinese cities. The partners will share knowledge and best practices as well as integrate and develop training, information, and booking systems. Meliá expects to learn more about Chinese customers, thus boosting its ability to expand further within China.

Relationship with Wyndham Melía's motivation for an agreement in 2010 with Wyndham was largely to facilitate North American expansion by using Wyndham's knowledge of that market and reputation with developers who are potential hotel investors. (Wyndham is the world's largest hospitality company and hotel franchisor, with 6900 hotels and 15 brands in 50 countries.) Through the agreement, Meliá sold its TRYP brand to Wyndham, but sold no real estate. The hotels in the transaction accounted for about 13,000 rooms and were re-branded as TRYP by Wyndham. Meliá became the franchisee for all the hotels using the TRYP by Wyndham brand for a 20-year period. Wyndham gained by increasing its reservations offerings for a mid-market brand in Europe and Latin America, even though the same hotels are also included in Meliá's reservation system. Of the hotels in the 2010 agreement, Meliá maintains ownership of six, leases 49, has management contracts in 24, and re-franchises twelve to other parties. Subsequently, TRYP by Wyndham has opened hotels in the United States, Canada, Turkey, and Colombia.

INTERNATIONAL HOTEL OPERATING MODES

The hotel industry is included in the so called "soft services" sector because production and consumption cannot be separated. Companies' operations abroad create service rather than product exports and imports, and there is usually a need to adapt the operations to meet local requirements. Further, tourist clientele usually want an ambiance that resembles their perceptions of the foreign country where they're staying. At the same time, they expect a similar threshold level of service and amenities wherever a hotel brand operates.

The industry presents some unique characteristics, such as high investment costs and the possibility of separating ownership and management through contractual operating modes. Thus, firms have a wide range of feasible operating modes, especially management by third parties, for all or a part of necessary hotel services.

To classify hotel operating modes, it is necessary to look at a chain's degree of exercised control over the foreign operation. This control involves four non-mutually-exclusive dimensions:

1. The daily operation of the hotel, e.g., the hiring and scheduling of personnel and the securement of supplies
2. Physical assets (primarily property ownership and the maintenance thereof)
3. Organizational routines and tacit elements of the company, such as the culture and systems to gain both efficiency and effectiveness
4. Codified assets, such as the brand and reservations system

The responsibility for controlling these elements may lie with the international hotel chain or with contractual parties, depending on the operation mode used. The capital contribution for each of the above four dimensions may be categorized as controlling ownership (usually direct investment), shared ownership (usually equity joint ventures), and no ownership (licensing, management contracts, turnkey operations, non equity joint ventures, and franchising).

Operating modes can be combined. For instance, for the TRYP by Wyndham brand, Meliá owns some hotels, pays a franchise fee to Wyndham for using the brand name, and depends both on its own and Wyndham's reservation systems. In some other cases, it has no property ownership, may lease the facility or not, and is paid for managing the operation. The Gran Meliá Shanghai is a joint venture between Chinese and Cuban organizations that, in turn, granted a management contract to Meliá for day-to-day operations and signed a franchise contract with it to use its name and reservations services.

Despite combining international operating modes within the hotel industry, direct investment, particularly if the ownership is 100 percent, normally gives the owner the right to control the four dimensions identified above. In joint ventures, two or more organizations agree on how to divide responsibilities and contribute assets and income between/among them. In management contracts, the hotel chains serving as contractors are responsible for the entire operation of the hotel, so they adopt their systems and procedures while recruiting hotel managers and enacting their human resource and quality policies. In short, the hotel is managed as if it were owned by the chain, and the chain usually agrees, as well, to use its brand name and reservation services. In license agreements the chain gives the rights to its brand name to the owner of the hotel. In franchise agreements, the chain not only gives brand name rights but also assists the hotel on an ongoing basis, most likely by contributing the chain's sales, marketing and quality control systems, and activities. Any of these modes may exist from the start, such as participation in a new hotel (start-ups are known as *greenfield)* or through acquisition of an ongoing operation, either by owning or leasing.

In partnering with other companies, regardless of operating mode, one increases the chance of developing competitors because partners may gain access to critical and core resources, especially knowledge. Thus, companies seek ways to prevent partners' opportunistic behavior. One way, of course, is through contracts. But control of some knowledge-based resources is more difficult. Meliá's main control is over its codified resources, especially brands and reservations system, which are protected legally and which Meliá does not cede to other companies. Meliá has developed the recognition and reputation of its brands over decades, so new ones cannot easily overcome the advantage. The codified resources are tied closely as well to Meliá's tacit resources because the value of the brands is dependent on clients' hotel experience, and both physical resources and human behavior influence their opinions. Competitors can easily copy the former if they have enough money. However, the latter is harder to emulate because learning must take place on a person-to-person basis (tacitly). Such learning in hotel operations is substantial—everything from greeting guests to making beds to assuring the flow of supplies—and affects efficiency and reputation. Over time, the actions become the essence of the company's culture.

MELIÁ'S EVOLVING OPERATING MODES

As we have seen, Meliá has made and continues to make use of various operating modes. (Figure 15.2 shows the evolution of its international entry modes.) However, it has not always had discretion in choosing a mode. When Gabriel Escarré established his first hotels, he had no track record that could entice other hotel owners to pay him to manage their facilities or use his brand name and reservations system. He developed a positive reputation through his successful greenfield and acquisition expansion over nearly

FIGURE 15.2 Meliá's Entry Modes by Time Periods

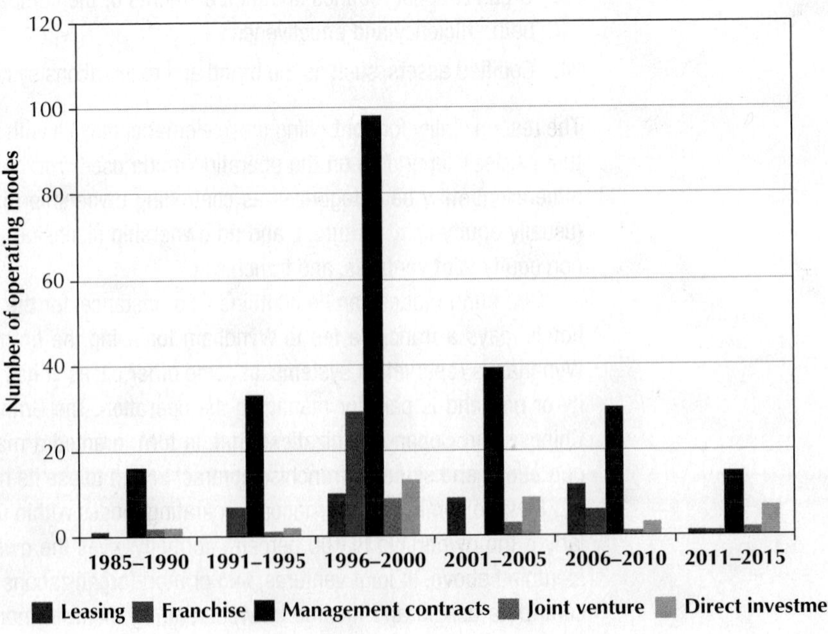

30 years in Spain before moving internationally. During its history, the company has had four names, finally settling on one that includes "Meliá" because the name has long been associated with luxury hotels and thus brings a certain cachet to the company.

Nevertheless, most of Meliá's early international growth resulted from acquisitions, such as its purchase of the Spanish chain TRYP that already had foreign operations and of Inside Inns in Germany. The success of these ventures has built Meliá's reputation as a quality hotel operator, allowing it to keep expanding its hotel portfolio with shared or no capital investment. This expansion has also occurred in China and Cuba, which place restrictions on foreign ownership.

Why grow? There are economies in handling larger hotel portfolios because of the clout and logistics in dealing with suppliers and the spreading of reservation and training system costs over more properties. There are also sales advantages because potential customers are more familiar with the larger chains.

MELIÁ NOW AND IN THE FUTURE

Currently, Meliá Hotels International comprises strong brands such as Meliá, Gran Meliá, ME by Meliá, Paradisus, Innside by Meliá, TRYP by Wyndham, Sol Hotels, and Club Meliá. The maintenance of different brands is important because of brand acquisitions that already had recognition and value. Nevertheless, Meliá is linking that recognition with its name (hence Innside by Meliá and Meliá White House). Additional linkage is due to all the brands being handled through one reservations system. Further, the different brands are aimed at different market niches.

Meliá expects more international growth by entering additional countries and adding hotels in those where it now operates. The latter includes the brands it already uses within those countries as well as the addition of its other brands. It has also indicated an interest in linking with brands held by other companies, such as the Hard Rock Café and Flintstones. Its ambitions seem too great to do everything alone. And it might not want to, even if it has the capital resources. For instance, it has so far been reluctant to make big commitments in countries, such as those in Southeast Asia, where it perceives the operating environment to be too different from its European (especially Spanish) experience. Thus, the use of non-equity operations seems to be the crux of Meliá's future.

As part of its growth strategy in high-potential markets, Meliá has recently entered Africa with operations in Cape Verde, Tanzania, and Egypt, and has indicated an interest in South Africa, Morocco, Kenya, Mauritius, Maldives, Mozambique, Senegal, and Tanzania. As for the Middle East, Meliá has recently entered Dubai by focusing on both the leisure and business traveler. In Latin America, recent growth has been carried out through the TRYP by Wyndham brand in Brazil, which has wide experience in that market.

Fast-forwarding to nearly a year since Li Feng returned to Beijing, we find that she has worked almost non-stop and has taken no more trips. Contractually, physically, and emotionally, she is ready for a vacation. She looks back at the hotel directory she brought from London and focuses on a picture showing a hotel half hidden among the foliage in front of a white sand beach and turquoise waters. "Who knows?" she thought. "Maybe I should forget my laptop and spend some time in such a beautiful place." ■

CRN
Case Review Note

QUESTIONS

15-1. After reading the chapter, explain the advantages for Meliá to own its hotels versus managing them for other organizations.

15-2. After reading the chapter, discuss the advantages and risks for Meliá in its non-equity joint venture with Jin Jiang.

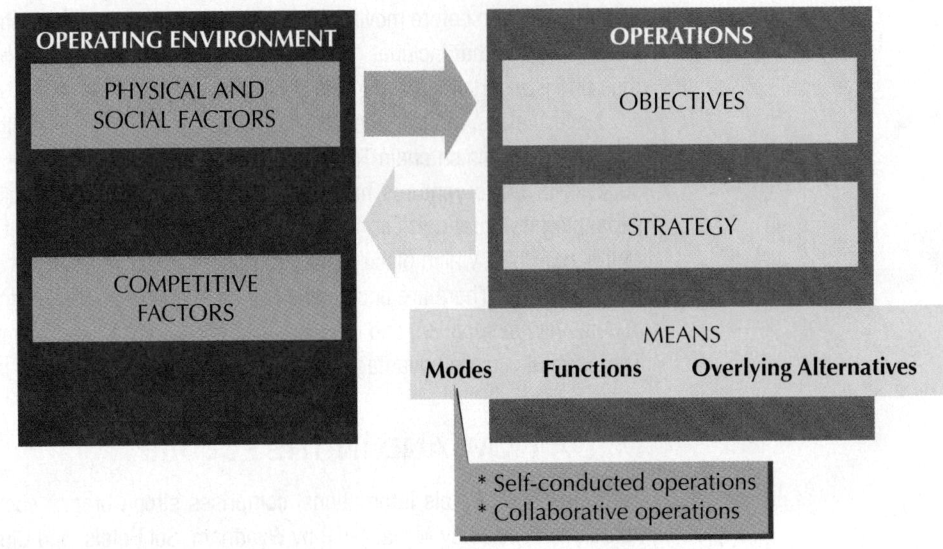

FIGURE 15.3 Factors Affecting Operating Modes in International Business

Companies may conduct international business operations independently or in collaboration with other companies. The choice will be determined both by external factors in the firm's operating environment and by internal factors that include its objectives, strategies, and means of operation (e.g., such modes of international business as exporting, franchising, etc.).

INTRODUCTION

As Figure 15.3 shows, companies must choose an international operating mode to fulfill their objectives and carry out their strategies. The preceding chapter examined exporting and importing—the preferred and most common modes of international business. Nevertheless, compelling factors can make these choices impractical. When companies depend, instead, on foreign production, they may own it in whole or in part, develop or acquire it, and/or use some type of collaborative agreement with another company.

Figure 15.4 shows the types of operating modes associated with each of these options, categorized by whether the company has foreign ownership, whether collaboration is involved, and whether production is located at home or abroad. The truly experienced MNE with a fully global orientation commonly uses most of the operational modes available, selecting them according to company capabilities, specific product, and foreign operating characteristics. The modes may also be combined, as with the Meliá's contract to manage the Shanghai hotel for a joint venture between Chinese and Cuban organizations. This chapter examines exporting/importing versus other options, the associated operating modes, and the advantages and problems with each, then concludes by discussing the management of these modes, particularly as foreign operations evolve over time.

FIGURE 15.4 Foreign Expansions: Alternative Operating Modes

A firm may choose to operate globally either through equity arrangements (e.g., joint venture) or through non-equity arrangements (e.g., licensing). Exporting operations are conducted in the home country, while all other modes entail production in foreign locations. The modes listed in the shaded area are collaborative arrangements. Note that, in any given location, a firm can conduct operations in multiple modes.

*Joint ventures may also be non-equity, but equity joint ventures are by far the more common.

PRODUCTION OWNERSHIP	PRODUCTION LOCATION Home country	Foreign country
Equity arrangements	a. Exporting	a. Wholly owned operations b. Partially owned with remainder widely held c. Joint ventures* d. Equity alliances
Non-equity arrangements		a. Licensing b. Franchising c. Management contracts d. Turnkey operations

WHY EXPORTING MAY NOT BE FEASIBLE

Companies may find more advantages by producing in foreign countries than by exporting to them. The advantages occur under six conditions:

1. When production abroad is cheaper than at home
2. When transportation costs to move goods or services internationally are too high
3. When companies lack domestic capacity
4. When products and services need to be altered substantially to gain sufficient consumer demand abroad
5. When governments inhibit the import of foreign products
6. When buyers prefer products originating from a particular country

WHEN IT'S CHEAPER TO PRODUCE ABROAD

Although companies may offer products or services desired by consumers abroad, producing them in their home markets may be too expensive, especially if other companies can make reasonably similar substitutes abroad at a lower cost. For example, Turkey has been a growing market for the sale of automobiles. However, it is generally less expensive to produce the vehicles in Turkey than to export them there because the country's skilled laborers and sophisticated engineers cost less and are willing to work more days per year and longer hours per day than workers in the home countries. Thus, the automakers and many of their parts suppliers have established Turkish production to serve that market.[2]

WHEN TRANSPORTATION COSTS TOO MUCH

Transportation raises costs so much that it becomes impractical to export some products.

The cost of transportation added to production costs makes some products and services impractical to export. Generally, the more distant the market, the higher the transportation costs, and the higher those are relative to production costs, the harder it is for companies to develop viable export markets. For instance, the international transportation cost for a soft drink is a high percentage of the manufacturing cost, so a sales price that includes both would be so high through exporting that soft-drink companies would sell very little of the product. In our opening case, it is obvious that if Meliá wishes to tap the market for visitors to New York, it must provide rooms in New York.

CRN Case Review Note

However, products such as watches have low transportation costs relative to production costs, so watch manufacturers lose few sales through exporting. The result is that companies such as Universal Genève and Seiko export watches from Switzerland and Japan, respectively, into the markets where they sell them.

Keep in mind that transport costs are dynamic, depending on fuel prices, new infrastructure (e.g., a widened Panama Canal cutting export distances), risk factors (e.g., ship piracy increasing security costs), and climate changes (e.g., warming making the Northwest Passage a viable option).

CONCEPT CHECK

In Chapter 5, we explain the concept of non-tradable goods—products and services that are seldom practical to export because of high transportation costs. Nevertheless, as we showed in Chapter 1, companies provide customers abroad with these non-tradable goods by locating near them.

WHEN DOMESTIC CAPACITY ISN'T ENOUGH

Excess capacity

- usually leads to exporting rather than new direct investment.
- may lead to competitive exports because of variable cost pricing.

As long as a company has excess capacity, it may compete effectively in export markets despite high transport costs. This occurs when domestic sales cover fixed operating expenses, enabling the company to set foreign prices on the basis of variable rather than full (variable + fixed) costs. In fact, its average cost of production per unit usually falls as foreign sales increase, but this decrease continues only as long as there is unused capacity.

Thus, companies typically produce in one location, from which they export before establishing plants in more than one country. Volkswagen, for instance, located its first plant to build the new Beetle at its facilities in Mexico, which served global markets. It wasn't until demand pushed that plant toward capacity that Volkswagen built a second plant in Europe to serve the markets there, thus freeing Mexican capacity to serve nearby markets while reducing transport costs for European sales.[3]

WHEN PRODUCTS AND SERVICES NEED ALTERING

Product alterations for foreign markets may lead to foreign production of the products.

Altering products to gain sufficient sales in a foreign market affects production costs in two ways. First, firms must make an additional investment, such as an automobile company adding an assembly line to put steering wheels on the right as well as on the left. Second, they lose some of the economies from large-scale production. As long as they must run an added assembly line anyway, they may place this line near the market they wish to serve.

The more a product must be altered for foreign markets, the more likely some production will shift abroad. Appliance maker Whirlpool finds that most U.S. demand is for top-loading, large-capacity washing machines using 110 electrical voltage, whereas most European demand is for front-loaders (more efficient in energy and water usage) with less capacity using 220 volts.[4] Given the differences in product preferences, Whirlpool produces in both the United States and Europe.

WHEN TRADE RESTRICTIONS HINDER IMPORTS

CONCEPT CHECK

In Chapter 7, we explain why governments are currently reducing trade restrictions, whether through bilateral integration (in which two countries agree to cooperate), regional integration (in which a group of geographically related countries agrees to cooperate), or agreements reached by the WTO, which serves as a multilateral forum. Here we observe that importers still face certain regulatory restrictions, some of which are designed to encourage forms of direct investment.

Although governments have been reducing import barriers, they still restrict many imports. As a result, companies may find that they must produce in a foreign country if they are to sell there. This has been the case with many auto companies—Volkswagen, Mercedes Benz, BMW, Renault, and Fiat—which decided to manufacture in India because it charged over 100 percent duty on fully built imported cars.[5]

Managers must view import barriers along with other factors, such as the market size of the country imposing the barriers and the scale of technology used in production. For example, import trade restrictions have been highly influential in enticing automobile producers to locate in Brazil because of its large market. Similar restrictions by Central American countries have been ineffective because of their small markets. However, Central American import barriers on products requiring lower amounts of capital investment for production, such as pharmaceuticals, have successfully enticed direct investment because these industries can be efficient with smaller-scale technologies and markets.

Regional or bilateral trade agreements may also attract direct investment, possibly because they create an expanded market that may justify scale economies and an ability to export part of the production.

WHEN COUNTRY OF ORIGIN BECOMES AN ISSUE

Consumers sometimes prefer domestically produced goods because of

- nationalism.
- a belief that these products are better.
- a fear that foreign-made goods may not be delivered on time.

If consumers prefer to buy goods produced in their own country rather than another (perhaps because of nationalism), exporting to them will be difficult.[6] They may push for identification labels showing that goods are domestically produced, such as those for many Australian-made products.[7] They may require labels showing where products originate, as with U.S. labeling of agricultural products.

Consumers may prefer goods from certain countries, believing them to be superior, like German cars and Italian fashion.[8] They may also fear that service and replacement parts for imported products will be more difficult to obtain. Finally, companies using just-in-time manufacturing systems favor nearby suppliers who can deliver quickly and reliably. In any of these cases, companies may find advantages in placing production where their output will best be accepted.

NONCOLLABORATION: FDI

In situations where exporting is not feasible, a company may choose to contract with another company to produce or provide services on its behalf or it may choose to "go it alone." Recall the four types of equity arrangements in Figure 15.2. In this section, we discuss the reasons and methods for making FDI for the two arrangements that do not involve collaboration: wholly owned operations and partially owned with the remainder widely held.

REASONS FOR FOREIGN DIRECT INVESTMENT

CONCEPT CHECK

Recall that in discussing global strategy as a type of international strategy in Chapter 12, we explain why some companies treat the world as a single market, preferring to integrate and measure performance on a global basis rather than on a country-by-country basis. Here we observe that the strategy of having wholly owned subsidiaries supports a global strategy.

Generally, the more ownership a company has, the greater its control over decisions, although if equity shares are widely held a company may be able to effectively control with even a minority interest. However, governments often protect minority owners so that majority owners do not act against their interests; thus, companies may opt for 100 percent ownership if they want control. There are four primary explanations for companies to take a controlling interest: *market failure, internalization theory, appropriability theory,* and *freedom to pursue global objectives.*

Market Failure Collaboration involves a transaction across the market between unrelated entities. Given liability of foreignness and the extra costs of investing abroad (along with other factors to be discussed later), collaboration is appealing, but only if management can find a collaborator at acceptable terms. For instance, they may not be able to find a contractor who is familiar enough with the company's unique technology to deal with it efficiently. In these instances, companies must control foreign activities within their own management structures (internal hierarchies) rather than depending on the external market to do it for them.[9] The extent to which companies take controlling ownership equity (FDI) in foreign operations—such as in warehousing, sales offices, or production facilities—indicates market failure.

Internalization Control through self-handling of operations is known as **internalization.**[10] The concept comes from *transactions cost theory,* which holds that companies should seek the lower cost between conducting operations internally and contracting another party to do so for them. In other cases, self-handling may reduce costs for a number of reasons:

1. *Different operating units within the same company are likely to share a common corporate culture, which expedites communications.* Executives participating in a Thought Leadership Summit on Digital Strategies concluded that a lack of trust, common terminology, and knowledge is a major obstacle to successful collaboration.[11]
2. *The company can use its own managers, who understand and are committed to carrying out its objectives.* When GE acquired a controlling interest in the Hungarian company Tungsram, it was able to expedite control and changes because it put GE managers in key positions.[12]
3. *The company can avoid protracted negotiations with another company on such matters as how each will be compensated for contributions.* The U.S. and Russian automakers GM and AvtoVAZ shut down production in their Russian joint venture while negotiating a higher price for critical components supplied by AvtoVAZ.[13]
4. *The company can avoid possible enforcement problems.* Tommy Hilfiger sued Mountain High Hosiery, manufacturer of its socks, for selling cheaply to unauthorized distributors, who cheapened the brand image.[14]

Companies may want to operate through FDI to lessen the chance of developing competitors.

Appropriability The idea of denying rivals access to resources is called the **appropriability theory.**[15] Companies are reluctant to transfer vital resources—capital, patents, trademarks, and management know-how—to another organization for fear of their competitive position being undermined. In fact, Chinese automakers—such as SAIV, Dongfeng, and Changan—that have collaborative arrangements with major global auto competitors—such as GM, Volkswagen, Nissan, and Ford—make no secret of their desire to learn from their partners so as to become global competitors in their own right.[16] Nevertheless, companies are less concerned about appropriability in countries they perceive as having a strong rule of law.[17] At the same time, they are less concerned about appropriability of non-strategic than of strategic resources. For instance, Coca-Cola, which is committed to a variety of collaborative operating forms with partners all over the world, steadfastly refuses to collaborate in the production of its concentrate. The formula is simply too critical to the company's competitive viability.

Freedom to Pursue a Global Strategy A company that has a wholly owned foreign operation may find it easier to allow the operation to participate in a global strategy. For instance, a U.S. company that owns 100 percent of its Brazilian operation might be able to take actions that, although sub-optimizing Brazilian performance, could deal more effectively with actual or potential competitors and customers globally, such as by decreasing prices to an industrial customer in Brazil to gain that customer's business in Germany. Or it might standardize its product to gain global cost savings even though this might result in some lost sales in Brazil. But if the company shared ownership in Brazil, either action might be detrimental to the Brazilian owners, who would balk at such practices.

ACQUISITION VERSUS GREENFIELD

FDI ownership takes place by transferring abroad financial and/or other tangible or intangible assets. Firms have two ways to use these assets to invest in a foreign country: either acquire an interest in an existing operation or make a greenfield investment. The reasons for each are below.

Acquisition Whether a company makes a direct investment by acquisition or start-up depends, of course, on which companies are available for purchase and at what terms.

The advantages of acquiring an existing operation include
- adding no further capacity to the market,
- avoiding start-up problems,
- making financing easier at times.

There are many reasons for seeking acquisitions. One is to obtain some vital resource that may otherwise be slow or difficult for the investor to secure.[18] Let's say a company has knowledgeable personnel that the investor cannot easily hire at a good price on its own.[19] Or perhaps an investor could hire the personnel, but lacks experience in managing them effectively. For instance, many Russian companies have recently expanded internationally through acquisition. They have had good scientific inventions and innovative products, but many have lacked experience in managing the transformation from R&D to market success.[20] By buying a company, the buyer gets not only labor and management but also an existing organization with experience in coordinating such functions as products' development and subsequent sales.

In addition, a company may gain the goodwill, brand identification, and access to distribution that are important to marketing its products, especially if the cost and risk of breaking in a new brand are high. Recently, much Chinese investment in the United States has been by acquisition, seemingly because of Chinese companies' desire to secure well-known brand names that will help them sell.[21]

There are also financial considerations. A company depending substantially on local financing rather than on transferring capital may find local capital suppliers more willing to put money into a known ongoing operation than to invest in a less familiar foreign enterprise. A foreign firm also may merge with an existing company through an exchange of stock.

In other ways, acquisitions may reduce costs and risks—and save time. A company may be able to buy facilities, particularly those of a poorly performing operation, for less than the cost of new operations. Brazil's José Batista Sobrinho (JBS), the world's largest meat company, bought U.S. companies Swift and Pilgrim's Pride at opportunistically low prices because they were in financial trouble.[22] If an investor fears that a market does not justify added capacity, acquisition enables it to avoid the risk of depressed prices through overcapacity. Finally, by buying a company, an investor avoids start-up inefficiencies and gets an immediate cash flow rather than tying up funds during construction.

Companies may choose greenfield expansion if

- no desired company is available for acquisition,
- acquisition will lead to carryover problems,
- acquisition is harder to finance.

Making Greenfield Investments Although acquisitions offer advantages, foreign companies may opt for greenfield investments if they face local roadblocks. For example, local governments may prevent acquisitions because they want more competitors in the market and fear market dominance by a single foreign enterprise. In addition, a foreign company may find local financing easier to obtain from development banks if it builds facilities because of being able to show that it is creating employment. Finally, companies frequently invest in sectors where there are few, if any, companies operating in their lines of business.

Even if acquisitions are available, they often don't succeed.[23] First, turning around a poorly performing operation is difficult because of potential personnel and labor relations problems, ill will toward its products and brands, and inefficient or poorly located facilities. Second, managers in the acquiring and acquired companies may not work well together because of different management styles and organizational cultures or because of conflicts over decision-making authority.[24] For instance, after acquiring IBM's PC division, Lenova had to overcome cultural differences between its Chinese and U.S. managers; e.g. the former thought the Americans talked without listening even when they had nothing to say, and the latter balked at mandatory exercise breaks and the public shaming of latecomers to meetings.[25] Nevertheless, there is some evidence that acquiring firms' success increases with more international acquisition experience.[26] Intuition tells us that acquisitions in more culturally distant countries would perform less well than those in more culturally similar countries; however, evidence shows the contrary, likely due to a combination of factors: organizational gains from added diversity, greater care in selection in dissimilar countries (particularly to get a better match between organizational cultures), and less of an attempt to integrate these operations into the corporate culture.[27]

Leasing We saw in our opening case that Meliá began by leasing a hotel in Majorca, and it has since used this operating mode extensively. This mode is much like an acquisition, but one that forgoes the need to invest. While common in the hospitality industry, it is not common in others. Although companies in other industries might lease certain assets abroad—computers, vehicles, buildings—such arrangements are quite different from leasing an entire operating facility.

WHY COMPANIES COLLABORATE

Companies collaborate (use alliances that are often called *strategic alliances*) abroad for much the same reasons they do domestically. In our opening case, we saw that Melía gains revenue by managing hotels both domestically and internationally. However, there are other reasons for collaborating abroad. For example, Melía's motive to collaborate with Jin Jiang is to learn more about the nuances of the Chinese market. Figure 15.5 shows both the general and internationally specific reasons for collaborative arrangements.

CONCEPT CHECK

We introduce the idea of the value chain in Chapter 12, where we explain how a company configures its global value chain by organizing a series of both primary and secondary activities—activities that naturally include the operations of its overseas partners. Needless to say, its global alliances must accommodate the structure of each firm's value chain.

ALLIANCE TYPES

Different terms are used to describe alliances based on their objectives and where they fit in a firm's value chain. In terms of objectives, *scale alliances* aim to provide efficiency by pooling similar assets so that partners can carry out business activities in which they already have experience. In our ending case on the oneworld alliance, airlines have gained economies by combining their lounges. *Link alliances* use complementary resources so that participating companies can expand into new business areas.[28] Nokia, once a producer of such products as toilet paper and rubber boots, has used a network of collaborators to develop and market cellular phones.[29] An example of a *vertical alliance* is the link between a food franchiser with

FIGURE 15.5 Collaborative Arrangements and International Objectives

A company may enter into an international collaborative arrangement for the same reasons that it does so domestically (e.g., to spread costs). In other cases, it may enter into a collaborative arrangement to meet objectives that are specific to its foreign-expansion strategies (e.g., to diversify geographically).

OBJECTIVES OF INTERNATIONAL BUSINESS
- Sales expansion
- Resource acquisition
- Risk minimization

MOTIVES FOR COLLABORATIVE ARRANGEMENTS

General
- Spread and reduce costs
- Specialize in competencies
- Avoid or counter competition
- Secure vertical and horizontal links
- Learn from other companies

MOTIVES FOR COLLABORATIVE ARRANGEMENTS

Specific to International Business
- Gain location-specific assets
- Overcome legal constraints
- Diversify geographically
- Minimize exposure in risky environments

a franchisee because they each operate in a different segment of the value chain. An example of a *horizontal alliance* is the joint venture between GM and Toyota because each partner extends its product offerings on the same level of the value chain.[30] *Coopetition*, such as the GM-Toyota example, refers to collaboration between competing firms.

GENERAL MOTIVES FOR COLLABORATIVE ARRANGEMENTS

Why do companies collaborate in either domestic or foreign operations? As explained in this section, reasons include spreading and reducing costs, the ability to specialize in their competencies, avoiding competition, securing vertical and horizontal links, and gaining knowledge.

Sometimes it's cheaper to get another company to handle work, especially
- at small volume.
- when the other company has excess capacity.

To Spread and Reduce Costs To produce or sell abroad, a company must incur certain fixed costs. At a small volume of business, contracting to a specialist rather than self-handling may be cheaper because a specialist can spread the fixed costs to more than one company. If business increases enough, the contracting company may then be able to handle the business more cheaply itself.

A company with excess production or sales capacity can use that excess to handle the activities for a client company. This may lower its average costs by covering its fixed costs more fully, and can prevent the client from having to incur fixed costs and longer delays for start-up and receipt of cash flows.

Individual companies may lack the resources to"go it alone"—especially small and young ones.[31] By pooling their efforts, they may be able to undertake activities that otherwise would be beyond their means. But large companies may also benefit when the cost of development and/or investment is very high. Disney's theme park in Hong Kong cost so much to develop that Disney and the Hong Kong government share ownership and expenses.[32]

One of the fastest-growth areas for collaborative arrangements has been in industries with projects too large, both in capital and technical-resource needs, for any single firm to handle, such as new aircraft and communication systems. From such an arrangement's inception, different firms (sometimes from different countries) agree to take on the high cost and high risk of development work for different components needed in the final product.

Then a lead company buys the components from the companies that did parts of the development work. A good example of this is the Boeing 787 aircraft, which involves component development and production by companies from around the globe.

Granting another company rights to an asset can yield a return on a product that does not fit the company's strategic priority based on its best competencies.

To Specialize in Competencies The **resource-based view** of the firm holds that each company has a unique combination of competencies. A company may seek to improve its performance by concentrating on those activities that best fit its competencies, depending on other firms to supply it with products, services, or support activities in which it is less competent. This concentration may lead to horizontal or vertical collaboration. However, a collaborative arrangement has a limited time frame, which may allow a company to exploit a particular product, asset, or technology itself at a later date if its core competencies change.

To Avoid or Counter Competition When markets are not large enough to accommodate many competitors, companies may band together so as not to compete. Companies may also combine resources to combat competitors, such as Sony and Samsung did to move faster in the development of LCD technology.[33] Or they may simply collude to raise everyone's profits. For example, Canpotex is made up of a group of Canadian companies that joined together rather than compete with each other to sell potash outside the United States and Canada: the group accounts for more than a quarter of the product's world market.[34] Only a few countries take substantial actions against the collusion of competitors.[35]

To Secure Vertical and Horizontal Links Potential cost savings and supply assurances can be attained through vertical integration. However, companies may lack the competence or resources necessary to own and manage the full value chain of activities. A study of small and medium-sized Argentine furniture manufacturers showed that they gained from both vertical and horizontal alliances. By allying horizontally, they pooled resources to gain manufacturing efficiencies and were able to deal more effectively in vertical alliances to access global markets and gain supplies.[36]

Horizontal links may provide economies of scope in distribution, such as by having a full line of products to sell, thereby increasing the sales per fixed cost of a visit to potential customers. For example, in many parts of the world Avon representatives market such products as books and crayons in addition to the company's usual fare to gain economies of scope.

To Gain Knowledge Many companies pursue collaborative arrangements to learn about a partner's technology, operating methods, or home market so that their own competencies will broaden or deepen, making them more competitive in the future.[37] An example is Chinese authorities allowing foreign companies to tap the Chinese market in exchange for their transference of technology. Sometimes each partner can learn from the other, a motive driving joint ventures between U.S. and European winemakers—such as the Opus One Winery owned by Constellation Brands' Robert Mondavi from the United States and Baron Philippe de Rothschild from France.[38]

INTERNATIONAL MOTIVES FOR COLLABORATIVE ARRANGEMENTS

In this section, we continue discussing why companies enter into collaborative arrangements, covering those reasons that apply only to international operations. Specifically, the reasons are to gain location-specific assets, overcome legal constraints, diversify geographically, and minimize risk exposure.

To Gain Location-Specific Assets Cultural, political, competitive, and economic differences among countries create barriers for firms abroad. Those ill-equipped to handle these differences may seek collaboration with local firms that will help them. When Walmart first tried to enter the Japanese market on its own, it gave up after having disappointing sales. It has since returned with a Japanese partner, Seiyu, which is more familiar with Japanese tastes and rules for opening new stores.[39] In fact, most foreign companies in Japan need to collaborate with Japanese firms that can help in securing distribution and a competent workforce—two assets that are difficult for MNEs to gain on their own there.

In addition to having a local partner advise and handle cross-national differences, a collaboration may facilitate international companies' learning about these differences. However, there is some danger that they assume wrongly that they can apply this learning effectively when entering subsequent countries—even those that appear to be similar to their previous entries.[40]

CRN Case Review Note

To Overcome Governmental Constraints Recall that in centrally planned economies (e.g., China and Cuba) Meliá cannot own its hotels, so it must collaborate with local organizations. Though centrally planned economies are very restrictive, virtually all countries limit foreign ownership in some sectors. India and Russia exemplify countries that are particularly restrictive in that they set maximum foreign percentage ownership in an array of industries.[41] They also usually require lengthy negotiations with governments to determine the operating terms; a savvy local partner can help in this regard. Our ending case on the airline passenger industry demonstrates that international collaboration has become very important, partly because, with few exceptions, governments allow only domestically owned airlines to carry passengers on domestic routes.

Legal factors may be
- direct prohibitions against certain operating forms.
- indirect (e.g., regulations affecting profitability).

Government procurement is another area that may encourage companies to collaborate because preference is often given to bids that include national companies or foreign firms that provide evidence that they will transfer technology to a local company so that it becomes more internationally competitive in the future. Taiwan does this with purchases by the state enterprise monopoly, Taiwan Power (Tai Power).[42]

Collaboration hinders nonassociated companies from pirating the asset.

Protecting Assets Many countries provide little de facto protection for intellectual property rights such as trademarks, patents, and copyrights unless authorities are prodded consistently. To prevent pirating of these proprietary assets, companies sometimes make collaborative agreements with local companies, which then monitor the market so that no one else uses the asset locally.

CONCEPT CHECK

In discussing a firm's allocation of operational emphasis among countries in Chapter 13, we consider the factors that contribute favorably to a geographic diversification strategy: growth rate, sales stability, and program-control requirements are low in each market; competitive lead time is short; and spillover effects among markets are high.

In addition, some countries provide protection only if the internationally registered asset is exploited locally within a specified period. If not, then whatever entity first does so gains the right to it. Burger King must sell under the Hungry Jack brand in Australia for this reason.[43] Thus, companies may need to follow a geographic diversification strategy to protect assets; doing so may necessitate collaboration to enter multiple markets quickly.

In other cases, local citizens, known as *trademark squatters*, register rights to the unused trademarks, then negotiate sales to the original owners when they do try to enter the market. One Russian company registered over 300 foreign trademarks, including Starbucks's trademark. Foreign companies then had to pay to regain their rights or go through lengthy and potentially expensive court proceedings.[44]

To Diversify Geographically For a company wishing to pursue a geographic diversification strategy, collaborative arrangements offer a faster initial means of entering multiple markets because other companies contribute resources. However, the arrangements will be less appealing for companies whose activities are already widely extended or for those that have ample resources for such extension.

Collaborative arrangements allow for greater spreading of assets among countries.

To Minimize Risk Exposure Companies worry that political or economic changes will affect the safety of assets and earnings in their foreign operations. One way to minimize loss from foreign political occurrences is to minimize the base of assets located abroad—or share them. A government may be less willing to move against a shared operation for fear of encountering opposition from multiple companies, especially if they are from different countries and can potentially elicit support from their home governments. Another way to spread risk is to place operations in a number of different countries, which firms may be unable to afford alone. This strategy reduces the chance that all foreign assets will encounter adversity at the same time.

TYPES OF COLLABORATIVE ARRANGEMENTS

The higher managers' perception of the risk of being in a foreign market, the greater their desire to form collaborative arrangements in that market.

The forms of foreign operations differ in the amount of resources a company commits and the proportion of the resources located abroad. Licensing, for instance, may result in a lower additional capital commitment than a foreign joint venture will. Exporting commits fewer resources abroad than does FDI.

Throughout this discussion, keep in mind that there are *trade-offs*. A decision, let's say, to take no ownership in foreign production, such as by licensing to a foreign company, may reduce exposure to political risk. However, learning about that environment will be slow, delaying (perhaps permanently) the ability to reap the full profits from producing and selling the product abroad.

Companies have a wider choice of operating form when there is less likelihood of competition.

Furthermore, when a company has a desired, unique, difficult-to-duplicate resource, it is in a good position to choose the operating form it would most like to use and to increase its compensation from the arrangement. When it lacks this bargaining strength, competition or governmental actions may force it to settle on a form that is lower on its priority list.

A further constraint is finding a desirable collaboration partner. For example, if the collaboration includes a transfer of technology, it may be impossible to find a local company familiar enough with the technology or having sufficiently similar values and priorities as the company making the transfer.[45] In effect, costs are associated with transferring technology to another entity, which include the time spent in cooperating to ensure that partners are trustworthy and cognizant of technologies and that they agree on objectives and means of implementing practices.[46]

SOME CONSIDERATIONS IN COLLABORATIVE ARRANGEMENTS

Some factors influencing companies' choice of arrangement type are their desire for control over foreign operations, prior foreign expansion, and expected compensation in one versus another.

Control The more a company depends on collaboration, the more likely it is to lose decision-making control, such as on quality, new-product direction, and expansion. This is because each partner favors its own performance and has its own objectives, which necessitates compromises.

Prior Company Expansion When a company already has operations (especially wholly owned ones) in place in a foreign country, some of the advantages of collaboration are no longer as important. It knows how to operate within that country and may have excess plant or human resource capacity it can use for new production or sales.

However, much depends on the compatibility between existing foreign operations and the new ones the company is planning abroad. If there is similarity, as with production of a new type of office equipment already made there, the new production will likely be handled internally. If product, function, or location is dissimilar, collaborating with an experienced company may be more advantageous.

Internal handling of foreign operations usually means more control and no sharing of profits.

Compensation Collaboration also implies sharing revenues and knowledge—an important consideration when profit potentials are high. Although there is a need to share revenue when collaborating, how to divide the revenue is not clear-cut because many variables influence the outcome. Certainly, the bargaining power of the collaborative partners is important in any agreement, but such factors as government mandates, partners' perception of risk, and competitive constraints are all important.[47] Further, the mode of collaboration guides normal practices. As we discuss the different modes, we will introduce some of these practices.

Point

Should Countries Limit Foreign Control of Key Industries?

Point **Yes** I believe they should, because a key industry affects a very large segment of the economy by virtue of its size or influence on other sectors. I'm not talking about either foreign control of small investments or non-controlling interest in large investments. If countries need foreign firms' resources—technology, capital, export markets, branded products, and so on—they can get them through collaborations without ceding control to foreigners. In turn, the foreign companies can still achieve their objectives, such as gaining access to markets.

Of course, each country should—and does—determine for itself what a key industry is. Mexico limits foreign control in its oil industry because it is such a dominant part of the Mexican economy. The United States is primarily concerned about security, so the government can halt any foreign investment that endangers national security.

The United States also prohibits foreign control of television and radio stations because they could be used as foreign propaganda instruments. It protects domestic transportation, a vital sector for national security, by prohibiting foreign control of domestic airlines and by preventing foreign airlines and ships from transporting passengers and cargo directly from one U.S. city to another.

The rationale for protecting key industries is supported by history, which shows that home governments have used powerful companies to influence policies in the foreign countries where they operate. During colonial periods, firms such as Levant and the British East India Company often acted as the political arm of their home governments.

More recently, governments, especially the United States, have pressured their companies to leave certain areas and to prohibit their subsidiaries from doing business with certain countries (Cuba, North Korea), even though the prohibition is counter to the interests of the countries where the subsidiaries were located.[48]

At the same time, some companies are so powerful that they can influence their home-country governments to intercede on their behalf. Probably the most notorious example was United Fruit Company (UFC) in so-called banana republics, which persuaded the United States to overthrow governments to protect its investments. Miguel Angel Asturias, a Nobel laureate in literature, referred to UFC's head as the "Green Pope" who "lifts a finger and a ship starts or stops. He says a word and a republic is bought. He sneezes and a president...falls....He rubs his behind on a chair and a revolution breaks out."[49]

Whenever a company is controlled from abroad, its decisions can be made there. Such control means that corporate management abroad can decide such factors as personnel staffing, export prices, and the retention and payout of profits. These decisions might cause different rates of expansion in different countries as well as possible plant closings, sometimes with subsequent employment disruption.

Finally, by withholding resources or allowing strikes, MNEs may affect other local industries adversely. In essence, the MNE looks after its global interests, which may not coincide with what is best for an operation in a given country.

Should Countries Limit Foreign Control of Key Industries?

Counterpoint

Counterpoint **No** The passionate arguments against foreign control of key industries don't convince me that such control leads to corporate decisions that are any different from those local companies would make. Nor do they convince me that limits on foreign ownership are in the best interests of people in host countries.

Certainly, companies make strategic global decisions at headquarters, but typically they depend on a good deal of local advice beforehand. Further, MNEs staff their foreign subsidiaries mainly with nationals of the countries where they operate, and these nationals make most routine decisions.

Regardless of the decision makers' or companies' nationalities, managers decide based on what they think is best for their firms' business, rather than based on some home-country or local socioeconomic agenda. At the same time, their decisions have to adhere to local laws and consider the views of their local stakeholders. Of course, MNEs sometimes make locally unpopular decisions, but so do local companies. In the meantime, governments can and do enact laws that apply to both local and international companies, and these laws can ensure that companies act in the so-called local interest.

Although preventing foreign control of key industries may be well intentioned, the resultant local control may lead to the protection of inefficient performance. Further, the key-industry argument appeals to emotions rather than reason. That's why arguments in the United States for security make little sense on close examination. Although foreign propaganda through foreign ownership of radio and television stations is the rationale for ownership restrictions, there are no such restrictions on foreign ownership of U.S. newspapers or on material appearing on the Internet. (Is this because people who read the news are presumed to be less swayed by propaganda?) The protection of U.S. domestic transportation for security reasons is a sham, just to protect the shipbuilding industry and maritime employees. For instance, U.S. merchant flagships must employ only U.S. citizens as crews because of the vulnerability to bombs on ships in U.S. waters, but foreign flag carriers regularly use U.S. ports, while foreigners can join the U.S. Navy.

The banana-republic arguments are outdated and go back to ***dependencia* theory**, which holds that emerging economies have practically no power in their dealings with MNEs.[50] More recent ***bargaining school* theory** states that the terms of a foreign investor's operations depend on how much the investor and host country need each other.[51] In effect, companies need countries because of their markets and resources, while countries need MNEs because of their technology, capital, access to foreign markets, and expertise. Through a bargaining process, they come to an agreement or contract that stipulates what the MNE can and cannot do.

I completely disagree that either countries or companies can necessarily gain the same through collaborative agreements as through FDI. Although collaborative agreements are often preferable, there are company and country advantages from foreign-controlled operations. For example, with wholly owned operations, companies are less concerned about developing competitors, so they are more willing to transfer essential and valuable technology abroad.

LICENSING

Licensing agreements may be
- exclusive or nonexclusive.
- used for patents, copyrights, trademarks, and other intangible property.

Under a licensing agreement, a company (the licensor) grants intangible property rights to another company (the licensee) to use in a specified geographic area for a specified period. In exchange, the licensee ordinarily pays a royalty to the licensor. The rights may be for an *exclusive license* (the licensor can give rights to no other company for the specified geographic area for a specified period of time) or a nonexclusive one.

The U.S. Internal Revenue Service classifies intangible property into five categories:

1. Patents, inventions, formulas, processes, designs, patterns
2. Copyrights for literary, musical, or artistic compositions
3. Trademarks, trade names, brand names
4. Franchises, licenses, contracts
5. Methods, programs, procedures, systems

Usually, the licensor is obliged to furnish sufficient information and assistance, and the licensee is obliged to exploit the rights effectively and pay compensation to the licensor.

Licensing often has an economic motive, such as the desire for faster start-up, lower costs, or access to additional resources.

Major Motives for Licensing Frequently, a new product or process may affect only part of a company's total output, and then only for a limited time. In such a situation, the company may foresee insufficient sales volume to warrant establishing its own foreign manufacturing and sales facilities. Meanwhile, it may find a licensee that can produce and sell at a low cost and within a short start-up time. In turn, the licensee's cost may be less than if it developed the new product or process on its own.

For industries in which technological changes are frequent and affect many products, companies in various countries often exchange technology or other intangible property rather than compete with each other on every product in every market—an arrangement known as **cross-licensing**. An example is Kodak (U.S.) and NEC Technology (Japan) entering a cross-licensing agreement for access to each other's patent portfolio.[52]

Payment Considerations The amount and type of payment for licensing arrangements vary, as each contract is negotiated on its own merits. For instance, the value to the licensee will be greater if potential sales are high. Potential sales depend, in turn, on such factors as the geographic scope of the sales territory, the length of time the asset will have market value, and the market experience of using the asset elsewhere.

Putting a Price on Intangible Assets Valuing partners' contributions and rewards is complex and always subject to negotiation. Companies commonly negotiate a "front-end" payment to cover technology transfer costs. Licensors of technology do this because there is usually more involved than simply transferring *explicit* knowledge, such as through publications and reports. The move requires the transfer of *tacit* knowledge, such as through engineering, consultation, and adaptation. The licensee usually bears the incurred transfer costs so that the licensor is motivated to ensure a smooth adaptation. Of course, the license of some other assets, such as copyrights or brand names, has much lower transfer costs.

Intangible assets may be old or new, obsolete or still in use at home when a company licenses it. Many companies transfer rights to assets at an early or even a developmental stage so products hit different markets simultaneously. This is important when selling to the same industrial customers in different countries and when global advertising campaigns can be effective. On one hand, a licensee may be willing to pay more for a new intangible asset because it may have a longer useful life. On the other hand, a licensee may be willing to pay less for a newer one, particularly one in the development phase, because of its uncertain market value.

Selling to Subsidiaries Although we think of licensing agreements as collaborative arrangements among unassociated companies, licensing is also common between parents and their foreign subsidiaries. One reason is that operations in a foreign country, even if 100 percent owned by the parent, are usually subsidiaries, which are legally separate companies. When a company owns less than 100 percent, a separate licensing arrangement may be a means of compensating the licensor for contributions beyond the mere investment in capital and managerial resources.

FRANCHISING

Franchising includes providing an intangible asset (usually a trademark) and continually infusing necessary assets.

Franchising is a specialized form of licensing in which the franchisor not only grants a franchisee the use of the intangible property (usually a trademark), but also operationally assists the business on a continuing basis, such as through sales promotion and training. In many cases, the franchisor provides supplies, such as the concentrate Coca-Cola sells to its bottlers. In a sense, the two parties act almost as a vertically integrated company because they are interdependent and each creates part of the product or service that ultimately reaches the consumer.

Many types of products and many countries participate in franchising.

Today, franchising is mostly associated with U.S. fast-food operations, although many international franchisors are from other countries and in many other sectors, such as Meliá's hotel franchises discussed in the opening case. To illustrate how diverse franchising can be, a Danish company, Cryos International, even franchises sperm banks in about 40 countries. It initially supplied the frozen sperm only from donors in Denmark (In 2012 more than 500 British women were artificially inseminated in Denmark), but it now uses local donors, such as in India.[53]

Franchisors once depended on trade shows and costly visits to foreign countries to promote their expansion. While such trade shows are still important (see the adjacent photo), especially for young franchising operations that are not well-known, the Internet has given companies another channel to send and receive information.

Franchise Organization A franchisor may penetrate a foreign country by dealing directly with individual franchisees or by setting up a *master franchise* and giving that organization the rights to open outlets on its own or to develop subfranchisees in the country or region. In the latter case, subfranchisees pay royalties to the master franchisee, which then remits some

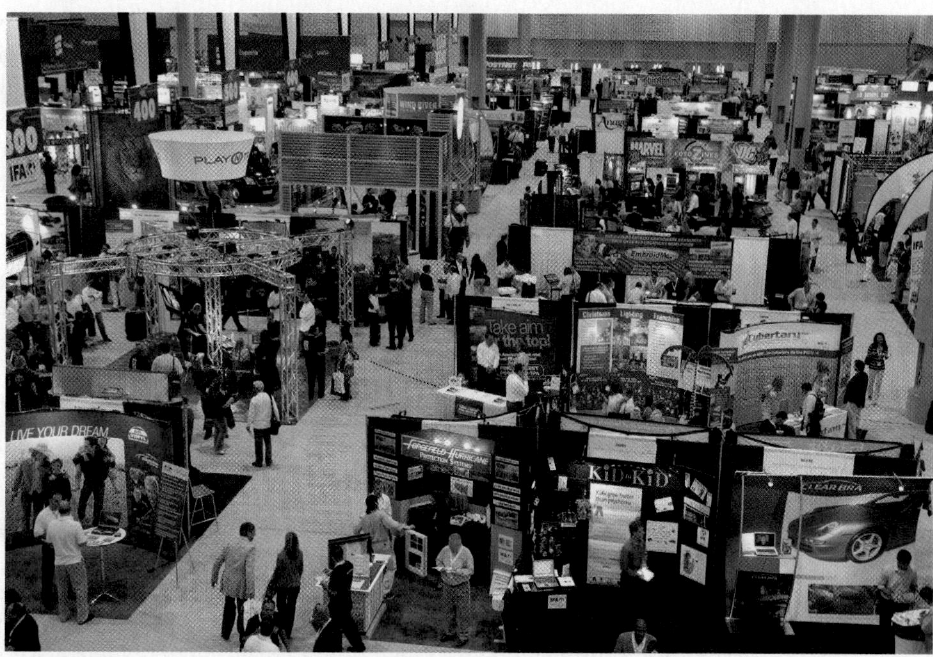

The Franchise Expo in Miami Beach (U.S.) brings franchisors and potential franchisees together.
Source: Jeff Greenberg/Alamy

predetermined percentage to the franchisor. Companies are most apt to use a master franchise system when they are not confident about evaluating potential individual franchisees and when overseeing and controlling them directly would be too expensive.[54]

If the franchisor is not well-known to many local people, or if local people are unsure about its market commitment, convincing them to make investments may be difficult. In effect, people are usually willing to invest only in known franchises because the name is a guarantee of quality that can attract customers. Therefore, if franchisors are not well-known in the foreign market they wish to enter (recall the Burger King case in Chapter 13), they may begin with some company-owned outlets that serve as a showcase to attract franchisees.

Operational Modifications Finding suppliers can add difficulties and expense for food franchisors. McDonald's, for instance, had to build a plant to make hamburger buns in the United Kingdom, while in Thailand it had to help farmers develop potato production.[55]

Franchisors face a dilemma:
- The more global standardization, the less acceptance in the foreign country.
- The more adjustment to the foreign country, the less the franchisor is needed.

Franchisors' success generally depends on three factors: product and service standardization, high identification through promotion, and effective cost controls. A dilemma when operating abroad is that the first of these may be difficult to transfer. In food franchising, for example, standardization is important so that consumers know what to expect. But when a company enters a foreign country, taste preferences may differ—even within regions of large countries. In response to such differences in China, Yum! Brands offers regionally different food in its KFC and Pizza Hut outlets.[56]

At the same time, the more adjustments made for the host consumers' different tastes, the less a franchisor has to offer a potential franchisee. U.S. food franchisors' success in Japan is mostly due to Japan's enthusiastic assimilation of Western products. Even so, food franchisors have had to make adjustments there. Pizza Hut, for instance, offers squid, oysters, and duck breast as pizza toppings.[57]

MANAGEMENT CONTRACTS

Foreign management contracts are used primarily when the foreign company can manage better than the owners.

In a foreign management contract, a company is paid a fee to transfer management personnel and administrative know-how abroad to assist a company. An organization may pay for managerial assistance when it believes another can manage its operation more efficiently than it can. This ability is most apt to occur because of industry-specific capabilities. An illustration is the British Airport Authority (BAA), which has contracts to manage some airports in the United States, Italy, and Australia because of its successful airport management skills.[58]

International management contracts diminish ownership control by foreign companies while allowing host countries to receive foreign expertise. In turn, the management company receives income without having to make a capital investment. This pattern has been important in hotel operations where hotel chains have been shying away from property ownership abroad because of risk and where some host-country property owners know more about real estate than about managing a hotel.[59] Recall the opening case whereby Meliá's demonstrated hotel management skills have attracted property owners to contract its services. At the same time, Meliá is able to expand more rapidly and to more foreign countries than if it had to contribute the capital itself.

TURNKEY OPERATIONS

Turnkey operations are
- most commonly performed by industrial-equipment, construction, and consulting companies.
- often performed for a governmental agency.

Turnkey operations are an arrangement in which one company, usually an industrial-equipment manufacturer, a construction company, or a consulting firm, contracts with another to build complete, ready-to-operate facilities. Manufacturers also sometimes provide turnkey services if they believe an investment on their own behalf is infeasible. The customer for a turnkey operation is often a governmental agency. Recently, most large projects have been in those developing countries that are moving rapidly toward infrastructure development and industrialization.

Contracting to Scale One characteristic that sets the turnkey business apart from most other international business operations is the size of many of the contracts, frequently for hundreds of millions into the billions of dollars. This means that a few very large companies—such as Vinci (France), Bechtel (U.S.), and Hochtief (Germany)—account for a significant share of the international market. The most notable change in leadership has been by Chinese firms. In 2003, none were among the world's 10 largest, but by 2012, they had five places there.[60] Often, smaller firms either serve as subcontractors for primary turnkey suppliers or specialize in a particular sector, such as the handling of hazardous waste. The following photos illustrate both the existing Panama Canal and a current large turnkey project to build an additional wider channel in order to accommodate larger ships that now must go around South America for routes between the Atlantic and Pacific Oceans. This project is being handled by a consortium of turnkey operators, led by Spain's Sacyr Vallehermoso.

Making Contacts The nature of these contracts places importance on hiring executives with top-level governmental contacts abroad, as well as on ceremony and building goodwill, such as opening a facility on a country's independence day or getting a head of state to inaugurate a facility. Although public relations is important to gain contracts, other factors—price, export financing, managerial and technological quality, experience, reputation, and so on—are necessary to sell contracts of such magnitude.

Marshaling Resources Many turnkey contracts are for construction in remote areas, necessitating massive housing construction and importation of personnel. Projects may involve building an entire infrastructure under the most adverse conditions, such as Bechtel's complex for Minera Escondida high in the Andes, so turnkey operators must have expertise in hiring people willing to work in remote areas for extended periods and in transporting and using supplies under very adverse conditions.

If a company holds a monopoly on certain assets or resources, such as the latest refining technology, other companies will find difficulty in competing to secure a turnkey contract. As the production process becomes known, however, the number of competitors for such contracts increases. Companies from developed countries have moved largely toward projects involving high technology, whereas those from such countries as China, India, Korea, and

Source: Chris Howey/Shutterstock

Source: Thinkstock

The two photos show a ship passing through the present Panama Canal and construction by a consortium of turnkey operators, led by Spain's Sacyr Vallehermosa SA, that will increase capacity and allow larger ships to pass through instead of having to sail around South America.

Turkey can compete better for conventional projects requiring low labor costs. The Chinese companies China State Construction Engineering and Shanghai Construction Group, in fact, have worked on subway systems in Iran and Saudi Arabia, a railway line in Nigeria, a tourist complex in the Bahamas, an oil pipeline in Sudan, and office buildings in the United States.

Arranging Payment Payment for a turnkey operation usually occurs in stages as a project develops, with final payment made once the facility is operating in accordance with the contract. Because currency fluctuations can occur between conception and completion, contracts commonly include price escalation clauses or cost-plus pricing.

The final payment is usually made only if the facility is operating satisfactorily, so disagreements sometimes arise on what constitutes "satisfactorily." For this reason, many turnkey operators insist on performing a feasibility study as part of the contract so they don't build something that, although desired by a local government, may be too large or inefficient.

JOINT VENTURES

Joint ventures may have various combinations of participants and ownership.

A type of operational sharing popular among MNEs is the joint venture (JV). While they are sometimes non-equity arrangements, JVs usually involve equity ownership by more than one organization. We emphasize this latter type in our discussion. Though usually formed to achieve particular objectives, JVs may continue to operate indefinitely as objectives are redefined. Thought of as 50/50 companies, JVs may nonetheless involve more than two companies, one of which may own more than 50 percent. Global Alumina, a joint venture in Guinea for bauxite extraction and processing, has four partners—two from Dubai and one each from Australia and Canada.[61] When more than two organizations participate, the venture is sometimes called a **consortium**.

Possible Combinations An international joint venture may contain any combination of partners, as long as at least one partner is foreign. Examples include:

- Two companies from the same country joining together in a foreign market, e.g., NEC and Mitsubishi (Japan) in the United Kingdom
- A foreign company joining with a local company, e.g., Great Lakes Chemical (U.S.) and A. H. Al Zamil in Saudi Arabia
- Companies from two or more countries establishing a joint venture in a third country, e.g., Tata Motors (India) and Fiat (Italy) in Argentina
- A private company and a local government forming a joint venture, or *mixed venture*, e.g., that of Gazprom (Russia) with the Bulgarian government
- A private company joining a government-owned company in a third country, e.g., BP Amoco (private British-U.S.) and Eni (government-owned Italian) in Egypt

The more companies in the joint venture, the more complex its management becomes. Development of the long-delayed Boeing 787 (the Dreamliner) was a joint effort among numerous companies from eight countries.[62] In essence, the project was hard to control, and a delay or performance hitch by any one of the participating companies delayed the others and caused overall project problems. Figure 15.6 shows that as a company increases the number of partners and decreases the amount of equity it owns in a foreign operation, its ability to control that operation decreases.

Certain types of companies favor JVs more than others, such as those new at foreign operations or having decentralized domestic decision making. Because they are accustomed to extending control downward in their organizations, it is easier for them to do the same thing in a JV.

EQUITY ALLIANCES

Equity alliances help solidify collaboration.

An **equity alliance** is a collaborative arrangement in which at least one of the companies takes an ownership position (almost always minority) in the other(s). For instance, the Port of Antwerp (Belgium) took a minority position in Essar Ports (India) when the two signed a long-term alliance to mutually improve quality and productivity.[63] In some cases, each party takes an ownership, such as by buying part of each other's shares or by swapping some shares with each other. Panama-based Copa and Colombia-based AeroRepublic (airlines) took equity in each other.[64]

The purpose of the equity ownership is to solidify a collaborating contract, such as a supplier-buyer contract, so that it is more difficult to break—particularly if the ownership is large enough to secure a board membership for the investing company.

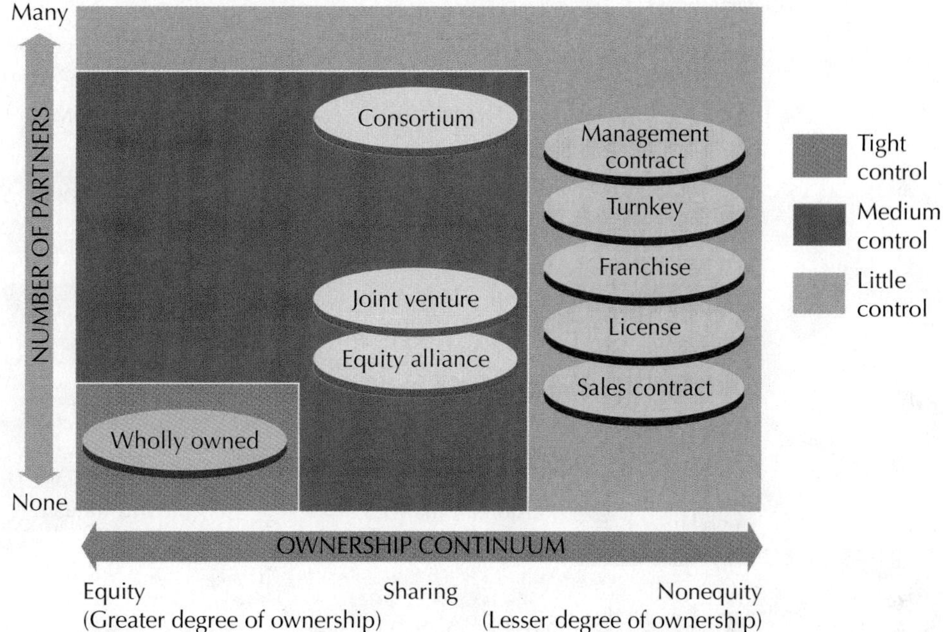

FIGURE 15.6
Collaborative Strategy and Complexity of Control

The more equity a firm puts into a collaborative arrangement, coupled with the fewer partners it takes on, the more control it will have over the foreign operations conducted under the arrangement. Note that non-equity arrangements typically entail at least one and often several partners.

Source: Based on Shaker Zahra and Galal Elhagrasey, "Strategic Management of International Joint Ventures," European Management Journal 12:1 (March 1994): 83–93. Reprinted with permission of Elsevier.

PROBLEMS WITH COLLABORATIVE ARRANGEMENTS

Keep in mind that all parties to a collaborative arrangement must be satisfied with performance. Otherwise, the arrangement may fail. Problems can develop that lead partners to renegotiate in terms of responsibilities, ownership, or management structure. Despite new relationships, many agreements break down or are not renewed at the end of an initial contract period, often because at least one partner becomes dissatisfied with the venture. Frequently, a partner buys out the other's interest and the operation continues as a wholly owned foreign subsidiary. In other breakups, companies agree to dissolve the arrangement or they restructure their alliance.

Figure 15.7 shows that joint venture divorce (and divorce from other collaborative arrangements) can be planned or unplanned, friendly or unfriendly, mutual or non-mutual. The major strains on the arrangements are due to five factors:

- Relative importance to partners
- Divergent objectives
- Control problems
- Comparative contributions and appropriations
- Differences in culture[65]

In spite of our focus on these problems, we do not mean to imply that there are no success stories. There are. The JV between Xerox (U.S.) and Rank (U.K.) is a case in point: not only has it performed well for a long period of time, it even has a JV in Japan with Fuji Photo, which has also performed well.

RELATIVE IMPORTANCE

One partner may give more management attention than the other to a collaborative arrangement. If things go wrong, the active partner blames the less active partner for its lack of attention, while the latter blames the former for making poor decisions. The difference in

FIGURE 15.7 How to Dissolve a Joint Venture

There's more than one way to dissolve a joint venture—and to influence the future of its erstwhile operations.

Source: Based on Manuel G. Serapio Jr. and Wayne F. Cascio, "End Games in International Alliances," *Academy of Management Executive* (May 1996): 67.

DIVORCE SCENARIOS	EXAMPLES
Planned	General Motors (U.S.) and Toyota (Japan)
vs.	
Unplanned	AT&T (U.S.) and Olivetti (Italy)
Friendly	Vitro (Mexico) and Corning (U.S.)
vs.	
Unfriendly	Coors Brewing Co. (U.S.) and Molson Breweries (Canada)
Mutually agreed upon	Ralston Purina (U.S.) and Taiyo Fishery (Japan)
vs.	
Disputed	Sover S.P.A. (Italy) and Suzhou Spectacles No. 1 Factory (China)

OUTCOMES	EXAMPLES
Termination by acquisition	Daewoo Motors (South Korea) and General Motors (U.S.)
Termination by dissolution	Meiji Milk (Japan) and Borden (U.S.)
Termination by reorganization/restructuring of the alliance	Matsushita Electric Industries Co. (Japan) and Solbourne Computer (U.S.)

attention may be due to the partners' different sizes. For example, a JV between a large and a small company uses a larger portion of operations for the small company than for the large one, so the small company may take more interest in the venture.

In addition, if disagreements need to be settled legally, the smaller firm may be at a disadvantage because it lacks the resources to fight its bigger partner. After Igen, a small U.S. firm, licensed its technology to Boehringer Mannheim of Germany, a company with sales of more than 100 times those of Igen, the two companies began to disagree over royalty payments. Igen fought for four years and spent $40 million in legal fees (about the amount of one year of its sales) to win a settlement of over a half billion dollars.[66] This example is unusual, however, because most small firms cannot or will not fight a larger company so effectively.

DIVERGENT OBJECTIVES

Although companies enter into collaborative arrangements because they have complementary goals and capabilities, these may evolve differently over time because one or both change as a result of competitive forces and product dynamics. Thus, a partner may no longer perceive collaboration to be in its best interest. (This is shown humorously in Figure 15.8.) For instance, IBM and Toshiba partnered until IBM's shift in product line required a type of monitor with which Toshiba had little expertise.[67] Further, one partner may want to reinvest earnings for growth while the other wants to receive dividends. Or one partner may want to expand the product line and sales territory while the other may see this as competition with its wholly owned operations (a point of disagreement between BP and its Russian partner, TNK.)[68] If one partner wants to sell or buy from the venture, the other may disagree with the price.

Partners also may differ over performance standards. GM and Fuji Heavy Industries' disagreements in Thailand over quality standards led to both of them performing time-consuming and expensive inspections that even included paint jobs.[69]

"Norman won't collaborate."

FIGURE 15.8 All parties must perceive that their objectives are best met by collaborative arrangements.

Source: Robert Weber/New Yorker Cartoon Bank/www.cartoonbank.com

QUESTIONS OF CONTROL

Sharing assets with another company may generate confusion over control, as happened when the Israeli company Remedia partnered with the German firm Humana Milchunion to make baby formula. Humana Milchunion removed Vitamin B1 from the formula concentrate without notifying its partners, which led to the deaths of three infants.[70] Moreover, when companies license their logos and trademarks for use on products they do not make, they may lack the ability to discern and control quality, with a detrimental effect on sales of all products in various countries using the brand name and logo. Pierre Cardin's licensing of its label for hundreds of products—from clothing to clocks to toilets—led to poor-quality goods that hurt the image of the high-quality ones.[71]

In collaborative arrangements, even though control is ceded to one of the partners, both may be held responsible for problems. Further, the question of control is rife with gray areas and may cause anxiety among employees. In a proposed JV between Merrill Lynch and UFJ, a Japanese senior manager queried, "Who is going to be in charge—a Japanese, an American, or both?"[72] When no single company has control of a collaborative arrangement, the operation may lack direction. At the same time, if one partner dominates, it must still consider the other's interests.

COMPARATIVE CONTRIBUTIONS AND APPROPRIATIONS

Partners' relative capabilities of contributing technology, capital, or some other asset may change over time. Relative contributions may also change when partners alter their strategy. In addition, Partner A may suspect that Partner B is taking more from the operation (particularly knowledge-based assets) than Partner A is, which would enable Partner B to become a competitor. (Recall our discussion of appropriability.) In the face of such suspicions, information may be withheld, eventually weakening the operation. There are many examples of companies "going it alone" after they no longer needed their partner—particularly if the purpose of the collaboration was to gain knowledge.

CULTURE CLASHES

Differences in Country Cultures Managers and companies alike are affected by their national cultures, and collaborative arrangements bring them directly together. For instance, they may vary in preferences in the method, timing, and frequency with which they report on project management progress.[73] Further, there are national differences in whether they evaluate primarily on the operations' effect on shareholders versus stakeholders in general.[74] These differences may mean that one partner is satisfied while the other is not. Such a clash led to the dissolution of a joint venture between Danone and its Chinese government-owned partner because the latter put employment maximization ahead of efficiencies and profits.[75]

Finally, the trust that companies have toward foreign partners is influenced by the general level of trust that exists within their home markets; some companies don't like to collaborate with those of very different cultures.[76] Nevertheless, JVs from culturally distant countries can thrive when partners learn to deal with each other's differences.[77]

Differences in Corporate Cultures Similar corporate cultures aid companies' ability to communicate and transfer knowledge to each other, whereas collaborations can experience problems when these cultures differ.[78] One partner may be accustomed to internal managerial promotions while the other opens its searches to outsiders. One may use a participatory management style and the other an authoritarian style. One may be entrepreneurial, the other risk-averse. This is why many companies delay JV collaboration until they have had long-term positive experiences with each other, such as through distributorship or licensing arrangements. In fact, there is evidence that a gradual increase in commitment, such as developing an alliance with a company before acquiring it, is a means of improving performance.[79] Of course, as with marriage, a good prior relationship between two companies does not guarantee a good match in a joint venture.[80]

MANAGING INTERNATIONAL COLLABORATIONS

The evolution to a different operating mode may

- be the result of experience.
- create organizational tensions.

As collaborative arrangements evolve, partners need to reassess certain decisions. For example, alterations in a company's resource base may render collaborations either more or less advantageous as a mode of operation. Or a country's risk and government ownership requirements may change. Finally, the relationship among partners may evolve positively or negatively. Because of such changes, a company needs to continually reexamine the fit between collaboration and its own strategy.

We now discuss the fit between the attractiveness of countries and the modes of operation, the problem of switching from one mode to another, the importance of learning from experience, and the necessity of dealing with partners.

COUNTRY ATTRACTIVENESS AND OPERATIONAL OPTIONS

Figure 15.9 illustrates a type of matrix that relates country attractiveness with operating forms. A company should ordinarily make a higher level of commitment, such as wholly owned operations, in the countries that appear in the top left corner, which are very attractive and fit best with its capabilities.

Country attractiveness is also high in the top right corner, but a company has weak competitive strength for those markets if, say, it lacks the knowledge of operating therein. If the cost is not too high, the company might attempt to gain greater domination in those markets by partnering with another whose assets are complementary.

A company might divest in countries in the bottom right corner or "harvest" by pulling out all possible cash it can generate while not replacing depreciated facilities. It could also engage in non-equity arrangements, thereby generating some income without investment outlays. In other areas, it must analyze situations individually to decide which approach to take. These are marginal areas that do not fit as neatly in the analysis.

FIGURE 15.9 Country Attractiveness/Company Strength Matrix

In a given scenario, a country in the upper left-hand corner may be the most attractive place for a company to locate operations. Why? Because its market is well suited to the company's greatest competitive strength and thus to its highest level of commitment (e.g., establishing a wholly owned subsidiary). A country in the upper right-hand corner also boasts an attractive market but poses a problem for a company whose competitive strengths don't quite match the opportunity (perhaps it has no experience in this particular market). It needn't forgo the opportunity, but it will probably prefer a joint venture or some other form of collaborative operation. Finally, note that because everything is subject to change—both a company's capabilities and the features of a country's market—firms try to be dynamic in their approach to potential operating modes.

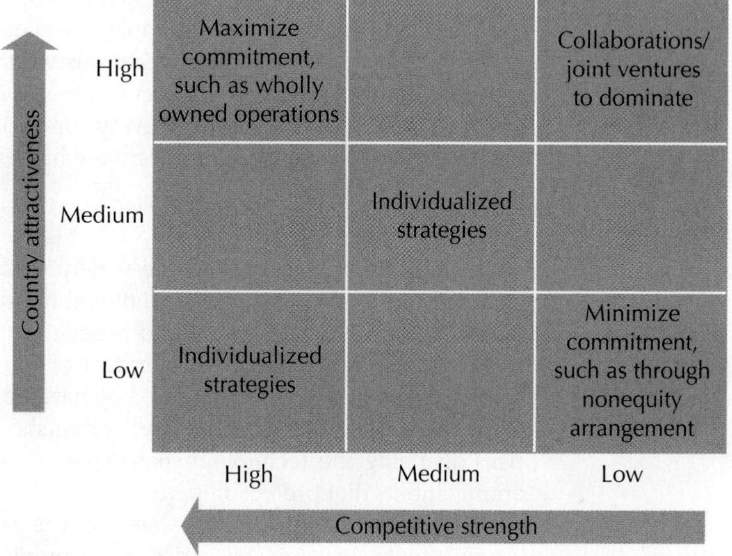

Although such a matrix may serve to guide decision making, managers must use it with caution. First, separating the attractiveness of a country from a company's position is often difficult; the country may seem attractive because it fits with the company. Second, some of the recommended actions take a defeatist attitude toward competitive position. Many companies have built competitive strength in markets previously dominated by competitors or built profitable positions without being the competitive leader.

PROBLEMS OF SWITCHING MODES

As companies switch from one mode of international operations to another, some individuals gain and others lose responsibilities. For example, moving from exporting to foreign production may reduce the size of domestic marketing and manufacturing divisions, thus disadvantaging those people who lost responsibilities if bonuses and promotions are based largely on the size of their sales or profits. Given that lower performance is due to decisions outside their control, companies will need to revise performance evaluations.

LEARNING FROM EXPERIENCE

Some evidence indicates that as companies gain experience by entering more collaborative arrangements, they perform better within them. However, improved performance is most associated with similar types of collaborations, such as JVs, from one place to another and with management approaches that are similar in a series of alliances.[81] In essence, companies may choose partners better and learn how to improve synergies between their partners and themselves. At the same time, effective alliance management has been undergoing significant changes; thus, companies cannot necessarily replicate what has succeeded for them in the past.[82]

DEALING WITH PARTNERS

Finding and Evaluating Potential Partners Whether a company seeks a collaborative partner or reacts to a request for partnership, it must evaluate the potential partner's resources, motivation, and compatibility.

Managers can identify potential partners by monitoring journals, attending technical conferences, developing links with academic institutions—even through social acquaintances.[83] Company visibility and partnership potential can be boosted through trade fairs, brochures, Web sites, and contacts in the potential collaboration locale.

The proven ability to handle similar types of collaboration is a key professional qualification. A good track record may indicate trustworthiness that could negate the need for expensive control mechanisms to carry out interests. Once into a collaboration, partners can also build trust through actions.[84] But every company has to start somewhere. Without a proven track record, a firm may have to negotiate harder and make more concessions.

In technology agreements,

- a seller does not want to give information without assurance of payment.
- a buyer does not want to pay without evaluating information.

Negotiating the Arrangement: The Question of Secrecy The value of many technologies would diminish if they were widely used or understood. Contracts historically have included provisions that the recipient will not divulge such information, while some sellers have held onto the ownership and production of specific components so recipients would not have full knowledge of the product or the capability to produce an exact copy. Often companies want to sell techniques they have not yet used commercially. A buyer is reluctant to buy what it has not seen, but a seller that shows the work in process to the potential buyer risks divulging the technology. For these and other reasons, it is common to set up pre-arrangements that protect all parties.

A controversial negotiation area is the secrecy surrounding the financial terms of arrangements. In some countries, for example, licensing contracts must be approved by governmental agencies, which consult their counterparts in other countries about similar agreements in order to improve their negotiating position. Many MNEs object to this procedure, believing that contract terms between two companies are proprietary information with competitive importance, and market conditions usually dictate the need for very different terms in different countries.

CONCEPT CHECK

In discussing "Behavioral Factors" with regard to international business in Chapter 2, we observe that there are substantial differences in the degrees of trust that people in different cultures extend to others. We go on to explain that when trust is high, managers tend to spend more time focusing on operational issues and less fussing over every little detail. Not surprisingly, the cost of doing business tends to be lower in this scenario.

Controlling Through Contracts and Trust Contracts with other companies entail some loss of control over the asset or intangible property being transferred. This creates two concerns that are not necessarily analogous—the partner's performance competency and the partner's integrity so as not to act opportunistically.[85] Choice of partner is, of course, important. Additionally, a host of potential problems must be settled as well as possible by setting mutual goals and spelling out all expectations in the contract. Of course, not everything can be included in a contract. The parties need to develop sufficient rapport so that common sense also plays a part in running the collaboration.[86] Partnering with a firm that highly values its reputation is probably a plus as well, inasmuch as it may prefer to settle differences quietly rather than having them exposed in the press. Frank communications may help determine potential partners' underlying expectations, which may otherwise come as a surprise. One study of local firms in China and Russia discovered that they had expected their foreign partners to deal much more with the Chinese and Russian governments (such as to alleviate bribery payments) than the foreign partners actually did.[87]

Although contracts have limits, their provisions should at least address the following issues:

- Will the agreement be terminated if the parties don't adhere to the directives?
- What methods will be used to test for quality?
- What geographic limitations should be placed on an asset's use?
- Which company will manage which parts of the operation outlined in the agreement?
- What will be each company's future commitments?

- How will each company buy from, sell to, or otherwise use intangible assets that result from the collaborative arrangement?
- How will revenues be divided?

In addition to contract terms, trust in the management of another company must be considered in choosing a partner. At the same time, trust is affected by national culture and, in turn, influences how much a partner wants to cover in a contract. Thus, if parties from cultures with similar levels of trust come together, they can more likely agree on what must be incorporated in detailed contractual arrangements and what must be left to trust.[88]

When collaborating with another company, managers must

- Continue to monitor performance,
- Assess whether to change the form of operations,
- Develop competency in managing a portfolio of arrangements.

Improving Performance Contracting with a capable and compatible partner is necessary but insufficient to ensure success. An agreement, once operational, must be run effectively. Management should estimate potential sales and costs, determine whether the arrangement is meeting quality standards, and assess servicing requirements to check whether goals are being met and whether each partner is doing an adequate job.

In addition to continually assessing partners' performance, a company must periodically assess the need for change in the type of collaboration, such as whether to replace a licensing agreement with a joint venture. At the same time, as its number of collaborations grows, it should consider developing competency in managing the portfolio of arrangements so that it applies what it learns in one situation to others.[89]

Looking to the Future
Why Innovation Breeds Collaboration

More than a half century ago, John Kenneth Galbraith wrote that the era of cheap invention was over, noting that "because development is costly, it follows that it can be carried out only by a firm that has the resources associated with considerable size."[90] The statement seems prophetic in terms of the estimated billions of investment dollars needed to bring a new commercial aircraft to market, eliminate death from diseases, develop defenses against unfriendly countries and terrorists, guard against cyberspace intrusions, and commercialize energy substitutes for petroleum. However, it overlooks the ability of companies to pool resources through collaboration—and that such collaboration will likely continue to grow.

Markets must be truly global if high development costs are to be recouped. The sums needed to develop and market solutions to major global problems are out of reach of most companies acting alone. Even if the companies grow ever larger through internal growth or mergers and acquisitions, governments nevertheless place limits because of antitrust concerns.

Moreover, with the realization that the costs of integrating a merged or acquired company can be very high, collaborative arrangements will likely become even more important in the future, involving both horizontal and vertical linkages among firms from many industries in many countries. However, some evidence indicates that collaborations slow the speed of innovation because of internalization and appropriation factors.[91] At the same time, although business strategists have advised companies for some time to specialize on what they do best, there is growing evidence that many customers prefer to deal with one rather than multiple suppliers. The result, especially in emerging economies, may be the return in popularity of conglomerates.[92] Thus, large companies that have the resources to go it alone may have advantages over small companies that do not.

Although some product development requires huge sums, most is much more modest. Nevertheless, companies lack all the product- and market-specific resources to go it alone everywhere in the world, especially if national differences dictate operating changes on a country-to-country basis. Such situations present opportunities for alliances that employ complementary resources from different companies.

Collaborative arrangements will bring both opportunities and problems as MNEs move simultaneously to new countries and to contractual arrangements with new companies. Differences must be overcome in a number of areas:

- Country cultures that may cause partners to obtain and evaluate information differently
- National disparities in governmental policies, institutions, and industry structures that constrain companies from using operating forms they would prefer
- Distinct underlying ideologies and values affecting corporate cultures and practices that strain relationships
- Different strategic directions resulting from partners' interests that cause disagreement over objectives and contributions
- Diverse management styles and organizational structures that cause partners to interact ineffectively[93]

The more partners in an alliance, the more cumbersome the decision-making and control processes. ■

CASE The oneworld Airline Alliance

Following approval by U.S. and Japanese authorities for antitrust immunity, American Airlines (AA) and Japan Airlines (JAL) began sharing routes in 2011 that connect mainland North America with East Asia through a non-equity joint venture.[94] Map 15.2 shows these routes and also illustrates that flights between Honolulu and Japan are not included in the agreement. This JV is similar to one forged among AA, British Airways (BA), and Iberia for trans-Atlantic travel that began operating in 2010. In both cases, the agreements allow representatives from each airline to jointly manage capacity, sell and promote space on flights operated by each other, divide revenues, and schedule connecting flights. The major thrusts for these ventures are to cut operating costs by better controlling capacity, to avoid disruptive price competition, and to improve scheduling so that there are more and better departure times and connections for passengers.

The proposals are merely extensions to a historical series of alliances linking international airlines. In fact, the airline industry is unique in that its need to form collaborative arrangements has been important almost from the start of international air travel because of regulatory, cost, and competitive factors. In recent years, this need has accelerated because of airlines' difficult profit performance.

In effect, the airlines have been squeezed. First, costs have risen, particularly due to oil prices and the need for greater security since 9/11. While pre-departure airport passenger-security checks are well publicized, some other costly airline security processes are not, such as providing governmental agencies with advance passenger information and working with freight forwarders and supply-chain operators to ensure the safety of cargo shipments carried on passenger aircraft. Second, a long-term trend toward greater price competition hinders airlines' ability to pass on increased costs to passengers—a situation exacerbated by the emergence of discount airlines and customers' ability to search the Internet for lower fares. Third, with the global recession curtailing passenger demand the airline industry has added capacity sparingly. Although the growth in international passenger jet travel has largely spurred globalization, no airline has sufficient finances or aircraft to serve the whole world. Yet passengers are traveling the whole world and perceive an advantage in booking on airline connections that will minimize both distances and connecting times at airports while offering reasonable assurance of reaching destinations with checked luggage more or

MAP 15.2 American Airlines and Japan Airlines: Trans-Pacific Routes

Note that the joint activity involves only flights from mainland North America into East Asia.

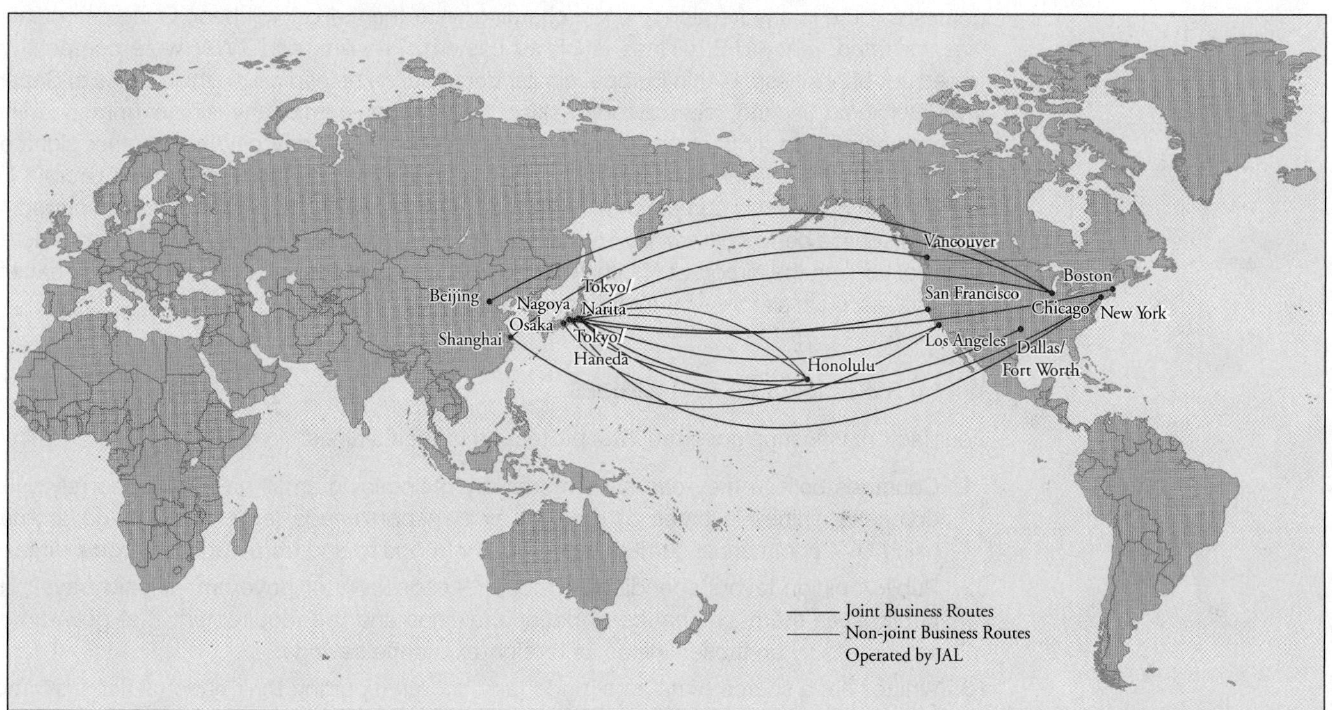

less on schedule. Thus, airlines have increasingly worked together to provide more seamless experiences for passengers and to cut costs.

This discussion, however, should not imply that all cost cuts necessitate collaboration. For example, in recent years, airlines have implemented a number of cost-saving changes that cover the gamut from ticket purchase to arrival at destination. Online purchases of electronic tickets have largely replaced airlines' need to pay hefty commissions to travel agencies and to issue and maintain costly inventories of paper tickets. Self-service check-in at airports reduces the need for agents. On board, especially on short flights, less is included in the price of the ticket, such as food, pillows, and headphones. In fact, the trip may be on one of the airlines' discount subsidiaries.

A Bit of History: Changing Government Regulations

Historically, governments played a major role in airline ownership. Many government-owned airlines were monopolies within their domestic markets, money losers, and recipients of government subsidies. However, there has been a subsequent move toward privatization.

What Governments Can Regulate

Despite the move toward privatization, governments still regulate airlines and agree on restrictions and rights largely through reciprocal agreements. Specifically, they control:

- Which foreign carriers have landing rights
- Which airports and aircraft the carriers can use
- The frequency of flights
- Whether foreign carriers can fly beyond the country (for instance, whether Iberia, after flying from Spain to the United States, can then fly from the United States to Panama)
- Overflight privileges
- Fares airlines can charge

Several notable regulatory changes have occurred in recent years. First, the U.S. domestic market has been deregulated, which means that any approved U.S. carrier can fly any U.S. domestic route in any frequency while charging what the market will bear. Once deregulation was instituted, many U.S. airlines (such as Eastern, Pan Am, and TWA) were competitively forced out of business. Within Europe, similar deregulation helped cause the demise of Sabena from Belgium. Second, several open-skies agreements permit any airline from countries in an agreement to fly from any city in one signatory area to any city in the other signatory area. Further, these flights have no restrictions on capacity, frequency, or type of aircraft. For instance, an open-skies agreement in 2010 between the United States and Japan spurred AA to begin service between New York and Haneda International Airport, which is closer to downtown Tokyo than the airport at Narita. Third, European countries have permitted cross-national acquisitions, such as those by Air France of KLM and Lufthansa of Swissair.

Why Governments Protect Airlines

Four factors influence governments' protection of their airlines:

1. Countries believe they can save money by maintaining small air forces and relying on domestic airlines in times of unusual air transport needs (e.g., the U.S. government using U.S. commercial carriers to help carry troops to and from Iraq and Afghanistan).
2. Public opinion favors spending "at home"—especially for government-paid travel. The public sees the maintenance of national airlines and the requirement that government employees fly on those airlines as foreign-exchange savings.
3. Airlines are a source of national pride, and aircraft (sporting their national flags) symbolize a country's sovereignty and technical competence. This national identification is less important than it used to be, but it is still important in some developing countries.
4. Worries about protecting airspace for security reasons are less of a concern today because foreign carriers routinely overfly a country's territory to reach inland gateways, such as JAL's flights between Tokyo and Chicago. Further, overflight treaties are quite common, even among unfriendly nations (e.g., Cubana overflies the United States en route to Canada, and AA overflies Cuba en route to South America).

Regulatory Obstacles to Expansion

Even if airlines had the financial capacity to expand everywhere in the world, national regulations would limit this expansion. With few exceptions, airlines cannot fly on lucrative domestic routes in foreign countries. For example, JAL cannot compete on the New York to Los Angeles route, nor can AA fly between Tokyo and Nagoya. Further, the U.S. government limits foreign ownership in a U.S. airline to 25 percent of voting stock.

Thus, airlines cannot easily control a flight network abroad that will feed passengers into their international flights. JAL has no U.S. domestic flights to take passengers into Chicago for connections to Tokyo, while AA has scores of such flights. However, JAL does have an advantage within Japan.

Finally, airlines usually cannot service pairs of foreign countries. AA cannot fly between Brazil and South Africa because those governments give landing rights on such routes only to Brazilian and South African airlines. To avoid these restrictions, airlines must ally themselves with carriers from other countries.

Collaboration Examples Related to Motives

Cost Factors

Certain airlines have always dominated certain international airports, thereby amassing critical capabilities in them, such as baggage handlers and aircraft-handling equipment. Sharing these capabilities with other airlines may spread costs. For example, BA has long handled passenger check-in, baggage loading, and maintenance for a number of other airlines at London's Heathrow Airport.

The high cost of maintenance and reservations systems has led to JVs involving multiple airlines from multiple countries, such as ownership in the Apollo and Galileo reservation systems. Actually, the reservations systems are motivated by more than cost savings, inasmuch as the pooling of resources provides customers with better service.

Connecting Flights

Given that governments restrict domestic or regional routes to their own carriers, airlines have long had agreements whereby passengers can transfer from one to another with a through ticket. However, people tend to select from among the first routings that show up on computer screens, and routings from one airline to another often appear on screens after those involving only one airline. Further, when passengers see that they must change airlines, they worry more about making those connections across great distances within ever-larger airports. To help avoid this worry, airlines have agreed to code sharing—a procedure whereby the same flight may have a designation for more than one carrier. For instance, the same flight operated by BA from New York-JFK to London Heathrow is listed as AA 142, BA 1507, and Iberia 4240. Hence, AA passengers originating in, say, Tampa and connecting at JFK to Heathrow may worry less about the JFK connection because they see themselves on the same airline all the way. However, they may still need to go from one terminal to another to make the plane-change. In such a situation, airlines must adhere to a longer minimum connecting time when showing a through/connecting flight.

The oneworld Alliance

The oneworld Alliance comprises 12 airlines: airberlin, American Airlines, British Airways, Cathay Pacific, Finnair, Iberia, Japan Airlines, LAN, Malaysian Airlines, Qantas, Royal Jordanian, and S7 Airlines. (The adjacent photo shows several of these parked alongside each other at Tokyo's Narita Airport.) oneworld competes largely with two other alliances: Star and SkyTeam. Airlines in these alliances cooperate on various programs, such as allowing passengers to earn credits for free or upgraded travel on any one of them. In the case of oneworld, all members flying into Narita Airport in Tokyo have moved into terminal 2, which shortens legal connecting times among them. They also advertise their affiliation; you may have seen aircraft painted with the airline's name and logo along with the oneworld name. These alliances allow for considerable cooperation, such as code-sharing; however, antitrust regulations (unless given immunity) prohibit their members from coordinating routes, schedules, and prices.

The Trans-Atlantic Joint Venture

Three airlines—AA, BA, and Iberia—have a combined network of over 400 destinations in over 100 countries and account for more than 6,000 daily departures. When their JV and antitrust immunity were approved, they collectively had 48 different routes between Europe and North America that included 22 North American and 13 European cities. Of these 48 routes, they competed directly on only nine.

In the short time since the airlines entered this JV, they have been able to coordinate schedules better for the convenience of passengers. For instance, whereas AA and BA used to have flights leaving between New York-JKF and London-Heathrow within minutes of each other, they now operate 16 flights per day between those two airports and have been able to coordinate departure times so that the flights leave approximately one hour apart. This gives passengers more options in finding a departure time convenient to them and allows for more connecting flight alternatives in either direction. Further, the participating airlines can now designate their own flight numbers on domestic connections when they connect

Aircraft from several oneworld alliance members parked at Narita Airport, Tokyo.
Source: Kyodo/AP Images

to trans-Atlantic destinations. For instance, Iberia shows one of its routes as San Diego to Madrid, even though both the San Diego–Chicago and Chicago–Madrid flights are operated by AA.

Because of dual or multiple designations and the sharing of revenue, more than one airline's sales force is trying to fill seats on the same route. The result is boosted sales, which allows the JV members to offer new routes, such as non-stop service between Chicago and Helsinki and between New York and Budapest that have come about since the JV's formation.

The AA–JAL Joint Venture

JAL is also a large airline, serving 85 cities in 20 countries and territories. Its joint venture with AA has the same advantages and objectives as the JV across the Atlantic. Some changes are notable. By altering each company's flight times between Chicago O'Hare and Tokyo Narita and tweaking schedules of connecting flights in both cities, many more passengers can make connections within two hours. For instance, 22 more flights from 20 more departure cities can make such connections for travel from O'Hare to Narita.

JAL has moved its O'Hare flights from the international terminal to be adjacent to AA. Meanwhile, AA has moved its Japanese offices to JAL's headquarters building, a move that eases communications between the two airlines. Both are helping each other with cultural questions, such as JAL aiding AA with public address announcements in Japanese to make them more meaningful to Japanese passengers. Meanwhile, plans are afoot for greatly increasing code sharing between the two airlines, especially to points beyond gateway cities, such as showing a JAL flight as Tokyo–Salt Lake City and as an AA flight beyond Tokyo to JAL-served cities such as Hanoi.

At this writing, JAL and BA are discussing a similar arrangement to connect flights between Japan and the United Kingdom. If this comes to fruition, it will create an effective around-the-world agreement.

Why Not a Merger or an Acquisition?

To begin with, government regulations such as ownership requirements would prevent a merger or acquisition between U.S. and non-U.S. carriers. Even if they didn't, fusing companies together creates daunting problems, even for domestic mergers and acquisitions. At this writing, discussions are underway for a merger between AA and US Airways. Their respective pilots' unions are strong and function under different operating and compensation systems. Although US Airways has no trans-Pacific routes, it does fly trans-Atlantic, and those routes will have to interface with the existing agreement that AA has with BA and Iberia. US Airways is a member of the Star Alliance, thus it will have to sever that relationship and figure out how accrued passenger points will be handled.

In the JVs, each company keeps its own identity and operates independently except for the coordination of the trans-oceanic routes. In addition, each airline in the JVs and within oneworld has developed its own culture and brand to appeal to its own nationality. BA is still strongest with British passengers, JAL with Japanese passengers, etc. By keeping separate identities, despite sharing flights, the member airlines can capitalize on the differences. Nevertheless, natural extensions are possible by strengthening collaboration, such as having check-in counters worldwide that handle all oneworld passengers and combining more airport lounges as a cost-saving measure. It is probably safe to say that future cooperation will strengthen rather than weaken among oneworld members.

QUESTIONS

✪ **15-3.** Companies within the oneworld, Star, and Sky Team alliances have also engaged in major mergers and acquisitions (M&A): Frontier and US Air (Star), Delta and Northwest (Sky Team), and Continental and United (Star). What are the advantages and disadvantages of M&A versus non-equity alliances in this industry?

15-4. Some airlines, such as Southwest, have survived as niche players without extensive international connections. Can they continue this strategy?

15-5. Why should an airline not be able to establish service anywhere in the world simply by demonstrating that it can and will comply with the local labor and business laws of the host country?

✪ **15-6.** The U.S. law limiting foreign ownership of U.S. airlines to no more than 25 percent of voting shares was enacted in 1938. Is this law an anachronism, or are there valid reasons for having it today?

15-7. What will be the consequences if a few large airlines or networks dominate global air service?

15-8. Many airlines have recently been no more than marginally profitable. Is this such a vital industry that governments should intervene to guarantee their survival? If so, how?

15-9. What methods could JAL and AA use to divide revenue and expenses on code-shared routes?

SUMMARY

- Selling abroad by exporting home-country production may not be advantageous because of lower production costs abroad, high transport costs, the need to alter products substantially, protectionist barriers, lack of domestic capacity, and consumer preferences to buy from specific countries.
- Companies often operate with FDI, especially wholly owned, because of inability to find an acceptable partner and because such operations may lower operating costs, lessen the possibility of developing competitors, and free them to follow global strategies.
- Some advantages of collaborative arrangements, whether a company is operating domestically or internationally, are to spread and reduce costs, allow a firm to specialize in its primary competencies, avoid certain competition, secure vertical and horizontal links, and learn from other companies.
- Some motivations for collaborative arrangements that are specific to international operations are to gain location-specific assets, overcome legal constraints, diversify among countries, and minimize exposure in risky environments.
- The forms of foreign operations differ in the amount and type of resources a company commits and the proportion of resources committed at home rather than abroad. Collaborative arrangements reduce such commitment.
- Although the type of collaborative arrangement a company chooses should match its strategic objectives, the choice often means a trade-off among objectives.
- Licensing is granting another company the use of some rights (such as patents, copyrights, or trademarks), usually for a fee. It is a means of establishing foreign production and reaching foreign markets that may minimize the licensor's capital outlays, prevent the free use of assets by other companies, allow the receipt of assets from other companies in return, and allow for income in some markets in which exportation or investment is not feasible.
- Franchising differs from licensing in that granting the use of intangible property (usually a trademark) requires the franchisor to assist in operations on a continuing basis.
- An international management contract is a means to secure income by managing a foreign operation while providing little of the capital outlay.
- Turnkey projects are contracts for construction of another company's operating facilities. Historically large and diverse, they necessitate specialized skills and abilities to deal with top-level government authorities.
- Joint ventures are a special type of collaborative arrangement in which two or more organizations share an operation or project, usually with each taking equity in it.
- There are various combinations of joint venture participants, including governments and private companies and two or more participants from the same or different countries.
- Equity alliances occur when a company takes an equity position in the company with which it has a collaborative arrangement so as to solidify the collaborating contract.
- A common motive for collaboration is to take advantage of different companies' complementary resources.
- Problems occur in collaborative arrangements when partners place different levels of importance on them, have different objectives, encounter control problems, worry that their partner is putting in too little or taking out too much from the operation, and misunderstand each other as a result of their different country or company cultures.
- Contracting performance by another company does not negate management's responsibility to develop objectives and assess performance.
- Companies may use different types of collaborative arrangements for their foreign operations in different countries or for different products. As diversity increases, coordinating and managing the foreign operations becomes more complex.

KEY TERMS

appropriability theory (p. 621)
bargaining school theory (p. 629)
consortium (p. 634)
cross-licensing (p. 629)
***dependencia* theory (p. 629)**
equity alliance (p. 634)
internalization (p. 621)
resource-based view (of the firm) (p. 625)

ENDNOTES

1 ***Sources include the following:*** Fidel León-Darder is Associate Professor and Cristina Villar is Assistant Professor, both in the Department of Management, Universitat de València (Spain). They used information from the following sources: J. Pla-Barber, F. León-Darder, and C. Villar, "The Internationalization of Soft-Services: Entry Modes and Main Determinants in the Spanish Hotel Industry." *Service Business* 5:2 (2011): 139–154; M. M. Massot, L.M. Vegas, and M.A. García, (1997): "Sol Meliá: Un Nuevo Paradigma en la Gestión Hotelera". In J. J. Durán (ed.): *Multinacionales Españolas II: Nuevas Experiencias de Internacionalización* (Madrid: Pirámide, 1997): 73–110; www.meliahotelsinternational.com (retrieved April 19, 2013); "Sol Meliá Absorbe la Cadena TRYP en una Operación Valorada en 72,500 Millones," *Cinco Días* (August 22, 2001) at www.cincodías.com (retrieved January 5, 2013); "Sol Meliá Compra una Cadena en Alemania por 16.5 Millones," *Cinco Días* (November 9, 2007) at www.cincodias.com (retrieved February 7, 2013);

"La Cadena Sol Meliá Vende la Marca TRYP al Grupo Hotelero Americano Wyndham: La Operación, Cifrada en unos 32 Millones, No Implica la Transacción de Establecimientos," *Diario de Mallorca* (June 9, 2010) at www.diariodemallorca.es (retrieved March 21, 2013); F. Contractor and S. Kundu, "Modal Choice in a World of Alliances: Analyzing Organizational Forms in International Hotel Sector," *Journal of International Business Studies* 29:2 (1998): 325–57; F. León-Darder, C. Villar, and J. Pla-Barber, "Entry Mode Choice in the Internationalization of the Hotel Industry: A Holistic Approach," *Service Industries Journal* 31:1 (2011): 107–122; "La Primera Aventura Británica de Escarrer – Meliá White House, un Hotel en Londres 'Made in Spain'," *Actualidad Económica* (September 23, 2002) at www.actualidad-economica.com (retrieved February 7, 2013); "Sol Meliá Renueva su Portfolio en el Exterior con Siete Altas y Ocho Bajas," *Alimarket* (March 1, 2008) at www.alimarket.es (retrieved January 19, 2013); "Sol MeliáControla Ya el 32% del Mercado Turístico Cubano," *El País* (May 16, 2005) at www.elpais.com (retrieved March 21, 2013); "Sol Meliá Busca una Alianza para Crecer en EE.UU," *La Vanguardia* (September 18, 1999) at www.lavanguardia.es (retrieved February 7, 2013); "Sol Meliá, Barceló y Blau Hotels Entrarán en China con la Gestión de Hoteles en Shanghai," *Cinco Días* (May 5, 1999) at www.cincodias.com (retrieved January 5, 2013); "Sol Meliá, Barceló y Riu Descartan Nuevas Inversiones en Asia a Corto Plazo por la 'Complejidad' del Mercado," *Europa Press* (February 6, 2006) at www.europapress.es (retrieved January 5, 2013); "Barceló Abandona la Gestión de su Primer Hotel en China," *Cinco Días* (January 5, 2001) at www.cincodias.com (retrieved January 5, 2013); "Sol Meliá Entra en China de la Mano de un Grupo Local y otro de Cuba," *Cinco Días* (July 10, 2010) at www.cincodias.com (retrieved January 5, 2013); "Meliá Apuesta por la Internacionalización en 2013 Para Reforzar su Liderazgo y Hacer Frente al Entorno," at www.meliahotelsinternational.com/es/sala-de-prensa/30012013/melia-apuesta-internacionalizacion-2013-reforzar-su-liderazgo-hacer-frente (retrieved April 19, 2013); "Meliá Hotels International Anuncia en Kenia su Interés de Expansión en África Subsahariana," at www.meliahotelsinternational.com/es/sala-de-prensa/26092012/melia-hotels-international-anuncia-kenia-su-interes-expansion-africa.

2 "Looking to the Future," *Business Europe* 50:18 (October 1, 2010): 7.

3 John Griffiths, "VW May Build Beetle in Europe to Meet Demand," *Financial Times* (November 11, 1998): 17.

4 Peter Marsh, "The World's Wash Day," *Financial Times* (April 29, 2002): 6.

5 "India-EU FTA to Include Tariff Reduction on Import of Vehicles," *Accord Fintech* [Mumbai] (May 20, 2011).

6 Jill Gabrielle Klein, "Us versus Them, or Us versus Everyone? Delineating Consumer Aversion to Foreign Goods," *Journal of International Business Studies* 33:2 (2002): 34563.

7 "'Made in Australia' Label Confuses Shoppers: Choice Survey," *Asia Pulse* (May 18, 2011).

8 John S. Hulland, "The Effects of Country-of-Brand and Brand Name on Product Evaluation and Consideration: A Cross-Country Comparison," *Journal of International Consumer Marketing* 11 (1999): 23–39; Ali Riza Apil and Erdener Kaynak, "Georgian Consumers' Evaluation of Products Sourced from European Union Member Countries," *International Journal of Commerce and Management* 20:2 (2010): 167–87.

9 An excellent overview of the literature is Jean-François Hennart, "Transaction Cost Theory and International Business," *Journal of Retailing* 86:3 (September 2010): 257–69.

10 *Internalization theory*, or holding a monopoly control over certain information or other proprietary assets, builds on earlier market-imperfections work by Ronald H. Coase, "The Nature of the Firm," *Economica* 4 (1937): 386–405. It has been noted by such writers as M. Casson, "The Theory of Foreign Direct Investment," Discussion Paper No. 50 (Reading, UK: University of Reading International Investment and Business Studies, November 1980); Alan M. Rugman, *Inside the Multinationals: The Economics of Internal Markets* (New York: Columbia University Press, 1981); David J. Teece, "Transactions Cost Economics and the Multinational Enterprise," Berkeley Business School International Business Working Paper Series No. IB-3 (1985); B. Kogut and U. Zander, "Knowledge of the Firm and the Evolutionary Theory of the Multinational Corporation," *Journal of International Business Studies* 24:4 (1993): 625–45; Peter W. Liesch and Gary A. Knight, "Information Internalization and Hurdle Rates in Small and Medium Enterprise Internationalization," *Journal of International Business Studies* 30:2 (1999): 383–96.

11 Eric M. Johnson, "Harnessing the Power of Partnerships," *Financial Times* (October 8, 2004): Mastering Innovation, Section 4.

12 Paul Marer and Vincent Mabert, "GE Acquires and Restructures Tungsram: The First Six Years (1990–1995)," *OECD, Trends and Policies in Privatization* III: 1 (Paris: OECD, 1996): 149–85; and their unpublished 1999 revision, "GE's Acquisition of Hungary's Tungsram."

13 James Mackintosh and Arkady Ostrovsky, "Partners Settle Lada Parts Dispute," *Financial Times* (February 21, 2006): 16.

14 Matthew Lynch, "Hilfiger Sues Former Sock Licensee," *WWD* 198:73 (October 7, 2009): 18.

15 Stephen Magee, "Information and the MNC: An Appropriability Theory of Direct Foreign Investment," in Jagdish N. Bhagwati (ed.), *The New International Economic Order* (Cambridge, MA: MIT Press, 1977): 317–40; C. W. Hill, L. P. Hwang, and W. C. Kim, "An Eclectic Theory of the Choice on International Entry Mode," *Strategic Management Journal* 11 (1990): 117–18; Ashish Arora and Andrea Fosfuri, "Wholly Owned Subsidiary versus Technology Licensing in the Worldwide Chemical Industry," *Journal of International Business Studies* 31:4 (2000): 555–72.

16 Peter Wonacott, "Global Aims of China's Car Makers Put Existing Ties at Risk," *Wall Street Journal* (August 24, 2004): B1+; Norihiko Shirouzu and Peter Wonacott, "People's Republic of Autos," *Wall Street Journal* (April 18, 2005): B1+.

17 Jean-Paul Roy and Christine Oliver, "International Joint Venture Partner Selection: The Role of the Host-Country Legal Environment," *Journal of International Business Studies* 40:5 (2009): 779–801.

18 Anne-Wil Harzing, "Acquisitions versus Greenfield Investments: International Strategy and Management of Entry Modes," *Strategic Management Journal* 23:3 (2002): 211–27.

19 Jaideep Anand and Andrew Delios, "Absolute and Relative Resources as Determinants of International Acquisitions," *Strategic Management Journal* 23:2 (2002): 119–34.

20 Sergery Filippov, "Innovation and R&D in Emerging Russian Multiantionals," *Economics, Management and Financial Markets,* 6:1 (March 2011): 182–206.

21 Geoff Dyer, Francesco Guerrera, and Alexandra Harney, "Chinese Companies Make Plans to Join the Multinational Club," *Financial Times* (June 23, 2005): 19.

22 "Beefed Up – The World's Largest Meat Company is Brazilian, But Mostly Operates Abroad," *The Economist* (September 24, 2011): Special Report on the World Economy, 16.

23 Two such indications are from studies by Alan Gregory, which is cited in Kate Burgess, "Acquisitions in U.S. 'Disastrous' for British Companies," *Financial Times* (October 11, 2004): 18; and Ping Deng, "Absorptive Capacity and a Failed Cross Border M&A," *Management Research Review* 33:7 (2010): 673–82.

24 John Child, David Faulkner, and Robert Pitethly, *The Management of International Acquisitions* (Oxford: Oxford University Press, 2001); Peter Martin, "A Clash of Corporate Cultures," *Financial Times* (June 2–3, 2001): Weekend section, xxiv.

25 "From Guard Shack to Global Giant," *The Economist* (January 12, 2013): 55–56.

26 Vlatka Bilas and Vedran Baci, "Utjecaj Akvizicijskog Iskustva Na Uspjesnost Medunarodnih Spajanja I Preuzimanja U Farmaceutskoj Industriji 2001–2009," *Ekonomska Misao* 19:2 (2010): 187–209.

27 Rajesh Chakrabarti, Swasti Gupta-Mukherjee, and Narayanan Jayaraman, "Mars-Venus Marriages: Culture and Cross-Border

M&A," *Journal of International Business Studies* 40:2 (2009): 216–36; See also Mary Yoki Brannen and Mark F. Peterson, "Merging Without Alienating: Interventions Promoting Cross-Cultural Organization and Their Limitations," *Journal of International Business Studies* 40:3 (2009): 468–89.

28 Pierre Dussauge, Bernard Garrette, and Will Mitchell, "Asymmetric Performance: The Market Share Impact of Scale and Link Alliances in the Global Auto Industry," *Strategic Management Journal* 25 (2004): 701–11; and Candace E. Ybarra and Thomas A. Turk, "Strategic Alliances with Competing firms and Shareholder Value," *Journal of Management and Marketing Research* 6 (January 2011): 1–10.

29 Koen Dittrich and Geert Duysters, "Networking as a Means to Strategy Change: The Case of Open Innovation in Mobile Telephony," *Journal of Product Innovation Management* 24:6 (November 2007): 510–21.

30 Barry J. Dickinson, "Symbiotic Marketing: A Network Perspective," *Journal of Management and Marketing Research* 11 (September 2012): 1-27 offers many examples of horizontal alliances.

31 Gabriel Baffour Awuah, Amal Mohamed, "Impact of Globalization: The Ability of Less Developed Countries' (LDCs') Firms to Cope with Opportunities and Challenges," *European Business Review* 23:1 (2011): 120–32; Rodney C. Shrader, "Collaboration and Performance in Foreign Markets: The Case of Young High-Technology Manufacturing Firms," *Academy of Management Journal* 44:1 (2001): 45–60.

32 Rahul Jacob, "Hong Kong Banks on New Disney Park for Boost," *Financial Times* (August 31, 2001): 6.

33 Paavo Ritala, "Coopetition Strategy – When Is It Successful? Empirical Evidence on Innovation and Market Performance," *British Journal of Management* 23:3 (September 2012): 307–24.

34 Phred Dvorak and Scott Kilman, "BHP Roils Potash Cartel," *Wall Street Journal* (August 25, 2010): 1.

35 John M. Connor, "Global Antitrust Prosecutions of Modern International Cartels," *Journal of Industry, Competition and Trade* 4:3 (2004): 239.

36 Luiz F. Mesquita and Sergio G. Lazzarini, "Horizontal and Vertical Relationships in Developing Economies: Implications for SMEs' Access to Global Markets," *Academy of Management Journal* 51:2 (2008): 359–80.

37 Destan Kandemir and G. Tomas Hult, "A Conceptualization of an Organizational Learning Culture in International Joint Ventures," *Industrial Marketing Management* 34:5 (2005): 440.

38 Robert F. Howe, "The Fall of the House of Mondavi," *Business 2.0* 6:3 (2005): 98.

39 Yumiko Ono and Ann Zimmerman, "Wal-Mart Enters Japan with Seiyu Stake," *Wall Street Journal* (March 15, 2002): B5.

40 Yuping Zeng, Oded Shenkar, Seung-Hyun Lee, and Sangcheol Song, "Cultural Differences, MNE Learning Abilities, and the Effect of Experience on Subsidiary Mortality in a Dissimilar Culture: Evidence from Korean MNEs," *Journal of International Business Studies* 44 (2013): 42–65.

41 Peter Wonacott and Eric Bellman, "Foreign Firms Find Rough Passage to India," *Wall Street Journal* (February 1, 2007): A6; Neil Buckly, "Russia Sets New Rules for Investors in Key Sectors," *Financial Times* (May 6, 2009): 3; Amy Kazmin, "Ikea Ditches Plans for India after New Delhi Refuses to Change Law," *Financial Times* (June 12, 2009): 13.

42 Jia-Ruey Ou, "An Analytical Model for Innovating Localization Policy," *International Journal of Electronic Business Management* 8:2 (2010): 110–19.

43 Julie Bennett, "Road to Foreign Franchises Is Paved with New Problems," *Wall Street Journal* (May 14, 2001): B10.

44 "H&M Wins Back Name in Russia," *Managing Intellectual Property* (April 2007): 1; and Steven Seidenberg, "Trademark Squatting on the Rise in U.S." *Inside Counsel* (May 2010): n.p.

45 Peter J. Lane, Jane E. Salk, and Marjorie A. Lyles, "Absorptive Capacity, Learning, and Performance in International Joint Ventures," *Strategic Management Journal* 22 (2001): 1139–61.

46 Steven White and Steven Siu-Yun Lui, "Distinguishing Costs of Cooperation and Control in Alliances," *Strategic Management Journal* 26 (2005): 913–32.

47 For an extensive discussion of these variables, see Farok J. Contractor and James Woodley, "How Do Alliance Partners Share the Value They Create? Determinants of the Value Split in International Technology Transfer Alliances," *Proceedings of the 54th Annual Meeting of the Academy of International Business* (Washington: 2012): n.p.

48 Melissa Maleske, "OFAC's Global Reach," *Inside Counsel* (August 2012): n/a.

49 Miguel Angel Asturias, *Strong Wind,* trans. Gregory Rabassa (New York: Delacorte Press, 1968): 112.

50 For an extensive treatise on the theory, see Robert A. Packenham, *The Dependency Movement: Scholarship and Politics in Development Studies* (Cambridge, MA: Harvard University Press, 1992). For some different national views of its validity, see Ndiva Kofele-Kale, "The Political Economy of Foreign Direct Investment: A Framework for Analyzing Investment Laws and Regulations in Developing Countries," *Law & Policy in International Business* 23:2/3 (1992): 619–71; and Stanley K. Sheinbaum, "Very Recent History Has Absolved Socialism," *New Perspectives Quarterly* 13:1 (1996).

51 Ravi Ramamurti, "The Obsolescing 'Bargaining Model'? MNC-Host Developing Country Relations Revisited," *Journal of International Business Studies* 32 (2001): 23; Yadong Luo, "Toward a Cooperative View of MNC-Host Government Relations: Building Blocks and Performance Implication," *Journal of International Business Studies* 32 (2001): 401.

52 "Kodak Enters into Technology Cross-Licensing Agreement with NEC," *Asia Pulse* (December 28, 2010).

53 Lauren Collins, "Danish Postmodern," *New Yorker* (January 7, 2013): 22; Lizette Alvarez, "Spreading Scandinavian Genes, without Viking Boats," *New York Times* (September 30, 2004): A4; and "Cryos Sets Up Sperm Banks in Mumbai," *Businessline* (September 25, 2008).

54 Fred Burton, Adam R. Cross, and Mark Rhodes, "Foreign Market Servicing Strategies of UK Franchisors: An Empirical Enquiry from a Transactions Cost Perspective," *Management International Review* 40:4 (2000): 373–400.

55 John K. Ryans, Jr., Sherry Lotz, and Robert Krampf, "Do Master Franchisors Drive Global Franchising?" *Marketing Management* 8:2 (1999): 33–38.

56 Janet Adamy, "Chinese Food the KFC Way," *Wall Street Journal Asian Edition* (October 20–22, 2006): 14–15.

57 Julie Bennett, "Product Pitfalls Proliferate in a Global Cultural Maze," *Wall Street Journal* (May 14, 2001): B11; Jane Wooldridge, "Fast Food Universe," *Miami Herald* (November 28, 2004): J1.

58 British Airport Authority, "International Airports" (2007), retrieved July 6, 2007, from www.baa.com/portal/page/Corporate%5EAbout+BAA%5EWho+does+what%5EInternational+airports/b0ccadc5c5c72010VgnVCM100000147e120a__/448c6a4c7f1b0010VgnVCM200000357e120a__/.

59 "Four Seasons Signs Management Contract with Three C Universal Developers," *Mint* [New Delhi] (April 21, 2011).

60 "Great Wall Builders," *The Economist* (October 27, 2012): 66.

61 "Global Alumina Releases Third Quarter 2010 Results," *PR Newswire* (November 2010).

62 Peter Sanders, Daniel Michaels, and August Cole, "Boeing Delays New Jet Again," *Wall Street Journal* (June 24, 2009): A1+; Peter Sanders, "Boeing Settles In for a Bumpy Ride," *Wall Street Journal* (October 7, 2009): B1+.

63 "Essar Ports Announces Strategic Alliance With Port of Antwerp International," *PR Newswire* (May 31, 2012): n.p.

64 Luis Zalamea, "AeroRepublica, Copa Offer Details of New Alliance," *Aviation Daily* (March 11, 2005): 5.

65 There are many different ways of classifying the problems. Two useful ways are found in Manuel G. Serapio Jr. and Wayne F. Cascio, "End

Games in International Alliances," *Academy of Management Executive* 10:1 (1996): 62–73; and Joel Bleeke and David Ernst, "Is Your Strategic Alliance Really a Sale?" *Harvard Business Review* (January–February 1995): 97–105.

66 Terrence Chea, "No Perfect Partnership," *Washington Post* (June 3, 2002): E1.

67 Anna Shaojie Cui, Roger J. Calantone, and David A. Griffith, "Strategic Change and Termination of Interfirm Partnerships," *Strategic Management Journal* 32:4 (April 2011): 402–23.

68 Mikhail Fridman, "BP Has Been Treating Russians as Subjects," *Financial Times* (July 7, 2008): 9.

69 Gregory L. White, "In Asia, GM Pins Hope on a Delicate Web of Alliances," *Wall Street Journal* (October 23, 2002): A23.

70 Ramit Plushnick-Masti, "German Firm Faulted for Taking Vitamin out of Baby Formula," *Miami Herald* (November 12, 2003): 19A.

71 William H. Meyers, "Maxim's Name Is the Game," *New York Times Magazine* (May 3, 1987): 33–35; Cristina Passariello, "Pierre Cardin Ready to Sell His Overstretched Label," *Wall Street Journal* (May 3, 2011): 1.

72 David Ibison, "Culture Clashes Prove Biggest Hurdle to International Links," *Financial Times* (January 24, 2002): 17.

73 Diana Elena Ranf, "Cultural Differences in Project Management," *Annales Universitatis Apulensis Series Oeconomica* 12:2 (2010): 657–62.

74 Marshall Geiger and Joyce van der Laan Smith, "The Effect of Institutional and Cultural Factors on the Perceptions of Earnings Management," *Journal of International Accounting Research* 9:2 (2010): 21–43.

75 James T. Areddy, "Danone Pulls Out of Disputed China Venture," *Wall Street Journal* (October 1, 2009): B1.

76 Gokhun Ertug, Ilya R. P. Cuypers, Niels G. Noorderhaven, and Ben B. Bensaou, "Trust Between International Joint Venture Partners: Effects of Home Countries," *Journal of International Business Studies* 44 (2013): 263–82.

77 Seung Ho Park and Gerardo R. Ungson, "The Effect of National Culture, Organizational Complementarity, and Economic Motivation on Joint Venture Dissolution," *Academy of Management Journal* 40:2 (April 1997): 279–307; Harry G. Barkema, Oded Shenkar, Freek Vermeulen, and John H. J. Bell, "Working Abroad, Working with Others: How Firms Learn to Operate International Joint Ventures," *Academy of Management Journal* 40:2 (April 1997): 426–42, found survival differences only for differences in uncertainty avoidance.

78 Rikka M. Sarala and Eero Vaara, "Cultural Differences, Convergence, and Crossvergence as Explanations of Knowledge Transfer in International Acquisitions," *Journal of International Business Studies* 41:8 (October-November 2010): 1365–90.

79 Akbar Zaheer, Exequiel Hernandez, and Sanjay Banerjee, "Prior Alliances with Targets and Acquisition Performance in Knowledge-Intensive Industries," *Organization Science* 21:5 (September-October 2010): 1072–91+.

80 Mike W. Peng and Oded Shenkar, "Joint Venture Dissolution as Corporate Divorce," *Academy of Management Executive* 16:2 (May 2002): 92–105.

81 Bharat Anand and Tarun Khanna, "Do Firms Learn to Create Value? The Case of Alliances," *Strategic Management Journal* 21:3 (March 2000): 295–315; Anthony Goerzen and Paul W. Beamish, "The Effect of Alliance Network Diversity on Multinational Enterprise Performance," *Strategic Management Journal* 26 (2005): 333–54; and Maurizio Zollo and Jeffrey J. Reuer, "Experience Spillovers Across Corporate Development Activities," *Organization Science* 21:6 (November-December 2010): 1195–1212.

82 Rachelle C. Sampson, "Experience Effects and Collaborative Returns in R&D Alliances," *Strategic Management Journal* 26 (2005): 1009–31.

83 Doug Cameron, "U.S. Airline Merger to Affect Alliances," *Wall Street Journal (Online)* (February 14, 2013): n.p.; Adrian Schofield, "JAL, British Airways Code-Share Another Step Toward Joint Venture," *Aviation Daily* 389:46 (September 5, 2012): n.p.; Anne Smith and Marie-Claude Reney, "The Mating Dance: A Case Study of Local Partnering Processes in Developing Countries," *European Management Journal* 15:2 (1997): 174–82.

84 Sanjiv Kumar and Anju Seth, "The Design of Coordination and Control Mechanisms for Managing Joint Venture–Parent Relationships," *Strategic Management Journal* 19:6 (June 1998): 579–99; T. K. Das and Bing-Sheng Teng, "Between Trust and Control: Developing Confidence in Partner Cooperation in Alliances," *Academy of Management Journal* 23:3 (July 1998): 491–512; Arvind Parkhe, "Building Trust in International Alliances," *Journal of World Business* 33:4 (1998): 417–37; Prashant Kale, Harbir Singh, and Howard Perlmutter, "Learning and Protection of Proprietary Assets in Strategic Alliances: Building Relational Capital," *Strategic Management Journal* 21:3 (March 2000): 217–37; and Dina Preston-Ortiz, "The Effects of Trust in Virtual Strategic-Alliance Performance Outcomes," unpublished doctoral dissertation (Phoenix: University of Phoenix, 2010).

85 Linda H.Y. Hsieh and Suzana B. Rodrigues, "Partner Trustworthiness and Ex Post Governance Choice in International Joint Ventures: The Role of Performance Satisfaction," AIB 2012 Proceedings of 54th Annual Meeting (Washington: June 30–July 3, 2012).

86 Africa Ariño and Jeffrey J. Reuer, "Designing and Renegotiating Strategic Alliance Contracts," *Academy of Management Executive* 18:3 (2004): 37–48.

87 Gary D. Burton, David Ahlstrom, Michael N. Young, and Yuri Rubanik, "In Emerging Markets, Know What Your Partners Expect," *Wall Street Journal* (December 15, 2008): R5.

88 Srilata Zaheer and Akbar Zaheer, "Trust across Borders," *Journal of International Business Studies* 37:1 (2006): 21.

89 Prashant Kale and Harbir Singh, "Managing Strategic Alliances: What Do We Know Now and Where Do We Go from Here?" *Academy of Management Perspectives* 23:3 (August 2009): 45–62.

90 John Kenneth Galbraith, *American Capitalism* (Boston: Houghton Mifflin, 1952): 91–92.

91 Eric H. Kessler, Paul E. Bierly, and Shanthi Gopalakrishnan, "Internal vs. External Learning in New Product Development: Effects of Speed, Costs and Competitive Advantage," *R & D Management* 30:3 (2000): 213–23.

92 Adrian Wooldridge, "Return of the Giants," *The Economist* (The World in 2013 edition): 25.

93 These are adapted from Arvind Parkhe, "Interfirm Diversity, Organizational Learning, and Longevity in Global Strategic Alliances," *Journal of International Business Studies* 22:4 (1991): 579–601.

94 ***Sources include the following:*** We wish to acknowledge the assistance of several American Airlines and oneworld executives, who, although wishing to remain anonymous, supplied useful information for and feedback on this case. Additional information came from "American Airlines to Operate Only Service between New York and Japan's Tokyo International Airport at Haneda After Historic Open Skies Agreement," *Entertainment Newsweekly* (March 4, 2011): 172; Andrea Ahles, "American Airlines, Japan Airlines Announce Joint Venture," *McClatchy–Tribune Business News* (January 12, 2011): n.p.; Julie Johnsson, "American Airlines Combining Pacific Flights with Japan Airlines," *McClatchy–Tribune Business News* (January 12, 2011): n.p.; "American to Move Its Asia-Pacific Regional Office to the Japan Airlines Building in Tokyo," *Journal of Transportation* (September 18, 2010): 26; "Japan Airlines and American Airlines Announce Joint Business Benefits for Trans-Pacific Consumers," *The Pak Banker* (January 11, 2011): n.p.; "Airline Profits to Tumble in 2011: IATA," *The Pak Banker* (June 8, 2011): n.p.; "Europe: Trans-Atlantic Alliances Are Set to Tighten," *Oxford Analytica Daily Brief Service* (January 3, 2008): 1; Alfred Kahn and Dorothy Robyn, "The Sky Must Be No Limit to Global Competition," *Financial Times* (February 15, 2006): 17; Bruce Bernard, "American Airlines Seeks OK for Trans-Atlantic Tie-up," *Journal of Commerce Online* (August 15, 2008); International Air Transport Association, *Annual Report* (2008).

CHAPTER 16
The Organization and Governance of Foreign Operations

OBJECTIVES

After studying this chapter, you should be able to

1. Profile the evolving process of organizing a company for international business
2. Describe the features of classical structures
3. Describe the features of neoclassical structures
4. Compare and contrast the idea of the hierarchy versus the hyperarchy
5. Discuss the systems used to coordinate international activities
6. Discuss the systems used to control international activities
7. Profile the role and characteristics of organizational culture
8. Profile the role and characteristics of corporate universities

Words have no wings but they can fly many thousands of miles.

—South Korean proverb

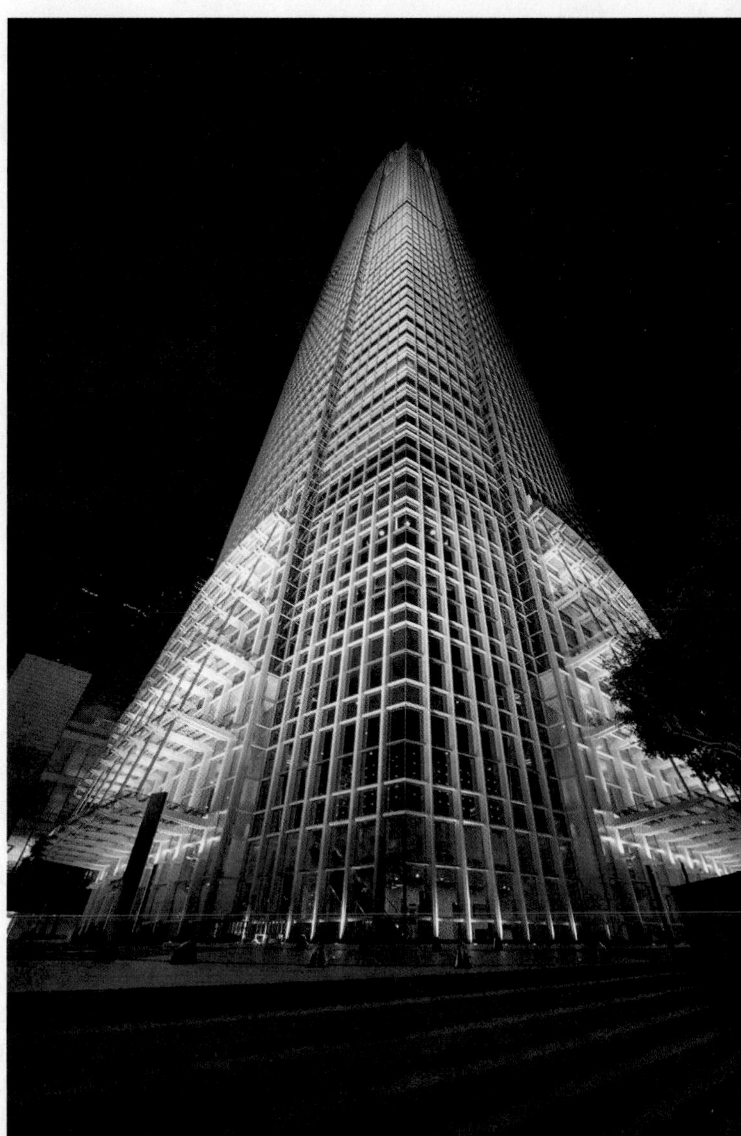

Source: © leeyiutung - Fotolia.com

CASE Building a Global Organization at Johnson & Johnson[1]

The typical pharmaceutical MNE relies on global integration, given its steep product development costs and potential scale economies. Meanwhile, it must respond to local market conditions, obtaining government approval for each product in each country, and establishing local sales and distribution systems. Consequently, headquarters and subsidiaries jointly implement the company's strategy. Building an organization that can meet this mission is tough. One standout that does is Johnson & Johnson (J&J).

Since the start of its U.S. operations in 1886, J&J has evolved into the most broadly based healthcare company in the world. International activity began in 1919 with J&J Canada. Headquartered in New Brunswick, New Jersey, J&J now lists some 250 operating companies across the world, sells products in more than 175 countries, and employs about 115,000 people worldwide, with nearly 70,000 working in 57 countries outside the United States. The company's steady success is renowned. Sales in 2012 passed $67 billion, while dividends increased for the 51st consecutive year. J&J has a portfolio of anti-infective, cardiovascular, dermatology, immunology, and oncology products whose quality is legendary—it owns more than 55,000 U.S. and foreign patents. Some, though, believe the intricacy of the company's organization, in terms of its decentralized structure, sophisticated coordination and control systems, and Credo-based culture, anchors its superior performance.

THE MAGIC OF DECENTRALIZATION

Decentralized management is the heart of J&J's organization. It allows managers who are closest to customers and competitors to make decisions. As the company says, it aims to be big and small all at once, building its global reach from the integration of many small units. By design, each of its 250 units operates with substantial autonomy, commanding the authority to act as it believes best given local conditions. Each is its own business, entrepreneurial in character, and aware that success depends on anticipating local customers' needs and delivering solutions.

Decentralization, explains Ralph Larsen, former CEO, "gives people a sense of ownership and control—and the freedom to act more rapidly."[2] His successor, William Weldon, concurs, adding that reducing bureaucracy, liberating initiative, and rewarding enterprise—the hallmarks of a decentralized organization—is the wellspring of the "magic around J&J."[3] Moving decision-making from headquarters to the front lines helps a large, globe-spanning MNE to capture qualities typically found in smaller companies. Certainly, a top-down hierarchy delivers benefits. Still, J&J reasoned that centralization reduces the magic cast by entrepreneurial drive, close contact with customers, and agile decision-making. Shortening chains of command, increasing spans of responsibilities, and breaking down boundaries in a decentralized organization gives everyone a strong sense of ownership of action and accountability for outcomes.

These outlooks, Larsen explains, makes the managers running J&J's 250 operating units worldwide intensely competitive, both with each other as well as other companies. Furthermore, he adds, managers that directly shape their future are driven to innovate, moving to translate ideas into new products and insights into better processes the bring greater value to the marketplace. Backstopping their efforts was the deep pools of products, processes, and people that one finds in a large, successful MNE.

J&J's successful decentralization appealed to talented, bright, and motivated people. Giving bright, ambitious people the authority to make decisions, Weldon noted, encouraged them to dream big dreams, keen to test new ideas that developed their skills, gave them room to grow, and powered big careers. While often found in small companies, these entrepreneurial outlooks and orientations are seldom seen in large MNEs. As such, senior leadership believes the company's ability to simultaneously achieve local effectiveness and global efficiencies supported its commanding competitiveness.

THE DILEMMA OF DECENTRALIZATION

J&J's enduring philosophy held that people who understand how the company creates value, are familiar with the company's competencies, and are culturally and physically close to the market ought to run the local business. Thus, for example, baby oil managers in Italy decide how big a bottle to use, even if that bottle differs from the one sold in Germany, Japan, or Mexico, given their sense of the local marketplace. J&J entered new markets by adding subsidiaries through investment, alliance, or acquisition. New units did not fear being overrun by legions of expatriates directed by headquarters-based generals because, with few exceptions, host country citizens direct local subsidiaries—indeed, a common view holds that "companies love to be acquired by J&J because they don't mess with you."[4] Granted, headquarters installed coordination and control systems and negotiated financial targets. Then, however, it stepped aside, supporting subsidiaries as needed, patiently awaiting superior results, yet always prepared to intervene in the event of shortfalls.

This high degree of autonomy created dilemmas for local management. At one point, the centralization-decentralization balance had tipped so unevenly that the directors of J&J's foreign subsidiaries acted as kings of their own countries. For example, J&J launched Tylenol in 1960 as an over-the-counter pain reliever in the United States. Although it was available to local operating units shortly thereafter, the Japanese unit did not begin local sales until 2000.[5] This sort of situation no longer exists. Yes, the company's commitment to decentralization endorses delegating authority to local managers. Headquarters, however, has increasingly relied upon coordination and control systems to ensure that subsidiaries optimize local activities while supporting global performance.

COORDINATION AND CONTROL SYSTEMS

Unquestionably, decentralization enabled J&J to respond quickly to local needs but slowed the global diffusion of products and programs. Preserving the magic of decentralization, in the face of the contest between local autonomy and global integration, led headquarters to tighten coordination and control systems. Channels of communication cut across the organization, thereby helping far-flung units share ideas. Self-directed councils—for research, engineering, and operations, among others—meet regularly to swap ideas. Headquarters negotiated planning formats, scheduled mandatory reports, and formally reviewed budgets and interim results. Senior executives pushed a global perspective into local decision-making. Likewise, local objectives influenced global discussions.

Intensifying pressures to integrate operations due to market trends, competitors' moves, and changing technologies tested J&J's commitment to decentralization. The resulting centralization, while understood, was not entirely welcome by local units. Some units resisted integration, arguing that global standards poorly fit their circumstances. Senior management acknowledged these concerns and reiterated their commitment to decentralized decision-making. They argued, however, that the imperatives of the company's strategy coupled with the tough standards of the global market meant that when J&J rolls out a product, country operations worldwide roll with it.

Significantly, J&J began recentralizing some activities from operating units. Senior executives set standards for issues common to all operating units, such as finance, science and technology, government affairs, and quality management. The company has installed more centralized reporting processes for key business functions, including manufacturing and quality control. Centrally managing common support activities, senior executives reasoned, freed operating units to concentrate on their day-to-day performance. J&J installed an Executive Committee and Group Operating Committees to formalize this change.

CULTURE AND THE CREDO

Inconsistent market development and duplicated efforts fanned friction between headquarters and subsidiaries. Tempting as it was to adopt a policy of "beating will continue until morale improves," J&J's proud legacy encouraged otherwise. Inspiring local entrepreneurialism while ensuring a global sensitivity relied on J&J's culture to socialize its workers. From the CEO to the employees of the smallest unit, management believes that the people and their values are the firm's greatest assets. Senior executives often note that employees have created product breakthroughs, management innovations, and customer insights. In and of itself, such praise is not terribly unusual. Many companies—perhaps even some that you have worked for—have likely expressed similar sentiments. However, separating J&J from the pack is the explicit primacy of its organization culture, as embodied in "Our Credo." Crafted in 1943 by Robert Wood Johnson, company chair from 1932 to 1963, this one-page ethical code of conduct states how J&J fulfills its responsibilities. Former CEO Larsen referred to it as the "glue that binds this company together."[6]

Originally set in 1943, Johnson & Johnson's Credo has been periodically updated to refine the company's sense of responsibilities. Presently, the Credo is available in more than 36 languages across Johnson & Johnson's global enterprise. The values codified in the Credo challenge every employee to put the needs and well-being of stakeholders first. This 'ethics oath' communicates the mission, vision, and accountability that every employee holds to each other and the communities they serve.

Source: Johnson & Johnson,"Our Company: Our Credo" (November 14, 2005), at www.jnj.com.

The Credo specifies who and what to care about and in what order. J&J's "first responsibility is to the doctors, nurses, patients, mothers and fathers who use our products and services." It addresses the communities where J&J operates and the roles and duties of employees. Notably, shareholders come last, long after customers, suppliers, and distributors. It declares that shareholders will get a fair return if other stakeholders are treated fairly. Collectively, the "Credo underscores J&J's personal responsibility to put the needs…of the people we serve first. It liberates our passion and deepens our commitment to delivering meaningful health innovations."[7] J&J steadfastly maintains that the Credo is more than just a moral compass; it is the basis of its long-running success. The proof, reasoned executives, is unequivocal: J&J is one of a handful of MNEs that has flourished through a century of change.

The Credo is available in more than 36 languages across the MNE's global enterprise. Despite its direct message, executives have worried that differing outlooks in different markets might blur its interpretation. Consequently, J&J periodically surveys employees on how well they practice the spirit and duties of the Credo. Where there are shortcomings, senior management steps in. They have, for example updated some of the language of the Credo given the rising visibility of the environment and work/family balance tensions. Despite occasional revisions, though, management believes the founding spirit of the Credo endures.

THE POWER OF ORGANIZATION

J&J believes the basis of its continued success is building an organization flexible enough to exploit each employee's knowledge. A long line of accomplishments by senior executives, through developing, adjusting, and improving its structure, systems, and culture, has built an organization that confidently leverages bright ideas, no matter if they are championed by global executives or local subsidiary leaders. Ultimately, the magic of decentralization, the balance of coordination and control systems, and the clarity of the Credo anchors an organization that lets employees capitalize on their initiative, develop their capabilities, enrich their perspectives, and quite possibly change the game. ■

CRN
Case Review Note

QUESTIONS

16-1. Identify and explain three to five benefits of decentralized decision-making within Johnson & Johnson. Discuss how these benefits might create strategic and operational difficulties.

16-2. Would you prefer to work in a decentralized or centralized company? What outlooks and competencies would make you a high-performing executive in your preferred choice?

INTRODUCTION

Artfully engineering an organization that adeptly runs global activities is a frontier of international business operations. Superior performance has a clear mandate: Create value by standardizing some activities to maximize global efficiency while simultaneously adapting other activities to optimize local effectiveness. This understanding, as we saw in Chapter 12, sets the strategy of a company. Once done, managers then construct, piece by piece, the requisite organization that implements their strategy.[8] This chapter examines how this is done.

Think of it this way: If formulating strategy is the first step of a long march, then the ensuing steps implement it. Indeed, advised GE's Jack Welch, "In real life, strategy is actually very straightforward. You pick a general direction and implement like hell."[9] Getting operations up and running directs managers' attention to the issue of organizing international operations.

Questions run the gamut: How should they balance global standards with local contingencies? How should they deploy knowledge and skills around the world? How might they help people communicate with workmates spanning the world? How do they adjust the organization to the changing geography of growth? J&J exemplifies how a large, complex, geographically dispersed MNE productively engages these sorts of issues. Its strategy of delivering superior healthcare required building a network of decentralized subsidiaries, tailoring technology, human resources, and information systems to coordinate and control activities, and relying on its Credo to sustain a meaningful culture. Separately and combined, these elements of its organization convert J&J's ambition into accomplishment.

Like many other firms profiled in this chapter, J&J shows how an MNE sets its structure, specifies its systems, and shapes its culture to implement its strategy. Organizing operations for international business, therefore, is not merely fine-tuning the ingenuity of an MNE's strategy. Rather, it is the process of organizing how employees contribute to its mission, minding how to coordinate interdependent activities, applying controls when situations go awry, and sponsoring values that create a common cause. This task, as we see in Figure 16.1, requires specifying a structure that arranges the MNE's workflow, installing the systems that get and keep the MNE moving, and promoting the culture that sustains the MNE.[10]

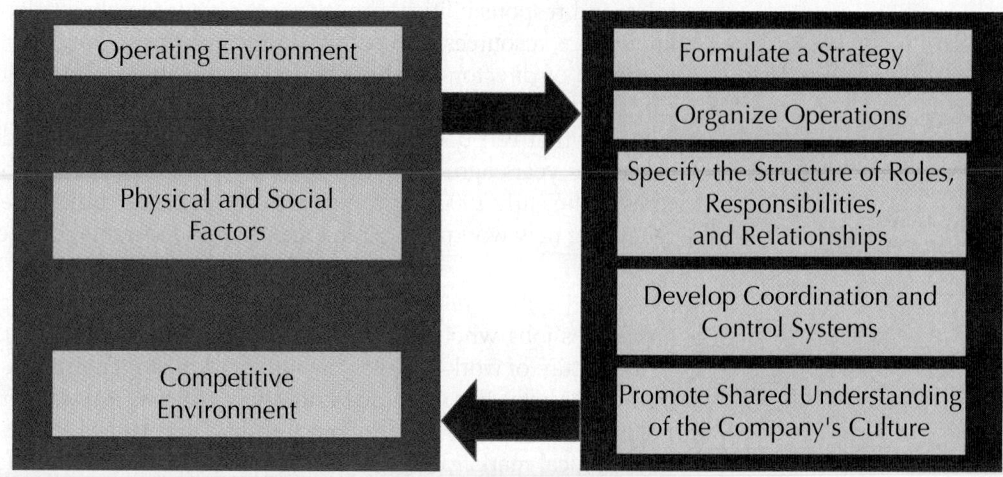

FIGURE 16.1 Factors Affecting Organizing Operations

The idea of an organization refers to the activities through which managers build the structure, systems, and culture needed to implement their strategy. The resulting organization, by arranging roles, responsibilities, and relationships, imposes order and clarity upon the MNE's worldwide operations.

CHANGING SITUATIONS, CHANGING ORGANIZATIONS

Environmental differences, technology trends, executive practices, and labor markets are challenges faced when organizing the MNE.

In the early 20th century, companies responded to the emerging technologies of railroads, telephone, and telegraph by engaging then heretical ideas.[11] The global titans of the day, such as General Motors, Ford, DuPont, and Sears, developed hierarchical structures, reasoning that this new, novel organization would best implement their new, novel strategies. Succeeding generations of managers refined these designs. Managing the changing scale and scope of their operations helped them better understand how to build an organization that specified who did what job, who could make which decision, who worked in which unit, who reported to whom, and who told whom what to do. The output of these analyzes, formally codified in the "lines and boxes" that commonly represent a MNE's formal structure, instituted a system of command, controls, constraints, and contracts that directed the efforts and ensured the compliance of workers worldwide.[12] Since then, this outlook has routinely organized the international operation of MNE. For many, it defines the nature of the life in in the modern-day corporation.

Contemporary environmental trends, industry conditions, and market opportunities prod managers to rethink this approach. Specifically:

Implementing increasingly sophisticated strategies requires increasingly sophisticated organizations.

Expanding International Business The growth and diffusion of global business changes MNEs' opportunity sets and efficiency frontiers. Markets once predominant, like the United States, Japan, and Germany, make the transition to new positions. Markets once on the periphery, such as Brazil, Russia, China, and India, move toward center stage. Indeed, the McKinsey Global Institute suggests that 400 midsized emerging-market cities, many unfamiliar in the West, will generate about 40 percent of global growth over the next 15 years.[13] MNEs, by choice or by force, respond. They engage unprecedented strategies that demand far more sophisticated organizations than any used in the past. For example, IBM, moving into its third organizational phase, is building a "globally integrated enterprise" that puts investments, people, and work anywhere in the world. This plan spurs it to make decisions "based on the right cost, the right skills, and the right business environment [with] work flow[ing] to the places where it will be done…most efficiently and to the highest quality."[14] Therefore, managing an increasingly sophisticated strategy calls for managing a commensurately sophisticated organization.

The Internet as a Design Standard The invention of the telephone and telegraph, by improving global communication, reset the standards of organizing activities in the early 20th century. Corporations at the time responded with formats that reflected the organizing logic of these technologies. We see the same processes in play today. The Internet as an organization metaphor pushes managers to rethink their assumptions of how they arrange work, roles, and responsibilities. The Internet is a supremely efficient and effective organization of knowledge, resources, and people. In the height of irony, however, it has no formal structure, no board of directors, and no central administrator. Its self-organizing and self-regulating capabilities prompt rethinking conventional notions of design, coordination, and control. Consider that Facebook, Red Hat, Yandex, PayPal, Naver, Baidu, and Alibaba could not have existed 20 years ago. Therefore, as had context novel strategies called for innovative structures in the early 1900s, so too do we see similar circumstances in the early 2000s. Therefore, managing new workplace arrangements calls for managing new structural formats.

Managerial Standards The evolving nature of work changes the conduct and context of employees' jobs, whether done at the biggest headquarters or the smallest subsidiary. Change in the nature of work changes the nature of management. Historically, the higher one's level in the hierarchy, the more one knew about the various jobs in the company. That no longer holds true. Similarly, at one time frontline employees at the subsidiary level were masters of their local marketplace but far removed from the global drama. That too no longer holds.

Real-time access to information, facilitated by cheap, powerful telecommunications, eliminates knowledge gaps. As a result, there are far fewer jobs that senior managers can script or that subsidiary managers cannot do. Furthermore, employees working with information technologies create value of astonishing variability, problem solving, and intellectual content. It is difficult and usually counterproductive to control workers charged with reasoning or problem-solving tasks; the bright, self-motivating, self-organizing people who staff these sorts of slots usually oppose direct supervision. Effectively, whether referred to as "knowledge workers" or the "creative class," these individuals aim to behave as if they are the CEO.[15] Therefore, managing new workplace standards calls for managing novel coordination and control systems.

Changes in the market environment and nature of work push managers to evaluate the effectiveness of their organization.

Social Contract Competitive changes and performance expectations alter the social contract between high-potential executives and MNEs. Traditional concerns for security, pay, and benefits have expanded to expectations of participating in decision-making, devising solutions to unique problems, and receiving challenging assignments.[16] Moreover, social contracts increasingly rely on the compatibility of company values and personal outlooks. Google's worries about brain drain to rivals, for instance, led it to identify why people typically quit; it found that executives flee when they go longer feel connected to the company's mission.[17] Consequently, MNEs develop organization cultures that people do not want to merely work for, but aspire to belong to. Therefore, managing new expectations calls for managing the social dynamic of organization cultures.

BUILDING A "MAGICAL" ORGANIZATION

CONCEPT CHECK

Designing an organization's structure requires fitting it to conditions in the external environment. These conditions involve, among many others, legal regulations on ownership structures, degree of economic freedom, location economics, and expectations of alliance partners.

These trends push MNEs to rethink the best mix of structure, systems, and values when building, as J&J called it, a "magical" organization. The payoff is clear: helping employees perform creatively, responsibly, and entrepreneurially. Some firms, like Nestlé in Switzerland, Cemex in Mexico, Toyota in Japan, Infosys in India, and DuPont in the United States, apply and improve classical formats. They fine-tune their organizations, process-map activities to clarify the work environment and improve system standards. Reengineering workflows, streamlining information technology, tightening planning sequences, and minimizing duplication are some of their tools of change.

Others, like Oticon in Sweden, Cisco in the United States, Grupo Empresarial Antioqueño of Colombia, Mitsui of Japan, and Li & Fung in Hong Kong, engage unprecedented formats. They design flexible models that replace the command-and-control ethos of the classical hierarchy with the goal of coordinating and cultivating in the context of neoclassical formats. Cross-functional task forces, network designs, Web-based collaboration, virtual formats, and social networking methods are some of their tools of change.

Organizing is the process of building the structure, systems, and culture that managers reason are needed to implement the MNE's strategy.

We examine the intricacies of each approach, as well as their respective tools, throughout this chapter. We begin by studying how an MNE builds an **organization** in terms of its choices on the (1) structure it specifies to arrange its workplace, (2) the systems it installs to coordinate and control what it does, and (3) the culture it promotes to shape and sustain its collective effort.

ORGANIZATION STRUCTURE

The formal arrangement of roles, responsibilities, and relationships in the MNE represents its **organization structure**. The various elements of the company are configured to identify the lines of authority and communication, assign rights and duties, stipulate flows between and among units, and indicate how the company aims to use its resources. This can spell the difference between success and failure for a firm as well as its workers.[18] In the case of J&J, managers believe their decentralized structure was the bedrock of their "magical" organization. Similarly, the profile of Zara in Chapter 11 emphasized its CEO's view that the company's structure creates tremendous advantages over its competition. Innovatively combining vertical integration, tech-choreographed coordination, just-in-time manufacturing, finely tuned logistics, and state-of-the-art merchandising poses tough challenges. Zara's structure, by arranging jobs, roles, rules, and responsibilities in ways that implemented this strategy, imposed clarity upon activities that otherwise would trend toward disorder.

Structure is the formal arrangement of jobs that specifies roles, responsibilities, and relationships.

Step one in building an organization is determining the ideal structure for arranging individuals and units to implement the strategy. Choice depends on many factors. The environmental and workplace trends discussed earlier highlight general conditions. Then there are the inevitable constraints that uniquely affect an MNE. Designing the ideal structure for international operation faces more complexity than designing for the company focused on a domestic marketplace. Designing a structure for the latter lets one reasonably set economic development, cultural orientation, and workplace practices as constants; organizing internationally requires one to interpret them as variables.

Differentiation means that the company is composed of different units that work on different kinds of tasks with different degrees of authority.

Various conditions influence an MNE's situation. Has it configured its value chain, for instance, to emphasize global integration or local adaptation? Alternatively, have location economics led it to concentrate value activities within nations or disperse them across countries? These and similar questions endorse the usefulness of some, while rejecting other, forms of structure. Managers resolve them by resolving two fundamental structural issues: the degree of **vertical differentiation** (the balance between the centralization and decentralization of authority) and the degree of **horizontal differentiation** (the task of specifying which people do which jobs in which units).

VERTICAL DIFFERENTIATION

CONCEPT CHECK

International business is marked by recurring dialectics; for example, global versus local, pro- vs. anti-globalization, democracy vs. totalitarianism, economic freedom vs. state capitalism, standardization vs. adaptation. Here we add another, namely, centralization vs. decentralization. Strong performance requires MNEs to strike and sustain a balance between competing pressures.

No matter the particular mix of markets, types of products, or executive ambitions, MNEs face competing calls for global integration and local responsiveness. Questions run the operational gamut: Who should decide to close a factory in Switzerland or open one in Malaysia? Does only headquarters decide whom to hire and whom to fire, both at home and overseas? How often and in what format do foreign subsidiaries report to headquarters? The company's structure reconciles these pressures by specifying who has the authority to make what decisions. More formally, managers vertically differentiate the company's structure in terms of the **centralization** (how high up) versus the **decentralization** (how low down) of decision-making. These factors, profiled in Table 16.1, endorse different principles, advocate different practices, and emphasize different objectives.

As a rule, decisions made above the subsidiary level are considered centralized, whereas those made at or below that level are decentralized. A centralized structure concentrates decision-making power among the executives staffing top levels. In contrast, a decentralized structure pushes decision-making authority down to the folks running the local subsidiaries. Strategic circumstances determine the appropriate degrees of autonomy. The MNE implementing an international or global strategy, for instance, sets centralization as the standard. Headquarters, in its role as the "imperialist corporate centre," makes decisions that the troops running the local subsidiaries then implement.[19] Alternatively, the MNE implementing a multi-domestic strategy decentralizes authority to the troops in the field, reasoning that those closest to the action have a superior understanding of the situation than do far-removed generals.

A DYNAMIC BALANCE

Centralization is the degree to which high-level managers, usually above the country level, make strategic decisions and delegate them to lower levels for implementation.

Research often represented the centralized-versus-decentralized choice as an either-or proposition. Arguably, a generation ago, MNEs could function effectively if big decisions were made by a select group of senior executives or local managers. Today, few, if any, can. The intrinsic dynamism of the global market requires a continual balancing of authority between headquarters and subsidiaries. Much like the swings of a pendulum, centralization and decentralization tend toward dynamic balance.[20]

TABLE 16.1 The Principles and Practice of Centralization and Decentralization

Centralization	Decentralization
Premise	**Premise**
Decisions should be made by senior managers who have the experience and expertise to set the optimal strategy.	Decisions should be made by the employees who are closest to and, arguably, most familiar with the situation.
The effective configuration and coordination of the value chain depends on headquarters' retaining authority over activities.	The effective configuration and coordination of the value chain depends on local managers' tailoring it to local conditions.
Centralized decision-making ensures that local operations support global objectives.	Local operations' success achieving national objectives boosts global performance.
Advantages	**Advantages**
Facilitates the coordination of the value chain.	Decisions are made by managers who directly deal with customers, competitors, and markets.
Ensures that decisions are consistent with strategic objectives.	Encourages lower-level managers to exercise entrepreneurial initiative.
Gives senior executives the authority to direct major change.	Motivates greater effort from lower-level employees.
Preempts duplicating activities across subsidiaries.	Enables more flexible response to rapid environmental changes.
Reduces the risk that lower-level employees make strategic mistakes.	Permits holding subsidiary managers more accountable for their unit's performance.
Promotes consistent relationships with stakeholders.	
Disadvantages	**Disadvantages**
Discourages initiative among lower-level employees.	Puts the organization at risk of lower levels' consistently making poor decisions.
Demoralized lower-level employees simply wait to be told what to do.	Impedes cross-country coordination as national concerns trump global objectives.
Information flows top down, thereby preempting possible bottom-up innovations.	Subsidiaries often champion local interests at the expense of global performance.
Factors Encouraging More Centralization	**Factors Encouraging More Decentralization**
Environment and industry conditions push for worldwide uniformity of products, methods, and policies.	Environment and industry conditions push for adapting products, methods, and policies to local circumstances.
Interdependent subsidiaries share value activities, have similar market segments, and compete with common rivals.	Economies of scale result from national production.
Need for the company to move resources efficiently from one value activity to another.	Lower-level managers are capable and experienced at making decisions.
Lower-level managers are less experienced decision-makers than are upper-level executives.	Decisions are relatively minor yet must be made quickly.
Decisions are important and the risk of loss is great.	Low necessity to develop foreign nationals for executive positions outside their home country.

Decentralization is the degree to which lower-level managers, usually at or below the country level, make and implement strategic decisions.

Significantly, the Internet changes the calculus of who should have the authority to make which decision. Technology progressively makes it easier for executives at both headquarters as well as subsidiaries to track global conditions and local performance in real time. Not too long ago, each relied upon reports provided by the other. Now, email, VoIP, teleconferencing, social networks, and related technologies eliminate the lag. Economical, off-the-shelf technology platforms, such as Microsoft's Skype, Google's Hangout, or Cisco's TelePresence, make video magic happen effortlessly today. Now, the click of a mouse lets one meet anyone, anywhere in the "world." These benefits, though, do impose consequences. For instance, MNEs must fine-tune the location of authority for a state of **globality** in which "business flows in every direction. Companies have no centers. The idea of foreignness is foreign. Commerce swirls and market dominance shifts."[21] Competing with everyone from everywhere for everything turns historically blunt decisions to centralize this activity or decentralize that responsibility into far more intricate questions.

In principle, decision-making should occur at the level of those who (1) are most directly affected by its outcome and (2) have the most direct knowledge of the situation.

The interdependency of activities requires that executives running headquarters understand the subtleties of country operations. Likewise, those running subsidiaries respect global imperatives. Recall our opening profile of J&J, in which headquarters had reasoned that local managers' improving real-time access to global and local information supported decentralizing decision making. Besides tracking local developments, subsidiary managers can efficiently monitor global trends and conditions.

HORIZONTAL DIFFERENTIATION

Vertical differentiation deals with how an MNE sets its chain of command from the top to the bottom of the organization. Besides vertically, companies also run sideways from function to function, such as operations to marketing to finance. The task of horizontal differentiation turns managers' attention to how to divide the firm into discrete functional groups, such as marketing and manufacturing, that are then responsible for their specialized tasks.

Vertical differentiation deals with the chain of command that runs from the "top to the bottom" of the organization. Horizontal differentiation deals with the separate tasks or skills that run "sideways" in the organization.

Setting horizontal systems makes manageable the otherwise immense scale and scope of international operations. More precisely, an MNE horizontally differentiates its structure to (1) specify the set of tasks that must be done; (2) divide those tasks among strategic business units (SBUs), divisions, subsidiaries, departments, committees, teams, jobs, and individuals; and (3) stipulates superior and subordinate relationships.

Typically, managers horizontally differentiate a structure in terms of three criteria: business function, type of business, geographic area, or a combination of the preceding. Differentiating on the basis of business activity anchors the *functional* structure; differentiating on the basis of product or geography installs a *divisional* or *area* structure; differentiating on the basis of a combination results in a *matrix* or *mixed* structure. The long-running use of these formats by MNEs worldwide designates them as classical structures. By no means does that characterization suggest they are relics. Rather, a surprising number of MNEs rely on the same sort of structure they used 50 years ago.[22] As we now see, such structures have enduring strengths that lead MNEs worldwide to use them.

FUNCTIONAL STRUCTURE

Functional structures:

- Group people based on common expertise nd resources.
- Fit the organizational demands of MNEs that have narrow product lines.

A **functional structure**, as depicted in Figure 16.2 (a), is the ideal way to organize work for the MNE that sees global integration trumping local responsiveness given an industry structure that compels configuring value chains to implement a global or international strategy. It helps managers maximize scale economies by efficiently arranging responsibilities and relationships. It creates specific departments that arrange work by business functions—i.e., production people work with production people, marketing people work with marketing people, finance people work with finance people, and so on. Functional structures are popular among MNEs with a narrow range of products, particularly those whose capital-intensity creates steep economies of scale. Energy and extraction MNEs, such as ExxonMobil, Vale, or Rio Tinto, as well as aircraft manufacturers such as Airbus, Boeing, or Bombardier commonly use this structure.

A functional structure does have drawbacks. The goal to maximize efficiency, by driving standardization of activities worldwide, may misinterpret local opportunities. Differentiating people and processes by business function also slows the development of broader knowledge-generating and decision-making relationships within the company. As a result, coordinating activities between departments, perhaps in response to an environmental change or market disruption, is difficult. The often-extreme vertical differentiation, represented by a long chain of command that spans many levels of the company's hierarchy, adds a deliberate pace to activity. As the volume of data expands faster than the processing capacity of the multi-layered hierarchy, the flow of information progressively slows. Finally, classical structures such as the functional format often unleash zero-sum battles for control among divisions, groups, and people. Separation of business tasks makes knowledge power. Hence, the all-too-often imperative of organizational survival within a compartmentalized functional hierarchy can suppress entrepreneurialism.

Divisional structures:

- Divide employees based on the product, customer segment, or geographical location.
- Duplicate functions and resources across divisions.
- Fit the organizational demands of the MNE that manages many different products.

DIVISIONAL STRUCTURES

Whereas executives specify roles and relationships in a functional structure in terms of inputs (e.g., oil, natural gas, and coal for an energy producer), they use a **divisional structure** to specify them according to product (e.g., soap, toothpaste, and cosmetics for a consumer

FIGURE 16.2 Classical Organizational Structure for International Business

Although shown here in simplified forms, these types of classical structures have been adopted by many MNEs. A key takeaway from these depictions is that organizational structure, whatever the type, is about definition and clarity. Many find it helpful to think of the structure as the "skeleton" that supports the organization; the characteristics of the particular shapes, whether set by function, produce, area, or a mix, institute the company's preferred configuration of activities.

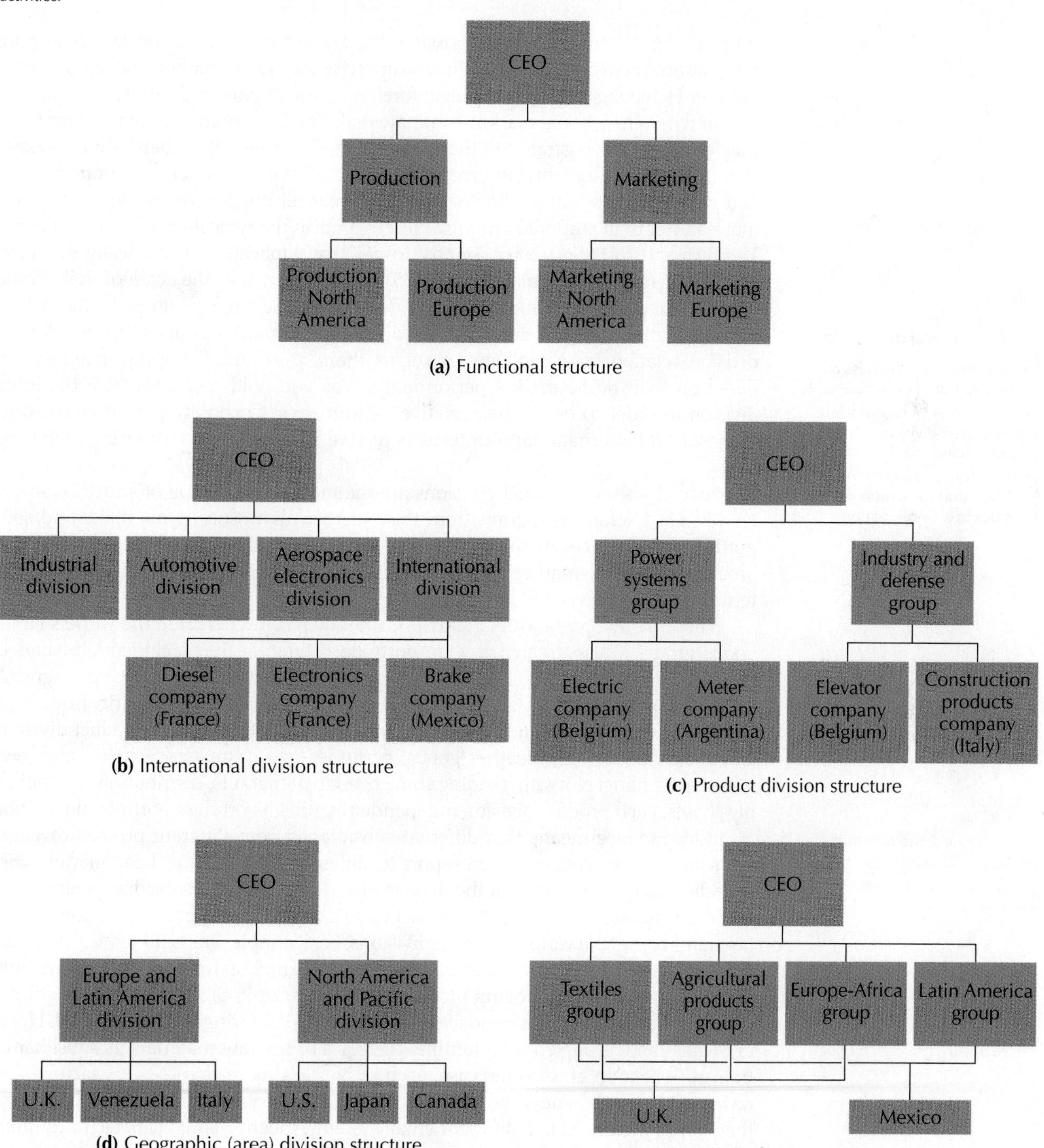

products firm) or markets (e.g., North America, Europe, and Asia). Each division then has responsibility for its assigned products or markets. Presuming a fit between a divisional format and the demands of its strategy, an MNE decides among installing an international-division, a global-product, or a worldwide-area structure.

International Division This format installs a separate operating group responsible for international activities. Domestic units supervise the home market, leaving the international division to manage the less strategic foreign sector (Figure 16.2[b]). Companies prefer this format when their home market dominates sales and international sales are far less. As such, this format supports strategies that demand modest integration between domestic and foreign operations. Clustering international personnel within a single unit improves monitoring and managing international activities; effectively, all the people needed to act are division mates rather than scattered among different units in the typically far larger domestic division. The format also limits costly country-to-country duplication. Historically the international division has proven popular among U.S. MNEs, given that the scale of their home market overwhelms their international activity. It finds less use among European and Asian MNEs.

An international division:

- Creates a critical mass of international expertise.
- Competes with powerful domestic divisions for resources.
- Fits the demands of the MNE that generates most sales in a single nation.

Segregating an MNE into discrete domestic-international divisions, by blocking cross-division relationships, can fan "us versus them" tensions. Domestic managers, evaluated based on their home market performance, may withhold resources from the international division in order to boost their relative performance. Corporate performance suffers when domestic and international counterparts receive little credit for supporting each other.

Product Division Product divisions are the most popular type of structure among MNEs worldwide. Usefulness follows from the fact that many such firms make and sell a broad portfolio of products in multiple markets that span multiple countries.[23] Effectively, the broader its product-market portfolio, the more likely an MNE looks to arrange its structure in terms of product divisions.

When the merger of Moët Hennessy and Louis Vuitton created the world's largest luxury goods group, it also created a wide portfolio of brands that included Christian Dior perfume, Tag Heuer watches, Louis Vuitton bags, and Moët & Chandon champagne. Although each product targets the same high-end market segment, the dissimilarity from fragrances to watches to luggage to liquor led managers to split LVMH into five product divisions: wines and spirits, fashion and leather goods, perfumes and cosmetics, watches and jewelry, and selective retailing. Notwithstanding some overlap in markets, distribution channels, and supply chains, each product division independently runs its product portfolio on a global basis.

If unchecked, the different product divisions may inefficiently administer systems.

Independence means that different subsidiaries from different product divisions within the same foreign country often report to different executives at headquarters. Figure 16.2 (c) indicates, for example, that the Belgian electric and elevator subsidiaries report to different units at headquarters. Unless safeguarded, MNEs struggle to coordinate common company programs across the various product divisions. For example, financial service institutions often have units that are unaware that customers who signed up for one service were already customers for other services being provided by another unit. Similarly, at one point Nestlé had more than 500 factories in nearly 90 countries manufacturing its 8,000 brands. Headquarters in Switzerland struggled to determine the costs of the raw materials its subsidiaries bought from suppliers. In an extreme case, each of Nestlé's more than 40 U.S. factories purchased raw materials independently. Lack of cross-division coordination, compounded by the fact that Nestlé then used five different email systems, meant that its U.S. factories unknowingly paid more than 20 different prices for vanilla extract to the same supplier.[24]

Geographic (Area) Division An MNE uses geographic divisions, as depicted in Figure 16.2 (d), when it has significant international sales that are not dominated by a single country or region (including the home country). Therefore, it horizontally differentiates activities based on geography—Division 1 is responsible for country X/region A, Division 2 takes country Y/region B, and so on. Historically, the area structure has proven more useful to European companies than their U.S. counterparts. European firms, usually based in small countries inevitably expanded into bigger markets worldwide. The proximity of their key foreign markets, such as Canada, United States, and Mexico comprising North America, supported organizing operations by geography.

Geographic divisions fit the demands of MNEs who have extensive international operations that are distributed across many countries.

The emergence of fast-growing developing markets pushes MNEs to tweak the geographic structure. For example, the rising strategic importance of China and Eastern Europe led Nike to reset its four-region structure into six areas: North America, Western Europe, Eastern/Central Europe, Japan, Greater China, and Emerging Markets. Nike also announced that China and Eastern Europe would operate separately from the other divisions. Their growing share of the company's total sales, comparatively faster growth rates, and superior long-term potential led Nike to reset its structure accordingly.

The geographic division structure is commonly associated with MNEs pursuing multidomestic strategies—as seen in Nike's reorganization to better respond to Eastern Europe and China. Generally, the intrinsic decentralization of the area structure—North America tends to North America, Europe tends to Europe, etc.—gives area managers more authority to adapt value activities for local conditions. As Nike explained regarding its new structure, "We are confident these changes will best position us for future growth.... This model allows our global categories to connect directly with consumers at the local level."[25]

Similar moves by other MNEs highlight a key trend afoot, whereby traditionally West-centric companies rethink the horizontal differentiation of their structures given the emergence of larger, faster-growing markets. For example, Panasonic adjusted its structure given its sales trends in emerging versus developed economies. Historically, Panasonic had maintained a conventional geographic format, such as area divisions—e.g., North America, Europe, and Asia. Now, given the equatorial proximity of many emerging economies, it differentiates operations by organizing in terms of temperature and tropical climate zones—longitude, not latitude, now matters more in setting its structure. Operationally, executives from Brazil, who previously conferred with colleagues in South America, now swap ideas with those in Malaysia, who previously conferred with colleagues in Asia.[26]

The key limitation of the geographic structure is administrative inefficiency due to configuring similar activities in several places. Each area essentially builds its own mini-me operation that shadows the home-office setup. Replication is unwieldy and expensive. However, one should note that this inefficiency is the expense that some MNEs, such as J&J, accept as the cost of a locally responsive organization. Rather than a structural deficiency, the requirements of its corporate strategy necessitate replicating administrative functions.

MATRIX STRUCTURE

A matrix organization:

- Institutes overlaps among functional and divisional forms.
- Gives functional, product, and geographic groups a common focus.
- Has dual-reporting relationships rather than a single line of command.
- Fits the demands of MNEs that cannot easily reconcile competing market pressures.

Some MNEs pursue strategies that simultaneously face high pressures for global integration and local responsiveness. This choice often leads some MNEs to install a **matrix structure**, as depicted in Figure 16.2 (e). Simultaneously targeting the strengths of the functional and divisional structures, it horizontally differentiates the organization such that a subsidiary reports to two different executives. Arguably, this approach best positions MNEs to reconcile opposing pressures for integration and adaptation. Superimposing geographical divisions across traditional business units formally blends units that are sensitive to competing pressures—presumably, the reasoning goes, this improves the odds that decision-making can simultaneously resolve both.

Operationally, a subsidiary now has two bosses: one representing the interests of, say, a business function like manufacturing, the other representing the interests of a sales region. The matrix structure requires that the two units build relationships, coordinate resources, and share rewards.[27] As a matter of course, each manager must approve key business proposals. As such, the matrix installs compelling incentives to build communication and collaboration systems.

The matrix structure fans competition by requiring the different groups to compete for resources and rewards. Disputes among lower-level managers often progress through the hierarchy. Besides delaying decisions, upper management involvement may favor a group, such as manufacturing and its call to standardize activities, to the annoyance of its matrix counterpart, such as the Asian sales group, which champions adapting products to local preferences. Others in the firm, monitoring the contest, may conclude that the true locus of power lies with the victor. Unchecked, gamesmanship threatens collaboration, thereby short-circuiting the knowledge-generating and decision-making relationships that were the original promise of the matrix.

A matrix structure also institutes a dual hierarchy that runs afoul of the **unity-of-command principle**. This notion holds that an unbroken chain of command should flow through the levels of the hierarchy, beginning with the CEO down to the entry-level employee. Giving one worker two bosses, by blurring lines of responsibility, creates conflicting lines of command and nebulous accountability.[28] The CEO of Dow Chemical, an early adopter of the matrix structure, explained, "We were an organization that was matrixed and depended on teamwork, but there was no one in charge. When things went well, we didn't know whom to reward; and when things went poorly, we didn't know whom to blame."[29] Persistent problems coordinating responsibilities and resources have led many MNEs to question the usefulness of this format.

MIXED STRUCTURE

In reality, the odd MNE has a structure that neatly applies the specific characteristics of a functional, divisional, or matrix format. For many, different growth rates and market conditions prevent applying a single organizing logic to all operations—recall, for example, Nike's dilemma organizing its various regions. Thus, some MNEs combine features of the functional, geographic, and product structures into the aptly titled **mixed structure**. Again, Nike illustrates the situation: It installed vertical and horizontal arrangements for China and Eastern Europe that were unsuitable for organizing its activities in North America, Western Europe, and Japan. Likewise with others: Dell Computers horizontally differentiated its Asian headquarters in Singapore by business function, aiming to improve its regional financial, operational, and tax efficiency; Halliburton, a U.S.-based energy MNE, set up a second headquarters in Dubai to better serve its customers throughout the Middle East; and Diageo, the British multinational alcoholic beverages company, responded to slowing European growth with a structure that moved strategic decisions to the regional level while handling customer relations nationally.[30]

CONCEPT CHECK

Discussion of the "Types of Economic Systems" in Chapter 4 noted that a mixed economy combines some of the characteristics of a free market with certain features of command systems. A mixed organizational structure reflects a similar choice to sacrifice purity to practicality. Managers customize "model" organizational configurations to accommodate their mix of businesses and countries.

Each MNE's structure reflects its particular:

- Market circumstances,
- Strategic choice,
- Value chain configuration,
- Administrative legacy,
- Executive preferences.

The mixed structure is not a tacit indication of indecision but rather the fact that no single method of horizontal differentiation optimizes organizational effectiveness. In reality, no single organizational model is ideal for all MNEs given their differences in industry conditions, strategic capabilities, and company legacies; some conditions support some formats while rejecting others. For example, when IBM reorganized its European operations to move decision-making staff closer to customers, it had to reduce the scale of its EMEA (Europe, Middle East, and Africa) headquarters in Paris, a major unit in place since the end of World War II. Many of its responsibilities moved to smaller hubs in Madrid and Zurich.[31] Meanwhile, IBM's North American and Asian operations, implementing different programs given different opportunities, adopted different structures. Hence, although a company may prefer structural consistency worldwide, adapting to market conditions often results in mixed structures.

NEOCLASSICAL STRUCTURES

Some MNEs find that the hierarchical architecture of classical structures struggles implementing their increasingly sophisticated strategies.[32] Environmental, organizational, and workplace trends create stress points that limit the usefulness of structures designed to maximize command, control, contracts, and compliance. Instead, some MNEs move to radically different configurations, so-called **neoclassical structures**, to set their organization. Certainly, neoclassical formats serve the same purpose as do their classical counterparts, stipulating how

CONCEPT CHECK

"The Forces behind Globalization" in Chapter 1 explains that market drivers such as expanded technology, liberalized trade, and increased cross-national cooperation reset the external environment of international business. Recognizing changes as opportunities moves MNEs to experiment with neoclassical structures that reset degrees of vertical and horizontal differentiation.

the MNE organizes its workplace, utilizes resources, administers communication systems, and specifies authority, rights, and responsibilities. However, neoclassical structures apply different horizontal and vertical methods to resolve those shortcomings—most notably conformity, rigidity, and bureaucracy—that limit the effectiveness of classical formats.

Increasingly intricate workflow patterns, social networking dynamics, and emergent workplace behaviors call for new approaches to coordination, collaboration, and control. Ever-improving telecom capabilities, from 4G to VoIP to teleconferencing and beyond, let globally dispersed executives manage activities as effectively as those at headquarters did a generation ago. Consequently, MNEs' increasingly sophisticated strategies require they design increasingly ambitious structures; these designs apply neoclassical, rather than classical, standards.[33]

CHANGING TIMES, CHANGING STRATEGIES, CHANGING STRUCTURES

A generation ago, technology, costs, and skills meant people in a particular country could economically serve customers—hence, companies could rely on multi-domestic strategy and geographic structure. Steadily, changing markets and transforming technologies pushed MNEs to reboot their organization. IBM's transition into its third organizational phase illustrates the dynamic in play. Top management's read of market conditions and corresponding organizational requirements spur them to build a "globally integrated enterprise" that puts investments, people, and work anywhere in the world based on the optimal mix of costs, skills, and environment. Explained IBM's vice president of global strategy for growth markets, "Instead of taking people to where the work is, you take work to where the people are."[34] Although a simple statement, this radical reversal of workflow pushes IBM to rethink the functionality of vertical and horizontal differentiation, a rethink that moves them from a classical to neoclassical structure.

Classical structures emphasize the principles of command and control. Neoclassical structures emphasize the principles of coordinate and cultivate.

Significant change is already apparent; for example, more than 40 percent of its 433,000 plus employees worldwide are "mobile," meaning that they do not report daily to an IBM site.[35] Too, IBM relies on its workers in Shanghai to process accounts receivables, specialists in Manila to oversee human resources, accountants in Kuala Lumpur to keep the books, buyers in Shenzhen to procure components, and customer specialists in Brisbane to run its help desk. Each unit, responding to IBM's quest to move work to places where it will be done most efficiently and to the highest quality, manages projects that arise throughout the global market without missing a beat.

Customers, meanwhile, couldn't care less where work is done as long as the results meet contract specifications. Within this context, IBM's decision to reset its structure to reflect its changing workflow speaks to the simple fact that markets and technologies meant it now could build a globally integrated enterprise. Instead of a precisely specified classical hierarchy, one could reasonably interpret IBM as a conglomeration of loosely connected, transient suppliers of IT services. Implementing this vision—intensified by competitors such as SAP, Infosys, Wipro, Cognizant, and others traveling the same path—spurs IBM to champion the coordination, collaboration, and control features of a neoclassical structure. Redesigning its organization to suit its changing workflow greatly improved its ability to manage its strategy, costs, people, and risk on a global basis.[36]

CONCEPT CHECK

A recurring theme of the text is the changing environment of international business. Here, we note that managers build organizations to align their strategy to the changing marketplace; the classical and neoclassical structures provide them a range of powerful options.

Likewise, consider the choices made by Cisco. Changing markets and enterprising rivals put it at a structural crossroad. Rather than give a classical divisional hierarchy another go, Cisco developed an elaborate system of cross-functional, cross-market, and cross-business committees, some of which do without a formal leader and behave more like a sports team, building a culture of collaboration. Indeed, Cisco fires so-called "lone rangers" and promotes those who work well with others. Asked why he led Cisco into uncharted organizational territory, its CEO replied that he had no choice. He needed a structure that would react quickly to new opportunities, develop entire solutions rather than stand-alone products, and help Cisco "to become a globally integrated company by making it easier for executives from all around the world to weigh in."[37] Going forward, he adds, as technology makes communicating cheaper, executives will continue migrating from the classical standards of command and control to the neoclassical ideals of coordinate and cultivate.

THE IDEAL OF BOUNDARYLESSNESS

Transitioning from a classical to a neoclassical structure directs MNEs, like IBM and Cisco, to the issue of boundaries. In practical terms, **boundaries** are (1) vertical divisions that separate employees into specific slots in the hierarchy and (2) horizontal divisions that follow from having specific employees do only specific jobs in specific units.[38] They are created when classical structures vertically and horizontally differentiate activities to arrange rules, responsibilities, and relationships. Think of, for example, the schematic of boxes and lines shown in Figure 16.2; each demarcates boundaries that segregate the people who run the various functions, markets, and businesses in a company. Boundaries, by instituting divisions between people, impede knowledge flows and interrupt coordination.

Increasingly sophisticated strategies require removing the internal structural, systemic, and interpersonal boundaries that constrain collaboration in the MNE.

The increasing diversity of markets, customers, and rivals brought on by expanding international operations calls for fewer organization boundaries. Likewise, increasingly sophisticated strategies require improving collaboration, sharing, and engagement across the MNE. The boundaries imposed by vertically and horizontally differentiating a structure, by hampering these activities, inevitably constrain performance. For example, Sony's CEO blames his company's poor turnaround not on the wrong strategy, but the sad reality that divisions, rivalries, and conflict between its differentiated businesses undermines efforts.[39] The globally integrated enterprise resets its organization to preempt these threats. Failure, as Sony shows, prolongs poor performance.[40]

Global expansion makes organization, unsurprisingly, more complicated and difficult to manage. The boundaries that establish the command-and-control usefulness of classical structures can turn from advantages to liabilities. If tolerated, companies futilely struggle to transfer lessons learned in one market to another. If unchallenged, the records of MNEs from Nokia to Sony indicate that boundaries undermine a shared vision, discourage communication and collaboration, promote decision rigidity, and worsen demotivating complexity. If ignored, boundaries consign the MNE to deteriorating performance precisely because the "models and frameworks that shaped our leading organizations from the end of the second world war through the conclusion of the cold war are clearly obsolete in this new era of e-business, perpetual innovation and global competition."[41]

Tools and Techniques The design of today's complex enterprises requires thinking about organizations in ways that bust boundaries between vertical ranks and roles; between horizontal units in different functions, products, and areas; and between the firm and its suppliers, distributors, JV partners, strategic allies, and customers.

General Electric's boundary busting, under the leadership of its former CEO Jack Welch, highlights the process. Directing GE's far-flung global operations led Welch to experiment with organizational formats that continue influencing interpretations. Reflecting on his 20-year run as CEO, he explained that his goal had been to build an organization that eliminated the vertical and horizontal boundaries that put barriers between company, managers, customers, suppliers, and stakeholders. As Welch explained,"The simplest definition of what we are trying to create—what our objective is—is a **boundaryless** company, a company where the artificial barriers and walls people are forever building around themselves or each other—for status, security, or to keep change away—are demolished and everyone has access to the same information, everyone pulls in the same direction, and everyone shares in the rewards of winning—in the soul as well as in the wallet."[42] Radical than, less so today, Welch pioneered the transformation of Organization Man into Network Person.

Boundarylessness refers to eliminating vertical, horizontal, and external boundaries that hinder the flow of information and formation of relationships.

Others pointed to W. L. Gore's unique flat"lattice" structure and its egalitarian workforce philosophy as exemplifying many of these practices. Gore, believing that no hierarchy fuels creativity and innovation, officially has few job titles. Indeed, it has no traditional organizational charts, no chains of command, nor predetermined channels of communication. It expects workers to share information eagerly, as opposed to jealously controlling it; in fact, collaborating in small, ever-changing, multidisciplinary teams is standard operating policy. Rather than telling people what to do, teams organize around opportunities and leaders gradually emerge."We work hard at maximizing individual potential, maintaining an emphasis on product integrity, and cultivating an environment where creativity can flourish," says CEO Terri Kelly. She added,"A fundamental belief in our people and their abilities continues to be the key to our success, even as we expand globally."[43]

Neoclassical structures move an MNE toward these outcomes. They promote loosely connected networks of self-organizing and self-governing agents. They develop less rigid structural forms that are marked by fewer rules, regulations, and processes, as well as better knowledge coordination and relationship cultivation. They persuade employees to behave as entrepreneurial owners rather than as risk-averse drones—at Gore, for example, every employee is a shareholder of the company after one year. Unlike classical structures, in which the formal attributes of managers (i.e., title, location, and number of direct reports) matter most, neoclassical formats make the managers' relationships with other agents in the network matter more—again, at Gore, team members evaluate one another. Neoclassical structures, quite simply, spur people to share rather than control information; collaborate rather than compete on projects; promote rather than suppress innovation; cultivate rather than command relationships; and engage rather than resist change.

Leading examples of neoclassical structures include the network structure and virtual organization.

CONCEPT CHECK

The notion of a *network* shapes discussions of international business: Chapter 7, for instance, describes the *trade networks* formalized by the WTO, Chapter 9 discusses financial networks composed of *global capital markets*, and Chapter 14 analyzes the effort of MNEs to network with partners through *collaborative alliances*.

A network structure anchors a dynamic organization that outsources value activities to firms whose core competency supports greater innovation at lower cost.

NETWORK STRUCTURE

The **network structure** provides an efficient and dynamic format for managing interdependent activities. Bringing to bear multidimensional perspectives in a flexible, integrative process, it arranges elements in a patterned flow of activity that allocates people and resources to decentralized projects.[44] Figure 16.3 depicts a simplified profile of a network.

FIGURE 16.3 A Simplified Network Structure

A network structure connects people, products, and processes into a coherent, competitive system. At the center of the network structure is a core unit that aims to "do what it does best and outsource the rest." Similarly, fellow network partners focus on their core competencies. A network structure uses extensive communication channels to maximize collaboration throughout the system. Dynamic coordination and control methods set, regulate, and integrate the typically vibrant interactions among the members of the network who share general goals yet target specific objectives.

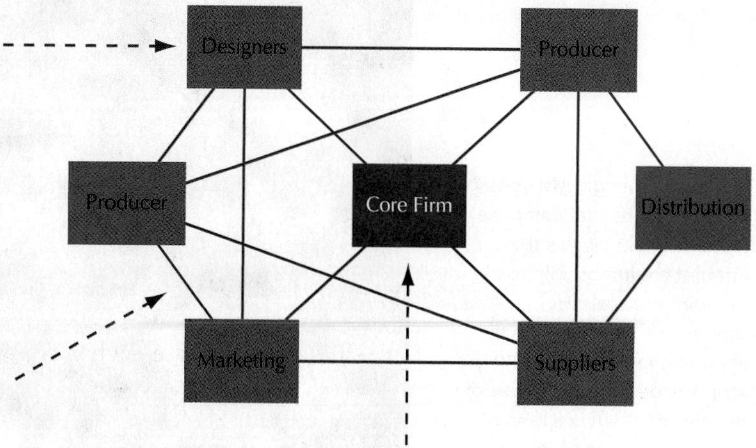

Differentiated units to which headquarters delegates decision-making authority. These units, whether a local marketing subsidiary, international production center, or suppliers, are the front line of the network. They have responsibility for sensing, processing, and acting upon specialized as well as generalized information in entrepreneurial fashion.

The channels of exchange that facilitate and fine-tune the volume, content, and flow of hard data and soft information. These linkages animate the network by setting paths of interaction, coordination, collaboration, and integration among the differentiating yet interdependent functional, area, and product units.

The formal center of the network that coordinates and controls strategic objectives and operational policies across the differentiated units. This unit ensures the efficient flow of resources, supplies, components, and funds throughout the network. It creates value by effectively collecting, sorting, and distributing the network's accumulated wisdom, knowledge, and experiences.

This format is anchored by a core organization unit that outsources activities in which it has no core competency to firms that do. Or, as the saying goes, "Do what you do best and outsource the rest."[45] For example, companies like Nike, Apple, Qualcomm, and Cisco concentrate on improving core competencies in R&D, product design, or marketing. They then contract other companies that excel in manufacturing, like Yue Yuen Industrial, Foxconn, Kyocera, or Flextronics, to make their products. Relationships in the network are not solely designed to improve transactional efficiency. Rather, the firms cultivate specialized decision-making relationships based on long-term common interests. Improving coordination and collaboration, rather than boosting transactional efficiency, energizes the network.

As for the activities of Qualcomm, Nike, and Cisco, each is essentially a research, development, and marketing MNE that uses outside suppliers and independent manufacturers to assemble its products. Operationally, each enters joint ownership arrangements with other companies to share production, distribution, and technology-development facilities. Each contracts with other MNEs to produce and distribute goods and components. And each organizes its many alliances with the latest and greatest communication technology, using the Internet, email, file sharing, social media, and teleconferencing to link partners.

Networks Aren't New Although a novel format to some, the network structure is not unprecedented. Japanese MNEs have long used the so-called *keiretsu* format, an integrated collective of nominally independent companies in which each owns a share of the others.[46] *Keiretsus* rely on long-term personal relationships among the companies' executives. Sometimes they are vertical, such as the *seisan keiretsu,* a manufacturing network in which managers connect the factors of production of a certain product (e.g., Toyota and its parts suppliers), or the *ryūtsū keiretsu,* a distribution network. Or they can be horizontal, like a *kigyō shūdan*, essentially a diversified business group that links companies across related and different industries. At the center of this type of network is a *sogo shosha* (trading company), like Mitsubishi, or a financial institution, like Sumitomo. In both vertical and horizontal *keiretsus*, the network center coordinates marketing and controls financing among the allied units.

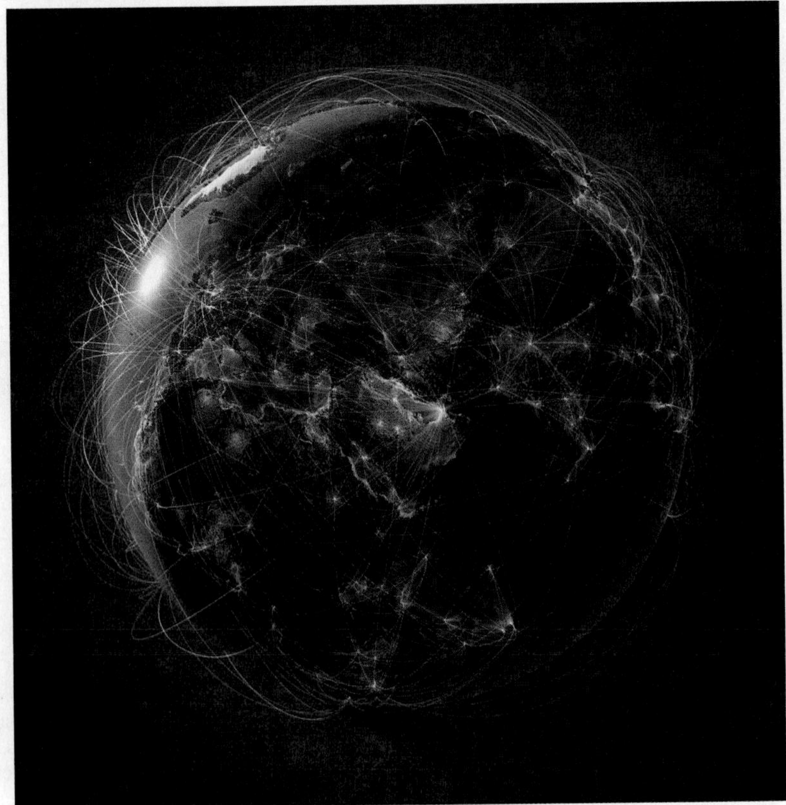

The ever-expanding billions of connections that comprise the network known as the Internet are impossible to pinpoint precisely. Here, though, we see a take on the likely configuration of links atop key geographic nodes of the airport network spanning Africa, Europe, the Middle East, and Asia. The principles that organize the arrangement of the elements of this map overlap with those that define a generic network.
Source: Anton Balazh/Shutterstock

MNEs worldwide use various forms of the neoclassical network structure.

Worldwide, MNEs exhibiting the *keiretsu* form of network structure include the Virgin Group, Cisco, and Grupo Empresarial Antioqueño. South Korean companies, like Samsung, LG, or Hyundai, share some of the characteristics of the *keiretsu* in their *chaebol* format; the ten main chaebols list nearly 600 affiliated companies.[47] German firms, such as Deutsche Bank, are similarly intertwined, but there is no formal term to describe the relationship.[48] Like their Japanese counterparts, these groups have extensive, self-sustaining connections; unlike the Japanese, they formalize centralized control.

VIRTUAL ORGANIZATION

A virtual organization is a dynamic arrangement among partners that efficiently adapts to market change.

A **virtual organization** is a temporary arrangement among independent companies, suppliers, customers, and even rivals that "works across space, time, and organizational boundaries with links strengthened by webs of communication technologies."[49] Deemphasizing formal rules, responsibilities, procedures, and relationships within the group promotes informal communication that disregards the presumptions of the hierarchy. Improving technologies support coordination among people working from different locations, making it easier to cultivate relationships, acquire resources, and develop strategic capabilities.[50]

The flexibility of virtual organizations enables easy replacement of poor performers.

The film industry provides a popular model of a virtual organization. Spread worldwide, "employees" are free agents who move from project to project applying their skills (i.e., directing, talent search, animation, costuming, and set design) as needed. Temporary arrangements let them organize, disband, and reorganize as projects evolve.[51] Market mechanisms, typically in the form of contracts, formalize relationships. Strong performers replace poor performers.

Operationally, a virtual organization consists of a core of full-time employees that rely on outside specialists to work on opportunities. The international advertising agency StrawberryFrog illustrates the process. Its peculiar name was inspired by a rare amphibian with a red body and blue legs—a nimble creature that, as the firm's CEO explains, represents the opposite of the existing "dinosaur agencies, established in the industrial age as monoliths, which have the greatest difficulty in adapting to the new era."[52] Competing with MNEs employing thousands, StrawberryFrog has a small staff, known as "frogs," based in New York, Sao Paulo, Amsterdam, and Mumbai. It bulks up as needed by hiring freelancers from around the world.[53] Free of the overhead, constraints, and complexity of hierarchies, it develops the agility and cost-effectiveness of a high-powered, loosely coupled organization.[54]

Finally, we see MNEs use variants of the virtual organization to transition from classical to neoclassical structures. Recall that 400 midsized emerging-market cities, many unfamiliar in the West, will generate nearly 40 percent of global growth over the next 15 years. Some MNEs are responding in kind, opening high-profile corporate centers in places that, although far from home, are close to the action. Company history, CEO preference, or legal constraints make others prefer less dramatic change, opting instead to create a global virtual headquarters from which to locate key functions in high-priority markets: finance and tax may go to Singapore, as Dell did, while global procurement goes to Shenzhen, as IBM chose.[55] Even as its opens subsidiaries far and wide, the MNE looks to the home-country headquarters to anchor its increasingly virtual organization.

PITFALLS OF NEOCLASSICAL STRUCTURES

Like its classical counterparts, neoclassical structures have limits. First is the difficulty of formatting something that, by definition, is evolving. Networks are intrinsically dynamic structures, thereby making adaptive reconfiguration, responsive coordination, and reasonable control challenging.[56] Cisco worries that the internal workings of its many management committees may prove too socially complex as well as physically tiring. It also struggles to manage teams amid its ongoing acquisitions and divestures. Nokia's consensus-seeking leaders promoted tremendous *esprit de corps* among its loosely bounded units; that, though, did not stop the company's gradual collapse.

Similarly, the general egalitarianism of network formats works well organizing small firms but struggles doing the same for larger ones. We see some firms devising means to preempt these threats. Srijan, an Indian software company, lets employees monitor coworkers' compensation. Others, such as SumAll, a U.S. software startup, institute a corporate constitution that formalizes the rights of employees to involve them in decision-making. The jury is still out on the effectiveness of such measures. Some fear that the resulting clarity from boundary-busting could prove detrimental in knowledge-intensive firms, like McKinsey or Google, that struggle to measure individual productivity.[57]

Neoclassical structures, like their classical counterparts, run into operational problems.

Lastly, there are executives who champion self-organization to the troops yet cannot resist the temptation to micromanage decision-making. When push comes to shove, they quickly pull rank, intervening in workers' creative independence and self-direction. Recurring gaps between policy and practice fans motivational problems. In addition, hidden hierarchies can arise as workers forsake management's rhetoric and organize around the reality of their rules, rewards, and punishments.[58] Said one observer, "I've been inside a lot of companies that espouse flat organizational structures and self-management. But when you really start looking at how things actually work, you find that there is in fact a hierarchy—just one that is not explicit."[59]

COORDINATION SYSTEMS

The MNE uses coordination and control systems to synchronize, integrate, and regulate value activities across the units of its organization.

Shifting pressures for global integration and local responsiveness, fueled by dynamic industry structures and evolving market conditions, push MNEs to devise sophisticated strategies. The resulting path-breaking plans require commensurately innovative coordination methods and control measures. The importance of **coordination** follows from the reality of life in the MNE. Designing products in Taiwan, sourcing inputs from Australia into production processes in China, and distributing them to consumers worldwide creates interdependencies among many parts of the company. Coordination systems synchronize rules, responsibilities, and relationships so that these parts, both in isolation as well as interactively, use resources efficiently and make decisions effectively.

Without the means to coordinate activities, the competitiveness of a strategy, no matter how ingenious, erodes. Therefore, designing an organization, whether the format is classical or neoclassical, requires that managers develop the requisite coordination methods. Today, prevalent coordination frameworks emphasize the ideas of *standardization, planning,* or *mutual adjustment*.

COORDINATION BY STANDARDIZATION

An MNE leverages its core competency by standardizing rules and routines that compel operational consistency. **Coordination by standardization** helps attain this goal by precisely specifying the way employees do their jobs, work with one another, and deal with customers. Aspects range from the mundane (i.e., dress and decorum requirements stipulated in employee manuals) to the strategic (i.e., decision-making heuristics, protocols for entering new markets). Asked why Starbucks standardizes its products, processes, and procedures for worldwide markets, its CEO notes the need to replicate the aesthetics, operations, and aura of the atmosphere of its U.S. coffee shop concept in thousands of Starbucks shops around the world—Starbucks in Seattle must be operationally interchangeable with Starbucks in Sydney. Coordination by standardization, by setting workplace standards and scripts, achieves this goal.

Coordination by standardization

- Sets universal rules and procedures that apply to units worldwide.
- Enforces consistency of activities among dispersed units.

Coordination by standardization is ideally suited for the MNE implementing an international or global strategy. Each strategy's imperative for worldwide consistency compels prescribing a universal approach. For an international strategy, transferring, applying, and protecting core competencies promotes mandating rules and regulations. In the case of the global strategy, running densely linked, interdependent activities leaves little slack for deviations. Clear lines of authority accountability, centralized decision-making, and codified

Point — Hierarchy: The Superior Structure?

Point **Yes** Proponents of the classical hierarchy argue that it is the enduring foundation for how an MNEs optimally arrange the roles, responsibilities, and relationships of its structure. The hierarchy supports a clear unity of command, functional span of control, effective allocation of authority, and precise assignment of tasks while specifying the ideal degree of rules, routines, policies, and procedures. As modestly depicted in Figure 16.4, it applies vertical and horizontal differentiation to spell out who's who in the organization chart.

Imposing clarity on chaos supports sophisticated planning, information, and control systems. One of the strongest advocates of the hierarchy, Harold Geneen of ITT, believed it helped "make people as predictable and controllable as the capital resources that they're responsible for."[60] The hierarchy's strengths have made it the *sine qua non* of the professional management model since the early decades of the 20th century. And given the strong preference for hierarchical organizations in countries such as India and China, we fully expect this format to flourish through the 21st century. Indeed, while neoclassical structures emerge in the West, the East has many companies that are commandeered by a lofty leader who is many rungs removed from the factory floor.

Ongoing Refinements Contemporary technological, regulatory, and competitive trends have interesting implications to organizing a company. We realize that as environments change, so too must companies' strategies and structures. However, the call to discard the classical principles of the hierarchy, akin to throwing the baby out with the bathwater, is reckless. Rather, where gaps emerge in the hierarchy, managers need only reengineer processes to fill them through such programs like Total Quality Control, the Balanced Scorecard, and Six Sigma. Fine-tuning workplace arrangements through these and similar methods more than meets the challenge of changing markets.[61]

What then, you ask, do we think of the neoclassical alternative of a hyperarchy that is championed in the Counterpoint? We see radical tinkering with the day-to-day reality of organizing international operations demonstrating commendable courage but questionable judgment. Avoiding costly falls calls for thoughtful adjustment to the way organizations run, not the wistfulness of a brave new cyberworld powered by newfangled social networking tools.

Leading Indicator Google, we submit, foreshadows the approach to designing a classical hierarchy that respects the past but engages the future. Specifically, Google organizes its senior executives and work groups by business function, with the largest functions represented by engineering, product management, and marketing divisions. Despite the founders' description of Google as engineering-centric, they see virtue in chaos by design. Insiders' tales of orderly disorder, purposeful disarray, and certain uncertainty signal Google's plans to thrive on the edge of controlled chaos, all the while firmly anchored in the functional order of a classical hierarchy.

Rather than retreat to the hierarchical conventions commonly found in engineering-centric companies, such as DuPont and General Motors in earlier times, Google stretches its hierarchy as much as possible. Asked why, Larry Page, Google's co-founder, CEO, and unofficial thought leader, explained, "I want to run a company where we are moving too quickly and doing too much, not being too cautious and doing too little. If we don't have any of these mistakes, we're just not taking enough risk." [62]

FIGURE 16.4 A Classical Hierarchy

Although quite simple, this depiction effectively communicates the organizing logic of a hierarchy—different people of different rank at different levels do different jobs. As such, the various shades of folks speak to the matter of horizontal differentiation while the top-down flow highlights the idea of vertical differentiation.

Source: Paperboat/Shutterstock

Hierarchy: The Superior Structure?

Counterpoint **No** Emerging technologies in the early 1900s supported then-heretical hierarchy. Emerging technologies in the twenty-first century endorse new organization heresies. Put simply, an expanding range of digital infrastructures allows MNEs to organize their activities in new ways. The business world demands organizations that efficiently diffuse information and effectively integrate its flows in accessing new markets, new suppliers, and new partners. Today, just as back then, bright executives break free of the shackles of conventionality, finding ways to build organizations that leverage the expanding waves of information flowing in, through, and out of the MNE.

The Crux of Change Unquestionably, the tried-and-true classical hierarchy has virtues. Nevertheless, market trends spotlight its growing limits. Notably, it organizes workplace activities and information flows in ways that thwart integration. Even when turbocharged with matrix overlays and mixed adjustments, the hierarchy slows relationships, confuses accountability, and complicates activities.[63] McKinsey & Company, for example, report that struggling MNEs' reliance on traditional organization formats imposes a steep globalization penalty. By leashing the intrinsic motivation of employees, stifling adaptation, and squelching entrepreneurialism, hierarchies lead to poor performance on several dimensions of organizational health such as establishing a shared vision, encouraging innovation, and building productive relationships with governments and business partners.[64]

The Hyperarchy Looking around today one sees examples of *social networks*, *virtual organizations*, *flat hierarchies,* or *peer-to-peer formats*. These neoclassical forms exhibit the general properties of a **hyperarchy**: namely, "a large-scale, self-organizing community that sets free unusually high degrees of energy and engagement—despite the lack of clear or direct economic payoff for participants."[65] In echoes of the network, the hyperarchy is a constellation of actors and relationships that follow from the interactions of technology, knowledge, social relations, administrative routines, and legal ties. Figure 16.5, albeit simply, illustrates these properties.

The hyperarchy is "infinitely large, never balanced, never optimal and has unique perspectives for all members."[66] Actors connect to others through direct and indirect channels. "Information flows along multiple and intermediate paths; this allows for multiple and overlapping points at which information can be sorted and interpreted. It makes it possible to process an abundance of information

Counterpoint

effectively."[67] By remedying the bias toward instituting enervating boundaries, the hyperarchy provides the framework to build a truly integrated enterprise.

A noteable hyperarchy is the open source model, a software movement in which program source code is given away to volunteers who fix bugs and design new features with no direct compensation. Operationally, it applies basic rules to increase transparency, coordinate efforts, and control performance. Programers' ability to monitor peers' production encourages bartering and collaboration. Similar situations unfold with the intriguing ecosystems that power the Apple and Android "app" phenomena. Others point to Technology, Entertainment, Design (TED), a non-profit devoted to "Ideas Worth Spreading," which hosts conferences that are then distributed in video format via the Internet. Absent central direction, an informal, loosely coupled network of some 8,000 volunteers has translated subtitles for thousands of videos into more than 90 languages.[68]

The Test Unquestionably, we are witnessing a fundamental shift in our idea of organization. The precision of vertical and horizontal differentiation, we argue, slowly but surely gives way to loosely coupled, less bounded neoclassical formats.[69] Moreover, in our opinion, it's a tad delusional to think that one need merely apply organizational band-aids, such as Six Sigma or the Balanced Scorecard, to update the increasingly anachronistic command-and-control systems of classical structures. Indeed, concluded an analyst, "Today's big companies do very little to enhance the productivity of their professionals. In fact, their vertically oriented organizational structures, retrofitted with ad hoc and matrix overlays, nearly always make professional work more complex and inefficient."[70]

Andy Grove, CEO of Intel for many years, foreshadows how the "chaos" of the hyperarchy will reset the "order" of the hierarchy. He reasons that a structure must encourage and energize constructive confrontation in ways that let workers agree and disagree but, ultimately, commit to the same goals. The challenge, he says, is developing a structure that will "let chaos reign and then rein in chaos."[71] In our view, quickly changing market situations, technological frontiers, and radical workflows indicate that the neoclassical hyperarchy, not the classical hierarchy, meets this mission.

Identify three defining features of a classical hierarchy as well as three defining features of a neoclassical hyperarchy. Which type would you prefer to work in, and why?

FIGURE 16.5 A Neoclassical Hyperarchy

This depiction of a hyperarchy, again quite simplified, highlights key features. Rather than the ranks and divisions found in a classical hierarchy, we see dynamic patterns of relationships, aided and abetted by technologies, that outline lines of communication, coordination, and collaboration among equivalent "blue" managers.

Source: Paperboat/Shutterstock

knowledge specified in detailed manuals prescribes who, when, why, and how one does his job. Resources and components, for instance, are needed at specific plants at specific times. Standardizing coordination methods—such as the format for processing information and supervising logistics—preempts irregularities that would otherwise interrupt activities.

Standardizing activities reduces the operational influence of national cultures. The performance of an integrated value chain depends on links between interconnected activities that satisfy precise schedules. An office in a monochronic culture may see deadlines as hard promises while its counterpart in a polychronic culture might regard them as guidelines. Coordination by standardization synchronizes how both interpret time in the workplace. Similarly, an MNE might have factories in Japan and Mexico that manufacture the same product but, because of cultural legacies and location economics, apply different production philosophies. The Mexican factory uses a traditional assembly-line operation because of inexpensive local labor, patchy transportation infrastructure, and a high marginal cost of technology. The Japanese factory, in contrast, uses a lean production system due to local labor competency, manufacturing expertise, efficient logistics, and high warehouse expense. Coordination by standardization, in synchronizing their activities, enables the MNE to harmonize different manufacturing orientations.

CONCEPT CHECK

In Chapter 2, we note that managers deal with differences in the ways in which colleagues and subordinates, especially those from foreign cultures, respond when it comes to issues like task motivation, relationship preferences, and workplace behavior. Here we observe that, to accommodate these differences, MNEs mind cultural orientations when setting coordination systems.

Differences in industry conduct and host-government attitudes complicate coordination by standardization. Market circumstances, strategic goals, or workflow patterns often prevent specifying universal rules and procedures. MNEs, especially those implementing a multidomestic strategy, decentralize authority so that subsidiaries can adapt activities to local conditions. Few rules and procedures are universal, applying to every situation in every unit in every country. Ongoing calls to adjust this rule or change that procedure undermine the authority of standardization. Hence, MNEs implementing a multidomestic strategy cautiously engage methods of coordination by standardization.

COORDINATION BY PLAN

Optimizing, as oppose to maximizing, organization effectiveness leads an MNE to use **coordination by plan**. This approach relies on general objectives, extensive guidelines, and precise schedules to coordinate activities. In turn, the resulting plans define critical success

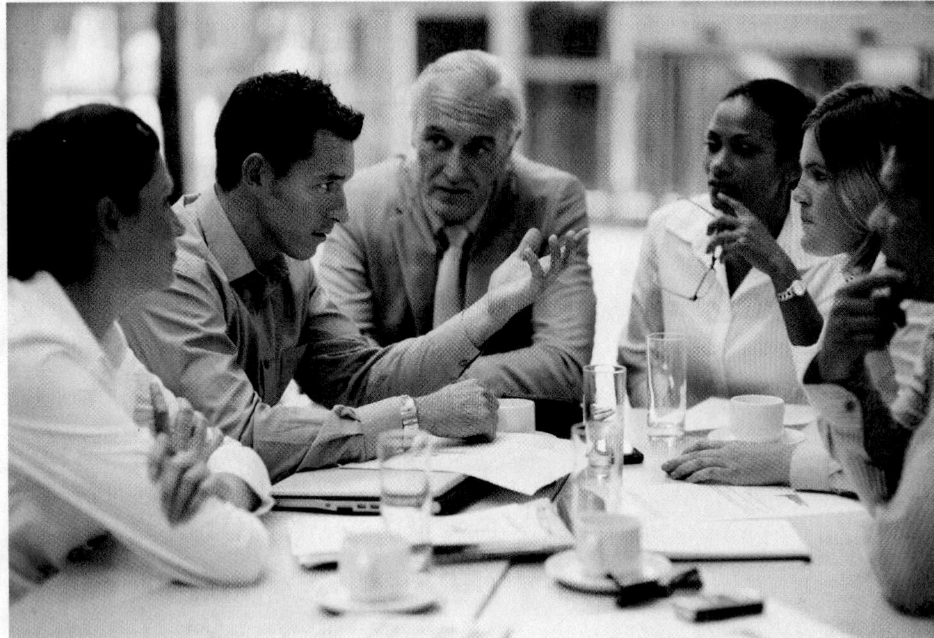

Technology create immense possibilities to connect, communicate, and coordinate with other folks without actually being in the same physical location. Still, an enduringly popular choice is face-to-face interaction that help coworkers set standards, discuss plans, and make adjustments.
Source: Yuri Arcurs/Fotolia

factors, specify expectations, and set hard deadlines. Managers rely on their planning systems to regulate how units accept, adopt, and, where legitimate, adapt plans. They also identify participating managers and programs, establish timing and format, and set communication methods. Optimizing objectives, as opposed to maximizing them, leads an MNE to use coordination by plan. In the key difference from coordination by standardization, managers of interdependent units have the latitude to mutually adjust goals and schedules—provided they still meet deadlines and hit targets.

Coordination by plan requires that interdependent units meet common deadlines and objectives.

Notwithstanding the brilliance of the plan, the unexpected is ever-present; recall, for example, "the best-laid plans of mice and men often go awry." Market disruptions, government regulations, and personnel moves, to name just a few, cause changes that require adjusting objectives and schedules. These sorts of anomalies complicate coordination by plan. Furthermore, managing objectives and schedules depends on extensive communication among different groups spanning multiple borders. Geographic distance and cultural divergence increase the time, expense, and errors in cross-national exchange.

Improving technologies steadily fortify the effectiveness of coordination by plan. Quantum leaps in information technology boost the ease of analyzing, synthesizing, and exchanging information. Faster travel, easier voice options, and better videoconferencing overcome long-running barriers to multinational planning. Teleconferencing, for instance, easily lets those who prefer dealing with counterparts through face-to-face contact still capture the non-verbal nuances of body language. Indeed, the historic bane of international business has been the necessity of visiting far-away colleagues, partners, and customers, often at a moment's notice, high expense, and considerable effort. Now, teleconferencing creates the magical ability to be many places at once, thereby boosting the practicality of coordination by plan.

Innovative management methods further bolster coordination by plan. Six Sigma, a rigorous and disciplined planning process, uses data and statistical analysis to coordinate practices and systems. Credit Suisse, Siemens, GE, Korea Telecom, Wipro, Nortel Networks, Air Canada, and DuPont have all used it to improve their planning processes. The parameters and analytics of similar programs, such as the Balanced Scorecard, are used worldwide.

Coordination by plan requires synchronizing people and processes across countries.[72] Hence, cultural differences pose complications. Often workers differ in their orientations toward trust, exchange, and collaboration.[73] Units anchored in individualistic cultures may disagree over information sharing or collaboration responsibilities with their collectivist counterparts; ensuing conflicts muddle coordination. These differences, which grow less disruptive in standardized situations as rules regulate relationship, significantly shape the effectiveness of coordination by plan.

MNEs apply various methods to reinforce coordination by plan. Some locate international and domestic personnel in proximity to each other—say, by placing the international division in the same building as product divisions—to promote networks that facilitate collaboration and communication. Others build cross-national teams of people with different responsibilities to debate objectives, resolve problems, and improve multinational planning.[74]

COORDINATION BY MUTUAL ADJUSTMENT

Coordination by mutual adjustment depends on managers interacting extensively with counterparts.

Some MNEs coordinate value activities through less formal mechanisms than standards or plans. They opt for the personal touch, socially engineering their systems to cultivate relationships among employees that, in turn, support coordination. Rather than rules and routines in the context of standardization, or objectives and schedules in the context of planning, they rely on social networking tools in the context of mutual adjustment. Aggressively cultivating collaboration among coworkers, goes the reasoning, builds systems that support sophisticated strategies. This outlook endorses **coordination by mutual adjustment**.

Consider 3M's technology experts in its 100-plus laboratories worldwide. Success, 3M believes, depends on these folks developing robust knowledge-generating and decision-making relationships that support exchanging ideas, coordinating programs, and integrating results. The abstraction of the research process along with the complexity of product development prevents standardizing impersonal coordination methods. Rather, productive communication among bright, independent-minded folks requires robust, personal, and frequent interactions to build trust and promote collaboration. Hence, 3M uses coordination by mutual adjustment.

Key tools include a Technical Council, which comprises the heads of the major labs, meets monthly, and has a three-day annual retreat to boost exchanges across units. A broader-based Technical Forum, composed of scientists and technical experts chosen as representatives of various units, extends the social network.[75] Both methods cultivate the personal exchange of ideas, a key precondition of coordinating activities by mutual adjustment.

Although 3M's design suggests a straightforward process, coordination by mutual adjustment imposes tough demands. It requires collaboration among associates in different parts of the world. The scale and scope of the typical MNE, naturally, poses many logistical obstacles; newfangled, robust social networking technologies provide only a partial solution. Ordinary geographic constraints, for example, require that teams alternate meetings between early morning and late evening to accommodate various time zones. It is not unusual, over the course of the day, for a manager in the United States to teleconference with folks in Asia at 2 AM, colleagues in Western Europe at 9 AM, and coworkers and South America at 3 PM. For example, Cisco averages nearly 6,000 teleconferences a week. Senior executives working on three to five coordination groups, and often many more, may have teleconferencing meetings around the clock.

Besides logistics, coordination by mutual adjustment often runs into behavioral obstacles. Decision making typically slows as views adjust and readjust. Managers' commitment may waver as some tire of ongoing negotiation. The personalized dynamic of coordination by mutual adjustment challenges the official trappings set by formal roles, status, and power. Its processes blur positional relationships among superiors, colleagues, and subordinates, whereas coordination by standardization or plan explicitly recognize and reinforce vertical and horizontal differentiation. Coordination by mutual adjustment, therefore, puts big demands on senior executives: Innovations can arise anywhere within the firm's global network, not just at the center. The role of headquarters changes fundamentally.[76] The necessity of breaking boundaries requires resetting executives' roles from telling people what to do to facilitating their success. Hence, the system is philosophically and practically compatible with forms of neoclassical structures.

FIGURE 16.6 Once Inconceivable, Now Ordinary.

Source: P. C. Vey/New Yorker Cartoon Bank/www.cartoonbank.com

Using coordination by mutual adjustment requires a range of management methods. Commonly, MNEs assess opportunities or check threats by building cross-national, cross-functional, and cross-business teams. Assembled and charged with collaborating, these teams share viewpoints and champion cooperative efforts while establishing liaisons among subsidiaries to integrate actions among different groups. Similarly, MNEs rotate managers among various slots in the company, reasoning that personal familiarity cultivates relationships that promote collaboration. In addition, rotation across divisional, business, or functional lines promotes relationships that weaken insular thinking and reinforce idea sharing.

CONCEPT CHECK

No matter the coordination approach adopted by an MNE, none are immune to the complications posed by national cultures. Different national cultures differently influence the social, workplace, political, legal, and economic contexts. Differences in cultural conditions also influence a company's strategic options, shaping its choices regarding coordination by standardization, planning, or adjustment.

A Case in Point Although difficult, coordination by mutual adjustment processes can productively move an MNE's strategy forward. Red Hat's Global Support Services, for example, solves complex technical problems facing users of the company's software products. Its technical support engineers, technical account managers, and software maintenance engineers work from 16 countries, support 3,600 coworkers in 65 offices distributed across 28 countries, and provide round-the-clock customer service in nine languages.[77]

Given the intricate technical architecture of Red Hat's software, many questions from customers were unique in nature and necessitated personal consultations. Improving their performance, management realized, depended on finding ways to leverage Red Hat's collective knowledge. The fact that solutions were often unique to a particular technical problem ruled out standardization and reduced the effectiveness of planning scripts. Still, even though many answers were unique to a particular client, overlapping aspects meant that Red Hat's consultants often reinvented parts of the software wheel. Improving the ability of its globally dispersed and diverse technical support associates, it decided, depended on improving collaboration among them through processes of mutual adjustment.

Over the course of a year or so, Red Hat relied on cross-national teams to bust the structural, cultural, and procedural boundaries that separated colleagues. Social-network analyses mapped the frequency and effectiveness of communications, thereby clarifying the flow of information among personnel. Red Hat's coordination by mutual adjustment systems

CONCEPT CHECK

In discussing measures for "Dealing with Cultural Differences" in Chapter 2, we explain how different attitudes toward *cultural distance* and different responses to *culture shock* frustrate the efforts of managers to coordinate value activities that span different cultural environments. Here, we add that they can create problems beyond the corrective capacity of a coordination system. In such cases, managers use control measures to impose order.

ultimately connected people from several different functional roles, across sixteen countries, through nine languages, and in dozens of areas of domain knowledge. Red Hat also created its Knowledge Centered Support unit and fostered its intelligent swarming model to resolve complicated problems more quickly as well as handle greater call volumes without adding staff. Resulting improvements in accuracy, consistency, and responsiveness boosted customer satisfaction, improved retention, and increased profitability.[78]

CONTROL SYSTEMS

MNEs monitor performance to make sure employees are appropriately doing what needs to be done. If plants are performing poorly, responses are slowing, schedules are slipping, or resources are wasted, then managers step in and impose forceful change. **Control systems**, the methods and means of forceful change, are part of a well-designed organization.[79] They define how managers compare performance to plans, identify differences, and, where found, assess the basis for the gap and impose corrections. Control systems regulate executive efforts, resource allocation, and self-interest. They directly complement coordination processes and structural designs. Prominent systems of control include bureaucratic, market, and clan.

BUREAUCRATIC CONTROL

Bureaucratic control emphasizes organizational authority and relies on rules and regulations.

Imposing explicit rules and routines to govern activities installs **bureaucratic control**. This system of control supports operations that lend themselves to absolute rules and exact scripts and, importantly, workplaces that require rules to regiment behaviors. It is highly effective in some situations, such as those applying Six Sigma or Total Quality Management, which rely on precise standards to regulate activities. Clear controls also clarify authority and accountability, thereby improving communication and coordination among the relevant workers. While tempting to think that MNEs do not suffer such difficulties, fewer rather than more executives believe their organizations have blurry rules and regulations; bureaucratic controls reduce this problem.[80] Bureaucratic control shares organizing principles with coordination by standardization and fits the principles of the classical forms of structure.

MARKET CONTROL

Market control uses external market mechanisms to set standards that regulate performance.

The MNE that uses external market mechanisms, such as profitability or market share, to establish performance benchmarks installs **market controls**. Objective standards, not subjective interpretations, regulate performance. Control systems, ever vigilant, escalate when a unit deviates from independent benchmarks. Relying on market standards creates universal metrics that work in all countries—e.g., profitability and market share are measured the same everywhere.

For example, MNEs such as Gore, Nestlé, Infosys, and Nike decentralize considerable authority to the local subsidiaries, preferring that citizens of the host country run local operations. Headquarters then supports subsidiaries and waits for superior results. If not forthcoming, control systems activate and senior executives step in. Absent objective indicators such as market share, senior executives would struggle to assess a subsidiary's performance. The principles of market control overlap with those of coordination by plan and fit the principles of the classical and neoclassical structures.

CLAN CONTROL

Clan control uses shared values and ideals to moderate employee behavior.

An MNE that relies on **clan control** aims to enforce its preferred way of doing business by developing shared values among employees. It promotes a collective ethos that aims to influence individual employees' workplace behavior. Operationally, clan control relies on values,

CONCEPT CHECK

Chapter 12 explains that MNEs face "Operational Obstacles" in building communication channels among the links in their value chains. It also explains that in deciding where to locate production operations, Not long ago, inefficient transportation and expensive communications hindered efforts to coordinate global activities. Today, improving social networking tools make clan control an increasingly practical option.

beliefs, and norms to regulate employee behaviors. The operative goal is socializing employees to personally identify with the MNE's strategic vision as they go about their day-to-day routines.[81]

Clan control is difficult in any context but particularly in the MNE. The ideal of a unifying vision within a dispersed, diverse global enterprise inevitably conflicts with some employees' values and norms. Certainly, there are notable successes, like the social aspects of renowned clan control systems, such as J&J's Credo or the Toyota Way. Clan control shares organizing principles with coordination by mutual adjustment and fits the principles of neoclassical structures.

CONTROL MECHANISMS

Ceteris paribus, effective control encourages engineering objective mechanisms. A generation ago, the comparatively costly economics of travel, data exchange, and communication technologies endorsed certain control mechanisms. Improving economics, courtesy of declining communication and transportation costs, make monitoring situations cheaper, faster, and easier. This process has reduced the usefulness of some tools, boosted the usefulness of others, and created the possibility for new mechanisms. MNEs often support their control system with the following tools.

Timely reports allow managers improve the speed and insight of decision-making.

Reports The intricacies of international business make reports a vital control method. Managers rely on frequent, accurate, and real-time reports to allocate resources, monitor performance, and reward successes. Reports also function as an early warning system, alerting managers to deviations from plans. Often, MNEs use report formats for foreign operations that resemble those used domestically, reasoning that they have worked here so they should work there. The global diffusion of standardized software packages from SAP, Oracle, IBM, Microsoft, and Red Hat supports this outlook. Standardizing the format of reports worldwide, by leveraging corporate management's familiarity, lessens the need for new types of reporting mechanisms. Also, reports that share the same format ease comparing the performance of units in different markets.

Visits to Subsidiaries Formal reports only go so far. Many senior managers, especially in those MNEs applying coordination by adjustment and clan control, regularly visit subsidiaries. Face-to-face meetings, formal budget reviews, and planning seminars fortify control systems. Old-school subsidiary visits promote direct, credible communication between headquarters and local managers.[82] Increasingly, technologies like teleconferencing expand managers' options. Ongoing teleconference innovations, supported by wikis, social networking, and web-based collaboration services, help MNEs reduce travel, save time, boost productivity, and tighten controls. Recall that Cisco averages about 6,000 teleconferences a week; those have cut its annual travel budget by more than half while significantly increasing face time among managers.[83]

A system that relies on a combination of measurements is more reliable than one that does not.

Evaluation Metrics Headquarters evaluate subsidiaries and their managers on many measures. Financial metrics dominate evaluations, particularly when an MNE relies on coordination by plan and control by bureaucracy. Important internal metrics look at budget, productivity, and profitability performance. MNEs adjust evaluation metrics to avoid penalizing or rewarding managers or subsidiaries for conditions beyond their control. For example, headquarters may decide not to expand further in a country because of its slow growth. Punishing managers for the country's adverse situation, independent of their performance, is demotivating. Effective metrics qualify evaluation for local conditions and global trends.

Information Systems Technology platforms, by expediting information systems, provide useful control tools. Most MNEs use enterprise resource planning to monitor activities, such as product planning, parts purchasing, maintaining inventories, customer service, and order fulfillment.[84] MNEs face constraints in acquiring information, notably the cost of that information compared to its value and the difficulty of identifying redundancies and excluding the irrelevant. MNEs regularly reevaluate the sources they use to preempt information overload. The preferred approach to coordination and control guides triage.

WHICH CONTROL SYSTEM WHEN?

An MNE tailors its control system to support its strategy. MNEs following a global strategy prefer market controls, given that they can use objective benchmarks to evaluate performance in any market. Transnational companies find value in clan control. The vitality of open exchange among geographically diffuse people fits the idea that common values, beliefs, and norms facilitate collaboration.

Still, like most operational decisions in international business, there are few hard and fast rules. Complications posed by the competing pressures of integration and responsiveness, along with evolving industry structures, make for dynamic value chain configurations. Likewise, supporting increasingly sophisticated strategies pushes managers to act in kind, fine-tuning established, and experimenting with promising, control methods. In practice, few MNEs enjoy the luxury of relying on a single method of control. J&J, for instance, uses market and clan control to regulate performance. Certainly, it would prefer a single universal solution. But, like those of other astute MNEs, its control systems fit the contingencies imposed by its structure, methods of coordination, and as we now see, its culture.

ORGANIZATION CULTURE

Having examined the roles played by structure and systems in organizing an MNE, we now turn to the final element of design: its organization culture. In theory, one could profile this idea from an applied perspective, specifying it as the way things are done in an MNE and evaluating how workers organize around rules, rewards, and punishments.[85] Alternatively, we could follow the suggestion of Chapter 2 and adopt a philosophical view and assess how organization culture, as an embedded set of shared normative principles, guides actions and sanctions behaviors within the MNE.

Organization culture is the shared meaning and beliefs that shape how employees interpret information, make decisions, and implement actions.

We opt to integrate these perspectives and define **organization culture** as the coherent set of assumptions about an MNE and its goals and practices that are shared by its employees. This system of shared values determines what is important, endorses common beliefs about how the world works, and frames how managers make decisions, take actions, and sustain a common cause.

A KEY PIECE OF THE PERFORMANCE PUZZLE

Analyses and anecdotes of corporate performance indicate that building a resourceful organization involves a difficult balancing act: inspire employees worldwide to develop and apply new ideas but ensure that they implement them ever mindful of the MNE's global objectives. Few companies strike and sustain balance solely through their structure and systems. Instead, they look to their organization culture to complete the trick. On this point, Jack Welch of GE cautioned, "Objectives don't get you there. Values do."[86] On the other side of the globe, South Korea's Hyundai Motor Company has strengthened its foothold in the Asian region and is fast expanding its cult of value-based operations on a large scale. The importance and intricacies of promoting, supporting, and sustaining common values among employees worldwide turns our attention to how an MNE develops, diffuses, and sustains its culture.

MNEs proactively develop their organization culture, just as they purposefully design their structure and systems.

Executives have long appreciated the strategic significance of organization culture. Over the past generation or so, they have applied a progressively expansive view, seeing it as a powerful tool to drive performance. Their zeal follows from a series of studies confirming a significant link between an MNE's organization culture and its success. Facets of its culture, such as the values and principles of management, nature of the work climate and atmosphere, and traditions and ethical standards, always and everywhere influence a firm's performance.[87]

Research shows that successful MNEs develop a culture that instills in their employees the enthusiasm beyond that justified solely by economic rewards. Pay certainly motivates performance but an effective organization culture stimulates people to engage the company's vision, do their jobs well, and collaborate with others while lessening the need to regulate their behaviors with elaborate structures and systems. Its capacity to power individual performance beyond that motivated by monetary incentives puts the onus on managers to build a company that people do not want to merely work for, but aspire to belong to; employees no longer check in to get a check but become mission-led and principle-driven.

The shared values that enact an organization's culture, goes the reasoning, influence what employees perceive, how they interpret, and what they do to respond to their world. J&J, for example, anchors its strategic purpose and ideas of value creation in the principles of its Credo. This ethics manifesto unequivocally champions the values that embody the company's responsibilities to its stakeholders worldwide. When employees anywhere are confronted with opportunities or threats in the world, the Credo helps them define, analyze, and resolve them in ways that respect and reinforce J&J's culture and, by extension, its strategy.

A vibrant organization culture accelerates an MNE's transition from "good" to "great" status. Unquestionably, product development, marketing ingenuity, and financial stewardship moderate progress. Research indicates that attaining greatness, however, depends on a culture of unwavering faith and passion; rigorous discipline and focus; clearly communicated and practiced core values and timeless principles; strong work ethics; and finding and promoting people with the right outlook.[88] Great companies purposefully promote an integrated system of overarching values, perspectives, and practices—much as J&J does with its Credo or Toyota with its Toyota Way—in order to give employees a consistent way to relate to their jobs, to each other, to customers, to shareholders, and to business partners. Perhaps most decisively, it legitimates the company's mission in the eyes of employees worldwide.

CULTURE'S INCREASING IMPORTANCE

Historically, uncertainty about the dynamic of social engineering led managers to adopt a benign perspective, letting culture naturally emerge and evolve. Information and advice on "how things work around here" spread by word of mouth on factory floors and lunch-time chats. Today, MNEs proactively manage culture's emergence and evolution.[89] Organizing a globally integrated enterprise requires extensive coordination and collaboration among workers. Convergent cultural values ease the exchange of ideas between people.

The importance of organization culture will grow as the rise in emerging economies and maturing growth in the West push managers to rethink strategies and reset operations. For example, GE has reconfigured its value chain to reflect market trends. Notably, these changes have required adjusting its historically West-centric orientation for the accelerating rise in emerging economies. Asked about GE's future, its CEO replied, "We've globalized around markets, not cheap labor. The era of globalization around cheap labor is over. Today we go to Brazil, we go to China, we go to India because that's where the customers are."[90] On a related front, emerging rivals from fast-growing economies devise strategies to navigate bustling markets that run the gamut from the Base of the Pyramid to surging affluence. Companies from both the East and the West pursue new, often astounding opportunities. Capturing them involves reinventing systems of production and distribution as well as experimenting with new business models.

Increasingly sophisticated value chain configurations escalate demands on MNEs' structure and systems. These demands have lower odds of success without a supportive organization culture. In the least, competing cultural values impose boundaries that distort the communication and collaboration that gird coordination and control systems. Certainly, MNEs could opt to develop elaborate constraints, controls, and contracts in order to compel employees to step up to the challenge. And, granted, the notion that"beatings will continue until morale improves" may boost short-term performance. But improving compatibility between an MNE's culture and its strategy has proven a far more powerful driver of superior performance.[91]

BUILDING AN ORGANIZATION CULTURE

Key features of a company's organization culture include
- Values and principles of management
- Work climate and atmosphere
- Patterns of "how we do things around here"
- Traditions
- Ethical standards

Despite its pivotal function, few MNEs have been able to parlay their culture into consistently high performance. A survey of 1,200 international executives found that fewer than 10 percent believe they are currently successful at building high-performance cultures.[92] Ongoing struggles repeatedly pinpoint the epic challenge of starting, shaping, and sustaining an organization's culture to fit the market, fit the company, and fits employees' ideals. Explained IBM's vice president of global strategy for growth markets, "Changing organization charts can take a few mouse clicks. Changing business processes can take months. Changing a culture and the way employees adapt to new ways of working takes years."[93] Despite the challenge, few question the usefulness of the quest: nine of ten CEOs acknowledge that "corporate culture is as important as a strategy for business success."[94] Ongoing failure to develop executives who are mission-led and principle-driven imposes penalties that threaten organizational health.

Techniques and Tools In reality, the values and outlooks of managers, especially those from culturally dissimilar countries, often differ.[95] Furthermore, many workers, especially those working in markets far removed from the home office, have slight, if any, exposure to the idealized values held by senior managers. Even on the standards of the strategy, a far more objective concept, MNEs struggle to unify interpretations; barely half of the managers in a cross section of MNEs believed that they communicated their strategy clearly to their workers worldwide.[96]

CONCEPT CHECK

The accelerating comeback of emerging economies indicates an "inflection point" at which old strategic patterns of thought give way to new. Our discussion of different national perspectives on *value creation* in Chapter 12 argues that such problems challenge coordinating increasingly sophisticated value chains. Evidence indicates that developing a supportive organization culture provides a powerful tool.

Managers use a variety of techniques to preempt these threats. Many advocate arranging closer contact among managers from different countries to unify values. Cross-national teams are a prevalent tool.[97] Developing a consensus depends on members' engaging common values, rather than mechanical compliance with coordination routines or control codes.

Others prefer a more interpersonal approach, rotating high-performing executives from headquarters and subsidiaries throughout global units. Wipro, an Indian technology company, employs 54,000 people in 35 countries, more than 11,000 of whom work for units outside of India and more than 90 percent of whom are Indian. Explained the chief executive of global programs, "We sprinkle Indians in new markets to help seed and set up the culture and intensity."[98] Some use more focused means. GE's Leadership Development Center, for example, puts managers from different businesses and different parts of the world into a classroom setting; there, they challenge and clarify the principles of the company's culture.

Mattel highlights a variation of this approach. It has more than 25,000 employees based in 36 countries who oversee toy sales in 150 nations. Although you would think selling the fun of toys would unify employees' cultural ideals, transcending different values has proven problematic. As a result, Mattel runs executive development programs via a global e-learning system that puts its people and its principles directly into play. Improving managers' understanding at both headquarters and subsidiaries means that "global management is more closely aligned with the corporate strategies and goals. This, in turn, produces innovative and creative products, reduces costs, and improves employee satisfaction."[99]

MNEs from other cultures share parallel outlooks and apply similar practices. Toyota relies on its Technical Skills Academy, its corporate university in Toyota City, to fortify its culture as well as firmly anchor its next generation of leadership in it. Some sessions teach factory controls and assembly procedures, others develop management skills, but all inculcate the principles of the esteemed "Toyota Way."[100] Socializing employees with renowned management secrets, top management believes, enables employees to base decisions on a "philosophical sense of purpose, to think long term, to have a process for solving problems, to add value to the organization by developing its people, and to recognize that continuously solving root problems drives organizational learning."[101] Toyota posts graduates to its offices worldwide, acting as missionaries who spread the Toyota Way. Long a fundamental feature of the company, the Toyota Way steadily plays a bigger part in developing the organization. Increasing international operations, particularly in the emerging economies, fueled concern among senior management that the key principles of its organization culture were weakening.[102] Now, the company relies on the Toyota Way to harmonize its organization culture throughout its global operations.

Instead of simply letting culture emerge naturally, many managers do as they do with structure and systems: purposefully and proactively develop the system of shared values they reason girds strategic success. As we just reviewed, they use a variety of approaches to socialize employees to the common cause. An intriguing development, showcased in our *Looking to the Future* box, is the rising prominence of corporate universities.

ORGANIZATION CULTURE AND STRATEGY

An organization's culture shapes the success of its strategic moves.

Strategy imposes organization requirements that call for certain configurations of structures and systems. Likewise, the preferred principles and practices of organization culture vary with the requirements of the MNE's strategy (see Figure 16.7). Although overlapping at the edge, each strategy sets critical operating standards that dictate organizational imperatives. Moreover, the quest for operational consistency calls for socially engineering the organization culture to spur employees' acceptance of the MNEs strategic standards.

FIGURE 16.7 Strategy and Organizational Culture in International Business

The four strategies mapped here correspond to the four strategic archetypes of strategies covered in Chapter 11. Each has specific indications for the features and forms of the company's organization. Strategic success depends on developing the requisite structure, systems, and culture. Absent that, MNEs struggle to convert ambition into accomplishment.

Pressure for Global Integration	Pressure for Local Responsiveness: Low	Pressure for Local Responsiveness: High
High	**GLOBAL** Strategic Objectives: Productivity and efficiency Strategic Emphasis: Integration and consistency Dominant Attributes: Standardized goal achievement, global competitiveness Leadership Style: Production achievement oriented, decisive control orientation Collaboration Standards: Objective goal orientation, efficiency driven	**TRANSNATIONAL** Strategic Objectives: Integration responsiveness, learning Strategic Emphasis: Innovation, ideas, and collaboration Dominant Attributes: Creativity, dynamism, flexibility Leadership Style: Visionary, entrepreneurial, risk affinitive Collaboration Standard: Multicultural, teambuilding
Low	**INTERNATIONAL** Strategic Objectives: Leverage core competencies Strategic Emphasis: Control, stability, predictability Dominant Attributes: Formal order, rules regulations uniformity Leadership Style: Director, administrator, enforcer Collaboration Standards: Rules, policies and procedures, clear expectations	**MULTIDOMESTIC** Strategic Objectives: Local market responsiveness Strategic Emphasis: Philosophical consensus, operational commitment Dominant Attributes: Cohesiveness, trust, affiliation Leadership Style: Adaptive, facilitator, mentor Collaboration Standard: Egalitarianism, tolerance, mutual respect

An MNE implementing a global strategy, for example, engineers a forceful culture that insists on universal goals, priorities, and practices. Standardizing value activities calls for standardizing employees' views on the specification of tasks, the arrangement of work, and the stipulation of rules, rewards, and punishments. Competing interpretations are not an option. The imperative of consistency calls for socially engineering an organization culture that spurs employees worldwide to accept and adopt the firm's standards. This, in turn, endorses coordinating through standardization and controlling through bureaucracy.

Features of organization culture vary with the strategy the MNE pursues.

Alternatively, the MNE implementing a multidomestic strategy encourages greater variety in the local interpretation of global goals. Adapting value activities to local standards requires decentralization, which in turn necessitates looser values and higher tolerance for different perspectives in order to sustain the vitality of local outlooks. Consequently, people in different units share fewer common values. Sustaining the vitality of local outlooks, in turn, necessitates a higher tolerance for different perspectives. One may wonder, given the preceding emphasis of the importance of a cohesive organization culture, does tolerating differentiation then reject this goal? The short answer, no, rests on the presumption that management adroitly adapts the organization to aggressively promote an integrative perspective among its workers, no matter where they are or what they do.

CRN
Case Review Note

Differentiation does not necessarily impose organizational penalties provided the MNE can rely on a common perspective to unify workers' interpretations. J&J provides a compelling case in point. Its multidomestic strategy led it to organize a decentralized area structure, install coordination by planning, and apply control through market metrics. However, J&J relied on its Credo to provide the values and visions that diffuses this mix throughout its family of interdependent yet also independent local subsidiaries. Recall that its Credo specifies who and what to care about and in what order. Without it, J&J would likely see its organization of 250 subsidiaries fracture into autonomous fiefdoms that overlapped less and less. With it, J&J reinforces the capacity of its structure and systems to unify its quasi-independent business units into a globally integrated enterprise.

Looking to the Future

The Rise of Corporate Universities

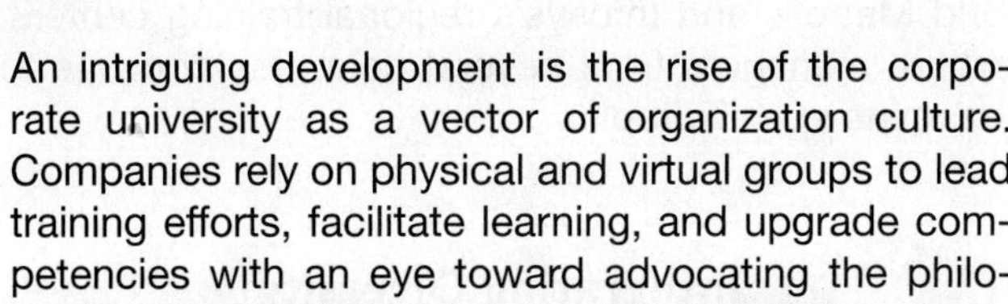

An intriguing development is the rise of the corporate university as a vector of organization culture. Companies rely on physical and virtual groups to lead training efforts, facilitate learning, and upgrade competencies with an eye toward advocating the philosophical ideals that anchor the organization's culture.

Worldwide, more than a thousand new corporate universities have opened over the past decade. By region, they are steadily expanding in the United States, thriving in Europe, and accelerating in Asia. The number of U.S. corporate universities grew from around 400 in 1993, to 2,000 in 2001, to nearly 4,000 today. Many of the *Fortune* 500, including Walt Disney, Boeing, Motorola, General Electric, J.P. Morgan Chase, and Southwest Airlines, run one.[103]

The first big one, McDonald's Hamburger University, began operating in 1961 in a restaurant basement in Elk Grove, Illinois. By 2013, it had trained nearly 85,000 managers and owner/operators in 28 languages from 119 countries in "hamburgerology." In 2010, McDonald's opened a Hamburger University in Shanghai, China, to support its goal of eventually launching up to 5,000 Chinese outlets. Elsewhere, similar changes are afoot. Infosys's 35-acre campus houses the world's largest corporate university. Its 250 faculty members annually socialize thousands of new hires to the ways of Infosys as well as align the ongoing education of tens of thousands of existing employees with its evolving strategy.

Whereas some companies attach their universities to headquarters, others sprinkle them worldwide. Unisys, for example, has campuses in its key market regions. Some break free of geography, running virtual online universities where employees e-learn via live webcasts, online discussion groups, webinars, videoconferences, and interactive sessions. Going forward, the issue of who teaches what and where will test unprecedented platforms and pedagogies. The potential disruptive innovation of massive open online courses—dubbed MOOCs—could reset our understanding of corporate universities. Presently, we see emerging players such as Udacity, Coursera, and edX offering a variety of services to students, institutions, and, increasingly, companies.[104] Vendors offer courses, designed by or tailored to the specific company, through their proprietary Internet platform. Increasingly, the compelling economics of online education question the practicality of the traditional infrastructure—classrooms, hotels, and transportation—of corporate universities.

An Expanding Mission

Originally, corporate universities aimed to teach practical skills and workplace systems. The founding goal of McDonald's Hamburger University, for instance, was preparing people to run the day-to-day operations of a franchise. Today, reports the American Society for Training and Development, "training isn't just a nice thing to do anymore. Companies are now thinking of training as a strategic imperative."[105] The challenges of changing global markets require continually upgrading managers' competencies. Companies use their universities to instill new hires with a big-picture view of global operations and to re-energize current workers' commitment. Others amplify this theme, declaring that their corporate university "inculcates everyone, from the clerical assistant to the top executive, in the culture that makes the organization unique and special and defines behaviors that enable employees to 'live the values.'"[106]

The Crucible of Change

Corporate universities run programs that engage high-potential executives on key topics. They push executives to develop the insights and cultivate the personal relationships that organize the globally integrated enterprise. Its rise as the forum of the future increasingly makes it the crucible of company strategy. Some foresee the corporate university becoming the MNE's thought center that formulates, rather than follows, strategy.

Linking executive learning with the company's strategy drives the recent and projected growth of corporate universities. The CEO of Unipart, a British auto parts maker, notes that his center "is at the very heart of the business" and a "key enabler for future growth of the business."[107] Like many other CEOs, he runs a monthly course on the philosophy and principles of Unipart's approach to business. Jack Welch probably set the standard. Over his 20-year role as GE's CEO, he appeared more than 300 times at the company's training center at Croton-on-Hudson. Holding forth in "the Pit," he socialized some 20,000 GE managers to the ways of the company.[108]

Senior executives who take on the hat of teacher generate great benefits. The director of LVMH's university believes that putting top people into the pit "gives them access to people they would never get access to....It is the role of our top senior executives to get a feel for what is going on."[109] Benefits accrue to attendees too. Activities, seminars, and training sessions build business skills, promote social networks, and improve operational analytics. Attendees return home with new ideas and a better sense of how their professional development stacks up to global counterparts.

Lastly, sophisticated strategies push MNEs to involve more employees, both those staying home and those heading abroad, in general international development. Few question the need to generate, transfer, and adopt ideas from wherever they originate to wherever they add value. This goal, particularly compelling in MNEs building a globally integrated enterprise, calls for preparing all employees to do so. Indeed, growing globalization spurs MNEs to help employees, both national and international, to understand worldwide operations, opportunities, and constraints. International business content once reserved for expatriates is added to the coursework irrespective of whether attendees plan to work abroad. Examples include Procter & Gamble's training on globalization issues; programs at Honda of America to improve cultural awareness; and Mattel's and Infosys's regional training centers, where managers from several countries convene to examine specific topics.

Integrating Diversity

Unquestionably, a mandate for corporate universities is integrating diverse workforces. Hiring people from around the world expands the mix of nationalities and ethnicities. Hiring engineers in Mumbai or Sophia to collaborate with folks in Redmond makes compelling economic sense. Preempting a Tower of Babel requires socializing the resulting mix of people to the sensitivities and skills needed to navigate cross-national teams.

Tempting as it is to rely upon happenstance to manage the process, benign neglect is risky. Executives turn to corporate universities, seeing in them a robust platform for managing the process in a controlled, purposeful setting. The vice president of Unisys University explains that getting people into the classroom aligns employee development with the company's strategy and fortifies their connection with the organization's culture.[110]

Expanding operations into more dissimilar emerging markets challenges sustaining common values. Toyota, for example, saw the globalization of its business steadily diluting the principles of the Toyota Way. When the firm was primarily Japan-centric, it relied upon spontaneous chats on the factory floor and informal networking in the executive suite to sustain its organization culture. "Before, when everyone was Japanese, we didn't have to make these things explicit," said the director of Toyota Institute, its corporate university. "Now we have to set the Toyota Way down on paper and teach it."[111] To that end, it relies on its Toyota Institute in Toyota City, Japan along with its satellite centers in Thailand and the United States.

Filling Gaps

The global financial crisis has boosted the role of corporate universities—but for less than charitable reasons. Analysts and educators debate whether the manner of teaching business students in traditional university settings may have aggravated the crisis.[112] Critics hold that conventionally designed MBA programs grew too scientific, too detached from real-world issues, and too isolated from the moral implications of choice and consequence. The orthodoxy of MBA programs, some contend, distorted students' view of the moral, ethical, and social considerations of business leadership.[113] These shortcomings poorly prepared graduates to do the right thing for their company and for society. Consequently, more companies increasingly look to their universities to develop socially responsible outlooks. ■

CASE Hyundai Motor Company: Expanding Organizational Excellence

The global automobile industry includes more than 50 different companies that produced a record 84 million vehicles[114] in 2012. This industry, dominated by firms such as Toyota and General Motors, has changed considerably since the first modern car was built in 1885. Instead of the initial manufacture of automobiles for the local market, firms today have been expanding their operations to span the globe through facilitating more exports and setting up international production factories in key regional markets. This expansion has forced companies to come to grips with unique structural, cultural, and control issues. One firm that has risen from obscurity to preeminence by successfully overcoming these challenges is the Hyundai Motor Company (HMC).

Hyundai Overview

Based in Seoul, South Korea, HMC was founded in 1968 and initially served as a complete knock down assembler for Ford Motors. Growing from its humble beginnings, HMC, with its sister company, Kia Motors, has become the largest automaker in South Korea and the fifth largest automaker in the world based on 2012 car sales totaling 1.26 million units.[115] The firm currently owns and operates not only its automotive division, but also possesses a 32.8 percent stake in Kia Motors as well as a full spectrum of vertically oriented subsidiaries that supply Hyundai with goods and services ranging from raw materials and parts to logistics and financing. The company employs over 75,000 people worldwide.

Establishment and Growing Pains

Founded in 1968 by the Hyundai business group, one of Korea's largest chaebols or family-owned conglomerates, HMC initially served as an automotive assembler for Ford Motor Company. However, Chung Ju-Young, the founder of Hyundai had big plans for the future direction and growth of the firm in hopes that it would help the chaebol to both diversify and to maximize its economies of scale and scope. In 1974, HMC took the next step and began producing and selling its first wholly designed model, the Pony. The following year, Chung firmly set his company's future in motion by beginning the export of the Pony to Ecuador and the Benelux countries and eventually exported worldwide utilizing a low cost strategy. Despite the growing international sales of the Pony and subsequent models, these times were not without their issues. Some of Hyundai's early models elicited ridicule for its shoddy construction, underpowered engines and boring designs.[116] Recognizing the barriers before them, HMC went on to expand its range of market offerings and especially worked on improving vehicle quality, which, over time, began to bear fruit by greatly improving sales.

Perhaps the greatest impact on Hyundai was felt when Chung Mong-koo, the founder's eldest son, was made the chief executive officer. The Chairman contributed his relentless drive to push HMC into world class status by adopting flashier designs and driving quality improvements necessary to stand behind a U.S. product warranty that was dubbed "America's Best Warranty" for its extensive coverage and other manifestations of quality aspirations.[117]

Global Growth

Another major contributor to Hyundai's spectacular growth has been its efforts to expand overseas through both export and the push to produce vehicles in key foreign markets. Although its first attempt at an international assembly plant built in Canada failed, HMC internalized and implemented the new knowledge they gained in the form of new ventures. Today, the company runs three domestic assembly plants in South Korea and other facilities in Brazil, Czech Republic, China, India, Turkey, Russia, and the United States. Foreign annual vehicle production has far outstripped domestic capabilities, producing 57 percent of its 4.4 million vehicles outside of Korea.[118] This growth is expected to continue for the foreseeable future as Hyundai continues to add additional overseas facilities as well as refine its approach to the global market and its quality capabilities.

Organizational Success Factors

There are several organizational pillars that have proven to strengthen or support Hyundai's ability to continue to adapt to and overcome often adverse market conditions. However, in some cases, these same success factors have also created issues when applied to foreign operations. These factors refer to Hyundai's unique yet locally-responsive centralized organizational structure, the control methods used both domestically and especially in its expansive overseas production facilities, and HMC's highly developed and strong corporate culture.

Hyundai: Centralized yet Locally-Responsive

Although HMC assembly plants and subsidiaries are spread out across the world, the organizational structure and approach remains similar throughout the company footprint. Like many Korean firms, Hyundai is a top-down, hierarchical company which employs a very hands-on authoritative management style. CEO Chung widely known for his "Bulldozer" leadership style,[119] could often be seen at surprise, on-site visits to Hyundai plants, pulling executives from their offices to directly show them issues. He was reported to have

Some observe that Japanese car firms are quickly learning by following Hyundai Motor Corporation's example.

Source: © Alma_sacra - Fotolia.com

conducted monthly meetings, pounding on tables and generally being a fastidious boss.[120] Furthermore, the decision-making style of the Hyundai CEOs could also be characterized as quick and decisive. Se-young Chung, the second CEO of the company, made a snap decision on an aggressive, new warranty policy during a car ride that would fundamentally revolutionize HMC's commitment towards quality. Regarding the quickness of the decision, it was widely believed that Koreans were cowboys unlike the Japanese, and that at the rival Japanese firm Toyota, a similar warranty policy might have taken at least eighteen months to get past consensus.[121]

Beyond the direct control of the president, Hyundai's Seoul executives maintain full control over all of their operations, which has implications regarding the ability for local country executives to autonomously operate. Critics of the centralized control note Seoul's propensity for micromanagement, unwillingness to listen to country level managers and an intolerance for any disagreements to Hyundai's often "feudal" approach to management. Reports from many of HMC's foreign operations, such as Russia, India, and the U.S., reveal similar situations.

However, despite the high degree of centralization, Hyundai has learned the necessity of relying on their international non-Korean teams to pick up on local market needs and opportunities and rapidly turn them into tangible products. One example of this intelligent usage of non-Korean employee assets has proven to be one of the success factors for the Chinese market. Understanding the essence of Chinese culture has allowed them to better anticipate which designs, products, and equipment would appeal to their target audience in that country. The firm goes as far as encouraging the local teams to take risks in the form of ambitious schedules, designs, and unconventional solutions. This reliance and trust can be seen especially in HMC's older and more established assembly plants.

In India, one of Hyundai's oldest international operations, headquarters realized the need for the host country official's authority and made commitments for all management staff to become Indian nationals by 2014.[122] Despite this practice in India, however, it appears that HMC management does not lightly award trust. As of 2012, their Russian operations were still stratified into Koreans representing management, whereas Russians got positions of manual workers and clerks.[123]

Control Systems

HMC's competition-based and bureaucratic control systems make up the second organizational success factor. Hyundai is well known for its competitive, team-based approach in the marketplace. Different teams regularly vie against each other to determine product or feature designs or even technology to identify the most effective or innovative solutions to the firm's challenges. The output of these internal competitions are said to often produce some of Hyundai's most spectacular results. However, they often engender mistrust and disunity amongst the personnel.

HMC's bureaucratic controls can be equally beneficial and disruptive. Working alongside the managers in Hyundai's international plants are Korean coordinators. These coordinators are typically young, Western-educated Korean workers whose job is to bridge the language and cultural gaps with the international managers and help them operate with their Korean counterparts. Decisions made in the Korean headquarters are relayed through these coordinators and followed without exception. It has been noted that coordinators often possess even more decision-making power than the foreign executive that they serve.[124] This degree of hands-on, long distance supervision has often been a serious issue between home and local offices.

Culture

HMC is well known for its vibrant corporate culture that heavily focuses on traditional Korean cultural attitudes such as collectivism and paternalism. Due to its history of Confucianism, Korea possesses a culture still highly aligned with collectivism which is embedded in the core of HMC beliefs. This belief has imbued HMC with a very strong work ethic and intolerance for deviation from the group. Workers at Hyundai facilities around the globe are known for their frantic pace and long hours (often working without extra compensation) as is the norm with most employees of the HMC family.

Like Hyundai's collective approach, the firm's paternalistic focus has also both benefited and hurt the company. Decisions by management, and especially the chairman, are often unquestioned, and executed instantly.[125] The term "Hyundai Speed" became part of HMC culture when the chairman stressed the importance of reaching operational status during the 2002 setup of Hyundai's first operation plant in China.[126] Only after Herculean efforts by the Korean and Chinese workers, the plant began manufacturing.

Another cultural area that often makes little sense to foreigners is the virtual cult of leadership and control that surrounds the Chung family's grip on the firm. When Chung Mong-koo, the founder's eldest son and CEO from 1987, was convicted by the South Korean government for embezzling $106 million from the company in a securities transaction, he was not only able to professionally survive the conviction, but he was granted a presidential pardon by President Lee, a former Hyundai executive, and continues to maintain the CEO position today with the blessings of most Hyundai managers and workers. The Chung family leadership of HMC is also expected to continue into the future as the CEO's only son, Chung Eui Sun, now 41 years old, is being groomed as the heir apparent.

A third area of constant contention in HMC's global organization that is contrary to the cultural approach management has tried to install regards the creation of independent employee unions. Most of the firm's global operations are periodically affected by labor talks and strikes. Labor strikes in Korea alone in 2012 resulted in $1.5 billion in lost production and have affected domestic production in 23 of the last 27 years.[127] These strikes have often caused spillover effects with work slowdowns or stoppages in other international plants due to parts shortages, but have also encouraged a greater amount of localized part production in some markets. International facilities show similar patterns as workers resorting to a strike in protest of practices like obligatory overtime, management harassment and intimidation, and poor working conditions. Despite the historically poor track record with labor groups however, Hyundai has seen some progress in terms of improving its overall relationship with its unions.

Next Steps

The future of Hyundai is far from determined. Although sales are fairly constant and well distributed worldwide and the organization appears to be well-prepared for most contingencies, many factors are yet unknown. Some believe the company is overreaching itself by continuing to develop its luxury brands, while others observe that Japanese car firms are quickly learning by following HMC's examples. Additionally, there is constant debate about the firm's growing emphasis on hydrogen fuel cell technology and whether this green technology is taking the firm in the correct direction.

However, through the firm's focus on quality, innovation and the growth and maintenance of its strong structural, cultural, and organizational strengths, HMC hopes to maintain its continued growth and profitability in the world market. Eventually, HMC might just reach the goals outlined in its management philosophy of realizing the dream of mankind by creating a new future through ingenious thinking and continuously challenging new frontiers.

QUESTIONS

16-3. Is it possible for Hyundai to retain its core culture and structure as it continues to expand? Is it even desirable for HMC to try?

16-4. Would it have been possible to resolve Hyundai's initial quality issues without the use of a strong, central figure making the decisions?

16-5. Evaluate the dangers of HMC's centralized approach versus a more decentralized path?

16-6. Identify the issues with using a competition-based control mechanism. Is there an alternative?

16-7. Often times, Korean culture doesn't lend itself to being easily understood by members of other cultures. What could Hyundai do to better communicate its core beliefs?

16-8. Hyundai management always has issues with unions. What could be done to promote a more cooperative and mutually beneficial working environment?

16-9. Which organizational shortcomings do you feel are the most necessary for Hyundai to address? How would you address the issues?

SUMMARY

- An MNE's organization is a function of how the company defines the structure that specifies the framework for work, develops the systems that coordinate and control what is done, and cultivates shared values among employees.
- Environmental and workplace trends, along with the fallout of the global financial crisis, push managers to refine their customary approaches to organizing their companies. Managers compare the classical command-and-control model versus the potential of the coordinate-and-cultivate approach of neoclassical formats.
- Vertical differentiation is the matter of how the company balances centralization versus decentralization in decision-making. Horizontal differentiation is the matter of how the company opts to divide itself into specific product, functional or area units.
- Effectively balancing the asymmetric demands of centralization and decentralization is strongly influenced by the pressures for global integration versus local responsiveness, the competence of headquarters versus subsidiary personnel, and the importance, expediency, and quality expectations of the decision at hand.

- Classical structures, like the functional, product, area, and matrix formats, rely on the formally specified hierarchy to arrange roles, responsibilities, and relationships.
- Neoclassical structures, like the network or virtual format, arrange work roles, responsibilities, and relationships in ways that bypass the horizontal and vertical boundaries that would otherwise hamper the development of knowledge-generating and decision-making relationships.
- Coordination can take place via standardization, plans, and mutual adjustment. Standardization relies on specifying standard operating procedures; planning relies on general goals and detailed objectives; mutual adjustment relies on frequent interaction among related parties.
- Control systems help managers compare performance to plans, identify differences, and, when found, assess the gap and implement corrective action.
- Companies exercise control through market, bureaucratic, and clan mechanisms. Market control relies on external market mechanisms; bureaucratic control relies on extensive rules and procedures; clan control relies on shared values among employees.
- Organization culture refers to the set of values shared among employees. Values express themselves as the behavior patterns or style of an organization that workers encourage new hires to follow.
- Firms engaging different strategies build different organizations. Firms engaging international, multidomestic, global, or transnational strategies tailor their structures, systems, and cultures to the respective demands of their choices.

KEY TERMS

boundaries (p. 668)
boundaryless (p. 668)
bureaucratic control (p. 679)
centralization (p. 660)
clan control (p. 679)
control systems (p. 679)
coordination (p. 672)
coordination by mutual adjustment (p. 677)
coordination by plan (p. 675)
coordination by standardization (p. 672)
decentralization (p. 660)
divisional structure (p. 662)
functional structure (p. 662)
globality (p. 661)
horizontal differentiation (p. 660)
market controls (p. 679)
matrix structure (p. 665)
mixed structure (p. 666)
neoclassical structure (p. 666)
network structure (p. 669)
organization (p. 659)
organization culture (p. 681)
organization structure (p. 659)
unity-of-command principle (p. 666)
vertical differentiation (p. 660)
virtual organization (p. 671)

ENDNOTES

1 ***Sources include the following:*** www.jnj.com; J&J's 2007, 2008, 2009, 2010, and 2011 Annual Reports; "J&J shares climb after upbeat update on its drugs" *Businessweek*, www.businessweek.com/ap/financial-news/D9NFV7U00.htm, (June 1, 2011); Avi Salzman, "J&J Now the 'Best Biotech Play' Says Goldman," Barrons.com, blogs.barrons.com/stockstowatchtoday/2011/05/27/jj-now-the-best-biotech-play-says-goldman/, (June 1, 2011); Margaret Cronin Fisk and Beth Hawkins, "Johnson & Johnson Hid Antibiotic Levaquin Risk, Lawyer Says - Bloomberg," www.bloomberg.com/news/2011-06-01/johnson-johnson-hid-risks-of-antibiotic-levaquin-lawyer-says-at-trial.html, (June 1, 2011). "Patients Versus Profits at Johnson & Johnson: Has the Company Lost Its Way?" View of Cowen & Co. analyst Ian Sanderson, Knowledge@Wharton, retrieved January 2, 2013 from knowledge.wharton.upenn.edu/article.cfm?articleid=2943.

2 "A Big Company That Works," *Businessweek*, retrieved February 25, 2013 from www.businessweek.com/stories/1992-05-03/a-big-company-that-works.

3 "Johnson & Johnson CEO William Weldon: Leadership in a Decentralized Company," Knowledge@Wharton, retrieved February 25, 2013 from knowledge.wharton.upenn.edu/article.cfm?articleid=2003.

4 "Patients Versus Profits at Johnson & Johnson: Has the Company Lost Its Way?" View of Cowen & Co. analyst Ian Sanderson, Knowledge@Wharton, retrieved January 2, 2013 from knowledge.wharton.upenn.edu/article.cfm?articleid=2943.

5 "Tylenol (Acetaminophen) To Be Available In Japan In Early Fall, 2000," retrieved June 15, 2011 from www.pslgroup.com/dg/1d9dfa.htm.

6 J&J's 2008 Annual Report.

7 J&J's 2007 Annual Report.

8 "The Organization Man, Dead at 76," *Journal of Business Strategy* 18 (1997): 6.

9 Jack Welch and Suzy Welch, *Winning*, HarperCollins Publishers (2005).

10 Lowell Bryan and Claudia Joyce, "Better Strategy through Organizational Design," *The McKinsey Quarterly* (May 2007).

11 Alfred P. Sloan, John McDonald, ed., *My Years with General Motors* (New York: Doubleday, 1964).

12 Chris Bartlett, "MNCs: Get Off the Reorganization Merry-Go-Round," *Harvard Business Review* (March–April 1983): 88–101.

13 Martin Dewhurst, Jonathan Harris, and Suzanne Heywood, "The Global Company's Challenge," *McKinsey Quarterly*, December 31, 2012, from www.mckinseyquarterly.com/The_global_companys_challenge_2979.

14 "Hungry Tiger, Dancing Elephant: How India Is Changing IBM's World," *The Economist* (April 4, 2007): 58–61; "A Survey of Globalisation: The Empire Strikes Back," *The Economist*, June 5, 2011, from www.economist.com/node/12080723: 72.

15 Peter Drucker, "Managing Oneself," *Harvard Business Review* (1999).

16 As some have suggested: Before: "Thanks for letting me work here." Today: "Improve my professional mobility or I will find a company that will."

17 Adam Bryant, "Google's 8-Point Plan to Help Managers Improve," NYTimes.com, retrieved March 12, 2011, from www.nytimes.com/2011/03/13/business/13hire.html?hp.

18 Craig W. Fontaine, "Organization Structure," Human Resource Management Knowledge Base, Northeastern University (August 2007).

19 "Identity Crisis: What Is the Corporate Center's Role in a Globalized Business?" BCG.perspectives, retrieved January 3, 2013 from www.bcgperspectives.com/content/articles/role_of_center_globalization_identity_crisis_corporate_centers_role_globalized_business/.

20 The Tao offers insight on this standard: The second principle of Taoism is that of Dynamic Balance. There are always two basic distinctions in nature, symbolized by the yin and yang (sun and moon, heaven and earth, dark and light, chaos and order, etc.), but Taoism sees balance as the basic characteristic underlying these distinctions.

21 Harold Sirkin, James Hemerling, Arindam Bhattacharya, *Globality: Competing with Everyone from Everywhere for Everything* (New York: Business Plus, 2008).

22 "Identity Crisis: What Is the Corporate Center's Role in a Globalized Business?" Bcg.perspectives.

23 Julian Birkinshaw, "The Structures behind Global Companies," *Financial Times* (December 4, 2000): 2–4.

24 "Nestlé Is Starting to Slim Down at Last," *Businessweek* (October 27, 2003): 56–58; "Daring, Defying, to Grow," *The Economist* (August 7, 2004): 55–57.

25 Andria Cheng, "Nike Reorganizes into Six Geographic Regions: Faster-Growing China, Eastern Europe regions to be Managed Separately," *MarketWatch* (March 20, 2009).

26 "Japanese Firms Push into Emerging Markets: The New Frontier for Corporate Japan," *The Economist*, April 19, 2011, from www.economist.com/node/16743435

27 John W. Hunt, "Is Matrix Management a Recipe for Chaos?" *Financial Times* (January 12, 1998): 10.

28 More precisely, Christopher Bartlett and Sumantra Ghoshal identified several key limitations of the matrix format, suggesting that: "Dual reporting led to conflict and confusion; the proliferation of channels created informational log-jams as a proliferation of committees and reports bogged down the organization; and overlapping responsibilities produced turf battles and a loss of accountability. Separated by barriers of distance, language, time, and culture, managers found it virtually impossible to clarify the confusion and resolve the conflicts." Many years after their article was published, many MNES are still trying to break free; C. Bartlett and S. Ghoshal, "Matrix Management: Not a Structure, a Frame of Mind," *Harvard Business Review*, July–August 1990.

29 Richard Hodgetts, "Dow Chemical CEO William Stavropoulos on Structure," *Academy of Management Executive* (May 30, 1999): 30.

30 "Companies and the Euro Crisis: Iron Enters the Soul," *The Economist* (October 6, 2012): 74.

31 "Axe to Fall Heavily at IBM, Unions Fear," *New York Times* (May 6, 2005): A1.

32 The *strategy-structure-systems model* was first adopted by General Motors, DuPont, Sears, and Standard Oil in the 1920s. Not until the post–World War II era did many companies began to develop divisional structures that then led to the rapid adoption of diversification strategies. Some reason that the network structure and its variants will follow the same pattern, moving from the few in the early 2000s to the many over the ensuing decades.

33 Just as these demands trigger the emergence of the transnational strategy, they likewise spur what some broadly call the *transnational organization.*

34 "Hungry Tiger, Dancing Elephant: How India Is Changing IBM's World," *The Economist* (April 4, 2007): 58–61.

35 "The New Organisation," *The Economist*, retrieved January 3, 2013 from www.economist.com/node/5380483.

36 "Hungry Tiger, Dancing Elephant: How India Is Changing IBM's World," *The Economist* (April 4, 2007): 58–61.

37 "The World According to Chambers," *The Economist* (August 27, 2009): 81–84.

38 For example, in the case of the latter, people see that the more senior executives have specialized knowledge that gives them personal respect as well as positional power. Hence, the more power their knowledge gives them, the less incentive they have to share with others. This develops boundaries between different levels of hierarchy.

39 Hiroko Tabuchi and Brooks Barnes, "Sony Chief Is Still in Search of a Turnaround," *New York Times*, (May 26, 2011): A1.

40 Sony adds another angle of analysis. In Chapter 11, we described how Sony ran big losses as markets, weakened by the global crisis, exposed weaknesses in its system. Fighting to rescue the company, CEO Sir Howard Stringer felt the need to revitalize the company's culture in order to jump-start new relationships and trigger new ways of thinking. Reorganization began in spring 2009. Senior executives opposed to restructuring efforts were replaced by four young, loyal lieutenants—dubbed "the Four Musketeers"—to lead Sony's redesigned businesses. Ironically, explained Sir Howard, "When this crisis came along, for me it was a godsend, because I could reorganize the company without having to battle the forces of the status quo"; "Game on: Sir Howard Stringer Believes He Is Finally in a Position to Fix Sony," *The Economist* (March 5, 2009): 73.

41 "The New Organisation," *The Economist*, (February 24, 2013): 63

42 Statement from Jack Welch's Letter to Shareholders, "Boundarylessness Company in a Decade of Change," reported in GE's 1990 *Annual Report.*

43 "Gore: Our Culture" retrieved May 1, 2013 from www.gore.com/en_xx/aboutus/culture/; "W. L. Gore & Associates - Best Companies to Work For 2012," *Fortune*, retrieved May 1, 2013 from money.cnn.com/magazines/fortune/best-companies/2012/snapshots/38.html.

44 W. Baker, the Network Organization in Theory and Practice. In N. Nohria and R. Eccles (Eds.), *Networks and Organizations,* (Cambridge, MA: Harvard Business School Press, 1992), 327–429.

45 Yves Doz and Keeley Wilson, *Managing Global Innovation: Frameworks for Integrating Capabilities around the World,* Harvard Business Press Books, 2012.

46 The keiretsu appeared in Japan during the "economic miracle" following World War II. Before Japan's surrender, Japanese industry was controlled by large family-controlled vertical monopolies called zaibatsu.

47 "Presidential Politics in South Korea: Bashing the Big Guys," *The Economist* (October 13, 2012): 49.

48 "A Tangled Web," *Financial Times* (June 12, 2001): 7.

49 J. Lipnack and J. Stamps, *Virtual Teams: Researching across Space, Time, and Organizations with Technology* (New York: John Wiley and Sons, 1997); Sonny Ariss, Nick Nykodym, and Aimee Cole-Laramore, "Trust and Technology in the Virtual Organization," *SAM Advanced Management Journal* 67 (Autumn 2002): 22–26; William M. Fitzpatrick and Donald R. Burke, "Competitive Intelligence, Corporate Security and the Virtual Organization," *Advances in Competitiveness Research* 11 (2003): 20–46.

50 Manju Ahuja and Kathleen Carley "Network Structure in Virtual Organizations," June 10, 2011, from jcmc.indiana.edu/vol3/issue4/ahuja.html.

51 Alf Crossman and Liz Lee-Kelley, "Trust, Commitment and Team Working: The Paradox of Virtual Organizations," *Global Networks: A Journal of Transnational Affairs* 4 (October 2004): 375–91; Philip J. Holt and James E. Lodge, "Merging Collaboration and Technology: The Virtual Research Organization," *Applied Clinical Trials* 12 (October 2003): 38–42.

52 Scott Goodson, Strawberry Frog, "Special Report: Global Players," *Advertising Age* (January 26, 2004): S4; Juliana Koranteng, "Virtual Agency Goes Global via the Web," *AdAgeGlobal* 1 (2000): 46.

53 Theresa Howard, "Strawberry Frog Hops to a Different Drummer," *USA Today* (October 10, 2005): C1.

54 Similar trend are afoot in other industries. The legal field, for example, increasingly rewards efficiency. "Clearspire, a virtual origination, relies on some 20 or so lawyers who work mostly from home, collaborating on a multi-million-dollar platform that mimics a virtual office.

A lawyer checking in on a colleague automatically sees a picture of her on the phone when she is, in fact, on the phone. Clients use the platform too, commenting on and even changing their own documents as they are being drawn up. Conventional lawyers are far less open"; "Bargain Briefs," *The Economist* (August 13, 2011): 64.

55 Toby Gibbs, Suzanne Heywood, and Leigh Weiss, "Organizing for an Emerging World," *McKinsey Quarterly*, June 2012.

56 Dmitry Ivanov, Boris Sokolov, and Joachim Kaeschel, "Structure Dynamics Control-Based Framework for Adaptive Reconfiguration of Collaborative Enterprise Networks," *International Journal of Manufacturing Technology and Management* 17 (2009): 23.

57 "Schumpeter: Corporate Burlesque," *The Economist* (November 3, 2012): 68.

58 Nicolai J. Foss. "Selective Intervention and Internal Hybrids: Interpreting and Learning from the Rise and Decline of the Oticon Spaghetti Organization," *Organization Science* 14 (May–June 2003): 331–50.

59 Patrick Kiger, "Hidden Hierarchies," *Workforce Management* (February 27, 2006): 24.

60 Karen Beaman, "An Interview with Christopher Bartlett," *Boundaryless HR: Human Capital Management in the Global Economy* (San Francisco: IHRIM Press, June 2002).

61 Darrell Rigby, "Bain & Company's 2005 Management Tools & Trends," August 2, 2005, from www.bain.com/management_tools.

62 Adam Lashinsky, "Chaos by Design," *Fortune* (October 2, 2006); Geoffrey Colvin, "Managing in Chaos," *Fortune* (October 2, 2006).

63 Lowell Bryan and Claudia Joyce, "The 21st-Century Organization," *The McKinsey Quarterly* 3 (2005).

64 Martin Dewhurst, Jonathan Harris, and Suzanne Heywood, "The Global Company's Challenge," *McKinsey Quarterly*.

65 Loren Cary, "The Rise of Hyperarchies," *Harvard Business Review* (March 2004).

66 Karl-Heinrich Grote and Erik K. Antonsson (Eds.), *Springer Handbook of Mechanical Engineering* (New York: Springer, 2009): 1344.

67 The Boston Consulting Group, "Reorganized Information Processing Vital to Improving U.S. Intelligence Capabilities," *BCG Media Releases*, May 6, 2007, from www.bcg.com/news_media/news_media_releases.jsp?id=928.

68 "Lessons from TED: Corporate TEDucation," *The Economist* (November 3, 2012): 67.

69 In contrast, one could precisely design a structure that looks great on paper but struggles in the stress test of reality.

70 "The New Organisation," *The Economist*.

71 More specifically, Grove reasoned: "Let chaos reign, then rein in chaos. Does that mean that you shouldn't plan? Not at all. You need to plan the way a fire department plans. It cannot anticipate fires, so it has to shape a flexible organization that is capable of responding to unpredictable events"; Michael E. Rock, "Case Example: Intel's Andy Grove," *CanadaOne*, October 31, 2007, from www.canadaone.com/magazine/mr2060198.html.

72 Michel Domsch and Elena Hristozova, (Eds.), *Human Resource Management in Consulting* (New York: Springer, 2006).

73 Anoop Madhok, "Revisiting Multinational Firms' Tolerance for Joint Ventures: A Trust-Based Approach." *Journal of International Business Studies* (2006): 30–43.

74 Daniel Erasmus, "A Common Language for Strategy," *Financial Times* (April 5, 1999): 7–8.

75 Sumantra Ghoshal and Christopher Bartlett, "Changing the Role of Top Management: Beyond Structure to Process," *Harvard Business Review* 73 (January–February 1995): 93–94.

76 Jennifer Spencer, "Firms' Knowledge-Sharing Strategies in the Global Innovation System: Empirical Evidence from the Flat Panel Display Industry," *Strategic Management Journal* 23 (March 2003): 217–33.

77 "Red Hat Global Support Services: The Move to Relationship-based Customer Servicing and Knowledge-centered Support," *Harvard Business Review*, retrieved January 3, 2013 from hbr.org/product/red-hat-global-support-services-the-move-to-relati/an/W11543-PDF-ENG.

78 Sam Folk-Williams, "Designing Open Collaboration in Red Hat Global Support Services," Management Innovation eXchange, June 2, 2011, from www.managementexchange.com/story-36.

79 Ultimately, every MNE regulates what people do. If they don't, the consequences can be grave. Failure, as we saw in the global credit crisis, permits opportunistic managers to take actions that crash the MNE. Experiences at several companies, such as Citibank, UBS, Siemens, Merrill Lynch, Lehman, Royal Bank of Scotland, AIG, and Société Générale, dramatize how weak controls enable destructive opportunism.

80 Toby Gibbs, Suzanne Heywood, and Leigh Weiss, "Organizing for an Emerging World," *McKinsey Quarterly*, June 2012.

81 Clan control represents humanist values that contrast with the scientific norms of bureaucratic control.

82 If conducted poorly, visits fan tension. Experience suggests "rules" for optimizing such visits. If subsidiary managers overload social activities and underplay hard business reviews, corporate personnel will see the trip as wasteful. If corporate personnel visit warm-weather subsidiaries during their home's cold-weather seasons, locals may perceive the trips as diversions. Further, if visitors arrive only when upset about local performance, subsidiary folks may be defensive.

83 "The World According to Chambers."

84 For instance, the Japanese retailer Ito-Yokado, which owns and operates the 7-Eleven convenience store franchise in Japan, links stores' cash registers into an ERP system. It records sales and monitors inventory as well as scheduling daily and weekly tasks. It also benchmarks managers' use of analytical tools, graphs, and forecasts; N. Shirouzu and J. Bigness, "7-Eleven Operators Resist System to Monitor Managers," *Wall Street Journal* (June 16, 1997): B1.

85 In some companies, few matters are left untouched. For generations, managers of IBM wore only dark blue suits, white shirts and dark ties, symbols of their lifetime allegiance to Big Blue.

86 Sumantra Ghoshal, Gita Piramal, Christopher A. Bartlett, *Managing Radical Change* (Penguin Books India, 2002): 318.

87 Eric Flamholtz and Rangapriya Kannan-Narasimhan, "Differential Impact of Cultural Elements in Financial Performance," *European Management Journal* (February 2005): 50–65; Ursula Fairbairn, "HR as a Strategic Partner: Culture Change as an American Express Case Study," *Human Resource Management* 44 (Spring 2005): 79–84.

88 Jim Collins, *Good to Great: Why Some Companies Make the Leap…and Others Don't* (New York: HarperCollins, 2001). For example, on the importance of technology, Collins reports "80 percent of the good-to-great executives—from more than 1400 companies over a 15 year span—we interviewed didn't even mention technology as one of the top five factors in the transition."

89 Dinker Raval and Bala Subramanian, "Effective Transfer of Best Practices across Cultures," *Competitiveness Review* (Summer–Fall 2000): 183.

90 David Wessel, "Big US Firms Shift Hiring Abroad," *Wall Street Journal* (April 19, 2011): B1.

91 H. Schwartz, "Matching Corporate Culture and Business Strategy," *Organizational Dynamics* (1981). Andrew Klein, "Corporate Culture: Its Value as a Resource for Competitive Advantage," *Journal of Business Strategy*, (2011): 21–28.

92 Bain & Company, "Executives Are Taking a Hard Look at Soft Issues" (March 27, 2007), October 31, 2007, from www.bain.com/bainweb/publications/printer_ready.asp?id=25728.

93 Toby Gibbs, Suzanne Heywood, and Leigh Weiss, "Organizing for an Emerging World," *McKinsey Quarterly*, June 2012.

94 Bain & Company, "Executives Are Taking a Hard Look at Soft Issues."

95 The severity of this problem is proportional to the importance of knowledge-generating and decision-making relationships to the MNE's organization; Alison Maitland,"Bridging the Culture Gap," *Financial Times* (January 28, 2002): 8.

96 Martin Dewhurst, Jonathan Harris, and Suzanne Heywood,"The Global Company's Challenge,"*McKinsey Quarterly.*

97 Tatiana Kostova,"Transnational Transfer of Strategic Organizational Practices: A Contextual Perspective,"*Academy of Management Review* 24 (1999): 308–24; Nitin Nohria and Sumantra Ghoshal,"Differentiated Fit and Shared Values: Alternatives for Managing Headquarters-Subsidiary Relations,"*Strategic Management Journal* 15 (July 1994): 491–502. For a discussion of how capabilities improve with experience, see Andrew Delios and Paul Beamish,"Survival and Profitability: The Roles of Experience and Intangible Assets in Foreign Subsidiary Performance,"*Academy of Management Journal* 44 (2001): 1028–38.

98 "Staffing Globalisation: Travelling More Lightly,"*The Economist* (June 23, 2006): 55.

99 Leslie Gross Klaff,"Many People, One Mattel,"*Workforce Management* (March 2004): 42–44.

100 Martin Fackler,"The 'Toyota Way' Is Translated for a New Generation of Foreign Managers,"*New York Times,* retrieved August 5, 2010 from www.nytimes.com/2007/02/15/business/worldbusiness/15toyota.html.

101 *The Toyota Way,* May 25, 2011, from secure.wikimedia.org/wikipedia/en/wiki/The_Toyota_Way.

102 Martin Fackler,"The 'Toyota Way' Is Translated for a New Generation of Foreign Managers,"*New York Times,* retrieved August 5, 2010 from www.nytimes.com/2007/02/15/business/worldbusiness/15toyota.html.

103 Rebecca Knight,"Corporate Universities: Move to a Collaborative Effort,"*Financial Times* (March 19, 2007).

104 Melissa Korn and Jennifer Levitz,"Online Courses Look for a Business Model - WSJ.com."retrieved January 2, 2013 from online.wsj.com/article/SB10001424127887324339204578173421673664106.html?mod=googl news_wsj.

105 Donna Fenn,"Corporate Universities for Small Companies,"Inc.com, May 6, 2007, from www.inc.com/magazine/19990201/730.html.

106 Jeanne C. Meister, *Corporate Universities: Lessons in Building a World-Class Work Force* (New York: McGraw-Hill, 1998).

107 John Griffiths,"Unipart University,"*Financial Times* (March 21, 2002).

108 The Pit is the well of a bright, multi-tier lecture hall.

109 Della Bradshaw,"LVMH,"*Financial Times* (March 21, 2002).

110 Steve Trehern,"More Than Just Learning Process,"*Financial Times* (March 21, 2002).

111 Martin Fackler,"The 'Toyota Way' Is Translated for a New Generation of Foreign Managers,"*New York Times,* retrieved August 5, 2010 from www.nytimes.com/2007/02/15/business/worldbusiness/15toyota.html.

112 Kelley Holland,"Is It Time to Retrain B-Schools? *New York Times* (March 14, 2009): A1.

113 "MBA Programs Are Failing in Ethics."*Businessweek,* retrieved January 2, 2013 from www.businessweek.com/debateroom/archives/2011/11/mba_programs_are_failing_in_ethics.html;"Dose of Humility with a Harvard MBA,"WSJ.com, retrieved January 2, 2013 from online.wsj.com/article/SB1000142405311190456390457658583893732362.html.

114 OICA,"2012 Production Statistics," October 22, 2013, from http://oica.net/category/production-statistics/.

115 Good Car Bad Car,"2012 Car Sale Statistics," October 22, 2013, from www.goodcarbadcar.net/2013/01/2012-usa-auto-sales-brand-rankings.html.

116 John Reed,"Hyundai reaps rewards of quality push,"*Financial Times* (May 7, 2012).

117 William J. Holstein,"Hyundai's Capabilities Play," October 22, 2013, from www.strategy-business.com/article/00162?pg=all&tid=27782251.

118 "Unions of Hyundai Motor, Kia authorize strikes," *The Korea Herald* (August 14, 2013).

119 Mooweon Rhee,"Hyundai Motor Company," Stanford University Graduate School of Business, Case SM-122.

120 William J. Holstein,"Hyundai's Capabilities Play," October 22, 2013, from http://www.strategy-business.com/article/00162?pg=all&tid=27782251.

121 William J. Holstein,"Hyundai's Capabilities Play," October 22, 2013, from www.strategy-business.com/article/00162?pg=all&tid=27782251.

122 Hyundai India,"Hyundai Introduces Indian Executive in Top Management Criteria,"October 22, 2013, from www.hyundaicarsindia.in/2013/01/hyundai-introduces-indian-executive-in-top-management-criteria.html.

123 Yulia Kubyshkina,"Development of Intercultural Competence in Russian Employees in Korean Companies (the Case of Hyundai Motor Company in Saint-Petersburg),"11th IACCM Annual Conference Proceedings (June 20-22, 2012).

124 Anonymous employee interview (October 16, 2013).

125 Anonymous employee interview (October 16, 2013).

126 John Reed,"Hyundai reaps rewards of quality push," *Financial Times* (May 7, 2012).

127 "Unions of Hyundai Motor, Kia authorize strikes," *The Korea Herald* (August 14, 2013). David Welch, David Kiley and Moon Ihlwan,"My Way or the Highway at Hyundai,"March 5, 2008 from http://www.businessweek.com/stories/2008-03-05/my-way-or-the-highway-at-hyundai; John Lippert, alan Ohnsman and Rose Kim,"Billionaire Chung Proving Hyundai No Joke Aiming for BMW,"March 2, 2012 from http://www.bloomberg.com/news/2012-03-01/billionaire-chung-proving-hyundai-luxury-no-joke-in-drive-to-top-bmw-cars.html

CHAPTER 17
Global Marketing

OBJECTIVES

After studying this chapter, you should be able to

1. Understand a variety of international marketing strategies/policies and their appropriate circumstances
2. Discuss the pros and cons of product alterations when deciding between standardized and differentiated marketing programs among countries
3. Appreciate the pricing complexities when selling in foreign markets
4. Recognize country differences that may necessitate alterations in promotional marketing practices
5. Comprehend the different branding strategies companies may employ internationally
6. Discern effective practices and complications of international distribution
7. Perceive why and how emphasis within the marketing mix may vary among countries
8. Anticipate the ways that international marketing segmentation may evolve

Source: © Nmedia - Fotolia.com

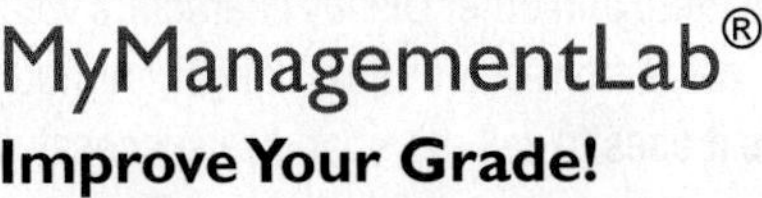

Improve Your Grade!

When you see this icon, visit **www.mymanagementlab.com** for activities that are applied, personalized, and offer immediate feedback.

Markets have customs and communes have traditions.

—Vietnamese proverb

CASE Tommy Hilfiger

For it's Tommy this, an' Tommy that

—Rudyard Kipling, "Tommy"

Mark Twain said, "The finest clothing is a person's skin, but, of course, society demands more than this."[1] Tommy Hilfiger, one of the notable international brands within the highly competitive clothing industry, exemplifies efforts to develop and respond to these demands. Retail sales from 90 countries in 2011 were $5.6 billion. Hilfiger has added other lines, but our discussion centers on the clothing brands using the Hilfiger name. Before we examine its international marketing practices, let's look for a moment at the company's description and history.

A BRIEF HISTORY

The early success of the Hilfiger brand was largely due to two men: U.S. designer Tommy Hilfiger and Indian textile magnate Mohan Murjani. Hilfiger designed blue jeans for Jordache, but in 1984, Murjani sought him out to be a designer for Murjani International. As one of the instrumental people in bringing about the designer blue-jeans craze of the 1970s, Murjani wanted to develop a new brand of clothing by offering a line of slightly less preppy and less expensive clothes than those offered by Ralph Lauren that he thought would attract a young mass-appeal audience.

Sales success came quickly for the Hilfiger brand, but Murjani International faced financial problems along with difficulty in separating its attention among its different brands, which it sold to the same department stores. Hilfiger, Murjani, and two other investors bought out Murjani International in 1988 and changed the name to Tommy Hilfiger. In 2009, Phillips-Van Heusen (now PVH) bought the company.

Hilfiger began with only a men's line but has since added women's and children's wear. Tommy Hilfiger's sales outside the United States now account for more than half its world total. Europe accounts for the largest portion of Hilfiger's international sales, although stores are also located in Asia, South America, and the Middle East. The opening photo shows a Tommy Hilfiger store in Berlin, Germany.

PROMOTION AND BRANDING

Hilfiger's promotion and branding have been so intertwined that it is almost impossible to separate them. At the beginning, Murjani saw two primary needs: to convince stores to stock a new brand and to convince customers to want it. Although his ad budget for the first year (1985) was U.S. $1.4 million—quite small for selling in a mass consumer market, especially for an unknown brand—the ads were aimed strictly at getting Tommy Hilfiger's name known. He placed two-page ads in leading magazines and newspapers, along with a billboard in New York's Times Square without showing any clothes or any models. The ads included Hilfiger's face, the logo for the clothes, and words describing him as being on a par with such well-known designers as Ralph Lauren, Perry Ellis, and Calvin Klein.

The ads were so unusual that the brand received free publicity through newspaper write-ups. Even Johnny Carson quipped about Hilfiger on his popular late-night TV show. Within a short time, surveys in New York revealed that people thought of Hilfiger as one of the four or five most important U.S. designers. and the logo-loving public was rushing to buy the brand, while many young managers were eager to be seen in upscale sportswear during the newly popular "casual Friday" workdays.

Early on, Hilfiger received much publicity in newspaper and magazine columns around the world that mentioned or showed celebrities wearing its clothes. An eclectic group, they included Bill Clinton, the Prince of Wales, Michael Jackson, Elton John, and Snoop Dogg. This fed into the image that Hilfiger clothes had cachet; thus the company's image was fairly well established internationally before the company expanded abroad.

Hilfiger has used celebrity advertising, including Sheryl Crow, Jewel, Beyoncé, and the husband-wife team of entertainer David Bowie and supermodel Iman. Film actresses Renée Zellweger and Claudia Gerini and France's first lady Carla Bruni helped the company sell a limited edition bag to support Breast Health International. Bollywood actor Shah Rukh Khan promoted Indian sales. The company has even used "delebs" (dead celebrities), such as Grace Kelly and James Dean. To help advertise its children's line, Disney artists have drawn Pluto and other Disney characters wearing the line. However, aside from celebrities, Hilfiger learned that the type of models it uses to sell merchandise successfully in the United States may not work well in Europe. For example, its models for men's underwear in Europe, including those on point-of-purchase package displays, must be thinner and less muscular than those in the United States. But it augments these thinner models by adding scantily clad, seductive-looking women who stand behind the men in the photos. Hilfiger also found that its average consumer in Germany was older than that in the United States, so it dropped the Tommy Jeans name because it sounded too much like a teen product.

Advertising has been a cornerstone of Hilfiger's success, depending on multimedia campaigns that include print and indoor and outdoor placements. Increasingly, it has depended on digital and social media promotions. In 2013, it introduced its first webisode.

PRODUCT AND PRICE

Although early promotion with the brand name has been instrumental in Hilfiger's success, logo and image are not enough. From the start, Hilfiger clothes have been casual, of good quality, and distinctive enough in color and shape so the public can usually distinguish them from clothing made by competitors (along with the little red, white, and blue logo visibly displayed on most merchandise). Nevertheless, this is an industry in which product lines must evolve. Maintaining that "Fashion brands have to reinvent themselves, just like Madonna does," Hilfiger has gone from preppy to urban and back again.

Hilfiger initially encountered some negative reactions abroad to its image of being a U.S. brand. Although some U.S. clothing products have been well received abroad (such as jeans), many have encountered problems among Europeans who tend to see France and Italy as the upscale fashion centers—an opinion clothing brands from other countries find difficult to overcome. However, Hilfiger has since played up its Americanism, and the perception that the brand and price are a step below the pure luxury brands have successfully helped its European sales find a niche.

In addition, Hilfiger has encountered some differing national preferences. In Germany, for example, its largest European market, men don't mind paying $50 more than the highest-priced Hilfiger shirts in the United States, but they want them in a higher-quality cotton. To accommodate European tastes, Hilfiger has switched to wool sweaters, adjusted to the European preference for slimmer-looking jeans and smaller shirt logos, and created a line of added-luxury items, such as leather jackets and cashmere sweaters for the Italian market.

To make these changes and adapt its look to the European demands, Hilfiger set up a design staff in Amsterdam that includes almost 30 different nationalities. The success in Europe has led to more harmonization in the products offered in the United States and Europe, a move more upmarket in the United States, and a greater dependence on the European design team.

Although its line is clearly identifiable as Hilfiger, the firm makes some adjustments to fit country preferences—brighter colors for Italy, tartans and plaids for Japan, and sleeker designs for Chile.

DISTRIBUTION

In the United States, Hilfiger traditionally relied mainly on wholesaling to about 1,800 department stores, many of which contained stand-alone Hilfiger departments. It has stayed away from chains considered more low-end, such as JCPenney and Sears, though it does sell its outdated stock to discount chains T.J. Maxx and Marshalls. However, in 2007, Hilfiger gave Macy's exclusive rights to sell its sportswear lines. Although Macy's has about 800 stores, the move required Hilfiger to pull sales from other department stores, such as Dillard's.

Distribution is perhaps the biggest difference Hilfiger found when entering Europe. Because the company succeeded in the United States by first going into department stores, it put an early European emphasis on them as well, which led to its entry into such leading chains as Galeries Lafayette in France and El Corte Inglés in Spain. Hilfiger's CEO has described the U.S. market as one of concentration (sending a lot to department stores) and the European market as one of fragmentation (sending small amounts to small stores that carry select pieces). European operational costs are about three times those in the United States because of this more fragmented retail and wholesale system. Hilfiger now has about 5,000 wholesale accounts in Europe—much more than in the United States. On top of that, the margins at the final consumer level in Europe run from 50 to 100 percent higher than at home, with the result that prices for Hilfiger merchandise are much higher in Europe.

Hilfiger entered most Asian countries through licensing agreements; however, as sales grew substantially in China and Japan, it turned to self-ownership within those markets.

In recent years, Hilfiger has inaugurated large flagship stores in prime locations within large markets, such as in New York City, Paris, and Tokyo. These stores serve not only to make sales, but also to demonstrate the variety of merchandise under the Hilfiger label. The foreign stores are decorated to emphasize an American image, while simultaneously connecting the United States to the host country. In the Paris store, this includes a poster of a U.S. magazine with the Eiffel Tower on the cover. By locating in prestige areas, Hilfiger promotes an aura of having high-end products, yet its aim is to be a high-margin brand with prices a notch lower than luxury brands.

There is an old adage that clothes make the man. Hilfiger, while making and selling clothes, has succeeded in convincing customers that its merchandise will help boost (or make) their positions. ■

CRN Case Review Note

QUESTIONS

17-1. The chapter explains five international marketing orientations. Which one most applies to Tommy Hilfiger? Explain why.

17-2. The chapter explains five elements in the marketing mix (product, pricing, promotion, branding, and distribution). In which of these have Tommy Hilfiger's operating practices been the most standardized globally? Explain why this has been possible and desirable.

INTRODUCTION

As the Hilfiger case points out, similar marketing principles apply in domestic and foreign markets and hold that regardless of where a company operates, it must have desirable products and services, tell people about them, and offer them at acceptable prices and accessible locations favored by consumers. However, country differences may cause companies to apply these principles differently abroad, such as by offering product variations to correspond with local preferences—as Hilfiger has done by offering higher-quality cotton for shirts in Germany. Hilfiger's experience also emphasizes the need to find the right balance between the benefits of local responsiveness and the efficiency gains of standardization.

CONCEPT CHECK

Recall that we devote an entire section of Chapter 12 to the issue of "Global Integration versus Local Responsiveness." As we point out, when expanding into foreign markets, a company can save money by standardizing many of its policies and practices and—particularly if it's pursuing a global strategy of expansion— its products. Here we observe that a strategy of marketing standardized products—marketing the same or similar versions to specific global segments—falls at one end of the global integration/local responsiveness spectrum.

Whatever marketing approach a company takes abroad should be compatible with its overall aims and strategies. This does not imply that it must follow the same strategy for every product or every country. Such factors as cost leadership or differentiation may matter more in some markets than in others. Choosing to follow the same tactics globally may lead to, say, a mass-market orientation in one country and a focused strategy in another. Finally, the degree of global standardization versus national responsiveness may vary within elements of the marketing mix, such as standardizing the product as much as possible while promoting it differently among countries.

Figure 17.1 shows marketing's place in international business. Here, we discuss the application of different marketing strategies to international operations, examine the marketing mix elements of product, pricing, promotion, branding, and distribution, and explain the major factors to consider for each element when operating internationally. Finally, we consider the need to vary the emphasis within the marketing mix to fit the conditions of each country.

MARKETING STRATEGIES

Overall international marketing strategies should depend on the company's
- Marketing orientation.
- Target market.

We first discuss the worldwide application of the orientations that commonly describe companies' marketing strategies. Keep in mind that they are not entirely mutually exclusive. We then examine market segmentation and targeting and how they relate both to the orientations and to the marketing mix elements. We emphasize product policy in our discussion because it is central to a firm's strategy, whereas the other elements in the marketing mix are supportive to it.[2]

FIGURE 17.1 Marketing as a Means of Pursuing an International Strategy

Recall that we used Figure 15.1 to introduce the various modes and means by which a company can pursue its international objectives and strategy. Among those means we included functions, and here we focus on one of the most important of those functions: *marketing*.

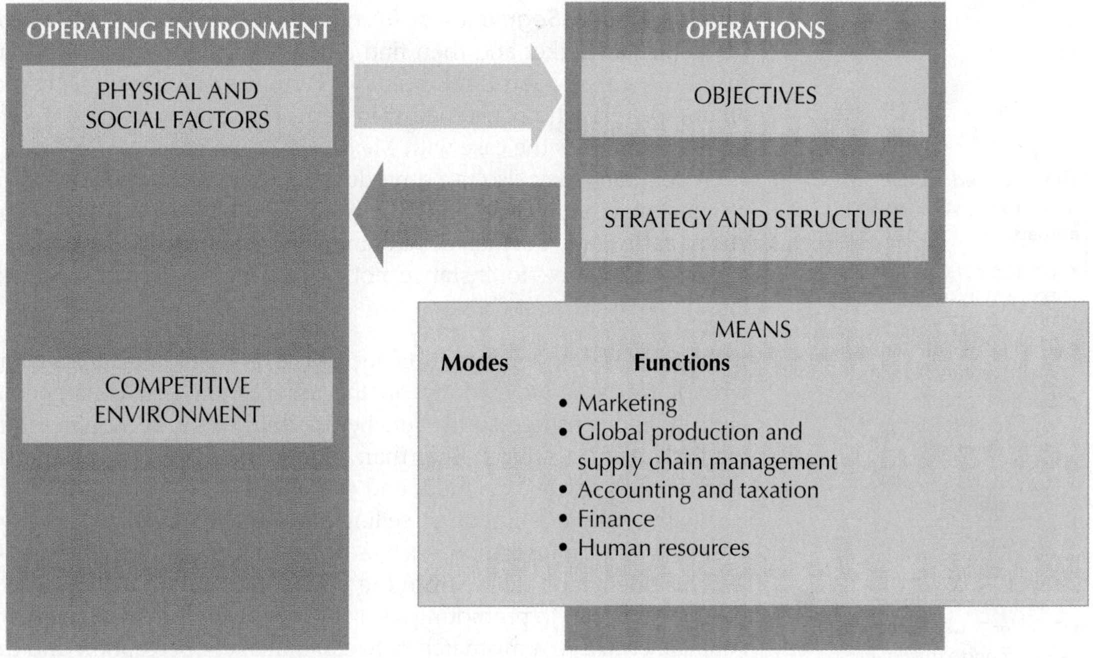

MARKETING ORIENTATIONS

Five common marketing orientations can be applied around the world: *production, sales, customer, strategic marketing,* and *social marketing.* Each is discussed below.

Price is the most important factor in selling many commodities.

Production Orientation A company may focus primarily on production—either efficiency or high-quality—with little emphasis on marketing. Rather than analyzing consumer needs to a high degree, managers assume that customers simply want lower prices or higher quality. Although this approach has largely gone out of vogue, it is used internationally for certain cases:

- *Commodity sales,* especially those for which there is little need or possibility of product differentiation
- *Passive exports,* particularly those that serve to reduce surpluses within the domestic market
- *Foreign-market segments or niches* that may resemble segments targeted domestically

CONCEPT CHECK

In explaining "Commodity Agreements" in Chapter 7, we define commodities as raw materials or primary products (e.g., crude petroleum, copper, coffee). Commodities account for a significant portion of global merchandise trade.

Commodity Sales Companies sell many undifferentiated raw materials and agricultural commodities primarily on the basis of price because of universal demand. However, even for commodities, companies have sometimes had positive international sales results through differentiation that builds favorable consumer perceptions such as with the Chiquita brand on bananas.

In addition, oil producers, such as PDVSA, LUKoil, and Aramco, have bought branded gasoline-distribution operations abroad to help them sell an otherwise undifferentiated product. Commodity producers also put effort into business-to-business marketing by providing innovative financing and ensuring timely, high-quality supplies.

Passive sales occur when foreign buyers seek new products.

Passive Exports Many companies begin exporting very passively by filling unsolicited requests from abroad. At this point, they adapt their products very little, if at all, to foreign consumers' preferences. This suffices for many companies that view foreign sales simply as a means to dispose of excess inventory they can't reasonably sell domestically. In fact, if fixed costs are covered from domestic sales, they can quote lower export prices to liquidate inventories without disrupting their domestic markets.

Foreign-Market Segments or Niches A company may aim a product at a large share of the domestic market and then find a few consumers abroad who are also willing to buy it. Inca Kola, a major soft drink brand in Peru, has only small niche markets abroad, primarily among people who consumed it in Peru. However, a niche market abroad may become a mass market, as is the case with Mexico's Corona beer.

The unaltered product may have appeal at home and abroad

- Because of spillover in product information from its home country,
- Through a simultaneous multi-country launch,
- Because of foreign and domestic input in development.

A company may also use a production orientation when selling in countries with only a minimal market potential and little competition from firms that adapt to local market preferences, particularly in small developing nations. In effect, the market size does not justify the alteration expense—for instance, not even changing electrical plugs to fit local sockets, which local purchasers must convert.

Sales Orientation Internationally, a sales orientation means a company tries to sell abroad what it can sell domestically on the assumption that consumers are sufficiently similar globally. Hilfiger successfully launches its children's collection in multiple countries this way.[3] Similarly, some products other than commodities need no international adaptation, such as razor blades, aircraft, cat food, and cameras. For others, however, a company may succeed best with a sales orientation by selling to culturally similar countries with a great deal of spillover in product information, such as between the United States and Canada.[4]

CONCEPT CHECK

In Chapter 2, we discussed that companies may gain competitive advantages by nurturing cultural diversity. By bringing different nationalities together, usually in teams to handle a specific project, their diverse backgrounds, perspectives, and experiences often enable companies to gain a deeper knowledge of products and services and how to create and deliver them.

This orientation differs from the production orientation because of its active rather than passive approach to promoting sales. However, there is much evidence of foreign-marketing failures because of a mismatch between managers' perception and the reality of what will be accepted abroad,[5] or because they believe heavy sales efforts can overcome negative foreign attitudes. To help alleviate this mismatch, companies may engage product development teams comprising people from different countries to share information so as to create customer solutions that apply globally from the start.[6] Additionally, a strong information exchange between foreign subsidiaries and headquarters can help develop products that can be sufficiently standardized and still fit the needs of consumers in different countries.[7]

Customer Orientation In a company that operates according to a sales orientation, management is usually guided by answers to such questions as: Should the company send some exports abroad? Where can it sell more of product X? That is, the product is held constant and the sales location is varied.

A customer orientation takes geographic areas as given.

In contrast, a customer orientation asks: What and how can the company sell in country A or to a particular type of consumer? In this case, the country or type of consumer is held constant and the product and marketing method vary. An MNE may most likely take this approach because it finds the country's size and growth potential or the consumer type attractive. In an extreme case, it would move to completely different products—an uncommon strategy that some MNEs nonetheless have adopted. Compañía Chilena de Fósforos, a Chilean match producer, wanted to tap the Japanese market because of its growth and size. However, because the company's matches were not price competitive in Japan, it successfully entered the market by making chopsticks, a product that would use its poplar forest resources and wood-processing capabilities.[8]

Business-to-business suppliers may be concerned primarily with promoting their production capabilities, prices, and delivery reliability rather than determining what will sell in foreign markets. Instead, they depend on other companies' purchasing agents to give them product specifications. For example, Hong Kong's Yue Yuen Industrial is the world's largest branded-footwear manufacturer, making athletic shoes to the specifications of companies such as Nike, New Balance, and Adidas.

The most common product strategy is to adapt by degree.

Strategic Marketing Orientation Most companies committed to continual rather than sporadic foreign sales adopt a strategy that combines production, sales, and customer orientations. Companies that don't make changes to accommodate foreign customers' needs may lose too many sales, especially if aggressive competitors are willing to adapt to those needs. At the same time, firms must consider their competencies, lest they deviate too much from what they do well. Thus, they rely on product variations. Hermès, known for its luxury silk products, has introduced limited edition silk saris for the Indian market that sell upwards of $6,000 each.[9] Thus, Hermès has used its competency in prestige design clothing to produce something that fits the unique Indian market.

Companies consider the effects on all stakeholders when selling or making their products.

Social Marketing Orientation Companies with social marketing orientations pay close attention to the potential environmental, health, social, and work-related problems that may arise when selling or making their products abroad. For instance, Tesco is building "green" stores and has introduced carbon labeling on its products.[10] Such groups as consumer associations, political parties, labor unions, and NGOs are becoming more globally aware—and vocal. They can quell demand when they believe a product somehow violates their concept of social responsibility.

Companies must increasingly consider not only how a product is purchased but also how it is made and disposed of and how it might be changed to be more socially desirable. Such considerations have led Coca-Cola to develop a vitamin-enriched beverage for Botswana, distribute rehydration salts in its packing crates in several countries, and use returnable glass containers for Argentina and Brazil.[11] Our ending case deals with a joint venture that aims to use social responsibility as a competitive advantage.

SEGMENTING AND TARGETING MARKETS

Companies must decide on their target markets, which may include segments that exist in more than one country.

Seldom can a company convince virtually an entire population to consume its product. Thus, based on the orientations just discussed, companies must segment markets for their products and services and then decide which to target and how. The most common way to do this is through demographics, such as income, age, gender, ethnicity, religion, or a combination of factors (say, a segment consisting of women age 20 to 30 earning $30,000–$40,000 per year). Companies may further refine these segments by adding psychographics (attitudes, values, lifestyles). Internationally, there are three basic approaches to segmentation.[12]

CONCEPT CHECK

In Chapter 13, we describe the importance of economic demographic variables in the process whereby companies evaluate and select countries as locations for international operations. Many of the demographic data considered in international marketing decisions are the same. In addressing the question "Will Prime Locations Change?" for example, we point out that while populations in such high-income countries as Japan are declining, those in many developing countries are growing.

By Country Let's say a company decides to go only to the Japanese market for the time being because of its population size and purchasing power. The firm will then need to decide whether to target one or multiple segments there, whether to use the same marketing mix to sell to all segments, whether to tailor the products separately to each segment, and whether to vary the promotion and distribution separately as well. However, although this approach may lead to success in Japan, it overlooks the possible similarities of various Japanese market segments with those in other countries, leaving little opportunity to gain economies through standardization in order to serve market segments that cut across countries.

By Global Segment An MNE may identify some segments around the world, such as those based primarily on some demographic or cultural attributes that transcend countries.[13] Red Bull targets a global, athletically minded, young-adult market.[14] Ferrari targets high-net-worth individuals who want the exclusivity of having a product whose demand exceeds supply.[15] Thus, each country may have some people within the same segment, but the proportional size of each segment will vary by country. Although this may bring about economies of standardization, the company may still need to prioritize by country of entry, delay tapping bigger markets in some countries, and face high entry costs in other countries where the targeted segment is small.

By Multiple Criteria MNEs can combine these choices by looking at countries as segments, identifying segments within each country, and comparing them with those in other countries. They can then determine similarities for targeting the most promising cross-country segments, gain efficiencies through standardization, and still tailor other marketing mix aspects—product offerings, promotion, branding, and distribution—to be compatible with the needs of each country's market.

In effect, a company may hold one or more elements of these marketing functions constant while altering the others. For instance, Chanel aims its cosmetics sales at a segment that transcends national boundaries. It uses branding, promotion, pricing, and distribution globally, but adapts the cosmetics to local ethnic and climatic norms.[16]

Mass Markets Versus Niche Markets At the same time, most companies have multiple products and product variations that appeal to different segments; thus, they must decide which to introduce abroad and whether to target them to mass markets or niche segments. For example, General Motors aims at most income levels in the United States with models ranging in price from its Chevrolet Sonic through its Cadillac Escalade SUV, but it entered China by aiming only at a high-income segment—first with Buicks and later with Cadillacs.

Because the percentage of people who fall into any segment may vary substantially among countries, a niche market in one country may be a mass market in another. An MNE may be content to accept a combination of mass and niche markets; however, if it wishes to appeal to mass markets everywhere, it may need to change elements in its marketing program. U.S.-based Bell South successfully managed to reach a much larger Venezuelan market by selling fewer minutes on phone cards—it added \$4 phone cards to the \$10 and \$20 cards it customarily sold.[17]

PRODUCT POLICIES

Although cost is a compelling reason to globally standardize any part of a company's marketing mix, it is product standardization that generally gains the biggest savings.[18] Nevertheless, product adaptations are common. We now consider the reasons for making them for foreign markets, their costs, the extent and mix of product lines, and product life-cycle considerations.

WHY FIRMS ALTER PRODUCTS

Companies have legal, cultural, and economic reasons for altering their products to fit the needs of customers in different countries. Each is examined in turn below.

Legal factors are usually related to safety or health protection.

Legal Considerations Explicit legal requirements, usually meant to protect consumers, are the most obvious reason to alter products for foreign markets. If you don't comply with the law, you won't be allowed to sell. Pharmaceuticals and foods are particularly subject to regulations concerning purity, testing, and labeling, while automobiles must conform to diverse safety, pollution, and fuel-economy standards.

When standards (such as for safety) differ among countries, MNEs may either conform to the minimum standards of each country or make and sell products fabricated to the highest global standard everywhere. Managers must consider cost along with any ill will that may result by having lower standards in some countries. Critics have complained, for example, about companies' sales abroad—especially in developing countries—of such products as toys, automobiles, contraceptives, and pharmaceuticals that did not meet safety or quality standards elsewhere.

Labeling Requirements One of the more cumbersome product alterations for companies concerns laws on labeling, such as for origin, ingredients, and warnings. Among the different requirements for food product labels are listing any bioengineered content and indicating whether a product is organic or fairly traded. Countries have varying requirements for warnings on cigarette packages (some show gruesome pictures); Australia requires all companies to use the same drab dark brown packages and standardized type for their brand names.[19]

Environmental-Protection Regulations Another problem concerns laws that protect the environment, such as Denmark's onetime ban on aluminum cans and current refundable deposit on them. Other countries restrict the volume of packaging materials to save resources and decrease trash. There are also differences in national requirements as to whether containers must be reusable and whether companies use packaging materials that must be recycled, incinerated, or composted.

Indirect Legal Considerations Indirect legal requirements also affect product content or demand. In some nations, companies cannot easily import certain raw materials or components, forcing them to construct an end product with local substitutes that may substantially alter the final result. Legal requirements such as high taxes on heavy automobiles also shift companies' sales to smaller models, thus indirectly altering demand for tire sizes and grades of gasoline.

Point

Should Home Governments Regulate Their Companies' Marketing in Developing Countries?

Point **Yes** MNEs advertise, promote, and sell products in developing markets that their home countries have banned. If we've made a decision not to sell these products domestically because of their dangers or ethical implications, we have a moral obligation to prevent the same consequences abroad. This statement may smack of extraterritoriality, but let's face it: Too many consumers in developing countries lack the education and reliable information to make intelligent decisions about products, and/or they are saddled with corrupt political leaders who don't look after their interests. We must ensure that they spend on needs rather than on wants engendered by MNEs' clever promotion programs. If developed countries don't regulate to protect consumers in developing countries, who will?

Companies also export products that don't meet quality standards at home or are potentially dangerous. Take DDT: It's so dangerous to the environment that all developed countries banned its use, but they allowed production and export for years afterward. Or consider battery recycling: Developed countries have pretty much abandoned that business because of strict antipollution requirements to prevent lead poisoning, which shows up only after slow, cumulative ingestion through the years. So now companies export the batteries to developing countries that have either weak or weakly enforced pollution laws.[20]

With the World Health Organization (WHO) estimating that tobacco is the leading cause of preventable death in the world, we have also attempted to limit tobacco use through warning labels and ads, restrictions on sales to minors, and smoking bans in certain public areas. While tobacco use has been declining in developed countries, it is burgeoning in developing ones, especially those in Africa, where tobacco companies have increased their promotions.[21]

There are also examples of products suitable for most customers in the developed world but not for poorer countries. The most famous case involves infant-formula sales, in which infant mortality rates rose in developing countries when bottle-feeding supplanted breast-feeding. Because of low incomes and poor education, mothers frequently over-diluted formula and gave it to their babies in unsanitary conditions. And the governments did little to stop the sales. Global publicity about the situation led WHO to pass a voluntary code to restrict formula promotion—but not sales—in such areas. Critics hit Nestlé hardest because it had the largest share of infant-formula sales in developing countries and because its name-identified products facilitated the organization of a boycott. Nestlé ceased advertising that could discourage breast-feeding, limited free formula supplies at hospitals, and banned personal gifts to health officials.[22]

MNEs also pay too little attention to the needs of consumers in developing markets. Instead, they primarily create products suitable to the needs of wealthier consumers who can afford them, but superfluous for low-income consumers, to whom MNEs introduce and promote them heavily. Thus, the poor end up buying products they don't need instead of spending their money on nutritional and health items. Bottled water, sold mainly in plastic bottles by such companies as Nestlé, Danone, Coca-Cola, and PepsiCo, is an example. It is often no better than tap water (in fact, it often *is* tap water), but it sells for 10,000 times more in bottles that are thrown out and take 1,000 years to biodegrade.

Finally, MNEs spend little to make products to fit the needs of developing countries. Consider that little of the global health research budget is spent on diseases that account for most of the global disease burden—mainly those that largely bypass developed countries.[23] Instead of spending heavily on life-threatening illnesses like malaria, Chagas disease, and sleeping sickness, they spend on lifestyle treatments, such as penile erectile dysfunction and baldness. The U.S. Food and Drug Administration (FDA) did institute an incentive in 2008—faster approval of potential "blockbuster drugs"—for pharmaceutical companies that research previously neglected diseases. However, there is skepticism about whether faster approval is enough of an incentive.[24] Surely we can find the regulatory means to force companies to meet real needs in the developing world rather than concentrating on selling dangerous and superfluous products there.

Should Home Governments Regulate Their Companies' Marketing in Developing Countries?

Counterpoint

No The answer here is education rather than limiting people's choices by regulating MNEs. In fact, there are many examples of behavior change in both consumers and governments when they learn the facts. Pakistan, for instance, has taken a number of actions to restrict tobacco use.[25]

Your argument that products banned at home should not be sold abroad assumes that the home government knows best. This may reflect a difference in morals rather than a problem of creating physical danger. For instance, some countries have banned the sale of the morning-after pill RU-486 on moral grounds. But to ban sales in other countries that accept a different morality would smack of cultural imperialism.

Conditions between rich and poor countries are sometimes so different that they need different regulations. Take your example of DDT exports. Developing countries are aware of DDT's adverse long-term effect on the environment, but in the short term many of them face a malaria crisis. When South Africa was persuaded to ban the use of DDT and turned instead to a different pesticide, the number of new malaria cases tripled in four years; renewing DDT spraying brought that number down again.[26] Until there is a better solution for malaria, DDT bans will do more harm than good. Certainly, if one government has found a product dangerous, it should pass on this information to other governments; in terms of DDT and toxic materials exports, this is already being done.

Yes, tobacco companies are promoting more heavily in developing countries. Keep in mind, though, that a good part of that promotion is for smokeless tobacco products, which are safer than cigarettes and can help smokers stop.[27] However, if other governments were to limit their companies' sales or promotion of tobacco, their citizens would still be able to buy it. Many developing countries have indigenous tobacco companies, some of which are even government-owned, such as the China National Tobacco Company.

The infant formula situation truly shows the complexity of this issue. Other factors also influenced the rise in bottle-feeding—specifically, more working mothers and fewer products and services originating in the home.

Counterpoint

Together, they led to feeding babies "home brews" that, sadly, were also often unsanitary. Promoting infant formula may simply have persuaded them to give up the home brews in favor of the most nutritious breast-milk substitute available. Moreover, well-intentioned anti-formula groups succeeded in replacing bottle-feeding with breast-feeding. However, the HIV virus is transmitted through breast milk—a particular problem in HIV/AIDS-plagued southern Africa.[28] This starkly shows the futility of trying to legislate what is good for people.

How far can we go to try to protect people? Obesity, considered a growing health problem in the developed world, is being attacked through education—the same way we should attack problems in developing countries. I can't imagine a widespread rationing or banning of sugars, fats, and carbohydrates. Certainly, products such as soft drinks and bottled water seem superfluous when people are ill-nourished and in poor health. But the lack of access to sanitary water is one of the world's biggest health problems, which the sale of soft drinks and bottled water are helping in the short term. In a longer term, Coca-Cola is working to distribute small scale purifying systems to mitigate the problem.[29] Moreover, there is no clear-cut means of drawing a line between people who can and can't afford these so-called superfluous products.

Companies *do* alter products to fit the needs of poor people—everything from less expensive packages to less expensive products. The pharmaceutical firms you criticized for not attacking low-income health needs spend heavily to find solutions to diseases that attack all people, such as cancer and diabetes. In fact, they have seen, and expect to see, huge prescription drug growth in emerging markets.[30] However, they must recoup their expenses if they are to survive, so they concentrate on drugs for which they can be paid. Governmental research centers and nonprofit foundations are better candidates for solving the developing countries' health problems. Some are working jointly with pharmaceutical firms to find solutions, while the National Institutes of Health (NIH) in the United States has instituted a program to find treatments for some of the 6,800 diseases for which there is likely insufficient revenue to recoup research expenditures.[31]

Although some standardization of products would eliminate wasteful alterations, there is resistance because

- A changeover would be costly.
- People are familiar with the "old."

Issues of Standardization A recurring issue is the need to arrive at international product standards and eliminate some of the wasteful product requirements for alterations among countries. Although governments have reached agreements on some products (technical standards on mobile phones, bar codes to identify products), other products (railroad gauges, power supplies) continue to vary. A global standard has usually resulted from companies wanting to emulate a dominant producer, such as making blades to fit Gillette razors.

In reality, there is both consumer and economic resistance to standardization—such as the U.S. reluctance to adapt to the metric system. Economically, a complete changeover would be more costly than simply educating people and relabeling. Containers would have to be redesigned and production retooled so that sizes would be in even numbers. (Would U.S. football have a first down with 9.144 meters to go?) Even for new products or those still under development, companies and countries are slow to reach agreement because they want to protect the investments they've already made. At best, international standards will come very slowly.

Examination of cultural differences may pinpoint possible problem areas.

Cultural Considerations Religious differences obviously limit the standardization of product offerings globally, such as food franchises limiting sales of pork products in Islamic countries and meat of any kind in India. However, cultural differences affecting product demand may not be so easily discerned. Toyota initially failed to sell enough pickup trucks in the United States until it redesigned the interior with enough headroom for drivers to wear cowboy hats. Home Depot pulled out of the Chinese market after discovering that it could not overcome consumers' preference for hiring people to do jobs rather than embracing the do-it-yourself concept.[32] International food marketers substantially alter ingredients (especially fat, sodium, and sugar) to fit local tastes and requirements, such as Kellogg's All-Bran bar having three times as much salt in the United States as in Mexico.

Economic Considerations

Personal incomes and infrastructures affect product demand.

Income Level and Distribution If a country's average consumers have low incomes, few of them may be able to buy products that MNEs sell domestically. But this creates an opportunity to sell to those with sufficient income while designing cheaper alternatives for those with lower incomes. In Peru, Unilever sells deodorants in aerosol cans to more affluent consumers and small containers of cream sachet to those with lower incomes. Often, consumers buy personal items in small quantities as they use them usually because of low incomes, but also because of difficulty in transporting and storing large amounts. In another Peruvian example, Kimberley Clarke sells Huggies (disposable diapers) in regular boxes along with a single Huggies in a small package.[33] Diageo and SABMiller have lowered beer prices in several African countries by brewing with local ingredients such as yams and convincing governmental authorities to remove excise taxes because of the agricultural jobs created by the ingredient change.[34] When segmenting sales to different economic levels, a company may need to differentiate its products with different brand names, such as what Procter & Gamble does in China with both a Duracell and Nanfu brand of batteries.[35] The adjacent photo shows a high-frequency store catering to the type of consumer who buys in small quantities.

CONCEPT CHECK

In Chapter 13, we list the factors that companies consider when "scanning" potential overseas locations to determine what conditions in the host country's environment are likely to affect the success of international operations. Under "Cost Considerations," we point out that poor internal infrastructure inflates operating costs and can in fact negate cost savings afforded by low labor rates.

Infrastructure Poor infrastructure may also require product alterations, such as the ability to withstand rough terrain and utility outages. The washing machine models Whirlpool sells in remote areas of India have rat guards to protect hoses, extra-strong parts to survive transportation on potholed roads, and heavy-duty wiring to cope with electrical ebbs and surges.[36] Japan, despite having an excellent infrastructure, is characterized by crowded conditions and high land prices. Some large foreign automobile models are too wide to fit into elevators that carry cars to upper floors to be parked, or to make narrow turns on back streets.

ALTERATION COSTS

Companies can usually cut production and inventory costs through product standardization. Nevertheless, as you've just seen, there can be compelling reasons to alter products for different national markets. Some alterations, such as package labeling, are cheaper to make than others, such as designing a different car model. Further, some will do more to increase sales than others, thus companies need to evaluate the potential cost savings versus sales generation for each type of change.[37] However, even packaging changes may necessitate costly research if the aim is to convey a particular product perception to a target market with different characteristics than

Some alterations cost less than others.

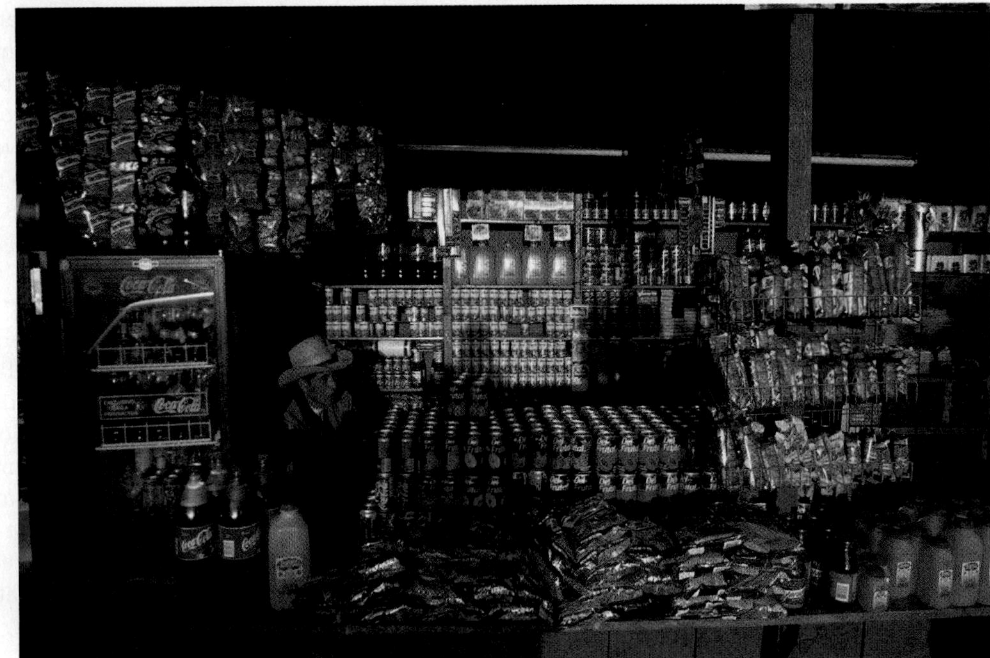

High-frequency stores in developing countries, including this one in the Guatemalan highlands, often crowd small packages into small areas to serve customers who shop frequently because they cannot afford to buy, transport, or store in large quantities.

Source: © Jon Crwys-Williams / Alamy

those at home. For example, there is evidence that packaging can partially sway consumers in buying decisions, but the image needed to do this may differ by target market.[38]

MNEs can compromise between uniformity and diversity by standardizing products a great deal while altering some components. Whirlpool does this by putting the same basic mechanical parts in all its refrigerators while changing such features as doors and shelves for different countries.[39]

THE PRODUCT LINE: EXTENT AND MIX

Broadening the product line may gain distribution economies.

When introducing a full range of its products abroad, a firm's percentage share for each product commonly differs from those in its home country. For instance, a tire manufacturer may sell all its tire sizes everywhere, but the share for each size depends on automobile models in each market. Cultural factors may also be important. Most of Nike's shoes for specialty sports have sold well in China, but not its running shoes because running there is associated with unpopular school exercising programs and with people being chased.[40]

In many other cases, it is doubtful that all of an MNE's multiple products could generate sufficient sales to justify the cost of penetrating each market with each product. Even if they could, the company might offer only a portion of its product line, perhaps as an entry strategy or because of limited space and high inventory costs when handling a very broad product line. Walmart's Canadian stores, for instance, have only 20 percent of the merchandise available in its U.S. stores.[41]

Sales and Cost Considerations In reaching product-line decisions, managers should consider the possible effects on sales and the cost of having a large versus small family of products. Sometimes a firm must produce and sell a wide variety of products to gain distribution with large retailers. Further, if the foreign sales per customer are small, selling costs per unit may be high because of the associated fixed distribution costs. In such a case, the company can broaden the product line it handles, either by introducing a larger family of products or by grouping sales of several manufacturers.

Product Life-Cycle Considerations Countries may differ in either the shape or the length of a product's life cycle. Thus, a product facing declining sales in one country may have growing or sustained sales in another. Consider cars: They are a mature product in Western Europe, the United States, and Japan, in the late growth stage in South Korea, and in the early growth stage in India. At the mature stage, automobile companies must emphasize characteristics that encourage people to replace their still-functional cars, such as lifestyle, speed, and accessories. In the early growth stage, they need to appeal to first-time buyers who worry about cost, so they emphasize fuel consumption and price.[42] Firms must also consider competition from other products. Best Buy closed its Chinese operations largely because consumers put off buying the electronics in which it specialized, such as stereos and large flat-screen TVs, in order to buy large appliances, such as washing machines and refrigerators.[43]

PRICING STRATEGIES

Within the marketing mix, a price must be low enough to gain sales but high enough to guarantee the flow of funds required to cover such expenses as R&D, production, and distribution. A competitive strategy, such as cost leadership versus product differentiation, also affects pricing decisions. The proper price not only ensures short-term profits but also provides the resources necessary to achieve long-term competitive viability.

POTENTIAL OBSTACLES IN INTERNATIONAL PRICING

Pricing is more complex internationally than domestically because of various factors that we'll now examine.

Governmental price controls may

- Set minimum or maximum prices.
- Prohibit certain competitive pricing practices.

Government Intervention Every country has laws that affect the prices of goods, such as price controls. Minimum prices are usually set to prevent companies from eliminating competitors and gaining monopoly positions or may be set simply to maintain an industry. Maximum prices are usually set so that poor consumers can buy products and services.

The WTO, under its antidumping regulations, permits countries to establish restrictions against any import entering at a price below cost. But why would a company wish to sell below its cost? First, it may want to induce customers to try a product, such as by offering a low price or even free samples. Second, it may be testing the market. Nestlé did this when it exported Lean Cuisine products from Canada to the United Kingdom at a price below cost, then sold them temporarily at the consumer price it would charge if it produced them in the United Kingdom. The loss was small compared to the value of the information gained and the amount of Nestlé's eventual commitment. However, antidumping regulations may prevent companies from fully utilizing the advantages from such temporary below-cost selling.

Consumers in some countries simply like certain products more and are willing to pay more for them.

Market Diversity Although a company can segment the domestic market and charge different prices in each segment, country-to-country variations create even more natural segments. A seafood company would sell few sea urchins or tuna eyeballs in the United States at any price, but it can export them to Japan, where they are considered delicacies.

Pricing Tactics In some places, a company may have many competitors and thus little discretion in setting its prices. Elsewhere, a near-monopoly situation may allow it to exercise considerable pricing discretion by using any of the following tactics:

- A **skimming strategy**—charging a high price for a new product by aiming first at consumers willing to pay that much, then progressively lowering the price to sell to other consumers
- A **penetration strategy**—introducing a product at a low price to induce a maximum number of consumers to try it
- A **cost-plus strategy**—pricing at a desired margin over cost

Country-of-origin stereotypes also limit pricing possibilities. For example, exporters in developing economies must often compete primarily through low prices because of negative perceptions about their products' quality. The danger is that a lower price may weaken the product image even further.

Cash versus credit buying affects demand.

Diversity in buying on credit affects sales, especially through impulse buying.[44] Credit buying raises costs and may also give some individuals a feeling of insecurity by incurring debt. They may also forgo purchases because of a preference to save. On average, consumers in some countries, such as Japan, are less willing to undertake debt than consumers in other countries, such as the United States. In the former, it is harder to generate sales by offering credit.

CONCEPT CHECK

In discussing "Export Strategy" in Chapter 14, we discuss the importance of export intermediaries in the international business transaction chain and explain their place in a carefully considered export business plan. In turning to "The Export Process," we describe the process of indirect selling and explain the central role of home-country intermediaries—independent companies that facilitate the international trade of goods.

Export Price Escalation If standard markups occur within distribution channels, lengthening the channels or adding expenses somewhere in the system will further raise the price to the consumer—a situation known as *export price escalation.* If a product's markup is 50 percent and its production cost is $1.00, the price to the consumer would be $1.50. However, if expenses in the system, such as extra transport expenses, were to raise costs to $1.20, the 50 percent markup would make the price $1.80, not $1.70 as might be expected.

Figure 17.2 shows price escalation in export sales, which occurs for two reasons:

1. Channels of distribution usually include additional intermediaries because exporters need to contract with organizations that know how to sell in foreign markets.
2. Tariffs and transport are added costs that may be passed on to consumers.

There are two main implications of price escalation. Seemingly exportable products may turn out to be noncompetitive abroad if companies use cost-plus pricing—which many do. To become competitive in exporting, a company may have to sell its product to intermediaries at a lower price to lessen the amount of escalation.

Price generally goes up by more than incremental costs for transport and duty.

Fluctuations in Currency Value For companies accustomed to operating with one (relatively) stable currency, pricing in highly volatile currencies can be extremely troublesome. Managers should price to ensure the company enough funds to replenish its inventory and still make a profit. Otherwise, it may be making a "paper profit" while liquidating itself—that is, what shows on paper as a profit may result from the failure to adjust for inflation while the merchandise is in stock.

Two other pricing problems occur because of inflationary conditions:

1. The receipt of funds in a foreign currency that, when converted, buy less of the company's own currency than had been expected
2. The frequent readjustment of prices necessary to compensate for continual cost increases

In the first case, the company sometimes (depending on competitive factors and governmental regulations) can specify an equivalency in some hard currency in sales contracts. For example, a U.S. firm's sale to a company in Venezuela may specify that payment be made in dollars or in bolivars at an equivalent price in terms of dollars at the time payment is made.

CONCEPT CHECK

We define foreign exchange in Chapter 9 as the currency of one country denominated in the currency of another country or group of countries. We point out that most foreign-exchange transactions stem from the activities of commercial banks, but we also observe that exporters and importers are players on the foreign-exchange market and explain how such factors as exchange rates affect certain international business activities, especially the process of making foreign payments.

FIGURE 17.2 Why Cost-Plus Pricing Pushes Up Prices

Let's say that a product is being exported from Country A and imported into Country B for purchase by consumers there. Let's also say that both the producer/exporter and the importer/distributor tack on 50 percent markups to the prices they pay for the product. If you add in the costs of transport and tariffs, the product is substantially more expensive in Country B than in Country A—perhaps too expensive to be sold competitively.

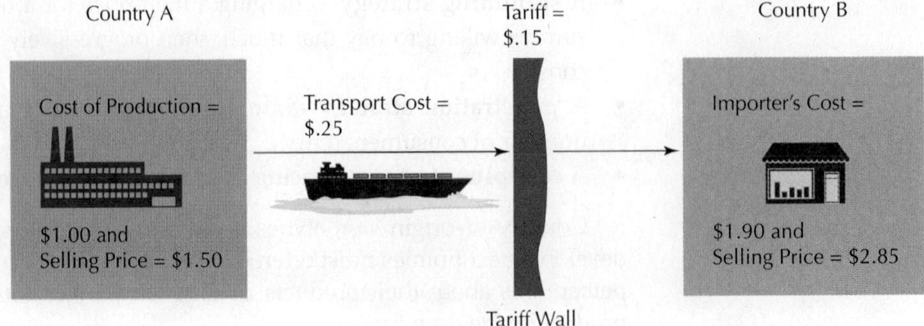

In the second case, frequent price increases may hamper the ability to quote prices in letters or catalogs, or even what the company would otherwise prefer for distribution. For instance, price increases in vending-machine sales are often difficult because of the need to recalibrate machines and come up with coins or tokens that correspond to the new prices. Another alternative is to change the product's quality, which few firms are willing to do, or its size, which is what Coca-Cola did to its soft-drink cans in Hong Kong when aluminum prices rose.[45]

Currency-value changes also affect pricing decisions for any product that has potential foreign competition. For example, when the U.S. dollar is strong, companies can sell non-U.S.-made goods more cheaply in the U.S. market because their prices in dollars decrease. In such a situation, U.S. producers may have to accept a lower profit margin to be competitive. When the dollar is weak, however, producers in foreign countries may have to adjust their margins downward.

When companies sell similar goods in multiple countries, price differences among them must not greatly exceed the cost of bringing the goods in from a lower-priced country, or spillover in buying will occur. Ice cream manufacturers, let's say, can vary their prices by a large percentage from country to country because the transportation costs compared to product price render large-scale movements across borders impractical. However, if the transportation costs compared to price are low, consumers can feasibly buy abroad and import when prices vary substantially from country to country.

The Gray Market The **gray market**, or **product diversion**, is the selling and handling of goods through unofficial distributors. Such unauthorized selling can undermine the longer-term viability of the distributorship system, induce a company's operations in different countries to compete with each other, and prevent companies from charging what the market will bear in each country. Let's say a firm's product is sold in Asia at a lower price than in the United States because of different market conditions. If an unauthorized distributor buys it in Asia and resells it at a lower price in the United States, the U.S. seller either loses sales or can no longer sell at the price the market will bear. One consulting firm estimates that U.S. companies lose $63 billion a year because of the gray market.[46] Traditionally, publishers sold texts at substantially different prices in different countries, but a U.S. Supreme Court ruling said it is legal to buy lower-priced textbooks abroad to re-sell in the United States. In essence, maintaining price differences among countries has become more difficult as consumers have gained access to more global information because of sources like the Internet and more access to buying abroad because of factors like lower trade barriers and more foreign travel.

There are country-to-country differences in

- Whether prices are fixed or bargained in stores.
- Where bargaining occurs.

Fixed Versus Variable Pricing MNEs often negotiate their export prices with importers. Small firms, especially those from developing countries, frequently give price concessions too quickly, limiting their ability to negotiate on a range of marketing factors that affect their costs:

- Discounts for quantity or repeat orders
- Deadlines that increase production or transportation costs
- Credit and payment terms
- Service
- Supply of promotional materials
- Training of sales personnel or customers

Table 17.1 shows ways in which an exporter (or other marketers as well) may deal more effectively in price negotiations.

Some people, regardless of culture, avoid price negotiation even when they know they may gain economically by doing so, such as because they fear the loss of face.[47] This could occur because of fear of being perceived as too aggressive or too poor. Other explanations include not wanting to take the time and preferring to develop long-term relationships that bargaining might upset. Regardless of cause, there is a substantial variation in whether,

TABLE 17.1 Negotiating Import-Export Prices

Exporters export because they want to sell their products in foreign markets, and pricing is a key factor in selling products profitably. MNEs and other veteran exporters have learned that negotiating prices—both their own and those of their import partners—is an effective way of considering all the factors that should go into pricing decisions.

The goal is to delay a pricing commitment while discussing a whole package of other commitments.

Importer's Reaction to Price Offer	Exporter's Response
1. Your offer is too expensive.	- Ask what is meant by too expensive. - Find out what is considered acceptable and on what basis. - Respond by providing justification. - Avoid lowering your price until you learn more about what the other party is looking for. - Find out if the objection is due to your price offer or if it reflects other factors. - Ask yourself, "If I'm too expensive, why are they negotiating with me?"
2. We don't have that kind of budget.	- Find out how large the budget is and for what time frame. - Explore whether your offer can fit within the overall budget by combining several budget lines. - Propose deferred-payment schedules. - Confirm the order and postpone deliveries until a new budget is allocated. - Split your order into smaller units or mini-orders to meet current budget limitations.
3. That's not what we are looking for.	- Ask what they are looking for, and insist on specifics. - Keep questioning until you understand the real needs. - Repackage your offer in light of the new information received.
4. Your offer is not competitive.	- Ask what "not competitive" means. - Find out if competitors' offers are comparable to yours. - Find weaknesses in other offers and emphasize your strengths. - Reformulate your offer by avoiding direct comparison with competition. Stress the unique features of your products/ services.

Source: Business Negotiations: Making the First Offer by Claude Cellich ©International Trade Centre, International Trade Forum, Issue 2/2000.

where, and for what products consumers bargain in order to settle on an agreed price. In the United States, consumers commonly bargain for automobiles, real estate, and large orders of industrial supplies but not for grocery items. However, some auto dealerships sell only on a fixed-price basis, while bargaining for smaller items is growing, as the Internet allows consumers to confront distributors with easily obtained alternative prices. In contrast, consumers in most developing countries commonly bargain for both large and small items, but more routinely in traditional markets than in retail stores.[48]

Supplier Relations Dominant companies with clout can get suppliers to offer lower prices, thereby gaining cost advantages over competitors. But they may lack this clout in foreign markets because of not being dominant there. Walmart, Marks & Spencer, and Carrefour have such clout in their respective domestic United States, United Kingdom, and French markets, but they have been hard pressed to gain the same advantage when entering the others' home markets.

The Internet is also causing more companies to compete for the same business, especially for sales of largely undifferentiated materials. Thus, many industrial buyers are claiming large price decreases through Internet buying. However, sellers can improve their positions by negotiating and by combining the Internet with face-to-face interaction.[49]

PROMOTION STRATEGIES

Promotion is the presentation of messages intended to help sell a product or service. The types and direction of messages and the methods of presentation may be extremely diverse, depending on the company, product, and country of operation.

THE PUSH-PULL MIX

Promotion may be categorized as **push**, which uses direct selling techniques, or **pull**, which relies on mass media. Most companies use combinations of both. For each product in each country, a company must determine its total promotional budget as well as the mix between push and pull. The photo in Tokyo shows pull ads by a number of Japanese and international companies.

Push is more likely when

- Self-service is not predominant.
- Advertising is restricted.
- Product price is a high portion of income.

Factors in Push-Pull Decisions Several factors help determine the mix of push and pull among countries:

- Type of distribution system
- Cost and availability of media to reach target markets
- Consumer attitudes toward sources of information
- Price of the product compared to incomes

Generally, the more tightly controlled the distribution system, the more likely a company is to emphasize a push strategy to distributors because it requires a greater effort to get them to handle a product. This is true where most distributors can carry few brands because they are small and highly fragmented, thereby forcing companies to concentrate on making their goods available.

Also affecting the push-pull mix is the amount of contact between salespeople and consumers. In a self-service situation, in which customers have few or no salespeople to turn to for opinions on products, it is more important for the company to use a pull strategy by advertising through mass media or at the point of purchase.

Most large cities have areas with large numbers of neon signs advertising products from both domestic and international companies. The photo shows such signs in the Shinjuku area of Tokyo, Japan.
Source: © STEVE DUCHESNE/Fotolia

Finally, consumers react to word-of-mouth opinions, especially where uncertainty avoidance is high.[50] Thus companies need to establish appropriate means to persuade existing customers that their purchases have been of high quality and at reasonable prices, such as by providing after-sales support and service. Social media platforms are rapidly becoming more important in conveying independent experiences for products and services because they allow users to interact, such as by rating their recent hotel stays and sharing information about their experiences.

SOME PROBLEMS IN INTERNATIONAL PROMOTION

Because of diverse national environments, promotional problems are quite varied and often problematic. For example, over 50 percent of China's population is rural, most are poor, and many lack access to traditional media to view advertisements. Thus, PC makers such as Lenova and Hewlett Packard promote in rural areas by providing variety shows and films to demonstrate their products. They also demonstrate at rural markets where customers visit a few times per month.[51] In rural Nigeria, Kuwait's Mobile Telecommunications Company found that its billboards were stolen to use in construction and that its direct marketers faced too many dangers. The company then turned successfully to small shop owners—tailors, retailers, etc.—and established a mini-franchise system with them.[52]

In many countries, government regulations pose an even greater barrier, such as in Scandinavia where television cannot broadcast commercials aimed at children. In China, ads cannot interrupt dramas, thus they are all bunched together between shows, which companies claim make the ads less effective. Other countries may put legal constraints on what a company says. For instance, the United States and New Zealand allow pharmaceutical firms to advertise prescription drugs directly to consumers, but European countries and Australia do not. Thus, in the former countries, pharmaceutical companies describe physical symptoms, such as erectile dysfunction, in television ads and tell viewers to ask their physicians about a particular brand, such as Viagra or Cialis. However, Pfizer's and Eli Lilly's European ads simply tell TV viewers, without mentioning their brands, to talk with their physicians about erectile dysfunction.[53]

Advantages of standardized advertising include

- Some cost savings,
- Better quality at the local level,
- A common image globally,
- Rapid entry into different countries.

Finally, when a product's price compared to consumer income is high, consumers will usually want more time and information before making a decision. In these situations, information is best conveyed in a personal selling situation that fosters two-way communication. Thus, in developing economies MNEs will often use push strategies for more products because of lower incomes.

Standardization: Pro and Con There are cost savings from using the same advertising programs among countries. In addition, advertising standardization may improve the quality of ads at the local level (because local agencies may lack expertise), prevent internationally mobile consumers from being confused by different images, and speed the entry of products into different countries.

However, globally standardized advertising usually refers to a program that is *similar* from market to market rather than one that is *identical* in each. An example is Red Bull's ad campaign that focuses on different sports in different countries.[54] Standardization also usually implies using the same ad agency globally. By doing this, MNEs such as IBM, Colgate, and Tambrands can take good ideas from one market and quickly introduce them into others without worrying about legal and ethical problems over agency copying. Other companies, like Procter & Gamble, prefer to use more than one agency to keep them in a state of perpetual competition and to cover one agency's weak spots by drawing on the ideas of another.

Finally, the issue of standardization in advertising raises problems in a few other areas—namely, *translation, legality,* and *message needs.*

CONCEPT CHECK

In Chapter 2, we emphasize that the effort to apply language practices across cultures can have an entirely different effect. We discuss why internationally minded companies should be careful in translating a message conceived in one language into a message to be delivered in another. We also emphasize that words may have different meanings even among countries using the same language. As for advertising in visual media, we also discuss a variety of potential pitfalls in "Silent Language"—nonverbal communication ranging from body language to the use of colors.

Translation When media reach audiences in multiple countries, the ads cannot be translated because viewers watch the same transmission. An additional problem is that the product may not be available everywhere it is advertised.

When a company is going to sell in a country with a different language, translation is usually necessary unless the advertiser is trying to communicate an aura of foreignness. The most audible problem in commercial translation is dubbing because words on an added sound track never quite correspond to lip movements. Companies can avoid this problem by creating commercials in which actors do not speak and add a voice or print overlay in the appropriate language.

Another type of advertisement dubbing involves product placement in books, movies, and television shows, especially those that are widely distributed internationally. Again, the product may not be available everywhere. So technology now permits the products to be removed and replaced for given markets. *Spider-Man 2* had Cadbury Schweppes's Dr. Pepper logo on a refrigerator for U.S. screenings and PepsiCo's Mirinda logo in Europe.[55]

On the surface, translating a message would seem to be easy. However, some messages, particularly plays on words, simply don't translate—even between countries that have the same language. Sometimes an acceptable word or direct translation in one place is offensive, misleading, or meaningless in another. In an Apple commercial, the U.S. version used the word "doozy" and the U.K. version used the word "humdinger." Another issue lies in choosing the language when a country has more than one, such as using Creole in Haiti to reach the general population but French to reach the upper class.

Legality What is legal advertising in one country may be illegal elsewhere. The differences result mainly from varying national views on consumer protection, competitive protection, civil rights promotion, standards of morality and behavior, and nationalism. For example, there are many products that some societies view as being in sufficiently bad taste that they restrict their advertising.[56]

In terms of consumer protection, policies differ on the amount of deception permitted and what can be advertised to children. The United Kingdom and the United States allow direct comparisons with competitive brands, while the Philippines prohibits them. Only a few countries regulate sexism in advertising. Elsewhere, governments restrict ads that might prompt misbehavior or law-breaking (such as promoting automobile speeds that exceed the speed limit), as well as those that show barely clad women.[57]

Message Needs An advertising theme may not be appropriate everywhere because of country differences in consumers' product awareness and perception, the people who make the purchasing decision, and what appeals are most important. At one time fewer Italians owned dishwashers than you would have expected from Italian income levels because the housewives felt that buying for the sake of convenience reduces cleanliness; hence, a group of dishwasher manufacturers teamed up to advertise that dishwashers clean better because they use hotter water.[58] Because of economic differences, Home Depot promotes its U.S. stores by appealing to hobbyists, whereas in Mexico it promotes the cost savings for do-it-yourselfers.[59]

The reaction to how messages are presented may also vary. Leo Burnett Worldwide produced a public service ad to promote breast exams that showed an attractive woman being admired in a low-cut sundress, with a voice-over message saying, "If only women paid as much attention to their breasts as men do…" Japanese viewers found this a humorous way to draw attention to breast cancer, whereas French viewers found it offensive because cancer should not be viewed humorously.[60] Given the increase in television transmissions that reach audiences in multiple countries, advertisers must find common themes and messages that will appeal to potential consumers everywhere their ads are viewed.

BRANDING STRATEGIES

A *brand* is an identifying mark for products or services. A legally registered brand is a trademark. A brand gives a product or service instant recognition and may save promotional costs. From a consumer standpoint, it conveys a perception of whether firms will deliver what they promise; however, the importance is more crucial in countries with strong cultural characteristics of uncertainty avoidance.[61]

The importance of brand can be illustrated by comparing examples of two companies. Our opening case illustrates how Tommy Hilfiger built a following for its brand even before consumers were familiar with its product offerings. In contrast, Chinese appliance maker Haier has had trouble with U.S. sales because its brand name is not well-known in the United States.[62]

Keep in mind, though, that a company may use the same brand globally while altering the brand image for different markets. For example, individualistic cultures offer greater advantages in creating an image of innovativeness than collectivist cultures. However, within the latter, images of social responsibility apparently contribute more to brand commitment than in the former.[63]

Because companies have spent heavily in the past to create brand awareness, *Marketing Week* estimates that 79 global brands in 2012 were worth at least $10 billion. U.S. companies accounted for 39 of the top 100.[64]

WORLDWIDE BRAND VERSUS LOCAL BRANDS

In addition to the same branding decisions every producer has to make, international marketers must decide whether to adopt a worldwide brand or use different brands for different countries. In this section, we discuss some of the ways in which the international environment affects this decision.

Advantages of a Worldwide Brand Some companies, such as Apple, have opted to use the same brand and logo for most of their products around the world. This helps develop a global image, especially for customers who travel internationally. In addition, there is evidence that the use of global brands helps identify companies as global players. Within the United States, consumers (especially ethnic minorities) view products of global players more favorably.[65] Other companies, such as Nestlé, associate many of their products under the same family of brands, such as Nestea and Nescafé, to share the positive perception of the Nestlé name.

Using the same brand name globally is hampered by
- Language differences
- Acquisitions

Some Problems with Uniform Brands Nevertheless, a number of problems are inherent in trying to use uniform brands internationally.

Language One problem is that brand names may carry a different association in another language. GM renamed its Buick LaCrosse to Allure in Canada after it discovered through a pre-entry focus group that the word was slang in Quebec for masturbation.[66] Coca-Cola tries to use global branding wherever possible but discovered that the word *diet* in Diet Coke had a connotation of illness in Germany and Italy. The brand is now called Coca-Cola Light outside the United States.

Pronunciation presents other problems, since a foreign language may lack some of the sounds of a brand name, or give it a different meaning. Marcel Bich dropped the *h* from his name when branding Bic pens because of the fear of mispronunciation in English. Microsoft changed the Chinese name of its search engine Bing to Biying so that it sounded like the word for "seek and ye shall find" instead of "illness." IKEA, which uses Scandinavian names for its products, hired a group of Thai speakers to modify its catalogue so that names would not be misinterpreted when pronounced in Thai.[67] Different alphabets present still other problems. For example, consumers judge brand names by whether they sound appealing; those in Chinese need to have visual appeal as well because the Chinese alphabet consists of pictograms. MNEs have taken great pains to ensure not only that the translation of their names is pronounced roughly the same in Mandarin or Cantonese Chinese as elsewhere but also that the brand name is meaningful in pictograms. Coca-Cola is pronounced *Ke-kou-ke-le* in Mandarin Chinese and means "tasty" and "fun." Tide became Tai-zi in Mandarin, which means "gets rid of dirt."[68] Companies seek names considered lucky in China, such as one with eight strokes in it and displayed in red rather than blue. Similarly, the digit 8 is overrepresented in product prices.[69]

Brand Acquisition Much international expansion takes place by acquiring foreign companies with branded products, such as Sara Lee acquiring various Brazilian coffee roasters. Although this has made Sara Lee the coffee-market leader in Brazil, it has been challenging to stretch the promotional budget over many brands.[70] Overall, the proportion of local to international brands is decreasing; however, there are many examples of strong local brands that companies cannot easily displace.[71] Similarly, having a combination of global and local brands that appeal to different segments can sometimes be advantageous, such as those used by the beer company Anheuser-Busch InBev.[72]

Images of products are affected by where they are made.

Country-of-Origin Image Marketers have long noted products' country-of- origin influences on consumers' opinions of their quality. But this influence is complex, depending on such factors as the type of product, consumers' national cultural attributes (such as individualism versus collectivism), and their individual personality differences (such as whether they are materialistic), along with the economic development and nearness of the country-of-origin.[73] In addition, consumers have diverse emotional affinity toward certain countries.[74] Despite the complexity, companies may play up positive and play down negative country-of-origin images. For example, because many Japanese believe that clothing made abroad is superior to that made in Japan, Burberry has created separate labels for its products made there and those made in the United Kingdom (Burberry London brand). In addition, both the country of origin and the brand have positive and negative images that interact. Evidence suggests that a positive brand image can help overcome negative perceptions of the country where the product is made.[75]

- The brand image may help overcome the country image.
- Country of origin images can change.

Still, images can change. Consider that for many years various Korean firms sold abroad under private labels or under contract with well-known companies. Some, such as Samsung, now emphasize their own trade names and Korean product quality. At the same time, the Korean LG Group, best known for its Gold Star brand, has introduced a line of high-end appliances with a European-sounding name, LG Tromm.[76] Nevertheless, there is evidence that consumers have limited knowledge of the country of origin of most brands and that they often misclassify the origins.[77] Such confusion is compounded with the increased mixed origin of the components that make up products.

One ongoing international legal debate concerns product names associated with location. The EU protects the names of many European products based on location names, such as Roquefort and Gorgonzola cheeses, Parma ham, and Chianti wine. It has also pushed for protection against the foreign use of regulated names associated with wines, such as *clos, chateau, tawny, noble, ruby,* and *vintage*.[78]

If a brand name is used for a class of product, the company may lose the trademark.

Generic and Near-Generic Names Companies want their product names to become household words, but not so much that competitors can use trademarks to describe their similar products. In the United States, the brand names Xerox and Kleenex are nearly synonymous with copiers and facial tissue, but they have nevertheless remained proprietary brands. Some other names that were once proprietary—cellophane, linoleum, Cornish hens—have become **generic** and available for anyone to use.

In this context, companies sometimes face differences among countries that may either stimulate or frustrate their sales. For example, *aspirin* and *Swiss Army knives* are proprietary names in Europe but generic in the United States—a situation that impairs European export sales of those products to the United States, since U.S. companies can produce them.

DISTRIBUTION STRATEGIES

A company may accurately assess market potential, design goods or services for that market, price them appropriately, and promote them to probable consumers. However, it will have little likelihood of reaching its sales potential if it doesn't make the goods or services conveniently available to customers. Goods need to be placed where people want to buy them. **Distribution** is the course—physical path or legal title—that goods take between production and consumption. In international marketing, managers must decide on distribution methods among countries as well as within the countries where final sales occur.

We've already discussed operating forms for foreign-market penetration. Chapter 14 discussed distribution channels: moving goods among countries and transferring titles. Rather than reviewing these aspects of distribution, this section discusses distributional differences and conditions within foreign countries that an international marketer should understand.

DECIDING WHETHER TO STANDARDIZE

Distribution reflects different country environments:

- It may vary substantially among countries.
- It is difficult to change.

Within the marketing mix, MNEs find distribution one of the most difficult functions to standardize internationally, for several reasons. Each country has its own distribution system, which an MNE finds difficult to modify because it is entwined with the country's cultural, economic, and legal environments. In fact, wholesalers and retailers have lagged manufacturers and service companies' entries into foreign markets because of the difficulty of breaking into these systems. Nevertheless, many retailers have more recently moved successfully internationally.

Some factors that influence the distribution of goods in a given country include citizens' attitudes toward owning their own store, the cost of paying retail workers, legislation restricting store sizes and operating hours, different effects of laws on chain stores and individually owned stores, the trust owners have in employees, the efficacy of delivery systems, the quality of the infrastructure system, and the financial ability to carry large inventories. A few examples should illustrate how widespread differences are. Compare Hong Kong with the United States: Hong Kong supermarkets carry a higher proportion of fresh goods, are smaller, sell less per customer, and are closer to each other, which means that companies selling canned, boxed, or frozen foods there encounter less demand per

Does Geography Matter?

Is Necessity the Mother of Invention?

You've probably heard the saying, "that's as difficult as selling a refrigerator to Eskimos." Climate is a great influence on the demand for many products—clothes, sporting equipment, snow tires, air conditioners, and sunscreen, to name a few—and is a variable when identifying market segments. Seasonal changes that occur at opposite times in the northern and southern hemispheres allow you to spread your sales more evenly throughout the year, such as by focusing ski sales in Switzerland from December through March and in Chile from June through September. This hemispheric difference may also lead to your making adjustments. Films aimed at young audiences sometimes debut months apart between the northern and southern hemispheres so as to be viewed during school vacation periods that usually correspond to the hot months.

Natural conditions, such as mountains, waterways, and deserts, create both barriers and expediencies to distribution. For example, countries can more easily build infrastructure where there are flat areas without obstructions; thus, other things being equal, these areas provide better internal distribution possibilities.

Immigration is largely clustered because people move where others of their ethnic group have gone before, thus forming subcultures. Understanding where these groups exist can help identify potential markets aimed at ethnic niches.[79]

Because transportation cost roughly correlates with distance, it is usually higher when the distance between production and market is greater. This extra cost must either be passed on to consumers or be absorbed by the selling company. Moreover, if markets are close to each other, it is more difficult to maintain different price schedules between them because promotion likely reaches both markets. In turn, consumers will buy from the less expensive location. In fact, the closeness of most Canadians to the U.S. border has influenced Canadian stores to stay open longer and operate on more days, lest Canadians cross the border to buy in the United States.

Although geography does play a role in product demand, higher disposable income and technology help overcome many geographic constraints. Some people in hot climates do buy winter clothes and skis because they travel to snowy areas for recreation. People in Dubai even enjoy an indoor ski resort complex. And there's even a market for refrigerators among the Eskimos. ■

store, have to make smaller deliveries, and have a harder time fighting for shelf space. Elsewhere, Finland has few stores per capita because general-line retailers predominate there, whereas Italian distribution has a fragmented retail and wholesale structure. In the Netherlands, buyers' cooperatives deal directly with manufacturers. Japan has cash-and-carry wholesalers for retailers that do not need financing or delivery services. Mail-order sales are very important in Germany, but not in many developing countries with less reliable delivery systems.

How do such differences affect marketing activities? Here's an example. A company targeted most of its European sales through grocery stores but varied the method for getting its products to those stores. In the United Kingdom, a national distributor gained sufficient coverage and shelf space so that the company could concentrate on other aspects of its marketing mix. In France, a single distributor had good coverage in the larger supermarkets but not in smaller retailers, so the company had to explore ways to get secondary distribution without upsetting its relationship with the primary distributor. In Norway, regional distributors predominated, so the company found it difficult to effect national promotion campaigns. In Belgium, the company could find no acceptable distributor, so it had to assume that function itself.

At the same time, a company's system of distribution may give it strategic advantages not easily copied by competitors, such as Avon's strategy of selling directly through independent reps and Amazon.com's Internet sales. Even these companies have had to adjust to national nuances. For instance, Avon does a thriving mail-order business in Japan because of the popularity of that distribution, has beauty counters in China because of regulations on house-to-house sales, has franchise centers in the Philippines because of infrastructure inefficiencies, and has beauty centers in Argentina because many customers want services when they purchase cosmetics.

SELF-HANDLING OR NOT?

Should companies handle their own distribution? Or should they contract other companies to do it for them? In Chapter 15 we discussed factors that favor internalization versus collaboration, and these all apply as well to distribution decisions. Thus, we will not elaborate on these except to comment on some cost considerations.

Distribution may be handled internally
- When volume is high,
- When companies have sufficient resources,
- When there is a need to deal directly with the customer because of the product's nature,
- When the customer is global,
- When the distribution form is a competitive advantage.

Sales Volume and Cost When sales volume is low, a company usually finds reliance on external distributors to be more economical. As sales grow, it may handle distribution itself to gain more control. However, such self-handling may still be difficult for small firms that lack necessary resources.

Nevertheless, companies may limit early distribution costs if they are able to sell regionally before moving nationally. Many products and markets lend themselves to this sort of gradual development. For example, many foreign companies enter the Chinese market by first going to Beijing, Shanghai, and Guanghou, then to provincial capitals, then to other large cities, and finally to smaller cities. Often, geographic barriers and poor internal transportation systems divide countries into very distinct markets. In fact, very little wealth or few potential sales may lie outside the large metropolitan areas.

A company may enter a market gradually by limiting geographic coverage.

Factors Favoring Self-Handling Circumstances conducive to the internal handling of distribution include not only high sales volume but also the following factors:

- When a product has the characteristic of high price, high technology, or the need for complex after-sales servicing (such as aircraft), the company will probably have to deal directly with the buyer. It may simultaneously use a distributor within the foreign country to identify sales leads.
- When the company deals with global customers, especially business-to-business (such as an auto-parts manufacturer selling original equipment to the same automakers in multiple countries), sales may go directly to the global customer.

- When the company's main competitive advantage is its distribution methods, it may control distribution abroad, such as Avon's direct selling through independent representatives. In addition, food franchisors typically maintain some restaurants of their own to serve as "flagships."

DISTRIBUTION PARTNERSHIP

If a company wishes to collaborate with a distributor abroad, it can usually compare a number of potential foreign organizations. While trying to find the best distributors, it must also convince them to handle its products.

Which Distributors Are Best Qualified? By using these common criteria (also useful for domestic options), a company can improve its choice of distributors:

- *The distributor's financial strength:* This helps determine the potential long-term relationship and whether money will be available for such things as maintaining sufficient inventory.
- *Its good connections:* These are particularly important if sales must be directed to certain types of buyers, such as governmental procurement agencies, and in societies where connections and mutual loyalty are often more important than product and price for making sales.[80]
- *Extent of its other business commitments:* These can signify whether the distributor has time for the company's product and whether it currently handles competitive or complementary products.
- *Current status of its personnel, facilities, and equipment:* These suggest its ability to deal with the product, to start up quickly, and to stay in business.
- *Its reliability as an honest performer:* This helps establish whether the use of trust can help enforce performance.[81]

Distributors choose which companies and products to handle. Companies

- May need to give incentives,
- May use successful products as bait for new ones,
- Must convince distributors that product and company are viable.

Promoting to Potential Distributors Companies must evaluate potential distributors, but distributors must choose which companies and products to represent and emphasize. Wholesalers and retailers alike have limited storage facilities, display space, money for inventories, and transportation and personnel to move and sell merchandise, so they try to carry only those products with the greatest profit potential.

In many cases, distributors are tied into exclusive arrangements with manufacturers that impede new competitive entries. This is true in Japan, where many manufacturers have arrangements with thousands of distributors to sell only their products.

Any company that is new to a country and wants to introduce products that competitors are already selling may meet difficulty in finding distributors to handle its brands. Even established companies can find distribution difficult for new products, although they have the dual advantage of being known and being able to offer existing profitable lines only if distributors accept the new unproven goods. Managers wanting to use existing distribution channels may need to analyze competitive conditions carefully to offer effective handling incentives (higher profit margins, after-sales servicing, promotional support, and so on), or identify distributors' problems so as to gain their loyalty by offering assistance. In the end, however, incentives will be of little use unless the distributors believe the company is reliable and its products viable.

DISTRIBUTION CHALLENGES AND OPPORTUNITIES

Although international distribution involves many challenges and opportunities, the following discussion highlights three: the need for after-sales service, the often overlooked cost advantages and disadvantages, and the use of Internet sales.

Replacement parts and service are important for sales.

How Reliable Is After-Sales Service? Consumers are reluctant to buy products that may require replacement parts and service in the future unless they feel sure that these will be readily available in good quality and at reasonable prices. This reluctance is especially keen for imported products because of concerns that distance and customs clearance will delay needed replacement parts. For fairly mature products, there are usually multiple service companies to which consumers can turn in case of problems. However, for products encompassing new technology, especially complex and expensive products, it is more important for producers to develop after-sales servicing. Thus, companies may need to invest in service centers for groups of distributors that serve as intermediaries between producers and consumers. Earnings from sales of parts and after-sales service may sometimes exceed that of the original product.

The question of after-sales service is important for technologically oriented entrepreneurial companies from developing countries, which have been growing, especially those from the BRICs. They face multiple problems in selling abroad because they are young, small, fairly unknown, likely suffering negative country-of-origin effects, and often assumed to be laggards in technological development.[82]

Hidden Distribution Costs and Gains A company considering launching products in foreign markets must approximate final consumer prices to estimate sales potential. Five factors that often contribute to distribution cost differences among countries are *infrastructure conditions, the number of levels in the distribution system, retail inefficiencies, size and operating-hour restrictions,* and *inventory stock-outs.*

Many countries' roads and warehousing facilities are in such bad condition that getting goods to consumers quickly, cheaply, and with minimum damage or loss en route is problematic. For example, Nigeria has no rail links to its ports, has fallen behind in road construction, and has poor connections between big and small cities.[83]

Some countries also have multi-tiered wholesalers that sell to each other before the product reaches the retail level. National wholesalers sell to regional ones, which sell to local ones, and so on. Japan, though changing rapidly, has had many more levels of distribution than, say, France and the United States. As each intermediary adds a markup, prices escalate.

In some countries, particularly developing ones, low labor costs and owners' basic distrust of nonfamily members cause many retailers to engage in practices that are less productive in serving customers, such as using counter- rather than self-service, and forcing customers to a cashier before picking up merchandise. On the one hand, the additional personnel add to retailing costs, and the added time people must be in the store means fewer people being served in the given space. On the other hand, because the retailers tend to be small and highly dispersed, they reduce the time, cost, and effort for customers to shop.[84] In contrast, most retailers in some (mainly economically developed) countries have equipment that improves the efficiency of handling customers and reports, such as electronic scanners and payment systems linked to inventory-control records and to credit-card companies.

France, Germany, Japan, and many other nations have laws protecting small retailers, effectively limiting the number of large retail establishments and the efficiencies they bring to sales. Most countries have patchwork systems that limit days or hours of operations for religious purposes or to protect employees from having to work late at night or on weekends. At the same time, the limits keep retailers from covering the fixed cost of their space over more hours, so the cost is usually passed on to consumers.

Where most retail establishments are small, there is little space to store inventory. Wholesalers must incur the cost of making small deliveries to many more establishments, sometimes visiting each retailer more frequently because of stock outages. However, these latter costs may be overcome through labor and transport cost savings resulting from low-paid delivery personnel who may carry small quantities of merchandise on bicycles. Further, the retailers themselves incur lower costs because their inventory-carrying costs are low compared to sales.[85]

E-COMMERCE AND THE INTERNET

The growth in online availability creates new distributional opportunities and challenges in selling globally over the Internet.

Estimates vary widely on the current and future number of worldwide online households and the electronic commerce generated through online sales. Nevertheless, they all indicate substantial growth. Further, the adjacent photo shows that people may generally access the Internet through publicly available facilities even though they have no online connections in

This solar-powered Internet café within a shipping container in a rural area of Kenya enables people in an impoverished village to have access to the rest of the world.
Source: Tony Karumba/Stringer/Getty Images

their households and even if they reside in remote areas. Through e-commerce, customers worldwide can quickly compare prices from different distributors, which drives prices down. Through the growing use of social media, they can obtain better information to compare the quality and reliability of products and distributors. There is evidence that online shoppers universally have some similar characteristics: they want convenience, use email and the Internet heavily, and have favorable attitudes toward direct marketing and advertising.[86]

Opportunities E-commerce offers firms an opportunity to promote products globally. It does not, however, relieve them of the need to develop the marketing tools discussed throughout the chapter. For some products and services, such as airline tickets and hotel space, the Internet has largely replaced traditional sales methods. But even here, companies may need to adapt to country differences, such as providing access through various languages.[87] There are certainly many e-commerce success stories. One is the New Zealand prefab housing company Tristyle International, for which about 95 percent of sales are export and 40 percent are through the Internet.[88]

The Internet also permits suppliers to deal more quickly with their customers. Lee Hung Fat Garment Factory of Hong Kong and Bangladesh produces for apparel companies abroad and flashes pictures of merchandise samples to them over the Web. Customers can tinker with the samples and transmit new versions so that Lee Hung Fat produces exactly what the apparel companies want.

Problems Global Internet sales are not without glitches. A company that wants to reach global markets may need to supplement its Internet sales with other means of promotion and distribution, which can be very expensive. Figure 17.3 shows humorously the need to capture Internet sales by convincing people to visit Web sites. Further, a switch to Internet sales may upset existing distribution and, if unsuccessful, make future sales more difficult.[89]

On the Internet, an MNE cannot easily differentiate its marketing program for each country in which it operates. The same Web ads and prices reach customers everywhere, even though different appeals and prices for different countries might yield more sales and profits. If the MNE makes international sales over the Internet, it must expeditiously deliver what it sells, which may require warehouses and service facilities abroad.

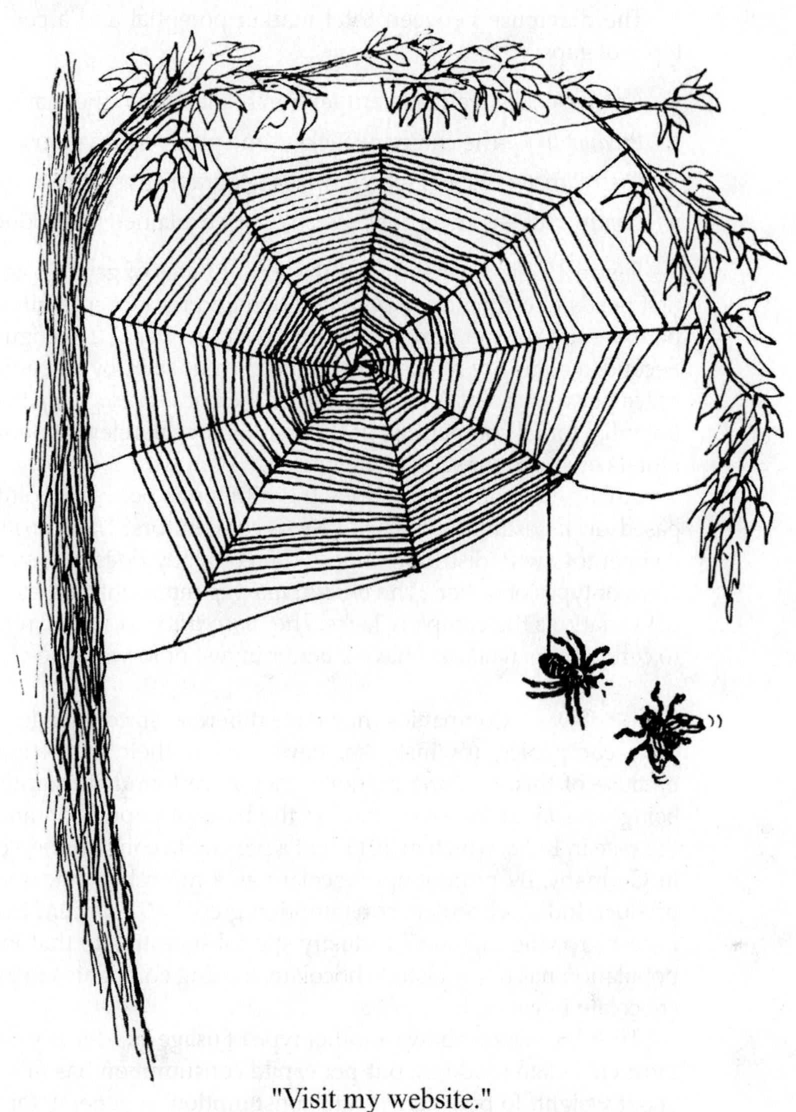

FIGURE 17.3 To capture sales from the Internet, it is first necessary to entice people to connect to the Web site.

Source: Joseph Farris/CartoonStock

Finally, the MNE's Internet ads and prices must comply with the laws of each country of sales. This is problematic because of the Web's global reach. Clearly, although the Internet creates opportunities for companies to sell internationally, it also creates challenges for them.

MANAGING THE MARKETING MIX

Although every element in the marketing mix—product, price, promotion, brand, and distribution—is important, the relative importance of one versus another may vary from place to place and over time. Thus, management must monitor and adjust its marketing programs accordingly.

GAP ANALYSIS

Once a company estimates a country's market potential, it must calculate how well it is doing there and how it might do better. A useful tool in this respect is **gap analysis,** a method for estimating a company's potential sales by identifying prospective customers it could serve more adequately.[90] When sales are lower than the estimated market potential for a given type of product, the company has the possibility to increase them.

The difference between total market potential and a company's sales is due to several types of gaps:

- *Usage*—collectively, all competitors sell less than the market potential;
- *Product line*—the company lacks some product variations;
- *Distribution*—the company misses geographic or type of outlet coverage;
- *Competitive*—competitors' sales are not explained by product line and distribution gaps.

Figure 17.4 is a bar showing these four types of gaps. To construct such a bar, a company first needs to estimate the potential demand for all competitors in the country for a relevant period—say, for the next year or the next five years. This figure gives the height of the bar. Second, a company needs to estimate current sales by all competitors, which is point A. The space between point A and the top of the bar is a *usage gap,* meaning that this is the growth potential for all competitors in the market for the relevant period. Third, a company needs to plot its own current sales of the product, point B.

Finally, the company divides the difference between points A and B into types of gaps based on its estimate of sales lost to competitors. The *distribution gap* represents losses to competitors who distribute where the company does not, such as to additional geographic areas or types of outlets. The *product line gap* represents losses to competitors who have product variations the company lacks. The *competitive gap* is the remaining unexplained sales lost to competitors who may have a better image or lower prices.

Usage Gaps Companies may have different-sized gaps in different markets. Large chocolate companies, for instance, have altered their marketing programs among countries because of this. In some markets, they have found substantial usage gaps—less chocolate being consumed than expected on the basis of population and income levels. This has been the case in India, which in 2011 had a per capita consumption of less than one percent of that in Germany. By promoting chocolate as a more hygienic and longer-lasting confectionary product, India's chocolate consumption grew by 75 percent from 2008, making it the world's fastest-growing market.[91] Industry specialists estimate that in many countries, much of the population has never tasted chocolate, leading companies to promote sales in those areas for chocolate in general.

The U.S. market shows another type of usage gap. Nearly everyone in this market has tried most chocolate products, but per capita consumption has fallen because of growing concern about weight. To boost chocolate consumption in general, for a short time Nestlé promoted

FIGURE 17.4 Gap Analysis

Why aren't sales as high as they could be? That's the question asked by a company's managers when they undertake gap analysis. The arrow at the top represents total sales potential for all competitors during a given period. The arrow at A indicates actual sales. Notice that there's a gap between the product's potential and actual sales—the so-called usage gap. But there are other gaps as well. The arrow bracketing points A and B, for example, designates all sales lost by the company to its competitors—the gap, that is, between what the company did sell and what it could have sold if, for a variety of reasons, it hadn't lost so many sales to competitors. Finally, remember that in the real world, gap sizes will fluctuate.

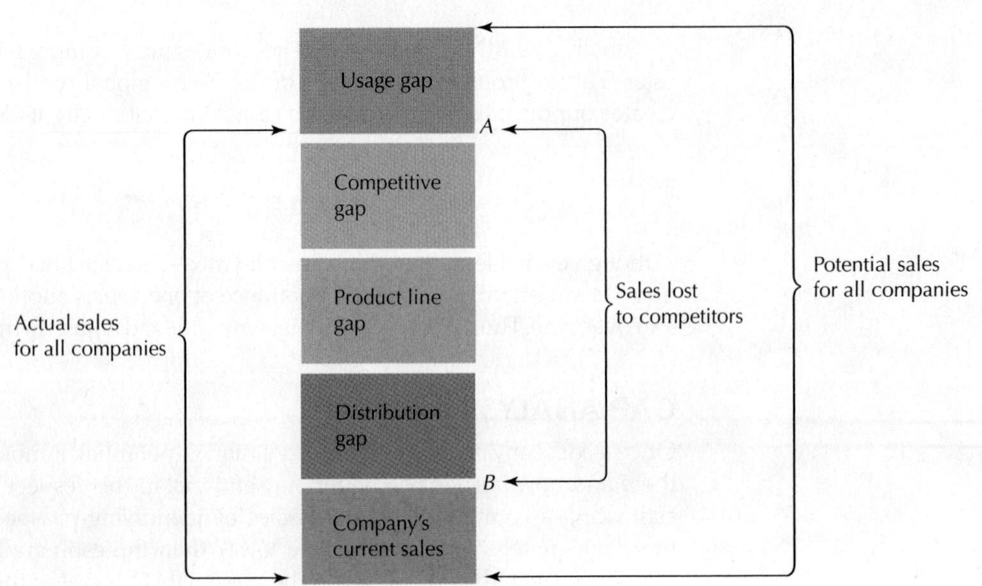

chocolate as an energy source for the sports-minded. Note, however, that building general consumption is most useful to the market leader. With U.S. chocolate sales below those of Mars and Hershey, Nestlé actually benefited its competitors during the short-lived campaign.

Product Line Gaps Chocolate companies have also found that they have product-line gaps. Some lack sugar-free chocolate products, which boosts competitors' sales. Kraft (brands include Cadbury, Dairy Milk and Oreo Cookies) has pursued global sales of fair-traded chocolate, a product once favored only by a small global niche and served by a fragmented group of small producers.[92] It has also added flavors, such as green tea, to its Oreo Cookies for sale in China.[93] Godiva has introduced specialty products in China to compete with local companies selling themed products for the Chinese Zodiac year and for the Mid-Autumn Festival.[94]

Distribution and Competitive Gaps Companies' products may be sold in too few places, creating a gap in distribution. To combat this, Ferrero Rocher has recently emphasized product placement in more mainstream outlets. There also may be competitive gaps—sales by competitors that cannot be explained by differences between product lines and distribution. That is, competitors are selling more because of their prices, advertising campaigns, goodwill, or any of a host of other factors. In markets where per capita chocolate consumption is high, companies exert most of their efforts in gaining sales at the expense of competitors. For instance, Switzerland has one of the world's highest per capita consumption rates of chocolate. In that market, such competitors as Migros, Lindt, and Nestlé's Cailler go head to head in creating images of better quality.[95]

Aggregating Countries' Programs Although gap analysis is primarily a means of prioritizing elements in the marketing mix within given countries, it is also possible to use the tool by aggregating needs among countries. Let's say the product-line gap is too small in a single country to justify the expense of developing a specific new product, such as a heat-resistant chocolate bar. Nevertheless, the combined market potential among several countries for this product may justify the product- and promotional-development costs. Thus, gap analysis may help managers improve country-level performance along with enhancing synergies among the countries where they operate.

Looking to the Future

Evolving Challenges to Segment Markets

Recall the discussion earlier in the chapter on three approaches to segmentation. While all three involve the geographic unit of the nation as one of the key components, such segmentation also involves both demographics and psychographics. How both of these will unfold in future years will likely affect international marketing. There are, of course, many more global trends that may affect future international marketing than we can possibly highlight—e.g. an aging population, growing obesity, increase in the use of social media—thus the following discussion highlights only one key demographic and psychographic area.

Income Demographics

Most projections are that disparities between the "haves" and "have-nots" will grow in the foreseeable future, both within and among countries. Furthermore, because haves will be more educated and more connected to the Internet, they will be better able to search globally for lower prices. Therefore, around the world, the affluent segment will have even more purchasing power than their incomes indicate.

As discretionary income increases, some luxury products will become more commonplace (partly because it will take less work time to purchase them), and seemingly dissimilar products and services (such as cars, travel, jewelry, and furniture) will compete with each other for the same discretionary spending. Japan was the premier importer of luxury goods during the 1980s and early 1990s, but competition from an array of other luxury products and services, such as spas and expensive restaurants, eroded those imports.[96] In addition, many Japanese consumers have moved down-market during the global economic crisis, and there is speculation that they may not move up-market again when the economy improves. Nevertheless, because of better communications and rising educational levels of the haves, they will want more choices. However, market segments may not fall primarily along national lines. Rather, companies will identify consumer niches that cut across country lines.

At the other extreme, because of growing numbers of poor people with little disposable income, companies will have opportunities to develop low-cost standardized products to fit the needs of the have-nots. In reality, low-income households collectively have considerable purchasing power, as we discussed in Chapter 4, and will likely spend mainly on housing, food, healthcare, education, communications, finance charges, and consumer goods.[97] Thus, companies will have conflicting opportunities: develop luxury to serve the haves and cut costs to serve the have-nots. The president of the Wine Academy of Spain pointed out this market split for Chinese wine sales. He indicated that there is no middle market; rather there is a high-end where people spend thousands of dollars per bottle as an investment or to drink at restaurants and a low-end where people spend no more than the equivalent of a few dollars per bottle while buying in large containers.[98] Similarly, some producers are already responding to this market dichotomy. Frito-Lay calls it the "bifurcation" of the snack market and is emphasizing new products for the high and low ends, but not the middle.[99] Despite the growing proportions of haves and have-nots, demographers project that the actual numbers of people moving out of poverty levels and into middle-income levels will increase. This is largely because of population and income growth in some low-income countries, especially in Asia. Such a shift will likely mean that companies' sales growth in poorer countries will mainly be for products that are mature in industrial countries, such as many consumer electronics and household appliances.

Will National Markets Become Passé?

In addition to demographic differences, especially regarding income, attitudinal differences affect demand in general as well as for particular types of products and services. Although global communications are reaching far-flung populations, different people react differently to them. At least three, not mutually exclusive, types of personality traits interact and affect how potential consumers react.[100] They exist in all countries (thus creating a segment that cuts across the globe), but the portion of people who are strongly influenced by one versus the other presently varies by country. How these factors evolve will likely have a profound influence on the future of international marketing.

The first of the traits is **materialism**, which refers to the importance of acquiring possessions as a means of self-satisfaction and happiness, as well as for the appearance of success. There is evidence of a growing and spreading global materialistic culture. However, there is also some evidence that people who have always been affluent may exhibit lower materialistic behaviors than those who have recently become affluent. The second of these traits is **cosmopolitanism**, which refers to openness to the world. While there is debate on whether this is a learned or an inborn trait, some of the characteristics include comparing oneself with the world rather than with the local situation. Cosmopolitanists may actually seek out foreign products and services. The third of these traits is **consumer ethnocentrism**, which refers to preference for local to global, such as seeking out local alternatives when buying products and services. ■

CASE Grameen Danone Foods in Bangladesh

Professors Jon Jungbien Moon and John D. Daniels

In 1932, U.S. President Franklin D. Roosevelt referred to an impoverished person as "the forgotten man at the bottom [base] of the economic pyramid." Later, the term—shortened to "BoP"—became business jargon after publication in 2010 of *The Fortune at the Bottom of the Pyramid*.

Few places have more impoverished people than Bangladesh.[101] With 161 million people in 2012, its per capita GDP at PPP was only $2,002, with 31.5 percent of the population below the poverty line and the bottom 10 percent living on less than $1 per day. Thus, Bangladesh has many conditions that correlate closely with poverty: an adult illiteracy rate of 43 percent, a high incidence of infectious diseases, a poor infrastructure, high underemployment, crowded conditions (imagine half the U.S. population squeezed into the state of Iowa), and more than its share of natural disasters, especially periodic flooding, that impede development. In the face of these ominous conditions, two companies—the Grameen Foundation from Bangladesh and Groupe Danone from France—have formed a joint venture social business to serve Bangladesh's BoP.

What Is a Social Business?

Mohammad Yunus, founder of the Grameen Bank in 1974 and winner of the Nobel Peace Prize in 2006, originated the concept of a social business, which aims to generate social benefit by creating a sustainable business. The Grameen Danone Foods JV was established as a social business to make a profit but pay no dividends. All earnings are reinvested, except that investors may recoup their original capital input. Unlike NGOs, charities, and not-for-profit organizations, a social business must sustain itself by earning profits competitively rather than receiving continual new contributions to carry on.

The Grameen Bank and Foundation

The Grameen Bank (GB) began when Yunus lent $27 to a group of indigent villagers who repaid the money even though he had required no collateral from them. This small beginning, which was contrary to Bangladeshi bank practices, led to GB's microfinancing program. It has competed primarily with usurious money lenders who charge as much as 10 percent interest per day. GB's typical rate of 20 percent per year may sound high, but Bangladesh has had an inflation rate of nearly 9 percent, and GB supports many non-interest loans as well. Some banks outside Bangladesh, such as Citigroup and Deutsche Bank, have since used GB's example as a model.

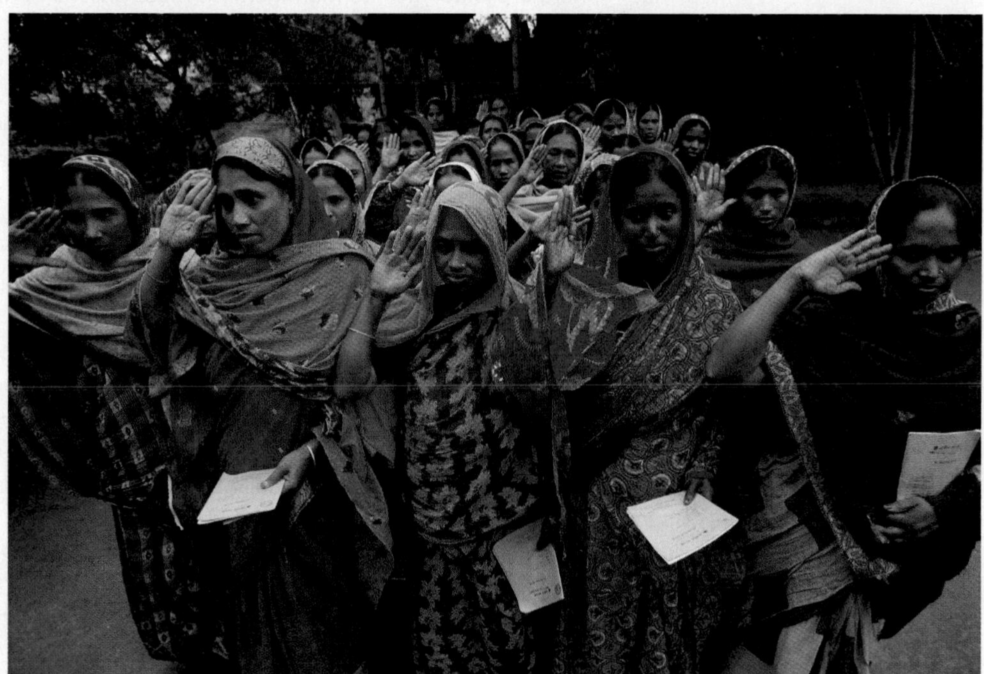

Women salute the Grameen Bank when repaying micro loans in Bangladesh.
Source: © RGB Ventures LLC dba SuperStock/Alamy

Before GB, hardly any Bangladeshi loans went to women, and Yunus had to convince religious opposition that the Prophet Mohammad would have supported what he was doing. Today, about 97 percent of GB's loans go to women, and audits show a repayment rate of 98 percent. (Borrowers must repay a loan in order to get a new one.) The adjacent photo shows women saluting GB as they make loan payments. GB uses repayments and interest to make additional loans and to support the Grameen Foundation's poverty-fighting projects. Its loans, which in 2011 came to almost $1.5 billion, have included initial financing for street vendors and construction of more than 600,000 houses. It provides more than 20,000 student loans and 50,000 scholarships per year. It has given non-interest loans to more than 70,000 beggars so they can sell trinkets during their house-to-house begging. The Foundation's activities have expanded into a variety of businesses, such as telephone service, solar power generation, and healthcare.

Groupe Danone

France's largest food company, Groupe Danone (spelled "Dannon" for the U.S. market) operates in four product divisions: dairy (world's largest, with Danone being almost a generic word for yogurt); bottled water (ranked second globally, including such brands as Evian and Volvic); baby food (second globally under the Blédine brand); and medical nutrition (largest in Europe). It operates worldwide and had 2012 sales of almost €21 billion ($27 billion). Before its JV with Grameen, it had no operations in Bangladesh. In fact, it aimed most of its products, such as its Activia and Actimel brands of yogurt, at higher-end consumers.

Why Invest in a Social Business?

Why would Danone, or anyone, want to invest in an operation that yields them no dividends or capital gains? Yunus contends that people are multidimensional and thus may desire more than economic gains for themselves, such as a craving to help the less fortunate. He points to business leaders (e.g., Carnegie, Gates, Rockefeller) who turned their attention to philanthropy after amassing large fortunes. Danone's JV participation fits this multidimensional vision. In fact, it has a history of socially responsible behavior, with a corporate mission "to bring health through food to as many people as possible." Further, it is the world's largest food company devoted to producing and selling only healthy foods. Nevertheless, Danone must generate profits, and its management must answer to shareholders. The Bangladeshi JV could offer several potential economic advantages.

Maturing of Traditional Markets

The demand for Danone's lines of business has been maturing in wealthier countries, which have been Danone's traditional markets. Hence, its management has been shifting more emphasis to poorer countries. Between 1999 and 2010, the share of its sales coming from LDCs increased from 6 percent to 49 percent. Yet even there its sales have centered on affluent segments, about which its chairman, Frank Riboud, said, "It would be crazy to think only about the peak of the pyramid." Thus, Bangladesh could serve as a laboratory for learning about customers and ways of operating at the BoP.

Promoting LDC Growth

Critics complain that MNEs' sale of superfluous products in developing countries contributes to economic underdevelopment because poor consumers lack the means to purchase nutritious food to make them more physically productive. Danone's products are all healthful and sanitary. Although one company's successful marketing of such products is not likely to have any significant impact on development, it is nevertheless a potential catalyst, which perhaps also leads to favorable publicity. Further, as BoP consumers move upward economically, they will have more to spend on other Danone products and may favor them because of their earlier experience. Riboud said, "When poverty is on the rise, my own growth prospects shrink. [This] means that combating poverty is good for my business."

Building Sales and Loyalty Abroad

Being perceived as socially responsible, such as helping needy causes, may improve business performance in various ways. However, there are an almost infinite number of competing needy causes toward which to contribute. The amount Danone invested in the JV was $500,000, a small outlay for a company of that size, and Danone stood to get the money back if the operation became sufficiently profitable. Moreover, the fact that it would become one of the first major corporations to invest in a social business could generate free positive publicity. In retrospect, Riboud has indicated that Danone's employees in France feel they are part of this project, so the small initiative has revitalized the company's culture.

Preceding the Bangladeshi JV

At a 2005 lunch in Paris, Riboud asked Yunus what Danone might do to help the poor. When Yunus explained the social business concept, Riboud immediately said, "Let's do it," and the two shook hands on setting up their JV. Although this JV is one of the first social businesses established in partnership with a major MNE, Roosevelt's "forgotten man" was not completely forgotten in the interim. Many organizations have marketed to the BoP (most notably in the 1970s' heyday of the appropriate technology movement), with such devices as crank-operated cash registers, dung-powered stoves, and bicycle-propelled water pumps. Nor is this JV the first effort aimed at nourishing the poor. A notable example is Central America's protein powder (Incaparina), which, though more nutritious and less expensive than milk, has had mixed success.

These experiences offer the following lessons for companies wishing to tap the BoP, especially with a nutritious product:

- ***Price***—Low and stable prices help create and sustain sales, so companies gain an advantage by finding new means to cut and stabilize their own costs, which they then pass on to customers.
- ***Product compatibility***—High nutrition at a low price alone is insufficient. Products must be compatible with the target market's accustomed habits and visually appealing and flavorful to buyers, so it is vital to pick the right products and adapt them to local markets.
- ***Education***—Within some countries the BoP is largely illiterate, has low access to popular media, and is unconvinced about cause-effect scientific relationships. Hence, it may be important to reach people in this segment by nontraditional means, convince them that changes from nutrition are important and take time, and convey information that they will believe.
- ***Promotion***—Publicity prior to the start of sales is quite valuable, so the use of opinion leaders (those that this group accepts) is essential in developing credibility.
- ***Competition***—Given efforts to help the poor, competition may come from government programs, not-for-profit organizations, and charities. Thus, companies need to outperform this competition or find means of working cooperatively with it.

Strategic Thrust and Orientation

After their 2005 Paris handshake, Grameen and Danone began production in less than two years, during which time they planned and carried out preliminary work. The partners started with a small rural factory to serve only its surrounding poverty-stricken area. Given their JV's social objective, the partners agreed that product and production would be as green as possible. Even though the factory is the size of only one percent of Danone's standard factories elsewhere, it has the latest equipment, treatment of both incoming and outgoing water, and solar panels to generate renewable energy.

Product Policies

The introductory plant makes only yogurt, a product of high nutritional value for children. It relies on efficient small-scale production and nearby supplies of the main ingredient (milk).

Through market testing, Danone decided to sell a sweeter and thinner yogurt, drinkable directly from the container (subsequent market feedback led the JV to sell spoons as well). It fortifies the yogurt with 30 percent of the daily need for vitamin A, zinc, and iodine, and it uses biodegradable technology so that containers can be converted to fertilizer.

Pricing

To keep costs and prices low, the plant uses only local ingredients, mainly from small suppliers such as farmers with only one or two cows, who collect and deliver milk in jugs (thus saving refrigeration and transportation costs). Fixed sales costs are kept low by selling only on commission (about 20 percent to saleswomen and 80 percent to small local stores). Personnel costs have been kept limited since completion of its start-up phase by using only Bangladeshis. Although the yogurt plant lacks scale economies, its unit costs are equivalent to Danone's larger plants elsewhere.

Two factors created temporary cost problems. First, milk prices rose by about 40 percent between initial planning and the plant's opening. Management subsequently negotiated longer-term contracts with farmers to better stabilize prices; hence, the JV pays higher than market price sometimes and less at other times. Second, management and saleswomen expected higher sales than what materialized. Rather than raising commissions to maintain the sales force, the company successfully suggested selling additional products during house-to-house visits.

Promotion

Most promotion is word of mouth; however, one promotional event was noteworthy. Riboud arranged for the best-known Frenchman in Bangladesh, the soccer star Zinédine Zidane (Zizou), to visit the plant's opening, an event that made large headlines in newspapers throughout the country. While in Bangladesh, Zizou played with youth in the national stadium, signed the cornerstone of the plant, and contributed to instant national recognition for the new JV and its yogurt.

Branding

The JV name put Grameen first because of its established high recognition. The yogurt brand is Shokti Doi, meaning "yogurt for power." The brand's symbol is a muscled lion that appears on the product and in ads. Lion-dressed mascots also visit youth areas to describe the value of eating yogurt.

Distribution

Bangladesh's high underemployment attracted more than enough women to work part-time selling yogurt. These were mainly poor mothers from the JV's target sales market. However, the JV had to contend with a backlash similar to the one GB faced when lending to women; the complaint this time was about the impropriety of women going house-to-house. The next big task was to train the saleswomen on (1) the significance of selling yogurt other than to earn a commission and (2) the essentiality of the yogurt's quality and how to maintain it.

Nourishment was the prime reason for selling. The company engaged doctors to explain that children's consumption of only two cups of yogurt per week enables them to regain within 9 to 10 months any physical loss from previously deprived nutrition. The second significance was to improve the economy, such as helping suppliers who would then hire more people and spend within the community.

Maintaining yogurt quality was essential because few homes had refrigeration and eating a spoiled product could cause illness and future sales losses. The company demonstrated to saleswomen how it makes yogurt, provided them with insulated bags, showed them how to use the bags properly, and stressed the need for them to carry only a minimum inventory to lessen the chance of spoilage.

Evaluation

Evaluating the JV's financial performance is straightforward; however, assessing its social effects is challenging. For this, the JV has hired a Swiss-based nutrition organization (GAIN) to develop, test, and validate its performance in terms of meeting the objectives for poor people. Preliminary findings have compared children who have consumed yogurt with and without micronutrient fortification and conclude that the former have grown more in height. In addition, psychometric tests show that the former are significantly better at important mental functions such as planning, concentration, problem solving, and conceptual flexibility.

The Future

Grameen Danone Foods' sales have increased steadily, from 150,000 cups in 2008 to 22.5 million cups in 2011. The number of saleswomen employed at the end of 2011 was 821. Further, Danone has learned much in Bangladesh about running small-scale production

MAP 17.1 Grameen Danone Foods Joint Venture

Groupe Dannon from France joined the Grameen Foundation to form a social business joint venture in Bangladesh. Subsequently, Group Dannone learned about serving the base of the pyramid and has transformed this knowledge to help it operate in Indonesia and Senegal.

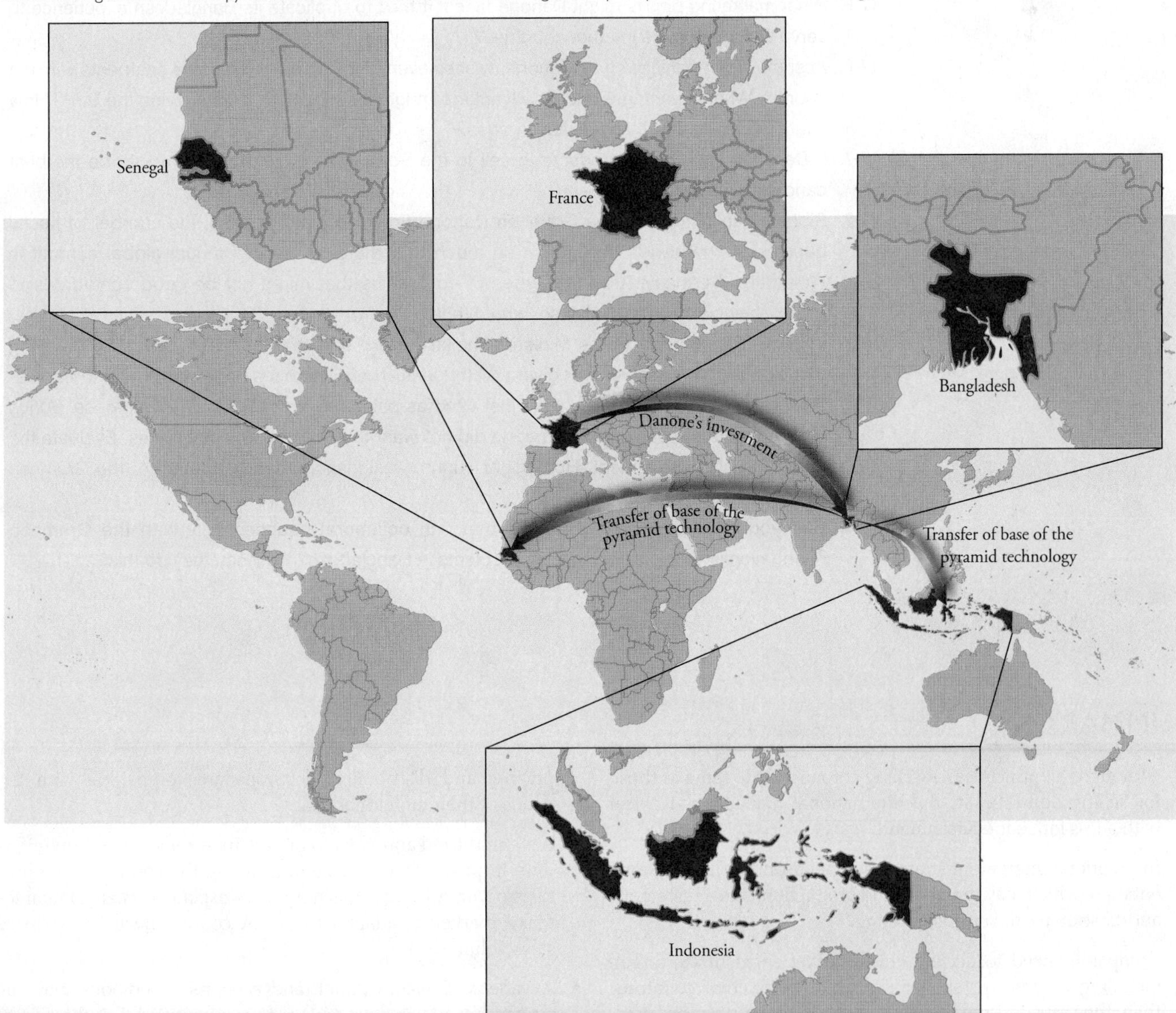

efficiently and is transferring this knowledge to help with its operations in Indonesia and Senegal. (Map 17.1 illustrates the international connections.) Inspired by this new model of collaboration, other major MNEs are establishing social businesses with Grameen Foundation. Grameen Intel Social Business Ltd. was founded in 2011 to create software applications on handheld computing devices that address such social problems as low agricultural output and lack of prenatal care. BASF, a German chemical company, formed BASF Grameen Ltd. and inaugurated production in 2012 of long-lasting insecticide-impregnated nets to fight the spread of malaria. Despite all the publicity and promise of these high-profile collaborative ventures, however, Danone will need to evaluate how brand recognition and good-will at the BoP can be harnessed for sales farther up the pyramid in order to expand to more affluent market segments.

QUESTIONS

17-3. What advantages might Danone receive from the Grameen Danone joint venture?

17-4. How much do you think Danone's decision to set up a social business was motivated by wanting to be socially responsible versus believing the move would help its performance? Does the answer to this make any difference?

17-5. What marketing pitfalls might Danone face if it tries to duplicate its Bangladesh experience to serve BoP customers in other countries?

17-6. Assume a company, such as Danone, wishes eventually to serve all income segments within a country. What advantages and disadvantages might it encounter by first serving the BoP? How might it later deal with any disadvantages?

17-7. If Danone were to add products to sell to the BoP, which of its products would be the best candidates? Why?

17-8. Since establishment of the Grameen Danone Foods social business, the number of social businesses worldwide has grown so much that there is now an annual global summit in Wolfsburg, Germany. Are there types of companies that might not be good candidates to establish social businesses? If so, what are they and why?

17-9. In 2010, Bangladeshi Prime Minister Sheikh Hasina said that Grameen had been "sucking money out of the people after giving them loans. There has been no improvement in the life-style of the poor so far. They were just used as pawns to get more aid." In response, Yunus resigned from the bank, saying that he did not want to distract from its activities. Evaluate the Prime Minister's statement. How might Yunus's resignation affect the future of the Grameen Danone Foods JV?

17-10. Can you think of any other MNEs that can collaborate successfully with the Grameen Foundation and help solve specific problems in Bangladesh? How can they do this?

SUMMARY

- Although the principles for selling abroad are the same as those for selling domestically, the international manager must deal with a less familiar environment.
- International marketing strategies depend on a company's orientation, which may center around production, sales, customers, and/or strategic or social marketing.
- Companies need to decide which market segments to target, including different or similar groups from different countries; then, they must ensure that their product, branding, promotion, pricing, and distribution decisions are compatible with the needs of their target markets.
- A standardized approach to marketing means maximum uniformity in products and programs among the countries in which sales occur. Although this minimizes expenses, most companies make marketing adaptations to fit country needs to increase sales volume.
- A variety of legal, cultural, and economic conditions may call for altering products to capture foreign demand, but the cost of

alteration relative to additional sales potential should be considered. In addition to determining when to alter products, companies also must decide how many and which products to sell abroad.

- Government regulations may directly or indirectly affect the prices that companies charge. International pricing is further complicated because of currency value fluctuations, differences in product preferences, price escalation in exporting, and variations in fixed versus variable pricing practices.
- For each product in each country, a company must determine not only its promotional budget but also the mix between push and pull strategies and promotions. The relationship between push and pull should depend on the distribution system, the cost and availability of media, consumer attitudes, and the product's price compared to incomes.
- Major problems for standardizing advertising among countries include translation, legality, and message needs.
- Global branding is hampered by language differences, expansion by acquisition, nationality images, and laws concerning generic names. Nevertheless, global brands help develop a global image.
- Distribution channels vary substantially among countries. The differences may affect not only the relative costs of operating but also the ease of making initial sales.
- Companies need to choose distributors carefully on the basis of both their abilities and their trustworthiness. At the same time, companies have to sell themselves to get distributors to handle their products and services.
- Although the Internet offers opportunities to sell internationally, using it does not negate companies' needs to develop sound programs within their marketing mix.
- Gap analysis is a tool that helps companies determine why they have not met their market potentials for given countries and to decide what part of the marketing mix to emphasize.
- Two future changes may greatly affect how companies segment markets in terms of demographics and psychographics: the economic schism between the haves and have-nots; and the composition of people in terms of their tendencies to be materialistic, cosmopolitan, or ethnocentric.

KEY TERMS

cosmopolitanism (p. 726)
cost-plus strategy (p. 709)
distribution (p. 717)
consumer ethnocentrism (p. 726)
gap analysis (p. 723)
generic (p. 717)
gray market (p. 711)
materialism (p. 726)
penetration strategy (p. 709)
product diversion (p. 711)
pull (p. 713)
push (p. 713)
skimming strategy (p. 709)

ENDNOTES

1 *Sources include the following:* "Tommy Thriving Under PVH Ownership," *Women's Wear Daily* 203:82 (April 19, 2012): n/a.; "Tommy Hilfiger Announces Global Spring 2013 Ad Campaign," *Business Wire* [New York] (January 28, 2013): n.p.; Lisa Lockwood, "Tommy Hilfiger," *Women's Wear Daily* 200:94 (November 3, 2010): n.p.; Ray A. Smith, "A Designer Changes His Stripes," *Wall Street Journal* (June 2, 2011): D1+; Drew Fitzgerald, "Phillips Van Heusen Swings to Profit," *Wall Street Journal* (May 31, 2011): n.p.; Rachel Dodes, "Macy's Buying Clout Drives Supplier Consolidation," *Wall Street Journal* (March 22, 2010): n.p.; "Tommy Hilfiger Group," *Entertainment News Weekly* (October 2, 2009): 105; "Tommy Hilfiger to Assume Direct Control of Distribution in China," *PR Newswire* (March 31, 2010): n.p.; Joe Fernandez, "Fashion: Hilfiger to Use 'Delebs' for Silver Anniversary," *Marketing Week* (June 10, 2010): 4; Miles Socha and Joelle Diderich, "Hilfiger: American in Paris," *Women's Wear Daily*, 200:107 (November 18, 2010): n.p.; "Tommy Hilfiger," *Investment Weekly News* (April 23, 2011): 898; Neha Dewan, "We Will Expand in Smaller Cities," *The Economic Times*, October 12, 2010): n.p.; Michael Barbaro, "Macy's and Hilfiger Strike Exclusive Deal," *New York Times* (October 27, 2007): 1; Cathy Horyn, "Still Tommy after All These Years," *New York Times* (December 7, 2008): Sec. M3, 182; Teri Agins, "Costume Change," *Wall Street Journal* (February 2, 2007): A1+; Miles Socha, "Tommy Takes Paris," *DNR* (October 23, 2006): 26; Miles Socha, "Tommy's Latest Take," *WWD* (October 20, 2006): 1; Julie Naughton, "Hilfiger and Lauder Aim for Perfect 10," *WWD* (June 23, 2006): 4; Lisa Lockwood, "CEO Says Tommy to Now Trade Up," *WWD* (May 11, 2006): 3.

2 Stefan Schmid and Thomas Kotulla, "50 years of Research on International Standardization and Adaptation—From a Systematic Literature Analysis to a Theoretical Framework," *International Business Review* 20 (2011): 491–507.

3 "Tommy Hilfiger Thriving Under PVH Ownership," *WWD* (April 19, 2012): n.p.

4 Constantine S. Katsikeas, Saeed Damiee, and Marios Theodosiou, "Strategy Fit and Performance Consequences of International Marketing Standardization," *Strategic Management Journal* 27 (2006): 867–90.

5 Stefan Schmid and Thomas Kotulla, loc. cit.

6 Karina R. Jensen, "Creating Global Innovation Opportunities through Cross-cultural Collaboration," *The International Journal of Knowledge, Culture and Change Management* 10:10 (2011): 33–42.

7 Ruby P. Lee, Qimei Chen, Daekwan Kim, and Jean L. Johnson, "Knowledge Transfer between Multinational Corporations' Headquarters and Their Subsidiaries: Influences on and Implications for New Product Outcomes," *Journal of International Marketing* 16:2 (2008): 1–31.

8 Matt Moffett, "Learning to Adapt to a Tough Market, Chilean Firms Pry Open Door to Japan," *Wall Street Journal* (June 7, 1994): A10.

9 Margarita Stancati and Preetika Rana, "Hermès Goes Local with India Sari Launch," *Wall Street Journal* (October 12, 2011): n.p.

10 Andrea Felsted, "Tesco," *Financial Times* (December 3, 2009): 39.

11 Betsy McKay, "Drinks for Developing Countries," *Wall Street Journal* (November 27, 2001): B1+; McKay, "Coke's Heyer Finds Test in Latin America," *Wall Street Journal* (October 15, 2002): B4; and "Vitamin

Angels," retrieved July 1, 2011, from www.vitaminangels.org/blogs/results/taxonomy%3A84?page=5.

12 Manoj K. Agarwal, "Developing Global Segments and Forecasting Market Shares: A Simultaneous Approach Using Survey Data," *Journal of International Marketing* 11:4 (2003): 56.

13 Rosalie L. Tung, "The Cross-Cultural Research Imperative: The Need to Balance Cross-National and Intra-National Diversity," *Journal of International Business Studies* 39:1 (2008): 41–46; James Agarwal, Naresh Malhotra, and Ruth N. Bolton, "A Cross-National and Cross-Cultural Approach to Global Market Segmentation: An Application Using Consumers' Perceived Service Quality," *Journal of International Marketing* 18:3 (2010): 18–40.

14 Ed Hammond, "Red Bull: Where marketing Goes into Overdrive," *Financial Times* (September 27, 2011): n.p.

15 "Ferrari Makes India Debut," *Wall Street Journal* (May 27, 2011): n.p.

16 Rebecca Rose, "Global Diversity Gets All Cosmetic," *Financial Times* (April 10–11, 2004): W11.

17 Allen L. Hammond and C. K. Prahalad, "Selling to the Poor," *Foreign Policy* (May–June 2004): 30–37.

18 Constantine S. Katsikeas, Saeed Damiee, and Marios Theodosiou, "Strategy Fit and Performance Consequences of International Marketing Standardization," *Strategic Management Journal* 27 (2006): 867–90.

19 "Look What They've Done to My Brands," *The Economist* (November 17, 2012): 60.

20 "CEC Finalizing Report on SLAB Exports," *Business Wire* [New York] (November 30, 2012): n.p.; Don Hopey, "Rachel Carson's Book Turned the Environmental World on Its Ear 50 Years Ago," *McClatchy - Tribune Business News* [Washington] (September 27, 2012): n.p.

21 Robert Kennedy, "Tobacco Firms Accused of Thwarting Controls," *McClatchy - Tribune Business News* [Washington] (May 30, 2012): n.p.

22 "Cause for Concern with Nestlé in the Spotlight Again over Its Advertising Tactics," *Marketing Week* (February 11, 1999): 28–31.

23 Andrew Jack, "Economic Reality Spurs Intervention: More Is Being Done to Tackle 'NTDs' as Research Reveals Their Impact on Countries' Growth," *Financial Times* (October 11, 2012): 2.

24 Andrew Jack, "FDA to Stimulate Tropical Disease Research," *Financial Times* (May 1, 2008): 6.

25 Muhammad Arsalan Khan, Tanvir A. Jafri, Asif Shahzad, and Riftat Abbas Rizvi, "Strategic Response of Cigarette Manufacturing Companies to the Implementation of Anti-smoke Measures in Pakistan, *Interdisciplinary Journal of Contemporary Research In Business*3: 12 (April 2012): 69–82.

26 Michael Finkel, "Bedlam in the Blood: Malaria," *National Geographic* (July 2007): 63; and Richard Tren and Roger Bate, "Malaria and the DDT Story," *SSRN Working Paper Series* (April 2012).

27 Kevin Helliker, "Smokeless Tobacco to Get Push by Venture Overseas," *Wall Street Journal* (February 4, 2009): B1+.

28 Pierre M. Barker, Kedar Mate, "Eliminating Mother-To-Child HIV Transmission Will Require Major Improvements In Maternal And Child Health Services," *Health Affairs* 31:7 (July 2012): 1489–97.

29 "Coca-Cola Releases 2011–2012 Global Sustainability Report," *Professional Services Close-Up* (November 11, 2012).

30 Avery Johnson, "Drug Firms See Poorer Nations as Sales Cure," *Wall Street Journal* (July 7, 2009): A1+.

31 Andrew Jack, "Anti-Malaria Drug to Sell at Cost Price," *Financial Times* (March 2, 2007): 3; Jennifer Corbett Dooren, "Research to Target Neglected Diseases," *Wall Street Journal* (May 21, 2009): 16.

32 Laurie Burkitt, op cit.

33 Louise Lucas, "Multinationals Try to Make the Most of their Local Credentials," *Financial Times* (September 22, 2010): Peru section, 10.

34 Paul Sonne, Devon Maylie, and Drew Hinshaw, "With West Flat, Big Brewers Peddle Cheap Beer in Africa," *Wall Street Journal* (March 20, 2013): A1+.

35 Orit Gadiesh and Till Vestring, "The Consequences of China's Rising Global Heavyweights," *MIT Sloan Management Review* 49:3 (Spring 2008): 10–11.

36 Keith Bradsher, "India Gains on China among Multinationals," *International Herald Tribune* (June 12–13, 2004): 13.

37 Stefan Schmid and Thomas Kotulla, "To What Degree Should Firms Standardize or Adapt Their Product Mix Across Countries? New Empirical Results Based on the Strategic-Fit Approach," Paper presented at the Academy of International Business annual meeting, Washington, DC (2012).

38 Yonca Limon, Lynn R. Kahle, and Ulrich R. Orth, "Package Design as a Communications Vehicle in Cross-Cultural Values Shopping," *Journal of International Marketing* 17:1 (2009): 30–57.

39 "The World's Wash Day," *Financial Times*, 6.

40 "Nike Faces Marketing Challenge in China: Make Running Cool," *Advertising Age* (October 20, 2011): n.p.

41 Ian Austen and Stephanie Clifford, "North of the Border," *New York Times* (November 15, 2012): B1+.

42 Arvind Sahay, "Finding the Right International Mix," *Financial Times* (November 16, 1998): Mastering Marketing section, 2–3.

43 Laurie Burkitt, loc. cit.

44 James A. Roberts and Chris Manolis, "Cooking Up a Recipe for Self-Control: The Three Ingredients of Self-Control and Its Impact on Impulse Buying," *Journal of Marketing Theory and Practice* 20:2 (Spring 2012): 173–88.

45 Jenny Wiggins and Chris Flood, "Coke to Shrink Size of Cans in Hong Kong," *Financial Times* (July 25, 2008): 18.

46 Carol Wolf, "Losing $63 Billion in Diverted U.S. Goods Is Sleuth Obsession," Bloomberg.com (accessed April 9, 2009), referring to a study by Deloitte & Touche.

47 Edward W. Miles, "The Role of Face in the Decision Not to Negotiate," *International Journal of Conflict Management* 21:4 (2010): 400–14.

48 C. Gopinath, "Fixed Price and Bargaining," *Business Line* (July 15, 2002): 1.

49 Claude Cellich, "FAQ...about Business Negotiations on the Internet," *International Trade Forum* 1 (2001): 10–11.

50 Jan H. Schumann, Florian V. Wagenheim, Anne Stringfellow, Zhilin Yang, Vera Blazevic, Sandra Praxmarer, G. Shainesh, Marcin Komor, Randall M. Shannon, and Fernando R. Jiménez, "Cross-Cultural Differences in the Effect of Received Word-of-Mouth Referral in Relational Service Exchange," *Journal of International Marketing* 18:3 (2010): 62–80.

51 Loretta Chao, "PC Makers Cultivate Buyers in Rural China," *Wall Street Journal* (September 23, 2009): B1.

52 Jamie Anderson, Martin Kupp, and Ronan Moaligou, "Lessons from the Developing World," *Wall Street Journal* (August 17, 2009): R6.

53 Owen M. Bradfield, Caroline Parker, and Leonie Goodwin, "Sustaining Performance: Learning from Buyers' Experience," *Journal of Medical Marketing* 9:4 (October 2009): 343–53.

54 Ed Hammond, loc cit.

55 Charles Goldsmith, "Dubbing in Product Plugs," *Wall Street Journal* (December 6, 2004): B1+.

56 Ouidade Sabri, Delphine Manceau, and Bernard Pras, "Taboo: An Underexplored Concept in Marketing: RAM," *Recherche et Applications en Marketing* 25:1 (2010): 59–85.

57 Gemma Charles, "Don't Be a Code Breaker," *Marketing* (March 17, 2010): 17; Ernest Cyril De Run, "Attitudes Towards Offensive Advertising: Malaysian Muslims' Views," *Journal of Islamic Marketing* 1:1 (2010): 25–36.

58 Deborah Ball, "Women in Italy Like to Clean but Shun the Quick and Easy," *Wall Street Journal* (April 25, 2006): A1+.

59 Andrew Ward, "Home Improvements Abroad," *Financial Times* (April 6, 2006): 8.

60 Sarah Ellison, "Sex-Themed Ads Often Don't Travel Well," *Wall Street Journal* (March 31, 2000): B7.

61 Tulin Erdem, Joffre Swait, and Ana Valenzuela, "Brands as Signals: A Cross-Country Validation Study," *Journal of Marketing* 70:1 (2006): 34; Desmond Lam, "Cultural Influence on Proneness to Brand Loyalty," *Journal of International Consumer Marketing* 19:3 (2006): 7.

62 Mei Fong, "Chinese Refrigerator Maker Finds U.S. Chilly," *Wall Street Journal* (March 18, 2008): B1+.

63 Andreas B. Eisingerich and Gale Rubera, "Drivers of Brand Commitment: A Cross-National Investigation," *Journal of International Marketing* 18:2 (2010): 64–79.

64 Jo Roberts, "The 100 Most Valuable Global Brands," *Marketing Week* (May 24, 2012):1+.

65 Claudiu V. Dimofte, Johny K. Johansson, and Richard P. Bagozzi, "Global Brands in the United States: How Consumer Ethnicity Mediates the Global Brand Effect," *Journal of International Marketing* 18:1 (2010): 81–106.

66 Andrews Adugudaa Akolaa, "Cultural Diagnosis and By Passing; The Effect on Successful Internationalizaton," *Review of Business & Finance Case Studies* 3:1 (2012): 69–84.

67 James Hookway, "IKEA's Products Make Shoppers Blush in Thailand," *Wall Street Journal* (June 5, 2012): n.p.

68 Michael Wines, "Picking the Pitch-Perfect Brand Name in China," *New York Times* (November 12, 2011): A4.

69 Lee Simmons and Robert M. Schindler, "Cultural Superstitions and the Price Endings Used in Chinese Advertising," *Journal of International Marketing* 11:2 (2003): 101.

70 Miriam Jordan, "Sara Lee Wants to Percolate through All of Brazil," *Wall Street Journal* (May 8, 2002): A14+; "Sara Lee Buys Brazilian Out-of-Home Player Expresso Coffee: Sara Lee Reinforces its Leadership in Fast-Growing Sao Paulo and Rio de Janeiro Markets," *PR Newswire* [New York] (April 10, 2012): n.p.

71 Isabelle Schuiling and Jean-Noël Kapferer, "Executive Insights: Real Differences between Local and International Brands: Strategic Implications for International Marketers," *Journal of International Marketing* 12:4 (2004): 197.

72 Jan-Benedict, E.M. Steenkamp, and Martijn G. de Jong, "A Global Investigation into the Constellation of Consumer Attitudes Toward Global and Local Products," *Journal of Marketing* 74 (November 2010): 18–40.

73 P. Sharma, "Country of Origin Effects in Developed and Emerging Markets: Exploring the Contrasting Roles of Materialism and Value Consciousness," *Journal of International Business Studies*, 42:2 (2012): 285-306; Terence Motsi and Ji Eun Park, "Consumer Evaluation of Developing Country Products: The Moderating Role of Product Ethnicity," Paper presented at the Academy of International Business annual meeting, Washington, DC (2012); Zhongqi Jin, Richard Lynch, Samaa Attia, Bal Chansarkar, Tanses Gulsoy, Paul Lapoule, "Antecedents of Home and Foreign Product Country Images in Developed and Developing Countries: A Comparative Study," Paper presented at the Academy of International Business annual meeting, Washington, DC (2012); Stephen Gould, Mike Chen-Ho Chao, Andreas Grein, and Rania Semaan, "The Biasing Effects of Country-of-Origin: A Cross-Cultural Application of Preference Reversals," Paper presented at the Academy of International Business annual meeting, Washington, DC (2012).

74 Eva M. Oberecker and Adamantios Diamantopoulos, "Consumers' Emotional Bonds with Foreign Countries: Does Consumer Affinity Affect Behavioral Intentions?" *Journal of International Marketing* 19:2 (2011): 45–72.

75 Daniel Laufer, Kate Gillespie, and David H. Silvera, "The Role of Country of Manufacture in Consumers' Attributions of Blame in an Ambiguous Product-Harm Crisis," *Journal of International Consumer Marketing* 21 (2009): 189–201.

76 Seah Park, "LG's Kitchen Makeover," *Wall Street Journal* (September 22, 2004): A19.

77 Saeed Samiee, Terrence A. Shimp, and Subash Sharma, "Brand Origin Recognition Accuracy: Its Antecedents and Consumers' Cognitive Limitations," *Journal of International Business Studies* 36 (2005): 379–97; George Balabanis and Adamantios, "Gains and Losses from the Misperception of Brand Origin: The Role of Brand Strength and Country-of Origin Image," *Journal of International Marketing* 19:2 (2011): 95–116.

78 Kevin McCallum, "Grape Debate," *Miami Herald* (March 27, 2009): 1C+.

79 "Opportunities in Sub-Culture," *Business Line* (February 12, 2004): 1.

80 Gary F. Keller and Creig R. Kronstedt, "Connecting Confucianism, Communism, and the Chinese Culture of Commerce," *Journal of Language for International Business* 16:1 (2005): 60–75.

81 S. Tamer Cavusgil, Seyda Deligonul, and Chun Zhang, "Curbing Foreign Distributor Opportunism: An Examination of Trust, Contracts, and the Legal Environment in International Channel Relationships," *Journal of International Marketing* 12:2 (2004).

82 Susanna Khavul, Mark Peterson, Drake Mullens, and Abdul A. Rasheed, "Going Global with Innovations from Emerging Economies: Investment in Customer Support Capabilities Pays Off," *Journal of International Marketing* 18:4 (2010): 22–42.

83 Mobolaji Olaseni ND Wale Alade, "Vision 20:2020 and the Challenges of Infrastructural Development in Nigeria," *Journal of Sustainable Development* 5:2 (February 2012): 63–76.

84 Tomasz Lenartowicz and Sridhar Balasubramanian, "Practices and Performance of Small Retail Stores in Developing Economies," *Journal of International Marketing* 17:1 (2009): 58–90.

85 Ibid.

86 Thomas G. Brashear, Vishal Kashyap, Michael D. Musante, and Naveen Donthu, "A Profile of the Internet Shopper: Evidence from Six Countries," *Journal of Marketing Theory and Practice* 17:3 (Summer 2009): 267–81.

87 Rita Marcella and Sylvie Davies, "The Use of Customer Language in International Marketing Communication in the Scottish Food and Drink Industry," *European Journal of Marketing* 38:11/12 (2004): 1382.

88 *New Zealand Business* 18:11 (2004): 21–27.

89 Moen Øystein, Iver Endresen, and Morten Gavlen, "Executive Insights: Use of the Internet in International Marketing: A Case Study of Small Computer Software Firms," *Journal of International Marketing* 11:4 (2003): 129–44.

90 J. A. Weber, "Comparing Growth Opportunities in the International Marketplace," *Management International Review* 1 (1979): 47–54; Van R. Wood, John R. Darling, and Mark Siders, "Consumer Desire to Buy and Use Products in International Markets: How to Capture It, How to Sustain It," *International Marketing Review* 16:3 (1999): 231–42.

91 "Mintel: India's Craving for Chocolate to Create Business Opportunities for Manufacturers," *Entertainment Close - Up* (November 17, 2012): n.p.

92 Nina Kruschwitz, "Why Kraft Foods Cares About Fair Trade Chocolate," *MIT Sloan Management Review* 54:1 (Fall 2012): 1–4.

93 Colum Murphy and Laurie Burkitt, "Hershey Launches New Brand in China," *Wall Street Journal* (May 21, 2013): B8.

94 Dermot Doherty, "Godiva's Sweet on China," *Miami Herald* (June 12, 2012): 6B.

95 Haig Simonian, "Nestlé Enriches Its Choc Value," *Financial Times* (March 24, 2006): 9.

96 Michiyo Nakamoto, "Japanese Fall out of Love with Luxury," *Financial Times* (June 3, 2009): 15.

97 Allen L. Hammond and C. K. Prahalad, "Selling to the Poor," *Foreign Policy* (May/June 2004): 30–37.

98 Kelvin Chan, "Foreign Vineyards Keen to Tap China Wine Market," *Miami Herald* (November 7, 2011): n.p.

99 Stephanie Strom, "New Tack on Snacks," *New York Times* (June 13, 2012): B1+.

100 For an excellent discussion of these traits and their interactions, see Mark Cleveland, Michel Laroche, and Nicolas Papadopoulos, "Cosmopolitanism, Consumer Ethnocentrism, and Materialism: An Eight-Country Study of Antecedents and Outcomes," *Journal of International Marketing* 17:1 (2009): 116–46.

101 Information for the case was taken from Muhammad Yunus, *Creating a World Without Poverty* (New York: Public Affairs, 2007); C. K. Prahalad, *The Fortune at the Bottom of the Pyramid* (Upper Saddle River, NJ: Wharton School Publishing 2010); Grameen Danone Foods Ltd. PowerPoint (Jan. 2012) available at www.danonecommunities.com; www.grameen-intel.com (accessed on Jan. 16, 2013); Social Business: BASF Grameen Ltd. available at www.basf.com (accessed on Feb. 7, 2013); GAIN and Grameen Danone:a study about nutrition, available at www.youtube.com/watch?v=EQJ0Qco7JhE, (accessed on Feb. 8, 2013); Sheridan Prasso, "Saving the World With a Cup of Yogurt," *Fortune* 155:2 (March 15, 2007): 44; John F. Jones, "Social Finance: Commerce and Community in Developing Countries," *International Journal of Social Economics* 37:6 (2010): 415–28; Nevin S. Scrimshaw, "History and Early Development of INCAP1, 2," *The Journal of Nutrition* 140:2 (February 2010): 394–96; Sarah Murray, "Yogurt Maker's Recipe for funding Social Businesses," *Financial Times* (July 7, 2008): 16; Christina Passariello, "Danone Expands Its Pantry to Woo the World's Poor," *Wall Street Journal* (June 29, 2010): A1; Paul Bennet, "The Biggest Idea Might Be Learning to Think Small," *Financial Times* (December 31, 2009): 10; Michael Fitzgerald, "As the World Turns," 133 *Fast Company* (March 2009): 33–34; Scheherazade Daneshkhu, "The Off-the-Wall Executive," *Financial Times* (November 22, 2010): 12; "Top CEOs Talk on Global Social Business in Germany," *The Global Express* [Dhaka] (November 12, 2010): n.p.; and Dean Nelson, "Pioneer Bank in Turmoil," *The Sunday Telegraph* [London] (February 13, 2011): 3.

CHAPTER 18

Global Production and Supply Chains

OBJECTIVES

After studying this chapter, you should be able to

1. Describe the different dimensions of a global manufacturing strategy
2. Examine the critical factors in successful global supply-chain management
3. Show how supplier networks function
4. Explain how quality affects global supply and effective inventory management
5. Discuss how to establish successful transportation networks as part of the global supply chain

Source: © kangshutters - Fotolia.com

A cheap thing doesn't lack defect, nor an expensive thing quality.

—Afghan proverb

CASE Apple's Global Supply Chain

How long does it take to get an iPhone?[1] In September 2012, Apple, the largest consumer electronics company in the world and the largest company in the U.S. in market capitalization, formally announced the iPhone 5, the sixth generation of the iPhone and successor to the popular iPhone 4S. The hype over the new phone was so high that pre-orders swamped Apple's ability to get enough phones from its factory in ZhengZhou, a city in the north-central region of China. Mandy Xiao was living in Provo, Utah at the time and wanted to get the phone by Christmas of 2012, so she ordered the phone directly from Apple.com on December 5. The factory in ZhengZhou is actually owned by Taiwan-based Hon Hai Precision Industry Co. Ltd., also known as the Foxconn Technology Group. Given the Christmas rush and the fact that ZhengZhou was a little over 6,500 miles away, Mandy wasn't sure how long it would take to get her phone. But Apple's supply chain was fast. Mandy was able to track her phone's journey by UPS online from ZhengZhou to Inchan International Airport in Korea to Anchorage, Alaska to her door in Provo, Utah—only two days after it was ordered. If you are going to compete today, you need to get the product to the consumer as soon as possible, and Apple excels at this, even when it's 6,500 miles away from the consumer.

APPLE'S ORIGINS

Apple's initial supply chain was relatively simple. In 1976, Steve Jobs and Steve Wozniak ("Woz") sold their first product, the Apple I computer, out of the Jobs' family garage in Cupertino, California. Woz was the designer and Jobs ran the business in the up-and-coming microcomputer industry. Jobs and Woz had to design the product, develop the operating system that made it work, manufacture it, and market it. Large auto companies like Ford and GM had the same issues, but they invested significant resources into building massive manufacturing facilities to supply the market. Unlike the auto companies, the new Apple Computer company was not a major manufacturer of products, but primarily an assembler of components supplied by other companies. However, Apple was extremely successful with this new venture, although the cost of the computer was quite high (since the company was in its infancy), volumes were not very high, and competition was not very strong.

What really changed the game was the entry of IBM into the market. IBM knew that to beat Apple, it needed to drive down costs as low as possible. Initially, IBM was a large vertically integrated company that produced most of its parts and components itself within the U.S. In the early 1980s, however, IBM realized that it needed to use external suppliers for key components in an effort to create a cheaper alternative to the Apple II computer, the successor to Jobs' and Woz's successful Apple I computer. Then IBM outsourced its operating system to Microsoft and its microprocessor to Intel, and the race was on. By taking a close look at the value chain, IBM was able to modularize the industry so that Microsoft, for example, could sell its operating system to any company that wanted to use it, and Intel could develop semiconductors for a wide range of products for many different companies. This allowed them to achieve even greater economies of scale.

APPLE'S ADAPTATION

Apple adapted in many different ways, as did the entire consumer electronics industry. Apple's strength was in the design of new products that consumers wanted. However, it realized that it had to go far beyond just computers. Rather than just stick with personal computers, it branched off into a variety of mobile communication and media devices, portable music players, software, and cloud storage. Its products include the iPhone, iPad, Mac, iPod, and the Apple TV, and it designs and manufactures its own products. Apple always comes up with cool stuff, and it is being pushed by new entrants in the market like Samsung. But it is still known for new ideas and new products, the strength of Steve Jobs and the organization he created before he died.

The big challenge is how do you manufacture this wide range of products? Apple has assembly operations in Freemont, California, Cork, Ireland, and Singapore using components supplied by other companies. In 2012, it even announced that it was "reshoring" or bringing the manufacturing of some of its Macs back to the U.S. by investing $100 million in new facilities to assemble the computers. Even though Apple no longer manufactures its own components, it buys them from suppliers, what is also called supply-chaining. Apple's decision to reshore some of its production is partly due to lower energy costs, rising wages in countries like China, a weaker U.S. dollar, quality control issues, and proximity to the large U.S. market. However, this is not a major shift in the way Apple manufactures all of its products.

THE RISE OF CONTRACT MANUFACTURING

Most of the components Apple uses come from multiple sources, but some are from single or limited sources, which can create supply problems. This is especially true when Apple uses some custom components that are not widely used in the industry but are used only for its products. Apple's search for reliable suppliers coincided with the emergence of Hon Hai Precision Industry Company, Ltd., widely known as Foxconn Technology Group. Foxconn was founded in Taiwan in 1976 by Terry Gou, about the same time Apple was founded. Gou began his company with a loan of $7,500 from his mother with a goal of to increasing the affordability of electronics products by combining his expertise for mechanical and electrical parts with a low-cost solution. He started supplying parts to Atari and then traveled to the U.S. to develop relationships with U.S. companies. One of the companies that he won orders from was IBM. Gou arrived at just the right time. IBM's supply chain moved from being vertical to horizontal and from sourcing only domestically to sourcing internationally.

When Apple assembles products at its factory in Singapore, it is offshoring, meaning that it is moving a factory offshore from the U.S. to assemble products. The factory still belongs to Apple, but it may still get parts and components from a variety of suppliers, mostly from Asia. Apple's relationship with Foxconn is different. As wages began to rise in Taiwan, many companies moved to the Philippines and Malaysia, but Foxconn invested in China, initially in Shenzhen but later to other cities where labor was plentiful and cheap. As it picked up more orders from abroad, it rose from a small company in Taiwan to the largest contract electronics manufacturer in the world, employing over 1 million people in China.

Although Foxconn supplies components to a variety of companies from all over the world, it is clear that Apple is its #1 customer. In fact, when concerns arose in the first few months of 2013 over Apple's first quarter results, shares of Hon Hai fell by 14 percent, with simliar results for shares of other Apple suppliers. However, when the first quarter results were released and Apple appeared to be doing just fine, the shares recovered their losses and posted gains. Such is the relationship between Apple and its suppliers.

When Tim Cook, the current CEO of Apple and successor to Steve Jobs, was brought into the company in 1997, he was asked by Jobs to clean up the manufacturing process. Manufacturing problems and excess inventory were a drag on corporate profits, cash flow, and therefore on funds available for investment in new products. As Cook worked to strengthen manufacturing, he developed strong supplier relations with companies throughout Asia, including Foxconn. The difference with Foxconn is that Apple was able to outsource the assembly of entire products, such as the iPhone5 mentioned above, instead of just sourcing components that Apple could assemble at its own facilities. Rather than manufacture the product through offshoring in Ireland or Singapore, Apple was able to outsource the entire production process to Foxconn as a contract manufacturer. Apple designed the product with very tight specifications and worked with Foxconn and their suppliers to roll out new products, but Foxconn was responsible for the manufacture and delivery of the product to Apple. Now nearly all of Apple's hardware products are manufactured by outsourcing partners located primarily in Asia. A significant amount of the manufacturing is currently performed by a small number of outsourcing partners, like Foxconn, in single locations. Some of these partners are sole-sourced suppliers of components and manufacturers of many of Apple's products.

Although Foxconn became a very trusted contract manufacturer, Apple still has to work hard to make sure the quality of the product and components are exactly what it is looking for. It's one thing to control quality at your own assembly facilities, and it's quite another thing to make sure Foxconn's quality is high enough. Apple's strong relationship with Foxconn and other suppliers is the envy of the industry. However, contract manufacturing is not without its problems. News of Foxconn's problems with its employees at its facilities in China created PR problems for Apple. Workers were accusing Foxconn of forcing them to work long hours in poor conditions, and some employees even committed suicide by jumping from Foxconn buildings. As a result, Mr. Cook visited factories in China and insisted that Foxconn and other suppliers comply with Chinese labor laws and even higher international standards of worker safety. Apple became the first technology company to join the Fair Labor Association, and Apple began publishing the results of its audits on worker conditions in 2007. In 2012, Apple listed the names of 156 companies that supplied it with parts and other services used by the Company in manufacturing its products. Any company that outsources to a company in a developing country faces similar challenges. It is important for companies like Apple to set high expectations, monitor compliance, and disclose information to its stakeholders.

THE LAST PART OF THE SUPPLY CHAIN

In addition to designing and manufacturing good products, Apple needs to worry about marketing, the last part of the supply chain. When Mandy decided to buy her iPhone, she had lots of options. Apple sells its products worldwide through its retail stores, online stores (Mandy's choice), a direct sales force, and third-party cellular network carriers, wholesalers, retailers, and value-added retailers. The photo at the beginning of the chapter is an Apple retail store opened in Shanghai in 2011, only the second Apple store opened in China. As of 2013, there were 8 Apple stores in China, three of which are in Shanghai. It sells its digital content through a variety of sources, including the iTunes Store. The key is to get the products from the point of manufacture to the final consumer, over 50 percent of whom are located outside of the United States. Clearly Apple's geographic spread was helping it to continue to grow and remain at the top in consumer electronics. ■

CRN
Case Review Note

QUESTIONS

18-1. Although Apple's inbound logistics began with Apple controlling the assembly of its computers, it shifted to having suppliers acquire raw materials with contract manufacturers handling most of the production and assembly of final products. Why did they do this, and what are the major challenges Apple faces?

18-2. Foxconn, a major contract manufacturer for Apple, is by far the largest ODM/EMS (original design manufacturer/Electronics Manufacturing Services) company in the world, dwarfing U.S.-based Flextronics, which is the major manufacturer and assembler of Samsung phones. In 2013, Foxconn was contemplating opening operations in the United States. In what way could this be a challenge for Apple, Inc.?

INTRODUCTION

Most companies agree that effective supply-chain management is one of their most important tools in reducing costs and boosting revenue.[2] Our opening case on Apple illustrates dimensions of these supply-chain networks that link suppliers with manufacturers and customers. Throughout this chapter we will explore the different networks and examine the links in an effective global supply chain. As illustrated in Figure 18.1, the core of an effective global supply chain strategy is operations. In the chapter, we will discuss the international dimensions of the global supply chain—from input to operations to final distribution to the consumer—through the following perspectives: the upstream processes of the purchasing function and supplier networks; operations strategy; the role of information technology in global supply-chain management; operations management including quality, total quality management and just-in-time inventory management; and downstream processes including effective transportation networks.

We must note here that effectively managing a supply chain is as important for services as it is for manufacturing. While our opening case on Apple traces developments in the supply-chain strategy of a traditional manufacturer, the closing case on Samsonite focuses on the company's continued efforts to reduce costs in the supply chain and the repeated reconfiguration employed to achieve that end.

CRN
Case Review Note

WHAT IS SUPPLY-CHAIN MANAGEMENT?

Supply chain—the coordination of materials, information, and funds from the initial raw-material supplier to the ultimate customer.

The **supply chain** is the network that links together the different aspects of the value chain (defined in Chapter 12) and coordinates materials, information, and funds from the initial raw-material supplier to the ultimate customer.[3] As determined by the Council of Supply Chain Management Professionals,

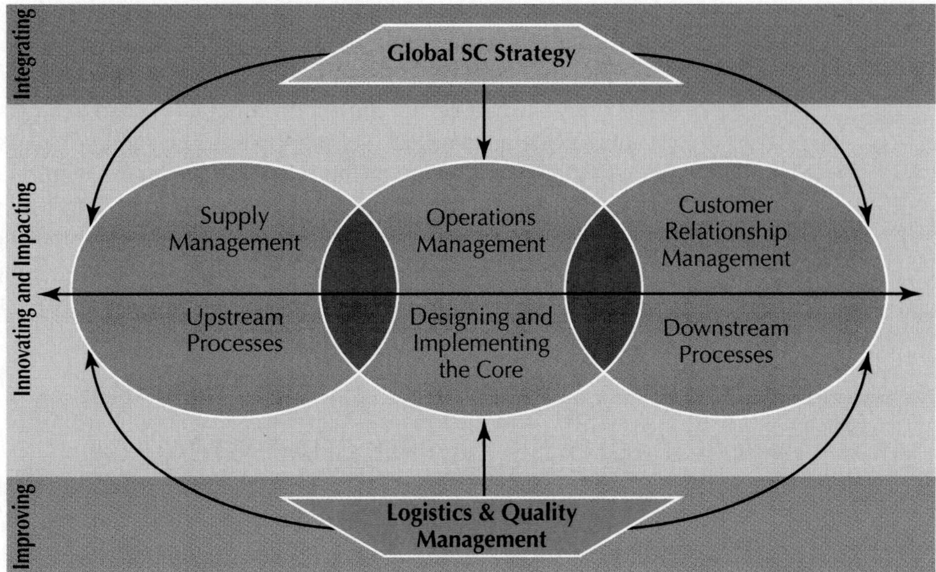

FIGURE 18.1 An integrated supply chain and operations model.

Source: Tom Foster, Jr.

> …supply chain management encompasses the planning and management of all activities involved in sourcing and procurement, conversion, and all logistics management activities. Importantly, it also includes coordination and collaboration with channel partners, which can be suppliers, intermediaries, third party service providers, and customers. In essence, supply chain management integrates supply and demand management within and across companies.[4]

Supply-chain management refers to activities in the value chain that occur outside the company, whereas **operations management** (also known as **logistics management**) often refers to internal activities. For example, Toyota assembles parts into a car. The assembly is part of the operations of the company, and the supply chain gets the parts to the factory and the final product to consumers worldwide.

Logistics (also called materials management)—that part of the supply-chain process that plans, implements, and controls the efficient, effective flow and storage of goods, services, and related information from the point of origin to the point of consumption in order to meet customers' requirements.

Suppliers can be part of the company's organizational structure, such as in a vertically integrated company, or they can be independent of it. Direct suppliers, in fact, have their own networks. For example, Foxconn, a contract manufacturer for Apple, has its own network of suppliers used in the manufacturing of Apple products in its factories in China. In a global context, they can be located in the country where the manufacturing or assembly takes place, or they can be located elsewhere and ship materials to the final assembly facility or to an intermediate storage point. Manufacturing process output can be shipped directly to the customers or to a warehouse network and sold directly to the end consumer or to a distributor, wholesaler, or retailer, then on to the final consumer. As is the case in the supplier network, the output can be sold domestically or internationally.

Most MNEs have excelled in their ability to manage their supply-chain networks. Examples exist all over the world, such as Apple (U.S.), Tesco (UK), Samsung (Korea), Nokia (Finland), Toyota (Japan), H&M (Sweden), and Zara (Spain). The companies we study in this chapter are considered part of a global network that links together designers, suppliers, subcontractors, manufacturers, and customers. The supply-chain network is quite broad, and its coordination takes place through interactions between firms in the network.[5]

GLOBAL SUPPLY CHAIN STRATEGIES

CRN Case Review Note

Recall from our opening case that Apple set up manufacturing facilities in China because of *location-specific advantages* (notably, cheap labor and associated costs), choosing to enter the country through an agreement with Foxconn, its future contract manufacturer. This allowed

CONCEPT CHECK

In Chapter 12, we explain **value** as the underlying principle of strategy, defining it as "the measure of a firm's capability to sell what it makes for more than the costs incurred to make it." Here, while further refining our discussion of strategy to enumerate factors contributing to a successful strategy, we hasten to repeat our definition of **strategy** as the effort of managers to build and sustain the company's competitive position within its industry to create value.

Apple to focus on its *firm-specific assets* (innovation, product development, and marketing) and thus move away from vertical integration to become more effective by giving up more of the elements of the value chain to Foxconn.

Apple is, of course, not the only company to outsource manufacturing to others. Examples abound. Nike subcontracts its manufacturing, remaining basically a design and marketing firm. Rather than owning facilities in China to manufacture Barbie dolls, Mattel instead outsources the manufacturing to a Hong Kong-based company that has investments in China. Some of the toys in McDonald's Happy Meals or Burger King meals are also subcontracted to a Hong Kong-based manufacturer. And as we note in Chapter 19, H&M purchases all of its fashion merchandise from external suppliers in Europe and Asia, rather than vertically integrating and establishing its own facilities.

FACTORS IN SUPPLY CHAIN STRATEGY

One piece in the supply chain strategy for both manufacturing and services is **operations**: the conversion of inputs into outputs. The success of a global operations strategy depends on four key factors: *compatibility, configuration, coordination,* and *control.*[6]

Compatibility Compatibility in this context is the degree of consistency between the foreign investment decision and the company's competitive strategy. Apple, for instance, realized that although direct manufacturing made sense initially, its strategy dictated that it was more effective at innovation and distribution. Here are some factors that companies must consider as they align their overall strategy with operations:

CONCEPT CHECK

In discussing the process of "Creating Value" in Chapter 12, we explain that a firm that aspires to a position of "Cost Leadership" strives to be the low-cost producer in an industry for a given level of quality. This strategy, we observe, means that the firm adopts one of two tactics, both of which must be compatible with the structure of its value chain: (1) earning a profit higher than industry rivals by selling products at average industry prices or (2) capturing market share by selling products at prices below the industry average.

- *Efficiency/cost*—reduction of operational costs
- *Dependability*—degree of trust in a company's products, its delivery, and its price promises
- *Quality*—performance reliability, good service, speed of delivery, and dependable product maintenance
- *Innovation*—ability to develop new products and ideas
- *Flexibility*—ability of the production process to make a variety of products and adjust the volume of output[7]

Efficiency/Cost Strategies *Cost-minimization strategies* and the drive for global efficiencies force MNEs to establish economies of scale in manufacturing, often by producing in areas with low-cost labor. This is a major reason why many MNEs have established operations in lower-cost emerging markets—a type of FDI known as **offshore manufacturing** or simply "offshoring" (which, again, includes services as well as manufacturing).

Compatibility—the degree of consistency between FDI decisions and a company's competitive strategy.

Total Cost Analysis When employing a cost-minimization strategy, companies tend to overlook important elements—and extra costs—of offshoring, such as shipping distances, extra inventory, political and security risks, and the availability of skilled and educated workers. In other words, when deciding to source abroad, companies should consider the total cost of facilitating the strategy, as opposed to merely the acquisition cost.

Total cost analysis—an in-depth assessment of the complete cost of a transaction that takes into account acquisition, ownership, and disposal costs.

A *total cost analysis* takes into account ownership expenses, such as storing, transporting, and disposing of inventory. In some instances, wages may be such a small percentage of overall costs that employing cheap labor abroad does not effectively save the company money. For example, Nike decided to employ a small contractor in San Francisco to produce some of its made-to-order goods—despite the $15-per-hour rates that were 20 times those of contractors in China—because the overhead costs, such as managing the flow of goods from halfway around the world and the risk of stock-outs and high inventories, were so much higher in China.[8]

Dependability Strategies Many factors besides cost must also be considered. The growing customer demand for *dependability* and prompt deliveries has led companies such as Dell Computer to locate plants closer to customers rather than only in low-wage areas. When a longer supply chain risks late deliveries of components or finished goods, shortening the distance can improve dependability.

Innovation and Quality Strategies Many companies are also responding to the importance of *innovation* and *quality.* One example of innovation is a new technology known as 3D printing. Instead of ink cartridges, 3D printers are filled with materials such as plastic and titanium. After you create a blueprint on your computer you press print and the printer builds up your object one layer at a time. These printers are able to do the job of a manufacturing machine in about the same time, with less waste, and with more opportunities to customize the product.[9] When first investing abroad to take advantage of low-cost labor, companies are not as concerned about innovation. But as more and more of them establish offshore R&D facilities, they are able to move beyond low-end manufacturing.

Quality is a major issue—one that is discussed later in more detail. As long as foreign operations ensure high quality and contribute to innovation, companies will keep setting up operations abroad. However, offshoring and outsourcing requires significant work with partners to ensure high quality products. This is true in any industry, but it is especially true in electronics, as illustrated in the Apple case.

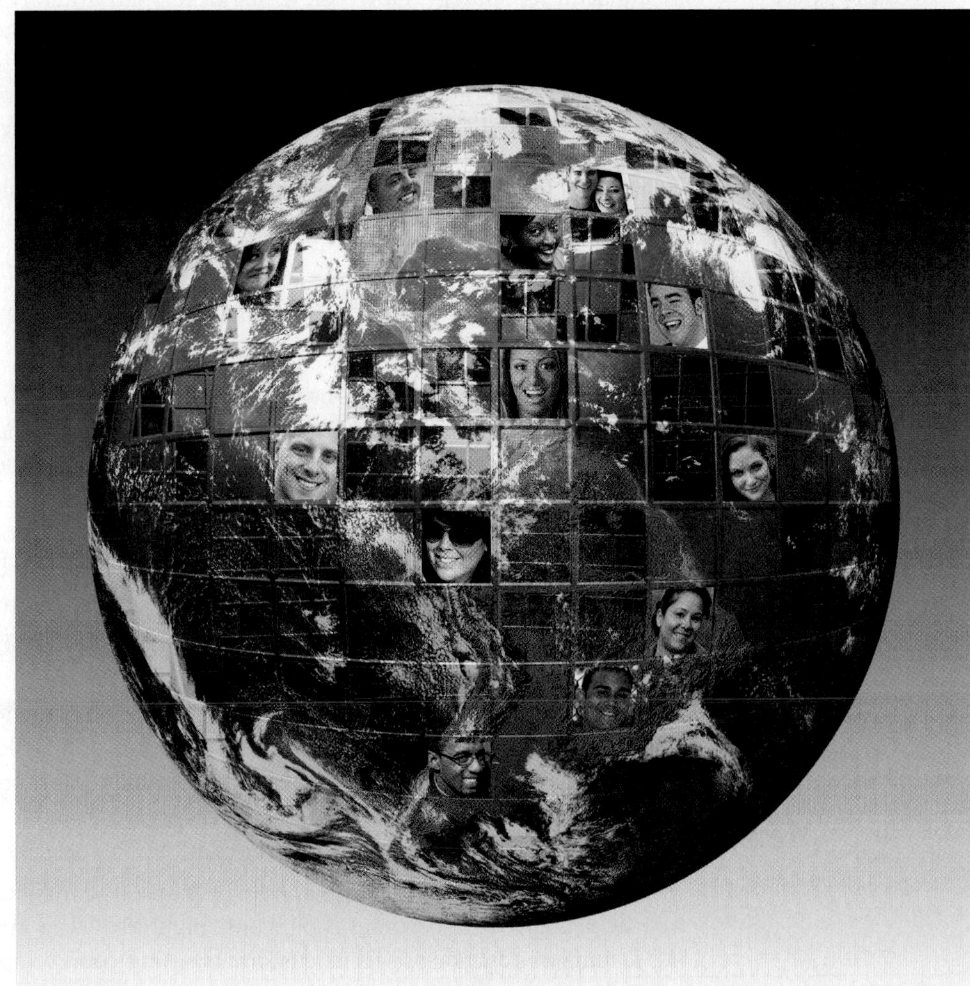

The key to effective offshoring and outsourcing is having a global network of partners with whom to work. Sometimes the network is essential for global teams; other times it's essential to determine where to source inputs, establish operations, or penetrate new markets. The bottom line is: the effectiveness of a company's global supply chain strategy depends on a good network of contacts.

Source: ARENA Creative/Shutterstock

CONCEPT CHECK

In Chapter 12, in discussing "Configuration" as a factor in creating a **value chain,** we explain the importance of identifying the best location economies—those in which operations can be most effective given prevailing economic, political, and cultural conditions. We also analyze several factors that may influence a company's decisions in configuring its value chain (e.g., cost, logistics, economies of scale, buyers' needs).

Flexibility Strategies The need for responsiveness or *flexibility* in the face of national market differences may result in regional manufacturing to serve local markets. It may not be possible to create all products in one location and ship them around the world. Wall's of Unilever, for example, makes ice cream in China, so it is able to develop products that are unique to the Chinese market as well as produce such global brands as the Magnum Bar and the Cornetto. However, Wall's has found that it can produce some of its global brands during the winter when demand is down and ship them to South Africa and Australia during their summer, enabling the use of excess production facilities and reducing costs in markets outside China.[10] Still, despite such flexibility, differences in measurement systems, time zones, and problem-solving approaches can also add unnecessary complexity to the supply chain.

Changes in Strategy As a company's competitive strategies change, so do its manufacturing strategies. In fact, it may adopt different strategies for different product lines, depending on their competitive priorities. For example, to reduce the cost and complexity of its products, Finnish mobile-phone maker Nokia designs phones that contain fewer parts and bases its different models on the same basic components, allowing it to maintain 17 percent profit margins on its low-end phones and 19 percent on its higher-end models—substantial numbers in the highly competitive market for cellular phones.[11] When Apple realized it had to control costs to remain competitive, it changed from being a vertically-integrated company to one that relied on contract manufacturers for managing the flow of materials and the manufacture of hardware.

Priding itself on high quality, Toyota has traditionally relied on manufacturing in Toyota City, Japan, where it is close to suppliers and can ensure high quality and adherence to its manufacturing strategy. However, it has developed a family of vehicles based on a single low-cost platform that is targeted to emerging markets. To keep the prices low enough to compete in the developing world, Toyota has abandoned its traditional practice of sourcing key components from its Japanese plants and is locating factories for these parts in low-wage areas such as South America, Africa, and Southeast Asia, which has helped reduce the costs by 20 to 25 percent. Still, managers are concerned that they may lose control over quality, a situation that became ever more real when Toyota faced significant recalls due to safety matters.[12] Many suggested that the drive for global market share caused the automaker to sacrifice quality and safety.

CONCEPT CHECK

Recall from Chapter 12 our extended discussion of "Global Integration versus Local Responsiveness" as an issue in configuring and coordinating a firm's value chain. We then proceed to explain how efforts to resolve this issue may contribute to the formulation of a **global** strategy or a **multidomestic** strategy for international operations. Here we analyze ways in which this same issue can put pressure on specific strategic decisions about the configuration of manufacturing facilities.

Manufacturing Configuration MNEs must consider three basic configurations in establishing a global manufacturing strategy:

- *Centralized Manufacturing*—Basically a manufacture-and-export strategy that offers a selection of standard, lower-priced products to different markets, centralizing is common for companies new to exporting, and is typically done through their home-country facilities. It is also important for expensive items for which economies of scale in manufacturing are important and for which there is little need for localization for consumption in different markets, such as aircraft. Samsonite, which will be described in more detail in the closing case, is a U.S. based luggage maker that has recently but steadily established itself in Asian markets as a brand to contend with, closely following its conquest of the European baggage market.

Manufacturing configuration:
- Centralized manufacturing in one country
- Manufacturing facilities in specific regions to service those regions
- Multidomestic facilities in each country

- *Regional Manufacturing*—These facilities serve customers within a specific region, as Samsonite initially did in Europe with its production facilities in Belgium, and as Toyota is doing in developing countries. Dell assembles computers in Brazil and exports them to different markets in South America—another example of a regional strategy, since it doesn't assemble computers in every country where it sells them.
- *Multidomestic Manufacturing*—Market expansion in individual countries, especially when the demand there becomes significant, might entail this approach in which a firm manufactures products close to its customers, using country-specific manufacturing facilities

It is far more efficient for Boeing to utilize its manufacturing facilities in Everett, Washington (U.S.) to assemble the 777 and 787 Dreamliner (shown in this photo) than it would be to set up final assembly in multiple plants in different countries.
Source: Stephen Brashear/Stringer/Getty Images

to meet local needs.[13] This is the approach that Philips, the Dutch electronics company, used after World War II. Because there were barriers to entry in European countries, and in order to maintain market share in the individual countries, Philips had to manufacture on a country-by-country basis. The reduction of trade barriers lessens the need to have manufacturing facilities in every country, but country size may result in firms establishing manufacturing facilities to supply the local market. Unless an MNE has such facilities in every country it operates in, it must combine exporting with manufacturing. In reality, MNEs choose a combination of these approaches depending on their product strategies.

Offshore manufacturing—any investment that takes place in a country other than the home country.

Offshore Manufacturing Once a company decides to manufacture outside its home market, it is engaging in offshore manufacturing, as was the case when Apple set up manufacturing facilities in Cork, Ireland and Singapore. The 1960s and 1970s saw a sharp escalation in offshore manufacturing as one electronics company after another set up production facilities in the Far East, mostly in Taiwan and Singapore. Those locations were attractive because of low labor costs, the availability of cheap materials and components, and proximity to markets. Even the athletic-shoe market left the United States for Korea and Taiwan. As wages rose in Korea, however, manufacturing began to shift to other low-cost countries, such as Indonesia, Malaysia, Thailand, and Vietnam. Piaggio, for instance, could have manufactured Vespa motorbikes in Italy and exported them to Vietnam, but it made more sense to manufacture them in Vietnam, with its cheaper costs, manageable transportation and tariffs, and a good market for the product.

China in particular has become the hot spot for manufacturing. Often called the world's factory, its output is so large and wide-ranging that it exerts deflationary pressure around the world on products such as textiles, TVs, furniture, auto parts, and mobile phones. As the world's largest manufacturer, China accounted for over 20 percent of world manufacturing in 2011, followed by the United States, Japan, Germany, and Italy. This is a big jump since 1991, when it ranked only #8 in the world.[14] Many MNEs set up operations there in the 1980s to capitalize on its huge population and growing demand.

Luggage manufacturer Samsonite is among the companies that have found it more cost-effective to manufacture products in China—and not just for the Chinese market, but for export to the rest of the world as well. More recently, it shifted a majority of its manufacturing

to India. As will be explained in the closing case, in India Samsonite works with a chosen few strategic partners to achieve its ends. Still other companies, such as Hewlett-Packard, Microsoft, and Motorola, have looked beyond simply outsourcing manufacturing to China and have established R&D centers within the country. IBM and General Motors are even using the country as a global center for their procurement operations.[15]

Countries also often specialize in the production of parts or final goods—a process known as *rationalization.* When Samsonite opened a new factory in the 1980s in Hénin-Beaumont, France, to manufacture the Prestige Attaché and a few other products, it was able to remove their production from its facility in Oudenaarde, Belgium, where it could then focus on its new Oyster product line. This strategy of specializing the manufacture of certain products in certain plants eventually made it feasible to export all production to a centralized European warehouse, from which Samsonite could then distribute its whole product line to retailers all over Europe. As the scale of production increases, it is common for companies to specialize in the production of certain products rather than make all of its product lines in one facility.

CONCEPT CHECK

We discuss control in Chapter 16 from the perspective of organization structure, coordination and control systems, and organizational culture. In explaining "Coordination and Control Systems," we explain that, regardless of its structure, the MNE must develop coordination and control mechanisms to prevent duplication of efforts, to coordinate resource allocation, and to ensure that company-wide operations benefit from ideas generated anywhere in the organization.

Corporate management often requires additional data to coordinate and control operations. In Chapter 16, we discuss some of the key types of information supplied by IT.

Coordination is linking or integrating activities into a unified system.

Control systems, such as organizational structure and performance measurement systems, ensure that managers implement company strategies.

Sourcing—the process of a firm having inputs supplied to it from outside suppliers (both domestic and foreign) for the production process.

Coordination and Control Coordination and control fit well together. *Coordination* is the linking or integrating of activities into a unified system.[16] The activities include everything along the global supply chain, from purchasing to warehousing to shipment. It is hard to coordinate supplier relations and logistics activities if those issues are not considered when the manufacturing configuration is set up.

Once the company determines the manufacturing configuration it will use, it must adopt a control system to ensure that company strategies are carried out. *Control* can be the measuring of performance so a firm can respond appropriately to changing conditions. Another aspect of a control structure is the organizational structure, discussed in more detail in Chapter 16.

SUPPLIER NETWORKS

Global sourcing and production strategies can be better understood by taking a look at Figure 18.2. **Sourcing** is the process of obtaining a supply of inputs (raw materials and parts) for production. The figure illustrates the basic operating-environment choices (home country or any foreign country) by stage in the production process (sourcing of raw materials and parts, manufacture and assembly of final products). Global sourcing is the first step in the process of materials management, which includes sourcing, inventory management, and transportation between suppliers, manufacturers, and customers. Figure 18.2 is a simplified version of Figure 18.1 in that it focuses on the domestic vs. international options of sourcing, operations, and sales. From a supplier network perspective, auto companies are good examples. Ford assembles some of its models in Hermosillo, Mexico and ships them into the United States for end-use consumers. For many years, some of these models were designed by Mazda, a Japanese company, and used some Japanese parts. U.S.-made parts were shipped to Mexico for final assembly and sale in the United States and Mexico. For Mexican assembly, some of the parts came from the United States, some from Japan, and a small percentage from Mexico. However, the alliance between Ford and Mazda became a casualty of the global financial crisis, and the two companies have basically parted ways.

Case: A Loaf of Whole-Grain White Bread Although global sourcing is often linked with high-tech and complex products, the process affects even the low-cost products we use and consume every day. Take U.S.-based Sara Lee's whole-grain white bread. To make this bread, Sara Lee acquires ingredients from a variety of suppliers, nearly a third of which are located in foreign countries. Its guar gum, used to keep the bread moist, is a powder that comes from the guar-plant seedpods grown in India. Calcium propionate, a powdery mold inhibitor that is manufactured in several countries, is sourced in the Netherlands. Honey, used as a natural sweetener, is purchased from suppliers in the United States, China, Vietnam, Brazil, Uruguay, India, Canada, Mexico, and Argentina. Sara Lee sources from several different countries besides the United States because the U.S. supply can often run short. Flour enrichments to

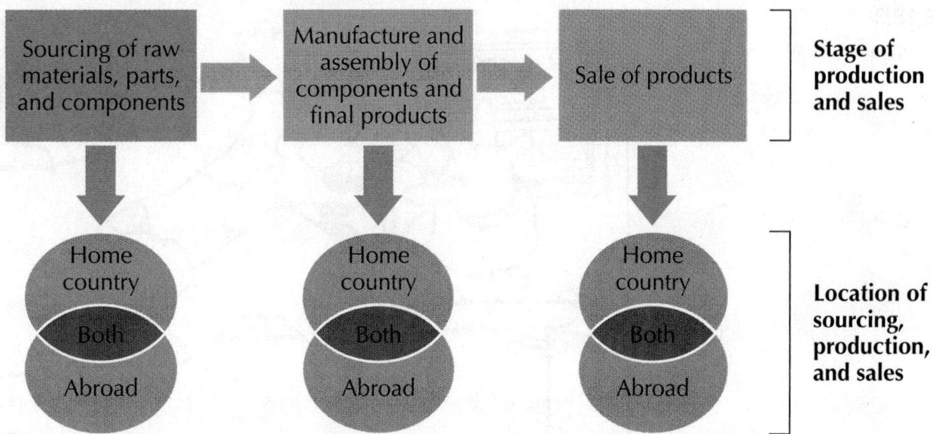

FIGURE 18.2 When a company wants to *source* raw materials, parts, or components as a function of its global strategy, it's faced with some key decisions. It may, for example, decide to source components at home, assemble them abroad, and then export the final product to the home market, to foreign markets, or to both.

replenish the vitamins lost in the milling process come from China. Due to industry consolidation, suppliers of flour enrichments are limited. Beta-carotene, an artificial coloring used to provide color to the bread and crust, is sourced from Switzerland, though it is available in many countries. Vitamin D3 is sourced from China, while wheat gluten comes from several countries, including France, Poland, Russia, the Netherlands, and Australia.[17]

With its ingredient sources spread all over the globe, Sara Lee must manage its supply chain carefully to ensure timeliness, safety, and quality. So it has centralized its global ingredients purchasing by consolidating its previously scattered procurement operations into a single division known as the "nerve center" located at company headquarters. Purchasing specialists monitor weather patterns, commodity trends, and energy prices. They also communicate and work closely with Sara Lee's diverse base of suppliers—in some cases, even investing money in suppliers' operations to ensure that they are complying with U.S. food safety standards.[18]

GLOBAL SOURCING

Companies can manufacture parts internally or purchase them from external manufacturers.

The book *The World is Flat* notes three flatteners relevant to this discussion: #5, Outsourcing; #6, Offshoring; and #7, Supply-Chaining. Flattener #6, which was discussed above, related to manufacturing configuration whereby a firm could decide where to set up its manufacturing operations worldwide. Once the company decided to move offshore from its home country and manufacture abroad, it was engaged in "offshoring." That is what Apple did when it shifted some of its manufacturing to a factory in Cork, Ireland. In Figure 18.2, that is illustrated by the decision to manufacture and assemble components and final products abroad.

On the sourcing side, a company can manufacture parts internally. Of course, a company can purchase parts from external (unrelated) manufacturers as well. It can also assemble its own products internally or subcontract to external firms; the manufacture of parts and final assembly may take place in its home country, the country in which it is trying to sell the product, or a third country.[19]

The term *sourcing* is used in a variety of ways. **Outsourcing**, for instance, refers to a situation in which one company externalizes a process or function to another business. This most often occurs with the IT function but is also being used in other areas, such as research, service centers, and even accounting and tax functions. In addition to *offshore manufacturing*, another type of offshoring occurs when a company moves part of its business processes outside its home country but internalizes the function rather than outsourcing it to another firm. An example would be setting up its own R&D facilities in another country, or, say, a U.S.-based public accounting firm setting up a branch of its tax practice in India. Outsourcing can be domestic or offshore. Sometimes the entire operations can shipped offshore using talent hired in that location, but the people who were working in the operations don't necessarily go offshore. They might be reassigned in the company or let go.

FIGURE 18.3

Source: Jack Corbett/CartoonStock, Ltd.

"No, no, Eddy- it's your job that's moving to Mexico, not you!"

Another way to look at outsourcing is Flattener #7, supply chaining. This is where a company decides to outsource its parts, or components, or products—even its manufacturing—to an external company. One example is Walmart, which buys its products from external suppliers, both domestic and international. Another example is an auto company, such as Toyota, buying its parts from external companies, such as Japanese parts-manufacturer DENSO. Supply chaining is slightly different from traditional outsourcing, which focuses more on a business process, but far more extensive and complicated since it relates more directly to the final product sold to customers. Apple's use of Foxconn as a **contract manufacturer** is technically supply-chaining, although it is similar to outsourcing since the entire manufacturing process is being handled by someone else. In Figure 18.1, a contract manufacture like Foxconn not only assumes the upstream processes, but it also takes on most of the operations management functions since it also does the assembly.

Using domestic sources for raw materials and components allows a company to avoid problems with language differences, distance, currency, politics, and tariffs, as well as other problems.

Sourcing in the home country enables companies to avoid numerous problems such as language differences, long distances, lengthy supply lines, exchange-rate fluctuations, wars and insurrections, strikes, politics, tariffs, and complex transportation channels. However, for many companies, domestic sources may be unavailable or more expensive than foreign sources. In Japan, foreign procurement is critical because nearly all of the country's uranium, bauxite, nickel, crude oil, iron ore, copper, and coking coal are imported, as well as about 30 percent of its agricultural products. Japanese trading companies came into being expressly to acquire the raw materials needed to fuel Japan's manufacturing.

Procter & Gamble has also found that sourcing chemicals from a variety of suppliers abroad is necessary to provide flexibility in a global environment of volatile energy prices. By diversifying its chemical supplier base, P&G plans on being able to switch procurement between different suppliers as energy prices shift in different regions.[20]

Companies outsource abroad to lower costs and improve quality, among other reasons.

Why Global Sourcing? Companies pursue global sourcing strategies for a number of reasons:

- To reduce costs through cheaper labor, laxer work rules, and lower land and facilities costs
- To improve quality
- To increase exposure to worldwide technology
- To improve the delivery-of-supplies process

- To strengthen the reliability of supply by supplementing domestic suppliers with foreign ones
- To gain access to materials that are only available abroad, possibly because of technical specifications or product capabilities
- To establish a presence in a foreign market
- To satisfy offset requirements
- To react to competitors' offshore sourcing practices[21]

These reasons are similar to the benefits to FDI discussed in Chapter 15. Whether the suppliers are company-owned or independent firms, MNEs can take advantage of the location-specific advantages in foreign countries.

In some ways, however, global sourcing is more expensive than domestic sourcing. For example, transportation and communications cost more, and companies may have to pay broker and agent fees. Given the longer length of supply lines, it often takes more time to get components from abroad, and lead times are less certain. This problem increases inventory carrying costs and makes it more difficult to get parts to the production site in time. If imported components come in with errors and need to be reworked, the cost per unit will rise, and some components may have to be shipped back to the supplier.

Concerns in Global Sourcing One concern with global sourcing is quality and safety. In April 2013, more than 1,000 people were killed when a garment factory collapsed in Bangladesh, the second-largest clothing exporter after China. The factory which housed many garments that supply the "fast fashion" industry popularized by Zara and Mango had been given the green light by the government to continue operating even though cracks were showing up in the walls and foundation. Now every retailer that buys fashions built in factories like the one that collapsed are trying to figure out what they can do to pick their suppliers better and disclose what they are doing to help protect workers. As the U.S. government announced that it was suspending preferential trade treatment for Bangladesh due to poor labor practices, several U.S. companies such as Walmart and the Gap were preparing to set up a $50 million fund to improve worker conditions in Bangladesh's garment factories over a five-year period. In Bangladesh, however, the anger was over the government's failure to enforce safety codes, not the actions of the companies buying the garments that were being manufactured.

A major challenge with these issues is finding the source of a given problem. Supply chains have become so long and complex that buyers can't be sure who the original producer is.[22] In Chapter 11, we mentioned the problem IKEA faced when it was accused of exploiting child labor by purchasing carpets in India and Pakistan from suppliers who employed children. IKEA had to make a more concerted effort to find out what suppliers were doing and require them to live up to high hiring standards so as to eliminate child labor abuse.

CONCEPT CHECK

In discussing "Taking Control: Foreign Direct Investment" in Chapter 15, we define internalization as the self-handling of operations (that is, by keeping them internal to the company). We point out the genesis of this concept in transactions cost theory, which holds that when there's a decision to be made between handling something internally and contracting with someone else to handle it, companies should opt for the lower-cost alternative. As we suggest later in this chapter, make-or-buy decisions invite the application of this principle.

Companies must also pay attention to natural disasters that can affect countries where they get their goods. The earthquake and tsunami that hit Japan in 2011 had an ill effect on those who relied on goods from factories that were destroyed. The auto industry was hit particularly hard. For example, many automakers—including General Motors, Peugeot-Citroën, and Ford—relied on a supply of airflow sensors from the Hitachi factory in Japan, which incurred a great deal of damage during the disaster. Other parts, such as the LCD chips used to monitor fuel, were also hard to come by. One estimate claimed that "about one-third of vehicle production globally [was] expected to grind to a halt." Automakers soon realized how quickly their supply chain could be disrupted due to forces outside their control.[23]

MAJOR SOURCING CONFIGURATIONS

Vertical Integration **Vertical integration** occurs when a company owns the entire supplier network, or at least a significant part of it as was the case with Apple before it began to outsource to suppliers and use contract manufacturers. The company may have to purchase raw materials from outside suppliers, but it produces the most expensive parts itself.

Major outsourcing configurations include
- Vertical integration
- Outsourcing through industrial clusters
- Other outsourcing

Integrating vertically can reduce transaction costs (finding suppliers, selling output, negotiating contracts, monitoring contracts, settling disputes with unrelated companies) by internalizing the different levels in the value chain.[24]

Industrial Clusters Outsourcing through **industrial clusters** is an alternative way to reduce transportation and transaction costs. Under clustering, buyers and suppliers locate close to each other to facilitate doing business. For example, Dell established an assembly operation in the Multimedia Supercorridor in Malaysia, where it is close to its key suppliers.

Keiretsus Japanese *keiretsus* are groups of independent companies that work together to manage the flow of goods and services along the entire value chain.[25] Toyota's highly coordinated supplier network is among the most successful and well known of the Japanese keiretsus and a good example of industrial clustering. It borders on vertical integration because parts suppliers tend to set up shop close to Toyota's assembly operations, and Toyota usually has an ownership interest in them. The trusted relationships among companies in the keiretsu allow the companies to work closely together from the design phase onward, often sharing proprietary technology but also allowing each other the first right of refusal when new technology is developed. The system began to unravel when France's Renault purchased a struggling Nissan, and the new owner disbanded the Nissan keiretsu and shifted to open-source bids. Toyota followed suit to a limited extent. Changes in its global markets and price pressures resulting from the high cost of steel and the strong yen forced Toyota to start looking beyond its closely knit supplier base in Japan by pressuring its *keiretsu* suppliers to benchmark against China's cheaper suppliers. If the suppliers can't achieve low enough pricing, Toyota will be forced to court suppliers outside Japan.[26]

CONCEPT CHECK

As we explain in Chapter 15, the **resource-based view** of the firm holds that every company has a unique combination of competencies. Here we suggest that make-or-buy decisions may depend on the extent to which a firm embraces this view, which may prompt it to concentrate internally on those activities that best fit its competencies while depending on other firms to supply products, services, or support activities for which it has lesser competency.

THE MAKE-OR-BUY DECISION

Make or buy—outsource or supply parts from internal production.

If MNEs outsource parts instead of sourcing them from internal production, they need to determine the degree of involvement with suppliers.

When it comes to production activities, MNE managers struggle with a *make-or-buy decision*: Which should be performed internally and which could be subcontracted to independent companies? In the case of subcontracting, a company must also decide whether the activities should be carried out in the home market or abroad. This involves developing a strategy that involves the three flatteners: outsourcing, offshoring, and supply-chaining.

In deciding whether to make or buy, MNEs can focus on those parts of production that are critical to the product and that they are particularly good at making. They can outsource parts when suppliers have a distinct comparative advantage, such as greater scale, lower cost structure, or stronger performance incentives. They can also use outsourcing as an implied threat to underperforming employees: Improve, or we move the business elsewhere.[27] The MNE must determine the design and manufacturing capabilities of potential suppliers compared to its own capabilities. If the supplier has a clear advantage, management needs to decide what it would cost to catch up to the best suppliers and whether it would make sense to do so.

Point **Should Firms Outsource Innovation?**

Point **Yes** A firm should outsource innovative processes if it can maintain focus and position itself effectively in the roiling high-tech and electronics industries. More and more companies are coming to realize the advantages of doing so. Suppliers are taking on such responsibilities as designing and manufacturing prototypes, converting them into workable products, upgrading mature products, conducting quality tests, putting together user manuals, and selecting parts vendors. The designs of 65 percent of PC notebooks and those of 70 percent of PDAs are outsourced. Companies such as Dell, Motorola, and Philips are buying complete designs from Asian developers. Even Boeing collaborated with an Indian company to develop software for its 787 Dreamliner jet.

Companies willing to outsource some R&D and technological designs can experience enormous cost savings. Although innovation is key to remaining competitive, more and more firms find that their internal R&D teams aren't producing results that justify the large investments in them. Thus, in the face of demanding customers and relentless competition that pressures margins, managers must find a way to reduce costs or increase R&D productivity.

Outsourcing is a viable solution. Companies can save millions by simply buying designs rather than developing them in-house. For instance, using a predesigned platform for cell phones can reduce the costs of developing them from scratch—which takes approximately $10 million and 150 engineers—by 70 percent. Furthermore, demands by retailers and customers as well as uncertain future market trends require developing a costly range of product models. Third-party developers are better equipped to handle such costs, spreading them over many buyers and possessing the expertise to develop a variety of models from a single basic design.

Outsourcing also helps get products to market faster, which is crucial where products become commodities in a matter of months. Hewlett-Packard claims that by working with partners and suppliers on designs, it now gets a new concept to the market in 60 percent less time. Critics worry that by outsourcing technology, companies are outsourcing their fonts of competitive advantage; still, outsourcing certain design and development processes allows firms to focus more on their true core competencies. Few, if any, companies plan on completely eliminating their own R&D forces, and most insist they will continue with the more proprietary R&D work.

No one company can manage everything in-house. Even the Chief Technology Officer of Nokia—a company that once prided itself on developing almost everything on its own—has stated, "Nobody can master it all." In fact, a recent survey of MNEs found that almost three-quarters of respondents believed they could boost innovation dramatically by collaborating with outsiders, even competitors.[28] The companies that will survive in the future are those able to efficiently and effectively control a network of partners and suppliers around the world.

Should Firms Outsource Innovation?

Counterpoint

No When it comes to outsourcing R&D, design, and development work, how does a firm know where to draw the line? How does it determine what is core intellectual property and what is commodity technology? The truth is, outsourcing turns the former into the latter, which becomes available to most anyone. Look at Toshiba. By working with South Korean chipmakers to develop its DRAM memory chips, it allowed the technology behind these components to become commoditized and is now struggling to stay ahead.[29]

Competitive advantage often depends on trade secrets that set a firm apart from its rivals. Outsourcing innovation enhances the risk that it will pass on these proprietary technologies to suppliers and partners, thereby fostering new competitors. Because suppliers rarely cooperate solely with one customer, the R&D they do for one can easily be transferred to another. Such was the case for Japanese company Sharp, which worked closely with suppliers to develop a "sixth-generation" plant for making larger flat panels for televisions. Unfortunately, its suppliers also work closely with Sharp's rivals, many of them Taiwanese companies, and not long after the completion of the plant, these competitors were constructing their own "Gen-6" facilities. Sharp now takes extra precautions, such as secretly rewriting software on some equipment and fixing machinery in-house rather than having suppliers do it. However, it may be too late since Foxconn of Taiwan bought 10 percent of Sharp in 2012 and one of its factories in Japan that manufactures LCD displays.[30]

Suppliers and partners might also take the information and technology that have been shared with them and become competitors themselves. After Motorola hired Taiwanese company BenQ Corp. to design and manufacture its mobile phones, BenQ began selling the phones under its own brand

Counterpoint

name in the highly competitive Chinese market, causing Motorola to terminate the contract.

Perhaps more important than giving rise to new competitors is losing competitive edge and investment incentive. Although some assert that outsourcing certain development and design work allows companies to focus more on new innovative technologies, it more often prompts companies to decrease internal R&D investments and become lazy in their pursuit of future breakthroughs, relying too much on suppliers to do their work. Jim Andrew, senior vice president of Boston Consulting Group, warns, "If the innovation starts residing in the suppliers, you could incrementalize yourself to the point where there isn't much left."

High-tech and electronics firms that outsource their innovative processes risk losing the essence of their actual business, becoming mere marketing fronts for others. It also sends a bad message to investors, who might have difficulty finding intrinsic value in a company that owns little true intellectual property and whose profits from successful products are most likely being paid out in licensing fees to the companies that actually developed them.

Much has been made of manufacturing outsourcing in the past few decades, but outsourcing innovation poses a potentially greater threat to high-tech firms that see it as a shortcut to cost savings. Looking to immediate savings is shortsighted, and firms that do so will ultimately damage their competitive positions and lose viability as true industry players.[31]

1. Now that Apple purchases its iPhones and iPads from Foxconn, should it let Foxconn develop the new technology that goes in Apple's products so that they can focus more on marketing? Why or why not?

SUPPLIER RELATIONS

Supplier relationships are very important but sometimes complicated, especially for MNEs trying to manage them around the world. As noted on the Web site of John Deere, the company's supplier base is broad, reflecting the diversity of its global markets. In order to maintain a good relationship with suppliers, John Deere has a supplier code of conduct that is translated into 18 different languages. It seems like most MNCs with significant supplier bases outside of their home countries, especially in developing countries, have supplier codes of conduct. Apple's supplier responsibility report for 2012 focuses on empowering workers, labor & human rights, health & safety, the environment, and accountability. The foundation of the supplier code of conduct is to ensure that workers have the right to safe and ethical working conditions. The report discusses supplier accountability, including their audit program, and it also discloses its 17 final assembly facilities, including who the supplier is and what they assemble, and its top 200 suppliers which represent 97 percent of its procurement expenditures worldwide.

Of course, not all supplier relationships are as collaborative as those of Apple and Foxconn. Sometimes large customers can use their strong market presence and buying power to place additional demands on suppliers. For many years, GM has pressured its U.S. suppliers to lower costs by certain set percentages each year and then pass those cost savings on to GM via lower prices. As it moved to increase production in China, some suppliers felt pressured to set up facilities in China to accommodate GM.[32]

The relationships MNEs establish with their suppliers are based largely on their individual competitive strategies, the nature of their products, the competitive environment they face, supplier capabilities, and the level of experience and trust they share with them. MNEs must consider these factors as they determine what kind of supplier relationship will best meet their needs.

THE PURCHASING FUNCTION

Global progression in the purchasing function:

- Domestic purchasing only
- Foreign buying based on need
- Foreign buying as part of a procurement strategy
- Integration of global procurement strategy

The purchasing agent is the link between a company's outsourcing decision and its supplier relationships. Just as companies go through stages of globalization, so does the purchasing agent's scope of responsibilities. Typically, purchasing goes through four phases before becoming "global":

1. Domestic purchasing only
2. Foreign buying based on need
3. Foreign buying as part of procurement strategy
4. Integration of global procurement strategy[33]

Phase 4 occurs when the company realizes the benefits that result from the integration and coordination of purchasing on a global basis and is most applicable to the MNE—as opposed to, say, the exporter.

When purchasing becomes this global, MNEs often face the centralize/decentralize dilemma. Should they allow each subsidiary to make every purchasing decision, or should they centralize all or some of them? The primary benefits of decentralization include increased production-facility control over purchases, better responsiveness to facility needs, and more effective use of local suppliers. The primary benefits of centralization are increased leverage with suppliers, better prices, eliminating administrative duplication, allowing purchasers to develop specialized knowledge in purchasing techniques, reducing the number of orders processed, and enabling purchasing to build solid supplier relationships.[34]

Case: Electrolux Swedish appliance manufacturer Electrolux has adopted a global purchasing strategy. Despite the worldwide downturn in 2009, Electrolux had a good second quarter due largely to its cost-reduction efforts. One aspect of the strategy was offshoring production to low-cost countries. Another was the reduction of personnel costs. Still another was lowered purchasing and product costs through efficient global purchasing, which cut the cost of buying raw materials and components.[35]

Sourcing strategies in the global context:

- Assign domestic buyers for foreign purchasing
- Use foreign subsidiaries or business agents
- Establish international purchasing offices
- Assign the responsibility for global sourcing to a specific business unit or units
- Integrate and coordinate worldwide sourcing

Major Sourcing Strategies Companies pursue five major sourcing strategies as they move into phases 3 and 4 in the preceding list. Moving from the simple to the complex (where there is no difference between domestic and foreign sources), they are:

1. Assigning domestic buyer(s) for international purchasing
2. Using foreign subsidiaries or business agents
3. Establishing international purchasing offices
4. Assigning responsibility for global sourcing to a specific business unit or units
5. Integrating and coordinating global sourcing[36]

INFORMATION TECHNOLOGY AND GLOBAL SUPPLY-CHAIN MANAGEMENT

A key to making the global supply chain work is a good information system.

A comprehensive supply-chain strategy is most effective with a strong commitment to information technology (IT), which aids in quick and efficient production, proficient inventory management, effective supplier communication, and customer satisfaction. In *The World is Flat*, Flattener #3 is workflow software.[37] Basically encompassing the standard protocols such as HTTP that allow computers to work with each other and business processes such as SAP, workflow software is critical for the supply-chain management process. We'll discuss some of these protocols and processes below and then examine how other "flatteners" that build on the technology platform are important in global supply chain management.

ELECTRONIC DATA INTERCHANGE (EDI)

EDI (electronic data interchange)—the electronic linkage of suppliers, customers, and third-party intermediaries to expedite documents and financial flows.

The key to making a global information system work is getting the relevant information in a timely manner. Apple, for example, has established a B2B (business to business) gateway that all of its suppliers are required to use, which basically allows suppliers to share electronic data with Apple. Many companies use **electronic data interchange (EDI)** to link suppliers, manufacturers, customers, and intermediaries, especially in the food-manufacturing and car-making industries, in which suppliers replenish in high volumes.

In a global context, EDI has been used to link exporters with customs to facilitate the quick processing of customs forms, thus speeding up cross-border deliveries. Walmart is known for its revolutionary use of EDI to connect its global suppliers to its inventory ordering system.[38]

ENTERPRISE RESOURCE PLANNING/MATERIAL REQUIREMENTS PLANNING

ERP (enterprise resource planning)—software that can link information flows from different parts of a business and from different geographic areas.

The next wave of technology affecting the global supply chain was the implementation of IT packages known as **enterprise resource planning (ERP)**. Companies such as Oracle, Baan, PeopleSoft, and German software giant SAP introduced software to integrate everything in the back office (the part of the business dealing with internal matters, as opposed to the front office, which deals with the customer). ERP is essential for bringing together the information inside the firm and from different geographic areas, but its inability to tie in to the customer and take advantage of e-commerce has been a problem.

Material requirements planning (MRP)—computerized information system that addresses complex inventory situations and calculates the demand for parts from the production schedules of the companies that use the parts.

An extension of ERP is *material requirements planning* (MRP), a computerized information system that addresses complex inventory situations and calculates the demand for parts from the production schedules of the companies that use them. DENSO, the Japanese auto parts supplier for Toyota, uses MRP extensively to calculate the demand for parts from the production schedules of the non-Toyota companies it supplies.

RADIO FREQUENCY ID (RFID)

A newer wave has recently swept the technology scene in the form of *radio frequency ID (RFID)*, a system that labels a product with an electronic tag that stores and transmits information on the product's origin, destination, and quantity. When electronic readers scan the tags by means of radio waves, the data can be rewritten or captured and sent to a computer-network database, which collects, organizes, stores, and moves the data—often in conjunction with an ERP system.

Radio frequency ID (RFID)—a system that labels products with an electronic tag, which stores and transmits information regarding the product's origin, destination, and quantity.

Such real-time information allows manufacturers, suppliers, and distributors to keep track of products and components throughout their manufacturing processes and transportation networks, resulting in greater efficiency and more visibility along the supply chain. The use of RFID in the Las Vegas airport to track luggage has resulted in more accurate sorting, better tracking, and fewer lost bags.[39] In 2003, Walmart mandated that its top suppliers use RFID tags at the pallet level, predicting it could save billions of dollars for the entire retail industry through supply-chain efficiencies.[40] In 2010, it announced it would experiment with placing removable "smart tags" on individual garments such as jeans and underwear that would allow workers to use handheld scanners to identify exact inventory on the shelves or in the backroom. There are concerns over privacy, but RFID tags placed on removable labels or packaging is not as invasive as imbedding them in the clothing, which could then be tracked anywhere.[41] Apple even has an RFID app which can be purchased on iTunes and downloaded to an iPhone or iPad to display the location status of taggable items.

E-COMMERCE

E-commerce—the use of the Internet to join together suppliers with companies and companies with customers.

The next technological wave linking together the parts of the global supply chain is **e-commerce.** To illustrate, Dell's factory in Ireland supplies custom-built PCs all over Europe. Customers transmit orders to Dell via call centers or its Web site, and the company relays the demand for components to its suppliers. Trucks deliver the components to the factory and haul off the completed computers within a few hours. All of this activity, of course, is made possible by the Internet. Since Walmart moved its EDI-based infrastructure from traditional but expensive value-added networks (VANs) to the Internet, it has been good news for thousands of worldwide vendors. All of their transactions with Walmart are now on the Web—a substantial cost savings for the MNE and its vendors.[42]

CONCEPT CHECK

In discussing "Contemporary Approaches to Organizational Change" in Chapter 16, we observe that the Internet, which accelerates the spread of ideas throughout an organization, has become a "metaphor" for organization structure. In other words, as a supremely efficient and effective means of organizing global knowledge, resources, and people, the Internet has inspired many people to imagine new ways of effectively organizing a company's resources (especially its people). We also point out the ironic attractiveness of a self-regulating organizational model that features no formal organizational hierarchy.

Most experts agree that the Internet has revolutionized communications across all levels of the global supply chain, though at different speeds in different areas. The number of worldwide Internet users rose from 420 million in 2000 to more than 2.4 billion in 2013, a growth of 566 percent. There are more internet users in Asia than any other region of the world, but given the large populations in Asia and the small percentage of internet users to the total population, there should be significant growth in Asia in the future.[43]

Extranets and Intranets Dell has established an **extranet** for its suppliers—a linkage to its information system via the Internet—so they can organize production and delivery of parts. Plugged into Dell's customer database, the suppliers can keep track of changes in demand; plugged into the ordering process, they can track the progress of their orders from factory to doorstep.[44]

The real attraction of the Internet in global supply-chain management is that it not only helps automate and speed up internal processes in a company through an **intranet**, but also spreads efficiency gains to the business systems of its customers and suppliers.[45] The new technology wave is **private technology exchange (PTX)**, an online collaboration model that brings manufacturers, distributors, value-added resellers, and customers together through the Internet to execute trading transactions and share information about demand, production, availability, and more.

Private technology exchange (PTX)—an online collaboration model that brings manufacturers, distributors, value-added resellers, and customers together to execute trading transactions.

"The Digital Divide" The challenge in global supply-chain management is that although some networks can be managed through the Internet, others—particularly in emerging markets—cannot because of the lack of technology or low Internet speeds. The use of the

Internet varies by location and by industry. North America is at least five years ahead of some countries in Europe, especially Eastern Europe, but it is behind Asia, especially in some key infrastructures. Industries such as computing and electronics, aerospace and defense, and motor vehicles are blasting ahead; industrial equipment, food and agriculture, heavy industries, and consumer goods are lagging.

This so-called "digital divide" has created difficulties for companies such as U.S.-based Newmont Mining Corporation. Newmont has struggled to implement its ordering and inventory management information system with its suppliers in Indonesia, who have to rent computers in different towns to even access the Internet and whose managers are typically former farmers who likely have never even used email.[46] It is no coincidence that the leaders in e-commerce are those who have invested significant amounts of money over the years in IT—notably in the defense and motor-vehicle industries.

The preceding discussion shows that IT can help companies manage their global supply chains but it must be carefully integrated into their overall strategy. Because IT is highly technical as well as a support to a company's lines of business, it is often difficult to align it with company strategy. This is especially true in the international arena, where personnel in different countries may be accustomed to their own IT systems and may have difficulty adopting a global IT format that will allow them to achieve some economies of scale as well as fully integrate it in the overall strategy.

QUALITY

Quality—meeting or exceeding the expectations of a customer.

An important aspect of all levels of the global supply chain is quality management, for service firms as well as manufacturers. **Quality** can be defined here as meeting or exceeding customer expectations. More specifically, it is conformance to specifications, value, fitness for use, support (provided by the company), and psychological impressions (image).[47] Quality involves careful design of a product or service and ensuring that an organization's systems can consistently produce the design.[48] For example, no one wants to buy computer software that has a lot of bugs, but the need to get software to market quickly may mean speeding it there as soon as possible and correcting errors later. In the airline industry, service is key. Some airlines, such as Singapore Air, have developed a worldwide reputation for excellence in service—a distinct competitive advantage, especially when trying to attract the business traveler.

Case: Car Quality Quality—or the lack thereof—can have serious ramifications for a company. Ford lost around $1 billion in 2001 due to faulty Firestone tires on its Explorers. Because of this and other quality problems, many automakers began to look at the way the Japanese firms, especially Toyota, manufactured their automobiles with higher efficiency and fewer defects. In the mid-2000s, accidents resulting from the sudden acceleration of Toyota cars called even its defect-free reputation into question. Although no final source of the problem was found (including potential driver error), this was the first of many defects Toyota admitted to. Nevertheless, its nearly perfect report card set off a flight to quality by all auto manufactures trying to emulate its success in ridding autos of defects. In 2011, J.D. Power & Associates named three assembly plants as recipients of its highest award for producing models yielding the fewest defects and malfunctions: Toyota plants in Canada and Japan that produced the Lexus, and a Honda plant in Greensburg, Indiana (U.S.) that makes the Civic. Although all three plants are Japanese-owned, it is interesting that two of the three are outside Japan.[49]

Each year, J.D. Power releases its Vehicle Dependability Study (VDS), which measures automobile quality after three years of ownership. In the 2013 Dependability Ratings, Lexus was the highest nameplate in vehicle dependability, followed by Porsche, Lincoln, Toyota, and Mercedes-Benz. Toyota, which also includes Lexus as one of its brands, led all manufacturers with awards in several different segments. GM earned four, while Honda earned three. Japanese automakers have long dominated the rankings, but these 2013 results exhibited marked improvements for American carmakers, though they still lag the Japanese models. The steady improvement in initial quality ratings for U.S. automakers should be translated into higher dependability rates after three years, so it appears that the focus on quality is narrowing the gap among the top auto manufacturers worldwide.[50]

Zero defects—the refusal to tolerate defects of any kind.

ZERO DEFECTS

Quality now refers to **zero defects**, an idea perfected by Japanese manufacturers who refuse to tolerate flaws of any kind. Before this strong emphasis on getting rid of defects, many companies operated according to the premise of **acceptable quality level (AQL)**, which held that a few faulty products would be dealt with through repair facilities and service warranties. This type of manufacturing/operating environment required buffer inventories, rework stations, and expediting, with the goal of pushing through products as fast as possible and then dealing with the mistakes later. However, world class companies prefer zero defects and they realize that taking quality seriously is the only way to beat the competition.[51]

Deming's 14 Points encompass the idea that the responsibility for quality resides within the policies and practices of managers.

In the late 1970s, when Japanese companies began to seriously outpace those in the United States in achieving high-quality products and processes, a new emphasis was placed on actively managing the operations that affect quality. One contributor to this focus on *quality management,* and one of the people who trained the Japanese in quality, was W. Edwards Deming. To espouse the idea that the responsibility for quality resides within the policies and practices of managers, Deming developed several suggestions on how companies could improve. His focus on quality was designed to reduce the variance in the manufacturing process through statistical control, design, and training and through the policies and practices of managers. He felt that higher quality would lead to lower costs and better acceptance by the consumer.

The emphasis on quality management has continued to provide a major source of competitive advantage and play a major role for companies across the globe. However, just as different countries possess different cultures, product preferences, and business practices, various regions of the world have approached the concept of quality management in various ways. The Japanese have long focused on lean production processes that eliminate waste and boost visibility, whereas the American approach has historically been more statistically based, and the Europeans have opted to concentrate more on quality standards.[52] These varying attitudes toward quality create a high level of complexity for MNEs with global operations. As we will see, however, many of the best practices concerning quality have been perfected in Japan and are being used worldwide.

CONCEPT CHECK

Compare the concept of employee involvement as it's characterized here with the idea of coordination by mutual adjustment, which we discuss in Chapter 16. Both approaches to coordination signal a willingness to coordinate value activities through a range of informal mechanisms, including means by which employees are encouraged to engage one another in decisions about matters of mutual importance.

LEAN MANUFACTURING AND TOTAL QUALITY MANAGEMENT (TQM)

One reason why companies might hesitate when considering whether to source parts from foreign suppliers is because of *lean manufacturing,* the process of reducing waste in all areas of the supply chain.[53] This concept was popularized by the Japanese, especially Toyota, and has been copied or emulated worldwide. Because it relies on the efficiencies gained by reducing waste and defects, lean manufacturing is also closely tied to quality management.

Lean manufacturing—a productive system whose focus is on optimizing processes through the philosophy of continual improvement.

The Japanese approach is known as **total quality management (TQM)**, a process that stresses three principles: *customer satisfaction, continuous improvement,* and *employee involvement.*[54] The goal is to eliminate all defects. TQM often focuses on benchmarking world-class standards, product and service design, process design, and purchasing.[55] The center of the entire process, however, is customer satisfaction, the achievement of which may raise production costs. In TQM, quality means the product is so good that the customer wouldn't think of buying from anyone else.

Total quality management (TQM)—a process that stresses customer satisfaction, employee involvement, and continuous improvement of quality. Its goal is to eliminate all defects.

TQM is a process of continuous improvement at every organizational level—from the mailroom to the boardroom. It implies that the company is doing everything it can to achieve quality at every stage of the process. For example, if management accounting systems are focused strictly on cost, they will preclude measures that could lead to higher quality. The key is to understand the company's overall strategy.

TQM does not use any specific production philosophy or require the use of other techniques, such as a just-in-time system for inventory delivery. It is a proactive strategy. Although benchmarking—determining the best processes used by the best companies—is an important part of TQM, it is not intended to be a goal. In essence, TQM means that a company will try to be better than the best.

Executives who have adopted the zero-defects philosophy of TQM claim that long-run production costs decline as defects decline. The continuous improvement process is also known as *kaizen,* which means identifying problems and enlisting employees at all levels to help eliminate those problems. The key is to make continuous improvement a part of every employee's daily work.

Just-in-time (JIT) approach to inventory management—a system that sources raw materials and parts just as they are needed in the manufacturing process.

An important element of lean manufacturing is just-in-time (JIT) inventory management, which focuses on "reducing inefficiency and unproductive time in the production process to improve continuously the process and the quality of the product or service."[56] The JIT system gets raw materials, parts, and components to the buyer"just in time"for use, sparing companies the cost of storing large inventories.

That is what Dell hoped to accomplish in its Irish plant by having parts delivered just as they were to enter the production process and then go out the door to consumers as soon as the computers were built. However, the use of JIT means that parts must have few defects and must arrive on time. That is why companies need to develop solid supplier relationships to ensure good quality and delivery times if JIT is to work—and why industrial clustering is a popular way of linking more closely with suppliers.

It is hard to combine foreign sourcing and JIT production without having safety stocks of inventory on hand, which defeats the concept of JIT.

Risks in Foreign Sourcing Foreign sourcing can create big risks for companies that use lean manufacturing and JIT because interruptions in the supply line can cause havoc. MNEs are becoming expert at meeting the requirements of JIT: ships that take two weeks to cross the Pacific docking within an hour of scheduled arrival, factories that are able to more easily fill small orders, and so on. However, because of distances alone, the supply chain is open to more problems and delays.[57]

As mentioned earlier in the chapter, companies such as Toyota that have set up manufacturing and assembly facilities overseas to service local markets have practically forced their domestic parts suppliers to move overseas as well to allow them to continue with JIT manufacturing. That is why so many Japanese parts suppliers have moved to the United States and Mexico to be near their major customers.

A company's inventory management strategy—especially in terms of stock sizes and whether JIT will be used—determines the frequency of needed shipments. The less frequent the delivery, the more likely the need to store inventory somewhere. Because JIT requires delivery just as the inventory is to be used, some concession must be made for inventory arriving from foreign suppliers. Since DENSO, one of Toyota's major suppliers, is very close to Toyota's assembly plants in Japan, JIT allows the DENSO components to arrive a matter of a few minutes but no more than a few hours from when they are used. However, Kawasaki Motors Corp., U.S.A., carries a minimum of three days' inventory on parts coming from Japan, with an average inventory of five days.[58]

U.S. Synthetics, a company based in Utah, used to ship some of their parts from Eastern Africa. However, these shipments became unreliable when Somalia pirates began taking ships hostage and demanding a ransom in return for the stolen goods. U.S. Synthetics now makes these parts in-house so they don't have to worry about when the shipments will arrive.

A *kanban* system facilitates JIT by using cards to control the flow of production through a factory.

The Kanban System One system pioneered by Toyota to facilitate its JIT strategies is the *kanban system,* named after the Japanese word for"card"or"visible record."Kanban cards are used to control the flow of production through a factory. In the system used by Toyota, components are shipped to a plant just before they need to go into production, where they are kept in a bin with an attached card identifying the quantity of items in the bin. When the assembly process begins, a production-order card signifies that a bin needs to be moved to the assembly line. When the bin is emptied, it is moved to a storage area and replaced with a full bin. The kanban card is then removed from the empty bin and is used to order a replacement from the supplier.

Six Sigma—a quality control system aimed at eliminating defects, slashing product cycle times, and cutting costs across the board.

SIX SIGMA

Six Sigma is an effective statistical approach to quality management developed by Motorola and popularized by General Electric. As a highly focused system of quality control that scrutinizes a company's entire production system, it aims to eliminate defects, slash product cycle times, and cut costs across the board. The system uses data and rigorous statistical analysis to identify "defects" in a process or product, reduce variability, and achieve as close to zero defects as possible.[59] General Electric has operationalized Six Sigma on a project basis using the acronym DMAIC. This refers to define (especially customers and their priorities), measure (the process and its performance), analyze (determine the most likely cause of defects), improve (determine how to remove the causes of the defects), and control (maintain the improvements).[60]

Since being introduced by Motorola in the 1980s, Six Sigma has been adopted by many MNEs, including GE, GlaxoSmithKline, and Lockheed Martin. Although some have accused the program of diverting attention away from customers and squashing innovation, most of the 100 largest companies in the United States have embraced it.[61] Its main goal is defect reduction, and fewer defects should cause an improvement in yields, which should improve customer satisfaction and then lead to enhanced income. Given that Six Sigma is a metric designed to measure defects, some argue that it is most effective when used in conjunction with the Baldrige Criteria for Excellence or the European Quality Award.[62]

QUALITY STANDARDS

There are three different levels of quality standards: *general, industry-specific,* and *company-specific.* The first is a general standard, such as the Deming Award, which is presented to firms that demonstrate excellence in quality, or the Malcolm Baldrige National Quality Award, which is presented annually to companies that demonstrate quality strategies and achievements. However, even more important than awards is certification of quality.

Levels of quality standards:
- General level—ISO 9000, Malcolm Baldrige National Quality Award
- Industry-specific level
- Company level

General-Level Standards The **International Organization for Standardization (ISO)** in Geneva was formed in 1947 to facilitate the international coordination and unification of industrial standards. From the beginning, it has partnered with the IEC (International Electrotechnical Commission), which is the originator of global technical standards. It also collaborates with the International Telecommunications Union and the World Trade Organization. As an NGO, the ISO represents a network of standard setters in 162 countries and has established over 19,500 international quality standards.[63]

ISO 9000—a global set of quality standards intended to promote quality at every level of an organization.

ISO 9000 and ISO 14000 Even with more than 19,000 standards in the ISO, new ones are being published every year, including nearly 1,300 in 2012. The two main families of standards are ISO 9000, which describes the fundamentals of quality management systems, and ISO 14000, which addresses what the company does to improve its environmental performance. However, many different areas have ISO standards.

ISO 14000—a quality standard concerned with environmental management.

ISO 9000 is a set of universal standards for a quality assurance system that is accepted around the world. Applying uniformly to companies in any industry and of any size, it is intended to promote the idea of quality at every organizational level. Initially it was designed to harmonize technical norms within the EU. Now it is an important part of business operations throughout Europe. Under the ISO 9000 family of standards, companies must document how workers perform every function affecting quality and install mechanisms to ensure that they follow through on the documented routine. The documentation is generic and applicable to any organization that makes products or provides services. A major advantage of ISO 9000 is the documentation process, which not only requires workers to examine what they do to improve quality but also ensures continuity as workers change positions.

ISO certification entails a complex analysis of management systems and procedures, not just quality-control standards. Rather than judging the quality of a particular product, ISO evaluates the management of the manufacturing or service process according to the standards it has created in 20 domains, from purchasing to design to training. The operational principles of its management-system standards are: plan, do, check, and act (correct and improve plans). A company that wants to be ISO-certified must fill out a report and submit to certification by a team of independent auditors.[64] The process can be expensive and time-consuming, as each site of a company must be separately certified. The ISO 14000 family of standards is designed to help companies establish high-quality environmental standards in terms of air, water and soil, ensure that environmental standards are followed, and develop products and services that are environmentally friendly.

Most MNEs claim ISO certification, but ISO is not the solution to all quality issues. One estimate holds that in some places, including China, as much as 40 percent of ISO certifications are falsified.[65] However, being certified will help suppliers obtain more business, especially with European companies.

Non-European companies operating in Europe need to become ISO certified in order to maintain access to that market.

U.S. companies that operate in Europe seek ISO certification to maintain access to its market. When DuPont lost a major European contract to an ISO-certified European company, it decided to become certified. By doing so, not only was it able to position itself better in Europe, it also benefited from the experience of going through the certification process and focusing on quality in and of itself. Some European companies are so committed to ISO that they will not do business with a certified company if its suppliers are not also ISO-certified. They want to be sure that quality flows back to every level of the supply chain.

Industry-Specific Standards In addition to the general standards described earlier, there are industry-specific standards for quality, especially for suppliers to follow. Since ISO standards are relatively generic, some industries, such as the auto industry, have developed more specific ones to fit the industry. One such example is QS9000, which was initially required for any supplier of Ford and General Motors. However, it was eventually replaced by ISO/TS 16949:2009, which was more applicable to the auto industry. It is supposed to be used in conjunction with ISO 9001, and it defines the quality management system requirements for the design, development, production, installation, and service of automotive-related products. [66]

Company-Specific Standards Individual companies also set their own standards for suppliers to meet if they are going to continue to supply them. Apple, for example, sets safety and employment standards for its suppliers, and in 2013 it conducted 393 audits at all levels of the supply chain, including 40 specialized process safety assessments to evaluate suppliers' operations and business practices.[67] In the service sector, global public accounting firms, such as KPMG and PWC, have set high audit practices that it expects its affiliates around the world to use. This is always complicated since public accounting firms are an association of individual national partnerships operating under one name. However, the audit of a multinational client must be performed to high standards.

FOREIGN TRADE ZONES

Foreign trade zones (FTZs)—special locations for storing domestic and imported inventory in order to avoid paying duties until the inventory is used in production or sold.

Once products are manufactured and ready to be shipped to customers, they can be shipped directly or they can be stored in warehouses until they are ready to be used. One way to store products is to use a foreign trade zone to shield products from tariffs. In recent years, **foreign trade zones (FTZs)** have become more popular as an intermediate step in the process between import and final use. FTZs are areas in which domestic and imported merchandise can be stored, inspected, and manufactured free from formal customs procedures until the goods leave the zones. They are intended to encourage firms to locate in the country by allowing them to defer duties, pay fewer duties, or avoid certain duties completely. Sometimes inventory is stored in an FTZ until it needs to be used for domestic manufacture. As noted earlier, one problem with JIT is the length of the supply line when relying on global sourcing, possibly causing either the buyer or the supplier to stockpile inventory somewhere until it is needed in the manufacturing process. One place to stockpile inventory is in a warehouse in an FTZ.

GENERAL-PURPOSE ZONES AND SUBZONES

A general-purpose FTZ is usually established near a port of entry, such as a shipping port, a border crossing, or an airport, and usually consists of a distribution facility or an industrial park used primarily for warehousing and distribution. A subzone is usually physically separate from a general-purpose zone but under the same administrative structure, commonly located at a manufacturing facility. Since 1982, the major growth in FTZs has been in subzones rather than in general-purpose zones because companies have sought to defer duties on parts that are foreign-sourced until they need to be used in the production process.

Dubai in the United Arab Emirates has established 18 different free zones, including Jebel Ali Free Zone Authority, Dubai Healthcare City, Dubai International Financial Center, Dubai Media City, and Dubai Internet City. The advantage of these free zones is that they allow 100 percent ownership of an enterprise, 100 percent repatriation of capital and profits, no minimum capital investment, no corporate or personal tax, and no need for a local partner. Different zones focus on different industries. For example, the major banks, financial, and law firms are in the DIFC; CNN, BBC, CNBC, and Dow Jones Thomson Reuters are in the Media Center; and Cox Internet, Hughes Satellite and Internet, and ATT Internet are in Internet City. Jebel Ali Free Zone includes standard assembly operations that one would find in any similar free zone. For instance, Unilever has a major tea factory in the Free Zone that is one of their largest in the world. It receives raw materials from different countries, packages them in the Free Zone, and ships them around the world.[68]

The major growth in subzones in the United States has been in the automobile industry, especially in the Midwest. Subzone activity is spreading to other industries, especially shipbuilding, pharmaceuticals, and home appliances, and is becoming more heavily oriented to manufacturing and assembly than was originally envisioned. Merchandise in U.S. FTZs may be assembled, exhibited, cleaned, manipulated, manufactured, mixed, processed, relabeled, repackaged, repaired, salvaged, sampled, stored, tested, displayed, and destroyed.[69]

The United States has about 250 general-purpose zones and more than 500 subzones in all 50 states and Puerto Rico. Over $300 billion a year in merchandise is handled in the FTZs, and $19 billion is exported from them each year.[70] FTZs in the United States have been used primarily as a means of providing greater flexibility as to when and how customs duties are paid. However, their use in the export business has been expanding.

The benefits to a zone user are:

- No duties or quota charges on goods imported into a zone and re-exported
- Customs duties and federal excise tax deferred on imports until taken from the zone and used in the domestic market
- Duties reduced if foreign inputs that enter the zone at one duty are higher than the duty would have been on the finished product leaving the zone for domestic sales (called an *inverted tariff*)
- Streamlined customs procedures
- Elimination of state and local inventory taxes if the goods are held in the zone for export[71]

TRANSPORTATION NETWORKS

Transportation links together suppliers, companies, and customers.

Just as Apple used UPS to ship Mandy her iPhone in the opening case, companies have to figure out the best way to ship goods from supplier to factory and from factory to customer. For a firm, transporting goods in an international context is extremely complicated in terms of documentation, choice of carrier (air or ocean), and the decision of whether to establish its own transportation department or outsource to a third party intermediary. Transportation is a crucial element of a logistics system. The key is to link together suppliers and manufacturers on the one hand and manufacturers and final consumers on the other. Along the way, the company has to determine its warehouse configuration. For example, in providing food items to its franchises around the world, McDonald's has warehouses in different countries to service different geographic areas.

Case: Panalpina As outsourcing of both manufacturing and other supply-chain functions grows ever more popular, third-party intermediaries are essential in storing and transporting goods. They constitute an important dimension of transportation networks. Panalpina is a Swiss forwarding and logistics services provider that focuses on intercontinental airfreight and sea freight, as well as other aspects of supply-chain management. Using its main hub in Luxembourg to connect to 500 offices in 80 countries throughout the world and partners in another 60 countries, Panalpina seeks to simplify the complexity of its customers' supply chains by handling their transportation, distribution, customs brokerage, warehousing, and inventory control, as well as providing door-to-door transport insurance and real-time track-and-trace systems.[72]

An example of how Panalpina services its clients involves IBM and its operations in Latin America. Through its selected airfreight services provider, ASB-Air, and through the management of its local branches, Panalpina coordinates vehicles to pick up IBM products in Europe and transport them to Luxembourg. From there, the goods travel by air to the cargo center in Miami, where products destined for various locations in South America are split and reconsolidated into pallets that are then loaded directly into Panalpina's space-controlled aircraft and transferred to its own company warehouses operated by its own staff. The warehouse personnel complete all customs details, taking advantage of the on-site offices of customs authorities, and update the company's information systems with current status messages.

Once customs has been cleared, an electronic data transfer is sent to IBM while the goods are shipped to IBM warehouses. Panalpina maintains control of the goods throughout the entire process, using electronic documentation and tracking to maintain real-time data and keep IBM informed. In this example, you can see all of the elements of transportation networks that are so essential in international logistics.[73]

The logistics management that companies like Panalpina engage in is very detail-oriented, requiring the ability to gather, track, and process large quantities of information. To be effective, logistics companies need to implement key technologies, including communication systems, satellite tracking systems, bar-coding applications, and automated materials-handling systems.[74] It is interesting to note how important the "Flatteners" are in this part of the supply chain network and how critical the third-party logistics companies are to ensuring the smooth flow of products around the world.

Looking to the Future

Uncertainty and the Global Supply Chain

Two competing ideas have been emphasized in this chapter: First, globalization has pushed companies to establish operations abroad or to outsource to foreign suppliers to reduce costs and be closer to markets; second, the longer the supply line, the greater the risk. Since September 11, 2001, the risks of longer supply lines have increased dramatically. At any time, global political events could completely disrupt a well-organized supply chain and put a company at risk. This was demonstrated more recently in 2011 with the earthquake and tsunami in Japan.

Because some of Sara Lee's suppliers have consolidated, there are fewer options for purchasing key ingredients for Sara Lee products. What if no supplier could deliver because of political events or safety/quality concerns? Ford Motor Company's announcement that the economic slowdown was forcing it to cut its suppliers by 50 percent created a ripple effect throughout the auto industry, since suppliers tend to supply many different companies.

As a supply chain stretches and uncertainty grows, companies have to become much better at scenario building so that viable contingencies are available. Maybe this means they will pursue more multidomestic strategies to insulate their foreign operations from other countries and allow them to be more responsive to local consumers. However, as MNEs in the developed countries respond to competitive pressures to reduce costs, they will be forced to continue sourcing abroad, either in company-owned facilities or from third parties—at least until nobody can source abroad.

That's probably a little extreme, but the important thing is to continue to look at the "what-ifs." What if there is no secure air or ocean transportation available to move goods? What if the goods can move, but there are delays? What if terrorists begin to use the global supply chain of legitimate companies to contaminate products or move hazardous materials? Clearly, the future appears much more complicated than current or past conditions, so let the manager beware. These uncertainties as well as high oil and other transportation costs plus escalating costs in China, the manufacturing floor of the world, are causing many firms to look closer to home for their sourcing decisions. ■

CASE Samsonite's Global Supply Chain[75]

Samsonite is the world's biggest luggage maker. Founded in 1910 in Denver, Colorado in the United States and headquartered in Luxembourg, the company took many years to become the global manufacturer and distributor of luggage that it is today. In 1963, Samsonite set up its first European operation in the Netherlands, and later, began production in Belgium. Shortly thereafter, it erected a joint-venture plant in Mexico to service the growing but highly protected Mexican market. By the end of the 1960s, Samsonite was manufacturing luggage in Spain and Japan as well. In addition to its manufacturing operations, Samsonite was selling luggage worldwide through a variety of distributors.

In the 1970s, business began to take off in Europe. In 1974, Samsonite developed its first real European product, called the Prestige Attaché, and business began to expand in Italy, causing the country to rival Germany as Samsonite's biggest market in Europe. Although the U.S. market began to turn to soft-side luggage in the 1980s, the European market still demanded hard-side luggage, so Samsonite developed a new hard-side suitcase for Europe called the Oyster case. At that point, soft-side luggage began to increase in importance, although Europe was still considered a hard-side market. In the 1980s, Samsonite opened a new plant in France to manufacture the Prestige Attaché and other key products. With the fall of the Iron Curtain in the early 1990s, Samsonite purchased a Hungarian luggage manufacturer and began to expand throughout Eastern Europe. During this same time period, Samsonite established several joint-venture companies throughout Asia, including China, to extend its reach there. Samsonite's key strategies for the 1990s have been detailed below.

The Quality Initiative

To establish products of high quality, Samsonite embarked on two different programs. The first was an internal program in which Samsonite conducted drop, tumble, wheel, and handle tests to determine if its products were strong enough and of sufficient quality for customers. The second was composed of two different, independent quality-assurance tests:

- The European-based ISO 9002 certification
- The GS Mark is the number-one government regulated third-party product test mark (similar to brand) of Germany or *Gepruefte Sicherheit* (translated "Tested for Safety"). It is designed to help companies comply with European product liability laws as well as other areas of quality and safety. To enhance quality, Samsonite introduced state-of-the-art CAD-CAM machinery in its plants. Samsonite also introduced a manufacturing technique in which autonomous cells of about a dozen employees assembled a product from start to finish.

Samsonite had three company-owned production facilities and two headquarters in Europe by the late 1990s. In addition, it had subsidiaries, joint ventures, retail franchises, distributors, and agents set up to service the European market. Although Samsonite initially serviced the European markets through exports, the transportation costs were high, and as the demand for luggage soared in Europe, Samsonite decided to begin production in Belgium in 1965. When Samsonite began its operations in Europe the products it sold there were made at production facilities located in the continent. At the time, six of the facilities were company owned, and one was a joint venture. In order to serve its European market, the company maintained subsidiaries and retail outlets, dealing with distributors and agents. Asia has overtaken Europe in terms of net sales, but the early experience of Samonsite in Europe has affected its supply chain strategy worldwide.

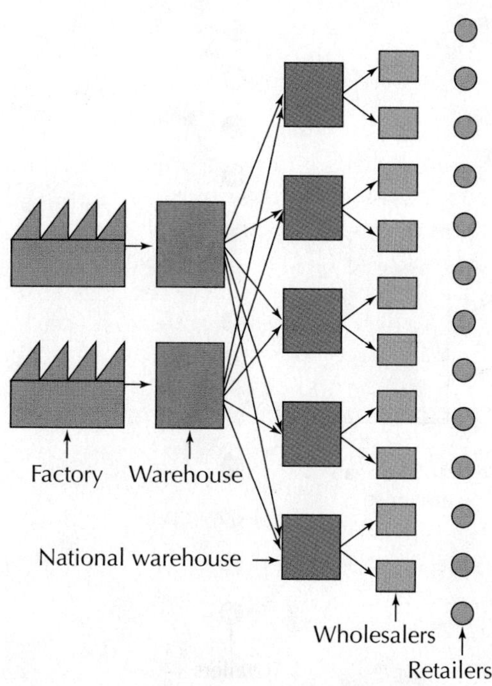

FIGURE 18.4 The Samsonite European Supply Chain (I): Decentralized, 1965–1974

For about a decade after it had first penetrated the European market, Samsonite shipped products from *factories* to *factory warehouses* and then to *national warehouses*. From there, products went to *wholesalers* and, at long last, to *retailers*. Needless to say, the system was cumbersome, lengthening the factory-to-retailer process and bumping up costs at every step of the way.

Source: F. De Beule and D. Van Den Bulcke, "The International Supply Chain Management of Samsonite Europe," Discussion Paper No. 1998/E/34 (Centre for International Management and Development, University of Antwerp, 1998):13.

Supply-Chain Decentralization

In the early years, Samsonite had a decentralized supply chain, as illustrated in Figure 18.4, whereby it operated through different wholesale layers before it finally got the product to the retailers. As Samsonite's business grew, management decided to centralize its supply chain so that products were manufactured and shipped to a central European warehouse, which then directly supplied retailers upon request (see Figure 18.5).

This centralized structure was put into place to eliminate the need to rely on wholesalers. Samsonite had to worry about transporting manufactured products to the warehouse, storing them, and transporting them to the retailers in the different European markets. The company invested heavily in information technology to link the retailers to the warehouse and thereby manage its European distribution system more effectively. Retailers would place an order with a salesperson or the local Samsonite office, and the order would be transmitted to the warehouse and shipping company by modem. The retail market in Europe began shifting at the turn of the new century, so Samsonite responded by opening franchised retail outlets in October 2002, beginning in Antwerp and spreading to other areas. As the vice-president of marketing and sales put it, "We are anticipating a shift in the market, in which the traditional luggage channel will no longer be at the forefront and a wide new retail opportunity will emerge."

R&D and Product Innovation

As noted earlier, Samsonite sold two basic types of suitcases: hard-side and soft-side. Most of the R&D was initially done in the United States, but the need to develop products for the European market led the company to establish R&D facilities in Europe. Samsonite invested heavily in R&D and in the manufacture of specialized machinery to help maintain a competitive edge. To facilitate the transportation and storage of suitcases, Samsonite located its production facilities close to the centralized warehouse.

Soft-side luggage is less complex technologically than hard-side, and Samsonite purchased Oda, the Belgium soft-side luggage company, to enter that market. Then it licensed its technology to other European companies. By the mid-1990s, 48 percent of Samsonite's sales came from hard-side luggage, 22 percent from soft-side, and 30 percent from attaché cases

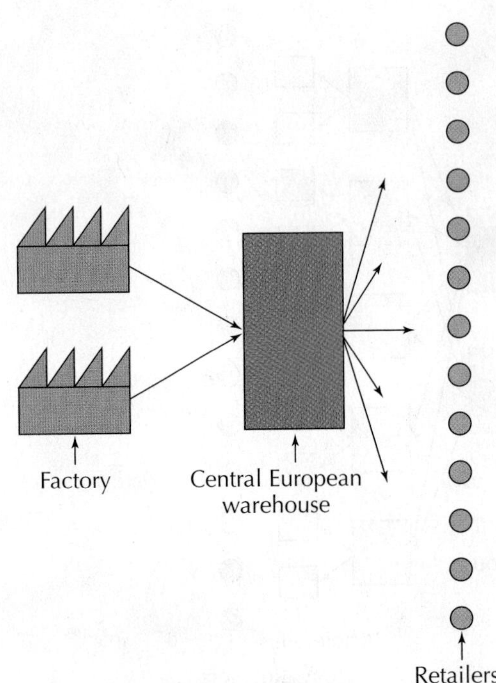

FIGURE 18.5 The Samsonite European Supply Chain (II): Centralized, 1975–Mid-1980s

In the mid-1970s, Samsonite decided to streamline the cumbersome supply chain illustrated in Figure 18.4. For the next decade or so, the company shipped products from *factories* to a *central European warehouse*, which then shipped them, upon request, to *retailers* located across the continent.

Source: F. De Beule and D. Van Den Bulcke, "The International Supply Chain Management of Samsonite Europe." Discussion Paper No. 1998/E/34 (Centre for International Management and Development, University of Antwerp, 1998):14.

and travel bags, some of which were hard-side and others soft-side. However, by fiscal 2000, soft-side luggage comprised 51 percent of European sales. In 2001 and 2002, sales of soft-side luggage continued to increase as a percentage, and hard-side luggage sales declined.

Outsourcing

As Samsonite expanded throughout the world, it continued to manufacture its own products and license production to other manufacturers. Then Samsonite entered into subcontract arrangements in Asia and Eastern Europe. In Europe, the subcontractors provide final goods as well as the subassemblies used in Samsonite factories. The trend to outsource more and more of its production has been steadily increasing.

By 2007, Samsonite had shut down several of its plants in Europe and decreased internal manufacturing of soft-side luggage from 23 percent in 2004 to just under 10 percent in 2007. Although it still produces the majority of its hard-side luggage internally, the company now sources 90 percent of its soft-side luggage from third-party manufacturers to consolidate its manufacturing capacities and to achieve cost savings. Figure 18.6 illustrates Samsonite's coordination of outsourced parts and finished goods, along with its own production in Europe.

The Shift to Asia

The slowdown in international travel and consumer spending in 2008 to 2009 nearly drove Samsonite under. Private equity firm CVC and the Royal Bank of Scotland (RBS) injected enough cash in the business to save the company. In addition, top management was forced to cut headcount 50 percent in the United States and 30 percent in Europe, closing 115 shops. To further reduce costs, Samsonite cut out some lines of business that didn't make much sense in a falling travel market. CVC's goal was to push Samsonite more aggressively into Asia, where a growing middle class loves to travel. As a result of this push and a global recovery in the travel industry, Samsonite saw a 45 percent increase in sales in Asia during 2010, which accounted for 42 percent of its group profits.

Consistent with its focus on Asia, Luxembourg-based Samsonite listed in Hong Kong in June 2011 in an IPO (Initial Public Offering), about the same time that luxury goods maker Prada

FIGURE 18.6 The Samsonite European Supply Chain (III): Globalized, 1996–1999

As it expanded production throughout Europe, Samsonite was soon obliged to establish arrangements with subcontractors (who provided both final products and subassemblies). Because the company now had to coordinate outsourced goods and parts in addition to production from its own factories, it reconfigured its supply chain once again. Today, all products and parts, whether company produced or outsourced, go to a central European warehouse and, from there, straight to retailers.

Source: F. De Beule and D. Van Den Bulcke. "The International Supply Chain Management of Samsonite Europe," Discussion Paper No. 1998/E/34 (Centre for International Management and Development, University of Antwerp, 1998):21.

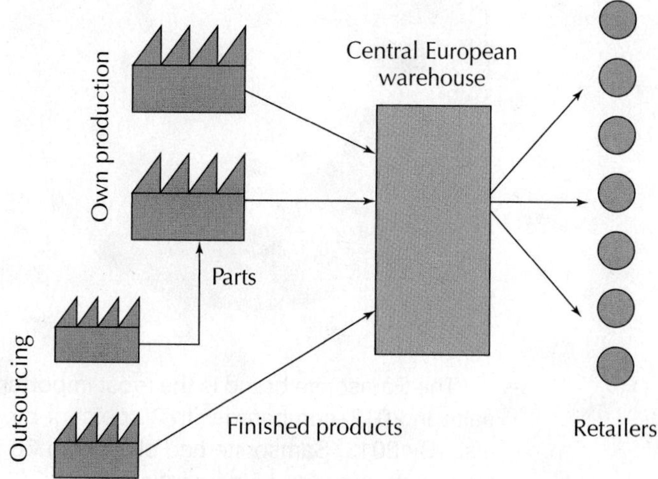

floated an IPO in Hong Kong to gain access to high liquidity and help build the brand name in China. This move resulted in Samsonite raising $1.25 billion in cash, which it could use to reduce its debt. CVS Capital and RBS jointly raised about $821 million by selling into the IPO and with the cash they raised, they exited completely their holdings in Samsonite.

In order to move forward, Samsonite established the following strategies to sustain revenues and earnings growth and generate free cash flow:

- "Leverage brands—continue to gain market share by leveraging the strength of the company's brands
- Innovate—introduce new and innovative product designs, adapted to the needs of consumers in different markets, while staying true to the company's core values of lightness, strength and functionality
- Product diversification—allocate more resources to the product categories that present the greatest opportunity for the Company to diversify its product offerings and gain market share
- Improve efficiency—continually improve the efficiency and effectiveness of the Company's supply chain and global distribution network
- Invest in R&D—increase the company's investment in R&D and marketing broadly in line with sales growth
- Growth—focus on achieving growth organically, and at the same time making acquisitions that have a compelling strategic and financial rationale"[76]

As described on its Web site and in its annual report, Samsonite's key brands are Samsonite, American Tourister, High Sierra, and Hartmann. The latter two brands are more recent additions to Samsonite's brand portfolio, in line with the growth strategy of making acquisitions that have a compelling strategic and financial rationale. They are interesting acquisitions. The High Sierra acquisition was made to allow Samsonite to enter the North American casual bag market, whereas Hartmann (HL Operating Corp.) is in the luxury luggage and leather goods markets. High Sierra offers a product line very different from anything Samsonite has done, even though some of the products are wheeled bags or wheeled backpacks. The products target the outdoors, active market rather than the traditional business traveller and is expected to help increase revenues in the United States and Latin America, which generates a small percentage of Samsonite's revenues.

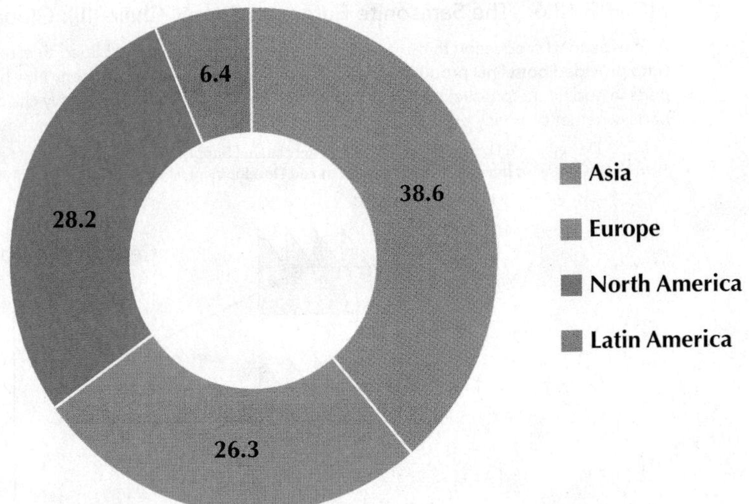

FIGURE 18.7 Net Sales by Region, 2012

The Samsonite brand is the most important brand for the group, generating 75 percent of sales in 2012, compared with 20 percent by American Tourister, and 5 percent by everyone else. By 2013, Samsonite had slipped to 68 percent, and new acquisitions High Sierra and Hartmann generated 5 percent of sales.

Although the first part of the case focused on Samsonite's operations in Europe and the evolution of its supply chain, it's obvious that those same issues exist around the world. Note in Figure 18.7 that revenues are pretty close in all three major regions of the world—Asia, Europe, and North America—even though Asia as a region has the lead.

A major factor leading to the growth in Samsonite's business in recent years is the overall increase in worldwide travel. As travel has recovered from the global slowdown, sales of luggage have also recovered.

Samsonite's Supply Chain

Given that Samsonite generates strong revenues in Asia, Europe, and North America, how does it get the product to the consumer? In 2012, Samsonite used two main distribution channels, wholesale (80%) and retail (19%). Samsonite went through a period when it closed down company-owned stores to save costs, but now they have opened up company stores again. However, the major points of distribution of products are department and speciality retail stores, mass merchants, catalogue showrooms, and warehouse clubs (such as Walmart, Costco, etc.). Samsonite expanded its sales in 2012 to 45,000 different points of sale in over 100 countries. Most of the growth in 2012 came in the United States and Asia. In Asia, China is the major market for growth, leading South Korea, India, Japan, and Hong Kong. Germany is still the leading market for Samsonite in Europe, but sales are pretty evenly spread among France, Belgium, and Italy, with Spain, Russia, and the UK a little below. However, sales in China are nearly three times that of any country in Europe. The market in the United States is by far the single largest market in the world for Samsonite—nearly 8 times that of China.

The supply chain for Samsonite is complicated, as it is for any MNE, because the company has to design, manufacture, and source the product and get it to different distribution points around the world. It's like taking Figures 18.4–18.6 and expanding them to a global system. This is especially an issue when considering that products are not exactly standardized for every market in the world.

Samsonite is organized along regional lines, with presidents in charge of each region. However, due to the complexity of the supply chain, there is a Chief Supply Officer responsible for Samsonite's supply chain and the development of supplier partnerships. In addition, Samsonite has a Vice President for Global Design and Development, which is consistent with one of their strategic goals of innovation.

Samsonite has developed strong relationships with its major suppliers. Samsonite purchases 10.8 percent of its products from its largest supplier, and the five largest supply 35.2 percent of the products to Samsonite. One of its largest strategic partners is Ramesh Dungarmal Tainwala, one of Samsonite's executive directors and President for Asia-Pacific and the Middle East. The Tainwala Group is involved in many facets of Samsonite in India. One of the companies controlled by certain members of the Tainwala Group purchases raw materials and components from Samsonite India and manufactures hard-side luggage products on behalf of Samsonite India. Another company, Bagzone Lifestyle Private Limited, is controlled by members of the Tainwala Group and is the preferred dealer of Samsonite and American Tourister products in India. The products are sold through 87 exclusive Samsonite retail outlets operated by Bagzone. Bagzone also purchases products from Samsonite India to sell in its own multi-brand outlet stores. And this is just a small part of the connection between the Tainwala Group and Samsonite. It is clear that the Group wields significant influence on Samsonite. As part of its organizational structure, Samsonite also has production/distribution operations in Chile, Belgium, Mexico, and India, but it appears that India alone is stepping up as a major supplier of Samsonite products.

One of Samsonite's strategic goals is to reduce costs in the supply chain. These increases in costs are due largely to increasing labor costs, product costs, and inventory carrying costs as well as import restrictions, especially in India.

TUMI—The Competition[77]

Tumi, one of Samsonite's recent competitors, was founded only in 1975. Like Samsonite, Tumi is sold worldwide, although on a smaller scale. At the close of 2012, Tumi distributed its products in 75 countries through approximately 1,700 points of distribution, including retail, wholesale, and e-commerce. Some of its channels include partner stores—local distributors or retailers that carry only Tumi products—its global wholesale distribution network of speciality luggage retailers, and department stores. Its products are designed in its U.S. design studios, whereas Samsonite has design facilities in different countries to fit local trends. Production of Tumi products takes place mostly in Asia (especially China and Thailand) and the Caribbean, rather than Europe, India, and Mexico as is the case with Samsonite.

One interesting dimension of Tumi's supply chain that is totally lacking in Samsonite's annual report is that Tumi has signed the California Transparency in Supply Chains Act. The law was designed to help eradicate human trafficking and slavery from supply chains. This also includes forced labor, illegal child labor, sweat shop conditions, and sexual exploitation. Tumi adopts a strict policy to enforce its product supply chains, including audits of suppliers to evaluate supplier compliance with company standards. In addition, Tumi is a member of the Fair Labor Association as well as the Leather Working Group, an industry group dedicated to assess compliance and environmental performance in the leather industry.

QUESTIONS

✪ **18-3.** What are the major reasons why Samsonite changed its supply chain organization over the years?

18-4. Compare the supply chain issues faced by Apple in the opening case and Samsonite in the closing case.

✪ **18-5.** Why do you think Samsonite does not mention the California Transparency in Supply Chains Act, and the Fair Labor Association, or the Leather Working Group in its annual report or on its Web site? What could pressure Samsonite to address those issues in the future?

18-6. What are the similarities and differences between Samsonite and Tumi in their supply chains?

18-7. How would you redraw Figure 18.6 to reflect the reality that Samsonite is a global company?

SUMMARY

- A company's supply chain encompasses the coordination of materials, information, and funds from the initial raw-materials supplier to the ultimate customer.
- "Operations" refers to the processes internal to the company, such as manufacturing, inventory control, etc. The supply chain and operations bring together supplier inputs, prepare the product for the consumer, and ensure delivery.
- The success of a global operations strategy depends on compatibility, configuration, coordination, and control.
- Cost-minimization strategies and the drive for global efficiencies often force MNEs offshore to low-cost manufacturing areas, especially in Asia and Eastern Europe.
- Manufacturing can be configured as centralized, regional, and multidomestic facilities. Offshoring is where the facilities are moved from the home country to another country.
- Global sourcing is the process of supplying raw materials and parts to a firm from domestic and foreign sources. Outsourcing means engaging another company to perform a limited function that was being done in-house, such as payroll, whether domestic or offshore. Supply-chaining is the process in which another company makes the firm's goods, such as Walmart purchasing goods from suppliers that it sells in its stores. Suppliers can be domestic or offshore.
- Domestic sourcing allows a company to avoid problems related to language, culture, currency, tariffs, and so forth. Foreign sourcing allows the company to reduce costs and improve quality, among other things.
- Under the make-or-buy decision, companies have to decide whether to make their own parts or buy them from an independent company.
- Companies go through different purchasing phases as they become more committed to global sourcing.
- When a company sources parts from suppliers around the world, distance, time, and the uncertainty of political and economic environments can make it difficult to manage inventory flows accurately.
- The key to making a global supply-chain system work is information. Companies are rapidly turning to the Internet as a way to link suppliers with manufacturing and eventually with end-use customers.
- Total quality management (TQM) is a process that emphasizes customer satisfaction, employee involvement, and continuous improvements in quality while aiming for zero defects.
- Lean manufacturing and just-in-time systems focus on reducing inefficiency and unproductive time in the production process to continuously improve the process and the quality of the product or service.
- Quality is defined as meeting or exceeding the expectations of customers. Quality standards can be general level (ISO 9000), industry-specific, or company-specific (zero defects, TQM, and Six Sigma).
- The transportation system links together suppliers with manufacturers and manufacturers with customers.

KEY TERMS

acceptable quality level (AQL) (p. 756)
contract manufacturer (p. 748)
e-commerce (p. 754)
electronic data interchange (EDI) (p. 753)
enterprise resource planning (ERP) (p. 753)
extranet (p. 754)
foreign trade zones (FTZs) (p. 759)
industrial clusters (p. 750)
International Organization for Standardization (ISO) (p. 758)
intranet (p. 754)
logistics (or materials management) (p. 741)
offshore manufacturing (p. 742)
operations (p. 742)
operations management (p. 741)
outsourcing (p. 747)
private technology exchange (PTX) (p. 754)
quality (p. 755)
Six Sigma (p. 757)
sourcing (p. 746)
supply chain (p. 740)
total quality management (TQM) (p. 756)
vertical integration (p. 749)
zero defects (p. 756)

ENDNOTES

1 Sources for the case: Philip Elmer-DeWitt, "What's Really Going on at Apple's iPhone 5 Factory in Zhengzhou, China," *Fortune* (October 7, 2012), http://tech.fortune.cnn.com/2012/10/07/whats-really-going-on-at-apples-iphone-5-factory-in-zhengzhou-china/ (accessed June 15, 2013); Kenneth L. Kraemer, Greg Linden, and Jason Dedrick, "Capturing Value in Global Networks: Apple's iPad and iPhone," pcic.merage.uci.edu/papers/2011/Value_iPad_iPhone.pdf; Dedrick, Kraemer, and Linden, "The Distribution of Value in the Mobile Phone Supply Chain," pcic.merage.uci.edu/papers/2010/CellPhoneProfitability_Oct2010.pdf; G. Froud, S. Johal, A. Leaver, & K. Williams, "Apple Business Model: Financialization Across the Pacific," University of Manchester, Centre for Research in Socio-cultural Change (CRESC), Working Paper no. 111 (2012); B. Ganges & A. Van Assche, "Product Modularity and the Rise of Global Value Chains: Insights from the Electronics Industry," CIRANO Scientific Series, Montreal, (2011): S64; Apple Inc., Form 10-K, September 29, 2012; Nick Wingfield, "Fixing Apple's Supply Lines," *The New York Times* (April 2, 2012): B1; Catherine Rampell and Nick Wingfield, "In Shift

of Jobs, Apple Will Make Some Macs in U.S.," *The New York Times* (December 7, 2012): A1; "When the Jobs Inspector Calls," *The Economist* (March 31, 2012): 73.

2 "The Fourth Annual Global Survey of Supply Chain Progress," Computer Sciences Corporation (CSC) and *Supply Chain Management Review* (2006); Darrell Rigby, "Management Tools 2005," *Bain & Company* (2005): 58.

3 Deloitte & Touche, "Energizing the Supply Chain," *The Review* (January 17, 2000): 1.

4 Council of Supply Chain Management Professionals," cscmp.org/about-us/supply-chain-management-definitions (accessed June 1, 2013).

5 Homin Chen and Tain-Jy Chen, "Network Linkages and Location Choice in Foreign Direct Investment," *Journal of International Business Studies* 29:3 (1998): 447.

6 Stanley E. Fawcett and Anthony S. Roath, "The Viability of Mexican Production Sharing: Assessing the Four Cs of Strategic Fit," *Urbana* 3:1 (1996): 29.

7 See S. C. Wheelwright, "Reflecting Corporate Strategy in Manufacturing Decisions," *Business Horizons* (1978): 21; S. C. Wheelwright, "Manufacturing Strategy: Defining the Missing Link," *Strategic Management Journal* 5 (1984): 77–91; Frank DuBois, Brian Toyne, and Michael D. Oliff, "International Manufacturing Strategies of U.S. Multinationals: A Conceptual Framework Based on a Four-Industry Study," *Journal of International Business Studies* 24:2 (1993): 313–14; Robert H. Hayes, Steven C. Wheelwright, and Kim B. Clark, *Dynamic Manufacturing* (New York: Free Press, 1988): 10–11.

8 See James P. Womack and Daniel T. Jones, "Lean Consumption: Locating for Lean Provision," *Harvard Business Review* (March 2005): 66–67.

9 "Print Me a Stradivarius," *The Economist* (February 12, 2011): 11.

10 Interview by author of Wall's Unilever personnel in Beijing, China (June 2006).

11 Jack Ewing, "Why Nokia Is Leaving Moto in the Dust," *Businessweek* (July 19, 2007), at www.businessweek.com/globalbiz/content/jul2007/gb20070719_088898.htm (accessed November 9, 2007): 1.

12 Norihiko Shirouzu and Jathon Sapsford, "Heavy Load—For Toyota, a New Small Truck Carries Hopes for Topping GM," *Wall Street Journal* (May 12, 2005): A1.

13 Michael E. McGrath and Richard W. Hoole, "Manufacturing's New Economies of Scale," *Harvard Business Review* (May–June 1992): 94.

14 Daniel J. Meckstroth, "China is the World's Largest Manufacturer, and by an Increasing Margin," MAPI, February 7, 2013, www.mapi.net/research/publications/china-world%E2%80%99s-largest-manufacturer-and-increasing-margin (accessed June 10, 2013).

15 Jim Hemerling, "China: Ready for the Next Sourcing Wave?" *Businessweek* (April 4, 2007): 1.

16 Fawcett and Roath, "The Viability of Mexican Production Sharing," 29.

17 Amy Schoenfeld, "A Multinational Loaf," *New York Times* (June 20, 2007), at www.nytimes.com/imagepages/2007/06/15/business/20070616_FOOD_GRAPHIC.html (accessed November 9, 2007).

18 Alexei Barrionuevo, "Globalization in Every Loaf," *New York Times* (June 16, 2007), at www.nytimes.com/2007/06/16/business/worldbusiness/16food.html?partner=rssnyt&emc=rss (accessed November 9, 2007).

19 Masaaki Kotabe and Glen S. Omura, "Sourcing Strategies of European and Japanese Multinationals: A Comparison," *Journal of International Business Studies* (Spring 1989): 120–22.

20 David Hannon, "Procter & Gamble Puts a New Spin on Global Chemicals Sourcing," *Purchasing* (February 15, 2007), accessed on June 1, 2013 at www.highbeam.com/doc/1G1-159694856.html.

21 Robert M. Monczka and Robert J. Trent, "Global Sourcing: A Development Approach," *International Journal of Purchasing and Materials Management* (Spring 1991): 3.

22 Nicholas Zamiska and David Kesmodel, "Tainted Ginger's Long Trip from China to U.S. Stores," *Wall Street Journal* (November 19, 2007): A1.

23 Miek Ramsey and Sebastian Moffett, "Japan Parts Shortage Hits Auto Makers," *The Wall Street Journal* (March 24, 2011): B1; Andrew Pollack and Steve Lohr, "The Chip that Powers Cars," *The Walls Street Journal* (April 28, 2011): B1.

24 R. D'Aveni and D. Ravenscraft, "Economies of Integration versus Bureaucracy Costs: Does Vertical Integration Improve Performance?" *Academy of Management Journal* 37:5 (1994): 1167–206; O. Williamson, "Vertical Integration and Related Variations on a Transaction-Cost Theme," in J. Stiglitz and G. Mathewson (eds.), *New Developments in the Analysis of Market Structure* (Cambridge, MA: MIT Press, 1986): 149–95; O. Williamson, *The Economic Institutions of Capitalism* (New York: The Free Press, 1985): 85–130.

25 Russell Johnston and Paul R. Lawrence, "Beyond Vertical Integration—The Rise of the Value-Adding Partnership," *Harvard Business Review* (July–August 1988): 98.

26 Chester Dawson, "A 'China Price' for Toyota," *Businessweek* (February 21, 2005): 50–51.

27 John McMillan, "Managing Suppliers: Incentive Systems in Japanese and U.S. Industry," *California Management Review* (Summer 1990): 38.

28 Rigby, "Management Tools 2005."

29 "Still Made in Japan," Economist.com (April 7, 2004), at www.economist.com/printedition/displayStory. cfm?Story_ id=2571689 (accessed November 9, 2007).

30 "Still Made in Japan," Economist.com.

31 Adapted from Pete Engardio and Bruce Einhorn, "Outsourcing Innovation," *Businessweek* (March 21, 2005): 84–94.

32 Lee Hawkins Jr., "GM Is Pushing Its U.S. Suppliers to Reduce Prices," *Wall Street Journal* (April 7, 2005): A2.

33 Monczka and Trent, "Global Sourcing: A Development Approach," 4–5.

34 Stanley E. Fawcett, "The Globalization of the Supply Environment," *The Supply Environment 2* (Tempe, AZ: NAPM, 2000): 11.

35 "Electrolux Delivers Strong Results in a Very Tough Market," *National Post* (June 25, 2009): FP 9.

36 Monczka and Trent, "Worldwide Sourcing," 17–18.

37 Thomas L. Friedman, *The World is Flat: a Brief History of the Twenty-First Century*, Release 3.0 (New York, NY: Picador, 2007): 77.

38 Richard Karpinski, "Wal-Mart Mandates Secure, Internet-Based EDI for Suppliers," Internetweek.com (September 12, 2002), at www.internetweek.com/supplyChain/INW20020912S0011 (accessed October 1, 2002); R. Sridharan and Shamni Pande, "Surviving Wal-Mart," *Business Today* (July 29, 2007): 166.

39 Scott McCartney, "A New Way to Prevent Lost Luggage," *Wall Street Journal* (February 27, 2007): D1.

40 Vlad Krotov and Iris Junglas, "RFID as a Disruptive Innovation," *Journal of Theoretical and Applied Electronic Commerce Research* 3:2 (August 2008): 44.

41 Miguel Bustillo, "Wal-Mart Radio Tags to Track Clothing," *The Wall Street Journal* (July 22, 2010), www.wsj.com (accessed July 25, 2011).

42 Karpinski, "Wal-Mart Mandates Secure, Internet-Based EDI for Suppliers."

43 www.internetworldstats.com/stats.htm (accessed June 10, 2013).

44 Check the Dell *Annual Report* for 2002 at www.dell.com (accessed April 20, 2002) and as updated in subsequent *Reports*, (accessed October 15, 2009). Go to "About Dell" at the bottom of the Web page, select "Investors," and search under "Year" to access annual reports.

45 "You'll Never Walk Alone," 17.

46 Jeremy Wagstaff, "Digital Deliverance; Asia's Technology Conundrum," *Asian Wall Street Journal* (July 27, 2007): W8.

47 Lee J. Krajewski and Larry P. Ritzman, *Operations Management: Strategy and Analysis*, 4th ed. (Reading, MA: Addison-Wesley, 1996): 141–42.

48 Jacobs and Chase, 134.

49 J.S. Power, "2011 U.S. Initial Quality Study," www.jdpower.com/news/pressrelease.aspx?ID=2011089 (accessed July 25, 2011).

50 J.D. Power & Associates Press Releases, "2013 Vehicle Dependability Study Results," at autos.jdpower.com/ratings/2013-VDS-Study.htm (accessed June 10, 2013).
51 Hayes, Wheelwright, and Clark, *Dynamic Manufacturing*, 17.
52 Foster, *Managing Quality*, 70–90.
53 Foster, *Managing Quality*, 87.
54 Krajewski and Ritzman, *Operations Management*, 140.
55 Krajewski and Ritzman, *Operations Management*, 156.
56 Krajewski and Ritzman, *Operations Management*, 732.
57 Gabriel Kahn, Trish Saywell, and Quenna Sook Kim, "Backlog at West Coast Docks Keeps Christmas Toys at Sea," *Wall Street Journal* (October 21, 2002), www.wsj.com (accessed October 25, 2002).
58 Shawnee K. Vickery, "International Sourcing: Implications for Just-in-Time Manufacturing," *Production and Inventory Management Journal* (1989): 67.
59 "Six Sigma Definition," at www.sixsigmasurvival.com/SixSigmaDefinition.html (accessed November 9, 2007).
60 Jacobs and Chase, 142.
61 Brian Hindo and Brian Grow, "Six Sigma: So Yesterday?" *Businessweek* (June 11, 2007): 11.
62 Robert McClusky, "The Rise, Fall and Revival of Six Sigma Quality," *Quality Focus* 4:2 (2000): 6.
63 International Organization for Standardization, "ISO Standards," www.iso.org (accessed May 1, 2013).
64 See Jonathan B. Levine, "Want EC Business? You Have Two Choices," *Businessweek* (October 19, 1992): 58; International Organization for Standardization, "ISO 9000:2000" (2007), at www.iso.org/iso/catalogue_detail?csnumber=21823 (accessed November 9, 2007).
65 Foster, *Managing Quality*.
66 International Organization for Standardization, "ISO/TS 16949:2009," at www.iso.org/iso/catalogue_detail?csnumber=36155 (accessed July 30, 2009).
67 "Supplier Responsibility Progress Report," at www.apple.com/supplierresponsibility/reports.html (accessed June 10, 2013).
68 Government of Dubai, "Free Zones" at www.dubai.ae (accessed June 1, 2013).
69 International Trade Administration, "What Activity Is Permitted in Zones?" at ia.ita.doc.gov/ (accessed July 26, 2011).
70 Foreign-Trade Zones Board, "How Many Zones Exist Now?" ia.ita.doc.gov/ftzpage/info/zonestats.html (accessed June 29, 2013).
71 Foreign-Trade Zones Board, "What Are the Benefits to a Zone User," under FAQ at ia.ita.doc.gov/ftzpage/info/ftzstart.html (accessed July 26, 2011).
72 Panalpina, www.panalpina.com, various pages (accessed June 29, 2013).
73 Panalpina, "Transporting IBM Products to Latin America" (2005), www panalpina.com/press/casestudies (accessed June 15, 2007).
74 Fawcett, "The Globalization of the Supply Environment," 11.
75 ***Sources include the following:*** Nikhil Kumar, "Samsonite IPO Size Rises to $1.3 bn," *The Independent* (London), July 11, 2011, p. 34; James Ashton, "The Pounds 90 Million Man in a Suitcase," *Sunday Times* (London), June 19, 2011, p. 6; F. De Beule and D. Van Den Bulcke, "The International Supply Chain Management of Samsonite Europe," Discussion Paper No. 1998/E/34, Centre for International Management and Development, University of Antwerp (1998); "About Samsonite: History," at www.corporate.samsonite.com/samsonite/about/history (accessed October 15, 2009); "Company Briefing Book," *Wall Street Journal*, www.wsj.com (accessed January 27, 2000); *Samsonite Quarterly Report*, SEC Form 10-Q, 2002; "Samsonite to Be Sold," *New York Times* (July 6, 2007): C4; "Samsonite Fiscal Year 2007 Annual 10-K," Samsonite (January 31, 2007); "Samsonite Introduces POINT A Franchise Concept," *Samsonite: Life's a Journey* (October 1, 2002), at www.samsonite.com/samsonite/?404= www.samsonite.com/global/globl_pressrelease_europ5.jsp; Helia Ebrahimi, "Samsonite Bags Debt-for-Equity Rescue Deal," *Sunday Telegraph* (May 31, 2009); Godfrey Deeny, "Y-3 Seals Luggage License with Samsonite," *Fashion Wire Daily* (May 7, 2009); Samsonite Corporation, *Hoover's Company Records*, 40046 (retrieved July 30, 2009), from *Entrepreneurship* (Document ID 168172041); Chris V. Nicholson, "IPO values Samsonite at $1.5 Billion," *The New York Times* (June 1, 2011): B9; Samsonite International S.A. 2012 Annual Report; Ven Sreenivasan, "Samsonite Confident About Maintaining Double-Digit Growth," *Business Times Singapore*, November 14, 2012 (retrieved November 5, 2013 from global.factiva.com).
76 Samsonite International S.A. 2012 Annual Report, p. 3.
77 Tumi Web site: www.tumi.com

CHAPTER 19
Global Accounting and Financial Management

OBJECTIVES

After studying this chapter, you should be able to

1. Examine the major factors influencing the development of accounting practices in different countries
2. Examine the global convergence of accounting standards
3. Explain how companies account for foreign-currency transactions and translate foreign-currency financial statements
4. Explain how companies include international factors in the capital budgeting process
5. Discuss the major internal sources of funds available to the MNE and show how they are managed globally
6. Describe how companies protect against the major financial risks of inflation and exchange rate movements

Even between parents and children, money matters make strangers.

—Japanese proverb

Source: © Springfield Gallery - Fotolia.com

CASE Parmalat: Europe's Enron

In January 2002, a European magazine published an article entitled "Enron: Could It Happen Here?" At the time the article was published, perhaps most people outside the United States would have answered "no" to that question.[1] In the wake of massive corporate frauds at Enron and WorldCom, there was a feeling outside the U.S. that such scandals were "an American problem" caused by the more aggressive business environment and practices there. However, a family-owned Italian firm was about to show the world that massive corporate scandals can happen anywhere.

A BRIEF BACKGROUND CHECK

In 1961, when Calisto Tanzi inherited his father's company at age 22, he directed it into dairy products and created the Parmalat brand. Inside two years, Parmalat had become the first Italian manufacturer of branded milk. In 1966, using packaging technology from Tetra Pak, Parmalat created its signature product: milk pasteurized at ultra high temperatures (UHT), which gave it a shelf life of over six months. UHT milk provided the company with a technological competitiveness in the dairy industry, placing it ahead of its competition. In 1970, the law permitted the sale of whole milk in grocery stores, removing the limitation of specialty milk shops, and Parmalat quickly became Italy's dominant milk supplier.

The "Champion's Milk"

Parmalat also became known as the "champion's milk" after sponsoring the Ski World Cup and world-champion Formula One race-car driver Nicki Lauda in the 1970s.The company moved into new markets with the production of cheese, butter, and a variety of desserts near the end of the decade. As it increased in popularity, Parmalat also began international expansion through acquisitions in Germany and France, which marked the beginning of a global dairy empire.

The Pious Pioneer Sports Marketer

Calisto Tanzi, an almost legendary figure in Italy, was the author of this growth. It was he who discovered the power of sports marketing to make Parmalat a famous brand. He had friends in important government positions who helped pass laws favoring Parmalat. A pious Catholic, Tanzi was a generous benefactor who sponsored the restoration of Parma's eleventh-century basilica and funded its professional soccer team. And he seemed modest about his achievements. He didn't smoke, he drank little, and he drove his own Lexus. All throughout Parmalat's expansion, Tanzi maintained a paternalistic approach to the business.

Going Public and Going Global

In 1989, the firm was acquired by a holding company and changed its name to Parmalat Finanziaria SpA. Profits were healthy every year, and the balance sheet appeared strong, with large amounts of cash on hand. This allowed the milk giant to go public in Italy and raise capital in the United States and other countries by selling shares and issuing bonds. Parmalat used this new capital to expand into Latin America, where it dominated the dairy markets in Brazil, Argentina, Venezuela, and several other countries.

By the early 1990s, Parmalat was popular not only among grocery shoppers but also among investors and creditors, who deemed the firm a profitable business partner. Large international banks collected hefty fees by helping the company issue bonds, list stock in foreign markets, and raise capital to fund international acquisitions. As CFO Alberto Ferraris put it, "Outside my office, there was always a line of bankers, asking about new business." There was one problem, though: The profits that Parmalat reported were only an illusion created by a set of accounting manipulations.

ACCOUNTING ISSUES

One of the most interesting aspects of Parmalat's case is the simplicity of its fraudulent accounting (which was not *quite* as simple as the scheme suggested in Figure 19.1). The purpose of the fraud was straightforward: to hide operating losses so as not to disappoint investors and creditors. The core of the scheme was double billing to Italian supermarkets and other retailers. By standard accounting procedures, every time a product is shipped to a customer, a company records a receivable that it later expects to collect as cash. Because receivables count as sales revenue, Parmalat billed customers twice for each shipment, thus greatly enlarging its sales. The company used these inflated revenues as a means of securing loans from several international banks.

"Off-Balance-Sheet Financing"

By 1995, Parmalat was losing more than $300 million annually in Latin America alone. These continued operating losses caused company executives to search for more complex ways of masking the firm's true performance. Using a trick called "off-balance-sheet financing," executives set up three shell companies based in the Caribbean that pretended to sell Parmalat products. Parmalat would send them fake invoices and charge costs and fees to make the "sales" look legitimate, then write out a credit note for the amount the subsidiaries supposedly owed and use it to raise money at the banks.

FIGURE 19.1

Source: Leo Cullum/The New Yorker Collection/www.cartoonbank.com

"New from accounting, sir. Two and two is four again."

Off-balance-sheet financing was also used to hide debts. The company transferred over half of its liabilities to the books of small subsidiaries based in offshore tax havens such as the Cayman Islands. This allowed Parmalat to present a "healthy" balance sheet and a profitable income statement to investors and creditors by hiding large amounts of debt and overstating sales revenue. In 2002, Parmalat reported liabilities of close to $8 billion on its consolidated balance sheet. In reality, the company had roughly $14 billion in debt.

The Art of Milking Growth

Taking advantage of its image, Parmalat issued bonds in the United States and Europe that were backed up by falsified assets, especially cash. "It was a reversal of logic," said the chief investigating magistrate after the scheme was discovered. Usually, companies take on debt to grow. But in Parmalat's case, "they had to grow to hide the debt." In other words, the company would obtain loans to pay off previous loans (which sounds a little like Greek sovereign debt). Investigators report that without the accounting manipulations, the company would have reported operating losses every year between 1990 and 2003. Clearly, Parmalat's milk carton was full of financial holes.

The circle of hiding operating losses by incurring increasingly larger amounts of debt eventually became hard to sustain. To perpetuate the fraud, Parmalat needed to continue incurring debt, paying interest on old debts with no real cash of its own, and finding new ways to create false sales. Alberto Ferraris, who was appointed CFO in March 2003, mentioned that "he couldn't understand why the company was paying so much to service its debt; the interest payments seemed far higher than warranted for the €5.4 billion in debt on the books."

By the late 1990s, auditors in Argentina and Brazil raised several red flags that pointed to problems with Parmalat's accounting. In early December 2003, the company failed to make a €150 million bond payment. This puzzled those familiar with the company because, according to the 2002 financial statements, Parmalat had plenty of cash on hand.

The fraud became public on December 19, 2003, when Grant Thornton LLP, the company's auditor, made a startling discovery. While auditing Bonlat, a fully owned subsidiary of Parmalat based in the Cayman Islands, the auditors contacted Bank of America to confirm a letter held by Bonlat in which the bank allegedly certified that the company had €3.95 billion in cash. Bank of America responded that such an account didn't exist. Investigators then swooped into Parmalat's headquarters to confiscate documents and computer hard drives, which uncovered the accounting tricks. On one hard drive, prosecutors found clues to the deception: "Account 999" contained details of secret transactions amounting to more than €8 billion.

THE CONSEQUENCES

Parmalat filed for bankruptcy protection on December 24, 2003. CEO Tanzi resigned and was detained by Italian authorities three days later and sent to prison, then subsequently confined to house arrest until September 27, 2004. Also accused of wrongdoing were Fausto Tonna, CFO during most of the period under investigation; Giovanni, Stefano, and Francesca Tanzi, the brother, son, and daughter of Calisto Tanzi; and other key employees believed to have been involved in the scheme.

Convicted

Initially, it was thought that misstatements were created only to hide operating losses; however, prosecutors demonstrated that the Tanzi family benefited financially from the fraud. For example, Calisto revealed that $638 million was moved to "a family-owned tourism business." In December 2008, he was finally sentenced to 10 years in jail for market rigging in a Milan court. In 2010 he was sentenced to another 18 years in prison by a judge in Parma for contributing to the company's demise. In 2012, the Public Prosecutor filed a motion for indictment against Calisto for hiding several valuable paintings from the prosecution that have since been seized to help pay for claims against him. Others have served or are serving jail time, and Stefano, Calisto's son, was tried and convicted in Switzerland on fraud and money-laundering charges and sentenced to 14 years in prison.

Enrico Bondi was appointed by the government as CEO of Parmalat to direct recovery efforts. As part of his campaign, he brought lawsuits against Grant Thornton and Deloitte, the auditors, for not performing the audit with proper care and not bringing their suspicions to the attention of management. In 2009 a judge in New York dismissed the case against Grant Thornton; in early 2011 the case was revived, but it was thrown out again.

Lawsuits, Rounds I and II

The lawsuits accuse the banks of ignoring the fraud to obtain fees from doing business with Parmalat. As mentioned earlier, these banks were instrumental in helping the company raise capital to fund its international expansion. The banks and the auditors deny any wrongdoing and claim they were victims of the scheme. Citigroup Inc., UBS AG, Deutsche Bank AG, and Morgan Stanley were involved in the Milan trial for "failing to have procedures that would have prevented crimes that contributed" to Parmalat's failure. As of mid-June 2007, Bondi has collected almost $900 million in settlements in Italy and the United States, but Parmalat lost its case against Citigroup and actually had to pay it damages.

Parmalat, in turn, has been sued by investors, banks, and other organizations. In the United States, the SEC filed a complaint against it on December 29, 2003, alleging that the company fraudulently raised money through bonds in the United States by overstating assets and understating liabilities. On July 30, 2004, Parmalat agreed to settle with the SEC without admitting or denying the claims. Parmalat won't be fined but has agreed to make changes to strengthen its board of directors and improve governance.

Restructuring

Besides the legal battles that have resulted from the fraud, Bondi's restructuring campaign calls for aggressive changes in Parmalat's organization. On March 29, 2004, the company announced it would narrow its focus in markets in Italy, Canada, Australia, South Africa, Spain, Portugal, Russia, and Romania and would pull out of other regions. However, in May 2007 Parmalat "agreed to sell its Spanish assets to Lacteos Siglo XXI." Latin American countries "with strong and profitable positions," such as Colombia, Nicaragua, and Venezuela, would be retained. In addition, Parmalat would cut its workforce from 32,000 to fewer than 17,000, slash the number of brands from 120 to 30, and concentrate on "healthy lifestyle" products.

By 2010 Parmalat had moved into Botswana, Cuba, Ecuador, Mozambique, Paraguay, Swaziland, and Zambia. It also has a presence through licensees in a number of countries. Recently the company has been focusing on higher value added products and has scheduled market testing to determine how much potential new products have in different geographic locations.

SO, WHAT'S THE BOTTOM LINE?

In Europe, the Parmalat scandal created deep concern among authorities. The European Commission suggested it would like to strengthen auditing standards by insisting that member countries introduce accounting-oversight boards similar to those in the United States. Many organizations have proposed reforms to prevent another scandal of such magnitude. One such reform considered was more transparency in the bond market in Europe—in other words, bond-price disclosure. However, "the [European Commission] has indicated that it will allow traders to police themselves instead of requiring the same data about bonds as for stocks."

From an accounting perspective, Parmalat joined the ranks of other European companies by adopting International Financial Reporting Standards published by the International Accounting Standards Board and adopted by the European Commission for their consolidated financial statements. In addition, global auditing firm PricewaterhouseCoopers has now become Parmalat's independent auditors. The hope is that these two moves will help convince investors that the company is moving in the right direction on the accounting side. Since the restructuring, Parmalat has risen from the ashes, is now listed again on the Milan stock exchange, and is Italy's biggest listed food company. At least it hasn't suffered Enron's fate.

Plus a Little Corporate Misgovernance

Even though the accounting moves described above were taken to help Parmalat recover, they are not enough. The fraud may have been perpetrated through a set of accounting tricks, but several issues converged to allow such manipulations to happen. One of the clearest deficiencies at Parmalat was its corporate governance system. As a family-owned business, the company was tightly controlled by insiders, especially Calisto Tanzi, who held the positions of CEO and chairman of the board of directors.

Most of the other board members were family members or managers of Parmalat, which prevented the company from having a strong, independent voice to stop the actions taken by management. In addition, Italian law allowed Parmalat to have two auditors instead of one. Grant Thornton was the main auditor, but Deloitte audited some of the subsidiaries, including Bonlat, where the fraud was uncovered. This arrangement made it more difficult for the auditors to have one clear, coherent picture of Parmalat's financial condition. (Neither of these auditors is used by Parmalat now.) Finally, and perhaps most importantly, management integrity failed. In the end, a manager determined to commit fraud will most likely succeed even in a very good governance system.

Parmalat is now taking the necessary steps to provide better corporate governance. Its managers are working hard to comply with the Italian Corporate Governance Code along with other general principles. The company has also created its own Code of Ethics, Code of Conduct, and Internal Dealing Code of Conduct. All employees are required to abide by the codes set in place. The 2012 Annual Report was audited by PricewaterhouseCoopers according to the rules set down by CONSOB, the Italian regulatory body that supervises companies and stock exchanges. Financial statements were prepared according to Italian accounting standards and IFRS as adopted by the European Union. The report was originally prepared in Italian, signed by Italian partner Massimo Rota, and translated into English for the convenience of international readers.

In the aftermath of Parmalat's fraud, investigators were left wondering how a few accounting numbers could fool so many people. One thing, however, was clear: Europe now had its very own version of Enron. ■

CRN
Case Review Note

QUESTIONS

19-1. How much of Parmalat's problems were due to bad accounting, and how much were due to fraud on the part of individuals in the company?

19-2. In the chapter, we discuss the difference in accounting standards in the U.S. and the rest of the world through IFRS. Do you think that it made a difference that Parmalat used IFRS instead of U.S. GAAP?

INTRODUCTION

As noted in Chapter 10, the Chief Financial Officer (CFO) of a company is responsible for the controller and treasurer functions. The controller tends to handle the accounting side, whereas the treasurer is responsible for the broader area of finance. International business managers cannot make good decisions without relevant and reliable information, and that is the responsibility of the controller. Whereas Chapter 10 discussed the role of capital markets in financing company operations, this chapter focuses on the CFO's role and examines not only the importance of accounting but also how the treasurer manages a company's financial flows.

THE CROSSROADS OF ACCOUNTING AND FINANCE

The accountant is essential in providing information to financial decision makers.

The accounting and finance functions are closely related, with each relying on the other to fulfill its responsibilities. The CFO of any company is responsible for procuring and managing the company's financial resources. Usually a member of the top management team, the CFO relies on the controller, or chief accountant, to provide the right information for making decisions, while the internal audit staff ensures that corporate policies and procedures are followed. The internal auditors, the controller, and the CFO work closely with the external auditor to try to safeguard the assets of the business. As you can see from our opening case on the Parmalat scandal, however, things can go wrong, especially when topmost management is willing to shirk its fiduciary responsibility and the external auditor may see a different sort of value in the company's assets.

The actual and potential flow of assets across national boundaries complicates the finance and accounting functions. So MNEs must learn to cope with differing inflation rates, exchange-rate changes, currency controls, expropriation risks, customs duties, tax rates and methods of determining taxable income, levels of sophistication of local accounting personnel, and local as well as home-country reporting requirements.

CONCEPT CHECK

We discuss **foreign currency exchange rates** and the ways in which they affect the operations of an MNE in Chapter 8. Here we explain the responsibilities of the CFO in overseeing a company's closely related financial and **accounting** functions. As we'll see, financial management deals with the effects of exchange rates on such financial-statement items as receivables and payables.

What Does the Controller Control? The role of the company controller is critical to providing useful and timely information to management and external stakeholders. Figure 19.2 illustrates some of the key responsibilities of the controller as part of a firm's financial team.

Today's controller is engaged in a variety of activities outside the typical accounting and reporting functions that support the firm's general strategy. These can include managing the supply chain, evaluating potential acquisitions abroad, disposing of a subsidiary or a division, managing cash flow, hedging currency and interest-rate risks, tax planning, internal auditing, and helping to plan corporate strategy. In fact, today's accountants overall must have a much broader perspective of business in general—and international business in particular, for our purposes—than the old stereotypes of accountants as bean counters (see Figure 19.3).

The controller of an international company must be concerned about a range of issues dealing with corporate strategy broader than just accounting issues.

As noted in Chapter 16 and elaborated here, foreign managers and subsidiaries are usually evaluated at headquarters on the basis of data generated in the company's reporting system as set up and coordinated by the controller's office. The controller generates

FIGURE 19.2 The Responsibilities of the Controller

We have our controller reporting to either a VP of finance or a chief financial officer. Note that our controller's area of responsibility, like that of many contemporary controllers, is twofold. He or she oversees not only activities in accounting, but also those in financial management as well.

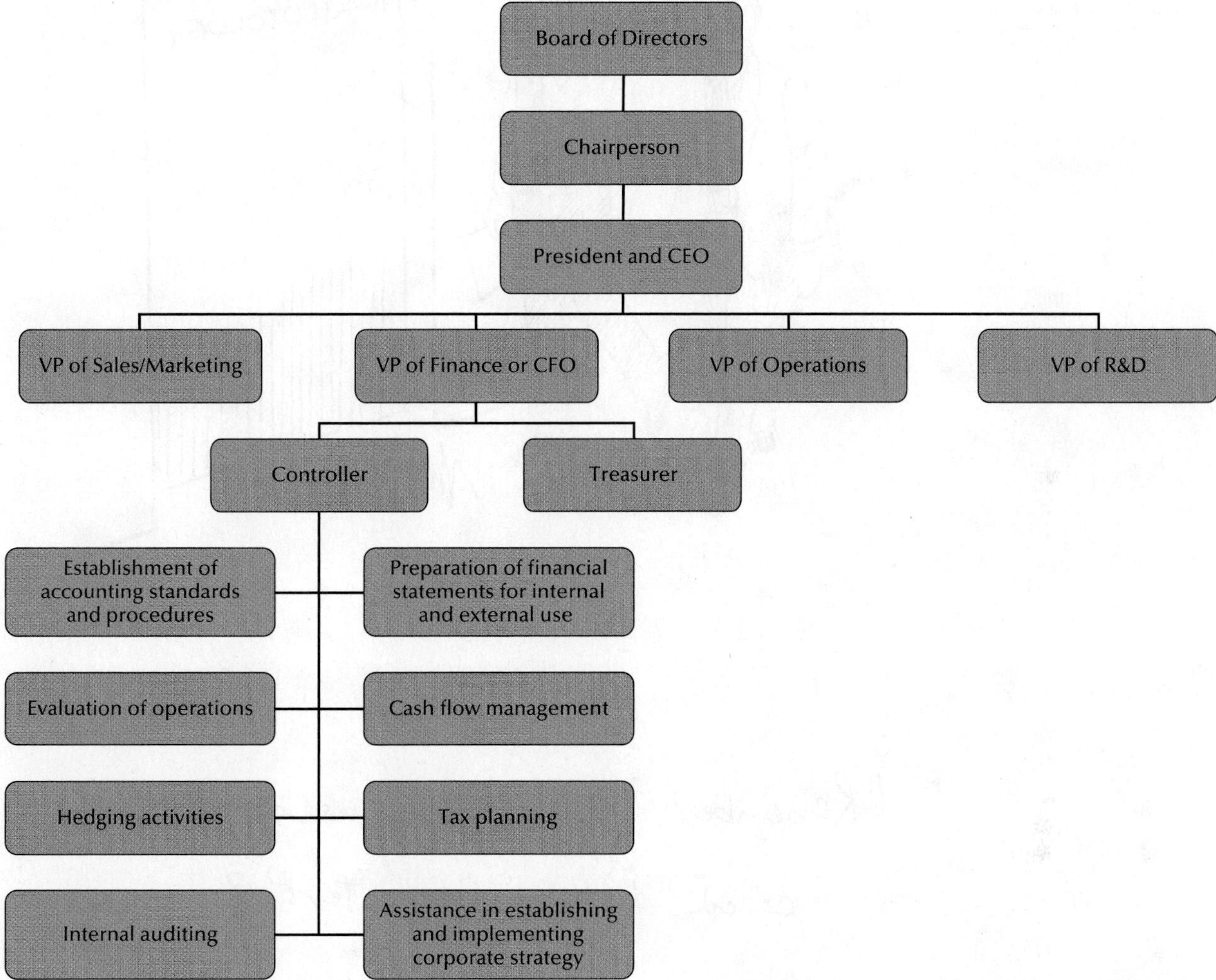

reports for internal consideration, local government needs, creditors, employees, suppliers, stockholders, and prospective investors while handling the effect of many different currencies and inflation rates on the statements and becoming familiar with different countries' accounting systems.

In discussing some key accounting issues facing MNEs, this chapter initially examines how accounting differs around the world and how global capital markets are forcing countries to consider converging their accounting and reporting standards in the attempt to move to one set of globally accepted standards. It then examines some unique issues facing MNEs, such as accounting for foreign-currency transactions, translating foreign-currency financial statements, reporting on foreign operations to shareholders and potential investors, and evaluating the performance of foreign operations and managers.

Although the focus here is on MNEs' problems, many of these issues affect any company doing business overseas, even a small importer or exporter. Foreign-currency transactions, such as denominating a sale or purchase in a foreign currency, must be accounted for in the currency of the parent company. This is true of both large and small companies, as well as service and manufacturing firms.

G. EDWIN PINKSTON
HARICOTOLOGY
"Remember when they used to be called 'bean counters'?"

FIGURE 19.3 Accountants Get a Little Semantic Respect

Source: From the Wall Street Journal/ Permission Cartoon Features Syndicate

DIFFERENCES IN FINANCIAL STATEMENTS INTERNATIONALLY

Both the form and the content of financial statements are different in different countries.

One problem an MNE faces is the varying accounting standards and practices around the world. Financial statements among countries differ in both form (or format) and content (or substance). For example, the balance sheets for U.S. companies are in the *balance format:*

Assets = Liabilities + Shareholders' equity

The balance sheet varies in the order of liquidity of the accounts presented. Some companies start with the least liquid assets (those that are harder to convert into cash quickly) and go to those that are most liquid (such as cash), whereas other companies go from the most to the least liquid assets (such as property, plants, and equipment). The former practice is very common among European companies; the latter is used by U.S.-based firms. Parmalat, for example, uses the following format:

Noncurrent assets + Current asset = Shareholders' equity + Noncurrent liabilities + Current liabilities

The balance sheet for British retailer Marks and Spencer uses the following format, which is very different from both the traditional U.S. format as well as the one used by Parmalat:

$$\text{Noncurrent assets} + \text{Current assets} - \text{Current liabilities} - \text{Noncurrent liabilities} = \text{Total equity}$$

Some of the terminology used in presenting financial statements varies for companies around the world. What is referred to by U.S. companies as inventories is called stocks in other English-speaking countries, whereas stocks in the U.S. are called shares elsewhere. U.S. firms, for example, present only a set of consolidated financial statements (also called group statements by European companies), whereas European firms like Marks & Spencer present both company (also called parent company) and group financial statements.

Major reporting issues:

- Language
- Currency
- Type of statements
- Financial statement format
- Extent of footnote disclosures
- Underlying GAAP on which the financial statements are based

DIFFERENCES IN THE PRESENTATION OF FINANCIAL INFORMATION

The types of financial information required in different countries can differ, while companies also have to consider who their audience is: are they providing financial information only for the local market (such as Brazilian firms for users in Brazil), or also for users from the broader global capital markets? Companies that list on stock exchanges usually provide an income statement, a balance sheet (also known as a statement of financial position), a statement of shareowners' equity, a cash-flow statement, and detailed footnotes in their annual report. Providers of financial information for the broader investing community need to consider the following four factors:

1. Language
2. Currency
3. Statement type (including format and extent of footnote disclosure)
4. Underlying GAAP on which the statements are based

Language Differences English tends to be the first choice of companies choosing to raise capital abroad. For example, German company Daimler issues financial statements in both German and English, while Sweden's H&M provides its annual reports in Swedish and English. Parmalat is interesting because its registered office is in Italy, its shares are traded on the Online Stock Market operated by the Borsa Italiana, and it is controlled by a French company that is part of the Lactalis Group, a French multinational dairy products company. It provides an annual report in English, although its financial statements are in euros, its major reporting currency.

Many companies also provide a significant amount of information on their Internet home pages. Managers can just click on the desired language button and all the information is provided in that language. Parmalat's home page is full of information for people all over the world. It even has a link, www.parmalat.com.br, that gives general information in Portuguese for Brazilian readers.

Currency Differences Companies around the world prepare their financial statements in different currencies—Daimler's are in euros, H&M's in Swedish kronor, Coca-Cola in U.S. dollars, and so on. In its 2012 annual report, Adidas provided its financial information in euros, disclosed information on the firm's currency-translation policies, and gave average exchange rates for the U.S. dollar, the British pound, the Japanese yen, the Russian ruble, and the Chinese yuan to allow investors to make convenient translations from euros.[2]

Differences in Types of Statements As noted earlier in the chapter, financial-statement format is not a big issue, but it can be confusing to read a balance sheet prepared in an analytical format when one is used to seeing it in the balance format. A major area of difference is the use of footnotes. Footnote disclosures in countries with strong equity markets, such as the United States, tend to be very comprehensive. Greater transparency is synonymous with more extensive footnote disclosures. Companies that list on multiple stock exchanges, such as Daimler AG, have extensive footnotes as well because they have to comply with the reporting requirements of a global investing community.

GAAP Usage Differences A major hurdle in raising capital in different countries is dealing with widely varying accounting and disclosure requirements. Although this problem is decreasing as more stock exchanges and countries allow the use of IFRS, some countries care more about those differences than others. Most countries also may apply one set of accounting standards for consolidated groups while using another set for the individual companies in the group. In this situation, the individual companies must use local accounting standards that are usually tied to legal requirements and are the basis for tax accounting. Consolidated financial statements, which are used for capital markets and not for tax purposes, are prepared by a different set of standards, such as IFRS. U.S. companies do not have the same situation. They disclose only consolidated financial statements, not individual company financial statements. There are some differences for tax accounting, but those differences are reconciled in the financial statements rather than as separate statements for each company in a group.

ACCOUNTING OBJECTIVES

The accounting process identifies, records, and interprets economic events.

The Financial Accounting Standards Board (FASB) sets accounting standards in the United States.

It is important in the accounting process to identify, record, and interpret economic events. Every country needs to determine the objectives of the accounting system it has put into place. According to the **Financial Accounting Standards Board (FASB)**, the private-sector body that establishes accounting standards in the United States, and the **International Accounting Standards Board**, a London-based organization that sets accounting standards for the broader global community, general purpose financial reporting should "provide financial information about the reporting entity that is useful for potential investors, lenders, and other creditors in making decisions about providing resources to the entity." As noted in Figure 19.4, there are many users of general financial information, but the primary users are existing and potential investors, lenders, and other creditors.

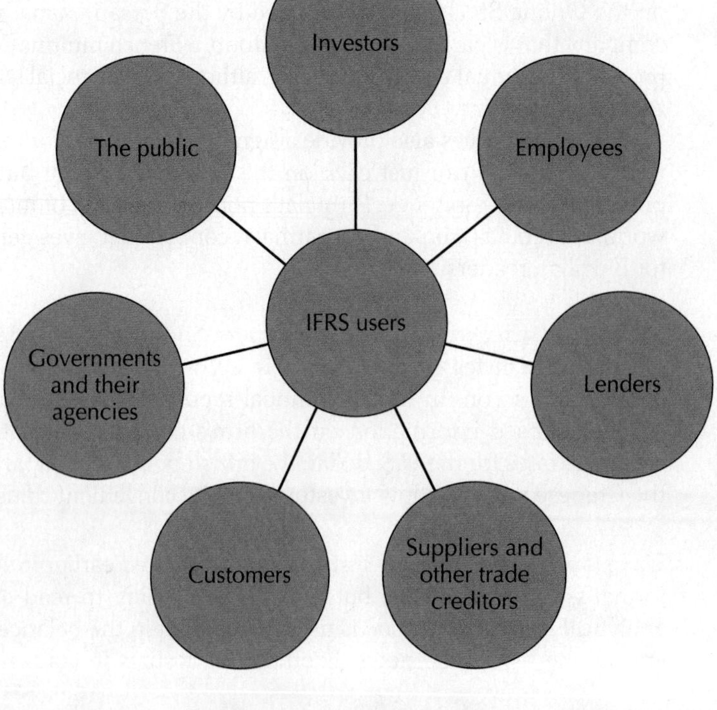

FIGURE 19.4 Who Uses Accounting Information?

Although there are many important users of accounting information as illustrated in this figure, the key users as identified by FASB and the IASB are current and potential investors, lenders, and other creditors. In some countries, such as the United States, investors might be more important than lenders, and in other countries, such as Germany, lenders (primarily the banks) have historically been the most important source of funding.

Source: Based on Financial Accounting Standards Board, Conceptual Framework: Statement of Financial Accounting Concepts, No. 8, Chapter 1, The Objective of General Purpose Financial Reporting, paragraph OB2-OB11.

Critical users of accounting information are investors, employees, lenders, suppliers, other trade creditors, customers, governments and their agencies, and the public.

It's important to identify primary users because a focus on different users might result in different financial information being reported. For example, because Germany's major users have historically been banks, accounting has focused more on the balance sheet, which contains a description of the company's assets. In the United States, however, the major users are investors, so accounting has focused more on the income statement. Investors see the income statement as an indication of the future success of the company, affecting stock price (or share price) and the flow of dividends.

CONCEPT CHECK

In discussing "Legal Issues in International Business" in Chapter 3, we survey the various ways in which local legal standards can affect foreign firms in operational concerns—in the ways in which they function on a day-to-day basis. Naturally, these standards include **accounting** standards, and here we emphasize that attitudes toward—and, more importantly, regulations concerning—accounting practices vary widely from country to country. Remember, too, that although standard-setting bodies may be public or private organizations, policies such as those pertaining to **FASB** and **GAAP** are strongly influenced by local governments.

FACTORS AFFECTING ACCOUNTING STANDARDS AND PRACTICES

Figure 19.5 identifies some of the forces leading to the development of international accounting standards and practices. Although all the factors shown are significant, their importance varies by country. For example, investors are influential in the United States and the United Kingdom, but creditors—primarily banks—have traditionally had more influence in Germany and Switzerland. Figure 19.5 is comprehensive because it focuses on *all* elements of the accounting process: national and international influences, users, regulators, auditors, and educators.

As we will discuss in more detail below, cultural issues cut across all countries and strongly influence the development of accounting. Institutional factors such as legal and tax

FIGURE 19.5 Sources of Influence on Accounting

Every aspect of the accounting process is influenced by a variety of internal and external factors, and they're all potentially important. The degree of importance will vary by country.

Source: Based on The International Journal of Accounting, Vol. 10, No. 3, Lee H. Radebaugh, Environmental Factors Influencing the Development of Accounting, Objectives, Standards, and Practices, p. 41, 1975.

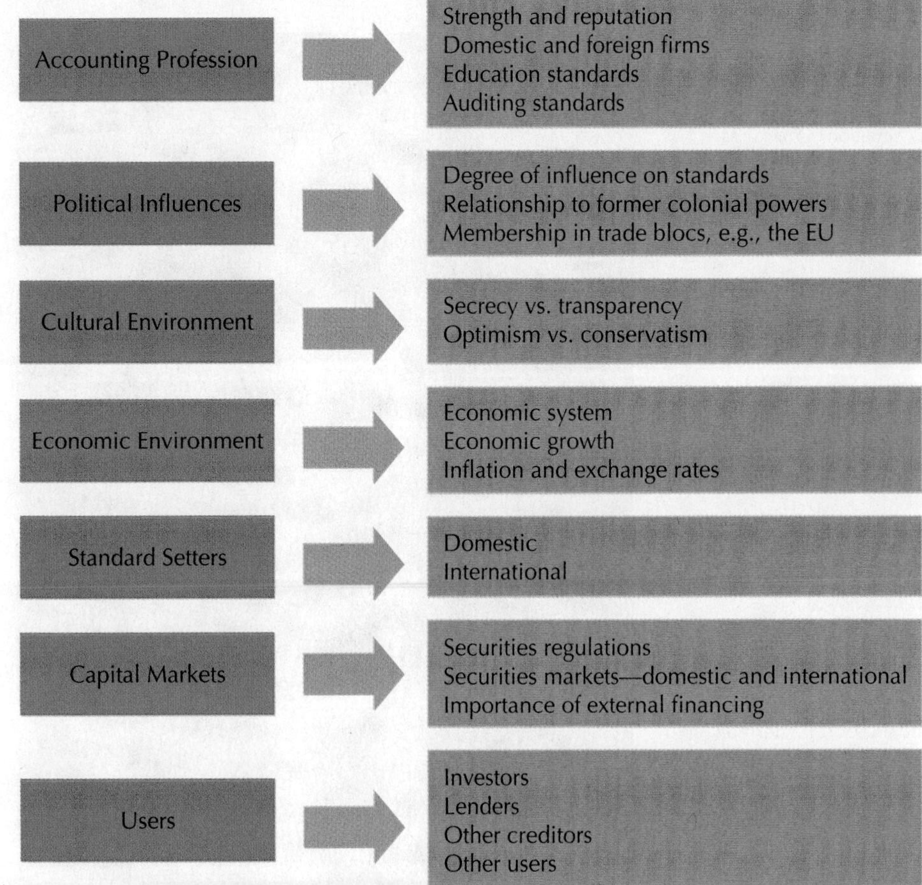

systems have a big influence on accounting standards and practices in most of the world. Certain international factors also have weight, such as former colonial influence and foreign investment. For example, most countries that are current or former members of the British Commonwealth have accounting systems similar to the United Kingdom's, former French colonies use the French model, and so forth. As shown later, however, the convergence of accounting standards being led by the IASB will eventually reduce many of these differences.

International public accounting firms, such as Deloitte, E&Y, KPMG, and PricewaterhouseCoopers, are also important sources of influence because they transfer high levels of accounting and auditing practices worldwide. As we observe in our opening case on Parmalat, public accounting firms are also responsible for ensuring that proper accounting practices are followed and that publicly released financial statements accurately represent a firm's financial position.

CONCEPT CHECK

Chapter 2 is devoted to illustrating the many ways in which local culture shapes the environment in which international business is conducted from country to country. Here we point out that culture also affects differences in approaches to **accounting** systems and policies. In Chapter 2, we cite Geert Hofstede among the researchers who've studied national differences in managerial attitudes and preferences, and here we use applications of Hofstede's findings to studies of work-situation behavior as a means of shedding light on the effect of cultural differences on accounting standards and practices.

Culture influences measurement and disclosure practices:

- Measurement—how to value assets
- Disclosure—the presentation of information and discussion of results

CULTURAL DIFFERENCES IN ACCOUNTING

The differences in measurement and disclosure practices among countries are of special interest to international investors. *Measurement* means how companies value assets, including inventory and fixed assets, whereas *disclosure* refers to how and what information companies provide and discuss in their annual and interim reports for external financial data users.

As noted in Chapter 2, culture refers to learned norms based on the values, attitudes, and beliefs of a group of people. Much of the work on culture and accounting is initially based on Hofstede's research on the structural elements of culture, particularly those that most strongly affect behavior in the work situations of organizations and institutions.[3] Hofstede's work was extended into the accounting area by Gray, which resulted in country classifications according to disclosure and measurement principles—specifically, secrecy/transparency and optimism/conservatism.[4]

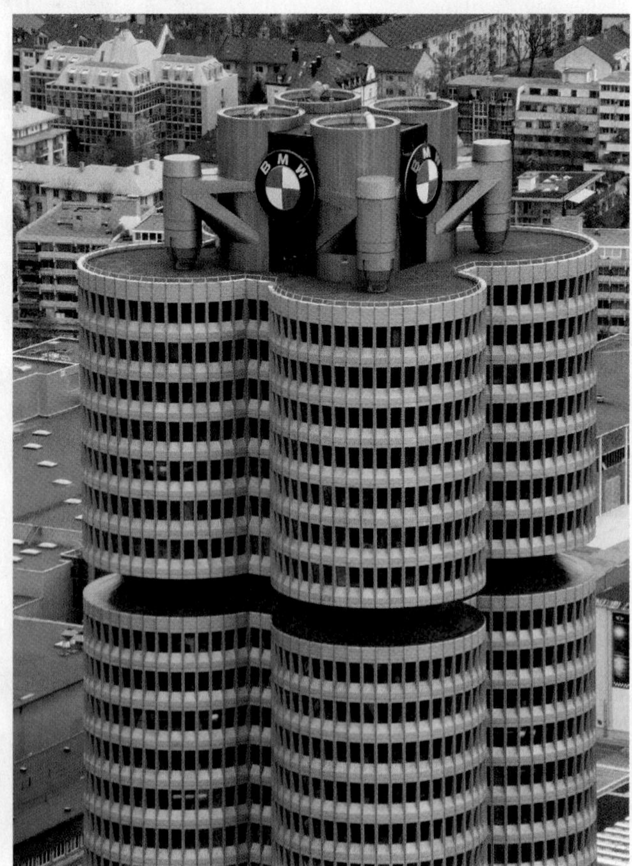

Global auto manufacturer BMW is headquartered in Munich, Germany, publishes its annual report in German and English, uses the euro as its reporting currency, and prepares its financial statements in IFRS.
Source: Ninelle/Shutterstock

Secrecy and transparency refer to the degree to which corporations disclose information to the public. Optimism and conservatism refer to the degree of caution companies display in valuing assets and recognizing income.

The Secrecy–Transparency/Optimism–Conservatism Matrix Figure 19.6 depicts the accounting practices of various groupings of countries within a matrix of the cultural values of secrecy–transparency and optimism–conservatism. With respect to accounting, secrecy and transparency indicate the degree to which companies disclose information to the public. Countries such as Germany, Switzerland, and Japan tend to have less disclosure (illustrating the cultural value of secrecy) than do the United States and the United Kingdom (Anglo-American countries, which are more transparent or open with respect to disclosure). The classification of countries in Figure 19.6 assumes how countries would fit, not how countries actually fit. In addition, the classifications represent a point in time, and countries are always changing, especially as their companies move closer to listing on capital markets, both locally and globally. However, it's still interesting to consider how countries fit on the matrix depending on their general cultural tendencies. The opening case on the Parmalat scandal demonstrates that even companies that list on global exchanges, borrow money from the largest banks in the world, and turn their financial statements over to the world's best auditing firms can have secretive corporate cultures.

Generally Accepted Accounting Principles In addition, as companies from the upper-right quadrant of secrecy and conservatism use capital markets more extensively, they move closer to the Anglo-American mode. This is especially true of companies like Deutsche Bank and Daimler, which adopted U.S. **Generally Accepted Accounting Principles (GAAP)** for reporting purposes, as allowed under German law, before moving to **International Financial Reporting Standards (IFRS)** as adopted by the **International Accounting Standards Board**. IFRS is to IASB as GAAP is to FASB; all refer to standards and practices that must be adopted. As companies headquartered in the European Union and other countries throughout the world adopt IFRS, they should become more transparent and optimistic.

Optimism and conservatism (in an accounting sense, not political) are the degrees of caution companies exhibit in valuing assets and recognizing income—an illustration of the measurement issues mentioned earlier. The more conservative countries tend to understate assets and income, whereas optimistic countries tend to be more liberal in their recognition of income. Banks primarily fund French companies, as they do in Germany and Japan, and are concerned with liquidity. So French companies tend to be very conservative both when recording profits that keep them from paying taxes and when declaring dividends to pile

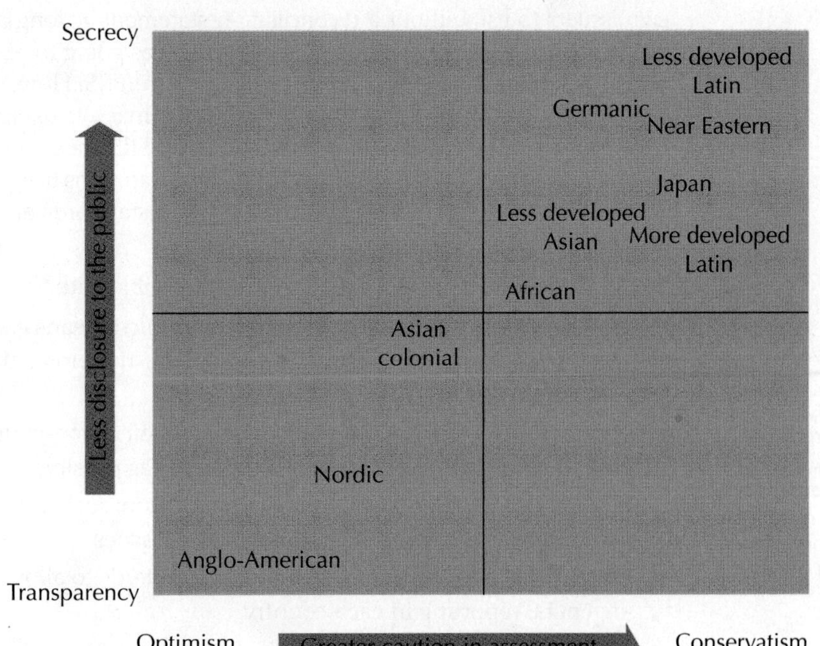

FIGURE 19.6 A Disclosure/Assessment Matrix for National Accounting Systems

The vertical axis reflects practices according to transparency-secrecy (the extent to which companies in a country disclose information to the public). The horizontal axis reflects practices accounting to optimism-conservatism (the degree of caution taken by companies when it comes to valuing assets and recognizing income). Note that, not surprisingly, transparency and optimism tend to go hand-in-hand, as do secrecy and conservatism.

Source: Based on Lee H. Radebaugh, Sidney J. Gray and Ervin L. Black, International Accounting and Multinational Enterprises, 6th ed. (New York: John Wiley & Sons, 2002) 6, p. 51.

British companies are optimistic when recognizing income. U.S. companies are slightly less optimistic. Japanese and continental European companies are even less optimistic than U.S. companies.

up cash reserves to service their bank debts. However, as German MNCs in particular outgrew the ability of banks to provide the majority of their funding needs, they were forced to adopt accounting standards and reporting practices more in line with global capital markets, becoming less secret and more transparent.

In contrast, U.S. companies want to show earning power to impress and attract investors. British firms tend to be more optimistic in earnings recognition than their U.S. counterparts, but the latter are much more optimistic than continental European and Japanese companies.

INTERNATIONAL STANDARDS AND GLOBAL CONVERGENCE

MUTUAL RECOGNITION VERSUS RECONCILIATION

Major approaches to dealing with accounting and reporting differences:

- Mutual recognition
- Reconciliation to local GAAP
- Recasting of financial statements in terms of local GAAP

Convergence is the process of bringing difference national Generally Accepted Accounting Principles (GAAP) into line with International Financial Reporting Standards (IFRS) issued by the IASB.

Before the rise in importance of global capital markets and the move to a common set of accounting standards, it was common for many countries to apply the principle of **mutual recognition**, whereby a regulator, such as the German stock exchange, would accept financial statements provided in U.S. GAAP of a U.S. company wanting to list securities in Germany. Prior to the requirement in 2005 that EU companies provide financial statements prepared according to IFRS, some German companies such as Daimler and Deutsche Bank prepared their consolidated financial statements according to U.S. GAAP, as permitted at the time by German law. This made it easier for them to list on the New York Stock Exchange. However, they dropped this practice and moved to IFRS in 2007. In their 2010 annual report, they stated that "the consolidated financial statements of Daimler AG and its subsidiaries have been prepared in accordance with Section 315a of the German Commercial Code (HGB) and International Financial Reporting Standards (IFRS) and related interpretations as issued by the International Accounting Standards Board (IASB) and as adopted by the European Union."

The United States uses two approaches: adoption of U.S. standards or the use of IFRS (in this original IASB version). If a foreign company prefers to list according to their home country GAAP instead of U.S. GAAP or IFRS, they must provide a statement of **reconciliation**. In this case, the company usually lists American Depositary Receipts (ADRs) on a U.S. exchange and then reconciles its home-country GAAP with U.S. GAAP in a special statement called Form 20-F on net income and shareholders' equity. This is the approach Daimler used before it adopted U.S. GAAP for its consolidated financial statements. Since 2007, however, the SEC permits foreign issuers to list without a reconciliation statement as long as their financial statements are prepared in accordance with full IFRS. The EU was going to require U.S. firms that want to list on European exchanges to list in accordance with IFRS. However, it announced in 2008 that it would allow U.S. firms to continue to list on EU markets using U.S. GAAP, given the progress of convergence and the fact that U.S. GAAP and IFRS are essentially equivalent. In addition, the SEC's dropping the 20-F reconciliation for European firms using IFRS was a contributing factor.[5]

Major forces leading to convergence:

- Investor orientation
- Global integration of capital markets
- MNEs' need for foreign capital
- Regional political and economic harmonization
- MNEs' desire to reduce accounting and reporting costs
- Convergence efforts of standards-setting bodies

Despite the many differences in accounting standards and practices around the world, a number of forces are leading to convergence:

- A movement to provide information compatible with the needs of investors
- The global integration of capital markets, which means easier and faster access to investment opportunities around the world and, therefore, the need for more comparable financial data
- The need of MNEs to raise capital outside their home-country capital markets while generating as few different financial statements as possible
- Regional political and economic harmonization, such as the efforts of the EU, which affect accounting as well as trade and investment issues
- Pressure from MNEs for more uniform standards to allow greater ease and reduced costs in general reporting in each country.

THE FIRST STEPS IN CONVERGENCE

Established in 1973, the International Accounting Standards Committee (IASC), the forerunner of the IASB, began working toward harmonizing standards by issuing a set of International Accounting Standards (IAS) that they hoped anyone in the world could use. Its original standards had a strong capital-markets focus so that they could be used worldwide to facilitate the free flow of capital. With such a goal, the IASC tended to lean more toward the traditions of the United States and the United Kingdom rather than the legal- and tax-based systems of Germany and France, where funding was more the domain of banks than broadly based capital markets. This engendered some hostility in other countries, which disliked the similarity to U.S. standards. In addition, these standards were often very superficial, with too many options to capture the support of everyone.

The International Organization of Securities Commissions accepted a core set of accounting standards issued by the IASB in which securities regulators can be confident.

The turning point in the significance of IAS came in 1995, when the **International Organization of Securities Commissions (IOSCO)** announced publicly it would endorse IAS if the IASC developed a set of core standards acceptable to it. IOSCO is significant because it comprises the regulators of most of the world's stock markets, including the SEC in the United States. In May 2000, the IASC completed a core set of standards acceptable to IOSCO, and securities market regulators began the process of convincing their standard setters to adopt these standards, called International Financial Reporting Standards (IFRS).

THE INTERNATIONAL ACCOUNTING STANDARDS BOARD

In March 2001, the IASC was reorganized into the International Accounting Standards Committee Foundation (now called the IFRS Foundation) and the International Accounting Standards Board (IASB). The IFRS Foundation is the parent entity of the IASB, which assumed the major standard-setting functions of the old IASC.[6]

Trustees of the Foundation search for and appoint members of the IASB. They serve for three years and come from different regions of the world. Six must be selected from the Asia/Oceania region, six from Europe, six from North America, one from Africa, one from South America, and two from the rest of the world.[7]

The IASB is attempting to harmonize accounting standards through issuing International Financial reporting Standards (IFRS).

International Financial Reporting Standards (IFRS) When the IASB was organized, all of the old standards from the IASC were adopted, and the Board began to go through each one to upgrade them. Then the Board began to issue the new International Financial Reporting Standards; thus, when we use the term *IFRS*, we refer to the new standards as well as the old IAS.

The objectives of the IFRS Foundation and the IASB are:

> (a) To develop a single set of high-quality, understandable, enforceable, and globally accepted international financial reporting standards (IFRSs) through its standard-setting body, the IASB; (b) to promote the use and rigorous application of those standards; (c) to take account of the financial reporting needs of emerging economies and small and medium-sized entities (SMEs); and (d) to promote and facilitate adopting of IFRSs, being the standards and interpretations issued by the IASB, through convergence of national accounting standards and IFRSs.[8]

As of 2013, the EU and more than 100 other countries either require or permit the use of IFRS. Of course, there is a difference between permitting and requiring, and that is a major issue. The IASB is conducting a detailed study of countries to determine the level of acceptance and usage of IFRS. It began with the G20 and 46 other countries. The goal is to profile every country that has adopted IFRS or is moving toward adoption.

FASB and IASB are trying to converge their standards through a variety of different activities.

The Relationship Between the FASB and the IASB The FASB and IASB have been working closely to achieve a convergence of accounting standards. In 2002, they issued the Norwalk Agreement, pledging their best efforts to:

a. undertake a short-term project aimed at removing a variety of individual differences between U.S. GAAP and International Financial Reporting Standards (IFRS, which include International Accounting Standards, IAS);

b. remove other differences between IFRSs and U.S. GAAP that existed on or before January 1, 2005, through coordination of their future work programs; that is, through the mutual undertaking of discrete, substantial projects which both Boards would address concurrently;

c. continue progress on the joint projects that they are currently undertaking; and,

d. encourage their respective interpretative bodies to coordinate their activities.[9]

Convergence implies a goal and a path to achieving it. The goal is to eliminate differences in accounting standards between FASB and the IASB. The convergence process (or path) takes several forms. Initially, the two Boards identified standards that could easily be converged. Now that they have joint projects to establish new standards, they are trying to eliminate existing differences in a short-term convergence project for standards that should be easy to converge, and the FASB is explicitly considering the effect of IFRS on every standard it sets. Some more complicated standards are part of a long-term convergence process.[10] However, some of the issues the two boards are trying to resolve are very difficult, in particular revenue recognition, leases, and financial instruments.

However, standard-setting in the United States depends on the cooperation of the SEC, whose mission is to "protect investors, maintain fair, orderly, and efficient markets, and facilitate capital formation."[11] Although the SEC does not set accounting standards, it empowers the FASB to do so because companies—both foreign and domestic—that want to raise capital in the United States must follow the SEC guidelines. It appeared as if the SEC were moving toward allowing U.S. companies to issue financial statements according to IFRS, but that was delayed in 2012. In July 2012, however, an SEC staff report was issued which recommended several areas of work and concern. In general, even though the staff found that IFRS were getting stronger, there were too many reasons why it was not yet the right time for U.S. companies to give up US GAAP and move to IFRS. IFRS are just not comprehensive enough with good implementation help and consistency across countries. It makes no sense to incur the cost to switch to IFRS when the adoption of the standards is not consistent worldwide. In addition, there is little difference in IFRS and U.S. GAAP where final standards exist. The challenge is not knowing what IFRS could be set in the future and whether or not they would be appropriate for the U.S. environment.

The European Response to Convergence The main body of financial reporting requirements for limited liability companies in the EU consists of two directives issued by the European Council. Thus, it is important to understand that IFRS and interpretations must be approved by the European Parliament and the European Council and adopted as an official regulation by the European Commission to have legal standing in the EU.[12] This illustrates the importance of the political process in IFRS adoption. Prior to the development of the IASB, the EU was working to harmonize reporting practices to better coordinate financial markets. To enhance that process, it supported the efforts of the IASB and, in the spring of 2002, directed its member countries to adopt IFRS by 2005. In the case of the EU, this meant that 7,000 publicly listed companies started using IFRS for their consolidated financial statements in 2005.[13] The two main reasons for the EU to push IFRS were to allow it to influence IASB standards and to avoid funding and developing a competing standard-setting body.[14] By working with the IASB, the EU would avoid relying on standards developed in the U.S. for capital market reporting.

The EU has adopted most of the standards as written, but has "carved out" or suspended the standard on financial instruments due largely to political pressure from French banks in response to the global financial crisis when banks would have been forced to write down the value of their derivatives to reflect changes in market value. As a result, the fear is that the EU could end up with its own version of IFRS, resulting from such political pressures rather than sound accounting judgment. Thus, the EU has ruled that it must officially approve any IFRS before it can have the force of law and has set up its own advisory process to review the standard and recommend whether or not it would be acceptable. As a result, European companies must state that they adopt IFRS "as adopted by the EU." That means that upon the EU's recommendation, its member companies can "opt out" or "carve out" certain standards, meaning that they could end up with their own versions of IFRS. The convergence process has been very unsettling to some Europeans because they feel the close cooperation of the IASB and FASB is making the new IFRS suspiciously similar to standards issued by FASB.

Full application of IFRS in various countries and under various regulatory regimes is difficult to judge. Not all countries require companies to adhere to all IFRS.

Enforcement of IFRS is a major concern.

Initial reactions of various parties to European firms' 2005 adoption of IFRS have been interesting. In fact, various interpretations and applications exist. Some firms use wide judgment in applying IFRS, while others use an adapted form with changes or alternative interpretations based on individual country accounting treatments. Moreover, the adapted versions are not the full IFRS as approved by the EU.

The SEC may soon allow U.S.-listed firms to report financial results using IFRS.

Convergence and Mutual Recognition The move to convergence adds an interesting twist to mutual recognition. Today's version of mutual recognition in the United States is that foreign issuers are allowed to list securities using full IFRS without reconciliation to U.S. GAAP. EU members can use the EU form of IFRS and still be exempted from such reconciliation. However, mutual recognition does not extend to companies that generate financial statements in their home-country GAAP. They are still required to issue Form 20-F and provide a reconciliation between their GAAP and U.S. GAAP for the income statement and owner's equity.

The landscape for convergence has changed since 2008. The global economic crisis diverted attention away from convergence to trying to resolve the credit crisis and global recession. In 2011, the path to convergence became even more complicated as the governments in Europe and the United States seemed more concerned about financial regulation and budget crises than convergence. However, the G20 has strongly recommended the adoption of IFRS worldwide, which lent even greater support to the work of the IASB. In December 2010, the Chief Accountant of the SEC came up with the idea of "condorsement"—a combination of convergence and endorsement—as the approach the SEC might follow in the future. The convergence part would refer to the completion of the MOU outlined in the Norwalk Agreement, and the endorsement part would involve having FASB endorse future IFRS as deemed appropriate in the context of U.S. capital markets.[15]

Point

Should U.S. Companies Be Allowed to Close the GAAP?

Point **Yes** A major issue for investors around the world is obtaining reliable, comparable financial-statement information for company evaluation and comparison. Creditors and other users also need this information for making well-informed decisions on a global basis. As the composition of the business world has shifted from domestic economies to a global economy, the need for a single set of financial reporting standards has never been greater. IFRS are required for listed entities in many countries, such as all countries in the European Union, Canada, Australia, and New Zealand.

U.S. GAAP and IFRS are the two most recognized sets of standards today, and they are steadily becoming nearly identical to each other. The combined efforts of the IASB and the FASB in their convergence project have brought the two closer than ever before. The SEC currently allows foreign firms that list on U.S. exchanges to use IFRS for financial reporting and should allow U.S. firms as well. Not only would this make the United States more a part of the global economy, its companies could also raise more capital because investors in countries that use it would be more familiar and able to keep up with the single international set of standards.

U.S. investors would also benefit. They would become more familiar with the international standards and would feel more apt to invest in international companies. As the gap between IFRS and U.S. GAAP shrinks, the quality of the financial information presented under IFRS will not be lower than it has been under GAAP.

The "principles-based" approach of IFRS may actually enhance the quality of financial information and help the economy avoid some of the scandals that have occurred due to manipulation of loopholes in the more "rules-based" system that is U.S. GAAP. Principles-based accounting means that the standard-setters identify key principles in a conceptual framework used to set standards and then try to establish rules that are simple but conform to those principles. A rules-based system is very legalistic, with lots of detail and difficulty. Finally, if the U.S. does not adopt IFRS, it runs the risk of being left out of the debate for setting new standards. The rest of the world will be responsible for those.

Should U.S. Companies Be Allowed to Close the GAAP?

Counterpoint

Counterpoint **No** It is unrealistic to assume that IFRS would be appropriate for the unique U.S. economic environment. As the largest economy in the world, with the largest and most sophisticated capital market, the United States should have the most stringent and transparent financial reporting standards in the world. Many companies around the globe continue to prepare their financial information in accordance with U.S. GAAP because it has historically been the world's most reliable set of standards, designed to present information that is both relevant and trustworthy. IFRS are far less comprehensive than GAAP, and the standards, though oriented to capital markets, cannot take into account specific issues important to U.S. capital markets.

Allowing U.S. companies to use IFRS would impose tremendous costs on the nation's economy. Publicly traded firms would need trained employees proficient in IFRS application. U.S. accounting firms would be responsible for training their existing auditors in IFRS, hiring new employees and training them, or hiring existing IFRS experts. This training and/or hiring would impose tremendous burdens in both time and money on these important firms, which would still be held responsible for meeting all the rigorous standards of the Public Company Accounting Oversight Board (PCAOB) and the Sarbanes-Oxley Act of 2002. Many contracts in the U.S. are based on U.S. GAAP, and it would be necessary to change nearly all of them to allow for the use of IFRS.

The differences between IFRS and U.S. GAAP, though growing more insignificant, still exist. The standards are not directly comparable, which could mean trouble for investors who may have difficulty seeing the differences. In addition, more than one set of IFRS seems to exist: (1) IFRS as issued by the IASB, (2) IFRS as adopted by the EU, and (3) IFRS as applied/adopted on an individual-country basis. How will investors ascertain which set is being used by various companies, and how will this information be comparable?

Valuable invested money may leave the United States and be invested in foreign corporations not even listed in the country as U.S. investors become more expert in analyzing financial statements prepared in accordance with IFRS. And with more room for interpretation and discretion when applying IFRS, more accounting scandals could result when U.S. companies use the more "principles-based" system instead of the more "rules-based" U.S. GAAP.

TRANSACTIONS IN FOREIGN CURRENCIES

When a company operates outside the domestic market, it must concern itself with the proper recording and subsequent accounting of assets, liabilities, revenues, and expenses that are measured or denominated in foreign currencies. These transactions can result from the purchase and sale of goods and services as well as the borrowing and lending of foreign currency.

RECORDING TRANSACTIONS

Any time an importer has to pay for equipment or merchandise in a foreign currency, it must trade its own currency for that of the exporter to make the payment. Assume that Sundance

Ski Lodge, a U.S. company, imports skis from a French supplier for €5,000 and agrees to pay in euros when the exchange rate is $1.4500/euro. Sundance records the following in its books:

Purchases	7,250	
Accounts payable		7,250
€ 5,000 @ 1.4500		

If Sundance pays immediately, there's no problem. But what happens if the exporter extends 30 days' credit to Sundance? If the rate changed to, say, $1.5000/euro by the time the payment was due, Sundance would record a final settlement as:

Accounts payable	7,250	
Foreign-exchange loss	250	
Cash		7,500

Foreign-currency receivables and payables give rise to gains and losses whenever the exchange rate changes. Transaction gains and losses must be included in the income statement in the accounting period in which they arise.

The merchandise stays at the original value of $7,250, but there is a difference between the dollar value of the account payable to the exporter ($7,250) and the actual number of dollars the importer must come up with to purchase the euros to pay the exporter ($7,500). The difference between the two accounts ($250) is the loss on foreign exchange and is always recognized in the income statement.

The company that denominates the sale or purchase in the foreign currency (in this case, the importer) must recognize the gains and losses arising from foreign-currency transactions at the end of each accounting period—usually quarterly. In the example here, assume that the end of the quarter has arrived and Sundance has still not paid the French exporter. The skis continue to be valued at $7,250, but the payable has to be updated to the new exchange rate of $1.5000/euro. The journal entry would be:

Foreign-exchange loss	250	
Accounts payable		250

The payable would now be worth $7,500. If settlement were made in the month following the end of the quarter and the exchange rate remained the same, the final entry would be:

Accounts payable	7,500	
Cash		7,500

If the U.S. company were an exporter and anticipated receiving foreign currency, the corresponding entries (using the same information as in the example here) would be:

Accounts receivable	7,250	
Sales		7,250
Cash	7,500	
Foreign-exchange gain		250
Accounts receivable		7,250

In this case, a gain results because the company received more cash than if it had collected its money immediately.

CORRECT PROCEDURES FOR U.S. COMPANIES

The FASB requires that U.S. companies report foreign-currency transactions at the original spot exchange rate and that subsequent gains and losses on foreign-currency receivables or payables be put on the income statement. The same procedure must be followed according to IFRS.

The procedures U.S. companies must follow to account for foreign-currency transactions are found in FASB Statement No. 52, "Foreign Currency Translation," which requires them to record the initial transaction at the spot exchange rate in effect on the transaction date and to record receivables and payables on subsequent balance-sheet dates at the spot exchange rate on those dates. Any foreign-exchange gains and losses that arise from carrying receivables or payables during a period in which the exchange rate changes are recognized in the income statement in that period.[16] This is basically the same procedure required by the IASB as well as in IAS 21.

TRANSLATING FOREIGN-CURRENCY FINANCIAL STATEMENTS

Translation—the process of restating foreign-currency financial statements

Consolidation—the process of combining the translated financial statements of a parent and its subsidiaries into one set of financial statements.

Even though U.S.-based MNEs receive reports originally developed in a variety of different currencies, they eventually must end up with one set of financial statements in U.S. dollars to help management and investors understand their worldwide activities in a common currency. The process of restating foreign-currency financial statements into U.S. dollars is called **translation**. The combination of all of these translated financial statements into one is **consolidation**. The same concept exists for other countries, such as a British-based MNE that has to come up with a set of financial statements in British pounds. For the sake of illustration, we use a U.S.-based MNE.

Translation in the United States is a two-step process:

1. *Companies recast foreign-currency financial statements into statements consistent with U.S. GAAP.* This occurs because a U.S. company with a subsidiary in Brazil, for example, must keep the books and records in Brazil according to Brazilian GAAP. For consolidation purposes, however, the resulting financial statements have to be issued according to U.S. GAAP in format as well as content. As an example of content, Brazil might require that inventories be valued a certain way. For the U.S. consolidated financial statements, however, inventories must be valued according to U.S., not Brazilian, standards. This is a big issue when local GAAP is very different from U.S. GAAP. As more foreign countries adopt IFRS, the differences between IFRS financial statements and U.S. GAAP financial statements will be less significant.
2. *Companies translate all foreign-currency amounts into U.S. dollars*. FASB Statement No. 52 describes how companies must translate their foreign-currency financial statements into dollars. All U.S. companies, as well as foreign firms that list on a U.S. exchange, must use Statement No. 52.

TRANSLATION METHODS

Statement No. 52 and IAS 21, the relevant translation standards issued by the FASB and the IASB, respectively, are basically the same in how they require MNEs to translate their foreign-currency financial statements into the currency of the parent's country. For simplicity's sake, we continue to use the example of a U.S.-based MNE that must translate its foreign-currency financial statements into dollars. It would use FASB Statement 52, while a British-based MNE would use IAS 21. The two standards yield the same result.

The functional currency is the currency of the primary economic environment in which the entity operates.

Two Methods: Current-Rate and Temporal Both standards allow companies to use either of two methods in the translation process: the **current-rate method** (called the *closing rate method* under IFRS) or the **temporal method**. The one the company chooses depends on the **functional currency** of the foreign operation, which is the currency of the primary economic environment in which that entity operates. Whichever method a company uses, it has to determine the proper exchange rate to translate the foreign-currency balances into U.S. dollars.

For example, one of Coca-Cola's largest operations outside the United States is in Japan. Its primary economic environment is Japan, and its functional currency is the Japanese yen. The FASB identifies several factors that can help management determine the functional currency: cash flows, sales prices, sales market data, expenses, financing, and transactions with other entities within the corporate group. So if, say, the cash flows and expenses are primarily in the foreign operation's currency, that is the functional currency; if they are in the parent's currency, that is the functional currency.

The current-rate method applies when the local currency is the functional currency.

If the functional currency is that of the local operating environment, the company must use the current-rate method, which provides that it translates all assets and liabilities at the current exchange rate, which is the spot exchange rate on the balance-sheet date.

All income-statement items are translated at the average exchange rate, and owners' equity is translated at the rates in effect when the company issued capital stock and accumulated retained earnings.

The temporal method applies when the parent's reporting currency is the functional currency.

If the functional currency is the parent's currency, the MNE must use the temporal method, which provides that only monetary assets (cash, marketable securities, and receivables) and liabilities are translated at the current exchange rate. The company translates inventory, property, plants, and equipment at the historical exchange rates (the transaction rate in IASB terminology), which are the rates in effect when the assets were acquired. In general, the company translates most income-statement accounts at the average exchange rate, but it translates cost of goods sold and depreciation expense, as well as owners' equity, at the appropriate historical exchange rates.

Because companies can choose the translation method—current-rate or temporal—that's most appropriate for a particular foreign subsidiary, they don't have to use one or the other for all subsidiaries. Coca-Cola sells its products in over 200 countries and uses 75 different functional currencies.[17] This practice is typical of many MNEs.

Figure 19.7 summarizes the selection of translation method, depending on the choice of functional currency. As in the preceding explanation, if the functional currency is the currency of the country where the foreign subsidiary is located, the current-rate method applies. If it is the reporting currency of the parent company, the temporal method applies.

The Translation Process Tables 19.1 and 19.2 show a balance sheet and income statement developed under both approaches to compare the differences in translation methods. The beginning balance in retained earnings for both methods is assumed to be $40,000. Using the explanation above, the following exchange rates are used to perform the translation process in Tables 19.1 and 19.2:

- $1.5000—Historical exchange rate when fixed assets were acquired and capital stock issued
- $1.6980—Current exchange rate on December 31, 2012
- $1.5617—Average exchange rate during 2013
- $1.5606—Exchange rate during which the ending inventory was acquired
- $1.5600—Historical exchange rate for cost of goods sold

Because the foreign currency was rising in value (strengthening) between the time the capital stock was issued ($1.500) and the end of the year ($1.6980), the balance sheet reflects a positive accumulated translation adjustment under the current-rate method. This is consistent with the idea that net assets were gaining value in a strong currency.

Note that under the temporal method, the ending retained earnings balance of $68,652 in Table 19.1 is found by subtracting the translated values of accounts payable, long-term debt, and capital stock from total assets. In Table 19.2, net income is found by subtracting the beginning retained earnings balance ($40,000) from the ending retained earnings balance ($68,652). When translating the income-statement accounts in Table 19.2, however, it is necessary to plug in the translation loss of $9,633 to get the net-income figure of $28,652. In the

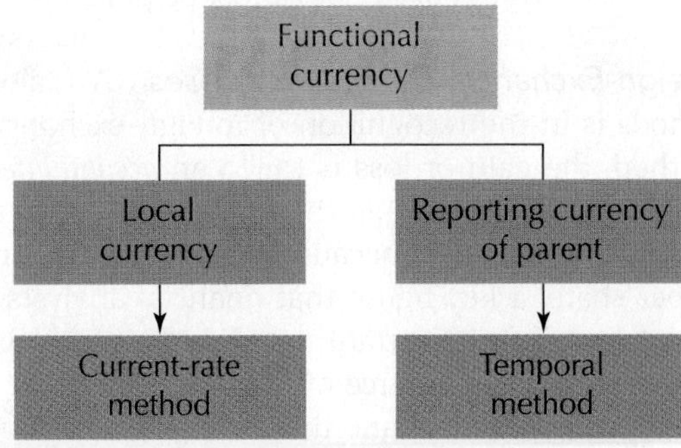

FIGURE 19.7 Selecting a Translation Method

When an MNE receives reports from subsidiaries or branches located in different countries, the accounting department is faced with financial figures stated in different currencies. Accountants must translate these foreign-currency figures into amounts stated in the currency of the parent's home country. The functional currency, which may be either the currency of the economic environment in which the subsidiary or branch operates or the parent firm's currency, will determine the translation method that the company will use.

TABLE 19.1 Translating Foreign Currency: The Balance Sheet

		Temporal Method		Current-Rate Method	
	Foreign Currency	Rate	Dollars	Rate	Dollars
Cash	20,000	1.6980	33,960	1.6980	33,960
Accounts receivable	40,000	1.6980	67,920	1.6980	67,920
Inventories	40,000	1.5606	62,424	1.6980	67,920
Fixed assets	100,000	1.5000	150,000	1.6980	169,800
Accumulated depreciation	(20,000)	1.5000	(30,000)	1.6980	(33,960)
Total Assets	**180,000**		**284,304**		**305,960**
Accounts payable	30,000	1.6980	50,940	1.6980	50,940
Long-term debt	44,000	1.6980	74,712	1.6980	74,712
Capital stock	60,000	1.5000	90,000	1.5000	90,000
Retained earnings	46,000	*	68,652	*	77,481
Accumulated translation adjustment					12,507
Total Liabilities and Owners' Equity	**180,000**		**284,304**		**305,640**

**Retained earnings* is the U.S. dollar equivalent of all income earned in prior years retained in the business rather than distributed to shareholders plus this year's income. There is no single exchange rate used to translate retained earnings into dollars.

TABLE 19.2 Translating Foreign Currency: The Income Statement

		Temporal Method		Current-Rate Method	
	Foreign Currency	Rate	Dollars	Rate	Dollars
Sales	230,000	1.5617	359,191	1.5617	359,191
Expenses:					
Cost of goods sold	(110,000)	1.5600	(171,600)	1.5617	(171,787)
Depreciation	(10,000)	1.5000	(15,000)	1.5617	(15,617)
Other	(80,000)	1.5617	(124,936)	1.5617	(124,936)
Taxes	(6,000)	1.5617	(9,370)	1.5617	(9,370)
Translation gain (loss)			(9,633)		
Net Income	**24,000**		**28,652**		**37,481**

case of the current-rate method, net income is found in Table 19.2 by subtracting translated expenses from revenues. There is no translation gain or loss on the income statement, as will be explained below. On the balance sheet in Table 19.1, the retained earnings balance of $77,841 is found by adding net income ($37,481) to the beginning retained earnings balance ($40,000). However, total assets must equal total liabilities and owners' equity, so the accumulated translation adjustment of $12,507 must be plugged in to get the right total balance.

With the current-rate method, the translation gain or loss is recognized in comprehensive income rather than net income, and therefore it goes to owners' equity. With the temporal method, the translation gain or loss is recognized on the income statement.

Disclosing Foreign-Exchange Gains and Losses A major difference between the two translation methods is in the recognition of foreign-exchange gains and losses. Under the current-rate method, the gain or loss is called an *accumulated translation adjustment* and is taken to comprehensive income rather than net income, so it appears as a separate line item in owners' equity. This is important because the accumulated translation adjustment does not affect earnings per share, a key figure that financial analysts monitor. From a cultural perspective, this points out how important net income is to U.S.-based companies, which rely on the stock market as a major source of funding. Under the temporal method, the gain or loss is taken directly to net income and thus affects earnings per share.

INTERNATIONAL FINANCIAL ISSUES

In Chapter 10, we examined the finance function from the standpoint of global capital markets. In this section, we will discuss some of the important treasury functions, including capital budgeting, cash flows and global cash management, and foreign exchange risk management.

CAPITAL BUDGETING IN A GLOBAL CONTEXT

Capital budgeting—the process whereby MNEs determine which projects and countries will receive capital investment funds.

Capital budgeting is the technique that helps the MNE determine which projects and countries will receive its capital investment funds. The parent company must compare the net present value or internal rate of return of a potential foreign project with that of its other projects around the world to determine the best place to invest resources.

Methods of Capital Budgeting

Capital budgeting techniques:

- Payback period
- Net present value of a project
- Internal rate of return

Payback Period One approach to capital budgeting is to determine the **payback period** of a project, or the number of years required to recover the initial investment made. This is typically done by estimating the annual after-tax free cash flow from the investment, determining the present value of the future cash flow for each year, and then determining how many years it will take to recoup the initial investment.

Net Present Value A second approach is to determine the **net present value (NPV)** of a project, which is defined as follows:

$$NPV = \sum_{t=1}^{n} \frac{FCF_t}{(1+k)^t} - IO$$

where FCF_t = the annual free cash flow in time period t
k = the appropriate discount rate; that is, the required rate of return or cost of capital
IO = the initial cash outlay
n = the project's expected life

MNEs need to determine free cash flows based on cash flow estimates and tax rates in different countries and an appropriate required rate of return adjusted for risk.

The required rate of return is the rate the company must get from the project to justify the cost of raising the initial investment or at least maintaining the value of its common stock. If the NPV is positive, the project is also considered positive. If the NPV is negative, the company should not enter into the project.

CONCEPT CHECK

Later in this chapter, we discuss *hedging strategies*—strategies by which companies can protect themselves from the losses to which they may be exposed in foreign-exchange transactions. Some of these strategies make use of the kinds of *foreign-exchange instruments* that we explain in Chapter 8, such as **forward contracts** (agreeing to exchange currency at a future date), **options** (agreeing to the right to trade currency at a later date), and **futures contracts** (agreeing to trade currency at a particular price on a specific date).

Internal Rate of Return A third approach is to compute the internal rate of return (IRR) of the project—the rate that equates the present value of future cash flows with the present value of the initial investment—and compare it with the required rate of return. If it is greater than the required rate of return, the investment is considered positive. However, the company then needs to compare the IRR with that of competing projects in other countries.

Several things are common about each of the methods. First, the firm needs to determine the free cash flows, which involves estimating those flows as well as bringing into the equation different tax rates from different countries. Second, in the case of both NPV and IRR, the company needs to determine what the required rate of return is.

Complications in Capital Budgeting Several aspects of capital budgeting are unique to foreign-project assessment:

- Parent cash flows (those from the project back to the parent in the parent's currency) must be distinguished from project cash flows (those in local currency from the sale of goods and services). Will the decision be based on one, the other, or both?
- Remittance of funds to the parent, such as dividends, interest on loans, and payment of intracompany receivables and payables, is affected by differing tax systems, legal and political constraints on the movement of funds, local business norms, and differences in

how financial markets and institutions function. In addition, tax systems affect free cash flows on the project, irrespective of the remittance issue.

- Differing rates of inflation must be anticipated by both the parent and the subsidiary because of their importance in causing changes in competitive position and cash flows over time.
- The parent must consider the possibility of unanticipated exchange-rate changes because of their direct effects on the value of cash flows and their indirect effects on the foreign subsidiary's competitive position.
- The parent company must evaluate political risk in a target market because political events can drastically reduce the value or availability of expected cash flows.
- The terminal value (the value of the project at the end of the budgeting period) is difficult to estimate because potential purchasers from host, home, or third countries—or from the private or public sector—may have widely divergent perspectives on the project's value. The terminal value is critical in determining the total cash flows from the project. The total cash outlay is partially offset by the terminal value—the amount of cash the parent company can get from the subsidiary or project if it eventually sells.[18]

Determine difference cash flow scenarios or adjust the hurdle rate (the minimum required rate of return for a project).

Because of all the forces listed here, it's very difficult to estimate future cash flows, both to the subsidiary and to the parent company. There are two ways to deal with the variations in future cash flows. One is to set out several different scenarios and then determine the payback period, net present value, or internal rate of return of the project. The other less appropriate approach is to adjust the hurdle rate, which is the minimum required rate of return the project must achieve for it to receive capital. The adjustment is usually made by increasing the hurdle rate above its minimal level. This is easier than estimating cash flows, but it is also the easy way out.

Once the budget is complete, the MNE must examine both the return in local currency and the return to the parent in dollars from cash flows. Examining the return in local currency will give management a chance to compare the project with other investment alternatives in the country. However, cash flows to the parent are important, since dividends are paid to shareholders from those flows. If the MNE cannot generate a sufficient return to the parent in the parent's currency, it will eventually fall behind in its ability to pay shareholders and pay off corporate debt. Finally, the decision must be made in the strategic context of the investment, not just the financial context.

INTERNAL SOURCES OF FUNDS

Funds are working capital, or current assets minus current liabilities.

Although the term *funds* usually means "cash," it is used in a much broader sense in business and generally refers to working capital—that is, the difference between current assets and current liabilities. From a general perspective, funds come from the normal operations of a business (selling merchandise or services) as well as from financing activities, such as borrowing money, issuing bonds, or issuing shares. They are used to purchase fixed assets, pay employees, buy materials and supplies, and invest in marketable securities or long-term investments.

Sources of internal funds:

- Loans
- Investments through equity capital
- Intercompany receivables and payables
- Dividends

Cash Flows and the MNE Cash flows in an MNE are significantly more complex than for a company that operates in a strictly domestic environment. An MNE that wants to expand operations or needs additional capital can look not only to the domestic and international debt and equity markets but also to sources within itself. The complexity of its internal sources is magnified because of the number of its subsidiaries and the diverse environments in which they operate.

Figure 19.8 shows a parent company that has two foreign subsidiaries. All three may be increasing funds through normal operations that may be used on a company-wide basis, perhaps through loans. The parent can lend funds directly to one subsidiary or guarantee an outside loan to the other. Equity capital from the parent is another source of funds for the subsidiary.

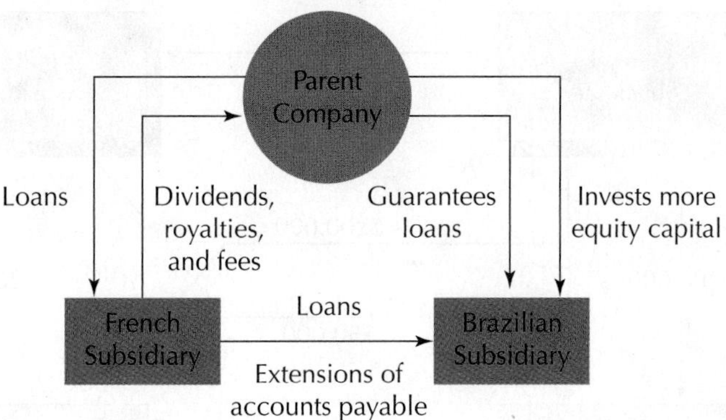

FIGURE 19.8 How the MNE Handles Its Funds (I): Internal Funds

Funds consist of working capital that comes from normal business operations and that may be used to purchase assets and materials, to pay employees, and to make investments. If the company is an MNE, funds may come from either parent or subsidiary operations, or both, and can be used by the parent to support either its own operations or those of its subsidiaries.

Funds can also go from subsidiary to parent. A subsidiary could declare a dividend to the parent as a return on capital, or lend cash directly to it. If the subsidiary declared a dividend, the parent could lend the funds back. The dividend would not be tax deductible to the subsidiary, but it would be included as income to the parent, so the parent would have to pay tax on the dividend. If the subsidiary lent money to the parent, the interest paid by the parent would be tax-deductible for the parent and taxable income for the subsidiary.

Merchandise, people (in service firms), and financial flows can travel between subsidiaries, giving rise to receivables and payables. Companies can move money between and among related entities by paying quickly, or they can accumulate funds by deferring payment. They can also adjust the size of the payment by arbitrarily raising or lowering the price of intercompany transactions in comparison with the market price—a transfer pricing strategy.

GLOBAL CASH MANAGEMENT

Managing cash effectively is a chief concern of the CFO, who must answer the following three questions:

1. What are the local and corporate system needs for cash?
2. How can the cash be withdrawn from subsidiaries and centralized?
3. Once the cash has been centralized, what should be done with it?

The 21st Annual Conference on International Cash and Treasury Management was held in September 2012 in Monte Carlo, Monaco. The Conference gave Treasurers of companies the opportunity to visit with cash management service providers.

Source: Dan Breckwoldt/Shutterstock

FIGURE 19.9 How the MNE Handles Its Funds (II): Multilateral Cash Flows

As the various subsidiaries of the MNE go about their business, cash can be transferred among them for a variety of reasons (e.g., in the form of loans or as proceeds from the sale of goods). Cash, of course, can flow in any direction, and if the MNE doesn't maintain some kind of cash-management center, each subsidiary must settle its accounts (receivables, payable, etc.) independently.

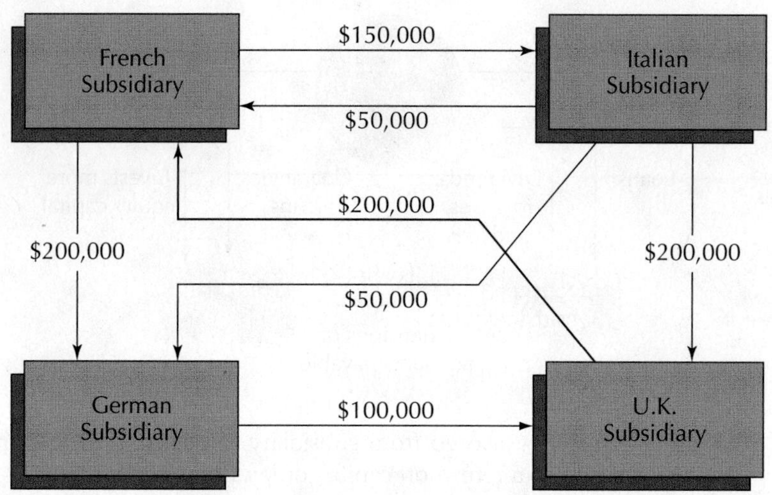

Cash budgets and forecasts are essential in assessing a company's cash needs.

The cash manager, who reports to the treasurer, must collect and pay cash in the company's normal operational cycle and then deal with financial institutions, such as commercial and investment banks, when generating and investing it. Before remitting any cash into the MNE's control center—whether at regional or headquarters level—the cash manager must first assess local cash needs through cash budgets and forecasts. Because the forecast projects the excess cash that will be available, the cash manager will know how much can be invested for short-term profits.

Dividends are a good source of intercompany transfers, but governments often restrict their free movement.

Once local cash needs are met, the cash manager must decide whether to allow the local manager to invest any excess cash or have it remitted to a central cash pool. If the cash is centralized, the manager must find a way to make the transfer. A cash dividend is the easiest way to distribute cash, but government restrictions may interfere. For example, foreign-exchange controls may prevent the company from remitting as large a dividend as it would like. Cash can also be remitted through royalties, management fees, and repayment of principal and interest on loans.

Multilateral netting—the process of coordinating cash inflows and outflows among the subsidiaries so that only net cash is transferred, reducing transaction costs.

Multilateral Netting An important cash-management strategy is **netting** cash flows internationally. For example, an MNE with operations in four European countries could have several different intercompany cash transfers resulting from loans, the sale of goods, licensing agreements, and so forth. In the illustration in Figure 19.9, for example, there are no fewer than seven different transfers among four subsidiaries. Among its special services, GPS Capital Inc., the foreign-exchange company profiled in the opening case in Chapter 10, helps clients determine their foreign-currency cash flows and assists them in developing strategies to net cash flows by minimizing the number of their foreign-currency transactions.

Table 19.3 identifies the total receivables, payables, and net position for each subsidiary. Rather than have each subsidiary settle its accounts independently with subsidiaries in other countries, many MNEs are establishing cash-management centers in one city (such as Brussels) to coordinate cash flows among subsidiaries from several countries.

TABLE 19.3 How the MNE Handles Its Funds (III): Net Positions

Assume that these data are from the same MNE as the one introduced in Figure 19.4. Because the company has no cash-management center, *net positions*—the difference between *total receivables* and *total payables*—must be determined on a subsidiary-by-subsidiary basis.

Subsidiary	Total Receivables	Total Payables	Net Position
French	250,000	350,000	(100,000)
German	250,000	100,000	150,000
Italian	150,000	300,000	(150,000)
U.K.	300,000	200,000	100,000

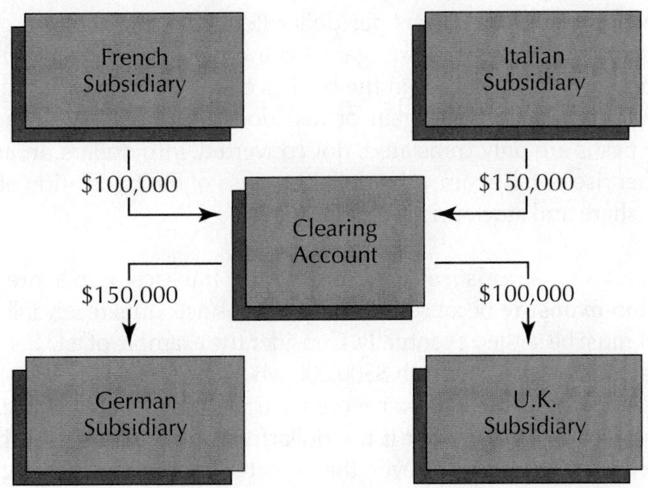

FIGURE 19.10 How the MNE Handles Its Funds (IV): Multilateral Netting

Dissatisfied with the process represented in Figure 19.9, our MNE has now established a cash-management center—a *clearing account*—into which each subsidiary transfers its net cash. Naturally, the MNE may in turn distribute the total to support subsidiary operations.

Netting requires sophisticated software and good banking relationships in different countries.

Figure 19.10 illustrates how each subsidiary in a net payable position transfers funds to the central clearing account. The account manager then transfers funds to the accounts of the net receiver subsidiaries. In this example, only four transfers need to take place. The clearing account manager receives transaction information and computes the net position of each subsidiary at least monthly, then orchestrates the settlement process. The transfers take place in the payor's currency, and the foreign-exchange conversion takes place centrally. For netting to work, the company needs to match its cash needs with software that can track and transfer funds and with banking relationships that allow money to be moved among corporate entities.

CONCEPT CHECK

In Chapter 8, we explain why it's important for MNEs to anticipate exchange-rate changes and make decisions about business activities that may be sensitive to those changes—decisions, for instance, about the sourcing of raw materials and components or the location of manufacturing and assembly facilities. We take up the same theme in Chapter 13, where we cite exchange-rate movement as just one factor that can affect wages in a particular country—and thus any advantage in labor-cost differences that a company might hope to gain from locating operations in that country.

FOREIGN-EXCHANGE RISK MANAGEMENT

As illustrated earlier, global cash-management strategy focuses on the flow of money for specific operating objectives. Another important objective of an MNE's financial strategy is to protect against the foreign-exchange risks of investing abroad. The strategies an MNE adopts to do this may mean the internal movement of funds as well as the use of one or more of the foreign-exchange instruments described in Chapter 8, such as options and forward contracts.

TYPES OF EXPOSURE

If all exchange rates were fixed in relation to one another, there would be no foreign-exchange risk. However, rates are not fixed, and currency values change frequently. Instead of infrequent, one-way changes, currencies fluctuate often and both up and down. A change in the exchange rate can result in three different exposures for a company: *translation exposure, transaction exposure,* and *economic* or *operational exposure.*

Three types of foreign-exchange exposure:

- Translation
- Transaction
- Economic or operational

Translation Exposure Foreign-currency financial statements are translated into the reporting currency of the parent company (assumed to be USD for U.S. companies) so they can be combined with financial statements of other companies in the corporate group to form the consolidated financial statements. **Translation exposure** occurs because exposed accounts—those translated at the balance-sheet rate or current exchange rate—either gain or lose value in dollars when the exchange rate changes.

Translation exposure arises because the dollar value of the exposed asset or liability changes as the exchange rate changes.

Consider the example of a U.S. company with a subsidiary in Mexico. The subsidiary keeps its books in pesos, but it has to translate the financial statements into dollars so the parent can combine the results of the Mexican subsidiary with its operations from around the world. Assume the subsidiary has 900,000 pesos in the bank. So what is the effect of a change in the exchange rate on the dollar equivalent of the cash? If the exchange rate before the change was 9.5 pesos per dollar ($94,737) and the rate changes to 10 pesos per dollar (a weakening of the peso against the dollar), the cash would only be worth $90,000. The subsidiary still has pesos in the bank account, but the dollar equivalent of the peso has fallen, resulting in a loss. The gain or loss does not represent an actual cash flow effect because the pesos are only translated, not converted, into dollars. In addition, reported earnings can either rise or fall against the dollar because of the translation effect, which can affect earnings per share and stock prices.

Transaction exposure arises when a transaction is denominated in a foreign currency and where the settlement gives rises to a cash flow gain or loss.

Transaction Exposure Denominating a transaction in a foreign currency gives rise to **transaction exposure** because the company has accounts receivable or payable in foreign currency that must be settled eventually. Consider the example of a U.S. exporter delivering merchandise to a British importer worth $500,000 when the exchange rate is $1.9000 per pound (equivalent to £263,158). If the exporter were to receive payment in dollars, there would be no immediate effect on the exporter if the dollar/pound exchange rate changed. If payment were to be received in pounds, however, the exporter might incur a foreign-exchange gain or loss. If the exchange rate when the exporter receives the pounds from the importer falls to $1.8800, the exporter would only receive $494,737, which would be a loss of $5,263. In this case, because the pound is falling in value, the exporter would receive fewer dollars from the sale after the change in the exchange rate. This would be an actual cash flow gain or loss to the exporter.

Economic, or operating, exposure arises from the effects of exchange-rate changes on

- Future cash flows,
- The sourcing of parts and components,
- The location of investments,
- The competitive position of the company in different markets.

Economic (or Operating) Exposure **Economic exposure,** also known as **operating exposure,** is the potential for change in expected cash flows that arises from the pricing of products, the sourcing and cost of inputs, and the location of investments. Pricing strategies have both immediate and long-term effects on cash flows. In the example above, if the exporter decides to receive payment in dollars, the foreign exchange risk would pass to the importer. However, the *importer* would have to come up with more pounds at the new exchange rate (£265,957) than at the original exchange rate. Now, the importer can either sell the product at the original price and not earn as much profit, or it can raise the price and hope that consumers will be willing to pay it. The *exporter,* however, also has two choices. It can continue to sell the merchandise at the same price, or it can lower it. If it lowers the price, it will incur a lower profit margin. If it continues to sell at the same price, the importer will have to pay more for the merchandise, then decide what to do.

Another economic-exposure decision involves how to make investment decisions. In 2011, Volkswagen AG decided to open a factory in the United States to take advantage of the strong euro vs. the dollar. Because of the strength of the euro, it had not been cost-competitive in the U.S., and it realized that by opening a factory in Tennessee, the southern part of the country, it could take advantage of the strong euro as well as lower labor costs. Following BMW's example of investing in the U.S. in 2005, VW hopes to not only be competitive in the U.S. but also use the U.S. as an export platform to other countries. Both VW and BMW found that exporting to the U.S. was complicated because costs were generated in euros (most of its manufacturing facilities were in Europe) while revenues in the United States were in dollars. Thus they were generating revenues in a weak currency and costs in a strong currency, severely affecting earnings. One of the economic solutions was to expand manufacturing operations in the United States to balance revenues and expenses in the same currency.[19]

EXPOSURE-MANAGEMENT STRATEGY

To protect assets from exchange-rate risk, management needs to

- Define and measure exposure,
- Establish a reporting system,
- Adopt an overall policy on exposure management,
- Formulate hedging strategies.

To adequately protect assets against the risks from translation, transaction, and economic exposure to exchange-rate fluctuations, management must do the following:

- Define and measure exposure
- Organize and implement a reporting system that monitors exposure and exchange-rate movements
- Adopt a policy assigning responsibility for minimizing—or hedging—exposure
- Formulate strategies for hedging exposure

All three types of exposure must be monitored and measured separately.

Define and Measure Exposure Most MNEs see all three types of exposure: translation, transaction, and economic. To develop a viable hedging strategy, an MNE must forecast the degree of exposure in each major currency in which it operates. Because the types differ, the actual exposure by currency must be tracked separately. For example, the firm should keep track of the translation exposure in Brazilian reais separately from the transaction exposure because it will result in an actual cash flow, whereas the translation exposure may not. Thus, the company generates one report for each type of exposure. It may also adopt different hedging strategies for the different types. Recall from the opening case in Chapter 10 that GPS developed proprietary software, called FXpert, which not only conducts specialized audits of clients' foreign-exchange cash flows but proposes effective hedging strategies for improving them. Solutions may include such well-known hedging strategies as forwards, options, and futures contracts, but GPS has designed FXpert to tailor strategies to clients' specific needs.

Exchange-rate movements are forecasted using in-house or external experts.

A key aspect of measuring exposure is forecasting exchange rates. A company should estimate and use ranges within which it expects a currency to vary over the forecasting period by developing in-house capabilities to monitor exchange rates or using economists who also try to obtain a consensus of exchange-rate movements from the banks they deal with. Their concern is to forecast the direction, magnitude, and timing of an exchange-rate change. As we note in Chapter 9, however, forecasting is imprecise.

The reporting system should use both central control and input from foreign operations.

Organize and Implement a Reporting System Once the company has decided how to define and measure exposure and estimate future exchange rates, it must create a reporting system that will assist in protecting it against risk. To achieve this goal, substantial participation from foreign operations must be combined with effective central control. Foreign input is important to ensure that the information the company uses in forecasting is effective.

Let's take the example of Dell investing in Brazil. Because exchange rates move frequently, Dell's management must obtain input from its operating and financial staff in Brazil since they understand the local economy better. Central control of exposure protects resources more efficiently than letting each subsidiary and branch manage its own. Each organizational unit may be able to define its own exposure, but the company also has an overall exposure. To set hedging policies on a separate-entity basis might not take into account the fact that exposures of several entities (that is, branches, subsidiaries, affiliates, and so on) could offset one another.

Once each basic reporting unit has identified its exposure, the data should be sent to the next organizational level for preliminary consolidation, which enables the region or division to determine exposure by account and by currency for each time period. The resulting reports should be routine, periodic, and standardized to ensure comparability and timeliness in formulating strategies. Final reporting should be at the corporate level, where top management can see the amount of foreign-exchange exposure. Specific hedging strategies can be taken at any level, but each level of management must be aware of the size of the exposure and the potential effect on the company.

Hedging strategies can be operational or financial.

Formulate Hedging Strategies Once a company has identified its level of exposure and determined which exposure is critical, it can hedge its position by adopting operational and/or financial strategies, each with cost-benefit as well as operational implications. The safest position is a balanced one in which exposed assets equal exposed liabilities.

Operational strategies include

- Using local debt to balance local assets,
- Taking advantage of leads and lags for intercompany payments.

Operational Hedging Strategies The use of debt to balance exposure is an interesting strategy. Many companies "borrow locally," especially in weak-currency countries, because that helps them avoid foreign-exchange risk from borrowing in a foreign currency and balances their exposed position in assets and earnings. One problem with this strategy is that, because interest rates in weak-currency countries tend to be high, there must be a trade-off between the cost of borrowing and the potential loss from exchange-rate variations.

Protecting against loss from transaction exposure becomes complex. In dealing with foreign customers, it is always safest for the company to denominate the transaction in its own currency to avoid any foreign-exchange exposure. The risk shifts to the foreign customer that has to come up with the company's currency. Or the company could denominate purchases in a weaker currency and sales in a stronger one. If forced to make purchases in a strong currency and sales in a weak one, it could resort to contractual measures such as forward contracts or options, or it could try to balance its inflows and outflows through astute sales and purchasing strategies.

A lead strategy means collecting or paying early. A lag strategy means collecting or paying late.

Leads and Lags Other operational strategies protect cash flows among related entities, such as a parent and subsidiaries. A **lead strategy** means either collecting foreign-currency receivables before they are due when the foreign currency is expected to weaken, or paying foreign-currency payables before they are due when it is expected to strengthen. With a **lag strategy**, a company either delays collection of foreign-currency receivables if that currency is expected to strengthen, or delays payables when it is expected to weaken. In other words, a company usually leads into and lags out of a hard currency and leads out of and lags into a weak one.

Sometimes an operational strategy means shifting assets overseas to take advantage of currency changes. As mentioned earlier, when the euro strengthened against the U.S. dollar, BMW shifted some of its manufacturing to the United States.

Using Derivatives to Hedge Foreign-Exchange Risk In addition to the operational strategies just mentioned, a company may hedge exposure through *derivative* financial contracts such as forward contracts and options, with the most common hedge being a forward contract.

Forward contracts can establish a fixed exchange rate for future transactions. Currency options can ensure access to foreign currency at a fixed exchange rate for a specific period of time.

Consider a U.S. exporter selling goods to a British manufacturer for £1 million when the exchange rate is $1.90 per £. If the exporter could collect the money right away and convert it into dollars, it would receive $1.9 million. However, if the exporter were not expected to receive payment for 90 days, it would be exposed to an exchange-rate change. One way to protect against this is to enter into a forward contract with a bank to deliver pounds and receive dollars at the forward rate of, say, $1.8500. In 90 days, the exporter would convert the pounds into dollars at $1.8500 and receive $1,850,000, which is less than it would have received at the initial spot rate. But if the pound had deteriorated even more in value, the exporter would still receive the $1.85 million, which is not a bad deal.

A foreign-currency option is more flexible than a forward contract because it gives its purchaser the right, though not the obligation, to buy or sell a certain amount of foreign currency at a set exchange rate within a specified amount of time. In the same situation described above, the exporter would enter into an option contract with a trader to convert pounds into dollars at a certain exchange rate. For the cost of protection, the exporter pays a premium to the trader, which is like insurance. When the exporter receives the cash from the importer, it can decide whether to exercise the option. If the option gives it more money than the spot rate, the exporter will exercise the option. If not, it won't.

Looking to the Future
Will IFRS Become the Global Accounting Standard?

With the adoption of IFRS by the EU, Australia, Brazil, New Zealand, and others, more than 100 countries on six continents will be requiring or permitting its use for some or all domestic listed companies. The adoption has been a steady process, and the key will be how the U.S. responds to the call. From an accounting standpoint, the key question is this: What will become the Coca-Cola of accounting standards: U.S. GAAP or IFRS? In other words, which will have the most recognized "brand name"?

IFRS has a lot going for it, and its proponents are working hard to ensure that it is accepted around the world. The IASB reaches through its board members and committees to various regions of the world by assignment to help them with adopting or converging with IFRS. The SEC simply sets guidelines and expects companies that wish to list in the United States to abide by them and the laws.

IFRS is being set by collaboration with many of the major countries in the world, so it is the product of a great deal of negotiation, compromise, and broad-based input. It's appealing to Europeans because they have a lot of influence in the development of the standards and it's free of regulation by the SEC. It also has EU backing, as noted earlier. Even with the strong support of IOSCO, the G20, the World Bank, and the EU, it is doubtful that the U.S. will give up setting accounting standards and let the IASB do it. However, the process of convergence is far more appealing in the U.S. than outright adoption with no opportunity to second-guess IFRS.

The major vote in favor of U.S. GAAP is that half the world's stock market capitalization is located in the United States, and companies that want access to U.S. capital must play by U.S. rules. Americans have always felt that their standards were the best in the world and that it would be unfair for U.S. companies competing for cash in the U.S. market to allow foreign companies to list using IFRS, which is perceived as more flexible and less comprehensive than U.S. GAAP. Foreign companies that want to list outside their national markets typically look to the United States first and thus have to adopt U.S. reporting requirements. However, the decision by the SEC to allow foreign firms to list in the U.S. if they use IFRS is a major game changer. As European stock markets continue to grow in importance, more European companies are choosing to list in Europe instead of the United States.

An additional complication to combining or converging IFRS and U.S. GAAP is the Sarbanes-Oxley Act of 2002. Requiring companies to establish solid internal controls over financial reporting, this legislation limits the types of services that may be performed by primary auditors in addition to the financial-statement audit, and requires the managers of publicly traded companies to assess internal controls and make a statement on this assessment, which must be examined and opined on by external auditors.

All of these requirements add additional costs to those already related to complying with U.S. GAAP. Although perhaps good for companies in the long term, as they must establish effective controls over financial reporting, the initial costs of complying with Sarbanes-Oxley may be too great for some firms to consider listing on U.S. exchanges. In addition, the United States has strict laws on granting stock options to managers, and the U.S. market has a heightened sensitivity to wrongdoing because of recent major accounting scandals.

The convergence project between the FASB and IASB may solve some of these problems in the long run. To its credit, the IASB has expanded coverage of key topics and has narrowed the alternatives available to companies. It has sold itself as based on *principles* rather than *rules,* although it is more accurate to say that the standards are simpler and less comprehensive. Anytime you have a standard, you have to have a rule. It's just that U.S. GAAP is very rule-based and complicated and covers far more topics and industries. However, the FASB and IASB are narrowing the differences in existing standards and developing new ones together. Now they jointly write new standards so that even the wording is the same. In addition, public accounting firms and publicly traded companies have five years of experience in adopting the requirements of Sarbanes-Oxley. Maybe the future of accounting standards will be like a merger of Coca-Cola and Pepsi—although accounting is a lot more complicated than soft drinks. ■

CASE Dell Mercosur: Getting Real in Brazil[20]

On October 29, 2013, Michael Dell, Dell's founder, Chairman and CEO, entered into a partnership with Silver Lake Partners to acquire the stock of Dell and turn it from a public to a private company. Why did that happen? Initially a successful personal computer company, Dell found that the market had drastically changed since it was founded. The demand for Dell computers had been falling for several quarters, resulting in a 30 percent drop in share prices over a five-year period. The market had shifted more to mobile phones and other internet-based devices such as tablets like the iPad and Microsoft Surface. As a result, Dell began to

With the Brazilian economy rebounding from the global economic crisis and the Brazilian real relatively strong against the U.S. dollar, the future looked bright for Dell's business in Brazil.

Source: © tashatuvango - Fotolia.com

shift its business to providing software and services for corporate clients. In order to stop the plunge in stock prices and allow him to focus on his new strategy, Michael Dell felt that he had no choice but to take the company private.

In spite of Dell's difficulties, the company had long been bullish about emerging markets, especially Brazil. With the Brazilian economy rebounding from the global economic crisis and the Brazilian real relatively strong against the U.S. dollar, the future looked bright for Dell's business in Brazil.

In 2013, Dell announced that it was going to open a solutions center in Sao Paulo as part of its strategy to increase Dell Software in Brazil. New software and products were constantly being released in Latin America. In addition to Brazil, Dell announced that it was going to make significant investments in R&D, capital expenditures, and personnel in its bid to become an integrated provider of IT solutions, including hardware and software.

With its global expansion, Dell has always had to worry about managing exchange rate risk. 2002 was an interesting year in Brazil, and Dell's challenges and strategies then, are still relevant today.

Dell in 2002

In 2002, Todd Pickett, CFO of Dell Mercosur, was facing the end of the year with conflicting predictions of the value of the Brazilian real and what to do to hedge Dell's operation in Brazil. Although Pickett was concerned about Dell's exposure in the other Mercosur countries, Brazil was clearly the largest concern. The year began with shocks resulting from the Argentine financial crisis, which started at the end of 2001, and ended with the election of Luiz Inácio Lula da Silva (known simply as "Lula") as president of Brazil in late 2002. Lula, the leader of the Workers' Party and a long-time leftist politician, held the lead throughout the year. The markets were sceptical of Lula's potential leadership, a factor that caused the real to weaken from 2.312 reais per U.S. dollar at the end of 2001 to a record 4 reais just prior to the election. After the election, the real began to strengthen somewhat, but Pickett had to base his strategies on whether the real would continue to strengthen or weaken again.

Dell's Entry into Brazil

In 2002, Dell was operating in 34 countries with 36,000 employees, of which about 14,400 were outside the United States. In the preceding five years, Dell had expanded beyond PCs to servers, storage, and communications equipment. Most PC manufacturers claimed poor results since the technology bubble burst in 2000; IBM left the industry in 2000 and Compaq and HP merged in 2001 in hopes of boosting their competitive position. Unlike its competitors, Dell had thrived in the previous few years, moving from a market share of 12 to 15 percent in 2001, the number-one spot in the industry. Fiscal year 2002, however, was one of the toughest years to date in the PC industry. Because of the softening of the global economy and the events of 9/11, demand for PCs was down sharply. Dell responded with an aggressive price strategy, reducing costs through workforce reductions and facility consolidations. Although global industry shipments fell by 5 percent in 2002, Dell's unit shipments increased by 15 percent and thus enabled Dell to retain its number-one position. Dell based its success on its build-to-order, direct-sales model. Dell had eliminated resellers and retailers, and it sold directly to the customer by phone or over the Internet. Dell customized every computer to the customer's needs and waited to build the computer until it was ordered. As a result, Dell required little inventory (four days on average) and was able to deliver the newest technology to its customers. Costs were kept to a minimum compared with its competitors because it had no costly retail outlets and little inventory. Dell began assembling computers in Texas, in 1985, and expanded its global production units as follows:

1990: Opened manufacturing plant in Ireland.
1996: Opened manufacturing plant in Malaysia.
1998: Opened manufacturing plant in China.
1999: Opened manufacturing plants in Tennessee and Brazil.
[By 2013, Dell's manufacturing facilities were in Texas, Malaysia, China, Brazil, India, and Poland.]

MERCOSUR and Dell's Decision to Locate in Southern Brazil

Dell's business center in Brazil initially was in southern Brazil. In addition, its call center services both Brazil and Argentina. Because of the tariff-free provisions of Mercosur and the proximity of Dell's manufacturing facilities in the south of Brazil, Dell is well positioned to service all of Mercosur with its Brazilian manufacturing operations. Although Dell is divided into products and customers, it is managed generally geographically. In 2002, Terry Kahler, the general manager of Dell Mercosur, reported to Rosendo Parra, the Vice President of the Americas/International Group in Austin, Texas. Pickett worked closely with Kahler to decrease currency risk and meet budget targets in dollars, but he also reported directly to the CFO staff in Austin to coordinate hedging strategies.

Dell's revenues in Brazil are denominated in reais, and most of its operating costs are also denominated in reais. However, about 97 percent of Dell's manufacturing costs in Brazil are denominated in U.S. dollars because Dell imports parts and components from the United States. Most general and administrative costs are in U.S. dollars. It translates its financial statements according to the current-rate method, which means that assets and liabilities are translated into dollars at the current exchange rate, and revenues and expenses are translated at the average exchange rate for the period. Because of business development loans from the Brazilian government, Dell's net exposed asset position in Brazil is quite small, but it is subject to foreign-exchange gains and losses as the rate changes.

How Dell Hedges Its Bets

In its Form 10K for the fiscal year 2002, Dell describes its foreign-currency hedging strategy as one that aims to minimize the impact of fluctuations on earnings and cash flows associated with foreign currency exchange rates. It establishes that Dell uses purchased option contracts and forward contracts designated as cash flow hedges to protect against the foreign currency exchange risk inherent in its forecasted transactions denominated in currencies other than [the] U.S. dollar. Hedged transactions include international sales by U.S. dollar functional currency entities, foreign currency denominated purchases of certain components, and intercompany shipments to certain international subsidiaries.

Dell's strategy is to hedge all foreign exchange risk, which is an aggressive hedging strategy. Because there is no options market for the real, Pickett uses forward contracts to hedge the foreign-exchange risks in Brazil. Corporate financial management monitors currency movements worldwide and provides support to Pickett's Brazilian financial-management group in terms of currency forecasts and hedging strategies. Within the broad strategy approved by corporate finance, the Brazilian group establishes a strategy and then works with corporate on specific execution of the strategy.

The Two-Part Strategy

There are two key parts to the strategy. One has to do with forecasting exposure, and the other deals with designing and executing the strategy to hedge the exposure. Although the balance sheet exposure is not material, it still must be forecast and is partly a function of the cash flows generated by revenues. Because the revenue side is more difficult to forecast, Pickett hedges about 80 percent of forecasted revenues. However, the Dell team in Brazil has become adept at forecasting revenues and in executing a strategy to reach its target forecast. The team works hard at identifying the challenges for reaching its target and in devising policies to overcome those challenges. Its execution strategies vary widely quarter by quarter, and the management team has become good at meeting its targets by working closely together and being flexible.

The second key to the strategy is designing and executing the hedging strategy. Because revenues vary every day, Pickett does not enter into contracts all at once. Instead, he works with corporate finance to enter into contracts of different amounts and maturities, depending on when they expect to generate the operating revenues. Revenues are generally lower at the beginning of the quarter and are always higher in the last week or two of the quarter, so he enters into contracts accordingly. Timing is a crucial issue. The gain or loss on a forward contract is the difference in exchange rates between when the contract is entered into and when it is settled. The key is to unwind (or settle) the contracts while the rate is still favorable. Pickett noted that if Dell began to unwind the contracts in the last week or two of the quarter instead of the last day or two of the quarter, it could get much more favorable foreign-exchange gains.

His strategy was so successful that in some quarters, Dell was generating more financial income than operating income. Although Pickett and his finance team have some flexibility in designing and implementing strategy, corporate finance keeps in close touch, depending on their forecasts of the exchange rate and the strategy that Dell Brazil is following. Corporate finance uses a consensus forecast of exchange rates that is provided by a group of banks, but banks have different scenarios. For example, in the last quarter of 2002, corporate was relying on bank forecasts that the real would revalue even more by the end of the year. Pickett's dilemma was that his gut feeling was telling him the real would actually fall instead of rise, and that would indicate a different hedging strategy. He was resisting entering into hedges, whereas corporate was pressuring him to do just that. But he was closely watching the forward market, and when it began to move, he decided it was time to enter into the contracts. He was also considering entering into operating strategies that would provide natural hedges for Dell in Brazil. Dell has significant market opportunities in Mercosur, but the financial risks will make for exciting times in years to come.

QUESTIONS

✪**19-3.** Given how Dell translates its foreign-currency financial statements into dollars, how would a falling Brazilian real affect Dell Mercosur's financial statements? What about a rising real?

19-4. Dell imports about 97 percent of its manufacturing costs. What type of exposure does that create for it? What are its options to reduce that exposure?

19-5. Describe and evaluate Dell's exposure management strategy.

✪**19-6.** Track the value of the real at the end of each year since 2002. How would the trend have changed Pickett's hedging strategy over that time period?

SUMMARY

- MNEs must learn to cope with differing inflation rates, exchange-rate changes, currency controls, expropriation risks, customs duties, tax rates and methods of determining taxable income, levels of sophistication of local accounting personnel, and local as well as home-country reporting requirements.
- A company's accounting or controllership function is responsible for collecting and analyzing data for internal and external users.
- Culture can have a strong influence on the accounting dimensions of measurement and disclosure. The cultural values of secrecy and transparency refer to the degree of information disclosure. The cultural values of optimism and conservatism refer to the valuation of assets and the recognition of income. Conservatism results in the undervaluation of both assets and income.
- Financial statements differ in terms of language, currency, type of statements (income statement, balance sheet, etc.), financial-statement format, extent of footnote disclosures, and the underlying GAAP on which the financial statements are based.
- Important users of financial statements that must be considered in determining accounting standards are investors, employees, lenders, suppliers and other trade creditors, customers, governments and their agencies, and the public.
- Some of the most important sources of influence on the development of accounting standards and practices are culture, capital markets, regional and global standard-setting groups, management, and accountants.
- The International Accounting Standards Board is charged with developing a single set of high-quality, understandable, and enforceable global accounting standards. Standards developed by the IASB require transparent and comparable information in general-purpose financial statements.
- In cooperation with national standard-setters around the world, especially the Financial Accounting Standards Board (FASB) in the United States, the IASB hopes to achieve convergence in accounting standards.
- The elimination of reconciliation information in the Form 20-F requirement for foreign companies listing in the United States and different methods of adopting IFRS are major issues that could affect the global convergence of accounting standards.
- When transactions denominated in a foreign currency are translated into dollars, all accounts are recorded initially at the exchange rate in effect at the time of the transaction. At each subsequent balance-sheet date, recorded dollar balances representing amounts owed by or to the company that are denominated in a foreign currency are adjusted to reflect the current rate.
- Companies enter foreign-exchange gains and losses arising from foreign-currency transactions on the income statement during the period in which they occur. Companies enter gains and losses arising from translating financial statements by the current-rate method as a separate component of owners' equity. Companies enter gains and losses arising from translating according to the temporal method directly on the income statement.

KEY TERMS

accounting (p. 776)
consolidation (p. 790)
convergence (p. 784)
current-rate method (p. 790)
economic exposure (operating exposure) (p. 798)
Financial Accounting Standards Board (FASB) (p. 780)
functional currency (p. 790)
Generally Accepted Accounting Principles (GAAP) (p. 783)
International Accounting Standards Board (IASB) (p. 780)
International Financial Reporting Standards (IFRS) (p. 783)
International Organization of Securities Commissions (IOSCO) (p. 785)
lag strategy (p. 800)
lead strategy (p. 800)
mutual recognition (p. 784)
net present value (NPV) (p. 793)
netting (p. 796)
payback period (p. 793)
reconciliation (p. 784)
temporal method (p. 790)
transaction exposure (p. 798)
transfer pricing (p. 795)
translation (p. 790)
translation exposure (p. 797)

ENDNOTES

1 ***Sources include the following:*** Vincent Boland, "The Saga of Parmalat's Collapse," FT.com (accessed April 1, 2009); Catherine Boyle, "Parmalat's Founder Is Sentenced to Ten Years' Jail for Market-Rigging," *The Times* (accessed April 1, 2009): 64; Judith Burns, "Parmalat to Settle SEC Charges of Fraud for U.S. Bond Offering," *Wall Street Journal* (Europe) (July 30, 2004): A6; "The Pause after Parmalat," *The Economist* (January 17, 2004): 13; Alessandra Galloni and Yaroslav Trofimov, "Tanzi's Power Games Helped Parmalat Rise, but Didn't Cushion Fall," *Wall Street Journal* (Europe) (March 8, 2004): A1; Mark Tran, "The Milk Sheikh Whose Dream Curdled," *The Guardian* (December 31, 2003), www.guardian.co.uk/business/2003/dec/31/italy.parmalat1 (accessed October 19, 2009); Peter Gumbel, "How It All Went So Sour," *Time* (Europe) (November 29, 2004): 44; Hoover's Online, "Parmalat," at www.hoovers.com (accessed April 19, 2005); Michelle Perry, "Enron: Could It Happen Here?" *Accountancy Age* (January 25, 2004), www.accountancyage.com/accountancyage/analysis/2040660/enron-happen-here (accessed October 19, 2009); David Reilly and Alessandra Galloni, "Spilling Over: Banks Come under Scrutiny for Role in Parmalat Scandal," *Wall Street Journal* (September 28, 2004): A1; David Reilly and Matt Moffett, "Parmalat Inquiry Is Joined by Brazil," *Wall Street Journal* (Europe) (January 7, 2004): A1; Susannah Rodgers and Kenneth Maxwell, "Parmalat Fallout Hits Farmers; Dairies Worry about Their Future as Milk Seller Misses Payments," *Wall Street Journal* (Europe) (January 15, 2004): B6; Securities and Exchange Commission

(SEC): Complaint #18527 (December 29, 2003);"Parmalat to Trim Key Operations in 10 Countries," *Wall Street Journal* (Europe) (March 29, 2004): A4;"How Parmalat Differs from U.S. Scandals,"Knowledge@ Wharton (January 28, 2004), at http://knowledge.wharton.upenn.edu (accessed November 15, 2007); Adrian Michaels,"Parmalat Case Leads to First Jail Sentences,"*Financial Times* (June 29, 2005): 28; Bruce Johnston and Caroline Muspratt,"Court Frees Daughter of Parmalat Founder,"*The* [London] *Daily Telegraph* (March 9, 2004): 29;"Daughter of Founder of Parmalat Is Freed," *Wall Street Journal* (Eastern Edition) (March 9, 2004): 1; Eric Sylvers,"In First Trial, Parmalat's Founder Charges That Banks Led Him Astray,"*International Herald Tribune* (March 9, 2006): 13; John Hooper,"Parmalat Fraudsters to Avoid Prison," *The Guardian* (June 29, 2005): 18; Giada Zampano and Sabrina Cohen, "Parmalat Trial to Focus on Banks," *Wall Street Journal* (Eastern Edition) (June 14, 2007): C3;"Parmalat Settles Suits with Three Financial Firms," *International Herald Tribune* (June 19, 2007): 16;"Parmalat SpA,"*Wall Street Journal* (Europe) (May 18, 2007): 6; Steve Rothwell and Sebastian Boyd,"EU Backing Off Effort on Bond Transparency,"*International Herald Tribune* (November 22, 2006): 13; Eric Sylvers,"Judge Clears Banks in Parmalat Case, "*New York Times,* (April 18, 2011): dealbook.nytimes.com/2011/04/18/judge-clears-banks-in-parmalat-case/ (accessed July 5, 2011); Bob Van Voris,"Parmalats Suits Against Grant Thornton Revived by Court,"*Bloomberg,* (January 18, 2011), www.bloomberg.com/news/2011-01-18/parmalat-claim-against-grant-thornton-revived-by-court-update1-.html (accessed July 6, 2011); Parmalat (2011), *Annual Report 2010,* (accessed July 6, 2011).

2 Adidas Group, *Annual Report 2010,* adidas-group.corporate-publications.com/2010/gb/files/pdf/en/ADS_GB_2010_En.pdf (accessed July 5, 2011).

3 Geert Hofstede, *Culture's Consequences: International Differences in Work-Related Values* (Beverly Hills: Sage, 1980): 327; Hofstede and Michael H. Bond,"The Confucius Connection: From Cultural Roots to Economic Growth,"*Organizational Dynamics* 16:4 (1988): 4; Hofstede, Geert, Gert Jan Hofstede, and Michael Minkov, *Cultures and Organizations: Software of the Mind,* Third Edition (Maidenhead, England: McGraw-Hill, 2010): 561.

4 Sidney J. Gray,"Towards a Theory of Cultural Influence on the Development of Accounting Systems Internationally,"*Abacus* (March 1988): 1.

5 European Union,"Third Countries/Convergence,"ec.europa.eu/internal_market/accounting/third_countries/index_en.htm, (accessed June 12, 2013).

6 "IFRS: About the Organisation,"www.ifrs.org/The+organisation/IASCF+and+IASB.htm (accessed July 11, 2011).

7 IFRS Foundation, The Organisation, Trustees, www.ifrs.org/The+organisation/Trustees/Trustees.htm (accessed June 12, 2013).

8 IFRS Foundation,"About the IFRS Foundation and the IASB," www.ifrs.org/The-organisation/Pages/IFRS-Foundation-and-the-IASB.aspx (accessed June 12, 2013).

9 Financial Accounting Standards Board,"Memorandum of Understanding, - The Norwalk Agreement,"in International Convergence of Accounting Standards – Overview,"www.fasb.org/jsp/FASB/Page/SectionPage&cid=1176156245663 (accessed July 11, 2011).

10 FASB,"Convergence with the International Accounting Standards Board."

11 Securities and Exchange Commission,"About the SEC: What We Do," www.sec.gov/about/whatwedo.shtml (accessed October 21, 2009).

12 European Union,"Regulations Adopting IAS,"ec.europa .eu/internal_market/accounting/legal_framework/regulations_adopting_ias_en.htm (accessed June 12, 2013).

13 "Finance and Economics: Speaking in Tongues,"*The Economist* (May 19, 2007): 77–78.

14 "Uniform Rules for International Accounting Standards from 2005 Onwards,"*European Parliament Daily Notebook,* Report on the Proposal for a European Parliament and Council Regulation on the Application of International Accounting Standards, (COM 2001) 80-C5-0061/2001–2001/004 (COD), Doc.: A5-0070/2002, www.europarl.europa.eu/sides/getDoc.do?pubRef=-//EP//TEXT+PRESS+DN-20020312-1+0+DOC+XML+V0//EN&language=EN#SECTION5 (accessed October 21, 2009).

15 Paul A. Beswick,"Remarks Before the 2010 AICPA National Conference on Current SEC and PCAOB Developments," December 8, 2010, www.sec.gov/news/speech/eo10/spch120610pab.htm (accessed June 15, 2011).

16 FASB,"Foreign Currency Translation,"Statement of Financial Accounting Standards No. 52 (Stamford, CT: FASB, December 1981): 6–7.

17 The Coca-Cola Company, 2010 Form 10-K (February 28, 2011): 34, 81.

18 Michael H. Moffett, Arthur I. Stonehill, and David K. Eiteman, *Fundamentals of Multinational Finance,* 4the edition (Pearson Prentice Hall: Upper Saddle Ridge, NJ:, 2012): Chapter 16.

19 Mike Ramsey,"VW Chops Labor Costs in U.S.,"*The Wall Street Journal* (May 23, 2011): B1; Stephen Power,"BMW's Profit Softened in Quarter,"*Wall Street Journal* (May 4, 2005): A12.

20 ***Sources include the following:*** Author interview with Todd Pickett (2002); Dell Computer Corp., *Form 10-K,* 2002 (April 28, 2003), retrieved November 20, 2007, from http://phx. corporate-ir.net/phoenix.zhtml?c=101133&p=irol-sec& control_ selectgroup=Annual%20Filings; Michael Schrage, "The Dell Curve," *Wired Magazine* (July 2002), retrieved October 23, 2009, from www.wired.com/wired/archive/10.07/dell; Bridget Carey, "Dell Adds Products in Latin America: Dell Is Amping Up Its Product Line in Latin America, Giving Consumers More Choices Than They Had Before," *Miami Herald* (July 29, 2009), accessed October 23, 2009, from www.miamiherald.com/business/technology/story/1161587.html. Michael J. De La Merced and Quentin Hardy,"Long Battle for Dell Ends in Victory for Founder,"http://dealbook.nytimes.com/2013/09/12/dell-shareholders-approve-24-9-billion-buyout/?_r=0 (accessed on November 2, 2013). Dell Inc., Form 10-K, February 1, 2013, Note 6, p. 84. Joachim Bamrud, "Dell Bets on Latin America," Latin Trade (January–February 2012), p. 64.

CHAPTER 20

Global Management of Human Resources

OBJECTIVES

After studying this chapter, you should be able to

1. Discuss the importance of human resource management
2. Explain the types of expatriates
3. Profile the staffing frameworks used by MNEs
4. Assess how MNEs select, prepare, compensate, and retain expatriates
5. Consider the role of language in the international assignment

A person does not seek luck; luck seeks the person.

—Turkish proverb

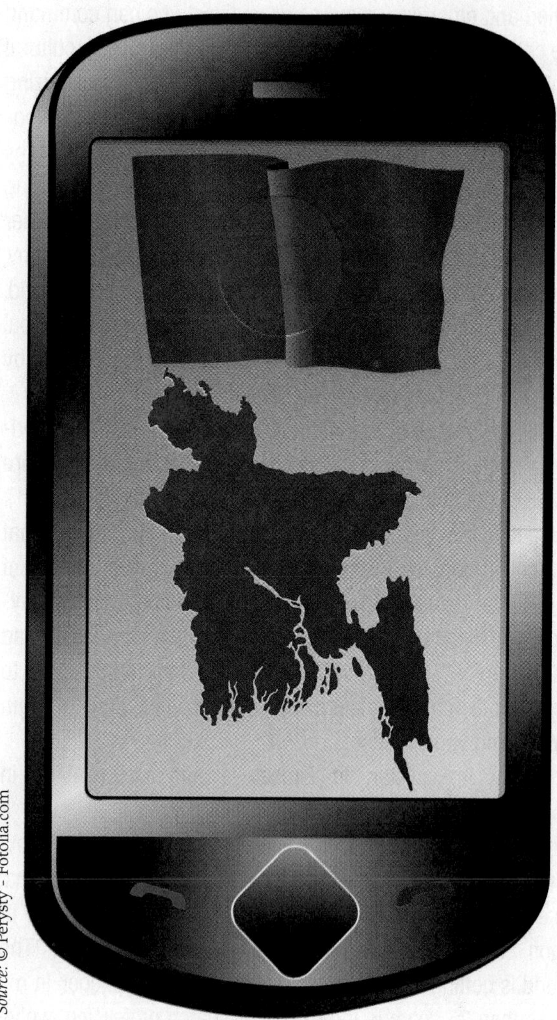

Source: © Perysty - Fotolia.com

CASE Globalizing Your Career

Companies have been moving people around for centuries, capturing the benefits of putting the right person into the right job at the right place at the right time at the right pay for the right stretch. Contemporary market trends, strategic imperatives, and executive performance standards intensify this task. Hence, professional success requires, in the least, expanding your global awareness, and, ideally, your experiential knowledge of ways that the world works.

Globalization, by spurring trade, capital, and investment flows, expands the scope of the hundreds of thousands of existing subsidiaries. Moreover, we see tens of thousands of units opening in fast-emerging markets. Each unit, established and emerging, requires executives who can command the competencies to navigate economic complexities, cultural ambiguities, and political challenges, all the while maximizing the MNE's global efficiency and optimizing its local responsiveness. GE's Jeffrey Immelt says, "A good global company does three things: It's a global sales company—meaning it's number one with customers all over the world, whether in Chicago or Paris or Tokyo. It's a global products company, with technologies, factories, and products made for the world, not just for a single region. And, most important, it's a global people company—a company that keeps getting better by capturing global markets and brains."[1]

By no means must one immediately pack up, say goodbye, and head abroad. But those who do, fear not, for there are many benefits to an expatriate assignment (see Figure 20.1). Moreover, this secret is out: A Gallup World Poll reports that 1.1 billion people, or one-quarter of the earth's adults, want to move temporarily to another country to find a higher paying job, while another 630 million people aim to move abroad permanently. Still, even if your career plans anchor you to your home market, globalizing markets spur you to begin globalizing your mindset.

From Afghanistan to Zimbabwe and all countries in between, effective leadership increasingly calls for such a global mindset. "You have to have an intuitive sense of how the world works and how people behave," says Paul Laudicina, vice president of A. T. Kearney.[2] Observed Daniel Meiland of Egon Zehender International, an executive search firm, "The world is getting smaller, and markets are getting bigger. In my more than 25 years in the executive search profession, we've always talked about the global executive, but the need to find managers who can be effective in many different settings is growing ever more urgent. In addition to looking for intelligence, specific skills, and technical insights, MNEs are also looking for executives who are comfortable on the world stage."[3]

THE EXPATRIATE

MNEs often send people to live and work in another country to run their foreign operations. Some, such as FedEx and J&J, send only a few. Others, like Royal Dutch Shell and Wipro Technologies, send many employees abroad. Unfortunately, few standards straightforwardly stipulate why, when, and where MNEs should use these **expatriates**, or "expats." Moreover, ambiguity extends to the matters of selecting the right expatriates, developing the right predeparture programs, designing the right compensation packages, setting the right stretch of time for the assignments, and determining the right way to reintegrate them into the home company when they complete their tour of duty.

The consequences of success and failure press MNEs to manage their human resources proactively. Honeywell, like many, begins nurturing potential expatriates years before they might head abroad, briefing candidates on their cross-cultural skills and prescribing training paths that address likely points of culture shock. "We give them a horizon, a perspective, and, gradually, we tell them they are potentially on an international path," says the company's vice president of HR. "We want them to develop a cross-cultural intellect, what we call strategic accountability."[4] To this end, Honeywell might advise employees to network with experienced expatriates, study another language, or assess where they might struggle while living abroad.

The pace of globalization, particularly for MNEs in emerging economies like India, China, and Brazil, accelerates preparation—indeed, some managers identify candidates upon hire. Sanjay Joshi, chief executive of global programs at India's Wipro Technologies, notes, "A big part of our recruiting is telling people that they will get a chance to work abroad." This approach, he believes, improves the quality of new hires while fortifying the company's growing cadre of expatriates.[5]

NEW PLACES AND NEW WAYS

Figure 20.1 lists the top benefits of working abroad. Accomplished expatriates testify to the merits of the quest, describing how the experience changed their perception of business and their sense of self. Many note that working abroad pushed them, sometimes nicely, sometimes harshly, to interpret situations differently. Galina Naumenko, of PwC Russia, says an international assignment "spurs global networking among employees, gives them an understanding of different cultures, and gets them thinking about alternative

FIGURE 20.1 Top Benefits of the Expatriate Experience

Executives identify many benefits of their international assignments. Here we see leading personal and professional motivations that make working abroad an enriching experience.

Source: HSBC EXPAT EXPLORER SURVEY 2010, p.11, www.expatexplorer.hsbc.com/files/pdfs/overall-reports/2010/experience.pdf (accessed June 10, 2013).

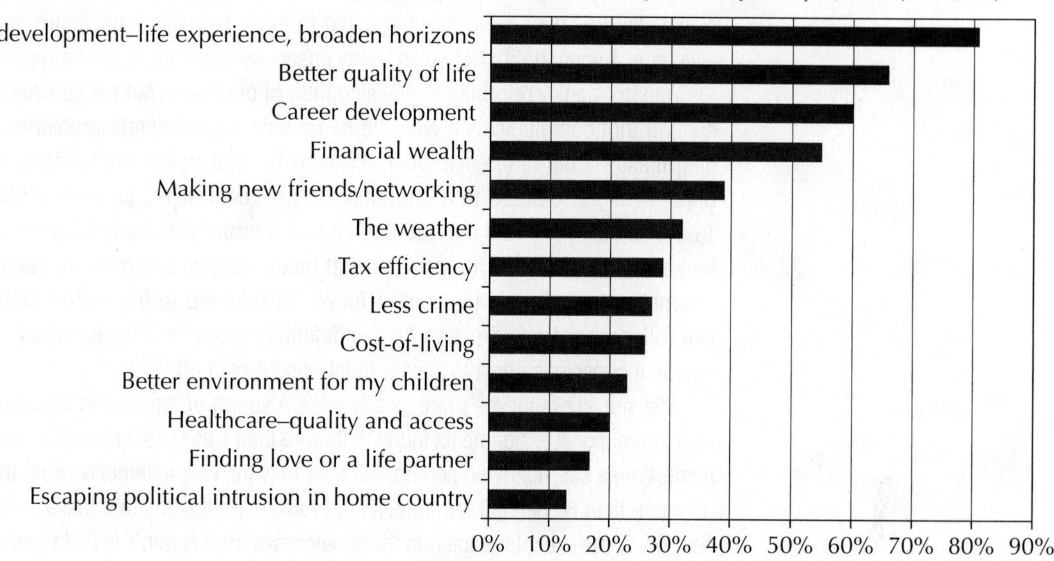

ways of approaching problems and solving them." Adds Michael Cannon-Brookes, head of strategy for IBM's Growth Markets, "You get very different thinking if you sit in Shanghai or São Paulo or Dubai than if you sit in New York."[6]

Working internationally compels employees to develop richer management repertoires. Consider Joan Pattle, a Microsoft marketing manager who worked at headquarters in Seattle before accepting a post as product leader in Great Britain. Her U.K. job came with wider responsibilities, as she explains: "At home, my job was very strictly defined. I basically had to know everything about managing a database. But when I got to London, I was also in charge of direct marketing and press relations. I was exposed to a much broader set of experiences."[7] Similarly, Laura Anderson, a spokesperson for Intel, explains that an assignment in Hong Kong improved her sense of the company's business. In fact, several Asian media relations encounters opened her eyes. "For me," she says, "it was a tremendous growth experience."[8]

NEW PROBLEMS AND NEW STRESSES

Notwithstanding the lure of excitement and rewards, the expatriate lifestyle is not for everyone. Difficulty adapting, no matter how strong the intent, is the primary cause of nearly half of failed foreign assignments. Put simply, living and working abroad can be tough. Cultural clashes, language difficulties, murky business practices, and harsh environments rule out anything beyond a short-term visit for many executives. Other problems arise when a company asks an executive to transfer to a second- or third-tier city in a less preferred country. Persuading someone to move from paradise to the wastelands is a hard sell.

The gap between life at home versus "over there" often fans professional, family, and personal problems. Many expatriates struggle with foreign cultures. Difficulty understanding and respecting differences, no matter how mundane, spiritual, or philosophical, often causes expensive failures. To top it off, international business travel "is perhaps the most dangerous form of travel. Tourists wouldn't consider flying into a Colombian war zone for a week, yet folks from oil, computer, pharmaceutical, agricultural, and telecom MNEs do it regularly."[9] Once there, merely frequenting high-profile hotels and restaurants with colleagues puts one into the crossfire.

COMING HOME

Floating around the world today are so-called "expat lifers." Moving from assignment to assignment, whether with the same company or another, they plan never to return "home." The majority, however, eventually do—they pack their bags, bid farewell to colleagues, board the plane, and return to a hero's welcome. A snap, right? Not so. In many cases, everything but the hero's welcome happens.

Repatriation— returning to one's country of origin—is not necessarily disappointing. Tales of success confirm that communication with the home unit helps preempt problems. Likewise, careful career planning makes a big difference when it's time to head home. Following a four-year assignment in Tokyo, Bryan Krueger returned to a promotion to president of Baxter Fenwal North America. When he left for Tokyo, his company had not guaranteed him a promotion upon his return. While he was away, however, he kept up to date with the goings-on at headquarters, and now credits his smooth return to this intensive networking. During his stint in Tokyo, he returned to the United States four to five times a year to see colleagues. As he explains, "I was definitely proactive. Anyone who is not, does himself a disservice. I made a conscious effort to stay in touch, and it paid off."[10]

Still, not all executives share victory tales. A survey of repatriated executives who successfully completed their international assignments found that more than a third held temporary posts three months after returning home. Worse still, nearly 80 percent felt their new job was a demotion from their foreign assignment. To top it off, more than 60 percent felt they did not have opportunities to transfer their international expertise to their new job. Some executives tolerate these outcomes. Others don't. In 2011, nearly 40 percent left their company within one year of returning from abroad, while another 25 percent left between the first and second years.[11]

RISKS AND RETURNS

The choice to work abroad, we see, has a high upside and a steep downside. On balance, the former usually tips the scale. The allure of an international assignment creates growing numbers of expat-lifers. While overseas, an expatriate is typically well-paid, has big responsibilities, and enjoys professional prestige. The adventure of living abroad makes an international career irresistible to some, effectively creating so-called "global nomads" who travel from one country to the next. For example, after stints in Singapore and London, a Morgan Stanley expat in India said, "I still don't want to go back to the United States. It's a big world—lots of things to see."[12]

Still, the risks of a career detour loom large. MNEs regularly tout a foreign assignment as a meaningful development experience that prepares managers for broader responsibilities. As the reasoning goes, it improves skills and expertise, fosters cultural awareness, increases confidence in overcoming challenges, and enhances creativity through exposure to new ways of doing things. Until recently, however, the odds were on a neutral or negative career outcome. As Tom Schiro of Deloitte & Touche observes, "Some MNEs just send somebody overseas and forget about them for two years."[13] Then, after returning, the company may be slow in rewarding a manager's successful international experience with an expanded leadership role.

EMERGING STANDARDS

With the expanding scale and scope of globalization come supply shortages of talented executives. MNEs report difficulty finding skillful candidates, investing more time interviewing and hiring, and worrying more about rivals poaching their high performers. Despite the global economic slowdown, skill shortages are getting worse. Manpower, a multinational human resource consulting firm, found that 34 percent of employers worldwide struggle to fill slots. According to the global consultancy McKinsey & Company, (1) only 43 percent of employers in leading markets such as Brazil, Germany, India, Mexico, Saudi Arabia, Turkey, and the United States can find enough skilled workers, (2) the world will be short 40 million college-educated workers in 2020, and (3) "there will be far too few workers with the advanced skills needed to drive a high productivity economy."[14] Shortages will amplify the value of a global mindset.

By changing the game, globalization changes performance standards. Increasingly, MNEs regard international experience as the cornerstone of a high-impact career. Nearly 33 percent of *FTSE 100* companies have a foreign national as CEO, and about 70 percent have had a foreign assignment. Among the *Fortune 100*, the figures clock in at 10 percent and 33 percent, respectively.[15] At Procter & Gamble, 39 of the company's top 44 global officers have had a foreign assignment, and 22 were born outside the United States. Global awareness and experience are "ingredient[s] you must have if you aspire to be a global player in the long term," says P&G's HR director.[16] P&G expects its leaders to be both innovative and worldly; they cannot rise to the top without running operations in a foreign market and managing a product around the world.[17] Its German rival, Henkel, insists on the same, requiring executives to live in at least two different countries prior to promotion.[18]

Boyden, an executive search firm, notes that seven of ten clients request international experience when seeking C-suite executives or board members; of those, roughly half now expect candidates' career records to show a few years' tenure in various countries.[19] Bluntly put, multinational experience is as essential as multifunctional and multiproduct experiences in developing high-performance executives. Consequently, MNEs post high-potential executives overseas, giving them the opportunity to step up to the challenge, battle test their skills, and improve their global mindset.

In summary, aspiring executives increasingly look abroad to move ahead. And, while perhaps overly hyped, personal ambition, environmental trends, market conditions, and workplace standards steadily move us toward situations where "the people with the top jobs in large corporations, even in the United States, will be those who have lived in several cultures and who can converse in at least two languages. Most CEOs will have had true global exposure, and their MNEs will be all the stronger for it."[20] ■

CRN
Case Review Note

QUESTIONS

20-1. From the text and tabular material presented in the case, select three compelling reasons to pursue a career in an international business.

20-2. Identify and discuss three benefits that you believe would follow from working as an expatriate in a foreign market (benefits can be related to career aspirations, personal goals, or general interests).

INTRODUCTION

CONCEPT CHECK

Recall our discussion in Chapter 1 of "The Forces Driving Globalization," in which we identify several factors that create connections among people worldwide. The convergence of cultures, politics, and markets diminish the physical and psychic distances between countries. Here we suggest that this trend has begun to make the prospect of moving from one country to another a more attractive career plan.

Indisputably, successful MNEs have insightful strategies, great supply chains, sharp financial systems, and the like. Ultimately, though, success is a function of the people who start and sustain the company. The expanding global web of commerce calls for executives who can manage complex, interconnected operations across a diversity of dissimilar markets. Running global operations from the sanctuary of the home office is no longer an option. The dispersion of design, manufacturing, and supply jobs worldwide requires managers with experience in several functions in several regions—for example, overseeing a product from its design phase in Silicon Valley to early production stages in China and then rolling it out for retail customers in Brazil.

The challenge of putting the right person into the right job in the right place at the right time for the right compensation for the right stretch takes us to the front lines of international business. From opening markets to returning home, international business careers take many directions. At the center is the person facing challenges that often lead to transformational opportunities. The contest between opportunity and challenge, the focus of this chapter, is the spirit of a career in international business.[21]

HUMAN RESOURCE MANAGEMENT

HRM refers to activities that staff the MNE.

Human resource management (HRM) shepherds an organization's most valued assets—its people. Opening and operating a business, whether a small-scale micronational or a vast multinational, requires finding people to implement the strategy, motivating them to perform well, upgrading their skills so they can move onto more challenging tasks, and, ultimately, retaining them.[22] HRM directs these functions.

Here we elaborate these issues, building on themes introduced in Chapter 12 and applied since to business functions and operating activities. We evaluate HRM from the perspective that the successful MNE must staff its operations with people who are mission-led and principle-driven to leverage the company's core competencies while reconciling pressures for local responsiveness and global integration. This perspective emphasizes that HRM activities, like the discrete activities that comprise the company's value chain, perform best when managers link them to the strategy of the firm (see Figure 20.2).

HRM AND THE GLOBAL COMPANY

HRM is far more difficult for the MNE than for its domestic counterpart. Besides dealing with situations in the home market, the firm must adjust its HRM practices for the political, cultural, legal, and economic differences in foreign markets. For example, leadership styles and management practices vary from country to country, causing difficulties between people at different units—say, headquarters and a local subsidiary.[23] The differences can turn great managers at home into ineffective ones overseas, as their struggle to adapt dampens performance.

HRM is more difficult for the MNE than its domestic counterpart due to
- Environmental differences,
- Strategic contingencies,
- Organizational challenges.

Similarly, labor markets vary in the mix of workers, costs, productivity, and regulations. Regarding the latter, national labor laws often require MNEs to reset their local workplace standards. In Malaysia, for instance, foreign engineers cannot work on building projects unless the hiring company demonstrates to the Malaysian Board of Engineers that a native engineer cannot do the job.[24] It's harsher in Thailand—the country's Alien Occupation Act reserves many architecture and engineering services jobs for Thai nationals.[25] Adjusting labor-management practices for these and similar regulations complicates decision-making. Consequently, MNEs continually evaluate how to staff international operations and fine-tune the mix of recruitment, training, compensation, transfer, and retention programs that persuade and prepare executives to work abroad.

One may wonder why MNEs and executives put up with these aggravations. The short answer is that the megatrend of globalization demands doing so. The long answer is that in the face of globalization, navigating these challenges creates competitive advantages and sustains the MNE's profitability. Both answers highlight HRM's mandate: Develop methods

FIGURE 20.2 Factors Influencing HRM in International Business

Successful MNEs consistently show that managing human resources, like managing finance, marketing, and supply chains, follow the requirements of the company's strategy. In the case of HRM, the key task centers on putting the right person in the right job in the right place at the right time for the right compensation for the right stretch—with the standard of "right" determined by the particular imperatives of the MNE's strategy.

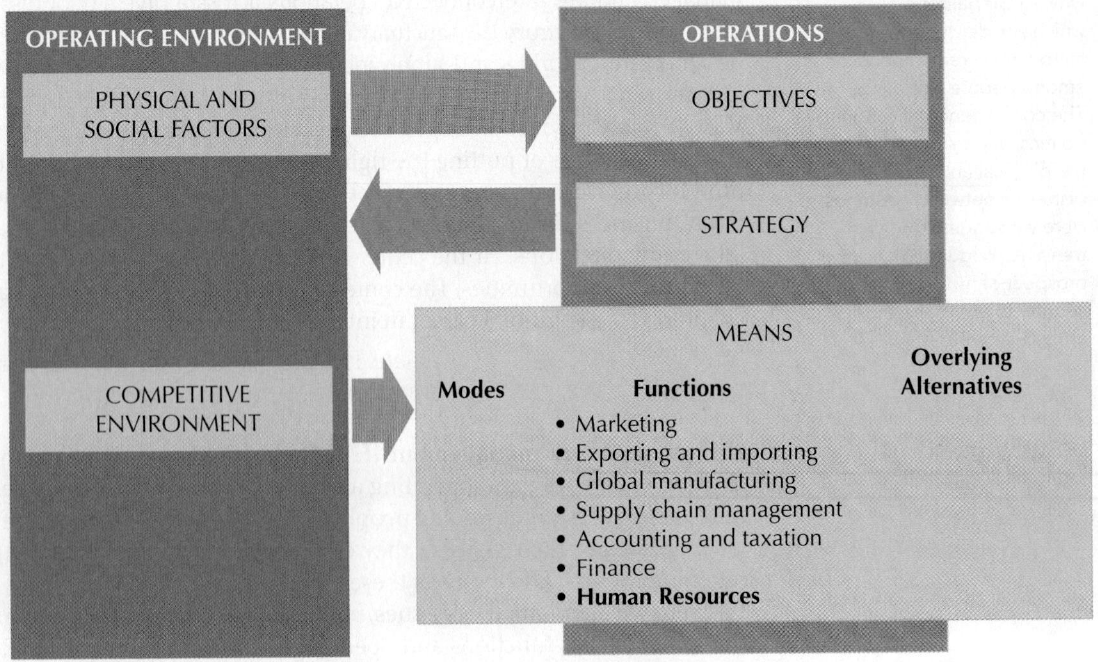

to build, develop, and retain the cadre of managers that will lead the company.[26] We now profile how HRM does so in organizing the selection, development, compensation, and retention of international managers.[27]

STRATEGIZING HRM

Anecdotes suggest, and research confirms, a powerful relationship between HRM processes, management productivity, and strategic performance.[28] Chapter 12, for instance, reported that GE's CEO believes success in becoming global is "truly about people, not about where the buildings are. You've got to develop people so they are prepared for leadership jobs and then promote them. That's the most effective way to become more global."[29] No matter the scale or scope of GE's international operations, it relies on superior human resources to sustain high productivity, competitive advantage, and value creation.

HRM policies that support the MNE's strategy generate high productivity and competitive advantage.

The Human Capital Index, synthesized from the practices of 2,000 MNEs in Asia, Europe, and the United States, found that superior HRM positively correlated with a firm's financial returns. It was also a leading indicator of increased shareholder value.[30] MNEs with superior human capital practices, on average, created more shareholder value than those with run-of-the-mill practices. Improving understanding of the link between human resources and company performance is correspondingly changing the thesis that superior financial outcomes lead MNEs to develop superior HRM practices. Analysis reveals the reverse: Superior HRM is a key determinant of corporate financial performance. Furthermore, the interaction between a firm's strategy and its HRM practices accounts for more variation in strategic performance than HRM in isolation.[31]

CONCEPT CHECK

A recurring theme of the text is the usefulness of adopting a strategic perspective. No matter if the topic involves political, legal, economic, or cultural dimensions of the marketplace, the quest for superior performance compels the MNE to link these trends, challenges, and consequences to its strategy.

The direct relationship between superior HRM and high productivity, competitive advantage, and value creation confirms the significance of people to performance. The power of these relationships highlights the HRM's role. No longer is it a glorified euphemism for personnel management, concerned with administering routine employee processes and setting short-term employment policies. HRM is now a performance driver, developing the executive talent that steers an MNE into a brave new world.

Our earlier look at the strategies that MNEs follow elaborates this view. Chapter 11 profiled commonly implemented choices: the international strategy and its quest to leverage core competencies abroad; the multidomestic strategy and its quest to maximize the local responsiveness of foreign operations; the global strategy and its quest to maximize worldwide integration; and the transnational strategy and its quest to optimize all three tasks simultaneously. Each strategy imposes unique standards for configuring and coordinating value activities. Hence, each strategy calls on HRM to find, staff, compensate, and retain the executives that command the requisite skills and outlooks. Struggling to do so, irrespective of the brilliance of its strategy, undercuts an MNE's performance. Getting it right, by integrating strategy and HRM, powers superior performance.

A CASE IN POINT: GE'S EVOLUTION

Looking at the role of HRM in the context of GE's evolution elaborates these ideas. Beginning in the 1980s, GE focused on globalizing its markets by selling existing products abroad (the international strategy). In the late 1980s, it began globalizing its material sources to acquire higher-quality inputs for lower prices in the quest to minimize costs (the global strategy). In the mid-1990s, it began globalizing its intellect by seeking, learning, and transferring ideas throughout its operations (the transnational strategy).

Each stop along its strategic evolution saw GE reset its HRM philosophy and practices to make sure it developed the requisite human capital. The key to its international strategy was staffing people who used GE's core competencies to build competitive operations in foreign markets. Local operations lacked the necessary knowledge and skills to implement the international strategy; hence, GE sent expats to fill the gap. The key to its global strategy was developing executives who optimized location economics in directing global supply chains.

Growing linkages among local operations required coordinating the expanding web of global product relationships; short supplies of the requisite executive talent in many subsidiaries spurred GE to send expats to fill the gap. Lastly, the key to its transnational strategy is staffing executives throughout its global operations who develop, transfer, and engage ideas, irrespective of the business, function, or market source. This goal required posting different people to different operations in different countries to develop the requisite executive outlook and leadership skills; hence, GE posted its best managers, no matter their nationality, to expat slots.

MNEs use expatriates for various reasons, including
- Filling a skills gap in the local market,
- Transferring competencies to coordinate activities,
- Executive development.

As you see, an MNE's strategic evolution resets how it engages international business. Each stage in GE's evolution required that HRM align executive selection, development, and compensation policies with the unique requirements of its strategy. Moreover, as GE's strategy evolved, so did its understanding of the role of expatriates. Jeffrey Immelt explains, "When I first joined General Electric [in 1982], globalization meant training the Americans to be global thinkers. So, Americans got the expat assignments. We still have many Americans living around the world, and that's good, but we shifted our emphasis in the late 1990s to getting overseas assignments for non-Americans. Now you see non-Americans doing new jobs, big jobs, important jobs at every level and in every country."[32] Today, GE has a cadre of international managers with the expertise to leverage its core competencies in developing and diffusing ideas around the world.

GE's success in international business, like that of many other MNEs profiled throughout this chapter, highlights HRM's mission: find, staff, compensate, and retain executives with the qualifications needed to support and sustain the company's strategy. Done well, HRM supports higher productivity, stronger competitiveness, and improving profitability. Done poorly, people problems fan frustrations that undermine firm performance and ruin careers.

THE PERSPECTIVE OF THE EXPATRIATE

An executive perspective directs attention to the tasks required to run international business operations.

You can evaluate HRM from many perspectives. Two reasons motivate an executive perspective. First, in the MNE, the tip of the operational spear is the executive running international operations. Indeed, virtually any successful (or, for that matter, struggling) international strategy has an executive drama at its core. Executives drive critical tasks of the company's strategy: they launch new ventures, build local management expertise, fill local skills gaps, transfer core competencies, assemble technology platforms, and diffuse the organization culture. Second, an executive perspective speaks to your likely interest in working internationally. Students routinely ask teachers about the why, how, when, where, and what of careers in international business.

This chapter provides some guidelines, suggestions, and insights into these questions, concerns, and issues. An executive perspective directs attention to the principles and practices HRM uses to specify the selection, role, responsibility, development, compensation, and retention of expatriates.

WHO'S WHO

An expatriate leaves her or his native country to live and work in another.

First, though, some definitions. Our discussions focus on two types of executives: *locals* and *expatriates*. A local is hired by the MNE in his or her home country to staff the local operations; no special provisions apply to the work contract. An **expatriate** (or "expat") is sent to work temporarily in a country that is not his or her legal residence. There are two classes of expatriates. One is a **home-country national**, a citizen of the country where the firm is headquartered, such as a Brazilian national running the German operations of her Brazilian company. The other is a **third-country national**, namely, a citizen of another country altogether, such as an Estonian national running the Russian subsidiary of his Australian company.

TRENDS IN EXPATRIATE ASSIGNMENTS

A third-country national is an employee who is a citizen of neither the home nor the host country.

We are witnessing a burst in worldwide demand for expatriates.[33] The emergence of fast-growing economies has led to opening many new subsidiaries. Western MNEs, besides running their existing operations, struggle to staff startup operations in new markets. Emerging

A sight common throughout airports worldwide—a smartphone-armed executive rushing to catch the next connection to the next stop on his globalization circuit.
Source: © Santiago Cornejo/Fotolia

MNEs similarly build operations in foreign markets. More precisely, there are approximately 22,000 multinationals based in the emerging world. Few of these existed a decade ago.[34] Each unit of each MNE requires executive talent.

Short-term expatriate assignments, such as commuter and flexpatriates, are more common today than a decade ago.

Staffing the latest wave of globalization also refines the characteristics of an expatriate. Unquestionably, the long-running standard of the executive sent from his home to work abroad endures. Furthermore, expatriates have usually been posted to a particular host country for a three- to five-year assignment, with the plan of ultimately returning home. Today, different circumstances reset these standards. For example, the notion of "a few years" increasingly gives way to a few days, few weeks, or a few months. So-called **commuter assignments** post an executive across different cultural or national borders for a short span; in an extreme case, it comprises the workweek, with the expat returning home to family and personal life for the weekend. Notes an HR director, "Commuter assignments were non-existent until ten years ago, but now they are much more common."[35]

Short-term assignments, besides being far more economical than long-term tours, quickly transfer skills and resources to local subsidiaries.[36] Moreover, research suggests that working solo increases productivity but personal interactions catalyze innovations.[37] Hence, a trip abroad to foreign colleagues, no matter how brief, promotes social relations that support innovation. Increasingly, common commuter assignments give rise to so-called **flexpatriates**, executives who run the commuter cycle for a longer span.[38]

The Young, Old, and Restless In addition to time frames, big changes reset who heads abroad. Traditionally, expatriates were mid-level executives being groomed for higher levels of responsibility. Essentially, international assignments were midcareer stepping-stones for the MNE's future leaders. At many companies, that mindset persists. Xerox, for instance, rotates its rising stars through two- to four-year assignments; successfully passing this "litmus test" makes one a C-level contender.[39] Increasingly, several trends and constraints push HRM to expand search criteria to include older employees whose children have grown and whose spouses regard an international assignment positively. In addition, HRM looks to younger employees who are single, more mobile, and eager to experience life in foreign places.

Changing markets, growing cost consciousness, and evolving strategies are resetting notions of who is an expatriate—now, we see growing interest in the young, the old, and the restless.

In terms of posting younger managers to international assignments, MNEs increasingly trade performance track records for long-term potential. For example, PricewaterhouseCoopers offers its Early PwC International Challenge program (EPIC) to accelerate international assignments for its younger employees. EPIC identifies promising workers who are interested in living abroad and have established a promising record of accomplishment. Operationally, candidates jump start the process by completing an online assessment and consulting PwC's career pages. EPIC encourages them to choose their preferred destination, then posts them abroad for two-year assignments with the goal of developing them for senior leadership roles.[40] Candidates benefit by skipping a rung or two on the career ladder as well as escaping slower-growth job markets. Likewise, HRM benefits by identifying high performers who command leadership, entrepreneurial zest, and a tolerance for uncertainty.

CONCEPT CHECK

MNEs' search for superior competitive advantage pushes many to build a globally integrated enterprise that can implement increasingly sophisticated strategies. Consequently, they adjust their idea of an expatriate, fine-tuning the traditional notion of someone posted abroad for a lengthy tour as well as experimenting with novel formats that tinker with duration and design.

Increasingly, university programs both respond to and accelerate these trends. Schools worldwide internationalize their curricula, expand study-abroad options, offer joint degrees with foreign campuses, and recruit students from different nations. Similarly, some students take the big plunge, heading abroad for college. Hong Kong University of Science and Technology's Business School, for example, had 16 nationalities in 2001, and almost all of them hailed from Asia. By 2012, it had 28 nationalities and half came from outside Asia.[41] Similar change is afoot elsewhere, with Americans increasingly heading to overseas MBA programs. Explained one enrolled in ESADE in Barcelona, "If you look at the world today, at the state of business, you see that bridges are being built and borders broken down. I desired to focus on global business to expand both my knowledge and my network."[42] This sort of self-initiated expatriate, with a quest to pursue cultural, personal, and career development experiences abroad, will refine our interpretations.[43]

Rising Role of Women The gender dimension of expatriate selection is similarly evolving. In absolute terms, females comprise roughly 20 percent of expatriates.[44] Relative growth has been far more dramatic. Since 2001, MNEs in the Asia-Pacific region have seen a sixteen-fold increase in women on international assignment, MNEs in North America have seen nearly a fourfold rise, and Europe has doubled its count. Surveys indicate that more than half of MNEs expect the number of female expatriates to increase, about a third believe the number will hold steady, and a handful see it declining. Reasoned an observer, "Going on expatriate placements can be an important step on the career ladder, and women are increasingly interested in taking these assignments."[45]

Growing Scope of Third-Country Nationals MNEs establish operations abroad in increasingly dissimilar markets—say, from the United States to Canada to England to India to Singapore to China to Vietnam. The changing workplace of globalization elevates the role

A situation once odd, but now increasingly prevalent—young folks heeding the siren call of opportunity in emerging economies. Here we see Mick Xomir, a junior at a U.S. university, on his way to a summer internship in Beijing.

Source: SHIHO FUKUDA/The New York Times/Redux Pictures

of third-country nationals, who often have the particular outlook and versatile competencies needed to run operations in diverse locales.[46] Longer term, the supply of skilled third-country nations will expand, especially in high-growth emerging economies. In 2013, for example, China added another $250 billion to its university infrastructure, on top of already doubling its number of universities over the previous decade. It plans to produce 195 million college graduates by 2020.[47]

The move toward short-term assignments boosts the logistical appeal of third-country nationals—an executive living in London yet working for a U.S. MNE, for instance, may spend Monday through Friday working in Zurich, then return home for the weekend. Then, as the need arises for help in the MNE's Stockholm office, she can easily reset her commute. Such mobility lets an MNE adroitly adapt its strategy, confident it has well-positioned executives to implement it. Data increasingly document the growing use of third-country nationals. A generation ago, the vast majority of expatriates were selected from managers working in the MNE's home country operations. In 2011, a little over 50 percent of international assignees, an all-time low, relocated to or from the headquarters country.[48]

Reverse Expatriates The rising importance of emerging markets refines our evolving ideas of expatriates. Historically, MNEs selected them from the pool of executives in richer countries and sent them to staff operations in developing countries. Now, well-educated executives from emerging economies—so-called **reverse-expats**—are sent straight to the richer countries to accelerate their development, spending anywhere from a few weeks to a year in an operational unit.[49] Eventually they return home, often replacing a traditionally defined—and usually much higher-priced—expatriate. Some tweak this option further. Goldman Sachs relies on its Growth Markets Opportunity Program to hire high-potential Asians and Latin Americans who have earned an MBA from Western universities, then posts them to its New York or London offices for up to a year before assigning them to leadership positions in local operations in Singapore, Hong Kong, China, Brazil, India, and other emerging economies.[50]

COST CONSIDERATIONS

The slow-growth legacy of the global financial crisis pushes MNEs to rethink the economics of expatriates. Sending workers abroad, as we discuss later, is quite expensive. In recourse, MNEs design short-term and cross-border commuter assignments and endorse frequent international business travel in lieu of traditional permanent assignments. Rather than moving to foreign markets, executives travel far more often to far more places that lie farther from their home base. Today, for example, just 35 percent of expats report living in their host country for more than five years, compared to 58 percent in 2009.[51] Likewise, cost concerns accelerate deploying third-country nationals in place of executives from the home office. The latter often demand richer compensation packages and impose higher relocation costs.

Economic pressures and cost concerns spur companies to emphasize frequent business travel in lieu of a longer-term international assignment.

General cost concerns push MNEs to localize assignments. **Localization** is the process whereby an expatriate retains the foreign assignment but accepts the status of a local hire and, correspondingly, the lower host-location salary. Effectively, one consents to lower compensation in order to work abroad. IBM's "Project Match" adds an interesting twist to localization, offering terminated employees in the United States the option to move to a local unit in India, China, Brazil, Nigeria, Russia, or other developing country provided the candidate has been a "satisfactory performer" and is "willing to work on local terms and conditions."[52] In other words, you have the option to move abroad and preserve your job but your compensation will be set by the local pay scale. Granted, a few perks may be added to the package. Inevitably, though, the total will fall short of the previous compensation package.

THE ENDURING CONSTANT

Ideas on staffing international operations change as market opportunities and cost pressures alter the global environment. As a result, the types and mechanics of expat assignments change as well. Nevertheless, there is an enduring constant: Running the hundreds of thousands of subsidiaries throughout the world requires talented, enterprising locals as well as home-country and third-country expatriates. So keen is the demand that MNEs report historic shortages of expatriate talent and, consequently, the increasing consideration of the young, old, and restless for international assignments.[53]

Furthermore, while the global financial crisis may have relieved some staffing pressure, the accelerating growth in emerging economies has begun picking up the slack. No matter how costly or complex, MNEs must continue staffing the right person in the right job in the right place at the right time for the right compensation for the right stretch. Success drives strategy and sustainability. Failure ruins careers and jeopardizes profitability.

STAFFING FRAMEWORKS IN THE MNE

Three perspectives anchor an MNE's staffing policy:

- Ethnocentrism
- Polycentricism
- Geocentricism

MNEs use **staffing frameworks**—basic conceptual structures that help HRM solve complex issues—to guide their decision-making. First, a staffing framework identifies the optimal mix of local workers from the host nation, expatriates sent from the home country, and third-country nationals. Second, it sets selection, training, compensation, and repatriation guidelines. Organizing key staffing frameworks leads us to revisit earlier discussions of ethnocentrism, polycentrism, and geocentrism.

THE ETHNOCENTRIC FRAMEWORK

CONCEPT CHECK

"Company and Management Orientations" in Chapter 2 introduced the idea of polycentrism, ethnocentrism, and geocentrism to describe how MNEs and their managers approach foreign cultures. Here, we reintroduce these terms, highlighting the ways these "attitudes or orientations" influence a MNE's staffing framework.

Ethnocentrism occurs when one group places itself at the top of an imagined hierarchy of relevant groups, thereby regarding others as inferior. Hence, the **ethnocentric framework** signifies the belief that the management principles and business practices used by headquarters are superior to those used by rivals in other countries. The proven success of the company's way of doing things, goes this reasoning, means there is little call to adapt it to foreign markets.[54] Thus, the MNE applying an ethnocentric framework aims to staff expatriate slots with executives from its home operation.

Advantages of the Ethnocentric Framework Those MNEs that link competitiveness to transferring core competencies abroad find value in this framework. Consider that a firm earns success in its home market doing something exceptional—what we earlier had referred to as a core competency. Such a legacy of success leads the firm to see its way of doing business as the superior means of creating value. Logically, it sees its international success dependent on controlling the transfer and regulating the use of its core competencies. With this in mind, headquarters understandably concludes that executives who had already successfully done a job should do the same overseas.

The ethnocentric framework fills key management positions with home-country nationals.

Look at India's Wipro Technology, which employs 54,000 people in 35 countries, more than 11,000 of whom are expatriates, and more than 90 percent of those Indian. Wipro posts Indian executives internationally who then run business development and train local staff in order to spread the "Wipro Way" throughout the world. "We sprinkle Indians in new markets to help seed and set up the culture and intensity," explained Sanjay Joshi, chief executive of global programs.[55]

Staffing overseas operations with people from the home country enables the MNE to regulate the transfer of its core competency.[56] This is particularly vital when it is difficult to articulate, specify, or standardize, such as Apple's product-design and media expertise, Walmart's information-management and product-distribution systems, or Honda's understanding of engine technology. Posting a home-country manager with direct experience in developing, applying, and protecting the company's core competency puts it in trustworthy hands. The HSBC Group long epitomized this outlook. For generations, most top executives came from a tight-knit cadre of elite expatriates who, in circulating among foreign operations, dispersed the "DNA of the organization."[57]

Home office executives commonly note there is no shortage of brainpower in a particular country, just a shortage of people with the ideal mix of technical skills, experience with the particular business methods, and fluency with the company's preferred way of doing business. The mounting importance of protecting ownership advantages spurs an MNE to safeguard its core competency. With it, the firm prospers; without it, the firm struggles. This stark reality spurs headquarters to entrust control of the company's "crown jewels" to those who will best protect them: namely, colleagues from the home country. Earlier discussion of intellectual property explained that safeguards deter but by no means prevent theft. The ethnocentric framework fortifies defenses by posting home country executives who vigilantly protect corporate assets.

Drawbacks of the Ethnocentric Framework As the adage goes, vices are simply virtues taken to extreme. The same applies to the ethnocentric framework. Force-fitting foreign operations with a standardized staffing policy risks pounding circular pegs into square slots. Certainly, an MNE can make its foreign operations mirror the outward appearance of the home office. Moreover, as we saw above, MNEs have compelling rationales when asked why they rely on home-country nationals to run foreign operations. However, assigning home office executives to foreign operations does not automatically create a successful "mini-me" subsidiary. Consequently, an ethnocentric framework can prove detrimental, blinding the MNE to different, possibly better, business methods.

In 2001, for example, Toyota aspired to sell 1 million cars a year in China within a decade. By 2012, many believed the world's biggest carmaker had sorely misread the world's largest market; it offered cars priced too high with too little *daqi* (Chinese consumers' perception of road presence). Toyota's solution to its ongoing China problem, a reflection of its traditional ethnocentric staffing policy, likely complicated problems. Explained a senior Toyota executive, "Our way of beefing up operations in China is to bring in more people from Japan. We should be localizing our business here, promoting Chinese managers, and listening more attentively to Chinese consumers. But we don't."[58]

Unless checked, the ethnocentric outlook can misinterpret local innovations.

Ethnocentric staffing policies often demotivate local executives. The implicit assumption that all the smart, capable people live within a 25-mile radius of headquarters sends the message that the home office does not value subsidiary personnel. Unless a foreign assignment is intended to develop unique skills, local employees may resent the expat, whom they see as no more qualified than themselves. Unchecked, resentment can lower productivity and increase turnover as locals see a glass ceiling capping their careers.

Finally, an ethnocentric staffing policy can prove impractical. Host governments, alert to the importance of developing and employing their nation's workforce, prefer that subsidiaries hire locals. MNEs' plea that the unique nature of their operations prevents their doing so is often ignored. Governments impose immigration laws or workplace regulations that prod MNEs to hire locals. Again, recall our earlier example about employment law in Thailand and Malaysia, to say nothing of similar situations in others, like India, Saudi Arabia, the European Community, and the United States that regulate the use of expatriates in place of natives.

THE POLYCENTRIC FRAMEWORK

Polycentrism is the principle of organizing around different political, social, or economic centers. A **polycentric framework** acknowledges the business practices of foreign centers as philosophically and practically equivalent to those at home. Anchored in the thesis that because the circumstances of the home country differ from those of local subsidiaries, and neither is intrinsically superior, a company accordingly adapts its HRM policies to local standards. Thus, staffing operating units, from headquarters to foreign subsidiaries, draws from the local environment—Chinese run the China operations, Mexicans run the Mexico operations, Austrians run the Austria operations, and so on. In rare cases where home-office executives are posted to foreign subsidiaries operations, the working assumption is that their effectiveness requires immersing themselves in the local culture.

Advantages of the Polycentric Framework Staffing foreign operations with locals has economic, political, and cultural advantages. Johnson & Johnson (J & J), which applies the polycentric framework, highlights some of them. With few exceptions, home-country nationals run J&J's subsidiaries. Each unit operates with substantial autonomy, commanding the freedom to act as it believes best given local market conditions. Thus liberated, each acts as a small business, entrepreneurial in character and aware that success depends on its superior sense in anticipating local customers' needs and delivering meaningful solutions. More formally, J&J's CEO explained that relying on locals to staff local operations "is a tremendous magnet for talent because it gives people room to grow and room to explore new ideas, thus developing their own skills and careers."[59]

The polycentric framework uses host-country nationals to manage local subsidiaries.

A compelling motivation of the polycentric approach is its implications for the economics of staffing international operations. Hiring local managers eliminates the typically exorbitant expense of posting expatriates to local slots. It is difficult to pinpoint the total cost of an expat assignment due to the range of relevant variables. A general rule is that the total annual cost is three times the expat's annual compensation. Indirect administrative expenses boost this sum. For example, an expat slot generates far more paperwork than a comparable domestic executive slot. Consequently, supporting expatriates requires, on average, twice as many HR professionals (1 HR professional to 37 expats) versus home-country executives (1 HR professional to 70 managers).[60]

These costs are far more dramatic when qualified by the comparative expense of a local hire. Typically, an expat costs the employer three to five times as much as an equivalent local worker, after taking into account financial incentives, relocation costs, cost-of-living allowances, local tax differentials, and so on. These stark economics increasingly encourage the staffing of local operations with home country nationals. A decade ago, for instance, HSBC Group had more than 1,000 expats out of 312,000 worldwide employees. Its concern for rising costs spurred local hires; it now has about 380 expatriates.[61]

Using host-country managers boosts local motivation and morale. Still, likely costs include gaps with global operations due to problems with accountability and allegiance.

Host governments typically see local managers as better citizens than expatriates, given the belief that locals will champion national interests over global objectives. Hiring local managers also boosts employee morale.[62] Too, it neutralizes impediments to using expats, such as licensing requirements that prohibit expatriate accountants and lawyers or visa regulations that put a hard cap on the number of foreigners who can staff a local subsidiary.

Finally, proponents of polycentrism reason that local managers are stronger performers given their keener understanding of local customers, markets, and institutions. Interviews of 300 senior executives at global companies found that fewer than 40 percent believed they better understood the local operating environment and customers' needs than did their local competitors.[63] For Toyota, fixing its Chinese market problems has spurred it to rethink its HR policy, deemphasizing its traditional ethnocentric approach in favor of greater localization; explained a Toyota spokesperson, "We're promoting more local Chinese employees to management ranks and will continue to do so."[64]

Microsoft's HR philosophy elaborates this perspective. When operating outside the United States, Microsoft aims to hire home-country nationals. As its former COO explains, "You want people who know the local situation, its value system, the way work gets done, the way people use technology in that particular country, and who the key competitors are....If you send someone in fresh from a different region or country, they don't know those things."[65] More philosophically, Bill Gates, Microsoft's chairman, reasons that a polycentric policy is a moral obligation of international business, declaring that when staffing an international office, "It sends the wrong message to have a foreigner come over to run things."[66]

Drawbacks to the Polycentric Framework A polycentric policy requires the MNE to decentralize authority to locals to run operations. This can confuse accountability and blur allegiance. Accountability problems escalate as local units depend less and less on the home office for resources. Moreover, as local managers develop their skills, they often build thriving local operations. Success supports growing resource independence from the home office and, in turn, transition of the local subsidiary into a quasi-autonomous unit and the MNE into a federation of loosely connected, largely autonomous national operations. Unchecked, these local subsidiaries pay less mind to headquarters. For instance, when J&J launched Tylenol in 1960 as an over-the-counter pain reliever in the United States, the product was available to worldwide units shortly thereafter. However, the quasi-independent Japanese unit, despite duress from headquarters, did not begin selling it until 2000.[67]

The polycentric staffing framework calls upon headquarters to unite the often loosely-coupled subsidiaries.

Likewise, dilemmas over where to pay allegiance emerge when host-country nationals in charge of a subsidiary are loyal to local colleagues instead of to the foreigners running the faraway headquarters. In theory, local managers balance the competing demands of making sense of events from a local and home office view. In practice, however, national concerns often take precedence given the immediacy of local marketplace pressures.[68]

Compounding this situation is a subtle drawback of polycentric staffing—namely, the potential disengagement of local staff from the parent company. By definition and design, there are few slots for expatriates in the polycentric framework; hence, locals have scant opportunities to work outside their home country. This outcome constrains the international mobility of enterprising host-country nationals. As a result, there may be little incentive for local managers to study business and cultural practices in other markets. Unaddressed, the resulting single-country focus can isolate national subsidiaries as well as push ambitious executives to quit.

THE GEOCENTRIC FRAMEWORK

Geocentrism is a world-oriented set of attitudes and values that regards humanity as a single entity sharing universal outlooks and orientations. Hence, the **geocentric framework** does not heed national boundaries. Rather, it regards the blunt split of home-, host-, and third-country managers as needless divisions. HRM's task, then, is developing the best people for key jobs throughout the organization, regardless of their home nationality or eventual host market. On this theme, reasoned GE's CEO, "It's more important to find the best people, wherever they may be, and develop them so that they can lead big businesses, wherever those may be."[69]

Advantages of the Geocentric Framework Geocentrism develops global executives who move between countries and cultures without forfeiting their personal effectiveness.[70] Top managers with varied cultural backgrounds and life experiences broaden a company's strategic perspective. Executives commanding a geocentric mindset better enable MNEs to pursue global and, especially, transnational strategies. Both strategies aim to exploit learning opportunities around the world in improving and leveraging core competencies. Resetting staffing frameworks to look beyond traditional talent pools for leadership supports these goals. As the CEO of Schering-Plough explains, "Good ideas can come from anywhere…the more places you are, the more ideas you will get. And the more ideas you get, the more places you can sell them and the more competitive you will be. Managing in many places requires a willingness to accept good ideas no matter where they come from—which means having a global attitude."[71]

The geocentric framework posts the most-qualified executives, regardless of nationality, to expatriate slots.

Performance data confirm these effects, showing that MNEs with diverse top teams were top financial performers, particularly those implementing ambitious global strategies with strong cross-cultural dimensions.[72] Similarly, others report that promoting a geocentric outlook in the executive ranks helps build teams that collaborate effectively, better capitalizes on global perspectives, adapts to a wider range of environments, and bridges differences of opinion.

Drawbacks to the Geocentric Framework A geocentric framework is tough to develop and costly to maintain. Certainly, the notion of a world-oriented set of attitudes and values is intellectually engaging. The multinational composition of senior management reduces cultural myopia, improves team representativeness, and enhances market responsiveness. Difficulty plagues adoption, however, given the need for executives to retain a sense of identity in the face of increasing diversity. At one point, for instance, J. P. Morgan housed managers of more than 50 nationalities in its London office, reasoning that putting the best people together, regardless of nationality, powered strategic insights.[73]

Economic factors, decision-making routines, and legal contingencies complicate implementing the geocentric framework.

Research reports that working with groups marked by cultural diversity takes on a different vibe than with groups made up of people of similar ethnicities and nationalities.[74] Often, the mix of different perspectives generates creative breakthroughs. However, the task of making sense of the various outlooks that potentially bear on a decision can prove

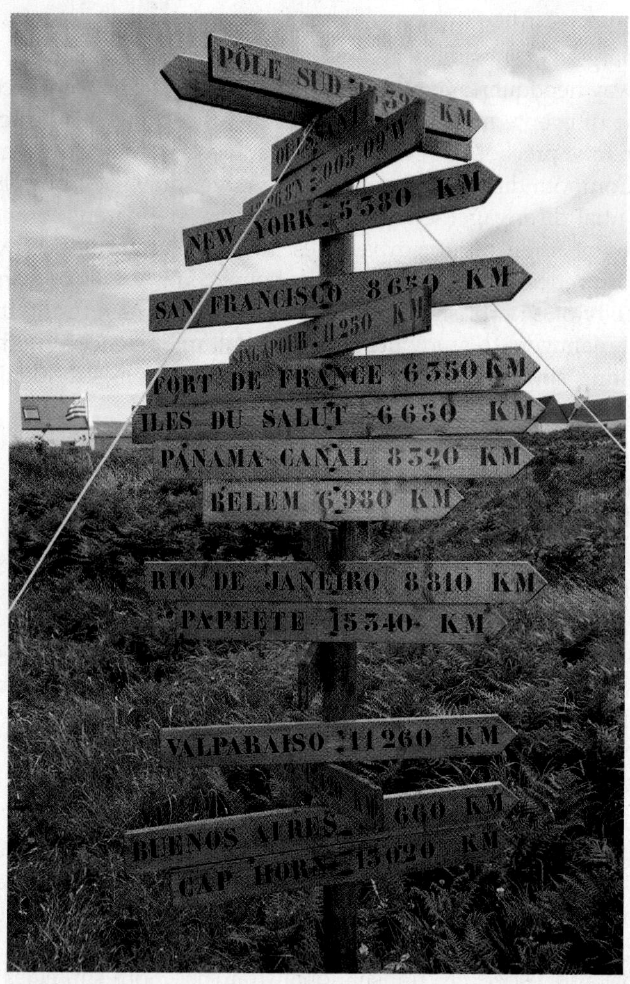

Where one goes inevitably shapes the game one then plays. Here we see a range, from a decidedly South American perspective, of a smattering of international game spots open to the enterprising individual.
Source: Stephane Bidouze/Shutterstock

overwhelming. Akin to the Tower of Babel, geocentrism can erode common cause as the clarity of the task is lost in a hodgepodge of competing perspectives.

The logistics of the geocentric framework are costly. Exposing people to different ideas in diverse places is expensive. Compensation and relocation costs quickly escalate when transferring high-priced executives from country to country. Often the higher pay and prestige enjoyed by those in the expatriate vanguard triggers resentment. Current cost sensitivities, aggravated by the global financial crisis, pressure firms to economize. In recourse, they experiment with short-term engagements, commuter relationships, and extended business travel in lieu of multi-year assignments.

WHICH FRAMEWORK WHEN?

CONCEPT CHECK

Table 20.1 demonstrates a principle that we develop throughout this book: Although most of us are prone to look for the "one best way" of doing things, it's seldom a promising approach in any area. This outlook applies to formulating a staffing strategy for international operations.

Table 20.1 summarizes the merits and constraints of the three staffing frameworks. Suggesting that there is no theoretically superior approach, it endorses a contingency perspective that calls for optimizing staffing policies in terms of the specific demands of the MNE's strategy. Earlier we noted that expatriates drive the critical tasks of the company's strategy; they launch new ventures, build management expertise, fill local skills gaps, transfer technology, and diffuse organization culture. Each strategy, whether international, multidomestic, global, or transnational, imposes different requirements to run these activities. Therefore, HRM devises the staffing framework that develops executive resources contingent upon the demands set by the MNE's strategy.[75] More to the point, a survey of MNEs noted that nearly 90 percent prepared for global expansion by determining strategic goals and needs. They then assessed their pool of potential expatriates, looking for the requisite outlooks and skills and filling gaps as needed.[76]

TABLE 20.1 Frameworks to Staff International Operations: Principles and Practices

The assumptions, advantages, drawbacks, and strategic fit of the leading staffing frameworks run the gamut. HRM, keen to the requirements of the MNE's strategy, applies the most appropriate staffing framework. As they do, they keep in mind the following conditions and the tradeoffs built into each choice.

Framework	Assumptions	Advantages	Drawbacks	Strategic Fit
Ethnocentric	• The leadership ideals, management values, and workplace practices of one's company are superior to those in foreign markets. • Headquarters makes key decisions and foreign subsidiaries follow orders.	• Leverages a company's core competence. • Promotes executives' international outlook. • Fills local skills gap quickly. • Protects the preferred principles and practices of the company's culture.	• Fans dissent and demotivation among locals. • Discourages cultural empathy. • Blinds managers to local innovations. • Posted expats prone to culture shock. • Alienates locals who prefer national development.	International Strategy given its quest to leverage and safeguard the company's core competencies in foreign markets.
Polycentric	• Headquarters makes broad strategic decisions that local units adapt to their marketplace. • Adapts to differences, real or imaginary, between home and host countries. • Superior competitiveness requires understanding local customers, markets, and institutions in the host market.	• Respects the unique merits of the local environment. • Local hires demand less compensation. • Local managers holding top jobs attract, motivate, and retain local employees. • Reduces the odds of executive/expat failure. • Appeases host governments that prefer locals who champion local goals.	• Complicates coordinating and controlling value activities. • Isolates country operations. • Reduces incentive among locals to engage a global perspective. • Creates agency dilemmas for quasi-autonomous country operations. • Promotes a single nation focus among local staff.	Multidomestic Strategy given its quest to maximize the local responsiveness of foreign operations by fitting people, products, and processes to local standards.
Geocentric	• All nations are created equal and possess inalienable characteristics that are neither superior nor inferior but simply there. • Headquarters and subsidiaries collaborate to identify, transfer, and diffuse best practices. • Ideas and innovations are found anywhere and everywhere—provided one is open to the insight.	• Adept way to deal with different people in different counties. • Streamlines activities by efficiently configuring operations and expat staffs. • Leverages the company's strategic scale and operational scope. • Promotes learning dynamics that develop, transfer, and leverage local ideas worldwide.	• Tough to develop, costly to run, hard to maintain. • Contrary to many countries' market development plans to champion local causes. • Difficult to find and fund qualified expatriates that effectively move from country to country. • High status of global expats demotivates supporting players.	Global and Transnational Strategies given the quest to optimize worldwide integration and local responses.

MANAGING EXPATRIATES

Developing high-performance expatriates requires that MNEs identify candidates who are interested in an international assignment, prepare them for the adventure, devise ways to motivate them, post them to the appropriate job, and capitalize on their improved skills when they are ready for their next position. Over years of trial and error, HRM has systematized programs to deal with these key matters. Let's look at each.

EXPATRIATE SELECTION

Screening executives to find those with the greatest inclination and highest potential for a foreign assignment is the process of **expatriate selection**. Always difficult, it grows increasingly so for a variety of reasons, most notably talent shortages and rising expenses of international assignments.[77]

CRN
Case Review Note

Some people enjoy the thrill of living and working abroad. Our opening case profiled a Morgan Stanley expatriate who has worked in Britain, Singapore, and India and welcomes the prospect to see the "big world." Others, however, prefer to achieve their career ambitions within the boundaries of their home market. Certainly, there are many potential candidates for an overseas assignment, particularly as economic slowdowns make jobs less secure. The problem, however, is not the supply of candidates who are ready and willing but the supply of candidates who are also able. And therein lies the challenge of expatriate selection. HR executives, try as they might, cannot consult a battery of technical indicators that consistently predict the likely performance of a potential expatriate.[78]

CONCEPT CHECK

In Chapters 2, 3, and 4, we analyze the environments—cultural, political, legal, and economic—that frame international business operations. The variability in each context prevents setting absolute standards for running international operations. Here, we observe the implications of that variability to selecting expatriates. General guidelines more often than not take the place of absolute standards.

One option is to rely on chance; that, though, can prove prohibitive. The enduring need for mobile, economical, and experienced expatriates to run international operations, along with the rising cost of failure, spurs systematizing selection processes. Therefore, HRM evaluates career, cultural, and psychological measures, anchored in the company's staffing framework, to identify good candidates. These measures, applied through objective evaluations and in-depth interviews, screen candidates on many dimensions. Anecdotes and analysis emphasize the importance of *technical competence* and *adaptiveness*.

Technical competence, adaptiveness, and leadership ability are leading determinants of who is selected for an international assignment.

Technical Competence Asked to rank the important objectives of an international assignment, HR directors commonly identify the goal of filling a skills gap in the foreign subsidiary. Implementing a software system, orchestrating a marketing campaign, or organizing new ventures may exceed the subsidiary's competencies. Headquarters reasons that assigning a high-performance expatriate quickly transfers the necessary expertise. Nearly one of four expats sent abroad, estimates indicate, are posted to fill skills gaps rather than run the foreign unit.[79] Therefore, an enduring precondition of selection for an international assignment is the executive's functional expertise and an understanding of how to apply it in the foreign operation.[80]

The importance of professional expertise means managers often have several years of work experience before moving into an international assignment. The fact that expatriate selections regularly follow line managers' recommendation, based on the candidate's operational track record, reinforces this routine. Finally, rightly or wrongly, outstanding technical competence is often seen as signifying the self-confidence needed to work well abroad.

In summary, HR executives, expats, and local staff agree that technical competence, usually indicated by past job performance, has been and continues to be the leading selection criterion.[81] However, this predisposition is slowly relaxing; recall that some MNEs seek younger employees to staff international slots, rebalancing the trade-off between performance and potential. Figure 20.3 depicts an extreme take on this scenario.

Adaptiveness Professional success in one's home country is a necessary but insufficient basis for success abroad. Effective expatriates, if anything, are adaptive.[82] Thrust into new, unusual situations, they develop the knowledge, skills, and outlook needed to thrive. Facing ambiguities, they quickly identify factors that organize interpretation and speed decision-making. Challenged by the physical, emotional, and intellectual stress of a tough assignment, they resolve their choices and consequences. The vitality of adaptiveness moves MNEs to evaluate candidates in terms of:

Adaptiveness refers to a person's potential for

- Self-maintenance and personal resourcefulness,
- Interpreting the immediate environment,
- Developing productive workplace relationships.

Self-Maintenance Personal qualities, such as industriousness, resourcefulness, and self-reliance, are useful when things do not go as planned—which is not unlikely in the zone of international business. For example, HSBC's selection process uses tests, interviews, and exercises to gauge a candidate's capacity for self-maintenance; throughout each assessment, reliable measures anchor objective evaluation. Still, HSBC also evaluates intrinsically

"You'll be perfect for heading up our new push into the global market place but what's this about you still living at home with your mother?"

FIGURE 20.3 The Promise and Problem of Potential

Changing circumstances in staffing international slots directs attention to younger employees, though rarely this youthful.

Source: Peter C. Vey/Cartoon Bank/www.cartoonbank.com

intangible indicators. Its CEO explains, "We don't look so much at what or where people have studied but rather at their drive, initiative, cultural sensitivity, and readiness to see the world as their oyster. Whether they've studied classics, economics, history, or languages is irrelevant. What matters are the skills and qualities necessary to be good, well-rounded executives in a highly international institution operating in a diverse set of communities."[83]

Empathy Living in different cultures calls for understanding and accepting diversity. This outlook enhances an expat's interactions with people and, importantly, an understanding of why some go well and others do not. Two factors anchor cultural empathy: the ability to develop sincere, honest friendships with foreign nationals and the willingness to use, no matter how rudimentary, the host-country language. The records of successful expats indicate that they did not recoil from the differences they encountered. Rather, they developed the necessary tools of communication, motivation, self-reliance, risk-taking, and diplomacy.

Tolerance As anyone who has traveled abroad understands, new situations in new settings challenge one's values and outlooks. Interpreting how colleagues, customers, and competitors in the local market see events, rather than unduly criticizing them for dissimilarities, supports strong performance. Interpreting events in ways that reject stereotypes, preconceptions, and unrealistic expectations helps one go far in international business.[84]

For example, fast-growing markets have attracted many foreign firms and, by extension, their expatriates. More than a few of the firms hail from a rule of law environment (where rules governing business are straightforward directives, as in Germany), and move into a rule of man setting (where rules are seen more as flexible guidelines, as in China). One expat noted that in the West, "everything is transparent. If you want to obtain a license to do something, you don't need to spend money bribing an official or hiring a go-between: You just download the form from the Internet and apply."[85] Moving from the transparency of Germany to the opacity of China can prove daunting for those accustomed to following the straight and narrow. The ability to adapt to the ways of the host country, whether it involves cultures, laws, or simply getting around town, shapes an expatriate's effectiveness.

Executives in foreign subsidiaries usually assume a greater range of leadership roles than do managers of similar-size home-country operations.

Versatility The precise job descriptions found in the job bank of the home office inevitably give way to far broader responsibilities in foreign subsidiaries. Furthermore, the expat director of a foreign subsidiary usually lacks the battery of resources he commanded at the home office. The call to do many jobs simultaneously requires finding ways to interpret how locals approach the workplace in terms of problem solving, tolerance for uncertainty, use of power, and consensus building. In addition, the expat will confront different trade rules, investment regulations, and business practices.

Microsoft's Joan Pattle found that working abroad imposed new demands. At home, her job in marketing meant working in her department with little responsibility for other business functions. Her expatriate assignment in the United Kingdom pushed her beyond the customary tasks of marketing. Posting a specialist, such as an engineer or finance officer, guarantees an expat will face a range of technical and behavioral situations, and the efficient administration of matters will likely fall short. Unusual circumstances may require switching from established management practices to more innovative methods. Effective resolution, HRM reasons, depends on the expat's versatility. Figure 20.4 elaborates this perspective, highlighting the importance of an eclectic set of talents to succeeding in an expat slot.

Studies indicate that successful expatriates see not a barren landscape, but rather a cornucopia of choices upon entering foreign markets.

Figure 20.4 also highlights the important facets of adaptiveness and technical competency. It particularly emphasizes the role of mindset and cultural sensitivity. These soft dimensions of the management process point out that the expatriate assignment is rife with technical circumstances. It is also marked by ambiguity, uncertainty, and risk. Hence, expatriate selection is a fine art that balances an intricate set of constraints and requirements. On this note, McKinsey & Co. concluded that whereas technical competence is a given, today's expatriates must have a particular mind-set. Specifically, "When you look behind the success stories of leading globalizers, you find MNEs that have learned how to think differently from the herd. They seek out different information, process it in a different way, come to different conclusions, and make different decisions. Where others see threats and complexity, they see opportunity. Where others see a barren landscape, they see a cornucopia of choices."[86]

FIGURE 20.4 Key Competencies of Expatriates

Surveys of the preferred competencies of expatriates steadily emphasize facets that we commonly associate with an executive outlook. Effectively, survey data indicates that technical skills typically open the door to an international assignment, but leadership skills and outlooks, power your move through it.

Source: Karen Beaman, 2010–2011 Going Global Report, Jeitosa Group International, Adapted from Table 7, page 5.

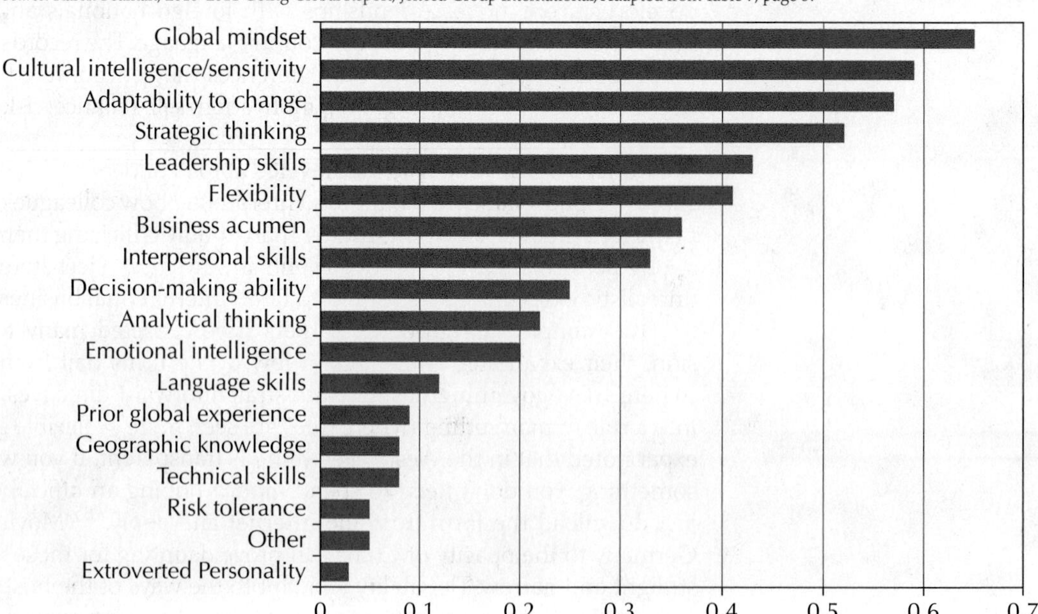

CONCEPT CHECK

Improving understanding of the intricacies of international business operations along with increasingly sophisticated HRM programs have steadily reduced the rate of expatriate failure. Evidence confirms the importance of commanding a broad band of knowledge about institutions, markets, companies, and consumers.

EXPATRIATE ASSESSMENT AND PREPARATION

Sometimes failure is the result of poor assignment planning putting the wrong person in the wrong job at the wrong time with the wrong expectations. Other times it comes as a surprise, as personal circumstances disrupt what many saw as a sure thing. Both situations spur MNEs to continue refining their assessment and pre-departure preparation programs.

Assessment typically focuses on the expat's technical expertise, along with the ability to cope with challenging environments, resolve personal or emotional difficulties, and adjust family life to the foreign environment. HRM's growing sophistication has reduced the rate of expatriate failure due to inadequate technical expertise. Indeed, rare is the foreign assignment that fails because HRM misjudged a candidate's technical qualifications. Likewise, common is the failure due to a poorly prepared executive.

Improving understanding shifts HRM's attention toward preparing the expat for the highs and lows of the assignment. Figure 20.1 identifies the highs; Figure 20.5 identifies recurring stress points. Reestablishing a social life, feeling lonely, and missing friends and family top the list. The challenge of building working relationships with new, different colleagues, to say nothing of interacting with host nationals within a new cultural milieu, further aggravates stress levels. HRM extrapolates from these long-running concerns a simple yet powerful moral: improving cultural sensitivities and interpersonal skills improves the odd of successful adjustment and, by extension, a successful expat assignment.[87]

A leading cause of expatriate failure is the difficulty the partner/spouse and family experience in adapting to the host country.

Today, most MNEs provide predeparture preparation in the form of cross-cultural training, destination familiarization, and language lessons. The operative rule is unequivocal: preparing expats in any or all ways helps them thrive abroad. HRM encourages individuals to understand both their home and host cultures, identifying how each shapes outlooks, influences interactions, and regulates relationships. Increasingly, MNEs use CD-based or Web-based programs to ease preparation. Some 35 percent of MNEs provided media-based or Web-based training in 2010—an all-time high.[88] Their economical convenience provides excellent predeparture preparation, as well as in-country reinforcement tools.

FIGURE 20.5 Leading Concerns of Expatriates Ahead of Moving to their Foreign Assignment

A foreign assignment is rich with opportunity yet, at the same time, fraught with challenges. Prior to heading abroad, executives worry about a host of issues. Data indicate their concerns run the gamut. Anticipating and adjusting for the sorts of tests shown here improves the odds of a successful expatriate experience.

Source: HSBC EXPAT EXPLORER SURVEY 2010, Page 8. Retrieved June 10, 2013 from www.expatexplorer.hsbc.com/files/pdfs/overall-reports/2010/experience.pdf

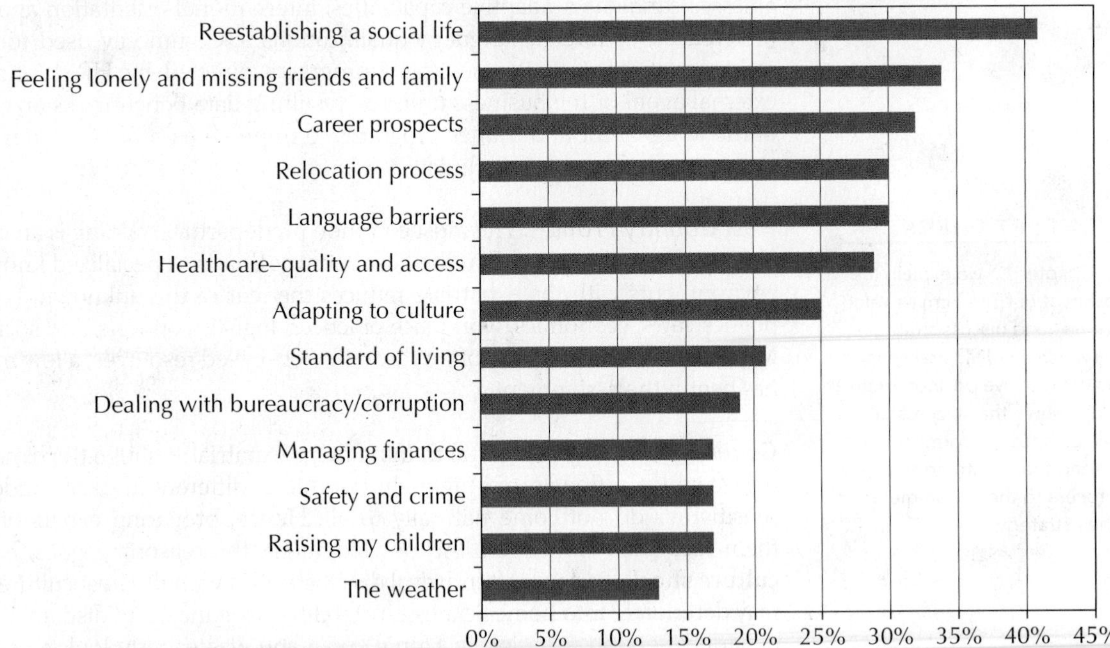

The Matter of Family Generally, a foreign assignment is more stressful for the family than for the expat. Indeed, a persistent cause of expatriate failure is the inability of a spouse and children to adapt to their new home.[89] Challenges include the children's education, family adjustment to different routines, and the spouse's resistance to and regret about moving abroad. Increasingly, the struggle of a previously employed spouse to find local employment complicates preparation and impedes adjustment.

Expats warn of a recurring dynamic. Abrupt separation from friends, family, and career isolates the spouse and children. Many then look for companionship and reassurance from the expatriate—whose job demands leave scant time to provide such support. Sometimes slowly, sometimes quickly, but almost always, family harmony suffers as stress escalates. Unchecked, the expat's work performance declines because, "If the family starts to unravel, the employee will at some time start to unravel too."[90]

Pre-departure preparations can lower the probability of expatriate failure. Increasingly, preparation activities include the spouse and family members.

The sad predictability of this cycle compels HRM take a proactive approach to prepare the expat, spouse, and family. HRM often monitors families' adjustment process. Increasingly, HRM tinkers with potential means to minimize family disruption. Recent innovations endorse posting executives on short-term or commuter assignments, thereby preempting the need to uproot families. Moves to send younger or older folks speak to other solutions. Younger candidates are more likely single, motivated by adventure, career, and money, and less risk-averse,[91] whereas older candidates have grown children and agreeable partners.[92] Combined, these sorts of solutions are changing the demography of expatriates. For instance 47 percent of expats had children 18 years or younger accompany them on foreign assignments in 2010; the ongoing decline dropped it to 40 percent in 2012.[93]

MNEs usually anchor training programs to transfer specific information about the host country as well as improve the executive's cultural sensitivity.

Preparation Programs Traditionally, the greater concern for the expat's functional performance led HRM to tailor predeparture programs toward improving technical skills and administrative competencies; the matter of developing adaptiveness was largely left up to the individual. Presumably, the manager interested in an international career would, through personal choices, travel abroad, monitor world events, and socialize with people of different ethnicities, cultures, and nationalities.[94] When eventually posted to a foreign assignment, these sorts of managers often outperformed their less worldly counterparts.

The variability in performance among expatriates, by consistently highlighting gaps in predeparture training, has led MNEs to expand formal preparation beyond technical capabilities. Honeywell, for instance, begins developing potential expats early and focuses on cross-cultural skills, including those necessary for dealing with culture shock. HRM routinely assesses candidates' adaptive capabilities, international orientation and outlook, geographic preferences, or foreign-language qualifications.[95] Commonly used tools include candidate self-assessment, formal assessment programs directed by HRM, and assessments by an external agent or the business unit. The resulting data benchmarks an expat's understanding of the assignment and frames programs to improve cultural awareness and refine practical skills. Areas of emphasis include:

CONCEPT CHECK

In Chapter 12, we explain the concept of "The Firm as Value Chain" and discuss strategies by which an MNE strengthens its competitive position. Here, we observe that successful MNEs boost performance by linking the expatriate selection process to the requirements of their strategy.

Host Country Profile The most common predeparture training is an informational briefing about the way things work in the host country. Sharing specialized knowledge about foreign environments with the expatriate reduces the fear of the unknown. Topics typically include politics, laws, economics, workplace practices, logistics options, and social situations.[96] Some MNEs refresh this training, often through Web-based resources, a few months after the expat has begun the assignment.

Cultural Sensitivity Cultural training helps expatriates gauge the dynamic of working with host-country nationals and highlight the role of different ideas, attitudes, and beliefs. These sensitivities do not come naturally to all. Hence, preparing expats often requires helping them recognize blind spots. Acknowledgment, the reasoning goes, helps them withstand **culture shock**—a soon-after-arrival dissatisfaction with the host culture that, if unaddressed, may deteriorate into homesickness, irritability, arrogance, and disdain. When Michelle Brown departed London for a job in Hong Kong, she was eagerly looking forward to immersing herself in the new culture. The day-to-day practicalities of her new life, however, proved daunting. "I suppose I was quite naive, but Hong Kong was a complete culture shock," she says. "The humidity was insane, the smells made me ill, there was just so much to take in and not all of it pleasant."[97]

Research confirms that developing interpersonal awareness in the context of cross-cultural sensitivity training tends to make people more receptive to and tolerant of foreign environments.[98] Hence, the MNE that does not offer some sort of cross-cultural preparation for international assignments is the outlier; expats appreciate the support, with recent surveys indicating that more than 80 of respondents rated cross-cultural training as having good or great value.[99] An emerging trend is including families in the prep program; data indicate that their involvement improves the expatriate's potential performance and reduces the odds of failure.

Key to successfully transitioning to a foreign assignment is mastering the new ways of schooling, socializing, and shopping.

Practical Skills Familiarizing expatriates and their families with features of the host country helps them develop an understanding of the realities of daily life. The sooner they develop useful, productive patterns of schooling, socializing, and shopping (to some, the 3S's of successful adjustment), the higher the odds of withstanding culture shock. Regrettably, this is easier said than done for many countries. Expatriates report big challenges in setting up finances, healthcare, accommodations, and utilities in India, China, Brazil, Qatar, Russia, and Saudi Arabia. Notably easier are South Africa, Canada, Thailand, and Australia.[100] Consulting former expats on their successes and struggles and, once abroad, socializing with local community groups help improve transitions.

Point

English: Destined to Be the World's Language?

Point **Yes** The prevalence of English throughout the world indicates that learning a foreign language is arguably worthwhile but ultimately unnecessary. Inexorably, English ably performs as the *lingua franca* of the business world, providing a universal means that enables people who speak mutually unintelligible languages to communicate. Presently, about a quarter of the world's population speaks some English, including the 400 million who speak it as their mother tongue and about the same number for whom it is a second language; moreover, both counts are rising.[101] Finally, when you get down to hard dollars, English rules. It accounts for a much larger share of world output than that represented by the proportion of native speakers in the world. Though the first language of only 6 percent of the world's population, its speakers generate more than 40 percent of world output.

The Preferred Choice Situations in the European Union, where more than half the population claims to be reasonably conversant in English, highlight common trends. Among Europeans born before WWII, English, French, and German are almost equally common. But 15- to-24-year-olds are five times more likely to speak English as a foreign language than either German or French. Add native speakers to those who have learned it, and some 60 percent of young Europeans speak English "well or very well."[102] Many envision improving their competency; more than 70 percent in a survey of 16,000 people living in the European Union agreed, "Everybody should speak English."

We see similar trends elsewhere. India now has the second-largest fluent English-speaking population, after the United States. It expects to have the world's largest number of fluent English speakers within a decade. Today, Hindi films, most advertising billboards, and higher education are in English. Virtually every well-paying job in India requires an understanding of English. To top it off, Indian firms pay workers who are fluent in English a third more than those who are not.[103] We see similar trends elsewhere. In China, state employees younger than 40 must master a minimum of 1,000 English phrases. Likewise, the prevalence of English throughout the Arab world fans worry about the decline of Arabic. American universities reflect these general trends as well. Although they are aggressively internationalizing their curricula, fewer require foreign language training—currently 37 percent versus 53 percent in 2001.[104]

The Default Choice Although English is not an official language in many countries, it is most often taught as the second language. In the EU, English is studied by schoolchildren (89 percent), followed by French (32 percent), German (18 percent), and Spanish (8 percent).[105] More than 200 million students in China are learning English; some begin as young as two, but all by kindergarten. Likewise, more than a fifth of Japanese 5-year-olds study English conversation. Argentina requires students from the fourth grade throughout high school take two hours of English every week. Chile mandates public schools begin teaching English in fifth grade. English is the language of choice in the classrooms of many African countries. Countries worldwide aim to become bilingual in English in the next decade or two in the belief that "it's the language for international teaching. English allows students to be able to come from anyplace in the world and for our students to go everywhere."[106] In sum, with 2 billion people speaking or studying it today, we are on the verge of a massive diffusion of English language competency.[107]

The Online Choice The prevalence of English is best seen in its predominance on the Internet; ever so easily, one can conduct business worldwide using the English interface of one's preferred browser.[108] More than 80 percent of home pages on the Web are in English. Heavyweight publications around the world, like *Der Spiegel* and *China Daily*, offer English-language websites that list translated news stories and opinion pieces. On a related front, the growing sophistication of translation software makes foreign language competency a moot point for those who prefer using their local language on the Internet. Offline, workable, almost flawless simultaneous-translation devices are now close-at-hand. Technology may one day make language learning unnecessary.[109]

Then again, the online choice may reset our notion of language. Rather than the phonetics or morphology of German, English, or Mandarin, people will master the semantics and syntax of Python, Java, or Ruby. The latter, prominent examples of high-level programming language, better prepare people for a future in which the Internet is the foundation for nearly everything. Facebook, for instance, serves more than a billion customers in more than 150 nations through a website interface that is automatically translated into more than 100 languages.[110] Speaking a programming language that fits the digital pieces together, rather than conversing with foreigners in their native tongue, may prove to be the path to meaningful linguistic competency. As the director of government affairs of the Computing Research Association notes, "To be successful in the modern world, regardless of your occupation, requires a fluency in computers."[111]

The Only Choice Many MNEs respond in kind. *The Economist* reports that just under half of employers rate language skills as important—a tendency linked to the laborious struggle to master a foreign language. Language competency ranked well behind technical competencies, leadership skills, and career development when evaluating a potential expatriate; it barely edged the importance of the ambition to work abroad.[112] Airbus, SAP, Daimler-Chrysler, Fast Retailing, Nokia, Renault, Samsung, SAP, Technicolor, and Microsoft, to name a few, mandate English as the common corporate language.[113] And growing interest in programming languages, long considered arcane as well as uncool, may reset standards.

Finally, some say language proficiency is an easy but ultimately misleading proxy of an expatriate's potential. As the CEO of Schering-Plough notes, "I've met many people who speak three or four languages yet still have a very narrow view of the world. At the same time, I've come across people who speak only English but have a real passion and curiosity about the world and who are very effective in different cultures."[114]

English: Destined to Be the World's Language?

Counterpoint

No Proponents of foreign language competency maintain that learning another tongue is an undeniably enriching experience. Studying another culture, through the prism of its language, clarifies one's values and outlooks. Ultimately, international cooperation and exchange depend on people who are proficient in foreign languages.

New Networks Expatriates who are averse to learning a foreign language, besides signifying cross-cultural illiteracy, exclude themselves from influential business networks, complicate relations with local officials, and slow socializing with workmates.[115] Working abroad is itself a challenge; language limitations make it further isolating.[116] Microsoft's Joan Pattle noted that her inability to speak

Counterpoint

Turkish made her seven-month stint in Istanbul very lonely, explaining, "You can't really mix with the locals... use local transportation because you can't read any of the signs."[117]

Symbolically, the effort to speak the local language, no matter how poorly, sends a subtle but essential cultural message. Just making an effort to say a few words in the native tongue can make a good impression, sending a subliminal message that "We are equal."[118] Moreover, as anyone who has struggled to learn a foreign language can attest, unexpected benefits include a good dose of humility.

New Ways of Thinking Learning a foreign language changes the way you think, teaching you that there are several ways to express a concept, interpret an abstraction, and make sense of a situation.[119] Thinking differently, besides improving exchanges with suppliers, buyers, officials, and stakeholders, sharpens your business skills and refines your global mindset. When asked about the importance of employees' foreign-language needs, many respond that such competency adds professional and personal value.[120] Surveys report that managers who learn one or more foreign languages find new ways to make innovative contributions. Even if they are far from fluent, their willingness to communicate in the language of the locals builds rapport with colleagues, thereby improving their effectiveness. Proponents point out that countries have different cultural and business expectations that can only be deciphered through the local language.

More directly, research suggests that learning a language makes you smarter.[121] Bilingualism fortifies the brain's so-called executive function—basically, the command system that each of us uses to plan, solve problems and puzzles, and manage cognitively demanding tasks. Bilinguals demonstrate sharper sensitivity to environmental circumstances and show greater efficiency solving problems; they are better able to focus despite distractions, can easily switch attention from one matter to another, and shine at organizing the information at hand.[122]

Cultural Imperatives Language allows people to build, understand, and express emotions, values, and intentions. A vibrant national language, besides defining and sustaining culture, fortifies nationalism. Rising linguicide—the killing of a language—spurs cultures and countries to protect their national languages. First, the death rate is accelerating: on average, every 14 days a language dies. By 2100, more than half of the 7,000 languages presently used will likely disappear.[123] Second, linguicide commonly follows from a community of speakers of the native language becoming bilingual in another language, then gradually shifting allegiance to the latter language until they cease using the former.

Rather than promoting English, the threat of linguicide moves nations to defend their language. Canada's Official Languages Act promotes and protects the equal status of French with English. France relies on its *L'Académie française*, its official authority on the usages, vocabulary, and grammar, to prevent the Anglicization of French. Proliferating *Arabizi*-—switching back and forth from Arabic to English—finds concern throughout the Middle East. In mid-2012, for example, Saudi Arabia prohibited the use of English to answer telephone calls in hotels, private companies, and government offices. Explained an observer, "There is a feeling that Arabic is fast becoming a second language in the Gulf, as people need to use English as a common language with the huge number of expatriate workers who make up most of the private sector, and as the wealthy and educated youth increasingly speak to each other in English."[124]

Likewise, China's General Administration of Press and Publication holds that the invasion of English words and abbreviations in Chinese texts is "abusing the language;" as a result, it has "severely damaged the standard and purity of the Chinese language and disrupted the harmonious and healthy language and cultural environment, causing negative social impacts."[125] The country has banned mixing foreign language phrases, such as English words or abbreviations like GDP (gross domestic product), CPI (consumer price index), or WTO (World Trade Organization), in Chinese publications. Lastly, deanglicization is a matter of national pride for some; India, for example, regarded Bombay as the corrupted English version of Mumbai and an unwanted legacy of British colonial rule. Hence, we now have Mumbai—and, for that matter. Kolkata, Bengaluru, and Chennai rather than Calcutta, Bangalore, and Madras.

New Requirements Besides mere enrichment, learning a foreign language will soon be a competitive necessity, some say. The expanding international links and intercultural connections of a globalizing world make linguistic skills crucial for getting many jobs and accelerating careers. In the context of the persistent unemployment resulting from the global financial crisis, any means to differentiate one's competencies, such as that demonstrated by linguistic skills, creates opportunities.

Inevitably, some respond that the spread of English competency worldwide means those who already speak it need not worry. Critics counter that marketplace trends will punish, not privilege, English-only speakers. Eventually, they will lose the advantages that once came with being among the small number of native Anglophones who could speak the language of business. Bilinguals or multilinguals will offer the same as English monoglots but also provide innovative cognitive outlooks and broader international perspectives. Officials have begun institutionalizing incentives to support this movement. For instance, the EU's official language policy is "mother tongue plus two," whereby citizens are encouraged to learn two additional languages.

Which One? Ultimately, one wonders, which foreign language should I study? As we see in Table 20.2, one has many choices that are shaped somewhat by their popularity and prevalence. Figure 20.6 suggests that to the native English speaker, choice entails different degrees of difficulty. Market trends clarify options for players in the business world. Local entrepreneurs may look around their hometown and go for fast-spreading languages such as Spanish, Mandarin, or Arabic. Those looking abroad quickly recognize that expatriate slot positions are migrating from Western Europe and North America to the booming emerging economies. As MNEs struggle to place expatriates in these high-growth markets, proficiency in languages like Mandarin, Portuguese, or Hindi will open opportunities and improve marketability.

TABLE 20.2 A Look at Languages in our World

Communication takes place in different countries with different languages through different mediums. Here we see the most prevalent forms and formats, in terms of the number of countries that speak a particular language as well as the numbers of users of that language in the physical as well as the cybernetic world.

Rank	Language	Countries[1]	Rank	Most Spoken Language	Speakers (million)	% of World	Rank	Countries	Internet Users[2] (million)	% of World
1	English	53	1	Mandarin	845	12.1	1	English	565	26.8
2	French	29	2	Spanish	328	4.7	2	Mandarin	509	24.2
3	Arabic	25	3	English	328	4.7	3	Spanish	164	7.8
4	Spanish	14	4	Arabic	221	3.2	4	Japanese	99	4.8
5	Portuguese	8	5	Hindi	181	2.6	5	Portuguese	82	3.9
6	German	7	6	Bengali	181	2.6	6	German	75	3.6
7	Albanian	4	7	Portuguese	177	2.5	7	Arabic	65	3.3
8	Italian	4	8	Russian	143	2	8	French	59	3
9	Russian	4	9	Japanese	122	1.7	9	Russian	59	3
10	Serbian	4	10	German	90	1.3	10	Korean	39	2

Notes
[1] Languages officially spoken in the most countries (independent states, excluding overseas territories and dependencies).
[2] Percentage of all Internet users based on 2011 estimate of world total of 2,071, 972, 363 users.

Sources: Based on Ethnologue; www.internetworldstats.com.

FIGURE 20.6 Learning a Foreign Language

While all languages are equal in legitimacy, not all are created equal in terms of their degree of difficulty. Here we see a sliding scale indicating that the choice of learning another language carries different degrees of difficulty for a native English speaker.

Source: Based on data compiled from the United States Foreign Service Institute School of Language Studies and the United States Defense Language Institute for Language Center.

The Degree of Difficulty for Native English Speakers

Least Difficult ⟵		⟶	Most Difficult
Afrikaans	Bulgarian	Amharic	Arabic
Danish	Dari	Bengali	Cantonese
Dutch	Farsi (Persian)	Burmese	Mandarin
French	German	Czech	Japanese
Haitian	Greek (Modern)	Finnish	Korean
Creole	Indonesian	Hebrew (Modern)	
Italian	Malay	Hindi-Urdu	
Norwegian		Hungarian	
Portuguese		Khmer (Cambodian)	
Romanian		Lao	
Spanish		Nepali	
Swahili		Pilipino (Tagalog)	
Swedish		Polish	
		Punjabi	
		Russian	
		Serbo-Croatian	
		Sinhala	
		Thai	
		Tamil	
		Turkish	
		Uzbek	
		Vietnamese	

"Keeping employees whole" spurs HRM to offset features of the international assignment that negatively affects an expatriate's standard of living.

COMPENSATING EXPATRIATES

MNEs must resolve a host of compensation questions in ways that accommodate the different types of expatriates—long-term, short-term, commuter, flexpatriates, third-country nationals—moving around the world to work in a variety of assignments. Setting effective compensation systems that fairly reward workers worldwide requires HRM deal with a range of issues regarding differing pay levels, benefits, tax programs, and prerequisites. India's Wipro Technology, for instance, employs 54,000 people in nearly 40 countries, more than 11,000 of whom are expatriates, and more than 90 percent of those being Indian.[126] Managing this pool requires Wipro's HRM to engage a series of compensation issues: Should it pay executives in different countries according to the prevailing standards in each locale? Or should it set pay for each position on a global basis? What sorts of allowance should it offer? What might be the qualification standards? How should it resolve the impact of different tax policies on compensation?

Although wide-ranging, HRM is mindful of fundamental principles. First, an effective compensation scheme must "keep employees whole," resolving the circumstances of the international assignment so that the task of working abroad does not upset one's standard of living. Second, HRM must prevent the already high costs of an expatriate assignment from spiraling out of control. MNEs in the United States spend nearly $1.3 million per expatriate during the course of a typical three-year foreign assignment; if unchecked, compensation costs exhibit a remarkable tendency to escalate.[127] Finally, an effective compensation scheme pays the executive enough to motivate him as well as incent his family to move abroad.

Ceteris paribus, compensation can make or break an expatriate's motivation.

All things being equal, compensation can determine the likelihood and success of expatriate assignments. Pay too little, and people decline to go; if in fact they do go, their likely regret may prove demotivating. Pay them too much, and costs escalate, returns fall short, and pay inequities fan dissension. Further complicating the pay-performance link is the dubious relationship between pay and performance. More often than not, the higher the pay, the longer an expatriate assignment tends to last. Some managers, quite content to prolong a munificent lifestyle, are less than eager to return home.[128]

Compensation must neither overly reward nor unduly punish a person for accepting a foreign assignment.

The task facing HRM, then, is straightforward: Devise compensation packages that convince executives to go abroad, enable them to maintain their standard of living, reflect the responsibility of the foreign assignment, and ensure that their after-tax income will not fall because of the foreign assignment. Throughout it all, HRM devises compensation plans that preserve pay equity among peers, promotes parity among expatriates, makes sure the plans compete with packages offered by industry rivals, and are easily administered.

Types of Compensation Plans Many MNEs, especially those in the United States, manage expatriate compensation with the **balance sheet approach.**[129] It develops a salary structure that equalizes purchasing power across countries so expatriates have the same living standard in their foreign posting that they had at home, no matter where their assignment happens to place them.[130] Its fundamental principle is equalization: an expatriate should neither overly prosper nor unduly suffer from working abroad. The strength of this approach follows from tailoring financial incentives to offset the differences in living standards between the home and host locale.

The most common approach to expatriate pay is the balance sheet approach.

Various methods implement a balance sheet compensation plan: notably, the home-based, headquarters-based, and host-based methods.

Home-Based Method This method bases expatriates' compensation on the salary of a comparable job in their home cities, thereby preserving equity with home-country colleagues as well as simplifying their eventual return. The evolving dynamics of globalization challenge the practicality of a home-country balance sheet approach. Originally designed to compensate employees and families transferred from Western-headquartered MNEs to slots throughout the world, it based its cost of living indices and support allowances on moves from high-cost countries, such as England or the United States, to countries like Argentina or Saudi Arabia.

Today's global environment is marked by expatriates of many different nationalities, different home and host combinations, varying salary levels and transfers to or from headquarters, and a growing number of transfers between subsidiaries. Difficulties arise when executive flows reverse—say, transferring an executive from inexpensive Santiago to costly San Francisco. For example, Chinese expatriates tend not to enjoy lavish pay and benefits. China Unicom's managing director in Europe received his modest Chinese salary plus a small cost-of-living allowance during his foreign assignment. Combined, they totaled to 30 percent of the local entry-level salary for his firm.[131] Hence, MNEs applying the home-based method struggle to maintain pay equity and benefit consistency given the changing locales and demography of their expatriate populations. Nevertheless, the home-based method is currently the most prevalent compensation plan.

The changing demography of expatriates increasingly complicates efficiently administering the home-based method.

Headquarters-Based Method A useful way to tweak the home-based method is to set the expatriate's salary in the terms of a comparable job in the city where the MNE has its headquarters. For example, if a Boston-headquartered MNE posts expats to its offices in London, Santiago, and Jakarta, it would give each executive a salary structured in terms of the going wage in Boston. This plan recognizes the disruption of a foreign assignment and helps expatriates live as they had in their home country. Adjustment resolves a move from a low- to a high-cost posting.

Host-Based Method Sometimes called *destination pricing* or *localization*, this method fine-tunes expatriate compensation by basing it on the prevailing pay scales of the foreign locale. HRM starts by setting the expatriate's salary equivalent to that of a local executive with similar responsibilities. The expat then negotiates additional compensation in the form of foreign-service premiums, extra allowances, home-country benefits, taxation relief, and so on.

The host-based method typically compensates expatriates, relative to the home and headquarters-based methods, the least. A key benefit of doing so is reducing tension between the expatriate and her typically lower-paid, host-country colleagues. Given the lower compensation paid to the expatriate, this method improves the company's return on its investment. At present, PwC uses the host-based method for expats involved in its EPIC program. Recognizing the constraint imposed by local pay levels, PwC assists its expatriates with immigration aid, relocation planning, language study, and intercultural training.

Key Aspects of Expatriate Compensation Figure 20.7 enumerates a simplified compensation package. The home, headquarters, and host-based methods apply different goals and guidelines to set total compensation. Commonly, expatriates improve their packages by negotiating their base salary, foreign-service premium, various allowances, fringe benefits, tax differentials, and benefits. Each dimension can significantly influence the total compensation. Let's look at each.[132]

Designing compensation packages for expatriates leads HRM to consider a variety of issues, such as

- Base salary,
- Foreign-service allowances,
- Fringe benefits,
- Tax differentials.

Base Salary An expat's base salary normally falls in the same range as that for a comparable job in the home country. It is paid either in the home-country currency or in the local currency.

Foreign Service Premium A *foreign service premium*, sometimes called a *mobility premium*, is a cash incentive to compensate an individual for the inconvenience of moving to a new country, living away from family and friends, dealing with the day-to-day challenges of the new culture, language, and workplace practices, and the reality that he will ultimately have to disrupt this life upon return. Long-term assignments usually qualify for a mobility premium; short-term assignments rarely do. Typically, the premium is expressed as a percentage of the annual base salary and varies depending on whether it is an intra-regional transfer (say, Canada to Mexico) or an intercontinental transfer (say, Germany to Japan).

Tax Differentials Varying tax polices require that MNEs adjust compensation so that expatriates' after-tax income does not suffer from the taxes incurred during the foreign assignment. Tax equalization often proves a costly component of expatriate compensation.

FIGURE 20.7 Compensating an Expatriate: A Sample Wage and Benefits Package

Consider the following scenario: An Atlanta-based MNE assigns an U.S.-based executive to run its local subsidiary in Mexico City. In the United States, the executive, who has a working spouse and two children, earns an annual income of $250,000. This balance sheet profiles how HRM typically organizes the compensation package for his foreign assignment.

Direct Compensation	
Base salary	$250,000
Foreign-service premium	25,000
Cost-of-living allowances	120,000
Housing	97,000
U.S. Taxes	(38,000)
Education (schooling for two children)	30,000
Mexican income taxes (presuming no reciprocity)	115,000
Transfer moving costs	47,000
Miscellaneous benefits (i.e., shipping and storage; home sale or property management fees; cultural, practical, and language training; pre-assignment orientation trip, destination assistance)	85,000
Working spouse allowance	75,000
Annual home leave (airfare for family of four, hotel, and meals)	15,000
Additional health insurance, pension supplements, evacuation coverage	20,000

The absence of a reciprocal tax treaty between the home and host countries obligates the expat to pay income tax to both governments. In such circumstances, the MNE ordinarily pays the host country tax bill. Compliance concerns requires HRM to monitor tax code revisions.

Tax differentials fundamentally shape the compensation plans of long-term assignments. They also influence the logistics of commuter and short-term assignments. For example, Chinese tax authorities stipulate that an expatriate who has spent fewer than 30 continuous days inside or more than 90 cumulative days outside China per tax year is not considered as having been in China for that year. Consequently, executives monitor their time there, tracking arrival and departure dates to minimize tax liability.

Fringe Benefits Various benefits supplement the expatriate's base salary. They run the gamut, including health insurance, life coverage, education reimbursement, childcare and assistance reimbursement, and so on. Wide variations in healthcare standards across countries is an enduring concern among expats. Care in a second-tier city in an emerging market is often far less desirable than care in one's home country. Hence, MNEs provide expatriates with access to medical resource benefits abroad equivalent to those available at home. They customarily expand these benefits to deal with local contingencies, such as bearing the cost of transferring ill expats or family members to suitable medical facilities.

Allowances give HRM the flexibility to tailor compensation plans to deal with special situations.

Allowances Sending an executive on an international assignment imposes expensive logistics and considerable stress. MNEs adjust the total compensation package with a variety of allowances, described below, that help reduce the difficulties facing the expatriate and her family.

Cost-of-Living Allowance A cost-of-living allowance (sometimes called a "goods-and-services differential") ensures that expats don't suffer a decline in their standard of living due to the steep expense of a particular city (London or Lagos) or nation (Switzerland).[133] Some companies progressively reduce the cost-of-living differential over time, reasoning that as the expatriate adapts to her environment, she should adopt local purchasing practices, such as substituting items from a neighborhood market in place of imported packaged goods.[134]

Allowances assign extra compensation to the expatriate to offset the difficulties of

- Different standards of living,
- Replicating preferred housing,
- Supporting a trailing spouse,
- Extraordinary safety or security hardships.

A fair, consistent compensation package reflects the cost of living in the assigned foreign city. HRM considers the prevailing cost of goods and services, including housing, transportation, food, clothing, household goods, and entertainment in a particular location.[135] Setting New York as the benchmark, cost-of-living estimates for 214 cities around the world indicate Tokyo as the world's most expensive city for expatriates, followed by Luanda, Osaka, Moscow, and Geneva.[136] Karachi ranks as the world's least expensive city for expatriates, less than one-third as expensive as Tokyo. Just above it are Tunis, Mumbai, Tehran, New Delhi, and Jeddah.[137]

Housing Allowance Moving from, say, mid-priced Salt Lake City to high-priced Singapore is a tough sell to potential expatriates. Housing costs vary because of crowded conditions that boost land prices as well as shortages of homes that are acceptable to expatriates.[138] In addition, Westerners pay steep premiums in some parts of Asia to rent accommodations with Western-style bathrooms and kitchens.[139] A housing allowance enables the expatriate to duplicate his accustomed standard of housing.

Spouse Allowance It is not unusual for an expatriate to have a spouse, who may then receive cross-cultural preparation. Previously employed spouses/partners typically struggle to find employment during an international assignment. In some cases, the company supports the spouse's search for employment.[140] About a quarter of MNEs provide trailing spouses with job-search assistance, often through networks with other MNEs. In 2011, for example, 60 percent of spouses/partners were employed before, but just 12 percent during the assignments.[141] Difficulties arise due to economic conditions, locations, and language and cultural differences. Immigration and visa complications further discourage potential local employers.

MNEs often provide additional compensation to expats who work in remote or dangerous locations.

Hardship Allowances An expatriate assigned to a difficult environment or dangerous location typically negotiates a hardship allowance—sometimes called combat pay. This allowance offsets the costs of ransom insurance, crisis response safeguards, threat management programs, or security systems.[142] He may also receive miscellaneous allowances that offset the burden of particular local difficulties. Popular options include travel allowances that let him and his family come home periodically, or education allowances for schools that resolve language difficulties or quality concerns.[143]

Trends in Allowances Spurred by cost pressures and competitive job markets, MNEs have begun reducing the range and extent of expatriate allowances. Foreign service premiums, for example, have been phased out by many companies. Moreover, the growing use of commuters and flexpatriates alters the compensation calculus. Short-term assignments typically do not trigger a change in pay or benefits. Rather, assignees receive their regular pay plus a per diem for related expenses.[144]

Globalization pushes many employees to sustain their careers by working abroad. Similarly, individuals see international assignments as a chance to develop business expertise and leadership skills. These folks are quite willing to go abroad for less compensation. Most believe that broadening their horizons and gaining life experience, not financial gain, are the most important benefits of a foreign assignment.[145] Consequently, international assignments in many MNEs have "gone from being special and unique, with piles of money thrown at them, to being an everyday part of the company."[146]

Cost-reduction techniques have gradually redefined the parameters of an international assignment. Increasingly, MNEs reduce benefits and cut allowances. For instance, many MNEs with operations in Europe now treat the continent as if it were one country. Also, many have cut hardship allowances for locales that are far more hospitable than they once were, such as Prague, Shanghai, and Rio de Janeiro. Ironically, increasing globalization reduces the number of hardship destinations. Indeed, many employees are quite willing to go most anywhere nowadays, motivated by career ambitions and personal quests. The combination of pressures to economize pay and prerequisites, the expanding supply of competent executives from emerging economies eager to work worldwide, and fewer "hard" locales increasingly cap the largess of expatriate compensation.

MNEs struggle to determine the proper degree to which they should equalize pay for the same type of job that is done by different people in different countries.

Compensation Complications Systematizing pay and benefit programs while removing inconsistencies ideally makes for fair and equitable compensation plans. Considerable progress has been made in the past decade; salaries for similar jobs vary less substantially among countries. Still, legal, cultural, and regulatory differences require tailoring performance-based pay by country and region.

Differences particularly challenge companies applying a geocentric staffing framework. Global and transnational strategies depend on cadres of international managers, which usually include multiple nationalities. HRM must determine if all managers who perform the same job but in different locations receive the same compensation. For China Mobile, say, this would require compensating its foreign nationals, no matter where they worked, in terms of Chinese salary levels. If China Mobile opts not to develop an equitable arrangement, it will likely result in underpaid expatriates resenting their higher-paid counterparts.

CONCEPT CHECK

The expanding scale and scope of globalization, driven by the increasing physical and cybernetic connectivity of some countries discussed throughout this text, increasingly blur the idea of expatriates. Where once foreigners seemed foreign, today they seem almost commonplace in many hometowns. Consequently, there is less and less need to pay people premiums to go to places that are more and more similar.

HRM, mindful of national differences, tries to avoid paying someone more than necessary to persuade him to go abroad. Besides reducing the company's return on its investment, extreme pay disparity among managers doing similar jobs weakens coworkers' motivation. Lastly, a MNE with an ethnocentric or polycentric staffing policy may have few expatriates today but expanding internationalization complicates administering compensation packages on a case-by-case basis. Hence, even if few in number, effective HRM calls for developing standards and systems.

Total, as well as forms of, executive compensation vary substantially among countries.

Compensating CEOs Generally, pay practices at the top set standards throughout the company. On average, CEOs in the United States enjoy the most comprehensive pay packages, both in terms of base compensation and total remuneration. CEOs in France, Germany, Italy, Switzerland, and the United Kingdom command higher levels of total compensation than their peers elsewhere. This model inspires emulation; Asian and South American MNEs have begun instituting similar pay practices, particularly the use of performance-based pay that ties compensation to business results.

Long-term incentives, such as options on restricted stock, are popular in the United States but not in Germany. However, German managers often receive compensation that U.S. managers do not, such as housing allowances and partial payment of salary outside Germany, neither of which is taxable. Similarly, countries with aggressive personal income tax rates privileges pay plans that reduce taxable base salaries in favor of tax-exempt fringe benefits. Ultimately, as MNEs from more countries broaden operations, they compete globally for executive talent. Likewise, local firms must tailor compensation to retain executives. Therefore, convergence in compensation practices is the order of the day.

REPATRIATING EXPATRIATES

MNEs apply staffing frameworks that drive a cycle of events: expatriate selection, predeparture preparation, compensation design, and a plan to bring the executive back home intact and in good spirits. The latter task, **repatriation,** is the process of reintegrating the expatriate into the home company upon completion of her foreign assignment. Success at each stage in the cycle, not just early on, is vital. Consistent success supports a self-sustaining cycle whereby returning employees share their knowledge, experiences, and enthusiasm with colleagues. High-performing coworkers, seeing the rewards of an international assignment, are then more receptive to the prospect of working abroad.

The repatriation system works for many. Roughly a third of returning expatriates believe their international experience boosted their career trajectory. Faster promotions and obtaining new positions more easily are commonly cited benefits. Indeed, nearly one in four expats who returns home is promoted in her first year of repatriation.

Returning home from a foreign assignment can be professionally rewarding. It is also fraught with difficulties.

For others, the repatriation process falls short. Problems arise on a variety of fronts. Promotions are rare, support for career progression is absent, opportunities for applying new knowledge and skills are scant, and previously strong networks are feeble.[147] A survey of repatriated executives who had successfully completed their overseas assignments found that more than a third held temporary assignments three months after returning home, nearly

80 percent believed their new jobs were demotions from their foreign assignments, and more than 60 percent felt they did not have opportunities to transfer their international expertise to their new jobs. A surprising share of these former high flyers switched to other companies. In 2010, nearly 40 percent left their firms within one year of returning from abroad (the 15-year average is 22 percent), whereas another 25 percent left between the first and second year.[148]

Explanations for these anomalies commonly cite MNEs' greater concern for preparing and paying workers for the foreign assignment than supporting them upon their return. Anticipation, opportunity, and preparation prior to departure earn the expatriate attention from a host of support functions. The backside of the cycle is less supportive.[149] Returning home can deteriorate into a disappointing part of the assignment. Ironically, many companies are well aware of this shortfall. Most MNEs see repatriation as important, yet just 20 percent conclude they manage it effectively.[150]

Unquestionably, job placement dominates repatriation concerns. Stress also arises in fitting back in with the home-country organization, changes in personal finances, and readjusting to life at home. Let's take a closer look at each.

Repatriation tends to cause work, financial, and social adjustment difficulties.

Readjustment to Home-Country Organization Completing the foreign assignment and returning to one's former office poses several problems. "People who have spent two years working in different ways across varied markets and cultures are not always happy to return to the same desk and the same prospects," concludes one report. "In this vacuum of direction, many have a career 'wobble,' then leave via a recruitment market in which their experience is seen as increasingly valuable."[151] Likewise, returnees may find that their former peers have been promoted above them. They enjoy less autonomy as they return to being a "little fish in a big pond." Colleagues may question whether they've maintained cutting-edge market knowledge and technical skills during their exotic "vacation." They may struggle to rejoin an office network that might not know quite what to do with them. In such situations, resentment often builds as executives reason that they have worked hard to progress professionally, sacrificed much for the company, and rightfully deserve praise and promotion.

A key cause of tension is the suspicion that "out of sight overseas" deteriorates into "out of mind back home." This fear has led many fast-tracking executives to decline an expatriate assignment. In their view, going abroad effectively means leaving the power center for the far-removed periphery. Explains one executive, "MNEs station people abroad and then forget about them. If anything, advancement is even more difficult for the expat when he returns to headquarters, having missed out on opportunities to network with top management."[152] This situation plays havoc in business cultures, particularly those anchored in collectivism, where face time with powerful people is critical to winning promotions.

More than half of returning expatriates report that their company had been vague about the repatriation process, their pending jobs, and future career progression. Concerns commonly emphasize returning home to a job that does not challenge them, leverage their international experience, or match their expertise. MNEs reply that repatriation jams them in a difficult situation. The expat's office cannot sit vacant while she is abroad. Cost-cutting measures, mergers, or acquisitions change a company's plans and, by extension, those it had for the expatriate. Likewise, permitting repatriated employees to bump their "replacements" on return solves one problem but creates another.

Expats are likely to stay with their company if it creates opportunities to apply their hard-won expertise.[153] Increasingly, headquarters pushes them to manage their return. Many encourage expats to revisit their home offices before completing their foreign assignments in order to recharge networks and regain visibility.

Changes in Personal Finances Returning home can significantly alter personal finances. Most expatriates enjoy rich benefits during their foreign assignments. While abroad, many live in exclusive neighborhoods, send their children to prestigious schools, employ domestic help, socialize with elites, and still save a good amount. Returning home to a reasonable compensation plan with far fewer rewards and privileges can prove demoralizing.

One wonders, considering the rise robots in workplaces worldwide, how these trends might reset our understanding of the role of globe-trotting expatriates. If, one day, executives can "overseer" robot-run operations from any screen from anywhere in the world, then our idea of an expatriate is in for big change.
Source: ©Vladimir Vydrin/Fotolia

Personal Readjustment Return can also challenge repatriates to readjust to home life.[154] Troubles emerge as they and their families experience reverse culture shock. One repatriate upon return to the United States said, "I loved the culture so much in Peru. My feelings don't fit my own beliefs anymore. This is my home, but it doesn't make sense."[155] Depending on the length of the foreign assignment, repatriates may need to relearn what they once took for granted about hometown life. Meantime, children may struggle to fit into the local school system while spouses may feel isolated or out of touch with the career or friends they left behind.

MANAGING REPATRIATION

MNEs are not blind to repatriation problems. Most decisively, ignoring them is not an option. The greater the difficulties that repatriates confront, the greater the difficulty convincing others to accept international assignments. Some MNEs, like Dow Chemical, pledge that repatriated employees will return to jobs at least as good as those they left behind. Others integrate foreign assignments into career planning and develop mentoring programs to look after the expats' domestic interests. Surveys report that three of four MNEs have written repatriation policies, whereas 95 percent have identified new jobs within the company for returning expats.[156]

CONCEPT CHECK

Chapters 3 and 4 note political, legal, and economic factors that contribute to the changing profile of high-growth markets. Chapter 17 discusses new wrinkles in global manufacturing strategies and strategies in supply-chain management that respond to this changing profile. These trends lead some MNEs to preempt repatriation problems by changing their expatriate-staffing policies to recruit more locals to run local operations.

PwC's EPIC program installs several safety nets, promising participants "unrivaled support mechanisms" to safeguard their careers.[157] Prior to an international assignment, EPIC participants are linked to a mentor at home and a colleague awaiting their arrival overseas to smooth the transition. Both share responsibility for supporting the expat's career development. Similarly, Avaya charges the manager who originally sponsored the expatriate with the job of helping his protégé find a job upon repatriation. Avaya monitors the expat's career plan for a simple reason: it has "invested in this person. To leave him overseas or to lose him to another company is a waste of money."[158]

The principal cause of repatriation frustrations is finding the right job for the returning executive.

In sum, research confirms that many expats struggle upon return. Pressed to pinpoint where repatriation breakdown begins, they target the difficulty of returning to the right job. Analyses and anecdotes highlight that personal career management is as vital to being

selected for a foreign assignment as it is to returning home triumphantly. Recall from our opening case the experience of Bryan Krueger, who accepted a four-year assignment in Tokyo without guarantee of a promotion when he got home. Krueger was conscientiously "proactive," networking avidly, keeping up with events at headquarters, and visiting the home office. Passivity is hazardous; navigating repatriation requires a keen sense of its positive and negative aspects—before departure, while abroad, and particularly before coming home.[159]

EXPATRIATE FAILURE

The best-laid plans, as we all know, often go awry. Similarly, MNEs fall prey when they select their best and brightest executives, invest in their preparation, post them to the foreign market, compensate them well, and watch them fail. **Expatriate failure**, narrowly defined, is a manager's premature return home due to poor operational performance. Broadly defined, it is the breakdown of the MNE's expatriate selection process. In both cases, it is an enduring concern among MNEs. In the 1980s, research reported that nearly a third of American managers assigned to advanced countries returned early; the failure rate was twice that for those posted to slots in less hospitable developing countries. Today, surveys report that 5 to 10 percent of expats fail to complete their international assignments; top causes include spouse/partner dissatisfaction, family stress, quitting in order to work elsewhere, and rejecting unacceptable local workplace conditions.[160]

Expatriate failure is operationally costly, professionally detrimental, and personally stressful.

The Costs of Failure The fall in the rate of expatriate failure testifies to the improving sophistication of HRM's selection processes to identify, prep, and post the right individual to the right job. While this drop may be cause for celebration, it does not signify mission accomplished. The financial and personal costs of failure, no matter how infrequent, are destructive. Some even anticipate a surge in the failure rate. Companies' expansion into emerging economies puts executives into market spots that severely test their abilities to deal with fundamental business, cultural, and lifestyle differences. Already, we see evidence of the challenge. China and India, today's leading hotbeds of expat slots, top the list of locations with the highest failure rates.[161]

The improving sophistication of selection processes has reduced the rate of expatriate failure.

The average cost per failure can be as high as three times the expat's annual domestic salary plus the cost of relocation.[162] Total financial costs are often eye-opening when one accounts for the time and money spent in selection, preliminary visits to the location, lost productivity as things fall apart, and eventually shutting down the slot. An incalculable cost is the personal implications of professional failure to the formerly high-performing executive's self-confidence and leadership potential. Finally, there is the consequence of the hardship on the spouse and family.[163]

Exceptions and Anomalies *Ceteris paribus,* the immediacies of the business world mean that MNEs tend to under-rather than over-prepare expatriates. In some circumstances, managers receive cursory predeparture training, often scanning reports and reviewing resources on the flight to their new home. Usually an MNE will blame this circumstance on the urgency of the situation, noting there was insufficient time for the expat to take a familiarization trip to the host country, let alone engage a comprehensive profile of its history, culture, politics, economy, religion, and business environment. Typically, the home office fears the rapid deterioration in subsidiary performance or swift fade of an opportunity. Speed and dexterity, not prudence and preparation, take precedence. Hence, the MNE quickly dispatches help, worrying more about technical competency than cultural IQ.

The Wildcard Ultimately, it is important to note that some causes of expatriate failure are intractable simply because some people do not adjust well to working abroad. In theory, the expatriate ideal champions solitary, self-confident, mobile individuals who, besides not being tied to any particular place, feel at home anywhere in the world.[164] For some, this ideal rings hollow in the face of rising difficulty adapting to the socializing, logistics, and safety standards of their new home. Also, an awareness of differences, as one might hear from an executive about to depart Boston for Bangkok, does not necessarily signify the ability to adapt to the practicalities of day-to-day life.[165] Displacement can lead to nostalgia, culture shock, and depression. Notwithstanding the glamour and rewards, the expatriate lifestyle moves some far beyond their comfort zone. For some, no matter the degree of preparation, a sought-after adventure devolves into a nerve-wracking sentence.

Looking to the Future

I'm Going Where? The Changing Locations of International Assignments

A generation ago, expatriates, by and large, flocked to the premier business centers of the flourishing markets of Europe, North America, and Japan. Certainly, some were scattered throughout Africa, Asia, South America, and the Middle East. Generally, though, these technical folks worked in primary or extractive industries, such as a petroleum engineer posted to Saudi Arabia to support ExxonMobil's drilling operations.

Changing Company Strategies

Looking down the road signals big changes in the geography of expatriate assignments. First and foremost, Western MNEs are increasingly reorienting their strategies toward national markets that used to be far off the beaten path. The rising importance of emerging economies, particularly in fast-expanding Asia and Africa, leads Western MNEs to relocate a larger share of operations there. In Europe, MNEs such as HSBC, Nokia, and Volkswagen downscale their European activities as they ramp up Asian operations. At Unilever, for example, emerging markets already make up 56 percent of the business. In the United States, companies such as GE, Microsoft, Walmart, and Caterpillar reset operations, moving more activities to emerging markets. IBM, for example, forecasts earning 30 percent of its revenues in emerging markets by 2015, up from 17 percent in 2009.

Changing corporate configurations also drives change in related areas. Consider, for a moment, the matter of hotel rooms in Africa. Its long-dormant but now fast-growing markets attract an increasing number of expats of all sorts, including commuters, flexpatriates, and long-termers. Consequently, hotel chains are constructing facilities across Africa. Marriott, a U.S. hotel group, plans 50 hotels in Africa by 2020, a 600 percent increase. Accor, a French counterpart, plans another 5,000 rooms in 30 hotels spanning the continent. Other global hotel brands are scouting sites in African capitals.[166]

As multinationals redeploy their operations, they reset their labor force. In the 1990s, for example, U.S. companies added 4.4 million workers in the United States versus 2.7 million abroad. In contrast, during the 2000s they cut their workforces in the United States by nearly 3 million while concurrently increasing employment overseas by 2.4 million. Asked about the shift, GE's chief executive replied, "Today we go to Brazil, we go to China, we go to India, because that's where the customers are."[167] Correspondingly, MNEs reorganize their executives, moving those that had worked in the West to business centers in the East. Change has been slow but it is accelerating. Specifically, executives at 17 leading global companies reported that "just 2 percent of their top 200 employees were located in Asian emerging markets that would, in the years ahead, account for more than one-third of total sales."[168]

Changing Career Strategies

The allure of emerging markets appeals not only to companies. Graduates face slow-growing business and saturated executive markets in mature Western economies. Many see a better chance of being promoted, to say nothing of just getting a job, in São Paulo, Shanghai, Lagos, or Mumbai than in New York, Tokyo, Paris, or London. "A lot of my friends are going to Asia and Latin America to do their internships," said a student at a leading U.S. business school. "It may be outside their comfort zone, but they see getting some experience there as helpful, since that's where many of the jobs will be."[169] Then again, let's not forget about the seemingly magnetic appeal of working abroad among young people; a survey of 4,200 graduates in 44 countries found that 80 percent wanted to work internationally.[170]

Rather than patiently waiting for opportunities, students jump-start the process and head straight to markets they see powering the future. This is particularly true for graduates with cultural links to foreign locales as well as those with relevant language fluency. The siren call of opportunity attracts even those with limited cultural experience and linguistic skills.[171] Surging economies, lower costs of living, higher after-tax compensation, and the chance to bypass years of dues-paying entry jobs prove irresistible.

Full Speed Ahead

Therefore, as sales, growth, labor, and executive opportunity migrate from the West to faster-growing emerging economies, we anticipate a radical reset of the geography of expatriate assignments and activities. Data already confirm the trend is underway: China, Brazil, India, Russia, and Singapore are leading destinations for expats.[172] Not far behind are Thailand, Malaysia, Kenya, and Nigeria. Finally, the flow is not one way. Consider, for example, the Aditya Birla Group, a multinational conglomerate based in India, operates in 40 countries and earns more than half its revenue outside India. Its expanding international operations, like those of many emerging market MNEs, work the expat model the other direction. It, like counterparts in China, Brazil, or Mexico, posts expatriates to markets in the West. ■

CASE Banglalink: Staffing the Bangladeshi Operation[173]

About Banglalink

Banglalink, established in 1996, is a leading mobile service operator in Bangladesh with over 25 million subscribers. Banglalink was acquired by Orascom Telecom Holding (OTH), an Egypt-based telecom multinational operator. In 2004, OTH purchased 100 percent of Sheba Telecom in and subsequently rebranded and launched its services as Banglalink, which started an aggressive campaign to become a leader in the mobile sector in Bangladesh rapidly expanding its network to provide mobile services at affordable prices. It offers mobile telephony products and services such as prepaid and postpaid services for individuals as well as corporates. Banglalink continues to invest in its infrastructure to ensure the best quality service to its customers.

The mission of Banglalink is to deliver optimum value to it customers, employees, attract and retain human resource and a firm commitment to the society and the growth of the national economy while ensuring good corporate governance. Banglalink has a clear commitment to its various stakeholders: customers, employees, society, and its leaders.

Banglalink: An Early Success Story

Banglalink has been growing rapidly since its first operations in 2005. Their growth was marked by the rapid rise in the number of customers. Banglalink began offering its services to a wide range of market segments. Customers were able to purchase mobile telephony service at an affordable price, as per the company's mission of bringing mobile telecommunications to the masses. Banglalink achieved much success in a short period of time, elevating the mobile phone's status from an object of luxury to one of utter necessity. This forged an emotional bond with millions of customers nationwide, and heralded positive change in Bangladesh. Banglalink always positioned itself as a brand that impacted people's lives. Their slogan, "making a difference". This was a very effective one. Banglalink's rapid growth of subscribers

MAP 20.1 Bangladesh

Banglalink, established in 1996, is one of the top mobile service operators in Bangladesh with over 20 million subscribers. The country's population was 154.7 million (2012, World Bank estimate). The official language of the country is Bengali and currency is Bangladeshi taka. Banglalink operates out of its headquarters in the capital of the country, Dhaka.

Source: Central Intelligence Agency, "Bangladesh," The World Factbook 2011, (accessed February 17, 2014).

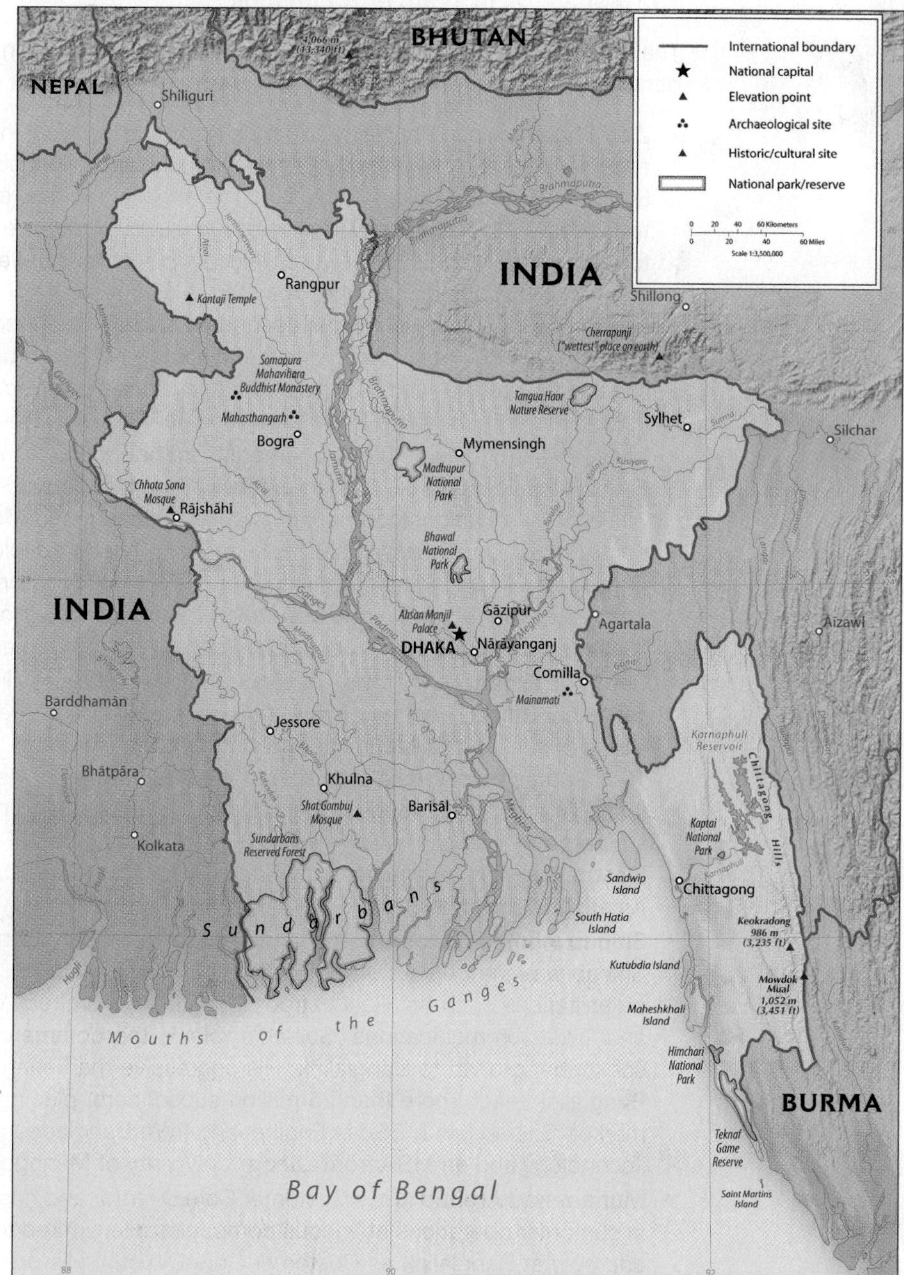

was highly impressive. They had more than 1 million customers at the end of the first year, 3 million in 2006, 7 million in 2007, and more than 27 million in June 2013, quickly representing a market share of more than 25 percent.

While the success of Banglalink is primarily because of its ability to offer unique services at a reasonable price, its true success can be attributed to a highly proactive staff. By providing unique IT services to the business, the team at Banglalink is able to solve more than 90 percent of customers' issues within the same day. Banglalink scores high on customer service and has evolved long, trusting relationships—a key differentiator in the mobile phone industry. The staff are customer-oriented, proactive, passionate, and transparent in all their work. The management team of Banglalink are staffed with experienced professionals who have extensive experience in various telecommunication operators around the world. They use their experience in other markets to examine the smartest way to launch mobile services in the Bangladeshi market.

The Management Team of Banglalink

The following section introduces members of the management team of Banglalink. The credentials of each member are also presented.

- **Ziad Shatara** joined Banglalink as its Chief Executive Officer in 2013. Ziad's extensive regional and international experience in the telecommunications industry make him well-suited to lead Bangalink. He has worked in the fixed line, mobile services, and broadband networks of the telecommunications industry. He has accumulated experience by working with various operators across the world such as Wind Telecommunications in Italy, Fastlink in Jordan, Wataniya Telecom in Kuwait, among other operators. He currently has almost 18 years of extensive experience working across various departments: information technology, network architecture, customer service, retail management and has a solid background in telecom operations from a technical, financial, commercial, and administrative perspective. Ziad holds a BSc and MSc in Electrical and Computer Engineering from the Technical University of Budapest in Hungary.
- **Yasser Hakim** joined the management team of Bangalink in July 2013 as the interim Chief Financial Officer. Yasser has an extensive experience working for more than 16 years in 7 telecommunications companies, namely: Telecom and Mobinil in Egypt, Wataniya Telecom in Iraq, Dubai, and Maldives, Orascom Telecom Holding in Egypt, and Beeline in Cambodia. His experience is mainly in the finance area where he held various roles starting from an accountant, revenue assurance, operations controller, and chief financial officer. Yasser Hakim received his accounting degree from Ain Shams University in Cairo.
- **Perihane Elhamy** joined the management team of Banglalink in March 2013 as the Chief Technical Officer. Perihane has extensive experience in the telecommunications industry with a focus on the technical and network management. Her experience in more than 10 countries across Asia, Africa, and the Middle East gives her very good knowledge on managing technical issues at Banglalink. She was able to handle the high growth in subscribers and load on network to its 25 million subscribers. Perihane received her degree in Electronics and Communications Engineering from Cairo University and an MBA from the American University in Cairo.
- **Shihab Ahmed** joined the management team of Banglalink in June 2013. Prior to that, Shihab was the Senior Director of Marketing at Banglalink. Shihab has worked at various organizations such as: Rahimafrooz Bangladesh Limited, Value Plus Computer Systems and True Communications. Shihab's role in the commercial area was key to drive the subscriber growth to Banglalink. His aggressive marketing and pricing campaigns made Banglalink reach more than 25 million subscribers, placing it second in the Bangladeshi market. Shihab has a BSc in Engineering from Bangladesh University of Engineering and Technology and an MBA from Lahore University of Management Sciences.
- **Muhammad Arshad** is the Customer Care Director and has extensive experience working in customer operations at various companies. He worked for Paktel in Pakistan, Mobilink, and now at Banglalink as Customer Care Director. His previous roles included managing customer operations, quality assurance, and customer retention. Muhammad managed Banglalink's customer operations which included more than 1,500 customer touch points. Muhammad received his BSc in Mathematics and Physics and IBA and MBA from the University of Punjab in Lahore.
- **Riviera ho Rathore** joined Banglalink as Human Resources and Administration Director in June 2012. Riviera has more than 15 years of experience in human resource administration in various organizations and industries. She has worked in human resources operations, performance management, safety and security, talent acquisition, employee engagement, and talent management. Her work was especially recognized in employee engagement, successfully helping operations of start-ups and spreading a smooth integration of processes across different environments and cultures.

Riviera was a member of the employer's federation and the national tripartite consultative group that develop policies for social protection and employment. She is also a founding member of the Asia-Pacific knowledge sharing network, which is affiliated with the ILO (International Labor Organization). Riviera received her diploma and master's degrees in labor management relations from the School of Labor and Industrial Relations, University of the Philippines.

- **Zakiul Islam** is currently the Regulatory and Legal Affairs Senior Director at Banglalink. Prior to that, he worked at various organizations such as Warid Telecommunications and Enast Telecom Manzur Industries, and Philips in Bangladesh, and Hicap in Saudi Arabia. He accumulated more than 20 years of experience in telecommunication and information technology. He has also participated in many conferences and seminars conducted by the International Telecommunication Union, GSM Association, South Asian Telecommunication Regulatory Council, and the South Asia Mobile Forum. He completed his Bachelor's in Electrical and Electronic engineering from the Bangladesh University of Engineering and Technology, an MBA from Royal Roads University in Canada, and the executive management program from INSEAD.
- **Nizar El Assaad** was the Technology Director at Banglalink in November 2004. Prior to that, he was the Senior Manager of Infrastructure and Operations at Banglalink. He also gained experience working in Anzima as Customer Support Manager and Support Engineer, and as IT administrator at Cablevision. He was well regarded in the IT industry in Lebanon. Nizar holds a bachelor's in Computer and Communication from the American University of Beirut. He then received the TGM certification from INSEAD, France.
- **Mahmoud Hosny** joined the management team of Banglalink in March 2013 as the Strategy and Business Planning Director. Prior to Banglalink, Mahmoud gained extensive experience working in various organizations such as: Orascom Telecom Holding, Mobinil, and KPMG. Mahmoud received his Bachelor's in Accounting from Cairo University, Egypt and his MBA from Maastricht School of Management.
- **M Nurul Alam** joined Banglalink in November 2007 as the Company Secretary. He has prior experience as a company secretary at GlaxoSmithKline in Bangladesh. He has accumulated over 30 years of experience in various multinational companies. He took various courses in internal audit, commercial contracts and agreements. He is a member of the Institute of Internal Auditors of Bangladesh and the Institute of Accounting Technicians of Bangladesh.

The Future of Banglalink

Banglalink's management team has scripted the success story of the company over a short period of time. Its diverse management team, mostly comprising expatriates, offered extensive experience in this new market. Their different ideas, methodologies, and innovations have helped to bring value added services to the Bangladeshi market. The main question becomes, how will the management team change in 5 years, and what further changes will come about in the operations of Banglalink.

QUESTIONS

✪ **20-3.** Identify some advantages of the managing director, human resources director, and director of strategy. Identify their liabilities.

✪ **20-4.** What operational as well as personal challenges might the CFO encounter?

20-5. How will the management team for Banglalink, especially the expats, manage to deal with the Bangladeshi language?

20-6. What are the benefits from the overall background of the entire management team at Banglalink?

20-7. How would the compensation package differ if Banglalink opted for a short-term versus long-term expatriate assignment?

20-8. What do you expect the ratio of locals to expats in the top management of Banglalink will be in 10 years time?

SUMMARY

- The task of HRM is putting the right person into the right job at the right place at the right time at the right pay for the right stretch. Effective HRM policies explicitly support the MNE's strategy.
- Market developments, workforce demographics, globalization, and technology drive demand for expatriate talent.
- MNEs use expatriates to transfer technical competence and home-country business practices, control foreign operations, develop leadership skills, and diffuse the organization culture.
- Market trends and competitive challenges encourage MNEs to use short-term assignments, cross-border commuter assignments, flexpatriates, and extended business travel in lieu of traditional longer-term assignments.
- The changing circumstances of international business operations lead MNEs to consider the "young, the old, and the restless" in staffing expatriate slots.
- HRM relies on three approaches to organize expatriate management: the ethnocentric, polycentric, and geocentric staffing frameworks.
- The ethnocentric framework fills foreign management positions with home-country nationals. The polycentric framework uses host-country nationals to manage local subsidiaries. The geocentric framework seeks the best people for key jobs throughout the organization, regardless of nationality.
- MNEs often prefer locals rather than expatriate managers because the former better understand local circumstances and demand less compensation. In addition, they demonstrate to coworkers that opportunities are open to hardworking people.
- The selection of an individual for an expatriate assignment is influenced by the candidate's technical competence, adaptiveness, and leadership ability.
- Training and predeparture preparations include general country orientation, cultural sensitivity, and practical training. They reduce the odds of expatriate failure. Increasingly, preparations include the expatriate's spouse and family.
- Expatriate failure, narrowly defined, is the manager's premature return home due to poor operational performance. Broadly defined, it is the failure of the MNE's selection policies to identify individuals who succeed abroad.
- The primary causes of expatriate failure are difficulty adjusting to a new environment and a spouse/family struggling with the foreign assignment.
- Hardship allowances, cost-of-living differences, and tax equalization, among other aspects, are key elements of an expatriate's compensation package.
- Compensation must neither overly reward nor unduly punish the expat. Most MNEs use the balance sheet approach to manage this dilemma. Compensation practices by emerging market MNEs, given their typically lower salary scales, complicate application.
- Effectively managing repatriation is a significant challenge for MNEs.
- Some expats are promoted upon repatriation while others are not; not surprisingly, the former typically regard repatriation as a positive process.
- Repatriation, the act of returning home from a foreign assignment, is difficult. Finding the right job for the expatriate to assume upon return is a consistent challenge.

KEY TERMS

balance sheet approach (p. 833)
commuter assignment (p. 815)
culture shock (p. 828)
ethnocentric framework (p. 818)
expatriate (p. 808)
expatriate selection (p. 824)
expatriate failure (p. 840)
flexpatriates (p. 815)
geocentric framework (p. 821)
home-country national (p. 814)
human resource management (HRM) (p. 811)
localization (p. 817)
polycentric framework (p. 819)
repatriation (p. 837)
reverse-expat (p. 817)
staffing framework (p. 818)
third-country national (p. 814)

ENDNOTES

1 S. Green, F. Hassan, J. Immelt, M. Marks, & D. Meiland, "In Search of Global Leaders," *Harvard Business Review* 81(8) (2003): 44.

2 Mark Schoeff Jr., "P&G Places a Premium on International Experience, *Workforce*, www.workforce.com/apps/pbcs.dll/article?AID=/20060412/NEWS02/304129985&template=printarticle (accessed February 25, 2013).

3 Ibid, Green, Hassan, Immelt, Marks & Meiland.

4 Barbara Ettorre, "A Brave New World," *Management Review* 82, no. 4 (April 1993): 10–16.

5 "Staffing Globalisation: Travelling More Lightly," *The Economist* (June 23, 2006): 67

6 "Globalisation: The Empire Strikes Back," *The Economist* (September 18, 2008): 51.

7 Melinda Ligos, "The Foreign Assignment: An Incubator, or Exile?" *New York Times* (October 22, 2000).

8 Mark Larson, "More Employees Go Abroad as International Operations Grow," *Workforce Management* (June 1, 2006): 12.

9 Joe Sharkey,"Global Economy Is Leading To More Dangerous Places," *New York Times* (April 19, 2005): C3.

10 Sandra Jones,"Going Stateside: Once the Overseas Hitch is Over, Homeward-Bound Expats Hit Turbulence,"*Crain's Chicago Business* (July 24, 2000): 23.

11 Global Relocation Trends, *GMAC Global Relocations Services 2012*, www.gmac.com (accessed December 23, 2012).

12 Newman, Barry,"Expat Archipelago,"*Wall Street Journal* (December 12, 1995): A1.

13 Ibid. Ligos.

14 "*The World at Work*,"McKinsey Global Institute, www.mckinsey.com/insights/ (accessed December 27, 2012).

15 "Routes to the Top: How CEOs embrace Global Mobility,"Global Mobility Articles and Studies, www.articles.totallyexpat.com/routes-to-the-top-how-ceos-embrace-global-mobility (accessed June 6, 2011); "Routes to the Top - How CEOs Embrace Global Mobility,"*Global Mobility*, www.articles.totallyexpat.com/routes-to-the-top-how-ceos-embrace-global-mobility/ (accessed April 18, 2013).

16 Ibid, Mark Schoeff Jr.

17 "Schumpeter: The Tussle for Talent,"*The Economist* (January 6, 2011): 58.

18 "Schumpeter: Davos Man and His Defects,"*The Economist* (January 26, 2013): 63.

19 Leslie Kwoh,"One Foreign Posting Isn't Enough for Managers Seeking Top Jobs,"WSJ.com, online.wsj.com/article/SB10001424052702303630404577390573349379782.html?mod=WSJ_Careers_CareerJournal_4 (accessed December 27, 2012).

20 S. Green, F. Hassan, J. Immelt, M. Marks, & D. Meiland,"In Search of Global Leaders,"*Harvard Business Review* 81(8) (2003): 44.

21 Paula Caligiuri and Victoria Di Santo,"Global Competence: What Is it, and Can It Be Developed through Global Assignments?"*Human Resource Planning* (September 2001): 27–36; Mark Morgan,"Career-Building Strategies: It's Time to Do a Job Assessment: Are Your Skills Helping You up the Corporate Ladder?"*Strategic Finance* (June 2002): 38–44.

22 Hoon Park,"Global Human Resource Management: A Synthetic Approach."*The Journal of International Business and Economics* (2002): 28–51.

23 William Judge,"Is a Leader's Character Culture-Bound or Culture-Free? An Empirical Comparison of the Character Traits of American and Taiwanese CEOs,"*Journal of Leadership Studies* 8 (Fall 2001): 63–79.

24 U.S. Trade Representative, 2010 National Trade Estimate Report on Foreign Trade Barriers, 2010; www.ustr.gov/about-us/press-office/reports-and-publications/2010 (accessed April 21, 2013).

25 U.S. Trade Representative, 2010 National Trade Estimate Report on Foreign Trade Barriers, 2010; www.ustr.gov/about-us/press-office/reports-and-publications/2010 (accessed April 21, 2013).

26 Keith Brouthers,"Institutional, Cultural and Transaction Cost Influences on Entry Mode Choice and Performance,"*Journal of International Business Studies* 33 (Summer 2002): 203–22.

27 Ben Kedia, Richard Nordtvedt, and Liliana M. Perez,"International Business Strategies, Decision-Making Theories, and Leadership Styles: An Integrated Framework,"*Competitiveness Review* 12 (Winter–Spring 2002): 38–53.

28 Sully Taylor, Schon Beechler, and Nancy Napier,"Toward an Integrative Model of Strategic International Resource Management,"*Academy of Management Review* 21 (1996): 959–85.

29 S. Green, F. Hassan, J. Immelt, M. Marks, & D. Meiland,"In Search of Global Leaders,"*Harvard Business Review* 81(8) (2003): 44.

30 Watson Wyatt Worldwide,"Human Capital Index: Human Capital as a Lead Indicator of Shareholder Value,"www.watsonwyatt.com/research/resrender.asp?id=w-488&page=1 (accessed November 27, 2007); H. B. Gregersen, A. J. Morrison, & J. S. Black,"Developing Leaders for the Global Frontier,"*MIT Sloan Management Review* 40(1) (1998): 22.

31 See, for example, N. Khatri,"Managing Human Resource for Competitive Advantage: A Study of MNEs in Singapore," *International Journal of Human Resource Management* 11:2 (2000): 336.

32 S. Green, F. Hassan, J. Immelt, M. Marks, & D. Meiland,"In Search of Global Leaders,"*Harvard Business Review* 81(8) (2003): 44.

33 "Travelling More Lightly,"*The Economist* (June 22, 2006): 67.

34 "A Special Report on Innovation in Emerging Markets: The World Turned Upside Down,"*The Economist*, www.economist.com/node/15879369 (accessed December 21, 2011).

35 "Up or Out: Next Moves for the Modern Expatriate,"*The Economist Intelligence Unit*, graphics.eiu.com/upload/eb/LON_PL_Regus_WEB2.pdf (accessed December 31, 2012); Leslie Klaff,"Thinning the Ranks of the Career Expats,"*Workforce Management* (October 2004): 84–87.

36 Statement by Yvonne Sonsino, reported in"Travelling More Lightly," *The Economist* (June 22, 2006): 67.

37 Sven Hemli, Carl Allwood, and Ben Martin,"Creative Knowledge Environments,"*Creativity Research Journal* (April-June 2008): 20; Claire Cain Miller and Catherine Rampell,"Yahoo Orders Home Workers Back to the Office, *The New York Times* (February 25, 2013): A1. David Wessel,"Chinese Firm Experiments With Telecommuting," *The Wall Street Journal* (December 19, 2012,): C3;"The Future of Telecommuting: Corralling the Yahoos,"*The Economist* (March 2, 2013): 61–62.

38 H. Mayerhofer, L. Hartmann, G. Michelitsch-Riedl, & I. Kollinger, "Flexpatriates Assignments: A Neglected Issue in Global Staffing," *International Journal of Human Resource Management* 15 (2004): 1371–89.

39 Leslie Kwoh,"One Foreign Posting Isn't Enough for Managers Seeking Top Jobs."

40 PwC International Challenge (EPIC), www.pwc.com/extweb/career.nsf/docid/9204374F898F3E5A8525748F00741E9D (accessed May 4, 2009).

41 Peter Saalfield and Rebecca Appel,"Business Schools: Looking Local for a Global Reach,"*New York Times* (May 17, 2012): B3.

42 "Americans Look Overseas for Global MBA Courses and Diversity," *TOPMBA*, www.topmba.com/articles/north-america/americans-look-overseas-global-mba-courses-and-diversity (accessed December 27, 2012).

43 Margaret Shaffer, Maria Kraimer, Yu-Ping Chen, and Mark Bolino, "Choices, Challenges, and Career Consequences of Global Work Experiences: A Review and Future Agenda,"*Journal of Management* 38 (2012): 1282–1327.

44 Global Relocation Trends, *GMAC Global Relocations Services 2012*, www.gmac.com (accessed April 21, 2013).

45 "More Females Sent on International Assignment than ever Before, Survey Finds,"www.mercer.com/pressrelease/details.htm?idContent=1246090 (accessed April 25, 2009).

46 Calvin Reynolds,"Strategic Employment of Third Country Nationals: Keys to Sustaining the Transformation of HR Functions,"*Human Resource Planning* 20 (March 1997): 33–50.

47 Keith Bradsher,"China's Ambitious Goal for Boom in College Graduates,"*The New York Times* (March 21, 2013): A1.

48 *Global Relocation Trends: 2012 Survey Report*, Brookfield Global Relocation Services, knowledge.brookfieldgrs.com/content/insights_ideas-2012_GRTS (accessed December 23, 2012).

49 Jeffrey Joerres,"Beyond Expats: Better Managers for Emerging Markets,"*McKinsey Quarterly* (May 2011): 5

50 "Financial Careers: Go East, Young Moneyman,"*The Economist* (April 16, 2011): 79–80.

51 *Global Relocation Trends: 2011 Survey Report*, Brookfield Global Relocation Services, www.brookfieldgrs.com/insights_ideas/grts (accessed June 15, 2011).

52 Karina Frayter, "IBM to Laid-off: Want a Job in India?" money.cnn.com/2009/02/05/news/MNEs/ibm_jobs (accessed April 29, 2009).

53 Adrian Wooldridge, "The Battle for the Best," *The Economist: The World in 2007*: 48.

54 Chi-fai Chan and Neil Holbert, "Marketing Home and Away: Perceptions of Managers in Headquarters and Subsidiaries," *Journal of World Business* 36 (Summer 2001): 205.

55 "Staffing Globalisation: Travelling More Lightly," *The Economist* (June 23, 2006): 67.

56 Tsun-yan Hsieh, Johanne Lavoie, and Robert Samek, "Are You Taking Your Expatriate Talent Seriously?" *The McKinsey Quarterly* (Summer 1999): 71.

57 "Staffing Globalisation: Travelling More Lightly," *The Economist* (June 23, 2006): 67.

58 "Why Toyota Has Flopped In China," *Business Insider*, www.businessinsider.com/why-toyota-has-flopped-in-china-2012-10 (accessed January 6, 2013).

59 William C. Weldon, "Chairman's Letter: To Our Shareholders," *Annual Report 2006* (Johnson & Johnson, 2007), jnj.v1.papiervirtuel.com/report/2007030901 (accessed November 27, 2007).

60 PricewaterhouseCoopers LLP and Cranfield School of Management, "Measuring the Value of International Assignments" (November 9, 2006), www.som.cranfield.ac.uk/som/news/story.asp?id=329 (accessed May 15, 2008).

61 S. Green, F. Hassan, J. Immelt, M. Marks, & D. Meiland, "In Search of Global Leaders," *Harvard Business Review* 81(8) (2003): 44.

62 Vijay Pothukuchi, Fariborz Damanpour, Jaepil Choi, Chao Chen, and Seung Park, "National and Organizational Culture Differences and International Joint Venture Performance," *Journal of International Business Studies* 33 (Summer 2002): 243–66.

63 Martin Dewhurst, Jonathan Harris, and Suzanne Heywood, "The Global Company's Challenge," *McKinsey Quarterly*, www.mckinseyquarterly.com/The_global_companys_challenge_2979 (accessed December 31, 2012).

64 "Why Toyota Has Flopped In China," *Business Insider*, www.businessinsider.com/why-toyota-has-flopped-in-china-2012-10 (accessed January 6, 2013).

65 J. Kahn, "The World's Most Admired MNEs," *Fortune* (October 11, 1999): 267.

66 Kahn, "The World's Most Admired MNEs."

67 "Tylenol (Acetaminophen) to Be Available in Japan in Early Fall, 2000," *Doctor's Guide*, www.pslgroup.com/dg/1d9dfa.htm (accessed June 15, 2011).

68 David Ahlstrom, Garry Bruton, and Eunice S. Chan, "HRM of Foreign Firms in China: The Challenge of Managing Host Country Personnel," *Business Horizons* 44 (May 2001): 59.

69 S. Green, F. Hassan, J. Immelt, M. Marks, & D. Meiland, "In Search of Global Leaders," *Harvard Business Review* 81(8) (2003): 44.

70 "High-Tech Nomads: These Engineers Work as Temps on Wireless Projects All over the World," *Time* (November 26, 2001): B20; B. Kedia and A. Mukherji, "Global Managers: Developing a Mindset for Global Competitiveness," *Journal of World Business* 34 (Fall 1999): 30.

71 S. Green, F. Hassan, J. Immelt, M. Marks, & D. Meiland, "In Search of Global Leaders," *Harvard Business Review* 81(8) (2003): 44.

72 Thomas Barta, Markus Kleiner, and Tilo Neumann, "Is There a Payoff from Top-team Diversity? *McKinsey Quarterly*," www.mckinseyquarterly.com/Is_there_a_payoff_from_top-team_diversity_2954 (accessed December 27, 2012).

73 A. Wendlandt, "The Name Game Is a Puzzle for Expats at Work," *Financial Times* (August 15, 2000): 3.

74 Alex Pentland, "The New Science of Building Great Teams," *Harvard Business Review*," hbr.org/2012/04/the-new-science-of-building-great-teams (accessed December 27, 2012).

75 Margaret Schweer, Dimitris Assimakopoulos, Rob Cross, and Robert Thomas, "Building a Well-Networked Organization, *MIT Sloan Management Review*," sloanreview.mit.edu/the-magazine/2012-winter/53211/building-a-well-networked-organization (accessed December 27, 2012). For instance, the type of ownership of its foreign operations influences an MNE's staffing policy. Expatriates transferred abroad to a foreign joint venture, for example, may find themselves in ambiguous situations, unsure of whom they represent and uncertain of whether they report to both partners or to the partner that transferred them. Typically, MNEs insist on using their own executives when they're concerned that local personnel may make decisions in their own interest rather than that of the joint venture.

76 Global Relocation Trends, *GMAC Global Relocations Services*, www.gmac.com (accessed April 21, 2011).

77 Wooldridge, "The Battle for the Best."

78 Again, recall how Honeywell screens candidates years before they might go abroad in order to maximize the probability of success.

79 M. Tahvanainen, D. Welch, and V. Worm, "Implications of Short-Term International Assignments," *European Management Journal*, 2005 (23): 663–73.

80 Caligiuri and Di Santo, "Global Competence"; Hsieh et al., "Are You Taking Your Expatriate Talent Seriously?"

81 Susan Schneider and Rosalie Tung, "Introduction to the International Human Resource Management Special Issue," *Journal of World Business* 36 (Winter 2001): 341–46.

82 J. Ramsey, J. Leonel, G. Gomes, and P. Monteiro, "Cultural Intelligence's Influence on International Business Travelers' Stress," *Cross Cultural Management*, 2011 (18): 21–37.

83 "In Search of Global Leaders: View of Stephen Green, Group CEO, HSBC," *Harvard Business Review* (August 1, 2003): 44.

84 S. Jun, J. Gentry, and Y. Hyun, "Cultural Adaptation of Business Expatriates in the Host Marketplace," *Journal of International Business Studies* 32 (Summer 2001): 369.

85 "Business in China and the West: A Tale of Two Expats," *The Economist* (December 29, 2010).

86 Tsun-yan Hsieh, Johanne Lavoie, and Robert Samek, "Are You Taking Your Expatriate Talent Seriously?" *The McKinsey Quarterly* (Summer 1999): 71.

87 M. Shaffer, D. Harrison, M. Gilley, and D. Luk, "Struggling for Balance amid Turbulence on International Assignments: Work-Family Conflict, Support and Commitment," *Journal of Management* 27 (January–February 2001): 99; Chris Moss, "Expats: Thinking of Living and Working Abroad?" *The Guardian* (October 19, 2000): 4.

88 "In Search of Global Leaders: View of Stephen Green, Group CEO, HSBC," *Harvard Business Review* (August 1, 2003): 44.

89 *Global Relocation Trends: 2012 Survey Report*, www. reloroundtable.com/blog/trends-in-relocation/brookfield-reports-2012-relocation-trends/ (accessed April 21, 2012).

90 Diane E. Lewis, "Families Make, Break Overseas Moves," *Boston Globe* (October 4, 1998): 5D; "Expat Spouses: It Takes Two," *Financial Times* (March 1, 2002): C1.

91 J. Selmer and J. Lauring, "Self-initiated Academic Expatriates: Inherent Demographics and Reasons to Expatriate," *European Management Review* 7 (2010): 169–79.

92 "Expat Spouses: It Takes Two."

93 *Global Relocation Trends: 2011 Survey Report; The Expat Explorer Survey 2010*, HSBC Bank International, survey of 4,127 expatriates form more than 100 countries.

94 Lisa Littrell, Eduardo Salas, Kathleen Hess, Michael Paley and Sharon Riedel"Expatriate Preparation: A Critical Analysis of 25 Years of Cross-Cultural Training Research," *Human Resource Development Review* 5 (2006): 355–388; Margaret Shaffer, Maria Kraimer, Yu-Ping Chen, and Mark Bolino, "Choices, Challenges, and Career Consequences of Global Work Experiences: A Review and Future Agenda," *Journal of Management* 38 (2012): 1282–1327.

95 D. Ones and C. Viswesvaran, "Relative Importance of Personality Dimensions for Expatriate Selection: A Policy Capturing Study," *Human Performance* 12 (1999): 275–94.

96 Valerie Frazee, "Send Your Expats Prepared for Success," *Workforce* 78 (March 1999): S6.

97 Jessica Twentyman, "An Expat Job Can Be a Move Too Far," FT.com, www.ft.com/cms/s/0/c1d1b668-d22b-11df-8fbe-00144feabdc0.html (accessed February 25, 2013).

98 Margaret Shaffer, Maria Kraimer, Yu-Ping Chen, and Mark Bolino, "Choices, Challenges, and Career Consequences of Global Work Experiences: A Review and Future Agenda," *Journal of Management* 38 (2012): 1282–1327.

99 S. Larson, "More Employees Go Abroad as International Operations Grow," Workforce.com, www.workforce.com/index.html (accessed April 27, 2009);

100 *Global Relocation Trends: 2011 Survey Report*, www. relocatemagazine.com/relocation-news-blog-format/3-general-relocation-news/2212-brookfield-grs-2011-global-relocation-trends-survey-report (accessed March 31, 2011); *Global Relocation Trends: 2012 Survey Report*, www. reloroundtable.com/blog/trends-in-relocation/brookfield-reports-2012-relocation-trends/ (accessed April 21, 2012).

101 Suzy Harris, *The University in Translation: Internationalizing Higher Education* (New York: Continuum International Publishing Group, 2011).

102 "English Is Coming: The Adverse Side-Effects of the Growing Dominance of English," *The Economist* (February 14, 2009): 85.

103 M. Joseph, "India Faces a Linguistic Truth - English Spoken Here," *New York Times* (February 16, 2011): B1."Schumpeter: New Rules for Schools," *The Economist* (March 26, 2013): 74.

104 "Language-teaching Firms: Linguists Online," *The Economist* (January 5, 2013): 52.

105 European Commission, "Languages of Europe," *Education and Training*, europa.eu. int/comm/education/policies/lang/languages/index_en.html (accessed July 18, 2007).

106 Doreen Carvajal, "In many Business Schools, the Bottom Line is in English," *The New York Times* (April 10, 2007), www.nytimes. com/2007/04/10/world/europe/10iht-engbiz.2.5212499.html?pagewant ed=all (accessed June 12, 2007).

107 "Global Spread of English Poses Problems for UK," *People's Daily Online* (February 18, 2006): B3.

108 A. Sitze, "Language of Business: Can E-Learning Help International MNEs Speak a Common Language?" *Online Learning* (March 2002): 19–23.

109 "Machine Translation: Conquering Babel," *The Economist* (January 5, 2013): 63.

110 "Facebook Will Be Hiring Number of Employees by 2017," techblog.weblineindia.com/news/facebook-will-be-hiring-number-of-employees-by-2017 (accessed January 11, 2013).

111 Jenna Wortham, "A Surge in Learning the Language of the Internet," NYTimes.com, /www.nytimes.com/2012/03/28/technology/for-an-edge-on-the-internet-computer-code-gains-a-following.html?_r=1&hpw (accessed December 26, 2012).

112 PricewaterhouseCoopers, *International Assignments: European Policy and Practice* (1997), www.pwcglobal.com/extweb/ncsurvres.nsf (accessed April 3, 2000)

113 Tsedal Neely, "Global Business Speaks English," *Harvard Business Review*, hbr.org/2012/05/global-business-speaks-english/ar/1 (accessed December 27, 2012).

114 "In Search of Global Leaders: View of Fred Hassan, Chairman and CEO, Schering-Plough," *Harvard Business Review* (August 1, 2003).

115 S. Baker, "Catching the Continental Drift: These Days, English Will Suffice for Americans Working in Europe," *Businessweek* (August 14, 2001): 35.

116 C. Cole, "Bridging the Language Gap: Expatriates Find Learning Korean Key to Enjoying a More Satisfying Life," *The Korea Herald* (August 16, 2002): B1.

117 M. Ligos, "The Foreign Assignment: An Incubator, or Exile?" *New York Times* (October 22, 2000): A1.

118 View of the American Council on the Teaching of Foreign Languages, reported in Tanya Mohn, "All Aboard the Foreign Language Express," *New York Times* (October 11, 2000): A1.

119 "Lera Boroditsky, "How Language Shapes Thought," *The Long Now*, longnow.org/seminars/02010/oct/26/how-language-shapes-thought/ (accessed December 27, 2012).

120 C. Panella, "Meeting the Needs of International Business: A Customer Service-Oriented Business Language Course," *The Journal of Language for International Business* 9 (1998): 65–75; M. Inman, "How Foreign Language Study Can Enhance Career Possibilities" (Washington DC: ERIC Clearinghouse on Languages and Linguistics, 1987), www.ericdigests.org/pre-927/career.htm (accessed November 27, 2007); C. Randlesome and A. Myers, "Cultural Fluency: Results from a UK and Irish Survey," *Business Communication Quarterly* 60:3 (1997): 9–22.

121 Yudhijit Bhattacharjeethe, "Benefits of Bilingualism," NYTimes.com, www.nytimes.com/2012/03/18/opinion/sunday/the-benefits-of-bilingualism.html?_r=1&src=me&ref=general (accessed December 31, 2012).

122 "Learning a New Language Makes the Brain Grow," *Psych Central News*, psychcentral.com/news/2012/10/09/ learning-a-new-language-makes-the-brain-grow/45761.html (accessed December 27, 2012).

123 "Enduring Voices Project," *National Geographic*, travel.nationalgeo-graphic.com/travel/enduring-voices/ (accessed December 27, 2012).

124 D.D. Guttenplan, "Battling to Preserve Arabic from English's Onslaught" NYTimes.com, www.nytimes.com/2012/06/11/world/ middleeast/11iht-educlede11.html?src=rechp (accessed December 26, 2012).

125 "It's Time to Protect Chinese Language," *China Daily*, www.chinadaily.com.cn/life/2011-01/06/content_11803112. htm (accessed December 27, 2012); "Breaking News English ESL Lesson Plan on Chinese," www.breakingnewsenglish. com/1012/101225-chinese.html (accessed December 27, 2012); "Protecting Chinese Characters – New Regulations Ban English Words in Chinese Publications," *BeijingToday*, www.beijingtoday. com.cn/debate/protecting-chinese-characters-new-regulations-ban-english-words-in-chinese-publications (accessed December 27, 2012).

126 "Staffing Globalisation: Travelling More Lightly," *The Economist* (June 23, 2006): 67.

127 Estimate reported in the second annual study of expatriate issues, conducted from January through March 2002, sponsored by CIGNA International Expatriate Benefits; the National Foreign Trade Council, an association of multinational MNEs that supports open international trade and investment; and WorldatWork, www.prnewswire.com/ micro/CI9 (accessed September 2, 2005).

128 "Measuring the Value of International Assignments, PricewaterhouseCoopers, www.pwc.fi/fi_FI/fi/palvelut/tiedostot/pwc_ measuring_the_value.pdf, (accessed March 12, 2013).

129 C. Gould,"What's the Latest in Global Compensation?" *Global Workforce* (July 1997): 28.

130 G. Latta,"Expatriate Policy and Practice: A Ten-Year Comparison of Trends," *Compensation and Benefits Review* 31:4 (1999): 35–39, quoting studies reported by Organization Resources Counselors.

131 "Business in China and the West: A Tale of Two Expats," *The Economist* (December 29, 2010): 65.

132 "Designing Competitive Expatriate Compensation Packages," Mercer, www.mercer.com/referencecontent.htm?idContent=1303865 (accessed May 3, 2009).

133 This practice, however, appears to be disappearing, especially for assignments in so-called world capitals like New York, London, and Tokyo, in which many executives are interested and where there is (relatively) little "deprivation." In addition, the number and nature of "hardships" resulting from foreign assignments are in decline, particularly as advances in transportation and communications enable expatriates to keep in closer contact with home countries; the openness of economies allows them to buy familiar goods and services; and the general level of housing, schooling, and medical services increasingly meets their needs.

134 A U.S. family based in China, for example, commonly spends more money to get the same goods than they would buy back home. Why? Because they prefer Western items that must be imported and have thus been subjected to high tariffs. Expatriates often obtain food and housing at rates higher than going local rates because they don't know the language well, where to buy, or how to bargain.

135 Towers Perrin and CIGNA, for example, specialize in international compensation. In addition, MNEs rely on estimates of cost-of-living differences—even if they are imperfect. MNEs commonly use such sources as the U.S. State Department's cost-of-living index, published yearly in *Labor Developments Abroad,* the UN *Monthly Bulletin of Statistics,* and surveys by the *Financial Times,* P-E International, Business International, and the Staff Papers of the International Monetary Fund.

136 "Cost of Living Survey 2012," *Mercer,* www.mercer.com/costoflivingpr#City_rankings (accessed December 27, 2012).

137 "Worldwide Cost of Living June 2011," *Economist Intelligence Unit,* www.eiu.com/public/topical_report.aspx?campaignid=wcol_June2011 (accessed December 27, 2012).

138 "Home Away from Home: Expatriate Housing in Asia," *The Korea Herald* (May 2, 2002): B1.

139 "Tokyo Tops in H.K. Survey on Living Cost for Expatriates," *Japan Economic Newswire* (January 24, 2002).

140 A. Maitland,"A Hard Balancing Act: Management of Dual Careers," *Financial Times* (May 10, 1999): 11.

141 *Global Relocation Trends: 2012 Survey Report,* Brookfield Global Relocation Services, knowledge.brookfieldgrs.com/content/insights_ideas-2012_GRTS (accessed December 23, 2012).

142 Joe Sharkey,"Global Economy Is Leading to More Dangerous Places," NYTimes.com, query.nytimes.com/gst/fullpage.html?res=9C06E0DD1F3EF93AA25757C0A9639C8B63 (accessed December 26, 2012).

143 "Education: Move over, Dalton," *The Economist,* www.economist.com/node/21561896 (accessed December 28, 2012). Also, visit International School Services www.iss.edu, the U.S. Department of State www.state.gov/m/a/os/, or the European Council of International Schools www.ecis.org for a sense of the situation.

144 For those interested, please visit ERI's Relocation Assessor at www.erieri.com and head to Sample Sceenshots to get a sense of the going rates.

145 "The Expat Explorer Survey 2010,"HSBC Bank International, www.expatexplorer.hsbc.com/files/pdfs/overall-reports/2010/experience.pdf (accessed April 4, 2011).

146 "International Assignments Increasing, Mercer Survey Finds," *Mercer,* www.mercerhr.com/summary.jhtml?idContent=1222700 (accessed May 6, 2006).

147 G. Stahl, C. Chua, P. Caligiuri, J. Cerdin, and M. Taniguchi,"Predictors Of Turnover Intentions In Learning-Driven And Demand-Driven International Assignments: The Role Of Repatriation Concerns, Satisfaction With Company Support, And Perceived Career Advancement Opportunities," *Human Resource Management,* 2009 (48): 89–109.

148 "In Search of Global Leaders: View of Stephen Green, Group CEO, HSBC," *Harvard Business Review* (August 1, 2003): 81.

149 Margaret Shaffer, Maria Kraimer, Yu-Ping Chen, and Mark Bolino, "Choices, Challenges, and Career Consequences of Global Work Experiences: A Review and Future Agenda," *Journal of Management* 38 (2012): 1282–1327.

150 PricewaterhouseCoopers LLP and Cranfield School of Management, "Understanding and Avoiding Barriers to International Mobility," *Geodesy* (October 2005), www.pwc.extweb/pwcpublications.nfs/docid/7ACA93FA424E80E88525121E006E82C/$file/geodesy.pdf (accessed November 27, 2007).

151 "Abroad but Not Forgotten: Improving the Career Management of Employees on International Assignments," *Human Resource Management International Digest* 15 (2007): 29–31.

152 "In Search of Global Leaders: View of Daniel Meiland, Executive Chairman, Egon Zehender International," *Harvard Business Review* (August 1, 2003): 81.

153 "Global Relocation Trends 2008,"GMAC Global Relocations Services, www.gmac.com (accessed June 1, 2008).

154 M. Lazarova and P. Caligiuri,"Retaining Repatriates: The Role of Organizational Support Practices," *Journal of World Business* 36 (Winter 2001): 389–402.

155 Liz Bleacher,"Students Return from Study Abroad, Experience Reverse Culture Shock," *Delaware Review* (February 19, 2013): 8.

156 "In Search of Global Leaders: View of Stephen Green, Group CEO, HSBC," *Harvard Business Review* (August 1, 2003): 81.

157 PwC International Challenge, www.pwc.com/extweb/career.nsf/docid/9204374F898F3E5A8525748F00741E9D (accessed May 4, 2009).

158 Leslie Klaff,"Thinning the Ranks of the Career Expats," *Workforce Management* (October 2004): 84–87.

159 I. Varner and T. Palmer,"Successful Expatriation and Organizational Strategies," *Review of Business* 23 (Spring 2002): 8–12; J. Selmer, "Practice Makes Perfect? International Experience and Expatriate Adjustment," *Management International Review* 42 (January 2002): 71–88.

160 John Daniels and Gary Insch,"Why Are Early Departure Rates from Foreign Assignments Lower Than Historically Reported?" *Multinational Business Review* 6:1 (1998):13–23.

161 Global Relocation Trends 2010, *GMAC Global Relocations Services* www. reloroundtable.com/blog/trends-in-relocation/brookfield-reports-2012-relocation-trends/ (accessed April 21, 2011).

162 Data provided by National Foreign Trade Council; Maria L. Kraimer, Sandy Wayne, and Renata Jaworski,"Sources of Support and Expatriate Performance: The Mediating Role of Expatriate Adjustment," *Personnel Psychology* 54 (Spring 2001): 71.

163 *Global Relocation Trends,* GMAC Global Relocations Services, www.gmac.com (accessed April 21, 2011).

164 Susan J. Matt, *Homesickness: An American History: The Story of How We Became a Nation of Nostalgic Homebodies* (Oxford: Oxford University Press, 2011).

165 N. Doherty, M. Dickmann, M. and T. Mills,"Exploring the Motives of Company-Backed and Self-Initiated Expatriates," *International Journal of Human Resource Management* 22 (2011): 595–611.

166 "African Hospitality: No Vacancy," *The Economist*, www.economist.com/news/business/21566017-race-build-new-hotels-africa-no-vacancy (accessed December 31, 2012).

167 "Big US Firms Shift Hiring Abroad," *Wall Street Journal* (April 19, 2011): B1.

168 Martin Dewhurst, Jonathan Harris, and Suzanne Heywood, "The Global Company's Challenge," *McKinsey Quarterly*, www.mckinseyquarterly.com/The_global_companys_challenge_2979 (accessed December 31, 2012).

169 "Financial Careers: Go East, Young Moneyman," *The Economist* (April 16, 2011): 79–80.

170 "Up or Out: Next Moves for the Modern Expatriate," *The Economist Intelligence Unit*, graphics.eiu.com/upload/eb/LON_PL_Regus_WEB2.pdf (accessed December 31, 2012).

171 H. Seligson, "Shut Out at Home, Americans Seek Opportunity in China," NYTimes.com, www.nytimes.com/2009/08/11/business/economy/11expats.html (accessed May 4, 2011).

172 *Global Relocation Trends: 2011 Survey Report.*

173 ***Sources include the following:*** www.banglalink.com "Banglalink enhances staff productivity and safeguards customer services with proactive IT support," www.ca.com/us/collateral/success-stories/na/banglalink-enhances-staff-productivity-and-safeguards-customer-services-with-proactive-t-support.aspx; "Banglalink prepares employees to face 3G," Abdullah Mamun, www.thedailystar.net/beta2/news/banglalink-prepares-employees-to-face-3g/.

Glossary

Absolute advantage: A theory first presented by Adam Smith, which holds that because certain countries can produce some goods more efficiently than other countries, they should specialize in and export those things they can produce more efficiently and trade for other things they need.

Acceptable quality level (AQL): A concept of quality control whereby managers are willing to accept a certain level of production defects, which are dealt with through repair facilities and service centers.

Accounting: The process of collecting and analyzing data for internal and external users of information.

Acquired advantage: A form of trade advantage due to technology rather than due to the availability of natural resources, climate, etc.

Acquired group membership: Affiliation not determined by birth, such as religions, political affiliations, and professional and other associations.

Active income: Income of a CFC that is derived from the active conduct of a trade or business, as specified by the U.S. Internal Revenue Code.

Ad valorem duty: A duty (tariff) assessed as a percentage of the value of the item.

Advance import deposit: A form of foreign-exchange convertibility control where the government tightens control of import licenses and requires importers to make a deposit with the central bank.

Agglomeration: A theory that competitive companies may gain efficiencies by locating near each other.

American Depositary Receipt (ADR): A negotiable certificate issued by a U.S. bank in the United States to represent the underlying shares of a foreign corporation's stock held in trust at a custodian bank in the foreign country.

American terms: The practice of using the direct quote for exchange rates.

Andean Community (CAN): A South American form of economic integration involving Bolivia, Colombia, Ecuador, Peru, and Venezuela.

Appropriability theory: The theory that companies will favor foreign direct investment over such nonequity operating forms as licensing arrangements so that potential competitors will be less likely to gain access to proprietary information.

Arab League: A group similar to PAFTA but with more representative countries and political rather than economic objectives.

Arbitrage: The process of buying and selling foreign currency at a profit that results from price discrepancies between or among markets.

Arm's-length price: A price between two companies that do not have an ownership interest in each other.

Ascribed group membership: Affiliation determined by birth, such as those based on gender, family, age, caste, and ethnic, racial, or national origin.

Asia Pacific Economic Cooperation (APEC): A cooperation formed by 21 countries that border the Pacific Rim to promote multilateral economic cooperation in trade and investment in the Pacific Rim.

Association of South East Asian Nations (ASEAN): A free trade area involving the Asian countries of Brunei, Indonesia, Malaysia, the Philippines, Singapore, and Thailand.

Balance of payments: Statement that summarizes all economic transactions between a country and the rest of the world during a given period of time.

Balance sheet approach: Compensation plan that sets expatriate salaries to equalize purchasing power across countries.

Bank for International Settlements (BIS): A bank in Basel, Switzerland, that facilitates transactions among central banks; it is effectively the central banks' central bank.

Bargaining school theory: A theory holding that the negotiated terms for foreign investors depend on how much investors and host countries need each other's assets.

Base currency: The currency whose value is implicitly 1 when a quote is made between two currencies; for example, if the Brazilian real is trading at 1.9 reals (reais) per dollar, the dollar is the base currency and the real is the quoted currency.

Bicultural: An individual who has internalized two national cultures because of holding dual nationalities, having parents from another country, or having lived abroad at an impressionable age.

Bid (buy) rate: The amount a trader is willing to pay for foreign exchange.

Bilateral integration: A form of integration between two countries in which they decide to cooperate more closely together, usually in the form of tariff reductions.

Black market: The foreign-exchange market that lies outside the official market.

Born global: *See* Born-global company.

Born-global company: A company that adopts a global orientation from inception.

Base of the Pyramid: The billions of people living on less than a few dollars per day yet who some see as the next market frontier of the global economy.

Boundaries: In terms of political environments, an official or perceived point of separation that defines the boundary of a nation. In terms of organization structure, horizontal constraints that follow from having specific employees only do specific jobs in specific units as well as the vertical constraints that separate employees into specific levels of a precisely stipulated command-and-control hierarchy.

Boundarylessness: State whereby companies build organizations that eliminate the vertical, horizontal, and external boundaries that impede information flows and hinder developing relationship.

Brain drain: A condition whereby countries lose potentially productive resources when its bright people migrate to other countries.

Bretton Woods Agreement: An agreement among IMF countries to promote exchange-rate stability and to facilitate the international flow of currencies.

BRICs: An acronym referring to the nations of Brazil, Russia, India, and China; aims to reflect their vanguard status as newly advanced economies.

Bureaucratic control: System whereby an organization uses centralized authority to install rules and procedures to govern activities.

Capitalism: An economic system characterized by private ownership, pricing, production, and distribution of goods.

Caribbean Community (CARICOM): A customs union in the Caribbean region.

Carry trade: Borrow a currency at a low interest rate and invest it in a currency with a higher interest rate.

Centralization: The degree to which high-level managers, usually above the country level, make strategic dicisions and delegate them to lower levels for implementation.

Chicago Mercantile Exchange (CME) Group: The CME Group is the world's largest derivatives marketplace, dealing in future and options products for a wide variety of asset classes, including foreign exchange.

Choice-of-law clause: A provision in a contract that allows the parties to agree that a particular country's laws will apply to the agreement.

Civil law: A body of rules that delineate private rights and remedies, and govern disputes between individuals in such areas as contracts, property, and family.

Civil law system: A legal system based on a detailed set of laws that are organized into a code; countries with a civil law system, also called a codified legal system, include Germany, France, and Japan.

Clan control: System whereby an MNE relies on shared values among employees to idealize and enforce preferred behaviors.

Cluster effects: Follows from the congregation of buyers and sellers of a particular good or service in a certain locale; they, in turn, induce other buyers and sellers to relocate there.

Clustering: The location of companies where there are many competitors and suppliers.

Code of conduct: A set of principles guiding the actions of MNEs in their contacts with societies.

Collaborative arrangement: A formal, long-term contractual agreement among companies.

Collectivism: Perspective that the needs of the group take precedence over the needs of the individual; encourages dependence on the organization.

Command economy: An economic system in which the political authorities make major decisions regarding the production and distribution of goods and services.

Commercial law: The area of law that governs the broad areas of business, commerce, and consumer transactions.

Common law system: A legal system based on tradition, precedent, and custom and usage, in which the courts interpret the law based on those conventions; found in the United Kingdom and former British colonies.

Common market: A form of regional economic integration in which countries abolish internal tariffs, use a common external tariff, and abolish restrictions on factor mobility.

Communism: A form of totalitarianism initially theorized by Karl Marx in which the political and economic systems are virtually inseparable.

Commuter assignment: One where the expatriate travels between his home and host country at frequent intervals.

Comparable access argument: Companies and industries often argue that they are entitled to the same access to foreign markets as foreign industries and companies have to their markets.

Comparative advantage: The theory that there is global efficiency gains from trade if a country specializes in those products that it can produce more efficiently than other products regardless of whether other countries can produce those products even more efficiently.

Compound duty: A tax placed on goods traded internationally, based on value plus units.

Concentrated configuration: The design of a value chain whereby a particular activity is performed in one geographic location and serves the world from it.

Concentration strategy: A strategy by which an international company builds up operations quickly in one or a few countries before going to another.

Configuration: To set up, arrange, and disperse value activities to the ideal locations around the world so that the company can start and sustain operations.

Confirmed letter of credit: A letter of credit to which a bank in the exporter's country adds its guarantee of payment.

Consolidation: An accounting process in which financial statements of related entities, such as a parent and its subsidiaries, are combined to yield a unified set of financial statements; in the process, transactions among the related enterprises are eliminated so that the statements reflect transactions with outside parties.

Consortium: The joining together of several entities, such as companies or governments, in order to strengthen the possibility of achieving some objective.

Constitutional law: Law that is created and changed by the people.

Consumer ethnocentrism: Refers to preference for local to global, such as seeking out local alternatives when buying products and services.

Contract manufacturer: A company that is responsible for manufacturing and delivering a product on behalf of another company with which it is contracted.

Control systems: Process by which managers compare performance to plans, identify differences, and, where found, assess the basis for the gap and implement corrective action; ensure that activities are completed in ways that support the company's strategy.

Controlled foreign corporation (CFC): A foreign corporation of which more than 50 percent of the voting stock is owned by U.S. shareholders (taxable entities that own at least 10 percent of the voting stock of the corporation).

Convergence: Efforts by the FASB and IASC to move toward a common global set of accounting standards.

Coordination: Systems that synchronize the work responsibilities of the value chain so that the company uses its resources efficiently and makes decisions effectively.

Coordination by mutual adjustment: System whereby managers interact extensively with counterparts in setting common goals.

Coordination by plan: System that relies on general goals and detailed objectives to coordinate activities.

Coordination by standardization: System whereby universal rules and procedures that apply to units worldwide, thereby enforcing consistency in the performance of activities in geographically dispersed units.

Core competency: A special outlook, skill, capability, or technology that runs through the firm's operations, weaving together disparate value activities into an integrated value chain.

Cosmopolitanism: This refers to openness to the world; also refers to a situation in which people seek out foreign alternatives.

Cost leadership: Strategy whereby a firm sells its products at the average industry price to earn a profit higher than that of rivals or below the average industry prices to capture market share.

Cost-plus strategy: The strategy of pricing at a desired margin over cost.

Countertrade (or offsets): A requirement that an exporter create value in the importing country, such as by transferring technology or receiving payment in the importing country's merchandise. An umbrella term for several sorts of trade, such as barter or offset, in which the seller accepts goods or services, rather than currency or credit, as payment.

Country of origin: Where products or services are created, which affects trade in that consumers may prefer to buy goods produced in one country rather than another usually because of quality perceptions or because of nationalism.

Country-similarity theory: The theory that a company will seek to exploit opportunities in those countries most similar to its home country because of the perceived need to make fewer operating adjustments.

Criminal law: Body of laws dealing with crimes against the public and members of the public.

Cross-licensing: The exchange of technology by different companies.

Cross rate: An exchange rate between two currencies used in the spot market and computed from the exchange rate of each currency in relation to the U.S. dollar.

Cultural collision: A condition that occurs when divergent cultures come in contact with each other.

Cultural distance: The degree to which countries differ from each other as measured by different cultural factors; the greater the difference, the greater the distance.

Cultural imperialism: Cultural change by imposition.

Culture: The specific learned norms of a group's attitudes, values, and beliefs.

Culture shock: A generalized trauma one experiences in a new and different culture because of having to learn and cope with a vast array of new cues and expectations.

Currency swap: The exchange of principal and interest payments.

Current-rate method: A method of translating foreign-currency financial statements that is used when the functional currency is that of the local operating environment.

Customs broker: The profession that involves helping importers and exporters clear shipments through a nation's customs agencies.

Customary law system: A legal system anchored in the wisdom of daily experience or great spiritual or philosophical traditions.

Deal-focus (DF) culture: A culture where people are primarily task-oriented rather than relationship-oriented.

Debt: The total of a government's financial obligations, measures what the state borrows from its citizens, foreign organizations, foreign governments, and international institutions.

Decentralization: The degree to which lower-level managers, usually at or below the country level, make and implement strategic decisions.

Deflation: A decrease in the general price level of goods and services; often caused by a reduction in the supply of money or credit.

Democracy: A political system that relies on citizens' participation in the decision-making process.

Deontological approach: An approach which asserts that moral reasoning occurs independent of consequences.

***Dependencia* theory:** This holds that emerging economies have practically no power in their dealings with MNEs.

Derivative: A foreign-exchange instrument such as an option or futures contract that derives its value from the underlying currency.

Diamond of national competitive advantage theory: A theory that says countries usually need four conditions (demand; factors; related and supporting industries; and strategy, structure, and rivalry) to develop and sustain a product's competitive advantage.

Differentiation: A business strategy in which a company tries to gain a competitive advantage by providing a unique product or service, or providing a unique brand of customer service.

Digitization: The conversion of paper and other media in existing collections to digital form.

Direct exports: Products sold to an independent party outside of the exporter's home country.

Direct quote: A quote expressed in terms of the number of units of the domestic currency given for one unit of a foreign currency.

Dispersed configuration: The design of a value chain whereby a particular activity is performed in many geographic locations and serves the world market from any to all of its units.

Distribution: The physical path or legal title that goods take from production to consumption.

Diversification strategy: A term used in international business to describe a strategy whereby a company moves rapidly into many markets and gradually increases its commitments within each one.

Divisional structures: An organization that contains separate divisions based around individual product lines or based on the geographic areas of the markets served.

Draft (or commercial bill of exchange): An instrument of payment in inter-national business that instructs the importer to forward payment to the exporter.

Dumping: The underpricing of exports, usually below cost or below the home-country price.

Dynamic effect: The overall growth in the market and the impact on a company of expanding production and achieving greater economies of scale.

E-commerce: The use of the Internet to join together suppliers with companies and companies with customers.

Economic exposure (operating exposure): The potential for change in expected cash flows that arises from the pricing of products, the sourcing and cost of inputs, and the location of investments.

Economic freedom: The absence of government coercion or constraint on the production, distribution, or consumption of goods and services beyond the extent necessary for citizens to protect and maintain liberty.

Economic Freedom Index: The systematic measurement of economic freedom in countries throughout the world. The survey is sponsored by the Heritage Foundation and the *Wall Street Journal*.

Economic integration: The abolition of economic discrimination between national economies, such as within the EU.

Economic system: The system concerned with the allocation of scarce resources.

Economies of scale: The lowering of cost per unit as output increases because of allocation of fixed costs over more units produced.

Effective tariff: The real tariff on the manufactured portion of developing countries' exports, which is higher than indicated by the published rates because the ad valorem tariff is based on the total value of the products, which includes raw materials that would have had duty-free entry.

Electronic data interchange (EDI): The electronic movement of money and information via computers and telecommunications equipment.

Embargo: A specific type of quota that prohibits all trade.

Emerging economies: Countries with developing economies, often experiencing rapid growth and offering lucrative investment opportunities, but also characterized by political instability and high risk.

Enterprise resource planning (ERP): Software that can link information flows from different parts of a business and from different geographic areas.

Equity alliance: A situation in which a cooperating company takes an equity position (almost always a minority) in the company with which it has a collaborative arrangement.

Escalation of commitment: The more time and money companies invest in examining an alternative, the more likely they are to accept it regardless of its merits.

Essential-industry argument: The argument holding that certain domestic industries need protection for national security purposes.

Ethnocentric framework: A staffing approach in which all key management positions, whether in the home country or abroad, are filled by home country nationals.

Euro: The common currency of the European Union; as of 12/31/09, 16 EU members had adopted the euro, and others were in the process of qualifying for adoption.

Eurobond: A bond sold in a country other than the one in whose currency it is denominated.

Eurocredit: A loan, line of credit, or other form of medium- or long-term credit on the Eurocurrency market that has a maturity of more than one year.

Eurocurrency: Any currency that is banked outside of its country of origin.

Eurocurrency market: An international wholesale market that deals in Eurocurrencies.

Eurodollars: Dollars banked outside of the United States.

Euroequity market: The market for shares sold outside the boundaries of the issuing company's home country.

European Central Bank (ECB): Established July 1, 1998, the ECB is responsible for setting the monetary policy and for managing the exchange-rate system for all of Europe since January 1, 1999.

European Monetary System (EMS): A cooperative foreign-exchange agreement involving many members of the EU and designed to promote exchange-rate stability within the EU.

European Monetary Union (EMU): An agreement by participating European Union member countries that consists of three stages coordinating economic policy and culminating with the adoption of the euro.

European terms: The practice of using the indirect quote for exchange rates.

European Union (EU): A form of regional economic integration among countries in Europe that involves a free trade area, a customs union, and the free mobility of factors of production that is working toward political and economic union.

Exchange rate: The price of one currency in terms of another currency.

Expatriate failure: The premature return of an expatriate manager to the home country.

Expatriates: Noncitizens of the country in which they are working.

Expatriate selection: The process of screening executives to find those with the greatest inclination and highest potential for a foreign assignment.

Exporting: The sale of goods or services produced by a company based in one country to customers that reside in a different country.

Export intermediaries: Individuals or companies that assume responsibility for different combinations of finding overseas buyers, sourcing and shipping products, and getting paid on the behalf of a manufacturer. The export intermediary may be a commissioned agent, an export management company (EMC), an export trading company (ETC), an export agent, or a re-marketer.

Export-led development: An industrialization policy emphasizing industries that will have export capabilities.

Export plan: Specification of the key issues that shape the success of exporting.

Export tariff: A tax on goods leaving a country.

Extranet: The use of the Internet to link a company with outsiders.

Extraterritoriality: The extension by a government of the application of its laws to foreign operations of companies.

Factor-mobility theory: The movement of factors of production such as labor and capital from one location to another.

Factor-proportions theory: The theory that differences in a country's proportionate holdings of factors of production (land, labor, and capital) explain differences in the costs of the factors and that export advantages lie in the production of goods that use the most abundant factors.

Favorable balance of trade: An indication that a country is exporting more than it imports.

Financial Accounting Standards Board (FASB): The private-sector organization that sets financial accounting standards in the United States.

First-mover advantage: A cost-reduction advantage attained through moving into a foreign market ahead of competitors.

Fisher Effect: The theory about the relationship between inflation and interest rates; for example, if the nominal interest rate in one country is lower than that in another, the first country's inflation should be lower so that the real interest rates will be equal.

Five-forces model: A framework used to assess industry structure and business strategy in estimating the potential for profitability.

Flexpatriates: An employee who conducts an international assignment through frequent international business travel from his home market rather than relocating to the host market.

Foreign bond: A bond sold outside of the borrower's country but denominated in the currency of the country of issue.

Foreign Corrupt Practices Act (FCPA): A law that criminalizes certain types of payments by U.S. companies, suchas bribes to foreign government officials.

Foreign direct investment (FDI): An investment that gives the investor a controlling interest in a foreign company.

Foreign exchange: Checks and other instruments for making payments in another country's currency.

Foreign-exchange control: A requirement that an individual or company must apply to government authorities for permission to buy foreign currency above some determined threshold amount.

Foreign-exchange market: The market where foreign exchange is traded; usually banks, non-bank financial institutions, and exchanges, such as the CME.

Foreign trade zone (FTZ): A government-designated area in which goods can be stored, inspected, or manufactured without being subject to formal customs procedures until they leave the zone.

Forward discount: The amount by which the forward rate in a foreign currency is less than the spot rate, that is, the foreign currency is expected to weaken in the future.

Forward premium: The amount by which the forward rate in a foreign currency is greater than the spot rate, that is, the foreign currency is expected to weaken in the future.

Franchising: A specialized form of licensing in which one party (the franchisor) gives permission to an independent party (the franchisee) the use of a trademark that is an essential asset for the franchisee's business and also gives continual assistance in the operation of the business.

Freight forwarder: A company that facilitates the movement of goods from one country to another.

Functional currency: The currency of the primary economic environment in which an entity operates; useful in helping a firm determine how to translate its foreign currency financial statements into the current of the parent company.

Functional structure: An organization that is structured according to functional areas of business.

Fundamental forecasting: A forecasting tool that uses trends in economic variables to predict future exchange rates.

Future orientation: An orientation where people invest for the future and delay instant gratification.

Futures contract: An agreement between two parties to buy or sell a particular currency at a particular price on a particular future date, as specified in a standardized contract to all participants in that currency futures exchange.

FX swap: A simultaneous spot and forward transaction in foreign exchange.

Gap analysis: A tool used to discover why a company's sales of a given product are less than the market potential in a country; the reason may be a usage, competition, product line, or distribution gap.

General Agreement on Tariffs and Trade (GATT): A multilateral arrangement aimed at reducing barriers to trade, both tariff and nontariff ones; at the signing of the Uruguay round, the GATT was designated to become the World Trade Organization (WTO).

Generally Accepted Accounting Principles (GAAP): The accounting standards accepted by the accounting profession in each country as required for the preparation of financial statements for external users.

Generic: Any of a class of products, rather than the brand of a particular company; also relates to pharmaceutical products which have lost patent protection and can be sold by any company under a name that is different from the original branded name.

Geocentric framework: Staffing perspective that seeks the best people for key jobs throughout the organization, regardless of nationality.

Gini coefficient: A measure of the extent to which the distribution of income deviates from a perfectly equal distribution.

Globality: The state of affairs where one competes with everyone, from everywhere, for everything.

Global integration: The unification of distinct national economic systems into one global market.

Globalization: The broadening set of interdependent relationships among people from different parts of a world that happens to be divided into nations. The term sometimes refers to the integration of world economies through the reduction of barriers to the movement of trade, capital, technology, and people.

Global strategy: A strategy that increases profitability by achieving cost reductions from experience curves and location economies.

Glorecalization: A portmanteau of **Glo**balization-**Re**gionalization-**Localization**; champions consistent global values and customized local tactics within a regional context.

Go-no-go decision: A decision is based on a proposal's meeting a specific threshold rather than comparing it with other alternatives.

Gray market: The handling of goods through unofficial distributors.

Great by choice: The principle that managers' choices are the basis of building and sustaining a high-performance enterprise in unpredictable, tumultuous, and fast-moving times.

Green economics: Transdisciplinary field that studies the interdependence and coevolution of human economies and natural ecosystems.

Gross national income (GNI): Formerly referred to as Gross national product.

Gross national product (GNP): The total of incomes earned by residents of a country, regardless of where the productive assets are located.

Gulf Cooperation Council: A subset of the Arab League countries that basically includes Bahrain, Saudi Arabia, Kuwait, Oman, Qatar, and the UAE.

Happynomics: Evaluating a country's performance and potential by directly considering peoples' life satisfaction.

Hard currency: A currency that is freely traded without many restrictions and for which there is usually strong external demand; often called a freely convertible currency.

Harvesting (or divesting): Reduction in the amount of investment. Also known as divestment.

Hedge fund: An investment fund available to a limited number of investors that is managed more aggressively than mutual funds.

Hierarchy-of-needs theory: A well-known motivation theory stating that there is a hierarchy of needs and that people must fulfill the lower-order needs sufficiently before they will be motivated by the higher-order ones.

High-context culture: A culture in which most people consider that peripheral and indirect information is necessary for decision making because such information bears on the context of the situation.

Home-country nationals: Expatriate employees who are citizens of the country in which the company is headquartered.

Horizontal differentiation: The process of specifying, dividing, and assigning organizational tasks.

Human resource management (HRM): The staffing function of the organization; includes the activities of human resources planning, recruitment, selection, performance appraisal, compensation, retention, and labor relations.

Idealism: Trying to determine principles before settling small issues.

Importing: The purchase of products by a company based in one country from sellers that reside in another.

Import (or export) license: A method of government control of the exchange rate whereby all recipients, exporters, and others who receive foreign exchange are required to sell to the central bank at the official buying rate.

Import substitution: An industrialization policy whereby new industrial development emphasizes products that would otherwise be imported.

Import tariff: A tax on goods entering a country.

Income distribution: The distribution of national income among groups of individuals, households, social classes, or factors of production.

Incremental internalization: The view that as a company gains experience, resources, and confidence, it progressively exports to increasingly distant and dissimilar countries.

Indirect exports: Exports that are not handled directly by the manufacturer or producer but through an export agent, freight forwarder, or 3PL.

Indirect quote: An exchange rate given in terms of the number of units of the foreign currency for one unit of the domestic currency.

Individualism: An emphasis on the importance of guaranteeing individual freedom and self-expression. Encourages fulfilling leisure time and improving skills outside the organization.

Industrial clusters: When buyers and sellers locate close to each other to facilitate doing business.

Industrialization argument: A rationale for protectionism that argues that the development of industrial output should come about even though domestic prices may not become competitive on the world market.

Industry organization (IO) paradigm: Field of economics that studies the strategic behavior of firms, the structure of markets, and their interactions.

Industry structure: The makeup of an industry: its number of sellers and their size distribution, the nature of the product, and the extent of barriers to entry.

Infant-industry argument: The position that holds that an emerging industry should be guaranteed a large share of the domestic market until it becomes efficient enough to compete against imports.

Inflation: A general and progressive increase in prices.

Integration-Responsiveness (IR) Grid: Schema that helps managers measure the global and local pressures that influence the configuration and coordination of value chains.

Intellectual property (IP): Property in the form of patents, trademarks, service marks, trade names, trade secrets, and copyrights.

Intellectual property rights: Ownership rights to intangible assets, such as patents, trademarks, copyrights, and know-how.

Interbank transactions: Foreign-exchange transactions that take place between commercial banks.

Interest arbitrage: Investing in debt instruments in different countries to take advantage of interest differentials. The investment is "covered" if the investor converts money into foreign exchange at the spot rate, invests it in the foreign market at a higher interest rate, and enters into a forward contract so that it can convert principle and interest back into the home currency and earn more than if that money had been invested in the home currency.

Internalization: Control through self-handling of foreign operations, primarily because such control is less expensive to deal with in the same corporate family than to contract with an external organization.

International Accounting Standards Board (IASB): The international private-sector organization that sets financial accounting standards for worldwide use.

International business: All commercial transactions involving of two or more countries.

International Financial Reporting Standards (IFRS): A set of accounting standards often known by the older name of International Accounting Standards (IAS). They are issued by the International Accounting Standards Board (IASB).

International Fisher Effect (IFE): The theory that the relationship between interest rates and exchange rates implies that the currency of the country with the lower interest rate will strengthen in the future.

International Monetary Fund (IMF): A multigovernmental association organized in 1945 to promote exchange-rate stability and to facilitate the international flow of currencies.

International Organization of Securities Commissions (IOSCO): An international organization of securities regulators that supports the efforts of the IASB to establish comprehensive accounting standards.

International Organization for Standardization (ISO): An international non-governmental organization headquartered in Geneva that publishes industrial and commercial standards.

International strategy: The effort of managers to create value by transferring core competencies from the home market to foreign markets in which local competitors lack those competencies.

Intranet: The use of the Internet to link together the different divisions and functions inside a company.

Jamaica Agreement: A 1976 agreement among countries that permitted greater flexibility of exchange rates, basically formalizing the break from fixed exchange rates.

Joint venture: An investment in which two or more companies share the ownership.

Kyoto Protocol: The international agreement among countries to reduce the emission of green house gasses.

Lag strategy: An operational strategy that involves either delaying collection of foreign-currency receivables if the currency is expected to strengthen or delaying payment of foreign-currency payables when the currency is expected to weaken; the opposite of a lead strategy.

Laissez-faire: The concept of minimal government intervention in a society's economic activity.

Lead strategy: An operational strategy that involves either collecting foreign-currency receivables before they are due when the currency is expected to weaken or paying foreign-currency payables before they are due when the currency is expected to strengthen; the opposite of a lag strategy.

Legal system: The rules that regulate behavior, the processes that enforce the laws of a country, and the procedures used to resolve grievances.

Letter of credit (L/C): A precise document by which the importer's bank extends credit to the importer and agrees to pay the exporter.

Leverage: The amount of debt used to finance a firm's assets.

Liability of foreignness: Foreign companies' lower survival rate in comparison to local companies for many years after they begin operations.

Licensing agreement: Agreement whereby one company gives rights to another for the use, usually for a fee, of such assets as trademarks, patents, copyrights, or other know-how.

Liquidity preference: A theory that helps explain capital budgeting and, when applied to international operations, means that investors are willing to take less return in order to be able to shift the resources to alternative uses.

Local content: A term used in trade agreements which refers to the percentage of a product which is produced in the member countries to the agreement. Preferential tariff provisions often depend on the amount of local or regional content included in a product.

Localization: Process whereby an expatriate retains a foreign assignment provided she accept the status, and corresponding compensation, of a local hire.

Local responsiveness: The process of disaggregating a standardized whole into differentiated parts to improve responsiveness to local market circumstances.

Location economies: Cost advantages arising from performing a value activity in the optimal location.

Logistics (or materials management): That part of the supply chain process that plans, implements, and controls the efficient, effective flow and storage of goods, services, and related information from the point of origin to the point of consumption, to meet customers' requirements; sometimes called materials management.

London Inter-Bank Offered Rate (LIBOR): The interest rate for large interbank loans of Eurocurrencies.

Low-context culture: A culture in which most people consider relevant only information that they receive firsthand and that bears very directly on the decision they need to make.

Management contract: An arrangement whereby one company provides management personnel, who perform general or specialized management functions, to another company for a fee.

Market capitalization: A common measure of the size of a stock market, which is computed by multiplying the total number of shares of stock listed on the exchange by the market price per share.

Market control: System whereby an MNE uses external market mechanisms to establish internal performance benchmarks and standards.

Market economy: An economic system in which resources are allocated and controlled by consumers who "vote" by buying goods; emphasizes minimal government involvement.

Masculinity–femininity index: An index comparing countries' norms on empathy for successful achievers versus the unfortunate, preference for being better than others versus being on a par with them, belief that it's better "to live to work" versus "to work to live," preference for performance and growth versus quality of life and the environment, and belief that gender roles should be different versus similar.

Materialism: Motivation for material wealth or gains; also refers to the importance of acquiring possessions as a means of self-satisfaction and happiness, as well as for the appearance of success.

Matrix structure: An structure in which foreign units report (by product, function, or area) to more than one group, each of which shares responsibility over the foreign unit.

Mercantilism: An economic philosophy based on the beliefs that a country's wealth is dependent on its holdings of treasure, usually in the form of gold, and that countries should export more than they import in order to increase wealth.

Merchandise export: A good sent out of a country.

Merchandise import: A good brought into a country.

MERCOSUR: A major subregional group established by Argentina, Brazil, Paraguay, and Uruguay, which spun off from ALADI in 1991 with the goal of setting up a customs union and common market. Venezuela has applied for membership.

Misery index: The sum of a country's inflation and unemployment rate.

Mixed economy: An economic system characterized by some mixture of market and command economies; balances public and private ownership of factors of production.

Mixed legal system: A legal system that emerges when two or more legal systems function in a country.

Mixed structure: A structure that integrates various aspects of classical structures.

Monochronic (approach to multitasking): A culture in which most people prefer to deal with situations sequentially (especially those involving other people), such as finishing with one customer before dealing with another.

Most-favored-nation (MFN) clause: A GATT (and now a WTO) requirement that a trade concession that is given to one country must be given to all other countries.

Multicultural: An individual who has internalized more than two national cultures because of holding dual nationalities, having parents from another country, or having lived abroad at an impressionable age.

Multidomestic strategy: An approach that emphasizes responsiveness to the unique conditions prevailing in different national markets.

Multinational corporation or company (MNC): A company that has operations in more than one country; sometimes used simultaneously with multinational corporation or company or transnational corporation.

Multinational enterprise (MNE): A company that has operations in more than one country; sometimes used simultaneously with multinational corporation or company or transnational corporation.

Multiple exchange-rate system: A means of foreign-exchange control whereby the government sets different exchange rates for different transactions.

Mutual recognition: The principle that a foreign registrant that wants to list and have its securities traded on a foreign stock exchange need only provide information prepared according to the GAAP of the home country.

NASDAQ OMX: The third-largest options market in the United States which pioneered a hybrid from of trading involving both traditional floor and online trading.

Natural advantage: Climatic conditions, access to certain natural resources, or availability of labor, which gives a country an advantage in producing some product.

Neoclassical structure: Applies different devices to resovlve the shortcomings, such as conformity, rigidity, bureaucracy, and authoritarism, often found in the classical formats of functional and divisional structures.

Neomercantilism: The approach of countries that apparently try to run favorable balances of trade in an attempt to achieve some social or political objective.

Net present value: The sum of the present values of the annual cash flows minus the initial investment.

Netting: The transfer of funds from subsidiaries in a net payable position to a central clearing account and from there to the accounts of the net receiver subsidiaries.

Network structure: Neoclassical structure whereby a small core organization outsources value activities to linked firms whose core competencies support greater innovation.

Nontradable goods: Products and services that are seldom practical to export, primarily because of high transportation costs.

Normativism: A theory stating that universal standards of behavior (based on people's own values) exist that all cultures should follow, making nonintervention unethical.

North American Free Trade Agreement (NAFTA): A free trade agreement involving the United States, Canada, and Mexico that went into effect on January 1, 1994, and will be phased in over a period of 15 years.

NYSE Liffe: The global derivatives business of the NYSE Euronext Group.

Offer (sell): The amount for which a foreign-exchange trader is willing to sell a currency.

Offshore financial centers (OFCs): Cities or countries that provide large amounts of funds in currencies other than their own and are used as locations in which to raise and accumulate cash.

Offshore financing: The provision of financial services by banks and other agents to nonresidents.

Offshoring: The process of shifting production to a foreign country.

Offshore manufacturing: Any investment that takes place in a country other than the home country.

Oligopolistic reaction: The process in oligopoly industries for competitors to emulate each other, such as going to the same locations.

Optimum-tariff theory: The argument that a foreign producer will lower its prices if an import tax is placed on its products.

Option: A foreign-exchange instrument that gives the purchaser the right, but not the obligation, to buy or sell a certain amount of foreign currency at a set exchange rate within a specified amount of time.

Operations: The conversion of inputs into outputs.

Operations management: Activities in the value chain that occur within the company.

Organization: The specification of the framework for work, development of the systems that coordinate and control what work is done, and the cultivation of common workplace culture among employees.

Organization culture: The shared meaning and beliefs that shape how employees interpret information, make decisions, and implement actions.

Organization of Petroleum Exporting Countries (OPEC): A producers' alliance among 12 petroleum-exporting countries that attempt to agree on oil production and pricing policies.

Organization structure: The formal arrangement of roles, responsibilities, and relationships within an organization.

Outright forward transaction: A forward contract that is not connected to a spot transaction.

Outsourcing: Where one company contracts with another company to perform certain functions, including manufacturing and back office operations. May be done in or close to the company's home country (nearshoring) or in another country (offshoring).

Pacific Alliance: An alliance initially comprising the relatively open and free market economies of Mexico, Columbia, Peru, and Chile with hopes of appearing more hospitable to trade and investment.

Pan Arab Free Trade Area (PAFTA): An FTA of Arab countries created to reduce trade barriers among its member countries. Its members span North Africa (Egypt, Tunisia, Sudan, Libya, and Morocco) and the Middle East (UAE, Bahrain, Jordan, Saudi Arabia, Syria, Iraq, Oman, Palestine, Qatar, Kuwait, Lebanon, and Yemen).

Par value: The benchmark value of a currency, originally quoted in terms of gold or the U.S. dollar and now quoted in terms of Special Drawing Rights.

Payback period: The number of years required to recover the initial investment made.

Peg: To fix a currency's exchange rate to some benchmark, such as another currency.

Penetration strategy: A strategy of introducing a product at a low price to induce a maximum number of consumers to try it.

Pluralism: Belief that there are multiple opinions about an issue, each of which contains part of the truth, but none that contain the entire truth.

Political freedom: The right to participate freely in the political process.

Political ideology: The body of complex ideas, theories, and aims that constitute a sociopolitical program.

Political risk: Potential changes in political conditions that may cause a company's operating positions to deteriorate.

Political spectrum: A conceptual structure that specifies and organizes various types of political ideologies.

Political system: The system designed to integrate a society into a viable, functioning unit.

Polycentric framework: A staffing policy whereby a company relies on host country nationals to manage operations in their own country, while parent-country nationals staff corporate headquarters.

Polychronic (approach to multitasking): A culture in which most people are more comfortable dealing simultaneously with multiple situations facing them.

Portfolio investment: An investment in the form of either debt or equity that does not give the investor a controlling interest.

Poverty: Multidimensional condition in which a person or community lacks the essentials for a minimum standard of well-being and life.

Power distance: A measurement of preference for consultative versus autocratic styles of management.

Pragmatic: Settling small issues before deciding on principles.

Primary activities: The line activities that comprise the value chain. Specifically, inbound logistics, operations, outbound logistics, marketing, and service.

Private technology exchange (PTX): An online collaboration model that brings manufacturers, distributors, value-added resellers, and customers together to execute trading transactions and to share information about demand, production, availability, and more.

Product diversion: *See* Gray market.

Product life cycle (PLC) theory: The theory that certain kinds of products go through a cycle consisting of four stages (introduction, growth, maturity, and decline) and that the location of production will shift internationally depending on the stage of the cycle.

Protectionism: Government restrictions on imports and occasionally on exports that frequently give direct or indirect subsidies to industries to enable them to compete with foreign production either at home or abroad.

Pull: A promotion strategy that sells consumers before they reach the point of purchase, usually by relying on mass media.

Push: A promotion strategy that uses direct selling techniques.

Purchasing power parity (PPP): A theory that explains exchange-rate changes as being based on differences in price levels in different countries. Also, the number of units of a country's currency to buy the same products or services in the domestic market that U.S. $1 would buy in the United States.

Quality: Meeting or exceeding the expectations of a customer.

Quota: A limit on the quantitative amount of a product allowed to be exported from or imported into a country.

Reconciliation: The process of a foreign country reconciling its home country GAAP with U.S. GAAP.

Reflation: The act of increasing the money supply.

Regional integration: A form of integration in which a group of countries located in the same geographic proximity decide to cooperate.

Relationship-focus (RF) culture: A culture where people put dealings with friends ahead of business dealings.

Relativism: A theory stating that ethical truths depend on the groups holding them, making intervention by outsiders unethical. The belief that behavior has meaning and can be judged only in its specific cultural context.

Repatriation: An expatriate's return to his or her home country.

Reshoring: A situation in which a firm brings operations *back* to its home country from abroad.

Resource-based view (of the firm): A perspective that holds that each company has a unique combination of competencies.

Reverse-expat: A local manager who directs a Western-based company's emerging-market business and is rotated through some of the company's established operations outside of that market before returning home.

Reverse culture shock: The experience of culture shock when returning to one's own country that is caused by having accepted what was experienced abroad.

Royalty: Payment for the use of intangible assets.

Rule of law: The principle that every member of a society must follow the same laws.

Rule of man: Notion that the word and whim, no matter how arbitrary, of the ruler are law.

Scanning: Examining a variety of variables for different countries that may affect foreign investment alternatives.

Serendipity: Refers to the trigger of so-called accidental exporters who, responding to happenstance or odd circumstances, enter overseas markets by chance.

Service export: Internationally paid earnings other than those derived from exporting a tangible good.

Service import: International payments for an import other than for a tangible good.

Sight draft: A commercial bill of exchange that requires payment to be made as soon as it is presented to the party obligated to pay.

Silent language: The wide variety of cues other than formal language by which messages can be sent.

Six Sigma: A highly focused system of quality control that uses data and rigorous statistical analysis to identify "defects" in a process or product, reduce variability, and achieve as close to zero defects as possible.

Skimming strategy: Charging a high price for a new product by aiming first at consumers willing to pay that price and then progressively lowering the price.

Small and medium-sized enterprise (SME): Companies whose headcount or sale turnover falls below certain thresholds; in the United States, companies that employ fewer than 500 employees. Commonly expressed as "SME."

Smithsonian Agreement: A 1971 agreement among countries that resulted in the devaluation of the U.S. dollar, revaluation of other world currencies, a widening of exchange-rate flexibility, and a commitment on the part of all participating countries to reduce trade restrictions; superseded by the Jamaica Agreement of 1976.

Socialism: A system based on public ownership of the means of production and distribution of wealth.

Soft (or weak) currency: A currency that is usually not fully convertible. Often these currencies are unstable and not very liquid.

Sourcing: The strategy that a company pursues in purchasing materials, components, and final products; sourcing can be from domestic and foreign locations and from inside and outside the company.

Sovereignty: A nation's intrinsic freedom from external (foreign) control.

Sovereign wealth fund (SWF): A pool of money from a country's reserve which is set aside for investment purposes.

Special drawing right (SDR): A unit of account issued to countries by the International Monetary Fund to expand their official reserves bases.

Specific duty: A duty (tariff) assessed on a per-unit basis.

Speculation: The buying or selling of foreign currency with the prospect of great risk and high return.

Spillover effect: Situation in which the marketing program in one country results in awareness of the product in other countries.

Spot rate: An exchange rate quoted for immediate delivery of foreign currency, usually within two business days.

Spot transactions: Foreign exchange transactions involving the exchange of currency the second day after the date on which the two foreign-exchange traders agree to the transaction.

Spread: In the forward market, the difference between the spot rate and the forward rate; in the spot market, the difference between the bid (buy) and offer (sell) rates quoted by a foreign-exchange trader.

Staffing framework: A systems view that articulates the internal structures and mechanisms of human resource management.

Stakeholders: The collection of groups, including stockholders, employees, customers, and society at large, that a company must satisfy to survive.

State capitalism: An economic system whereby the state decides how, when, and where assets will be valued and resources allocated.

Static effect: The shifting of resources from inefficient to efficient companies as trade barriers fall.

Strategic alliance: An agreement between companies that is of strategic importance to one or both companies' competitive viability.

Strategic trade policy: The identification and development of target industries to be competitive internationally.

Strategy: Management's idea on how to best attract customers, operate efficiently, compete effectively, and create value. Guides building and sustaining the company's competitive position within its industry.

Subpart F (or passive) income: Income of a CFC that comes from sources other than those connected with the active conduct of a trade or business, such as holding company income.

Subsidy: Direct assistance from governments to companies to make them more competitive.

Supply chain: The coordination of materials, information, and funds from the initial raw material supplier to the ultimate customer.

Support activities: The general infrastructure of the firm that anchors the day-to-day execution of the primary activities of the value chain.

Sustainability: The ability to meet the needs of the present without compromising the ability of future generations to meet their own needs, while taking into account what is best for the people and the environment.

Sustainable development: Use of resources use that meet present needs while preserving ability of future generations to do the same.

Syndication: Cooperation by a lead bank and several other banks to make a large loan to a public or private organization.

Tariff (or duty): A government tax levied on goods, usually imports, shipped internationally.

Technical forecasting: A forecasting tool that uses past trends in exchange rates themselves to spot future trends in rates.

Teleological approach: An approach based on the idea that decisions are made based on the consequences of the action.

Temporal method: A method of translating foreign-currency financial statements used when the functional currency is that of the parent company.

Terms currency: In a foreign exchange quote, the base currency is 1 and the terms currency gives you the number of units of that currency per one unit of the base currency. If a foreign exchange trader quotes USD/JPY, the dollar is the base currency and the yen is the terms currency. The quote will give you the number of Japanese yen per U.S. dollar. The quote is also shown as USDJPY=X.

Terms of trade: The quantity of imports that can be bought by a given quantity of a country's exports.

Theocratic law: A situation whereby a nation's legal system is based on whatever religious text the ruling religion abides by.

Theory of country size: A theory holding that large countries usually depend less on trade than small ones.

Third wave of democratization: Expression to capture the collective set of nations that moved from nondemocratic to democratic political systems during the 1970s through the 1990s.

Third-country nationals: Expatriates who are neither citizens of the country in which they are working nor citizens of the country where the company is headquartered.

Third-party logistics (3PL): Agents that develop state-of-the-art technology to help companies understand trade practices, identify opportunities, manage risks, and shepherd exports and imports from buyers to sellers.

Time draft: A commercial bill of exchange calling for payment to be made at some time after delivery.

Total quality management (TQM): The process that a company uses to achieve quality, where the goal is elimination of all defects.

Totalitarian system: A political system characterized by the absence of widespread participation in decision making and suppression of political and civil freedoms.

TQM: *See* Total quality management.

Trade deficit: A situation in which a country imports more than it exports.

Trade surplus: A situation in which a country exports more than it imports.

Transaction exposure: Foreign-exchange risk arising because a company has outstanding accounts receivable or accounts payable that are denominated in a foreign currency.

Transfer price: A price charged for goods or services between entities that are related to each other through stock ownership, such as between a parent and its subsidiaries or between subsidiaries owned by the same parent.

Transit tariff: A tax placed on goods passing through a country.

Translation: The restatement of foreign-currency financial statements into the currency of the parent company.

Translation exposure: Foreign-exchange risk that occurs because the parent company must translate foreign-currency financial statements into the reporting currency of the parent company.

Transnational company (TNC): Usually used as a term that is synonymous with multinational enterprise.

Transnational strategy: Configuring a value chain to exploit location economies as well as coordinate activities to leverage core competencies while simultaneously responding to local pressures.

Treaty of Lisbon: Effective December 1, 2009, this treaty was created to strengthen the EU's governance process and improve its ability to make and implement decisions.

Triad: Refers to the three major economic regions of the world—Europe, North America, and Asia.

Turnkey operation: An operating facility that is constructed under contract and transferred to the owner when the facility is ready to begin operations.

Uncertainty avoidance: A cultural trait where individuals are uncomfortable with uncertainty and prefer structure to independence.

Unemployment rate: The percentage of the workforce that is unemployed at any given date.

Unfavorable balance of trade: An indication of a trade deficit—that is, imports are greater than exports. Also called deficit.

United Nations Conference on Trade and Development (UNCTAD): A UN body that has been especially active in dealing with the relationships between developing and industrialized countries with respect to trade.

Unity-of-command principle: An unbroken chain of command and communication should flow from the CEO to the entry-level worker.

Utilitarianism: A consequences-based approach to moral reasoning that judges an action to be right if it does the most good to the most people.

Value: A measure of a firm's capability to sell what it makes for more than the costs incurred to make it; the ultimate purpose of strategy.

Value chain: The collective activities that occur as a product moves from raw materials through production to final distribution; the disaggregation of value creation.

Vertical differentiation: The specification of the degrees of centralization and decentralization of decision-making in an organization.

Vertical integration: The control of the different stages as a product moves from raw materials through production to final distribution.

Virtual organization: A form of company that acquires strategic capabilities by creating a temporary network of independent companies, suppliers, customers, and even rivals.

Voluntary export restraint (VER): A negotiated limitation of exports between an importing and an exporting country.

World Trade Organization (WTO): A voluntary organization through which groups of countries negotiate trading agreements and which has authority to oversee trade disputes among countries.

Zero defects: The elimination of defects, which results in the reduction of manufacturing costs and an increase in consumer satisfaction.

Company Index

Page references with "*f*" refer to figures, page references with "*m*" refer to maps, page references with "*n*" refer to endnotes cited by number, and page references with "*t*" refer to tables.

3G Capital, 526
3M, 169
7-Eleven, 694n84

ABB, 131
Abbott Laboratories, 169, 233
ABN AMRO, 364
Accenture, 499
Accor, 841
Adidas, 61, 169, 702, 779
Aditya Birla Group, 842
AeroRepublic, 634
African Development Bank, 153
Agatec, 289
A.H. Al Zamil, 634
Ahold, 576
AIG, 694n79
Air Canada, 676
Air France, 60, 247, 644, 767
Airberlin, 645
Airbus, 246, 287, 306, 509, 662, 830
Aldi, 215
Alfred Dunhil, 435
Alibaba, 578, 658
Alliance Oil Company, 419–420, 424
Alsea, 528
Amazon, 433, 498, 587, 604
Amcor, 419
American Airlines (AA), 263, 642, 643*m*, 644–647
American Express, 504
Analytic Graphics, 572, 590, 597
Anheuser-Busch, 717
Apple, 47, 172n8, 173n38, 285, 483, 485, 487, 496, 499, 503–505, 509, 545, 579, 670, 674, 715, 738–742, 745, 747, 749, 751–753, 759, 818
Aramco, 701
ArcelorMittal, 486
Areva, 224n49, 578
Armani, 487
Asian Development Bank, 153
A.T. Kearney, 808
AT&T, 355
Atari, 739
ATT Internet, 760
Avaya, 839
Avon, 625, 719
AvtoVAZ, 621

Baan, 753
Baden-Württemberg, 491
Baidu, 511, 658
Bain Capital Partners, 526
Balanced Scorecard, 676
Bangko Sentral ng Pilipinas (BSP) (Central Bank of the Philippines), 570
Banglalink, 842–846
Bank of America, 773–774
Bank of Japan, 401
Bank of Montreal, 364
Barceló, 614
Barclays Capital, 343, 345
Barings PLC, 360
Baron/Philippe de Rothschild, 625
BASF, 732
BASF Grammeen Ltd., 732
Baxter, 233
Baxter Fenwal North America, 810
BBC, 760
Bechtel, 60, 567, 632
Beijing Orient Electronics, 507
Bembos, 527
Benson & Hedges, 169
Bertelsman, 51
Best Buy, 709
BHP Billiton, 469
Biogas Technology, 442
Blockbuster, 541
Bloomberg, 345, 352, 355, 409, 410
BMP Recycling, 582
BMW, 398, 482, 620, 782*f*, 800
BNP Paribas, 419
The Body Shop International, 463
Boehringer Mannheim, 636
Boeing, 65, 246, 287, 306, 357, 562, 568, 601, 625, 662, 685, 745
Bombardier, 662
Bonlat, 773
Bosch, 482
Boston Consulting Group, 498, 751
Boston Red Sox, 46
BP, 443, 634, 636
Bridgestone, 542
British Airways (BA), 642, 644, 645
British American Tobacco, 151
British East India Company, 628
Bundesbank, 386

Burberry, 169, 717
Burger King, 526–528, 527*m*, 531, 538, 540, 542, 552, 626, 631

Cadbury, 535, 715, 725
Cadbury Schweppe's, 715
Calvin Klein, 698
Canon, 46
Canpotex, 625
Car Shoe, 435
Carlsberg, 46
Carpesian Capital Group, 529
Cartier, 435
Caterpillar, 131, 562
Catfish Institute, 273
Cathay Pacific, 645
Cemex, 486, 659
Center Rock, 50
Chanel, 704
Changan, 622
Chevron Texaco, 468
Chi Mie Optoelectronics, 507
China
Ford Motor, 494
China National Tobacco Company, 706
Chiquita Brands, 538, 701
Chloé, 435–436
Christian Dior, 435, 664
Chrysler, 64, 151, 292
Church's Group, 435
CIGNA, 850n135
Cisco, 184, 503, 659, 667–668, 670–671, 680
Citibank, 343, 355, 367, 508, 513, 694n79
Citigroup Inc., 364, 486, 727, 774
Claimpower, 56–57
CME (Chicago Mercantile Exchange) Group, 345
CNBC, 760
CNN, 760
Coca-Cola, 64, 218, 260, 285, 468, 536, 601, 622, 630, 703, 711, 716, 779, 790–791
Coeur D'Alene Mines, 151
Coffee & More, 569, 597
Cognizant, 667
Colgate, 714
Colgate-Palmolive, 468

Colorplast, 233
Comerci, 424
Compañía Chilena de Fósforos, 702
Cooper Industries PLC, 430
Copa, 634
Corona, 702
COS, 802
Costco, 320, 500, 767
Coty Beauty, 88
Coursera, 686
Cox Internet, 760
Crédit Agricole Corporate and Investment Bank, 419
Credit Suisse, 343, 421, 676
Cryos International, 630
Cummins Engine, 117

Daimler, 779, 780, 784
Daimler-Chrysler, 830
Danone, 638
Dell Computers, 666, 671, 743–744, 750, 754, 757, 799, 801–805
Deloitte, 439n34, 782
Deloitte & Touche, 810
Denso, 753, 757
Dentsu, 508, 567
Deutsche Bank, 343, 345, 355, 364, 366, 419, 671, 727, 774, 784
Deutsche Börse, 422
DHL, 602
Diageo, 526, 666, 707
Dillards, 699
Disney, 60, 115, 454, 624, 685, 698
Disney Channel, 115
Domes International, 570
Domino's Pizza, 528
Dongfeng, 622
Dow Chemical, 666, 839
Dow Jones Thomson Reuters, 760
Dr Pepper, 715
Dubai Ports World, 67–70
Du Pont, 444
Duke Energy, 443
DuPont, 443, 658, 673, 676, 693n32, 759
Duracell, 707

E-Discovery, 497
E&Y, 782
Eastern, 644

Eaton, 430
eBay, 602
EBS, 345, 355
EDF, 224n49
edX, 686
Egon Zehender International, 808
El Al, 99
El Corte Inglés, 699
Eli Lilly, 714
Eni, 634
Enron, 432, 434, 447, 772–776
Ericsson, 59
Essar Ports, 634
Evergreen Solar, 185, 490, 494
Everstone Capital, 529
Evertek Computer, 573
Export Salva Free Zone, 373
Exxon Mobil, 131, 662, 841

Facebook, 466, 658, 830
Fast Retailing, 830
Fedex, 587, 602, 808
Ferrero Rocher, 725
Fiat, 64, 620, 634
Finnair, 645
Firestone, 755
First Security Bank, 409
First Security Corporation, 408
Flextronics, 670
Floating Island International (FII), 457
Foley & Corinna, 170
Ford Motor Corporation, 289, 468, 494, 596, 622, 658, 755, 759, 761
ForEveryBody, 579
Fortis, 513
Foxconn, 172n8, 486, 670, 739, 741, 744, 751, 752
Fresco Group S.A., 373
Fuji Heavy Industries, 636
Fuji Photo, 635
FXConnect, 345

GAIN, 730
Galeries Lafayette, 699
Gap, Inc., 463, 465, 540, 749
Garmine Marine, 590
Gazprom, 419
GCL-Poly Energy, 184, 197
GDF Suez, 224n49
GE Hitachi, 442
General Electric Company (GE), 131, 140, 158, 214, 442–444, 443*m*, 450, 456–457, 466, 489, 499, 513–514, 530, 562, 621, 681, 685, 686, 757–758, 813–814, 821, 841
General Motors (GM), 64, 292, 398, 458, 494, 533, 621, 622, 624, 636, 658, 673, 693n32, 704, 716, 746, 749, 752, 755
Gigante, 533
Gillette, 107, 706
GlakoSmithKline (GSK), 429, 460–461, 465, 470
Glencore International PLC, 436
Global alumina, 634
Global Positioning Solutions (CPS), 409–410
Godiva, 725
Goldman Sachs, 172n5, 343, 355, 526, 567, 817
Goodyear, 482
Google, 314, 421, 430, 433, 499, 500, 509, 511, 672, 673
GPS Capital Markets Inc. (GPS), 352*f*, 408–409, 796
Grameen Bank (GB), 727, 728
Grand Metropolitan, 526
Great Lakes Chemical, 634
Greenland, 614
Groupe Danone, 727, 728, 729
Gruner + Jahr (G + J), 117
Grupo Empresarial Antioqueño, 659, 671
Grupo Hilasal, 373
Gucci, 424, 435, 480
Guinness, 526

Haier, 215, 486
Halliburton, 666
Harvard Law School, 497
Harvey Nichols, 88, 91
Heineken, 45
Hennes & Mauritz (H&M), 478–479, 741, 742, 779
Hermès, 703
Hersheys, 110, 725
Hewlett Packard, 714
Hitachi, 749
Hochtief, 632
Holcim, 538
Home Depot, 707, 715
Hon Hai Precision Industry Co., 568, 738, 739
Honda, 686, 755
Hoteles Sol. *See* Meliá Hotels International
HSBC, 343, 364, 367, 511, 818, 820, 824, 841
Huawei, 163, 167, 504
Hughes Satellite and Internet, 760
Hugo Boss, 168
Humana Milchunion, 637
Hydraulx Visual Effects, 567
Hyundai, 671, 687–691
Iberia, 645–646
IBM, 57, 59, 169, 184, 218, 318, 487, 494, 499, 515, 521n62, 623, 636, 666–668, 671, 680, 694n85, 714, 738, 746, 761, 809, 817, 841
Idealab, 214
IKEA, 94, 134, 161, 464, 506, 716, 749
Inditex Group, 477–478, 480–481
Industrial Perception, 498
Infosys Technologies Limited (Infosys), 57, 508, 659, 667, 679, 686
ING, 360, 364
Intel, 492, 674
International Baseball Federation, 45
Intesa SanPaolo, 435
Invest AD, 420
InvestCorp, 424
Ito-Yokado, 694n84

Japan Airlines (JAL), 642, 643*m*, 644–647
Jarden Zinc Products, 570–571
Java Lounge, 91, 111
JCPenney, 699
J.D. Power & Associates, 755
John Deere, 752
Johnson & Johnson, 508, 511–512, 654–657, 661, 665, 681, 682, 685, 808, 820
José Batista Sobrinho (JBS), 622
JP Morgan, 343, 419, 685

Kajima, 567
Kawasaki Motors Corp., 757
Kellogg's, 707
KFC, 631
Kia, 45
Kimberley Clarke, 707
KINCO, 528
Kleenex, 717
KLM, 644
Kodak, 285
Korea Telecom, 676
KPMG, 759, 782
Kraft, 725
Kyocera, 670

LaCoste, 45, 169
Lactalis Group, 779
LAN, 357, 645
Land Rover, 289
Lean Production, 484
Leap Wireless, 215
Lee Hung Fat Garment Factory, 722
Lego, 554–557, 560n78
Lehman Brothers, 383, 694n79
Lenova, 623, 714
Leo Burnett Worldwide, 715
Levant, 628
Levi Strauss & Co., 463
Lexadigm, 497
LG, 318, 435, 507, 671, 717
Li & Fung, 515, 659
LightInTheBox, 421
Limited Brands, 545
Lincoln, 755
Lindt, 725
Liverpool Football Club, 46, 61, 63
Lockheed Martin, 291, 543, 758
Logitec, 572
Lone Star Funds, 420
L'Oreal, 91
Louis Vuitton, 168, 664
Lucent Technologies, 454
Lufthansa, 644
LUKoil, 701
Luxottica, 435

Macy's, 699
Major League Baseball (MLB), 45
Malaysian Airlines, 645
Manchester United (Man U), 46
Mango, 749
Marks & Spencer, 120, 463, 712
Marriott, 538, 841
Mars, 725
Marshalls, 699
Marvel, 289
Masdar, 459, 460
Maserati SpA, 436
Mattel, 686, 742
McCall's, 117
McDonalds, 61, 88, 99, 392, 526–527, 529, 542, 685–686, 742, 760
McKinsey & Company, 508, 810, 826
Meliá Hotels International, 617, 623, 626, 630, 632
Mercedes-Benz, 482, 620, 755
Merck, 461
Mercosur, 801–805
Merrill Lynch, 637, 694n79
Michelin, 59, 482
Microsoft, 109, 168–169, 314, 451, 499, 680, 716, 738, 820, 826, 830
Migros, 725
Mitsubishi, 634, 670
Mitsui, 659
Mobile Telecommunications Company, 714, 837
Moët & Chandon, 664
Moët Hennessy, 664

Morgan Stanley, 343, 774, 810, 824
Motorola, 134, 214, 685, 750, 757
Mountain High Hosiery, 621
M-Pesa, 515–519
MTV, 115

Nalco, 486
Nanfu, 707
NASA, 188
NASDAQ OMX, 345
Nassional Association for Stock Car Auto Racing, 46
National Basketball Association (NBA), 48
National Intelligence Council, 172n5
Natures Way Foods, 59
Naver, 511, 658
NBC Universal, 442
NEC, 634
Nestlé, 59, 505, 506, 511, 659, 664, 679, 705, 709, 716, 725
Neuhauss, 47
New Balance, 702
New York and Mississippi Valley Printing Telegraph Company, 340. *See also* Western Union
New York Stock Exchange, 356, 400, 526, 784
New York Yankees, 46
New Zealand All Blacks, 46
Newmont Mining Corporation, 755
Nike, 46, 51, 168, 169, 464–465, 503, 670, 679, 702, 708, 742
Nissan, 118, 119, 622, 750
Nokero, 740, 744–745
Nokia, 214, 504, 623, 741, 744, 751, 830, 841
Nortel Networks, 676
North Face, 168
Novartis, 167, 462
Nu Skin, 416
NYSE Euronext, 356
NYSE Liffe, 345, 356

Oakley, 168
Office Tiger, 497
OfficeMax, 289
Old Navy, 478
Olympics, 90
Opus One Winery, 625
Oracle, 169, 680, 753
Oticon, 659
Overseas Private Investment Corporation (OPIC), 153

Pan Am, 644
Pan American Silver, 151
Panalpina, 760
Panasonic, 318, 401, 508, 514
Pangea3, 497
Paris Saint-Germain (PSG) football club, 47
Parmalat, 432, 434, 447, 772–776
PayPal, 658
PDVSA, 701
Pearson, 51
Penguin, 51
People's Bank of China (PBOC), 364, 366
PeopleSoft, 753
PepsiCo, 59, 596
Perdigão, 51
Perry Ellis, 698
Petronas, 66
Peugeot-Citroën, 316, 749
Pfizer, 170, 714
Philip Morris, 151
Philips Electronics, 498, 514, 745, 750
Phillips-Van Heusen (PVH), 698
Piaggio, 745
Pierre Cardin, 637
Pilgrim's Pride, 622
Pillsbury, 526
Pizza Hut, 631
Pollo Campero, 527, 533
Polo Ralph Lauren, 435
Porsche, 755
Prada, 168, 421, 434–437, 480
Price Waterhouse, 172n5
PriceSmart, 543
PricewaterhouseCoopers (PwC), 775, 815, 834
PricewaterhouseCoopers (PwC) China, 494
PricewaterhouseCoopers (PwC) Russia, 808, 839
Procter & Gamble (P&G), 59, 233, 500, 507, 510, 596, 686, 707, 748, 811
Progress Energy, 66
Protek, 233
Prudential Insurance Company of America, 416

Qantas, 645
Qualcomm, 503, 670
Quick, 527

Ralph Lauren, 57, 451, 698
Ranbaxy Laboratories, 486
Rank, 635
Rawlings, 59
Raytheon, 291
RBS Securities Japan Ltd., 225n100, 343
Real Madrid football team, 61
Red Bull, 714
Red Hat, 658, 678, 680
Reebok, 169
Reliability, 233
Remedia, 637
Renault, 118, 119, 224n49, 620, 750, 830
Richemont, 435
Rio Tinto, 662
Ritz-Carlton, 487
Robert Mondavi, 625
Rolex, 45
Royal Bank of Canada, 578
Royal Bank of Scotland, 364, 418, 513, 694n79
Royal Crown, 64
Royal Dutch Shell, 808
Royal Jordanian, 645
RSR, 583

S-Market, 121
S7 Airlines, 645
Sabena, 644
SABMiller, 707
Sacyr Vallehermosa SA, 633*f*
Sadia, 51
Safaricom, 214, 483, 515–519
SAFE Investment Company (China), 420
Safran, 224n49
Sainsburys, 120
SAIV, 622
Saks Fifth Avenue, 91
SAMA Foreign Holdings (Saudi Arabia), 420
Samsonite, 745, 746, 762–767
Samsung, 121, 200–201, 214, 318, 401, 500–501, 504, 568, 578, 625, 671, 741, 830
Sanyo, 318
SAP, 667, 680, 753, 830
Sara Lee, 717, 746–747, 761
Saudi Arabia Airlines, 88, 89
Saudi Arabian General Investment Authority (SAGIA), 91
Schering-Plough, 821, 830
Sears, 658, 693n32, 699
Seco/Warwick, 585
Seiko, 619
Seiyu, 626
Sensortronics, 233
Shanghai Construction Group, 633
Sharp, 46, 318, 751
Shisheido, 507
Shokolanitsa, 529
Siemens AG, 455–456, 676
Singapore Air, 755
Six Sigma, 484, 673–674, 676, 679, 757–758
Skanska AB, 567
Skype, 661
Société Générale, 360
Sol Hotels, 617
Sony, 59, 168–169, 318, 399–404, 500, 520n27, 625, 668, 693n40
SoundCloud, 51
South West Trading, 600
Southwest Airlines, 486, 685
Spectra Colors, 586
SpinCent, 562–564, 567–569, 571, 576–577, 586, 590
Squigle, 575, 576
Standard Chartered PLC, 432
Standard Oil, 693n32
Staples, 289
Starbucks, 88, 392, 433, 487, 504, 526, 567, 626, 672
Stifel Financial, 421
StrawberryFrog, 671
Subway, 526
SumAll, 672
Suzuki, 289, 533
Swift, 622
Swiss Bank Corporation, 355
Swissair, 644

Ta Ann Holdings, 553
Tambrands, 714
Target, 289, 320
Tata, 215, 219, 424, 487, 499, 566, 634
Technicolor, 830
Tesco, 59, 65, 121, 161, 511, 741
in Asia, 121–122
in UK, 121–122
Tesco SUB, 121
Tetra Pak, 772
Thai Union Frozen, 486
Thomson Reuters, 345, 355, 366, 409–410, 418
Tide, 716
T.J. Maxx, 699
TNK, 636
TNT, 587
Tokyo Star Bank, 420
Tokyo Tsushin Kogyo Corporation, 400
Tommy Hilfiger, 621, 698–700, 716
Toshiba, 401, 636, 751
Toxics-Link, 583
Toyota, 64, 302–304, 312, 316, 404, 424, 482, 533, 542, 624, 659, 670, 680, 682, 684, 687, 707, 741, 744, 750, 753, 755, 757, 819
TPG Capital, 526
TracFone, 215
Transparency International, 451, 451*f*

Tristyle Internationl, 722
TWA, 644
Twitter, 175n98, 466

UBS, 343, 345, 567, 694n79, 774
Udacity, 686
UFJ, 637
UGG, 168, 169
Unilever, 332–336, 507, 744, 760
Unipart, 686
Unisys, 686
United Airlines, 46, 111
United Fruit Company (UFC), 628
Universal Genève, 619
UPS, 486, 587, 596, 600, 602
US Airways, 646–647
U.S. Synthetics, 757

Vale, 662
Vellus, 575
Viagra, 169
Vinci, 632
Virgin, 671
Virgin Mobile, 486
Vistaprint, 62
Vodafone, 131
Volkswagen, 59, 319, 543, 553, 619–620, 622, 798, 841

Wall Street Journal, 65, 351, 352, 398
Walmart, 116, 160–161, 215, 304, 319, 333*f*, 424, 451, 499, 521n64, 540, 555, 576, 596, 708, 712, 748–749, 754, 767
Weibo, 175n98
Wells Fargo & Company, 408
Wendy's, 529
Western Union, 340–342, 345, 351
Whirlpool, 620
Wii, 168
Wilson, 45
Wimpy, 526
Wipro, 667, 676, 808, 818, 833
W.L. Gore, 668–669, 679
Wonder Auto, 494
World Bank, 160, 163, 180, 187, 199–201, 204, 212, 225n65, 225n69, 225n71
World Bank Group, 153
World Cup, 44, 46
World Economic Forum, 216
WorldCom, 772
Wyndham, 615

Xerox, 635, 717, 815

Yandex, 658
YouTube, 466
Yue Yuen Industrial, 670, 702
Yum Brands, 526, 529
Yves Saint Laurent, 435

Zara, 476–481, 477*f*, 478*m*, 482, 485–487, 496–500, 504, 507, 659, 741, 749,
Zeiss, 168
Zipcar, 215
ZTE, 163, 167

Name Index

Page references with "*f*" refer to figures, page references with "*m*" refer to maps, page references with "*n*" refer to endnotes cited by number, and page references with "*t*" refer to tables.

Abe, Shinzo, 403
Abu-Nasr, Donna, 126n1
Adamantios, 735n77
Adamy, Janet, 650n56
Aeppel, Timothy, 73n35
Agarwal, James, 734n13
Agarwal, Manoj K., 734n12
Agarwal, Vibhuti, 300n55
Agins, Teri, 733n1
Agle, Bradley R., 472n3
Ahles, Andrea, 651n94
Ahlstrom, David, 651n87, 849n68
Ahmad, Shihab, 845
Ahmed, Azam, 560n57
Ahuja, Manju, 693n50
Airbnb, 215
Akerlof, George, 55
Akolaa, Andrews Adugudaa, 735n66
al Jundi, Nora, 126n1
Alade, Wale, 735n83
Alessandri, Todd M., 558n5
Alfaro, Laura, 176n138
Ali, A.M., 472n22
Aljindi, Omar, 126n1
Allam, Abeer, 126n1
Alam, M Nurul, 846
Allen, Robert, 608n114
Allwood, Carl, 848n37
Alvarez, Lizette, 650n53
Anand, Bharat, 651n81
Anand, Jaideep, 649n19
Anderson, Jamie, 734n52
Anderson, Laura, 809
Andrew, Jim, 751
Andrews, Edmund L., 405n15
Andrews, R., 270n62
Anishchuk, Alexei, 227n143
Antonsson, Erik K., 694n66
Apil Ali Riza, 649n8
Apostopoulos, Yorghos, 269n48
Appel, Rebecca, 848n41
Arbour, Louise, 176n130
Areddy, James T., 651n74
Arendt, Hannah, 173n34
Ariño, Africa, 651n86
Ariss, Sonny, 693n49
Armario, Enrique, 606n27
Armario, Julia, 606n27
Armstrong, Richard, 608n113
Arnst, Catherine, 473n91
Arora, Ashish, 649n15
Arshad, Muhammad, 846
Arthur, W. Brian, 521n70
Asawo, Soye Peniel, 560n60
Asgary, Nader, 128n90
Ashill, Nicholas, 606n12
Assaad, Nizar el, 845
Assche, A. Van, 768n1
Assimakopoulos, Dimitris, 849n75
Asturias, Miguel Angel, 628, 650n49
Attia, Samaa, 735n73
Austen, Ian, 473n59, 734n41
Aviel, David, 560n77
Aw, B., 606n16
Awuah, Gabriel Baffour, 650n31
Axtell, Roger, E., 112*f*
Ayal, Igal, 560n62
Azarian, Mohammad, 175n115

Baci, Vedran, 649n26
Badenhausen, Kurt, 520n40
Bader, Benjamin, 560n59
Bagozzi, Richard P., 735n65
Bahree, Megha, 300n55
Bailey, Nicholas James, 558n11
Bailey, Ronald, 174n60
Bajaj, Vikas, 473n74, 520n29
Bakacsi *et al.*, 127n61
Baker, S., 850n115
Baker, W., 693n44
Balabanis, George, 735n77
Balassa, Bela, 338n11
Balasubramanian, Sridhar, 735n84, 735n85
Ball, Deborah, 734n58
Baluja, Tamara, 605n8
Bandler, James, 128n94
Banerjee, Sanjay, 607n84, 651n79
Barbaro, Michael, 733n1
Barber, Tony, 559n52
Barboza, David, 175n98, 473n71
Barkema, Harry G., 651n77
Barker, Pierre M., 734n28
Barnes, Brooks, 693n39
Barrionuevo, Alexei, 769n18
Barstow, David, 128n88, 176n132
Barta, Patrick, 269n49, 299n21, 338n40
Barta, Thomas, 849n72
Bartlett, Christopher A., 269n25, 522n85, 692n12, 693n28, 694n75, 694n86
Bartmess, Andrew, 559n17
Basañez, Miguel, 126n11,
Bate, Roger, 734n26
Batson, Andrew, 72n4
Battisti, Martina, 607n77
Bauerschmidt, Alan, 606n39, 607n78
Baulch, Helen, 607n61, 607n69
Bauza, Vanessa, 299n25
Beach, William W., 224n30
Beaman, Karen, 694n60, 826*f*
Beamish, Paul W., 559n27, 651n81, 695n97
Bean, Frank D., 270n56
Beattie, Alan, 406n50
Beechler, Schon, 848n28
Beer, Lawrence A., 128n78
Behfar, Kristin, 126n4
Belford, Aubrey, 175n100
Bell, John H. J., 651n77
Bellman, Eric, 650n41
Ben-Atar, Doron S., 176n160
Bendick, Marc Jr., 126n13
Benedict, Jan, 735n72
Bennet, Paul, 736n101
Bennett, Julie, 650n43, 650n57
Bensaou, Ben B., 651n76
Berenbeim, Ronald, 472n11
Berg, Nicola, 560n59
Bergman, Harriet, 128n85
Berk, Jonathan, 438n2
Bernard, Andrew, 606n20, 607n52, 607n54
Bernard, Bruce, 651n94
Bernhagen, Patrick, 174n61
Berry, Heather, 73n42
Bertelli, Patrizio, 434, 435
Bertrab, Alejandra Xanic von, 128n88, 176n132
Bertrand, Olivier, 73n30
Bertsch, Andy, 127n36
Beswick, Paul A., 806n15
Bettina, Merlin, 606n49
Beyonce, 698
Bhagwati, Jagdish, 72n25, 73n56, 649n15
Bhattacharjeethe, Yudhijit, 850n121
Bhattacharya, Arindam, 223n4, 521n50, 693n21
Bianchi, Alessandra, 608n117
Bierly, Paul E., 651n91
Bigness, J., 694n84
Bilas, Vlatka, 649n26
Bills, Steve, 369n22, 369n23
bin Laden, Osama, 432
Birkinshaw, Julian, 472n31, 559n20, 693n23
Birnbaum, Jeffrey H., 298n1
Black, Ervin L., 783*f*
Black, Fisher, 559n31
Black, Thomas, 406n50
Blackstone, Brian, 405n24
Blafour, Frederik, 368n1
Blair, C. Morris, 270n62
Blanc, Luis, 480
Blas, Javier, 299n32
Blazevic, Vera, 734n50
Blazona, Edgar, 600
Bleacher, Liz, 851n155
Bleeke, Joel, 651n65
Blitz, Roger, 72n1
Blossfeld, H.-P., 72n8
Boatright, John R., 472n18, 472n19
Bochner, Stephen, 128n93
Boddewyn, Jean J., 560n69
Bodoni, Stephanie, 338n20
Boland, Vincent, 806n1
Bolino, Mark, 848n43, 849n94, 849n98, 851n149
Bolton, Ruth N., 734n13
Bond, Michael Harris, 127n60, 127n62, 806n3
Bondi, Enrico, 774
Bonilla-Carríon, Roger Enrique, 268n10
Bonnin, A., 519n1
Boonstra, Jaap J., 127n62
Booth, William, 177n169
Borland, Rosilyne Mae, 268n10
Boroditsky, Lera, 850n119
Bouncken, Ricarda B., 128n68
Bowdidge, John S., 369n20
Bowen, Sally, 128n97
Bower, Joseph, 519n12, 521n54
Bowie, David, 698

Boyd, Jens, 519n10
Boyd, Sebastian, 806n1
Boyle, Catherine, 806n1
Bradfield, Owen M., 734n53
Bradshaw, Della, 695n109
Bradsher, Keith, 172n9, 223n14, 223n15, 520n24, 520n38, 521n56, 521n60, 558n11, 734n36, 848n47
Brady, Anne-Marie, 173n41
Brahm, Richard, 269n43
Brain, Cecelia, 73n48
Brannen, Mary Yoko, 120, 128n84, 128n85, 128n99, 128n100, 128n106, 650n27
Braunerhjelm, Pontus, 559n20
Bremmer, Ian, 224n60
Brett, Jeanne, 126n4
Brewer, Paul, 126n13
Bridgewater, Susan, 606n48
Brooke, James, 522n92
Brooks, Chad, 519n14
Brooks, Geraldine, 128n86
Brown, Alan S., 73n32
Brown, David E., 126n6
Brown, Drusilla K., 269n17
Brown, Michelle, 126n12
Browne, Andrew, 223n14, 223n19
Browning, E. S., 337n1
Bruner, Henry, 522n84
Bruni, Carla, 698
Bruton, Garry, 849n68
Bryan, Lowell, 692n10, 694n63
Bryant, Adam, 522n85, 692n17
Bryant, Christa Case, 226n129
Bryla, Pawel, 126n5
Buchholz, S., 72n8
Buckley, Peter J., 337n2, 338n13, 559n26
Buckly, Neil, 650n41
Bulkeley, William M., 72n27
Bull, Christopher, 73n38, 270n57
Burgess, Kate, 649n23
Burke, Donald R., 693n49
Burkitt, Laurie, 439n53, 734n32, 734n43, 735n93
Burns, Judith, 806n1
Burton, Fred, 650n54
Burton, Gary D., 651n87
Bush, George W., 193
Bustillo, Miguel, 769n41
Byrne, Jack A., 522n115, 522n116
Byrne, Patrick, 519n6

Calantone, Roger J., 651n67
Calhoun, David, 444
Caligiuri, Paula, 848n21, 849n80, 851n147, 851n154
Calvo, Guillermo A., 405n10
Cameron, Doug, 651n83
Cannon-Brookes, Michael, 809
Cantwell, John, 559n41
Capelli, Peter, 128n101
Caprar, Dan V., 126n5
Cardwell, Diane, 223n20
Carey, John, 473n55, 473n64
Carey, Susan, 72n17
Carley, Kathleen, 693n50
Carnegie, Dale, 728
Carruthers, R., 519n8
Carson, Johnny, 698
Carter, Ralph G., 300n57
Carter, S., 607n81
Carvajal, Doreen, 850n106
Cary, Loren, 694n65
Cascio, Wayne F., 636*f*, 650–651n65
Casey, Nicholas, 558n12
Cashin, Paul, 338n41
Casselman, Ben, 126n8
Casson, M., 649n10
Castellano, José Maria, 479
Castillo, Michelle, 607n67
Castle, Stephen, 338n21
Caulki, Simon, 520n44
Cavusgil, S., 606n13, 735n81
Cellich, Claude, 734n49
Cento, Arianne, 558n1
Cerdin, J., 851n147
Cerny, Keith, 559n17
Cerruti, Corrado, 559n17
Cervellati, Matteo, 175n95
Chaffin, Joshua, 338n28
Chaichalearmmongkol, Nopparat, 438n7
Chakrabarti, Rajesh, 649n27
Chaloupecky, Kurt E., 369n20
Chan, Chi-fai, 848n54
Chan, Christine M., 558n4, 560n63, 560n68
Chan, Eunice S., 849n68
Chan, Kelvin, 439n53, 735n98
Chandrashekhar, G., 299n35
Chang, Anita, 300n47
Chansarkar, Bal, 735n73
Chao, Chi-Chur, 299n36
Chao, Loretta, 734n51
Chao, Mike Chen-Ho, 735n73
Chari, Anusha, 176n138
Charles, Gemma, 558n1, 734n57
Chase, 769n48, 770n60
Chatterji, Aaron, 73n45
Chung, Se-young, 689
Chea, Terrence, 651n66
Chen, Chao, 849n62
Chen, Homin, 769n5
Chen, Qimei, 733n7
Chen, Tain-Jy, 769n5
Chen, Yu-Ping, 848n43, 849n94, 849n98, 851n149
Cheng, Andria, 560n55, 693n25
Cheosakul, Adith, 127n62
Chetty, Sylvie, 560n64
Ch'ien, Evelyn Nien-Ming, 126n24
Child, John, 649n24
Chintakananda, Asda, 558n5
Chipman, Kim, 471n1
Choi, Jaepil, 849n62
Choi, Yong-Seok, 269n13
Chon, Gina, 128n96
Chooi, Clara, 127n34
Chow, Dan, 173n22
Christensen, Clayton, 519n11, 519n12, 521n54
Chua, C., 851n147
Chung, Se-young, 689
Cienski, Jan, 559n22
Cimilluca, Diana, 73n43
Clagg, Jeremy, 337n2
Clark, Don, 128n71, 269n22
Clark, Kim B., 769n7, 770n51
Clarke, Phillip, 121
Clarke, Ronald V., 299n14
Cleeland, Nancy, 368n1
Clegg, Jeremy, 559n26
Cleveland, Mark, 736n100
Clifford, Stephanie, 176n144, 734n41
Clinton, Bill, 698
Coase, Ronald H., 649n10
Coats, Jack, 176n153
Cochrane, Lauren, 519n1
Cohen, Jack, 120
Cohen, Roger, 174n87, 225n80
Cohen, Sabrina, 806n1
Colchester, Max, 438n11, 438n13
Cole, August, 650n62
Cole-Laramore, Aimee, 693n49
Collier, Joe Guy, 337n1
Collier, Paul, 176n124
Collins, Jim, 520n18, 694n88
Collins, Lauren, 650n53
Colvin, Geoffrey, 694n62
Comer, Lucette B., 128n77
Comte, Auguste, 494
Confucius, 135
Connaghan, Clare, 406n35
Connor, John M., 650n35
Contractor, F., 649n1, 650n47
Cook, Tim, 496, 739
Cookson, Clive, 128n91
Coucke, Kristien, 73n29
Court, David, 226n130
Cowen, Tyler, 128n90
Cramer, Gail L., 299n27
Crawford, David, 472n43, 472n45, 472n49
Crick, D., 606n17
Cross, Adam R., 650n54
Cross, Rob, 849n75
Cross, Sam Y., 368n2, 368n3, 368n7, 368n10, 405n23, 406n40
Crossman, Alf, 693n51
Crow, Sheryl, 698
Crystal, David, 126n22, 350*m*
Cui, Anna Shaojie, 651n67
Cutler, Edward, 575, 576
Cuypers, Ilya R. P., 651n76

da Silva, Lulu, 146
Dada, M., 559n45
Daekwan, Kim, 72n1
Dalton, Mathew, 338n27
Damanpour, Fariborz, 849n62
Damiee, Saeed, 734n18
Daneshkhu, Scherazade, 736n101
Daniels, John D., 559n28, 726–732, 851n160
Darling, John R., 735n90
Das, T. K., 651n84
Da Silva, Luiz Inacio (Lula), 802
D'Aveni, R., 769n24
David, Paul A., 225n77
Davies, Sylvie, 735n87
Davis, Bob, 73n50
Davis, Donald R., 269n14
Davis, Lance, 299n16
Davis, Nick, 439n51
Dawson, Chester, 337n1, 769n26
de Jong, Abe, 438n4, 438n5
de Jong, Martijn, 735n72
de la Baume, Maïa, 128n89
de La Merced, Michael J., 438n11
De Marzo, Peter, 438n2
De Run, Ernest Cyril, 734n57
De Soto, Hernando, 176n125
Dean, James, 698
Dean, Jason, 177n171, 177n172, 223n14, 223n19
Dedrick, Jason, 768n1
Deeny,Godfrey, 770n75
DeGeorge, Richard T., 472n5, 472n6, 472n14
Delbufalo, Emanuela, 559n17
Deligonul, Seyda, 735n81
Delios, Andrew, 649n19, 695n97
Dell, Gillian, 472n33
Demain, Beth, 337n1
Deming, W. Edwards, 756
DeMorro, Christopher, 72n20
Demos, Telis, 438n24
Denbour, C., 559n23
Dermody, Joe, 605n4

Devereaux, Charlie, 406n30
Dewan, Neha, 733n1
Dewhurst, Martin, 173n9, 223n6, 223n18, 520n17, 521n61, 522n95, 692n13, 694n64, 695n96, 849n63, 851n168
Di Santo, Victoria, 848n21, 849n80
Diamantopoulos, Adamantios, 735n74
Dibble, Sandra, 338n29
Dickerson, Marla, 368n1
Dickinson, Barry J., 650n30
Dickmann, M., 851n165
Diderich, Joelle, 733n1
Dimofte, Claudiu V., 735n65
Dittrich, Koen, 650n29
Dobbs, Richard, 186*m*
Doherty, Dermot, 735n94
Doherty, N., 851n165
Dolan, Brian, 368n9
Dolan, Matthew, 299n41
Dollar, David, 269n30
Dolles, Harald, 72n1
Dolven, Ben, 369n20
Domhoff, William, 226n110
Domsch, Michel, 694n72
Donaldson, Thomas, 472n3
Donthu, Naveen, 735n86
Dooren, Jennifer Corbett, 734n31
Dorfman, Peter W., 126n11
Doukas, John A., 559n44
Dow, Douglas, 269n24
Doz, Y., 522n105, 693n45
Drucker, Peter, 692n15
Drummond, James, 560n66
Duanmu, J., 270n60
DuBois, Frank, 769n7
Dufey, Gunter, 406n37
Dunning, John H., 605n9
Durán, J. J., 648n1
Dussauge, Pierre, 650n28
Dutta, Madhumita, 583
Dutta, Soumitra, 520n44
Duysters, Guy, 650n29
Dvorak, Phred, 650n34
Dyer, Geoff, 649n21

Earley, P. Christopher, 127n56
Easterlin, Richard, 225n77
Eberts, Randall W., 298n2
Eccles, R., 693n44
Eden, Lorraine, 72n19, 300n57
Edmondson, Gail, 337n1
Egan, Mary Lou, 126n13
Eichengreen, Barry, 224n35
Einhorn, Bruce, 473n91, 769n31
Eisingerich, Andreas B., 735n63
Eiteman, David K., 806n18
el-Assaad, Nizar, 846
Elhagrasey, Galal, 635*f*
Elhamy, Perihane, 845
Elhamy, Perihane, 844
Ellis, Paul D., 559n32
Ellison, Sarah, 735n60
Elmer-DeWitt, Philip, 768n1
Enderwick, Peter, 558n6
Endresen, Iver, 735n89
Engardio, Pete, 769n31
Engerman, Stanley, 299n16
Enrich, David, 438n8, 438n11, 438n13
Ensinger, Dustin, 223n10, 223n12
Erasmus, Daniel, 694n74
Erdbrink, Thomas, 299n22
Erdem, Tulin, 735n61
Erece, Jonathan, 177n172
Erikson, T., 606n33
Ernst, David, 651n65
Ertug, Gokhun, 651n76
Escarré, Gabriel, 612
Esterl, Mike, 72n1, 73n43, 472n43, 472n45, 472n49
Estevadeordal, Antoni, 269n13
Etter, Lauren, 72n11
Ettorre, Barbara, 847n4
Evans, Ben, 298n1
Evans, Nathan, 176n156
Evans, Paul, 405n25
Evans-Pritchard, Ambrose, 227n143
Ewing, Jack, 338n24, 338n25, 472n47, 472n50, 473n61, 769n11
Ezema, Benedict, 299n6

Fackler, Martin, 695n100, 695n102, 695n111
Fairbairn, Ursula, 694n87
Fairgrieve, Duncan, 176n142
Fairlamb, David, 368n1
Fang, Ying, 369n24
Farrell, Diana, 521n58
Fassihi, Farnaz, 299n18
Fattah, Hassan, 175n96
Faucon, Benoît, 559n53
Faulkner, David, 649n24
Fawcett, Stanley E., 769n6, 769n16, 769n34, 770n74
Feenstra, Robert C., 73n31
Felsted, Andrea, 733n10
Feng, Li, 612
Fenn, Donna, 695n105
Fernandez, Dennis, 176n145, 733n1
Fernhaber, Stephanie A., 72n14
Ferraris, Alberto, 772
Field, Alan M., 338n35, 338n37
Filippov, Sergery, 649n20
Fingar, Courtney, 608n105
Finkel, Michael, 734n26
Fisher, Anne, 471n1
Fisk, Margaret Cronin, 692n1
Fitzgerald, Drew, 733n1
Fitzgerald, Michael, 736n101
Fitzpatrick, Jonathan, 558n1
Fitzpatrick, William M., 693n49
Flamholtz, Eric, 694n87
Fletcher, Owen, 177n171, 177n172
Flint, Robert, 406n50
Flood, Chris, 734n45
Flores, Ricardo Gabriel, 560n71
Florescu, Elizabeth, 225n88, 520n42, 522n83
Florida, Richard, 174n82
Flowers, Edward B., 559n47
Flyer, Fredrick, 559n49
Flynn, J. Laurie, 607n59
Fogel, Robert, 65, 172n5
Folk-Williams, Sam, 694n78
Follath, Erich, 172n6
Fong, Mei, 735n62
Fontaine, Craig W., 692n18
Forelle, Charles, 338n19, 438n6
Forsans, Nicolas, 337n2
Fortunato, Piergiuseppe, 175n95
Fosfuri, Andrea, 649n15
Foss, Nicolai J., 694n58
Foster, Robert J., 126n16, 770n52, 770n53, 770n65
Foster, Jr., Tom, 741*f*
Francis, June N. P., 128n81
Frangos, Alex, 338n40
Frankel, Jeffrey A., 269n28
Fraser, Jane, 226n132
Fraser, Matthew, 299n28
Frayter, Karina, 848n52
Frazee, Valerie, 849n96
Freeman, Susan, 560n64
Freeman, R. Edward, 472n3
French, Patrick, 173n37
Fridman, Mikhail, 651n68
Friedman, Milton, 135
Friedman, Thomas, 176n131, 223n1, 223n2, 769n37
Froud, G., 768n1
Frynas, Jedrzej George, 559n50
Fu, Ping Ping, 127n62
Fukuyama, Francis, 127n42, 174n56
Furnham, Adrian, 128n93

Gabel, Medard, 522n84
Gadiesh, Orit, 734n35
Gage, Jack, 520n16
Galbraith, John Kenneth, 641, 651n90
Galloni, Alessandra, 806n1
Gallup, J. L., 269n29
Galvão, Jorge Manuel Mendes, 127n42
Gama, Ana Paula Matias, 127n42
Gandhi, 135
Ganges, B., 768n1
Garcia, Dominie, 128n99
Garcia-Escribano, Mercedes, 405n10
García, M.S., 648n1
Garcia, Roberto P., 128n98
Gardella, Adrianna, 73n35
Garrette, Bernard, 650n28
Gates, Bill, 728, 820
Gauthier-Villars, David, 127n47, 369n21
Gavlen, Morten, 735n89
Geiger, Marshall, 651n74
Gemunden, Hans, 606n27
Geneen, Harold, 673
Gentry, J., 849n84
Gerini, Claudia, 698
Gesteland, Richard, 126n10
Ghemawat, Pankaj, 337n4, 338n12, 472n2, 519n5, 541*t*
Ghoshal, Sumantra, 472n31, 694n75, 694n86, 695n97
Ghosn, Carlos, 119
Gibbons, Ryan, 408, 410
Gibbs, Toby, 522n112, 694n55, 694n80, 694n93
Gibson, Christina, 126n4, 128n67
Giddy, Ian H., 406n37
Gilbert, Brett Anitra, 72n14
Gilbertson, Brian, 469
Gillespie, Kate, 607n78, 735n75
Gilley, M., 849n87
Glader, Paul, 558n2
Glenn, Jerome, 225n88, 520n42, 522n83
Gobry, Pascal-Emmanuel, 606n51
Godart, Benoit, 177n176
Goerzen, Anthony, 651n81
Goldsmith, Charles, 734n55
Goldstein, Andrea E., 269n44
Golovko, Elena, 606n21
Gomes, G., 849n82
Gomes, Leonard, 268n4
Gong, Yaping, 126n4
Gongshan, Zhu, 184, 197
Gonzalez, Carmen G., 299n35
Gonzalez, David, 558n7
Goodson, Scott, 693n52
Goodwin, Leonie, 734n53
Gopalakrishnan, Shanthi, 651n91
Gopinath, C., 734n48
Gopolan, Nisha, 439n53

Gordon, Theodore, 225n88, 520n42, 522n83
Gottfredson, Mark, 521n69
Gou, Terry, 739
Gould, C., 850n129
Gould, Stephen, 735n73
Gowen, Annie, 299n9
Graab, Alison, 473n58
Graham, Matthew, 72n1
Grant, Jeremy, 299n46
Gratchev, Mikhail V., 559n40
Gray, Alistair, 559n36, 782
Gray, H. Peter, 269n22
Gray, Sidney J., 783*f*, 806n4
Greaney, Theresa M., 269n45
Green, Matthew, 560n72
Green, S., 847n1, 847n3, 848n20, 848n32, 849n61, 849n69, 849n71
Greenberg, Paul, 298n1
Greene, Jay, 128n74
Greenhalgh, Christine, 520n41
Greenspan, Alan, 224n61
Greenway, D., 606n14
Gregory, Alan, 649n23
Grein, Andreas, 735n73
Grescoe, Taras, 298n1
Grevatt, Jon, 300n51
Griffith, David A., 651n67
Griffiths, John, 649n3, 695n107
Grillo, Ioan, 368n1
Gross, Daniel, 227n143
Grote, Karl-Heinrich, 694n66
Grove, Andy, 674, 694n71
Grow, Brian, 770n61
Guerrera, Francesco, 649n21
Guiso, Luigi, 127n44
Gullstrand, J., 606n14
Gulsoy, Tanses, 735n73
Guncavdi, Oner, 269n14
Guney, Y., 270n60
Gunter, Bernhard G., 72n24
Gupta-Mukherjee, Swasti, 649n27
Gupta, Vipin, 126n11

Habib, M., 472n29
Haerpfer, Christian, 174n61
Hajro, Aida, 126n4, 128n67
Håkanson, Lars, 269n24
Hakim, Yasser, 845
Hall, Edward T., 128n76
Hall, Peter, 560n75
Hall, Terry, 269n26
Halper, Stefan, 175n90
Hamel, Gary, 608n119
Hammond, Allen, 734n17, 735n97
Hammond, Ed, 734n14, 734n54
Hanges, Paul J., 126n11
Hanke, Steve H., 225n95, 225n96, 405n10
Hannon, David, 769n20
Hansel, Saul, 522n92
Hansen, James M., 299n27
Hansen, Suzy, 519n5
Hanson, Gordon H., 73n31, 268n11
Hanson, Terry, 298n1
Harding, James, 73n50
Harford, Jarrad, 438n2
Harney, Alexandra, 522n110, 649n21
Harrigan, James, 269n16
Harris, Gardiner, 72n9, 176n134, 176n157
Harris, Jonathan, 172n9, 223n6, 223n18, 520n17, 521n61, 522n95, 692n13, 694n64, 695n96, 849n63, 851n168
Harris, Suzy, 849n101
Harrison, D., 849n87
Hart, Michael, 298n3
Hart, S.L., 226n128
Hartmann, L., 848n38
Harvey, David, 298n1
Harzing, Anne-Wil, 126n12, 649n18
Hassan, F., 847n1, 847n3, 848n20, 848n32, 849n61, 849n69, 849n71
Hausmann, R., 269n21
Hawkins, BEth, 692n1
Hawkins, Lee Jr., 769n32
Hayashi, Yuka, 406n50
Hayes, Robert H., 769n7, 770n51
Haynes, Michelle, 560n69
Head, Keith, 269n54
Hebron, Lui, 522n101
Heckscher, Eli, 243, 268n12
Hedley, Hale E., 299n28
Heimann, Fritz, 472n33
Helleiner, Gerald K., 299n8
Heller, Richard, 519n1
Helliker, Kevin, 734n27
Hemerling, James W., 223n4, 693n21, 769n15
Hemli, Sven, 848n37
Hendricks, Tyche, 368n1
Hennart, Jean-François, 649n9
Henninger, Daniel, 72n10
Hensley, Scott, 473n91
Herbert, Bob, 226n109
Hernandez, Exequiel, 651n79
Herodotus, 135
Herring, Andrew Avery, 268n10
Hertz, Noreen, 225n79
Hess, Kathleen, 849n94
Hexiang, Hou, 299n7
Heywood, Suzanne, 172n9, 223n6, 223n18, 520n17, 521n61, 522n95, 522n112, 692n13, 694n55, 694n64, 694n80, 694n93, 695n96, 849n63, 851n168
Higashide, Hiro, 127n62
Hill, C. W., 649n15
Hill, Kenneth Hailey, 268n10
Hilsenbrath, Jon, 405n24
Hindo, Brian, 770n61
Hinshaw, Drew, 734n34
Ho, P. Sai-wing, 298n4
Ho, Prudence, 439n53
Hoag, Christina, 128n75
Hodgetts, Richard, 693n29
Hoeven, Rolph van der, 72n24
Hofacker, D., 72n8
Hofstede, Geert, 126n11, 126n14, 127n49, 127n53, 127n54, 127n57, 782*f*, 806n3
Hofstede, Gert Jan, 806n3
Holbert, Neil, 849n54
Holland, Kelley, 695n112
Holm, Ulf, 559n20
Holmes, Kim, 191*m*, 192*f*
Holstein, William J., 695n117
Holt, Philip J., 693n51
Hommes, Martin, 558n3, 560n65
Hookway, James, 438n7, 735n67
Hoole, Richard W., 769n13
Hooper, John, 806n1
Hope, Kerin, 559n52
Hopey, Don, 734n20
ho Rathore, Riviera, 846
Horch, Dan, 438n25
Horyn, Cathy, 733n1
Hosny, Mahmoud, 846
House, Karen Elliott, 126n1
House, Robert J., 126n11, 127n28
Howard, Theresa, 693n54
Howe, Robert F., 650n38
Howell, Jon P., 127n62
Howells, Geraint, 176n142
Hristozova, Elena, 694n72
Hsieh, Linda H.Y., 651n85
Hsieh, Tsun-yan, 849n56, 849n86
Hu, Patrick, 176n147
Hu, Yiyang, 298n5
Huang, Shicheng, 369n24
Hulland, John S., 649n8
Hult, G. Tomas, 650n37
Hunt, John W., 693n27
Huntington, Samuel P., 174n54, 175n97
Hussein, Saddam, 156
Hutchings, Kate, 560n64
Hutzschenreuter, Thomas, 558n3, 560n65
Hwang, L. P., 649n15
Hyun, Y., 849n84

Ibison, David, 651n72
Ignat, Ion, 269n36
Imaka, Isaac, 405n18
Immelt, Jeffrey, 442–443, 514, 808, 814, 847n1, 847n3, 848n20, 848n32, 849n61, 849n69, 849n71
Inglehart, Ronald, 126n11, 126n25, 127n37, 127n41, 127n57, 128n82, 174n61
Inman, Daniel, 406n50
Inman, M., 850n120
Insch, Gary, 851n160
Isla, Pablo, 481
Islam, Zakiul, 846
Isobe, Takehiko, 558n4, 560n63, 560n68
Ito, Kiyohiko, 269n33
Itzigsohn, Jose, 268n1
Ivanov, Dmitry, 694n56

Jabareen, Josef, 472n52
Jack, Andrew, 734n23, 734n24, 734n31
Jackson, Michael, 698
Jacob, Rahul, 650n32
Jacobs, 769n48, 770n60
Jacques, Martin, 175n90
Jafri, Tanvir A., 734n25
Jain, Sudeep, 406n41
James, Harold, 73n50
James, LeBron, 46
Jarvis, Steve, 126n1
Javidan, Mansour, 126n11
Jaworski, Renata, 851n162
Jayaraman, Narayanan, 649n27
Jefferson, Thomas, 142, 143f, 156
Jenkins, Wyn, 520n21
Jensen, B., 606n20
Jensen, Bradford, 607n52, 607n54
Jensen, Karina R., 733n6
Jensen, Michael C., 472n3
Jesino, Jorge Correia, 127n61
Jewel, 698
Jiang, Jin, 614
Jimenez, Alfredo, 126n5
Jiménez, Fernando R., 734n50
Jin, Zhongqi, 735n73
Jingjing, Jiang, 606n47
Jintao, Hu, 146
Jobs, Steve, 173n38, 496, 738
Joerres, Jeffrey, 848n49
Johal, S., 768n1

Johansson, Johny K., 735n65
John, Elton, 698
Johnson, Avery, 734n30
Johnson, Eric M., 649n11
Johnson, Jean L., 733n7
Johnson, Keith, 299n10
Johnson, Robert Wood, 655
Johnston, Bruce, 806n1
Johnston, David Cay, 439n36, 439n48
Johnston, Russell, 769n25
Jon, Wertheim, 72n1
Jones, Charles, 225n81
Jones, Daniel T., 769n8
Jones-Evans, D., 607n81
Jones, Geoffrey, 608n106
Jones, Harold B. Jr., 127n43
Jones, Sandra, 847n10
Jorda, Miriam, 473n77
Jordan-Jones, Victoria, 560n71
Jordan, Miriam, 269n52, 368n1, 735n70
Joseph, M., 850n103
Joshi, Sanjay, 808, 818
Jouanjean, Marie-Agnés, 299n49
Joyce, Claudia, 692n10, 694n63
Joyner, Nelson T., 608n105
Judge, William, 848n23
Jun, S., 849n84
Junglas, Iris, 769n40

Kabir, Resaul, 438n4
Kaeschel, Joachim, 694n56
Kafouros, Mario I., 559n26, 559n46
Kahle, Lynn R., 734n38
Kahler, Terry, 803
Kahn, Alfred, 651n94
Kahn, Gabriel, 770n57
Kahn, Jeremy, 72n1, 849n65, 849n66
Kahneman, Daniel, 520n34, 522n91, 522n94, 522n115
Kaka, Noshi, 521n58
Kale, Prashant, 651n84, 651n89
Kaletsky, Anatole, 224n40
Kalleberg, Arne, 72n23
Kan, Ozgur B., 559n44
Kandemir, Destan, 650n37
Kania, Bruce, 457
Kannan-Narasimhan, Rangapriya, 694n87
Kano, Liena, 73n48
Kanter, James, 127n30, 338n20
Kapferer, Jean-Noël, 735n71
Karatnycky, Adrian, 174n52
Karmin, Craig, 72n26
Karnitschnig, Matthew, 128n94
Karpinski, Richard, 769n38, 769n42
Kashyap, Vishal, 735n86
Katsaros, Steve, 39
Katsikeas, Constantine S., 733n4, 734n18
Kaufman, Daniel, 158*m*, 173*n29*, 607n74
Kaynak, Erdener, 649n8
Kazaz, B., 559n45
Kazmin, Amy, 650n41
Kedia, Ben, 848n27, 849n70
Keller, Gary F., 735n80
Kelly, Grace, 698
Kelly, Terri, 669
Kemp, Murray, 268n9
Kendall, Jerry, 175n115
Kennedy, Jeff, 127n62
Kennedy, Robert, 734n21
Kern, Mary C., 126n4
Kerr, John, 607n80, 608n90
Kerviel, Jérôme, 360
Kesmodel, David, 769n22
Kessler, Anna, 302, 304
Kessler, Eric H., 651n91
Ketelhöhn, Niels W., 268n1
Khalaf, Roula, 126n1
Khamenei, Ayatollah Ali, 155
Khan, Matthew, 607n65
Khan, Muhammad Arsalan, 734n25
Khan, Shah Rukh, 698
Khanna, Tarun, 651n81
Khatri, N., 848n31
Khavul, Susanna, 735n82
Khurana, Anil, 558n14
Kiger, Patrick, 694n59
Kilman, Scott, 650n34
Kim, Daekwan, 733n7
Kim, Quenna Sook, 770n57
Kim, W. C., 649n15
King, Colbert Il, 126n1
King, Ed, 473n60
King, Stephen, 223n21
Kipling, Rudyard, 698
Kirkpatrick, Colin, 559n27
Kitsantonis, Niki, 472n25
Klaff, Leslie Gross, 695n99, 851n158
Klein, Jill Gabrielle, 649n6
Klein, Lawrence, 65
Kleiner, Markus, 849n72
Kleinfeld, Klaus, 455–456
Klenow, Peter, 225n81
Kline, John M., 472n13
Knecht, G. Bruce, 559n18
Kneller, R., 606n14
Knepper, Paul, 562–564, 567, 586, 590
Knickerbocker, Frederick, 559n47
Knight, Gary A., 649n10
c, Rebecca, 695n103
Knippenberg, Daan van, 126n2
Kofele-Kale, Ndiva, 650n50
Kogut, B., 649n10
Kohlberg, Lawrence, 472n4
Kolk, Ans, 473n81 473n84
Kollinger, I., 848n38
Kolobov, Alex, 529
Komisar, Lucy, 439n49
Komor, Marcin, 734n50
Kong, Deborah, 368n1
Koopman, Paul, 127n62
Koranteng, Juliana, 693n52
Korn, Melissa, 695n104
Koseki, Mari, 337n1
Köster, Karen, 126n12
Kostova, Tatiana, 695n97
Kotabe, Masaaki, 769n19
Kotulla, Thomas, 733n2, 733n5, 734n37
Kraay, Art, 158*m*, 173n29
Kraemer, Kenneth L., 768n1
Kraimer, Maria, 848n43, 849n94, 849n98, 851n149, 851n162
Krainer, John, 559n31
Krajewski, Lee J., 769n47, 770n53, 770n54, 770n55, 770n56
Kramer, Andrew, 227n143, 227n145, 270n55, 299n32,
Krampf, Robert, 650n55
Krebsbach, Karen, 368n1
Kripalani, Manjeet, 128n74
Krishna, Pravin, 269n13
Krissoff, Barry, 298n1
Kristal, Tali, 73n36
Kronholtz, June, 270n58
Kronstedt, Creig R., 735n80
Krotov, Vlad, 769n40
Krueger, Anne O., 223n1
Krueger, Bryan, 810, 840
Krugman, Paul, 174n72, 268n7, 269n15, 269n16, 269n41, 521n51
Kruschwitz, Nina, 735n92
Kubyshkina, Yulia, 695n123
Kuchler, Fred, 298n1
Kucukcifi, Suat, 269n14
Kumar, Nagesh, 559n21
Kumar, Sanjiv, 651n84
Kumar, Vinod, 439n32
Kundu, S., 649n1
Kuper, Simon, 72n1
Kupp, Martin, 734n52
Kurian, Boby, 558n1
Kwoh, Leslie, 848n19, 848n39
Kwok, Alex K.F., 225n95, 225n96
Kwon, Jong-Wook, 126n27

Labelle, Huguette, 472n32
Lacassagne, Marie-François, 127n62
Laciak, K. J., 270n62
Lahart, Justin, 608n118
Lahiri, Nandini, 559n41
Lake, Maggie, 439n28
Lam, Desmond, 735n61
Lam, Willy, 173n15, 173n46
Lamont, Jame, 473n91
Lander, Mark, 473n62, 473n63
Landes, David S., 127n45
Lane, Peter, 650n45
Langston, Jason, 408, 410, 438n1
Lapoule, Paul, 735n73
Laroche, Michel, 736n100
Larsen, Ralph, 654, 655
Larson, Mark, 847n8
Larson, S., 849n99
Lashinsky, Adam, 694n62
Lateille, Luc, 582
Latta, G., 850n130
Lattman, Peter, 472n24
Laudicina, Paul, 808
Laufer, Daniel, 735n75
Lauricella, Tom, 369n24
Lauring, J., 849n91
Lavoie, Johanne, 848n56, 849n86
Law, Fiona, 438n16
Lawrence, John J., 127n56
Lawrence, Paul R., 769n25
Lawson, Robert, 224n34
Lazarova, M., 851n154
Lazzarini, Sergio G., 650n36
Leahy, Terry, 121
Leamer, Edward E., 559n49
Leaver, A., 768n1
Lee, Hyun-Jung, 127n66
Lee-Kelley, Liz, 693n51
Lee, Ruby P., 733n7
Lee, Seung-Hyun, 650n40
Lee, Yvonne, 439n53
Leeson, Nicholas, 360, 369n19, 369n20
Leeson, Nick, 369n20
Lemieux, Andrew M., 299n14
Lenartowicz, Tomasz, 126n7, 735n84, 735n85
Lenway, Stefanie, 72n19
Leon, Amos Vivancos, 300n42
León-Darder, Fidel, 648n1, 649n1
Leonel, J., 849n82
Leonidou, L., 607n77

Leung, Peter, 173n10, 520n26, 520n39
Levine, Jonathan B., 770n64
Levitz, Jennifer, 695n104
Lewis, Diane E., 849n90
Lewis, Geoff, 176n133
Li, Lee, 608n103
Liang, Hong, 338n41
Liesch, Peter W., 649n10
Ligos, Melinda, 847n7, 850n117
Limon, Yonca, 734n38
Lincoln, Abraham, 138
Linden, Greg, 768n1
Linder, Stefan B., 269n19
Lindsay, Vai, 606n12
Lindzen, Richard S., 473n56
Lipnack, J., 693n49
Littrell, Lisa, 849n94
Liviu-George, 269n36
Lockwood, Lisa, 733n1
Lodge, James E., 693n51
Lohr, Steve, 72n22
Lopez, Marcos, 480
Lotz, Sherry, 650n55
Lovallo, Dan, 520n34, 522n91, 522n94, 522n115
Lowe, Janet C., 520n36
Lowrey, Annie, 73n55
Lubin, Joann S., 338n27
Lucas, Louise, 734n33
Luce, Edward, 473n80
Luchnow, David, 559n15
Lui, Steven Siu-Yun, 650n46
Luiz, John Manuel, 558n13
Luiz Inacio (Lula) Da Silva, 802
Luk, D., 849n87
Lukashenko, Alexander, 158
Luo, Yadong, 126n21, 650n51
Lyles, Marjorie A., 650n45
Lynch, Matthew, 649n14
Lynch, Richard, 735n73
Lyons, John, 405n21

Ma, Jack, 603
Maalouf, Amin, 128n83
Mabert, Vincent, 649n12
MacDonald, Alistair, 369n21
MacDonald, Philip, 608n104
Machiavelli, 135
Mackintosh, James, 128n104, 649n13
Maddison, Angus, 223n1
Madhok, Anoop, 694n73
Madonna, 478, 699
Madsen, T. Koed, 606n32
Magee, Stephen, 649n15
Magnusson, Peter, 126n5
Maheshwar, Atul, 582
Maitland, Alison, 473n85, 695n95, 851n135
Makino, Shige, 558n4, 559n42, 560n63, 560n68
Maleske, Melissa, 650n48
Malhotra, Naresh, 734n13
Maling, Nick, 337n1
Manbeian, Ali, 408, 410, 438n1
Manceau, Delphine, 734n56
Mander, Benedict, 406n30
Mangaliso, Mzamo P., 128n95
Mankiw, N. Gregory, 72n29
Mann, James, 175n90
Manolis, Chris, 734n44
Manyika, James, 186*m*
Marcella, Rita, 735n87
Marcus, Alfred, 472n8
Marer, Paul, 649n12
Markllie, Paul, 73n34, 270n61
Markoff, John, 521n73, 521n74
Markowitz, Harry, 65
Marks, M., 847n1, 847n3, 848n20, 848n32, 849n61, 849n69, 849n71
Marsh, Peter, 521n49, 521n78, 649n4
Marshall, Alfred, 491
Martens, Pim, 72n8
Martin, Andrew, 175n109
Martin, Ben, 848n37
Martin, Daniel, 299n15
Martin, Justin, 608n117
Martin, Melissa, 298n1
Martin, Philippe, 559n49
Marx, Karl, 135, 224n55
Maslow, Abraham, 105, 127n50
Masson, Paul, 405n16
Massot, M. M., 648n1
Mastruzzi, Massimo, 158*m*, 173n29
Mata, Jose, 560n69
Mate, Kedar, 734n28
Mathewson, G., 769n24
Matlack, Carol, 338n20
Matt, Susan J., 851n164
Matthews, Christopher M., 472n40
Mauri, Alfredo J., 559n19
Maxwell, Kenneth, 806n1
Mayer, Peter, 73n52
Mayerhofer, H., 848n38
Maylie, Devon, 73n44, 299n19, 734n34
Mazda, 746
Mbeki, Thabo, 470
McCallum, Kevin, 735n78
McCartney, Scott, 769n39
McClusky, Robert, 770n62
McCrae, Robert R., 126n14
McDermott, C. John, 338n41
McDonald, John, 692n11
McDonald, Mark, 172n4
McDougall, Patricia P., 72n14
McDougall, Phillips, 72n12
McGahan, Anita, 520n20
McGeever, Jamie, 406n50
McGrath, Michael E., 769n13
McGraw, Dan, 72n15
McGregor, Richard, 172n2
McGroarty, Patrick, 405n28
McGuire, Patrick, 438n10
McGuire, Steven M., 269n44
McKay, Betsy, 733n11
McLaurin, Ian, 120
McMahon, Dinny, 369n24
McMillan, John, 769n27
McNeil, Donald Jr., 226n127
Meckstroth, Daniel J., 769n14
Meiland, Daniel, 808, 847n1, 847n3, 848n20, 848n32, 849n61, 849n69, 849n71
Meister, Jeanne M., 695n106
Mellah, Kamel, 559n50
Menon, Ravi, 297
Merrick, Amy, 473n84, 559n39
Merton, Robert C., 559n31
Mesquita, Luiz F., 650n36
Metters, Richard, 127n52
Meyers, William H., 651n71
Michaels, Adrian, 806n1
Michaels, Daniel, 269n23, 337n4, 650n62
Michelitsch-Riedl, G., 848n38
Mihov, I., 406n48
Miles, Edward W., 734n47
Miles, Marc A., 224n30
Miller, Claire Cain, 848n37
Miller, John W., 299n31, 337n4, 337n8
Miller, Scott, 473n91
Miller, Stewart R., 559n33
Miller, Terry, 191*m*, 192*f*
Millman, Joel, 269n49, 558n7, 559n51
Mills, T., 851n165
Milner, Mark, 337n1
Minder, Ralph, 300n46
Ming, Tang, 174n62
Minkov, Michael, 806n3
Miranda, Ana, 558n1
Mishan, E., 225n86, 225n87
Mitchell, Josh, 337n9
Mitchell, Matthew Coy, 126n26
Mitchell, Ronald K., 472n3
Mitchell, Will, 650n28
Moaligou, Ronan, 734n52
Moen, O., 606n33
Moens, Alexander, 300n42
Moffett, Matt, 733n8, 806n1
Moffett, Michael H., 806n18
Moffett, Sebastian, 406n50, 769n23
Mogollon, Francisco Suarez, 39
Mohamed, Amal, 650n31
Molin, Anna, 522n103
Mollenkamp, Carrick, 369n21
Møller, J. Ørstrøm, 73n56
Monahan, Andrew, 406n50
Monczka, Robert M., 769n21, 769n33, 769n36
Mong-koo, Chung, 688
Monteiro, P., 849n82
Moon, Jon Jungbien, 726–732
Moore, Stephen, 299n12
Moran, P., 472n31
Moreno, Alejandro, 126n11,
Morgan, Mark, 848n21
Morris, Ian, 175n119
Morse, Andrew, 438n8
Mosakowski, Elaine, 559n33
Moskowitz, H., 559n45
Moss, Chris, 849n87
Moss, David A., 406n39
Motsi, Terence, 735n73
Mtima, Lateef, 176n152
Muethal, Miriam, 127n60
Mughan, Terence, 120, 128n73, 128n106
Mukherji, A., 849n70
Mullens, Drake, 735n82
Mulligan, Mark, 72n1
Murjani, Mohan, 698
Murphy, Colum, 735n93
Murphy, John, 406n50
Murphy, Kim, 223n25
Murphy, Marina, 299n8
Murray, Brendan, 471n1
Murray, Sarah, 473n90, 736n101
Murthy, Raja, 176n161
Musante, Michael, 735n86
Muspratt, Caroline, 806n1
Mutsaka, Farai, 405n28
Myers, A., 850n120
Myrdal, Gunnar, 298n4

Nachum, Lilach, 559n41
Nackman, Mark J., 300n53
Naím, Moisés, 560n58
Nakamoto, Michiyo, 735n96
Napier, Nancy, 848n28
Narasimhan, Laxman, 226n130
Nash, John, 65
Naughton, Julie, 733n1
Naumenko, Galina, 808
Nayak, Debiprasasd, 406n41
Nazarbayev, Nursultan, 158
Neely, Christopher J., 406n37

Neely, Tsedal, 850n113
Negishi, Mayumi, 406n50
Nelson, Dean, 736n101
Nelson, Mark M., 337n1
Nelson, Roy, 268n1
Neogy, Abhijit, 227n143
Neuliep, James W., 126n15
Neumann, Tilo, 849n72
Neuwirth, Rostram J., 299n26
Newman, Barry, 847n12
Newmann, Matthew, 473n91
Nguyen, Thuy Thu, 438n4
Nicholson, Chris V., 770n75
Nie, Linlin, 369n24
Nisbett, Richard E., 128n69
Nishioka, Junko, 225n100
Nixon, Richard, 376
Nohria, Nitin, 693n44, 695n97
Noorderhaven, Niels G., 651n76
Nordtvedt, Richard, 848n27
Nosrat, R., 270n62
Nueno, Jose Luis, 519n5
Nwankwo, Sonny, 269n37, 269n39
Nykodym, Nick, 693n49

Obama, Barack, 196
Obe, Mitsuru, 338n26
Oberecker, Eva M., 735n74
O'Boyle, Thomas F., 337n1
O'Brien, Kevin J., 338n19
O'Connor, Sarah, 299n45
Ohlin, Bertil, 243
Olaseni, Mobolaji, 735n83
O'Leary, Christopher J., 298n2
Oliff, Michael D., 769n7
Oliver, Christine, 649n17
Omura, Glen S., 769n19
O'Murchu, Cynthia, 559n22
Ones, D., 849n95
Ong, Aihwa, 126n18, 128n102
Ono, Yumiko, 406n50, 650n39
Oppenheim, Jeremy, 226n132
Oppenheimer, Andres, 338n33
Ordish, Rebecca, 558n1
Orlick, Tom, 369n24
O'Rourke, Kevin H., 224n35
Orr, Gordon, 172n7
Ortega, Armancio, 480
Orth, Ulrich R., 734n38
Ortley, John, 573
Osland, Joyce S., 72n2
Oster, Shai, 223n14, 223n19, 369n24
Ostergard, Robert, 176n149
Ostrovsky, Arkady, 649n13
Ottaviano, Gianmarco I. P., 269n18, 559n49
Ou, Jia-Ruey, 650n42
Oviatt, Benjamin M., 72n12
Øystein, Moen, 735n89

Pack, Howard, 269n41
Packenham, Robert A., 650n50
Pacquiao, Manny, 46
Page, Larry, 673
Paine, Thomas, 175n122
Pakko, Michael, 406n33
Paley, Michael, 849n94
Paliwoda, S., 606n27
Pallazolo, Joe, 472n40
Palley, Thomas I., 268n8
Palmer, T., 851n159
Pande, Shamni, 769n38
Panella, C., 850n120
Papadopoulos, Nicolas, 736n100
Park, Hoon, 559n25, 848n22
Park, Ji Eun, 735n73
Park, Seah, 735n76
Park, Seung Ho, 651n77, 849n62
Parker, Caroline, 734n53
Parkhe, Arvind, 559n33, 651n84, 651n93
Parmar, Neil, 128n103
Parrish, Austen L., 472n20
Pasa, Selda, 127n62
Passariello, Cristina, 651n71, 736n101
Patillo, Catherine, 405n16
Pattle, Joan, 809, 826, 830
Pearce, J. M., 270n62
Pearl, Daniel, 128n80
Pearson, Thomas W., 176n152
Peel, Michael, 559n16
Peel, Quentin, 128n105
Peltokorpi, Vesa, 126n21
Peng, George Z., 559n27
Peng, Mike W., 651n80
Peng, Tai-Kuang, 127n62
Pentland, Alex, 849n74
Pepper, Suzanne, 174n69
Perez, Liliana M., 848n27
Perlmutter, Howard, 651n84
Perrin, Towers, 850n135
Perry, Joellen, 72n18, 72n21
Perry, Mark J., 439n27
Perry, Martin, 607n77
Perry, Michelle, 806n1
Petersen, Carol Dawn, 300n52
Peterson, Mark F., 650n27, 735n82
Pfanner, Eric, 439n40, 439n52
Pfeifer, Stuart, 472n38
Phatak, Arvind V., 559n19
Phillips, Kevin, 225n98
Phillips, Michael M., 405n10
Pichler, F., 127n51
Pickett, Todd, 802-805
Pico, Alejandro, 128n77
Pierer, Heinrich von, 455–456
Pieterse, Jan Nederveen, 522n101
Pieth, Mark, 472n32
Pigman, Geoffrey Allen, 559n50
Pilat, Dirk, 269n20
Piramal, G., 472n31
Piramal, Gita, 694n86
Pitethly, Robert, 649n24
Pittelko, Brian M., 298n2
Pla-Barber, J., 648n1, 649n1
Plato, 135
Pleskovic, B., 269n29
Pleven, Liam, 299n13
Plushnick-Masti, Ramit, 651n70
Politi, James, 223n8, 223n9, 299n33, 338n28
Pollack, Andrew, 473n79
Polland, Patricia, 406n33
Pollock, Andrew C., 406n38
Polman, Paul, 295
Pons, Corina, 406n30
Porter, Michael E., 251*f*, 268n1, 269n32, 519n9, 520n20, 520n33, 520n35
Portugal, Pedro, 560n69
Postolachi, Andre Teofil, 269n36
Pothukuchi, Vijay, 849n62
Potts, David, 120–121
Power, Stephen, 337n1
Prada, Miuccia, 434–436
Prada, Paulo, 73n35
Prada, Mario, 435
Prahalad, C. K., 226n128, 522n105, 734n17, 735n97, 736n101
Pras, Bernard, 734n56
Prasso, Sheridan, 405n27, 736n101
Praxmarer, Sandra, 734n50
Prebisch, Raul, 298n4
Preston-Ortiz, Dina, 651n84
Prestowitz, Clyde, 223n1, 223n3, 223n13
Prieto, Leonel, 127n62
Pucik, Vladimir, 269n33
Puddington, Arch, 174n64, 174n66
Pudelko, Markus, 126n3, 126n4, 128n67
Puga, Diego, 269n18
Pugh, Wendy, 226n125
Pulfer, Rachel, 471n1
Purushothaman, Roopa, 227n143
Pushkar, 174n77
Putin, Vladimir, 134, 221

Raab, M., 72n8
Radebaugh, Lee H., 781*f*, 783*f*
Radebe, Busi, 558n13
Ramamurti, Ravi, 650n51
Ramirez, Julio, 558n1
Rampell, Catherine, 768n1, 848n37
Ramsey, J., 849n82
Ramsey, Mike, 559n35, 769n23, 806n19
Rana, Preetika, 733n9
Randlesome, C., 850n120
Ranf, Diana Elena, 651n73
Rappoart, Liz, 439n50
Rasheed, Abdul A, 735n82
Rassweiler, Andrew, 607n58
Rastello, Sandrine, 226n125
Rathore, Riviera ho, 844
Rauwald, Christoph, 337n1
Raval, Anjji, 558n10
Raval, Dinker, 694n89
Ravenscraft, D., 769n24
Rawe, Julia, 368n1
Reade, Carol, 127n66
Reddy, Sudeep, 338n27
Reder, Melvin W., 225n77
Reed, John, 695n116
Regalado, Antonio, 72n11
Reilly, David, 806n1
Reilly, Kevin T., 337n2, 338n13
Reilly, Patrick M., 128n94
Reinhart, Carmen M., 405n10
Reinstaller, Andreas, 73n38, 270n57
Remes, Jaana, 186*m*
Reney, Marie-Claude, 651n83
Rentrope, Shantyana, 269n48
Reuer, Jeffrey J., 558n5, 651n81, 651n86
Reynolds, Calvin, 848n46
Rhee, Mooweon, 695n119
Rhoads, Chistopher, 405n14
Rhodes, Mark, 650n54
Riboud, Frank, 728, 729
Ricardo, David, 239, 268n6
Richards, Darlington, 269n37, 269n39
Richelieu, André, 72n1
Richtel, Matt, 519n13
Richter, Konstantin, 472n46, 472n48
Riedel, Sharon, 849n94
Ries, John, 269n54
Riesenberger, J.R., 406n46
Rigby, Darrell, 694n60, 769n2, 769n28
Ritala, Paavo, 650n33
Ritzman, Larry P., 769n47, 770n54, 770n55, 770n56
Rizvi, Riftat Abbas, 734n25
Roath, Anthony S., 769n6, 769n16
Roberson, Roy, 298n1
Roberts, James A., 734n44

Roberts, Jo, 735n64
Roberts, M., 606n16
Robinson, Sara, 300n56
Robyn, Dorothy, 651n94
Rock, Michael E., 694n71
Rockefeller, 728
Rodgers, Suzannah, 806n1
Rodrigues, Suzana B., 651n85
Rodríguez-Clare, Andrés, 268n1, 269n40
Rodriguez, Rosa Salter, 368n1
Rodrik, D., 269n21
Rogers, Mark, 520n41
Rogoff, Kenneth, 223n1, 225n99
Rohter, Larry, 73n54
Rohwedder, Cecile, 126n1, 559n43
Romer, David, 269n28
Romero, Simon, 338n50
Ronaldo, Cristiano, 46
Ronen, D., 73n53
Roosevelt, Franklin D., 726, 729
Rose, Rebecca, 734n16
Rosenthal, Elisabeth, 607n63
Rota, Massimo, 775
Roth, Kendall, 126n7
Rothbard, Murray, 225n90
Rothwell, Steve, 806n1
Rouhani, Hassan, 155
Rousseau, 135
Roxas, Hernan, 606n12
Roxburgh, Charles, 186*m*
Roy, Jean-Paul, 649n17
Rubanik, Yuri, 651n87
Rubera, Gale, 735n63
Rugman, Alan M., 73n48, 337n3, 649n10
Ruiz, David, 606n27
Ruland, M., 72n8
Rumelt, Richard, 520n20
Russell, Alec, 473n91
Rutigliano, Tony, 608n116
Ryan, Alan, 173n30
Ryans, John K. Jr., 650n55
Saalfield, Peter, 848n41
Sabar, Ariel, 126n20, 126n23
Sabri, Ouidade, 734n56
Sachs, Jeffery, 226n123, 269n29, 269n38
Saggi, Kamal, 269n41
Sahay, Arvind, 734n42
Saiad, I. H., 472n22
Said, Summer, 126n1
Salas, Eduardo, 849n94
Salk, Jane E., 650n45
Salk, Yoko, 128n85
Salorio, Eugene, 300n58
Salzman, Avi, 692n1
Samek, Robert, 848n56, 849n86
Samiee, Saeed, 735n77
Sampson, Rachelle C., 651n82
Samuelson, Paul A., 72n22, 200
Sanborn, Stephanie, 176n150
Sanchez, Alberto Rubio, 128n77
Sánchez, Francisco, 605n7
Sanders, Peter, 650n62
Sang-Hun, Choe, 126n19
Sapienza, Paola, 127n44
Sapsford, Jathon, 337n1, 769n12
Sarala, Rikka, 126n5, 651n78
Sarno, Lucio, 406n37
Saul, John Ralston, 73n50
Saunders, Carol, 128n78
Sawyer, Granville, 299n37
Saxena, Sanchita B., 299n11
Saywell, Trish, 770n57
Schaer, Fabian, 186*m*
Schechner, Sam, 128n89
Schellhas, John, 268n1
Schindler, Robert M., 735n69
Schiro, TOm, 810
Schmalensee, 519n10
Schmid, Stefan, 733n2, 733n5, 734n37
Schmidt, Lisa, 299n8
Schmitz, Hubert, 269n35
Schneider, Susan, 849n81
Schoeff, Mark Jr., 847n2, 847n16
Schoenberger, Karl, 607n65
Schoenfeld, Amy, 769n17
Scholes, Myron S., 559n31
Schonberger, B., 72n8
Schoofs, Mark, 473n91
Schott, Peter, 607n52, 607n54
Schuiling, Isabelle, 735n71
Schultz, Don E., 558n8
Schulze, Günther G., 72n5
Schumann, Jan H., 734n50
Schwartz, H., 694n91
Schwartz, S., 126n11
Schweer, Margaret, 849n75
Schweikart, James A., 559n28
Scott, Mark, 72n13
Scrimshaw, Nevin S., 736n101
Searcey, Dionne, 472n37
Segalla, Michael, 127n29
Sekiguchi, Toko, 338n26
Seligson, H., 851n171
Sell, Susie, 299n17
Selmer, J., 849n91, 851n159
Semaan, Rania, 735n73
Sen, Amartya, 102, 127n31, 174n73, 225n76
Serapio, Manuel G., 636*f*, 650–651n65,
Sermiento-Saher, Sebastian, 338n34
Servais, P., 606n32
Seth, Anju, 651n84
Sethi, S. Prakash, 472n15
Shaffer, Margaret, 849n87, 849n94, 851n149
Shah, Neil, 406n50
Shahzad, Asif, 734n25
Shainesh, G., 734n50
Shan, Chuanxuan, 126n27
Shan, Jordan, 268n3
Shane, Scott, 174n79
Shannon, Randall M., 734n50
Sharapova, Maria, 46
Sharkey, Joe, 847n9, 851n142
Sharma, Amol, 558n9
Sharma, P., 735n73
Sharma, Samidha, 558n1
Sharma, Subash, 735n77
Shatara, Ziad, 845
Shaver, J. Myles, 559n49
Sheinbaum, Stanley K., 650n50
Shenkar, Oded, 520n25, 520n37, 521n57, 522n111, 650n40, 651n77, 651n80
Shenon, Philip, 299n20
Sherer, Paul M., 269n42
Sherman, Stratford, 522n113, 522n114
Sheth, Niraj, 73n35
Shimamoto, Kenichi, 559n27
Shimoni, Baruch, 128n85
Shimp, Terrence A., 735n77
Shin, Jongtae, 73n42
Shirouzu, Norihiko, 694n84, 769n12
Shorto, Russell, 224n48
Shrader, Rodney C., 72n12, 650n31
Siders, Mark, 735n90
Siegmund, John, 605n7
Silvera, David H., 735n75
Simmons, Lee, 735n69
Simonian, Haig, 559n30, 735n95
Simpson, Glenn R., 472n42
Sims, G. Thomas, 405n14, 472n51
Singer, Hans, 298n4
Singer, Jefferson A., 127n55
Singh, Harbir, 128n101, 651n84, 651n89
Singh, Jitendra, 128n101
Sirkin, Hal, 223n4, 693n21
Sissell, Kara, 471n1
Sites, Dave, 298n1
Sitze, A., 850n108
Slater, Joanna, 405n21, 406n50
Slaughter, Matthew J., 73n30
Slavin, Barbara, 126n1
Sleuwaegen, Leo, 73n29
Sloan, Alfred P., 692n11
Sloane, Julie, 608n117
Slyke, Craig Van, 128n78
Smit, Sven, 186*m*
Smith, Adam, 135, 189, 195, 236, 268n6
Smith, Alasdair M., 269n41
Smith, Anne, 651n83
Smith, Benson, 608n116
Smith, Geoffrey T., 438n8
Smith, Geri, 368n1
Smith, Joyce van der Laan, 651n74
Smith, Vernon, 65
Snoop Dog, 698
Socha, Miles, 733n1
Söderman, Sten, 72n1
Sokolov, Boris, 694n56
Solinger, Dorothy, 298n5
Soloman, Jay, 299n18
Solomon, Deborah, 73n37
Song, Jaeyong, 73n42
Song, Sangcheol, 650n40
Sönmez, Sevil, 269n48
Sonne, Paul, 734n34
Sonsino, Yvonne, 848n36
Sorbeim, R., 606n33
Sorrentino, Constance, 226n105
Sosa, Sebastián, 405n10
Spencer, Jennifer, 694n76
Sridharan, R., 769n38
Srinivas, Ekkirala S., 127n62
St. Anthony, Neal, 471n1
Stack, John F., 522n101
Stahl, G., 851n147
Stam, Erik, 559n20
Stamps, J., 693n49
Stancati, Margarita, 733n9
Stearman, Kathy, 173n17
Steenkamp, E. M., 735n72
Stein, Mark, 607n41, 607n44
Stein, Peter, 369n24, 406n50
Stern, Robert M., 269n17
Stiglitz, Joseph, 225n75, 226n116, 226n117, 269n29, 299n31, 769n24
Stonehill, Arthur I., 806n18
Storper, Michael, 559n49
Stringer, Howard, 693n40
Stringfellow, Anne, 734n50
Strom, Stephanie, 736n99
Sturze, Sascha, 521n58
Subramanian, Bala, 694n89
Sugden, Roger, 73n56
Sullivan, Bartholomew, 298n1

Sullivan, Daniel, 168, 173n10, 173n17, 176n147, 520n26, 520n39, 606n39, 607n78
Sun, Fiona, 268n3
Sundaram, Anant, 438n19
Sunde, Uwe, 175n95
Suris, Oscar, 406n43
Sutton, Stephanie, 176n167, 176n168
Swagel, Phillip, 72n29
Swait, Joffre, 735n61
Swann, Christopher, 298n44
Sylvers, Eric, 806n1
Sylvester, Michael, 172n1

Tabuchi, Hiroko, 406n50, 693n39
Tabuchi, Takatoshi, 269n18
Tait, Nikki, 560n67
Takebe, Miyako, 406n50
Taleb, N., 227n143
Talmon, Jacob, 175n91
Tamimi, Talah, 126n1
Tamirisa, Natalia T., 406n31
Taniguchi, M., 851n147
Tanzi, Calisto, 772, 774–775
Tanzi, Francesca, 774
Tanzi, Giovanni, 774
Tanzi, Stefano, 774
Tao, Xiangnan, 268n3
Taras, Vas, 126n5
Tata, Jasmine, 127n62
Taylor, Alan M., 269n13
Taylor, Colleen, 472n43
Taylor, Sully, 848n28
Teece, David J., 649n10
Tejada, Carlos, 73n39
Teng, Bing-Sheng, 651n84
Tenzer, Helene, 126n3
Terazono, Emiko, 299n10
Teresko, John, 471n1
Terlep, Sharon, 559n35
Teweldemedhin, M. Y., 128n86
Theodosiou, Marios, 734n18
Thirani, Neha, 520n31
Thirwell, A. P., 268n7
Thisse, Jacques-François, 269n18
Thomas, Amy M., 72n3
Thomas, Anna, 606n48
Thomas, David C., 128n99
Thomas, Robert, 849n75
Thompson, Steve, 560n69
Thornton, Grant, 773, 774
Tian, Qing, 472n36
Tibballa, Sue, 126n1
Tichy, Noel, 522n113, 522n114
Timmons, Heather, 368n1, 521n71
Todaro, Michael, 224n46
Tofani, Roberto, 175n93
Tomlinson, John, 128n87
Tong, Tony W., 558n5
Tonna, Fausto, 774
Torres, Craig, 405n11
Toyne, Brian, 769n7
Trachtenberg, Jeffrey A., 72n11
Tracy, Tennille, 299n10
Tran, Diane, 269n48
Tran, Khanh T. L., 559n43
Tran, Mark, 806n1
Trehern, Steve, 695n110
Tren, Richard, 734n26
Trent, Robert J., 769n21, 769n33, 769n36
Triandis, Harry C., 126n17, 127n48
Triner, Gail D., 268n1
Trofimov, Yaroslav, 806n1
Trompenaars, Fons, 127n32, 128n79
Tröster, Christian, 126n1
Tsang, Eric W. K., 559n42
Tucci, Linda, 73n35
Tudor, Alison, 439n53
Tulder, Rob van, 473n81, 473n84
Tung, Rosalie L., 734n13, 849n81
Turk, Thomas A., 650n28
Twain, Mark, 698
Twentyman, Jessica, 849n96

Ucbasaran, Deniz, 606n30
ul Haq, Mahbub, 225n76
Ungson, Gerardo R., 651n77
Urbina, Ian, 522n117
Ursprung, Heinrich W., 72n5
Useem, Michael, 128n101

Vaaler, Paul M., 269n53
Vaara, Eero, 126n21, 651n78
Vaggi, Gianni, 268n2
Valentini, Giovanni, 606n21
Valenzuela, Ana, 735n61
Vance, Ashlee, 519n13
Varner, I., 851n159
Vecsey, George, 72n1
Vegas, L.M., 648n1
Venables, Anthony J., 269n15, 269n21, 269n27
Venaik, Sunil, 126n13
Verbeke, Alain, 73n48, 337n3
Vermeulen, Freek, 651n77
Vernon, Raymond, 269n30
Veseth, Michael, 522n101
Vestring, Till, 734n35
Vickery, Shawnee K., 770n58
Victorio, Antong, 606n12
Vidal, David J., 472n9
Villalonga, Belen, 520n21
Villar, C., 648n1, 649n1
Viswesvaran, C., 849n95
Vogel, Douglas, 128n78
Voris, Bob Van, 806n1
Voronov, Maxim, 127n55
Voyle, Suzanna, 560n66

Wagenheim, Florian V., 734n50
Wagner, Wieland, 172n6
Wagstaff, Jeremy, 769n46
Wahl, Grant, 72n1
Wailes, Eric, 299n27
Waldmeir, Patti, 126n9
Walker, Elaine, 558n1
Walker, Marcus, 73n47
Wallace, C., 127n51
Wallace, Irving, 472n12
Walle, Alf H., 128n90
Wallechinsky, David, 472n12
Walmsley, Julian, 350*m*
Walt, Vivienne, 519n3, 521n65, 521n79
Wang, Shirley, 127n63
Wang, Wynne, 369n24
Wang, Zhenmin, 176n148
Ward, Andrew, 560n56, 734n59
Warner-Soderholm, Gillian, 127n36
Waters, Richard, 72n28
Wayne, Leslie, 472n21
Wayne, Sandy, 851n162
Weber, J. A., 735n90
Weber, Max, 103
Weeks, John, 268n1
Wei, Lingling, 369n24
Weifang, He, 175n121
Weinberg, Carl B., 338n25
Weiner, Eric, 225n78
Weinstein, David E., 269n14
Weinstein, Veronica, 176n145
Weisberg, Jacob, 299n23
Weisman, Steven, 173n20
Weiss, Leigh, 522n112, 694n55, 694n80, 694n93
Welch, D., 849n79
Welch, Jack, 444, 489–490, 513–514, 522n115, 522n116, 657, 668, 681, 686, 692n9
Welch, Suzy, 692n9
Weldon, William, 654
Welzel, Christian, 174n61
Wendlandt, A., 849n73
Werdigier, Julia, 473n91
Wernerfelt, B., 520n20
Wessel, David, 73n47, 694n90, 848n37
Westhead, Paul, 606n30
Wheelwright, Steven. C., 769n7, 770n51
White, Gregory L., 651n69
White, Steven, 650n46
Whitehouse, Mark, 225n79
Whitley, Edward, 369n20
Whitney, Glen, 369n20
Whorf, Benjamin Lee, 127n64
Wiechman, Denis, 175n115
Wiesen, Jeremy, 269n34
Wiggins, Jenny, 734n45
Wild, J.J., 406n45
Wild, K.L., 406n45
Wilkie, Mary E., 406n38
Williams, K., 768n1
Williams, Serena, 60
Williams, Venus, 60
Williamson, J., 406n47
Williamson, O., 769n24
Wilson, Dominic, 227n143
Wilson, Duff, 175n106
Wilson, James R., 73n56, 128n105
Wilson, Keeley, 693n45
Wilson, Simon, 223n26
Windrum, Paul, 73n38, 270n57
Wines, Michael, 224n53, 735n68
Wingfield, Nick, 519n14, 768n1
Winkler, Viviane A., 128n68
Wolf, Carol, 734n46
Wollaston, Graham, 582
Womack, James P., 769n8
Wonacott, Peter, 649n16
Wong, Edward, 175n98
Wood, Donna J., 472n3
Wood, Van R., 735n90
Woodley, James, 650n47
Wooldridge, Adrian, 522n100, 651n92, 849n53, 849n77
Wooldridge, Jane, 650n57
Wonacott, Peter, 650n41
Worm, V., 849n79
Wortham, Jenna, 850n111
Wozniak, Steve, 738
Wozny, Meg, 522n85
Wright, Mike, 606n30
Wright, Robert, 559n29
Wucherpfennig, Julian, 174n75

Xiao, Mandy, 738, 740
Xiaochuan, Zhou, 223n7
Xomir, Mick, 816*f*
Xu, D., 606n16

Yang, Zhilin, 734n50
Ybarra, Candace E., 650n28
Yeganeh, Hamid, 127n46
Yeh, Reh-song, 127n56

Yester, Brenda, 39
Yoshikawa, Katsuhiko, 127n66
Young, Michael N., 651n87
Yu, Eden S. H., 299n36
Yu, Rose, 559n48
Yuki, Gary, 127n62
Yun, L., 606n15
Yung, Jean, 369n24
Yunus, Mohammad, 727, 728, 736n101
Zaheer, Akbar, 127n59, 651n79, 651n88
Zaheer, Srilata, 127n59, 559n33, 651n88
Zahra, Shaker, 635*f*
Zalamea, Luis, 650n64
Zamiska, Nicholas, 769n22
Zampano, Giada, 806n1
Zander, U., 649n10
Zaun, Todd, 337n1
Zedong, Mao, 218
Zelenika-Zovko, I., 270n62
Zellweger, Renee, 698
Zeng, Yuping, 650n40
Zestos, George K., 268n3
Zhang, Chun, 735n81
Zhang, Yajun, 406n42
Zhao, Shuming, 126n12
Zhou, Wenting, 128n72
Zidane, Zinédine (Zizou), 730
Zif, Jehiel, 560n62
Zimbalist, Andrew, 72n1
Zimmerman, Ann, 559n39, 650n39
Zingales, Luigi, 127n44
Zollo, Maurizio, 651n81
Zou, S., 606n13
Zulfikar, Yavuz Fahir, 127n43
Zurawicki, L., 472n29
Zywietz, Daniel, 72n8

Subject Index

Page references with "*f*" refer to figures, page references with "*m*" refer to maps, page references with "*n*" refer to endnotes cited by number, and page references with "*t*" refer to tables.

3D printing, 743
9/11 terrorist attacks, 761

Absolute advantage, 236
Abu Dhabi Investment Authority, 420
Abu Dhabi Securities Exchange, 423
Acceptable quality level (AQL), 756
Accounting (international accounting), 776, 797–800
  company controller and, 776, 777*f*
  cultural differences in, 782–784
  Dell Mercosur case and, 801–805
  finance and, 776–778
  finance issues and, 771–806
  foreign-currency financial statements, 790–792
  information, users of, 780*f*
  international financial issues, 793–797
  objectives, 780–781
  Parmalat case, 772–776
  practices, factors in, 781–784
  sources of influence on, 781*f*
Accumulated translation adjustment, 792
Achievement, masculinity-femininity index and, 105
Acquired advantage, 237
Acquired group membership, 102
Acquisitions
  FDI and, 622–623
  resource, 59, 534–536
Active income, 427
Ad valorem duty, 287
Adaptiveness, 824–826
Adjusting analytics, 201–204
  population size, 203
  purchasing power parity (PPP), 203–204
  rate of economic growth, 202
Adjustments, culture shock and, 113–114
Advance import deposit, 390
Advantages
  acquired, 237
  natural, 237
  reciprocal, globalization and, 52
Affiliation needs, 105, 105*f*
Africa
  cell phones in, 49
  common currency and, 384–385
  customary law and, 155
  regional economic integration in, 326–327, 326*m*
African Bond Fund, 421
African, Caribbean, and Pacific Group of States, 285
African Union (AU), 327, 384
AFTA, 308, 317, 332
agglomeration, 51
Agreement on Trade-Related Aspects of Intellectual Property Rights (TRIPS), 461
Agricultural subsidies, 287–288
Aid and Loans, 288
AIDS. *See* HIV/AIDS
Airline alliances case, 642–647, 643*m*
Airline routes, map of, 643*m*
Alibaba case, 575, 602–604
Alien Occupation Act (Thailand), 812
Allocating among locations, 548–552. *See also* Country evaluation and selection
Allowances, expatriate compensation, 835
Alternative gradual commitments, 549–550
American Chamber of Commerce (AmCham) in Cairo, 308
American Depositary Receipts (ADR), 400, 424
American Society for Training and Development, 686
American terms, 351
Americas, regional economic integration of, 320–322, 321*m*
Andean Community (CAN), 320, 322
Andorra, 175n116
Anglo American Corporation of South Africa, 468
Anglo American PLC case, 468–469
Antarctica, 53–54
Anti-Bribery Convention, 452
Anti-Bribery Recommendation, 452
Anti-Counterfeiting Coalition, 170
Antiglobalists, 66
Antiglobalization forces, 54
Antiglobalization groups, 546
Antiretroviral therapy (ART), 468–470
Antitrust issues, European Union (EU) and, 314
APEC (Asia Pacific Economic Cooperation), 325
Apparel industry cases, 477*f*
  Prada Group, 434–437
  Zara, 476–481, 478*m*
Apple supply chain case, 738–741, 743–744
Apple TV, 738
Appropriability theory, 621–622
aquaculture, 272
Arabian Gulf, 459–460
Arab League, 327
Arab Monetary Union, 384
Arab oil embargo, 377
Arab Spring, 147, 153, 466
Arbitrage, 358
Arbitrageurs, importers as, 358, 579
Area division structure, 664–665
Argentina
  bribery and, 451
  idealism and, 109
Arm's-length price, 428
Artic Sea Ice, passages through, 188–189, 189*f*
Ascribed group membership, 102
ASEAN (Association of Southeast Asian Nations), 317*t*, 324–325, 332
ASEAN Free Trade Area (AFTA), 317*t*, 324, 332
Asia
  Association of Southeast Asian Nations, 317*t*
  financial crisis in, 414
  regional economic integration in, 324–325
  Tesco PLC in, 121–122
Asia Pacific Economic Cooperation (APEC), 325, 332. *See* APEC (Asia Pacific Economic Cooperation)
Asian financial crisis of 1997, 414
Assembly plant, 494, 688–689, 755, 757
Assets
  location-specific, 625–626
  service exports/imports and, 60–61
Association of African Central Bank Governors, 384
Association of Southeast Asian Nations (ASEAN), 308, 324–325, 325*m*
Association of Tennis Professionals (ATP), 44–45
Australian Open, 44–45
Austrian School of Economics, 209
Authoritarianism, 139t
  democracy and, 146
  economic problems and, 145–146
  engines of, 145
  political economy of growth, 145
  rhetoric vs. reality, 145
  surge of, 145–146
Autonomous moral development level, 446

Balance of payments (BOP), 215, 215*t*, 227n137
Balance of trade
  adjustments, 279–280
  deficits, 376
  mercantilism and, 236
Balance sheet approach, 833
Balance sheets, foreign currency translations and, 792*t*
Balanced scorecard, 673–674
Baldridge Criteria for Excellence Award, 758
Bangladesh, 727
  child labor and, 463
  garment factory collapse in, 749
  Grameen/Danone Foods joint venture and, 731–732, 731*m*
  workers killed in fire in, 58

Bank for International Settlements (BIS), 343
 foreign-exchange market and, 346*f*
Bankruptcy, 162
Banks
 central, 386–387
 foreign-exchange trading and, 354–356, 355*t*
Barbados, 106
Bargaining school theory, 629
Barter, 601*t*
Base currencies, 351
Base of the Pyramid (Bop), 214–215, 219, 682, 732
 Grameen/Danone Foods joint venture and, 726–732, 731*m*
Base salary, expatriate compensation, 834
Basel Committee on Global Banking Supervision, 416
Basel Convention on the Transboundary Movement of Hazardous Wastes and Their Disposal, 584
Basis of rule, 156–160. *See also* Rule of law; Rule of man
 rule of law, 156–157
 rule of man, 156
Behavioral/cultural practices, affecting international business, 100–109
Beijing
 Consensus, 147
 Silk Market of, 168–169
BenQ, 751
Berlin Wall, 142, 148, 191
Berne Convention for the Protection of Literary and Artistic Works, 165, 167
Biases, forecasting and, 396
Bicultural, 95, 118
Bid, 351
Big Mac index, 392–393, 393*t*
Bilateral integration, 304
BIS (Bank for International Settlements), 388–389
Bitcoins, 170
Black markets, 389
Body language, 111–112, 112*f*. *See also* nonverbal communication
Bolivia, 223n16
Bombings, 545–546
Bonds, international, 418–420
Booking centers, 431
BoP, 727
Born global, 572–573
Born-global companies, 51, 572–573
Borsa Italiana, 779
Boundaries, 668–669
Boundaryless company, 514, 668–669
Boundarylessness, 668
Bracero program, 259
Brain drain, 257
Brand acquisition, 717
Brand image, 64
Branding strategies, 715–717
 marketing mix and, 715–717
 Tommy Hilfiger case, 698–699
 worldwide vs. local brands, 716–717
Brands, 715
 acquisition of, 717
 generic, 461
 professional sports players as, 45
 worldwide vs. local, 716–717
Brazil, 53, 180, 199, 421
 Amazon rain forest, 285
 automobiles and, 494
 BRICs and, 217–222
 Burger King in, 526–528
 Greenhouse gas (GHG) emissions, 459–460
 racial quotas in, 102
 state capitalism and, 198
 World Trade Organization (WTO) and, 306
Breast Health International, 698
Bretton Woods Agreement, 375, 377
Bribe Payers Index, 452
Bribery, 451. *See also* Corruption
 as business as usual, 451*f*
 corporate, 451
 corruption and, 451–454
 extortion and, 545–546
 Foreign Corrupt Practices Act (FCPA) and, 453–454
 point/counterpoint feature, 455–456
 Siemens AG and, 455–456
BRICs, 199–200, 217–222, 436, 452, 465. *See also* Brazil; China; India; Russia
 Burger King in, 528–529
 case, 217–222
 changing markets and, 218–219
 the dollar and, 221
 future of, 221
 IMF and, 375
 National Challenges, 220
 World Trade Organization (WTO) and, 306
British Airport Authority (BAA), 632
Budgeting, capital, 793–794
Bulgari SpA, 436
Bureau of Customs and Border Protection (CBP), 289, 593, 608n108
Bureau of Labor Statistics, 172n8
Bureaucratic control, 679
Burger King case, 526–528, 527*m*, 531, 539, 540, 552
Business dividend, economic growth and, 207
Buy Local, 290
Buyback, 601*t*
CAFTA-DR. *See* Central American Free Trade Agreement-Dominican Republic (CAFTA-DR)
Calyon, 419
CAN (Andean Community), 322
Canada-Israel RTA, 308
Canada-U.S. Free Trade Agreement of 1989, 317
Capital Asset pricing model (CAPM), 520n21
Capital budgeting, 793–794
Capital, factor-mobility theory and, 255
Capital markets, *see* global capital markets
Capital markets, accounting and, 781*f*
Capital structures, 413–416, 414*t*
 factors affecting, 414–416
 global capital markets and, 413–416
 leveraging debt financing, 413–414
 regulatory risk and, 415–416
Capitalism, 194, 224n41
 market economy and, 194
Capitalization, market, 422m
Carbon footprint, 55, 459, 460
Career globalization case, 810–811
Caribbean Basin Initiative, 232
CARICOM (Caribbean Community), 320–322
CARICOM Single Market and Economy (CSME), 321
Caribbean Community (CARICOM), 320–322
Carry trade, 348, 402
Cash flows
 capital budgeting and, 793–794
 capital structures and, 413–416
 MNEs and, 794–795, 796*f*, 797*f*
 multilateral netting and, 797*f*
Cash management, global, 795–797
Catastrophic political risks, 149*f*, 151
Catfish case, 272–274, 273*m*, 288, 292–293
Censorship, 175n98
Central African Republic, 162
Central American Common Market (CACM), 230–231, 320, 372
Central American Free Trade Agreement-Dominican Republic (CAFTA-DR), 320, 322–324, 372, 380, 384
Central Bank of Canada, 387
Central Bank of Japan, 387
Central Bank of the U.K., 387
Central banks, 386–387
Central European Free Trade Agreement (CEFTA), 313*m*
Central Intelligence Agency (CIA) *World Fact Book*, 317*t*
Centralization, 660
 decentralization *vs.*, 661*t*
 dynamic balance and, 660–661
 principles/practices of, 661*t*
Centralized manufacturing strategy, 744
Centrally planned economy. *See* Command economy
CEOs, expatriate compensation, 837
Certified Emission Reduction (CER), 459
CFA franc zone, 405n17
Chaebols, 671, 688
Change
 culture and, 95–96
 prime locations and, 553–554
 resistance to, 117
 value chains and, 500–501
Chartists, 396
Chase, 685
Chicago Mercantile Exchange (CME) Group, 356
Chief financial officer (CFO)
 global perspective of, 413
 role of, 413, 776
Child labor, 463, 749
Chilean miners, 2010 rescue of, 50
China, 145, 148, 156, 180, 199, 307, 324, 741
 Apple products manufacturing in, 744
 attraction of, 130

automobiles and, 494
bribery and, 451
BRICs and, 217–222
Burger King in, 528–529
business risks and opportunities, 130–133
carbon footprint, 219
car ownership in, 219
case, 130–133
Chinese yuan, 363, 366–367
contaminated food imported from, 290
cost leadership strategy, 486
counterfeiting and, 133
Cultural Revolution, 218
economic challenges, 365–366
Ford Motor in, 494
foreign laws and, 165
future of, 133
GCL-Poly Energy and, 197
Gini coefficient, 226n118
Global financial crises, 365
GM and, 494
Great Leap Forward era, 196
Infrastructure, 130
intellectual property and, 165
iPhones, 738–740
Law on Joint Ventures Using Chinese and Foreign Investment (1978), 130
legal system and, 132
legality of illegality, 132–133
luxury goods market and, 435–436
Mandate of Heaven, 173n16
manufacturing and, 745
map of, 131*m*
market potential, 130
mediation and, 173n15
Meliá Hotels International case, 614–615
multinational enterprises (MNEs) in, 130–131
one child policy, 93, 173n39
pay of manufacturing workers, 172n8
pearl farmers, 486
piracy, 132–133
political and legal environment, 132, 134
Prada Group case and, 434, 436–437
reality of, 131–132
resources, 130
risks and opportunities, 130–133
solar energy industry and, 184–185
state capitalism and, 131, 197–198
strategic positioning, 130–131
Tiananmen Square Protests of 1989, 225n92
working age population, 226n102
World Trade Organization (WTO) and, 306
China Daily, 830
China National Petroleum, 117
China Price phenomenon, 512
China State Construction Engineering, 633
Chinese Communist Party (CCP), 130, 140, 146–148, 156
Chinese currency case, 361–367
Chinese yuan, 366–367, 399
Choice, cultural change by, 96
CINDE (Coalición Costarricense de Iniciativas de Desarrollo), 232–233
Civil and commercial laws, 153
Civil law, 154*m*, 155
Civilizations, clash of, 147–148. *See also* Cultural differences
Clan control, 679–680, 694n81
Clash
of civilizations, 147–148
of cultures, 638
Classical approach. *See* Separate entity approach; Separate entity approach
Classical organizational structures, 662, 663*f*
Clean Development Mechanism (CDM), 459
Clearspire, 693n54
Climate Action Partnership, U.S., 443
Climate change
Artic sea ice and, 188–189
greenhouse gas (GHG) emissions, 457
Kyoto Protocol and, 312*t*, 457–458
Northwest Passage and, 189
Climate, product demand and, 718
Closing businesses, legal issues in, 162
Clothing industry cases. *See* Apparel industry cases
Cluster effect, 491
Clustering, 51
MNEs and, 491–492
value-chain configuration and, 491–492
CME (Chicago Mercantile Exchange) Group, 356
CNN, 115
Code of conduct, 464–466
Code of ethics, 464–465
Cold War, 142
Cold War Era, 199
Collaborative arrangements, 61, 611–651
airline alliances case, 642–647
alliance types, 623–624
compensation and, 627
control and, 627, 635*f*, 637
costs and, 624–625
dealing with partners, 640–641
equity alliances and, 618*f*, 634
exporting *vs.*, 619–620
franchising, 618*f*, 630–631
general motives for, 624–625, 624*f*
innovation and, 641–642
international, 640–641
international, managing, 638–641
international motives for, 624*f*, 625–627
joint ventures, 618*f*, 634, 726–732, 731*m*
learning from experience, 639
licensing agreements, 618*f*, 629–630
management contracts, 618*f*, 631–632
managing, 638–641
Meliá Hotels International case, 612–618, 613*m*
noncollaborative foreign equity arrangements *vs.*, 618*f*, 621–623
oneworld Alliance and, 642–647
operating modes and, 618*f*, 639
prior company expansion and, 627
problems with, 635–638
reasons for, 623–627, 624*f*
securing vertical and horizontal links, 625
switching modes, 639
turnkey operations, 618*f*, 632–634
types of, 618*f*, 627–635
Collectivism, 106–107, 135–136. *See also* Totalitarianism
family and, 106–107
Colombia, 538
Burger King in, 528, 531
Colors, silent language and, 111
Columbia, immigration and, 257*m*
Comeback of emerging economies. *See* Emerging economies
COMESA (Common Market for Eastern and Southern Africa), 317*t*, 326*m*
Command economy, 195–196
companies in, 224n44
Commercial Bills of Exchange, 357
Commercial invoice, 589*f*, 608n95
Committee on Foreign Investment in the United States (CFIUS), 282
Commodities
economic integration and, 329–331
global economy and, 328
sales, product orientation and, 701
Commodity agreements, 328–331
consumers and producers, 328–329
Common currency, Africa and, 384–385
Common law, 154*m*, 155
Common Market, 309
Common Market for Eastern and Southern Africa (COMESA), 308, 317*t*, 326*m*, 327, 384
Communications, 535–536
cultures and, 109–112
globalization and, 50
silent language and, 111–112
spoken and written language, 109–110
Communism, 195
Communist Bloc, 142
Commuter assignment, 815
Companies
born-global, 572–573
boundaryless, 668–669
company controllers, 776, 777*f*
country attractiveness/company strength matrix, 638–639, 639*f*
foreign exchange and, 356–358
orientations, cultures and, 114
quality standards, 759
Company attractiveness/company strength matrix, 639*f*
Comparable access argument, 280
Comparative advantage, 239
Comparative trade advantage, 239–240
production possibilities and, 239*f*

Compatibility, 742–744
  changes in strategy, 744
  global manufacturing strategies and, 742–744
  of international business operations, 539–543
Compensation, for expatriates, 833–839, 835*f*
Competencies, collaborative arrangements and, 625
Competition
  collaborative arrangements and, 625
  globalization and, 51, 65
  heading off, 542–543
  international business and, 65
Competitive advantage, 252
  diamond of national advantage and, 251
  diamond of national advantage theory, 250–252, 251*f*, 255
Competitive environment
  company resources and, 64
  competitors and, 65
  international business and, 64–65
  marketing and, 701*f*
  operating modes and, 618*f*
  organizations and, 657*f*
Competitive gap, 724
Competitive lead time, 550
Competitive Risk, 539–540
Composition of Official Foreign Exchange Reserves (COFER), 386
Compound duty, 287
Computing Research Association, 830
Concentrated, 489
Concentration strategy, 550
Conduct, code of, 464–465
Confidence, in exchange-rate determination, 395
Configuration, 489–496
  business environment quality, 490
  economies of scale and, 492
  innovation context, 490
  labor costs, 492–496
  sourcing, 749–750
  value chains and, 489–496
Confirmed letter of credit, 358, 369n18
Consolidation, 790
Consortium, 634
Constitutional law, 153
Consumer Price Index (CPI), 209, 225n93
Consumers
  divergent behavior of, 505–506
  globalization and, 51
  trade policies and, 276
Continuous improvement, 756
Contract, 176n135
Contract manufacturer, 748
Contract manufacturing, 738–740, 748
Contracts, making/enforcing, 161–162
Control. *See also* Control mechanisms
  bureaucratic control, 679
  clan control, 679–680
  collaborative arrangements and, 635*f*
  global manufacturing strategies and, 746
  market control, 679
  for organizations, 679–681
Control mechanisms, 680–681
  evaluation metrics, 680
  information systems, 680–681
  reports, 680
  visits to subsidiaries, 680
Control systems, organization, 672–681
Controlled foreign corporation (CFC), 426–427, 427*t*
Controllers, 776, 777*f*
Controlling convertibility, 390–391
  import deposits, 390
  licenses, 390
  multiple exchange rates, 390
  quantity controls, 391
Conventional fixed-peg arrangement, 380
Conventional moral development level, 446
Convergence
  European Union (EU) and, 786–787
  first steps in, 785
  International Accounting Standards Board (IASB) and, 784–787
  international standards and, 784–787
  mutual recognition *vs.*, 784, 787
Convertibility, 389–391
COOL (country-of-origin labeling), 163
Cooperation
  Antarctica and, 53–54
  cross-national, 52, 327–328
  oceans and, 53–54
  outer space and, 53–54
Coopetition, 624
Coordination, 497–500, 672
  core competency, 499
  global manufacturing strategies and, 746
  Johnson & Johnson case and, 655
  by mutual adjustment, 677
  operational obstacles, 500
  by plan, 675–677
  by standardization, 672
  subsidiary networks, 499–500
  value chains and, 497–500
Coordination systems, 672–679
  by mutual adjustment, 677–679
Copyright, 52, 61, 63, 132, 164–165
Core competency, 499, 522n82
Corporate bribery. *See* Bribery
Corporate code of ethics, 464–465
Corporate culture, 638, 688, 689
Corporate responsibility, 464–465
  motivations for, 465
Corporate taxation, 426
Corporate universities, 685–687
Corporation, controlled foreign, 426–427, 427*t*
Corruption, 451, 451*f*
  addressing, 452–454
  addressing with Industry initiatives, 454
  bribery and, 451–454
  consequences of, 452
  Foreign Corrupt Practices Act (FCPA), 453–454
  point/counterpoint feature, 455–456
  relativism and, 454
  responsibility and, 454
  rule of law and, 454
Corruption Perceptions Index, 135, 451
Cosmopolitanism, 726
Cost-benefit analysis, of change, 117
Cost leadership, 486
Cost-minimization strategies, 742
Cost-of-living allowance, expatriate compensation, 835–836
Cost-plus pricing strategy, 709–710, 710*f*
Cost-plus strategy, 709
Cost strategies, 64
Costa Rica, 231*m*
  CAFTA-DR and, 322–324
  CINDE and, 232, 233
  coffee/wheat example, 238–240, 238*f*, 239*f*
  comparative trade advantage example, 240
  foreign trade case, 230–233
  history of trade in, 230–232
  miscalculations and mixed results, 231–232
  natural advantage and, 237
  resource efficiency and, 240
  strategic trade policy and, 232
  trade evolution case, 233
Costs
  of globalization, 56
  governmental incentives and disincentives, 536
  scanning and, 534–536
Cotonou Agreement, 285
Council for Trade in Goods, 307
Council for Trade-Related Aspects of Intellectual Property Rights, 307
Council of Supply Chain Management Professionals, 740
Council of the European Union, 313
Counterfeiting, 133, 176n164
Counterparty risk, 410
Counterpurchase, 601*t*
Countertrade (offsets), 291, 601–602, 601*t*
Countries
  business operations regulated in, 161t, 163*t*
  current account balances of, 215*t*
  developing, 705–706
  needs hierarchy comparison, 105, 105*f*
  strategy and characteristics of, 163
  understanding, expatriates, 828–829
Country attractiveness/company strength matrix, 638–639
Country comparison tools, 545–548
  grids, 547, 547*t*
  matrices, 548
Country evaluation and selection, 525–560
  allocating among locations, 548–552
  Burger King case, 526–528, 527m
  competitive risk and, 539–543
  cost considerations, 534–536
  data collection and analysis, 543–545
  distance sensitivity and, 541*t*
  economic and demographic variables, 533–543
  natural disasters and, 540

noncomparative decision making, 552–553
prime locations and, 553–554
violent areas and, 545–546
Country-of-origin, 163
exporting and, 620
Country-of-origin image, 717
Country-of-origin labels, 314
Country-similarity theory, 246–247, 308
effects of cultural similarity, 247
effects of political relationships and economic agreements, 247
product differentiation, 246–247
specialization and acquired advantage, 246
Country size trade theory, 242
Crawling bonds, 373
Crawling pegs, 373
Creeping expropriation, 151
Creolization, 96
Cricket, 46
Criminal law, 153
Cross-border trade liberalization. *See* Trade
Cross-licensing, 629
Cross-national agreements (economic integration), 301–338. *See also* Regional economic integration; Regional trading groups; *specific agreements*; United Nations; World Trade Organization (WTO)
bilateral, 307–308
commodity agreements, 328–331
cross-national cooperation and, 52
European trade and, 313*m*
Toyota in Europe Case (SUB), 302–304
Unilever case, 332–336
Cross-national cooperation, 52, 327–328
Cross rate, 348
Cuba, 283
Meliá Hotels International (CASE), 612–613
work motivation and, 104
Cuba embargo case, 290
Cues, perception of, 108
Cultural awareness, 93–94
Cultural collision, 93
Cultural differences
in accounting, 781–784
clashes and, 638
dealing with, 112–115, 117–118
degree of, 112–114
Secrecy-Transparency/Optimism-Conservatism Matrix, 783, 783*f*
Cultural diffusion, 96
geography and, 101
Cultural distance, 113
Cultural diversity, 92–93
Cultural environments, 87–128. *See also* Cultures
Cultural factors, 533
accounting and, 781*f*, 783*f*
international operations and, 92*f*
Cultural homogeneity, 55
Cultural hybridization, 118–119
Cultural identity, 119
Cultural imperialism, 96
point/counterpoint feature, 115–117
Cultural values, 119, 275*f*
Cultural variables, 100
Culture
delineating, 95
people factor, 92–93
sensitivity and adjustment, 93
Culture clashes, 638
between corporate cultures, 638
between countries, 638
Culture shock, 113–114, 828
Cultures, 92–93
behavioral practices and, 100–109
change and, 95–96, 115–118
communications and, 109–112
cultural awareness, 93–94
defined, 92
formation of, 95–96
future of national cultures, 118–119
geography and, 101
hidden cultural attitudes in, 113
high-context, 108
host society acceptance, 112
information processing and, 108–109
languages and, 96–99
low-context, 108
monochronic, 109
nations *vs.*, 95
people factor, 92
polychronic, 109
punctuality and, 111
relationship preferences and, 106
religions and, 99–100
risk-taking behavior and, 107–108
Saudi Arabia case, 88–92
situational differences and, 106–107
social stratification issues and, 100–101
sports and, 44–46
Tesco PLC case and, 120–124
time and, 111
trust and, 107
Currency
Africa and, 384–385
Chinese, 366–367
dollarization of, 380
fixed or managed rate and, 385–386
floating rate and, 385–386
foreign-currency financial statements, 779–780, 790–792
functional, 791*f*
information and, 395
speculation and, 358, 359–360
value, fluctuations in, 711
Currency basket, 364
Currency board, 380
Currency pairs, 348
Currency swaps, 346, 346*f*
Current account balances, 215*t*
Current-rate method, 790–792
Customary law, 154*m*, 155, 175n116
Customer satisfaction, 756
Customers
competitors, following, 542
orientation, marketing strategies and, 702
satisfied, TQM and, 756–757
Customs brokers, 593–595
Customs Unions, 309
Customs valuation, 288–289
Cyprus, banking crisis in, 395

Danone Foods/Grameen joint venture (case), 726–732, 731*m*
DDT (pesticide), 449, 705–706
Deal-focus (DF) culture, 93
Debt, 211
exchange rates, capital structure and, 414–415
Debt crisis
Greek, 376
UN Conference on Trade and Development UNCTAD, 328
Debt financing, leveraging, 413–414
Debt markets, 416
Decentralization, 654, 660
centralization *vs.*, 661*t*
dynamic balance and, 660–661
Johnson & Johnson case and, 654–655
principles/practices of, 661*t*
Decision making
exchange-rate changes and, 397–398
make-or-buy, 750
Decline stage, product life cycle trade theory, 249*t*, 250
Deflation, 210
Deforestation, 458
Delisting, 424
Demand conditions, diamond of national advantage, 251
Deming Award, 758
Democracy, 138, 143–144, 159, 173n36
business implications of, 139
communication innovations and, 142
engines of, 142
ideology of, 173n35
prominent types of, 138*t*
recession/retreat of, 143–145, 157–158
regime legitimacy, 142
Denso, 748
Deontologicical approach, 446, 448
Department of Agriculture, 274
Department of Agriculture, U.S., 449
Department of Commerce, U.S., 545
International Trade Administration, 590
Department of Homeland Security, 593
Department of Justice, U.S., 454
Dependability strategies, global manufacturing, 743
Dependencia theory, 629
Der Spiegel, 830
Derivatives, 343, 800
Design, 478–479
Developed countries, 199–200
Developing countries, 199
marketing in, regulations and, 705–706
Development, 225n76
Diamond of National Advantage theory, 250–252, 251*f*, 255
facets of, 251
limitations of, 252
transformation and, 252
Diamond of national competitive advantage theory, 250
Differentiation, 486–487
competition and, 65
horizontal, 662–666
strategies, 64
Digital divide, 498, 754–755

Digitization, 496
Dim sum bonds, 419
Direct exporting, 576
Direct investment. *See* Foreign direct investment
Direct quotes, 351
Direction, forecasting and, 396
Disclosure, 782
Disclosure/assessment matrix, 783*f*
Discrimination, trade without, 305–306
Dispersed, 489
Dissolution, of joint ventures, 636*f*
Distance
  country-similarity theory and, 247
  power, 106
Distance, silent language and, 111
Distribution, 717
  of languages, 97*m*, 832*t*
  of legal systems, 154*m*
  of religions, 100*m*
  of rule of law, 158*m*
  of stock markets, 422*m*
Distribution gap, 724
Distribution strategies, 717–723
  challenges, 720–721
  choosing channels/distributors, 720
  e-commerce and the Internet, 721–723
  hidden costs and, 719–721
  marketing mix and, 717–723
  partnerships, 720
  reliability of after-sales service, 720–721
  self-handling, 719–720
  Tommy Hilfiger case, 698–700
Distributive political risks, 149*f*, 150–151
Diversification
  developing an industrial base and, 278–279
  exporting and, 570–571
  importing and, 580
  LEGO® Group case, 554–557
Diversification strategy, 550
Divesting, 552
Division of gains, 241
Divisional organization structure, 662, 664
Divisional structures, 662
DMAIC, 758
Doctors without Borders (Médecins Sans Frontières), 328, 545–546
Documentation, export, 588*t*, 589*f*
Dodd-Frank Wall Street Reform and Consumer Protection Act, 409–410
Doha Ministerial Declaration. *See* Doha Round
Dollar, U.S., 402
  dollarization, 373, 374
  El Salvador and, 372–374
  foreign-exchange market and, 347–348
  as safe-haven currency, 401
  yen and, 387–388
Dollar/yen currency pair, 348
Dollarization, of currency, 380
Domestic business, international business vs., 62–65
Domestic consumption, 236, 556
Domestic law, 63
Dominican Republic, 106
Double taxation, 429–430
Dow Jones Sustainability Index, 444
Draft (or commercial bill of exchange), 357
Drugs, generic, 461
Dubai, 760
Dubai Financial Market, 423
Dubai, Western Union and, 342
Due diligence, 175n110
Dumping, 281
  e-waste, 581–584, 581*m*
  prices, 281
  unfair competition: dumping, 273
Duty, 286
Dynamic balance, 660–661, 693n19
Dynamic effects, 309
  NAFTA, 317–318

e-Commerce, 577, 721–723, 754–755
E-waste, 581–584, 581*m*
Early PwC International Challenge Program (EPIC), 815
Earthquake, 402–403
Earthquake/tsunami, Japan, 540
East African Council of Ministers, 384
Ecomagination case, 442–447
Economic analysis, 209–217
  balance of payments, 215
  debt, 211
  Global Competitiveness Index (GCI), 216
  global indices and, 215–217
  Global Innovation Index (GII), 216
  income distribution, 211–212
  inflation, 209–210
  poverty, 212–213
  unemployment, 210–211
  Where to be Born Index (WTBBI), 217
  World Competitiveness Index (WCI), 216
Economic and Monetary Community for Central Africa (CAEMC), 384
Economic Community of Central African States, 384
Economic Community of West African States (ECOWAS), 326*m*, 384
Economic connections, business operations and, 234*f*
Economic development, assessing
  alternative methods, 204–205
  performance and potential, 199–206
Economic Development Board (EDB), 294, 295
Economic efficiency, specialization trade theories and, 240
Economic environments, 179–227, 184–186
  accounting and, 781*f*, 783*f*
  economic freedom, 189–194
  international economic analysis, 187–188
Economic exposure, 798
Economic factors, business operations in, 187*f*
Economic freedom, 189–194
  global distribution of, 191*m*
  Index, 190*t*, 196
  by region with population, 192*f*
  standard of living and, 192*f*
  state capitalism *vs.*, 197–198
  today, 190–191
  trends in, 191, 193
  value of, 191
Economic Freedom Index, 189
Economic growth
  environmental stress and, 55
  point/counterpoint feature, 207–208
Economic Integration Agreement, 309
Economic integration (cross-national agreements), 304. *See also* Regional trading groups; World Trade Organization (WTO)
  bilateral, 304, 307–308
  in Central America and the Caribbean, 320*m*
  commodity agreements, 328–331
  common market and, 309
  cross-national cooperation and, 52, 327–328
  European trade and, 313*m*
  global, 304
  local responsiveness *vs.*, 503–508
  regional, 304
  Toyota in Europe Case, 302–304
  Unilever case, 332–336
Economic motives, factor-mobility theory and, 256
Economic performance, measures of, 200
  gross domestic product (GDP), 203–204
  gross national income (GNI), 200–201
  gross national product (GNP), 201
Economic rationales, for government trade intervention, 279–282
Economic relationships with other countries, government intervention and, 279–282
Economic systems, 194–197
  command economy, 195–196
  market economy, 194
  mixed economies, 196–197
  test for, 193–194
  types of, 194–197, 194*f*
Economies of scale, 311, 492
The Economist, 392
Economist Intelligence Unit (EIU), 143–145, 157, 174n59, 174n67, 174n68, 174n74, 174n80
Ecuador
  currency of, 372–373
eCycling Leadership Initiative, 582
Education
  cultural awareness and, 94
  global distribution of university students (top 52 countries), 491*t*
  learning abroad, 118
  learning foreign languages, 829–831, 832*f*
  preparation programs for expatriates, 828–829
Educational toys, 556
Effective tariff, 287
Efficiency/cost global manufacturing strategies, 742
Efficiency, standardization and, 504–505
Egypt, 175n98
  Mubarak regime, 153
El Salvador case, 371–374
Electronic Data Interchange (EDI), 753
Electronic trading, 345, 355, 359, 366
Elephant poaching, 283, 284*f*
Embargoes, 290, 297*f*
  defined, 290

Emerging economies, 199, 199*t*
case, 180–183
economic situation, good/bad, 183*f*
emergence, 180–181
future of, 180
infant-industry argument, 277–278
leading, 183
map of, 181*m*
precedents in, 181–182
predictions for, 181–182
Emerging markets, 199
challenges of, 185
comeback of, 182*f*
differences in countries, 184–185
economic and political changes, 185
government and policies, 185–186
new perspectives and, 184
Employee involvement, TQM and, 756–757
Employment
full employment as government objective, 276
social stratification and, 100–101
specialization trade theories and, 240
Endaka, 400–401
Energy, 220, 325, 442, 444
English language, 116, 829–831
culture and, 98
misspeaking in, 110*t*
Enterprise Resource Planning (ERP), 753
Environmental and Natural Resources Defense Council, 442
Environmental issues
e-wastes and, 581–584, 581*m*
Ecomagination case, 442–445
economic growth and, 207
ethics and, 456–458
Environmental Protection Agency, U.S., 582
Environmental stress
economic growth and, 55
global growth and cooperation and, 55–56
Equilibrium exchange rate, 385*f*
Equity alliances, 618*f*, 634
Equity capital, 414
Equity-capital markets, 420–421. *See also* Stock markets
Equity securities, 420–421
Eritrea, 115
ESADE, 815
Escalation of commitment, 532
Essential-industry argument, 282–286
Established market economies, 200
Esteem needs, 105, 105*f*
Ethical behavior
companies interest in, 447
corporate bribery and, 451
cultural foundations of, 447–449
environmental issues and, 456–458
foundations of, 446–447
legal foundations of, 449–451
moral development levels, 446–447
pharmaceutical industry and, 460–462
relativism/normativism and, 448–450
workers and, 462*f*
Ethical dilemmas, 449
Ethical Trading Initiative (ETI), 462–463
Ethics, code of, 464–465
Ethnocentric framework, 818
Ethnocentric staffing framework, 818–819, 823*t*
Ethnocentrism, 114, 726
Euro, 315, 381–382, 402
conversion to, 382–384
European Union (EU) and, 314–315
foreign-exchange market and, 348–349
global financial crisis and, 383–384
pluses and minuses of conversion to, 383–384
Euro/dollar currency pair, 348
Eurobonds, 416, 419–420
Eurocredit, 417
Eurocurrencies, 416–418
Eurocurrency market, 416–418
interest rates and, 417–418
Eurodollar, 416, 417
Euroequity market, 416, 423–424
Euromoney, 355, 355*t*
Europe
debt crisis and, 315, 383, 399
economic crisis in, 414
Parmalat case, 772–776
Toyota case, 302–304
European Central Bank (ECB), 145, 312, 376, 382–383, 386–387, 394, 402, 415
European Commission, 312, 453, 543, 775
European Community (EC), 311, 382
European Council, 312
European Court of Justice, 313
European Economic Area (EEA), 313*m*
European Economic Community (EEC), 311
European Free Trade Association (EFTA), 308, 311, 313*m*
European Monetary System (EMS), 382
European Monetary Union (EMU), 382
European Parliament, 312–313, 316
European Quality Award, 758
European terms, 351
European trade, economic integration and, 313*m*
European Union (EU), 160, 169, 175n110, 280, 285, 290, 306, 308–309, 332, 376, 434, 545, 593, 717, 759, 784, 786
balancing "common denominators" with national differences, 316–317
bilateral agreements, 316
bribery and, 453
corruption and, 453
doing business with (implications for corporate strategy), 316
Euro and, 315
European trade and economic integration, 313*m*
governing bodies, 312–313
milestones, 312*t*
organizational structure, 312–313
predecessors, 311
Toyota in Europe case, 302–304
Evolution to floating exchange rates, 376–377
Jamaica Agreement, 377
Smithsonian Agreement, 377
Ex-Im Bank, 605n2
Exchange-rate changes
business implications of, 397–398
risk and, 539
Exchange rates, 343, 396
arrangements, 377–384, 378–379*m*
arrangements and anchors, 377*t*
business implications of changes in, 397–398
capital structure/debt and, 415–416
circumstances, 397
competition and, 341
confidence factors, 397
determination of, 371–406
equilibrium, 385*f*
factors to monitor, 396
floating, 376–377, 380–381
forecasting, 395–397
fundamental analyses of, 397
government intervention and, 388–389
interest rates and, 394–395
International Monetary Fund (IMF) and, 374–377
movement, diagram of, 385*f*
purchasing power parity (PPP) and, 391–394
Sony case and, 399–404
technical analyses, 397
Exchanges, foreign-exchange trading and, 354–356
Expansion
debt markets and, 416
European Union (EU) and, 315–317
Expatriate failure, 840–841
costs of, 840
exceptions and anomalies, 840
Expatriate selection, 824–826
adaptiveness, 824–826
technical competence, 824
Expatriates, 814
assignments, 814–817
benefits of the experience, 809*f*
compensating, 833–839
concerns of, 827*f*
demographics of, 815–816
failure of, 840–841
family and, 828
global career case and, 810–811
key competencies of, 826*f*
management of, 823–829, 833–841
perspectives of, 814–818
preparation programs for, 828–829
repatriating, 837–839
reverse, 817
selection of, 824–826
trends in assignments, 814–817
types of, 814
Expectation, of success and reward, 104
Export Assistance Center, 590
Export documentation, 588*t*, 589*f*
Export intermediaries, 591–593
Export Management Company (EMC), 591–592
Export Trading Company (ETC), 592–593
fees, 593
Export-led development, 279
Export license, 290
Export plan, 596–599
defined, 596
Export price escalation, 710–712

Export processing zone (EPZ), 232
Export quotas, 289
Export tariffs, 286
Export Trading Company Act, 592–593
Exporting, 561–609
  advantages of, 567–568
  Alibaba case and, 602–604
  approaches to, 575–578
  assistance/resources and, 590–596, 591*t*
  collaborative arrangements *vs.*, 619–620
  country of origin and, 620
  customer management, 585–586
  defined, 566
  direct, 575–576
  e-waste, 581–584, 581*m*
  exporter characteristics, 568–569
  exporter types, 567
  factors influencing, 566*f*
  feasibility of, 619–620
  government regulation, 586–587
  indirect, 576
  initiating/developing, 571–575
  International Business Expertise, 586
  leading barriers to, 585*t*
  marketing challenges, 586
  merchandise, 60
  problems and pitfalls, 584–588
  reasons for, 569–571
  resources and assistance, 588, 590–596, 591*t*
  serendipity in, 575
  services, 60
  SpinCent case and, 562–564
  technology and, 578, 599–600
  top management commitment, 586
  trade documentation, 587–588
Exports
  laissez-faire/interventionist approaches, 233–234
  passive, 701–702
  planning framework, 598*t*
  prices and, 330–331, 712
  quotas, 291
  Voluntary Export Restraint (VER), 289–290
Exposure, management strategy, 798–800
External convertibility, 390
External debt, 211
External sources, of information, 544–545
Extortion, 545–546
Extranet, 754
Extraterritoriality, 450
Facets of the Diamond (of National Competitive Advantage), 251
Facilitating payments, 453
Factor conditions, diamond of national advantage, 251
Factor mobility, 315
Factor-mobility trade theory, 252, 254–255, 260
Factor movements, 256–258
Factor-proportions theory, 243–246
Fair Labor Association, 466, 739
Families, family-based groups, 103
Fascism, 139*t*
Fatalism, 107–108
Favorable balance of trade, 236
FDI. *See* Foreign Direct Investment (FDI)
Federal Drug Administration, 170
Federal Reserve Bank (the Fed), U.S., 380, 417
Federal Rules of Civil Procedure, U.S., 497
Federation of International Trade Associations (FITA), 592
Fees, service exports/imports and, 60
Filière, 501
Finance, 771–806
  accounting and, 776–778
  decisions, exchange-rate changes and, 398
  GPS case, 408–411
Finance function (multinational finance function)
  capital budgeting, 793–794
  CFO's role and, 413
  foreign exchange risk management, 797–800
  global capital markets and, 412–413
  internal sources of funds, 794–795
  offshore financial centers (OFCs), 430–431
  taxation of foreign-source income, 425–426
Financial Accounting Standards Board (FASB), 780, 801
  International Accounting Standards Board (IASB) and, 786
Financial crisis. *See* Global financial crises
Financial hedging strategies, 408–411
  Dell Mercosur in Brazil case, 801–805
Financial institutions, 343
Financial risk, importing/exporting and, 584–585
Financial Stability Oversight Council, 410
Financial statements
  differences in, 778–781
  foreign currency, 779–780, 790–792
  language differences, 779
Financial Times, 850n135
Financial Times 500, 185, 514
Firm-specific assets, 742
Firms
  diamond of national advantage and, 251
  as value chains, 487–489
First-mover advantage, 543
Fiscal dividend, economic growth and, 208
Fisher Effect, 394–395
Five-forces model, 482
Fixed/managed floating rates, 386–387
Flexibility, strategies, global manufacturing, 744
Flexpatriates, 815
Floating, 379
Flow of goods and services, 275*f*. *See also* Trade
Fluctuations, in currency value, 711
Focus strategy, 64
Following customers/ competitors, 542
Food and Drug Administration (FDA), U.S., 274, 705
Football, 46
Foreign bonds, 418
Foreign-change trading, banks and, 355*t*
Foreign Corrupt Practices Act (FCPA), 450, 453–454, 456, 461
Foreign currency financial statements, 779–780, 790–792
Foreign currency transactions, 788–792
Foreign direct investment (FDI), 193, 304–305, 309–310, 621–623
  acquisitions and, 622–623
  defined, 61
  greenfield investments and, 622–623
  market failure and, 621
  as noncollaborative foreign equity arrangements, 618*f*
  pharmaceutical, India and, 461–462
  pursuit of global strategy and, 622
  reasons for, 621–622
Foreign exchange, 343
  cash flow and, 357–358
  controls, 389–391
  convertibility, 389–391
  defined, 343
  disclosing gains and losses, 792
  financial flows, 358
  risk, management of, 797–800
  risk, scanning and, 539
  usage of, companies and, 356–358
Foreign-exchange controls, 291
Foreign-exchange exposure, management strategy, 798–800
Foreign-exchange markets, 339–369
  aspects of, 345–349
  average daily volume 1998–2013, 347*f*
  composition of, 346–349
  daily volume, 346*f*
  forward market, 352–353
  future of, 353, 361
  location of, 346–349, 349*f*
  major, 351–353
  options, 346*f*, 353
  players on, 343
  size of, 346–349
  spot market, 351
  turnover, by counterparty, 344*f*
  turnover, by instruments, 346*f*
  types of, 797–798
  Western Union case, 340–342
Foreign-exchange risk, 539
  mobility of funds, 539
Foreign-exchange trading, 345, 353–356
  banks and, 354–356
  exchanges and, 354–356
  geography and, 349
  international time zones and, 349, 350*f*, 350*m*
  point/counterpoint feature, 359–360, 384–385
  process, 353–356, 354*f*
  top dealers, 355–356
  top exchanges, 356
Foreign Investment Advisory Service (FIAS), 233
Foreign languages, learning, 829–831, 832*f*
Foreign niches, product orientation and, 702
Foreign service premium, expatriate compensation, 834
Foreign sourcing, risks, 757
Foreign subsidiary, 426–428
Foreign taxing branch, 426–428

Foreign trade case, Costa Rica, 230–233
Foreign trade investment case, LUKOIL, 262–266
Foreign trade zones FTZs, 759–760
Fortune 100, 811
The Fortune at the Bottom of the Pyramid, 726
Forward discount, 352–353
Forward market, 352–353
Forward premium, 352–353
France, 104
Franchising, 61
  collaborative arrangements and, 618*f*, 630–631
  franchise organization and, 630–631
  operational modifications, 631
"Free" country, 141
Free markets. *See also* Economic freedom
  fear of, 193
  the market test, 193–194
Free Trade Agreements (FTA), 309
  impact of, 310*f*
Free Trade Area (AFTA), 308
Free trade theories, 236–237
Freedom, 174n51
  consequences of, 142
  gains/declines in, 144*f*
  map of, 141*m*
  standard of, 140–142
  in world, 144*f*
Freedom House, 140–141, 144, 174n51
Freight forwarders, 595
French Open tennis tournament, 60
Fringe benefits, expatriate compensation, 835
Frugal innovation, 483
Fukushima Dai-ichi nuclear power station, 458
Fully convertible currencies, 389
Functional currency, 791*f*
Functional structure, 662
Fundamental forecasting, 396
Funds, 794
  internal sources, finance function and, 794–795
  mobility, risk and, 539
  sovereign wealth, 420–421
Future directions
  collaboration and innovation, 641–642
  corporate universities, 685–687
  ethical dilemmas in the global economy, 466
  exports/imports and technology, 599–600
  foreign-exchange markets, 361
  GAAP (Generally Accepted Accounting Principles, U.S.), 800–801
  global currencies, 398–399
  global supply chain, 761
  government efforts to increase tax revenue, 433–434
  growth of capital markets, 433–434
  IFRS, 800–801
  international assignments, 841–842
  international business and, 65–66
  national cultures, 118–119
  political ideologies, 146–148, 159
  prime location changes, 553–554
  rise of robots (automation), 498
  robotics, 498
  segment markets, 725–726
  state capitalism, 197–198
  trade, 260–261
  trade agreements, 293–294
  trade restrictions, 293
  WTO and bilateral/regional integration efforts, 331–332
Future orientation, 107
Futures, 353
Futures contract, 346
FX swap, 346
FXpert software, 410–411, 79

G8 countries, 376, 458
GAAP. *See* Generally Accepted Accounting Principles (GAAP)
Gap, 59
Gap analysis, 723–725, 724*f*
  aggregating, 725
  distribution and competition, 725
  product line, 725
  usage, 724–725
GDP. *See* Gross domestic product (GDP)
Gender-based groups, 102–103
Gender roles, 90–91
General Administration of Press and Publication (China), 831
General Agreement for Trade in Services, 307
General Agreement on Tariffs and Trade (GATT), 305–306
  trade without discrimination, 305
  World Trade Organization (WTO) and, 305–306
General Electric Ecomagination Initiative, 442–445, 443*m*
General purpose FTZ, 759–760
Generally Accepted Accounting Principles (GAAP), 783–784, 787–788, 801
  future of, 800–801
  IFRS *vs.*, 787–788
  international tax practices and, 425–426
  point/counterpoint feature, 787–788
  reconciliation and, 784–787
  usage differences, 780, 783–784
Generic, 717
Generic brand names, 717
Generic brands, 461
Genuine Progress Indicator (GPI), 205
Geocentric staffing framework, 821–822, 823*t*
Geocentrism, 114
Geographic diversification, concentration *vs.*, 541–542, 550–551
Geographic division structure, 664–665
Geography
  Artic sea ice, 188–189
  culture and, 101
  foreign-exchange trading and, 349
  natural disasters and, 540
  product demand and, 247–248, 718
  trade flow and, 308–309
  value-chain configuration and, 491–492
German Commercial Code (HGB), 784
Germany
  economic policies of, 173n32
  reunification of, 48
Gini coefficient, 212
  China and, 226n118
  global, 226n119
Global Business Coalition on HIV/AIDS, Tuberculosis and Malaria, 470
Global Business Council on HIV/AIDS, 468
Global capital markets, 407–439
Global cash management, 795–797
Global competition, 51
Global Competitiveness Index (GCI), 216
Global convergence. *See* Convergence
Global economic crisis, 329
Global economic integration. *See* Economic integration; Economic integration (cross-national agreements)
Global economy
  commodities and, 328
Global financial crises, 218, 365, 410, 483, 507, 604
  emerging economies case and, 181–182
  Euro and, 383–384
  GPS case and, 410
  international business risk and, 59
  International Monetary Fund (IMF) and, 376
  state capitalism and, 198
Global Foreign-Exchange Markets. *See* Foreign-Exchange markets
Global Greening of General Electric case, 442–445
Global Innovation Index (GII), 216
Global integration, 304, 503–505
Global integration, local responsiveness *vs.*, 503–508
Global manufacturing strategies, 740–741. *See also* Manufacturing
Global marketing. *See* Marketing
Global Positioning Solutions (GPS) case, 408–411
Global purchasing, 752
Global rivalry, importing and, 580
Global sourcing. *See* Sourcing
Global sports case, 44–47
Global stock markets. *See* Stock markets
Global strategy, 512–513
Global supply chain. *See* Supply chain
Global supply-chain management. *See* Supply-chain management
Global warming, 457–458
  greenhouse gas emissions, 457
  Kyoto Protocol and, 312*t*, 457–458
Globality, 661
Globalization, 545–546. *See also* International business
  costs of, 54–58
  cultural imperialism and, 115–117
  defined, 47
  domestic vs. international business, 62–65
  ethical behavior and, 441–474
  forces driving, 48–54
  future of, 65–66
  government policies and, 52
  increased factors in, 49–52
  inevitableness of, 65
  international business and, 43–74

Globalization (*continued*)
- local objectives and policies, 55
- local responsiveness *vs.*, 505–507
- of markets, 504
- national sovereignty *vs.*, 55
- regionalism *vs.*, 65
- slowing down of, 65–66
- society and, 445
- sports case, 44–47
- technology and, 49–50

Globalizing career case, 810–811
GNI. *See* Gross national income (GNI)
GNM, 759
Go-no-go decision, 552
Government Accountability Office, U.S., 274
Government agencies
- import/export assistance and, 590–591
- for information, 545

Government intervention
- exchange rates and, 386–387
- pricing strategies and, 709

Government Pension Fund (Norway), 420
Government procurement, 626
Government trade intervention. *See* Trade intervention
Grameem Foundation, 727
Grameen/Danone Foods joint venture case, 726–732, 731*m*
Grameen Foundation, 728, 732
Grameen Intel Social Business LTD., 732
Grandchild subsidiaries, 428*f*
Gray market, 711
Grease money, 453
Great by choice, 484–485
Great Depression, 193
Great Leveling, 600
Greater Arab Free Trade Area (GAFTA), 308, 317*t*
Greek debt crisis, 375
Green economics, 204
Greenfield investments, 622–623
Greenhouse emissions, 442
Greenhouse gas (GHG) emissions, 457–458
Grids
- country comparison tools and, 547, 547*t*
- simplified market-penetration grid, 547*t*

Gross domestic product (GDP), 181, 201, 211
- population size, 203–204
- purchasing power parity (PPP), 203–204
- rate of economic growth, 202–203
- real growth rate, 202*f*
- of top ten economies, 218*f*

Gross National Happiness (GNH), 206
Gross national income (GNI), 200–201, 224n65, 226n108
- largest economies, 201*t*
- largest economies, adjusted for PPP, 204*t*
- per capita, 203*m*, 225n67
- per capita, adjusted for PPP, 205*m*
- population size, 203
- purchasing power parity (PPP), 203–204
- rate of economic growth, 202

Gross national product (GNP), 200
- population size, 203
- purchasing power parity (PPP), 203–204
- rate of economic growth, 202

Group of Twenty (G20), 53, 53*f*
Groups, social stratification and, 100–103
Growth stage, product life cycle trade theory, 249, 249*t*
Guernsey, 175n116
Gulf Cooperation Council, 327
Guttenplan, D.D., 850n124

Hanke-Krus hyperinflation table, 225n94
Happynomics, 206
Hard currencies, 390
Hard peg exchange rate arrangements, 380
Hardship allowances, expatriate compensation, 836
Harmonized Index of Consumer Prices (HICP), 209
Harvesting, 551–552
Hazardous e-waste, 581–584, 581*m*
Heading off competition, 542–543
Headquarters-based compensation, for expatriates, 834
Hedge funds, 347, 359
Hedging strategies, 408–411, 799–800, 803–805
Heritage Foundation, 189
Hierarchy
- classical, 673*f*, 675*f*
- hierarchy-of-needs theory, 105–106, 105*f*
- hyperarchy *vs.*, 673–674

Hierarchy-of-needs theory, 105–106, 105*f*
High collectivism, 106
High-context cultures, 108
High individualism, 106
High power distance, 106
Hiring/firing, legal issues in, 162
HIV/AIDS, 327, 461, 706
- Anglo American PLC and, 468–469
- antiretroviral therapy and, 468
- in South Africa, 467

Holding company income, 427, 428*f*
Home-based compensation, for expatriates, 833–834
Home-country national, 814
Homogeneity, cultural, 55
Hong Kong, Legislative Council of, 174n69
Hong Kong Monetary Authority, 366, 418
Hong Kong Stock Exchange, 421
Hong Kong University of Science and Technology, 816
Horizontal alliances/links, 624–625
Horizontal differentiation, 662–666
Horizontally extended family, 107
Host-based compensation, for expatriates, 834
Host-government policies, 506–507, 522n107
Housing allowance, for expatriates, 836
HR, 820, 824
HRM. *See* Human resource management (HRM)
Human Capital Index, 813
Human Development Index (HDI), 209
Human resource management (HRM), 807–851, 812*f*. *See also* Expatriates
- career globalization case, 810–811
- global company and, 812–813
- staffing frameworks and, 818–823, 823*t*
- strategizing, 813–814

Human trafficking, 284
Hybrid cultures, 118–119

Iceland, 315
Idealism, 109
IMF. *See* International Monetary Fund (IMF)
Immigration, 292
- Europe and, 315
- map of, 257*m*
- money-transfer market and, 340
- North American Free Trade Agreement (NAFTA) and, 319

Imperialism, cultural, 115–117
Import competition
- catfish case and, 272–274, 273*m*
- dealing with, 292

Import deposit requirements, 390
Import licensing, 290, 390
Import quotas, 289
Import substitution, 230
Import tariffs, 286
- imports, 286

Importing, 561–609
- assistance/resources and, 588–596, 591*t*
- characteristics of importers, 579
- customer management, 585–586
- diversification and, 580
- factors influencing, 566*f*
- global rivalry and, 580
- government regulation, 586–587
- importer types, 578–579
- International Business Expertise, 586
- local unavailability and, 580
- marketing challenges, 586
- merchandise, 60
- problems and pitfalls, 584–588
- reasons for, 579–580
- resources and assistance, 588
- resources/assistance and, 588–596, 591*t*
- services and, 578
- specialization of labor and, 580
- top management commitment, 586
- trade documentation, 587–588
- trade restrictions and, 620

Imports
- laissez-faire/interventionist approaches, 233–234
- prices, negotiating, 712*t*
- quotas, 289–290
- services, 60
- substitution, 258–260

Imposition, cultural change by, 96
Inaccuracy, 543
Income
- active vs. passive, 427
- determining subsidiary's, 428
- inequality, globalization and, 56

Income distribution, 211
- benefits and costs, 212
- distribution, 211–212
- GNI and, 211, 212

Income elasticity, 533
Income inequality, 212, 226n112, 226n123, 533

Incoterms, 608n94
Incremental internationalization, 571–572
Indentured, 463
India, 180, 199
  BRICs and, 217–222
  child labor and, 463
  Gini coefficient and, 212
  intellectual property and, 166–167
  leisure/productivity trade-off, 104
  offshoring and, 57
  pharmaceutical FDI in, 461–462
  World Trade Organization (WTO) and, 306
Indirect exporting, 576
Indirect quotes, 351
Individual qualifications, social stratification and, 101–102
Individualism, 106, 135–136
  family and, 106–107
Individualized reports, for information, 544
Industrial base development, government trade intervention and, 278–279
Industrial clusters, 750
Industrial revolution, 497
Industrialization argument, 278
Industry
  essential-industry argument and, 282–286
  infant-industry argument, 277–278
  key, foreign control of, 628–629
  quality standards, 759
Industry change, 483–484
Industry organization (IO) paradigm, 484–485
Industry structure, 482
  strategy/value and, 482–484
Infant-industry argument, 277–278
Inflation, 209–210
  cost of living and, 209
  deflation *vs.*, 209–210
  measuring, 209
Inflation rates, 225n99
Information
  accounting, users of, 780*f*
  collecting/analyzing, country selection and, 543–545
  exchange rates and, 395
  external sources of, 544–545
  internally generated data, 545
  scanning and, 532–544
Information processing, cultures and, 108–109
Information technology (IT), 753
  digital divide and, 754–755
  global supply-chain management and, 753–755
  magical organizations and, 676
Infrastructure, 480–481
Initial public offering (IPO), 420
  Prada Group case and, 436–437
Innovation
  collaborative arrangements and, 641–642
  outsourcing, 750–751
  strategies, global manufacturing, 743
Input optimizers, importers as, 578
Institutional setting, 396
Intangible assets, 630
Integrated system approach, taxation, 426
Integration-Responsiveness (IR) Grid, 507, 509–510, 509*f*
Intellectual property, 164–165, 168
  theft of, 168
Intellectual property rights (IPR), 164–166, 170–171, 751
Interbank transactions, 351
Intercontinental Exchange (ICE), 422
Interest arbitrage, 358
Interest rates, 223n24
  exchange rates and, 394–395
Interfaith Center on Corporate Responsibility (ICCR), 447
Internal debt, 211
Internal rate of return (IRR), 793
Internal Revenue Service (IRS), U.S., 162, 429
Internal sources of funds, 794–795
Internalization theory, 621, 649n10
Internally generated data, 545
International Accounting Standards Board (IASB), 775, 780, 783, 785–787, 801
  convergence and, 784–787
  Financial Accounting Standards Board (FASB) and, 786
  International Financial Reporting Standards (IFRS), 785
International Accounting Standards Committee (IASC), 785
International Anti-Counterfeiting Coalition (IACC), 168
International bond market, 419
International bonds, 418–420
International business
  behavioral/cultural practices, 100–109
  behavioral factors and, 63
  competitive environment and, 64–65
  cultural factors and, 92*f*
  cultural imperialism and, 115–117
  defined, 47
  domestic business *vs.*, 62–65
  economic forces and, 63–64
  environment/operations relationship and, 47–48
  future of, 65–66
  geographic influences and, 62–63
  globalization and, 43–74
  individualism vs. collectivism, 135–136
  legal issues in, 160–163, 164–165
  legal policies, 63
  marketing and, 701*f*
  modes of operations in, 60–62
  physical and social factors, 62–64
  political and economic environments facing, 129–177
  political and legal differences, 165–167
  political changes and, 52
  political policies and, 63
  reasons companies engage in, 58–59
  reasons for studying, 47–48
  services for supporting, 51
  slowing down of, 65
  social business *vs.*, 727
International business career case, 810–811
International Chamber of Commerce (ICC), 452
International Cocoa Organization, 329
International Coffee Organization (IC), 329
International collaborations. *See* Collaborative arrangements
International Commercial Terms (Incoterms), 588
International Copper Study Group, 329
International Court of Justice, 328
International division structure, 664
International economic analysis, 187–188
  data overload, 187
  market dynamism, 187
  market interdependence, 187
  system complexity, 187
International Electrotechnical Commission (IEC), 758
International Financial Reporting Standards (IFRS), 783, 787–788, 800
  future of, 800–801
  GAAP *vs.*, 787–788
  International Accounting Standards Board (IASB) and, 785
International Fisher Effect (IFE), 395
International human resources. *See* Human resource management (HRM)
International job market, sports and, 44–45
International Labor Organization (ILO), 323, 463, 495
International law, 63
International Monetary Fund (IMF), 180–181, 211, 225n65, 327, 380, 434, 545
  assistance programs, 375
  Bretton Woods and the Principle of Par Value, 375
  BRICs and, 375
  current status, 375–376
  evolution to floating exchange rates, 376–377
  exchange-rate anchors/arrangements, 377*t*
  exchange rates and, 374–377
  global financial crisis and, 376
  origin and objectives, 374–375
  quotas, 375
  special drawing rights (SDRs), 375–376
International Organization for Standardization (ISO), 758
International Organization of Securities Commissions (IOSCO), 785, 801
International organizations. *See also* Organizations
  types of, 61
International organizations and agencies, 545
International Red Cross, 328
International sports case, 44–47
International strategy, 509–511
International Tax Practices, 425–426
International Telecommunications Union, 758
International trade. *See* Trade
International Trade Administration, 590
International Trade Zones, 350*m*

International transaction chain, 597*f*
Internationalization. *See also* Country evaluation and selection
  born-global and, 572–573
  incremental, 571–572
  usual pattern of, 549*f*
Internet, 50, 219, 500
  communications and, 50
  e-commerce and, 721–723
  organizations' design and, 669*f*
  value chains and, 491–492
Intervention, 386–387
  attitude towards, 388
  central banks and, 387
  challenges of, 388
Interventionism, 235–236
Interventionist approach to exports/imports, 233–234
Interventionist trade theories, 235–236
  neomercantilism, 236
Intranet, 754
Inuits, 101
Investments, 61. *See also* Foreign direct investment
  inflows, 278–279
  international business and, 61
IO paradigm, 485
iPads, 579, 580, 738, 744, 751
iPhones, 47, 738–740, 744, 751
IPO, 421, 423–424
Iran, 175n98
  economic sanctions and, 283
Iron Curtain, 218
Islam, Saudi Arabia and, 88–89
ISO 14000, 758–759
ISO 9000, 758–759
Itaipu Dam, 53*f*
Italian Corporate Governance Code, 775
iTunes, 740
Ivory trade, 283, 284*f*

Jamaica Agreement, 377
Japan, 180, 744
  age-based groups and, 102
  Agency of Industrial SCIENCE and Technology, 608n102
  collectivism in, 106
  earthquake and, 399
  earthquake/tsunami, 540
  first Endaka and, 400
  international business risk and, 59
  kanban system, 757
  Ministry of International Trade and Industry (MITI), 608n102
  second Endaka and, 401
  Small and Medium Enterprise agency, 608n102
  Sony case and, 399–404
  Toyota in Europe Case (SUB), 302–304
  TQM and, 756–757
  tsunami and earthquake and, 399, 402–403, 761
  yen, 385
Japanese yen, 387–388
  Sony case and, 399–404
Jenbacher Biogas Engine, 443
Jensen index, 520n21
Jersey Islands, 175n116
Job market, international, sports case and, 44–45
Johnson & Johnson case, 654–657
Joint ventures (JV), 61, 634. *See also* Collaborative arrangements
  AA-JAL Joint Venture, 646–647
  collaborative arrangements and, 618*f*, 634
  dissolving, 636*f*
  Grameen/Danone Foods, 726–732, 731*m*
  Trans-Atlantic Joint Venture, 645–646
Just-in-Time (JIT) inventory management, 757

Kanban system, 757
Keiretsu, 670–671, 693n46, 750
Key industries, foreign control of, 628–629
Kidnapping, 545–546
Kinesics (body language), 111
Knowledge
  collaborative arrangements and, 625
  HDI and, 209
Korduglu, 529
Korea, 308
  intellectual property and, 166
  North Korea, 156
  U.S. Korea-FTA, 308
Kyoto Protocol, 312*t*, 457–458

La Familia, 169
Labels, 290
Labor
  child, 464
  conditions, ethical dilemmas and, 460–464
  costs of across the world, 492–496, 493*t*
  distribution of, 495*t*
  scanning and, 534–535
  specialization, importing and, 580
Labor Developments Abroad, 850n135
L'Académie française, 831
Lag strategy, 800
Laissez-faire, 135, 195, 224n41
  interventionist approaches *vs.*, 233–234
Land/people, factor proportions theory and, 244
Languages, 116. *See also* Communications; English language
  body language, 111
  brand names and, 716
  culture and, 96–99
  financial statements and, 790–792
  humor and, 110
  population/output, 98*f*
  silent, 111–112
  spoken and written, 109–110
  translation of, 109–110
  world distribution of, 97*m*, 832*t*
Latin America
  income per capita, 225n66
  regional economic integration and, 321*m*
Lead strategy, 800
Leads and lags, 800
Lean manufacturing, 756–757
Leapfrogging, of products, 533
Leasing, 623
Legal environments, 153–165
Legal issues, in international business, 153–165
  operational concerns, 160–163
Legal jurisdiction, 164
Legal systems, 153
  basis of rule in, 156–157
  trends in, 154–155
  types of, 154–155
  world map of, 154*m*
Leisure/productivity trade-off, 104
Letter of credit (L/C), 357–358
  confirmed, 358
Levels of moral development, 446–447
Leverage, 413–414
Liability of foreignness, 539
LIBOR Scandal, 418
Licensing, 629–630
  motives for, 629
  payment, 629–630
  selling to subsidiaries, 630
Licensing agreements, 61, 618*f*, 629–630. *See also* Collaborative arrangements
LIFFE CONNECT, 356
Link alliances, 623, 625
Liquidity preference, 539, 559n31
Lisbon Treaty, 314–315
Liz Claiborne Inc., 169, 540
Local brands, worldwide brand *vs.*, 716–717
Local content regulations, 163
Local economies, 489
Local responsiveness, global integration *vs.*, 503, 505–508
Local unavailability, importing and, 580
Localization, 817
Location advantages, exporting and, 568
Location decisions, 489–490, 495*t*
  allocating among locations and, 548–552
  competitive risk and, 539–543
  international operations and, 530*f*
  prime locations and, 553–554
  process, 531*f*
  violent areas and, 545–546
Location-specific assets, 741
Locations, 495*t*
Logging industry, 56
Logistics (materials management), 479, 496–497, 600
  digitization and, 496–497
  value chains and, 496–497
Logistics platforms, trade and, 600
London, foreign exchange markets and, 349
London Inter-Bank Offered Rate (LIBOR), 417–418
  LIBOR scandal, 418
London International Financial Futures and Options Exchange (LIFFE), 356
London Stock Exchange, 419
Longevity, economic growth and, 207
  HDI and, 208
Los Zetas, 169
Low-context cultures, 108
Low-cost strategy, 486, 487, 489–490
Low power distance, 106
Luggage, 762
Lukashenka, President (Belarus), 143
LUKOIL, 262–266
Luxury goods, 435–436, 512

M&A, 335
Magical organizations, 659
Magna Carta, 157
Magnitude, forecasting and, 396

Make-or-buy decision, 750
Malaysia, employment quotas in, 102
Malaysian Board of Engineers, 587, 812
Malcolm Baldridge National Quality Award, 758
Managed/fixed floating rates, 386–387
Management contracts, 60, 618*f*, 631–632. *See also* Collaborative arrangements
Management, orientations, cultures and, 114
Management team, 776, 804, 844–845
Manufacturing, 737–770
  configurations, 744–746
  factors in, 744–746
  foreign trade zones and, 759–760
  global, strategies for, 744–746
  global supply-chain management and, 753–755
  global supply chain strategies and, 741–746
  growth in manufactured goods, 279
  information technology and, 753–755
  locations, factor-proportions theory and, 244
  plant, 334, 496, 803
  quality, 755–759
  standards, 556
  supplier networks, 746–750, 752–753
  transportation networks and, 760–761
Margin, 369n19
Market capitalization, 421, 422*m*
Market control, 679
Market diversity, 709–710
  currency value fluctuations, 710–711
  export price escalation, 710
  pricing strategies and, 709–712
  pricing tactics, 709
  supplier relations, 712
Market economies, 194–195
  method and means of, 195*t*
Market-penetration grid, 547*t*
Marketing, 480, 697–736
  branding strategies, 715–717
  competitive environment and, 701*f*
  decisions, exchange-rate changes and, 397
  distribution strategies, 717–723
  gap analysis of, 723–725
  Grameen/Danone Foods joint venture and, 726–732, 731*m*
  international business and, 701*f*
  managing, 723–725
  physical factors and, 701*f*
  pricing strategies, 709–712
  product policies, 704, 708–709
  promotion strategies, 713–715
  regulation of, in developing countries, 705–706
  segment markets, 703–704, 725–726
  social factors and, 701*f*
  strategies, 700–704
  target, 408–409
  Tommy Hilfiger case, 698–700
Marketing mix
  branding strategies in, 715–717
  distribution strategies and, 717–723
  gap analysis of, 723–725
  managing, 723–725
  pricing strategies in, 709–712
  product policies in, 704, 708–709
  promotion strategies in, 713–715
Marketing orientations, 701–703
Marketing Week, 716
Markets
  eurocurrency, 416–418
  euroequity, 423–424
  globalization of, 504
  growth rate in, 550
  market penetration grid, 547*t*
  sales stability in, 550
  segment markets, 703–704, 725–726
  target, 408–409, 703–704
Masculinity-femininity index, 105
MASDAR, 459–460
Mass markets, 704
Massive open online courses (MOOCs), 685
Master franchise, 630
Material requirements planning (MRP), 753
Materialism, 726
  work motivation and, 103–106
Matrices, 693n28
  country attractiveness/company strength, 638–639, 639*f*
  country comparison tools and, 547
  disclosure/assessment, 783*f*
  matrix organizational structure, 665–666
  Secrecy-Transparency/Optimism-Conservatism Matrix, 783, 783*f*
Matrix structure, 665
Maturity stage, product life cycle trade theory, 249–250, 249t
McKinsey Global Institute, 158, 494, 567, 672
"McParity," 393*t*. *See also* Big Mac index
Measurement, 782
Mechanisms, 680–681
Médecins Sans Frontières (Doctors Without Borders), 545–546
Medicare, 290
Medicines, counterfeiting and, 169–170
Meliá Hotels International case, 612–618, 613m, 614*f*, 616*f*, 623, 632
Mercantilism, 235–236
Merchandise exports/imports, 60. *See also* Exporting
Mercosur, 322, 332, 534
Mexico
  bribery and, 451
  collectivism and, 107
  as a consumer market, 320
  drug cartels, 169
  family and, 107
  money-transfer market and, 340–342
  NAFTA and, 320
  time/punctuality and, 111
  Walmart and, 116, 160
Micro loans, 727
Micro-payments, 516
Migration. *See* immigration
Milan Stock Exchange, 435
Milk, Parmalat case, 772–776
Misery index, 210
Misspeaking, in English language, 110*t*
Mixed economies, 196–197, 224n50
Mixed legal system, 154*m*, 155
Mixed organizational structure, 666
Mixed structure, 666
Mobile banking, 515–518
Mobile money revolution, 515–518
Mobile telephony, 516, 842, 844
Mobility
  factor-mobility trade theory and, 252, 255–256
  of funds, risk and, 539
  specialization trade theories and, 241
Mobility premium, 834
Monetary Authority of Singapore, 296, 399
Monetary policy, 382, 398–399
Money center banks, 343
Money laundering, OFCs and, 432
Money-transfer market, 340–342
  converting currency, 340
Monochronic cultures, 109
Moral development levels, 446–447
Moral stability, economic growth and, 207
Morocco, 106
Most-favored-nation (MFN) clause, 305–306
Motivation
  hierarchy of needs theory, 105, 105*f*
  materialism and, 103–104
  work, behavioral practices and, 103–105
Mubarak, 153
Multicultural, 95, 118
Multidimensional Poverty Index, 213*t*
Multidomestic manufacturing strategy, 744–745
Multidomestic strategy, 511–512
Multilateral development banks (MDBs), 153
Multilateral netting, 796, 797*f*
Multinational corporation or company (MNC), 61
Multinational enterprises (MNEs), 58, 61, 151, 628
  cash flows and, 794–795, 796*f*
  in China, 130–131
  clusters and, 491, 492*f*
  defined, 61
  English language and, 98
  internal funds and, 795*f*
  net positions and, 796*t*
  offshoring and, 56–57
  piracy and, 170–171
  political ideologies and, 146–148
  staffing frameworks and, 818–823, 823*t*
  strategy types used by, 510*t*
  supply chain networks and, 741
  trade groups and, 304
Multinational problem-solving, 52–53
Multiparty democracy, 138*t*
Multiple exchange-rate system, 390
Multiple exchange rates, 390
Mutual adjustment, coordination by, 677–679
Mutual recognition, 784. *See also* convergence
Myanmar, 104, 324

NAFTA (North America Free Trade Agreement), 289, 304, 317*t*
NASDAQ OMX, 356, 420, 424
NASDAQ Options Market, 356
Nation, 95
  culture and, 95
Nation building, 279
National borders
  ethnic differences and, 119
  success/reward across, 104
National cultures, 95. *See also* Cultures
  future of, 118–119
  governmental trade intervention and, 282–286
  hybridization and, 118–119
National Football League (NFL), 46
National Institutes of Health (NIH), 706
National Retail Federation, 481
National sovereignty, globalization and, 55
National sports case, 44–45, 45*m*, 55
National territories, areas outside, 53–54
National Trade Data Bank, 545
Nations, cultures *vs.*, 95
Natural advantage, 237, 252
  diamond of national advantage theory, 250–252, 251*f*, 255
Natural disasters, 540
  Japanese earthquake/tsunami, 540, 761
Natural gas, 29, 50, 66, 261, 281
NatWest Bank, 355
NBA, 46, 48
Near-generic brand names, 717
Needs, hierarchy of, 105–106, 105*f*
Neoclassical organizational structures, 666–672
  change and, 667–668
  network structures, 669–671, 669*f*
  pitfalls of, 671–672
  virtual organization, 671
Neoclassical structures, 666
Neomercantilism, 236
Net National Product (NNP), 205
Net present value (NPV), 793
Netease.com, 175n98
Netting, 797*f*
Networks. *See also* Supply-chain management
  structure of, 669–671, 669*f*
  supplier, 746–750, 752
  transportation, 760–761
New York Federal Reserve Bank, 386
Nigeria, 44, 535, 538, 560n60
Nokero solar light case, 744, 746
Non-comparability of data, 544
Non-exporters, 567
Noncollaborative foreign equity arrangements, 618*f*
Noncontrolling financial interest, 61
Noneconomic rationales, for government intervention in trade, 282–286
Nonfinancial institutions, 343
Nongovernmental Organizations (NGOs), 328
Nonintervention, 385–386
Nonresident convertibility, 390
Nontariff barriers
  direct price influences, 287–289
  other direct-price influences, 289
  quantity controls, 289–292
Nontradable goods, 242
Normativism, 449
  relativism *vs.*, 448–450
North American Free Trade Agreement (NAFTA), 308, 311, 384, 398, 574, 593
  doing business with (implications for corporate strategy), 319
  immigration and, 319
  impact of, 319
  rationalization of production and, 319–320
  reasons for, 317–318
  rules of origin and regional content, 318
  special provisions, 318
  trade diversion and, 318
North Korea, 156
Northeast Passage, 188, 189*f*
Northern Sea Route, 187–188, 223n27
Northwest Passage, 188, 189*f*, 223n27
Not-for-profit services, 291
"not free country," 141
Nuclear energy, 458
Nuclear family, 107
Nuclear plant failure, Japan, 458
Obsolescence, of products, 533
Occasional exporters, 567
Oceans, 53–54
OECD, 288, 434, 545
OECD Centre for Tax Policy and Administration, 429
Off-balance-sheet financing, 772–773
Offer, 351
Office of Antifraud (OLAF), 453
Official Languages Act (Canada), 831
Offsets, 291, 601*t*
Offshore currency, 416
Offshore financial centers (OFCs), 430–431
Offshore financing, 425, 430–431
Offshore manufacturing, 742, 745–746, 747
Offshoring, 56–58
  point/counterpoint feature, 56–58
Oligopolistic reaction, 542
Olympics, 44, 46, 62
oneworld Airline Alliance case, 642–647, 643*m*
  AA-JAL Joint Venture, 643*m*
  Trans-Atlantic Joint Venture, 643*m*
oneworld Alliance, 646*f*
Online platforms, trade and, 599–600
OPEC. *See* Organization of the Petroleum Exporting Countries (OPEC)
Operating exposure, 798
Operating income, 804
Operating modes, 618*f*, 639. *See also* Collaborative arrangements
Operational centers, 431
Operational concerns, 160–162
Operational hedging strategies, 799–800
Operational obstacles, 500
Operations (international business operations), 480
  compatibility and, 539–541
  cultural factors in, 92*f*
  economic connections and, 234*f*
  economic factors in, 187*f*
  factors in, 47–48, 48*f*
  location decisions and, 530*f*
  regulation of, 163*t*
  supply chain and, 741*f*
Operations management, 741
Opportunistic, importers as, 579
Opportunities, scanning for, 532–533
Opportunity-risk matrix, 548*f*
Optimum tariffs, 281–282
Optimum-tariff theory, 281
Options, 346*f*, 353
Organization, 659
Organization culture, 681–685
  building, 683–684
  importance of, 682–683
  Johnson & Johnson case and, 654–657
  performance and, 681–682
  strategy and, 684–685, 684*f*
Organization for Economic Cooperation and Development (OECD), 452–453
  Anti-Bribery Convention, 452
Organization of the Petroleum Exporting Countries (OPEC), 289, 328–331
  exports and, 329–330
  prices and, 329–331
Organization structures, 659–661
  classical, 662, 663*f*
  divisional, 662, 664
  dynamic balance in, 660–661
  functional, 662
  hierarchy vs. hyperarchy, 673–674
  horizontal differentiation, 662–666
  Hyundai Motor Company case, 687–691
  international division, 664
  matrix, 665–704
  mixed, 666
  neoclassical, 666–672
  network structure and, 669*f*
  vertical differentiation, 660
Organizations, 653–695
  change and, 657–659
  competitive environment and, 657*f*
  control systems, 679–681
  coordination systems, 672–679
  corporate universities and, 685–687
  design, internet and, 658, 669*f*
  hierarchy vs. hyperarchy, 673–674
  international business expansion and, 658
  Johnson & Johnson case, 654–657
  magical, 659, 676
  management standards and, 658–659
  physical factors and, 657*f*
  size and, 61–62
  social contract, 659
  social factors and, 657*f*
  types of, 61
Orientations, marketing, 701–703

OTC (over-the-counter) foreign-exchange instruments, 345–349
Outer space, 53–54
Outright forward transactions, 345, 346*f*
Outsourcing, 57, 747
  innovation, 750–751
Over the counter bond, 419
Ownership advantages, exporting and, 568

Pacific Alliance, 322
Pakistan, 538
Pan Arab Free Trade Area (PAFTA), 316, 317*t*, 327
Papua New Guinea, 101
Par value, 375
Paraguay, 53
Paris Convention for the Protection of Industrial Property, 165, 167
Parliamentary democracy, 138*t*
Parmalat case, 772–776, 782, 783
"Partly free" country, 141
Partnering Against Corruption Initiative (PACI), 454
Partners, dealing with, 640–641
  controlling through Contracts and Trust, 640–641
  finding and evaluating, 640
  negotiating, 640
  secrecy and, 640
Passive exports, 701–702
Passive income, 427
Past patterns, political risk and, 538
Payback period, 793
Payment considerations, 629–630
Payroll to population, 211
Peace, dividend, economic growth and, 207
Penetration pricing strategy, 709
People
  factor-mobility theory and, 255–256
  land, factor-proportions theory and, 246
Perception of cues, 108
Performance, masculinity-femininity index and, 105
Persian Gulf War, 401
Personal stress, globalization and, 56
Pew Center on Global Climate Change, 442–443
Pharmaceutical industry, 507–507
  ethical dilemmas and, 460–462
Philadelphia Stock Exchange, 356
Philippines, child labor and, 464*f*
PHLX, 356
Photoshop, 168
Physical factors
  marketing and, 701*f*
  operating modes and, 618*f*
  organizing operations and, 657*f*
Physiological needs, 105, 105*f*
Piracy
  case, 168–171
  China and, 132–133
  counterfeiting and, 168–169
  fighting against, 169–170
  global health and safety and, 169
  intellectual property and, 169–170
  medication and, 169–170
  medicines and, 460
  pervasiveness of, 170–171
  software and, 169–170
Plan, coordination by, 675–677
Pluralism, 136, 173n33
Point/counterpoint feature
  Africa and common currency, 384–385
  CAFTA-DR, 322–324
  corruption/bribery, 455–456
  cultural imperialism and, 115–117
  economic growth, 207–208
  Exporting e-waste, 581–584, 581*m*
  foreign control of key industries, 628–629
  GAAP (Generally Accepted Accounting Principles, U.S.), 787–788
  hierarchy vs. hyperarchy, 673–674
  learning foreign languages, 829–831, 832*f*
  offshore financial centers and tax practices, 432–433
  offshoring, 56–57, 58
  outsourcing innovation, 750–751
  political risk management, 151–153
  regulation of marketing in developing countries, 705–706
  speculation on currency, 359–360
  strategic trade policies, 253–254
  value chains, 501–503
  violent locations, 545–546
Political and legal difference, basis of, 165–167
  cross-national convergence, 167
  cultural orientation, 166–167
  economic circumstances, 166
  historical legacies, 165
Political disruptions, 483–484
Political factors, accounting and, 781*f*
Political freedom, 137
Political ideologies, 136–140, 142–146
  authoritarianism, 145
  democracy, 138, 142–143
  spectrum analysis, 137–138
  totalitarianism, 139
Political motives, factor-mobility theory and, 256
Political risks, 148–151, 538–539
  classifying, 149–151
  management of, 151–153
  point/counterpoint feature, 151–153
  predicting, 538–539
  types and outcomes of, 149–151, 149f
Political spectrum, 137*f*
Political system, 135
Politics/political environments, 134–152
Polycentric framework, 819
Polycentric staffing framework, 823*t*
Polycentrism, 114
Polychronic cultures, 95, 109
POPClocks, 225n68
Population, 174n70
  language groups, 98*f*
Portfolio investment, 61
Postconventional moral development level, 446
Poverty, 212–215
  consequences of, 213–214
  economic growth and, 207
  Multidimensional Poverty Index, 213*t*
  potential and, 214
  prevalence of, 213–214
  success standards and, 214–215
Power distance, 94, 106
PPP. *See* Purchasing power parity (PPP)
PPR, 435
Prada Group case, 434–437
Prada SpA., 435
Pragmatism, 109
Preconventional moral development level, 446
Premium, 352–353
Preparation programs, expatriates, 828–829
Prestige, silent language and, 112
Price-control objectives, of government trade intervention, 280–281
Prices, 533
  import/export, negotiating, 712*t*
  OPEC (Organization of the Petroleum Exporting Countries) and, 330–331
Price stability, 68, 395
Pricing strategies, 709–712
  fixed vs. variable, 711–712
  marketing mix and, 709–712
  obstacles in, 709–712
  potential obstacles in international pricing, 709–712
  Tommy Hilfiger case, 699
Primary activities, 488
Prime locations, changes in, 553–554
Principled moral development level, 446
Prior company expansion, collaborative arrangements and, 627
Private technology exchange (PTX), 754
Privatization, 151, 195, 376, 506
Problem-solving, multinational, 52–53
Procedural political risks, 149*f*, 150
Process disruptions, 483
Process technology, 237
  factor-proportions theory and, 243–246
Product disruptions, 483
Product diversification, 551
Product diversion, 711
Product division structure, 663*f*
Product Life Cycle (PLC) trade theory, 248–250, 249*t*
  Changes over the cycle, 248–250
Product line
  extent and mix of, 708
  product life-cycle considerations, 708–709
  sales and cost considerations, 708
Product line gaps, 725
Product policies, 707–709
  altering products, 704–707
  marketing mix and, 704, 707–709
  The Product Line: Extent and Mix, 708
  Tommy Hilfiger case, 699
Product safety and liability, 164, 704
Product technology, 237
  factor-proportions theory and, 245–246

Production, 479
decisions, exchange-rate changes and, 398–399
Production factors, factor-mobility theory and, 255–256
Production, marketing orientation and, 701–702
Production networks, 241
Production orientation, 701–702
Productivity, exporting and, 570
Productivity/leisure trade-off, 104
Products, 704
altering, 704–707
competitive strategy for, 64
cultural considerations, 707
economic considerations, 707
environmental-protection regulations, 704
income level and distribution, 707
indirect legal considerations, 705
infrastructure, 707
issues of standardization, 706
labeling requirements, 704
legal considerations in altering, 704
Products, demand, climate and, 718
Professional sports players, as brands, 46
Profitability, exporting and, 569–570
Proletariat, 224n43
Prominent types of totalitarianism, 139*t*
Promotion
international, 714–715
sports/teamwork and, 46
strategies, 713–715
Tommy Hilfiger case, 698–699
Property rights, 157
Protectionism, 275
Protestant ethic, 103
Public Company Accounting Oversight Board (PCAOB), 787–788
PUIG Beauty and Fashion group, 435
Pull, 713
Punctuality, cultures and, 111
Purchasing function, 752
Purchasing power parity (PPP), 203–204, 225n70, 226n108, 405
Big Mac Index and, 392, 393*t*
exchange rates and, 225n71, 391–394
Starbucks Index and, 392–394
Push, 713
Push-pull mix, 713–714

Qatar Investment Authority, 47
Quality, 755, 755–759
standards, 758–759
strategies, global manufacturing, 743
Quantity controls, 289–292, 390
quotas, 289–290
Quotas, 289–290, 375. *See also* embargoes

R&D, 460
Race
in Brazil, 102
ethnic groups and, 102
ethnic/racial groups and, 102
ethnicity and, 102–103
social stratification and, 102
Radio Frequency Identification (RFID), 754
chips, 169
rationalization, 746
REACH (Registration, Evaluation, and Authorization of Chemicals) (in Europe), 586–587
Recession. *See* Global financial crises
Recession/retreat, of democracy, 143–145
Reciprocal advantages, globalization and, 52
Reconciliation, 784
mutual recognition *vs.*, 784
Recycling, e-wastes and, 581–584, 581*m*
Red Cross, 546
Reflation, 210
Regional economic integration, 304, 308–311
Africa, 326–327, 326*m*
Americas, 320–322, 321*m*
Asia, 324–325
economies of scale and, 310–311
effects of, 310–311
geography and, 308–309
increased competition and, 311
static and dynamic effects of, 309–310
trade creation and, 310
trade diversion, 310
Regional integration, 304
Regional manufacturing strategy, 744
Regional trade agreements (RTAs), 308, 317–318
Regional trading groups, 311–322. *See also* European Union
in Africa, 326–327
in the Americas, 320–322
in Asia, 324–325
comparisons of, 317*t*
European Union (EU), 311–317
NAFTA, 317*t*
North American Free Trade Agreement (NAFTA), 317–320
other forms of international cooperation and, 327–328
Regular exporters, 567
Regulation
of international business operations, 161t, 163*t*
of marketing, in developing countries, 705–706
wealth and, 162
Reinvestment, 551–552
Reinvestment decisions, 552
Relationship-focus (RF) culture, 109
Relationships
preferences, cultural environments and, 106–107
Relativism, 457
bribery and, 451
normativism *vs.*, 448–450
Religions
as cultural stabilizer, 99–100
Saudi Arabia and, 88–89
worldwide distribution of, 100*m*
Renewable energy, 458
Renminbi, 366–367
Repatriation, 837
Reporting dealers, 343, 344*f*
Representative democracy, 138*t*
Research and development (R&D), 51
Reserve assets, central bank, 386–387
Reshoring, 57, 58
Resource acquisition, 534–536
cost considerations, 534–536
scanning and, 534–536
Resource acquisition, international business and, 59
Resource-based view (of the firm), 625
Resource efficiency, 237–238
Resources. *See also* Human resource management (HRM)
assistance, for exporting/importing, 590–596
movements, liberalization of, 50–51
Responsibility, corporate, 464–466
Responsiveness-Integration Grid, 509–510, 509*f*
Retaliation, from government trade intervention, 276–277
Retreat/recession, of democracy, 143–145
Reverse culture shock, 114
Reverse engineering, 461
Reverse-expat, 817
Rewards, success and, 104
Risk-taking behavior, 107–108
Risks, 537–543. *See also* specific risks
factors to consider in analyzing, 537
foreign exchange risk, 539
foreign sourcing, 757
international business and, 59
mobility of funds and, 539
return and, 520n19
scanning and, 537–543
Robotics, 490, 496, 498
Rounds, 307
Royalties, 61
RQFII, 296
Rule of law, 156
basis of rule and, 156–157
implications of, 157
world distribution of, 158*m*
Rule of man, 156–157
Rules of origin, 318
Rules of regional content, 318
Russia, 180, 199
BRICs and, 217–222
Burger King in, 526–528
political environment in, 134
World Trade Organization (WTO) and, 306

Sales
expansion, scanning and, 532–533
international business and, 59
Sales income, 427
Sales, marketing orientation and, 702
Samsonite, 762–767
Sarbanes-Oxley Act (SOX), 424, 454, 787–788, 801
Saudi Arabia, 101, 180
background, 88
case, 88–92
cultural dynamics, 91
gender roles, 90–91
map of, 89*m*
religion and, 88–89
traditions, 89–90
Scale alliances, 623, 625
Scanning, 531–532
cost considerations and, 534–536
description of, 531–532
vs. detailed analysis, 532
economic and demographic variables, 533–543
foreign exchange risk and, 539
information and, 532–544
labor and, 534–535

opportunities and, 532–533
resource acquisition and, 534–536
risks and, 537–543
sales expansions and, 532–533
Schengen Agreement, 315
Schengen area, 314–315
Second-tier subsidiaries, 428*f*
Secrecy-Transparency/Optimism-Conservatism Matrix, 783, 783*f*
Secular totalitarianism, 139*t*
Securities and Exchange Commission (SEC), 454, 774, 784, 800
Security needs, 105, 105*f*
Segment markets, 703–704, 725–726
Seisan keiretsu, 670
Self-actualization, 105, 105*f*
Separate entity approach, taxation, 426
September 11, 2001 terrorist attacks, 761
Serendipity, in exporting, 575
Serious Fraud Office (UK), 418, 454
Service companies, for information, 544
Service income, 427
Services
exports, 60
imports, 60
international trade and, 51, 291–292
performance of, 60
Severe acute respiratory syndrome (SARS), 540
Shanghai Maritime Court, 110
Shari'a law, 155
Shipping, 596–597, 600
Sight draft, 357
Silent language, 111–112
Silk Market, of Beijing, 168
Sina.com, 175n98
Singapore International Monetary Exchange (SIMEX), 360
Singapore Stock Exchange, 419
Single European Act, 314–315, 381
Singularity Principle, 490
Six Sigma, 757–758
Skimming pricing strategy, 709
Small and medium-sized enterprise (SME), 408, 562, 568, 577
defined, 568
exporting and, 584
Small and mid-sized firms (SMMs), 59
Small Business Administration, 590
Small economies' overdependence, 55
Smart tags, 754
SMEs, 584–588, 590–591, 594
Smithsonian Agreement, 377
Soccer, 47
Social business, 727–728
Social connections, 102
Social democracy, 138*t*
Social factors
marketing and, 701*f*
operating modes and, 618*f*
organizing operations and, 657*f*
Social marketing orientation, 703
Social networks, 54, 175n98
Social stratification
ethnic/racial groups and, 102
family-based groups and, 103
gender-based groups and, 102–103
issues in, 100–101
Socialism, 196
Société Générale, 694n79
Societies
Ecomagination case, 443m
host society acceptance, 112
Soft currencies, 390
Soft peg exchange rate arrangements, 380
Software, piracy and, 169–171
Software platforms, trade and, 600
Solar energy, 184–185
China and, 184–185
Sony case, 399–404
Sourcing, 479, 746
concerns in, 749
configurations, 749–750
defined, 746
global, 747–749
production strategy and, 747*f*
strategies, 753
South Africa
AIDS in, 461
Anglo American PLC in, 466–471
Southern African Development Community (SADC), 326*m*, 327, 384
Southern Common Market (MERCOSUR), 308, 320, 322
Sovereignty, 55
Sovereign wealth funds (SWFs), 420–421
Soviet Union, 48, 196
Spain
map of, 478*m*
Meliá Hotels International case, 612
wine academy in, 726
Zara case, 476–481
Special Drawing Rights (SDRs), 375
Specialization
acquired advantage and, 246
labor, importing and, 580
Specialization trade theories, 240–246
Specialized studies, for information, 544
Specific duty, 287
Specific permission requirements, 290–291
Spectrum, political, 139
Speculation, 358
point/counterpoint feature, 359–360
Speed money, 453
Spider-Man 2, 715
Spillover effects, 551
SpinCent case, 562–564
Spoken language issues, 109–110
Sports case, 44–47
Spot market, 351
Spot rate, 345
Spot transactions, 346*f*
Spouse allowance, expatriate compensation, 836
Spread, 351
Stability, 206
Gross National Happiness (GNH), 206
Happy Planet Index (HPI), 206–207
Your Better Life Index (YBLI), 206
Stability and growth pact, 382
Staffing frameworks, 818–823, 823*t*
Stakeholders, 275
trade policies and, 275–276
Standardization, 714–715
coordination by, 672, 675
distribution strategies and, 718–719
efficiency and, 504–505
legality and, 715
message needs and, 715
promotion strategies and, 714–715
translation and, 714–715
Standards, 290, 291–292
of living, HDI and, 209
Stanley Cup, 45
Starbucks Index, 392–394
Stare decisis, 155, 175n114
Starting businesses, operational concerns, 160–161
State Administration of Foreign Exchange (SAFE), 364
State capitalism, 185, 197–198
State Department, U.S., 850n135
Statement of International Transactions. *See* Balance of payments (BOP)
Static effects, 309
NAFTA, 317–318
Stock markets, 421–424
delisting and, 424
emerging, 423
NASDAQ OMX, 356
size of, 421–424
trends in, 422–423
world distribution of, 422*m*
Stockholm Convention on Persistent Organic Pollutants, 449
Strategic alliances, 61, 623–627
Strategic concerns, legal issues in, 160–165
Strategic marketing orientation, 702–703
Strategic trade policies (industrial policies), 232, 253–254. *See also* Trade policies
Strategies for instituting change, 115–118
cultural bridges, 118
learning abroad, 118
opinion leadership, 117–118
participation, 117
resistance to change, 117
reward sharing, 117
value systems, 115
Strategizing HRM, 813–814
case in point: GE's Evolution, 813–814
Strategy (international business strategy), 475–523. *See also* Branding strategies; Distribution strategies; Value chains
apparel industry case, Zara, 476–481
characteristics of types used by, 510*t*
cost leadership, 486
differentiation, 486–487
global, 512–513
global manufacturing strategies, 740–741
hallmarks of, 485
industry structure and, 482–484
international, 509–511
marketing, 700–704
multidomestic strategy, 511–512
organization culture and, 684*f*
perspectives on, 484–485
role of, 482*f*
transnational, 513–514
types of, 508–514

Strategy-structure-systems model, 693n32
Strike price, 353
Subpart F income, 427
Subsidiaries
networks, 499
U.S.-owned foreign, tax status of, 428*f*
visits to, 694n82
Subsidies, 287–288, 305
agricultural, 287–288
overcoming marketimperfections and, 288
Substitution, 533
Substitution, import, 258–260, 279
Subzones, 759–760
Success and reward, across borders, 104
Suppliers
networks, 746–750, 752–753
relations, sourcing and, 752
Supply chain, 740, 741–746, 741*f*, 747
defined, 740
sources of worker-related pressures in, 462*f*
strategies, 741–746
Supply-chain management, 740–741
Apple case and, 738–740
defined, 740–741
foreign trade zones and, 759–760
future of, 761
global manufacturing strategies, 741–746
global strategies, 741–746
information technology, 753–755
quality and, 755
Samsonite case, 762–767
supplier networks and, 746–750, 752–753
transportation networks and, 760–761
uncertainty and, 761
Support activities, 489
Supported/related industries, diamond of national advantage, 251
Surplus workers, 278
Sustainability, 199, 204–206, 278, 398–399, 456
economic growth and, 208
ethical behavior and, 456–457
Genuine Progress Indicator (GPI), 205
Human Development Index (HDI), 206
Net National Product (NNP), 205
Sustainable development, 205
Swap trading, 601*t*
Switch trading, 601*t*
Syndication, 417
Synergy, 522n81
Systemic political risks, 149–150, 149*f*

Taliban, 196
Taoism, 693n20
Target markets, 703–704
GPS Capital Markets and, 408–409
segment markets and, 703–704
Tariffs, 286–287, 305
criteria for assessing, 287
import, 286
optimum, 281–282
as revenue source, 286
Tax credit, 429
Tax havens, 428*f*, 431
Tax haven subsidiary, 428*f*
Tax treaties, 429–430
Taxation, 834–835
dodging, 430
double, 429
international tax practices and, 425–426, 783–784
OFCs (offshore financial centers) and, 430–433
transfer prices and, 428–429
of U.S.-owned foreign subsidiaries, 428*f*
Technical forecasting, 396
Technology
foreign-exchange markets and, 361
globalization and, 49–50
Technology, Entertainment, Design (TED), 674
Telecommunication, 288, 398, 427
Teleological approach, 446
Televised sports, worldwide, 45–46
Temporal method, of translation, 790–792, 791*f*
Tennis, 44–45
Terms currency, 351
Terms of trade, 279
Terrorism
9/11 terrorist attacks, 761
bombings and, 546
kidnapping and, 546
Tesco PLC case, 120–124, 122*m*
Textbooks, 711
Theocratic law, 139*t*, 154*m*, 155
Theocratic totalitarianism, 139t
Theory of country size, 242
"Think globally, act locally," 55
Third-country national, 814, 816–817
Third-party logistics (3PL), 596
Third Wave of Democratization, 142, 145, 155, 159
Third World Countries, 199
Tiered pricing, 460–461
Time, cultures and, 111
Time draft, 357
Time zones, foreign exchange trading and, 349
Timing
of change, 118
forecasting and, 396
Tokyo Stock Exchange, 400
Tomatoes example, factor-mobility theory, 259*f*, 260
Tommy Hilfiger case, 698–700, 716
Torts, customary law and, 155
Total cost analysis, 742
Total Quality Management (TQM), 673, 679, 756–757
Totalitarian system, 139
Totalitarianism, 139–140, 142, 159
business implications of, 140
types of, 139t
Tourism
transportation and, 60
Toyota in Europe case, 302–304, 316
Trade
administrative delays, 291
choice of trading partner and, 246–247
Costa Rica foreign trade case, 230–233
countertrade and, 601–602, 601*t*
economy size and, 242
factor mobility and, 258–260
factor-mobility theory and, 229–270
foreign-exchange trading process, 353–356, 354*f*
foreign trade zones, 759–760
international, 565*f*
liberalization, 50–51
physical and social factors, 275*f*
product types, 243–246
reciprocal requirements, 291
services and, 51, 60, 241, 291
statics/dynamics of, 248–252, 317–318
strategic trade policies, 253–254
technology and, 599–600
without discrimination, 305–306
Trade agreements, regional, 318–319
Trade associations, 545
Trade barriers, 65
Trade control instruments, 286–292. *See also* Trade restrictions
Trade deficit, 236
Trade diversion, NAFTA and, 317–318
Trade intervention, governmental, 271–300
changes in the competitive environment, 293
dealing with, 292–293
decision makers, 292–293
economic rationales for, 276–282
economic relationships with other countries, 279–282
essential-industry argument and, 282–286
industrial base development, 278–279
infant-industry argument, 277–278
interventionist trade theories and, 235–236
noneconomic rationales for, 282–286
preserving national cultures and, 286
price-control objectives and, 280–281
promoting acceptable practices abroad, 282–284
reasons for, 276*t*
risks in designating industries, 277–278
Singapore model, 294–297
spheres of influence and, 285
unemployment and, 276–277
Trade-offs, 627
Trade pattern theories, 234, 242–248
Trade policies
conflicting results of, 275–276
strategic, 253–254
Trade-Related Aspects of Intellectual Property Rights (TRIPS), 165, 171
Trade restrictions, 275*f*, 594*t*
as a bargaining tool, 280
catfish case and, 272–274, 273*m*
trade-control instruments, 286–292
Trade surplus, 236
Trade theories, 252
absolute advantage, 236–237, 238*f*
business and, 234
checklist, 235*t*
comparative advantage, 239–240

country-similarity, 246–247
country size, 242
diamond of national advantage theory, 250–252, 251*f*, 255
factor mobility, 234, 252, 254, 255–256
factor-proportions, 243–246
free trade, 236–237
interventionist, 235–236
mercantilism, 235–236
product life cycle, 248–250
specialization, 240–246
trade pattern, 234, 242–248
Trademark squatters, 626
Trading blocs, 534
Traditional factors, Saudi Arabia, 89–90
Trans-Pacific Partnership (TPP), 325
Transaction exposure, 797–798
Transactions cost theory, 621
Transactions, foreign currency, 788–789
Transatlantic Trade and Investment Partnership (EU), 316
Transfer prices, 428–429
Transit tariffs, 286
Translation exposure, 797–798
Translation methods, 790–792
Translations, 790
foreign-currency financial statements, 790–792
Transnational company (TNC), 61
Transnational organization, 693n33
Transnational strategy, 513–514
Transparency
Secrecy-Transparency/Optimism-Conservatism Matrix, 783, 783*f*
Transparency International, 135
Transport costs, 241
Transportation, 535–536, 595, 596
globalization and, 50
networks, 760–761
tourism and, 60
Treasurer, role of, 412*f*
Treaty of Maastricht, 315, 381, 382
Triad, 304
Trust, cultures and, 107
Tsunami/earthquake, Japan, 402–403, 540, 761
Turkey, 315
Turnkey operations, 60, 618*f*, 632–634. *See also* Collaborative arrangements
UK Bribery Act, 454
UN Conference on Trade and Development (UNCTAD), 328
Special Unit on Commodities, 329
UN Framework Convention on Climate Change, 457
UNASUL. *See* Union of South American Nations (UNASUR)
Uncertainty avoidance, 107
UNCTAD. *See* UN Conference on Trade and Development UNCTAD
Unemployment
government trade intervention and, 276–277
measuring, 210–211
Unemployment rate, 210
UNESCO, 286
Unfavorable balance of trade, 236
UNICEF, 464
Union of South American Nations (UNASUR), 320
Unit of account, 375
United Kingdom (UK)
customary law and, 175n116
misspoken words and, 110*t*
Tesco PLC in, 121–122
uncertainty avoidance and, 107
United Nations, 55, 169, 185, 199, 327–328, 452, 503, 545. *See also* Nongovernmental Organizations (NGOs)
Committee on Non-Governmental Organizations (NGOs), 328
Conference on Trade and Development (UNCTAD), 328
cross-national cooperation and, 327–328
Economic and Social Council, 327–328
Food and Agriculture Organization, 226n126
General Assembly, 328
International Court of Justice, 328
organization and membership, 327–328
sanctions and, 285
Security Council, 328
World Bank and, 327
United Nations Convention against Corruption (UNCAC), 452
United Nations Convention on Contracts for the International Sale of Goods, 161
United Nations Development Programme, 540
United Nations General Assembly, 174n53
United Nations Global Compact, 465
United Nations Office on Drugs and Crime (UNCAC), 453
United Nations World Food Program, 115
United States (U.S), 306, 307, 385
Caribbean Basin Initiative, 232
collapse of housing market, 402
common law and, 155
Costa Rica/U.S. trade examples, 236–240, 238*f*
Cuba/U.S. Relations, 247
debt crisis and, 402
Foreign Corrupt Practices Act (FCPA) and, 453–454
import quotas, 289
individualism and, 106
Internal Revenue Service, 162
leisure/productivity trade-off, 104
misspoken words and, 110*t*
piracy laws and, 170
pragmatism and, 109
state economies compared to national, 243*m*
tax loopholes, 226n107
top trade partners of, 574*t*
Vietnam/U.S. catfish controversy, 272–274, 273*m*
wheat/coffee example, 238–240, 238*f*, 239*f*
Unity-of-command principle, 666
Universal Declaration of Human Rights, 174n53
Universal language, body language *vs.*, 111–112
Universities, corporate, 685–687
U.S. Commercial Service, 590
U.S. Commercial Service Export Assistance Center, 563
U.S. Customs Service. *See* Bureau of Customs and Border Protection (CBP)
U.S. Korea-FTA, 308
U.S. Population Clock, 225n68
Usage gaps, 724
Users, of accounting information, 780*f*
Utilitarianism, 446

Value, 485, 520n22
Value-added networks (VANS), 754
Value-added tax (VAT), 425
Value chains, 488, 488*f*
change and, 500–501
clusters and, 491–492
configuration and, 489–496
coordination and, 497–500
firms as, 487–489
Internet and, 502
logistics and, 496–497
managing, 489–500
point/counterpoint feature, 501–503
virtuality vs. reality, 501–503
Value creation, 476–481, 485–487
Values, 275*f*
industry structure and, 482–484
Vehicle Dependability Study (VDS), 755
Venezuela, 538
black markets in, 390
Vertical alliances/links, 623–625
Vertical differentiation, 660
Vertical integration, 749–750
Vertically extended family, 107
Vietnam/U.S. catfish controversy, 272–274, 273*m*
Violent areas, location and, 545–546
Virtual organization, 671
Virtuality, value chain and, 501–503
Voice-over-Internet-protocol (VoIP), 584
Voluntary Export Restraint (VER), 289–290

Walmart, 160, 304, 333
Washington Consensus, 146–148, 159
Web, 500
West African Economic and Monetary Union (WAEMU), 384
Western Union case, 340–342, 345, 351
Where to be Born Index (WTBBI), 217
Wine Academy of Spain, 726
Women
expatriates and, 816
micro loans and, 728
Saudi Arabia and, 90–91
Workflow software, 753
Working age population, 226n102
Workplace
motivation, behavioral practices and, 103–105
Saudi Arabian women and, 91
World Bank, 327
International Finance Corporation, 233

World Competitiveness Index (WCI), 216
World Competitiveness Project, 216
World Cup, 44, 46
World Economic Forum, 160
World Fact Book, CIA, 317*t*
World Health Organization, 448, 460, 466, 540, 705
World Intellectual Property Organization (WIPO), 164
The World Is Flat (Thomas Friedman), 747, 753
World Luxury Association, 434*f*
World maps
  economics, 186*m*
  GNI per capita, 203*m*
  immigration, 257*m*
  languages, 97*m*
  legal systems, 154*m*
  religions and, 100*m*
  rule of law, 158*m*
  stock markets, 422*m*
World Population Clock, 225n68
World Trade Organization (WTO), 133, 160, 167, 180, 304–305, 308, 314, 318, 461, 504–505, 545, 602, 709, 758
  Agreement on Trade-Related Aspects of Intellectual Property Rights (TRIPS), 461
  bilateral economic integration and, 331–332
  BRICs and, 306
  Council for Trade in Goods, 307
  Council for Trade-Related Aspects of Intellectual Property Rights, 307
  dispute settlement and, 306–307
  Doha Round and, 307
  functions of, 306–307
  GATT and, 306–307
  General Agreement for Trade in Services, 307
  global integration and, 305–307
  Most Favored Nation (MFN) and, 306
  regional economic integration and, 331
  Trade-Related Aspects of Intellectual Property Rights (TRIPS), 165, 171
World War II, 193, 304, 374
Worldwatch Institute, 219
Worldwide brand, local brands *vs.*, 716–717
Worldwide televised sports, 45
Worldwide Trade by Major Sectors (FIG), 246*f*

Yen, Japanese, 399, 402, 403–404
Your Better Life Index (YBLI), 206
Yuan, Chinese, 366–367, 402

Zara case, 476–481, 478m, 485
Zero Defects, 756
Zimbabwe, 389
  black market in, 389